FALK'S DICTIONARY OF CHINESE MARTIAL ARTS

Books available from **tgl books**

Jiang Rongjiao's Baguazhang
Li Tianji's The Skill of Xingyiquan
Yan Dehua's Bagua Applications
Di Guoyong on Xingyiquan: Vol. I Five Element Foundation
Di Guoyong on Xingyiquan: Vol. II Form and Theory
Di Guoyong on Xingyiquan: Vol. III Weapon and Partner Play
A Shadow on Fallen Blossoms
Falk's Dictionary of Chinese Martial Arts

www.thewushucentre.ca

FALK'S DICTIONARY OF CHINESE MARTIAL ARTS

CHINESE TO ENGLISH

Comprehensive vocabulary for techniques, training methods, applications, weapons, routines, styles, sayings and phrases relevant to the theory, practice, and study of the modern and traditional martial arts of China, plus many representative *zhaofa*. Also contains vocabulary helpful in reading martial arts reference books – anatomical terms, dynastic dates, historical, literary, and folklore references, military stratagem, and traditional Chinese medical terminology.
Compiled and translated by Andrea Mary Falk

Compiled and translated by Andrea Mary Falk.
Copyright © Andrea Mary Falk, 2019.

All right reserved. This book or any portion thereof may not be reproduced or used in any manner whatsoever without the express written permission of the publisher except for the use of brief quotations in a book review or scholarly work.

First printing: 2019.
Published by tgl books, Québec, Canada.

ISBN 978-0-9879028-5-6
This ISBN is for the deluxe soft-cover edition.
The dictionary is also available as hard cover, compact soft cover, and PDF.

Library and Archives Canada Cataloguing in Publication
Canadian CIP data is no longer done ahead of publication time for small publishers such as tgl books.
The library number is assigned after legal deposit of the published book.

The techniques described in this book are intended for experienced martial artists. The author, translator, and publisher are not responsible for any injury that may occur while trying out these techniques. Please do not apply these techniques on anyone without their consent and cooperation.

TABLE OF CONTENTS

Introduction	vii
Acknowledgements	viii
Notes on Using the Dictionary	ix
Character Index by *Pinyin* order	1

Dictionary in *Pinyin* Order

	A	āi to ào	13
	B	bā to bù	15
	C	cā to cuò	41
	D	dā to duò	63
	E	é to èr	91
	F	fā to fù	95
	G	gǎi to guò	111
	H	hā to huò	127
	J	jī to jūn	151
	K	kā to kuò	177
	L	lā to luò	185
	M	mā to mù	207
	N	ná to nuó	217
	O	o	226
	P	pā to pǔ	227
	Q	qī to qún	239
	R	rán to rùn	257
	S	sā to suǒ	263
	T	tā to tuǒ	303
	W	wā to wù	329
	X	xī to xùn	343
	Y	yā to yùn	363
	Z	zá to zuò	391

Notes on Looking up by Radicals	421
Standard Radical Index	423
Character Index by Radical Order	425
Notes on Looking up by Stroke Order	443
Radical Index for Stroke Order Lookup	444
Character Index by Stroke Order	446

Pronunciation Guide for Chinese Pinyin 463

INTRODUCTION

If you don't know what *zhaofa* means, but would like to, then you've picked up the right book. This is a comprehensive dictionary of Chinese martial arts terminology, with character lookup in Pinyin order from āi to zuò, Radical order from 一 to 龜, and Stroke order from 一 to 鸞.

Chinese martial arts terms use characters, words, and phrases that have meanings specific to martial artists. Sometimes, because of the oral transmission of so much of martial arts knowledge, characters are changed slightly or invented to suit the meaning of a word that everyone knew. For instance, changing the hand radical to a foot radical to indicate a technique done with the leg is much like an action normally done with the arm. This is part of what makes translating martial arts materials so much fun, and such a specialised profession. Trying to translate with only the use of a standard dictionary takes a lot of experience in the martial arts in addition to knowledge of Chinese – the martial meanings, and sometimes the characters themselves, are not there. The primary purpose of this dictionary is to give the martial arts meanings of the characters a reader will come across in a manual. A secondary purpose is to give the reader words that constantly occur in martial writings, but you can never remember, so have to look up again, like acupuncture points and dates of dynasties.

This dictionary is the culmination of almost fifty years of martial arts and language study. I started studying Chinese at the University of Victoria in about 1972, the same time I started training kungfu, and moved to Vancouver to be able to major in Chinese at the University of British Columbia and train kungfu with an excellent instructor. The Chinese course was an intensive course of modern Chinese with the practical vocabulary of the Cultural Revolution. We read newspapers, memorized Mao's speeches, and couldn't order a meal to save our lives. Fortunately, I also studied classical Chinese, which seemed a world unto itself, but turned out to be essential to the martial arts. I won a national scholarship to China, arriving in 1980, and immediately applied to the Beijing Sports University to major in wushu. The Chinese language course there consisted of my reading the wushu textbook out loud to the teacher, asking any time there was something I didn't understand. Since the only characters I couldn't read were specialised vocabulary, and he wasn't a wushu specialist, the course lasted about two weeks. From then on, my Chinese studies consisted of training, listening, reading, asking, and making notes.

My notes collected on scraps of paper and in notebooks, and years later started moving into my computer. Eventually I printed an unofficial edition of my dictionary in 2012. In this first official edition I have added a great deal more words and phrases, corrected the errors that my friends and I found in the earlier edition, and formatted as a normal Chinese dictionary, especially adding the indices to help find the characters, and a lot of cross referencing. Most of the contents are practical words – stances, strikes, kicks, controls, and throws – but there are also many words and phrases necessary to be able to read and understand a book about the martial arts. This is not just a list of words useful to me in my normal translations, or from books on my shelves. Once I decided to publish a proper dictionary I spent years working on making it as complete as possible. I made a concerted effort to find books on as many styles as possible, and spent a lot of time in the libraries in Beijing and Shanghai, learning quite a lot more as I compiled the dictionary.

This is not an encyclopedia. I do not attempt to explain why things are called the way there are or to explain the meanings. This dictionary is a tool to allow you to quickly access the words you need for your own research. I tried to define words and phrases without commentary, and with a relatively casual language, so that martial artists can enjoy and interpret for themselves. A few personal remarks slipped in, just to remind you that it is just a martial artist, not a learned committee, who has written this dictionary.

Another purpose of the dictionary is to gather together the imaginatively named *zhaofa* – moves – because of the playfulness and creativity that they show. There are too many to put them all in. They are like a secret code for each style – without having learned the move, the name only hints at the movement possibilities. During my research I found the first martial arts book I ever bought, on the tiger and crane routine that probably everybody learned at some point. Back then I had to look up Every. Single. Character. I put the entire routine in the dictionary, because it brought back to me the fun of the thing just for itself.

I hope that this dictionary will lighten the work of the next generation of translators. At the very least, it will cause less eye strain. I put the characters in a square, unpretty but functional font that has very clear strokes, and made them all large.

I also hope that anyone who wants to know more about the Chinese martial arts will enjoy flipping through the pages. Please take the time to wander through related phrases when you've looked something up. Sometimes unexpected treasures and new understandings are there waiting for you. I particularly like it when a character has clearly been written down and passed on wrong because it sounded like something else.

I've tried not to have any mistakes, but that is not possible, especially given the complexity of a dictionary. I know that there are words left out, especially for the names of moves, routines, and styles – the infinite variety made it impossible to include them all. As I find new words or make corrections, I will post a PDF addenda to the website www.thewushucentre.ca.

Andrea Mary Falk
Québec, Canada
July, 2019

Acknowledgements

Thanks to Neil Bates in Basingstoke for encouraging me to soldier on and for finding mistakes and omissions that snuck through my net during the proof-reading process. Thanks to James Saper, who yet again explained TCM terminology to me. Thanks also to Byron Jacobs in Beijing for having a look at my work in progress. And many thanks to Di Guoyong, for sharing his love of words with me over the years. Even for the word lá, which I found in his handwriting in the border of a Xingyiquan book after the 'final' proof had been printed.

And of course, infinite thanks to all my teachers for all the moves and words.

My favourite word in the dictionary is dōu. During my trip to Beijing in October 2018, when I thought I was almost done with word collection, in a training session with Lu Yan, she, in complete innocence, said, 'zhècì lánqiāng yào dōu', doing a cool sneaky kick. Just as my skills will never be perfect, and I will never know all the techniques out there, I will have mistakes and omissions in the dictionary, but it is still worth while to have a go.

Andrea Mary Falk
Québec, Canada
July, 2019

NOTES ON USING THE DICTIONARY

The order of the dictionary is by pronunciation, written in *pinyin*. The secondary order is determined thusly:

> The alphabetical order of pinyin goes by full syllable, as they represent characters. For instance, the phrase yǐn <u>jìn</u> luò kōng comes before yǐn <u>jǐng</u> because <u>*jin*</u> comes before <u>*jing*</u>, not <u>*jing*</u> before <u>*jin luo*</u>. For clarity, I have kept the *pinyin* syllables separate, as the characters are written. Normally *pinyin* is written in the appropriate full words, often linked.
>
> The tones are called 'first, second, third, and fourth', so first tone <u>jīn</u> comes first in order, then second tone <u>jín</u>, then third tone <u>jǐn</u>, and finally fourth tone <u>jìn</u>.
>
> When the pronunciation is the same, the order is by radical (see the radical chart).
>
> When the pronunciation and the radical are the same, then the order is by number of strokes, less coming before more.

When looking up from written material, and if you do not know the pronunciation of the character you see in writing, look it up using the Radical Order or Stroke Order in the back. Refer to the Character Indices by Radical Order or by Stroke Order. You need some familiarity with how to write characters in order to look them up. Use either the radical plus stroke order, or the total stroke order. To look up by Radical Order, look up the number of the radical first, then go to the radical and look up by stroke order. When the number of strokes is the same, then the list is in *pinyin* order. To look up by Stroke Order, use the stroke order table and count out the strokes. When the number of strokes is the same, the list is in radical order, then *pinyin* order. Even if you are new to Chinese characters, although looking them up takes a few steps, you soon get to know the radicals quite well and each step can be quickly done. This method is standard in Chinese to English dictionaries.

The dictionary includes both traditional and simplified characters. Within the *pinyin* index and main dictionary, the order is by the traditional characters, so they are listed first and the simplified characters follow. In the main dictionary, if the simplified differs from the traditional, it follows in square brackets, like this 單 [单]. The multi-character words and phrases are in simplified characters. Within the Character Indices, where there are two characters for one word, the traditional is first, followed by the simplified. When looking up in the Radical Order or Stroke Order Indices at the back, each character is included by its own radical and stroke order. The simplified characters are placed with the proper radical that makes most sense, I did not use the over-simplified radicals that were used for a while in China.

The final reference that I chose to confirm radical identification, number of strokes, and correspondence of simplified to traditional characters is the Far East Chinese-English Dictionary, Beijing, 1995. It is one of the few dictionaries to contain both simplified and traditional characters. It does not meld them to the extent that I have – I suspect I am the first to try to treat them equally.

There about a dozen characters that cannot be written by the computer input keyboard. I inputted them in separate parts, then condensed the parts together. They look a bit disjointed, like this 扌丐 .

Further help in looking up characters is in the Notes on Looking up Characters, just before each of the Radical and Stroke order Indices.

Abbreviations and short cuts used:
- TCM refers to Traditional Chinese Medicine.
- When cross referencing, the character is not written out when there are more than one or two repetitions of the character, a hyphen stands in for the repeated cross-referenced character. For example, "For techniques specific to the palms, see also under àn zhǎng, bǎi-, bān-, bào lián-, bào qiú-, bào yīng-..."

- 'From' means that a name or term is likely to be seen in written texts of that style. The name or term may certainly be used in other styles. Where no attribution is given, the name or term is commonly used.
- When an application is used to help describe a move, it is only one of many possibilities.

Character Index by Pinyin Order

Each column: Pinyin | Traditional character | Simplified | Page number

A — A

Pinyin	Trad	Simp	Page
āi	挨	挨	13
ǎi	矮	矮	13
ān	安	安	13
àn	按	按	13
	暗	暗	14
āo	凹	凹	14
ào	拗	拗	14

B — B

Pinyin	Trad	Simp	Page
bā	八	八	15
	巴	巴	17
	扒	扒	17
bá	拔	拔	17
bǎ	把	把	18
	鈀	钯	18
	靶	靶	18
bà	弝	弝	18
	欛把	把	18
	耙	耙	18
	霸	霸	18
bāi	掰	掰	19
bái	白	白	19
bǎi	擺	摆	22
	百	百	22
bài	敗	败	23
bān	扳	扳	23
	搬	搬	23
bǎn	板	板	24
bàn	半	半	24
	拌	拌	24
	絆	绊	24
bāng	幫	帮	25
bǎng	膀	膀	25
bàng	棒	棒	25
bāo	包	包	25
	胞	胞	25
bǎo	保	保	25
	寶	宝	25
bào	報	报	25
	抱	抱	25
	暴	暴	28
	爆	爆	28
	豹	豹	28
bēi	揹	揹	28
	臂	臂	28
běi	北	北	28
bèi	背	背	29
bēn	奔犇	奔	30
běn	本	本	30
bèn	夯笨	夯笨	30
bēng	崩	崩	30
	弸	弸	31
	繃繃	绷	31
bèng	蹦	蹦	31
bī	逼偪	逼	31
bí	鼻	鼻	31
bǐ	匕	匕	31
	彼	彼	31
	比	比	31
bì	庇	庇	32
	碧	碧	32
	避	避	32
	鉍	铋	32
	閉	闭	32
biān	編	编	32
	蝙	蝙	32
	邊	边	32
	鞭	鞭	33
biǎn	匾	匾	33
	扁	扁	33
biàn	卞	卞	33
	變	变	33
biāo	摽	摽	34
	標	标	34
	鏢	镖	34
biǎo	表	表	34
biē	憋	憋	34
bié	別	别	34
	蟞	蟞	34
biè	彆	别	34
bìn	髕	髌	35
	鬢	鬓	35
bīng	掤	掤	35
bǐng	丙	丙	35
	柄	柄	35
	秉	秉	35
bìng	並併立	并	35
bō	剝	剥	36
	撥	拨	36
	波	波	37
bó	搏	搏	37
	脖	脖	37
	鉢	钵	37
bǒ	跛	跛	37
bǔ	補	补	37
bù	不	不	37
	布	布	38
	步	步	38

C — C

Pinyin	Trad	Simp	Page
cā	擦	擦	41
cái	裁	裁	41
cǎi	採	采	41
	綵	彩	41
	踩	踩	41
cài	蔡	蔡	42
cān	參	参	42
cán	殘	残	42
cāng	蒼	苍	42
cáng	藏	藏	42
cāo	操	操	43
cè	側	侧	43
	策	策	44
cèng	蹭	蹭	44
chā	叉	叉	44
	扠	扠	44
	插	插	45
chá	查	查	46
chāi	拆	拆	46
chān	攙	搀	46
chán	禪	禅	46
	纏	缠	46
chǎn	鏟	铲	47
	闡	阐	48
cháng	嫦	嫦	48
	腸	肠	48
	裳	裳	48
	長	长	48
chǎng	場	场	49
chàng	暢	畅	49
chāo	抄	抄	49

1

Character Index by Pinyin Order

Each column: Pinyin | Traditional character | Simplified | Page number

	綽	绰	49	chǒu	丑	丑	55	cùn	寸	寸	60	dǎo	倒	倒	73
	超	超	49	chū	出	出	55	cuō	搓	搓	61		導	导	74
cháo	朝	朝	49		初	初	55		撮	撮	61		搗	捣	74
chē	車	车	50	chǔ	杵	杵	56		蹉	蹉	61	dào	倒	倒	74
chě	撦	扯	50		處	处	56	cuò	挫	挫	61		道	道	75
chè	徹	彻	50	chuāi	揣	揣	56		銼	锉	62	dé	得	得	76
	掣	掣	50	chuài	踹	踹	56		錯	错	62	dèn	扽	扽	76
	撤	撤	50	chuān	川	川	56					dēng	撑	撑	76
chēn	搋	抻	50		穿	穿	56	**D**		**D**			登	登	76
chén	晨	晨	50	chuán	傳	传	57	dā	搭	搭	63		蹬	蹬	76
	沈	沈	50	chuǎn	喘	喘	57	dá	達	达	63	děng	等	等	76
	辰	辰	51	chuàn	串	串	57	dǎ	打	打	63	dī	低	低	76
	陳	陈	51	chuǎng	闖	闯	58	dà	大	大	64		滴	滴	77
chèn	稱	称	51	chuí	垂	垂	58	dāi	呆獃	呆	67	dí	敵	敌	77
	趁	趁	51		捶搥	捶搥	58	dài	代	代	67		滌	涤	77
chēng	撐	撑	51		槌	槌	58		帶	带	67	dǐ	底	底	77
	稱	称	52		錘	锤	58		待	待	68		抵	抵	77
chéng	乘	乘	52	chūn	春	春	58		戴	戴	68		骶	骶	77
	成	成	52	chuō	戳	戳	58		袋	袋	68	dì	地	地	77
	承	承	52		踔	踔	59		逮	逮	68		的	的	78
chī	吃	吃	52	chuò	綽	绰	59	dān	丹	丹	68		第	第	78
	黐	黐	53	cǐ	跐	跐	59		單	单	68		遞	递	78
chí	持	持	53	cì	刺	刺	59		擔	担	71	diān	顛	颠	78
	遲	迟	53		次	次	59	dǎn	撣	掸	71	diǎn	典	典	78
	馳	驰	53	còu	腠	腠	59		膽	胆	71		踮	踮	78
chǐ	尺	尺	53	cuān	躥	蹿	59	dàn	彈	弹	72		點	点	79
	齒	齿	53	cuán	攢	攒	60		膻	膻	72	diàn	墊	垫	79
chì	瘛	瘛	53	cuàn	竄	窜	60	dāng	當	当	72		電	电	80
	翅翄	翅翄	53	cuī	催	催	60		襠	裆	72	diāo	刁	刁	80
	赤	赤	53		摧	摧	60	dǎng	擋	挡	72	diào	吊弔	吊	80
chōng	充	充	54	cuì	脆	脆	60	dàng	蕩盪	荡	72		掉	掉	81
	衝	冲	54	cún	存	存	60	dāo	刀	刀	73		調	调	81
chóng	重	重	54					dáo	捯	捯	73		釣	钓	81
chōu	抽	抽	54									diē	跌	跌	81

Character Index by Pinyin Order

Each column: Pinyin | Traditional character | Simplified | Page number

Pinyin	Trad	Simp	Page		Pinyin	Trad	Simp	Page		Pinyin	Trad	Simp	Page		Pinyin	Trad	Simp	Page
dié	疊	叠	81		dùn	盾	盾	89		fǎng	仿倣	仿	100			腹	腹	108
	蝶	蝶	82			鈍	钝	89		fàng	放	放	100			複	复	109
dīng	丁	丁	82			頓	顿	89		fēi	非	非	100			負	负	109
	釘	钉	82		duō	多	多	89			飛	飞	100			附	附	109
dǐng	頂	顶	83		duó	奪	夺	89		féi	腓	腓	101		**G**			**G**
	鼎	鼎	83		duǒ	躲	躲	89		fèi	肺	肺	101		gǎi	改	改	111
dìng	定	定	83		duò	剁	剁	89		fēn	分	分	102		gài	蓋	盖	111
	鋌	铤	84			挆	挆	89		fēng	封	封	103		gān	乾	干	111
diū	丟	丢	84			跺	跺	89			楓	枫	103			桿	杆	111
dōng	東	东	84								豐	丰	103			竿	竿	112
dǒng	懂	懂	84		**E**			**E**			鋒	锋	103			肝	肝	112
dòng	動	动	84		é	囮	囮	91			風	风	103		gǎn	橄	橄	112
dōu	兜	兜	85			峨峩	峨	91		fèng	縫	缝	105			趕	赶	112
dǒu	抖	抖	85			額	额	91			鳳	凤	105		gāng	岡	冈	112
	陡	陡	85			鵝鵞䳘	鹅	91		fó	佛	佛	106			剛	刚	112
dòu	鬥鬦鬪	斗	85		è	惡	恶	91		fū	敷	敷	106			扛	扛	112
dū	督	督	86			扼搤	扼	91			跗	跗	106			缸	缸	112
dú	毒	毒	86			餓	饿	91		fú	伏	伏	106			肛	肛	112
	犢	犊	86		ér	兒	儿	92			刜	刜	107		gàng	槓	杠	112
	獨	独	86		ěr	耳	耳	92			扶	扶	107		gāo	膏	膏	112
dǔ	堵	堵	87		èr	二	二	92			拂	拂	107			高	高	112
dù	杜	杜	87								服	服	107		gē	戈	戈	113
	肚	肚	87		**F**			**F**			浮	浮	107			格	格	113
duān	端	端	87		fā	發	发	95			蚨	蚨	107			歌謌	歌	113
duǎn	短	短	87		fá	乏	乏	95		fǔ	俯	俯	108			胳	胳	113
duàn	斷	断	88			伐	伐	95			府	府	108		gé	鞈	鞈	113
	段	段	88			法	法	95			弣	弣	108			格	格	113
duì	兌	兑	88		fā	翻	翻	95			斧	斧	108			膈	膈	113
	對	对	88		fǎn	反	反	97			腑	腑	108			隔	隔	114
	鐓	镦	88			返	返	99			輔	辅	108			頜	颌	114
	隊	队	88		fàn	犯	犯	99			釜	釜	108		gě	搹	搹	114
dūn	墩	墩	89		fāng	方	方	99		fù	副	副	108		gè	個	个	114
	蹲	蹲	89		fáng	防	防	99			復	复	108		gēn	根	根	114
											父	父	108					

Character Index by Pinyin Order
Each column: Pinyin | Traditional character | Simplified | Page number

	跟	跟	114		貫	贯	122		禾	禾	129	huà	化	化	142
gěn	艮	艮	114	guāng	光	光	122		和	和	129		畫	画	142
gēng	庚	庚	114	guī	歸	归	122		荷	荷	130	huái	懷	怀	142
	耕	耕	115		規	规	122		閤	阁	130		槐	槐	143
gěng	梗	梗	115		龜	龟	122		頜	颌	130		踝	踝	143
gōng	公	公	115	guǐ	癸	癸	122	hè	鶴	鹤	130	huān	驩	驩	143
	功	功	115		軌	轨	123	hēi	嘿	嘿	130	huán	環	环	143
	弓	弓	115	guì	跪	跪	123		黑	黑	130		還	还	143
	攻	攻	116	gǔn	滾	滚	123	hěn	狠	狠	132	huǎn	緩	缓	143
	肱	肱	116	gùn	棍	棍	124	hèn	恨	恨	132	huàn	換	换	143
	躬	躬	116	guó	國	国	125	hēng	哼	哼	132	huāng	慌	慌	144
gǒng	拱	拱	116		膕	腘	125	héng	恆	恒	132		肓	肓	144
	鞏	巩	116	guǒ	裹	裹	125		橫	横	132	huáng	黃	黄	144
gōu	勾	勾	117	guò	過	过	125		衡	衡	134	huǎng	晃	晃	145
	鉤	钩	117					hōng	轟	轰	134		謊	谎	145
gòu	構	构	118	**H**		**H**		hóng	洪	洪	134	huàng	晃	晃	145
gū	孤	孤	118	hā	哈	哈	127		紅	红	135	huī	揮	挥	145
gǔ	古	古	118	há	蛤	蛤	127		肛	肛	135	huí	迴	回	145
	穀	谷	118	hǎi	海	海	127		鴻	鸿	135	huì	喙	喙	146
	股	股	118	hài	亥	亥	127	hóu	喉	喉	135		會	会	146
	骨	骨	119	hán	含	含	127		猴	猴	135	hún	混	混	146
	鼓	鼓	119		寒	寒	128	hòu	後	后	136		渾	浑	147
gù	固	固	119		涵	涵	128	hū	嘑呼	呼	138		魂	魂	147
	顧	顾	119		韓	韩	128	hú	壺	壶	138	hùn	混	混	147
guā	刮	刮	119	hàn	漢	汉	128		弧	弧	138	huō	劐	劐	147
guà	掛	挂	119		頷	颔	128		蝴	蝴	138		攉	攉	147
guǎi	拐	拐	120	hāng	夯	夯	128	hǔ	虎	虎	138		秴	秴	147
guài	怪	怪	120	háng	行	行	128	hù	互	互	140		豁	豁	148
guān	觀	观	120	hāo	薅	薅	128		戶	户	140	huó	活	活	148
	關	关	121	hào	耗	耗	128		護	护	140	huǒ	火	火	148
guǎn	管	管	121		號	号	128	huā	花蘤	花	141	huò	攫	获	149
guàn	慣	惯	121	hé	合	合	128	huá	劃	划	141				
	摜	摜	121		核	核	129		華	华	141				
	灌	灌	122						滑	滑	141				

4

Character Index by Pinyin Order

Each column: Pinyin | Traditional character | Simplified | Page number

Pinyin	Trad	Simp	Page
J			
jī	基	基	151
	擊	击	151
	激	激	151
	箕	箕	151
	肌	肌	151
	雞	鸡	151
jí	急	急	152
	極	极	152
	疾	疾	152
	鈒	鈒	152
	集	集	152
jǐ	己	己	153
	戟	戟	153
	擠	挤	153
	脊	脊	153
jì	忌	忌	153
	技	技	153
	計	计	154
	記	记	154
jiā	夾	夹	154
	挾	挟	154
jiá	頰	颊	154
jiǎ	假	假	154
	甲	甲	155
	胛	胛	155
jià	架	架	155
jiān	尖	尖	156
	肩	肩	156
	間	间	157
jiǎn	剪	剪	157
	檢	检	157
	簡	简	158
	翦	翦	158
	鐧	锏	158
jiàn	劍劒劔	剑	158
	建	建	158
	濺	溅	159
	箭	箭	159
	見	见	159
	踐	践	159
	踺	踺	159
	間	间	159
jiāng	僵	僵	159
	江	江	160
jiàng	將	将	160
	降	降	160
jiāo	交	交	160
	教	教	160
	蛟	蛟	160
	跤	跤	161
	驕	骄	161
jiǎo	剿勦	剿	161
	攪	搅	161
	絞	绞	161
	腳	脚	161
	角	角	162
jiào	教	教	162
	較	较	162
jiē	接	接	163
	揭	揭	163
jié	刦劫刧	劫	163
	截	截	163
	節	节	164
jiě	解	解	164
jiè	借	借	164
jīn	斤	斤	165
	津	津	165
	筋	筋	165
	金	金	165
jǐn	緊	紧	169
	錦	锦	169
jìn	勁	劲	170
	禁	禁	170
	近	近	170
	進	进	170
jīng	京	京	171
	惊	惊	171
	睛	睛	171
	精	精	171
	經	经	171
jǐng	井	井	172
	警	警	172
	頸	颈	172
jìng	敬	敬	172
	競	竞	172
	脛	胫	172
	靜	静	173
jiū	揪	揪	173
	糾	纠	173
	鳩	鸠	173
jiǔ	九	九	173
jiù	就	就	174
	臼	臼	174
	舊	旧	174
jū	居	居	174
	拘	拘	174
jú	局	局	174
jǔ	舉	举	174
	巨	巨	175
jù	聚	聚	175
	距	距	175
	鋸	锯	175
juǎn	卷捲	卷	175
juē	撅	撅	176
jué	厥	厥	176
	抉	抉	176
	橛	橛	176
	決	决	176
	絕	绝	176
	角	角	176
juě	蹶	蹶	176
jūn	軍	军	176
K			
kā	抔	抔	177
	擖	擖	177
kǎ	卡	卡	177
kāi	開	开	177
kǎi	鎧	铠	178
kǎn	坎	坎	178
	砍	砍	178
kāng	糠	糠	178
káng	扛	扛	178
kàng	抗	抗	179
kào	靠	靠	179
kē	磕	磕	179
kě	可	可	180
kè	剋	克	180
kèn	掯	掯	180
kōng	空	空	180
kǒng	孔	孔	180
kòng	控	控	180
kōu	摳	抠	180
kǒu	口	口	181

Character Index by Pinyin Order
Each column: Pinyin | Traditional character | Simplified | Page number

kòu	扣鈕	扣	181	lǎo	老	老	187	liāo	撩	撩	196	lǔ	呂	呂	203
	敂	叩	182	lè	勒	勒	188	liáo	遼	辽	197		履	履	203
kū	枯	枯	182	lēi	勒	勒	188	liè	列	列	197		捋	捋	203
kǔ	苦	苦	182	léi	雷	雷	189		捌	捌	197		臍	臍	203
kù	庫	库	182	lèi	擂	擂	189		擸	擸	197	luán	鸞	鸾	204
kuà	挎	挎	182		肋	肋	189	līn	拎	拎	197	luàn	亂	乱	204
	胯	胯	182	lěng	冷	冷	189	lín	林	林	197	lüè	掠	掠	204
	跨	跨	183	lí	梨	梨	189		麐麟	麟	197	lūn	掄	抡	204
kuǎi	扨	扨	183		狸	狸	189	líng	凌	凌	197	lún	輪	轮	204
kuài	快	快	183		蠡	蠡	190		菱	菱	197	luō	捋	捋	205
kuān	髖	髋	183		離	离	190		靈	灵	197	luó	羅	罗	205
kuī	盔	盔	183	lǐ	李	李	190	lǐng	領	领	198		螺	螺	206
kuí	奎	奎	183		理	理	190	lìng	令	令	198	luò	絡	络	206
	魁	魁	184		禮	礼	190	liū	溜	溜	198		落	落	206
kūn	坤	坤	184		裡裏里	里	190	liú	劉	刘	199				
	昆	昆	184		鯉	鲤	191		流	流	199	**M**		**M**	
kǔn	捆	捆	184	lì	利	利	191		留	留	199	mā	媽	妈	207
kuò	廓	廓	184		力	力	191	liǔ	柳	柳	199	mǎ	馬	马	207
	闊	阔	184		厲	厉	192	liù	六	六	199	má	麻	麻	208
					立	立	192		碌	碌	200	mái	埋	埋	208
L		**L**			荔	荔	193	lóng	龍	龙	200	mài	脈衇	脉	208
lā	拉	拉	185	lián	廉	廉	193	lǒng	攏	拢	202		邁	迈	208
lá	剌	剌	185		臁	臁	193	lōu	摟	搂	202	mán	瞞	瞒	208
lán	攔	拦	185		連	连	193	lòu	漏	漏	202		蠻	蛮	208
	蘭欄	阑栏	186		鎌鐮	镰	194		露	露	202	mǎn	滿	满	208
lǎn	懶	懒	186	liǎn	斂	敛	194	lū	擼	撸	202	màn	慢	慢	208
	攬	揽	186		臉	脸	194	lú	顱	颅	202	máng	鋩	铓	209
	纜	缆	186	liàn	煉	炼	194	lǔ	擄	掳	202	mǎng	蟒	蟒	209
làn	爛	烂	186		練	练	195		櫓	橹	203	māo	貓	猫	209
láng	狼	狼	186		鏈	链	195	lù	路	路	203	máo	毛	毛	209
làng	浪	浪	187	liáng	梁	梁	195		轆	辘	203		矛	矛	209
lāo	撈	捞	187		樑	梁	195		露	露	203	mǎo	卯	卯	209
láo	勞	劳	187	liǎng	兩	两	195		鹿	鹿	203				
				liàng	亮	亮	195								

Character Index by Pinyin Order
Each column: Pinyin | Traditional character | Simplified | Page number

méi	梅	梅	209		目	目	215	nòng	弄	弄	224	pèng	搨碰	掽碰	231
	眉	眉	210		**N**	**N**		nǔ	努	努	224	pī	劈	劈	231
měi	美	美	210						弩	弩	224		批	批	232
mén	捫	扪	210	ná	拿挐	拿挐	217	nù	怒	怒	224		披	披	232
	門	门	210	nà	捺	捺	218	nǚ	女	女	224	pí	琵	琵	232
měng	猛	猛	210		納	纳	218	nuó	挪	挪	225		疲	疲	232
mī	瞇	眯	211	nǎi	乃	乃	218						皮	皮	232
mí	迷	迷	211	nài	耐	耐	218		**O**	**O**			脾	脾	232
mì	秘	秘	211	nán	南	南	218	ōu	O	O	226	pǐ	痞	痞	232
mián	綿	绵	212		男	男	218					piān	偏	偏	232
miǎn	勉	勉	212		難	难	218		**P**	**P**		piàn	片	片	233
	抿	抿	212	náo	撓	挠	218	pā	趴	趴	227		騙騙	骗	233
miáo	苗	苗	212	nǎo	腦	脑	219	pá	爬	爬	227	piāo	飄	飘	233
miǎo	秒	秒	212	nào	臑	臑	219		耙鈀	耙钯	227	piáo	瓢	瓢	233
miào	妙	妙	212	né	哪	哪	219	pāi	拍	拍	227	piǎo	瞟	瞟	233
mǐn	抿	抿	212	nèi	內	内	219	pái	排	排	228	piē,piě	撇	撇	233
	敏	敏	212	nèn	嫩	嫩	221	pài	派	派	228	píng	平	平	234
míng	名	名	212	ní	泥	泥	221	pān	攀	扳	228		瓶	瓶	235
	明	明	212	nǐ	你	你	221	pán	盤盘	盘	228		評	评	236
	瞑	瞑	212	nì	逆	逆	221		蟠	蟠	228	pō	坡	坡	236
mìng	命	命	213	niān	拈	拈	222	pàn	判	判	229		潑	泼	236
mō	摸	摸	213	nián	粘	粘	222	páng	旁	旁	229	pò	破	破	236
mó	摩	摩	213		黏	黏	222		膀	膀	229		迫迫	迫	236
	磨	磨	213	niǎn	撚	捻	222		螃	螃	229		魄	魄	236
mǒ	抹	抹	213		碾	碾	222	pāo	抛	抛	229	pū	仆	仆	236
mò	磨	磨	214		跈	跈	222	páo	刨	刨	230		撲	扑	237
	莫	莫	214	niǎo	鳥	鸟	222	pǎo	跑	跑	230		鋪	铺	238
mǔ	拇	拇	214	nie	捏	捏	222	pào	炮	炮	230	pǔ	樸	朴	238
	母	母	214	níng	凝	凝	223	pèi	沛	沛	230		譜	谱	238
	踇	踇	214		擰	拧	223	pēng	弸	弸	230				
mù	木	木	214	niú	牛	牛	223	péng	掤	掤	230		**Q**	**Q**	
	沐	沐	215	niǔ	扭	扭	224		鵬	鹏	230	qī	七	七	239
	牧	牧	215					pěng	捧	捧	230		期	期	239
													欺	欺	240

Character Index by Pinyin Order
Each column: Pinyin | Traditional character | Simplified | Page number

Pinyin	Trad	Simp	Page	Pinyin	Trad	Simp	Page	Pinyin	Trad	Simp	Page	Pinyin	Trad	Simp	Page
qí	奇	奇	240	qiè	怯	怯	248	ráo	橈	桡	257	shā	殺	杀	268
	臍	脐	240		鍥	锲	248	rào	繞	绕	257		沙	沙	268
	騎	骑	240	qín	擒	擒	249	rè	熱	热	257	shān	扇	扇	268
	麒	麒	240		秦	秦	249	rén	人	人	258		搧	搧	268
	齊	齐	241	qìn	撳	揿	249		仁	仁	258		膻	膻	269
qǐ	起	起	241	qīng	清	清	249		壬	壬	258	shǎn	閃	闪	269
qì	器	器	241		蜻	蜻	249	rěn	忍	忍	258	shāng	傷	伤	269
	棄	弃	241		輕	轻	249	rèn	任	任	258		商	商	269
	氣	气	241		青	青	249		刃	刃	258	shàng	上	上	269
qiā	掐	掐	242	qíng	擎	擎	251		韌	韧	258		尚	尚	272
qià	髂	髂	243	qǐng	請	请	251	rēng	扔	扔	258	shāo	弰	弰	272
qiān	千	千	243	qiū	丘	丘	251	rì	日	日	259		梢	梢	272
	扦	扦	243		秋	秋	251	róu	揉	揉	259	sháo	杓	杓	272
	牽	牵	243	qiú	求	求	251		柔	柔	259		芍	芍	273
qián	乾	乾	243		球毬	球	251	ròu	肉	肉	259	shǎo,shào	少	少	273
	前	前	244	qū	屈	屈	251	rú	儒	儒	260	shé	舌	舌	274
	拑	拑	245		曲麯	曲	252		如	如	260		蛇虵	蛇	274
	潛	潜	245		趨	趋	252		蠕	蠕	260	shè	射	射	274
	鉗	钳	245		軀	躯	252	rǔ	乳	乳	260	shēn	伸	伸	274
qiǎn	胁	胁	245	quān	圈	圈	252	rù	入	入	260		申	申	274
qiāng	槍	枪	246	quán	全	全	253	ruán	壖	壖	260		身	身	275
qiáng	強	强	246		拳	拳	253	also 日 inside, instead of 王				shén	神	神	275
qiǎng	強	强	246		顴	颧	254	ruǎn	軟	软	260	shěn	審	审	276
	搶	抢	246	quǎn	犬	犬	254	ruì	銳	锐	261	shèn	慎	慎	276
qiāo	蹺蹻	跷	247	quàn	勸	劝	254	rùn	潤	润	261		腎	肾	276
qiáo	樵	樵	247	quē	缺	缺	255	**S**				shēng	生	生	276
	橋	桥	247	què	雀	雀	255						聲	声	276
	翹	翘	247		鵲	鹊	255	sā,sǎ	撒	撒	263	shéng	繩	绳	276
qiǎo	巧	巧	247	qún	群	群	255	sāi	腮顋	腮	263	shī	失	失	277
qiào	撬	撬	248		裙	裙	255	sān	三	三	263		師	师	277
	撽	撽	248	**R**				sǎn	散	散	267		施	施	277
	窾	窍	248					sǎo	掃	扫	267		濕	湿	277
	鞘	鞘	248	rán	然	然	257	sēng	僧	僧	268		獅	狮	277
qiē	切	切	248	ràng	讓	让	257								

Character Index by Pinyin Order
Each column: Pinyin | Traditional character | Simplified | Page number

Pinyin	Trad	Simp	Page	Pinyin	Trad	Simp	Page	Pinyin	Trad	Simp	Page	Pinyin	Trad	Simp	Page
shí	十	十	278	shuān	栓	栓	287	suǒ	鎖	锁	302	téng	籐	藤	309
	實	实	280	shuàn	涮	涮	287						騰	腾	309
	拾	拾	280	shuāng	雙	双	288	**T**		**T**		tī	剔	剔	310
	時	时	280	shuǐ	水	水	293	tā	塌	塌	303		踢	踢	311
	石	石	281	shùn	瞬	瞬	294	tà	撻	挞	303	tí	提	提	311
	食	食	281		順	顺	294		撻	挞	303	tǐ	體	体	313
shǐ	矢	矢	281	shuō	說	说	296		踏	踏	303	tiān	天	天	313
shì	世	世	281	shuò	搠	搠	296		蹋	蹋	303	tián	填	填	315
	市	市	281		槊	槊	296	tāi	胎	胎	303		田	田	315
	勢	势	281	sī	撕	撕	296	tái	擡	抬	303	tiǎn	腆	腆	315
	式	式	282		絲	丝	296	tài	太	太	303	tiáo	條	条	315
	示	示	282	sǐ	死	死	296		泰	泰	305		調	调	315
	視	视	282	sì	四	四	296		鮐	鲐	305	tiǎo	挑	挑	315
	試	试	282		巳	巳	299	tān	攤	摊	306	tiào	跳	跳	316
shōu	收	收	282	sōng	嵩松	崧	299		癱	瘫	306	tiē	貼	贴	317
shǒu	手	手	283		鬆	松	299	tán	彈	弹	306	tiě	鐵	铁	317
	首	首	285	sǒng	聳	耸	299		潭	潭	306	tīng	聽	听	318
shòu	受	受	285	sòng	宋	宋	299		罈	坛	306	tíng	停	停	319
	獸	兽	285		送	送	300		錟	铩	306	tǐng	挺	挺	319
shū	樞	枢	285	sōu	搜	搜	300		鐔	镡	306	tōng	通	通	319
	殳	殳	285	sū	蘇	苏	300	tàn	探	探	306	tóng	同	同	319
	腧	腧	285	sù	宿	宿	300	tāng	蹚	蹚	307		瞳	瞳	319
	舒	舒	285		素	素	300	táng	堂	堂	307		童	童	320
	輸	输	285		速	速	300		唐	唐	307		筒	筒	320
shǔ	暑	暑	286	suān	酸	酸	300		膛	膛	307	tǒng	捅	捅	320
	蜀	蜀	286	suí	隋	隋	300		螳	螳	307	tōu	偷媮	偷	320
	鼠	鼠	286		隨	随	300	tǎng	躺	躺	308	tóu	頭	头	320
shù	束	束	286	suǐ	髓	髓	301		銻	锑	308	tòu	透	透	321
	樹	树	286	suì	碎	碎	301	tàng	趟	趟	308	tū	凸	凸	321
	竪	竖	286	sūn	孫	孙	301	tāo	掏	掏	308		突	突	321
	術	术	286	suō	娑	娑	301	táo	淘	淘	309	tú	圖	图	321
shuāi	摔	摔	286		縮	缩	301		陶	陶	309		徒	徒	321
shuǎi	甩	甩	287					tào	套	套	309	tǔ	吐	吐	321
shuài	率	率	287					tè	特	特	309				

Character Index by Pinyin Order
Each column: Pinyin | Traditional character | Simplified | Page number

Pinyin	Trad	Simp	Page	Pinyin	Trad	Simp	Page	Pinyin	Trad	Simp	Page	Pinyin	Trad	Simp	Page
	土	土	322	wēi	偎	偎	332	**X**					梟	枭	350
tù	兔	兔	322	wéi	圍	围	332						消	消	350
tuán	團	团	322		維	维	332	xī	吸	吸	343		銷	销	350
tuī	推	推	322		韋	韦	333		扱	扱	343	xiǎo	小	小	350
tuǐ	腿骸	腿	323	wěi	委	委	333		犀	犀	343	xiào	笑	笑	352
tuì	退	退	324		尾	尾	333		膝	膝	343	xiē	楔	楔	353
tūn	吞	吞	325	wèi	喂	喂	333		西	西	344		歇	歇	353
tún	囤	囤	325		未	未	333		郗	郗	344		蠍	蝎	353
	臀	臀	325		胃	胃	333	xí	襲	袭	344	xié	協	协	353
tùn	褪	褪	325		衛	卫	334	xǐ	喜	喜	344		挾	挟	353
tuō	托託	托	325		魏	魏	334		洗	洗	344		攜	携	353
	拖	拖	327	wēn	溫	温	334	xì	細	细	344		斜	斜	353
	脫	脱	327	wén	文	文	334	xiā	蝦	虾	345		脇脅	胁	354
tuó	砣鉈	砣铊	327	wěn	吻	吻	334	xiá	俠	侠	345		邪	邪	354
	駝	驼	327		穩	稳	334		暇	暇	345	xiè	卸	卸	354
	鼉	鼍	327	wèn	搵	揾	334		狹	狭	345		蟹蠏	蟹	354
tuǒ	橢	椭	328		問	问	334	xià	下	下	345	xīn	心	心	354
				wō	撾	挝	335		夏	夏	347		新	新	355
W					窩	窝	335	xiān	仙僊	仙	347		辛	辛	355
				wò	握	握	335		先	先	348	xìn	信	信	355
wā	哇	哇	329		臥	卧	335		掀	掀	348		囟顖	囟	356
	挖	挖	329		屋	屋	336	xián	弦	弦	349		芯	芯	356
wǎ	瓦	瓦	329	wū	烏	乌	336	xiǎn	顯	显	349	xíng	形	形	356
wāi	抓	抓	329	wú	吳	吴	337	xiàn	獻	献	349		行	行	356
	揺	揺	329		無	无	337		陷	陷	349	xiōng	胸臅	胸	357
	歪	歪	329		蜈	蜈	338	xiāng	相	相	349	xióng	熊	熊	357
wài	外	外	329	wǔ	五	五	338		香	香	349		雄	雄	357
wān	彎	弯	331		午	午	339	xiáng	祥	祥	349	xiū	休	休	357
wán	完	完	331		捂	捂	339		降	降	349		修脩	修	357
wǎn	挽輓	挽	332		武	武	339	xiàng	嚮向	向	349	xiù	袖	袖	357
wàn	腕	腕	332		舞	舞	341		相	相	350	xū	戌	戌	358
	萬	万	332	wù	悟	悟	341		象	象	350		虛	虚	358
wáng	王	王	332		戊	戊	341		項	项	350	xù	續	续	358
wàng	望	望	332		誤	误	341	xiāo	削	削	350		蓄	蓄	358

Character Index by Pinyin Order

Each column: Pinyin | Traditional character | Simplified | Page number

Pinyin	Trad	Simp	Page
xuān	宣	宣	359
xuán	懸	悬	359
	旋	旋	359
	玄	玄	359
	璇	璇	359
xuǎn	選	选	360
xuàn	眩	眩	360
	鏇	旋	360
xué	學	学	360
	穴	穴	361
xuě	雪	雪	361
xuè	血	血	361
xūn	薰	薰	361
xún	尋	寻	361
	循	循	361
xùn	巽	巽	361
	訓	训	361

Y ——— Y

Pinyin	Trad	Simp	Page
yā	壓	压	363
	鴉鵶	鸦	363
	鴨	鸭	363
yá	牙	牙	364
yǎ	啞	哑	364
yān	咽	咽	364
yán	研	研	364
	閻	阎	364
yǎn	偃	偃	364
	掩	掩	364
	演	演	365
	眼	眼	365
yàn	燕鷰	燕	365
	雁鴈	雁	366
yáng	佯	佯	366
	揚	扬	366
	楊	杨	367
	羊	羊	367
	陽	阳	367
yǎng	仰	仰	368
	養	养	368
	腰	腰	368
yāo	腰	腰	368
yáo	搖	摇	370
yǎo	齩	咬	370
yào	要	要	370
	鷂	鹞	370
yē	掖	掖	371
yě	野	野	371
yè	亱	夜	372
	液	液	372
	腋	腋	372
	葉	叶	372
yī	一	一	373
	醫	医	374
yí	拸	拸	374
	移	移	374
yǐ	乙	乙	374
	以	以	375
	倚	倚	375
yì	億	亿	375
	意	意	375
	易	易	376
	嗌	嗌	376
	義	义	376
	翳	翳	376
	藝	艺	376
	譩	譩	376
	殹	殹	376
yīn	陰	阴	377
yín	寅	寅	378
	銀	银	378
	齦	龈	378
yǐn	引	引	378
	隱	隐	378
yìn	印	印	378
yīng	應	应	378
	膺	膺	379
	鶯	莺	379
	鷹	鹰	379
	鸚	鹦	379
yíng	營	营	379
	迎	迎	379
yìng	硬	硬	381
yōng	擁	拥	381
yǒng	勇	勇	381
	永	永	381
	泳	泳	381
	涌	涌	381
	詠	咏	381
yòng	用	用	381
yōu	幽	幽	381
	悠	悠	382
yóu	游遊	游	382
yǒu	有	有	382
	酉	酉	382
yòu	右	右	382
	誘	诱	382
	瘀	瘀	382
yū	迂	迂	383
yú	漁	渔	383
	隅	隅	383
	餘	余	383
	魚	鱼	383
yǔ	羽	羽	383
yù	彧	彧	383
	御禦	御	384
	玉	玉	384
	慾	欲	385
	預	预	385
yuān	淵	渊	385
	鴛	鸳	385
yuán	元	元	386
	原	原	386
	圓	圆	386
	援	援	386
	猿猨	猿	386
	轅	辕	387
yuǎn	遠	远	387
yuè	岳嶽	岳	387
	月	月	388
	躍	跃	388
	鉞	钺	388
yūn	暈	晕	388
yún	紜	纭	388
	耘	耘	388
	雲	云	389
yùn	暈	晕	390
	運	运	390
	韻	韵	390

Z ——— Z

Pinyin	Trad	Simp	Page
zá	砸	砸	391
	雜	杂	391
zāi	栽	栽	391
zài	載	载	391
zǎn	攢	攒	391

Character Index by Pinyin Order

Each column: Pinyin | Traditional character | Simplified | Page number

Pinyin	Trad	Simp	Page	Pinyin	Trad	Simp	Page	Pinyin	Trad	Simp	Page	Pinyin	Trad	Simp	Page
zàn	暫	暂	391	zhē	遮	遮	396		忠	忠	405	zhǔn	準	准	411
	鏨	錾	391	zhé	折摺	折	396		鐘	钟	406	zhuō	拙	拙	411
zàng	臟	脏	391		蟄	蛰	396	zhòng	中	中	406		捉	捉	411
zào	燥	燥	391		輒	辄	396		重	重	406	zhuó	啄	啄	411
	造	造	391	zhēn	真	真	397	zhōu	周週	周	406		斫	斫	411
zè	仄	仄	391	zhěn	枕	枕	397		搊	搊	406		濁	浊	411
zhā	扎紮	扎	392	zhèn	震	震	397	zhóu	軸	轴	406		着	着	411
	揸	揸	392	zhēng	爭	争	397	zhǒu	肘	肘	406	zǐ	子	子	411
zhá	閘	闸	392	zhěng	拯	拯	397	zhū	朱	朱	407		紫	紫	412
zhà	乍	乍	392		撜	撜	397		柱	柱	407		釨	釨	412
	炸	炸	392		整	整	397		諸	诸	407	zì	字	字	412
	詐	诈	392	zhèng	掙	挣	397		豬	猪	407		自	自	412
zhāi	摘	摘	392		正	正	398	zhú	竹	竹	407	zōng	宗	宗	413
zhān	粘	粘	392		靜	静	399	zhǔ	主	主	407		綜	综	413
	霑	沾	393	zhī	之	之	399		拄	拄	407	zǒng	總	总	413
	黏	黏	393		支	支	400	zhù	注	注	407	zòng	縱	纵	413
zhǎn	展	展	393		肢	肢	400		筑築	筑	407	zǒu	走	走	413
	斬	斩	393	zhí	直	直	400	zhuā	抓	抓	407	zú	足	足	414
zhàn	占佔	占	393		蹠	蹠	401		撾	挝	408	zǔ	阻	阻	415
	戰	战	393	zhǐ	只	只	401	zhuǎ	爪	爪	408	zuān	躦	躜	415
	站	站	393		指	指	401	zhuāi	拽	拽	408		鑽	钻	415
	顫	颤	394		止	止	403	zhuān	甎	砖	408	zuàn	攥	攥	416
zhāng	張	张	394		紙	纸	403	zhuǎn	轉	转	408	zuǐ	嘴	嘴	416
	章	章	394		趾	趾	403	zhuàn	傳	传	409	zuì	最	最	416
zhǎng	掌	掌	394	zhì	志	志	403		轉	转	409		醉	醉	416
zhàng	丈	丈	395		擲	掷	403	zhuāng	樁	桩	409	zūn	鐏	鐏	417
	仗	仗	395		智	智	403		裝	装	409	zuǒ	左	左	417
	杖	杖	395		治	治	403	zhuàng	撞	撞	410	zuò	作	作	417
zhāo	招	招	395		滯	滞	403		狀	状	410		坐	坐	418
	着	着	395		秩	秩	403	zhuī	追	追	410				
zhǎo	爪	爪	395		室	室	403		錐	锥	410				
zhào	照炤	照	395		至	至	403	zhuì	墜	坠	411				
	趙	赵	395		製	制	403	zhūn	肫	肫	411				
				zhōng	中	中	403								

A

挨 (rad.64) **āi**　1. To be or get close to. 2. Close range techniques in general. 3. In wrestling, to lean on, a throwing technique. 4. To get in very close to the adversary's torso for a short strike, often used for a throw or control. From Bajiquan, one of its ten major techniques, see also shí dà jī fǎ.

āi shēn pào 挨身炮 Close Range Barrage: one of Xingyiquan's traditional partner routines, common to many branches, develops close range techniques, written up as twenty-one to twenty-three moves. Also called ān shēn pào.

矮 (rad.111) **ǎi**　Short of stature; low.

ǎi gōng bù 矮弓步 Low bow stance, the hip joint well set in and the torso often leaning onto the thigh. See also gōng bù.

ǎi zhuāng 矮桩 Low stake standing posture.

安 (rad.40) **ān**　1. Peaceful, calm. 2. At ease. 3. To pacify. 4. To arrange.

ān shēn pào 安身炮 Keep the Body Safe Barrage, see āi shēn pào.

按 (rad.64) **àn**　1. To push down with one or two hands, usually with the palm facing down: the technique is used to shut down an adversary. 2. To press forward, up then down, or down then up. 3. While taking the pulse, to press while looking for tenderness in the channels. From TCM. 4. To push down, one of the falling hands in Chuojiao, see also luò shǒu.

àn dāo 按刀 Press down with a broadsword, the left hand pressing on the spine of the blade or on the right wrist, edge down or pressing down with the flat of the blade.

àn fǎ 按法 Pressing methods 1. A twisting press, firm but not to the point of pain. From TCM. 2. As joint control or manipulation, to press down sharply with the palm against the natural movement of a joint.

àn jìn 按劲 The power and skill used to do a press forward and down, usually first controlling an adversary then pushing away.

àn ná fǎ 按拿法 Pressing grappling hold: press down on an adversary's arm to direct his attention there, in preparation for another attack. From wrestling.

àn qiú zhuāng 按球桩 Press the ball standing: standing up in an open stance, press the hands down at belly height as if pushing a ball down in water, an internal training stake standing of Taijiquan and other styles.

àn shì 按势 Pressing-down posture: sit into empty stance and push down with both palms. From Wu Taijiquan.

àn shǒu 按手 Press, push; double-handed push.

àn tán shì lì 按弹试力 Press and spring testing power: stand in sixty-forty stance with the palms facing down, alternating raising and lowering tha hands, feeling as if they are on springs. From Yiquan, one of its combat testing moves.

àn tiān gǔ 按天鼓 Press Down the Celestial Drum: a head lock. From behind, bring your hands up under your adversary's armpits and wrap them around his neck, pushing his head down.

àn tóu duàn jǐng 按头断颈 Press down the head to break the neck: move into an incoming attack, reaching around to grab the adversary's back and gouging his eyes with the other hand, pushing his head back.

àn zài yāo gōng 按在腰功 The key to the power and efficiency of the press down lies in the waist and back. A martial saying.

àn zhǎng 按掌 1. Press down with the palm or both palms. 2. Press down. From Baguazhang, one of its set circle-walking positions. See xià chén zhǎng. Also called shuāng àn zhǎng.

àn zhǒu 按肘 Press down with the elbow in close grappling situations.

àn zhù 按住 Press and control.

A

暗 (rad.72) àn Dark; obscure; covert.

àn dù chén cāng 暗渡陈仓 Take a Hidden Ford by way of Chencang: pretend to take one path while taking another. The eighth of the Thirty-six Stratagems of Warfare, which apply to many situations.

àn dù jīn zhèn 暗渡金针 Take a Hidden Ford with a Golden Needle: step forward with a large slicing action, continue the large circle to the rear, then drop to a cross legged stance and bring the sword through to snap up in the direction of travel. From Qingping sword.

àn jìn 暗劲 Hidden power. 1. A soft, supple application of power, light and coordinated power without recourse to strength. 2. Power within the body that is hidden from view.

àn qì 暗器 Hidden weapon: small weapons such as throwing knives, darts, metal balls.

àn tuǐ fǎ 暗腿法 Hidden leg techniques: kicks hidden in stepping. From Baguazhang. See tào tuǐ, gōu tuǐ, cuō tuǐ, cǎi jiǎo, and chuài tuǐ, among others. See also míng tuǐ fǎ.

àn yǎn fǎ 暗眼法 Hidden look method: to appear to be looking at obvious targets on an adversary, while actually looking for unprotected areas and weaknesses in defense.

凹 (rad.17) āo Concave, hollow, depressed, dented.

拗 (rad.64) ào 1. Bent, warped; bend or twist as to break. 2. Put a joint into an awkward position in controlling methods. An alternate dialect pronunciation is ǎo.

ào bù 拗步 Reverse stance, counter stance, offset stance; counter step, opposite step. 1. In most styles, a bow stance or step into stance with the opposite hand and foot forward. 2. In styles based on a sixty-forty stance, it is a sixty-forty stance with the opposite hand and foot forward. 3. A turned stance, a cross stance with the attention to the rear direction. 4. An empty stance with the opposite hand and foot forward.

ào bù mái fú 拗步埋伏 Reverse Stance Ambush. 1. A sharp turn from a bow stance to a reverse stance, bringing the blade around quickly to stab. 2. A drop from a straight stand into a reverse bow stance, intercepting across with the blade. Both from Qingping sword.

ào bù qiān jì 拗步谦计 A Modest Idea in Reverse Stance: in reverse bow stance, reach out the blade to stab to the front with the hand turned over, palm out. From Qingping sword.

ào dān biàn 拗单鞭 A reverse single whip: in a reverse bow stance, the arms extended at shoulder height in a relatively straight line, one forward one back. See dān biàn.

ào gōng bù 拗弓步 A reverse bow stance: see ào bù.

ào luán zhǒu 拗鸾肘 Obstinate Luan (a mythical bird) Elbow. 1. With the hands on the forearms, strike to the side with the elbow. From Chen Taijiquan. 2. In reverse bow stance, strike with the elbows bent, one forearm horizontal, the other elbow at its fist and angled in front of the chest. From Wudangquan. See also luán.

ào qiāng 拗枪 A half-circle vertically forward and up with a spear, releasing the hand.

ào shì 拗势 Position based on a reverse stance, opposite stance (opposite hand and foot forward).

ào shǒu 拗手 To face off with a practice or sparring partner with the same hands touching (right touching right or left touching left).

B

八 (rad.12) bā 1. Eight. 2. Often used in movement names to refer to the shape of the character.

bā bā liù shí sì zhǎng 八八六十四掌 Eight (times) Eight Sixty-four Palms. See liù shí sì shǒu. Also called bā duàn liù shí sì zhǎng, zhí tàng liù shí sì zhǎng.

bā bù táng láng quán 八步螳螂拳 Babu (eight step) Tanglangquan, a branch of Preying Mantis style, which specialises in close techniques.

bā dǎ bā bù dǎ 八打八不打 Eight allowed targets and eight disallowed targets. The eight allowed targets that hurt a lot are: between the eyebrows, the top of the lips, the ears, the shoulder blades, the ribs, the bone near the groin, the knee, and hitting any bone hard. The eight targets that do too much damage and so are disallowed are: the acupoint Taiyang at the temple, full on the chest plate, the walls in the body core, the ends of the floating ribs, the groin, the kidneys, the coccyx, and the ear openings. This is not competition rules, but rules of conduct.

bā dà zhǎng 八大掌 Eight great palms: eight palm changes to practice the principles and techniques of Baguazhang. Also called lǎo bā zhǎng, mǔ zhǎng.

bā dà zhāo 八大招 Eight main methods: The eight main concepts of Bajiquan, each containing a variety of techniques.

bā duǎn 八短 Eight short. 1. Eight short elbow strikes to eight sensitive parts of the body, see bèi zhǒu, bì zhǒu, bó zhǒu, gǔ zhǒu, tóu zhǒu, xié zhǒu, zuǐ zhǒu. From Tanglangquan 2. Eight close range techniques, see also dūn shēn bó chuí, kào shēn tún chuí, liǎng zhǒu liǎng xī sì chuí, yíng miàn tóu chuí, zhān ná xiōng chuí. From Tanglangquan.

bā duǎn zhī qiáng 八短之强 The strength of the eight short techniques. From Tanglangquan. See also qī cháng zhī qiǎo.

bā duàn jǐn 八段锦 Baduanjin (eight pieces of brocade), an internal strength training method, consisting of eight exercises.

bā duàn liù shí sì zhǎng 八段六十四掌 Eight sections, Sixty-four Palms. See liù shí sì shǒu. Also called bā bā liù shí sì zhǎng, zhí tàng liù shí sì zhǎng.

bā fǎ 八法 The eight methods: the eight basic skill sets that need to be mastered in any style. Hand techniques, eyes, body work, legs, spirit, *qi* control (some lists say breathing), strength, and effectiveness.

bā fān quán 八翻拳 Bafanquan (eight rolls fist), a style from Shandong province, developed during the Song dynasty. Also called bā shǎn fān, bā fān shǒu.

bā fān shǒu 八翻手 See bā fān quán.

bā fāng 八方 The eight directions: Four cardinal and four non-cardinal directions: East, West, South, North, South-west, North-west, North-east, South-east.

bā fēn jiàn quán 八分箭拳 Eight Parts Arrow Punch: from a right bow stance, sit to a horse stance and punch the right fist to the side with an upright fist, pulling the left to the waist. The 55th move of the tiger and crane routine.

bā fēng 八风 Extraordinary acupoint Bafeng (eight winds), EX-LE10. Four points at the foot (with two feet, eight altogether), at each web between the toes, where the darker skin meets the lighter skin. From TCM.

bā guà chuí 八卦捶 See bā guà quán.

bā guà dāo 八卦刀 Bagua broadsword, a single-edged sword about the length from floor to solar plexus or up to head height, with a handgrip about a foot long, and a blade that curves towards the end. The weight is usually as heavy as the player can handle.

bā guà gǔn shǒu dāo 八卦滚手刀 Bagua Rolling broadsword, a routine of Baguazhang, written up as thirty-two moves.

bā guà lián huán duì dāo 八卦连环对刀 Bagua

B

Connected partner broadsword, a partner routine of Baguazhang, written up as twenty-five moves.

bā guà quán 八卦拳 Baguaquan (eight trigrams fist), a style from Shandong province, developed during the Qing dynasty. Also called bā guà chuí.

bā guà tuǐ 八卦腿 Eight Trigrams kick: first do a hook kick from a half squat, retract the leg while standing up, then do a side kick. From Chuojiao.

bā guà yóu shēn lián huán zhǎng 八卦游身连环掌 Bagua Swimming Continuous Palms: a Baguazhang routine, written up as thirty-five moves.

bā guà zhàn shēn qiāng 八卦战身枪 Bagua Battle spear, a spear routine of Baguazhang, written up as sixty-four moves.

bā guà zhǎng 八卦掌 Baguazhang (eight trigrams palm), a style attributed to Dong Haichuan and first taught in Beijing in the mid 1880s. Based on walking and applying power while moving. Originally called zhuàn zhǎng.

bā guà zhuàn jiàn 八卦转剑 Bagua Turning sword: circle-walking and eight changes done with a sword. From Baguazhang.

bā guà zhuàn qiāng 八卦转枪 Bagua Turning spear: circle-walking and eight changes done with a spear. From Baguazhang.

bā guà zhuāng 八卦桩 Bagua stake standing. 1. Varies with style, may be sitting in a partial squat with the knees together, hands in front of the chest with palms in and fingers touching. 2. See zhuàn zhǎng shì.

bā jī 八击 Eight strikes, the eight targets of the staff: the head, the ears, the collarbones, the ribs, the solar plexus, the groin, the thighs, and the instep of the feet.

bā jí quán 八极拳 Bajiquan (eight extremes fist), developed in Hebei province, with forceful, straight forward, practical movements that include many short-range techniques. Also called bā jì quán, bā jì quán, bā zi quán, kāi mén quán, kāi quán.

bā jì quán 八忌拳 Bajiquan (eight dreaded fist), see bā jí quán.

bā jì quán 八技拳 Bajiquan (eight skills fist), see bā jí quán.

bā jiè qiē guā 八戒切瓜 Eight Rings Cut the Melon: chop down with both hands, pulling one back to the waist. From Shaolinquan.

bā mén 八门 The eight gates: the eight main techniques of Taijiquan. See also àn, cǎi, jǐ, kào, liè, lǚ, péng, zhǒu.

bā mén quán 八门拳 Bamenquan (eight gates fist), an old style from the western provinces of Gansu, Ningxia, Qinghai, and Xinjiang.

bā mén wǔ bù 八门五步 The eight gates and five stances. From Taijiquan. See bā mén, wǔ bù.

bā pán dāo 八盘刀 Eight basin broadsword: a curved, one edged blade a bit thicker than a normal broadsword.

bā pán tuǐ 八盘腿 The eight basin kicks, a series of short routines of Chuojiao. See also shàng pán tuǐ, xià pán tuǐ, zhōng pán tuǐ.

bā quán 八拳 The eight fists: see bā mén.

bā shǎn fān 八闪翻 See bā fān quán.

bā shí yī shì 八十一式 The Eighty-one moves, a Yang Taijiquan routine.

bā shì 八势 The Eight postures. See bā shì quán.

bā shì quán 八势拳 The Eight postures routine, a Xingyiquan routine. Written up as forty-two moves, made up of eight combinations, repeated out and back. Also called bā shì.

bā tǐ 八体 The eight parts of the body that play a key role in movement: top of the head, groin, heart, eyes, ears, hands, feet, waist.

bā xiān 八仙 The eight immortals, often used in movement and style names. Common in folklore, they are Cao Guojiu, Han Xiangzi, Han Zhongli, He Xiangu, Lan Caihe, Li Tieguai, Lü Dongbin, and Zhang Guolao.

bā xié 八邪 Extraordinary acupoint Baxie (eight evils), EX-UE9. At the back of the hand, four points, at the webs between the fingers, where the dark skin meets the lighter skin (eight points altogether, counting both hands). From TCM.

bā yào 八要 The eight essentials, body positioning requirements of Xingyiquan. See bào, chuí, dǐng, kòu, mǐn, qū, tǐng, yuán.

bā zhǎn dāo 八斩刀 1. Eight hacking blade, a short sabre with a broad blade and full hand guards. Commonly used as a pair. Called butterfly knives in English. A weapon used mainly in southern styles. 2. Eight hacking blades, the eight main techniques of the butterfly knives. From Wing Chun.

bā zhèn 八阵 Eight arrays, or formations. Refers to the formations of the eight trigrams, as they relate to natural phenomenon. Qián relates to the heavenly formation, kūn relates to the earthly formation, xùn relates to the wind formation, kǎn relates to the cloud formation, zhèn relates to the flying dragon formation, duì relates to the tiger flank formation, lī relates to the circling bird formation, and gèn relates to the coiling snake formation.

bā zì bù 八字步 Character eight stance: feet placed in the shape of a Chinese character eight (八), usually a foot-length apart, sitting on both legs, knees aligned with the feet. Toes inwards is dào bā zì bù or zhèng bā zì bù; toe to heel is fǎn bā zì bù.

bā zì gōng 八字功 The eight word skill: methods of Xingyiquan, mostly done as separate drills. See dǐng, guǒ, jié, kuà, lǐng, tiǎo, yún, zhǎn.

bā zì gōng fáng fǎ zé 八字攻防法则 The eight attack and defense models. See bī, dǎ, piàn, ràng, shǎn, suí, tàn, yíng.

bā zì jué 八字诀 The eight characters formula, a verse describing the essentials of Xingyiquan posture. See also bào, chuí, dǐng, kòu, mǐn, qū, tǐng yuán.

bā zì kòu bù 八字扣步 Character eight step. Step one foot hooked in to form a character eight stance with the other foot. See also bā zì bù.

bā zì mǎ bù 八字马步 Character eight horse stance: a horse stance with the feet turned slightly out.

bā zì zhǎng 八字掌 Character eight palm: a palm shape. 1. In some styles the index finger and thumb spread open to form the character eight 八, the other fingers bent. When in this shape it is also called lín jiǎo zhǎng, yáng jiǎo zhǎng. 2. The four fingers are straight and the thumb is spread open to form the character eight. From Duanquan and Chuojiao.

bā zì zhǐ 八字指 Character eight finger palm shape. From Chuojiao. See #2 of bā zì zhǎng.

巴 (rad.49) bā   1. Open, spread. 2. Close to, next to. 3. Stick to. 4. The Ba state, during the Zhou dynasty see also zhōu. 5. Abbreviation for eastern Sichuan province.

bā zǐ quán 巴子拳 Baziquan (close fist), see bā jí quán.

扒 (rad.64) bā   1. To cling onto with hands like raking. 2. To cling to, rake, a raking grab.

bā jiǎo 扒脚 Cling on with the feet: when in difficulty in close quarters, hook the feet around the legs of an adversary.

bā jìn 扒劲 Raking power. Front foot landing power. From Baguazhang and Xingyiquan.

bā lì 扒力 Raking power. See bā jìn.

拔 (rad.64) bá   1. To spread open, pull out. 2. To suck out; draw. 3. To pull up out of the ground. 4. To chose; select.

bá bèi 拔背 Expand the upper back.

bá bù 拔步 Uprooting step: from a horse stance, lift one knee then jump up, tucking the feet up into the groin, turning one-eighty degrees to land with the feet having switched places.

bá chū gōng 拔出功 Uprooting training: to pull up on a tree, about ten centimetres around, regularly every day, trying to uproot it. This can be done with a planted wooden or iron pole. This develops grip strength, wrist and arm strength.

bá dīng gōng 拔钉功 Pull out the nail training: a hard skills training drill. Pull up nails planted into a board, using the fingers.

bá dǐng 拔顶 Hold the neck straight to lift the top of the head.

bá gēn 拔跟 Uprooting the heel. 1. Letting the heel come off the ground in a stance where it is supposed to be set down. An error in most styles. 2. In Baguazhang, the error of letting the heel come up when stepping, instead of picking up the foot flatly.

bá gùn 拔棍 Open up the staff: in a bow stance, strike strongly with both hands out to the left side, tucking the shaft onto the body under the left armpit.

bá shān gōng 拔山功 Pull Up the Mountain

B

training. 1. Plant an eight-foot-long pole about three feet into the ground. The daily practice is to try to pull it out of the ground. 2. Often exercises that also train grip strength, such as lifting jars, are also called this.

bá shù jiù zhǔ 拔树救主 Pull Up the Tree to Save the Master: a straight filing cut. Step into a left bow stance and turn the sword blade to be able to do a filing cut at an angle in front, to cut an adversary's arm and prepare to stab in the belly. From Qingping sword.

bá shù shì lì 拔树试力 Pull up the tree testing power: stand, bring the hands up in front of the chest, palms facing each other, then press down, palms down. The feeling is like pulling up a tree then pushing it down. From Yiquan, one of its combat testing moves.

bá tiào 拔跳 Pulling out jumps: stand absolutely straight with the hands at the sides and jump up without bending the knees or hips.

bá zhǎng 拔掌 Spread out: with the arm slightly bent, rotate and bend the wrist to hook outwards to deflect a low attack.

把 (rad.64) bǎ   1. To hold, grasp; control. 2. Grabbing techniques. 3. Pronounced bà, the grip of a weapon, see bà.

鈀 [钯] (rad.167) bǎ   1. A rake. 2. A long handled weapon with a hard, flat rake end. Usually pronounced pá.

靶 (rad.177) bǎ   1. A target. 2. Hand-held target pads used in sparring training.

弝 (rad.57) bà   The arc of a bow, the central part of the bow grasped by the hand.

bà bèi 弝背 Hold the upper back slightly rounded as if it is the centre of a bow, with the hands forming the tips of the bow. A requirement in many styles, though more commonly described as bá bèi or yuán bèi.

把 欛 (rad. 64, 75) [把] (rad.64) bà   1. Hilt, handle, handgrip, grip of a short weapon. 2. Base of a long weapon. 3. Measurement of one hand width. 4. Character 把, pronounced bǎ, to grip, see bǎ.

bà duàn 把段 Aft-section of a long weapon, the quarter or third of the shaft nearest the butt.

bà fǎ 把法 1. Methods of gripping a weapon, changing to a grip appropriate to the action of the weapon. 2. Methods of using the base of a long weapon or the handgrip of a short weapon to strike or block.

bà wèi 把位 Grip placement. 1. The position of the hands on the shaft of a long weapon, which determines the effectiveness of the use of the weapon. 2. The placement of the hands to grab on an adversary in wrestling, which determines to a great extent the effectiveness of the throw.

耙 (rad.127) bà   1. A harrow, a tined plough. 2. To draw a harrow over a field. Pronounced pá, a rake; to smooth with a rake.

bà ná 耙拿 A harrow and grab throw: hook an adversary's ankle with yours, then grab it and pull up.

bà zǐ 耙子 A harrowing throw: hook your adversary's lower leg with your foot and push on his shoulder, switching his leg to your hand so you can lift the leg. Also called lǐ gòu jiǎo.

霸 (rad.173) bà   1. A leader of feudal lords. 2. Tyrant, despot, bully.

bà wáng 霸王 Hegemon King. 1. In movement names, the type of movement often channels the legendary viciousness and strength of the lord of Chu, during the Han dynasty. 2. The Hegemon King Xiang Yu, 232-202 BC.

bà wáng kāi gōng 霸王开弓 Tyrant Pulls a Bow. 1. Pull out an adversary's arm to strike with the elbow to the ribs under it. From Baguazhang. 2. Horse stance bracing palm. From Piguaquan.

bà wáng kǔn zhǒu 霸王捆肘 Tyrant Binds the Elbow. 1. Strike with the elbow, forearm vertical, holding the other hand at the elbow. 2. Strike with the elbow, forearm horizontal, holding the wrist with the other hand.

bà wáng kǔn zhū 霸王捆猪 Tyrant Binds the Pig: tie up an adversary's arms by pulling and crossing them, to enable punching over. From Baguazhang.

bà wáng jǔ dǐng 霸王举鼎 Tyrant Holds up the Pot: sitting in horse stance, push up over the head with the elbows bent, index fingers extended and pointing to each other. The 23rd move of the tiger and crane routine.

bà wáng liàng xuē 霸王亮靴 Tyrant Flashes his Boots: spin and stamp with swinging chopping arms. From Tongbeiquan.

bà wáng sòng kè 霸王送客 Tyrant Sees off a Guest: pull your adversary's arm down and back to jam it, then use it to push him away, twisting the elbow to lock it out. From Baguazhang, one of its sixty-four hands.

bà wáng tuī dǐng 霸王推鼎 Tyrant Pushes the Pot: push your adversary's jaw with one hand, while holding into his lower back with the other, to take him back. From Qinna.

bà wáng tuō kuī 霸王脱盔 Tyrant Casts off the Helmet. 1. An arm bar and takedown in response to a grab to the neck. From Shaolinquan. 2. Take a kicking step forward and lift with the hands up close to the chest, then reach out and pull down to the belly, and finally come back up and punch forward with backfists. From Wudangquan.

bà wáng yìng zhé jiāng 霸王硬折繮 Tyrant Pulls Firmly on the Reins: to press or hit the arm, shoulder, head or back, combining a grip with a strike, and combining softness with hardness. From Bajiquan, one of its eight main concepts, see also bā dà zhāo.

bà wáng yí dǐng 霸王移鼎 Tyrant Moves the Pot: control an adversary's arm and head from the side, pressing him back and down. From Baguazhang.

bà wáng zhǒu 霸王肘 Tyrant's elbows, a hard skills training method: to plank face up with the legs straight and elbows bent, with only the heels and elbows touching the ground. A further exercise is to plank on one side with one foot and one elbow on the ground.

掰 (rad.64) **bāi** 1. To pull apart with hands. 2. To break off a piece of something with the fingers and thumb; pry apart. 3. A takedown towards the back with both hands on the torso, one high and one low, pressing down and sliding the legs in, keeping upright.

bāi bù 掰步 Prying open step: stepping with the feeling of pulling apart with the legs, keeping power in both legs. Brace outward in both legs to set the knees, and may also turn the stepping foot out. From Baguazhang.

bāi gōng bù 掰弓步 Prying open bow stance: based on a bow stance, but with the front foot turned out and the rear heel off the ground. The body faces forward. From Tongbeiquan and Piguaquan. See also gōng bù.

bāi ná fǎ 掰拿法 Prying grappling hold: control your adversary's legs with your leg, hook around his head with one arm, and pull on his arm with your other hand. A simple pulling apart action will topple him. From wrestling.

bāi shǒu 掰手 Pull apart: open the hands to either side. From Duanquan.

白 (rad.106) **bái** White.

bái dǎ 白打 Barehanded sparring or fighting, especially wrestling.

bái é liàng chì 白鹅亮翅 White Goose Flashes its Wings. See bái hè liàng chì.

bái hǎi 白海 White Sea: Colloquial name for the Baichongwo acupoint. See bǎi chóng wō.

bái hè fǎn fēi 白鹤反飞 White Crane Flies Upside Down, a backward balance: supporting leg straight, lean back to horizontal, lifting the suspended leg straight in front to at least horizontal. This is the term used in southern styles for face up balance, see also yǎng shēn píng héng.

bái hè jīng fēng 白鹤惊风 White Crane Startles the Wind: take a number of steps forward, bringing the blade from the rear to finish with a straight lunging stab. From Qingping sword.

bái hè liàng chì 白鹤亮翅 White Crane Flashes its Wings: varies with style, but usually involves bracing out with both arms. 1. In Taijiquan, often a stance weighted to one leg and bracing the arms out, one high, one low. 2. In Xingyiquan, a movement that closes then opens the arms, moving through horse stance. 3. In Chaquan, a high empty stance with the arms spread out to the side above the shoulders, palms up. 4. In Shaolinquan. the same as Chaquan but in a raised knee stance. 5. In Baguazhang staff, to swing the staff around, finishing holding it hanging vertically in one hand, the hands spread out to the sides at shoulder height. 6. In Baguazhang deerhorn blades, to snap and rotate them down then up, staying in horse stance with the arms extended to the sides. 7. In Qingping sword, to stab out or to draw a vertical blade to the side, also extending the left arm straight to the other side.

bái hè liàng chì 白鹤晾翅 White Crane Dries its Wings. See bái hè liàng chì above. From Yang Taijiquan.

bái hè niǔ jǐng 白鹤扭颈 White Crane Twists its Neck: twist an adversary's arm by controlling his little finger and elbow, for a takedown. From Qinna.

bái hè shēn yāo 白鹤伸腰 White Crane Stretches its Waist: step aside and throw a heel kick to the flank, turning the body away.

bái hè zhuó shí 白鹤啄食 White Crane Pecks Food: lower the body and stab down, then rise and block up while pushing forward into a bow stance. From Liuhebafa.

bái hǔ dòu wēi 白虎抖威 White Tiger Shows off its Prowess: a straight elbow strike. From Xingyiquan.

bái hǔ xǐ liǎn 白虎洗脸 White Tiger Washes its Face: hands in front of the chest, place the palms together and push to one side, to in front of the shoulder. From Shaolinquan.

bái huán shū 白环俞 Acupoint Baihuanshu (white ring transport), BL30. At the sacrum, level with the fourth sacral foramen, 1.5 *cun* lateral to the midline (on each side). From TCM.

bái là gān 白蜡杆 White waxwood pole. The white ash tree, once cut and debranched, retaining its natural spring. See also bái là shù.

bái là shù 白蜡树 White Ash, colloquially called waxwood. A pliable tree from which staffs and spears are made. See also bái là gān.

bái mǎ dēng yuán 白马蹬猿 White Horse Kicks the Ape: if your adversary grabs your foot after you kick, give a quick jerk and kick to test him. If he doesn't release, quickly turn fully away, put your hands on the ground, and kick with the other leg. From Shaolinquan.

bái mǎ fǎn tí 白马反蹄 White Horse Turns Over its Hooves: a back cross step, slashing a sword back, followed by a straight front heel kick holding the grip at the hip, tip back. From Qingping sword.

bái mǎ guì dào 白马跪道 White Horse Kneels in the Road: retreat, drop to one knee, and drive up a reverse drilling punch. From Tongbeiquan.

bái mǎ gǔn tí 白马滚蹄 White Horse Rolls its Hooves, a controlling takedown: control an adversary's wrist and fingers, rolling the fingers into a fist and hyper-flexing them along with the wrist. From Baguazhang and Qinna.

bái mǎ jiǎn tí 白马剪蹄 White Horse Slashes with its Hooves: dodge a low kick, trap your adversary's foot by bending your knee, then sit down on that leg, also grabbing his knee with your hand.

bái mǎ wò cáo 白马卧槽 White Horse Lies in its Manger: tuck the deerhorn blades in front of the chest, flat, with the tips pointing outward. Then step into a crossed stance and sweep them across at shoulder and chest height, keeping them flat. From Baguazhang.

bái mǎ xiàn tí 白马献蹄 White Horse Presents its Hooves: from horse stance, take a front cross step and pull the fists to the waist. The thirtieth move of the tiger and crane routine.

bái mǎ xiè ān 白马卸鞍 White Horse Removes its Saddle: when your adversary grabs your shoulder, press his hand with both hands to set it, then twist the body and press down. From Qinna.

bái méi quán 白眉拳 Baimeiquan (white eyebrow fist). 1. An Emei style from Sichuan province. 2. A southern style from Guangdong province.

bái páo zhá cǎo 白袍铡草 White Gown Chops Hay: pull down an adversary's arm and press down on his wrist while pulling up on his hand. From Baguazhang, one of its sixty-four hands.

bái shé bō cǎo 白蛇拨草 White Snake Slithers through the Grass: a scoop with the arm, settling down in the legs. From Xingyiquan and Wudangquan.

bái shé chán shēn 白蛇缠身 White Snake Coils its Body. 1. Refers to a coiling action of the arms and body, often into a coiled stance in the legs as well. 2. In Baguazhang, to coil the arms around the body, one at the back, the other in front, without moving the feet. 3. In Xingyiquan, to coil the arms, one at the hip, one at the face, in a resting stance. 4. In Wudang sword, to sit into a coiled stance while brandishing a sword then stabbing. 5.

In Qingping sword, to hold a sword behind while stepping, and then to lunge with a pierce.

bái shé chū dòng 白蛇出洞 White snake shoots out of its cave: usually a stab straight out from a closed position. As a broadsword technique, first gathering the broadsword in close to the body. As a spear technique, first covering, then stabbing.

bái shé fú cǎo 白蛇伏草 White Snake Hides in the Grass. 1. A low horse stance, spreading the arms out, palms at the knees. From Baguazhang. 2. Squat into a drop stance, pressing a sword down close to the body. From Wudang sword.

bái shé nòng fēng 白蛇弄风 White Snake Plays with the Wind: do a lifting block with a spear, followed by a low chop.

bái shé rù dòng 白蛇入洞 White Snake Enters its Den: a low stab, palm down, arms extended so their line is angled. From Wu Taiji sword.

bái shé tù xìn 白蛇吐信 White Snake Spits its Tongue. Usually refers to many variations of a forward strike or knee strike. 1. In Baguazhang and Xingyiquan, a finger strike, usually palm up. 2. In Taiji sword, squat into a drop stance, then come up and forward with a pierce. 3. In Taijiquan broadsword and Qingping sword, step forward and stab. 4. With a spear, it is also to stab straight. 5. With a Bagua broadsword, spin under the blade, laying it on the chest, to stab out. 6. In some branches of Baguazhang, circle-walking in the spear carrying posture, inside hand palm up at shoulder height, outside hand holding up above. 7. In Piguaquan, a finger strike in a double bow stance.

bái shé tù xìn 白蛇吐芯 White Snake Spits its Tongue. 1. Sometimes written instead of the above bái shé tù xìn. 2. A sliding out stab with a spear laid out over a front kick, leaning back.

bái yuán dāo 白猿刀 White Ape Broadsword: a routine of Tongbeiquan, written up as twenty moves.

bái yuán káng qí 白猿扛旗 White Ape Shoulders the Pennant: grab your adversary's lower legs (one or both), hitting his knees with your shoulder, causing him to fall back. Continue on to roll over him or to the side. A throw. Also called qiǎng bèi wò niú.

bái yuán pān kōng 白猿攀空 White Ape Climbs to the Sky: spin around to a raised knee stance, bring the hands in to the waist, then stab the reverse side hand up to above head height, pulling the other back to the waist. From Shaolinquan.

bái yuán tōng bèi quán 白猿通背拳 Baiyuan (white ape) Tongbeiquan, the full name of Tongbeiquan, a northern style. Also called bái yuán tōng bèi quán, see below.

bái yuán tōng bèi quán 白猿通备拳 White Ape Tongbeiquan, see bái yuán tōng bèi quán above.

bái yuán tuō dāo shì 白猿拖刀式 White Ape Drags the Blade model. One of twenty-four classic spear moves. Most spear routines will have a move with a like name. In general, this name refers to a retreat, holding a spear at mid level.

bái yuán tuō dāo wǎng shàng kǎn 白猿拖刀往上砍 White Ape Drags the Blade and Hacks Upwards: with a halberd, do a back cross step, press down, then a jumping wheel over, swinging the blade up and over to hack downwards. From Chen Taijiquan.

bái yuán xiàn guǒ 白猿献果 White Ape Presents Fruit. Generally cupping with two hands near the face. 1. In Baguazhang and Xingyiquan, to cup the hands near the jaw then push upwards and forward with a knee strike. This is a strike to an adversary's jaw and groin. From Baguazhang, one of its sixty-four hands. 2. In Baguazhang, this posture is also held to circle-walk in this position (sometimes called hé zhǎng). 3. In Taijiquan, to circle a sword around, leaning back to allow it to pass by the head, bringing it back to the front to present with both hands on the grip. 4. In Qingping sword, to draw the hands in front of the chest, sword pointing forward, and then stab forward in bow stance.

bái yuán xiàn táo 白猿献桃 White Ape Presents a Peach: see bái yuán xiàn guǒ.

bái yuán zuò dòng 白猿坐洞 White Ape Sits in its Den: press a sword to the right side, then advance in a front cross step, turning the blade to cut across to the left, palm up. From Qingping sword.

bái yún gài dǐng 白云盖顶 White Clouds Cover the Peak. 1. An upper block with or without a simultaneous heel kick. 2. In Taijiquan, an upper block with a sword or broadsword.

B

bái yún gài dǐng chéng yīng háo 白云盖顶呈英豪 White Clouds Cover the Mountain Peak and Disclose the Hero: turning half flowers with a halberd, to shoulder the shaft along the back in single whip posture. From Chen Taijiquan.

擺 [摆] (rad.64) **bǎi** 1. To swing, an action like waving. 2. To place; arrange; put on, flaunt. 3. A kick: open the leg outwards to kick or throw. 4. An outward swinging category of kicks, middle-basin kicks in Chuojiao.

bǎi bù 摆步 Hook-out step. This differs by styles, and can be quite close or extended, quite turned or not very turned. From Baguazhang.

bǎi chǎng zǐ 摆场子 To set up a field: to set up a martial demonstration in a village as part of a celebration.

bǎi diǎn 摆点 Open and poke kick: an outside swinging kick to open up an entry point, followed by a poke kick. From Chuojiao, one of its middle-basin kicks.

bǎi hǎo mén hù 摆好门户 Place the Gate in Readiness: take a ready stance for fighting.

bǎi jiǎo diē chā 摆脚跌叉 Outer crescent kick followed immediately by a half split on the ground, dropping the kicking leg's thigh and lower leg on the ground, and extending the other leg on the ground. From Chen Taijiquan.

bǎi lèi tái 摆擂台 To issue an open challenge for a sparring match.

bǎi lián 摆莲 Lotus kick, see bǎi lián tuǐ.

bǎi lián tuǐ 摆莲腿 Lotus kick, also called outer crescent kick or outside crescent kick. 1. A swinging out kick, usually done without a slap to the foot. Also called guò tuǐ. 2. A jumping outer crescent kick.

bǎi lián pāi jiǎo 摆莲拍脚 Lotus kick, outer crescent slap kick: slapping the outward swinging foot with both hands. In the category of slap kicks, see jī xiǎng xìng tuǐ fǎ.

bǎi lián zhuàn tǐ yī bǎi bā 摆莲转体180 A Lotus one-eighty, a lotus kick with one full turn.

bǎi qiāng 摆枪 Swing a spear outwards horizontally then back across, keeping the right hand stable and sliding the left hand on the shaft.

bǎi quán 摆拳 1. A swinging inward punch, a widow maker. 2. To place the fist: swing a fist out to the side and hold it there, usually opening out the other arm as well or placing it at the waist, a dramatic placement of the arms. This is a posture common in Beijing opera, and is used in the martial arts as a spirited posture.

bǎi shēn qián jìn bù 摆身前进步 Step forward with the foot turned out to turn the body sideways, but still looking and moving forward.

bǎi tuǐ 摆腿 Outer crescent kick, swinging out to kick with the outside of the foot or leg. In Longfist, this refers specifically to the outer crescent kick without a slap. Either done straight, as a ballistic stretch, or slightly bent to kick with a stamp, trample, butt, or trap.

bǎi xī 摆膝 Outer knee swing: raise the knee and snap it outwards to parry an attack.

bǎi zhǎng 摆掌 Lash, swing the arm to throw or strike; a circular block from in front of the body to the side.

百 (rad.106) **bǎi** One hundred.

bǎi bǎ gōng 百把功 Hundred grip training: a training method to improve grip and wrist strength. Sit in horse stance and punch repeatedly, changing the fist to eagle claw after each punch, then clenching and returning to the waist.

bǎi bīng zhī jūn 百兵之君 The sovereign of weapons: the straight sword.

bǎi bīng zhī shī 百兵之师 The master of weapons: the halberd, the big cutter.

bǎi bīng zhī wáng 百兵之王 The king of weapons: the spear.

bǎi bīng zhī shuài 百兵之帅 The commander in chief of weapons: the spring and autumn cutter.

bǎi chóng wō 百虫窝 Extraordinary acupoint Baichongwo, EX-LE3. Near the knee, up along the inner thigh, three *cun* up from the inner edge of the patella, one *cun* above acupoint Xuehai. Colloquially called bái hǎi. From TCM.

bǎi hái 百骸 A hundred bones: refers to all the bones of the body.

bǎi hé quán 百合拳 Lily fist, a hand shape: see lóng xū quán.

bǎi huí 百会 Acupoint Baihui (hundred convergences), DU20. At the peak or crown of the head, seven *cun* up from the rear hairline, five *cun* back from the front hairline, on the midline. The meeting place of all *yang* meridians. From TCM. A sensitive point, striking causes dizziness. Striking too hard may cause brain injury or death. In internal styles, this point is pressed upwards so that the head feels as if suspended from above. Colloquially also called tiān líng gài.

bǎi wū cháo fèng 百乌朝凤 A Hundred Crows Face the Phoenix, a rope dart technique: tuck the dart under the right elbow so that it loops over the left shoulder, switch the right hand to that part of the rope and keep the dart circling counter-clockwise, turn and tuck the right hand under the right armpit, bring the dart around under the right armpit, continuing to circle it, coiling the rope around the upper arms held in front of the body, turn again and continue coiling the rope around the left elbow, changing the right grip to the rope at the elbow, turn again and continue to circle the dart, finally placing the dart on the left foot and sending it out.

败 [败] (rad.66) **bài** 1. To defeat. 2. To be defeated. 3. To fail; to lose.

bài bù 败步 Retreating step: when in hold, when you can't get in a technique, step sideways and back. From wrestling.

bài shì 败势 Retreat to a drop stance.

bài zhōng qǔ shèng 败中取胜 Wrest Victory from a Defeat. 1. A tactic that gains victory from what seemed like defeat. 2. A move that turns and comes back with a strong attack. 3. In Qingping sword, a combination of a series of unpredictable high and low strikes done while stepping away, finally jumping and spinning around to a full drop stance chop.

扳 (rad.64) **bān** 1. To pull; drag. 2. A grappling technique, controlling without grabbing. One of the sixteen key techniques of Baguazhang, see also shí liù zì jué. As simplified character, also pronounced pān, to clamber, climb by pulling oneself up.

bān shǒu 扳手 Pull, drag.

bān fǎ 扳法 Dragging grappling hold: a thread into a space to catch and drag. From wrestling.

bān tī 扳踢 Drag and trip: lift an adversary's leg, move in close, and trip while tilting his body and leg over. From wrestling.

bān tuī 扳推 Simultaneous drag and push. 1. A one-handed switch in direction such as a push with the heel of the hand that then twists to a different direction on contact (such as from upright push to sideways push down). 2. A two-handed technique with one hand pushing and the other pulling, such as controlling an adversary's wrist with pressure outwards while twisting his elbow with pressure inwards. From Baguazhang.

bān yāo 扳腰 Drag at the back: the lower back is arched, the chest puffed up, and the buttocks sticks out, so that the waist cannot act to coordinate the whole body. This is seen as a major error in most styles.

搬 (rad.64) **bān** To take away, remove, move something (the limbs of an adversary, a weapon) out of the way.

bān dǎo tài shān 搬倒泰山 Topple Mount Tai: a close range takedown, stepping in to trip, one hand behind an adversary's back, one arm across his chest. From Baguazhang.

bān fǎ 搬法 To grab and pull along the same side, pulling sharply and quickly across. Also called shùn shǒu bān zhǎng.

bān jiǎo cháo tiān 搬脚朝天 Leg hold face the sky. See bān tuǐ cháo tiān zhí lì. Also called cè cháo tiān dēng, cè tī bāo jiǎo.

bān lán chuí 搬拦捶 Deflect, Parry and Punch: alternating hands, moving in circular paths, deflect across with one hand, parry to control with the other, and finish with a punch from the original side. A common combination, specific actions vary.

bān lán zhǒu 搬拦肘 Deflect and trap with the elbows, then strike horizontally with the fists. From Chen Taijiquan.

bān ná fǎ 搬拿法 Removing grappling: combines getting out of a hold with a counter attack that shoves an adversary over with considerable force. From wrestling.

bān quán 搬拳 Deflect with the fist and forearm, circling the forearm to deflect to the side or front.

B

bān tuǐ 搬腿 Assisted stretch: stretching holding the leg up with your own hands or having a partner hold your leg up.

bān tuǐ cháo tiān zhí lì 搬腿朝天直立 Leg hold face the sky upright balance: stand with the supporting leg straight, the upheld leg at the side, foot on top of the head, holding the foot on the head. Also called bān jiǎo cháo tiān, cè cháo tiān dēng, cè tī bāo jiǎo.

bān wàn 搬腕 Wrist trap: grab the wrist area and press the hand palm down to flex the joint to the point of pain.

bān zhǎng 搬掌 Remove with the palm: a horizontal sweeping action of the arm, hand outstretched, to clear the way.

bān zhǒu 搬肘 Elbow trap: grab your adversary's wrist under his elbow with the other hand. Push on the wrist and lift the elbow, causing his elbow to bend and twist outwards. From Qinna.

bān zhǒu pāi wàn 搬肘拍腕 Elbow trap wrist slap, an escape from an elbow lock: slap the wrist of the grabbing hand with your free hand.

板 (rad.75) bǎn   1. A board, a plank. 2. A shutter. 3. Rigid, stern.

bǎn dèng 板登 A wooden bench. A regular bench, without backing or arm rests, used for seating, but also trained as a weapon.

半 (rad.24) bàn   Half, semi-.

bàn bǎi bù 半摆步 Half hook-out step: in Cheng Baguazhang, a hook-out step that turns ninety degrees, with the middle of the stepping foot on line with the toes of the other foot, making a T.

bàn biān diē fǎ 半边跌法 Half side Takedown: when kicked to the chest, grab the leg, control it, step in to attack and take down.

bàn dūn 半蹲 Half squat: sit down to squat, heels on the ground, so that the thighs are parallel to the ground, not lower.

bàn dūn qū zhǒu 半蹲屈肘 Half squat bend the elbow: in a half squat, strike upwards at the side with the elbow. From Bajiquan.

bàn gōng bù 半弓步 Half bow stance: a bow stance with the rear leg slightly bent (foot still flat on the ground) and the weight centered.

bàn kòu bù 半扣步 Half hook-in step: a hook-in step that turns ninety degrees to place the instep of the stepping foot on line with the toes of the standing foot, making a T. From Cheng Baguazhang.

bàn mǎ bù 半马步 Half horse stance. 1. A stance with the same construction as a horse stance but weighted slightly back, with one foot turned out relative to the other, making this the front, and the body faces the front. 2. Sometimes a sixty-forty stance the same as bù dìng bù bā, sì liù bù.

bàn mó jī 半膜肌 Semimembranosus muscle: in the inside posterior of the thigh, a hip extensor (one of the muscles in the group referred to as hamstrings).

bàn quān shǒu fǎ 半圈手法 Half-circle methods: against a straight attack, to step a half step to the angle to avoid the attack.

bàn xié dāng 半斜裆 See bàn xié dāng bù.

bàn xié dāng bù 半斜裆步 Half slanted crotch stance: sit with the feet open about one foot-length apart, the lead foot turned out about forty-five degrees. From Duanquan. This is a higher than the usual half horse stance, see bàn mǎ bù.

bàn zuò pán bù 半坐盘步 Half crossed-sit stance: cross legged, half sitting stance. Has the turning energy of the sitting stance, so is not quite the same as a mid-height crossed stance, see also xiē bù. Not as low as the full sitting stance, see also zuò pán bù.

拌 (rad.64) bàn   1. To mix, stir. 2. To set the heel at an adversary's foot, inside, outside, or behind.

bàn jiǎo 拌脚 Stir the foot: stick the foot to the outside of an adversary's foot then push him to the outside or shove with the shoulder. A throw or takedown.

绊 [絆] (rad.120) bàn   To loop, catch; cause to stumble; shackle. To trip someone.

bàn fǎ 绊法 Tripping methods: getting a foot in behind an adversary's heel to keep it from moving when a technique is applied to the upper body.

bàn jiǎo 绊脚 Trip, a stepping or kicking technique: step the front foot across to catch behind an adversary's heel and press his leg.

bàn zǐ 绊子 Tripping methods, takedown methods that attack the legs.

幫 [帮] (rad.50) bāng   1. To help or assist. 2. As a throwing technique, 'help' someone to fall.

bāng zhǒu 帮肘 Help the elbow: when doing an elbow strike, place the other hand on the fist to assist.

膀 (rad.130) bǎng   1. The upper arm, including the shoulder girdle; arm. 2. Pronounced páng, swelling.

bǎng dāo 膀刀 Wing arm with knives: lay the blade on the forearm while doing the wing bridge technique. Commonly done with butterfly knives.

bǎng qiáo 膀桥 Wing bridge, a forearm technique. See gǔn qiáo. From Wing Chun. Also called gǔn biān.

bǎng shǒu 膀手 Wing arm: Guarding or deflecting on the midline. 1. Turn the elbow upwards, forearm angled downwards, palm down and facing out, to cut inwards with the outside flat of the forearm. From Wing Chun. 2. The same idea or deflecting with the forearm, but the palm heel bracing out at groin height.

bǎng shǒu chén yāo 膀手沉腰 Wing Arm Settle the Waist: step to right open bow stance and brace the left arm in the middle of the stance, right hand protecting the jawline. The 68th move of the tiger and crane routine.

棒 (rad.75) bàng   A pole. Generally, longer than a staff, well above head height. See also gùn.

包 (rad.20) bāo   1. To wrap. To contain. 2. A parcel. 3. To surround. 4. To guarantee.

bāo gōng 包公 Lord Bao, a model of honesty among officials, lived in the Song dynasty. Also refers figuratively to any honest and upright official. Used in movement names.

bāo gōng pāi àn 包公拍案 Lord Bao Bangs the Table: strike an adversary's arm at wrist and elbow, pressing in opposite directions to break the elbow or shock it before grabbing. From Baguazhang.

bāo guǒ jìn 包裹劲 Enveloping power: a power that bundles up relentlessly without revealing oneself. From Xingyiquan.

bāo guǒ shì 包裹式 Wrap up, bind up, envelope. An action like wrapping up a parcel.

bāo mǎ bù 包马步 Wrap the horse stance. See shuāng kòu bù.

胞 (rad.130) bāo   1. Placenta. 2. Children of the same parents.

bāo huāng 胞肓 Acupoint Baohuang (placenta area), BL53. At the lower back, level with the second sacral foramina, three *cun* lateral to the midline (on each side). From TCM.

保 (rad.9) bǎo   1. To protect; defend. 2. To preserve, maintain. 3. To ensure.

bǎo biāo 保镖 Bodyguard, convoy guard. See also biāo jú, biāo kè, biāo shī, wèi duì.

bǎo jiàn gōng 保健功 Preserve the health training. See yǎng shēn gōng.

bǎo mén shì 保门势 Protect the Gate stance: sit in empty stance holding a bladed weapon over the head and extending the left hand forward.

bǎo shēn fǎ 保身法 Protect the body method: step in close behind an adversary to prevent him from using his full power.

寶 [宝] (rad.40) bǎo   Treasure. Precious; treasured.

bǎo yā chuān lián 宝鸭穿莲 Precious Duck Passes through the Lotus: sitting in horse stance, push both palms forward, palms with index fingers extended, thumbs and other fingers tucked in. The 17th move of the tiger and crane routine.

報 (rad.32) [报] (rad.64) bào   To report; announce; declare.

bào gào 报告 Report; make known.

bào gào yuán 报告员 The announcer at a competition or event.

bào míng dān 报名单 Sign up sheet (for competition).

抱 (rad.64) bào   1. The original, practical, meaning is to hold or cradle in one or both arms. 2. As a technique, to cradle in the crook of the arm, usually with both arms (looks like an embrace, so often translated as embrace or hug in movement names). Best translated as cradle when the arms are front/back or up/down, and hug when the arms are rounded equally. 3. A hold in wrestling, pinning an adversary's arms to his body in a hug. 4. One of the eight body requirements of Xingyiquan: for the *dantian*, mind, and ribs. 4. To use an arm as the fist, circling inwards or across left to right, or right to left, combining defense with attack. From Bajiquan, one of its six main striking techniques, see also liù dà kāi.

bào chán 抱缠 To tie up an adversary in a clinch.

bào dān tuǐ 抱单腿 Embrace a leg: grab one of an adversary's legs and pressure to take down, or lift to throw. From wrestling.

bào dāo 抱刀 Cradle a broadsword. 1. Cross the arms with the spine of the blade on the left arm, grip forward. 2. Hold a broadsword vertically at the left side of the body, cradling the guard in the left hand, as a position before commencing a routine.

bào dāo lǐ 抱刀礼 A salute while holding a broadsword. See bào jiàn lǐ.

bào gùn 抱棍 Cradle a staff. See bào qiāng.

bào hǔ guī shān 抱虎归山 Embrace a Tiger and Return to the Mountain: Turn step into a brush knee and push. From Yang Taijiquan.

bào hǔ tuī shān 抱虎推山 Embrace a Tiger and Push a Mountain: Step into a double push, bringing the rear foot in. From Sun Taijiquan.

bào jiàn 抱剑 Cradle a sword: to cradle a sword in front of the chest: the left hand is on the grip, not touching the blade to the arm.

bào jiàn cì hóu 抱剑刺喉 Cradle the Sword and Stab the Throat: support the right hand in the left, for a two handed strike with the blade tip at the throat. From Wudang sword.

bào jiàn lǐ 抱剑礼 A salute with the right hand holding a sword in reverse grip, placing the grip into the left palm (can substitute any weapon).

bào jiǎo shuāi fǎ 抱脚摔法 Cradling leg throws: throws which involve first grabbing the legs of an adversary. From wrestling.

bào lián zhǎng 抱莲掌 Embrace the Lotus palm, a circle-walking posture: the reverse of the *yin yang* fish palm, palms rotated to face in. From Baguazhang. See also yīn yáng yú zhǎng.

bào pāi shǒu 抱排手 Double palm strike: a high and low straight forward simultaneous palm strike, top hand to chest height, fingers up, bottom hand to solar plexus, fingers down. From Wing Chun.

bào pí pǎ shì 抱琵琶式 Hold the Pipa: in bow stance, pull the shaft of a spear in, holding the right hand a foot away from the butt and tucking the shaft in on the body with the left hand, tip high.

bào qiāng 抱枪 Cradle a spear: hold it steady in front of or beside the body, hands together, apart, or crossed.

bào qiú zhǎng 抱球掌 Hold the Ball palm, a circle-walking posture: the reverse of the moon embracing, arms in the same position, but palms in. From Baguazhang. See bào yuè zhǎng.

bào quán 抱拳 Cradle fists: 1. A double punch that closes in as if embracing someone or holding something with both arms. 2. To hold the fists up in front of the body, fists at the ready, rear fist at the front arm's elbow, fist hearts twisted in. 3. To hold the fists at the waist or hips, fists heels touching the body, palms up, elbows back.

bào quán lǐ 抱拳礼 A salute with the right fist placed into the left palm, the normal salute before a fight or performance, without a bow.

bào shì 抱式 Embracing position during *qigong* training. Standing with the legs open to shoulder width, hands facing in in front of the chest.

bào shuāng bì 抱双臂 Embrace both arms: wrap around both an adversary's arms, jamming them onto your body for leverage for a throw.

bào shuāng bì biè 抱双臂别 Hug both arms pin: wrap around both your adversary's arms, jamming them onto your body for leverage for a throw over the hip, swinging the leg though to lift his leg.

bào shuāng tuǐ 抱双腿 Hug both legs: encircle both an adversary's legs, lift and throw.

bào shǒu lián huán 抱手连环 Continuous alternating grip: changing from a double grip to a one-handed grip with the left hand on a broadsword blade, and back again.

bào tóu tuī shān 抱头推山 Hold the Head and Push the Mountain: turn, releasing from a head grip, and push. Settle and sink before the push, to uproot and push far, as if settling in to try to push a mountain away. From Chen Taijiquan.

bào tuǐ 抱腿 Hug the legs, a wrestling leg training exercise. Step forward, then step in and sit to a full hunkered squat, stand up and repeat on the other leg. Repeat.

bào tuǐ bàn shuāi 抱腿绊摔 Hug the legs and lift: grab an adversary's kicking leg and lift it, moving in and throwing him down. From wrestling.

bào tuǐ biè tuǐ 抱腿别腿 Hug the leg and pin: grab around your adversary's leg and step the leg in behind his supporting leg. Turn and lift, then pin his leg after he falls, pressing down with the chest. From wrestling.

bào tuǐ dǎ tuǐ 抱腿打腿 Hug the leg and hit the leg: grab your adversary's leg in both arms, lift it, and kick behind his other knee, turning and lifting his leg further, for a takedown. From wrestling.

bào tuǐ gēn 抱腿跟 Hug the leg and move in: grab your adversary's thigh, tucking your body in close to his body, and drive forward. From wrestling.

bào tuǐ guò xiōng 抱腿过胸 Leg holding pass the chest: from a clinch, as you have moved in to hug your adversary's thighs to avoid a punch, hold tight, stand up, and arch back, lifting him high, then allowing him to drop behind you and roll out. From wrestling.

bào tuǐ qián dīng 抱腿前顶 Hug the legs forward butt: encircle your adversary's legs in your arms and pull strongly back while pressing into his legs or belly with the shoulder for a takedown. From wrestling.

bào tuǐ shǒu biè 抱腿手别 Hug the leg and pin with the hand: grab your adversary's leg in both arms, lift it, sliding your hand along to the groin, lifting his foot and pressing into his groin for a takedown. A throw or takedown.

bào tuǐ shuāi 抱腿摔 Hug the leg throw: grab an adversary's leg or legs and quickly press in or hit to take down. From wrestling.

bào tuǐ yā 抱腿压 Hug the leg and press down: grab your adversary's thigh, tuck your body in close to his leg, and press down to take him straight down. From wrestling.

bào xuē 抱靴 Hug the shoes: self pulling stretches.

1. Standing straight with one foot up on something, holding that foot in both hands to pull the body towards it. 2. Standing straight up on one leg, hug the other, tucking the knee in tight to the body, holding the tucked shin with the same side arm and the foot with the other hand.

bào yāo guò bèi 抱腰过背 Waist hugging throw over the back: get in close to encircle your adversary's waist with one arm. Turn and get your hip in, grabbing his other arm, then extend your legs and put power in your hips, dropping your head to throw him over your back. From wrestling.

bào yāo guò xiōng 抱腰过胸 Waist hugging pass the chest: from a clinch, as you have moved in to embrace your adversary to avoid a punch, hold tight and arch back, lifting him high, then turning as you both go down, so that you land on top. From wrestling.

bào yāo shuāi fǎ 抱腰摔法 Waist hugging throws: throws which involve first holding around the waist of an adversary. From wrestling.

bào yāo wài gōu tuǐ 抱腰外勾腿 Waist hug and hook the leg from the outside: grab around the waist and step to the outside of your adversary's lead leg, pressing him back while preventing his leg from moving, or lifting it to assist the takedown. From wrestling.

bào yīng zhǎng 抱婴掌 Cradle the Baby palm, a circle-walking posture: the reverse of the millstone pushing palm, arms in the same position, but palms rotated to face in as if cradling a baby in the arms. From Baguazhang. See also tuī mò zhǎng.

bào yuán shǒu yī 抱圆守一 Embrace the Circle and Be Faithful to One: circle the hands in an embracing move, then push out to one side. From Wudangquan.

bào yuè zhǎng 抱月掌 Moon embracing palm. 1. Palms facing in, in front of the chest, with the arms rounded and fingers pointing to each other. The power both embraces and pushes outward. 2. Press the palms out in the same posture. Both meanings used in Baguazhang, especially for circle-walking, see also #2 of píng tuī zhǎng.

bào zhǎng 抱掌 Embracing palms. 1. Holding the arms rounded with the palms facing each other or facing inwards, as if cradling or hugging something in the arms. 2. An embracing power, but with the arms over the head.

暴 (rad.72) **bào**   Sudden and violent; savage, cruel, fierce.

bào yǎn fǎ 暴眼法 Savage look method: stare at an adversary, fixing him like a fierce tiger, to make him feel like your prey.

爆 (rad.86) **bào**   1. To explode; to burst. 2. To quick fry.

bào fā 爆发 Explosive, exploding. To explode.

bào fā jìn 爆发劲 Explosive power: hard and fast explosion of clearly focussed power such as a straight punch or a throw.

bào fā lì 爆发力 Explosive power: hard and fast explosion of clearly focussed power, combining strength, speed, and focus. One of the main requirements for many styles.

豹 (rad.153) **bào**   A leopard; a panther. Sometimes used in movement names that combine quickness with ferocity. For more movement names using the actions or qualities of the leopard, see also under jīn bào.

bào hǔ tuī shān 豹虎推山 Leopard and Tiger Push a Mountain: push forward in a reverse bow stance, pulling back with the other hand. From Wu Taijiquan.

bào pái quán 豹排拳 Leopard fist: see bào quán.

bào quán 豹拳 Leopard fist: fingers bent at the second joint, thumb tucked into the side of the index finger. This fist presents a small punching surface and can get through small spaces.

bào zhuā quán 豹爪拳 Leopard fist: see bào quán.

bào zǐ jiǎn wěi 豹子剪尾 Leopard Lashes its Tail: turn the body away, crouch down, and simultaneously throw a heel kick to the groin.

揹 (rad.64) **bēi**   1. To carry on the back or across shoulders. 2. In wrestling, getting an adversary onto your shoulder for a throw. 3. Throws using the body as leverage, hips throws in general. In simplified characters, often written 背, the meaning understood from the context.

bēi bāo fú 揹包袱 Carry baggage: to fear failure in a competition or performance, whether due to fear of loss of face or letting someone down. Fear of failure often leads to loss of focus during the event.

bēi dān měng hǔ 揹担猛虎 Carry a Fierce Tiger on the Back: curl your arm around your adversary's neck, step in and lift him on your back, pulling one of his legs in the opposite direction. From wrestling.

bēi dāo 揹刀 Carry a broadsword. 1. To raise the right arm with the spine of the blade along the arm and back. 2. To lift the blade in front of the body, resting the spine on the front of the shoulder. Also called bèi dāo.

bēi gùn 揹棍 Shoulder a staff: holding the butt end, lay the shaft on the shoulder.

bēi qiāng 揹枪 Shoulder a spear: lay the shaft flat on the back.

臂 (rad.130) **bēi**   The upper arm, or whole arm, arms. In combination with other characters, usually pronounced bì.

bēi chán lóng tóu 臂缠龙头 Coil the Arm around the Dragon's Head: step in behind your adversary, press the arm across his throat, then coil it behind his neck to choke and take down. From Qinna.

bēi yǐn shén jīng 臂隐神经 The hidden nerve in the arm, the funny bone. A sensitive target.

bì nào (xué) 臂臑(穴) Acupoint Binao (upper arm), LI14. At the outside of the arm, just above the insertion of the deltoid, seven *cun* above the acupoint Quchi (on each arm). From TCM.

bì zhǒu 臂肘 1. The elbow. 2. An elbow strike to the arm. From Tanglangquan, one of its eight short techniques.

bēi zǔ dǎng 臂阻挡 Arm block: with the arms held up in on guard position, take a kick on the outside of the shoulder and arm, keeping the forearms up to dissipate the force as well.

北 (rad.21) **běi**   North, Northern, northerly.

běi cháo 北朝 The Northern dynasties, Wei, Qi, and Zhou (386-585).

běi fāng 北方 The North. Sometimes written descriptions of routines use compass directions for orientation.

běi pài 北派 Northern styles, as differentiated from southern styles. This refers to geography, north of the Yangzi river. It often refers to an external type of style or Shaolin style that utilises many kicks, even though most internal styles come from the north.

běi qí 北齐 The Northern Qi (550-557), of the Northern Dynasties.

běi sòng 北宋 The Northern Song dynasty (960-1127).

běi wèi 北魏 The Northern Wei (386-534), of the Northern Dynasties.

běi yuè héng shān 北岳恆山 Mount Heng, the Northern of the sacred mountains. See also héng shān, wǔ yuè.

běi zhōu 北周 The Northern Zhou (557-581), of the Northern Dynasties.

背 (rad.130) bèi 1. The upper back. 2. The back of the body or an object. 3. The spine of a bladed weapon. 4. To carry on the back. With this meaning, may also be written 揹, pronounced bēi.

bèi biān zhuǎn tǐ 背鞭转体 Carry the whip on the back and turn, a steel whip technique: with vertical circles, bring the whip over the left shoulder, then turn and continue the circle.

bèi bù 背步 1. A back cross step: similar to a back insertion step but shorter. See also chā bù. 2. A backwards step to place the feet parallel, stepping tightly into an adversary while turning the back on him, often used in throws.

bèi chuān jiē qiāng 背穿接枪 Back thread and toss a spear: draw a spear back to lie behind the body then shoot it forward and catch. Also called bèi hòu chuān jiē qiāng.

bèi dāo 背刀 Place a broadsword at the back: either lifting the handgrip up over head with the tip down lying on the upper back, or placing the handgrip at the lower back, with the tip up across the back or shoulder. Also called bēi dāo.

bèi dà dāo 背大刀 Place a big cutter on the back: with the right hand at the hilt, let the shaft lie along the right arm and upper back behind the shoulder, blade edge to the rear.

bèi gōng 背弓 Arch back from the waist, used for some throwing techniques.

bèi hòu bēi dāo 背后背刀 Place a broadsword behind the back: lift the handgrip up over head with the tip down lying on the upper back.

bèi hòu bēi gùn 背后背棍 Place the staff behind the back: after swinging the staff, place it under the right arm and across the back.

bèi hòu chuān gùn (qiāng) 背后穿棍(枪) Thread the staff (or spear) from the back: tuck the shaft behind the back, then shoot out by snapping the rear wrist, shooting the staff (or spear) forward.

bèi hòu zhuàn shēn fǎ 背后转身法 Footwork to turn and get in behind an adversary.

bèi huā dāo 背花刀 Flowers, or figure eights, behind the back with a broadsword: vertical circles, alternating in front of and behind the body.

bèi jìn 背劲 Back power: to separate the strength of an adversary who comes directly, so that the attack cannot succeed on the direct line.

bèi kuà 背挎 Hoist over the back. Grab an adversary's incoming wrist and lift in your other hand, turning to throw over the back. A throw.

bèi kuò jī 背阔肌 Latissimus dorsi muscle: one of the muscles in the back of torso that attaches from the pelvis up the spine, and spreads to the arm. Assists in shoulder adduction, extension, and medial rotation.

bèi lā gōng 背拉功 Back strength training, combining upper body strength and whole body strength.

bèi pū dāo 背扑刀 Place a horse cutter on the back. See bèi dà dāo.

bèi rú wō niú 背如蜗牛 The upper back must be like a snail. From Tongbeiquan, one of its requirements.

bèi rù 背入 Back cross entry, to enter for a throw by stepping in crossing the foot behind, used for a turning throw.

bèi shēn kào 背身靠 Strike with the back: strike to the back with the shoulders, one after the other, snapping the waist and back and opening the shoulders. For this technique you need to first step into an adversary to be directly connected.

bèi shēn tàn zhǎng 背身探掌 Reverse reaching palm: strike with a flat reaching strike behind the body, turning to face behind without moving the feet. From Baguazhang.

bèi shēn tǔ xìn 背身吐信 Spit the Tongue behind the Body. 1. Stepping forward with the foot turned out, push each hand out to the opposite side of the body, one pushing back out from over the head, one pushing out at the armpit. 2. With a palm tucked in under the jaw, step around and send it out. From Baguazhang.

bèi shēn zhǎng 背身掌 Reversing change: one of the mother palms, usually involving hitting behind. From Baguazhang.

bèi shì 背势 To be caught on the back foot: to be caught off balance and out of position, necessitating the use of force. To not be able to use smooth, balanced methods against an adversary.

bèi shǒu shì 背手式 Hands on the back position: stand with the legs open to shoulder width, placing the back of the hands on the kidneys. Used during some *qigong* methods.

bèi tuō qiāng 背拖枪 Drag a spear behind the back: pull the spear behind the back with the palm reversed, tip forward.

bèi wàn 背腕 Reverse the wrist: control and rotate an adversary's forearm so that elbow is extended and under, and hyper-extend the wrist. From Qinna.

bèi yuè qiāng 背月枪 Back moon spear: retreating steps, snapping a low tip outwards.

bèi zhé kào 背折靠 Strike with the back, Bend and Strike with the body: in shifting horse stance, open the back by turning and raising the elbow, to strike with the back of the body. From Chen Taijiquan.

bèi zhǒu 背肘 An elbow to the back. From Tanglangquan, one of its eight short techniques.

奔 (rad.37) ancient form 犇 (rad.93) [奔]

(rad.37) **bēn** 1. To run, to move quickly. 2. To flee, run away. 3. To go straight for.

bēn mǎ chòng tí 奔马冲蹄 Galloping Horse Charges with its Hooves, a close-range technique: continuous advancing knee butts, hitting or jamming to any target on an adversary. Best done combined with continuous punches to the face.

本 (rad.75) **běn** 1. Root of a plant. 2. Origin, source, foundation. 3. Original. 4. We, our, me, my. 5. A book.

běn lì 本力 A person's natural, untrained strength. Also called tāi lì and xiān tiān lì.

běn mén 本门 Our school, our style.

běn shén 本神 Acupoint Benshen (root spirit), GB13. At the head, 0.5 *cun* in from the front hairline, in line with the pupil of the eye, three *cun* lateral to acupoint Shenting (on each side). From TCM.

夯 笨 (rad.37, 118) **bèn** Stupid, dull. Clumsy, awkward. Foolish.

bèn lì 笨力 Clumsy, awkward application of strength, thus hard and unskilled, unable to change according to the situation. Also called zhuō lì.

崩 (rad.46) **bēng** 1. Original meaning is to collapse; to burst. 2. To snap a weapon, usually upwards, but also to the side. Often translated as tilt. 3. A direct punch, usually with an upright, or sun, fist.

bēng bǔ 崩补 Burst and Repair: a Tanglangquan routine, written up as thirty-five moves.

bēng dāo 崩刀 Snap a broadsword. See bēng jiàn.

bēng dǒu 崩抖 Snapping shake, a wrestling training method with a long strap: cross the legs, then bring them together and sharply snap the belt ends in opposite directions in a half squat.

bēng gùn 崩棍 Snap, tilt, a staff. See bēng qiāng.

bēng huō 崩豁 A bursting strike that inserts accurately as if into a crack, like breaching a dam.

bēng kāi 崩开 To snap yourself free from a grab.

bēng jiàn 崩剑 Snap a sword: snap the blade up or to the side sharply, flicking so that the force reaches the tip. The grip may be held in one or both hands.

bēng jìn 崩劲 Bursting power: to use the body like a bow and arrow – when the bow is pulled the arrows (hand and feet) fly. This is mostly a directly forward and backward power. Its most valuable aspect is that the bow returns to normal immediately after shooting, returning to its original position with the same speed and power that it shot the arrow. The snap of the entire body is applied through to the fists. From Xingyiquan.

bēng qiāng 崩枪 Snap, tilt, a spear: using a short, sharp power, snap the tip upwards or to either side, sending power to the tip, so that the shaft vibrates.

bēng quán 崩拳 1. In general, a punch that extends and strikes with the knuckles, fist eye up. 2. The crushing fist, smashing fist, driving punch of Xingyiquan: a straight midline punch with an upright fist, combined with a step, usually forward, but also done moving backwards. It is related to the wood element, see mù. 3. In Duanquan: a straight, fast, one-inch punch.

bēng tuǐ 崩腿 Pop the legs: a short snapping power applied from the legs to complete a throw. From wrestling.

bēng zhǒu 崩肘 Elbow snap. 1. A hand technique followed closely by a popped elbow strike. 2. A short range elbow strike to the side.

bēng zǐ 崩子 To pop. See tú shǒu bèi.

绷 (rad.57) bēng   See pēng.

繃 繃 [绷] (rad.120) bēng   To stretch or draw tight. Spring; bounce.

bēng jiǎo 绷脚 To plantar-flex the ankle, point the toes.

bēng jǐn 绷紧 Stretch something tight. Used particularly for fully pointing the foot.

bēng zhǒu 绷肘 Stretch the elbow: techniques that involve wrapping around an adversary's arm and turning his elbow to control it by hyper-extending it and pressing firmly.

蹦 (rad.157) bèng   To leap, jump, spring. To jump from a standing start. Sometimes refers to vertical jumps, sometimes to jumps for distance.

bèng bù 蹦步 Jump stance: from a horse stance, jump up, bring the feet together and turn one-eighty degrees, landing back in horse stance facing the other direction.

逼 偪 (rad.162,9) [逼] (rad.162) bī   1. To force, compel. Press for, extort. 2. Press up to, close in on. 3. As one of the eight attack and defense models, press the attack forward, with more and more urgency. See also bā zì gōng fáng fǎ zé.

bī jìn 逼进 Close in on, tie up: drive into an adversary's space to shut him down.

bī shǒu 逼手 Close in on, press on: drive into an adversary's space while shutting him down with the hands.

鼻 (rad.209) bí   1. The nose. One of the main targets on the body. 2. One of the five sensory organs, see also wǔ guān.

bí kōng 鼻空 The nostrils. Also called bí kǒu.

bí kǒu 鼻口 See bí kōng.

bí liáng 鼻梁 The bridge of the nose. An easy target.

bí tōng 鼻通 Extraordinary acupoint Bitong (clear nose). At the face, beside the nose, at the top of the nasolabial groove. From TCM.

匕 (rad.21) bǐ   1. A ladle, a spoon. 2. A dagger.

bǐ shǒu 匕首 A double edged dagger. Usually used as a pair. Also called shuāng bǐ shǒu.

彼 (rad.60) bǐ   That; those; the other; another. Used in the martial arts to indicate an adversary or assailant.

bǐ bú dòng jǐ bú dòng, bǐ wēi dòng jǐ xiān dòng 彼不动己不动，彼微动己先动 Don't move if the adversary doesn't move, but if he initiates the slightest movement, move first. A martial saying.

比 (rad.81) bǐ   To compare. Compete. Copy. Compare to. Proportion.

bǐ huà 比画 See bǐ huà.

bǐ huà 比划 To run through a routine or combinations, not full out.

bǐ mù yú jī 比目鱼肌 Soleus muscle: a calf muscle, runs interior to the gastrocnemius. Assists in plantar flexion of the foot. Most active when the knee is flexed.

bǐ sài 比赛 A competition.

bǐ sài chǎng dì 比赛场地 Competition site, sports pitch. For modern wushu, the competition carpet is 14x8 metres for individual events and 16x14 metres for group events.

B

庇 (rad.53) **bì**   To shelter, protect, shield.

bì shēn chuí 庇身捶 Shield the Body: see pī shēn chuí. From Taijiquan. Also called piē chuí.

碧 (rad.112) **bì**   Light jade colour. When referring to leaves, light green, to water, light blue.

bì shuǐ yáng fān 碧水扬帆 Set Sail on Blue Water: control an adversary's arm then bend the elbow and push it up into his face. From Baguazhang.

避 (rad.162) **bì**   1. To avoid; to evade. 2. To prevent; to keep away.

bì kāi 避开 To evade, get out of the way, keep away from.

bì shí jī xū 避实击虚 Avoid the solid and hit the empty, avoid the strengths and attack the weaknesses: to evade an incoming attack and strike to an adversary's weak places.

bì zhèng dǎ xié 避正打斜 Avoid the straight and hit the angle: to evade an incoming direct attack and strike from the sides or back.

bì zhú sǎo yuè 避竹扫月 Avoid the Bamboo and Sweep the Moon: lift the right knee and present a sword at the chest, then step across and cut down and back, and then sit to the right leg and slice up to the front. From Qingping sword.

鉍 [铋] (rad.167) **bì**   The end of a weapon with a long shaft such as the pike or halberd. Usually used for the non-blade end of the shaft on a long bladed weapon.

閉 [闭] (rad.169) **bì**   1.To close, shut; stop up. 2. A controlling or grappling technique: to lock up. 3. Also can mean specifically parrying by closing to the right.

bì dì hū 闭地户 Close the ground door: lightly close the anal sphincter. See also shōu gāng, tí gāng.

bì mén shì 闭门势 Close the Doorways: take a closed defensive stance. 1. In Chen Taijiquan, sit in empty stance and raise a sword with the tip held down to the front. 2. In Duanquan, squat down and cover the midline with the arms, palms in.

bì mén tuī yuè 闭门推月 Close the Door and Push the Moon. 1. Step out to the side, moving both arms across along with the foot to brace out. Can be used as a double push or a pressure and push. From Baguazhang. 2. Press one forearm vertical and push out from underneath. From Liuhebafa.

bì qì 闭气 Close the breath, seal the breath. 1. Grab or compress the windpipe, or strike the Tiantu (RN22) acupoint to prevent an adversary from inhaling. See also tiān tū. 2. Strike cavities under the ribs to cause lungs to stop, but this is more difficult to be accurate.

bì qiāng 闭枪 Close with a spear: a circular cover outwards. See lán qiāng.

bì xué 闭穴 Block an acupoint: block the *qi* flow at an acupoint by pressure with the fingers or a blunt weapon.

編 [编] (rad.120) **biān**   1. A book or part of a book. 2. Organization and personnel. 3. To organize, arrange, group. 4. To write, compose.

biān pái 编排 1. A pairing in a sparring or wrestling competition. 2. The choreography of a routine.

biān pái bù jú 编排布局 The composition of the choreography of a routine.

biān pái chéng xù 编排程序 Pairing procedure in a Sanda or wrestling competition.

biān pái jié gòu 编排结构 The structure of the choreography of a routine.

biān pái nèi róng 编排内容 The content of the choreography of a routine.

biān zhě 编者 Editor; compiler.

蝙 (rad.142) **biān**   A bat (animal). Usually used in combination as biān fú for bat.

biān fú 蝙蝠 A bat (the animal).

biān fú luò dì 蝙蝠落地 Bat Lands on the Ground: drop into a resting stance, first lifting, then threading the arms out. From Baguazhang.

邊 [边] (rad.162) **biān**   Edge, margin, side, border.

biān lán shì 边拦式 Trap to the Side model. One of twenty-four classic spear moves. Most spear routines will have a move with a like name. In general, this name refers to a trap and cover inwards.

鞭 (rad.177) **biān** 1. To whip, to lash. 2. A hard whip, iron staff: a straight, thin weapon about one metre long, thirteen jointed bumps, a sharp end and a handgrip end that is also used to strike. 3. A jointed steel whip, with seven, nine, or thirteen segments lined together with rings. See also jiǔ jié biān.

biān dǎ xiù qiú 鞭打锈球 Whip Hits the Rusty Ball: lift an adversary's arm while cranking his head forward and down, pressing behind the neck. From Baguazhang.

biān fǎ 鞭法 Forearm techniques. The more common name for forearm techniques is qiáo fǎ.

biān gān 鞭杆 Short pole: a thin pole, about 1.1 to 1.4 metres long, slightly tapering. Both ends are used. Often called gān zi.

biān jīn fǎ 鞭劲法 Method for training forearms: to develop power in pressing down with the forearms. Attach bags to a rope and pulley arrangement on two supports, so that a pole is suspended between them attached to the ropes, needing to be pushed down by the forearms while in high horse stance.

biān quán 鞭拳 Whipping backfist punch: backfist. 1. To swing the arm (bent or straight) flat towards the front or rear, usually completing the technique with the fist below shoulder height. From southern styles. 2. In Sanda, usually refers to a full spinning backfist.

biān shí qǔ zhū 鞭石取珠 Whip a Stone to Get Pearls: lift the left knee and swing the blade over the head to dab forward at waist height. From Qingping sword.

biān wǔ ruò zhuàn lùn 鞭舞若转轮 The steel whip should spin like a wheel. A martial saying.

biān wǔ yī dǔ qiáng, zài shùn 鞭舞一堵墙,在顺 The steel whip should dance to form a wall, its essence lies in being smoothly handled. A martial saying.

扁 (rad.23) **biǎn** 1. In martial arts, this means awkward: movement is not full, not upright, power is not applied correctly. Generally, an error. 2. A specific error when occurs in Taijiquan push hands: hard inside but too soft in the arms, not able to react. One of the four defects, see sì bìng.

扁 (rad.63) **biǎn** Flat.

biǎn chuāi tuǐ 扁踹腿 Flat thrust kicks, thrust kicks that are rotated out and thrust forward. From Chuojiao, one of its middle-basin kicks.

biǎn xuàn zhǎng 扁旋掌 Flat spinning palm: a full circle into a horizontal cut with the palm edge. From Baguazhang.

卞 (rad.3) **biàn** Irritable; irascible. To be impatient, in a hurry.

biàn zhuāng qín hǔ 卞庄擒虎 Impatient Mr. Zhuang Catches the Tiger: set to a turned horse stance, more on the left leg, and pound out with the right fist, blocking up with the left. The 81st move of the tiger and crane routine.

變 (rad.149) [变] (rad.29) **biàn** 1. To change, alter, transform. 2. To change into; become.

biàn huà mò cè 变化莫测 Changes and actions are well calculated in application. A martial saying.

biàn jià zǐ 变架子 Changing movements and postures freely during practice, not following the usual order. From Baguazhang.

biàn jiāo 变跤 Adjust the throw: adjust position as an adversary moves out of position, to enable a throw.

biàn liǎn 变脸 To change the face: to snap the head to look in a different direction. The term is used in the sharp turns during performance of routines.

biàn shì yào kuài 变势要快 Changing moves must be done quickly. From Tongbeiquan, one of its requirements.

biàn xíng 变形 To change the shape of a weapon by hitting or otherwise causing it to bend. An error in performance.

biàn zhāo 变着 Changed movement: doing a movement slightly changed from in the form, as when doing applications, adjusting the movement a bit to get more effective applications.

B

摽 (rad.64) **biāo** 1. To wave off. 2. Pronounced biào, to throw out; push out; strike.

biāo tī 摽踢 Waving kicks. See zhí bǎi xìng tuǐ fǎ. From Mizongquan.

標 [标] (rad.75) **biāo** 1. The standard meaning is to mark; put a tag on; award. 2. To martial artists, usually means a dart shaped object or a dart-like action.

biāo bù 标步 Dart step: Step forward quickly, first the lead, then then the rear foot and then the lead foot, staying in the same forward-facing stance. From Wing Chun.

biāo dāo 标刀 Stab with a broadsword. From southern styles.

biāo quán 标拳 Dart punch: starting with the fist heart up, finish the punch with it down. The fist surface is straight forward throughout.

biāo tóu 标头 Dart head: the tip of a steel whip or the dart of a rope dart.

biāo zhǎng 标掌 Dart palm: with the muscles tense, extend the arm with a short, sharp strike to the finger tips. If a double strike, the palms are facing each other. From southern styles.

biāo zhǎng chén qiáo 标掌沉桥 Dart palm and sink bridge: follow a fingertip strike with an immediate drop of the elbow. From southern styles.

biāo zhǐ 标指 Dart fingers: a routine in Wing Chun.

biāo zhǐ shǒu 标指手 Dart fingers: thrust forward with the fingers held firmly. In Wing Chun, the arm is straight. From southern styles.

biāo zhǔn 标准 A standard, a criterion.

鏢 [镖] (rad.167) **biāo** 1. Any dart-like weapon. 2. The goods sent under protection, and so refers to the work of a bodyguard or convoy guarding.

biāo fā sì liú xīng, zài qiǎo 镖发似流星，在巧 A dart should shoot out like shooting star, its essence lies in being skillfully handled. A martial saying.

biāo jú 镖局 A bodyguard or convoy guard service.

biāo kè 镖客 A bodyguard or convoy guard. Also called biāo shī. See also bǎo biāo, wèi duì.

biāo shī 镖师 See biāo kè.

表 (rad.145) **biǎo** 1. Surface; external. 2. Show, express. 3. Model, example. 4. A table, form, list.

biǎo hán 表寒 Exterior cold, External cold: a disharmony caused by a pernicious influence. From TCM.

biǎo rè 表热 Exterior heat, External heat: a disharmony caused by a pernicious influence. From TCM.

biǎo xiàn 表现 To express; expression; manifestation. Behavior.

biǎo yǎn 表演 Demonstration, performance, exhibition; give a performance.

biǎo yǎn sài 表演赛 Exhibition match, exhibition competition. Awards are given more for participation than to differentiate places.

憋 (rad.61) **biē** 1. To suppress, hold back. 2. To feel oppressed. 3. In martial arts, the defense method of smothering an attack.

biē qì 憋气 1. Hold the breath by blocking it in the throat (in the martial arts). 2. To suppress resentment.

別 [别] (rad.18) **bié** 1. To leave; part. 2. Other; another. 3. Differentiate. Difference. 4. The simplified character is also pronounced biè, see biè below.

蹩 (rad.157) **bié** 1. To sprain (the ankle). 2. To limp.

bié zǐ 蹩子 Takedowns that involve moving in and putting pressure to the thigh while applying torque above.

彆 (rad.57) [别] (rad.18) **biè** 1. Original meaning in dialect is to persuade somebody to change his opinion. 2. To pin down (in wrestling), a pinning hold in wrestling. 3. Throws, usually those with the hips in contact, and swinging the leg straight to get leverage.

biè fǎ 别法 Pins: Various methods of taking down and pinning an adversary to the ground.

biè jiān 别肩 Shoulder pin: block an incoming punch and move in to control the shoulder, grab your hands together around his arm and lean into the shoulder to bring him down. From wrestling.

biè jiǎo 别脚 Foot pin, pressing the foot and lower leg into an adversary's leg in preparation for a tripping throw.

biè jǐng 别颈 Neck pin: pin the neck, control and twist an adversary's neck, immobilizing it. This may be in preparation for a throw.

biè shǒu fēng hóu 别手封喉 Arm bar choke hold: from the back, apply an arm bar with one hand while choking with the other.

biè tuǐ shuāi 别腿摔 Leg pin throw: pin an adversary's leg (especially after he kicks you) to your body with one arm and go for a takedown. A throw or takedown.

biè yāo 别腰 Waist pin: embrace all the way around an adversary's waist and pull, pressing into him with your head or chest to hyper-extend the spine for a takedown. From wrestling.

biè zhǒu 别肘 Elbow pin. 1. Bend and reverse an adversary's elbow, keeping control at the shoulder and wrist, to tuck the elbow up and onto his back. You may take him to the ground. 2. An elbow pin while on the ground. From wrestling.

biè zǐ 别子 Hip throws: throws involving getting the hip into an adversary for a throw or controlling the hip of an adversary for a takedown.

髌 [髌] (rad.188) bìn The kneecap; patella.

bìn gǔ 髌骨 The kneecap; patella.

鬓 [鬢] (rad.190) bìn The hairline or hair at the temples. Often means the temples. An easy target, but care should be taken.

bìn jiǎo 鬓角 Sideburns; hair on the temples.

bìn jiǎo chā huā 鬓角插画 Arrange Flowers on the Temples: a double strike to the temples with the backs of the hands. From Baguazhang.

掤 (rad.64) bīng 1. The quiver of an arrow. 2. A wrestling technique, to gather and pull on someone.

丙 (rad.1) bǐng 1. The third of the ten Celestial Stems, used in combination with the twelve Terrestrial Branches to designate years, months, days, and hours. See also dì zhī, tiān gān. 2. Third in a list when listing using the celestial stems, equivalent to C in English when listing alphabetically.

bǐng chén 丙辰 The years 1976, 1916, and so on, for sixty year cycles.

bǐng shēn 丙申 The years 2016, 1956, and so on, for sixty year cycles.

bǐng wǔ 丙午 The years 1966, 1906, and so on, for sixty year cycles.

bǐng yín 丙寅 The years 1986, 1926, and so on, for sixty year cycles.

bǐng xū 丙戌 The years 2006, 1946, and so on, for sixty year cycles.

bǐng zǐ 丙子 The years 1996, 1936, and so on, for sixty year cycles.

柄 (rad.75) bǐng Grip of a sword or broadsword (the specific part of the handgrip that is gripped).

秉 (rad.115) bǐng 1. To hold in the hand, grasp. 2. To take charge of. 3. Authority.

bǐng chí 秉持 Hold a weapon in the hand.

bǐng fēng 秉风 Acupoint Bingfeng (grasping the wind), SI12. At the scapula, in a cavity directly above acupoint SI11 (on each side). From TCM.

並 併 立 (rad.2, 9, 117) [并] (rad.2) bìng 1. On a level with. 2. To combine. 3. To stand or place side by side.

bìng bù 并步 1. Stand to attention. 2. Stance with the feet together, parallel, usually legs straight. 3. Step one foot in to place the feet together, to stand to attention.

bìng bù bǎi quán 并步摆拳 Stand to Attention Flaunt the Fists: step to a closed stance and open the arms out to the sides, looking to the front fist. From Chaquan.

bìng bù bào quán 并步抱拳 Stand to Attention Clench the Fists: stand in a parallel stance, clench the fists and bring them to the waist, fist centres turned up.

bìng bù chōng quán 并步冲拳 Stand to attention punch: step to a closed parallel stance and punch. From Chaquan.

bìng bù pāi dì 并步拍地 Feet together ground slap: with the feet together, squat and slap the ground with one or both hands. With low techniques, bìng bù is often used with this meaning.

bìng bù tuī gùn 并步推棍 Stand to Attention Push the Staff: with the feet together, push the vertical staff forward.

剥 [剥] (rad.18) **bō** To peel; to peel off; to shell.

bō jiǎn chōu sī 剥茧抽丝 To peel a cocoon to draw out silk: to lift one arm into the wrist and push down with the heel of the other, softly, repeating and alternating. From Meishanquan.

撥 [拨] (rad.64) **bō** 1. The original, practical, meaning is to move something, especially with a stick, but also with a hand or foot. 2. To flick the beads on an abacus. 3. The technique is to check, knock something aside. This involves a knocking action, not a heavy block.

bō bà 拨把 Check with the butt. 1. Check with the butt of a long weapon, a small circle to either side. 2. Strike with the butt of a staff, the shaft tucked under the right armpit. Sometimes bá 拔 and bō 拨 are used interchangeably.

bō biān 拨鞭 Check a steel whip: catching it fairly near the handle on your forearm to redirect it while circling it.

bō bù 拨步 Switchover step, pulling the feet up to the crotch during the jumping switch.

bō cǎo xún shé 拨草寻蛇 Push aside the Grass to Search for the Snake. 1. Step forward with a low intercept or sweep with a sword or butt of a staff. 2. Bring a broadsword over then push upwards, left hand supporting the blade. From Taijiquan. 3. A sideways interception, either low or high with the blade, stepping sideways into high empty stance. From Qingping sword. 4. Swing the shaft of a spear back and forth, tip low. 5. In a horse stance, tuck the right hand in to the waist, heel of palm on the body, fingers out to the side, thumb up. The 40th move of the tiger and crane routine.

bō dà dāo 拨大刀 Check with a big cutter: with the right hand near the blade and the left hand at mid-shaft, check downwards with the butt.

bō fǎ 拨法 A flicking grab: to grab and dig the thumb in close to the index finger, moving it hard back and forth, especially across long muscles or tendons.

bō gùn 拨棍 Check with a staff. See bō qiāng.

bō huā biān 拨花鞭 Checking flowers with a steel whip: while circling the whip, toss the whip from your right hand, catching it near the middle with the left and continuing the circles by twisting and releasing with the left hand.

bō jìn 拨劲 Checking power: a sharp knock to an adversary's attacking technique and power to knock the attack aside.

bō qiāng 拨枪 Check with a spear: snap the tip from side to side with a quick, short, and steady power that reaches the fore-section of the shaft.

bō quán 拨拳 Check with the fist.

bō tuǐ 拨腿 Check with the leg: a low jamming turned out kick to the ankle.

bō wù xún yōu 拨雾寻幽 Push aside the Fog to seek Quiet: step to the side and check up to the right with the blade, hand up, tip flat. This combines a dodge with a defensive check that can also cut an adversary's arm. From Qingping sword.

bō yè xún guǒ 拨叶寻果 Push aside Leaves to Seek Fruit: draw a small circle with a staff butt, then knock aside. From Baguazhang.

bō yè xún huā 拨叶寻花 Push aside Leaves to Seek Flowers: withdraw to a left empty stance with a sweeping interception on the right above the shoulder, extending the arm straight out with the tip slightly up. From Qingping sword.

bō yún jiàn rì 拨云见日 Push aside the Clouds to See the Sun. 1. Strike to an adversary's face to draw him to a high reaction, moving in to strike low with the other hand. From Baguazhang. 2. Grab and pull and press an adversary low and high, stepping in to trip and slice up. From Baguazhang, one of its sixty-four hands. 3. A combination of continuous moving pulls and presses. From Liuhebafa. 4. Draw a large circle with the hands, opening them out to the sides, then close them in front of the chest in a ready stance. From Wudangquan.

bō yún jiàn yuè 拨云见月 See bō yún wàng yuè.

bō yún wàng yuè 拨云望月 Push aside the Clouds to Gaze at the Moon. 1. In Taijiquan, a moving draw with a sword. 2. In Baguazhang, a hook with one deerhorn knife then a flat sweep to the front with the other. Also called bō yún jiàn yuè.

bō yún zhān rì 拨云瞻日 Push aside the Clouds to Look at the Sun: turn around and check up with the blade, a defense against a high strike from behind. From Qingping sword.

bō zhǎng 拨掌 Check with the forearm: with the elbow slightly bent, palm open. Rotate the hand inward or outward to check to the opposite or the same side.

波 (rad.85) bō   1. Waves, breakers. 2. To fluctuate, fluctuations. 3. To affect, implicate.

bō cháng jiàn 波长剑 A wavy long sword: a straight double-edged sword with a wavy blade.

bō yǎn fǎ 波眼法 Wave looking method: use peripheral vision to sweep for an adversary's weak spots while fighting.

搏 (rad.64) bó   To wrestle; fight; combat.

bó jī 搏击 Wrestling.

bó shǒu 搏手 Bare knuckle fighting. See also tú bó.

脖 (rad.130) bó   The neck.

bó zhǒu 脖肘 An elbow to the neck. From Tanglangquan, one of its eight short techniques.

bó zi 脖子 The neck, a common term when spoken rather than written.

鈸 [钹] (rad.167) bó   Cymbals. Used for music during lion dances, along with the drum. When cut in half with a grip, used as weapons.

跛 (rad.157) bǒ   Lame.

bǒ jiǎo 跛脚 Limping throw. See lǐng tī.

bǒ jiǎo bù 跛脚步 Limping steps: continuous steps to the side using a front crossing step that mimics limping. From Drunken fist.

bǒ tuǐ 跛腿 Limping kick: lift the leading foot slightly and charge forward a half step while simultaneously bringing the other foot along the ground, extending forward.

補 [补] (rad.145) bǔ   1. To repair, mend, patch. 2. To supplement. 3. To make up for. 4. Supplements. 5. To nourish. 6. To subsidize.

bǔ tī 补踢 Make up kick: hook up the foot (bending the knee to bring the foot up behind) when your adversary tries a sweep, then bring your foot back to kick his leg to throw him instead. From wrestling.

不 (rad.1) bù   Negation, no.

bù bǔ 不补 Not securing, a pattern applied in channel diagnosis. From TCM.

bù bù 不布 Not distributing, a pattern applied in channel diagnosis. From TCM.

bù dào wèi 不到味 To fall short in achieving the flavour of a movement.

bù dào wèi 不到位 To fall short, not achieve the final placement of a movement.

bù dé fēn 不得分 No point: no points awarded, a clash in a sparring match.

bù dīng bù bā 不丁不八 Neither a T stance nor a character eight stance: feet open to front and back, about shoulder width apart, front foot tucked in slightly, rear foot open about thirty degrees, weight sixty to seventy percent towards the rear leg. Sometimes called bàn mǎ bù, liù sì bù, sān qī bù, sān qī mǎ bù, sì liù bù.

bù diū bù dǐng 不丢不顶 Don't lose contact, don't fight against: neither slack nor resisting: follow an adversary's attacks exactly, neither losing contact with his arm nor resisting against it. From Taijiquan.

bù èr fǎ 不二法 Not two method: while one should always attack with a target in mind, if one misses the target, one continues with multiple attacks, each as accurate and decisive as if it is the only strike.

bù gù 不固 Not securing, a pattern applied in channel diagnosis. From TCM.

B

bù guī jīng 不归经 Not returning to the channels, a pattern applied in channel diagnosis. From TCM.

bù hé 不和 In disharmony, a pattern applied in channel diagnosis. From TCM.

bù jiāo 不交 Not interacting, a pattern applied in channel diagnosis. From TCM.

bù jiē chù shì fáng shǒu 不接触式防守 Non-contacting defense: any defensive move that involves making evasive moves to avoid contact with an incoming attack.

bù lì 不利 Inhibited, a pattern applied in channel diagnosis. From TCM.

bù néng lǎo bù néng nèn 不能老不能嫩 You must not be old, and you must not be immature. A martial saying: You need to wait to defend against a weapon when it is within your space, but not too close: not too late, not too early. From Xingyiquan.

bù níng 不宁 Not quiet, a pattern applied in channel diagnosis. From TCM.

bù pà qiān zhāo huì, jiù pà yī zhāo jīng 不怕千招会，就怕一招精 Don't fear someone who knows a lot of techniques, fear someone who has mastered one. A martial saying.

bù piān bù yǐ 不偏不倚 Don't tilt or lean. A common requirement describing an upright torso in many styles.

bù róng 不容 Acupoint Burong (not contained), ST19. At the abdomen, five *cun* up from the navel, two *cun* lateral to the midline (on each side). From TCM.

bù shēng 不升 Not up-bearing, a pattern applied in channel diagnosis. From TCM.

bù shōu 不绶 Not restraining, a pattern applied in channel diagnosis. From TCM.

bù tiáo 不调 Not regulating, a pattern applied in channel diagnosis. From TCM.

bù tōng 不通 Blocked, not transmitting *qi*.

bù xuān 不宣 Not diffusing, a pattern applied in channel diagnosis. From TCM.

bù zhàn rén xiān, bù luò rén hòu 不占人先不落人后 Don't try to take possession first, but don't land your technique last. A martial saying.

bù zhèn 不振 Devitalised, a pattern applied in channel diagnosis. From TCM.

bù zhí de zhí quán 不直的直拳 A not-straight straight punch: a jab, not quite straightening the arm. From Yiquan.

布 (rad.50) bù   Cloth, cotton cloth; textiles.

bù dài 布袋 A pouch, sack, bag. Filled with content giving various degrees of weight and hardness, such as rice or sand. Usually canvas, as a durable material for striking.

bù rén 布人 Canvas dummy: a training dummy with arms and legs used to practice wrestling techniques.

步 (rad.77) bù   1. A step; a pace. 2. To walk; to go on foot. 3. A stance. 4. To pace out to measure distance. 5. A pace: a traditional unit of length, 300-360 make up one *li*. See also shì lǐ.

For more stances and stepping terms, see also under ǎi gōng bù, ào-, ào gōng-, bā zì-, bā zì kòu-, bā zì mǎ-, bá-, bāi-, bāi gōng-, bǎi-, bǎi shēn qián jìn-, bài-, bàn bǎi-, bàn gōng-, bàn kòu-, bàn mǎ-, bàn xié dāng-, bàn zuò pán-, bāo mǎ-, bèi-, bèng-, biāo-, bìng-, bō-, bǒ jiǎo-, cǎi-, cǎi tuǐ-, cè gōng-, chuō dìng-, chuō jiǎo-, cǐ-, cuān-, cuī-, cùn-, cuō-, cuō-, cuò-, cuò-, dài-, dān dié-, dān guì-, dān huàn-, dào bā zì-, dào-, dào chā-, dà jí-, dēng jī-, dī nǎi zì-, diān-, diān qǐ-, diān tī-, diǎn-, diàn-, diào mǎ-, diào-, dié-, dié zuò-, dié-, dīng bā-, dīng xū-, dīng zì-, dīng zì gōng-, dīng zì kòu-, dǐng-, dìng-, dú lì-, dú lì dūn-, dú lì gōu tuǐ-, dūn-, èr zì mǎ-, fān bā zì-, fēi jiàn-, fú huàn-, gài-, gài chā-, gài tiào-, gǎn-, gāo tǐ-, gē dēng-, gēn-, gēn diǎn-, gōng-, gōng mǎ-, gòu-, guǎi-, guì-, guì dìng-, guì pū-, guì xī-, guò bǎi-, guò-, guò kòu-, hán-, hán jī-, hé tuǐ mǎ-, hè xíng-, hèn-, héng-, héng dāng-, héng kāi-, héng kuà-, héng rào-, hóu xíng-, hòu jiāo chā-, hòu guān-, hòu tuǐ-, hú xíng-, hù dāng-, huá-, huàn-, huàn tiào-, huí shēn xíng-, huó-, jī-, jī xíng-, jí-, jí zòng-, jiā jiǎn-, jiǎn-, jiǎn zi gǔ-, jiàn-, jiàn-, jiàn chuān-, jiàn-, jiàn cuàn-, jiāo chā-, jiāo cuò-, jiǎo-, jiǎo jiǎn-, jiǎo jiān-, jīn chā-, jīn jī-, jìn-, jiǔ gōng-, kāi-, kāi hé-, kāi lì-, kòu-, kuà-, kuài-, lā lā-, lā mǎ-, lǎo-, lǐ hé-, lǐ mǎ-, liǎn-, liù hé-, liù sì-, lóng xíng-, luò-, mǎ-, má què-, mài-, māo-, méi huā-, mó yǎn-, mó jìng-, nǎi zì-, nèi bā-, nì huàn-, niǎn-, níng-, niǔ-, nǚ zì-, nuó-, pá xíng-, pán chán-, pán gēn-, pǎo-, piān mǎ-, pò jiǎo-, pò-, pū-, pū-, qī xīng-, qī zì-, qí lóng-, qí lǔ-, qí lín-, qián diǎn-, qián jiāo chā-, qián jìn-, qián tǎng ào-, qián tàng ào-, qiǎng-, qiáo jiǎo-, qū dūn dīng-, qū xī-, qū-, qū gōng-, quān-, quān kòu-, quān tiào-, qué-, qué yuè-, rào-, rú-, rú xíng-, sān cái-, sān jiǎo-, sān jiǎo mǎ-, sān qī-, shǎn-, shǎn zhǎn-, shàng-, shàng bù cǐ-, shé xíng qián-, shí zhàn-, shuāng dié-, shuāng gōng-, shuāng huàn-, shuāng kòu-, shuāng zhuàn-, shùn-, sì liù-, sì píng-, sì píng mǎ-, suí-, suí xíng-, suì-, suō suō-, tā jī-, tà-, tàn-, tāng ní-, tāng shuǐ-, táng láng-, tàng ní-, tào-, téng kōng shù chā yuè-, tí-, tí xī dú lì-, tiào bìng-, tiào-, tiào chā-, tiào tī-, tōu-, tuì-, tuō-, tuō lì-, tuō tiào-, tuó xíng-, wā xíng-, wài chā-, wǔ-, xí-, xiāo bǎi-, xiē-, xié chèn-, xié dāng-, xié shēn rào-, xiè-, xíng-, xū-, xù-, xuán zhuǎn-, xuàn fēng-, yī zhì-, yī zì-, yī zì mǎ-, yí-, yòu gōng-, yòu xié-, yū huí-, yú-, yù huán-, yuán-, yuè-, zhān-, zhèn-, zhēng bā zì-, zhèng-, zhèng dāng-, zhèng dīng zì-, zhèng jí-, zhí xíng-, zhuǎn shēn-, zhuàn-, zhuāng-, zhuī mǎ-, zì rán-, zòng-, zòng tiào-, zǒu mǎ-, zuǒ gōng-, zuǒ xié-, zuò-, zuò dēng-, zuò liàn-, zuò pán-, zuò shān-.

bù bù wěn zé quán luàn, bù bù kuài zé quán màn 步不稳则拳乱，步不快则拳慢 If your footwork is unstable your hand techniques will be a mess, if your footwork isn't quick your hand techniques will be slow. A martial saying.

bù fǎ 步法 Footwork, step work.

bù jí dāo měng 步疾刀猛 The footwork is fast and the blade is fierce. A martial saying. The techniques of the broadsword should combine both speed and power.

bù láng 步廊 Acupoint Bulang (corridor walk), KI22. At the chest, at the fifth intercostal space, 2 *cun* lateral to the midline (on each side). From TCM.

bù sì zuàn 步似钻 Footwork like a drill: one of the basic qualities of many styles.

bù tíng yì bù tíng 步停意不停 The intent is not interrupted when the stepping pauses. From Baguazhang, one of the qualities sought in its methods.

bù xíng 步型 Stances, stance: the shape taken by the legs when static.

bù yǎn 步眼 The eyes of the feet: how the feet take the most advantageous placement, distance, and timing in a fight.

bù yào líng 步要灵 Footwork must be quick. Agility, ease of movement, and timing in footwork are necessities in fighting.

B

C

擦 (rad.64) cā   1. To rub, wipe. 2. To apply or spread something on.

cā jiǎo 擦脚 Rubbing slap kick. Tends to mean a lifted kick, or slightly snapping kick, rather than a fully cocked snap kick. The emphasis of the slapping hand is to move forward, rather than down onto the foot.

cā shāng 擦伤 A scrape, graze, abrasion; a surface, skin injury.

裁 (rad.145) cái   1. To judge; decide. 2. To cut into parts.

cái pàn 裁判 Officials. A referee, a judge.

cái pàn rén yuán 裁判人员 Officials. A referee, a judge.

cái pàn zhǎng 裁判长 Chief official, head judge of a judging team.

cái pàn zǔ 裁判组 Team of officials in a competition, jury: the team of head judge, A, B, and C judges for Taolu competition.

採 (rad.64) [采] (rad.165) cǎi To pick, pluck, or gather. To grab and pull with a twist. Pluck, which implies a double handed pull, one hand holding steady while the other pulls. Usually implies separating with a short power, to change the direction of an incoming attack.

cǎi jìn 采劲 Plucking power: the power and skill used to grab and pluck.

cǎi jiān 采肩 Pluck the shoulder: when an adversary is face down on the ground, lift his arm up with the other hand controlling at the shoulder.

cǎi shǒu 采手 Plucking hand: loop around an adversary's arm with the wrist to finish with a grab. From Tanglangquan.

綵 (rad.120) [彩] (rad.59) cǎi   Vari-coloured silk.

cǎi chóu 彩绸 Coloured silks or synthetic fabrics attached to the handles of broadswords, steel whips, etc. Usually called flags in English.

cǎi dié liàn huā 彩蝶恋花 Colourful Butterfly Yearns for Flowers: to escape from a double-handed grab on the wrist, reach through to use both hands as leverage to twist out of the grab.

cǎi fèng shū yǔ 彩凤舒羽 Colourful Phoenix Smooths its Feathers: a front cross step with a cut low behind, extending both arms, the left reaching up to the front. From Wu Taijiquan sword.

踩 (rad.157) cǎi   To trample, step on.

cǎi bù 踩步 Trampling step: a walking step that sets a root on landing – not rubbing forward. From Baguazhang.

cǎi fǎ 踩法 Trampling methods: using the foot to press any part of an adversary down.

cǎi jiān 踩肩 Trample on the shoulder: when an adversary is face down on the ground, pull his arm up behind with his arm twisted, kneeling or standing on his shoulder joint. From Qinna.

cǎi jiǎo 踩脚 Trample, a crushing kick. 1. A low kick, just under the knee, with the foot turned out. In the category of snap kicks, see qū shēn xìng tuǐ fǎ. 2. Landing with the foot turned out to stamp on an adversary's foot. In Baguazhang, is a hidden kick, appearing to step with a bǎi bù. 3. In some styles is a kick to the shin or a kick and slide down. Also called lán mén jiǎo. From Chuojiao, one of its middle-basin kicks.

cǎi jìn 踩劲 Trampling power: to reach out and land the foot as if trampling on a poisonous snake. One of Xingyiquan's five powers. See also guǒ jìn, jué jìn, pū jìn, shù jìn.

cǎi shāo jiǎo 踩梢脚 Stamp on the tip: same as a crushing kick, but more with the intent to stand on the foot to pin it to allow for another technique. From Xingyiquan. See also cǎi jiǎo.

cǎi shǒu ér rù shǒu 采手而入手 If grabbed with one hand, control an adversary's grabbing hand and attack his elbow. From Tanglangquan, one of its twelve soft counters, see also shí èr róu.

C

cǎi tuǐ 踩腿 See cǎi jiǎo.

cǎi tuǐ bù 踩腿步 Trampling step: stepping forward circling outward slightly, with the feet turned out to step on an adversary. Also called jiǎo bù.

cǎi xī 踩膝 Trample on the knee: from behind, reverse and control your adversary's arm and step on his knee, pushing it down (allowing it to bend naturally, not a knee break). From wrestling.

cǎi yī zhǎng 踩一掌 Trample with a Palm: a trampling low kick in combination with a rising palm strike. From Chen Taijiquan.

cǎi yóu shé 踩游蛇 Trample on a roving snake: a metaphor for the walking of Baguazhang. At each step, the feet must be firm, accurate, steady, and flat, as if trampling on the head and tail of a snake, not allowing it to escape or attack.

蔡 (rad.140) cài   A surname.

cài jiā quán 蔡家拳 Caijiaquan (Cai family fist), a southern style attributed to the Fujian province Shaolin temple and the Cai family, popular in Guangdong province. Known of since the mid 1700s. Also called cài quán.

cài lǐ fú quán 蔡李拂拳 Cailifujia (Cai, Li, and Fu fist), attributed to Chen Dianying in the 1800s, combining Fu family style, Li style, and Cai style. It is popular in Guangdong province. Known in English as Choylifut from the Cantonese pronunciation.

cài quán 蔡拳 Caiquan (Cai fist). See cài jiā quán.

參 [参] (rad.59) cān   1. To take part in.

cān chán 参禅 See zuò chán.

cān jiā 参加 To participate, as in to participate in a performance or competition.

cān jiàn 参见 Refer to, see, cf: used to indicated references in a book or article.

cān jūn 参军 To enlist, join up, sign up for the army.

cān kǎo 参考 Refer to; consult written materials.

殘 [残] (rad.78) cán   1. To destroy, injure. 2. Cruel, heartless. 3. Crippled, disfigured. 4. To kill. 5. Remnant, remaining.

cán xué 残穴 Crippling points: accurately striking these points can cause very severe injury, so they are to be avoided unless driven to extremity. See also chéng shān, dà líng, fēng shì, hè dǐng, huán tiào, láo gōng, nèi huái jiān, sān yīn jiāo, shén mén, shǒu sān lǐ, wài guān, wài huái jiān, wěi gōng, wěi zhōng, zhī zhèng, zú sān lǐ.

蒼 [苍] (rad.140) cāng   Dark blue or green (in evergreens). Grey (in hair or beard).

cāng lóng bǎi wěi 仓龙摆尾 Grey Dragon Slashes it Tail: step forward bringing the hands alternately across the face and down the body with a deflecting action. From Wudangquan.

cāng lóng bǎi wěi shì 仓龙摆尾式 Grey Dragon Slashes it Tail model. 1. One of twenty-four classic spear moves. Most spear routines will have a move with a like name. In general, this name refers to a technique that retreats, but wins by spinning. 2. Large coils with a spear, first to the left, laying the shaft along the chest, then to the right, tucking the body and tucking the right hand at the left armpit.

cāng lóng fú dì 仓龙伏地 Grey Dragon Lies on the Ground: a drop stance threading palm. From Piguaquan.

cāng lóng jiǎo hǎi 仓龙搅海 Grey Dragon Stirs the Sea: stepping backwards with rear cross steps cutting down to the rear, alternating with front steps chopping forward. From Qingping sword.

cāng lóng nào hǎi 仓龙闹海 Grey Dragon Roils the Sea: toss a sword up and catch the grip in the left hand. From Yangjia sword.

cāng lóng suō wěi 仓龙缩尾 Grey Dragon Tucks in its Tail: step one foot into a character eight stance and cross the arms, pressing out to the sides with the hands, keeping the shoulders open and the hips closed. From Baguazhang.

cāng lóng tàn zhǎo 仓龙探爪 Grey Dragon Reaches its Claws: withdraw with a shearing cut with a sword, tucking in the body while lifting and snapping the wrist to dip the blade tip. From Qingping sword.

藏 (rad.140) cáng   To hide, conceal.

cáng dāo 藏刀 Hide a broadsword: draw a broadsword back to hold it angled behind the body. The tip is usually, but not necessarily, at the knee.

操 (rad.64) **cāo** 1. To grasp; hold. 2. To do. 3. A drill; an exercise.

cāo jiǎo fǎ 操脚法 Leg training exercises such as kicking wooden dummies. From Tongbeiquan.

cāo shǒu 操手 Partner exercises, partner sparring drills, applications practice.

cāo shǒu fǎ 操手法 Hand and arm training exercises, such as hitting sandbags hitting leather bags, partner hitting. From Tongbeiquan.

側 [侧] (rad.9) **cè** 1. The side. 2. To incline to one side.

cè bǎi tuǐ 侧摆腿 Side outer crescent kick, an outward crescent kick turned to contact with the heel.

cè bān tuǐ 侧搬腿 Assisted side stretch: Holding the foot up straight up to the same side, either by yourself or partner assisted.

cè bēng quán 侧崩拳 Side snap punch: snap the heel of the fist out to the side.

cè biāo tuǐ 侧摽腿 Side waving leg: a straight swing kick up to the side. From Mizongquan. Also called shí zì tī.

cè chǎn tuǐ 侧铲腿 Side shovel kick: side kick to the knee, using the outer edge of the foot.

cè cháo tiān dēng 侧朝天蹬 Side hold kick on the head: stand with the supporting leg straight, the upheld leg at the side with the foot curling over the head, pressing the foot on the head with the hands. Also called bān jiǎo cháo tiān, cè tī bào jiǎo.

cè chēng tuǐ 侧撑腿 Side Propping kick: see cè chuài tuǐ.

cè chuài píng héng 侧踹平衡 Side thrust kick balance: extend the leg in a side kick position and hold it for two seconds.

cè chuài tuǐ 侧踹腿 A side thrust kick with the foot flat. A common name. One of Chuojiao's middle-basin kicks. Also called cè chēng tuǐ.

cè dēng 侧蹬 Side heel kick.

cè diǎn gùn 侧点棍 Side dab with the staff: with the hands a third of the way along the shaft, swing the staff to the side to dab downwards with the tip of the staff. You may lift the foot to tap it with the tip.

cè diǎn jiǎo 侧点脚 Sideways poke kick: lean to the side to touch down one hand and poke kick with the other leg, the foot angled upwards.

cè gōng bù 侧弓步 Side bow stance: a bow stance with the feet parallel but turned. Also called dǎ hǔ bù.

cè gōu shǒu 侧勾手 Sideways hooked hand: fingers pointing back, top of wrist pointing to the side. A positional reference, separate from the direction of the strike.

cè gǔn fān 侧滚翻 A side roll.

cè kōng fān 侧空翻 Aerial cartwheel: cartwheel without touching the hands down.

cè kōng fān zhuàn tǐ 侧空翻转体 Aerial cartwheel full twist: an aerial cartwheel with a full three-sixty rotation while vertical in the air.

cè kōng fān zhuàn tǐ qī bǎi èr 侧空翻转体720 Aerial cartwheel seven-twenty, an aerial cartwheel with a double twist.

cè kòng tuǐ 侧控腿 Side leg hold: standing holding the leg to the side without support.

cè kōng tuǐ píng héng 侧空腿平衡 Side leg raised balance: standing holding the leg to the side without support, holding for two seconds.

cè lì zhǎng 侧立掌 Side vertical palm: fingers up, palm heel forward, arm out and wrist flexed so that the fingers point up. A positional reference, not related to the direction of the strike.

cè mén 侧门 The side gate of an adversary: the flanks, which include the shoulders, ribs, waist and hips.

cè miàn 侧面 From the side: in illustrated books, the side view, looking at the posture from one side or the other. See also hòu miàn, zhèng miàn.

cè pī fā lì 侧劈发力 Release of power with a sideways cut, arms opening out to the side. From Yiquan.

cè shǎn 侧闪 Sideways dodge: dodge to the side, without stepping, to avoid an attack without contact.

cè shēn 侧身 As a positional description: positions and movements that present one side of the body.

C

cè shēn mǎ 侧身马 Side horse stance, diagonal stance: turn and sit from a high horse stance to extend one shoulder forward. From Wing Chun.

cè shēn píng héng 侧身平衡 Side balance: supporting leg straight, the body leans forward, tilted to the side, the suspended leg extended to the rear to at least waist level. The arms extend to the lower front and to the rear with the suspended leg.

cè shēn quán 侧身拳 Side punch: turn and punch simultaneously without moving the feet, turning the hips and shoulders to extend the punch. From Wing Chun.

cè shēn zhǎng 侧身掌 Sideways palm: turn and push/block across the body to the outside with the palm at the shoulder, fingers up, palm outwards. From Wing Chun.

cè shǒu fān 侧手翻 A cartwheel.

cè shuāi 侧摔 A side fall.

cè sī tuǐ 侧撕腿 Tear the legs: the side splits.

cè tī bāo jiǎo zhí lì 侧踢抱脚直立 Side straight hold: kick the leg up the side and hold the foot, keeping upright.

cè tī jiǎo 侧踢脚 A side kick. From Yiquan. Usually called cè chuài tuǐ.

cè tī tuǐ 侧踢腿 A side straight kick: a straight legged kick, swinging up to the same side ear. In the category of straight swinging kicks, see also zhí bǎi xìng tuǐ fǎ.

cè tí xī píng héng 侧提膝平衡 Side knee raised balance: raise one knee to the side of the body, the supporting leg straight.

cè tuō diǎn 侧托点 Poke kick to the side with the hands up to hold an adversary. From Chuojiao, one of its middle-basin kicks.

cè wò jié tuǐ 侧卧截腿 Cutting kick from side lying position: as an adversary comes at you, hook your lower foot on his ankle and cut with the other foot in the opposite direction at the knee.

cè wò tuǐ 侧卧腿 Side leg lying, a stretch: both legs straight with both feet on the ground, lie the body on the leg to put the foot to the same side ear.

cè xíng bù 侧行步 Side stepping: step one foot to the side, then step the other foot in.

cè yā tuǐ 侧压腿 Side stretch, both legs straight, foot to same ear, with the foot raised and supported on something.

cè yì 侧翼 The flank, flanks, sides. Includes the shoulders, armpits, ribs, and sides of the waist and hips.

cè zhǎng 侧掌 Side palm: the palm held sideways. A positional reference, separate from the direction of the strike.

cè zhuàng xī 侧撞膝 A knee strike to the side. From Chuojiao, one of its middle-basin kicks, and a common name in northern styles.

cè zǐ tiào 侧子跳 A side jump, jump to the side.

策 (rad.118) cè   1. A whip (for horses). 2. To whip; to spur; to urge.

cè mǎ fēi tí 策马飞蹄 Whip the Horse to Make its Hooves Fly: pull in the hands as if pulling on reins, kick, and push out to the sides. From Wudangquan.

蹭 (rad.157) cèng   To rub; smear; scrape.

cèng tuǐ 蹭腿 Smearing kick: with the foot hooked in, cut your adversary's shin with the outside edge of your foot and apply further pressure downwards. Also called duò zi tuǐ, xià qiē tuǐ.

叉 (rad.29) chā   A trident, fork: a long or short weapon with three tips pointing forward. To work with a fork. A stabbing hand strike with the fingers.

chā bù 叉步 1. A cross stance, cross bow stance; back cross step, inserting step. 2. Sometimes means an unaligned stance or stepping, when the opposite hand and foot move forward.

chā tuō 叉脱 Crossing release, an escape from a control: a leverage escape, crossing with and striking hard at the grabbing hand.

chā zǐ zhǎng 叉子掌 Stabbing palm, a circle-walking posture. See tuō qiāng zhǎng.

扠 (rad.64) chā   1. A harpoon. 1. To fork; to work with a fork.

chā chè 扠撤 Forking withdrawal, a takedown: slide the hand in under an adversary's armpit and step back, turning to take him down to his side.

chā fǎ 扠法 Forking hold. 1. As a hand technique

stab one arm through the armpit of an adversary in preparation to grab. 2. As an arm technique, thread the arm through the armpit to gain leverage. 3. As a leg technique, thread the thigh in between an adversary's legs. From wrestling.

chā shǎn 扠闪 Forking dodge, a takedown: a subtle movement of the body, sliding the arm in under the armpit and leveraging to take an adversary down to the side.

chā shǒu pō jiǎo 扠手泼脚 Fork the Hands and Spill the Feet: grab an adversary by the sleeve, then slide the arm in for more contact, sliding in to trip from the front of his leg. From wrestling.

chā tī 扠踢 Forking kick, a trip: a low kick using circular, withdrawing movement, drawing into emptiness and dodging.

chā yāo 扠腰 Hands on hips, a casual placement with thumbs behind, elbows out, often used during warm-ups. Chinese translators always call this arms akimbo.

chā zhǎng 扠掌 Palm strike with the fingers up, heel of palm forward.

chā zhāo 扠招 To spar.

插 (rad.64) chā 1. To stab, insert, stick in. 2. As a strike, is often downwards. 3. Inserting leg techniques.

chā bào tiāo dǎ 插抱挑打 Insert and embrace scooping throw: catch your adversary's arm and move in grasping his arm, stepping in and turning to tuck the hip into him. Catch his leg with yours and lift one leg high to take his leg up, at the same time bowing the back, so that he does a high-flying fall. A throw.

chā bù 插步 Back insertion step. 1. Step one foot behind the other, crossing the legs, touching the toes down. Usually fairly extended. The intention is to insert your foot between an adversary's legs in preparation for a throw. 2. To step directly in between an adversary's legs to control him close to the centre of balance, not crossing the legs.

chā bù dān biān 插步单鞭 Back cross step single whip: in a back cross step, extend upright fists out in a straight line at shoulder height, opposite hand forward.

chā bù shuāng bǎi zhǎng 插步双摆掌 Back cross step arm swings: step into a back cross step while swinging the arms over towards the back.

chā bù zhuā jiān 插步抓肩 Back cross step shoulder grab: step into a back cross step while placing the rear hand on the leading shoulder, hooking with the lead hand. This is a setup for a control. From Chaquan.

chā chuí 插捶 Stabbing fists: a routine of Mizongquan, written up as seventy moves.

chā dì lóng 插地龙 Dragon stabs the ground: fully squat on one leg, extend the other to the side, feet flat. Usually called pū bù.

chā diǎn 插点 A snap kick to the ankle, with the foot extended to strike with the top of the foot. From Chuojiao, one of its middle-basin kicks.

chā gān bù 插竿步 Insert the Stick step: lift the front knee and hop back on the rear foot, landing in a raised knee stance.

chā huā yē lèi 插花掖肋 Insert a Flower into the Ribs: step in, move an adversary's arm out of the way, and drive an extended turned over punch to his ribs. From Baguazhang, one of its sixty-four hands.

chā jiān guò bèi 插肩过背 Insert the shoulder throw over the back: get in close and slide the shoulder under your adversary's armpit. Turn to get the hip onto his body, with the knees bent. Extend the knees, lower the head, and push with the back to throw him over the back. From wrestling.

chā jiǎo 插脚 Stabbing kick, snap kick.

chā shā 插砂 Insert into sand: stab the fingers into sand or beans to train finger strength and hardness.

chā shǒu 插手 Insert the hand: stab with the palm and fingers straight.

chā tuǐ 插腿 Insert the leg: step in to an adversary's stance, catching the leg with the inside or outside of your leg.

chā zhǎng 插掌 To stab. 1. Extend the arm to apply power to the finger tips, usually downwards. 2. Stabbing palm: fingers down, wrist straight. A positional reference, separate from the direction of the strike. 3. In Baguazhang, often means to stab by sliding the hand along the extended leg into a drop stance.

C

查 (rad.75) chá   1. To check, examine. To look into, to investigate. 2. Pronounced zhā, a surname. The martial style, though from this surname, is usually pronounced Chaquan.

chá dāo 查刀 A broadsword routine of Chaquan, written up as forty-seven moves.

chá gùn 查棍 A staff routine of Chaquan, written up as forty-nine moves.

chá quán 查拳 Chaquan (Cha's fist), a Longfist style from the Hui nationality, considered to be from Shandong province. It has ten solo hand routines, weapons, and partner routines. It has quick, clean, open movements.

拆 (rad.64) chāi   To break, to rip open. To take down, to tear down; to dismantle.

chāi quán 拆拳 See chāi shǒu.

chāi shǒu 拆手 To break down techniques. 1. Analyze a technique with a partner to find its applications. 2. Break down a routine to find the power for each technique and figure out all the details for each technique.

攙 [搀] (rad.64) chān   To support something by the arm; support somebody with the hand.

chān guǎn 搀管 To jam with the lower leg, preventing an adversary from using his leg. From wrestling.

chān ná 搀拿 Supporting grappling hold: tuck the arm under the arm of an adversary, as if supporting them, but actually jamming the arm in preparation for a throw. From wrestling.

chān tī 搀踢 Supporting kick, a trip. See tāng hé.

禪 [禅] (rad.113) chán   1. Meditation; contemplation. 2. Chan Buddhism, called Zen in English, from the Japanese.

chán lín 禅林 See chán yuàn.

chán mén 禅门 Chan Buddhism, called Zen in English, from the Japanese.

chán wù 禅悟 Enlightenment, realization of truth though meditation or a shock.

chán yuàn 禅院 A Chan Buddhist temple. Also called chán lín.

chán zhàng 禅杖 A Buddhist monk's staff.

纏 [缠] (rad.120) chán   1. To wind around, bind up, coil around, twine. An action like a snake coiling around its prey, or a vine coiling around a branch. 2. A kick: coil the foot around to trap. 3. A grappling technique: wrap around, usually wrapping around the arm to pressure the wrist, elbow, or shoulder. 4. A winding strike used to clear the main gateway of an adversary. From Bajiquan, one of its six main striking techniques, see also liù dà kāi. 5. One of the sixteen key techniques of Baguazhang, see shí liù zì jué.

chán biān 缠鞭 Coil the whip. See chán qiáo.

chán dǒu jìn 缠抖劲 Coiling shaking power: a snapping power that also coils and keeps contact. From Tanglangquan.

chán fǎ 缠法 Coiling methods. 1. Twisting or wringing control methods. 2. Inward coiling. From Chen Taijiquan.

chán fēng shuāng zhǎng 缠封双掌 Coiling shut down, double palms: reach out with both hands to press down on an attack. From Tongbeiquan, one of its seven long range techniques.

chán má huā 缠麻花 Wind the Fried Dough Twist. Wrestling techniques that involve coiling one leg around the leg of an adversary in combination with the upper body and arm work. Also called chán.

chán qià shǒu 缠骱手 Wind the Waist strike: bring the hands directly from the hip, both on the same side, to strike with the heel of the palms to front and rear at shoulder height, the body turned into the front arm. From Tongbeiquan.

chán qiāng 缠枪 Circle a spear. 1. With the shaft level at chest height, draw smooth coiling circles with the tip. 2. The same, but specifically in a clockwise direction. See also jiǎo qiāng.

chán qiāng fǎn zhā 缠枪返扎 Coil a spear to stab behind. See huí mǎ qiāng.

chán qiáo 缠桥 Coil the bridge, a forearm technique: with the wrist as pivot point, coil in a small circle (either inwards or outwards) while grabbing and pulling. From southern styles. Also called chán biān.

chán rào 缠绕 Coil around, twine around, wind

around.

chán shēn dāo 缠身刀 Wind a broadsword around the body: wrap a broadsword around the body, the grip above the head, the blade vertical and close to the body. Used with long broadswords to protect the torso.

chán shǒu 缠手 Coil the hands around something.

chán shǒu kào dǎ 缠手靠打 Coil and Lean: an expressive term for the category of hand techniques using leading methods. See also lǐng fǎ.

chán shǒu yē zhuàng 缠手掖撞 Coil and Hidden Shove: coiling the fist in the palm, completing with a low punch. From Baguazhang, one of its sixty-four hands.

chán sī fǎ 缠丝法 The method of using coiling silk power.

chán sī jìn 缠丝劲 Coiling silk power, a spiraling throughout the body, sending power from the centre of the body to the extremities in a complex internal and external spiraling through all the segments and joints. Most often used to describe the power generation of Chen Taijiquan.

chán sī tuǐ 缠丝腿 Place your foot near your adversary's foot and control his lower leg by pressing with your knee.

chán tóu (dāo) 缠头(刀) Coil the head, around the head twining: wind a broadsword around the head/neck/ upper back, tip down, spine on the back, from left to right shoulder. The blade should stay close to the back and come out from over the shoulder and the left forearm should run along the spine of the blade as it curls around.

chán tóu guǒ nǎo 缠头裹脑 Coil the head and wrap the brain: wind a broadsword around the head/ neck/ upper back, tip down, spine on the back, from left to right shoulder. Continue on to wind the broadsword around the head, neck, and upper back from right to left shoulder. The blade should stay close to the back and come out from over the shoulder, and the left forearm should run along the spine of the blade as it curls out and back.

chán tóu pī dāo 缠头劈刀 Coil the head and chop: wind a broadsword around the head/neck/ upper back, tip down, spine on the back, from left to right shoulder, and continue on the action, opening to a full chop in front.

chán tuǐ 缠腿 Coil the leg: 1. A wrapping kick: first wrap the leg in then side kick or shovel kick. In the category of snap kicks, see also qū shēn xìng tuǐ fǎ. 2. A tripping takedown, done by wrapping the leg around an adversary's leg and snapping from the waist. Also called má huā bāi, wō gòu.

chán wàn 缠腕 Wrist wrap: trap an adversary's hand with your free hand when he grabs one wrist. Coil the little finger side of your grabbed hand around his wrist to press down. His wrist is extended and pressed down sideways. From Qinna.

chán wàn gǔn fān 缠腕滚翻 Rolling release from a wrist wrap, an escape from a control: move forward and roll the body.

chán yāo biān 缠腰鞭 Coil the whip around the waist: bring a steel whip in towards the waist while performing horizontal circles, release the handle and keep the whip circling with the middle at the waist.

chán zhǒu 缠肘 Arm wrap, a technique to control the arm of an adversary. From Qinna and wrestling.

chán zhǒu bǎi lián 缠肘摆莲 Wrap the arm and lotus kick: trap the adversary's elbow with your hands and do an outside crescent kick. From Baguazhang, one of its sixty-four hands.

铲 [铲] (rad.167) **chǎn** 1. A shovel, a spade. 2. When used as a long weapon, often has a blade at each end: a crescent moon shaped blade and a shovel shaped blade.

chǎn dào zhàng jiàn 铲道仗剑 Shovel the Road holding a Sword: slash upwards, first bringing the tip of the sword close to the ground. From Taijiquan.

chǎn shǒu 铲手 Spade hand: strike with the heel of the palm, fingers turned out. This shape sits nicely into the jaw line. From Wing Chun.

chǎn tuǐ 铲腿 Shovel kick: snap kick with the turned outer edge of the foot. In the category of snap kicks, see also qū shēn xìng tuǐ fǎ. Sometimes also called fǔ rèn tuǐ.

chǎn yuè 铲钺 A shovel axe: a long-handled battle axe with a shovel blade on the other end.

C

闡 [阐] (rad.169) **chǎn** 1. To explain, elucidate. 2. Evident.

chǎn mén 阐门 Sensitive point Chanmen (evident gate), the navel or just above the navel, on the midline. One of seven painful gateways to attack that are related to midline acupoints. Best hit with a straight punch, a knee or elbow butt, or a kick. Also called qí mén. See also qī chōng mén.

嫦 (rad.38) **cháng** Usually in combination as Chang'E, the Chinese Moon Goddess.

cháng é bēn yuè 嫦娥奔月 Chang'E Flies to the Moon: jump up, bending the knees to tuck the feet up behind, and do an upward slice with a sword. From Yangjia sword.

腸 [肠] (rad.130) **cháng** 1. The intestines. 2. Sausage.

cháng guǎn 肠管 The intestines.

萇 [苌] (rad.140) **cháng** A surname.

cháng jiā quán 苌家拳 Changjiaquan (Chang family fist). A style from Henan province, attributed to Chang Naizhou in the mid 1700s. Also called cháng mén quán.

cháng mén quán 苌门拳 Changmenquan (Chang's fist). See cháng jiā quán.

長 [长] (rad.168) **cháng** 1. Long (of space or time). Length. 2. A strong point; be good at. 3. To gradually develop; to gradually become good at.

cháng biān 长鞭 Long whip: see cháng qiáo.

cháng bīn 长兵 1. Long weapons in general, at least head height. As a competition category, staff and spear are the most common. 2. Weapons that can shoot a distance.

cháng gē 长戈 A long dagger: a thick dagger attached to a long wooden handle.

cháng gōng 长功 To gradually grow in skill while training.

cháng jìn 长劲 Lengthening power. 1. Lengthen the intent into an attack or defense, expanding the feeling into the whole structure of the body and ensuring an adversary cannot deal with you. 2. To initiate a long technique simultaneously with an adversary, making contact before him.

cháng jiàn duǎn dìng yào huǎn, duǎn jiàn cháng bì yào máng 长见短定要缓；短见长必要忙 When facing a short weapon with a long weapon, take your time; when facing a long weapon with a short weapon, move quickly. A martial saying.

cháng pái 长牌 A long tablet: a long shield, usually used by foot soldiers for full body protection.

cháng qì xiè 长器械 Long weapons. Refers to any long weapon. As a competition category, nowadays generally refers to staff and spear.

cháng qiāng duǎn yòng 长枪短用 Use a long spear close: spear techniques that use the tip as a dagger or use the butt in close work.

cháng qiáng 长强 Acupoint Changqiang (long strong), DU1. Under the pelvis, in the anal cleft, midway between the coccyx and the anus, 0.5 *cun* from the tip of the coccyx. From TCM. One of the main targets on the body. In internal styles, this point is kept relaxed and pointing downwards to align the body.

cháng qiáo 长桥 Long bridge: to apply forearm techniques with the arm straight or only slightly bent. Also called cháng biān.

cháng quán 长拳 Changquan (long fist), Longfist. 1. Long range styles, as differentiated from short range styles. Includes the northern styles of Chaquan, Huaquan, Paoquan, Hongquan. 2. A northern style that combined Chaquan, Huaquan, Paoquan, Shaolinquan and other northern styles, known by the Ming dynasty. 3. The modern competition style that combines these styles with performance elements. Now the term usually applies to the modern competition style, which is often referred to as wushu in English.

cháng shāo zǐ gùn 长梢子棍 Long handled flail: a two-section staff with longer and shorter parts, linked with metal links. The long is about 1.5 metres, the short about 0.36 metres. Also called dà shāo zi gùn.

cháng shé jiàn 长蛇剑 Long snake sword: a short tasselled sword routine of Mizongquan, written up as sixty-five moves.

cháng shēn 长身 Lengthen the torso, straighten the spine. Also means to shift and extend the body forward, the opposite of zuò shēn.

cháng shǒu pán qiáo 长手盘桥 Long hand basin bridge, a forearm technique: with straight arm, a vertical circle inwards rotating around the shoulder, the hand no higher than the head, and no lower than the groin. From southern styles.

cháng suō jiàn 长梭剑 Long tasselled sword.

cháng yāo 长腰 Lengthen the waist. 1. Straighten the back, used in throwing and takedown actions. From wrestling. Also called shēn yāo. 2. A back exercise to prepare for throwing: with the feet apart, turn in bow stance and turn the back fully, extending the arm to open up the back.

cháng zhēn 长针 Long needle: a fully extended pierce with a long pole, both hands at the butt end.

場 [场] (rad.32) **chǎng** 1. An open space, an area of level ground. 2. The stage. 3. An arena, a playground.

chǎng dì 场地 Training or competition area. In Taolu (routines) competition, the competition area is fourteen by eight metres, with a further two metres of surrounding safety area. In group events, it is sixteen by fourteen metres, with a one metre safety area. In Sanda, the competition area is six metres square. In wrestling, it is between eight to ten metres square.

暢 [畅] (rad.72) **chàng** Free, unimpeded, smooth (power or energy flow).

chàng xiōng 畅胸 Unimpeded chest: the shoulders settled and very slightly brought inwards, the chest relaxed and settled. This allows the chest cavity to lengthen and broaden while remaining contained.

抄 (rad.64) **chāo** To bend the elbow to lift up with the forearm; grab. Non-martial meanings are to copy or transcribe; to make a raid upon; to confiscate; to fold one's arms.

chāo quán 抄拳 An uppercut: with the elbow bent, strike upward, contacting with the knuckles.

chāo shǒu 抄手 See chāo zhǎng.

chāo zhǎng 抄掌 Forearm lift: lift the arm with the elbow bent at shoulder height (this may be in a circular movement, first dropping the palm, then bending and finishing with a lift). This is intended to catch and lift an adversary's arm or leg.

綽 [绰] (rad.120) **chāo** 1. To grab, take up, as in grabbing a weapon. Pronounced chuò, ample.

超 (rad.156) **chāo** To exceed; surpass; ultra-; go beyond.

chāo dà dāo 超大刀 Exceed with a big cutter: with the right hand at the butt, release the left hand and rotate the right hand to turn the blade edge up, jumping and turning to swing the entire weapon over to chop down. This is a long-range technique, exceeding the normal range of the weapon.

chāo tào xùn liàn 超套训练 Ultra-routine training, 'full routine plus' training session: train a whole routine followed immediately by another section. This trains endurance and lactic acid recovery, and is normally done only in final preparation for competition.

朝 (rad.74) **cháo** 1. An imperial court. 2. To face.

cháo tiān dēng 朝天蹬 Foot Faces the Sky. 1. A balance with the supporting leg straight, holding the other foot on top of the head, the leg straight and sole facing directly up. 2. A heel kick upwards.

cháo tiān shì 朝天式 Face the Sky model. One of twenty-four classic spear moves. Most spear routines will have a move with a like name. In general, this name refers to a high feint followed by a low strike.

cháo tiān yī zhù xiāng 朝天一柱香 Put an Incense Stick up to the Sky. 1. Standing up straight, stab a sword directly upwards. 2. Tuck a sword grip at the waist, the blade sticking straight up.

cháo tiān yù zhù 朝天玉柱 Put a Jade Stick up to the Sky. 1. Stand up in a one-legged stance and thrust a staff vertically, butt in the right hand at the chest, left hand extended along the shaft. From Baguazhang. 2. Stand up with the feet together and stab a sword blade directly upright, hands in front of the face. From Qingping sword.

cháo yáng jiàn 朝阳剑 Sword Faces the Sun: in a raised knee stance, block up with a sword above the head, pushing the left hand to the left side.

C

From Chen Taijiquan.

cháo yáng shǒu 朝阳手 Hand Faces the Sun: stand straight up and push one hand up directly over the head, the other at the armpit. From Wudangquan.

車 [车] (rad.159) **chē**   1. A vehicle. 2. A wheeled machine. 3. A lathe. 4. To lift water by waterwheel. 5. A surname.

chē lún 车轮 Wheeling: step forward with a full swinging chop with a sword. From Yang Taijiquan.

chē lún bù 车轮步 Wheel step: pivot on one foot and sweep the other in a circular withdrawing arc, used to trip an adversary. From wrestling.

chē lún fǔ 车轮斧 Wheel axe: a long handled axe with a wheel shaped blade.

chē lún zhǎng 车轮掌 Wheel arms: spin around a full one-eighty circle, swinging the arms horizontally with the turn.

chē mǎ 车马 Waterwheel stances: train a stance repeatedly, shifting to perform on both sides to train both stability and agility.

chē shì xíng yì quán 车式形意拳 Cheshi (Che's) Xingyiquan, attributed to Che Yizhai, from Shanxi province, who learned from Li Nengran and Dai Wenxiong.

撦 [扯] (rad.64) **chě**   To rip up, tear down; raise; haul. To pull and rip: an action like ripping a length of material off a roll.

chě qiāng 扯枪 Haul a spear: an upper whipping outer block.

chě zuān quán 扯钻拳 Ripping drilled punch: open the hand to an eagle claw then clench immediately as the punch extends. Open again as the hand pulls back to the body, clenching again. This is a drilling straight punch, usually done as combination punches, one extending while the other pulls back. From Xingyiquan.

徹 [彻] (rad.60) **chè**   1. Thorough; penetrating. Pervade. 2. As footwork, to penetrate the defenses of an adversary.

掣 (rad.64) **chè**   To pull; tug. To draw back.

chè chì 掣翅 Tug the wingtips: grab an adversary's hand in a reverse grip, turn it over and hyper-flex the wrist, taking him down. Also called wài bāi.

撤 (rad.64) **chè**   To withdraw; to take away.

chè bù 撤步 Withdraw: step the rear foot back or bring the front foot back to the rear foot.

chè bù jiǎo gùn 撤步绞棍 Withdraw while circling a staff: bring the leading foot back to a back cross stance, while continuously doing an entangling circle with the tip of a staff.

chè cì bù 撤跐步 Withdrawing stamp step: slide the front foot back a relatively long way, stopping sharply with a thump.

chè jiān 撤肩 Withdraw the shoulder: turn the body to withdraw the shoulder to avoid an incoming punch to that side, keeping the hands up to cover as well.

chè yāo 撤腰 Withdraw the waist: stepping back, setting down, and withdrawing the torso to initiate a throw.

搀 [抻] (rad.64) **chēn**   To pull out, stretch, like making hand-pulled noodles.

晨 (rad.72) **chén**   Morning; daybreak; dawn.

chén xīng luò dì 晨星落地 Stars at Dawn Land on the Earth: stand up straight with the feet together, and slice over with the blade to chop to the forward right, arm and blade fully extended. From Qingping sword.

沈 (rad.85) **chén**   To sink; settle down; lower; deep, profound; heavy. Settling, one of Ziranmen's nineteen main methods.

chén biān 沉鞭 Sinking whip. See chén qiáo.

chén hǎi shǒu 沉海手 Sink into the Sea: to strike an adversary's coccyx with the hand.

chén jiān 沉肩 Settled shoulders: relax the elevator muscles of the shoulders and settle down the collar bone, releasing through the joints of the shoulder girdle.

chén jiān zhuì zhǒu 沉肩坠肘 Settle the shoulders and elbows, drop the shoulders and sink the elbows.

chén jìn 沉劲 Settling power: relax and settle down throughout the body, lowering the centre of gravity and settling all the joints and *qi*. Combined with propping power, this keeps the body settled and stable. See also dǐng jìn.

chén qì 沉气 1. To settle the breath and energy down to the lower *dantian* (body core). 2. To stop the breath briefly after exhaling, to settle power for dropping movements.

chén qiáo 沉桥 Sinking bridge, a forearm technique: bend the elbow and settle the forearm down with a sharp action, tucking the elbow in close to the body. May continue to pull the hand palm down to the waist. From southern styles. Also called chén biān, chén shǒu.

chén qiáo chuàn zhǎng 沉桥串掌 Sinking Bridge Skewering Palm: in a right reverse bow stance, settle the left hand down then stab it forward, palm down. The 33rd move of the tiger and crane routine.

chén shǒu 沉手 Sinking hand: See chén qiáo.

chén zhǒu 沉肘 Settled elbow. 1. As a positional requirement: keep the elbow tips down and the arms slightly curved at most times. A requirement in many styles. 2. As a technique, a downwards elbow strike. 3. A settling block or jam with both elbows.

辰 (rad.161) **chén** The fifth of the twelve Terrestrial Branches, used in combination with the ten Celestial Stems to designate years, months, days, and hours. For the sixty year cycles, see also under bǐng chén, gēng-, jiǎ-, rèn-, wù-. The period of the day from 7:00 a.m. to 9:00 a.m. See also dì zhī, tiān gān.

chén shí 辰时 The period of the day from 7:00 a.m. to 9:00 a.m. (7:00 to 9:00).

陳 [陈] (rad.170) **chén** 1. To arrange. To tell. 2. A surname. 3. The Chen of the Southern dynasties (557-589).

chén shí tài jí quán 陈式太极拳 Chenshi (Chen's) Taijiquan, attributed to Chen Wangting, in Chenjiagou village, Henan province.

chén zhàn qiāng 陈战枪 Battle display spear: a routine of Yangjia style, written up as twenty-four moves.

稱 [称] (rad.115) **chèn** 1. To be equal to. 2. Symmetrical. 3. Well matched. 4. Pronounced chēng, a balance.

chèn shǒu 称手 Match the hands: to put power in the rear hand in the opposite direction when doing a strong strike, to maintain balance and give an assisting power to the front hand.

趁 (rad.156) **chèn** To take advantage of; avail oneself of.

chèn huǒ dǎ jié 趁火打劫 To Loot a Burning House: take advantage of someone's difficulties. The fifth of the Thirty-six Stratagems of Warfare, which apply to many situations.

撐 [撑] (rad.64) **chēng** 1. To brace; prop up; support. 2. A brace. 3. To brace the legs to withstand a hit or attempt at a throw and remain upright.

chēng bào zhuāng 撑抱桩 Brace and hug stake standing: sitting slightly with the arms rounded at chest height, palms in, alternating expanding and closing slightly. From Yiquan.

chēng chuán gāo 撑船篙 Brace a boat with a punt-pole: a metaphor for the mud wading step of Baguazhang. To imagine that the rear foot is a punt pole and the front foot is a boat, so that the rear foot digs into the ground to send the front foot forward.

chēng dà dāo 撑大刀 Brace with a big cutter: with the right hand near the hilt and the left along the shaft, hold the shaft vertically and brace to the side, blocking an attack with the shaft.

chēng quán 撑拳 Brace with the whole arm, hands clenched.

chēng tiān zhǎng 撑天掌 Brace up the sky palm. Extend the arms rounded above the head, palms angled up. This is used for circle-walking in some branches of Baguazhang. Also called mó tiān guàn yuè zhǎng.

chēng tuǐ 撑腿 Brace the leg. See diǎn tuǐ.

chēng tuǐ zhuāng 撑腿桩 Brace the leg stake standing. See jiāo lóng chū hǎi.

chēng xī 撑膝 Brace the knees: in horse stance, fix the feet and hip joints and brace the knees outwards to round the crotch and stabilise the stance. This method is used in some styles, in others, the requirement is to tuck in the knees, see also kòu xī.

chēng zhǎng 撑掌 Brace with the whole arm, hands open. Extend the arms slightly bent as if they were the buttresses of a building. The power is in the internal rotation of the arm and the horizontal movement.

chēng zhǒu 撑肘 Brace with the elbows: bend the arms in front of the body, then circle them down to strike them out and up to the sides, no higher than the shoulders.

稱 [称] (rad.115) chēng
1. A balance, a weight scale. 2. Pronounced chèn, symmetrical.

chēng liáng tǐ zhòng 称量体重 The weigh in: to weigh in for a Sanda or wrestling competition.

乘 (rad.4) chéng
To ride; to mount. To take advantage of; to seize an opportunity.

chéng shì shùn lì 乘势顺力 Use the momentum smoothly. A saying about staff techniques. Use the waist and arms with speed, power and balance to make the most of the momentum of the large motions.

成 (rad.62) chéng
1. To accomplish. 2. To become. 3. Achievement. 4. Fully grown.

chéng nián sài 成年赛 Senior category of competition: athletes eighteen and above.

chéng nián zǔ 成年组 Senior group of athletes in a competition: athletes eighteen and above.

承 (rad.64) chéng
1. To bear, hold, carry. 2. Undertake. 3. Continue, carry on.

chéng fú 承扶 Acupoint Chengfu (support), BL36. At the gluteus, at the crease of the buttocks, in the midline of the thigh (on each leg). From TCM.

chéng guāng 承光 Acupoint Chengguang (light guard), BL6. At top of the head, 2.5 cun up from the hairline, 1.5 cun lateral to the midline (on each side). From TCM.

chéng jiāng 承浆 Acupoint Chengjiang (sauce receptacle), RN24. At the face, in the depression between the jaw and the lower lip, on the midline. This is the final point of the Conception Vessel channel. From TCM.

chéng jīn 承筋 Acupoint Chengjin (sinew support), BL57. At the calf, in the middle of the two heads of the gastrocnemius, five cun below acupoint Weizhong (on each leg). From TCM.

chéng líng 承灵 Acupoint Chengling (spirit support), GB18. At the head, 4 cun in from the front hairline, 2.25 cun lateral to the midline (on each side). From TCM.

chéng mǎn 承满 Acupoint Chengman (assuming fullness), ST20. At the abdomen, five cun above the navel, two cun lateral to the midline (on each side). From TCM.

chéng qì 承泣 Acupoint Chengqi (tear container), ST1. At the face, directly under the pupil of each eye, on the infraorbital ridge (on each side). From TCM.

chéng shān 承山 Acupoint Chengshan (mountain support), BL57. At the calf, at the V formed by of the gastrocnemius when the foot is extended. From TCM. A crippling point, striking here may cause serious injury. See also cán xué.

吃 (rad.30) chī
1. To eat; take. 2. Annihilate. 3. Exhaust. 4. Absorb. 5. In martial arts, to press onto, take the place of, to control.

chī bù 吃步 Eating step: turn sideways to avoid a rushing attack and step your lead foot in behind your adversary's foot.

chī gēn 吃根 To Eat the Root: control the lower limbs with pressure, usually by hooking, tucking into, pressing onto, pinning, and sometimes by lifting the ankle. From Bajiquan, one of its ten major techniques, see also shí dà jī fǎ.

chī kǔ 吃苦 To eat bitter. Often used in the sense of suffering hardship in training in order to achieve mastery.

chī lǐ 吃里 To eat the inner: to make contact with an adversary's chest and/or belly and control them. See also nèi mén.

chī wài 吃外 To eat the outer: to make contact with an adversary's outer arms and/or legs and control them. See also wài mén.

chī zhāo huán zhāo 吃招还招 To eat a technique to get in the counter technique. Defend by absorbing and counter attack.

黐 (rad.115) chī 1. Bird lime. 2. In martial arts, it is used with its secondary meaning of to stick; sticky. See also nián.

chī dān shǒu 黐单手 Sticky single hands: single arm clinging exercise, a partner training for arm feeling. From Wing Chun.

chī gùn 黐棍 Sticky poles: pole clinging exercise, a partner training for feeling into the poles. From Wing Chun.

chī shǒu 黐手 Sticky hands: arm clinging exercise, a partner training for arm feeling. From Wing Chun.

chī shuāng shǒu 黐双手 Double sticky hands: partner training with both arms connected. From Wing Chun.

持 (rad.64) chí To hold, grasp.

chí dāo 持刀 Hold a broadsword: hold a broadsword behind the body in the right hand, or hold a broadsword at the left side of the body (hold indicates that it is not a technique as such, but a position taken).

chí jiàn 持剑 Hold a sword: hold a sword at the left side of the body, or in front of the body, cradling the guard in the left hand. Generally, as a position on commencing or upon completion of a routine.

chí gùn (qiāng, pū dāo) 持棍(枪,扑刀) Hold a staff (spear, or horse cutter) hold a staff vertically, at the right side of the body in the right hand, or in the left hand angled downwards. The butt may be on the ground. Generally, as a position on commencing or upon completion of a routine.

遲 [迟] (rad.162) chí 1. Late, tardy. 2. Slow; dilatory. 3. Stupid.

chí dāo 迟刀 Late broadsword: to block sharply after an adversary's weapon has arrived.

chí huǎn 迟缓 Sluggish: power and movements are slow and without meaning. An error in most styles.

馳 [驰] (rad.187) chí To go swiftly. Speed of vehicles, horses; gallop.

chí bù 驰步 A cross-step: stepping forward, backward, or to the side, tucking the knees in together with the leading foot turned out.

尺 (rad.44) chǐ 1. A Chinese foot. See shì chǐ. 2. A ruler. 3. Any instrument or weapon in the shape of a ruler.

chǐ cè wàn qū jī 尺侧腕屈肌 Flexor carpi ulnaris muscle: a forearm muscle, on the inside. Assists in wrist and finger flexion.

chǐ cè wàn shēn jī 尺侧腕伸肌 Extensor carpi ulnaris muscle: a forearm muscle, on the outside. Assists in wrist and finger extension.

chǐ gǔ 尺骨 1. Ulnar bone, ulna, one of the principle bones of the forearm. The ulna is the principle bone at the elbow and becomes smaller at the wrist, at the little finger side. The radius pivots around the ulna for palm supination and pronation. See also ráo gǔ. 2. Ulnar side of the forearm (little finger side).

chǐ zé 尺泽 Acupoint Chize (cubit marsh), LU5. At the bend of the elbow, in the depression on the radial side of the biceps brachii tendon (on each arm). From TCM. A sensitive point, pressing or striking here can cause numbness, loss of strength, pain, or even shock the Lung to cause unconsciousness.

齒 [齿] (rad.211) chǐ Tooth; teeth. Something tooth-like. See also yá chǐ.

瘛 (rad.104) chì Tugging, used as a noun.

chì mài 瘛脉 Acupoint Chimai (spasm vessel), SJ18. At the head, behind the ear lobe, at the centre of the mastoid process (on each side). May also be pronounced jì mài. From TCM.

翅 翄 [翅] (rad.124) chì 1. Wing, fin. 2. Wing tips. 3. In humans, refers to shoulder blades, especially when referring to the placement of shoulder blades. 4. Wing tips also refer to the wrist and fingers when applying control techniques to them.

赤 (rad.155) chì 1. Red. 2. Bare. 3. Sincere.

chì bì zhī zhàn 赤壁之战 The battle of Red Cliff: a battle famous in folklore, of the Three Kingdoms period, fought along a stretch of the Yangzi river in Hubei province, made famous in the Romance of the Three Kingdoms.

C

chì lóng dǒu lín 赤龙抖鳞 Red Dragon Shakes its Scales: sit into an empty stance with an upward snap of a spear.

chì lóng fēi tiān 赤龙飞天 Red Dragon Soars in the Heavens: tuck a spear flat along the back then shoot it out, running after it to catch it.

充 (rad.10) **chōng** Full; sufficient. To fill.

chōng shí 充实 Solid. This is a requirement at the basic level of training, strength must be full.

衝 (rad.144) [冲] (rad.15) **chōng** 1. To charge; rush, dash, surge; clash; collide. 2. As a hand technique: a straight punch.

chōng diǎn quán 冲点拳 A punch thrown directly from the waist.

chōng jī fǎ 冲击法 Charging techniques: methods of taking the initiative in a fight.

chōng jiǎo 冲脚 Collide with the foot: a short, sharp, low kick meant to cause an adversary to lift that leg. From wrestling.

chōng jìn 冲劲 A charging power. Impulsion.

chōng mài 冲脉 Extraordinary vessel Chongmai, Thrusting vessel, or Penetrating vessel. From the Mingmen, descends to connect with the Renmai and Dumai, and also rises up the spine, connecting the Qihai in the *dantian* with the Qihai in the chest. It integrates the flow of blood and disseminates original *qi* (see yuán qì) by connecting the torso.

chōng mén 冲门 Acupoint Chongmen (charging gate), SP12. At the groin, 3.5 *cun* medial to the pelvic crest, 3.5 lateral to the midline (on each side). From TCM.

chōng quán 冲拳 A straight punch. Generally, refers to a rotating punch that is thrown straight from the waist, hitting with the knuckles, fist heart down.

chōng tī 冲踢 Charging kicks: place the foot on the inside of your adversary's foot, then kick it to the outside and turn the other way, bringing the other foot in to kick his other shin to assist the throw. From wrestling.

chōng tiān chuí 冲天捶 Charge Heaven Strike: an uppercut. From Shaolinquan.

chōng tiān rù dì chuí 冲天入地捶 Charge Heaven and Enter the Ground: an uppercut followed by an advancing driving down punch. From Chuojiao.

chōng tuō 冲脱 Charging release, an escape from a wrist grab: first twist an adversary's wrist then suddenly charge forward, also brushing his hand with your free hand.

chōng xīn zhǒu 冲心肘 Charge the Heart elbow: to drive the point of the elbow directly into the chest of an adversary.

chōng yáng 冲阳 Acupoint Chongyang (charging yang), ST42. At the foot, the highpoint, between the extensor tendons of the big toe and second toe (on each foot).

重 (rad.166) **chóng** 1. To repeat, duplicate. 2. Again, once more. 3. Pronounced zhòng, heavy, see zhòng.

chóng dié 重叠 Overlapping.

chóng tuǐ pō jiǎo 重腿泼脚 Repeating spilling kick. See chòng tuǐ tī.

chóng tuǐ tī 重腿踢 Repeating kick: in hold, after your adversary steps in, lift a bit with a hooking foot so that he starts to take his foot away. Then attack that leg again with the same leg, lifting his leg for a throw. From wrestling. Also called chóng tuǐ pō jiǎo.

chóng zhǎng 重掌 Overlapping palms: press one hand on the back of an open palm, gripping the palm edge with the fingers and the thumb edge with the thumb.

chóng zuò 重作 1. To redo. 2. A restart in competition.

抽 (rad.64) **chōu** 1. To pull back, draw in. 2. To take a part from a whole. 3. To take out from in between something.

chōu biān 抽鞭 Draw the whip. See chōu qiáo.

chōu bō tuǐ 抽拨腿 Draw and check kick: lift the foot a bit off the ground with the knee bent and push quickly outward with the thigh, shin, and foot.

chōu dà dāo 抽大刀 Draw back with a big cutter: with the right hand near the blade, draw the blade back flatly, turning the edge upwards.

chōu gēn jiǎo 抽跟脚 Pull the heel: If an

adversary stands on your front foot, drive your rear foot forward.

chōu jiàn 抽剑 Pull back with the blade of a sword, specifically with the blade standing.

chōu kuà 抽胯 Draw in the hip. See shōu kuà.

chōu lā 抽拉 Lash, whip (as with a spear).

chōu liáng huàn zhù 抽梁换柱 Take Away the Roofbeam to Change the Pillar. 1. Fake high to draw an adversary's reaction, then strike to his armpit with the other hand and continue on to strike. From Baguazhang. 2. Move in with lifting palms, then drop them to stab down, and then lift again to stab forward. From Liuhebafa. 3. Do one forward kick and punch (opposite hand and foot), then jump up to switch to kick and punch the other side. From Chuojiao.

chōu qiān 抽签 To draw lots for pairing in Sanda or wrestling competition.

chōu qiáo 抽桥 Draw the bridge. 1. With the elbow bent, draw the forearm back or to the side with a scooping action. 2. Circle the arm straight then bend the elbow to block outwards with the forearm vertical. Also called chōu biān.

chōu shēn 抽身 Draw into the hips and waist.

chōu shēn huàn yǐng 抽身换影 Draw in the Body to Change for a Shadow: draw in the arm or weapon close to the body and step around to turn a full circle, back to the starting place. From Baguazhang.

chōu shǒu 抽手 Draw in: with the palm up, pull back and down. From Baguazhang.

chōu sī jìn 抽丝劲 Drawing silk power: a steady, unbroken power application, neither too slow nor too fast, too hard nor too soft, similar to the power used to draw the silk out of the cocoon. Most often applied to describe the power generation of Yang style Taijiquan.

chōu tuǐ 抽腿 Leg draws, a leg training exercise: from full squat crossed stance (see xiē bù), stand and lift the rear knee, then sit to the other side. Repeat.

chōu tuǐ biè 抽腿别 Leg draw throw: start with a hooking trip, then turn it into a swinging leg throw.

chōu yāo 抽腰 Pull back the lower back: flatten the lower back so that it is neither rounded nor arched.

chōu zhuàng quán 抽撞拳 Drawing ram: a low uppercut punch. From Wing Chun.

丑 (rad.1) chǒu The second of the twelve Terrestrial Branches, used in combination with the ten Celestial Stems to designate years, months, days, and hours. For the sixty year cycles, see also under dīng chǒu, guǐ-, jǐ-, xīn-, yì-. The period of the day from 1:00 to 3:00 a.m. See dì zhī. See also dì zhī, tiān gān.

chǒu shí 丑时 The period of the day from 1:00 to 3:00 a.m. (1:00 to 3:00).

出 (rad.17) chū 1. To go out, come out, exit. 2. To exceed, go beyond.

chū dòng rù dòng jǐn suí shēn 出洞入洞紧随身 The hands go in and out tight to the body like going in an out from a hole. A martial saying. This is a classic phrase that describes the tight actions of Duanquan and Xingyiquan.

chū qiāng 出枪 Get out with a spear: move the body to avoid an attack to the inside line to your chest.

chū shǒu 出手 Ordinary meaning is to hit. Specialised meaning is to extend one or both hands.

chū shǒu bù fán 出手不凡 Send out the hands out of the ordinary: to make a skillful opening move or to make an impressive start in a routine.

chū shǒu rú chuān suō 出手如穿梭 Send out the hands like throwing a shuttle (fast and direct).

chū shǒu rú fàng jiàn 出手如放箭 Send out the hands like shooting arrows. From Tongbeiquan, one of its requirements.

chū shǒu sì gāng cuò, huí shǒu rú gōu gān 出手似钢锉，回手如钩竿 Send out the hands like a steel file, and bring them back like a grappling pole. A martial saying from Xingyiquan.

初 (rad.145) chū 1. First (in order). 2. The beginning of; the early part of.

chū jí cháng (nán) quán 初级长(南)拳 Beginner's level standardised long (Southern) fist routine.

chū jí dāo (jiàn, gùn, qiāng) shù 初级刀(剑棍枪)

C

术 Beginner's level standardised broadsword (straight sword, staff, spear) routine.

chū jí tào lù 初级套路 Beginner's level routine. 1. Any routine considered to be at a basic level. 2. In standardised Longfist, the standardised C level routines specifically. These are fairly short routines, usually thirty to forty moves.

chū shōu 初收 Initial Gather: an on guard empty stance, the first of such moves in the Chen Taijiquan long routine.

杵 (rad.75) chǔ 1. A wooden club. The original meaning is a club used to beat clothes when washing, so it is a weapon similar to this. 2. A pestle.

chǔ bàng 杵棒 A double headed club with wolf-teeth spikes on elongated balls at both ends.

處 (rad.141) [处] (rad.34) chǔ 1. To dwell. 2. To get along with. 3. To be situated in. 4. To manage. 5. To punish; to sentence.

chǔ fá 处罚 A penalty in a competition. To penalize.

揣 (rad.64) chuāi A throw: a straight hip throw: hip throws that place an adversary directly on the back or buttocks and throw him over and directly forward to land on his back, usually bowing directly forward to do so. From wrestling. Also called dǎo kǒu dài.

踹 (rad.157) chuài A kick: a side thrust kick with heel or full bottom of foot.

chuài jiǎo 踹脚 Side thrust kick with heel or full bottom of foot. Also called simply chuài.

chuài tuǐ 踹腿 1. A side thrust kick with heel or full bottom of foot. Also called simply chuài. In the category of snap kicks, see qū shēn xìng tuǐ fǎ. 2. In Baguazhang, a hidden kick, appearing to step with a kòu bù or bǎi bù, but finishing as a low kick.

川 (rad.47) chuān 1. A river. 2. A plain. 3. Abbreviation for the province of Sichuan.

chuān liú bù xī 川流不息 River Flows without Cease: Stepping back and forth pulling with both hands in a circular manner, alternating between open stance and horse stance. From Liuhebafa.

穿 (rad.116) chuān To thread along or through. Pierce through; penetrate. To bore. One of the sixteen key techniques of Baguazhang, see also shí liù zì jué.

chuān bǎ 穿把 Thread the butt of a long weapon: bring the butt end in towards the body, then shoot it out the other side.

chuān bēi 穿臂 Thread the arm: extend the arm along an adversary's arm, sliding up to dissipate his force. From Baguazhang.

chuān bēi guò bèi 穿臂过背 Thread the arm throw over the back: slide along your adversary's arm, moving in and turning to tuck your hips into his, grabbing high and low on his arm, placing is over your shoulder. Then extend your knees, put power into your hips, and drop your head to throw him over your back. From wrestling.

chuān dāng kào 穿裆靠 Shoot: step behind your adversary's legs and thread your arm through in front, into his crotch, leaning into his hip with your shoulder.

chuān dāng kào shuāi 穿裆靠摔 Shoot: quickly step in between an adversary's legs to set your thighs on his, getting in tight and getting an arm in to grab and throw. From wrestling.

chuān huā jiǎo 穿花脚 Thread through flowers kick: snap kick to the front, then immediately thrust kick to the rear. From Mojiaquan.

chuān jiàn 穿剑 Thread a sword: circle the blade in past the chest/abdomen before stabbing out.

chuān lín bù 穿林步 Thread through the woods walking: to walk very quickly and smoothly in a curving pattern, as if threading around trees. Used in routines to go from one end of the carpet to the other. Also called S xíng bù.

chuān qiāng tuǐ 穿抢腿 Penetrating kick, turning the body to extend the hip fully into the kick, so that the body is almost prone and turned away from the kick. The hands line up, the same hand along the kicking leg, the opposite hand extended in front of the body, to draw a straight line with the kick. From Chuojiao, one of its middle-basin kicks.

chuān qiáo 穿桥 Thread the bridge. 1. A forearm technique: slide one hand forward under the other arm to circle out, pressing out with the wrist. Can also be a double threading forearm, stabbing forward with the palms pressed together. 2. A piercing arm: a straight stab, little finger side down. From southern styles.

chuān qiáo guī dòng 穿桥归洞 Thread the Bridge and Return to the Den: sit to horse stance and push the left hand to the side, elbow slightly bent, index finger extended. The 110th move of the tiger and crane routine.

chuān quán xià shì 穿拳下势 Low stance thread the fist. See xià shì. From Taijiquan.

chuān suō gùn 穿梭棍 Thread a staff. See chuān suō qiāng.

chuān suō liǎng jiǎo 穿梭两脚 Thread the Shuttle with Two Feet: a rubbing hook kick followed by a turn to a side kick. From Chen Taijiquan.

chuān suō qiāng 穿梭枪 Thread a spear like a weaving shuttle: thread the tip and shaft past the throat or waist, keeping the shaft level, close to the throat, waist, or arm, then shoot out to the other side.

chuān suō tōu diǎn 穿梭偷点 Thread the Shuttle Stealing in Poke kick: slide a kick through along the arm of an adversary to poke with the foot. From Chuojiao, one of its middle-basin kicks.

chuān tuǐ 穿腿 Thread the leg. 1. As a kick: shoot the front leg out along the ground into a drop stance (see also pū bù), kicking with the outer edge of the foot. 2. As a throw: shoot between the legs of an adversary to lift him up on your shoulders and throw.

chuān tuǐ kào shuāi 穿腿靠摔 Shoot the leg and butt throw: grab an incoming punch, step in and thread your other arm through your adversary's groin area to catch his leg. Controlling his arm and leg, lean for a takedown, falling on top of him.

chuān tuǐ zuò dì 穿腿坐地 Scoot through: From lying face down on the ground, brace on the hands to scoot the legs through the arms to finish sitting.

chuān xīn chuí 穿心捶 Punch threads to the heart: a simultaneous punch and kick to the midline. From Tongbeiquan.

chuān xīn jiǎo 穿心脚 Foot threads to the heart: a dorsi-flexed turned out thrust kick. From Meijiaquan.

chuān xīn zhǒu 穿心肘 Elbow threads to the heart: a straight strike to the side with the elbow, also stepping in.

chuān xiù tiǎo dǎ 穿袖挑打 Thread the Sleeve, Scoop up and Hit: slide the hand forward as if putting on an adversary's shirt, then lift the arm and come through to strike with the other hand. From Baguazhang.

chuān zhǎng 穿掌 1. Penetrating palm, piercing palm, spearing palm, threading palm: extend the arm to strike with the fingers, usually sliding under the leading arm. The palm may be up, down, angled, or sideways. 2. The hand shape used in the piercing palm, fingers almost straight, thumb tucked in.

chuān zhǎng sì liú xīng 穿掌似流星 Penetrating palm strikes like a meteor. From Tongbeiquan, one of its five requirements, see also wǔ zì yāo qiú.

chuān zhǎng xià shì 穿掌下势 Low stance thread the hand. See xià shì. From Taijiquan.

傳 [传] (rad.9) **chuán** 1. To pass on; hand down. To impart (knowledge, skill). Transmit. Spread. 2. To infect, spread disease. 3. Pronounced zhuàn: commentary, story. See zhuàn.

chuán tǒng 传统 Tradition. Traditional.

chuán tǒng wǔ shù 传统武术 Traditional styles of wushu.

喘 (rad.30) **chuǎn** To breath heavily, pant.

chuǎn qì 喘气 1. To pant, gasp for breath. 2. To take a breather.

chuǎn xī 喘息 1. To pant, gasp for breath. 2. A respite, a breather.

串 (rad.2) **chuàn** 1. To string together. 2. To conspire, gang up. 3. A bunch, a string of things.

chuàn huā quán 串花拳 String of Flowers fist: a routine from Mojiaquan, written up as fifty-one moves.

chuàn tóu bān tí 串头扳踢 String in the Head and Trip: duck the head into an adversary's armpit, grab under his leg, stand up, and lift. From wrestling.

chuàn xīn xiàn jiàn 串心献剑 String through the Heart Presenting the Sword: continuous alternating slices up and pierces with the blade, piercing directly to the heart. From Qingping sword.

闖 [闯] (rad.169) **chuǎng**   To charge; rush; dash.

chuǎng bù 闯步 Charging step: stamp with one foot on the spot to quickly charge forward with the other, sending the body quickly forward to shove in horse stance. From Bajiquan.

chuǎng hóng mén shì 闯鸿门式 Charge the Hongmen Feast model. 1. One of twenty-four classic spear moves. Most spear routines will have a move with a like name. In general, this name refers to chasing techniques like throwing out the tip. 2. Repeated stabs of a spear with both hands fixed, leaving about a metre of butt sticking out. See also hóng mén yàn.

chuǎng wáng dāo 闯王刀 Charge the King broadsword: a curved, one edged broadsword a bit thicker than a normal broadsword.

垂 (rad.33) **chuí**   1. To hang down, droop. 2. Dropped, settled. 3. To let fall, drop.

chuí dāo 垂刀 Hanging broadsword: the blade tip is down. A positional reference, separate from the direction of the strike.

chuí jiān 垂肩 Settle the shoulders down, lengthening the arms to allow free, relaxed movement.

chuí qì 垂气 Settle the *qi* to the *dantian* to stabilise and unify the body.

chuí shǒu 垂手 1. To grab the hand and elbow, circle and drag the hand down, a takedown. 2. To bring the hand up in a reverse slice, then snap the wrist down to snap the palm over.

chuí tóu 垂头 To hang the head, an error in most styles.

chuí zhǒu 垂肘 Settle the elbow or elbows down, protecting the ribs and allowing free movement of the shoulders.

捶 搥 [捶] (rad.64) **chuí**   To pound, thump, beat. Beat with a stick or fist; punch. Used in movement names for punches that are more beating than punching, often using the heel or backfist. Ofte translated as hammer fist punch, to distinguish from a normal corkscrew straight punch.

chuí fǎ 捶法 Punches, as a category of hand techniques. From Tanglangquan.

chuí quán 捶拳 A hammer fist punch: a punch that uses the meaty part of the fist rather than the knuckles. Usually also is a throwing punch, rather than a straight rotating punch.

槌 (rad.75) **chuí**   1. A mallet. 2. To beat with a stick or fist. Using the fist as a mallet or hammer, similar to chuí 捶.

錘 [锤] (rad.167) **chuí**   Usually called a hammer or mace, but is a weapon with a large ball on the end, so perhaps better called a club. Long handled or short handled. The short-handled mace is usually very heavy.

春 (rad.72) **chūn**   Spring, springtime.

chūn fēng fú liú 春风拂柳 Spring Breeze Rustles the Willow: trap an adversary's arm under your armpit and press the elbow inward to lock it out.

chūn fēng mā qí 春风摩旗 Spring Breeze Ruffles the Banner: bring the feet together and tuck a sword at the side, then step back into a bow stance, stabbing up to the rear right. From Qingping sword.

chūn qiú 春秋 The Spring and Autumn period (770-476 BC).

chūn qiú dāo 春秋刀 Spring and Autumn cutter. Also translated as big cutter, halberd, Guan's halberd. See guān dāo. Also called dà dāo, dìng sòng dāo, yuè shèng dāo.

chūn shān liè méi 春山列眉 Spring Mountain Arranges the Eyebrows: lift the left knee and lean into a low cut with a sword to the right. This is a cut in response to a mid height attack. From Qingping sword.

戳 (rad.62) **chuō**   1. To poke with a blunt weapon or a firm straight palm. Jab; poke; stab. 2. To strike soft parts of the torso with the fingers or end of the fist. From Bajiquan, one of its ten major techniques, see also shí dà jī fǎ.

chuō bà 戳把 Thrust with the butt of a long weapon.

chuō dì 戳地 Stab the ground: hit the ground with the foot with friction.

chuō dìng bù 戳丁步 Stab the ground to land in T stance: hit the ground with the ball of the foot, heel turned out, to stand in a reversed T stance, heel forward. From Chuojiao.

chuō gùn 戳棍 Poke with a staff: poke strongly in a straight line with either the tip or butt.

chuō jiǎo 戳脚 Chuojiao (jabbing foot), a northern style that uses a great variety of kicks. From Hebei province, some branches divide the routines into scholarly and martial.

chuō jiǎo bù 戳脚步 Jabbing stance: stand with the legs apart, the front foot slightly turned in, the rear heel off the ground, the body slightly turned.

chuō jiǎo fān zǐ 戳脚翻子 Chuojiao Fanzi (stabbing foot and overturning fist) style, a branch of Chuojiao.

chuō quán 戳拳 To poke the fist: to punch with the fist not aligned with the forearm. An error in many styles.

chuō xué 戳穴 Poke a pressure point with straight fingers. See also dǎ xué.

chuō zhǎng 戳掌 Poke: extend the arm to strike directly with the fingers, palm either up or down.

chuō zhǐ zhǎng 戳指掌 Slide one arm out from the waist past inside the other, striking directly forward with the fingers, palm up.

踔 (rad.157) **chuō** 1. To move quickly; go swiftly. 2. As a shield and broadsword technique, charge: jump over an adversary to land on the other side, combining with a chop, slice, or stab.

綽 [绰] (rad.120) **chuò** 1. Ample, spacious; graceful. 2. Pronounced chāo, to grab.

chuò hào 绰号 Nickname. People, particularly in the past, are often referred to by a given name (míng), private name (zì), literary name (hào) and/or nickname (chuò hào).

跐 (rad.157) **cǐ** 1. To step on. 2. To stand on tiptoe.

cǐ bù 跐步 Trample step. 1. Move forward staying in stance by pushing off the rear foot then the front foot, stamping forward rather than jumping. 2. A sliding retreating step that lands with a thump.

刺 (rad.18) **cì** 1. To pierce, stab, prick with a thin, sharp point. 2. A thorn; a splinter. 3. A short weapon with a thin, sharp point.

cì dà dāo 刺大刀 Pierce with a big cutter: with the right hand near the blade, stab forward with the blade edge down.

cì jiàn 刺剑 Pierce straight to the tip. 1. Prick or pierce with a sword, forming a straight line with the arm and blade. 2. A throw: drop to the ground and shoot the legs to trap an adversary, then turn to throw.

cì lèi jiǎo 刺肋脚 Pierce the ribs kick: a heel thrust kick to the ribs, the toes angled. From Tanglangquan.

cì quán 刺拳 A straight jab, on the same side as the forward foot.

cì qiāng 刺枪 Pierce with a spear. See zhā qiāng.

cì tòng gǎn 刺痛感 Pricking pain, especially on touching an acupoint, either in treatment, self massage, or internal training.

次 (rad.76) **cì** 1. Next in order. Secondary. 3. Inferior, lower. 4. Vice-, deputy. 5. A grade, sequence. 6. Each occasion of a recurring action.

cì liáo 次髎 Acupoint Ciliao (second bone-hole), BL32. At the sacrum, the second sacral formina, just below acupoint Shangliao, 0.7 *cun* lateral to the midline (on each side). From TCM.

腠 (rad.130) **còu** Interstices. Usually used in combination as còu lǐ.

còu lǐ 腠理 Interstices; the tissue and space between skin and muscles, or between skin and flesh.

蹿 [躥] (rad.157) **cuān** 1. Long jump, to jump for length. 2. To leap. 3. Throw; fling.

cuān bèng tiào yuè 蹿蹦跳跃 Jumps, as a category of physical fitness and basic skill.

cuān bù 蹿步 To jump forward.

cuān zòng shù 蹿纵术 Leaping skills training. For example, start with hill running, then walk on a tub full of water, gradually taking the water out of the

C

tub without tipping it. Or walk on upright bricks, gradually increasing their height and your speed.

攢 攅 (rad.64, 75) [攒] (rad.64) **cuán** 1. To collect together; assemble. 2. With radical 64, also pronounced zǎn, to accumulate.

cuán ná fǎ 攢拿法 Gathering grappling hold: grab both arms of an adversary and press them together. From wrestling.

cuán quán 攢拳 Gathered fist, as hand shape: clench the fist with the middle segment of the middle finger slightly extended and the thumb pressing on the distal joint. From Tongbeiquan.

cuán shǒu pō jiǎo 攢手潑脚 Collect the Hands and Spill the Feet, a tripping takedown. Fix an adversary's hands so they cannot move, then turn and trip.

cuán zhǎng sì àn jiàn 攢掌似暗箭 Punch like a arrow shot from hiding. From Tongbeiquan, one of its five requirements, see also wǔ zì yāo qiú.

竄 [窜] (rad.116) **cuàn** 1. To flee; scurry. 2. As a shield and broadsword technique, flee: when your shield is hit, leap to the side, striking with your broadsword.

cuàn máo 竄毛 High jump to front somersault. Also called gāo máo.

cuàn pū hǔ 竄扑虎 Pounce on the tiger. A high jump, landing with hands first to absorb softly, then smoothly through the belly, the rest of the body, and the legs. Also called zhí pū hǔ.

cuàn shēn 竄身 Charge in, cover distance to reach an adversary.

催 (rad.9) **cuī** 1. To urge, hurry, press. 2. Release a proximal joint to allow a distal segment to reach forward.

cuī bù 催步 Urging step: step one foot forward, sideways or backwards, bring in the other foot (see gēn bù), and, just as the second foot lands, take another step in the same direction.

cuī fā 催发 Release power by urging from a proximal segment to send the distal segment forward.

摧 (rad.64) **cuī** To break; destroy.

脆 (rad.130) **cuì** 1. Crisp. Held in common with many styles, one of Ziranmen's nineteen main methods. 2. Brittle; hard but easily broken. 3. Easy, quick, neat.

cuì gǔ 脆骨 Cartilage; gristle.

cuì jìn 脆劲 Crisp power, a hard power that strikes out quickly. Recoiling power. From Tongbeiquan, one of its nine types of power, see also jiū gōng jìn. Common also to Baguazhang.

存 (rad.39) **cún** 1. To exist, live. 2. To store, keep. 3. Accumulate, collect. 4. Reserve, retain. 5. Leave with, check.

cún lì fǎ 存力法 Reserve power method: keeping back some power when attacking, to avoid becoming under the control of an adversary.

cún qì kāi guān 存气开关 Reserve *Qi* to Open the Pass: brush a hand across high and push with the other to finish with the wrists together, moving forward to bow stance. From Liuhebafa.

寸 (rad.41) **cùn** 1. One Chinese inch: a proportional measurement on the body. See shì cùn. 2. 'Short' in relation to power generation or small movement. 3. In Xingyiquan, refers to footwork that advances a little bit, trampling firmly without lifting more than an inch.

cùn bù 寸步 One-inch step: to step the leading foot forward no more than a foot before stepping. From Xingyiquan.

cùn jìn 寸劲 One-inch power: a quick, short strike generated from within the body with very little visible movement.

cùn tī tuǐ 寸踢腿 One-inch kick: a short upward striking kick with the toe to the shin, digging the ground first with the heel. Xinyi Liuhequan also calls this kick dú hǔ jiǎo.

cùn tuǐ 寸腿 One-inch kick. 1. A short upward striking kick, digging the ground first with the heel. Used extensively in Chuojiao with a variety of hand technique combinations. Also called dīng tuǐ. From Chuojiao, one of its middle-basin kicks. 2. A short, low, snapping kick. From Tantui.

搓 (rad.64) cuō   1. To rub with the hands, thus, used for a sliding grab. 2. A chop in tennis, table tennis, etc., that hits with a slight rubbing.

cuō bù 搓步 Rubbing step: a step that has some forward impetus, so that the foot rubs into the ground as it lands. From Baguazhang.

cuō biè 搓别 Chopping throw: move the hip in and swing the leg to throw over the hip, grabbing around the neck. From wrestling.

cuō dòng jīn jiǎn 搓动金翦 Rub with the Golden Scissors: lift the right knee, bring a sword grip to the ribs with the tip angled forward, left hand also at the hilt. Then quickly land and step to a left bow stance, cutting down with a rubbing action, the tip angled upwards a bit. From Qingping sword.

cuō fǎ 搓法 Rubbing technique: grab tightly with both hands close together, jerk one forward and one backward.

cuō jìn 搓劲 Rubbing power: to stick to an adversary's attack and apply an opposing force to it (up, down, left or right).

cuō má shéng 搓麻绳 Rub a hemp rope: to walk with the feet close to but not touching the ground, with the feeling of rubbing the fibres of hemp between the palms to make a hemp rope. A metaphor for the hovering step circle-walking of Baguazhang.

cuō ná fǎ 搓拿法 Rubbing grappling hold: an abrupt shoving action to the face. From wrestling.

cuō shǒu 搓手 Rub: with the palms facing each other, extend one while pulling the other back. From Duanquan.

cuō tī 搓踢 A category of sliding or rubbing kicks. The ground strike is thought to increase the acceleration into, and thus the final force of, the kick. From Chuojiao.

cuō yāo 搓腰 Rubbing waist: a partner exercise. Sitting back and forth, with the hands on each other to assist in finding the powers of pushing and accepting. From Yiquan.

撮 (rad.64) cuō   To pinch, a pinch of something. To take with the fingers.

cuō huǒ 撮豁 Pinching takedown: press the back of the hand onto the outside of an adversary's knee while pulling on his neck in the opposite direction.

cuō shǒu 撮手 Pinched hand, as hand shape: the same as hooked hand. Different styles have different configurations. See also gōu shǒu.

cuō wō 撮窝 Throwing techniques that involve getting in close, pulling on an adversary and hooking his leg with your leg, usually pulling his leg up in an awkward position while applying an off-balancing technique above. From wrestling. Also called cuō, wài gōu jiǎo.

蹉 (rad.157) cuō   1. A failure, a miss. 2. This character is also often used to mean rubbing with the foot instead of using 搓, which means to rub, but has the hand radical.

cuō bù 蹉步 A step that uses the rubbing action of the foot.

cuō dì 蹉地 Land the foot with a rubbing action.

cuō tuǐ 蹉腿 Rubbing kick: a hidden kick, stepping into an adversary. From Baguazhang.

挫 (rad.64) cuò   1. Original meaning to defeat. 2. In martial arts, is a check, a short abrupt blocking or shoving action. 3. To push down with a circular or filing action. 4. To put torsion on the knee. From Qinna.

cuò gǔ 挫骨 File the bone: a quick strike that slides slightly, to a part of the body that has bone close to the surface, such as the shin. This kick shin rips the skin as it slides, and can break bone.

cuò jiǎo 挫脚 Checking kick: a short kick with the sole of the foot to an adversary's foot.

cuò jìn 挫劲 Checking power: a quick shake of the waist, applied directly to the arms, hands, or weapon. This power is short, hard, and direct. From Bajiquan.

cuò lā tuō wàn 挫拉脱腕 Filing pull wrist release: pull an adversary's wrist with your free hand and sharply drop the grabbed hand to release a one handed grab on the wrist. From wrestling.

cuò shāng 挫伤 A bruise, a contusion.

cuò shǒu 挫手 Repressing hand: an abrupt block. From Wing Chun.

cuò yāo 挫腰 Check the back: keep one side steady while abruptly putting power into the other side, tightening the abdomen and exhaling. Commonly used for shoulder techniques and for checking. See also cuò zhǎng.

cuò zhǎng 挫掌 Check: a short, abrupt shove.

锉 [锉] (rad.167) cuò   To rasp, file; to smooth with a file.

cuò bù 锉步 Rasping step. 1. A retreating step with both feet just slightly leaving the ground, completed with a simultaneous abrupt landing. 2. A switchover step without a jump.

cuò jìn 锉劲 Rasping power: a back and forth power similar to the movement of working with a file or rasp. From Xingyiquan.

cuò lì shì lì 锉力试力 Rasping testing power: stand, place the hands one on top of the other, strike out to the side with the elbows. From Yiquan, one of its combat testing moves.

错 [错] (rad.167) cuò   1. Interlocked, intricate, complex; grind; move out of the way; alternate; mistaken. 2. As a technique: rub, a reverse upper stabbing block. 3. As a controlling or grappling technique: to dislocate.

cuò bù 错步 1. Alternating stance: the feet point forward, front to back about one to two foot-lengths apart, the legs naturally bent. This is a common natural stance in sparring. 2. Switchover step: switch the place of the feet, staying in the same place, keeping down, not jumping. This changes the body orientation one-eighty degrees. Also called diào bù, huàn bù, jiāo cuò bù.

cuò dāo 错刀 Rub with a broadsword: a quick backward press followed by a forward push.

cuò gǔ 错骨 Displace or dislocate a joint control technique: bend or twist a joint in a way counter to its natural movement. This also tears the tendons and ligaments at the joint.

cuò gǔ fēn jīn 错骨分筋 Dislocate Bones and Split Tendons: a coiling movement in horse stance, twisting in the shoulders to extend the arms, then coiling to bring the forearms in. From Chen Taijiquan.

cuò pàn 错判 An error by a judge in competition, a misjudgement; to misjudge.

cuò wù 错误 An error, a mistake.

cuò zhǒu 错肘 Rub with the elbows: hold the elbows bent in front of the body, then strike outwards separately with both elbows.

cuò zōng bā zì bù 错综八字步 Interlocked character eight stance, feet parallel, heel to toe so that the feet point in opposite directions, knees aligned with the feet.

D

搭 (rad.64) dā 1. To build, put up, build. 2. To come into contact. 3. To take (a taxi).

dā bǎ 搭把 1. Touching hands or crossing arms before sparring. 2. Since it means the gesture of politeness before sparring, sometimes is used with the meaning of sparring. 3. Taijiquan push hands.

dā qiáo 搭桥 Build a bridge, a forearm technique: keep the forearm in contact to frame and press up (see also jià) as move in with an attack.

dā shǒu 搭手 See dā bǎ.

dā wàn zǒu quān 搭腕走圈 1. Prepare for circle-walking with a partner, by touching wrists. 2. Circle-walking with a partner, touching wrists. From Baguazhang.

達 [达] (rad.162) dá 1. To extend. 2. To reach, to attain. 3. To express, to communicate. 4. A surname.

dá mó 达磨 Da Mo, a monk from India purported to have developed kungfu training at the Song mountain Shaolin temple.

dá mó jiàn 达磨剑 Da Mo sword: a Tanglangquan routine, written up as thirty-eight moves.

dá mó zhàng 达摩杖 Da Mo cane, a Shaolinquan routine with a rod or cane, written up in forty-nine moves.

dá zūn quán 达尊拳 Dazunquan (attain respect fist): a style from Fujian province, which primarily uses palm techniques.

打 (rad.64) dǎ 1. To hit; strike. 2. To play a game or play a routine. To play a sport or play the martial arts. 3. The category of strikes using hands, arms, or body that exist in each move. See also sì jì. 4. As one of the eight attack and defense models, to initiate the attack as soon as there is an opportunity. See also bā zì gōng fáng fǎ zé.

dǎ bìn chuí 打鬓锤 Hit the hairline on the temple: a backfist. Also called fǎn bèi chuí.

dǎ cǎo jīng shé 打草惊蛇 Beat the Grass to Startle the Snake. The 13th of the Thirty-six Stratagems of Warfare, which apply to many situations.

dǎ fǎ 打法 Hits: category of strikes that use the upper limbs, including fists, open hand, elbows, forearms, and arms. Common to most styles are bēng, chōng, jǐ, pī, tiǎo, zá, zhuàng. See also sì jì.

dǎ gǔ 打鼓 Hit the Drum: an extended double strike to the head, reaching over and under. From Taiji Changquan.

dǎ héng 打横 See dǎ héng zhǎng.

dǎ héng zhǎng 打横掌 Hit with a crossing palm: bring the hand up on the opposite side then swing across to its own side, getting power from the waist, hitting with the palm edge or back of hand. From Tongbeiquan. Also called dǎ héng, héng zhǎng.

dǎ hǔ bù 打虎步 Hit the Tiger stance: a side bow stance, a bow stance with the feet parallel but turned. Also called cè gōng bù.

dǎ hǔ shì 打虎势 Hit the Tiger position: a double strike or block with the fist surfaces facing each other, one high and one low. The actual technique varies with styles. May be with the fist heels turned outwards, the arms curved, one arm over the head or near the temple, the other at chest or hip height. Often done with one fist over the head and one at the knee, either in a raised knee stance, an empty stance, a bow stance or a horse stance. The fists may be held close or far from each other. Also called fú hǔ, wān gōng shè hǔ. See also wǔ sōng, wǔ sōng dǎ hǔ.

dǎ jià 打架 Fighting, scuffling, brawling.

dǎ kāng bāo 打糠包 To hit a husk filled bag, a training method to develop hard skills, especially fist, palm, and forearm strikes. The bag is usually about a foot square.

dǎ lèi 打擂 Sparring by Chinese rules, allowing hitting, kicking, trips, and throwing, but not grappling on the ground.

dǎ lèi tái 打擂台 1. To accept a challenge for a sparring match. 2. To undertake a sparring match.

D

dǎ luàn chéng xù mō jìn 打乱程序摸劲 Seeking power with changing directions: without moving the torso outwardly, seek out power lines in random directions. May be done in different stances or stepping. From Yiquan.

dǎ lún 打轮 To play the circle: push hands with only the four basic techniques. From Taijiquan, see also àn, jǐ, lǚ, péng.

dǎ quán 打拳 To practice or play drills or routines. Also called xíng quán, yǎn liàn, yǎn quán.

dǎ quán róng yì zǒu bù nán 打拳容易走步难 It is easy to learn hand techniques, hard to get the stepping and stances. A martial saying.

dǎ sān xīng 打三星 To hit the three stars: a training method with a pole or a partner to develop the forearm strike. Hit with the forearm, alternating continuously between three strikes on each arm – thumb edge palm down, thumb edge palm up, and little finger edge palm down.

dǎ shǒu 打手 Play hands: old name for push hands. From Taijiquan. See also kā shǒu, tuī shǒu.

dǎ wǔ shù 打武术 To practice or play Chinese martial arts in general.

dǎ xué 打穴 To attack pressure points. This term includes five specific methods of striking: see also chuō xué, ná xué, pái xué, qín xué, zhuó xué.

dǎ yǎn shǒu 打眼手 Eye strike hands: a double palm strike to the eyes with the fingers turned out, the thumbs tucked to gouge the eyes. From Wing Chun.

大 (rad.37) dà 1. Big, large. 2. Major; main. 3. Old (of age). 4. Eldest. 5. Heavy (rain, wind).

dà bǎ lán qiāng 大把拦枪 Large outer trap with a spear: counter-clockwise circle with press down, bringing the base of the spear up to the right shoulder, the shaft on the chest. The spear tip draws a large half circle, between hip and head height. The left hand needs to slide along the shaft. Also called huó bǎ lán qiāng.

dà bǎ ná qiāng 大把拿枪 Large inner trap with a spear: clockwise circle with a press down, bringing the base of the spear from the right shoulder (after a large outer trap) down to the waist. The spear tip draws a large half circle, between head and hip height. The left hand needs to slide along the shaft. Also called huó bǎ ná qiāng.

dà bàng 大棒 A large stick, ninety centimetres long, seven centimetres thick. Used for wrestling training by gripping the ends while simulating wrestling throws.

dà bāo 大包 1. Acupoint Dabao (great embrace), SP21. At the chest, down from the armpit, at the sixth intercostal space (on each side). This is the final point of the Spleen meridian. From TCM. A sensitive point, striking it can cause breathlessness. 2. A large heavy bag used for training wrestling throws.

dà bù yīng zhuāng 大步鹰桩 Large stance eagle standing: sit in a half horse stance with the arms rounded above the legs at head height, palms angled forward and up. From Yiquan. Also called dà shì zhuāng.

dà chán shǒu 大缠手 Large arm wrap: grip an adversary's hand on your forearm and wrap your other arm around his to control the wrist and elbow. From Qinna.

dà chán sī tuǐ 大缠丝腿 Big coiling leg: swing the leg out then bend the knee to coil inwards to trap with the foot and lower leg. From Chuojiao, one of its middle-basin kicks.

dà chán zhǒu 大缠肘 Large elbow wrap: grip an adversary's wrist and bend the hand into the forearm to lift the elbow, thread your other arm under his elbow and wrap his upper arm, then turn and press down. From Qinna.

dà cháng 大肠 1. The large intestine. 2. The Large Intestine, the organ associated with the Shou Yang Ming channel. It is a *yang* organ.

dà cháng jīng 大肠经 The Large Intestine meridian. See shǒu yáng míng. From TCM.

dà cháng shū 大肠俞 Acupoint Dachang (large intestine transport), BL25. At the lower back, level with the depression below the spinous process of the fourth lumbar vertebra, 1.5 *cun* lateral to the midline (on each side). From TCM.

dà chéng quán 大成拳 Dachengquan (great achievement fist). See yì quán.

dà dān biān 大单鞭 Big single whip: a bow stance with the arms extended out to front and back at shoulder height, in fists. The 'big' is to distinguish it from a single whip position in horse stance. From Shaolinquan. Usually called dān biān.

dà dāo 大刀 Big cutter, halberd, Guan's halberd. See guān dāo. Also called chūn qiú dāo, dìng sòng dāo, yuè shèng dāo.

dà dāo kàn dǐng shǒu 大刀看顶手 (To judge the skill with) the big cutter, watch the propping hand (which is usually the left hand). A martial saying.

dà dāo wò dāo 大刀握刀 To hold a big cutter with the left hand at the butt and the right hand near the blade.

dà dé hé 大得合 Big gains takedown: in wrestling, while grabbing and pulling above, step in between the legs of an adversary, then take down with a hook behind his knee. Also called lǐ dāo gòu, lǐ gòu, sān dào yāo.

dà dǐng 大鼎 A head stand. Also called tóu shǒu dǎo lì, tóu shǒu fān.

dà dū 大都 Acupoint Dadu (great metropolis), SP2. At the inside of the foot, the proximal segment of the big toe (on each foot). From TCM.

dà dūn 大敦 Acupoint Dadun (large pile), LR1. At the foot, the lateral side of the distal end of the big toe, 0.1 cun proximal to the toenail (on each foot). From TCM.

dà fǔ 大斧 A long handled axe.

dà fù 大腹 The upper abdomen.

dà gān zǐ 大竿子 A pole, a rod: a wooden weapon, as long as a long spear.

dà gē zǐ 大个子 A tall and big person.

dà gǔ kōng 大骨空 Extraordinary acupoint Dagukong (thumb bone hollow), EX-UE5. At the back of the hand, the middle of the interphalangeal joint at the distal end of the proximal phalanx of the thumb. From TCM.

dà hé dāo 大合刀 Big harmony broadsword: a Xingyiquan routine, written up as seventy-two moves.

dà hè 大赫 Acupoint Dahe (great manifestation), KI12. At the abdomen, four cun below the navel, 0.5 cun lateral to the midline (on each side). From TCM.

dà héng 大横 Acupoint Daheng (great horizontal), SP15. At the abdomen, at navel height, four cun lateral to the midline (on each side). From TCM.

dà hóng quán 大洪拳 Big Resonant Fist: a Shaolinquan routine, written up as twenty-seven moves. Also called dà hóng quán, see below.

dà hóng zhuāng 大洪桩 Big Resonant Stake: A routine of Meishanquan, written up as sixty-four moves.

dà hóng quán 大红拳 Big Red Fist: A routine of Shaolinquan. Also called dà hóng quán, see above.

dà hóng 大肱 1. The upper arm. 2. Can also mean the thigh. Normally pronounced gōng, pronounced hóng in the martial arts.

dà hóng quán xiǎo hóng quán 大肱拳小肱拳 Big Arm Strike, Small Arm Strike: moving palm strikes, circling high and low. From Chen Taijiquan.

dà huā qiāng 大花枪 Big flowers spear: a routine of Yangjia style, written up as forty-three moves.

dà huán dāo 大环刀 A broadsword with rings attached to the spine of the blade.

dà huàn zhuāng 大换桩 Big changing stances. See dà zhuàn jiǎo.

dà huò quán shèng 大获全胜 1. To win a complete victory. 2. Cover, press, and stab with a spear, especially at the end of a routine. From Shaolinquan.

dà jià 大架 Large frame, refers to any style that has characteristic open and expansive postures.

dà jù 大巨 Acupoint Daju (great gigantic), ST27. At the abdomen, two cun below the navel, two cun from the midline (on each side). From TCM.

dà kāi dà hé 大开大合 Open and close with big movements. From Tongbeiquan.

dà kòu bù 大扣步 Big tucked in step: turn around with a tucked in step that is also placed well around. See also kòu bù.

dà líng 大陵 Acupoint Daling (great mound), PC7. At the wrist, on the inside at the crease, between the tendons of the flexor carpi ulnaris and the palmaris longus (on each arm). From TCM. A crippling point, striking here may cause serious injury. See also cán xué.

dà lǐng 大领 The back collar of a wrestling jacket.

dà lǚ 大将 Big pulling: push hands using only the bigger, or corner, techniques in moving step. From

D

Taijiquan, see also cǎi, kào, liè, zhǒu. Also called sì yú shǒu tuī shǒu.

dà mǎng fān shēn 大蟒翻身 Great Python Rolls Over. 1. In Baguazhang, a reach, then a roll under an extended arm or broadsword. 2. A rolling kick doing the same essential action, but rolling under the leg. From Chuojiao, one of its low-basin kicks.

dà mǎng yáo tóu 大蟒摇头 Great Python Sways its Head: shift a bit back and forth while circling the tip of the blade, finishing with a pierce. From Qingping sword.

dà mén 大门 The big gate. 1. The big gate of an adversary: between the arms, on the chest and abdomen. Also called hóng mén. 2. Big gate setup stance, each with the same foot forward so that you present a large frontal surface, standing chest facing chest.

dà ná gōu 大拿勾 Big grab hook: holding your adversary, step into him, hooking your leg between his and lifting to throw. From wrestling.

dà ná tī 大拿踢 Big grab kick: holding your adversary, either pull him in towards you or step into him, kicking his legs out from under him as you pull him to the side. From wrestling.

dà níng bǐ qiāng 大宁笔枪 Writing brush spear: a spear with the tip the shape of a writing brush – the tip a bit more rounded than usual.

dà pǎn tóu 大盘头 Big basin around the head: with a big cutter, right hand near the blade and left along the shaft, circle the blade over the head with a large, flat circle, bringing the edge around in cutting position.

dà péng zhǎn chì 大鹏展翅 Great Roc Spreads its Wings. 1. In Liuhequan, to raise the knee and swing both arms in opposing circles. 2. In Taijiquan, a paring slice outward and upwards with a sword. 3. In Baguazhang, open the arms out to the sides at shoulder height, palms up, with dual lifting and extending powers, see tuō tiān zhǎng. 4. Slice up the forward arm and come through with a rising push with the other arm. From Baguazhang, one of its sixty-four hands. 5. In Liuhebafa, to open the arms out to the sides, like drawing a bow, punching the front hand and pulling the rear hand higher than the head. 6. In wrestling, to press down on an adversary's shoulder and lift his arm, opening out extending his arm to the rear. 7. In Piguaquan, a bow stance with double reversed palm strikes. See also péng.

dà péng zhǎn chì zhǎng 大鹏展翅掌 Great Roc Spreads its Wings palm: to circle-walk with the posture arms open at shoulder height, palms up. Also called tuō tiān zhǎng. From Baguazhang.

dà qiāng 大枪 Long spear. 1. A spear four metres long, with a base circumference greater than a circle made with thumb and forefinger. Also called yǎn qiāng. 2. A spear six metres long. See also lián qiāng.

dà shāo zǐ gùn 大梢子棍 Long handled flail. See cháng shāo zi gùn.

dà shuàn yāo 大涮腰 Large waist circles, a warm up exercise.

dà shì zhuāng 大式桩 Large stake standing. See dà bù yīng zhuāng.

dà suō shēn 大缩身 Big Contraction: an empty stance with the front fist sitting on the front knee, the rear fist up at the side of the jaw. Here 'big' means 'more', to distinguish it from a normal sit back. From Shaolinquan.

dà sì tào chuí 大四套捶 Big Four Hits routine: the third routine of Chen Taijiquan.

dà tóu bàng 大头棒 A big headed pole: a short pole with a large round metal head.

dà tuǐ 大腿 The thigh, thighs.

dà tuǐ hòu qún jī ròu 大腿后群肌肉 The hamstrings, the group of muscles at the back of the thigh.

dà tuǐ yǐn shén jīng 大腿隐神经 The hidden nerves along the inner thighs, sensitive points. Good targets for striking. Beside the Xuehai points.

dà xiá cáng jiàn 大侠藏剑 Big Hero Hides his Sword: sit to empty stance and cut in with the reverse hand, hooking the other out then striking behind the back. From Shaolinquan.

dà xún huán fǎ 大循环法 Big cycle changeover: in Baguazhang, completing all eight circle-walking fixed postures in one direction, then changing from one side to the other and repeating all eight postures on the other side. See also xiǎo xún huán fǎ, zhōng xún huán fǎ.

dà yíng 大迎 Acupoint Daying (great reception), ST5. At the jaw, in front of the bulge made by the chewing muscles, on the mandible (on each side). From TCM.

dà yuè bù qián chuān 大跃步前穿 Pass Forward with a Big Leap: swing the arms and leap up and forward, opening up the chest. This should be a light and aesthetic leap.

dà yuán jī 大园肌 Teres major muscle: one of the muscles in the back of torso that attaches from the scapula to the arm, assists in shoulder adduction, extension, and medial rotation.

dà zhōng 大钟 Acupoint Dazhong (large goblet), KI4. At the ankle, on the inside, behind the ankle bone, at the depression made by the Achilles tendon (on each leg). From TCM.

dà zhōu tiān 大周天 The big heavenly circulation: moving the *qi* through the body in a big circle, down the front of the body, down the legs to the soles of the feet, then up the back, through the twelve meridians.

dà zhù 大杼 Acupoint Dazhu (great shuttle), BL11. At the back, level with the depression below the spinous process of the first thoracic vertebra, 1.5 *cun* lateral to the midline (on each side). From TCM.

dà zhuàn jiǎo 大转脚 Big turns of the feet, a leg training exercise: sit in bow stance and snap turn from one side to the other. Also called dà huàn zhuāng, dà zuān zi.

dà zhuàng bēi shǒu 大撞碑手 Big Shove to the Stele: a long driving step in to shove the chest directly. This is a long range move that only works when the opportunity presents and is taken immediately. From Shaolinquan.

dà zhuī 大椎 1. Acupoint Dazhui (great hammer), DU14. At the neck, in the depression below the spinous process of the seventh cervical vertebra, on the midline. From TCM. In internal styles, this point should align with the point Jianjing, to ensure the shoulders and neck are settled. See also jiān jǐng 2. The cervical vertebrae in general, as a target.

dà zhuō pào 大捉炮 Big Grab and Pound: a double grab and pull, then double strike towards the back, in a horse stance. From Chen Taijiquan. Also called dāng mén pào, which emphasizes the strike.

dà zuān zǐ 大钻子 Big drills. See dà zhuàn jiǎo.

呆 獃 (rad.30,94) [呆] (rad.30) dāi 1. Slow witted, dull, stupid. 2. Maladroit, clumsy.

dāi jià 呆架 A clumsy stance in sparring, placing the body or weight improperly so that one is in a poor situation for reacting.

dāi lì 呆力 Slow witted use of strength: the inability to react to a changing situation, resulting in using the inappropriate defense for a given situation, pitting strength against strength.

代 (rad.9) dài To take the place of; be in place of. Acting, substitute.

dài bù tuǐ 代步腿 Substituting kick: an edging side kick in a slight squat, arms crossed, landing to a horse stance double punch. From Chuojiao.

带 [带] (rad.50) dài 1. A belt; a band. 2. To bring; carry. 3. To lead. To draw, drag towards the rear, sometimes written 攦, to indicate use of the hands. This is one of the sixteen key techniques of Baguazhang, see also shí liù zì jué. 4. In Chaquan, a two-handed cutter, total length is body height, blade about a third of the length.

dài bù 带步 Dragging step: bring one foot in towards the other after a step. May step the rear foot up towards the lead foot after a step, or step the lead foot back after the rear foot retreats. Also called gēn bù.

dài dāng pī xīn quán 带裆劈心拳 Draw the Crotch and Chop the Heart, the third routine of Duanquan, written up as twenty-two moves.

dài fǎ 带法 Drawing, or dragging methods, grabbing and pulling along the line of attack with one or two hands. Also called shùn shǒu qiān yáng.

dài jiàn 带剑 Draw with a sword, pulling back at the side with the blade.

dài mǎ guī cáo 带马归槽 Lead the Horse back to the Manger: Step to a right reverse bow stance and strike across the front with the left elbow. The 65th move of the tiger and crane routine. The same as shǒu bān dān guī on the other side.

dài mài 带脉 1. Acupoint Daimai (belt vessel, girdling vessel), GB26. At the side of the abdomen, on a line with the navel and the eleventh, floating, rib, 1.8 *cun* below acupoint

D

Zhangmen (on each side). From TCM. 2. The extraordinary vessel the Belt Vessel, which surrounds the waist like a strap. From TCM.

dài qiāng 带枪 Draw with a spear, drawing it in a straight line with the shaft on the body.

dài shǒu 带手 Draw: use the oncoming force of an adversary to draw him to the side or back, palm down and open to grasp. A pulling drag on the smooth side of the stance. From Baguazhang.

dài zhǎng 带掌 Draw with the palm. See dài shǒu.

待 (rad.60) **dài** 1. To treat. Entertain. 2. To await, wait for.

dài jiǔ píng héng 待久平横 A controlled balance: a balance held in a routine for two seconds. Term used for competition training and judging.

戴 (rad.62) **dài** 1. To wear on the head. 2. To support; to sustain. 3. A surname.

dài shì xíng yì quán 戴式形意拳 Daishi (Dai's) Xingyiquan, attributed to Dai Longbang, from Shanxi province, who learned from Cao Jiwu.

袋 (rad.145) **dài** A bag, sack, or pouch. In martial arts, a narrow bag made to carry weapons. Made of cotton, canvas, nylon, or leather, usually closes with a pull tie or zipper.

逮 (rad.162) **dài** To catch; seize; reach.

丹 (rad.3) **dān** Cinnabar, red.

dān biàn 丹变 *Dantian* Transforms: an alternate manner of doing single whip, involving a turn from bow stance to angled horse stance. See dān biān.

dān fèng cháo yáng 丹凤朝阳 Red Phoenix Faces the Sun: hook your adversary's wrist by grabbing his hand, and press his elbow upward with your elbow, locking out his shoulder. From Baguazhang and Liuhebafa.

dān fèng shū yì 丹凤舒翼 Red Phoenix Smoothens its Wings: drop back and cut to the inside of an adversary's wrist, opening out both arms at waist height. From Qingping sword.

dān fèng tóu cháo 丹凤投巢 Red Phoenix Drops into the Nest. Extend the palms out to eyebrow height, palms up, combined with a poke kick.

From Baguazhang.

dān shān qǐ fèng 丹山起凤 Phoenix Rises from Cinnabar Mountain: extend the leg out to the front, leaning back to stab down to the foot behind. From Qingping sword.

dān tián 丹田 Cinnabar field. In martial arts, usually refers to the lower *dantian*, the body core area within the pelvic girdle. Specifically, three finger widths below the navel and a third of the thickness of the torso into the body. This is the energetic centre, where *qi* collects, disperses, and recirculates. See also shàng dān tián, xià dān tián, zhōng dān tián.

dān tián nèi zhuàn 丹田内转 Internal rotation of the *dantian*.

dān tián (zhī) qì 丹田(之)气 *Dantian*'s *qi*: the feeling of *qi* returning to and filling the lower belly, used to build and express power. Deep breathing into the belly.

單 (rad.30) [**单**] (rad.24) **dān** 1. One; single; alone; simple, plain. 2. To use the backfist with the meaty part of the fist or back of the fist to pound downwards. This is a hard strike with sudden power. From Bajiquan, one of its six main striking techniques, see also liù dà kāi.

dān bào zhǒu 单抱肘 Hold the elbow: while doing an elbow strike with the hand clenched, place the other hand at the fist to support (fingers on the outside, thumb in).

dān bēi rào huán 单臂绕环 Single arm swings, a warm-up exercise.

dān bēi shuāng shǒu ná 单臂双手拿 Double handed grab to one arm: a grip in wrestling or in practicing releases.

dān biān fú bù 单蝙蝠步 Single bat stance: a raised knee stance. From Shaolinquan.

dān biān bù 单鞭步 Single Whip stance: a drop stance. This stance is usually called pū bù.

dān biān 单鞭 Single whip. 1. A short rod, about the length of a sword, with a grip. Also called biān. 2. See dān biān shì.

dān biān shì 单鞭势 Single Whip posture. Sit in bow stance with the arms extended out at shoulder height, aligned with each leg. The exact posture varies with the style. In Chaquan, Shaolin, and

Taiji Changquan, the fists punch out level with the shoulders. In Taijiquan and Huaquan the rear hand is hooked and the front is a vertical palm (in TJQ the hook is down, in HQ the hook is reversed). In most styles it is in a bow stance. In Chen Taijiquan, the stance is usually a biased horse stance. Also called dān biān.

dān biè chì 单别翅 Single Wing Pin: a pin across with one elbow. From Tongbeiquan.

dān chā 单叉 Single split: fully squat on one leg, sitting in the inside of its thigh and lower leg, with the other extended along the ground. Both feet are flat on the ground. Also called pū bù.

dān dā shǒu 单搭手 Single hand contact: in partner training such as push hands, contacting with one arm only.

dān dāo 单刀 A broadsword, sabre: a sword with a relatively thick blade, curving towards the tip, sharp on one edge, with a single-handed grip. See also dāo.

dān dāo fù huì 单刀赴会 Broadsword Goes to the Meeting: a straight inverted punch. From Tanglangquan.

dān dāo kàn shǒu shuāng dāo kàn zǒu 单刀看手双刀看走 (To judge the skill of) the single broadsword, watch the empty hand, while for the double broadsword, watch the footwork. A martial saying.

dān dāo jìn qiāng 单刀进枪 Broadsword Attacks Spear: a popular category of two person routine.

dān dié bù 单蝶步 Single butterfly stance: squat on one leg and kneel on the other leg with the knee and inside of the shin of the rear leg on the ground. From southern styles.

dān fāng huà jǐ 单方画戟 One sided design crescent headed spear: a spear with a crescent hook on one side of the tip. See jǐ and shuāng fāng huà jǐ.

dān fèng cháo yáng 单凤朝阳 Lone Phoenix Faces the Sun. 1. A jump with a leg swung straight up. From Tongbeiquan. 2. A thrust kick that changes into a poke kick. From Wudangquan.

dān fèng guàn ér 单凤贯耳 Lone Phoenix Hits the Ear: a swinging hook punch to the ear with one fist. From Tongbeiquan and Wudangquan.

dān fèng tóu cháo 单凤投巢 Lone Phoenix Drops into the Nest: a direct extended rolled over punch to the ribs. From Baguazhang, one of its sixty-four hands.

dān gōng qián zì 单工千字 Single Worker Writes the Character Qian: from a reverse stance shift to horse stance and cut the right palm inwards, cutting with the edge of the palm and forearm, angled as if writing the first stroke of the character. The 49th move of the tiger and crane routine.

dān guì bù 单跪步 Single kneeling stance: see dān dié bù.

dān hǔ bào tóu 单虎抱头 Single Tiger Wraps the Head: step forward gathering the hands up the midline, bring the same side hand up close to the head, which presses forward. Grab and pull into a low kick. From Xingyiquan.

dān hǔ chū dòng 单虎出洞 Single Tiger Emerges from its Den: step forward to a left empty stance and push/grab through with the right hand in a tiger claw, left pulling back to the waist. Lean into the strike. The 62nd move of the tiger and crane routine.

dān huā 单花 Single handed flowers: circle the shaft of a big cutter flat over the head, switching hands.

dān huàn bù 单换步 Single change step: step forward with a hook-in step then turn the other foot out on the spot.

dān huàn zhǎng 单换掌 Single change: the first change of the eight mother palms, usually involving one tuck in and one brace out step, each paired with one upper body action. From Baguazhang.

dān jiā zhǒu 单挟肘 Single elbow press: hook inwards with the elbow to press to the neck or lock the arm of an adversary with one arm.

dān liàn 单练 1. Individual training, includes training individual techniques in a group. 2. A Bajiquan one-person routine, written up as fifty to fifty-six moves.

dān lóng chū hǎi 单龙出海 Single Dragon Emerges from the Sea: shift to left reverse bow stance and punch with the right fist to chest height, pulling the left fist to the waist. The 111th move of the tiger and crane routine.

dān lún chuí 单抡捶 Single swinging of the

D

mallet, a shoulder exercise: swinging each arm loosely from the shoulder in a full circle, both forwards and backwards. From Tongbeiquan.

dān lún guàn rì 单抡贯日 A Single Throw Pierces the Sun: from a raised knee stance, take steps forward as if falling forward, leaning forward and flicking the feet up behind, holding the hilt of a sword behind the right hip and tip down, then step firmly into a bow stance pierce. From Qingping sword.

dān ná 单拿 Single control: to grasp a small joint of an adversary (like a finger, wrist, elbow), or to poke a pressure point on the arm with a controlling grasp. From Qinna.

dān ná shǒu wàn zhǒu, shuāng ná jiān kuà zú 单拿手腕肘，双拿肩胯足 Single handed weapons use the hand, wrist, and elbow; double handed weapons use the shoulders, hip joints, and feet. A martial saying.

dān pāi jiǎo 单拍脚 Slap kick: single foot instep slap kick, slapping the foot with the same side hand. Usually is a straight swinging instep kick. In the category of slap kicks, see jī xiǎng xìng tuǐ fǎ.

dān qín 单擒 Single grasp: to grasp an adversary with one hand, often in preparation for a following control technique. From Qinna.

dān shǒu héng ná wàn 单手横拿腕 Single handed transverse catch to the wrist. Grasp the opposite side of an adversary, i.e.: your left hand grabs the adversary's right wrist, like holding a tennis racket. From wrestling.

dān shǒu huā 单手花 Single handed flowers, a steel whip technique: holding the whip in its middle with the right hand, circle it vertically to the left and right of the body.

dān shǒu jià qiāng 单手架枪 Framing block up single handed with a spear: lift the shaft above the head, right hand at the butt, shaft horizontal or angled. Normally the empty left hand will push out at shoulder height.

dān shǒu jiāo chā zhuā 单手交叉抓 Single handed crossing grab. Grab the same side of an adversary, i.e. your left hand grabs the adversary's left shoulder, arm, or hand. The arm crosses the other's body. From wrestling. See also dān shǒu shùn zhuā.

dān shǒu lì jǔ gùn 单手立举棍 Single handed present a staff vertically: Stand at attention, holding the base of the staff with the right hand in front or side of the body, staff vertical. This is usually at the beginning of a routine.

dān shǒu lì yuán tuī shǒu 单手立圆推手 Fixed step ppush hands with one arm connected, and following only a circular vertical path. From Taijiquan.

dān shǒu pāo qiāng huàn wò bà duàn 单手抛枪换握把端 Single handed spear toss to switch grip to the butt: holding the tip, toss and spin a spear in the air to catch the butt.

dān shǒu pāo qiāng huàn wò qián duàn 单手抛枪换握前端 Single handed spear toss to switch grip to the tip: holding the butt, toss and spin a spear in the air to catch just behind the tip.

dān shǒu píng lūn gùn 单手平抡棍 Single handed level swing of a staff: swing a staff in a full circle, passing in front and over the head.

dān shǒu píng yuán tuī shǒu 单手平圆推手 Fixed step push hands with one arm connected, and following only a circular horizontal path. From Taijiquan.

dān shǒu píng zhā qiāng 单手平扎枪 Single handed stab with a spear: straight stab holding the spear at the butt with the right hand only.

dān shǒu shuāi qiāng 单手摔枪 Single handed spear slap: Strike the shaft quickly and strongly flat on the ground, holding the butt in the right hand, in a bow stance.

dān shǒu shùn zhuā 单手顺抓 Single handed aligned grab. Grab the opposite side of an adversary, i.e., your left hand grabs the adversary's right shoulder, arm, or hand. You are both aligned smoothly, the arm does not cross the other's body. From wrestling. See also dān shǒu jiāo chā zhuā.

dān shǒu tí liáo biān 单手提撩鞭 Single handed rising flowers, a steel whip technique: holding the whip in the middle with the right hand, circle it upwards forward vertically to the left and right of the body.

dān tiào hòu kōng fān 单跳后空翻 Back flip with a single leg takeoff.

dān tóu gùn 单头棍 A one headed club: a short staff gripped only at the butt end, which is the thinner end.

dān tóu shí dàn 单头石担 A barbell with a stone weight on one end. Used for wrestling training, mostly for leg hooking techniques, holding the unweighted end.

dān tuī shǒu 单推手 Push hands practice with one arm connected. From Taijiquan and Yiquan.

dān tuī zhǎng 单推掌 A push with one hand.

dān tuī zhǐ 单推指 Push with the palm, the hand held in the single finger shape. This is a short way of referring to the technique.

dān xiàng 单项 Single event at a competition, for the title of a single event.

dān yún shǒu 单云手 Single cloud hands: a silk reeling practice, performing cloud hands with just one hand, the other set on the hip. See also yún shǒu.

dān zhǎn chì 单展翅 Stretch Out One Wing: settle back and bring a raised fist back in to meet the other fist at the belly. From Xingyiquan.

dān zhǐ 单指 Single finger, a hand shape. 1. The index finger extended, the others bent at the second and third joints, the first joints extended, the thumb bent. 2. The index finger extended and the thumb tucked onto the second joint of the middle finger, the fingers clenched. From southern styles. Also called dān zhǐ kuài, yī zhǐ méi.

dān zhǐ chā 单指插 To stab with a single finger.

dān zhǐ fān 单指翻 Grab a finger and flip over: grab one finger or the thumb and turn counter to the natural position. Backwards or sideways both work. From Qinna.

dān zhǐ kuài 单指筷 Single finger chopstick, a hand shape: see dān zhǐ.

dān zhǐ yǐn shǒu 单指引手 Single Finger Drawing Hand: shift into a right bow stance, and extend the left hand, index finger upright, pushing forward on the midline of the stance, right fist open behind. The 84th move of the tiger and crane routine.

dān zhū quán 单珠拳 Single pearl fist, a hand shape: the fingers tightly clenched, the index finger joint protruding and the thumb tucked onto its distal segment. From Shaolinquan.

dān zhuàn bù 单转步 Pivot on the ball of one foot.

dān zú zhèn jiǎo 单足震脚 Stomp, thump with one foot, a heavy stamp. See zhèn jiǎo.

擔 [担] (rad.64) dān
1. The original, practical meaning is to carry on a shoulder pole. 2. In martial arts, is a technique that gives this feeling. 3. A traditional unit of weight, 100 jin, or fifty kilograms.

dān shān gǎn rì 担山赶日 Chase the Sun Carrying a Mountain: block up overhead, flicking the left foot and hand behind, then land to a reverse stance chop. From Qingping sword.

dān zhǒu 担肘 Carry with the elbow. 1. An elbow strike: bent arm, lift the elbow to strike with the tip. A close-range strike, usually to the jaw. 2. To shoulder the elbow, a controlling technique: grab your adversary's wrist and reverse his arm, stepping in and turning to place his arm over your shoulder. Push down on his arm to break his elbow or throw.

撣 撢 [掸] (rad.64) dǎn
1. The original, practical, meaning is to flick off; whisk. 2. The technique is to brush lightly aside.

dǎn ná fǎ 掸拿法 Whisking grappling hold: a hard, crisp, fierce action that like whisking. Can be used as a sharp grab intended to initiate a reaction from an adversary, or to break a grip or to initiate an attack. From wrestling.

dǎn zhǎng 掸掌 To whisk with the palm. In some styles, throw the arm inwards to complete a sideways chop in front, snapping the wrist. In some styles, lift the arm then throw it down and forward to shoulder height, palm up.

膽 [胆] (rad.130) dǎn
1. The gallbladder. 2. The Gallbladder, the organ associated with the Zu Shao Yang channel. It is a *yang* organ. 3. Courage, guts.

dǎn dà 胆大 Brave, bold.

dǎn jīng 胆经 The Gallbladder meridian. See zú shào yáng. From TCM.

dǎn liàng 胆量 Courage, bravery, guts.

D

dǎn náng 胆囊 Extraordinary acupoint Dannang (gallbladder point), EX-LE6. At the calf, on the outside, two *cun* below the head of the fibula (on each leg). From TCM. The most sensitive point on the gallbladder channel.

dǎn qiè 胆怯 Timidity, fearfulness, fear. Considered a fault in most styles, and likely to lead to defeat in a fight.

dǎn shū 胆俞 Acupoint Danshu (gallbladder transport), BL19. At the back, level with the depression below spinous process of the tenth thoracic vertebra, 1.5 *cun* lateral to the midline (on each side). From TCM.

dǎn xiǎo 胆小 Timid, cowardly.

dǎn yào zhuàng 胆要壮 The gallbladder should be sturdy. To be fearless is a necessity in fighting.

dǎn zǐ 胆子 Courage, nerve.

彈 [弹] (rad.57) **dàn** 1. A ball; a pellet; a bullet; a bomb. 2. Pronounced tán, to shoot or send forth a pellet etc., see tán.

dàn gōng 弹弓 1. A catapult; a slingshot. 2. Pronounced tán gōng, a full-sized bow.

膻 (rad.130) **dàn** Most often seen in combination as dàn zhōng in TCM. Also pronounced shān.

dàn zhōng 膻中 Acupoint Danzhong (chest centre), RN17. See shān zhōng.

當 (rad.102) [当] (rad.42) **dāng** 1. Equal. 2. Should. 3. Just at. 4. Serve as. 4. To bear.

dāng kǒu 当口 The sweet spot for a throw. See jiāo kǒu.

dāng mén jiàn 当门剑 Pound the Door with the Sword. See wò hǔ dāng mén.

dāng mén pào 当门炮 Pound the Door: a double pull and strike towards the back, in a horse stance. From Chen Taijiquan. Also called dà zhuó pào, which emphasizes the pull.

dāng mén xué 当门穴 Sensitive point Dangmen, the solar plexus. The colloquial term for acupoint Jiuweixue, Conception Vessel #15. See jiū wěi xué.

dāng tóu pào 当头炮 Head on Punches, Hit to the Head, Pound the Head: a double punch to the front, applying power to the fist surfaces. May also be done with the top fist turned, and used as a block. From Chen Taijiquan and Wudangquan.

dāng yáng 当阳 Extraordinary acupoint Dangyang (equal *yang*), EX-HN2. On the top of the head, above acupoint Tongkong, one *cun* from the front hairline. From TCM.

襠 [裆] (rad.145) **dāng** Crotch area of the trousers, so a polite way of referring to the groin area. Sometimes is used to mean specifically the acupoint Huiyin, see also huì yīn.

dāng bù 裆部 The groin area, the crotch. One of the main targets on the body, a sensitive point. Best to hit with a drop and rise in stance, an upward slice, a groin punch, snap kick, or knee. Normally only attacked when in extremity. Disallowed as a striking area in Sanda. Also called dāng, qián yīn, xià yīn.

dāng gōng 裆功 Stance training methods to develop strength in the loins. As in strong stances through the hips and legs, not as in striking the groin.

dāng yāo jìn 裆腰劲 The power of the waist and groin area, referring to the entire inside groin/hip/*dantian* area.

擋 [挡] (rad.64) **dǎng** 1. To block; keep off; ward off. 2. To get in the way of. 3. A wrestling takedown that involves holding the upper body tightly, stepping in between an adversary's legs and tripping, keeping upright.

dǎng dà dāo 挡大刀 Block with a big cutter: with the right hand near the hilt and the left two thirds down the shaft, with the blade angled upwards, edge down, use the upper shaft to block.

蕩 盪 (rad.140, 108) [荡] (rad.140) **dàng** 1. To swing, sway; wave. 2. To sweep off.

dàng dāng 荡裆 1. To allow the thigh to drop below knee height in a horse or bow stance, bringing the knee angle to less than ninety degrees. From Chen Taijiquan, and considered an error. 2. A technique to attack the groin. From Baguazhang.

刀 (rad.18) **dāo** 1. A knife, a blade. 2. A broadsword, sabre: one of the standard short weapons, with a relatively thick blade, curving towards the tip, and one sharp edge. The standard length is to the top of the ear when cradling the grip down at the side. Also called dān dāo. 3. In wrestling, a swinging trip, called so because the action resembles that of using a sickle.

dāo bǎ 刀把 Broadsword's handgrip, handle, term usually used for broadswords with a longer handle.

dāo bèi 刀背 Broadsword's back: the spine of the blade, the edge that is not sharpened, used for blocking.

dāo bǐng 刀柄 Broadsword's grip, handle.

dāo cǎi 刀彩 The flags attached to a broadsword, a silk, cotton, or synthetic cloth. May be square or triangular, and usually two flags of different colours. Also called dāo páo and dāo piāo dài.

dāo dǔ 刀肚 Broadsword's belly: the thickest part of the blade.

dāo gōu 刀勾 A hooking, swinging trip.

dāo hù shǒu 刀护手 Broadsword's hand guard or protector: the cover in front of the grip.

dāo huán 刀环 A ring at the end of the grip of a horse cutter or halberd.

dāo jiān 刀尖 Broadsword's tip.

dāo kuài fǎ zhà 刀快法诈 The broadsword is quick and its methods are unpredictable. A martial saying.

dāo páo 刀袍 See dāo cǎi.

dāo piāo dài 刀飘带 See dāo cǎi.

dāo rèn 刀刃 Broadsword's edge: the sharp edge of the blade.

dāo rú měng hǔ jiàn rú fēi fēng 刀如猛虎剑如飞凤 A broadsword is like a fierce tiger, a sword is like a flying phoenix. A descriptor of the difference between the weapons.

dāo qiào 刀鞘 Scabbard, sheath, or case, for a broadsword.

dāo shēn 刀身 Broadsword's body, the whole of the blade.

dāo shǒu pèi hé 刀手配合 The broadsword and hand coordinate. A saying about the broadsword. This refers to the use of the left hand for balance and power.

dāo shǒu 刀首 Broadsword's head: the metal sheath at the end of the grip.

dāo shù 刀术 1. Broadsword skill. 2. Broadsword-play: a Taolu competition event, called Daoshu in English.

dāo tǐng bù bù tǐng 刀停步不停 The stepping does not stop when the broadsword stops. From Baguazhang, a quality sought in its broadsword methods.

dāo wěi 刀尾 Broadsword's tail: the end of the grip.

dāo zǒu hēi 刀走黑 The broadsword goes darkly. A martial saying. The broadsword, because of the solid blade, should move quickly and powerfully.

dāo zuàn 刀钻 Big cutter's drill: the butt end, tipped with metal of a long-handled cutter such as the big cutter or horse cutter.

捯 (rad.64) **dáo** To pull hand over hand.

倒 (rad.9) **dǎo** 1. To fall over; to collapse. 2. To knock down. 3. To throw down in wrestling. 4. Pronounced dào, to back up, see dào.

dǎo dì 倒地 1. To fall down (general term, not a specific fall). 2. Be taken down or thrown in a wrestling match. 3. A fall during performance of a routine, a major deduction (0.3) in Taolu competition, includes touching both hands or touching any part of the torso to the ground.

dǎo dì fǎ 倒地法 Tumbling techniques: techniques that involve deliberate falling to attack.

dǎo dì gōng 倒地功 Falling techniques: techniques for falling, such as break falls, rolls, side falls, front falls, back falls.

dǎo dì jiǎn shuāi 倒地剪摔 Drop to the ground and do a scissors grasp with the legs to throw an adversary.

dǎo dǐng 倒顶 Let the head drop or go crooked. A major error in most styles.

dǎo gēn 倒根 Knock down the root, term for stamping on the foot or toes, breaking the root of an adversary's stance.

D

dǎo gēn tóu 倒跟头 Backwards summersault, starting from a full squat.

dǎo gōu kūn lún 倒勾昆仑 Topple by Hooking the Kunlun: a strong, low sweep to the Kunlun acupoint, just outside the heel. Combined with a grab and pull, it takes an adversary down as well as causing pain and numbness to the lower leg.

dǎo jiǎo 倒脚 Throw down trip. See yuán bǎo jiǎo. Also called yáng wěi bǎ zhuì.

dǎo kǒu dài 倒口袋 Empty the pockets: hip throws that place an adversary directly on the back or buttocks and throw him over and directly forward to land on his back. Also called chuāi.

dǎo shān 倒山 Topple the Mountain. A common name for movements that push strongly, first settling to uproot.

dǎo shù fǎ 倒树法 Topple a Tree: stamp on an adversary's foot. From Shaolinquan.

dǎo tī jīn guān 倒踢金冠 Kick Off the Golden Hat: drop down and dodge to kick the back of an adversary's head.

導 [导] (rad.41) dǎo To lead, guide. Transmit, conduct.

dǎo qì 导气 Guide the *qi*. Guide the *qi* to the acupuncture needle by using fairly strong methods of needle manipulation. From TCM.

dǎo qì kāi xué 导气开穴 Open an acupuncture point by pressing and tapping the skin, to guide the *qi* to the area prior to inserting acupuncture needles. From TCM.

dǎo yǐn 导引 Leading and guiding energy.

dǎo yǐn gōng 导引功 *Qigong* exercises that lead and guide the energy within the body to cultivate *qi*.

dǎo yǐn tǔ nà 导引吐纳 Traditional *qigong* exercises to cultivate *qi*.

搗 [捣] (rad.64) dǎo 1. To pound (with a pestle). 2. To beat into the ground, a throwing technique in wrestling. 3. To stab with a blunt weapon.

dǎo chā dǎo chā 捣叉捣叉 Harass and Jam twice, Beat and Crosscut twice: moving forward twice, covering with the rear hand and stepping through to punch with the lead hand. From Chen Taijiquan.

倒 (rad.9) dào 1. To back up. 2. Backwards. 3. Upside down; inverted. 3. Pronounced dǎo, to fall over, see dǎo.

dào bā zì bù 倒八字步 Inverted character eight stance: feet form the shape of a Chinese character eight 八, toes pointing in. Also called bā zì bù, zhèng bā zì bù.

dào bá chuí liǔ 倒拔垂柳 Topple the Willow Tree: step behind and grab an adversary around the front of the waist with an inverted hold across the front, and throw over the hip. From Baguazhang.

dào bù 倒步 Back up, backing up steps. 1. The front foot steps directly through behind, usually more than one step. 2. A switching step, the rear foot coming up and the front foot stepping back into its place.

dào chā bù 倒插步 Back cross step: the foot steps behind, moving backwards.

dào chā huáng qí 倒插黄旗 Stab the Banner in Upside down: a reverse pierce with a sword, rolling the hand over to pierce upwards to head height. From Qingping sword.

dào chā shì 倒插式 Stab Backwards: pivot from a bow stance to bow stance on the other side, turning to look back, cutting to strike with what becomes the lead elbow. From Wudangquan.

dào chā shì 倒插势 Stab Backwards: insert the foot, then twist away to insert the fist also, to prepare for a throw or takedown. From wrestling.

dào chā tuǐ 倒插腿 1. Backwards insertion step: step your leg into your adversary's stance, turning your back so you are doing a cross step into him, pressing with your leg in preparation for a throw. 2. Backwards insertion kick. From Chuojiao, one of its middle-basin kicks.

dào fā wū léi 倒发乌雷 Throw Back Dark Thunder: turn around with a scooping palm and a chopping fist. From Piguaquan.

dào gōu shǒu 倒勾手 Inverted hooked hand. See fǎn gōu shǒu.

dào hòu jiān 倒后肩 Backup the rear shoulder: strike upwards to the rear with the head of the shoulder, using the whole body.

dào jí bù 倒疾步 Back cross quick step: foot steps behind, then the other foot quickly comes in to step forward. This step is used to move quickly and cover distance to the side.

dào jiē niú wěi 倒揭牛尾 Rip off the Oxtail: reach out to grab, then push the other hand through, simultaneously pushing and pulling. From Liuhebafa.

dào juǎn hóng 倒卷肱 Rolling Arms Retreat, Step back and Whirl Arms, Back up Rolling the Arms: retreating footwork combined with forward strikes simultaneously. May also be used as elbow strikes to the back or a throw. From Taijiquan. Also called dào niǎn hóng, dào niǎn niǎn hóu, dào niǎn 辇 hóu.

dào kāi miào mén 倒开庙门 Backup to Open the Door of the Temple: turn around with a reverse hack with a sword. Step back, turning around to the back, settling to a horse stance and chopping down. From Qingping sword.

dào lì zhǎng 倒立掌 Vertical palm with the fingers pointing down.

dào líu 倒流 To flow in reverse: to return the power of an attack like crashing breakers.

dào ná fǎ 倒拿法 Reverse grappling hold: grab an adversary's elbow then quickly switch it to your other hand, to facilitate pulling it in towards you. From wrestling.

dào niǎn hóng 倒捻肱 Rolling Arms Retreat, Backup Twisting the Arms. See dào juǎn hóng.

dào niǎn hóu 倒捻猴 Monkey Retreats, Rolling its Arms. From Wu and Yang Taijiquan. See dào juǎn hóng.

dào niǎn hóu 倒辇猴 Monkey Backs up the Handcart: similar to Rolling Arms Retreat but done more side to side. Name used in Sun Taijiquan. See dào juǎn hóng.

dào qí lóng 倒骑龙 Ride a Dragon Backwards. 1. With one hand pushing in front and one hand hooking behind, move forward continuously with a dragging step, staying in the same stance. From Chen Taijiquan. 2. Step to a reverse bow stance, doing a pounding punch down to shoulder height behind. From Wudangquan.

dào qí lóng bèi 倒骑龙背 Back Up the Dragon, Riding on its Back: sit back into empty stance, pressing one hand low behind, then roll that hand up and over the head while standing up to throw over and down. From Liuhebafa.

dào qián jiān 倒前肩 Reverse the front shoulder: tuck the shoulder up towards the jaw to protect it.

dào sǎo tuǐ 倒扫腿 Back sweep kick. From Chuojiao, one of its middle-basin kicks.

dào shuāi 倒摔 Backwards slap: to slap a long weapon flat on the ground, holding the tip.

dào tī tuǐ 倒踢腿 Back swinging kick: a swing kick up to the rear, touching the feet with the hands or touching the foot to the head. In the category of straight swinging kicks, see also zhí bǎi xìng tuǐ fǎ.

dào tí jīn lú 倒提金炉 Lift the Golden Oven Upside Down: a back cross step with a chop with a sword, then lift the foot high behind, leaning forward and holding the left hand out, and snap the blade up. From Qingping sword.

dào yǎo 倒咬 Reverse bite, a counter takedown: when grabbed, slide in tight to an adversary, hook his leg, wrapping around his calf to prevent a fall.

dào zhuā lí 倒抓梨 Reverse ploughing: grab an adversary's wrist with a reverse grip (thumb web forward, palm up) and rotate to twist it over. From Qinna.

dào zhuài fēng chē 倒拽风车 Drag a Windmill Backwards: do an elbow strike and then use the snap back to extend a backfist.

dào zhuài fēng zhōu 倒拽风舟 Drag a Sailboat Backwards: do a hooking punch strike then punch the other fist through with the arms crossed. From Wudangquan.

dào zhuàn qián kún 倒转乾坤 Spin Heaven and Earth in Reverse: circle each hand at its side of a circle drawn in front of the chest, palm up when lowering, palm down when rising. From Liuhebafa.

道 (rad.162) **dào** 1. A road; way; path. Channel; course. 2. Way; method. The Way, the Dao (Tao in the old Wade-Giles transliteration); Daoism (Taoism).

dào tóng jī zhǎng 道童击掌 Daoist Acolyte Claps his Hands: a takedown, stepping in to crowd an

D

adversary, pull his arm down, trap his foot, and push to his face. From Baguazhang.

得 (rad.60) **dé**   To gain, get, acquire. Can; may.

dé fēn 得分 Gain a point, score (in competition).

dé héng 得横 Get control over the transverse, crossing, line of an adversary's stance.

dé jī 得机 Gain the advantage: take the opportunity as it presents, get control through good timing.

dé jī dé shì 得机得势 Take the opportunity to gain the advantage in a fight.

dé qì 得气 Get the *qi*: to feel that the *qi* has taken the acupuncture needle, a feeling of the person getting needled. From TCM.

dé shí 得实 Gain control: get control of adversary's balance, movements, or rhythm.

dé shì 得势 Gain position: get behind or move in to cause an adversary to off-balance.

扽 (rad.64) **dèn**   To yank; pull with sharp tugs.

dèn tóu 扽头 Tug with the head: when in a choke hold, use the leverage of the head with a short, sharp tug to turn your position into one of throwing.

扥 (rad.64) **dēng**   To grab and give a short, abrupt, jerk.

登 (rad.105) **dēng**   1. To ascend; to mount; to scale (a mountain). 2. To press down with the foot, to step or tread on.

dēng zhǒu 登肘 Mounting elbow: an elbow strike. From Shaolinquan.

蹬 (rad.157) **dēng**   1. A heel kick: to thrust with the heel. 2. To press down with the foot. Step on. 3. The category of kicks that thrusts with the bottom of the foot or heel.

dēng jī bù 蹬基步 Thrusting stance: feet about three foot-lengths apart front to back, sitting down with the weight in between the feet, rear foot turned out a bit, front foot turned in a bit, knees tucked in a bit. Similar to an empty stance posture, but weighted evenly. From Chuojiao.

dēng jiǎo 蹬脚 1. A thrust heel kick: a front thrust kick, with foot dorsi-flexed, the toes up. In the category of snap kicks, see also qū shēn xìng tuǐ fǎ. 2. A strong push off from the rear leg when stepping, keeping the heel down. From Baguazhang and Xingyiquan.

dēng jìn 蹬劲 Power or energy of the forward thrust from the rear heel.

dēng pū diē 蹬扑跌 Extending takedown: type of takedown that puts the leg in between an adversary's legs, then extending with power thrusting into the heel.

dēng tā jiǎo 蹬踏脚 Stomping kick. From Yiquan. Usually called cǎi jiǎo.

dēng tuǐ 蹬腿 Thrust heel kick. See dēng jiǎo.

dēng xuē 蹬靴 Thrust the shoe self pulling stretch: standing straight, hold onto one foot, first bending the knee then extending the leg up in the air, still holding the foot.

dēng yī gēn 蹬一跟 A thrust heel kick. From Chen Taijiquan. See also dēng jiǎo.

等 (rad.118) **děng**   1. To wait. 2. A grade; rank. 3. A kind; sort. 4. Equal.

děng pāi 等拍 React, reactive fighting: wait for an adversary to attack, wait for an adversary to block your attack before attacking again, or wait for an adversary to make a mistake before attacking.

děng yú shì 等鱼势 Waiting for Fish: a reverse dip with the blade of a sword in front of the body, left hand at the right wrist. From Yang Taijiquan.

低 (rad.9) **dī**   Low. Let droop; hang.

dī bǎng shǒu 低膀手 Low wing arm: Guarding or deflecting low on the midline, turn the elbow upwards but below shoulder height, forearm angled downwards, palm down and facing out at about waist height. From Wing Chun.

dī cì jiàn 低刺剑 Low pierce straight to the tip with a sword, forming a straight line with the arm and blade, tip very near to the ground.

dī gōu 低勾 Low hook. See dī gōu tī tuǐ. Also called qiào tī.

dī gōu tī tuǐ 低勾踢腿 Low hook kick: a short, low hooking kick. May scrape the ground with the heel. Kicks no higher than the knee, and usually to the ankle.

dī mǎ 低马 Low horse stance: sit in horse stance, with the feet turned out a bit to allow your hips to sink below knee height.

dī nǎi zì bù 低乃字步 A full hunkered squat, sitting on one leg, the other foot extended, both feet flat on the ground. This stance is not as low or as extended as a drop stance, but the weight balance is about the same. See also nǎi zì bù, pū bù.

dī pán 低盘 The lower basin. 1. The lower body, the legs. 2. A low height used whilst training moving and stances, at the height of placing the hips at the level of the knees. From Baguazhang.

dī píng qiāng 低平枪 A low level stab with a spear: the shaft is horizontal, about twenty centimetres off the ground.

dī shì qián dēng cǎi jiǎo 低势前蹬踩脚 Stamping kick in low stance: fully squat on one leg and extend the other leg forward with the foot turned out. A held balance in modern competition Taijiquan.

dī shǒu 低手 Low hand. 1. An unskilled martial artist. 2. Used to refer to oneself with modesty.

dī tóu 低头 Tuck the head down. 1. To look down, an error in most performances. 2. In wrestling, to tuck the jaw in to prevent the head from hitting the ground – a requirement to protect the head during a fall. 3. Also in wrestling, to drop the head down prior to a throw that requires dropping the head and waist.

滴 (rad.85) dī 1. A drip (of liquid), a drop. 2. A descending pierce with a blade or tip.

dī shuǐ shì 滴水式 Dripping Water model. One of twenty-four classic spear moves. Most spear routines will have a move with a like name. In general, this name refers to a chop or dab that then lifts to stab.

dī shuǐ xiān huā 滴水献花 Drip water and Present Flowers, a pole technique. Hunker down in a squat and hit down with the pole.

敌 [敵] (rad.66) dí 1. Enemy, adversary, opponent. 2. To resist; to withstand.

dí shǒu 敌手 Match, opponent.

dí rén 敌人 Enemy, adversary.

涤 [滌] (rad.85) dí To wash; cleanse. To sweep.

dí kē 涤磕 Wash away (with a broadsword): wrap the head with the blade to knock the incoming attack away. See also chán tóu dāo, lǎo dāo.

底 (rad.53) dǐ Bottom, base.

dǐ chà 底岔 The lower edge of a wrestling jacket, at the opening.

dǐ pán 底盘 The base basin: the legs. Also called dī pán.

dǐ zhǎng 底掌 A low strike with the heel of the palm. From Wing Chun.

dǐ zhuāng 底桩 Base pillars: the legs.

抵 (rad.64) dǐ To support, prop; resist, withstand.

dǐ àn dāo 抵按刀 Supported press down with a broadsword: press down the blade edge close to the ground, the left hand pressing on the spine of the blade or on the right hand.

骶 (rad.188) dǐ The sacrum.

dǐ gǔ 骶骨 The sacrum bone, the largest of the pelvic girdle bones, the base of the spinal column.

地 (rad.32) dì The earth; land; soil; fields; ground, floor.

dì cāng 地仓 Acupoint Dicang (earth's granary), ST4. At the face, outside the corner of the mouth, on a vertical line with ST1, ST2, and ST3 (on each side). From TCM.

dì chèng 地秤 A ground balance: a barbell with the weight only on one end, used for a variety of training exercises, such as rolling with one arm, or simulating wrestling throws.

dì jī 地机 Acupoint Diji (earth's crux), SP8. At the calf, up the inside, about three *cun* below the knee, slightly behind the back edge of the tibia (on each leg). From TCM.

dì tāng biān 地趟鞭 Groundwork with the steel whip: lying on the ground, swing the whip horizontally above the body, also swinging it under the body, hopping up with the body to allow it to pass.

D

dì tāng quán 地趟拳 Ditangquan (ground fist), , from Shandong province. Mixes tumbling with techniques.

dì tǎng quán 地躺拳 See dì tāng quán.

dì wǔ huì 地五会 Acupoint Diwuhui (earth's fivefold convergence), GB42. At the foot, on the top, at the proximal end of the metatarsal of the fourth toe, inside the tendon of the little toe (on each foot). From TCM.

dì zhī 地支 The twelve Earthly Branches, used in combination with the ten Heavenly stems to designate years, months, days, and hours. See chén, chǒu, hài, mǎo, shēn, sì, wèi, wǔ, xū, yín, yǒu, zǐ. See also tiān gān.

的 (rad.106) dì   1. The original meaning is a target. 2. In the martial arts is a shout used in southern styles to gain or express power. The character is used to represent the sound. 3. The character is also a grammatical particle pronounced de.

第 (rad.118) dì   An affix that indicates numerals are ordinal numbers.

dì yī tāng 第一蹚 The first routine. Many styles name their routines in this way – Qingping sword among others. Subsequent routines would be second, third, etc.

dì yī tàng 第一趟 The first routine. 1. Many styles name their routines in this way – Chuojiao's martial routines (see also wǔ tàng zi), Sanhuang Paochui, Jingangchui, among others. Subsequent routines would be second, third, etc. 2. The first section of a routine. Subsequent sections would be second, third, etc.

dì yī zhǎng 第一掌 The first palm. Baguazhang often numbers the eight mother palm changes as well as naming them. Subsequent changes would be second, third, etc.

遞 [递] (rad.162) dì   To hand over; to pass; give.

dì shǒu 递手 To touch hands, usually in a practice or teaching sparring situation.

顛 [颠] (rad.181) diān   1. The crown; top, summit. 2. Jolt; topple down. 3. The crown of the head.

diān bù cè chuāi tuǐ 颠步侧踹腿 Upsetting step to side thrust kick. From Chuojiao, one of its middle-basin kicks.

diān bù cè pā chuāi 颠步侧趴踹 Upsetting step to leaning side thrust kick. From Chuojiao, one of its middle-basin kicks.

diān bù cè pā diǎn 颠步侧趴点 Upsetting step to leaning poke kick. From Chuojiao, one of its middle-basin kicks.

diān qǐ bù 颠起步 Upsetting leap: stride forward with one foot, push off with the other foot, lifting the knee, either kicking or threatening a kick. Land on the first foot and land the pushing off foot forward. Should have good height and distance. From Chuojiao.

diān tī bù 颠踢步 Upsetting kick step. 1. An upsetting leap to kick step: do the upsetting leap and on landing, kick up with the foot dorsi-flexed, striking the ground with the heel. From Chuojiao. 2. Used with the same meaning as diān qǐ bù, without the final kick.

diān tī tuǐ 颠踢腿 Upsetting kicks: category of kicks using the upsetting stepping with kicks and hand strikes. From Chuojiao, one of its middle-basin kicks.

diān tuǐ 颠腿 Upsetting step or kick: lift one knee, then the other while stepping.

diān xiōng tí fù 颠胸提腹 Topple the chest and pull in the belly. See tǐng xiōng shōu fù.

典 (rad.12) diǎn   1. A rule. 2. A standard work, a canon. 3. To take charge of.

diǎn xíng 典型   A typical case; model; representative.

diǎn xíng zhāo shì 典型招势 A representative move of a style or a model of a certain type of attack.

踮 (rad.157) diǎn   To stand on tiptoe.

diǎn bù 踮步 Take a quick step on the toes.

diǎn tiào 踮跳 Take a light jumping step on the toes.

點 (rad.203) [点] (rad.86) **diǎn** 1. A drop of liquid; a spot. The image is that of the movement a writing brush makes when it draws the dot of a character. 2. To dab, poke in, a hooking pierce, nod. 3. A kick: to lift and extend the leg to poke in with the toes. 4. Poking pressure points. From Qinna. 5. To strike a soft target with the finger tips or knuckles with a short, sharp pecking action. From Bajiquan, one of its ten major techniques, see also shí dà jī fǎ.

diǎn bù 点步 Dotting stance: similar to an empty stance, but with the front foot pointing straight down.

diǎn chuí 点捶 Dabbing fist: dab with a strong punch, a joint of the middle finger of the fist protruding. Commonly used to get in between the ribs.

diǎn dāo 点刀 Dab with the tip of a broadsword. See diǎn jiàn.

diǎn dà dāo 点大刀 Dab with a big cutter: with the right hand near the blade, drop the butt down to strike.

diǎn fǎ 点法 Poking methods: stabbing methods to sensitive points.

diǎn fēng dìng wèi 点风定位 Point into the Wind to Orient yourself: a low empty stance with a horizontal rolled over stab. From Qingping sword.

diǎn jiàn 点剑 Dab with the tip of a sword, lifting the wrist to drop sharply forward and down, cutting just behind the tip of the blade or digging the tip in.

diǎn jiǎo 点脚 Poking kick. 1. An extending kick, first lift the knee, then kick with the toes leading to poke them into an adversary. Also called diǎn tuǐ. 2. A short kick, just off the ground, extending to the toes. From Yiquan.

diǎn jiǎo mǎ 点脚马 Foot touch horse stance: with the feet about a foot-length apart, half squat and lift the heel of one leg, shifting the weight a bit to the flat foot leg. From southern styles.

diǎn jīng shǒu 点睛手 Eye poke: poke an adversary in the eye with the fingers. Often use the thumb, index and middle fingers as the striking point.

diǎn jīng zhǎng 点睛掌 Eye poking palm, a hand shape: index and middle fingers extended but not straight, and spread apart, the other fingers tucked under the thumb. Also called zhuó mù zhǐ.

diǎn gùn 点棍 Dab with a staff. See diǎn qiāng.

diǎn mài 点脉 Touch vessels: press, put pressure on a vein or artery to block it. Known as Dim Mak in English, from the Cantonese.

diǎn qì fǎ 点气法 Techniques for pressuring acupoints to block the flow of *qi*.

diǎn qiāng 点枪 Dab with a spear: drop the tip down from above with a short action, usually with the hands coming together at the butt to extend the tip.

diǎn quán 点拳 Poking fist shape: an upright fist with one joint of the middle finger extended.

diǎn tuǐ 点腿 Poking kick. 1. An extending kick with the toes. Also called diǎn jiǎo. In the category of snap kicks, see also qū shēn xìng tuǐ fǎ. 2. In Duanquan the kick uses this action but contacts with the outer edge of the foot.

diǎn xué 点穴 Press the cavities: press, put pressure on an acupoint cavity to disrupt *qi* circulation. Traditionally, there are considered to be thirty-six points that cause death and seventy-two points that cause numbness or unconsciousness.

diǎn xué fǎ 点穴法 Cavity press methods: techniques for pressuring acupoints. This is done to block the *qi*. Done with intent, pressuring causes numbness, unconsciousness, or even death. Done with just force and no intent, it is said that pressuring causes pain but usually no real damage. Also called yā xué fǎ.

diǎn xué shǒu fǎ 点穴手法 Specific hand techniques for pressuring acupoints.

diǎn xué zhēn 点穴针 Acupoint pressing needles: see tié kuài zi.

垫 [垫] (rad.32) **diàn** 1. To fill something in or up, put something under something else to level it out. 2. To advance money. 3. To advance in stepping, when one foot changes places with the other.

diàn bù 垫步 Hop or step up. 1. Bring the rear foot in, then lift the front foot so that the rear foot takes its place, advancing while remaining in the same stance. 2. A stamp drive: step forward then hop forcefully, lifting the other foot then landing it forward. 3. In Xingyiquan, to first step the front foot turned out, then step the rear foot through.

diàn bù dēng tuǐ 垫步蹬腿 Hop step heel kick: skip the supporting leg forward while doing a heel kick.

diàn shǒu 垫手 Act as a sparring partner for someone, feeding the handwork to help in training.

電 (rad.173) [电] (rad.73) **diàn** 1. Lightning. 2. Electricity. 3. Related to electrical things such as telegram. telephone.

diàn guāng qíng chè 电光擎掣 Lightning Lifts and Tugs: step forward to a right bow stance, stabbing down to about knee height with fully straight arm. Then hop forward on the left leg, spinning fully around to the right and landing back in a right bow stance, stabbing to head height with straight arm. From Qingping sword.

刁 (rad.18) **diāo** 1. Tricky, sly. 2. In the martial arts, sometimes is used instead of hook (see gōu 勾) for a hooking control, trapping without grabbing. One of the sixteen key techniques of Baguazhang, see also shí liù zì jué. 3. Sometimes means a surprise attack. Sometimes written 叼, which means to hold in the mouth.

diāo bà 刁把 Trap grip: hold a sword with the thumb and index finger firmly at the guard, other fingers straight, gripping with the palm.

diāo dǎ 刁打 Trap and hit. 1. A quick hook that turns into a palm heel strike. 2. To hook an adversary then rebound to strike with the same hand. 3. To first hook an adversary outwards then hit from the inside with the other hand.

diāo dāo 刁刀 Trapping broadsword: the blade is angled downward, the tip angled downward to the right. A positional reference, separate from the direction of the strike.

diāo fǎ 刁法 Trapping methods: techniques that first hook and control before striking, without grabbing.

diāo gōu 刁勾 1. To hook onto, trap. 2. A trapping hand shape: wrist flexed, thumb tucked onto the second segment of the index and middle fingers.

diāo ná 刁拿 To hook onto and trap an adversary's arm with one hand and grasp with the other to control or take down.

diāo shǒu 刁手 1. Hook onto and keep away. 2. Hook the wrist with the arm slightly bent, to trap. 3. A hand shape, some styles hold the five fingers together with the palm empty. Some styles bend the fingers as if holding a spiral shell – fingers bent, the little finger curled in, and each finger gradually curling in less. Also called diāo zhǎng.

diāo zhǎng 刁掌 Trapping hand, a cocked wrist, less hooked than a hook (see gōu). Refers to the hand shape, not a technique. See also #3 of diāo shǒu, gōu.

吊 弔 (rad.50, 57) [吊] (rad.50) **diào** To hoist with a rope; suspend; hang.

diào dāng 吊裆 A suspended crotch: a rounded and relaxed groin area combined with the buttocks slightly sent forward and the anal sphincter lifted so that the back is naturally straight. From Taijiquan.

diào dāo 吊刀 Hoist a broadsword: lift the grip so that the blade hangs angled down on line with the arm, edge out. The spine may lie along the arm.

diào jiàn 吊剑 Hoist a sword: lift the grip so that the blade hangs angled down on line with the arm, edge out. The blade must be held away from the arm.

diào jiǎo 吊脚 Hanging Foot stance: a squat with one foot touching down lightly near the instep of the supporting leg.

diào jiǎo qiān zì 吊脚千字 Hanging Foot stance and Write the Character Qian (千): squat to the right leg and touch down the toes of the left near the instep, cutting down the left forearm in front of the left thigh. The 57th move of the tiger and crane routine.

diào mǎ bù 吊马步 Hanging horse stance. 1. A one legged stance with the raised leg held as if still in horse stance. 2. An empty stance with the empty knee raised so only the toes touch the ground. 3. An empty stance.

diào máo 吊毛 A forward no-hands somersault.

diào shǒu 吊手 Hoist. 1. A quick, strong, and short hook to send an adversary off in any direction chosen. 2. A hook onto an adversary's wrist to lock onto it.

diào yāo 吊腰 Hoist the Waist: with a straight supporting leg, swing the torso and other leg keeping them in a straight line, leaning forward so the torso is on the supporting leg, so that the suspended leg swings up vertically, quickly drawing a full circle. Also called zhí fān shēn.

diào zhuāng 吊装 Hoist a Fake: extend a palm then punch with the other fist. In Tongbeiquan, the punching fist starts out as a palm, rubs the incoming palm, then clenches to punch, then the other fist punches again.

掉 (rad.64) **diào** 1. To fall, to drop. 2. To lose. 3. To lag behind. 4. To move. 5. To turn.

diào bù 掉步 Dropping step. 1. One foot comes in to land in the place that the supporting foot occupies. The other foot lifts at that instant so that this can happen. 2. A switchover step, changing the place of the feet quickly without lifting them. Also called cuò bù, huàn bù, jiāo cuò bù.

diào dāo 掉刀 A halberd with a wide double edged blade.

diào dì 掉地 To drop, to be dropped.

diào shēn 掉身 To turn fully around. Usually called huí shēn. From Baguazhang.

調 [调] (rad.149) **diào** 1. To transfer, to collect. 2. Pronounced tiáo, to regulate.

diào bà 调把 Transfer the grip: to switch the tip for the base of a staff.

diào hǔ lí shān 调虎离山 Lure the Tiger out of the Mountain. Try to get yourself set up with favourable terrain, especially against a strong adversary. The 15th of the Thirty-six Stratagems of Warfare, which apply to many situations.

釣 [钓] (rad.167) **diào** 1. To fish. 2. To lure. 3. A fishhook.

diào yú chuí 钓鱼锤 A fishing punch: a hooking punch to the ribs.

跌 (rad.157) **diē** 1. Tumbling. 2. To fall, tumble.

diē cén 跌岑 Leap the Hill: a direct drop to a hurdler stance. A drop, not a leap, but the stance looks like a leap. From Chen Taijiquan. Also called diē chā, diē chà.

diē chā 跌叉 1. Land from a jump into the front splits. Also called diē shù chā. In the category of the splits leg techniques, see also pī chā xíng tuǐ fǎ. 2. A hurdler stance, see diē cén.

diē chà 跌岔 Drop to a forked stance. See diē cén.

diē dàng qí lín 跌荡麒麟 Kylin Stumbles and Falls: Step in front cross steps, left and right, with the fists at the waist. The 67th move of the tiger and crane routine.

diē fǎ 跌法 Throws and tripping techniques.

diē pū 跌扑 Tumbling. The tumbling category of movements.

diē pū fān gǔn 跌扑翻滚 Tumbling. The tumbling category of movements.

diē shù chā 跌竖叉 Land from a jump into the front splits, also called diē chā. From Longfist.

疊 (rad.102) [叠] (rad.29) **dié** 1. To fold. 2. Pile up. 3. Repeat.

dié bì zāi bēi shì 叠臂栽碑式 Folding Arms Plant the Stele: forward straight break fall, bending the arms to land on the forearms.

dié bù 叠步 Squat on one leg, the other touching down beside. Like a T stance, but a more natural squat. See also dīng bù.

dié dǎo 叠倒 Folding fall leg technique, tucking the leg in to control a fall.

dié guān zhōng mén zhǎng 叠关中门掌 Fold the main gate closed: a double press down in a bow stance. From Chuojiao.

dié jīn 叠筋 Fold the tendons: kip up. Also called lǐ yú dǎ tǐng.

dié shǒu 叠手 Fold the hand: roll back after being blocked, and attack again with the same hand. From Tanglangquan.

dié wàn 叠腕 Folding wrist: turning and coiling with the wrist to combine pushes.

dié zhǒu 叠肘 Fold the elbow: with the elbow fully bent, press down with the forearm.

dié zuò bù 叠坐步 Folded sitting stance. See zuò lián bù.

D

蝶 (rad.142) **dié** Butterfly. For more movement names referencing the butterfly, see also under cǎi dié, dān-, fú -, shuāng -.

dié bù 蝶步 1. Butterfly stance: squat on one leg and place the lower leg of the other fully on the ground, or kneel on both knees with both whole lower legs on ground. 2. A folding step used in turning, when you first move the foot, then brace the knees, then open the hip. From Baguazhang.

dié shǒu 蝶手 Butterfly hands: starting with one hand palm to the side at the shoulder and the other palm forward at the same hip, circle both hands in opposition until they are in reverse position at the other side of the body. From southern styles.

dié zhǎng lián huán 蝶掌连环 Linking Butterfly Palms: step with front crossing steps, circling with butterfly hands, the 105th move of the tiger and crane routine. See dié shǒu.

丁 (rad.1) **dīng** 1. The fourth of the ten Celestial Stems, used in combination with the twelve Terrestrial Branches to designate years, months, days, and hours. See also dì zhī, tiān gān. 2. Fourth in a list when listing using the celestial stems, equivalent to D in English when listing alphabetically. 3. In martial arts names, often used for its shape: T, or like a nail.

dīng bā bù 丁八步 'T8' stance, a stance with the weight two thirds to the rear leg. the front foot turned slightly in, rear foot turned about thirty degrees, legs bent. Abbreviation for bù dīng bù bā, see also sì liù bù.

dīng bù 丁步 T stance. 1. In many styles: squatting on one leg, the toes of the light foot touching close to the supporting foot, at the middle of the foot. 2. In some styles: sitting while placing one foot in front of the other to draw the character T. 3. In Duanquan, the lead foot is turned in.

dīng chāi tuǐ 丁钗腿 Nail the Hairpin kick. See dīng tuǐ. From Xinyi Liuhequan.

dīng chǎng 丁场 Nail kick: see dīng tuǐ.

dīng chǒu 丁丑 The years 1997, 1937, and so on, for sixty year cycles.

dīng gāo tuǐ 丁高腿 Nailing High kick: a heel kick to the chest. From Xinyi Liuhequan.

dīng hài 丁亥 The years 2007, 1947, and so on, for sixty year cycles.

dīng mǎo 丁卯 The years 1987, 1927, and so on, for sixty year cycles.

dīng sì 丁巳 The years 1977, 1917, and so on, for sixty year cycles.

dīng tuǐ 丁腿 Nail kick: 1. Holding the ankle solidly, dorsi-flexed, knock the ground with the heel and kick up with the sole of the foot. Usually is below knee height. Also called cùn tuǐ, dīng chāi, dīng chǎng. From Chuojiao. 2. Kick with the foot plantar flexed, to contact with the point of the toes. From southern styles.

dīng wèi 丁未 The years 1967, 1907, and so on, for sixty year cycles.

dīng xū bù 丁虚步 T empty stance, see dīng bù.

dīng yǒu 丁酉 The years 2017, 1957, and so on, for sixty year cycles.

dīng zì bù 丁字步 T stance. 1. The legs straight, both feet flat on the ground, and the heel of one foot placed at the instep of the other to form a T. 2. In some styles (most notably Baguazhang), a stance that forms an open cornered L or a T with the feet flat on the ground and the toes tucked in.

dīng zì gōng bù 丁字弓步 T Bow stance: a bow stance with the front foot turned in across the line, the rear foot straight with the leg straight, both heels on the ground.

dīng zì kòu bù 丁字扣步 Hook in step to T stance: step one foot hooked in to form a T stance with the other foot.

dīng zì tuǐ 丁字腿 T kick: a front snap kick (see also tán tuǐ) with the hands performing an opening technique, one aligned with the kick, the other to the side, looking like a T from the top.

dīng zì zhǎng 丁字掌 T palm: thumb tucked, fingers straight and spread. A hand shape. From southern styles.

dīng zì zhuāng 丁字桩 Nail stake: a basic routine of Meishanquan, written up as twenty-eight moves, practising compact moves.

dīng zhǒu 丁肘 Nail with the point of the elbow. Also called dǐng zhǒu.

钉 [釘] (rad.167) **dīng** A nail.

dīng quán 钉拳 Nailing punch: a short, sharp

punch downwards with the elbow bent, striking with the fist surface or the fist back. From southern styles.

dīng xīn zhǒu 钉心肘 Nail the heart with the elbow: hold your ground and set the elbow as an adversary moves in, to strike the tip directly to his heart.

頂 [顶] (rad.181) dǐng 1. Crown of the head, peak of the head (not the top, but the sensitive point where the skull plates join). 2. To press up, prop up, support; push up. 3. To butt: a short strike with a pointed part of the body or the head. 4. To press: one of the body requirements of Xingyiquan: for the head, palm, and tip of tongue. 5. An error when used in push hands when used with the meaning of 'force against force'. From Taijiquan, one of the four defects in push hands, see also sì bìng. 6. In wrestling, when attempting to off balance an adversary, and both are on one leg and about to fall, press into his leg with the knee, reversing his throw so that he falls. 7. To use a prominent part of a body segment (such as an elbow joint) as the initial attack. From Bajiquan, one of its six main striking techniques, see also liù dà kāi.

dǐng bǎ 顶把 Hit with the butt of a short weapon: a short strike.

dǐng bù 顶步 Pressing step: advance the rear foot to send the front foot forward. From Xingyiquan.

dǐng dāng shuāi 顶裆摔 Butt the groin throw. See dǐng tuǐ shuāi.

dǐng fǎ 顶法 Strikes with the elbow.

dǐng gùn 顶棍 Prop up with a staff: stab up and forward with the butt held down. In some styles the butt is held steady on the ground.

dǐng jià 顶架 Butting face-off in wrestling, adversaries have the opposite feet forward (one right, one left).

dǐng jīn 顶筋 Butt a tendon: butt a tendon, artery or vein. From Qinna.

dǐng jìn 顶劲 1. Propping power, an energy put to prop up, support the head. 2. Energy put into a butting skill. 3. To use 'force against force' in fighting, an error in many styles, especially Taijiquan.

dǐng niú 顶牛 To fight stubbornly like an ox instead of using skill, agility, or intelligence.

dǐng quán 顶拳 Butting punch: a short, sharp, snapping punch to the fist surface with the wrist straight.

dǐng tóu 顶头 1. Butt with the head. 2. To press the head up, straighten the neck.

dǐng tuǐ shuāi 顶腿摔 Butt the legs throw: a quick throw used in Sanda. Quickly drop and grab an adversary's ankles, leaning into his shins with the shoulders. Also called dǐng dāng shuāi.

dǐng xī 顶膝 Knee butt, a knee technique. Strike forward or to the side with the knee.

dǐng xīn chuí 顶心锤 Butt the Centre Punch: step into a bow stance with an uppercut through the middle. From Shaolinquan.

dǐng yāo 顶腰 Butt the waist: control an adversary from behind, grabbing his throat and pressing the knee into his lower back. From wrestling.

dǐng zhèng 顶挣 Elbow butt: an inward elbow strike or control. From Wing Chun.

dǐng zì gōng 顶字功 Butting Skill, one of Xingyiquan's eight skills, striking with the head, knee, and elbow.

dǐng zhǒu 顶肘 Butt with the point of the elbow. Also called dīng zhǒu.

鼎 (rad.206) dǐng   A pot. An ancient cooking vessel with three or four legs. Often used when referring to a tripod structure.

dǐng gōng 鼎功 Tripod training methods to develop upper body strength. Includes head stands, hand stands, forearm stands.

dǐng zú zhǐ 鼎足指 Tripod fingers: to strike with three fingers held together. Also called sān yīn zhǐ.

定 (rad.40) dìng 1. Set, stable. Calm; decided. 3. Fixed; settled.

dìng bù 定步 Fixed stance, doing an action or exercise without moving the feet.

dìng bù fā lì xùn liàn 定步发力训练 Fixed stance power exertion training. From Yiquan.

dìng bù tuī shǒu 定步推手 Fixed step push hands: the feet may not move during the training. From Taijiquan.

D

dìng chuǎn 定喘 Extraordinary acupoint Dingchuan (panting stabiliser), EX-B1. At the back, level with the depression under the seventh cervical vertebra, one *cun* lateral to the midline (on each side). From TCM.

dìng diǎn dǎ fǎ 定点打法 Fixed point striking practice: Repeatedly practising a technique to perfect it on a bag or post.

dìng jià zǐ 定架子 Practise a routine stance by stance, carefully, stopping in each stance.

dìng jìn 定劲 To set an adversary so that he cannot control his movements, uprooting him and making him shift, putting him off balance.

dìng nán fǎ 定南法 Set to the south method: to set into the most advantageous place in a fight, avoiding obstacles and roughness of the ground, and getting the sun behind you. This helps to deal with multiple attackers.

dìng shì 定式 1. Fixed postures, training of stationary postures, holding them for a set time. 2. Circle-walking in fixed positions in Baguazhang.

dìng shì 定势 Fixed postures. See dìng shì above.

dìng sòng dāo 定宋刀 Pacify the Song cutter. Also translated as big cutter, halberd, Guan's halberd. See guān dāo. Also called chūn qiū dāo, dà dāo, yuè shèng dāo.

dìng xīn 定心 A direct elbow strike to the heart or solar plexus.

鋌 [铤] (rad.167) **dìng** 1. A unit of weight of fifty liang, for silver. See also liǎng. 2. Ingots, bars of metal. 3. A short pike made of metal.

丟 [丢] (rad.1) **diū** 1. To lose, mislay. 2. To lose contact with an adversary in a close-range sparring or push hands. A major error in push hands. From Taijiquan, see sì bìng. 3. To lose the impetus and become reactive in sparring. 4. To lose the feeling in practising a routine.

東 [东] (rad.75) **dōng** 1. East, Eastern, Easterly. 2. The host.

dōng chéng 东城 1. The Eastern part of a city. 2. In Baguazhang, the branch that trained in the Eastern part of Beijing in the old days.

dōng fēng xián rì 东峰衔日 Eastern Peak Holds the Sun: place a sword grip into the right hand in preparation for action. From Chen Taijiquan.

dōng fāng 东方 The East. Often written descriptions of routines use compass directions for orientation.

dōng hàn 东汉 Eastern Han dynasty (25 BC-220 AD).

dōng jìn 东晋 Eastern Jin dynasty (317-420).

dōng wèi 东魏 Eastern Wei of the Northern dynasties (534-550).

dōng yuè tài shān 东岳泰山 Mount Tai, the Eastern of the sacred mountains. See also tài shān, wǔ yuè.

dōng zhōu 东周 Eastern Zhou dynasty (770-256 BC).

懂 (rad.61) **dǒng** To understand; know.

dǒng jìn 懂劲 Understanding power: understand and feel the structure and movement of power within yourself and within an adversary, and be able to use this understanding to control the situation. From Taijiquan.

動 [动] (rad.19) **dòng** 1. Motion, activity. 2. Move; to get moving. 3. To touch.

dòng bù tuī shǒu 动步推手 Moving step push hands: push hands with set stepping patterns. Also called jìn tuì bù tuī shǒu. From Taijiquan.

dòng hé yú kōng 动合于空 Movement combines with emptiness. From Liuhebafa, one of its principles.

dòng jí zé jí yìng, dòng huǎn zé huǎn suí 动急则急应，动缓则缓随 When attacked at speed, react quickly, when attacked slowly, follow leisurely. A martial saying.

dòng jìng 动静 Motion and stillness; activity and inactivity.

dòng jìng shuāng xiū 动静双修 Combining movement and stillness within each action.

dòng jìng xiāng yīn 动静相因 Movement and stillness interact and grow from each other.

dòng mài 动脉 An artery, arteries; arterial.

dòng rú tāo 动如涛 Move like billowing waves: one of the twelve qualities of movement of

Changquan, though these descriptors apply to many other styles.

dòng xùn jìng dìng 动讯静定 Sudden movement and set stillness: a quality of rhythm and power of many styles. Movement should be like having no space between the lightning and the thunder, like pounding waves, giving no chance of defense. Stillness should be immovable like a mountain peak.

dòng zhōng qiú jìng 动中求静 Seek stillness in action.

dòng zuò 动作 A movement, a move.

dòng zuò yào jīng shén 动作要精神 Movement must be vigorous. From Tongbeiquan, one of its requirements.

dòng zuò zhì liàng 动作质量 The quality of movement.

兜 (rad.10) **dōu** 1. A pocket; bag; pouch. 2. To wrap up in a cloth.

dōu dāng tuǐ 兜裆腿 Leg in the pouch: a front straight swing kick to the groin with the foot dorsiflexed. This kick is common, but this term is from Chuojiao. Also called qián liāo yīn tuǐ.

dōu jiǎo 兜脚 Foot in the pouch: a rising, slightly swinging kick with the foot turned out and the knee bent. The foot is lifted to about knee height. It may be used as a hidden kick during a leap forward.

dōu zhǎng 兜掌 Cupping palm, slap with the palm cupped.

抖 (rad.64) **dǒu** To shake, often a full body shake off of a grab, or shaking the shoulders or hips.

dǒu chén shì 抖尘势 Shake the World Position: set into a half horse stance, shaking the fists to the side to strike with the meaty edge of the forward fist.

dǒu dāng 抖裆 Slice up with a strong shake into the groin.

dǒu gùn zǐ 抖棍子 Pole shaking, a training method to develop power.

dǒu jìn 抖劲 Shaking power: a sudden rotational power emanating from the pelvic and waist area (*dantian*). It is quick, strong, uses short movement for long power, and can be applied through the body to strike with just about any body segment. It is applied from a relaxed body. From Tongbeiquan, one of its nine types of power, see also jiǔ gōng jìn.

dǒu ná fǎ 抖拿法 Shaking grappling hold: while in hold, applying an abrupt snapping action, short and over a small range of motion. From wrestling.

dǒu pí tiáo 抖皮条 Snapping the leather strap: training exercises used in wrestling, holding each end of a leather strap or strong cotton belt from the wrestling uniform, and simulating wrestling throws.

dǒu quán 抖拳 Throw out a punch with a shake of the body. Also called tán quán.

dǒu shǒu 抖手 Shaking strike: snap out a wrist strike.

dǒu sǒu jìn 抖擞劲 Shaking, or arousing, power: the whole body combines in one expression, all parts moving as one.

dǒu tuǐ 抖腿 Shaking kick. 1. Move in and do a quick kick across outwards to the groin with the toes of the front foot. 2. A training technique of shaking leg: stand with one knee up, enduring the shaking of the suspended leg.

dǒu yāo 抖腰 Shake the back. A full torso shake while doing a technique, often with a wave moving through the body from one side to the other or from top to bottom or the reverse.

陡 (rad.170) **dǒu** Suddenly, abruptly. Steep.

dǒu qǐ jiān 陡起肩 Suddenly Lift the Shoulder, a shoulder technique: hit to the rear with the head of the shoulder. This is a close, leaning, technique, not a strike.

鬥 鬦 鬭 [斗] (rad.191) **dòu** To fight; tussle. Contend with.

dòu kǒu 斗口 See pán kǒu.

dòu qì 斗气 Quarrelsome, to quarrel on emotional grounds. Considered a fault in most styles, and likely to lead to defeat in a fight due to lack of attention to defense.

dòu zēng 斗曾 Douzeng (fighting) style, a Longfist style, a branch of Shaolinquan.

D

督 (rad.109) **dū**　To direct, supervise, regulate.

dū mài 督脉 Governor Vessel meridian, vessel, or channel, GV or DU. Flows up the back of the body from the Mingmen to the Huiyin. In most internal styles, at least, the back is held straight to allow the flow of *qi* in this important channel, which commands the *yang* channels of the body.

dū shū 督俞 Acupoint Dushu (governing transport), BL16. At the back, level with the depression below the spinous process of the sixth thoracic vertebra, 1.5 *cun* lateral to the midline (on each side). From TCM. A sensitive point, striking it can cause breathlessness.

毒 (rad.80) **dú**　1. Poisonous, poison. 2. This meaning is extended to mean fierce, ferocity, viciousness.

dú shé chuàn tuǐ 毒蛇串腿 Viper Shoots out a Leg: a thrusting kick with the ball of the foot to the stomach, snapping back as the hands follow through to complete the attack.

dú shé juǎn shé 毒蛇卷舌 Viper Rolls its Tongue: a dodge then a poking kick from the side to the navel.

dú shé tù xīn 毒蛇吐心 Viper Spits its Tongue: a direct, fully extended kick to the groin, leaning the body back to throw from the hip.

dú shé xún xué shǒu 毒蛇寻穴手 Viper Seeks the Hole: any straight finger strike to the throat.

dú xiē fǎn wěi 毒蝎反尾 Scorpion Snaps its Tail: from a low stance, reach the torso forward, shifting forward to a low bow stance, extending a sword blade forward to execute a quick scooping stab with a standing blade, coming from under to cut an adversary's arm. From Qingping sword.

犊 (rad.93) **dú**　A calf (as in a young animal, especially when referring to the calf used in a sacrifice).

dú bí 犊鼻 Acupoint Dubi (calf's nose), ST35. At the knee, outside and under the patella on the outside at the tendon (on each leg). From TCM.

獨 [独] (rad.94) **dú**　Solitary, alone, single; by oneself.

dú bì dān qiáo 独臂单桥 Single Arm does a Single Bridge: sit to a horse stance and push the left palm out to the side, index finger extended. The 47th move of the tiger and crane routine.

dú hǔ jiǎo 独虎脚 Single tiger kick. See cùn tī tuǐ.

dú jiǎo è hè 独脚饿鹤 Hungry Crane on One Leg: in a right raised knee stance, bring the hands to hook in front of the body, right higher and more forward. The 75th move of the tiger and crane routine.

dú jiǎo fēi hè 独脚飞鹤 Flying Crane on One Leg: lift the right knee and open the hands to the sides, elbows tucked down so that the arms are quite bent. The 74th move of the tiger and crane routine.

dú lì bù 独立步 One legged stance, raised knee stance. The suspended leg held at least at knee height, exact height varies with the style.

dú lì cháo yáng 独立朝阳 One legged stance Face the Sun: raise the knee and push the blade up overhead. If the right knee is lifted the hands are both at the hilt and the right palm faces in. If the left knee is lifted the left hand pushes forward and the right palm faces out. From Qingping sword.

dú lì dūn bù 独立蹲步 Squatting one legged stance. Squatting on one leg, the suspended leg held at ankle height, the thighs together, parallel to the ground.

dú lì gōu tuǐ bù 独立勾腿步 Hooked one legged stance. Standing on one leg, slightly bent, the suspended leg tucked behind the knee.

dú lì shàng tuō 独立上托 One legged stance and lift up with a sword or broadsword.

dú lì shì 独立势 1. A complete posture in a one-legged stance. 2. Just the one-legged stance.

dú lì tiǎo lián 独立挑帘 Stand on One Leg to Raise the Curtain. See dú lì shàng tuō.

dú lì tuō zhǎng 独立托掌 One legged stance and lift up and forward on the same side as the lifted knee.

dú lì zhuāng 独立桩 Stake standing on one leg: stand on one leg, raise the other knee. Extend the raised knee's side arm straight up and extend the standing leg's arm straight down. From Yiquan. Also called jīn jī dú lì.

dú yīn 独阴 Extraordinary acupoint Duyin

(solitary yin), EX-LE11. At the sole of the foot, under the distal end of the middle phalanx of the second toe (on each foot). From TCM.

dú zhàn áo tóu 独占鳌头 Head the List of Successful Candidates: from a raised knee cradling the sword position, advance four steps and stab. From Qingping sword.

堵 (rad.32) dǔ 1. To stop up, block up. 2. A wall.

dǔ jié fǎ 堵截法 Intercepting method: to receive and counter an attack simultaneously.

dǔ mén tuǐ 堵门腿 Stop up the Door Kick: a short upward striking kick to the shin, foot turned across, digging the ground first with the heel. Also called qī xīng diǎn zi.

杜 (rad.75) dù 1. Birch-leaf pear. 2. A surname. One of the four big family branches of Emeiquan, see sì dà jiā.

肚 (rad.130) dù 1. The belly; abdomen. 2. Pronounced dǔ, tripe.

端 (rad.117) duān 1. End; extremity. Beginning. 2. Item. 3. Carry in both hands.

duān dēng 端灯 Carry a Lantern: grab the ear of your adversary in one hand (pressing the point above the bone behind the ear) and pressing his opposite temple (getting a grip with the nose) in the other, twisting. This will render him unconscious. From Qinna.

duān ná fǎ 端拿法 Carrying grappling hold: any double handed grab that is intended to lift an adversary off the ground. From wrestling.

duān qiāng 端枪 Carry a spear, either in one hand or with both hands at the butt, holding it out horizontally.

duān tī 端踢 Carry and kick, a trip: holding the sides of the belt, lift your adversary to shift him, kicking his legs out from under him. From wrestling.

duān xuē 端靴 Carry the foot: a self pulling stretch. Standing straight on one leg, hold onto one foot with the leg extended upward in the air.

短 (rad.111) duǎn Short.

duǎn bà chuí 短把锤 A short handled mace.

duǎn biān 短鞭 Short whip: see duǎn qiáo.

duǎn bīng 短宾 Short weapons. 1. Short weapons in general. 2. As a competition category, generally refers to sword and broadsword.

duǎn dǎ 短打 Short range fighting, close range fighting.

duǎn dǎ mián shā zhǎng 短打绵沙掌 Short Range Continuous Sand Palm, the first routine of Duanquan, written up as forty-three moves.

duǎn dǎ shí bā shì 短打十八势 Eighteen Short Range Moves: a routine of eighteen sequences practiced in Shaolinquan.

duǎn jiàn cháng shě mìng máng 短见长舍命忙 A short weapon can be made long by throwing oneself in with quick footwork. A martial saying. From Xingyiquan.

duǎn jìn 短劲 Short power, a short application of power or strike generated with little movement, not fully extending the limbs.

duǎn qì xiè 短器械 See duǎn bīng.

duǎn qiáo 短桥 Short bridge: to apply forearm techniques with the elbow bent between ninety and one-thirty-five degrees. Also called duǎn biān.

duǎn quán 短拳 1. Short range styles, as differentiated from long range styles. 2. Duanquan (short fist), a style written up by general Qi Jiguang, possibly with Shaolin atecedents. Called Mian Zhang Duanda during the Ming dynasty, later called Mian Zhang Quan (Mian and Zhang are names of the creators), and finally Duanquan. Contains fist and weapons forms emphasising small close-range techniques. See also miǎn zhāng duǎn dǎ, miǎn zhāng quán.

duǎn shāo zǐ gùn 短梢子棍 Short handled flail, a two-section staff with one section longer than the other, linked with metal links, with a total overall length of seventy-five centimetres. Also called xiǎo shāo zǐ gùn.

duǎn shǒu 短手 To hit with close range hand techniques.

duǎn shǒu zhēn 短手针 Short handed needle: a pierce with a long pole, rear hand at the a third of

D

the shaft from the end, at the waist, front hand extended along the pole.

duǎn shǒu pán qiáo 短手盘桥 Short hand basin bridge, a forearm technique: with bent arm, a vertical circle inwards rotating around the shoulder, the hand no higher than the head, and no lower than the groin. From southern styles.

斷 [断] (rad.69) **duàn** To break, snap.

duàn jīn 断筋 Break the sinews; sever tendons and ligaments.

duàn jìn 断劲 Breaking power: to break the attack of an adversary.

duàn mài 断脉 To block or break a blood vessel. A Qinna term.

duàn mén qiāng 断门枪 Gate breaking spear, a spear routine of Tongbeiquan, written up as sixty-six moves.

duàn shǒu 断手 Disconnected hands: free sparring. From Yiquan.

段 (rad.79) **duàn** A section. In martial arts, a section of a routine. Usually a competition routine is divided into four sections: two passes to left and right of the training area. Traditional routines often have more sections or don't divide up the routine.

duàn wèi 段位 A rank; level.

兑 (rad.10) **duì** The Water-in-Lake Trigram, represented by one broken (*yin*) line over two solid (*yang*) lines, called 'upper missing'. Corresponds to the tiger flank formation or gate. An opening gate formation. Indicates the attribute of joyful.

duì duān 兑端 Acupoint Duiduan (mouth's extremity), DU27. At the face, at the dip in the upper lip, where the philtrum meets the skin of the lip, on the midline. From TCM.

對 [对] (rad.41) **duì** 1. Correct. 2. Facing; mutual. Opposed. 3. Answer. Cope with. 4. Aligned. 5. In martial arts, also means to make small adjustments to stick to an adversary's attack, dissipating the force to allow a counter attack.

duì dǎ 对打 Mutual hitting: a general term for a partner routine.

duì jiǎo mǎ 对角马 Angled horse stance: sitting in a high horse stance, shift to one leg and pivot the feet slightly. Sometimes translated as sideling stance. From Wing Chun.

duì kàng dòu zhēng 对抗斗争 Combat. Generally, means fighting rather than competitive Sanda.

duì kàng xìng xiàng mù 对抗性项目 Combative events. Includes Sanda, wrestling, boxing, etc.

duì liàn 对练 1. Training two-person drills with a partner. 2. The Taolu competition event category of a partner routine, duel event (two or more players), paired routine. Includes bare hand, bare hand vs weapons, and weapons. 3. A Bajiquan two-person routine, written up as forty-eight moves.

duì pī dāo 对劈刀 A Xingyiquan partner broadsword routine, written up as forty-six moves.

duì shǒu 对手 1. An adversary, an opponent. A competitor. 2. A match, as in, you have met your match, or he is no match for you.

duì quán 对拳 Facing fists: punch both fists towards each other, fist surfaces facing each other in front of the belly (the elbows will be out and the fist hearts down). From Chaquan and Chuojiao. In Chuojiao, also called duì xīn chuí.

duì xīn chuí 对心锤 See duì quán.

duì xíng zǒu 对行走 Mutual walking: walk while facing off, usually in a circle, commonly used in partner routines while preparing for the next move.

duì yáng jiàn quān 对阳剑圈 Palm up mutual circling with swords: circle one another, stepping around to the left, holding swords flat on the inside of the circle, angled towards each other, in a palm up grip.

duì yīn jiàn quān 对阴剑圈 Palm down mutual circling with swords: circle one another, stepping around to the right, holding swords flat on the outside of the circle, in a palm down grip.

錞 (rad.167) **duì** The flat bottomed metal sleeve that is slid onto the end of a pike or halberd.

隊 [队] (rad.170) **duì** 1. A row of people, a queue, a line. 2. A team.

墩 (rad.32) dūn A heap; a mound; a block of stone.

dūn bǎo bèi zhuāng 蹲宝贝桩 Hold the treasure stake stance: standing in sixty-forty stance with the arms held as if cradling a baby (though a bit further away than if really holding a baby). From Yiquan.

蹲 (rad.157) dūn 1. To squat on the heels. 2. As a shield and broadsword technique, squat: squat, holding the shield as protection, preparing to react to an attack.

dūn bù 蹲步 1. Full squat, both heels on the ground. 2. Hunker down squat – a squat with the front foot flat on the ground and the rear with the heel raised.

dūn shēn bó chuí 蹲身膊捶 Squat down and hit with the arm: pull your adversary's arm to extend it, then press your shoulder and upper arm into to it, turning to lock it out. From Tanglangquan, one of its eight short techniques.

dūn shēn cè diǎn 蹲身侧点 Side poke kick from a squatting stance. From Chuojiao, one of its middle-basin kicks.

dūn yāo 蹲腰 Squatting waist: sitting down to thighs horizontal while stake standing. From Yiquan.

盾 (rad.109) dùn A shield.

dùn pái 盾牌 A shield.

鈍 [钝] (rad.167) dùn 1. Blunt, dull. 2. Stupid, dull-witted.

dùn lián gē gǔ 钝镰割谷 Dull Sickle Cuts Millet 1. Drop to the ground, hook one leg and kick with the other. From Chuojiao, one of its low-basin kicks. 2. Bar the arm and press on the elbow for a takedown. From Baguazhang.

頓 [顿] (rad.181) dùn 1. Pause. 2. Suddenly.

dùn jìn 顿劲 A pause caused by a stamp, a settling power.

dùn wù 顿悟 Suddenly realize the truth, achieve enlightenment.

dùn zhǎng 顿掌 Stamp the palms: pull a foot in to stamp beside the other, also pulling the hands to the belly, pounding the backs of the hands into the belly.

dùn zhù 顿住 Stamp the foot.

多 (rad.36) duō Many; much; more.

duō rèn bīng qì 多刃兵器 Multi-edged bladed weapons such as, for example, chicken blade sickle, double hooks and deerhorn blades. See jī dāo lián, shuāng gōu, yuān yáng yuè.

奪 [夺] (rad.37) duó 1. To seize; wrest control of. 2. Compete for. 3. Force one's way through.

duó bù fēng bì qiāng 夺步封闭枪 Controlling step closing spear: a front step, lifting the foot up (see dōu jiǎo) with an outward cover, then step to bow stance with an inward cover and stab.

躲 [躲] (rad.158) duǒ To dodge; avoid. Hide oneself. One of Ziranmen's nineteen main methods.

duǒ shǎn 躲闪 Dodge.

剁 (rad.18) duò To pound, mince, hash; chop, cut.

duò dāo 剁刀 Pound with a broadsword: hack downwards with the blade, first pushing off the spine of the blade with the left hand to give more of a snap (used more often with a large bagua broadsword or a halberd).

duò zǐ tuǐ 剁子腿 Pounding kick. See cèng tuǐ. Also called xià qiē tuǐ.

扚 (rad.64) duò A wrestling technique, to grab the middle of the belt with both hands.

duò dài tī 扚带踢 Grab the belt and kick: grab your adversary by the belt, place your foot on the inside of his foot, then kick it to the outside and turn the other way, bringing the other foot in to kick his other shin to assist the throw. From wrestling. The kicking trip without the grab is also called chōng tī.

跥 (rad.157) duò 1. To stamp on top of someone's foot. 2. A low side kick that stamps on an adversary's knee.

D

duò jiǎo 跺脚 Stomping kick. From Chuojiao, one of its middle-basin kicks.

duò zǐ jiǎo 跺子脚 1. A stomp, thump with the foot, a heavy stamp. Can also be done with both feet. Can be used to stamp on an adversary's feet or to gain power for a power release movement. Also called hèn bù, zhèn bù, zhèn jiǎo. 2. A heel thrust kick to the belly. From Tanglangquan.

E

囮 (rad.31) é   1. To decoy. 2. To cheat.

é quán 囮拳 Equan (decoy fist): a style known of before the Ming dynasty, written up in general Qi Jiguang's book on martial arts.

峨 峩 [峨] (rad.46) é   Lofty; high.

é méi 峨嵋 Relating to Emei mountain or Emei temple.

é méi cì 峨嵋刺 Emei daggers. A double short weapon, about thirty centimetres long, sharp at both ends but not along its length, held with a ring in the middle.

é méi quán 峨嵋拳 Emeiquan (Emei mountain fist), Emei temple's category of styles.

é méi shān 峨嵋山 Emei mountain. One of the famous mountains in martial lore, in Sichuan province.

é méi shí èr zhuāng 峨嵋十二桩 Emei twelve posts: internal health training methods, twelve in all.

額 [额] (rad.181) é   1. The forehead. 2. A horizontal tablet.

鵝 鵞 䳘 [鹅] (rad.196) é   A goose. Sometimes used in movement names for the actions or qualities of wild geese, see also under bái é.

惡 [恶] (rad.61) è   Evil. Fierce. Wicked.

è hǔ bā xīn 恶虎扒心 Fierce Tiger Rakes out the Heart. 1. A short, strong strike down with the heels of the palms in a pouncing action towards the midsection. May also rake down the face or pull down the clothes at the chest. 2. A double palm out fixed position held in circle-walking: From Baguazhang. See bào yuè zhǎng.

è hǔ pū shí 恶虎扑食 Fierce Tiger Pounces on its Prey. 1. Step forward, reaching out and pulling down and back to the hips, leaning forward with the shoulder. From Wudangquan. 2. Jump the knee up into an adversary's chest while pulling or striking down with a double pouncing action. From Baguazhang.

è shé zuān xīn 恶蛇钻心 Fierce Snake Bores into the Heart: drop back and turn sideways while executing a kick to the navel.

扼 搤 [扼] (rad.64) è   1. To grip; grasp; clutch. 2. Control. 3. Choke, strangle. 4. To restrain.

è hóu 扼喉 Choke: grab an adversary's throat tightly with the fingers and thumb. From Qinna.

è hóu fǎ 扼喉法 Choking, strangling, throttling techniques: grabbing the throat with the palm stretched, thumb web on the larynx.

餓 [饿] (rad.184) è   1. Hungry; hunger. 2. Greedy.

è hè xún há 饿鹤寻虾 Hungry Crane Searches for Frogs: land to a left bow stance and strike with a left extended beak hand on line with the front leg, right hand hooking back at the body. The 76th move of the tiger and crane routine.

è hǔ bā xīn 饿虎扒心 Hungry Tiger Rakes Out the Heart: a double shove to the chest, prepared for with a deflection across to tie up an adversary or turn him sideways. From Baguazhang, one of its sixty-four hands. See also píng tuī zhǎng.

è hǔ pū shí 饿虎扑食 Hungry Tiger Pounces on its Prey. 1. From many styles, usually for a pouncing type of action striking or pushing with both hands. 2. A straight stab with a sword in Taiji sword. 3. A reverse grip reaching stab with a sword in Qingping sword.

è hǔ qín yáng 饿虎擒羊 Hungry Tiger Catches a Sheep: step to a right reverse bow stance and push/grab through with both palms in tiger claws, left further out at head height, right below near its elbow. Lean into the push. The 61st move of the tiger and crane routine.

è hǔ tāo xīn 饿虎掏心 Hungry Tiger Rips out the Heart, a knee technique: an outwards opening knee butt to the belly.

E

è hǔ zhú lù 饿虎逐鹿 Hungry Tiger Chases a Deer: twist an adversary's elbow and wrist over, pressing both joints in reverse.

兒 [儿] (rad.10) ér   Child; a youth.

ér tóng sài 儿童赛 Child category competition: competition for children under twelve.

ér tóng zǔ 儿童组 The children's age group at a competition: the under twelve group.

耳 (rad.128) ěr   1. Ear, ears. 2. Ear, as one of the five sensory organs, see also wǔ guān. 3. Ear shaped things.

ěr duǒ 耳朵 The ear; ears.

ěr gēn 耳根 A sensitive point, just in front of the base of the ears. Colloquial term for the Yifeng acupoint. Best to hit with the palm edge.

ěr hé liáo 耳和髎 Acupoint Erheliao (ear harmony bone-hole), SJ22. At the head, just above and in front of the ear, at the edge of the hairline (on each side of the head). From TCM.

ěr hòu 耳後 Behind the ears. As the ears in general are one of the main targets on the body, this can also mean in front of the ears.

ěr huán gēn dǎ 耳环跟打 Kick the Earrings: a jump front snap kick, dropping back to pull. From Chen Taijiquan.

ěr jiān 耳尖 Extraordinary acupoint Erjian (ear tip), EX-HN6. At the tip, the top of the ear. From TCM.

ěr mén 耳门 Acupoint Ermen (ear gate), SJ21. At the side of the head, just in front of the ear hole, in the small depression above the jawbone (on each side of the head). From TCM. A sensitive point. Hitting can cause tinnitus and dizziness. Best to hit with a head butt, hooking punch, covering strike, backfist, or swing punch.

ěr míng 耳鸣 Ringing in the ears, tinnitus.

ěr tīng bā fāng 耳听八方 The ears listen in eight (all) directions: to be aware of one's surroundings whilst training or playing a routine.

二 (rad.7) èr   Two.

èr bái 二白 Extraordinary acupoint Erbai, EX-UE2. At the forearm, on the inside, two points side by side, on either side of the brachioradialis tendon, four cun up from the wrist crease. From TCM.

èr hǔ cáng zōng 二虎藏踪 Two Tigers Hide their Tracks: standing up, pull the fists to the sides. The second move of the tiger and crane routine.

èr hǔ xiāng zhēng 二虎相争 Two Tigers Fight: a double pouncing strike, but with the backs of the fists. From Baguazhang.

èr huàn tuǐ 二换腿 Changeover jump: jump up and turn one-eighty degrees to replace the feet in the same position, switching places.

èr jí cái pàn yuán 二级裁判员 Level two judge: a basic level judge, qualified to judge at provincial level competitions. A classification within China.

èr jí jiào liàn yuán 二级教练员 Level two coach: a basic level coach, qualified to coach both full time and spare time athletes. A classification within China.

èr jí wǔ shì 二级武士 Level two martial artist, a mid level athlete: an athlete who has achieved high scores and placings in local competitions. A classification within China.

èr jiān 二间 Acupoint Erjian (second space), LI2. At the root of the radial side of the index finger, at the border of the darker and lighter flesh (on each hand). From TCM.

èr jié gùn 二节棍 Two-section staff, forearm length sticks attached by a short chain. Called nunchaku in English, from the Japanese for a similar weapon.

èr láng 二郎 Erlang, a warrior god.

èr láng dān shān 二郎担山 Erlang Shoulders a Mountain. 1. A rope dart technique: circling the dart counter-clockwise, turning the body multiple times and using the right elbow to loop the rope, lift the elbow to shoot the dart out. 2. Drop to a drop stance, bring the fists to the waist, then come up and step forward, extending the fists front and back. From Baguazhang (done with the palms) and Chuojiao. 3. In Shaolinquan, step forward into a bow stance (without the drop stance) bringing the fists in to in front of the chest, then extending a palm down stabbing palm forward and a slicing hook back. 4. In Wudangquan, sit into horse stance, bringing the arms over and down with covering backfist strikes. 5. In Kunlunquan, swing a staff to rest on the right shoulder, looking forward. 6. In Piguaquan, a double backfist in a high stance.

èr láng mén 二郎门 Erlang (warrior god) style: a style known from the Qing dynasty around Beijing that emphasizes two person routines.

èr lóng pěng zhū 二龙捧珠 Two Dragons Carry Pearls: circle-walking with the hands lifting at waist height, fingers pointing to the centre of the circle. From Baguazhang.

èr lóng tǔ xū 二龙吐须 Two Dragons Spit their Beards: step to closed parallel stance, presenting two carrying palms. From Piguaquan.

èr lóng xī shuǐ 二龙吸水 Two Dragons Draw Water: pull to off balance an adversary while stabbing his eyes with two extended fingers. From Baguazhang.

èr lóng xì zhū 二龙戏珠 Two Dragons Play with a Pearl: smearing sword cuts at shoulder height to alternate sides. From Qingping sword.

èr lù 二路 Second path, refers to the second routine of many styles. Used by Chen Taijiquan, Chaquan, Huaquan, Shaolinquan, among others.

èr mǎ pái duì 二马排队 Two Horses Stand in Line: sit in a left empty stance and chop down with a sword, then pivot around and shift to a right empty stance, bringing the blade over to chop down again. From Qingping sword.

èr mén 二门 The second gate in on an adversary: inside the elbows.

èr mén shǒu 二门手 The second gate hand: the elbow, used for closer techniques.

èr qǐ cǎi jiǎo 二起采脚 Jump front slap kick, pulling the rear hand in to the waist. The name used in Shaolinquan. Also written 踩脚.

èr qǐ cǎi jiǎo 二起踩脚 See èr qǐ cǎi jiǎo above.

èr qǐ jiǎo 二起脚 Two jump kick: jump up, swinging the left leg to kick, but only slapping the right. From Chen Taijiquan. Also called tī èr qǐ. Also called fān shēn èr qǐ when there is a turn before the jump.

èr shí sì shì tài jí quán 二十四式太极拳 Twenty-four move Taijiquan. A standardised beginner's level routine based on Yang style Taijiquan.

èr shí sì yào 二十四要 The twenty four essentials of martial arts foundation. These combine the four ways of hitting, the eight methods of the body, and the twelve models. See bā fǎ, sì jī, shí èr xíng.

èr xiān chuán dào 二仙传道 Two immortals Preach the Way. 1. A double hooking punch, stepping in from the side to strike the chest and back of an adversary simultaneously. From Baguazhang, one of its sixty-four hands. 2. A double hooking back beside the legs with deerhorn blades. From Baguazhang. 3. Move to a high empty stance and circle the palms to a ready stance in front of the chest. From Wudangquan.

èr xīng pāo chuí 二星抛捶 Second Star Throwing Punch: shift into a right bow stance and do a swinging rising punch almost on line with the front leg with the left fist, the right swinging behind. The 86th move of the tiger and crane routine. See also pāo chuí and yī xīng pāo chuí (the same move on the other side).

èr zhǐ 二指 Two finger palm shape: index and middle fingers extended straight, thumb tucked on the bent ring and little fingers.

èr zhǐ chán 二指禅 Two finger hand stand.

èr zì guǎi 二字拐 Character two crutch: a short wooden staff with crutch grips at each end, making it somewhat an H, or character 二, shape.

èr zì mǎ bù 二字马步 Character two horse stance, a stance that looks like the character two 二. A short horse stance with the feet straight, about two foot-lengths apart, knees tucked tightly in, sitting in the stance the same as a horse stance.

èr zì qián yáng mǎ bù 二字拑羊马步 Character two (looks like the character 二) clamping the sheep horse stance: a short horse stance with the knees in (the feet also turned in), as if clamping onto a sheep with the legs whilst sheering it. From Wing Chun.

E

F

發 (rad.105) [发] (rad.29) fā   1. To release (an arrow); send out; discharge, shoot. 2. Send out. From Taijiquan, one of its four principles of push hands, see also sì zé.

fā biāo 发镖 Launch a rope dart; release the dart of a rope dart, shooting it out.

fā hěn 发狠 To be savage, show anger. Considered a fault in most styles, and likely to lead to defeat in a fight due to excess tension. See also hěn.

fā hòu tuǐ 发后腿 Back kick, a swinging kick to the rear with the leg slightly bent. From Chuojiao. Also called yuān yáng jiǎo.

fā jìn 发劲 To launch power, issue force, initiate a hit, release a strike, throw a punch, shoot, explosive release of power. Involves first a subtle gathering power within the body then releasing with a coordinated expression through the body for the targeted strike. An efficiently timed, directed, and regulated energy burst. Some also call this fā lì.

fā lì 发力 1. Launch strength: most styles use fā lì interchangeably with fā jìn. See fā jìn. 2. Some use fā lì to mean an error, or using brute strength in a fā jìn attempt.

fā luò diǎn 发落点 Point of contact on an adversary where you are able to control and use a power launch.

fā shēng 发声 To shout: shout to gain or express power in a technique. Commonly used in southern styles, with the specific traditional sounds of dī, hēi, wā, yì.

fā shǒu 发手 To attack, an attack.

fā tōu shǒu dǎ èr shǒu 发头手打二手 Fake the first hand high and hit low with the other.

fā zhāo yào zhǔn 发招要准 The technique must be accurate. From Tongbeiquan, one of its requirements.

乏 (rad.4) fá   1. To lack; deficient. 2. Tired; exhausted.

fá lì 乏力 Tired, worn out.

伐 (rad.9) fá   1. To fell, to cut down. 2. To send an expedition against an enemy.

fá shù sòng yǒu 伐树送友 Fell a Tree to Send to a Friend: stab a sword up to the high right in a right raised knee stance, land and lift the left knee, slicing down and up to the other side with the palm down, then land into a reverse bow stance and chop down, the wrist cocked. From Qingping sword.

法 (rad.85) fǎ   1. A law. 2. A method; way; mode. 3. Standard; model.

fǎ lún dǎo zhuǎn 法轮倒转 The wheel of the Buddhist Law Spins Backwards: continuous horizontal inward bent arm pulling, moving forward. From Tongbeiquan.

fǎ lún yùn zhuǎn 法轮运转 The wheel of the Buddhist Law Spins: horizontal inward bent arm pulling, lifting the knee and shifting back. From Tongbeiquan.

翻 (rad.124) fān   1. To turn upside down or inside out. 2. To wheel around, wheel over, turn over, a turn which pivots rather than stepping around, often involves a rolling action or turning face up. One of the sixteen key techniques of Baguazhang, see also shí liù zì jué.

fān bà qiāng 翻把枪 Reverse grip spear: a spear routine that utilizes the butt more than usual for a spear.

fān bì chōng chuí 翻臂冲捶 Rolled over thrown punch. 1. An extended flicking backfist to between the eyes. 2. A crossing punch. From Baguazhang, one of its sixty-four hands. Also called fǎn bì pī chuí, fǎn bì shuāi chuí.

fān bì fá zhú 翻臂伐竹 Roll Over Fell the Bamboo: bring a sword around with a large slice up to throat height, palm up. From Wu Taijiquan.

fān chē 翻车 Flip the Cart: from a prone position, push off with hands and feet, flip over in the air, and land on the back with the body still straight.

F

From Ditangquan.

fān dòng yīn yáng 翻动阴阳 Flip Over *Yin* and *Yang*: lift the left knee and slice a sword up to head height, land and lift the right knee and rotate the wrist to block up with the blade, then land and lift the left knee and circle to slice up again to the same place. From Qingping sword.

fān gǔn 翻滚 Roll over, overturn by rotating.

fān huā pào 翻花炮 Overturn Flowers Punch: from a single whip posture, spring over with an elbow stab, land and punch. From Chen Taijiquan.

fān huā wǔ xiù 翻花舞袖 Overturn Flowers by Twirling the Sleeves: jump and turn while twisting and swinging the arms over. This refers to an action you would do with the long sleeves of an old-style Chinese robe. From Chen Taijiquan.

fān huán diǎn tuǐ 翻环点腿 Rolling continuous poke kicks. From Chuojiao, one of its middle-basin kicks.

fān jiāng dǎo hǎi 翻江倒海 Overturn Rivers and Turn Back the Sea. 1. Rising on one leg, coil the arms from close to the body to open up one high, one low, with opening power. From Chen Taijiquan. 2. Continuous vertical circling with the arms to come over and slap downwards with the back of each hand in succession. From Liuhebafa and Taiji Changquan. 3. Cross the forearm in front of the body then step back and roll the fist over to punch forward. From Wudangquan.

fān làng jìn 翻浪劲 Wave breaking power: to hit by rising and falling with an action like a breaking wave. One complete rise and fall is a breaking wave, so the power is initiated like the ocean moving in and the landing is like the wave breaking on the shore. From Xingyiquan.

fān shēn 翻身 Wheel around, turn over, a turn which pivots rather than steps around, often involving a rolling action, a jumping action, or turning through face up.

fān shēn dāo 翻身刀 Wheel around with a broadsword: extend the tip forward and roll under the handle, allowing the blade to turn naturally but not to move in space (used with the larger blade Bagua broadsword).

fān shēn duò zǐ 翻身跺子 Roll with a stamp: lean back and use a stamping kick to an adversary's body. From Baguazhang.

fān shēn èr qǐ 翻身二起 Turn to two jump kick. See èr qǐ jiǎo. Also called tī èr qǐ, though not necessarily with a turn.

fān shēn jí rù 翻身疾入 Wheel around quick entry, to step as if retreating, then turn to strike. From Tongbeiquan, one of its seven long range techniques. Also called huí mǎ quán.

fān shēn kǎn 翻身砍 Wheel around and hack: spin around, swinging the blade in a full circle, finishing with a hacking downward chop. May be done to either direction.

fān shēn pī chuí 翻身劈捶 Rolling turn to chopping backfists: turn through the back, bringing the fists over in backfists, one to the front, one behind. From Baguazhang, one of its sixty-four hands.

fān shēn pū hǔ 翻身扑虎 Back flip pouncing land: back flip, absorbing with the hands and landing on the chest.

fān shēn qǔ shèng 翻身取胜 Roll Over to Gain Victory: spin around to the back one-twenty degrees, landing to reverse bow stance stab. From Qingping sword.

fān shēn tuī dāo 翻身推刀 Roll over and push the broadsword: roll under the blade of a broadsword then push out with the blade.

fān shēn xiē 翻身楔 Flipping wedge: drop to a one-handed handstand and use your body to knock an adversary down. A throw.

fān shēn zhǎng 翻身掌 Wheeling Change: one of the mother palms, generally involving rolling the body around to turn. From Baguazhang.

fān shǒu 翻手 Wheeling hand: rotating at the elbow, roll the hand or fist over, going from palm up to down or visa versa, to directly strike. From Chuojiao.

fān tà 翻塌 Rolling tamp: from palm up, rotate the forearm to bring the palm through to finish with a palm down tamp to cave in an adversary. From Baguazhang.

fān tún 翻臀 Stick out the buttocks.

fān xiōng 翻胸 Wheel the chest. In wrestling, many throws involve a twisting roll of the chest.

fān xuán fēng tuǐ 翻旋风腿 Wheeling tornado kick: a jump full three-sixty turning outside crescent kick.

fān yāo 翻腰 Waist wheeling exercise. 1. Starting and finishing with legs crossed, swing the arms around to wheel over keeping the torso horizontal. 2. Standing with the legs astride, roll around, circling to roll back and coming around to the front.

fān yún fù yǔ 翻云覆雨 Overturn the Clouds and Rain: sit into a low crossed stance and slice a sword up to the back, shoulder rolled under, leaning on the upper leg to take the tip as straight up as possible. From Qingping sword.

fān zá chuí 翻砸锤 Downward backfist, coming in a circle up then down to shoulder height.

fān zhòng zhuān 翻重砖 Flip a brick, a training method using a large heavy rectangular brick or cement block, gripping it with the fingers, releasing and flipping it around, usually while sitting in horse stance.

fān zhuǎn 翻转 Wheel around.

fān zhuǎn tuō 翻转脱 Wheeling release, an escape: dissipate a grab by wheeling vertically to twist an adversary.

fān zǐ quán 翻子拳 Fanziquan (overturning fists), developed in Hebei province, with quick and strong movements.

反 (rad.29) **fǎn** To reverse, turn over; in reverse, inside out; return; counter. Turn against. Oppose.

fǎn bā zì bù 反八字步 Reverse Character Eight stance: form the character eight 八 with the feet toe to heel, usually a foot-length apart, sitting on both legs, knees aligned with the feet.

fǎn bǎ 反把 Reverse grip. 1. Holding the shaft of a long weapon with the palms down, thumb webs pointing towards each other. Also called yīn bǎ. 2. Holding a short weapon with the thumb web away from the guard, towards the base. Also called fǎn wò, yīn bǎ.

fǎn bǎ shàng zhā qiāng 反把上扎枪 Reversed grip high stab with spear: stab with the right hand in reverse grip, sending the spear straight out at head height, usually combined with a turn around.

fǎn bǎ xià zhā qiāng 反把下扎枪 Reversed grip low stab with spear: stab with the right hand in reverse grip (forearm rotated), sending the spear out from head height to a lower height, usually combined with a turn around.

fǎn bèi 反背 Strike from the back, or towards the back, or turn around and strike to the side.

fǎn bèi chuí 反背捶 or 锤 Backfist punch: hit with the back of the fist, whipping it out. Refers both to an extended punch and a dropping down strike, but is usually the extended punch.

fǎn bèi dǎ 反背打 Backfist punch.

fǎn bèi dāo 反背刀 Cut behind the back: a flat cut with a broadsword blade, reaching out to the rear in a horse stance.

fǎn bèi pī zhǎng 反背劈掌 Back hand chopping strike.

fǎn bèi quán 反背拳 Backfist punch hit with the back of the fist, whipping it out. Also called yī tiáo biān.

fǎn bèi zhǎng 反背掌 Back hand strike: hit with a backhand, whipping it out.

fǎn bèi zhuǎn 反背转 Reverse behind the back, twist the arm behind the back in a policeman's grip. From Qinna. Also called shǒu bào huàn xióng.

fǎn bì liāo zhǎo 反臂撩爪 Reverse lifting claw: swing a claw hand up strongly behind your body to grab an adversary's groin.

fǎn bì pī chuí 反臂劈捶 Reverse Chop. See fǎn bì chōng chuí. Also called fǎn bì shuāi chuí.

fǎn bì shuāi chuí 反臂摔捶 Rolled over thrown punch. See fǎn bì chōng chuí. Also called fǎn bì pī chuí.

fǎn chán shǒu 反缠手 Reverse wrap: grip the adversary's wrist and wrap your other arm under his to lift, pressing his elbow up with your elbow, controlling the elbow and shoulder. From Qinna.

fǎn chōng quán 反冲拳 Inverted punch: a straight punch with the arm internally rotated so the fist eye is down.

fǎn cì 反刺 Pierce with the weapon inverted.

fǎn cuò guān jié 反挫关节 Grasp and control methods using joint reversal.

fǎn cuò dāo 反错刀 Reverse rub with a broadsword: a quick backward press followed by

F

a forward push, palm down, tip to the left.

fǎn dǎ 反打 An inverted strike, general term for any inverted hit.

fǎn dīng zì bù 反丁字步 Reversed T stance: both feet flat on the ground, one foot pointing away from the instep of the other, feet about a foot-length apart. From Baguazhang.

fǎn duō dāo 反跺刀 Inverted cut with a halberd, cutting up using the hook on the spine of the blade.

fǎn è zhǎng 反扼掌 Inverted guarding palm: palm extended with the fingers down, palm facing away from the body, arm internally rotated. See also zhèng è zhǎng.

fǎn gài zhǎng 反盖掌 Inverted covering palm: a covering technique with the palm up.

fǎn gōng 反弓 Reverse the bow: use the body as leverage to take down an adversary.

fǎn gōng bèi shè 反弓背射 Reverse the Bow to Shoot Behind: sit to a crossed stance, tucking the forearms in front of the chest to point a sword blade up to the left. From Qingping sword.

fǎn gōng 反攻 Counter attack: to counter as an adversary attacks or to turn a defense into an attack, becoming the instigator of the attack.

fǎn gōu shǒu 反勾手 Inverted hooked hand: fingers pointing up, arm rolled under, usually behind the body. A positional reference, separate from the direction of the strike. Also called dào gōu shǒu.

fǎn gǔ fǎ 反骨法 Bone reversal: joint control and dislocation techniques.

fǎn guà mén 反挂门 Reverse grip (thumb down) on the chest front of a wrestling jacket, in preparation for a throw. From wrestling.

fǎn guān jié 反关节 Reverse the joint: any joint control technique that uses understanding of the natural movement of a joint to control an adversary by reversing that natural movement. May be used to throw, break, press to control, lock out, etc. Prohibited in competition Sanda. From Qinna.

fǎn guàn 反贯 Inverted hook punch.

fǎn huán tuǐ 反环腿 Inverted hoop kick: kick up behind, also reaching the head back so that the foot touches the back of the head, the bent leg and back forming a circle.

fǎn jī 反击 Counter attack, fight back: defend and counter against a multiple attack or counter after an adversary misses an attack.

fǎn jī zhāo fǎ 反击招法 Counter attacking methods: methods that strike back immediately after controlling an incoming attack (or move to directly counter attack).

fǎn jiā bó biè 反夹脖别 Reverse grip neck throw: when facing in opposite directions, wrap the arm around the neck from back to front, then throw the leg to throw with the hip.

fǎn jiā kuò 反夹廓 Reverse grip neck squeeze: when facing in opposite directions, wrap the arm around the neck from back to front.

fǎn jiàn jì 反间计 The Strategy of Sowing Distrust. The thirty-third of the Thirty-six Stratagems of Warfare, which apply to many situations.

fǎn jiǎo 反搅 Reverse stirring: circle the tip of a sword anti-clockwise.

fǎn kè wéi zhǔ 反客为主 Turn from Guest to Host. Gain the Initiative. The thirtieth of the Thirty-six Stratagems of Warfare, which apply to many situations.

fǎn kòng zhì 反控制 A counter attack power or technique. From Yiquan.

fǎn liāo dāo 反撩刀 Inverted upward slice with a broadsword. See fǎn liāo jiàn.

fǎn liāo jiàn 反撩剑 Inverted upward slice with a sword: slice up with the forearm internally rotated (turn thumb towards palm) until the thumb edge is on the bottom, cutting up with the little finger edge of the blade.

fǎn liāo zhǎng 反撩掌 Inverted upward slice with the forearm internally rotated to little finger side up, hitting with the knife edge of the palm and forearm.

fǎn liāo zhuā 反撩爪 Inverted upward slice with the forearm internally rotated to palm up, with the palm held in tiger claw.

fǎn lūn biān 反抡鞭 Reverse circles with a steel whip: swing the whip vertically at the right side of the body, the whip circling down behind, up in front.

fǎn pàn 反判 To reverse a judge's decision or score.

fǎn pī 反劈 Reverse chop: chop forward and down with the backhand.

fǎn pī huá shān 反劈华山 Turn Around and Chop Mount Hua: turn around and bring a sword over to chop down strongly, finishing with the sword level. From Wudang sword.

fǎn qín 反擒 Reverse seize, reverse grab: holding an adversary with your thumb web inside, your hand coming up to grab.

fǎn qǔ yuán yáng 反取元阳 Reverse and Take the Head: drop back, lowering and turning the torso to kick back high to the head.

fǎn shēn 反身 Reversed: sometimes used when a technique starts out towards the back.

fǎn shēn lūn bì 反身抡臂 Waist roll with arm swing: step one foot through behind and lean forward, preparing the arms, then swing the arms vertically, turning around and over, keeping the torso horizontal.

fǎn shǒu 反手 Inverted hand or grip (palm up).

fǎn shǒu jiàn 反手剑 Inverted grip sword: a sword that is manipulated with the hold continuously in reverse grip (like Ichiro the blind swordsman). When only temporarily taking a reverse grip, the grip is called fǎn bà, fǎn wò.

fǎn tán lì 反弹力 Rebound.

fǎn wò 反握 Reverse grip: holding a weapon such as a broadsword or steel whip with the blade or whip coming out from the little finger side. Also called fǎn bà.

fǎn wò wàn 反握腕 Reverse wrist grab. When differentiating types of grabs, this is with the tiger's mouth facing an adversary's wrist. See also wò wàn.

fǎn yā wàn 反压腕 Inverted wrist press: grab an adversary's wrist and press his hand to his forearm with both hands, taking his elbow down to the floor. From Qinna.

fǎn yìng 反应 Reaction; response. In martial arts, refers to reaction time and responses in a fight.

fǎn zhā dāo 反扎刀 Reverse stab with a broadsword: with the handgrip held with a reverse grip, usually in both hands, stab behind the body at waist height.

fǎn zhǎn dà dāo 反折大刀 Reverse cut with a big cutter: with the right hand near the blade, on top with palm down, cut across, tucking the shaft to the right side with the left hand.

fǎn zhǎng 反掌 1. The palm is turned over and moves to the rear or side. Used in certain strikes such as slice up or stab. A positional reference, separate from the direction of the strike. 2. As a technique: an inverted open hand strike, a backhand strike.

fǎn zuò yòng lì 反作用力 Reacting force.

返 (rad.162) fǎn   To return, come or go back.

犯 (rad.94) fàn   To violate (rules). To commit (crimes).

fàn guī 犯规 To commit a foul in a Sanda match. To break the rules in a game or competition.

方 (rad.70) fāng   1. Square. 2. Direction. 3. Place.

fāng bǎ 方靶 Square pad: a largish, square, hand held pad used by a trainer for kicking practice. Generally, with straps to slide onto the forearm.

fāng biàn chǎn 方便铲 A convenient shovel: a long weapon with a wooden shaft, a shovel shaped blade at one end and a crescent blade at the other.

fāng dāng 方裆 A square horse stance. See zhèng dāng bù. Also called zhèng dāng.

fāng xiàng 方向 Direction.

防 (rad.170) fáng   To guard against. Defend.

fáng shǒu 防守 Defend, defense: blocking, parrying, deflection, covering up, evasion, any technique that prevents attack from reaching its goal. Usually also sets up the counter.

fáng shǒu fǎn jī 防守反击 Counter attacks.

fáng shǒu huán jī 防守还击 Defend then attack: block, parry, deflect, cover up, or evade, and then counter attack.

fáng shǒu jì shù 防守技术 Defensive skills.

fáng shǒu zhàn shù 防守战术 Defensive tactics.

F

倣 仿 [仿] (rad.9) **fǎng** 1. To imitate, copy. 2. To resemble.

fǎng shēng quán 仿生拳 Imitative styles: styles that take on many of the characteristics of a specific animal, such as eagle claw, monkey, preying mantis, snake, etc.

放 (rad.66) **fàng** To release, let go, liberate, loosen, relax. To put, place. To put in, add.

fàng biān 放鞭 Release a whip: from holding a steel whip folded in the hand, release and throw out the whip, keeping the grip in the hand.

fàng cháng jī yuán 放长击远 Release long and hit far. A characteristic of long-range styles such as Longfist and Tongbeiquan.

fàng kāi 放开 To relax or loosen (a grip, unwanted tension). To let go. To release hold of.

fàng kuà 放胯 1. Send the hips, put the hips into a kick: getting reach from the hips. See also zhǎn kuà. 2. Slacken the hips: the rear leg leaves the hip splayed out in a bow stance, an error. Also called kāi kuà.

fàng sōng 放松 To relax; to loosen; to release tension. To let go of extra tension.

fàng sōng fā lì 放松发力 Relaxed release of power. From Yiquan.

非 (rad.175) **fēi** 1. Not, negative. 2. Wrong; faults. 3. To refute.

fēi dài jiǔ píng héng 非待久平衡 Non-held balance: a balance in a routine that does not need to be held for a full two seconds. The balance needs to be completed and have a brief pause to show control. Term used for competition routines.

飛 [飞] (rad.183) **fēi** 1. To fly, flying. 2. In martial arts, aerial techniques and jump kicks. 3. Guide the *qi* to an acupuncture needle by grasping the handle then releasing with a 'flying' motion. From TCM.

fēi biāo 飞镖 Flying dart: a throwing knife. A three-edged double-bladed dagger about twelve centimetres long. Also called tuō shǒu biāo.

fēi chā 飞叉 Flying fork. 1. A long fork weapon, intended for throwing. 2. The same shape of the long fork weapon but only six centimetres long, made for hiding and throwing.

fēi chuí 飞锤 Flying hammer: a heavy ball (about five hundred grams) on the end of a rope about five metres long. Also called liú xīng chuí.

fēi dài zǐ 飞逮子 Flying catch, a trip: to catch an adversary by surprise with a trip just as he is moving his front foot, not in hold, catching behind his ankle and swinging your leg up. From wrestling.

fēi dāo 飞刀 Flying knife: a throwing knife. Either double edged or single edged, usually about twenty-five centimetres long.

fēi diǎn tuǐ 飞点腿 Jumping poke kick: jump and poke kick with the leg turned in. From Chuojiao, one of its high-basin kicks.

fēi gē tuǐ 飞割腿 Flying Reaper kick: a snapping outside crescent kick, kicking with the outside edge of the foot.

fēi hè gōu 飞鹤勾 Flying Crane hook, a hand shape: thumb, index and middle fingers together, ring and little finger clenched. From southern styles.

fēi hóng héng jiāng 飞虹横江 Rainbow Flies over the River: a crossing sword chop behind, in a cross-over stance. From Qingping sword.

fēi hóng gù yǐng 飞鸿顾影 Flying Swan Admires its Reflection: Holding the sword up as if looking in a mirror, walk a full circle to parry, and finally turn the hand to snap out to the side. From Qingping sword.

fēi hóng liǎn yì 飞鸿敛翼 Flying Swan Restrains its Flanks: sitting in horse stance, pull the hands tight to the sides, hooking out with the palms down and fingers pointing out to the sides. The 24th move of the tiger and crane routine.

fēi hǔ quán 飞虎拳 Flying Tiger fist, a routine of Piguaquan.

fēi hǔ shí xīn 飞虎食心 Flying Tiger Eats the Heart: a jumping heel thrust kick.

fēi huáng shí 飞蝗石 Flying locust rock: an ancient weapon. Rocks about the size of peach pits, used for throwing. Also called fēi shí, sǎn shǒu dàn.

fēi jiàn bù 飞箭步 Flying arrow step: from a horse

stance, push off with both legs, jumping up and driving to one side a good distance. Land on both feet in the same stance. From Duanquan.

fēi lóng cháng quán 飞龙长拳 Flying Dragon Changquan, a traditional Longfist routine, written up as fifty moves.

fēi lóng sǎo wěi 飞龙扫尾 Flying Dragon Sweeps its Tail: a jumping back spin kick.

fēi lóng shēng tiān 飞龙升天 Flying Dragon Ascends to the Heavens: a jumping front slap kick. From Piguaquan. Also called téng kōng fēi jiǎo.

fēi mén 飞门 The philtrum. See fèi mén.

fēi niǎo shì 飞鸟式 Flying bird stance: slowly raise the arms up at the sides as if flying, then lower them back down. From Yiquan.

fēi quán 飞拳 Flying fist: punch out from the chest with an oblique arcing action on the same side of the body, contacting with the fist back or base. From Shaolinquan.

fēi shā fú miàn 飞沙拂面 Flying Sand Whisks the Face: slice a sword up in front while doing a swing up kick to the rear. From Yangjia sword.

fēi shé chuàn dòng 飞蛇串洞 Flying Snake Threads the Hole: a flying snap kick to the head.

fēi shí 飞石 Flying rocks. See fēi huáng shì. Also called sǎn shǒu dàn.

fēi shǐ 飞矢 A flying arrow, flying arrows.

fēi xíng shù 飞行术 Flying steps skill: the training of and skill of quickness and lightness. One way to train is to attach weights to the lower legs, gradually increasing the weight. Also called yè xíng gōng.

fēi yán zǒu bì gōng 飞檐走壁功 Flying eaves wall walking skill: the training and skill of running along a wall. One way to train is to attach weights to the lower legs and arms, running towards and up a wall, gradually adding weight and number of steps up, and reducing the runup. Also called héng pái bā bù.

fēi yàn chāo shuǐ 飞燕抄水 Flying Swallow Skims Over the Water: sit into a drop stance, extending the arms out to both sides, one following the extended leg, the other forming a straight line behind. From Baguazhang.

fēi yàn dā dì 飞燕搭地 Flying Swallow Hits the Ground, an escape from a shoulder grab: grab one of an adversary's hands in each hand, turn and bend the arms to press his wrists down with your upper arms and drop down.

fēi yàn rù lín 飞燕入林 Flying Swallow Enters the Woods: rotate and lower a sword grip while dropping the stance, circling the sword tip but keeping it high, to deflect with the blade. From Wudang sword.

fēi yàn tuǐ 飞燕腿 Flying swallow kick: a jumping snap kick that moves forward.

fēi yáng 飞扬 Acupoint Feiyang (taking flight), BL58. At the calf, under the lateral belly of the gastrocnemius, outside and below acupoint Chengshan, seven *cun* up from acupoint Fuyang, on the outer edge of the Achilles tendon (on each leg). From TCM.

fēi yún duò zǐ jiǎo 飞云跺子脚 Flying Cloud stamp kick. 1. A side kick with the toes up. 2. A flying side kick, landing on the side in a break fall holding the position. From Chuojiao, one of its high-basin kicks. Both meanings from Chuojiao.

腓 (rad.130) féi   The calf, the back and sides of the lower leg.

féi cháng jī 腓肠肌 Gastrocnemius muscle: a calf muscle, the largest and most exterior. Assists in knee flexion and plantar flexion of the foot.

féi gǔ 腓骨 The fibula: the smaller bone in the lower leg, beside the tibia.

féi gǔ cháng jī 腓骨长肌 Peroneus longus muscle: a shin muscle. Serves to evert the foot and help protect from excessive inversion.

féi gǔ duǎn jī 腓骨短肌 Peroneus brevis muscle: a shin muscle, shorter and interior to the peroneus longus. Serves to evert the foot and help protect from excessive inversion.

肺 (rad.130) fèi   1. The lungs. 2. The Lung, the organ associated with the Shou Tai Yin channel. It is a *yin* organ. See also shǒu tài yīn.

fèi jīng 肺经 The Lung meridian. See shǒu tài yīn. From TCM.

fèi mén 肺门 The philtrum, the spot just under the nose on the midline. One of seven painful gateways to attack that are related to midline acupoints. Sometimes called fēi mén. See also qī chōng mén.

fèi shū 肺俞 Acupoint Feishu (lung transport), BL13. At the back, in the depression below the spinous process of the third thoracic vertebra, 1.5 *cun* lateral to the midline (on each side). From TCM. Striking here can injure the arteries, veins, and nerves in the flank, and shock the heart and lungs.

分 (rad.18) **fēn**   Separate. To separate, divide, move two segments in opposite directions.

fēn bì 分臂 Separate the arms: when an adversary is on his back, sit on his chest (facing him) and pull both his arms out to the side, pressing them on your thighs to break the elbows.

fēn chā fǎ 分叉法 Separating methods: methods that grab and pull apart the fingers. From Qinna.

fēn dāo 分刀 Separate with a broadsword. 1. Starting with the blade down in front of the body, the left hand on the right wrist, swing both arms up then out to the sides, to chop down at shoulder height. 2. To open the arms out horizontally to cut flat to the right. The arms draw the same circle in opposite directions.

fēn duàn 分段 1. Sections of a routine. 2. To break a routine into sections for repeated practice.

fēn duàn xùn liàn 分段训练 Sections training: to train repetitions of a routine section by section.

fēn guà fā lì 分掛发力 Release of power with an opening hook. From Yiquan.

fēn jiàn 分间 To separate the spaces: to draw an adversary into letting down his guard or guarding in the wrong place.

fēn jiàn jī bái 分间击白 To separate the spaces and hit the white: fake an adversary into exposing a target and hit that.

fēn jiǎo 分脚 Separating kick, parting kick, a plantar flexed kick, opening the hands as well. In the category of snap kicks, see also qū shēn xìng tuǐ fǎ. From Taijiquan.

fēn jīn 分筋 Separate the tendons or muscles: grab and tear tendons, sinew, or muscles by twisting the joint or bones, squeezing with the fingers, or grabbing and pulling larger muscles or tendons. From Qinna.

fēn jīn jié mài 分筋截脉 Separate the tendons and cut the vessels. Strikes that cause blockage of the blood and *qi* vessels make an adversary lose strength and becomes dizzy, at the least. This method makes him give up without injuring him. Separating the tendons means striking the muscles, joints, and tendons so they lose the capacity for movement. From Qinna.

fēn jìn 分劲 Separating power: to separate and disperse the techniques and power of an adversary's attack, enabling you to apply a technique.

fēn mén yī jiǎo 分门一脚 Break Open the Door with One Kick: a heel thrust kick, pushing the palms out to the sides. From Chen Taijiquan.

fēn shuǐ é méi cì 分水峨眉刺 Separating water Emei daggers: a weapon the size of double hooks, with the same hand guard, but with wavy blades attached to extend from the tips instead of hooking tips.

fēn shuǐ gōng 分水功 Separate water training: in a large frame, attach bamboo poles at top and bottom. Standing between them push them apart, arms straight at shoulder height. Gradually increase the number of poles to increase the strength needed to separate them.

fēn shuǐ kāi lù 分水开路 Separate Water to Clear the Way: jump up and open both arms out to the side, cutting a sword outwards. From Yangjia sword.

fēn shuǐ shì lì 分水试力 Separate water testing power: stand in sixty-forty stance, open and close the arms to the sides at belly height, hands feeling as if working against water. From Yiquan, one of its combat testing moves.

fēn shuǐ zhuāng 分水桩 Separate water stake standing: sitting slightly with the arms out to the sides, palms down. From Yiquan.

fēn xīn jiǎo 分心脚 Separate the centre kick: a short, sharp, low kick with the instep. From Shaolinquan.

fēn xīng bào yuè 分星抱月 Separate the Stars and Carry the Moon: a jumping snap kick, landing into a forward stance punch. From Yangjia style.

fēn zhǎng 分掌 Separating palms. Varies with style, but the hands separate out to either side, usually at shoulder height. In Bajiquan, the palms are up, to slice with the forearms. In Taijiquan, the palms are out, to push with the palms.

fēn zhǐ 分指 Finger separation: grab an adversary's fingers, two in each hand, and lift and spread them open. From Qinna.

fēn zhuàng quán 分撞拳 Separating ramming punch: a strong double swinging punch with the arms straight, to just above shoulder height, one punching forward one punching behind the back. The forward fist's palm faces up, the behind fist's palm faces down.

fēn zōng dāo nán zhē nán dǎng 分鬃刀难遮难挡 Blade Splitting the Mane is Difficult to Block: three forward stepping rising slices with a halberd, stepping to smooth stances. From Chen Taijiquan.

封 (rad.41) **fēng** 1. To seal (an envelope); bank (a fire). 2. An envelope. 3. A controlling or grappling technique: to shut down, seal off.

fēng bǎ zhēn 封把针 Closed grip needle: to pierce with a long pole, rear hand at the butt end at the waist, front hand extended along the pole.

fēng bì 封闭 Seal off, close off.

fēng bì fǎ 封闭法 Sealing off methods: to keep the three gates closed from attack (the shoulders, elbows, and wrists above, and the hips, knees, and ankles below), using the body structure and footwork.

fēng bì qiāng 封闭枪 Seal and close with a spear. 1. Circular covers out and in, followed by a stab. This is the old term for outer trap, inner trap, stab. 2. Traditionally, this dual trapping action done as a mid-height defense with a spear. See also lán ná qiāng, lán ná zhā, tí lū qiāng.

fēng mén bì hù 封门闭户 Seal the door and close the door: set to horse stance, swing the forward arm out and prepare the fist at the shoulder, then swing it down to the knee and block across the face with the rear hand. From Meishanquan.

fēng qiāng 封枪 Seal with a spear: cover inwards and stab. See also ná qiāng, zhā qiāng.

fēng shǒu 封手 Seal off, shut down an adversary at the hands and elbows.

fēng xiōng shí zì diē 封胸十字跌 Close off the Chest and Crossing Takedown: when an adversary kicks, gather his leg into your chest, step to his rear side and sweep one arm through to his chest while holding his leg in the other, applying crossing pressure for a takedown.

fēng zhǒu xiè jiān 封肘卸肩 Close off the elbow and lay down the shoulder: grab an adversary's oncoming hand and twist it over, pressing down on the elbow with the other hand, crossing your hands to twist his wrist and elbow, forcing his shoulder down. From Qinna.

楓 [枫] (rad.75) **fēng** Chinese sweet gum tree. Maple tree.

fēng lín sǎo yè 枫林扫叶 Sweep the Leaves in the Maple Woods: step across behind and sit into a crossed stance, slicing the blade across and out low, reaching the left hand up to form a straight line with the right arm and sword. From Qingping sword.

豐 (rad.151) [丰] (rad.2) **fēng** Abundant, plentiful.

fēng lóng 丰隆 Acupoint Fenglong (bountiful bulge), ST40. At the shin, eight *cun* above the ankle bone, to the outside of acupoint ST38 (on each side). From TCM.

鋒 [锋] (rad.167) **fēng** 1. The sharp point or cutting edge of a blade. 2 Vanguard.

fēng dāo pō lín 锋刀泼林 Sharp Blade Spills the Forest: jump forward, landing in a drop stance, sweeping the hands down and across, palms down (hitting with the blade of the hands). From Shaolinquan.

風 [风] (rad.182) **fēng** 1. The wind. For more movement names evocatively using the wind, see also under chūn fēng, qīng-, shùn-, xuán-, xūn-, yíng-. 2. Wind: as one of the six *qi* of nature, environmental influences that can cause disease when in excess. See also liù qì, liù yín.

fēng bǎi hé yè 风摆荷叶 Wind Sways the Lotus Leaves: a double sweeping arm swing with a stepping hook sweep. From Xingyiquan. Also called fēng bǎi liú xù.

fēng bǎi hé yè jiǎo 风摆荷叶脚 Wind Sways the Lotus Leaves kick, an outside crescent kick. From Chuojiao and Duanquan.

F

fēng bǎi liú xù 风摆柳絮 Wind Sways the Willow Fronds. See fēng bái hé yè.

fēng chí 风池 Acupoint Fengchi (wind pool), GB20. At the back of the head, under the external occipital protuberance, in the depression between the tendons of the trapezius and sternocleidomastoid muscles, level with the point Fengfu (on each side). From TCM.

fēng dòng chē lún 风动车轮 Wind Moves the Windmill: advance with a hanging hook of a sword. From Taijiquan.

fēng fǔ 风府 Acupoint Fengfu (wind mansion), DU16. At the nape of the neck, the base of the skull, below the bony protuberance of the occipital bone, between the tendons of the neck, one *cun* into the hairline, on the midline. From TCM. A sensitive point, striking jars the occipital bone and may cause fainting, coma, or even death, so should not be hit hard.

fēng gé 风格 Flavour, character, of a style, routine, or area.

fēng juǎn cán huā 风卷残花 Wind Whirls the Broken Flowers: a rolling action with a broadsword, wrapping the blade from the right side around the head, but not bringing the blade as tight to the body as usual. From Chen Taijiquan. See also guǒ nǎo.

fēng juǎn cán yún 风卷残云 Wind Whirls the Scattered Clouds: cutting with the palm while stepping around with hooking out and in steps. From Baguazhang. See also bǎi bù, kòu bù.

fēng juǎn hé yè 风卷荷叶 Wind Whirls the Lotus Leaves: From Yang Taijiquan sword.

fēng làng yuè lǐ 风浪跃鲤 Carp Jumping in the Stormy Waves: advancing with large sweeping vertical hooks with a sword to both sides, then stepping through with a cross stance cradle to set up for a bow stance pierce. From Qingping sword.

fēng lún dāo 风轮刀 Windmill broadsword: sweep a large broadsword around the body, tip down, grip above the head, spinning the body around as well. From Baguazhang.

fēng lún fǎn zhǒu 风轮反肘 Windmill reversed Elbows. 1. Jump and spin to get to an adversary's back, striking with both elbows. 2. Step and turn to elbow strikes directly behind the body. From Baguazhang, one of its sixty-four hands.

fēng lún pī zhǎng 风轮劈掌 Windmill Chops: two swinging chops with one hand following the other, often also turning a full circle. From Baguazhang and Wudangquan, one of Baguazhang's sixty-four hands.

fēng mén 风门 Acupoint Fengmen (wind gate), BL12. At the back, level with the depression below spinous process of the second thoracic vertebra, 1.5 *cun* lateral to the midline (on each side). From TCM.

fēng piāo luò yè 风飘落叶 Falling Leaves Flutter in the Breeze: bring a sword tip from high to low, allowing the blade to sway back and forth following the gentle movement of the waist, keeping the tip pointing forward. From Wu Taijiquan.

fēng sǎo cán yún 风扫残云 Wind Sweeps the Fragmentary Clouds: turn around to the rear, swinging a staff in a full circle over the head, finishing with the butt tucked at the armpit. From Baguazhang.

fēng sǎo méi huā 风扫梅花 Wind Sweeps the Plum Blossoms. 1. Lift the palm in preparation for a lifting stamp. From Chen Taijiquan. 2. Sweep around with a sword. From Taijiquan.

fēng sǎo qiū shuǐ 风扫秋水 Wind Sweeps the Autumnal Waters (limpid eyes of a woman): lean back on the bent leg of a left bow stance, cutting a sword along the length of the extended leg. Then turn and jump towards the left, moving to a right bow stance and slice up to shoulder height in front of the right leg. From Qingping sword.

fēng shì 风市 Acupoint Fengshi (wind market), GB31. At the thigh, seven *cun* up from the popliteal crease, on the midline down the outside, where the middle finger touches when the arm hangs straight. From TCM. A crippling point, striking here may cause serious injury, see also cán xué. This point is sometimes touched during standing training or at the beginning of a routine, to stimulate the *qi*.

fēng shù 风俞 Acupoint Fengshu, BL13. At the back, level with the depression below the third thoracic vertebra, 1.5 *cun* lateral to the midline. From TCM.

fēng wǔ luò yè 风舞落叶 The Wind causes the

Fallen Leaves to Dance: resting stance press down with a sword. From Taijiquan.

fēng xiāng quán fǎ 风箱拳法 Bellows Punches: standing up, pull the left fist in and punch the right fist out with a hammer fist. The 12th move of the tiger and crane routine.

縫 [缝] (rad.120) fèng   Seam. Crack; fissure.

fèng jiàng jī 缝匠肌 Sartorius muscle: in the anterior of the thigh. Mainly a knee flexor, it is also a weak hip flexor, and assists in lateral hip rotation.

鳳 (rad.196) [凤] (rad.29) fèng The Phoenix, a splendid mythical bird, the king of birds. One of China's four divine creatures, along with the dragon, tortoise, and kylin. Often used in movement names. For more movement names using the actions or qualities of the phoenix, see also under cǎi fèng, dān- 丹, dān- 单, jīn-, shuāng-.

fèng chì tǎng 凤翅镗 Phoenix wing trident: a long handled weapon with three prongs, the middle straight and the outer curved like wings.

fèng huáng 凤凰 Phoenix. Often used in movement names.

fèng huáng dān zhǎn chì 凤凰单展翅 Phoenix Spreads a Wing: move into a horse stance opening out one arm to shoulder height, the other set at the elbow.

fèng huáng diǎn tóu 凤凰点头 Phoenix Nods its Head. 1. A dab with a sword, usually in empty stance or parallel stance. 2. Advancing repeated dabs with a sword. 3. In Shaolinquan, a dab with a spear, and can add a kick.

fèng huáng dié chì 凤凰叠翅 Phoenix Folds its Wings: spin from a crossed sitting stance around to another on the other side, bringing the blade in to tuck it in front of the chest. The left hand comes in to the hilt, elbow up behind. From Qingping sword.

fèng huáng duó wō 凤凰夺窝 Phoenix Fights for its Nest: a front kick, holding the palms up in front of the face, keeping the body upright. From Baguazhang.

fèng huáng mǐn chì 凤凰抿翅 Phoenix Smoothens its Wings: circle-walking with the hands pointing down on either side of the body, slightly behind, palms facing each other. From Baguazhang.

fèng huáng qǐ chì 凤凰起翅 Phoenix Lifts its Wings: circle-walking with the hands palms down on either side of the body, arms extended so the palms are about hip height, aligned on the circle. From Baguazhang.

fèng huáng tóu cháo 凤凰投巢 Phoenix Drops into its Nest: lift a knee and spin to the rear, lifting the handgrip of a sword up over the head to point the tip down to the side. From Baguazhang sword.

fèng huáng xuàn wō 凤凰旋窝 Phoenix Circles its Nest: circle-walking holding deerhorn blades with the upper blade hooks reversed and lower blade flat, pushing in the line of walking. From Baguazhang.

fèng huáng xué wō 凤凰踅窝 Phoenix Paces in its Nest: drive forward stabbing a sword, then jump and spin two-seventy degrees, landing in a half horse stance, ready to continue. From Wudangquan.

fèng huáng zhǎn chì 凤凰展翅 Phoenix Spreads its Wings. 1. A toe kick to the armpit. Usually a counter attack or an exploratory strike, not a finishing strike. 2. A straight crossing kick, opening out the arms: a toe kick to the groin, opening out an adversary's arms. 3. A move into a horse stance opening out the arms to shoulder height. 4. A circling move with both arms, completing with slices front and back. 5. Circle-walking with the arms extended at shoulder height on either side of the body, aligned on the circle, palms down. From Baguazhang. Sometimes also called fèng zhǎn chì, shuāng fèng zhǎn chì.

fèng míng lóng yín 凤鸣龙吟 Phoenix and Dragon Sing: drop to the knees and lean back to stab a sword overhead behind. From Yangjia sword.

fèng qī wú tóng 凤栖梧桐 Phoenix Perches in the Parasol Tree: smoothly reverse an adversary's wrist and extend his arm, locking out wrist and elbow.

fèng tóu fǔ 凤头斧 Phoenix head axe: a long handled axe with a phoenix head shaped blade.

fèng tóu quán 凤头拳 Phoenix head fist, a hand shape: middle finger knuckle extended from a

F

tight fist, with the thumb supporting it. From Chuojiao.

fèng yǎn gōu 凤眼勾 Phoenix eye hook, a hand shape: wrist bent, thumb and index finger connected, remaining fingers tucked slightly into the palm. From Tongbeiquan.

fèng yǎn quán 凤眼拳 Phoenix eye fist, a hand shape. 1. In most styles, one joint of the index finger is extended from a tightly clenched fist, with the thumb supporting it. Also called hè yǎn quán, kāi fèng yǎn. 2. In Xingyiquan, all four fingers are tightly clenched, and the thumb is tucked down to the middle finger so that the thumb does not stick out at all.

fèng zhǎn chì 凤展翅 Phoenix Spreads its Wings. See #5 of fèng huáng zhǎn chì.

fèng zuǐ dāo 凤嘴刀 Phoenix beak blade: a halberd with a deeply curved tip.

佛 (rad.9) **fó** Buddha; Buddhism; relating to Buddhism.

fó jiā quán 佛家拳 Fojiaquan (Buddhist, or Fu family fist), a southern style that combines hard and soft. Known since the early 1880s.

敷 (rad.66) **fū** 1. To apply (an ointment) on something. 2. To smear: connect with adversary such that he becomes passive or unable to move during push hands practice. From Taijiquan.

跗 (rad.157) **fū** The instep of the foot.

fū gǔ 跗骨 Tarsal bones, bones of the foot.

fū miàn 跗面 The instep of the foot.

fū yáng 跗阳 Acupoint Fuyang (instep yang), BL59. At the calf, on the outside of the gastrocnemius tendon, three *cun* up from the tip of the lateral malleolus, and the acupoint Hunlun (on each leg). From TCM.

伏 (rad.9) **fú** 1. To bend over; lie prostrate. 2. Hide; ambush. 3. As a shield and broadsword technique, ambush: cover your body with the shield, hiding the broadsword within, ready for ambush.

fú dì hòu sǎo 伏地后扫 Back sweep kick in full squat with the hands on the ground. In the category of sweep kicks, see also sǎo zhuàn xíng tuǐ fǎ.

fú dì tǐng shēn 伏地挺身 Pushups.

fú hǔ 伏虎 Ambush the Tiger, Subdue the Tiger, Tame the Tiger: a move where the fists come in towards the centre, one high, the other low, as if holding a tiger around the body and hitting it in the head. From many styles with slight variations. See also dǎ hǔ shì, wǎn gōng shè hǔ.

fú hǔ cáng lóng 伏虎藏龙 Tiger Ambushes and Dragon Hides, Crouching Tiger Hidden Dragon: standing up, left fist at the hip, brace the right hand down in front of the belly. The third move of the tiger and crane routine.

fú hǔ gōng 伏虎功 Fingertip pushups.

fú hǔ lián zhū 伏虎连珠 Ambush the Tiger with a Chain of Pearls: from cross stance, step to a right reverse bow stance and push the left hand down in front of the groin, thumb turned in, fingers pointing right. The 31st move of the tiger and crane routine.

fú hǔ shì 伏虎式 Ambush the Tiger model. One of twenty-four classic spear moves. Most spear routines will have a move with a like name. In general, this name refers to closing off, or sealing, techniques.

fú hǔ tīng fēng 伏虎听风 Hiding Tiger Listens to the Wind. 1. In an empty stance, sword in the left hand, pull it back in front of the chest to place the right hand on the grip. From Baguazhang. 2. Step forward, circle the hands around to come in front of the chest, pressing up and down, rotate and extend them out to the sides, circling back around to return, then stab forward. From Liuhebafa.

fú hǔ zhuāng 伏虎桩 Subdue the tiger post standing. 1. Stand in an open horse stance, bracing out over each leg with the arms, palms in. Done to lower the fire in the body and collect it as water in the kidney. From Xingyiquan. 2. In a sixty-forty stance with the front heel raised, hold the hands in a low strum the pipa position and do micro movements in all directions. From Yiquan. 3. Similar to #1 with the palms down. From Yiquan.

fú rè zài lǐ 伏热在里 Internal deep lying heat, a pattern applied in channel diagnosis. From TCM.

fú shēn 伏身 1. Lie prostrate, flatten prone. 2. When the body faces down in a movement, bent over face down, although not lying down.

fú shǒu 伏手 Shielding hand: hook the wrist and tuck in the elbow in front of the body, to connect and press down with the forearm. From Wing Chun.

fú tú 伏兔 Acupoint Futu (hiding rabbit), ST32. At the thigh, up six *cun* from the outer edge of the patella (on each side). From TCM.

fú zhǎng 伏掌 Lying palm. 1. Circle and rotate a bent arm out then in, to press down with the palm in front of the body, most usually as a defense against a groin strike. 2. A direct hook with the hand, elbow tucked, forearm on midline (sometimes called bridge-on arm). Both terms used mainly in southern styles. 3. A hand placement, a slightly open palm with the fingers naturally curved, palm down.

刜 (rad.18) fú   To chop, strike.

fú jiàn 刜剑 Chop with a sword: to cut flatly to the left and right. It is a cutting technique, done continuously back and forth. See also zhé jiàn.

扶 (rad.64) fú   To support with the hand.

fú àn shì 扶按式 Supporting position during *qigong* training. Standing with the legs open to shoulder width, hands facing down at belly height, as if pressing on something for support.

fú àn qiú fā lì 扶按球发力 Release of power as pressing down on a ball. From Yiquan.

fú dì hòu dēng tuǐ 扶地后蹬腿 Supported back thrust kick: Put the hands on the ground and do a thrust kick behind.

fú lán kàn huā 扶栏看花 Lean on the Fence to Look at Flowers, a shoulder throw: grab an adversary's shoulder with one arm and around his waist with the other (or both around the shoulders), step to the outside and hook one ankle to lift it inwards.

fú qǐ yù zhù 扶起玉柱 Support the Jade Pillar: stand up in a high T stance, raising the left hand and stretching and turning the torso, looking back as you cut down to the right with a sword, fully extending the right arm to draw a line with the blade. From Qingping sword.

fú tū 扶突 Acupoint Futu (protuberance assistant), LI18. At the outer edge of the neck, level with the Adam's apple, above the acupoint Tianding (on each side). From TCM.

拂 (rad.64) fú   To whisk. Stroke.

fú shǒu 拂手 Whisking arm: a strike to the side with the heel of the palm and wrist, extending the arm fully. From Wing Chun.

服 (rad.74) fú   1. Clothing, clothes. 2. To wear. 3. To serve.

fú zhuāng 服装 Clothing, costume, uniform. Competition or performance uniform.

浮 (rad.85) fú   1. To float; superficial, on the surface. 2. Lightness, one of Ziranmen's nineteen main methods. 3. In martial arts, usually floating, superficial power application or weighting, considered a fault.

fú àn zhuāng 浮按桩 Float and press stake standing: sitting with the arms rounded, hands in front of the belly, palms down, combining the powers of floating and pressing down. From Yiquan.

fú bào zhuāng 浮抱桩 Float and hug stake standing: sitting with the arms rounded, hands in front of the belly, palms up, combining the powers of floating and embracing. From Yiquan.

fú bái 浮白 Acupoint Fubai (floating white), GB10. At the head, on the temporal bone, on an arc with acupoints Tianchong and Wangu, two thirds up from Wangu (on each side). From TCM.

fú xī 浮郄 Acupoint Fuxi (superficial cleft), BL38. At the back of the knee, one *cun* above acupoint Weiyang, inside the tendon of the biceps femoris (on each leg). From TCM.

fú yún fǎn zhǎng 浮云反掌 Floating Clouds Reverse the Palms: stab the hands out, then snap them over to palms up. From Shaolinquan.

fú yún zhuāng 浮云桩 Floating clouds stake standing: standing in a sixty-forty stance with the hands up at chest height, forward hand over the forward leg, palms down. From Yiquan.

蚨 (rad.142) fú   A kind of water beetle.

fú dié fēn fēi 蚨蝶分飞 Water Beetle and Butterfly Fly Apart: step to a left open bow stance and push through with both palms with the elbows

F

tucked in and the palm heels close, right on top with fingers up, left below with fingers down. The 60th move of the tiger and crane routine. (See also hú dié.)

俯 (rad.9) **fǔ**   To bow the head.

fǔ chēng 俯撑 Pushups.

fǔ chōng dǎo dì 俯冲倒地 A shoulder roll.

fǔ quán 俯拳 Fist heart faces down, surface forward. Refers to the fist placement, not the direction of the strike.

fǔ shēn 俯身 Prone torso: the body faces down, usually means the torso approaches horizontal. Does not mean lying down., but leaning the torso while standing.

fǔ zhǎng 俯掌 Palm faces down, a prone palm. Refers to the hand placement, not the direction of the strike.

府 (rad.53) **fǔ**   A mansion. A government agency. Your home.

fǔ shě 府舍 Acupoint Fushe (bowel abode), SP13. At the belly, four *cun* down from the navel, four *cun* lateral to the midline (on each side). From TCM.

弣 (rad.57) **fǔ**   The grip of a bow.

斧 (rad.69) **fǔ**   An axe, hatchet. Also called yuè. In general, a fǔ is smaller and the blade has a flat back for pounding, a yuè is larger and the blade may have a decorative back.

fǔ rèn tuǐ 斧刃腿 Axe blade kick, a turned out kick to the knee. See chǎn tuǐ.

腑 (rad.130) **fǔ**   The *yang* organs of the body, using the Chinese meanings: Large Intestine, Gallbladder, Bladder, Triple Burner, Stomach, and Small Intestine. The *yang* organs open to the external environment, and are generally hollow conduits for substances produced and used by the *yin* organs. Can be referred to collectively as the bowels, as they receive, digest, transport and transform food. From TCM. See also dà cháng, dǎn, páng guāng, sān jiāo, wèi, xiǎo cháng, zàng.

辅 [辅] (rad.159) **fǔ**   To assist, complement, supplement.

fǔ shēn fǎ 辅身法 Method of supplementing the body: to fully utilize the whole body in conjunction with the torso.

釜 (rad.167) **fǔ**   A cauldron.

fǔ dǐ chōu xīn 釜底抽薪 Remove the Firewood from Under the Cauldron. The 19th of the Thirty-six Stratagems of Warfare, which apply to many situations.

副 (rad.18) **fù**   Deputy; assistant; vice-.

fù zǒng cái pàn zhǎng 副总裁判长 Assistant head judge; assistant chief referee.

復 (rad. 60) [复] (rad.34) **fù**   1. To turn around. 2. To turn over, come back. 3. To repeat. 4. To return to a normal state. 5. Again.

fù liū 复溜 Acupoint Fuliu (recover flow), KI7. At the ankle, on the inside, two *cun* above acupoint Taixi, just in front of the Achilles tendon (on each leg). From TCM.

父 (rad. 88) **fù**   1. Father. 2. Male relative of an elder generation.

fù zǐ gōng shǒu 父子恭手 Father and Son Show Respect: a salutation, feet together, forearms crossed in front of the chest, fingers up, right arm on the outside. Also written fù zǐ gǒng shǒu, see below.

fù zǐ gǒng shǒu 父子拱手 See fù zǐ gōng shǒu.

腹 (rad.130) **fù**   Abdomen, belly.

fù āi 腹哀 Acupoint Fu'ai (abdominal lament), SP16. At the bellow, three *cun* above the navel, four *cun* lateral to the midline (on each side). From TCM.

fù bì 腹壁 The abdominal wall.

fù gōu 腹沟 The trench of the belly, where it creases on bending.

fù jié 腹结 Acupoint Fujie (abdominal bind), SP14. At the abdomen, 1.3 *cun* below the navel, four *cun* lateral to the midline (on each side). From TCM.

fù nèi xié jī 腹内斜肌 Internal oblique muscle: a layer of muscle in the front of the abdomen, runs ninety degrees to the external oblique muscle. Used in compression, flexion, and rotation of the torso.

fù shì hū xī 腹式呼吸 Deep breathing into the belly.

fù shì nì hū xī 腹式逆呼吸 Reverse deep breathing: draw the belly in slightly when breathing in, expanding the lower ribs, protrude the belly slightly when breathing out. This is the natural breathing pattern for activity and power output. Also called nì shì fù hū xī.

fù shì shùn hū xī 腹式顺呼吸 Smooth deep breathing: expand the belly slightly when breathing in, draw the belly in slightly when breathing out. This is the natural breathing pattern for relaxed, health training.

fù tōng gǔ 腹通谷 Acupoint Futonggu (abdominal open valley), KI20. At the abdomen, five *cun* above the navel, 0.5 *cun* lateral to the midline (on each side). From TCM.

fù wài xié jī 腹外斜肌 External oblique muscle: a layer of muscle in the front of the abdomen, runs at ninety degrees to the internal oblique muscle. Used in compression, flexion, and rotation of the torso.

fù zhí jī 腹直肌 Rectus abdominus muscle: a muscle in the front of the abdomen, runs directly upwards.

複 (rad.145) [复] (rad.34) fù 1. To duplicate. 2. Compound, complex. 3. To repeat, to reiterate.

fù huàn bù 复换步 Duplicating change step. See shuāng huàn bù.

負 [负] (rad.154) fù 1. To carry on the back or shoulder, literally. 2. To bear, to shoulder, figuratively.

fù zhòng xíng 负重行 Walking with weights: to attach weights to the hands, feet, or body while circle-walking. From Baguazhang.

fù zhòng zhuǎn zhǎng gōng 负重转掌功 Circle-walking with palm weights: to hold or suspend weights from the palms while circle-walking. From Baguazhang.

附 (rad.170) fù To rely on; to be dependent on. To attach. Near to.

fù fēn 附分 Acupoint Fufen (attached branch), BL41. At the back, level with the depression below spinous process of the second thoracic vertebra, three *cun* lateral to the midline (on each side). From TCM.

fù jiā zhī chēng 附加支撑 Added support, placing a body part to support on the ground to prevent oneself from falling over or losing balance further. A serious deduction (0.2) in Taolu competition: includes using one hand, one elbow, one knee, the head only, one arm, the non-supporting foot, or a weapon to catch balance.

G

改 (rad.66) **gǎi** 1. To change; convert; transform. 2. To alter; revise; modify. 3. To correct; remedy. 4. To switch over.

gǎi pàn 改判 To alter a judge's decision or score.

蓋 (rad.140) [盖] (rad.108) **gài** 1. A cover, a lid. 2. The original, practical, meaning is to put a cover on a pot, reaching over to avoid the heat. 3. A hard striking or a controlling move downwards. 4. To cover an adversary's attack by adjusting your power first, such that he is unable to attack effectively.

gài bǎ 盖把 Cover with the butt of a long weapon: strike strongly downwards with the right hand along the aft-section of the shaft, the left hand along the fore-section.

gài bù 盖步 Cross-over step, cover step, front cross-over step: rear foot comes through to cross over in front, stepping forward.

gài bù biè 盖步别 Cross-over step throw: step the leg across both of an adversary's legs, getting in close, then swing that leg up, turn, and throw him over your hip. From wrestling, a throw.

gài bù rù 盖步入 Cross over step entry: to enter for a throw by stepping in crossing the foot in front, used for a turning throw.

gài chā bù 盖插步 See gài bù.

gài dǎ 盖打 Covering hit: cover with a palm and straight punch over the forearm with the other hand.

gài fǎ 盖法 See yā fǎ.

gài gùn 盖棍 Cover with a staff: slide a hand and swing one end to strike down with the shaft level.

gài lán chuān xīn 盖拦穿心 Cover and Trap, then Pierce to the Heart: retreat and draw back a sword, then step forward to pierce. From Taijiquan.

gài ná fǎ 盖拿法 Covering grappling hold: grab with the arms wrapped over and around an adversary's body, wrapping one arm over his shoulder and one under his arm to grip one wrist in the other hand to keep a strong hold. From wrestling.

gài pī gùn 盖劈棍 Cross-over chop: chop down with a staff, crossing the arms to tuck one in at the armpit.

gài quán 盖拳 Downward cover with the fist or forearm, a straight swinging punch (can also have the arm slightly bent) from behind and over the head. Can strike with the fist clenched with the palm down or with the knuckles. Normally used to strike the top of an adversary's head, like putting a cover on a pot.

gài shēn dāo 盖身刀 Cover the body with a broadsword: turn around, bringing the blade flat over the head to press down with the flat of the blade.

gài tiào bù 盖跳步 Covering jump: jump forward, bringing the rear foot across in front of the leading foot.

gài zhǎng 盖掌 Covering palm, pressing down with the palm down or forward, with the arm curved, thumb inside. The hand passes behind or past the head in its trajectory.

gài zhǒu 盖肘 Cover with the elbow, pressing down with the elbow or forearm.

乾 干 (rad.5,7) [干] (rad.7) **gān** 1. Clean. 2. Dry; dried. 3. In martial arts can also refer to a shield. 4. The traditional character is also pronounced qián, the heaven trigram, see qián.

桿 [杆] (rad.75) **gān** 1. A pole. 2. The shaft of a long wooden weapon. 3. The wooden shaft of a long weapon that has a metal sleeved tip.

gān shǒu 杆手 A straight punch, thrown directly with little corkscrewing.

gān zǐ 杆子 Short pole: a thin pole, about 1.1 to 1.4 metres long, slightly tapering. Both ends are used. Also called biān gān.

gān zǐ biān 杆子鞭 Pole whip, a soft weapon: rope with a section of wooden staff attached to one end and a metal spike attached to the other end.

G

竿 (rad.118) **gān** A pole or rod, usually bamboo.

gān zǐ 竿子 A pole or rod, usually bamboo.

肝 (rad.130) **gān** 1. The liver. 2. The Liver, the organ associated with the Zu Jue Yin channel. It is a *yin* organ.

gān jīng 肝经 The Liver meridian. From TCM. See zú jué yīn.

gān shū 肝俞 Acupoint Ganshu (liver transport), BL18. At the back, level with the depression below spinous process of the ninth thoracic vertebra, 1.5 *cun* lateral to the midline (on each side). From TCM.

橄 (rad.75) **gǎn** An olive, in conjunction with lǎn 榄.

gǎn lǎn quán 橄榄拳 Olive fist, a hand shape. See lì zhī quán. Also called lóng zhū quán.

趕 [赶] (rad.156) **gǎn** 1. To pursue, to try to catch. 2. To catch up with; to overtake. 3. To drive; to expel. 4. To hurry; to rush.

gǎn bù 赶步 Catch up step: stride forward with the front foot, bring the rear foot up to meet the front foot, then stride the front foot forward again.

岡 [冈] (rad.13) **gāng** Ridge of a hill.

gāng shàng jī 冈上肌 Supraspinatus muscle: in the shoulder girdle, attaches proximally along the whole upper part of the shoulder blade, runs under the acromion, to the humerus. Active in arm abduction.

gāng xià jī 冈下肌 Infraspinatus muscle: in the shoulder girdle, attaches proximally along the whole middle to lower part of the shoulder blade to the humerus. Active in arm lateral rotation.

剛 [刚] (rad.18) **gāng** Hard; rigid; strong.

gāng jìn 刚劲 Hard, obvious, unsubtle power (trained, not brute strength). Also called yáng jìn.

gāng róu xiāng jì 刚柔相济 Hard and pliant power interact and interchange, a characteristic of most Chinese styles.

gāng zhōng wú róu bù wéi jiān 刚中无柔不为坚 Hardness without pliancy is not in fact strong. A martial saying.

扛 (rad.64) **gāng** 1. To lift with both hands. 2. To carry between two people. 3. To carry someone's elbow, lifting it into an uncomfortable position. From Qinna. 4. Pronounced káng, to carry on the shoulder.

缸 (rad.121) **gāng** A vat; crock; large jar shaped vessel. Often used for training hand grip and arm strength.

肛 (rad.130) **gāng** The anus.

gāng mén 肛门 The anus.

槓 [杠] (rad.75) **gàng** A stout carrying pole. A bar.

gàng biè 杠别 Levered throw: grab an adversary on the sleeve and at the back belt, and lever him around your leg.

gàng gān tuō 杠杆脱 Lever release, an escape: use the joint of an adversary as leverage to escape.

gàng líng 杠铃 Barbells and weights, the general term for barbells and dumbbells.

膏 (rad.130) **gāo** 1. The region just below the heart. 2. Fat; grease. 3. A medicinal ointment for external use. 4. Padding or fatty substance within the body.

gāo huāng shū 膏肓俞 Acupoint Gaohuangshu (gaohuang area transport), BL43. At the back, level with the depression below the spinous process of the fourth thoracic vertebra, three *cun* lateral to the midline (on each side). From TCM.

gāo yào 膏药 Medicated plaster: for external application, to alleviate muscular soreness and pain from strains.

高 (rad.189) **gāo** 1. High. 2. Tall.

gāo gōu 高勾 A high straight hook kick. See páo tuǐ.

gāo máo 高毛 Traditional name for a high jump into a front somersault.

gāo shān liú shuǐ 高山流水 Water Flows from a High Mountain: Stepping forward and sitting back, circle to control, then press with the forearms, then open out. From Liuhebafa.

gāo shǒu 高手 A highly skilled athlete or martial artist.

gāo tàn mǎ 高探马 High Pat on Horse: varies with style, but generally ends in an empty stance with the hands in final posture as if holding the chin of a small horse and patting its forehead. From Taijiquan.

gāo tí bù 高提步 Lifted stance, suspended foot held at mid-shin. The knee is not as high a raised knee stance, see also tí xī.

gāo zhuāng 高桩 High stance stake standing.

gāo zhuàng jiǎo 高撞脚 High ramming kick: a jumping front thrust kick. From Chuojiao, one of its high-basin kicks.

戈 (rad.62) gē   1. A weapon with a long wooden shaft with a thick metal spike and a bladed crosspiece. 2. A dagger-axe, a short, thick dagger.

格 (rad.75) gē   Used together with dēng to make an onomatopoeic word. This character is usually pronounced gé, see gé.

gē dēng bù 格登步 Dadum step (makes the sound like the beating of the heart). See huá bù.

歌 謌 (rad.76, 149) [歌] (rad.76) gē   A song.

gē jué 歌诀 Verse, formula: the traditional way to state the important points about a style, not necessarily rhyming but concise to be easily remembered. Short, pithy explanations of martial theory, to aid understanding and memory. Usually have been passed down orally. Also called quán jué.

胳 (rad.130) gē   The arm, arms; armpit.

gē bó 胳臂 The upper arms.

gē bó rú pí biān 胳膊如皮鞭 The arms must be like leather whips. From Tongbeiquan, one of its requirements.

gē bó zhǒu 胳膊肘 The elbows.

掰 (rad.64) gé   To hold or embrace in two hands.

gé xī 掰膝 Hug with the knees: when the knees are spread, as in a horse stance, to have a rolling in power, but not to the extent that they are pulled together. From Baguazhang.

格 (rad.75) gé   1. The original meaning is crossed lines forming squares. 2. The technique meaning is a transverse outer block, hitting across with the forearm vertical, meeting force with force. 3. To fight. 4. The guard of a sword. 5. Also pronounced gē when used just for the sound, see gē.

gé dài 格带 Draw out and across (with a weapon), softening the impact of an attack.

gé dǎng 格挡 Block. A general term for any way of directly obstructing an attack.

gé dāo 格刀 Block with a broadsword: circle the blade around to block with the blade held vertically, with the tip up or down.

gé dà dāo 格大刀 Block with a big cutter: with the right hand at the butt and the left at two thirds down the shaft, with the blade angled downwards, edge down, use the shaft to block.

gé dòu 格斗 Sparring, fighting. To fight.

gé dòu yùn dòng 格斗运动 Sparring, including all categories: Sanda, push hands, wrestling, and weapons sparring.

gé gùn 格棍 Block with a staff: block to the left or right with the shaft near vertical, applying power to the whole shaft.

gé jié 格截 To block and cut with both arms.

gé kāi 格开 To block, knocking aside.

gé zhǒu 格肘 Elbow block with the forearm: with the forearm vertical, elbow bent, block either inwards or outwards with the forearm.

膈 (rad.130) gé   Diaphragm.

gé guān 膈关 Acupoint Geguan (diaphragm pass), BL46. At the back, level with the depression below the spinous process of the seventh thoracic vertebra, three cun lateral to the midline (on each side). May sometimes be written with the character 隔, also pronounced gé. From TCM.

gé mó 膈膜 Diaphragm.

gé shū 膈俞 Acupoint Geshu (diaphragm

G

transport), BL17. At the back, level with the depression below the spinous process of the seventh thoracic vertebra, 1.5 *cun* lateral to the midline (on each side). Sometimes be written with the character 膈, also pronounced gé. From TCM.

隔 (rad.170) gé   Be apart from, be at a distance from. Separate; cut off.

gé àn guān huǒ 隔岸观火 Watch the Fire from the Other Shore. The ninth of the Thirty-six Stratagems of Warfare.

gé guān 隔关 Acupoint Geguan (partition pass). See gé guān above. From TCM.

gé duàn shān hé 隔断山河 Partition Mountains and Rivers: dodge with a lifting interception. Evade while standing straight up, shifting to the forward right leg to get reach while slicing a sword up. Then lift the left knee, drawing the sword down to the right, pressing down with both hands at the hilt, in front of the body. From Qingping sword.

gé shān réng hǔ 隔山仍虎 Throw the Tiger from the Neighbouring Mountain: throws in which the body remains apart from the adversary. This is a category of throw, which are usually a combination of strike and throw.

gé shū 隔俞 Acupoint Geshu (partition transport). See gé shū above. From TCM.

頜 [颌] (rad.181) gé   Jaw, chin. Also pronounced hé.

扢 (rad.64) gě   1. To scrape. 2. Pronounced kā, to scrape with a knife.

個 [个] (rad.9) gè   A general measure word, can be used instead of the proper measure word. A measure word used informally for people.

gè rén dàn xiàng 个人单项 Individual competition for the title in individual events.

gè rén jìng sài 个人竞赛 Individual competition: competition for titles for the individual, not counting towards the team.

gè rén quán néng 个人全能 Individual competition for the title in the individual all round event.

gè rén sài 个人赛 See gè rén jìng sài.

根 (rad.75) gēn   1. The root of a plant. 2. Used in the martial arts to mean the foundation or root of the body, with the goal of rooting the lower legs well in the ground.

gēn jiē cuī 根节催 The root sections urges, or drives the movement. See also sān jié.

跟 (rad.157) gēn   Heel of the foot.

gēn bù 跟步 Following step, follow-up step, step up. 1. Bring one foot in towards the other after a step. Usually means to step the rear foot up towards the lead foot after a step. Also called dài bù. Sometimes called qí lín bù. 2. To step the lead foot back after the rear foot retreats. Also called suí bù. 3. A full step forward, plus the follow-up step, used as a charging step.

gēn diǎn bù 跟垫步 A step plus a following step. A stealing step.

gēn yāo 跟腰 Follow up the waist: a slight shift forward to get in tight with an adversary with the hips and torso during wrestling.

艮 (rad.138) gěn   The Mountain Trigram, represented by one solid (*yang*) line over two broken (*yin*) lines, called 'overturned bowl'. Corresponds to the coiling snake formation or gate. A closing gate formation. Indicates the attribute of resting.

庚 (rad.53) gēng   1. The seventh of the ten Celestial Stems, used in combination with the twelve Terrestrial Branches to designate years, months, days, and hours. See also dì zhī, tiān gān. 2. Seventh in a list when listing using the celestial stems, equivalent to G in English when listing alphabetically.

gēng chén 庚辰 The years 2000, 1940 and so on, for sixty year cycles.

gēng shēn 庚申 The years 1980, 1920 and so on, for sixty year cycles.

gēng wǔ 庚午 The years 1990, 1930 and so on, for sixty year cycles.

gēng yín 庚寅 The years 2010, 1950, and so on, for sixty year cycles.

gēng xū 庚戌 The years 1970, 1910, and so on, for sixty year cycles.

gēng zǐ 庚子 The years 1960, 1900, and so on, for sixty year cycles.

耕 畊 (rad.127, 102) [耕] (rad.127) gēng
To plough; to till.

gēng dāo 耕刀 Plough with a broadsword: a low sweeping block with the edge of the blade, putting power to the tip as if ploughing in the ground. Most effective with thick bladed broadswords such as the butterfly knives.

gēng lán 耕拦 Plough: cut with both forearms to the same side, leading edge to the outside (little finger side cutting), one forearm down, palm down, one forearm up, palm up. From Wing Chun.

梗 (rad.75) gěng
1. A stalk, stem. 2. To straighten the neck.

公 (rad.12) gōng
1. Public. Open to all. 2. Unselfish.

gōng sūn 公孙 Acupoint Gongsun (yellow emperor), SP4. At the foot, the root of the big toe (on each foot). From TCM.

功 (rad.19) gōng
1. Skill, work; 2. Achievement; result. 3. Usefulness; effectiveness.

gōng fǎ 功法 Training methods towards mastery, including body hardening, routines, sparring, and internal strength methods.

gōng fū 功夫 1. Mastery; skill developed over a long period of work; workmanship, effort devoted to a task. 2. Accomplishments. 3. Used colloquially for Chinese martial arts in general. In English, kungfu usually refers to the Chinese traditional martial arts. See also wǔ shù.

gōng fū jià zǐ 功夫架子 Practice of basics and forms to develop mastery.

gōng jià 功架 Posture and movement: includes stances, stepping, hand positions, handwork, body positions, bodywork, kicks, etc.

gōng lǐ 功理 Training theory, theory and principles behind training methods.

gōng lì 功力 1. Effectiveness. 2. Strength achieved from much training. 3. A traditional routine, known in Mizong and other styles. 4. A style that trains both internal and external power, developed in Cangzhou since the early 1800s.

gōng lì yào chún 功力要纯 The effectiveness (power, speed, endurance, agility, etc.) should be pure and simple.

gōng lì zhuāng 功力桩 Power stance training: a variety of stake stances that develop power. From Yiquan.

gōng yí chún 功宜纯 Mastery should be pure and simple: one of the basic qualities of many styles.

弓 (rad.57) gōng
A bow.

gōng bù 弓步 Bow stance: varies with style, but is always facing front, front knee bent (to varying degrees), and the rear heel must be on the ground. The front foot is sometimes on straight line and sometimes slightly turned in. In many styles the feet are about three to four foot-lengths apart and the front thigh parallel to the ground, in some styles the feet are less far apart and the stance is higher. Also called gōng dēng bù, gōng jiàn bù, jiàn mǎ, qián gōng bù.

gōng bù bá gùn 弓步拔棍 Bow stance open up a staff: in a bow stance, strike a staff strongly with both hands out to the left side, tucking the shaft onto the body under the left armpit.

gōng bù bèi gùn 弓步背棍 Bow stance shoulder a staff: in a bow stance, hold a staff across the back, the tip coming forward over the shoulder.

gōng bù chōng quán 弓步冲拳 Bow stance punch: set to a bow stance and punch with one fist. May refer to a same side punch, an opposite punch, a punch to front and back, or a punch to the middle of the stance.

gōng bù dǐng zhǒu 弓步顶肘 Bow stance elbow strike: strike straight forward with same side elbow in bow stance.

gōng bù jià chōng quán 弓步架冲拳 Bow stance framing block and punch: set to a bow stance, doing a framing block up with the smooth side hand and throwing a reverse punch.

gōng bù pī quán 弓步劈拳 Bow stance chopping fist: set to a bow stance and chop down with an extended arm, finishing at shoulder height with the elbow cradled in the other palm.

gōng bù shí zì quán 弓步十字拳 Bow stance cross fists: in an open bow stance, punch to the front and back, not aligned with the legs, but across the line of the stance to draw the character ten 十.

gōng bù shuāng gōu shǒu 弓步双勾手 Bow stance double hooks: set to a bow stance and hook both hands behind, looking forward. From Chaquan.

gōng bù shuāng tuī dān zhǐ 弓步双推单指 Bow stance push with hands in single finger shape, one pushes forward and the other pushes to the rear, across the line of the stance. Done either as a power move or quickly. From southern styles.

gōng bù tuī zhǎng 弓步推掌 Bow stance push: set to a bow stance and push with the opposite side palm, the same side palm usually at the knee. From Chaquan.

gōng dài 弓袋 A soft case or bag to carry a bow.

gōng dēng bù 弓登步 Bow stance. See gōng bù.

gōng jiàn bù 弓箭步 Bow stance. See gōng bù.

gōng mǎ 弓马 A bow stance. See gōng bù.

gōng mǎ bù 弓马步 A horse stance with the feet turned out.

gōng shǐ 弓矢 A bow and arrow.

gōng yāo 弓腰 To bow at the waist, a throwing technique. Not simply to lean over, but to use the hip and lean forward, keeping strong through the waist, to throw an adversary over the hip or back. More deeply bent than bending at the waist to throw. See also wān yāo.

攻 (rad.66) **gōng** To attack; take the offensive.

gōng biān 攻鞭 Attacking whip. See gōng qiáo.

gōng fáng 攻防 Attack and defense; offense and defense.

gōng jī 攻击 Attack; attacking strike.

gōng qiáo 攻桥 Attacking bridge, a forearm technique: with the elbow slightly bent, internally rotate the forearm to ram forward with the edge of the palm or fist. May be done with one or both arms at once. From southern styles. Also called gōng biān.

gōng zhǎng 攻掌 Attacking palm. From southern styles.

肱 (rad.130) **gōng** The upper arm (formal). Also pronounced hóng.

gōng èr tóu jī 肱二头肌 Biceps brachii muscle: an upper arm muscle. Runs from attachments in the scapula down to the radius. Assists in elbow flexion and supination. Colloquially called the biceps.

gōng gǔ 肱骨 Humerus: the long bone of the upper arm.

gōng jī 肱肌 Brachialis muscle: an upper arm muscle. Runs from attachments in the humerus down to the radius. Assists in elbow flexion. Colloquially included in the biceps.

gōng ráo jī 肱桡肌 Brachioradialis muscle: a forearm muscle. Runs from attachments in the humerus down to the wrist. Assists in elbow flexion and protects the elbow during extension.

gōng sān tóu jī 肱三头肌 Triceps brachii muscle: an upper arm muscle. Runs from attachments in the scapula and humerus down to the elbow. Active mainly as an elbow extensor. Colloquially called the triceps.

躬 躳 [躬] (rad.158) **gōng** To bend at the waist, to bow.

拱 (rad.64) **gǒng** 1. To fold the hands before bowing. 2. To encircle with the hands. 3. To raise up; to hump up; to arch. 4. In wrestling, a short, sharp movement, hitting an adversary's arm with your shoulder, whilst gripping his shoulder with your hand.

gǒng bèi 拱背 Open the upper back, arch the back like a cat.

gǒng yāo 拱腰 Bow the back, throw by using the buttocks and bowing the back.

gǒng zǐ 拱子 Bow: grab an adversary at the wrist and around the waist, and move the hips in tight to his, turning and bowing to throw him over your hips. A throw.

鞏 (rad.177) [巩] (rad.48) **gǒng** 1. To consolidate. 2. A throwing technique in wrestling.

勾 (rad.20) gōu   1. To cancel; draw; collude with. 2. The shorter leg of a right triangle. 3. A hooked hand shape, with the wrist bent. 4. In wrestling, a throwing technique: hook onto an adversary (with the arm or leg) and throw.

gōu bǎn 勾扳 Hook the Plank: trap an adversary by hooking the foot below and crossing his body or neck with a reverse arm above, so that he falls like a plank.

gōu bàn tuǐ 勾拌腿 Hooking trip: a low, short hook-in sweep kick, usually to an adversary's heel to trip him up. The stepping pattern of the throw is called guǎn.

gōu chuō 勾戳 Stab with a hook hand: swing downwards with the fingertips of a hooked hand.

gōu dài jiǎo 勾带脚 Hook and draw the foot, a trip: if you are in clench with an adversary, quickly dodge to the side and hook his foot with yours, pulling it strongly forward.

gōu diē 勾跌 Hooking throw: hook a foot in close to an adversary's foot, then shift forward to apply pressure to the ankle.

gōu dǐng 勾顶 Hook peak: the peak of the bent wrist of a hand held in a hooked shape.

gōu guà 勾挂 Hook the Plank: a trap and pull down on the arm if a throw did not succeed, and finally a high hook strike if the trap did not succeed.

gōu guà zhuāng 勾挂桩 Hooking stake standing: standing in a sixty-forty stance with the hands up at chest height, forward hand over the forward leg, palms in. From Yiquan.

gōu jiān 勾尖 Hook tip: the fingertips of a hand held in a hooked shape.

gōu jiǎo 勾脚 Hook foot. 1. The action of dorsi-flexion. 2. Hook your foot behind your adversary's heel.

gōu jiǎo shuāi fǎ 勾脚摔法 Hooking leg throws: throws which involve first hooking the leg or legs of an adversary. From wrestling.

gōu quán 勾拳 A hook: a hooking punch.

gōu shǒu 勾手 Hooked hand. See gōu zi shǒu.

gōu tān jiǎo fǎ 勾弹脚法 Hooking Snap Kick: grab and do a right low snap kick, then coil the foot around an adversary's leg and hook the foot back, pushing forward with the hands. Land in a left reverse stance with the hands pushing forward on line with the stance, fingers turned to the right. The 90th move of the tiger and crane routine.

gōu tī 勾踢 Hooking kick. 1. A category of low snap kicks with the foot hooking, usually to the ankle, intended to take down an adversary. In the category of snap kicks, see also qū shēn xìng tuǐ fǎ. 2. A low hook kick, a hidden kick done almost as a step. 3. A category of hook kicks and short sweep kicks. From Mizongquan. 4. Also in Mizongquan, specifically a mid height hook kick to the thigh. Also called zhōng gōu.

gōu tuǐ 勾腿 Hook kick: a low rising kick with the foot dorsi-flexed. From Baguazhang, may be done as a hidden kick, seeming to step into an adversary with a hook-in step. From Chuojiao, one of its middle-basin kicks.

gōu zǐ 勾子 A hooking throw using the leg.

gōu zǐ shǒu 勾子手 Hook shaped hand position. The exact configuration differs with styles, but usually the wrist is bent and three to five finger tips are touching the thumb. Also called gōu shǒu.

鈎 鉤 [钩] (rad.167) gōu   1. To hook, secure with a hooking action. 2. Hooks, a bladed short weapon, sharp on both edges, with a hook on the tip, a crescent moon guard at the handle, and an additional spike at the butt. Often used as a double weapon.

gōu dǐng 钩顶 Hook tip: the tip of the hooks on a weapon that has hooks.

gōu guà yù píng 钩掛玉瓶 Hang up the Jade Bottle: trap an adversary's arm and hyper-extend his wrist. From Baguazhang.

gōu guà fā lì 钩掛发力 Release of power with a hanging hook. From Yiquan.

gōu guà shì lì 钩掛试力 Hook and file testing power: stand in sixty-forty stance, push forward at chest height with the palms down, then pull back with the palms facing each other. From Yiquan, one of its combat testing moves.

gōu lián dāo 钩镰刀 A sickle hook blade: a halberd with a hook on the spine of the blade.

gōu lián qiāng 钩镰枪 A sickle hook spear, a spear with a long hook in the tip, the hook curling back towards the shaft. May be wielded as a pair.

G

gōu shǒu 钩手 Hooking hand: hook onto an adversary.

gōu qiāng 钩枪 1. A hooked spear, a spear with hooks in the tip. 2. Hook a spear outward (to the right side), down, and behind.

gōu qiāng guǎi 钩枪拐 A hooked spear crutch, a short spear with hooks in the tip and a crutch grip near the end.

gōu yuè 钩月 Hook crescent: the crescent shaped blade of a double hook, acts as a hand guard and additional blade. Also called yuè yá.

gōu zǐ 钩子 A hook: a hooked tool used as a weapon.

gōu zǒu làng shì 钩走浪势 The hooks should move like breaking waves. A martial saying.

构 (rad.64) gòu   1. To pull, drag. 2. To reach.

gòu bù 构步 Circling steps, plucking steps: circle the foot in then out when stepping forward. From Wing Chun.

gòu shǒu 构手 Circling block or deflection: circle the wrist outwards from inside an adversary's arm, lifting the elbow to do so. From Wing Chun.

孤 (rad.39) gū   1. Orphaned. 2. Solitary; alone.

gū shù pán gēn 孤树盘根 Lone Tree Winds its Roots: step around holding a sword blade up at an angle, then drop to a cross legged sit, continuing the line to cut behind. From Qingping sword.

gū yàn chū qún 孤雁出群 Lone Goose leaves the Flock. 1. Without moving the feet, turn fully around to look behind, placing the hands in a ready position, one up one down. From Baguazhang. 2. Sometimes the circle-walking in this position. From Baguazhang. Also called hōng yàn chū qún. 3. Stepping forward, a lift and twist to off balance an adversary. 4. Step in with a high framing block and a push or scoop to the armpit. From Baguazhang, one of its sixty-four hands. 5. Move forward to a seventy-thirty stance and stab the upper hand forward with the palm down, placing the other hand below, also palm down. From Liuhebafa. 6. Lift the knee with a double ramming palm. From Piguaquan.

gū zhàn qún dí 孤战群敌 Lone Fight Against a Hoard: step back with a back step then spin around one-eighty degrees, stepping again to a back step. Swing the lead hand over then block, then elbow strike, pushing the other hand out to the rear. From Shaolinquan.

古 (rad.30) gǔ   Ancient; age-old.

gǔ shù pǎn gēn 古树盘根 Ancient Tree Coils its Roots: resting stance combined with a technique such as a punch or a stab of a sword or broadsword. The technique can be a high or low strike, as long as the action follows the coiling of the stance. From Baguazhang, Shaolinquan, and Taijiquan.

gǔ téng chán shù 古藤缠树 Ancient Vine Coils around the Tree: to escape from a wrist grab, lower and twist the forearm, pressing with the other hand then pressing down with the forearm to reverse an adversary's elbow.

gǔ yuè chén jiāng 古月沉江 Old Moon Sinks in the River: step forward into a bow stance and sword chop, circle the sword on the left side, then, leaning the body forward and blocking up with the left hand, chop down at the right side, tip fairly close the ground. Then shift and lean back and pull the sword back online with the stance. From Qingping sword.

gǔ yuè lí huái 古月离怀 Old Moon Leaves the Bosom: cradle a sword in front of the belly in a raised knee stance, then land in horse stance, stabbing straight out in front, both hands still on the hilt. From Qingping sword.

穀 (rad.115) [谷] (rad.150) gǔ   Grain, cereal, corn.

gǔ dào 谷道 Grain route, alimentary canal: colloquial term for the anal sphincter. Often used instead of the term Huiyin, see also huì yīn.

gǔ qì 谷气 Grain *qi*, nourishing *qi*.

股 (rad.130) gǔ   Thigh, haunches, rump.

gǔ èr tóu jī 股二头肌 Biceps femoris muscle: in the posterior of the thigh, a hip extensor (the more outer of the muscles in the group referred to as hamstrings).

gǔ gǔ 股骨 Femur: the thigh bone.

gǔ nèi cè jī 股内侧肌 Vastus medialis muscle: in

the anterior of the thigh, a knee extensor (the medial of the muscles in the group referred to as quadriceps).

gǔ wài cè jī 股外侧肌 Vastus lateralis muscle: in the anterior of the thigh, a knee extensor (the lateral of the muscles in the group referred to as quadriceps).

gǔ zhí jī 股直肌 Rectus femoris muscle: in the anterior of the thigh, a hip flexor and knee extensor (the outer of the muscles in the group referred to as quadriceps).

gǔ zhōng jiān jī 股中间肌 Vastus intermedius muscle: in the anterior of the thigh, a knee extensor (the middle branch of the muscles in the group referred to as quadriceps).

gǔ zhǒu 股肘 An elbow to the thigh. From Tanglangquan, one of its eight short techniques.

骨 (rad.188) gǔ   A bone, bones. Pronounced gú in certain contexts.

gǔ gé 骨胳 A skeleton.

gǔ guān jié 骨关节 Joints (in the body).

gǔ mó yán 骨膜炎 Periostitis (swelling of the tissue around the bone), as in shin splints.

gǔ shāo 骨梢 The bone tip: the teeth. The visible outer parts of the body in which the energy of the bones is expressed.

gú tǒu 骨头 Bone, bones.

gú tǒu jià zǐ 骨头架子 A skeleton.

gǔ zhé 骨折 A bone fracture, a broken bone.

鼓 (rad.207) gǔ   1. A drum. To drum. 2. To vibrate, quiver. 3. In movement names, usually refers to the temples of an adversary.

gǔ dàng jìn 鼓荡劲 Drumming power: to combine internal power, breathing, and movement to cause the body to vibrate like a drum with a rhythmic wavelike power.

gǔ xiōng 鼓胸 Drum chest: to puff up the chest, an error in most styles.

固 (rad.31) gù   1. Solid; firm; strong. 2. Hard; solid. 3. Martial meaning is a lockout that fixes the limb solidly, such as arm bars on the ground.

gù dìng 固定 To make immovable. Fixed; regular.

顧 [顾] (rad.181) gù   To look at, watch; turn around to look at. 2. To take care of (as in a defense).

gù dǎ 顾打 Defend and attack.

gù fǎ 顾法 1. Defensive techniques. 2. To watch in all directions.

gù pàn 顾盼 Look / take care of (defend) to the left and right.

刮 (rad.18) guā   1. To scratch; scrape; shave. 2. Scratch an acupuncture needle to vibrate the tip, to guide the *qi* to the needle. From TCM.

guā jiǎo 刮脚 Scrape with the foot: a small trapping action of the foot. From wrestling.

guā lōu 刮搂 Scrape and brush with the foot: a trapping action of the foot and lower leg. From wrestling. Also called lōu zi.

掛 [挂] (rad.64) guà   1. To hook, entrap, downwards or upwards hooking parry. Often translated as to hang. 2. A kick: hook with the foot dorsi-flexed, to entrap.

guà bà 挂把 Hook with the butt of a long weapon: bring the butt down and back around the side.

guà chuí 挂槌 Hooking hammer fist. From southern styles.

guà chuí shuāng luò 挂搥双落 Hang and Beat Land Together: step to a right bow stance and pound the fists forward and down, using the backfists to hit the head or chest. The 52nd move of the tiger and crane routine. See shuāng guà chuí fǎ.

guà dāo 挂刀 Parry with a broadsword, catching with the spine of the blade. See guà jiàn.

guà dà dāo 挂大刀 Hook with a cig cutter: drill the blade towards the ground and back, hooking down with the shaft and spine of the blade.

guà dǎng 挂挡 Hooking block: bend and lift the elbow to protect the head.

guà diē 挂跌 Hooking takedown: takedowns done by hooking with the foot, generally taking down onto the back. From Tanglangquan.

guà gài quán 挂盖拳 Hook and cover punches; an alternating double swinging punch of a backfist with a following punch with the fist face. These punches are done with the arms almost straight, swinging overhead and continuing through. From southern styles.

guà gài sǎo quán 挂盖扫拳 Hook, cover, and sweeping punches: swinging upwards then downwards with the same fist, with a following covering punch with the other fist with the fist heel (fist centre down). These punches continue through. From southern styles.

guà gōu 挂钩 Hang with double hooks: hook downwards and to the rear with both blades, using the hooked side to catch.

guà jiàn 挂剑 Parry with a sword, hooking forward and up or backward and down, catching with the thumb side edge of the blade.

guà jiǎo 挂脚 Hook with the foot and ankle, dorsi-flexed.

guà méi jiǎo 挂眉脚 Hook the eyebrows kick: turn a full circle and swing up the leg to hit with the heel. From Mojiaquan.

guà pī quán 挂劈拳 Downward striking backfist, stopping.

guà pū dāo 挂扑刀 Hook with a horse cutter. See guà dà dāo.

guà qiāng 挂枪 Hook a spear inwards (to the left side), down, and behind.

guà quán 挂拳 Hook. 1. A downward striking punch with the knuckles. 2. A downward striking backfist, carrying through.

guà tuǐ 挂腿 Parrying kick. 1. Open the foot out to the side, keeping it on the ground, contacting with the calf. 2. A kick with the same movement, but off the ground. From Chuojiao, one of its middle-basin kicks. 3. A hooking with the leg in close contact, to throw.

guà zhǎng 挂掌 Hooking palms: flow with the line of attack to sweep an adversary's hand diagonally up, down, or back.

拐 (rad.64) guǎi   1. To turn. 2. Strange. 3. A corner. 4. To limp. 5. Crutches.

guǎi bàng 拐棒 Turning the stick, a training exercise. Standing straight holding the arm out level, holding a heavy stone tied to a short stick by a rope, twist the hand side to side. This is not the same as rollups, it is just twisting with one hand.

guǎi bù 拐步 Turned stance, a high front crossed stance. From southern styles.

guǎi fǎ 拐法 See rào fǎ.

guǎi tū qiāng 拐突枪 A crutch spear, a spear with a four edged tip and a crutch grip at the butt end.

guǎi tuǐ 拐腿 Turning kick: lift the knee in front, tucking it in to strike or protect with the outer edge of the knee and shin in close fighting.

guǎi zhǒu 拐肘 Turning elbow. 1. Do an elbow stab then press down, pushing a bit to the outside. 2. An elbow/forearm pressure towards the inside. 3. In wrestling, to control an adversary by pressing the elbow into his body to prevent his escaping from a takedown.

guǎi zǐ 拐子 A wooden flail, a weapon with a crosspiece either across the end in a T shape or along the shaft. A short flail is sixty-five to one hundred centimetres, while a long flail is about one hundred and thirty centimetres. Also called yáng jiǎo guǎi.

怪 怪 [怪] (rad.61) guài   1. Strange; odd. 2. Monster; demon. 3. To blame.

guài mǎng fān shēn 怪蟒翻身 Monstrous Python Rolls Over: upward slice, turning into a full turn with a swinging over chop with a sword. From Taijiquan.

guài mǎng huí tóu 怪蟒回头 Monstrous Python Looks Back: turn and do a reverse slice with a sword up behind, sitting into a cross stance. From Wudang sword.

觀 [观] (rad.147) guān   To look at, watch, observe. Outlook.

guān yīn 观音 Bodhisattva Guanyin, often used in movement names.

guān yīn zuò huà 观音坐化 Guanyin Sits to Beg, a sweep throw: when caught by a hugging grab from behind, circle your leg outside an adversary's calf (behind you), hooking onto his ankle and lifting it while grabbing his wrists. Sit down, leaning into him.

guān yīn zuò lián 观音坐莲 Guanyin Sits on a Lotus: when grabbed from behind, squat down and grab your adversary's legs, leaning back for a takedown. A release.

關 (rad.169) [关] (rad.37) **guān** 1. To shut, close. 2. A pass (in the mountains, etc.). 3. Turn off; close down. 4. A barrier. 5. Concern, involve. 6. A surname.

guān chōng 关冲 Acupoint Guanchong (passage hub), SJ1. At the hand, near the tip of the ring finger, 0.1 *cun* to the outside of the root of the fingernail (on each hand). From TCM. Pinching the side of the finger tip while applying a control can add considerable pain to the technique, even to the extent of causing unconsciousness.

guān dāo 关刀 Guan's blade, Guan's halberd. A halberd, a big cutter: a wide, curved, single edged blade, attached to a long wooden handle. The shaft is to about ear height, and the weapon is generally quite heavy. General Guan is famous for the use of this blade in popular fiction. Also called chūn qiú dāo, dà dāo, dìng sòng dāo, yuè shèng dāo.

guān gōng 关公 General Guan, see guān yǔ.

guān jié 关节 Joint, joints of the body.

guān jié yán 关节炎 Pain and swelling in the joints; arthritis.

guān mén 关门 Acupoint Guanmen (pass gate), ST22. At the abdomen, three *cun* up from the navel, two *cun* lateral to the midline (on each side). From TCM.

guān mén jìng jiǔ 关门敬酒 Close the Door and Propose a Toast: Drive the elbow up in a reverse bow stance. From Meishanquan.

guān mén zhuō zéi 关门捉贼 Close the Door to Catch the Thief. The twenty-second of the Thirty-six Stratagems of Warfare, which apply to many situations.

guān shèng tí dāo shàng bà qiáo 关圣提刀上霸桥 The Sage Guan Lifts his Blade and Mounts the Despot's Bridge: Open by kicking the shaft of a halberd to the side, stamp, step forward and shoulder the shaft, then front cross over step, slice up in reverse stance. From Chen Taijiquan.

guān yǔ 关羽 Guan Yu (-219), a general from the Three Kingdoms period, famous as one of the three blood brothers (with Liu Bei and Zhang Fei) in the novel Romance of the Three Kingdoms. Known for his virtue and loyalty as well as his skill with the halberd (though that is more legend than fact). Became a guardian god after his death. Often used in movement names. Also called guān gōng. See also guān dāo.

guān yǔ wǔ dāo 关羽舞刀 Guan Yu Plays with his Blade: press an adversary's hand to your chest and control his elbow to lock his arm on your body (not a halberd technique).

guān yuán 关元 Acupoint Guanyuan (head of the pass), RN4. At the abdomen, three *cun* below the navel, on the midline. From TCM. Striking shocks the arteries in the abdominal wall, the intercostal nerves, and the intestines, causing *qi* and blood stagnation.

guān yuán shū 关元俞 Acupoint Guanyuanshu (origin pass transport), BL26. At the lower back, level with the depression below the fifth lumbar vertebra, 1.5 *cun* lateral to the midline (on each side). From TCM.

管 (rad.118) **guǎn** 1. A short hook-in sweep step to an adversary's heel, used as a trip or kick. As a kick, also called gōu bàn tuǐ. 2. To jam with the lower leg, preventing an adversary from using his leg. As a wrestling jam, also called chān guǎn. 3. In wrestling, a type of throw with the upper body that works similar to a lean (see also kào), but trapping with the leg as well.

guǎn jiǎo 管脚 A hook with the ankle. From wrestling.

guǎn qiāng jìn 管戗劲 Combining a downward pull with an upward press, especially when pressing the head down into the body in close range fighting. From wrestling.

guǎn zhǒu 管肘 Elbow press: grabbing behind your adversary's head with both hands, press your elbows upwards into his chest, combining a downward pull with an upward press. From wrestling.

慣 [惯] (rad.61) **guàn** Be used to; in the habit of; custom.

guàn xìng 惯性 Inertia.

guàn xìng lì 惯性力 Inertial force.

摜 [掼] (rad.64) **guàn** To throw, toss; cast.

guàn quán 掼拳 A hook punch: to throw a punch

forward and in, hitting with the knuckles, usually palm down, turning to give it more power. Commonly used in competition Sanda.

灌 (rad.85) **guàn**   To irrigate. Pour; fill.

guàn xué 灌穴 Fill the holes: strike the hollow in the shoulder blade.

貫 [贯] (rad.154) **guàn**   1. To pass through; pierce. 2. In martial arts, used for punches to the ears, temple, and sensitive places.

guàn dǐng 贯顶 To send the intention to the top of the head, to keep it lively and upright.

guàn ěr 贯耳 Roundhouse punch to the ear. Also called guàn ěr chuí.

guàn ěr chuān chuí 贯耳穿锤 Roundhouse threading punch. See tiē ěr chuān chuí.

guàn ěr chuí 贯耳锤 Roundhouse punch to the ear. Also called guàn ěr.

guàn lì 贯力 Sequential power or force.

guàn mén 贯门 Sensitive point Guanmen, the solar plexus. One of seven painful gateways to attack that are related to midline acupoints. See qī chōng mén.

guàn quán 贯拳 Inside hook punch, roundhouse punch, usually circling downwards at the end. Strike with the fist rolled over to angle the thumb side down, wrist bent, hitting with the knuckles.

guàn táng chuí 贯堂锤 Upper framing block to clear for a punch to the armpit.

guàn táng shǒu 贯堂手 Upper block and hooking punch to the armpit.

guàn táng shǒu 贯膛手 Strike to the armpit.

光 (rad.10) **guāng**   1. Brightness; light. 2. Glory. 3. To exhaust. 4. Bare. 5. Alone.

guāng bǎn táng láng quán 光板螳螂拳 Guangban (smooth board) Tanglangquan, a branch of Preying Mantis style, which uses a tight hand shape and uses the hand like a plank.

guāng bèi 光背 Shirtless, bare chested (bare backed).

guāng míng 光明 Acupoint Guangming (bright light), GB37. At the calf, on the outside, five *cun* up from the ankle, on the forward edge of the fibula or the peroneus brevis muscle (on each leg). From TCM.

歸 (rad.77) [归] (rad.58) **guī**   1. To return, go back to. 2. Give back to. 3. Turn over to. 4. Converge.

guī lái 归来 Acupoint Guilai (return), ST29. At the abdomen, four *cun* under the navel, two *cun* lateral to the midline (on each side). From TCM.

guī táng tuǐ 归堂腿 Return to the Hall kick: hook the foot up then in to the supporting leg's knee, holding the knee up in front of the groin.

規 [规] (rad.147) **guī**   1. Regulation; rule. 2. To plan; map out.

guī dìng tào lù 规定套路 Compulsory routines: routines set by a committee, which must be followed exactly in Taolu competition.

龜 [龟] (rad.213) **guī**   Tortoise; turtle. One of China's four divine creatures, along with the dragon, phoenix, and kylin. Symbol of longevity and wealth. Breathing like a tortoise means to breathe slowly and evenly, almost imperceptibly. Since the tortoise lives a long life, its breathing pattern is thought to bring health and longevity. For more movement names using the turtle, see also jīn guī, shén-.

guī bèi 龟背 Turtle back. 1. A body condition gradually developed. The whole back is full of *qi* and strong, feeling like the shell of a turtle. 2. The upper back is arched like a rounded turtle shell.

guī bèi gōng 龟背功 Turtle back training, a combination of hard and soft skills training: to rub and strike the entire back, especially around the kidney area, with gradually increasing hardness, starting softly with the hands and moving gradually to wood then iron rods. This is combined with breathing skills to bring *qi* to the *dantian*.

guī shé jiāo zhàn 龟蛇交战 Turtle and Snake Fight: alternate stabbing palms with elbow strikes. From Wudangquan.

guī xíng 龟形 See tuó xíng. This is due to confusion with the simplified character.

癸 (rad.105) **guǐ**   1. The tenth and last of the ten Celestial Stems, used in combination with the twelve Terrestrial Branches to designate years, months, days, and hours. See also dì zhī, tiān gān. 2. Tenth in a list when listing using the celestial stems, equivalent to J when listing alphabetically.

guǐ chǒu 癸丑 The years 1973, 1913, and so on, for sixty year cycles.

guǐ hài 癸亥 The years 1983, 1923, and so on, for sixty year cycles.

guǐ mǎo 癸卯 The years 1963, 1903, and so on, for sixty year cycles.

guǐ sì 癸巳 The years 2013, 1953, and so on, for sixty year cycles.

guǐ wèi 癸未 The years 2003, 1943, and so on, for sixty year cycles.

guǐ yǒu 癸酉 The years 1993, 1933, and so on, for sixty year cycles.

軌 [轨] (rad.159) **guǐ**   Rail; track; course; path.

guǐ jī 轨迹 The course, trajectory of movements: the line taken by the arms and hands. See also lù xiàn.

跪 (rad.157) **guì**   To kneel, putting one or both knees to the ground.

guì bù 跪步 Kneeling squat, squat with the rear leg almost kneeling but knee not touching the ground, buttocks sitting on the rear leg.

guì dīng bù 跪丁步 Kneeling T stance, kneeling on the rear leg, buttocks sitting on the kneeling leg, front leg pointing forward bent with the shin vertical. The front foot and rear shin form a T shape about a foot-length apart.

guì fǎ 跪法 Kneeling methods: methods that involve getting the knee in to press on an adversary during a takedown.

guì pū bù 跪仆步 Kneeling drop stance: Kneel on one leg and extend the other straight to the side, full foot on the ground and hooked in. From southern styles.

guì tuǐ 跪腿 Kneeling leg. 1. In wrestling, a type of throw. See xiǎo dé hé. 2. To kneel on an adversary's leg to prevent his tripping you. 3. A back hook, flip the foot up lightly behind to bend the knee fully, kicking the buttocks, a leg loosening exercise.

guì xī 跪膝 1. Kneel, as a throwing technique: trap an adversary's heel with your foot and kneel into his shin. 2. A takedown from behind, apply a choke and kneel on an adversary's knee (it will bend naturally and go to the ground, this is not a knee break). From wrestling.

guì xī bù 跪膝步 Kneeling stance: to kneel without putting the knees on the ground, the rear knee by the foot of the front leg.

guì yāo 跪腰 Kneel on the back: with an adversary prone, do a neck lock and kneel on his back. From wrestling.

guì zhèng 跪睁 Kneeling elbow: a downward elbow strike, curving downward strike with the elbow or forearm. From Wing Chun.

guì zhǐ 跪指 Kneeling fingers, a hand shape: fingers bent at second joint, uses the second joint as contact.

滚 [滚] (rad.85) **gǔn**   1. To trundle, roll: usually a defensive move, turning and using the forearms to control. 2. Can mean specifically parrying by turning to the left. 3. As a shield and broadsword technique, roll: roll on the ground using the shield, combining this with a rolling or sweeping broadsword technique.

gǔn bāng diē 滚邦跌 Rolling clapper takedown: type of takedown that involves an arm bar, then uses the adversary's momentum trying to pull away, to jam his arm and throw away.

gǔn biān 滚鞭 Rolling whip. See gǔn qiáo.

gǔn chuí 滚捶 Roll the fists: with the forearms vertical, tuck and body and turn to intercept with the forearms or fists.

gǔn diē 滚跌 Rolling fall: tuck a foot behind to lower in a gentle back fall.

gǔn jiǎn tuǐ 滚剪腿 Rolling scissors sweep kick: drop to the ground and trap an adversary's legs with the legs, then roll over to take him down.

gǔn jìn 滚劲 Rolling power: a combination of turning the centre and rotating the extremities, so that movement is rounded and able to be applied in any direction. Used in conjunction with wrapping power, contending power, and drilling power to keep power balanced for any type of movement. See also guǒ jìn, zhèng jìn, zuān jìn.

G

gǔn léi quán 滚雷拳 Rolling Thunder fist: a routine of Piguaquan.

gǔn qiáo 滚桥 Rolling bridge, a forearm technique: extend the arm downwards to the front, arm bent, hand a bit across the body, with the palm down, contacting an adversary with the outside of the forearm. Then rotate the forearm and circle the hand up, keeping the elbow set, palm facing in, in front of its shoulder, contacting with the thumb side of the forearm. Also called bǎng qiáo, gǔn biān.

gǔn qiú 滚球 Trundle a ball: rolling the adversary.

gǔn qiú tuō zhǎng 滚球托掌 Trundle the Ball and Carry: roll the arms as if trundling a ball, completing with a lifting hand, lifting the knee so the hand is on the foot. From Taiji Changquan.

gǔn qiú zhǎng 滚球掌 Ball rolling palm: extending the palms as if holding a large ball in front of the chest, the lower arm at chest height, the upper arm above the head (especially while circle-walking). The power both holds and expands. From Baguazhang.

gǔn shēn 滚身 Trundle the body: step in to the side to present the body square to the side of an adversary. From Baguazhang.

gǔn shēn dāo 滚身刀 Trundle the body with a broadsword: with the left hand also at the grip, blade up, edge up, tip forward, roll under the blade keeping the left hand at the grip, rolling the edge over (used with the larger blade Bagua broadsword).

gǔn shǒu 滚手 1. Trundle, roll with both hands. 2. roll the arm around an adversary's arm.

gǔn shǒu dāo 滚手刀 Trundle a broadsword: place the left hand on the blade spine, grip at the chest, edge out, then step forward, push the blade forward and roll under the blade, pushing forward, keeping the edge out and the left hand on the grip (used with the larger blade Bagua broadsword).

gǔn shǒu pào 滚手炮 Trundle to control, then double strike. Also called shuāng gǔn chuí.

gǔn yā gùn 滚压棍 Trundle and press down with staff: gripping with both hands, draw it back and press it down, above the thigh turning the front arm palm up, with force reaching the fore section of the shaft.

gǔn zhǒu 滚肘 Trundle, roll using the elbow. 1. With the forearms vertical in front of the body, elbows bent, roll inwards or outwards to defend with the forearms and elbows. 2. To grab an adversary's arm and roll his elbow over, keeping it bent.

棍 (rad.75) gùn A staff, stave, cudgel, stick. Competition length for modern wushu is about the head-height of the athlete. More traditional is the length to the wrist of the upstretched arm. Longer than that is a pole, see bàng.

gùn bà 棍把 The base of a staff, the end of the aft-section. Also called gùn dǐ.

gùn dǎ yī piàn 棍打一片 The staff hits in a slice. A saying about the staff. This describes how most staff techniques are swinging and hitting strikes. This phrase differentiates staff methods from the spear, which mainly coils and stabs.

gùn dǐ 棍底 The base of a staff. See gùn bà.

gùn duān 棍端 The tip of a staff. See gùn shāo.

gùn pà diǎn tóu 棍怕点头 The worst thing for the staff is a dipping head. A martial saying.

gùn qián duān 棍前端 The fore-section of a staff, about the first third from the tip.

gùn sǎo yī dà piàn 棍扫一大片 The staff sweeps a large area in one blow. A martial saying that describes the essence of the staff.

gùn shāo 棍梢 The tip of a staff, the end of the fore-section. Also called gùn duān. Sometimes called gùn zhǐ.

gùn shēn 棍身 The body of a staff, the whole staff.

gùn shù 棍术 Staff skill. Cudgel play: a Taolu competition event, called Gunshu in English.

gùn tóu 棍头 The fore-section third of a staff, the third nearest the tip.

gùn wěi 棍尾 The aft-section third of a staff, the third nearest the tail, or butt.

gùn zhǐ 棍指 The staff finger. See gùn shāo. Also called gùn duān.

gùn zhōng 棍中 The mid-section of a staff, the middle third of the shaft.

國 [国] (rad.31) **guó**   Country; nation.

guó jiā jí cái pàn yuán 国家级裁判员 National level judge: a judge qualified to work at national level competitions.

guó jiā jí jiào liàn yuán 国家级教练员 National level coach: the highest standard coach within a country.

guó shù 国术 Chinese martial arts.

guó shù guǎn 国术馆 1. A Chinese martial arts hall or club. 2, Historically, the National Martial Arts College that operated from 1928 to 1937.

膕 [腘] (rad.130) **guó**   The back of the knee.

guó wō 腘窝 The back of the knee; the depression at the back of the knee.

裹 (rad.145) **guǒ**   To wrap around, enclose in the arms, bind.

guǒ biān pào 裹鞭炮 Wrapping Firecrackers: a double exploding strike. From Taijiquan.

guǒ chán jìn 裹缠劲 Wrapping coiling power, used in Qinna: a combination of wrapping and coiling, twisting an adversary's arm or leg to dislocate at the root.

guǒ dài 裹带 Wrapping draw, often with a weapon.

guǒ dāng 裹裆 Wrap the crotch area: when in stance, press in with the knees to create an enclosing feeling through the groin.

guǒ fǎ 裹法 Wrapping methods: rolling inwards to deal with a looping attack, using the inward action to strike. Also called nèi lán fǎ.

guǒ jìn 裹劲 Wrapping, enveloping power. 1. Power applied as movements come in towards the body, as if applying pressure to a bundle. 2. Used in conjunction with rolling power to keep the power balanced during closing movement. See also gǔn jìn. 3. As one of Xingyiquan's five powers, to wrap up without giving chance of escape. See also cǎi jìn, jué jìn, pū jìn, shù jìn.

guǒ kuà 裹胯 Wrap the hip joints: roll the knees in to roll the hip joints open at the back, closed in front.

guǒ nǎo (dāo) 裹脑(刀) Wrap the head: wind a broadsword around the head, neck, and upper back, tip down, spine on the back, from right to left shoulder. The blade spine should stay close to the back. Knocks an adversary's weapon out away from you. Often translated literally as 'wrap the brain', to differentiate it clearly from 'coil the head' (see also chán tóu), which is in the opposite direction.

guǒ shǒu pō jiǎo 裹手泼脚 Wrap and sprinkle: in an upright clinch, wrap the arms tightly around your adversary to pull him off balance, and step in to hook the foot outside his front foot to trip him sideways. From wrestling.

過 [过] (rad.162) **guò**   1. To pass, pass through. 2. To go past, or overdo something.

guò bǎi bù 过摆步 Extra-hook-out step: stepping past the line of the usual hook out step. This differs by style, depending on the angle of the usual step.

guò bèi huā 过背花 Over the back flowers, a steel whip technique: holding the whip in the middle with both hands, turn and switch to right handed grip in the middle, bring the whip behind the upper back.

guò bèi qiāng 过背枪 Around the back with a spear. 1. Roll the spear with the shaft on the back, coming around over the left shoulder to re-catch. 2. A full circle behind the back with the arms extended to either end of the shaft, keeping the spear on the back to that it finishes on the chest as the body turns.

guò bèi shuāi fǎ 过背摔法 Over the back throws: throws that involve putting an adversary over your back.

guò bù 过步 Pass through stepping. 1. To charge your lead foot through past the rear foot of an adversary to take over his place. 2. To step forward from the rear foot, passing your front foot.

guò dǐng lì 过顶力 Overhead strength: the strength involved in pressing a heavy object such as a stone lock straight above the head. Also called zhí lì.

guò guān zhǎn jiāng 过关斩将 1. The set phrase meaning is to go through a strategic pass by killing the garrison commander: to overcome one difficulty at a time. 2. A series of diagonal slashes

G

up and down. From Yangjia sword.

guò kòu bù 过扣步 Passing hook-in step: stepping with a hook in step around past the other foot, usually landing back where it started. This differs by style, depending on the angle of the usual step.

guò le 过了 To overextend, overdo, go past the position or place you should be in.

guò mén 过门 Go through the gate: in a partner routine, to switch places by having one partner sweep and the other jump over the sweeping leg or weapon.

guò qiáo 过桥 Pass the bridge: catch an adversary's wrist and advance with a reverse strike.

guò shǒu 过手 Passing hands: controlled fighting practice, training techniques with a partner.

guò tuǐ 过腿 Passing kick, outside crescent kick. Usually called bǎi lián tuǐ.

guò tuǐ biè zi 过腿别子 Passing leg throw: hook the leg behind, then move in, turn, and swing the leg up for a hip throw.

guò tuǐ tiào 过腿跳 Jump through the leg: hold onto one foot and hop, threading the hopping foot through the held leg.

H

哈 (rad.30) hā To breathe out strongly. with the mouth open. In martial arts, 'ha' is one of the specific sounds used to gain or express power in a technique, using the breath to assist the power. The use of this word originally comes from the temple doorway guardian Guhyapada, 'the blower', who blows a gust of yellow energy from his mouth. See also hēng, jīn gāng.

hā yāo 哈腰 Bend the back, stoop; bow slightly.

蛤 (rad.142) há Frog, toad, usually in combination with 蟆.

há mǎ shì 蛤蟆式 Frog posture. From Chuojiao, one of its low basin kicks.

海 (rad.85) hǎi Sea, ocean.

hǎi bào shēn yāo 海豹伸腰 Seal Stretches its Back: pin an adversary flat on the ground with his legs crossed to lock them and your arm around his neck, pressing down on his back with your knee. From wrestling.

hǎi dǐ 海底 The sea bottom: colloquial term for the Huiyin point, the groin, see also huí yīn.

hǎi dǐ fān huā 海底翻花 Turn Over Flowers at the Sea Bottom. From Taijiquan.

hǎi dǐ lāo yuè 海底捞月 Scoop up the Moon from the Sea Bottom. 1. In Taijiquan, continuous upward slicing with a sword. 2. In Baguazhang, to slice with a broadsword across close to the ground in a drop stance, then lift up. 3. In Baguazhang, to grab in incoming knee strike at the knee and ankle, to twist the bent leg outward. 4. In Baguazhang, to lift the knee and hook downward with a deerhorn blade, then step forward and scoop up with the other blade.

hǎi dǐ qín áo 海底擒鳌 Catch the Turtle at the Sea Bottom: turn and do a low reaching stab with a sword, held in a reverse grip. From Wu Taijiquan.

hǎi dǐ qǔ bǎo 海底取宝 Fetch Treasure from the Sea Bottom: a low horse stance punching one fist straight down in the middle, blocking up with the other.

hǎi dǐ rèn zhēn 海底纫针 Thread a Needle at the Sea Bottom: a low stab in an empty stance or a drop stance.

hǎi dǐ shēng yún 海底生云 Generate Clouds at the Sea Bottom: dodge with a sweeping scoop with a sword. Sweep the blade across to the right, turning and shifting right, then sweep across to the left, turning and shifting left. Finally shift again to the right and lift with the blade flat in front of the face. From Qingping sword.

hǎi dǐ zhēn 海底针 Needle to Sea Bottom. Varies with style, but is generally a low empty stance with one hand reaching out and down, a low strike or move into a throw. From Taijiquan.

hǎi quán 海泉 Extraordinary acupoint Haiquan (sea spring), EX-HN11. Inside the mouth, under the tip of the tongue, on the midline. From TCM.

亥 (rad.8) hài The twelfth of the twelve Terrestrial Branches, used in combination with the ten Celestial Stems to designate years, months, days, and hours. For the sixty year cycles, see also under dīng hài, guǐ-, jǐ-, xīn-, yǐ-. The period of the day from 9:00 p.m. to 11:00 p.m. See also dì zhī, tiān gān.

hài shí 亥时 The period of the day from 9:00 p.m. to 11:00 p.m. (21:00 – 23:00).

含 (rad.30) hán 1. To hold in the mouth. 2. To contain; to include.

hán bù 含步 Contained step: a type of circle-walking step – a careful, contained stepping, but not held back to be purposefully slow. From Baguazhang.

hán róu yuān yāng zhǎng 含柔鸳鸯掌 Soft Mandarin Duck Palms, the sixth routine of Duanquan, written up as twenty-four moves.

hán xiōng 含胸 Hollow, contain, the chest: keep the shoulders down and very slightly forward, so the chest is held in naturally. The chest feels broad and relaxed. This is a requirement in many styles.

H

hán xiōng tā yāo 含胸塌腰 Contain the chest and settle the waist.

寒 (rad.40) **hán**   1. Cold. 2. Cold: as one of the six *qi* of nature, environmental influences that can cause disease when in excess. See also liù qì, liù yín.

hán jī bù 寒鸡步 Cold Chicken stance: sitting on one leg, the other touching the toes in front but not weighted (as if not wanting to put the foot down in the cold). Usually called xū bù.

hán jiān 寒肩 Hunch the shoulders: hunch up the shoulders as if cold. An error in most styles.

hán jié 寒结 Cold binding, a pattern applied in channel diagnosis. From TCM.

hán máng chōng xiāo 寒鋩冲霄 Cold Point Shoots up into the Sky: sit into a low cross stance with a reverse grip slice up with a sword behind, to chase after an adversary to cut under his wrist. From Qingping sword.

涵 (rad.85) **hán**   1. To contain. 2. Damp and marshy.

hán jìn 涵劲 Contained power. From Tongbeiquan, one of its nine types of power, see also jiǔ gōng jìn.

hán xiōng 涵胸 Hold the chest without thrusting it out. The chest is relaxed, to store energy within, it is not collapsed.

hán xù 涵蓄 Reserved of manners and speech.

韓 [韩] (rad.178) **hán**   1. Korean. 2. South Korea. 3. The Han state during the Warring States period. 4. A surname.

hán tōng tōng bèi 韩通通背 Han Tong extends his back: a fully extended punch. From Tongbeiquan, one of its seven long range techniques.

漢 [汉] (rad.85) **hàn**   1. The Han ethnic group; the Chinese people; the Chinese language. 2. A man. 3. The Han dynasty (206 BC – 220 AD).

頷 [颔] (rad.181) **hàn**   1. The chin, the jaw. 2. A slight nod of the head.

hàn yàn 颔厌 Acupoint Hanyan (forehead fullness), GB4. At the head, above the hairline, at the widow's peak (on each side of the head). From TCM.

夯 (rad.37) **hāng**   1. A rammer, a tamper. 2. To ram; to tamp. To strike heavily as with a tamper. 3. Pronounced bèn, foolish or clumsy, see bèn.

hāng dì chuí 夯地捶 Tamp the Ground with a Mallet: go down into a full feet together forward weighted squat and punch towards the ground by the forward leg with a hammer punch. From Shaolinquan.

行 (rad.144) **háng**   1. A line, a row. 2. A trade, a profession; a line of business. A business firm. 3. Pronounced xíng, to go, see xíng.

háng jiā yī shēn shǒu, biàn zhī yǒu méi yǒu 行家一伸手, 便知有没有 As soon as someone moves it is obvious whether or not he has skill. A martial saying.

薅 (rad.140) **hāo**   1. To pull up (weeds). 2. In dialect also means to pull; tug; drag someone or thing, with an action similar to pulling up weeds.

hāo bàn 薅绊 Tugging takedown: move quickly to an adversary's side when he attacks, and use his incoming force to keep him moving forward, tucking your foot in to trip him as well.

耗 (rad.127) **hào**   1. Standard meaning is to consume or to dawdle. 2. In the martial arts, usually refers to static stretching, or holding postures.

hào jìn 耗劲 1. Basics practice holding a low posture or a static posture. 2. Competing by holding postures to outlast one another.

號 (rad.141) [号] (rad.30) **hào**   Literary name, assumed name. People, particularly in the past, are often referred to by a given name (míng), private name (zì), literary name (hào) and/or nickname (chuò hào).

合 (rad.9) **hé**   1. To close; connect. 2. Whole. 3. Combine; add up to.

hé bǎ 合把 Combined grip: holding a short weapon with both hands on the grip.

hé bào zhuàn zhǎng 合抱转掌 Embracing circle-walking: walking as if holding something up in one arm and controlling it from above with the other. Also called shī zi bào qiú. From Baguazhang.

hé fèng 合缝 Sensitive point Hefeng (the meeting fissure), at the space where the shoulder and arm meet. From TCM. The clavicle is easy to separate at this point. Best to hit with chopping strike.

hé gǔ 合谷 Acupoint Hegu (union valley), LI 4. At the depression where the thumb and index finger metacarpal bones approach each other (on each hand). From TCM. A sensitive point, pressing or striking here can cause numbness and loss of strength as well as pain. If more pain is applied it can injure the Large Intestine and cause unconsciousness.

hé jī 合击 Closing hit: slap the hands together in front of the body, swinging with straight arms in from the side.

hé jìn 合劲 1. Closing in power. 2. Connected power or unified power that it is expressed even in opening out or explosive actions.

hé jiān 合肩 Close the shoulders, bring the shoulders forward slightly.

hé pán zhǎng 合盘掌 Close the basin palms, training methods to improve wrist strength. 1. With a bundle of about thirty chopsticks tied together, hold at each end and twist, the hands working in opposite directions. 2. With the palms facing in the middle of the bundle, rub the bundle.

hé shǒu 合手 Close the hands together, palms facing, with closing in power but not touching. Term used in many styles, particularly in Sun Taijiquan.

hé shǒu quán 合手拳 Connect the hands routine: a partner routine of Tongbeiquan, written up as seven moves.

hé tuǐ mǎ bù 合腿马步 A closed horse stance: a horse stance with the knees tucked inwards.

hé wò dāng 合卧裆 Lying groin stretch: standing with the legs well apart, lean fully over from the hips, keeping the back flat. Grasp both feet to lie to the middle, and also move side to side grasping one foot with both hands, lying on each leg.

hé yáng 合阳 Acupoint Heyang (yang union), BL55. At the knee, in the middle two *cun* below the popliteal crease, two *cun* beneath acupoint Weizhong, between the heads of the gastrocnemius muscle (on each leg). From TCM.

hé zhǎng 合掌 Closed palms, closing palms. 1. A double shove with the wrists held together. Sometimes Baguazhang uses this in set position circle-walking. 2. To apply a closing force to an outstretched palm. 3. To move the hands together to close them. 4. The same as hé shǒu.

hé zhǎng bái lián tuǐ 合掌摆莲腿 Outside crescent kick slapping with both hands. From Duanquan.

hé zhǎng bài fó 合掌拜佛 Press the Palms together to Worship Buddha: bring the palms together in front of the chest, fingers up.

hé zhǎng pán 合掌盘 Combined palms training: see hé pán zhǎng.

hé zǐ zhǎng 合子掌 Combined palms. 1. Strike with the hands together, pressing the rear back of the hand into the front palm, striking with the back of the front hand. 2. Press the rear palm into the front horizontal forearm. Also called jǐ zhǎng.

核 (rad.75) hé   Nucleus.

hé xīn 核心 Nucleus; core; kernel.

禾 (rad.115) hé   Standing grain, especially referring to rice.

hé liáo 禾髎 Acupoint Heliao (grain bone-hole), LI19. From TCM. This is not always listed as a point.

和 (rad.115) hé   1. Gentle, mild, kind. Harmonious. 2. Together with; and.

hé shàng 和尚 A Buddhist monk.

hé shàng zhuàng zhōng 和尚撞钟 Monk Strikes a Bell: Step into a horse stance with an elbow strike. From Meishanquan and other southern styles.

hé shùn 和顺 Smooth and natural. This is a requirement at the basic level of training, movement must advance and retreat in a flowing manner.

H

荷 (rad.140) hé   Lotus, water lily.

hé yè zhǎng 荷叶掌 Lotus leaf palm shape: thumb and index finger spread and straight, the other fingers slightly bent.

闔 阖 [阖] (rad.169) hé   To shut; close; unite to the inside (formal). Usually hé 合 is used with the same meaning.

頜 [颌] (rad.181) hé   1. The chin, the jaw. 2. A slight nod of the head. Also pronounced gé.

鶴 [鹤] (rad.196) hè   A crane (the bird). For movement names using the actions or qualities of the crane, see also under bái hè, è-, fēi-.

hè dǐng 鹤顶 Extraordinary acupoint Heding, EX-LE2. At the knee, in the depression above the patella, at the middle of the thigh. From TCM. A crippling point, striking here may cause serious injury. See also cán xué.

hè dǐng fǎ 鹤顶法 Crane peak technique: in a left reverse bow stance, punch with the right fist in a crane peak fist, tucking the left fist at the face. This right side is the 77th move of the tiger and crane routine, the left side is the 78th.

hè dǐng quán 鹤顶拳 Crane peak fist, a hand shape: middle knuckle of the third finger protruding, with the thumb pressing on the distal segment. From southern styles.

hè dǐng shǒu 鹤顶手 Crane peak hand, a hand shape: finger tips together, wrist bent. From southern styles. Also called jīn gōu shǒu.

hè quán 鹤拳 Hequan (crane fist). There are many crane styles that imitate the hunting style of the crane. Usually considered to be from Fujian province. Four main branches are Shaking (zōng 宗), Hooting (wū 呜), Flying (fēi 飞), and Eating (shí 食).

hè xíng bù 鹤行步 Crane stepping. 1. Lifting the knee and foot up while stepping (both lifting and landing) with the feet flat. From Baguazhang. 2. In some branches of Baguazhang, circle-walking lifting the foot to knee height then heel kicking to chest height on the step.

hè yǎn quán 鹤眼拳 Crane eye fist, see fèng yǎn quán.

hè zhuā zhǎng 鹤爪掌 Crane palm, fingers bent, the palm slightly closed.

hè zuǐ 鹤嘴 Crane beak, a fist with the third finger slightly extended, supported by the thumb, used particularly for hitting pressure points. From Shaolinquan.

hè zuǐ chén zhǒu 鹤嘴沉肘 Crane Beak with Settled Elbows: shift to a right hanging stance and strike with the left hand to head height using a crane's beak, tucking the right crane's beak at the chest. Lean back a bit. The 72nd move of the tiger and crane routine. The same as huán hún bǎo hè on the other side.

hè zuǐ shǒu 鹤嘴手 Crane beak hand, a hand shape and a strike: finger tips together, wrist straight. From southern styles.

嘿 (rad.30) hēi   Colloquially, 'hey'. In martial arts, 'hei' is one of the specific sounds used to gain or express power in a technique. Commonly used in southern styles. The character is used to represent the sound, without any particular meaning.

黑 (rad.203) hēi   Black.

hēi gǒu zuān dāng 黑狗钻裆 Black Dog Drills into the Groin. 1. A rope dart technique: shoot out the dart then pull it back in again, catching it with the outside of the foot, then shoot it out again. 2. Squat with a slicing up palm into the groin. From Piguaquan.

hēi hǔ biān 黑虎鞭 Black tiger whip: a pointed iron bar, shorter than a staff, with notches along its length. From Piguaquan.

hēi hǔ chū dòng 黑虎出洞 Black Tiger Emerges from its Cave. Usually refers to an advancing straight-line punch, the exact configuration differs with styles. In Xingyiquan, a straight punch that specifically advances with an inch step (see also bēng quán, cūn bù).

hēi hǔ jiǎn wěi 黑虎剪尾 Black Tiger Cuts with its Tail: shuffle step to retreat and get around behind an adversary to throw a sidekick to the Mingmen point on the back.

hēi hǔ lán lù 黑虎拦路 Black Tiger Blocks the Road: step forward to a high empty stance, bringing a staff up to strike with the butt with a scooping action, tucking the left hand at the hip. From Baguazhang.

hēi hǔ pò dǎn 黑虎破胆 Black Tiger Destroys your Courage: step forward into a bow stance, brush aside with both hands, then drive the front elbow forward to strike.

hēi hǔ quán 黑虎拳 Heihuquan (black tiger fist). There are a few styles that go by this name, from Zhejiang, from Sichuan, and from Gansu provinces.

hēi hǔ sōu shān 黑虎搜山 Black Tiger Searches the Mountain: lift the left knee and hang a broadsword, continuing to finish with the blade edge up at the chest, the left hand on the spine of the blade. From Taijiquan.

hēi hǔ tāo xīn 黑虎掏心 Black Tiger Pulls out the Heart. 1. A driving step with a stamp combined with a strong punch. From Tongbeiquan. 2. A reverse punch with an upright fist. From Meishanquan.

hēi hǔ tōu dāng 黑虎偷裆 Black Tiger Steals the Groin, a leg grab throw: advance and squat, enveloping an adversary's knees or lower legs in your arms, pressing your head into his belly.

hēi hǔ yáo wěi 黑虎摇尾 Black Tiger Slashes its Tail: swing the arm upwards in an inverted slice up (thumb side down). From Xingyiquan.

hēi hǔ zhuā fǎ 黑虎抓法 Black Tiger Grabs: turn to a right reverse bow stance and push the palms forward in tiger claws, left on top, fingers up, right below, palm down. Lean into the technique but do not extend the arms. The 94th move of the tiger and crane routine.

hēi hǔ zhuā xīn 黑虎抓心 Black Tiger Grabs the Heart: step forward into a bow stance grab with the same side hand and pull back to the waist, pushing forward with the opposite hand. From Shaolinquan.

hēi hǔ zuò dòng 黑虎坐洞 Black Tiger Sits in its Den: sit in a low resting stance with the blade held out horizontally in front of the chest, left hand also at the hilt. From Qingping sword.

hēi lóng chū dòng 黑龙出洞 Black Dragon Emerges from its Cave: an advancing straight-line punch. From Xingyiquan.

hēi lóng rù dòng 黑龙入洞 Black Dragon Enters its Cave: a driving straight line punch. From Baguazhang.

hēi lóng qiāng 黑龙枪 Black Dragon spear: extend a spear and roll under it, finishing with a stab.

hēi xióng bēi guān 黑熊背冠 Black Bear Carries a Hat on its Back: circle-walking in the yinyang fish posture. From Baguazhang. See yīn yáng yú zhǎng.

hēi xióng chū dòng 黑熊出洞 Black Bear Comes out of its Cave: pivot and stamp, pulling down with both hands and leaning forward. From Shaolinquan.

hēi xióng dǎo gēn 黑熊倒根 Black Bear Topples the Root: stamp down on the instep or toes of an adversary.

hēi xióng fǎn bèi 黑熊反背 Black Bear Rolls Over. 1. In Baguazhang, to brace out with both arms above the knees, sometimes including a turn around. 2. In Taiji sword, a turning full swing chop with a sword.

hēi xióng jū gōng 黑熊鞠躬 Black Bear Takes a Bow: a kicking technique to deal with two adversaries. Drive a kick into one adversary's abdomen to knock him down, then approach the second in small steps, kicking to his shin.

hēi xióng pán zhǎng 黑熊盘掌 Black Bear Coils its Paws: shift back and forth in horse stance circling the hands in a flat figure eight to catch at the shoulder and reach out. From Wudangquan.

hēi xióng rù dòng 黑熊入洞 Black Bear Enters its Den: a kneeling stance with double ramming palms. From Piguaquan.

hēi xióng tàn bì 黑熊探臂 Black Bear Reaches out an Arm: extend one hand low to the front, fingers down in a lifting palm, keeping the other palm at the elbow. From Baguazhang. See also tuō zhǎng.

hēi xióng tàn zhǎng 黑熊探掌 Black Bear Reaches out a Paw. 1. In a raised knee stance, reach the hand in front. If in a horse stance, reach the arm to the side. From Baguazhang. See also tàn zhǎng. 2. In a raised knee stance, stab the hand out palm up. From Wudangquan.

hēi xióng yáo bǎng 黑熊摇膀 Black Bear Sways its Shoulders: shift back and forth in horse stance

H

with the hands pressing down near the knees, pushing more into one then the other, looking side to side. From Wudangquan.

hēi xióng yún zhǎng 黑熊云掌 Black Bear Brandishes its Paws: shift back and forth in horse stance circling the hands in a large figure eight to catch at the shoulder and down to the waist. From Wudangquan.

hēi xióng zhāng kǒu 黑熊张口 Black Bear Opens its Mouth: step into a reverse stance, lifting the same side hand and pressing forward with the rear hand, so that the palm heels are facing each other. From Wudangquan.

hēi yàn diǎn shuǐ 黑燕点水 Black Swallow Skims the Water: in smooth empty stance, dip a sword tip to an adversary's knee. From Qingping sword.

hēi yú juǎn cǎo 黑鱼卷草 Black Fish Rolls the Grass, a scissoring throw: usually used against a rear enveloping grab, roll to the front, side, or back, trapping and entwining an adversary's legs.

狠 (rad.94) hěn 1. Ruthless; relentless. Hard hearted. When used with negative connotation, means acting savagely, causing injury on purpose, without martial virtue. See also fā hěn. 2. Firm; resolute. When used with positive connotation, it means firm and unyielding in a fight.

恨 (rad.61) hèn 1. To resent; to hate. 2. To regret.

hèn bù 恨脚 A heavy stamp, see hèn jiǎo.

hèn jiǎo 恨脚 A heavy stamp. In Shaolinquan, a stamp to a full closed squat. Also called duō zi jiǎo, zhèn bù, zhèn jiǎo.

hèn jiǎo hǎi dǐ pào 恨脚海底炮 Stamp and Punch the Sea Bottom: stamp to a full closed squat, pounding the right fist into the left palm just in front of the knees.

哼 (rad.30) hēng A groan or snort. A strong exhalation with a closed mouth to set the body when throwing or striking. In martial arts, 'heng' is one of the specific sounds used to gain or express power in a technique, using the breath to assist the power. The use of this word originally comes from the temple doorway guardian Narayana, 'the snorter', who blows rays of energy from his nostrils. See also hā, jīn gāng.

hēng hā 哼哈 Using the 'hengha' breathing to protect the body and assist power output. See also hā.

恆 [恒] (rad.61) héng Permanent; lasting.

héng shān 恒山 Mount Heng, Heng Shan, in Shanxi province. The Northern of the five sacred mountains. See also běi yuè héng shān, wǔ yuè.

héng xīn 恒心 Perseverant. An expected character trait for martial artists.

横 (rad.75) héng Horizontal. transverse. Sideways. A horizontal, crossways or transverse movement or placement. Lateral movement.

héng bǎi sǎo tuǐ 横摆扫腿 A throwing roundhouse kick.

héng bēng 横崩 Horizontal snap punch: swing the fist, leading with the heel with the fist centre down, to the side at waist height. From Piguaquan.

héng bù 横步 Horizontal step: step out to the side.

héng cǎi 横踩 Crossing stamp step: bring the rear foot through and step forcefully down with the heel or sole, the foot turned out.

héng cǎi tuǐ 横踩腿 See héng cǎi.

héng cǎi tuǐ bō quán 横踩腿拨拳 Crossing stamp kick checking with the fists: bring the rear foot through and kick forcefully down with the heel or sole, the foot turned out. Simultaneously pull back to pull an adversary into the low kick.

héng chā 横叉 Side splits. Also called yī zì chā. In the category of the splits leg techniques, see also pī chā xìng tuǐ fǎ.

héng chā tiě mén shuān 横插铁门闩 Break the Bolt on the Iron Door Inserting a Crossbar: continuous swinging strikes. From Piguaquan.

héng chōng quán 横冲拳 Lateral punch: a blend of a swing and a snapped punch, out to the side. From Choylifut.

héng dài 横带 Lateral draw: catch and jerk an incoming attack in the same direction, sending an adversary off to the side.

héng dāng bù 横裆步 Side stance, crossways stance, open bow stance: a bow stance opened to the side to face square on, feet parallel, about three foot-lengths apart, squatting on one leg with the other extended, squatting thigh parallel to the ground, body facing directly forward (to the open side).

héng dāng bù liàng zhǎng 横裆步亮掌 Side stance flash palm: in a side stance, flash both palms or flash one and hook the hand that is over the extended leg. From Longfist.

héng dēng 横蹬 Transverse heel kick, kick forward with the foot opened and turned out.

héng dīng tuǐ 横钉腿 Crossing nail kick: with the foot dorsi-flexed, snap kick across the body, contacting with the outer edge of the sole of the foot. In the category of snap kicks, see qū shēn xìng tuǐ fǎ.

héng gǔ 横骨 Acupoint Henggu (pubic bone), KI11. At the abdomen, five *cun* below the navel, at the upper edge of the pubic bone, 0.5 *cun* lateral to the midline (on each side). From TCM.

héng hōng lì liàng 横轰力量 Horizontal throwing power, used in a flat wrestling throw.

héng jī bǎ 横击把 Lateral strike with the butt: strike with the base of a long weapon horizontally to either side.

héng jiǎo 横脚 A low sidekick.

héng jié 横截 A turned out intercepting foot to pressure and control an adversary's front leg.

héng jìn 横劲 Lateral power: power applied by a combination of the waist, back, and chest to apply a horizontal turning force and movement through the arms.

héng kāi bù 横开步 Sideways opening step: step to the side, sliding the foot slightly on the inside of the heel.

héng kòu quán 横扣拳 An inward hooking punch; a hook, a short, quick crossing punch.

héng kuà bù 横跨步 Step across, often involving a sideways action.

héng lán jìn zhǒu 横拦进肘 Crossing Armbar with the Elbow: extend and twist an adversary's arm and press the forearm to jam his elbow. From Baguazhang.

héng léi 横擂 Lateral pound, strike across with a backfist or outer edge of the fist.

héng lì 横力 Lateral strength: the force one is able to apply to right or left from the trunk, to beat straight attacks.

héng lì fáng shǒu 横力防守 Crossing defense: defending against a straight attack by changing its direction with a stepping aside with strong defensive technique such as an upper block, interception, scoop, or knock.

héng lì gù shǒu fǎ 横力固手法 Crossing set hands. See héng lì fáng shǒu.

héng liáng tuǐ 横梁腿 Swing the roof beam kick: a follow up to a missed kick, turn the body around to gain momentum and swing the other leg across at kidney height.

héng ná zhǎo 横拿爪 Crossing grab: bring the hand across strongly to seize an adversary's wrist, elbow, or upper arm.

héng pái bā bù 横排八步 Eight steps along: the ability to run eight steps along a wall. See fēi yán zǒu bì gōng.

héng pī 横劈 Crossways chop, cut across with the blade of the hand. Also called héng qiē.

héng piāo yù dài 横瓢玉带 Wave the Jade Belt back and forth: alternate stepping back in bow stance and forward in front cross stance, drawing the blade across low. From Qingping sword.

héng qiē 横切 See héng pī.

héng qiē zhǎng 横切掌 Crossing palm cuts: strike with both palms, with short power across the body. The palm in the direction you are going is palm down, power to the heel. The palm following is palm up, power also to the heel.

héng qiāng 横枪 Crossing spear: a sideways snap of a spear, using the power of the body.

héng quán 横拳 1. A swinging punch, a wide swinging or straight arm sweeping punch that strikes with the heel of the fist. 2. A crosscut, the crossing fist of Xingyiquan, cutting from inside to jam an attack. It is related to the earth element, see also tǔ. 3. A swing to the outside, straight on, hitting the outer edge of the fist. From Tongbeiquan. 4. An inside hooking punch. From Yiquan.

héng quán fā lì 横拳发力 A crossing punch. From Yiquan.

héng rào bù 横绕步 Crossing roundabout step:

H

Step the front foot diagonally forward, stepping the rear foot to follow, then step the front foot diagonally again. From Shaolinquan.

héng sǎo 横扫 Flat sweep. 1. A low strike with the forearm, using the thumb edge, palm down. From Choylifut. 2. A sweeping kick, see héng sǎo tuǐ.

héng sǎo qiān jūn 横扫千军 Sweep Aside an Army of a Thousand. 1. Hook out the foot and slice with the arm. 2. Step around with a large broadsword blade sweeping around at waist height. From Baguazhang. 3. Step to the side and slice a sword flat to the opposite side. From Qingping sword. 4. A back sweep kick. From Yangjia style.

héng sǎo tuǐ 横扫腿 Sweep across kick. 1. A throwing kick that cuts sharply across to the thigh of an adversary. 2. A sweeping kick where the kicking foot stays on the ground but the supporting leg does not do a full squat, and the hands do not touch the ground. Also called héng sǎo. In the category of sweep kicks, see also sǎo zhuàn xìng tuǐ fǎ.

héng sǎo xià lù 横扫下路 Sweep Aside the Low Route: spin and sweep with the butt of a long weapon at about knee height.

héng shēn 横身 Sideways dodge: step and turn sideways to an attack.

héng shǒu 横手 Sideways cut: stepping to avoid a direct attack, cut the arm across with power. From Chuojiao.

héng shǒu pào 横手炮 Sideways cutting pound: spin around two-seventy degrees, swinging the fist around hitting with the fist heel. From Tongbeiquan.

héng tī 横踢 Transverse kick, kick with the leg and foot turned out.

héng tuī bā mǎ 横推八马 Push Across Eight Horses: step around and push with a sword blade flat, palm down, left hand at the right wrist. From Baguazhang sword.

héng tuō 横脱 Crossing release: caught in a wrist grab, clench the fist and bend the elbow strongly, using power from the waist. At the same time, grab and pull with the other hand across.

héng wò 横握 Crossing grip: if right hand to right hand or wrist, a handshake grip. If left hand to right hand or wrist, a grip like on a tennis racquet.

héng xiàng jù lí 横向距离 Side to side distance. When describing foot placement, the width between the feet in a stance, as distinct from the length of the stance.

héng zhǎng 横掌 Sideways palm. 1. Crossways palm: fingers pointing across to the opposite side, palm down, wrist straight. A positional reference, separate from the direction of the strike. 2. As a technique: power applied to the palms in a horizontal turning plane or a crossing action. 3. To hit with a crossing palm: bring the hand up on the opposite side then swing across to its own side, getting power from the waist, hitting with the palm edge or back of hand, also called dǎ héng zhǎng.

héng zhé 横折 A strong lateral cut.

héng zhóu 横轴 Transverse, cross plane, divides the body into upper and lower parts.

héng zhǒu 横肘 Elbow cross: strike with the elbow, bent and flat, fist heart down. Strike to the head or ribs, stepping and turning into the strike.

héng zhuó 横啄 Sideways peck: to strike to the temple or ear with the fingers in a hooked hand.

héng zuǐ 横嘴 Sideways beak: strike to the side with the fingers in a hook hand.

衡 (rad.144) héng   1. Weighing apparatus. 2. To weigh. 3. To measure. 4. A surname.

héng shān 衡山 Mount Heng, Heng Shan, in Hunan. The Southern of the five sacred mountains. See also nán yuè héng shān, wǔ yuè.

轟 [轰] (rad.159) hōng   To rumble, to explode.

hōng dǎ chuí 轰打捶 Exploding hit: move into a bow stance, upper block, then punch in reverse stance. From Chuojiao.

洪 (rad.85) hóng   1. Big, vast. 2. Flood. 3. A surname. 4. One of the small family styles of Emei. See also sì xiǎo jiā.

hóng jiā quán 洪家拳 Hongjiaquan (Hong family fist), a southern style from Guangdong province, attributed to the Fujian province Shaolin temple during the Qing dynasty, at least the 1600s. Also called hóng quán.

hóng mén 洪门 The big gate of an adversary: between the arms, on the chest and abdomen. Also called dà mén.

hóng mén quán 洪门拳 Hongmenquan (big gate fist). 1. A style originally from Sichuan province. 2. A style from Hubei province, popular by the Ming dynasty.

hóng mén shā gùn 洪门杀棍 Hit the Big Gate with the pole: raise the pole strongly sweeping back behind, then strike downwards with a strong chop, then snap up. Essentially, a combination of chop and scoop. From Ziwu pole.

hóng quán 洪拳 Hongquan. See hóng jiā quán.

紅 [红] (rad.120) **hóng** Red.

hóng liǎn zhào jìng 红脸照镜 Red Face Looks in the Mirror: moving into a framing high block (jià) with a palm strike. From Tongbeiquan. Red face is usually a reference to General Guan, see guān gōng.

hóng quán 红拳 Hongquan (red fist). 1. A Longfist style from the west of China, popular in Shaanxi, Gansu, Ningxia provinces. Known as Western fist before the Qing dynasty. 2. The fourth routine of Chen Taijiquan.

hóng shā zhǎng 红砂掌 Red sand palm. See zhū shā zhǎng.

hóng yīng qiāng 红缨枪 Red tassel spear: a spear. This name is often used instead of just qiāng to differentiate the spear from a gun or rifle. See also qiāng.

肱 (rad.130) **hóng** 1. The arm. Normally pronounced gōng, usually pronounced hóng in the martial arts. Dà hóng is the upper arm, xiǎo hóng is the forearm. 2. Occasionally refers to the leg in the same manner: dà hóng being the thigh and xiǎo hóng being the lower leg.

hóng chuí 肱捶 A hammer punch, usually unfurling the arm rather than corkscrewing the punch. See also chuí.

鴻 [鸿] (rad.196) **hóng** A wild swan or wild goose. For more movement names using the actions or qualities of the wild swan, see also under fēi hóng, yún-.

hóng máo yù fēng 鸿毛遇风 Goose Feather in the Wind: withdraw to a high empty stance and slice a sword forward and up to intercept with a flat blade. From Qingping sword.

hóng mén yàn 鸿门宴 Hongmen feast: a feast at Hongmen at which a trap was set in an attempt to assassinate Liu Bang by Xiang Yu. In movement names, Hongmen feast refers to a trap.

hóng yàn chū qún 鸿雁出群 Wild Goose leaves the Flock. 1. Without moving the feet, turn fully around to look behind, placing the hands in a ready position, one up one down. A lift and twist to off balance an adversary. Also called gū yàn chū qún. 2. Circle-walking in this posture, see also tuī mò zhǎng. From Baguazhang.

hóng yàn shuāng fēi 鸿雁双飞 Wild Geese Fly as a Couple: Step forward, crossing the arms, then extending to a bow stance double strike forward and back to shoulder height. From Liuhebafa.

hóng yàn zhǎn chì 鸿雁展翅 Wild Goose Opens its Wings: in a horse stance, push out to the sides, fingers up, palms out. From Shaolinquan.

喉 (rad.30) **hóu** Larynx; throat. One of the main targets on the body.

hóu lóng 喉咙 The throat.

猴 (rad.94) **hóu** 1. Monkey. Monkeys are often referred to in martial arts, both in descriptive movement names and referring to their qualities of movement. For more movement names using the actions or qualities of the monkey, see also under xiǎo hóu, yuán-. 2. Monkey, as the ninth of the twelve animals from the Chinese zodiac, associated with a twelve year cycle symbolic of the earthly branches. The twelve animals make up a sixty year cycle when combined with the five phases. See also dì zhī, shēng xiào, wǔ xíng.

hóu gùn 猴棍 Monkey staff, a weapon of the Monkey style. A strong staff, enabling the player to hold balances on it.

hóu quán 猴拳 Houquan (monkey fist), an animal imitative style.

hóu tán tuǐ 猴弹腿 Monkey snap kick: a quick snapping kick, flicking out and back. From Chuojiao, one of its low basin kicks.

H

hóu xiāng 猴相 Monkey gaze: the eyes are bright and spirit full, and reactions quick. One of the body requirements of Xingyiquan.

hóu xíng 猴形 Monkey form: step around then move forward with a climbing kick and multiple soft palm strikes. From Xingyiquan.

hóu xíng bù 猴形步 Monkey stance: sitting in a half crouch on the rear leg, touch the toes of the front foot down lightly by the supporting foot.

hóu yǒu zòng shān zhī néng 猴有纵山之能 Monkeys have the ability to run over mountains. A quality sought in Xingyiquan's monkey form.

hóu zhǎng 猴掌 Monkey palm, a hand shape: elbow and wrist loosely bent, the fingers loosely bent and hanging down, tips not touching. From Chuojiao and Shaolinquan.

hóu zhuā quán 猴爪拳 Monkey claw fist, a hand shape: varies with style. In Xingyiquan, fingers loosely bent and touching, palm empty. In Shaolinquan, fingers together and bent and almost touching at the tips.

hóu zǐ pá gān 猴子爬杆 Monkey Clambers up the Pole: a step hop to move quickly forward with multiple soft palm strikes, raising the foot and knee to clamber onto an adversary. From Xingyiquan. Sometimes written gān 竿.

hóu zǐ pá gān 猴子爬竿 See hóu zi pá gān above.

hóu zǐ sāo jiǎo 猴子搔脚 Monkey Scratches its Foot: lift the knee and tuck in the foot near the buttocks, grabbing the heel with the same side hand, blocking up with the other hand. From Shaolinquan.

hóu zǐ tōu táo 猴子偷桃 Monkey Steals a Peach: turn to a left reverse bow stance and push the palms forward, right on top and pushing upwards, left below, pushing to the outer edge. The 93rd move of the tiger and crane routine.

hóu zǐ xún xué 猴子寻穴 Monkey Seeks the Den: step forward to bow stance and chop down strongly with the forward arm, slicing the other arm up behind and leaning into the strike. From Shaolinquan.

後 (rad.60) [后] (rad.27) **hòu** 1. Behind, rear, aft. 2. Afterwards, later.

hòu bǎi tuǐ 后摆腿 1. A back hook kick. 2. A spinning back kick. In the category of straight swinging kicks, see also zhí bǎi xìng tuǐ fǎ.

hòu bān tuǐ 后搬腿 Back partner stretch: Standing with the hands on a support, the partner lifts one leg up behind, keeping it straight.

hòu bào yāo 后抱腰 Hug from the back, around the waist: a grip in wrestling or to practice releases.

hòu biāo tuǐ 后摽腿 Back waving leg: a straight swing kick, leaning forward and turning to kick up. From Mizongquan. Also called hòu liāo tuǐ.

hòu chā tuǐ dī shì píng héng 后插腿低势平衡 Knee lock squat with extended leg balance: fully squat on one leg, fully extend the other leg through behind the supporting knee, horizontal to, but not touching, the ground.

hòu chuāi 后踹 Backwards thrust kick.

hòu cì jiàn 后刺剑 Backward pierce straight to the tip with a sword, forming a straight line with the arm and blade, either turning the body around or leaning backwards.

hòu dēng tuǐ 后蹬腿 Back thrust kick.

hòu diǎn bù 后点步 Back touch stance: standing with legs straight, withdraw and touch down the toes of one foot behind.

hòu diǎn gùn 后点棍 Back dab with a staff: stepping to a cross stance, swing a staff to the back to dab downwards with the tip of the staff.

hòu dǐng 后顶 Acupoint Houding (behind the peak), DU19. At the top of the head, 5.5 *cun* up from the rear hairline, three *cun* above acupoint Naohu, on the midline. From TCM.

hòu duàn 后段 Aft-section: the section of a multi sectioned weapon that usually stays closer to the body.

hòu guà tuǐ 后挂腿 Back hook kick, kicking with a bent leg to the rear, contacting with the heel. In the catagory of snap kicks, see qū shēn xìng tuǐ fǎ.

hòu gǔn fān 后滚翻 Back somersault.

hòu hàn 后汉 The Later Han dynasty (947-950) of the Five dynasties.

hòu jiāo chā bù 后交叉步 Back crossing step: starting from an open sparring stance, step the lead foot back, crossing behind the rear foot, stepping the rear foot immediately to take the original stance, futher back.

hòu jié dāo 后截刀 Intercept with a broadsword. See hòu jié jiàn.

hòu jié jiàn 后截剑 Intercept with a sword: a diagonal cut to the rear with the arm on a straight line with the blade, a flat blade, cutting with the fore-edge.

hòu jìn 后晋 The Later Jin dynasty (936-946) of the Five dynasties.

hòu jǐng 后颈 The back of the neck. See xiàng.

hòu kōng fān 后空翻 A back flip.

hòu kòng tuǐ 后控腿 Rear leg hold: standing holding the leg up to the rear without support.

hòu liáng 后梁 The Later Liang dynasty (907-923) of the Five dynasties.

hòu liǎng bēi bào 后两臂抱 Hug from the back, pinning both arms: a grip in wrestling or to practise releases.

hòu liāo tuǐ 后撩腿 Back swing kick, kicking up with the heel with the leg fairly straight. Sometimes called hòu biāo tuǐ, huí mǎ tán. In the category of straight swinging kicks, see also zhí bǎi xìng tuǐ fǎ.

hòu liāo yīn tuǐ 后撩阴腿 Back straight swing kick to groin level with the foot pointed. A common kick. From Chuojiao, one of its middle-basin kicks, where it is called xiē zi bèi zhuī.

hòu mén 后门 The Back Gate: the distance of an outstretched elbow.

hòu mén kǎn tuǐ 后门坎腿 Destroy the back door kick. See kòu tuǐ. See also mén kǎn tuǐ.

hòu miàn 后面 From behind: in illustrated books, the rear view, showing the posture from behind. See also cè miàn, zhèng miàn.

hòu nǎo 后脑 1. The back of the head. An easy target in real fighting, usually disallowed in Sanda. 2. General term for the acupoint Naohu, see nǎo hù.

hòu quān bù 后圈步 Back circling step: in a sparring stance, slightly lift the rear heel to reposition the foot, circling around without changing stance.

hòu ruǎn fān 后软翻 Back walkover: arch back to put the hands on the ground and walkover one leg, then the other to land behind.

hòu sǎo tuǐ 后扫腿 Back sweep kick: drop to the ground and sweep one leg around in the direction to contact with the heel. Sometimes called sì huán sǎo.

hòu shǎn 后闪 Backwards dodge: shift and lean back to avoid an attack without contact.

hòu shǒu 后手 The reactive fighter in a match, the one in the defensive position. Also called xià shǒu. See also xiān shǒu.

hòu shǒu fān 后手翻 Backflip, touching the hands down.

hòu suǒ hóu 后锁喉 Rear choke hold: grab your adversary from the back, wrapping one arm around his neck and controlling with your other hand. Press his head forward as you apply pressure to the neck. From Qinna.

hòu tán tuǐ 后弹腿 Back snap kick: a sharp, low kick to the rear with the heel.

hòu táng 后堂 The Later Tang dynasty (923-936) of the Five dynasties.

hòu tī bāo jiǎo zhí lì 后踢抱脚直立 Back held kick balance: supporting leg straight, swing the leg up behind the head, catch it, and stand motionless.

hòu tiān 后天 Post birth, post natal, acquired, refers to the effects of the world on a person after birth, environmental effects, nuture (vs nature).

hòu tiān bā guà 后天八卦 Acquired eight trigrams: using the trigram order of lí, kūn, duì, qián, kǎn, gèn, zhèn, xùn. See also xiān tiān bā guà.

hòu tiān qì 后天气 Refers to the *qi* that a person takes in, the air.

hòu tiǎo tuǐ 后挑退 Back raising kick: a straight swing kick behind the body kicking with the heel.

hòu tuì bù 后退步 Retreating step: push off the lead foot to step the rear foot backward, then follow in with the lead foot, to retreat without changing stance.

hòu tuì tiào bù 后退跳步 Retreating jump step: from a fighting stance, push off the front foot to jump back the rear foot, sliding the front foot back to arrive in the same stance.

hòu tuō zhǒu 后托肘 Lift the elbow from the rear:

H

when grabbed at the shoulder from the back, reach up to grab your adversary's hand and turn, twisting his arm over and placing it on your shoulder, pressing his elbow.

hòu xī 后溪 Acupoint Houxi (back ravine), SI3. At the hand, the outer edge near the little finger, where it protrudes when the hand is clenched, at the border of the darker and lighter skin (on each hand). From TCM.

hòu xià fā lì 后下发力 Release of power to the rear and downwards. From Yiquan.

hòu yā tuǐ 后压腿 Leg stretch to the rear: standing with foot supported behind the body to stretch the hip flexors.

hòu yǎng 后仰 1. To bend backwards. 2. Back arch: shift the lead foot back and lean back a bit to avoid an incoming high punch.

hòu yǎng yāo 后仰腰 Back arch kick: Arching the back, swing one leg to the rear and touch the hands to the foot over the head.

hòu zhāo 后招 Rear Provocation, Backward Beckoning, Maneuver to the Rear: raise one hand and lower the other to the sides, turning to the back, a throw, to defend from an attack coming from the back. From Chen Taijiquan.

hòu zhōu 后周 The Later Zhou dynasty (951-960) of the Five dynasties.

呼 嘑 [呼] (rad.30) hū To breathe out, exhale.

hū xī 呼吸 Breathing, breath.

壺 [壶] (rad.33) hú A pot, a jug; usually a pot bellied container with a small opening and a handle. Used for training lifting strength, specifically for leg throws.

弧 (rad.57) hú 1. A segment of a circle, arc. 2. A wooden bow.

hú xíng 弧形 A curve, an arc.

hú xíng bù 弧形步 Curving walk, curving run: walk quickly and smoothly along an arcing path. From Chaquan.

hú xíng lóng xíng héng 弧形龙形横 Circular Dragon form: stepping forward pressing with the arm down by the front knee, pull back and lift the same side foot to cut in, moving around in a full circle by about six steps. From Xingyiquan.

蝴 (rad.142) hú Butterfly, usually used in combination as hú dié.

hú dié chā 蝴蝶叉 Butterfly splits: side splits with the feet dorsi-flexed and tucked in, so the soles of the feet are on the ground.

hú dié chuān huā 蝴蝶穿花 Butterfly threads through the flowers. 1. Dodge an oncoming punch and thread the hand under your adversary's armpit across his chest, thread your other hand behind his leg. Press back with your upper arm and forward with your lower arm and move back so he falls forward. A quick throw used in Sanda. 2. A repeating double palm up stab, one hand fully extended, the other at its elbow. From Baguazhang.

hú dié jiǎo 蝴蝶脚 Butterfly kick: kick across the body with the edge of the foot at waist height with the foot dorsi-flexed and tucked in. From Chuojiao, one of its high-basin kicks.

hú dié shǒu 蝴蝶手 Butterfly hand technique: the parrying hand crosses the body and rotates out to block up above the head, the striking hand hits directly out from the waist. Also called yáo shān shǒu.

hú dié zhǎng 蝴蝶掌 Butterfly palms: circle the palms to alternate side to side, placing at the waist and shoulder, then shoulder and waist, preparing for a double palm strike.

虎 (rad.141) hǔ 1. A tiger. Often used in movement names, particularly those involving ferocity and/or a double attack. 2. Vigorous. 3. Tiger, as the third of the twelve animals from the Chinese zodiac, associated with a twelve year cycle symbolic of the earthly branches. The twelve animals make up a sixty year cycle when combined with the five phases. See also dì zhī, shēng xiào, wǔ xíng.

For more movement names using the actions or qualities of the tiger, see also under bái hǔ, dǎ-, dān-, dú-, è- (恶), è- (饿), èr-, fēi-, fú-, hēi-, lǎo-, měng-, shuāng-, wò-, xiǎo hēi-, yī péng-, yù-. For movement names fighting against tigers, see also under bào hǔ, bēi dān-, dǎ-, diào-, fú-, kuà-, pū-, zuò-. These, and shè hǔ, often occur within longer movement names as well.

hǔ bào 虎抱 Tiger hug or embrace: pounce forward with both arms acting together, circling then pushing forward and catching.

hǔ bào tóu 虎抱头 Tiger holds its head. 1. One of the body requirements of some branches of Xingyiquan: this refers to the way the tiger holds its head up with a fierce look in its eyes, and also the way it nestles its head in its paws before pouncing. 2. A knee strike with the forearms held up to protect the head (or have the hands up to grab an adversary's head). From Tongbeiquan. 3. A stance with the arms rounded, one arm up and the other across the chest, in fists. From Shaolinquan. 4. Holding a sword in a cradling position. Yang Taijiquan.

hǔ bào chū shān 虎豹出山 Tiger and Panther Come Out of the Mountain: an instep kick followed by landing forward with a double straight punch. From Chuojiao.

hǔ bào shuāng quán 虎豹双拳 Double Fists from Tiger and Panther: sit back to a right empty stance, pulling both fists back to the shoulders, elbows dropped and extended to the sides. The 109th move of the tiger and crane routine.

hǔ chēng 虎撑 Tiger brace: pounce forward with both arms acting together, shoving with the palms forward with the arms in a bracing posture.

hǔ cù shān 虎踧山 Tiger Presses the Mountain: double pounce, pull and low kick, then land forward into another double pounce.

hǔ hè qí míng 虎鹤齐鸣 Tiger and Crane Call Together: sit to left hanging stance and do a salutation with the left palm in front of the left shoulder and the right fist in front of the right shoulder. The 112th and last move of the tiger and crane routine.

hǔ hè shuāng xíng 虎鹤双形 The Tiger and Crane routine, a southern routine, written up as one hundred and twelve moves.

hǔ jié 虎截 Tiger intercept: pounce forward with both arms acting together, pulling to the side and cutting across the front simultaneously.

hǔ kǒu 虎口 Tiger's mouth: thumb web, the thumb to forefinger web of an open palm.

hǔ kǒu bá yá 虎口拔牙 Pull a Tooth from the Tiger's Mouth: on shaking hands, catch the adversary's thumb and press hard to take down.

hǔ lán 虎拦 Tiger trap: pounce forward with both arms acting together, the forearms vertical, cutting one forearm across the body and pulling to the side with the other.

hǔ mén 虎门 Tiger gate: the front of the torso, chest and arms, that uses the tiger-like power of enveloping and pulling in.

hǔ píng chái láng 虎凭豺狼 Tiger Leans against Jackals and Wolves: Step forward to a left reverse bow stance and push/grab through with the both hands in tiger claws, right forward and high, left near its elbow. Lean into the strike. The 64th move of the tiger and crane routine. The same as měng hǔ xià shān on the other side.

hǔ pū 虎扑 Tiger pounce. 1. A double dropping push or grab. 2. One of the body requirements of some branches of Xingyiquan: the hands go out as fiercely as a tiger charging out of its cave or pouncing on prey, also, the hands tend to stay together.

hǔ pū bà 虎扑把 Tiger pounce grab: pounce with both hands, then grab and pull back with a low turned kick. From Xingyiquan.

hǔ quán 虎拳 Huquan (tiger fist), a southern style from Fujian province.

hǔ rù qún yáng 虎入群羊 Tiger Enters the Flock of Sheep: a tripping takedown, wrap the arm around an adversary's neck from the front while stepping behind and controlling with the hip and leg. From Baguazhang and wrestling.

hǔ tiào 虎跳 Tiger leap: a cartwheel with the legs straight, landing the feet one at a time.

hǔ tóu gōu 虎头钩 Tiger head hooks: a type of double hook weapon. See shuāng gōu.

hǔ tóu chuí 虎头捶 Tiger head punch: in a bow stance, punch straight forward from the waist in a smooth stance. From Chuojiao.

hǔ tuō 虎托 Tiger carry, a low double strike with the palms facing up.

hǔ wěi jiǎo 虎尾脚 Tiger tail kick: a rear thrust kick, putting the hands on the ground and keeping the supporting leg fairly straight. From Mojiaquan.

hǔ wěi tuǐ 虎尾腿 Tiger tail kick. 1. Rear thrust

H

kick with the toes pointing down, hands may be on the ground. From southern styles. In the category of snap kicks, see also qū shēn xìng tuǐ fǎ. 2. A half circle turning slashing swing kick. Also called zhuǎn shēn biāo tuǐ.

hǔ wò fèng gé 虎卧凤阁 Tiger Lies in the Phoenix's Nest: do a sweeping slice into a low cut sitting stance. From Qingping sword.

hǔ xǐ liǎn 虎洗脸 Tiger Washes its Face: pull the hand in to smear in front of the face, also cutting with the forearm and dropping the elbow down. From Xingyiquan. Often also called māo xǐ liǎn. Sometimes called yuán hóu xǐ liǎn, zhé jié.

hǔ xíng 虎形 Tiger form: the standard form is a double push to the chest, catching and pulling down. There are alternate methods, all involving double palm strikes. From Xingyiquan.

hǔ xíng quán 虎形拳 Huxingquan (tiger form fist), a southern style.

hǔ yǎn bào chuí 虎眼豹搥 Tiger Looks and Panther Beats: shift forward to a bow stance and do a double punch to the ears. The 46th move of the tiger and crane routine.

hǔ yǒu pū shí zhī yǒng 虎有扑食之勇 Tigers have the ferocity of pouncing on prey. A quality sought in Xingyiquan's tiger form.

hǔ zhāng kǒu 虎张口 Tiger opens its mouth: allowing the outer edge of the foot to leave the ground in stances such as bow stance that should plant firmly into the ground. An error in most styles. Also called xiān zhǎng.

hǔ zhǎo 虎爪 Tiger claw, a hand shape: differs in different styles. In some, the five fingers are spread and bent at the second and third joints, the first joint stretched open to make the palm protrude. In some, all fingers are bent at all joints, thumb bent close to the thumb web.

互 (rad.7) hù   Mutual, each other.

hù jìn fǎ 互进法 Mutually advancing method: to release an attack and then counter.

hù zhòng 互中 Exchange with no points, mutual hits: sparring opponents make contact simultaneously, nullifying any points. Also applies when opponents wildly strike each other with no points given.

户 [户] (rad.63) hù   1. Door. 2. Household.

hù mén 户门 The point of the jaw. The sensitive point Humen, the doorway. One of seven painful gateways to attack that are related to midline acupoints. See also qī chōng mén.

護 (rad.149) [护] (rad.64) hù   To protect, guard, shield.

hù chǐ 护齿 Mouth guard.

hù dāng 护裆 Groin protector, cup, jock strap.

hù dāng bù 护裆步 Groin protecting stance: with the feet at shoulder width, turn the feet in and pull the knees together, so the knees are no more than ten centimetres apart. Tuck in the buttocks and keep the body straight. From southern styles.

hù jù 护具 Protective gear in general.

hù shān zǐ mén luó hàn shí bā shǒu 护山子门罗汉十八手 Guard the Mountain Gate Arhat Eighteen Hands: one of the Eighteen Arhat routines of Shaolinquan, written up as eighteen moves.

hù shēn zhǎng 护身掌 Guarding palm: protect the face or body, guarding with the palm.

hù shǒu 护手 Guard hand: palm on the centre line fingers up, either ready to push to the side, or the technique of pushing an incoming strike off the centre line. Considered a second line of defense in Wing Chun.

hù shǒu dāo 护手刀 Handguard broadsword: a curved, one edged blade with teeth on the spine and an added hand guard around the fingers.

hù shǒu pán 护手盘 Guard on a broadsword grip.

hù shǒu shuāng gōu 护手双钩 Hand protector double hooks: double hook with full hand guards at the grips. The guards have a sharpened edge and pointed tips, so can be used as blades as well. Usually used in pairs. See also shuāng gōu.

hù tóu 护头 A head protector, head guard.

hù tuǐ 护腿 A leg protector, shin guard.

hù xīn dāo 护心刀 Protect the Heart with a broadsword: sit in an empty stance, holding the blade near vertical in front of the body. From Chen Taijiquan.

hù xīn quán 护心拳 Protect the Heart. 1. A double strike or bracing with the forearms in front of the chest. From Chen Taijiquan. Also called shǒu tóu shì. 2. Multiple backfists in front of the chest.

hù xīn zhǎng 护心掌 Protect the Heart palm. See yīn yáng yú zhǎng.

hù xiōng 护胸 1. A chest protector, chest guard. 2. The technique of protecting the chest by turning sideways, covering with the hands or squeezing the elbows.

hù zhūn 护肫 Protect the throat: tuck the chin down to protect the throat.

花 蘤 [花] (rad.140) huā 1. A flower, blossom, bloom. 2. Something resembling a flower. 3. Patterned or coloured. 4. Flowery or fancy.

huā dāo 花刀 Flowery, useless, waving of a broadsword. This term can be used with any weapon, just substituting the weapon's name.

huā fǎ 花法 Flowery, useless moves.

huā jià 花架 See huā jià zi.

huā jià zǐ 花架子 Flowery postures or actions. Considered a fault in most styles, and likely to lead to defeat in a fight. As well as being useless, taking poses and showing off can create an opening for your adversary.

huā quán 花拳 Huaquan (flower fist). 1. A short fist style attributed to Gan Fengchi in Zhejiang province during the Qing dynasty. 2. A routine of Meishanquan, its only soft routine. Written up as forty-three moves. Also called nǔ rén quán.

huā zhàn qiāng 花战枪 Flowery battle spear: a routine of Yangjia style, written up as thirty-eight moves.

huā zǐ 花子 Flowers. See wǔ huā.

劃 [划] (rad.18) huá 1. To paddle, row. 2. Scratch, cut into the surface.

huá jìng 划劲 Scratching power, gliding energy: to issue power on contact with an adversary, with a rolling, almost rowing power.

huá ná fǎ 划拿法 Cutting grapple: cutting the hand up to avoid a grab, which places the hand ready to slide down an adversary's forearm for a grab. From wrestling.

華 [华] (rad.24) huá 1. Magnificent, splendid. 2. China, Cathay. Also refers to Chinese. 3. Pronounced huà, a surname. 4. One of the small family styles of Emei, see sì xiǎo jiā.

huá gài 华盖 Acupoint Huagai (florid canopy), RN20. At the chest, level with the first intercostal space, on the midline, where the sternum protrudes. From TCM. A good target. Best to hit with the head, shoulder, elbow, pouncing and shoving techniques.

huá quán 华拳 Huaquan (magnificent fist), a Longfist style from Shandong province, attributed to the Cai family, from the Tang dynasty. The style uses the best part, or cream, of the body, referring to the essence, qi, and spirit.

huá shān 华山 Mount Hua, Hua Shan, in Shaanxi province (the usual spelling in English for shǎn xī). The Western of the five sacred mountains. See also xī yuè huá shān, wǔ yuè.

huà tuō 华陀 Hua Tuo (140-208). A famous Chinese physician.

huà tuō bō jiàn 华陀拨剑 Hua Tuo Draws the Sword: drop the feet back, feet together, and stab forward with two fingers. From Shaolinquan.

huà tuō chā xiāng 华陀插香 Hua Tuo Plants the Incense Stick: a dabbing downward strike with two fingers extended. From Shaolinquan.

huà tuō jiā jǐ 华陀夹脊 Acupoint Huatuojiaji (Hua Tuo squeezes the spine), Ex B35. From the first thoracic vertebra to the fifth lumbar vertebra, on both sides, five fen apart, one at each vertebra. From TCM.

huà tuō jìng xiāng 华陀敬香 Hua Tuo Offers Incense: an upward scoop with both hands, with index fingers extended, the rear hand at the elbow of the front hand. From Shaolinquan.

滑 (rad.85) huá 1. Slippery, smooth. 2. Slip, slide. 3. Cunning, slippery. 4. A throwing technique in wrestling. 5. One of Ziranmen's nineteen main methods.

huá bǎ 滑把 Slide the grip. 1. With one hand firm, slide the other hand on the shaft of a long weapon. 2. Slide both hands on the shaft of a long weapon at the same time.

H

huá bù 滑步 Slide step: Sliding one foot then sliding the other to stay in the same stance, to shift position slightly. Commonly used in sparring and wrestling. Also called gē dēng bù.

huá chē 滑车 Sliding vehicle: a large frame with a pulley setup to use weights hanging from a rope. Used for training by pulling on the end of the rope, setting up angled downward pulls simulating wrestling throws.

huá cuò 滑锉 Sliding file: snap a sword tip down using the wrist with a sliding filing action downward.

huá dāo 滑刀 Slide a broadsword: to slide the blade along an adversary's weapon, until the guard is in close contact, preparing for a strong push.

huá gān 滑杆 Slide a pole: hold a pole and practice drawing back and forth, twisting and sliding the pole back and forth along a spot on a tree or on the vertically held pole of a partner. From Yiquan. Also called huá gān 竿.

huá gān 滑竿 Slide a pole: see huá gān 杆.

huá kuà 滑胯 To slide with the hips, changing place with a snap of the waist, in a tight clinch.

huá ròu mén 滑肉门 Acupoint Huaroumen (slippery flesh gate), ST24. At the abdomen, one *cun* above the navel, two *cun* from the midline (on each side). From TCM.

化 (rad.9) huà
1. To change, convert; reform. 2. As a body technique, to dissipate or neutralise. One of Ziranmen's nineteen main methods. 3. Neutralise. From Taijiquan, one of its four principles, see also sì zé.

huà jiě 化解 To dissolve or release the grip that an adversary has on you; to get out of a throw.

huà jìn 化劲 1. To dissolve or neutralize incoming power, engaging softly but with strong expanding power to deflect in many possible directions. 2. Transformed power, force dissolved into the body to become natural.

huà shēn 化身 Drop back, dissolving incoming power.

畫 [画] (rad.102) huà
1. To draw; paint. 2. Drawing, painting. 3. Stroke of a character.

huà dà dāo 画大刀 Stroke with a big cutter: start with the left hand palm up at the butt, raised above the head, and the right hand along the shaft, the tip angled downwards, the blade turned inwards. Step in, moving the tip as if drawing the character 之.

huà dì duàn shuǐ 画地断水 Draw a Line on the Ground to Cut off the Water: lift the right knee and a sword with the tip down, then land and step forward to a left bow stance, bring the sword in to the right ribs, then finally pierce straight on, on the apex of the triangle of the stance. From Qingping sword.

huà jǐ 画戟 A type of halberd: a long weapon with a long spear tip and a crescent hook blade near the tip.

huà méi shàng jià 画眉上架 Thrush Blocks Upwards: sit to an empty stance, pushing both hands forward, fingers up, palms facing each other, rear hand at the elbow of the front hand. From Shaolinquan.

懷 [怀] (rad.61) huái
1. Bosom. 2. To cradle to the bosom in the arms.

huái bào dān yú 怀抱单鱼 Cradle the Single Fish: a circle-walking posture, the arms forming one of the fishes of the *yinyang* fish. From Baguazhang. See tuī mò zhǎng.

huái bào jīn huā 怀抱金花 Cradle the Golden Flower: tuck the right knee up tight to the body and hold the hands together in front of the chest, right arm tucked inside the thigh, left elbow up behind, blade tip forward. From Qingping sword.

huái bào jīn shān 怀抱金山 Hug the Golden Mountain: tuck the right knee up to the body and hold the hands together in front of the belly, tilting the sword tip upwards. From Qingping sword.

huái bào pí pá 怀抱琵琶 Cradle the Pipa. 1. An arm bar, levering the arm across the body. From Baguazhang. 2. Hold a staff in front of the chest as if holding a pipa. From Baguazhang. 3. Circle-walking with the inside hand raised as if looking in a mirror, the outside hand at its elbow. From Baguazhang.

huái bào qī xīng 怀抱七星 Cradle the Seven Stars: a circle-walking posture, the inner hand at shoulder height and the outer hand at its elbow, both pointing to the centre of the circle. From

Baguazhang.

huái nèi chōu zhēn 怀内抽针 Draw a Needle from the Bosom: drop back to empty stance, chopping down with the front fist, guarding with the other palm. From Meishanquan.

huái zhōng bào yuè 怀中抱月 Cradle the Moon to the Bosom, often translated as Embrace the Moon. 1. Hold one or two arms in a cradling posture in front of the chest. A name in common in Baguazhang, Duanquan, Piguaquan, and Shaolinquan. 2. Pull the fists in to the belly, pulling an adversary in. From Baguazhang, one of its sixty-four hands. 3. In Taijiquan, cradle a broadsword in the left hand, when switching hands. 4. A double shoving palm. 5. In Shaolinquan, circle the hands to place the forearms crossed in front of the chest, left on the outside, fingers up, as a salutation. 6. In Qingping sword, sit in a low crossed stance with right arm tucked in, the left hand at the hilt, the blade held pointing forward ready to stab.

huái zhōng lǎn yuè 怀中揽月 Clasp the Moon to the Bosom: pull an adversary's arm across the chest, pulling his hand down to your hip and pressing his arm in reverse with the shoulder. From Baguazhang.

槐 (rad.75) **huái** A Chinese scholar tree, a Japanese pagoda tree.

huái chóng bù 槐虫步 Inchworm stepping: moving in the following foot towards the leading foot after it steps.

踝 (rad.157) **huái** The ankle.

huái guān jié 踝关节 The ankle joint.

驩 (rad.187) **huān** 1. A breed of horse. 2. A tractable, well behaved horse.

huān ěr dāo 驩耳刀 Horse ear blade: a long-handled broadsword with a heavy four sided blade. Used both for fighting and for digging through city walls.

環 [环] (rad.96) **huán** 1. Around; to surround. 2, A jade ring or bracelet. 3. A link.

huán shì 环视 To look around; to let the regard move around to take in the surroundings.

huán tiào 环跳 Acupoint Huantiao (jumping ring), GB30. At the buttocks, at the greater trochanter of the femur (on each side). From TCM. A crippling point, striking here may cause serious injury, see also cán xué. In internal styles, the *qi* connections between the legs and body core are through these points, which feel full when the body is properly aligned and relaxed.

huán zhōng 环中 Acupoint Huanzhong (ring centre). In the buttocks, one third of the way between the sacrococcygeal joint and the greater trochanter, midway between acupoints DU2 and GB30 (on each side). From TCM.

還 [还] (rad.162) **huán** 1. To go or come back, return. 2. To give back; repay.

huán hún bǎo hè 还魂饱鹤 Replete Crane Revived from the Dead. The 73rd move of the tiger and crane routine. The same as hè zuǐ chén bó, on the other side.

huán hún quán fǎ 还魂拳法 Revived from the Dead Punch: from a horse stance right punch, turn to a reverse bow stance and punch the left fist out, pulling the right back to the waist. The 56th move of the tiger and crane routine.

huán jī 还击 Riposte: fight back by counter attack, meeting head on, or returning fire.

huán jī zhāo fǎ 还击招法 Riposte: methods of fighting back that include immediate counter attack (see fǎn jī), meeting head on (see yíng jī), and returning fire (see huí jī).

緩 [缓] (rad.120) **huǎn** 1. Slow; gradual. 2. Unhurried. 3. To postpone.

huǎn màn 缓慢 Slow, slow-moving.

huǎn rú xuě 缓如雪 Unhurried like (drifting) snow. See huǎn rú yīng.

huǎn rú yīng 缓如鹰 Unhurried like an eagle (soaring): one of the twelve qualities of movement of Changquan, though these descriptors apply to many other styles. Also called huǎn rú xuě, màn rú yīng.

換 [换] (rad.64) **huàn** 1. To change for, exchange, trade. 2. Often used for continuous strikes alternating sides.

H

huàn bà 换把 Changeover grip. 1. To slide both hands on the shaft to switch their positions on a long weapon in order to change the technique or striking direction. 2. To switch hands on the grip of a short weapon.

huàn bà wǔ huā 换把舞花 Changeover grip flowers. 1. To twirl a weapon, bringing it behind the back with one hand, then continuing the flowers taking it in the other hand. 2. To walk forward, turning and switching hands with one handed flowers.

huàn bù 换步 Changeover step, switch step: trade places with the feet, front to back, maintaining the body position facing forward (will switch the forward hand). Also called cuò bù, diào bù, jiāo cuò bù.

huàn huā 换花 Changeover flowers: a wrist circle with a sword, a quick vertical circle with the grip held in a loose grip.

huàn jìn 换劲 Change the power: by attentive training, change one's ordinary direct strength and hard brute strength into a rounded, soft power.

huàn qiáo 换桥 Switch bridges, a forearm technique: keeping the forearms in contact with an adversary, switch one forearm that is in contact for the other forearm so that it can swing a block up. Also called xù qiáo.

huàn tī 换踢 Changeover kick: in hold, if your adversary avoids your sweep, sweep again from the other direction as soon as he replaces his foot to the ground. From wrestling.

huàn tiào bù 换跳步 Quick changeover, jumping switch step: trade places with feet with a jump.

huàn yāo 换腰 Changeover of the back: a quick change of direction, such as changing from a push to a pull, or from a hook to a trip.

huàn zhěn shǒu 换枕手 Switch the Pillow: get behind an adversary and slap the back of his head.

慌 (rad.61) **huāng** Hurried, flustered, confused. A teacher will say 'bié huāng' meaning 'don't rush the moves and make a mess of them.'

肓 (rad.130) **huāng** 1. The vitals: the region between the heart and the diaphragm. From TCM. 2. Spaces within the body, especially those around vital organs.

huāng mén 肓门 Acupoint Huangmen (huang area gate), BL51. At the back, level with the spinous process of the first lumbar vertebra, three *cun* lateral to the midline (on each side). From TCM.

huāng shū 肓俞 Acupoint Huangshu (huang area transport), KI16. At the abdomen, at the navel, 0.5 *cun* lateral to the midline (on each side). From TCM.

黄 (rad.201) **huáng** Yellow.

huáng fēng rù dòng 黄蜂入洞 Yellow Bee Enters the Nest: sweep the blade around then stab low. From Yang Taijiquan.

huáng lóng chū dòng 黄龙出洞 Yellow Dragon Emerges from its Den. 1. Stab out combined with a low kick, once each side. From Wudangquan. 2. A spear stab starting from crossed arms. See yè xià qiāng.

huáng lóng rù hǎi 黄龙入海 Yellow Dragon Enters the Sea: spin a full three-sixty degrees, swinging a sword to come back to the same place with a chop. From Wudang sword.

huáng lóng sān jiǎo shuǐ 黄龙三搅水 Yellow Dragon Agitates the Water thrice: move forward three times with a front cover crossing and striding steps, pulling back and bracing out with a single hand. From Chen Taijiquan.

huáng lóng wò dào 黄龙卧道 Yellow Dragon Lies in the Road: draw a sword back to finish with a lifting block up at the side of a transverse bow stance, left hand on the right forearm. From Qingping sword.

huáng lóng zhàn chǔ 黄龙占杵 Yellow Dragon Seizes the Pestle: curl a spear, tucking the right hand into the left armpit, closing the chest and crossing the left arm to the right shoulder. Then unroll and snap open, turning and laying the shaft along the chest.

huáng lóng zhuàn shēn 黄龙转身 Yellow Dragon Turns Around. 1. Step around, holding a sword angled across the body, then finishing with a stab. From Wudang sword. 2. Step around, slicing the arms downward vertically to the front, and up behind. From Liuhebafa.

huáng lóng zhuō bǎng 黄龙捉膀 Yellow Dragon Grasps the Shoulder: a full arm bar, twisting the shoulder joint. From Baguazhang.

huáng mǎng bǎi wěi 黄蟒摆尾 Yellow Python Swings its Tail: a throwing roundhouse kick from the rear leg.

huáng mǎng chū dòng 黄蟒出洞 Yellow Python Emerges from the Cave: a heel kick directly to the face from the rear leg.

huáng niú zhuǎn jiǎo 黄牛转角 Yellow Ox Turns its Horns: brandish the deerhorn blades around in front of the face then draw down to the side of the hip. From Baguazhang.

huáng yīng nié bó 黄莺捏嗦 Oriole Kneads the Neck. 1. A one handed choke and twist. Also called kǎ bō zi. 2. A initial grab to the throat, then a transfer to the other hand, to push or also grab.

huáng yīng shuāng bào zhuǎ 黄莺双抱爪 Oriole Grabs with both Feet: to attack with both hands simultaneously, and in the same direction. From Bajiquan, one of its eight main concepts, see also bā dà zhāo.

huáng yīng zhì suō 黄莺掷梭 Oriole Passes as Quickly as Throwing a Shuttle: a lifting interception with the blade, in a left bow stance, aligning the blade at an angle, shoulder height, angled a bit away. From Qingping sword.

huáng yīng ná tù 黄鹰拿兔 Yellow Eagle Grabs the Rabbit: drop and grab around an adversary's thighs, shoving your shoulder into his belly.

huáng yīng qiā bó 黄鹰掐嗦 Yellow Eagle Clutches the Neck: a one-handed choke. From Baguazhang.

huáng yīng shàng jià 黄鹰上架 Yellow Eagle Climbs the Frame: a wrist control, twisting both wrists of an adversary in opposite directions. From Baguazhang and Qinna.

晃 (rad.72) huǎng To dazzle; flash past.

huǎng shǒu 晃手 Flash the hand: a fake to the eyes to enable you to get in another technique while your adversary is thinking of protecting his eyes. Also called huǎng shǒu 慌手.

huǎng tóu tuī zhǒu 晃头推肘 Press the head on the elbow, in a wrestling clinch, such as grabbed by the collar, to release the grab.

huǎng xià qiāng shàng 晃下抢上 Fake low and attack high.

謊 [谎] (rad.149) huǎng Lie; falsehood.

huǎng shǒu 慌手 False hand: a feint to enable you get in another technique while your adversary is distracted. Also called huǎng shǒu 晃手.

揈 (rad.64) [晃] (rad.72) huàng 1. To rock, sway, shake. 2. To shake off an adversary or strike with shaking power.

huàng dòng 晃动 Sway, stand unsteadily. An error in most styles.

huàng shàng bāo tuǐ 晃上抱腿 Shake the upper body and go for a leg embrace throw, a combined fake and technique. From wrestling.

揮 [挥] (rad.64) huī 1. To wave; wield. 2. Wipe off. 3. Scatter; disperse.

huī dāo (jiàn) 挥刀(剑) To wield a broadsword (sword). Applies to any one handed weapon.

huī xiù qū fēng 挥袖驱蜂 Wave the Sleeves to Drive Away a Bee: circle the arms into a knee strike at the side. From Meishanquan.

huī zhū sǎo chén 挥麈扫尘 Brandish to Sweep the Dust: sweep a sword across to intercept in a low empty stance, sweeping the blade upwards at an angle. From Qingping sword.

迴 (rad.162) [回] (rad.31) huí To turn fully around, return, go back. Circle.

huí hé 回合 A round of a fight. See jú. Also called lún cì.

huí huán liàng zhǎng 回环亮掌 Winding flash palm: sweep the arms in full circles before taking the flash palm posture. From Huaquan. See also liàng zhǎng.

huí jī 回击 Return fire: to counter attack immediately following a defensive move. This is often a well-trained combination move that combines defense and attack.

huí lóng zhuǎn bì shì lì 回龙转臂试力 Dragon turning arms testing power: stand, stretch forward the hands, palms turning down. From Yiquan, one of its combat testing moves.

huí mǎ biān 回马鞭 Turn back the Horse Whip: with the right foot and the left arm up, bring a sword from the front to cut behind. From Wu

H

Taijiquan.

huí mǎ lì gōng 回马立功 Turn back the Horse to Win Honour: step through to a turned bow stance, swinging a sword from in front to line up with the extended leg with a hooking scoop. From Qingping sword.

huí mǎ qiāng 回马枪 Turn back the Horse Spear. 1. A back thrust, not necessarily with a spear. 2 Curl and stab a spear with the right hand tucked into the left armpit, the shaft along the extended left arm. Also called chán qiāng fǎn zhā.

huí mǎ quán 回马拳 Turn the horse punch. See fān shēn jí rù.

huí mǎ sháo 回马杓 Turn back the Horse to Scoop: step into a horse stance, nestling into an adversary, then turn smoothly for a takedown to the side.

huí mǎ tán 回马弹 Turn back the Horse Kick: a swing kick to the rear with the heel, the body leaning forward. From southern styles. Normally called hòu liāo tuǐ.

huí mǎ yī qiāng 回马一枪 Turn back the Horse with a Spear. From running away (see huí shēn xíng bù), jump up to turn and stab back. From Shaolinquan.

huí mǎ yín qiāng 回马银枪 Turn back the Horse with a Silver Spear: step across, turning the waist to strike out directly behind with the tip of a staff. From Baguazhang.

huí sǎo jīn huā 回扫金花 Turn around to Sweep the Golden Flower: from a crossed sit stance, step the left foot out to the side into a drop stance and sweep a sword across to align with the extended right leg. From Qingping sword.

huí shēn 回身 Return, turn back: turn around one-eighty degrees, stepping around in place. Also called diào shēn.

huí shēn pī dāo 回身劈刀 Turn back and chop: turn and chop a broadsword in a big swinging action to cut behind the body.

huí shēn tuō 回身脱 Turning release, an escape: change the direction of an adversary's grab by turning, thus releasing his grip.

huí shēn xíng bù 回身行步 Turned walk: holding a long weapon extended to the rear, looking at it, walk away a number of steps. In Shaolinquan, this stepping uses one-inch power, pressing into the ground then snapping up, as if kicking sand in someone's eyes.

huí shēn zhǎng 回身掌 Turning Change: one of the eight mother palms, usually involving repeated turning back. From Baguazhang.

huí shǒu zài chuí 回首载捶 Look Back to Plant a Punch: in a bow stance, block up in front and punch behind, turning to look behind (the punching arm is the same side as the forward leg). From Shaolinquan.

huí tóu wàng yuè 回头望月 Look Back to Gaze at the Moon. 1. With the arms extended to the sides at shoulder height, palms up, turn back and roll over the palms, lowering the rear palm to hip height. From Baguazhang. 2. Go to a full sit stance, cutting up behind with the sword rolled over. From Yangjia sword.

喙 (rad.30) **huì** 1. Beak; snout; mouth. 2. Often used for techniques that use the finger tips of a hooked hand or straight finger strike.

huì zhǎng 喙掌 Beak palm: an outward block with the forearms combined with a quick poke with the finger tips. From southern styles.

會 (rad.73) [会] (rad.9) **huì** 1. To meet. To assemble. 2. Meeting. 3. Association. 4. To be able to. Be good at. 5. Be sure to.

huì yáng 会阳 Acupoint Huiyang (meeting of yang), BL35. At the sacrum, just at the coccyx, 0.5 *cun* lateral to the midline (on each side). From TCM.

huì yīn 会阴 Acupoint Huiyin (meeting of yin), RN1. For men, between the anus and the scrotum. For women, between the anus and the pelvic diaphragm. From TCM. This is an easy target but should not be hit too hard, as causes extreme pain and could cause death. Colloquially also called hǎi dǐ.

huì zōng 会宗 Acupoint Huizong (convergence and gathering), SJ7. At the forearm, on the outside, three *cun* up from the wrist crease, just to the outside of acupoint Zhigou, on the edge of the ulna (on each arm). From TCM.

混 (rad.85) **hún** Used with the same meaning as 渾 hún. Pronounced hùn, to mix; confuse; pass for; turbid; muddy.

hún hé shì gé dòu 混合式格斗 Mixed martial arts, MMA, see zōng hé gé dòu. Also called hún hé shì wǔ shù, zōng hé bó jī.

hún hé shì wǔ shù 混合式武术 Mixed martial arts, MMA, see zōng hé gé dòu. Also called hún hé shì gé dòu, zōng hé bó jī.

hún yuán chuí 混元锤 Primordial punch: a straight driving punch with the other hand covering the forearm. From Xingyiquan. Also called jīn jī shí mǐ. See also bēng quán. The characters 浑 and 混 are both used for hún.

hún yuán dǎo qì gōng 混元导气功 Primordial *qi* leading training, an internal robustness training method: standing with the feet apart, place the arms in front of the chest, turning the palms inwards and outwards, or raising and lowering the hands in coordination with deep and relaxed breathing.

hún yuán yī qì 混元一气 Primordial One *Qi*: Standing with the feet together, hands at the sides. From Wudangquan.

渾 [浑] (rad.85) hún   1. Muddy, turbid. 2. Foolish. 3. Unsophisticated.

hún shēn 浑身 The entire body.

hún shuǐ mō yú 浑水摸鱼 Muddy the Water to Catch the Fish. The 20th of the Thirty-six Stratagems of Warfare, which apply to many situations.

hún yuán 浑元 Primordial, mixed essence, the time before heaven and earth began. Refers to the chaos before things were separated and organized. The characters hún 浑 and hún 混 are both used for hún yuán with the same meaning.

hún yuán zhuāng 浑元桩 Primordial stance training. 1. Standing in an open stance with arms settled down. 2. A stance sitting holding the arms rounded in front of the chest. The training cleanses the turbid elements in the body and brings out the latent abilities of its original nature. The stance is used by many styles to clear the mind and spirit, regulate breathing, and release excess tension in the body. 3. To stand in this posture and search for a feeling of power moving forwards and backwards within the body. This is a combat stance training. From Yiquan.

魂 (rad.194) hún   1. Ethereal soul. 2. Mood, spirit. 3. National spirit. 4. Associated with the Liver, and with the character attribute of balanced courage.

hún lǐng 魂灵 The soul.

hún mén 魂门 1. Acupoint Hunmen (gate of the ethereal soul), BL47. At the back, level with the depression below the spinous process of the tenth thoracic vertebra, three *cun* lateral to the midline (on each side). From TCM. 2. Colloquial term for the groin. One of seven painful gateways to attack that are related to midline acupoints. See also qī chōng mén.

hún pò 魂魄 The soul.

掍 (rad.64) hùn   1. The edging of a dress, hem. 2. Martial meaning is to strike with the blade of the hand.

hùn shǒu 掍手 An edging strike, a strike with the edge of the hand.

hùn shǒu ér lòu shǒu 掍手而漏手 If an adversary blocks your attack with a cut with the blade of his hand, control and do a reaching rolled punch. From Tanglangquan, one of its twelve soft counters, see also shí èr róu.

劐 (rad.18) huō   1. To slit or cut with a knife. 2. To hoe.

huō shǒu 劐手 Destroying hand: turned uppercut, a scooping punch or throw with the elbow bent, fist eye up.

huō tiǎo 劐挑 A body-hugging scoop with the arm or a long weapon.

攉 (rad.64) huō   1. The original, practical, meaning is to shovel to transfer something from one place to another. 2. To scull; a low dragging action that brings a long weapon through from behind.

huō tiǎo 攉挑 A dragging scoop with a long weapon, starting low behind, finishing high across.

耠 (rad.127) huō   To hoe, to plough: an upward punch, coming from below.

H

豁 (rad.150) **huō** 1. To slit; break; crack. Breach (a dam). 2. An action with the arm or a weapon that resembles getting into a fissure and opening it up. 3. A takedown that slides the back of the hand to an adversary (usually the side of the knee) and presses in the opposite direction of the upper hand.

huō bì tuō wàn 豁臂脱腕 Breaching wrist release: lift the forearm and press the elbow forward to release a one handed wrist grab. From wrestling.

huō dǎ 豁打 Breaching hit: a straight arm strike up with the fist eye up. From Bajiquan.

huō ná fǎ 豁拿法 Breaching hold: a strong, heavy pin, using the back of the hand. From wrestling.

huō tiǎo 豁挑 Breaching scoop: a tight scooping action with the forearm, keeping the upper arm close to the body.

活 (rad.85) **huó** 1. To live; to be alive. 2. Active, lively. 3. Movable, mobile, flexible.

huó bà 活把 Mobile grip: changing the positioning of the hands on a long weapon as necessary, according to the situation. The opposite of sǐ bà.

huó bà lán qiāng 活把拦枪 Mobile outer trap with a spear. See dà bà lán qiāng.

huó bà ná qiāng 活把拿枪 Mobile inner trap with a spear: clockwise circle with press down, bringing the base of the spear from the right shoulder (after a large outer trap) down to the waist. The spear tip draws a large half circle, between head and hip height. The left hand slides along the shaft. Also called dà bà ná qiāng.

huó bēi (or bì) gōng 活臂功 Arm mobility exercises, include stretching and moving.

huó bù 活步 Mobile step. 1. To slightly lift one foot, bring it to the other foot without touching down, then replace it in its original position. 2. To lift a foot and replace it.

huó bù tuī shǒu 活步推手 1. Random moving step pushing hands. From Taijiquan. 2. May be used for push hands stepping with set patterns.

huó dòng xìng dǎ fǎ 活动性打法 Mobile striking practice: varying the angle of attack on one or multiple punching or kicking bags.

huó jià zǐ 活架子 Moving frame: practicing a routine stance to stance, moving quickly and smoothly between the stances. From Baguazhang.

huó kuà gōng 活胯功 Hip mobility exercises, include stretching and moving.

huó jiān gōng 活肩功 Shoulder mobility exercises, include stretching and moving.

huó jìn 活劲 Flexible power, lively power: the ability to change with the situation when issuing power, the ability to rebound or adjust direction or amount. See also sǐ lì.

huó jìn bù 活进步 Moving step advancing: first advance the front foot forward a half-step, then immediately step the rear foot through forward.

huó yāo gōng 活腰功 Waist mobility exercises, include stretching and moving.

火 (rad.86) **huǒ** 1. Fire. 2. Fire, as one of the five elemental phases. Fire relates to the internal organ of the heart, to the sensing organ of the tongue, to the tissue of the blood vessels, and to the season of summer. Its *yang* expression is burning wood, and its *yin* is lamp flame. See also wǔ xíng. 3. Fire as one of the five phases techniques of Xingyiquan. The mindset of fire is fully committed, defensive moves charge in to cut off the attack, and attacking moves charge in with no thought of failure or return. See also pào quán. 4. One of the six *qi* of nature, an excessive dry heat that might occur in spring, summer, or fall. See also liù qì.

huǒ sēng kǎn chái 火僧砍柴 Angry Monk Cuts Firewood: take a staff with both hands at the tip and chop directly down to foot height with the butt. From Shaolinquan staff.

huǒ chā 火叉 Fire fork: a long handled, two tined fork with flat blades bent back in reverse hooks.

huǒ gùn 火棍 Fire staff: a Shaolinquan short staff routine, written up as twelve moves. The staff is thirteen hand grips long.

huǒ jī 火机 Opportunity (in a fight), the instant of opportunity.

huǒ lì 火力 Fire power. Originally in the military sense, but also used for a person's fighting skills and power.

huǒ pào chōng tiān 火炮冲天 Cannon Shoots to

the Sky. 1. Raise an adversary's arm to enable a fast, charging, straight punch to the body. From Baguazhang. 2. A raised knee stance with an uppercut on the same side arm. From Wudangquan.

huǒ shén fēn jīn 火神分金 God of Fire Parts Metal: step forward into an empty stance and circle the front fist or palm down to chop strongly. From Shaolinquan.

攉 (rad.64) [获] (rad.140) huò   1. To trap, to snare. 2. To catch, to seize.

huò shèng 获胜 To win (a competition or fight).

huò shǒu 获手 The rear guard hand: the palm or fist held at the elbow of the forward hand in an on guard position.

huò xīn quán 获心拳 Seize the heart: a double punch to the chest.

J

基 (rad.32) jī   1. Base, foundation. 2. An origin. 3. On the basis of.

jī běn 基本 Basic, fundamental.

jī běn dòng zuò 基本动作 Basic techniques, basic movements.

jī běn gōng 基本功 Basic skills, basic abilities.

jī chǔ 基础 Foundation, base; basics; underlying.

擊 (rad.64) [击] (rad.17) jī   To strike, to hit. To strike as if hitting a large bell.

jī bù 击步 Hitting step, skip step: push off the lead foot and jump forward, the rear foot tapping the lead foot in the air, then land the rear foot first. Often used to develop momentum for jump kicks.

jī dǎ lèi 击打类 Striking methods, the category of methods that include striking with any part of the body.

jī dǎ shā dài 击打沙带 Heavy bag training.

jī dǎ shǒu bǎ 击打手靶 Training by punching a small hand held target.

jī dà dāo 击大刀 Striking cut with a big cutter: with the right hand near the blade, palm down, cutting edge down, press down strongly, putting power into the shaft to press down with both the shaft and the blade.

jī dì chuí 击地捶 Pummel the Ground: a low punching action to the ground, a take-down or a follow through to an adversary on the ground. From Chen Taijiquan.

jī gǔ pào 击鼓炮 Bombard the Drum: a repeating, building one-two punch to the head. From Chen Taijiquan.

jī gùn 击棍 Strike with a staff: hit to either side with the tip or butt, with the shaft horizontal.

jī jiàn 击剑 Strike with the final few inches of a sword blade, striking strongly from the wrist, using either a dabbing action or a snapping action. The action may be done in any direction. See also bēng, diǎn.

jī sān quán 击三拳 Three quick punches: three punches in succession with the same fist, using the other hand to cover and scoop. From Chaquan and Fanzi.

jī shuǐ chōng yuè 击水冲月 Hit the Water to Charge the Moon: step back to hit a right bow stance, stabbing a sword forward. From Qingping sword.

jī xiǎng tuǐ fǎ 击响腿法 See jī xiǎng xìng tuǐ fǎ.

jī xiǎng xìng tuǐ fǎ 击响性腿法 Slap kicks: the category of kicks that involve slapping the foot. Also called jī xiǎng tuǐ fǎ. See for example, bǎi lián pāi jiǎo, dān pāi jiǎo, lǐ hé pāi jiǎo, xié pāi jiǎo.

jī xiǎng wài bǎi tuǐ 击响外摆腿 Outside crescent slap kick: an outside crescent kick contacting with the hand or hands to make a sharp sound.

jī zhǎng 击掌 A palm strike. 1. A straight pushing strike. 2. To clap the hands together.

jī zhǒu 击肘 An elbow strike: strike the elbow into the palm.

激 (rad.85) jī   To dash; to surge. As footwork, to surge in on an adversary.

箕 (rad.118) jī   A winnowing basket, a sieve.

jī mén 箕门 Acupoint Jimen (winnower gate), SP11. At the thigh, on the vastus medialis muscle, six *cun* above acupoint SP10, in line to SP12 (on each leg). From TCM.

肌 (rad.130) jī   Muscle, muscles; flesh.

jī ròu 肌肉 Muscle, muscles.

雞 (rad.172) [鸡] (rad.196) jī   1. A chicken, chickens; rooster. Often used in movement names, both for their fighting spirit and for the positioning of the legs. For more movement names using the actions or qualities of the chicken or rooster, see also under hán jī, jīn-, jǐn-, yě-. 2. Rooster, as the tenth of the twelve animals from the Chinese zodiac, associated with a twelve year cycle symbolic of the earthly branches. See also dì zhī, shēng xiào, wǔ xíng.

J

jī bù shì 鸡步式 Chicken stance: a high empty stance, front foot touching the toes down lightly.

jī dāo lián 鸡刀镰 Chicken blade sickle, Rooster sickle: a traditional weapon, a double-edged straight sword about eighty centimetres long with a double hooked tip that resembles a beak and a cockscomb. From Xinyiquan. Also called yōng huā yāo zi.

jī dēng tuǐ 鸡蹬腿 Chicken thrusts its legs, a combination kick: first an inch kick to an adversary's shin, then just on landing, a forward thrust kick with the other foot.

jī tuǐ 鸡腿 Chicken legs, a stepping pattern: the legs are neither overextended nor over flexed, the crotch is tucked in with the legs tight together, the feet grip the ground steadily, and pass close by each other when stepping. One of the requirements of Xingyiquan.

jī xíng 鸡形 Chicken form of Xingyiquan, involving a number of actions done in the way a chicken fights, combining soft moves with hard hits.

jī xíng bù 鸡形步 Chicken form stance or stepping. 1. A one legged stance, with the unweighted foot held dorsi-flexed midway at the shin or at the ankle. 2. Circle-walking with a specific method of lifting the rear leg, flicking the heel up behind. From Baguazhang.

jī xíng sì bǎ 鸡形四把 Chicken form Four Grips: a Xingyiquan routine, written up as fifteen moves.

jī yǒu zhēng dòu zhī xìng 鸡有争斗之性 Chickens have the instinct for fighting. A quality sought in Xingyiquan's chicken form.

jī zuǐ 鸡咀 Chicken beak: a fist with the third finger fully extended, the index and thumb together supporting it midway, the other fingers tightly clenched. Used particularly for striking pressure points. From Shaolinquan.

急 (rad.61) **jí** 1. Quick; quickly. 2. Urgent. Anxious.

jí dāo 急刀 Quick broadsword: to go to meet an adversary's weapon before his attack arrives.

jí jìn 急劲 Quick, urging power. From Tongbeiquan, one of its nine types of power, see also jiǔ gōng jìn.

jí jiù 急救 First aid; give first aid; give emergency treatment.

jí jiù yào xiāng 急救药箱 First aid kit.

jí jiù zhàn 急救站 First aid station.

jí mài 急脉 Acupoint Jimai (urgent pulse), LR12. At the groin, outside acupoint Qichong where the large artery is evident, 2.5 *cun* lateral to the midline (on each side). From TCM.

jí sān chuí 急三捶 Three Urgent Hits: three hits in quick succession, low, low, and high. From Chen Taijiquan.

極 [极] (rad.75) **jí** 1. Extreme, utmost point. 2. Pole (north, south). 3. Extremely.

jí diǎn 极点 The limit, 'the wall': the point in a fight when you reach the limit of your endurance, lacking breath and power. Usually this is a temporary phase, and can be got through by husbanding your forces for a while, going on the defensive.

jí quán 极泉 Acupoint Jiquan (highest spring), HT1. In the centre of the armpit, at the entrance of the major artery (on each side). From TCM. This is a good target to strike or grab, as an accurate strike can cause pain or numbness to that entire side of the body. It should not be hit too hard, as that may induce a heart attack.

疾 (rad.104) **jí** 1. Swift; quick. 2. Vigorous: a combination of speed, ferocity, and relentlessness (this term is often used with this meaning in Xingyiquan). 3. Disease. 4. To detest.

jí bù 疾步 Quick step, gallop. 1. To push off the rear foot to drive the lead foot forward, then quickly driving the rear foot forward. The feet stay close to the ground and make no sound. Also called zhèng jí bù. 2. Essentially the same as #1, but first stepping the rear foot in beside the lead foot.

jí zòng bù 疾纵步 Quick lengthwise step, similar to the quick step (see jí bù above), with more emphasis on moving forward a good distance.

鈒 (rad.167) **jí** A short pike, a short spear.

集 (rad.172) **jí** To assemble; to collect; to gather together.

jí tǐ 集体 Collective. See jí tǐ xiàng mu.

jí tǐ xiàng mǔ 集体项目 The group event in Taolu competition.

己 (rad.49) jǐ
1. Oneself, self. 2. The sixth of the ten Celestial Stems, used in combination with the twelve Terrestrial Branches to designate years, months, days, and hours. See also dì zhī, tiān gān. 3. Sixth in a list when listing using the celestial stems, equivalent to F in English when listing alphabetically.

jǐ chǒu 己丑 The years 2009, 1949, and so on, for sixty year cycles.

jǐ hài 己亥 The years 2019, 1959, and so on, for sixty year cycles.

jǐ mǎo 己卯 The years 1999, 1939, and so on, for sixty year cycles.

jǐ sì 己巳 The years 1989, 1929, and so on, for sixty year cycles.

jǐ wèi 己未 The years 1979, 1919, and so on, for sixty year cycles.

jǐ yǒu 己酉 The years 1969, 1909, and so on, for sixty year cycles.

戟 (rad.62) jǐ
A crescent headed spear: a long weapon with a long wooden handle, a long (may be wavy) spear tip, and one or two curved crescent blades attached just behind the tip. Sometimes translated as a halberd, but that is usually a guān dāo.

擠 [挤] (rad.64) jǐ
1. To press with the arms or trunk, crowding an adversary as he moves backwards. 2. To jostle; to push with the elbows. 3. To squeeze, to wring, to crowd an adversary. 4. To pressure the torso with the arm for a takedown with no strike. From Bajiquan, one of its ten major techniques, see also shí dà jī fǎ.

jǐ dǎ 挤打 Pressing hit. 1. Press with the rear palm assisting on the front horizontal forearm. 2. Crowd an adversary with the body as he moves backwards.

jǐ jìn 挤劲 The power and skill used in performing a press or squeeze. 1. The power and skill used to push forward with the forearm, assisting with the rear hand. 2. The power and skill used to crowd an adversary with the body as he moves backwards.

jǐ shǒu 挤手 Press: double armed press with forearms together.

jǐ zhǎng 挤掌 Press or squeeze: press with the rear palm on the front horizontal forearm. Also called hé zi zhǎng.

脊 (rad.130) jǐ
Spine, backbone.

jǐ zhōng 脊中 Acupoint Jizhong (spinal centre), DU6. At the back, below the spinous process of the eleventh thoracic vertebra, on the midline. From TCM.

jǐ zhù 脊柱 The spine, the backbone.

忌 (rad.61) jì
1. To fear; dread. 2. To avoid, abstain from.

jì fǔ 忌俯 Avoid bowing. Bowing the head down or bowing the back ruins the efficacy of techniques. From Baguazhang.

jì ná 忌拿 Avoid grabbing. Once you've grabbed someone your hands are also fixed. From Baguazhang.

jì yǎn 忌仰 Avoid arching back. In most internal styles at least, arching the back or puffing up the chest ruins the efficacy of techniques by preventing one from settling into the *dantian*. From Baguazhang.

jì zhàn 忌站 Avoid standing still. 1. Keep moving during a fight. 2. Train by walking rather than by standing. From Baguazhang.

技 (rad.64) jì
1. Skill, skills, ability, talent. 2. A trick.

jì fǎ 技法 1. Skill and technique. 2. Application of skills and techniques in fighting or defense.

jì jī 技击 Fighting, sparring.

jì jī zuò yòng 技击作用 Practical fighting or defense application.

jì jī zhuāng 技击桩 Fighting stance, a seventy-thirty stance used to train power with shifting weight movement. From Yiquan.

jì qiǎo 技巧 Skillful use of techniques.

jì yì 技艺 Skills, the artistry of skills.

J

計 [计] (rad.149) jì   To count; compute; calculate.

jì shí yuán 计时员 Timekeeper (at a competition).

記 [记] (rad.149) jì   1. To remember; commit to memory. 2. To record; note down.

jì lù yuán 记录员 Record keeper (at a competition).

夾 (rad.37,9) [夹] (rad.37) jiā   1. To be wedged between; to squeeze, to press. 2. In Xingyiquan, to squeeze the legs together like scissors.

jiā gùn 夹棍 To squeeze a staff: tuck a staff into the armpit, striking to the side.

jiā huā dà dāo 夹花大刀 Squeezed flowers with a big cutter: with the right hand near the blade and the left along the shaft, bring the blade over as a chop, tucking the left hand into the armpit. Continue to circle the blade vertically to left and right of the body, tucking each time.

jiā jí 夹脊 Extraordinary acupoints Jiaji (squeezing the spine), EX-B2. Seventeen (sometimes listed as 24 points on each side) pairs of points down the spine, from the depression under the first thoracic vertebra to that of the fifth lumbar vertebra, 0.5 *cun* on either side of the spine. From TCM.

jiā jí guān 夹脊关 Spine squeezing pass. See jiā jí . See also #2 of sān guān.

jiā jiǎn bù 夹剪步 Scissors stance: a cross stance with the front foot straight and the rear foot turned out, both feet flat on the ground, squatting to level, weight more to the rear leg.

jiā jiǎn tuǐ 夹剪腿 Scissors leg. 1. Trap an adversary with a scissors action of the legs around his body. 2. A scissoring action stepping pattern.

jiā jǐng chán tuǐ fān 夹颈缠腿翻 Neck squeeze coil the leg throw: get in close to squeeze around your adversary's neck, getting your leg into his groin area to then coil your leg around his leg, throwing with the leverage between his neck and leg. This type of throw is also called chán, or chán má huā in general.

jiā jǐng guò bèi 夹颈过背 Neck squeeze over the back throw: get in close to squeeze around your adversary's neck, getting your hip onto his body, with your knees bent. Extend your knees, lower your head, and push with your back to throw him over your back.

jiā jǐng tiǎo 夹颈挑 Neck squeeze scooping throw. See tiào gòu zi.

jiā mǎ 夹马 Squeezing horse: an empty stance with the empty leg fairly extended and the knees together.

jiā ná fǎ 夹拿法 Squeezing grappling hold. 1. Squeeze an adversary between both arms. Applies to anywhere, but especially the neck. 2. Using the arms, grab the rear collar and squeeze the throat with the arm. From wrestling.

jiā zhǒu 夹肘 Trap with the elbows, press inwards with both elbows to control.

挾 [挟] (rad.64) jiā   1. To press from both sides. 2. To carry something under one's arm. 3. Pronounced xié, to hold under the arm.

jiā bēi (bì) 挟臂 Arm pins, wrestling techniques involving arm locks.

jiā jǐng 挟颈 Head lock with choke: wrap the arm around an adversary's neck from behind or from the front, pushing his head into your body. From wrestling.

jiā yāo 挟腰 Waist lock: when on the ground, wrap your legs around an adversary's waist.

jiā zhǒu 挟肘 Elbow press: hook inwards with the elbow. A single press is to press to the neck or lock the arm of an adversary with one arm. A double press is to tuck the elbows together in front of the chest as a protective move.

頰 [颊] (rad.181) jiá   The cheeks.

jiá chē 颊车 Acupoint Jiache (cheek cart), ST6. At the jaw, at the prominence created when the teeth clench (on each side). From TCM. A sensitive point, striking it may induce unconsciousness. Extreme care should be taken, as a too hard a strike may cause death.

假 (rad.9) jiǎ   False, fake.

jiǎ chī bù diān 假痴不癫 Fake Dim-wittedness while Remaining Stable. The twenty-seventh of the Thirty-six Stratagems of Warfare, which apply to many situations.

jiǎ dào fá guó 假道伐虢 Obtain Safe Passage to Conquer the Kingdom of Guo. Use an ally to attack a common enemy. The twenty-fourth of the Thirty-six Stratagems of Warfare, which apply to many situations.

jiǎ dòng zuò 假动作 A fake, a feint.

jiǎ jìn gōng 假进攻 A fake attack, feint.

jiǎ quán 假拳 A feinted punch.

jiǎ shǒu 假手 A feint with the hand or hands. Also called yòu shǒu.

甲 (rad.102) jiǎ 1. The first of the ten Celestial Stems, used in combination with the twelve Terrestrial Branches to designate years, months, days, and hours. See also dì zhī, tiān gān. 2. First in a list when listing using the celestial stems, equivalent to A in English when listing alphabetically.

jiǎ chén 甲辰 The years 1964, 1904 and so on, for sixty year cycles.

jiǎ shēn 甲申 The years 2004, 1944 and so on, for sixty year cycles.

jiǎ wǔ 甲午 The years 2014, 1954, and so on, for sixty year cycles.

jiǎ yín 甲寅 The years 1974, 1914, and so on, for sixty year cycles.

jiǎ xū 甲戌 The years 1994, 1934, and so on, for sixty year cycles.

jiǎ zǐ 甲子 The years 1984, 1924, and so on, for sixty year cycles.

jiǎ zǔ 甲组 The A level athletes at a competition, if the competition is organized by skill level.

jiǎ zǔ cháng (nán) quán 甲级长（南）拳 Advanced, or A level standardised long (southern) fist routine.

jiǎ zǔ dāo (jiàn) shù 甲级刀(剑)术 Advanced, or A level standardised broadsword (straight sword) routine.

jiǎ zǔ gùn (qiāng) shù 甲级棍(枪)术 Advanced, or A level standardised staff (spear) routine.

jiǎ zǔ tào lù 甲组套路 The advanced, or A level standardised routines of the compulsory wushu routines.

胛 (rad.130) jiǎ Shoulder blade, scapula.

jiǎ gǔ 胛骨 Shoulder blade, scapula.

架 (rad.75) jià 1. Frame; rack (therefore a posture, the framework of a technique). 2. A shelf. 3. To put up; erect. 4. To support; prop up (therefore, to circle upwards to an upper framing or bracing block).

jià biān 架鞭 Blocking whip. See jià qiáo.

jià chòng quán 架冲拳 Combined upper framing block and straight punch. Also called jià dǎ.

jià dǎ 架打 1. See jià chòng quán. 2. The upper framing block combined with a different hit such as a scoop.

jià dāo 架刀 Framing block up with a broadsword: edge horizontal, facing up above the head. When blocking up with the blade, usually place the left hand on its spine to support it.

jià dà dāo 架大刀 Framing block up with a big cutter: with a two-handed grip, block up above the head with the shaft near horizontal.

jià gé 架格 To block or knock upward or aside an attack.

jià gòu 架构 Frame and construction; alignment and structure.

jià gùn 架棍 Framing block up with a staff. See jià qiāng.

jià jiàn 架剑 Framing block up with a sword: edge horizontal, facing up above the head. When blocking with a sword, the blade is higher than the head, but not directly above it.

jià lán tī 架拦踢 Propping trap kick: in clinch, keep close hold of your adversary, curl the leg around his leg and use leverage for a takedown. From wrestling.

jià liáng hóng chuí 架梁肱捶 Support the Roof Beam and punch: an upper block with a straight punch, in an open horse stance facing the attack. From Chen Taijiquan.

jià liáng jiǎo 架梁脚 Support the Roof Beam Foot: lift with the ankle on an adversary's shin while doing a throw. From wrestling.

jià liáng tī 架梁踢 Support the Roof Beam kick: pull your adversary strongly in towards you while advancing one foot in close to his foot, then twist and throw, kicking the outside of his ankle. From wrestling.

jià liáng zhǒu 架梁肘 Support the Bridge with the Elbow: contact the adversary's punching arm, pushing his arm up. Catch his forearm with the other elbow, pressing down. From Xingyiquan.

jià pū dāo 架扑刀 Framing block up with a horse cutter: with a two-handed grip, block up above the head with the right hand at the head so that the blade is behind the head, the shaft angled to the front.

jià qiāng 架枪 Framing block up with a spear: lift the shaft above the head, shaft near horizontal. This can be done with both hands, the left hand along the shaft, or single handed with only the right hand at the butt.

jià qiáo 架桥 Framing block up with the bridge, a forearm technique: block up above the head with the forearm, with the elbow bent. Also called jià biān.

jià quán 架拳 Framing block up above the head with a closed fist, circle the arm upward and finish with fist heart out. Tends to be more extended than the elbow framing block, see also jià zhǒu.

jià shì 架式 1. Posture, stance. 2. Ready stance. Term used more in northern styles.

jià zhǒu 架肘 Framing block up above the head with the elbow bent, circle the arm upward and finish with fist heart out. May also be used as an elbow strike.

jià zǐ 架子 Posture, stance.

尖 (rad.42) **jiān, jiānr** 1. The tip of a sharp weapon. 2. The tip of a sharp or pointed part of the body.

jiān quán 尖拳 Pointed fist, a hand shape: fingers tightly clenched, with the thumb tucked behind the first segment of the middle finger so that its second joint is extended. From Tongbeiquan.

肩 (rad.130) **jiān** Shoulder, shoulders.

jiān bǎng 肩膀 The shoulder girdle: the shoulder, inclusive of the whole shoulder structure, including the upper arm.

jiān bèi dāo 肩背刀 Shoulder a broadsword: raise the right arm to the side with the spine of the blade along the arm and back.

jiān dǐng 肩鼎 A shoulder stand.

jiān fā lì 肩发力 1. A shoulder strike. 2. Training for shoulder strikes. From Yiquan.

jiān fǎ 肩法 Shoulder techniques.

jiān gōng 肩功 1. Shoulder training exercises. 2. The trained result of the exercises on the shoulders.

jiān guān jié 肩关节 The shoulder joint.

jiān jiǎ gǔ 肩胛骨 Scapula, shoulder blade.

jiān jiǎ tí jī 肩胛提肌 Levator scapula muscle: a muscle in the neck that runs from the topmost vertebrae to the inner top of the scapula (shoulder blade). It helps to elevate and rotate the scapula.

jiān jǐng (xué) 肩井（穴）Acupoint Jianjing (shoulder well), GB21. At the shoulder, halfway between the spine and the high point of the acromio-clavicular articulation, at the level of the depression below the seventh cervical vertebra (on each side). From TCM. A sensitive point, pressure here can cause numbness in the shoulder. A sudden, strong strike may shock the brain and induce unconsciousness. In internal styles, awareness is placed on settling these points and keeping them level with each other, to enable power to transfer smoothly through the shoulders.

jiān liáo 肩髎 Acupoint Jianliao (shoulder bone-hole), SJ14. At the shoulder, just under and behind the acromion edge of the scapula (on each side). From TCM.0

jiān rú fēng lún 肩如风轮 The shoulders must be like windmills. From Tongbeiquan, one of its requirements.

jiān shàng bèi gùn 肩上背棍 Shoulder a staff: raise the right arm to the side with the shaft along the arm and back. The left hand may also grasp the staff.

jiān tiǎo piān dān 肩挑扁担 Carry a Pole over the Shoulder: grab your adversary's wrist, step behind his front leg, extend his arm, turn his arm palm facing out and place it over your shoulder, applying pressure to his arm and controlling with the other arm. From Qinna.

jiān wài shū 肩外俞 Acupoint Jianwaishu (outer

shoulder transport), SI14. At the back, below the spinous process of the first thoracic vertebra, three *cun* lateral to the midline (on each side). From TCM.

jiān wō 肩窝 Shoulder den: the depression seen at the shoulder joint, made when the arm is raised and the shoulder is set down.

jiān yào cuī zhǒu ér zhǒu bù nì jiān 肩要催肘而肘不逆肩 Power should flow from shoulders to elbows, the elbows should not run counter to the shoulders. A principle in Xingyiquan.

jiān yú kuà hé 肩与胯合 The shoulders harmonize, or work together with, the hips. One of the six harmonies. See also liù hé.

jiān yú 肩髃 Acupoint Jianyu (shoulder bone), LI15. At the shoulder, just below the acromio-clavicular articulation, found in the depression that the deltoid makes on the top of the shoulder when the arm is held out (on each side). From TCM. A sensitive point, pressure here can cause the arm to go numb.

jiān zhēn 肩贞 Acupoint Jianzhen (true shoulder), SI9. Behind the upper arm, near the armpit, one *cun* above and behind the armpit crease (on each arm). From TCM.

jiān zhōng shū 肩中俞 Acupoint Jianzhongshu (central shoulder transport), SI15. At the back, below the spinous process of the seventh cervical vertebra, two *cun* lateral to the midline (on each side). From TCM.

jiān zǔ dǎng 肩阻挡 Shoulder block: In on guard position, lift the shoulder to cover up, bending the elbow, turning and closing in the body as well. Used when there is not enough time for a more effective technique.

間 [间] (rad.169) jiān Between, among. Also pronounced jiàn.

jiān jù 间距 The distance between two points. The space between two objects.

jiān shǐ 间使 Acupoint Jianshi (intermediary courier), PC5. At the forearm, on the inside, on line with acupoints Ximen and Daling, three *cun* up from the wrist crease, between the long tendons of the wrist flexors (on each arm). From TCM.

剪 (rad.18) jiǎn 1. Scissors, shears. 2. Crossing strikes or traps with both arms or legs, as if opening and closing scissors. 3. In Xingyiquan, footwork that tramples, thrusting forward from the rear leg, with pressure between the legs like scissors.

jiǎn bù 剪步 Scissors stance or step: one foot crosses in front of the other so that the knees are crossed, the front foot turned out.

jiǎn dà dāo 剪大刀 Scissors cut with a big cutter: with the right hand near the blade and the left along the shaft, bring the blade over as a chop, then immediately turn it and slice horizontally.

jiǎn dāo zhǐ 剪刀指 Scissors fingers, a hand shape. See shuāng zhǐ.

jiǎn qiáo 剪桥 Scissors bridges, a forearm technique: with the arms fairly straight, cross them quickly and strongly. From southern styles.

jiǎn sǎo 剪扫 Scissors sweep: drop to the ground and use a scissors action to sweep an adversary's legs.

jiǎn shǒu 剪手 Scissors hands: open the hands and then bring them in to chop, striking the ribs, throat, or eyes. From Shaolinquan. Also called jīn chā shǒu, shuāng yáng tà shǒu.

jiǎn shǒu tiǎo dǎ 剪手挑打 Scissors hands with a hidden raised kick.

jiǎn wàn huā dāo (jiàn) 剪腕花刀(剑) Wrist flowers, figure eight with broadsword (or sword): wrist cutting vertical circles with the blade slicing forwards and down, pivoting around the wrist.

jiǎn zhǒu 剪肘 Scissor elbows. See jīn jiǎn jiǎo bì.

jiǎn zǐ gǔ bù 剪子股步 Scissors stance. See xiē bù.

檢 [检] (rad.75) jiǎn To check; inspect; examine.

jiǎn lù 检录 Roll call: call the list of contestants in a competition.

jiǎn lù yuán 检录员 The whip at a competition: the person responsible for assembling the athletes and bringing them on carpet.

jiǎn lù zhǎng 检录长 The chief whip at a competition.

J

jiǎn lù zǔ 检录组 The officiating team responsible for roll call and getting athletes on at a competition.

簡 [简] (rad.118) jiǎn Simple, brief, simplified.

jiǎn huà 简化 Simplified. As in simplified routines, developed to spread the martial arts by introducing more people to easier routines.

翦 (rad.124) jiǎn Scissors, shears. Clippers. To cut.

jiǎn shí xún jīn 翦石寻金 Cut Stone to Seek Gold: step forward with a spreading block with a sword, setting into horse stance, cutting across at shoulder height out to the side. Avoids a hacking attack and slides in to cut an adversary's wrist. From Qingping sword.

鐗 [锏] (rad.167) jiǎn A ruler, mace: a short iron weapon shaped like a ruler, with a rounded grip and a slightly rounded tip. Can also have a square shaped blade. Varies from sixty-five to eighty centimetres. Often translated as mace or baton. Usually a pair, see also shuāng jiǎn.

劍 剱 劔 [剑] (rad.18) jiàn A straight sword; a sword with a straight, relatively thin, double edged blade. The standard length is to the top of the ear when held down at the side of the body. Traditional styles often use longer swords.

jiàn bǎ 剑把 Sword grip, handle: includes the metal tip at the end, the grip, and the guard.

jiàn fēng 剑锋 The peak of a sword blade, the final few inches of the blade, including the narrowing of the blade to the tip.

jiàn jí 剑脊 Spine of a straight sword blade: the slightly raised middle on the flat of the blade.

jiàn jiānr 剑尖 The tip of a sword blade.

jiàn jué 剑诀 Sword-fingers, see jiàn zhǐ zhǎng.

jiàn miàn 剑面 Face of a straight sword blade: the flat of the blade.

jiàn qiào 剑鞘 Scabbard, sheath, or case, for a sword.

jiàn rēnr 剑刃 The sharp edges of a straight sword blade.

jiàn rú fēi fèng 剑如飞凤 The straight sword is like a soaring phoenix. A martial saying. The blade should be smooth and graceful, and move too quickly to be blocked.

jiàn shēn 剑身 The body of a sword blade, the whole blade.

jiàn shǒu 剑首 Head of a sword: the tip of the grip, usually a metal cap.

jiàn shù 剑术 1. Straight sword skill. 2. Swordplay: a Taolu competition event, called Jianshu in English.

jiàn suì 剑穗 Sword tassel, made of silk or synthetic.

jiàn tǐng bù bù tǐng 剑停步不停 The stepping does not stop when the sword stops. A quality sought in Baguazhang's sword methods.

jiàn wěi 剑尾 Tail, or end, of a sword grip, usually the grip is wood and the end is a metal cap.

jiàn zhé yuán tóu 剑折鼋头 Sword Cuts the Turtle's Head: sit to horse stance and pull one arm above the head in a block with the fingers in sword fingers shape. Cut the other hand across to outside the knee as if it were a sword blade. From Wudangquan.

jiàn zhǐ zhǎng 剑指掌 Sword-fingers, a hand shape: index and middle fingers extended, other fingers bent and pressed by the thumb. Usually the left hand is maintained in this position when holding the sword in the right hand. Also called jiàn jué.

jiàn zǒu qīng 剑走青 The straight sword goes freshly. A martial saying. The sword, because of its light blade, should move easily and with intelligence without making heavy contact.

建 (rad.54) jiàn To build; construct. Establish.

jiàn lǐ 建里 Acupoint Jianli (interior strengthening), RN11. At the abdomen, three *cun* above the navel, on the midline. From TCM.

jiàn shēn 建身 To strengthen the body.

jiàn shēn zhuāng 建身桩 Stance training to strengthen the body and health, may be standing, sitting, or lying.

濺 [溅] (rad.85) **jiàn**   To splash; to spatter.

jiàn bù 溅步 Splashing step: jump the rear foot up to or past the front foot, jumping the front foot forwards as well, to land in the same configuration. From Shaolinquan.

箭 (rad.118) **jiàn**   An arrow, arrows.

jiàn bù 箭步 Arrow step. 1. From an empty stance, step the lead foot forward and push off it to jump forward. The rear foot also jumps through, then the lead foot lands forward. 2. From a horse stance, bring one foot in towards the other, push off with the other and jump forward, tapping the feet together in the air, and landing in the same stance. From Duanquan. Also called jī bù (though that usually refers to a more running step).

jiàn chuān bù 箭穿步 Threading Arrows stepping. See jiàn cuàn bù.

jiàn mǎ 箭马 Arrow stance. See gōng bù. Also called gōng dēng bù, gōng jiàn bù, qián gōng bù.

jiàn quán 箭拳 Arrow punch: a fast and hard punch crossing the body. From southern styles.

jiàn sì lí xián 箭似离弦 Like Arrows Leaving the Bowstring: a side heel kick simultaneous with a cut of the sword.

jiàn tán qiǎng shǒu 箭弹枪手 Arrow kick stealing hand: a jump front snap kick with a finger stab with the opposite hand, not slapping.

jiàn tán tuǐ 箭弹腿 Arrow kick. 1. A front snap kick. From Chuojiao. Usually called tán tuǐ. 2. A jump front snap kick. From Chuojiao and Shaolinquan, one of Chuojiao's high-basin kicks.

jiàn tóng 箭筒 A quiver, a carrying bag for arrows.

見 [见] (rad.147) **jiàn**   To see; to perceive; to observe. To visit.

jiàn fèng chā zhēn 见缝插针 Stick in a Pin Wherever There is Room: a straight stab forward, palm down. From Shaolinquan.

jiàn gāng ér huí shǒu 见刚而回手 See hard and counter: elicit a hard response to your attack, then control your adversary's blocking arm and attack again. From Tanglangquan, one of its twelve soft counters, see also shí èr róu.

jiàn shì 见识 Insight, developed through knowledge and experience; sense.

jiàn sǐ fǎn huó fǎ 见死反活法 Turn Certain Death into Life: counter attack techniques practiced in Shaolinquan.

jiàn zhāo fān 见招翻 Reverse incoming attacks, a routine of Tongbeiquan, written up as eighteen moves.

踐 [践] (rad.157) **jiàn**   To trample, tread on, walk on.

jiàn bù 践步 Trample. 1. A stance squatting on one leg and touching the toes down behind (similar to a T stance, but with the foot behind rather than beside). 2. A galloping step used in Xingyiquan: the front foot steps forward, the rear foot steps through and forward, then the rear foot does a follow step (combines jìn bù, shàng bù, and gēn bù).

jiàn cuàn bù 践窜步 Full gallop: the rear foot steps through and forward, the lead foot steps forward, the rear foot then drives to make the front foot step forward again, then the rear foot does a follow step. From Xingyiquan. Also called jiàn chuān bù.

jiàn quán 践拳 Galloping punch, a continuous barrage of at least two punches to the same place. Usually straight punches to the ribs.

踺 (rad.157) **jiàn**   1. A cartwheel, somersault. 2. Head-over-heels.

jiàn zǐ 踺子 Cartwheel, landing on both feet simultaneously.

間 [间] (rad.169) **jiàn**   1. A crevice. 2. A space in between. Also pronounced jiān.

僵 (rad.9) **jiāng**   1. Stiff; rigid. Tense. 2. Deadlocked.

jiāng jìn 僵劲 Musclebound power, stiff and tense use of power.

jiāng lì 僵力 Musclebound strength: poor coordination from the wrong muscles contracting at the wrong time, agonists and antagonists fighting against each other to cause movements to be stiff and incorrect.

J

江 (rad.85) jiāng   A river.

jiāng hú 江湖 The society of rivers and lakes: the brotherhood (and sisterhood) of martial artists who live in the margins of society.

將 [将] (rad.41) jiàng   1. A general or admiral. Commander-in-chief. 2. To command, to lead. When in combination, and with other meanings, often pronounced jiāng.

jiāng jūn 将军 A general or admiral. Often used in movement names.

jiāng jūn chū jiàn 将军出简 General Fires an Arrow: a straight punch. From Wing Chun.

jiāng jūn guà xuē 将军挂鞋 General Hangs up his Shoes (takes retirement), a one-two kick with the same leg to two adversaries who are facing you, first the closest, then to the next one.

jiāng jūn liàng jiàn 将军亮剑 General Flashes his Sword: lean into a bow stance and raise the rear hand straight up with sword fingers, stabbing the front hand in at the waist. From Shaolinquan.

jiāng jūn piàn mǎ 将军片马 General Mounts a Horse, an inside swinging kick to the torso, like mounting a horse. Can kick with the instep or shin to the head or torso.

jiāng tái 将台 General's platform, commander's platform: sensitive points either side of the larynx. Best attacked with a grasping grip.

降 (rad.170) jiàng   1. To fall, drop. 2. To lower, reduce, cut down. 3. Descending treatment of channels. From TCM. 4. Pronounced xiáng, to surrender or subdue.

交 (rad.8) jiāo   1. To hand over; deliver. 2. Intersect. 3. Mutual. 4. Association with.

jiāo chā bù 交叉步 Crossed stance: stand upright with the legs crossed, feet about a foot-length apart, weight towards the front leg. Similar to resting stance but higher and longer, see also xiē bù. From southern styles. Also called jīn chā bù.

jiāo chā shǒu 交叉手 Crossed hands: hold the hands upright in front of the chest with the wrists crossed.

jiāo cuò bù 交错步 Switchover step: trade places quickly with the feet, keeping them close to the ground. Make the turn with a snap of the hips. Also called cuò bù, diào bù, huàn bù.

jiāo jiǎo mǎ 交脚马 Feet crossed horse stance: Squatting on one leg with the other foot hooked behind the knee. From southern styles. Also called kòu bù, kòu tuǐ píng héng.

jiāo shǒu 交手 Cross hands: to make initial contact with an adversary. Also called jiē.

jiāo xìn 交信 Acupoint Jiaoxin (intersection reach), KI8. At the calf, on the inside, two *cun* above acupoint Taixi, 0.5 *cun* in front of acupoint Fuliu, just behind the line of the tibia (on each leg). From TCM.

教 (rad.66) jiāo   1. To teach. 2. Pronounced jiào, to teach; religion.

蛟 (rad.142) jiāo   A flood dragon, the dragon that invokes storms and floods. With this meaning, usually in combination as jiāo lóng.

jiāo lóng chū hǎi 蛟龙出海 Flood Dragon Charges out of the Sea: stand on one leg with the other held up in a turned out kick position. Turn the torso to bring the opposite hand at chest height over the lifted leg, palms turned in, in a hugging position. From Yiquan. Also called chēng tuǐ zhuāng.

jiāo lóng chū shuǐ 蛟龙出水 Flood Dragon Charges out of the Water: jump forward with both feet to land in a right bow stance, leaning into the leg to stab a sword strongly forward. From Qingping sword.

jiāo lóng fān shēn 蛟龙翻身 Flood Dragon Rolls Over: step forward with a cut with the deerhorn blades, then turn and roll to bring the blades over the head to cut in the other direction. From Baguazhang.

jiāo lóng rù hǎi 蛟龙入海 Flood Dragon Enters the Sea. 1. Drop into a drop stance, sending a sword out along the extended leg. From Wudang sword. 2. Lift an adversary's arm and step in to strike to his groin. From Baguazhang. 3. Drop a sword tip low, then snap the wrist to bring the tip up to head height, not moving the grip. From Baguazhang sword.

跤 (rad.157) **jiāo**   To stumble, fall.

jiāo jià 跤架 Wrestling setup postures.

jiāo kǒu 跤口 The sweet spot for a throw, proper position that allows a throw to work on the best lines and with the least effort. Also called dāng kǒu.

jiāo shǒu 跤手 A wrestler.

jiāo shù 跤术 Wrestling. Also called shuāi jiāo.

jiāo wō zǐ 跤窝子 A wrestling den, a traditional term for a training place.

jiāo yī 跤衣 A wrestling jacket. In Chinese wrestling, this is a short, thick, cotton jacket with short sleeves.

驕 [骄] (rad.187) **jiāo**   Proud; arrogant; conceited.

jiāo ào 骄傲 Arrogant, conceited.

剿 勦 (rad.18, 19) [剿] (rad.18) **jiǎo**   To destroy; extirpate; annihilate.

jiǎo shǒu kǎn zhǎng 剿手砍掌 Destroying hand hacking palm: enter with a strong attack and hack with the follow-up hand. From Tongbeiquan, one of its seven long range techniques.

攪 [搅] (rad.64) **jiǎo**   1. To stir up, agitate, mix. 2. To stir, circle the tip of a weapon with the pivot point at the forward hand on a long weapon, and at a midpoint of the blade on a short weapon. 3. Circle with the hand or forearms.

jiǎo tuǐ 搅腿 Stir the legs. See wū lóng jiǎo zhǔ.

絞 [绞] (rad.120) **jiǎo**   1. To stir, entangle. 2. To wind around, envelop.

jiǎo bǎ 绞把 Trap with the butt: entangle, circle, and trap with the base of a long weapon. The height is between shoulder and hip.

jiǎo bàng gōng 绞棒功 Stick rollups, a training drill: with a weight attached to a short stick by a rope, hold the stick straight out from the shoulders and roll the weight up and down, using the forearms and wrists. See also qiān jīn bàng, tuó bàng.

jiǎo bù 绞步 Stirring step. See cǎi tuǐ bù.

jiǎo dài 绞带 Trap and draw back.

jiǎo dāo 绞刀 Stir with a broadsword: draw a small circle with the tip, usually bracing the left hand on the blade spine.

jiǎo dà dāo 绞大刀 Entangle, stir with a big cutter: with the right hand near the blade and the left hand keeping the shaft tight to the body, draw a circle with the blade, first turning the edge to the right then down.

jiǎo gùn 绞棍 Stir with a staff. See jiǎo qiāng.

jiǎo jiǎn bù 绞剪步 Twisted scissors stance: half sit with the legs crossed, more weight on the front leg, body turned around towards the back.

jiǎo jiàn 绞剑 Stir with a sword, envelope: draw a small circle with the sword tip, then draw back slightly with the elbow.

jiǎo qiāng 绞枪 1. Stir, encircle with a spear: draw vertical circles with the tip or butt, in either direction, as if stirring something in a bowl that is facing you in the air. The height is between shoulder and hip. 2. The same action, but specifically in an anti-clockwise direction. In this sense, chán qiāng will be the same action in a clockwise direction.

jiǎo sī jìn 绞丝劲 Stirring silk power: a coiling, spiraling, circular power. From Tanglangquan.

jiǎo shǒu pào 绞手炮 Stirring Hands, a basic partner routine of Xingyiquan, written up as seven moves.

腳 [脚] (rad.130) **jiǎo**   1. Foot, feet. 2. Base. For more kicks named by 'foot' rather than 'leg', see also under bā jiǎo, bǎi lián pāi-, bàn-, bēng-, biè-, bǒ-, cā-, cǎi-, cè diǎn-, cè tī-, chā-, chōng-, chōu gēn-, chuài-, chuān huā-, chuān xīn-, chuō-, cì lèi-, cuò-, dān pāi-, dǎo-, dēng-, dēng tā-, diǎn-, diào-, dōu-, dú hǔ-, duò-, èr qǐ cǎi-, èr qǐ-, fēi yún duò zi-, fēn-, fēn mén yī-, fēn xīn-, fēng bǎi hé yè-, gāo zhuāng-, gōu dài-, gōu guà-, guà-, guà méi-, guǎn-, hèn-, héng-, hú dié-, hǔ wěi-, jià liáng-, juě zǐ-, lán mén-, lǐ gòu-, lǐ hé pāi-, lián huán fēi-, liāo yīn-, lèi shǒu pō-, lōu-, luò bù-, niǎn-, pāi-, pāo-, pō-, pū-, qiē-, qiè-, sháo-, shí zì cǎi-, shí zì-, shí zì pāi-, shuāng hèn-, shuāng zhèn-, shuāng zú zhèn-, téng kōng fēi-, téng kōng lián huán fēi-, téng

J

kōng shān-, téng kōng shuāng fēi-, téng kōng xié pāi-, téng kōng zhuàn shēn fēi-, tiào bù fēi-, tiào dàn pāi-, wài bǎi pāi-, wài gòu-, xī niú biè-, xī niú gōng-, xī niú zhèng-, xiǎo zhuàn-, xié pāi-, xuàn fēng-, yáo chē-, yuān yāng-, yuán bǎo-, zhèn-, zhèng-, zhuǎn tǐ fēi-, zhuàng-, zuān-, zuān zǐ-.

jiǎo bèi 脚背 The back of the foot. See jiǎo miàn.

jiǎo bǎ 脚靶 Kicking pad: a small hand-held pad used by a trainer for kicking practice. Usually refers to the type that has straps to slide onto the forearm.

jiǎo dǎ qī fēn 脚打七分 The feet are seventy percent (of success). This saying is used in styles that rely heavily on stepping, such as Baguazhang and Xingyiquan.

jiǎo fā lì 脚发力 A kick, and training for kicks. From Yiquan.

jiǎo gēn 脚跟 The heel of the foot.

jiǎo jiān 脚尖 The tip of the foot, the point of the foot.

jiǎo jiān bù 脚尖步 Walking on the tips of the toes (not just tiptoe, but on the ends of the toes). From Monkey style.

jiǎo miàn 脚面 The instep, the top of the foot. Also called jiǎo bèi.

jiǎo rú zuān 脚如钻 The feet are like drills. From Tongbeiquan, one of its requirements.

jiǎo wài cè zǔ jié 脚外侧阻截 Jam with the outer foot: lift your knee and jam an incoming kick with the outer edge of your foot, either to the hip joint, thigh, or shin of an adversary, depending on opportunity.

jiǎo xià wú gēn 脚下无根 The feet have no root: footwork and stances are unstable.

jiǎo xià yǒu gēn 脚下有根 The feet are well rooted; footwork and stances are stable.

jiǎo xīn 脚心 The palm of the foot, just behind the ball of the foot.

jiǎo yào wěn 脚要稳 The feet must be stable. Stability and balance are necessities in fighting.

jiǎo yí dòng 脚移动 Unwanted movement of foot or feet, an error in Taolu competition, indicates loss of balance.

jiǎo zhǎng 脚掌 The pad of the foot, or just behind the ball of the foot.

jiǎo zhǎng zǔ jié 脚掌阻截 To jam with the sole of the foot: jam with the foot to prevent an adversary from lifting his leg to kick.

jiǎo zhǐ 脚趾 The toe, toes.

jiǎo zhuāng 脚桩 Kicking post: a short wooden pole (less than a metre high) for low kicking techniques.

角 (rad.148) **jiǎo** 1. Corner. 2. Horn. 3. Pronounced jué, a role; to contend or wrestle.

jiǎo dù 角度 Angle. Usually require exact positioning and directional angles in routines practice. An essential element of fighting strategy.

jiǎo sūn 角孙 Acupoint Jiaosun (angle vertex), SJ20. At the side of the head, at the hairline above the apex of the ear (on each side of the head). From TCM.

教 (rad.66) **jiào** 1. To teach, instruct, guide. Also pronounced jiāo. 2. A religion.

jiào bù yán quán bì wāi, xué bù zhuān quán bì làn, liàn bù kǔ quán bì kōng 教不严拳必歪，学不专拳必滥，练不苦拳必空 If the teaching isn't strict the skills will be incorrect, if the studying isn't dedicated the skills will be false, if the training isn't bitter the skills will be empty. A martial saying.

jiào cái 教材 Teaching materials.

jiào liàn 教练 A coach, trainer. To coach.

jiào liàn yuán 教练员 A coach, trainer.

jiào tóu 教头 The head instructor at a club, the chief trainer.

jiāo xué 教学 To teach.

jiào zhàn 教战 To teach martial arts.

較 [较] (rad.159) **jiào** To compare; contrast.

jiào dòu 较斗 To spar, fight.

jiào liàng 较量 To test each others skills; have a sparring contest. Testing specifies that the fighters will not try to inflict serious injury.

接 (rad.64) **jiē** 1. To receive; to accept; to take with the hand. 2. To welcome. 3. To join, to connect. 4. To come close to, to make contact with. 5. In martial arts, often means to make initial contact with an adversary, also called jiāo shǒu.

jiē bì 接臂 Contact the arm: when an adversary has grabbed high, take his wrist in a reverse grip with your opposite arm and under his arm with your same side arm, pressing down. From wrestling.

jiē chù 接触 To contact.

jiē chù shì fáng shǒu 接触式防守 Contacting defense: any defensive move that involves making direct contact with an incoming attack.

jiē dān bǔ shuāng fǎ 接单补双法 Take a Single to Remedy a Double. To control one hand of an adversary holding a double handed weapon, thus rendering his other hand useless. From Baguazhang.

jiē shǒu 接手 Connecting the hands: the first receiving of an attack, give the first indication of the comparative abilities of the fighters.

jiē tuǐ gōu tī 接腿勾踢 Intercepting leg hooking kick: catch your adversary's leg as he kicks, and move in to hook kick his supporting leg for a takedown.

jiē tuǐ lōu tuǐ 接腿搂腿 Intercepting leg raking leg: catch your adversary's leg as he kicks, and hook behind his supporting leg while pushing on his chest for a takedown.

jiē tuǐ shàng tuō 接腿上托 Intercepting leg lift: catch your adversary's leg as he kicks, and lift it up for a takedown.

jiē tuǐ shuāi 接腿摔 Intercepting leg throw: catch your adversary's leg as he kicks, and pull to the side for a takedown.

jiē tuǐ shuāi fǎ 接腿摔法 The category of throws and takedowns that involve catching and using the kick of an adversary.

揭 (rad.64) **jiē** 1. To tear off; take off. 2. To uncover. To expose.

jiē dǐ 揭底 Expose the bottom: lift the rear heel in mud stepping. From Baguazhang, where it is considered an error.

jiē qiāng 揭枪 Expose with a spear: knock an attacking weapon back and up, preparing for a chop.

jiē tí gōng 揭蹄功 Exposing the Hooves training methods. See jiù dì shí bā gùn.

刦 刧 刼 劫 (rad.18, 19) [劫] (rad.19) **jié** 1. To rob, plunder. 2. To coerce; compel. 3. As a hand technique, to exert pressure.

截 (rad.62) **jié** 1. To intercept, check, stop. 2. To cut, sever. 3. A cutting interception, a block that uses a cutting rotation rather than a hard hit. One of the sixteen key techniques of Baguazhang, see also shí liù zì jué. 4. A controlling or grappling technique: a quick cut to a pressure point.

jié bà 截把 Intercept with the base: encircle and trap with the butt of a long weapon.

jié biān 截鞭 Intercepting whip. See jié qiáo.

jié dāo 截刀 Cutting interception with a broadsword. See jié jiàn.

jié dà dāo 截大刀 Intercept with a big cutter: with the right hand near the hilt and the left along the shaft, rotate the right palm down and block down with the blade to intercept a low attack.

jié jiàn 截剑 Cutting interception with a sword: cut to the rear, lifting the grip with the arm straight to bring the blade at an angle, cutting edge down, tip angled down towards the body.

jié jìn 截劲 1. Cutting power: a short, quick expression of power, usually used after contact and drawing in of an adversary has been achieved. Once he has lost the initiative, then apply a quick power burst to his centre. 2. Jamming power: a hard, jamming strike to the attacking limb before an adversary has completed his strike.

jié qì fǎ 截气法 *Qi* cutting methods: using pressure points to block the flow of *qi* and blood. The general term for *qi* blocking, with various methods, is called diǎn xué fǎ.

jié qiáo 截桥 Intercepting bridge, forearm intercept, a forearm technique: with the arm slightly bent, rotate the forearm (either in or out, depending on the direction of the movement) and intercept upwards, downwards, left or right. From southern styles. Also called jié biān.

jié shǒu ér gǔn shǒu 截手而滚手 Deal with

J

intercept with a roll: if an adversary jams your attack with his forearm, roll around that arm to allow you to get in with the counter. From Tanglangquan, one of its twelve soft counters, see also shí èr róu.

jié tuǐ 截腿 Intercept with the leg: intercept an attack angling downwards with the ankle dorsiflexed to angle the foot forward and down to contact with the sole and outer edge of the foot. Can be done as an attacking kick as well as a block.

jié tuǐ gōu tī 截腿勾踢 Leg intercept, hooking kick: catch an adversary's incoming snap kick, hooking and embracing his leg. Then reach out to chop his neck and hook kick the ankle of his supporting leg. A throw.

jié tuǐ lōu tuǐ 截腿搂腿 Leg intercept, brush leg: catch an adversary's incoming throwing kick to the ribs, trapping it to your body, advance and catch his supporting leg behind the knee with your foot, placing your hand on his shoulder. Then hook his leg up and push forward to take down. A throw or takedown.

jié tuǐ shuāi 截腿摔 Leg intercepting throw. 1. The category of throws that involve intercepting a kick and manipulating the leg for a throw or takedown. 2. A specific leg intercepting throw: catch with both hands the adversary's foot when he kicks to your chest, bend the knees and bow, pulling and dropping, then lift his foot and push forward and up to take him down.

jié tuǐ shàng tuō 截腿上托 Leg intercept and lift: catch with both hands an incoming thrust kick to the chest, then lift your adversary's foot to take him down. A throw or takedown.

jié tuō 截脱 Cutting release, an escape from a wrist grab: Strike strongly down on an adversary's grabbing arm with your free fist, pulling in your grabbed arm at the same time.

jié wàn 截腕 Wrist cut, cut to the wrist. Either with a weapon or the blade of the hand.

jié zhǎng gōu wàn 截掌勾腕 Cut the hand to hook the wrist: if, for example, your right wrist is grabbed by an adversary's left hand, press your left hand on his grabbing hand, open your right hand, rotate and sit the wrist to sit out from his little finger side, twisting his wrist over.

jié zhǒu 截肘 Elbow cut. 1. As a defense: with the arm bent, cut the elbow down and across, crossing the body and turning the palm in. 2. As a Qinna technique: control an adversary's attacking hand, get his arm extended, and cut across at his elbow with your forearm, twisting and reversing the elbow.

jié zì gōng 截字功 Skill of intercepting, one of Xingyiquan's eight skills, involving a double interception with a smooth follow-up attack.

節 (rad.118) [节] (rad.140) **jié** 1. A joint; section; node; knot. 2. A move or an action when describing routines action by action. 3. A section of a routine.

jié jié guàn chuān 节节贯穿 All joints connect through and through, power threads through all the joints. Once one joint moves, all other joints of the body move in a fully coordinated and connected manner.

jié quán 节拳 Jiequan (jointed fist). Based on the foundations of the Tantui style, a style with many kicks, known of since the Qing dynasty.

jié zòu 节奏 Rhythm. Important to both routine performance and fighting.

解 (rad.148) **jiě** 1. To untie, undo. 2. To separate. 3. To dismiss. 4. To explain. 5. To understand.

jiě fǎ 解法 Release techniques, escapes from control methods or from grappling. Also called jiě tuō, pò jiě, tuō ná.

jiě tuō 解脱 Release technique. See jiě fǎ.

jiě xī 解溪 Acupoint Jiexi (ravine divide), ST41. At the ankle crease, in the depression at the midline, between the tendons of the extensor digitorum longus and the extensor hallicis longus muscles (on each leg). From TCM.

借 (rad.9) **jiè** 1. To lend. 2. To borrow. 3. To make use of.

jiè dāo shā rén 借刀杀人 Kill Someone with a Borrowed Blade: use one person to get rid of another. The third of the Thirty-six Stratagems of Warfare, which apply to many situations.

jiè jìn 借劲 Borrowing power: to borrow the

jiè lì dǎ rén 借力打人 Borrow an adversary's strength to hit him.

jiè lì fā lì miào zài cùn jìn 借力发力妙在寸劲 Whether borrowing an adversary's strength or initiating an attack, one inch power is the best way. A martial saying.

jiè shī huán hún 借尸还魂 Borrow a Corpse to find Reincarnation. The 14th of the Thirty-six Stratagems of Warfare, which apply to many situations.

jiè shì dǎ shì 借势打势 Borrow a position to hit a position: Utilize the positioning and power of an adversary to get yourself in for a strong attack, through use of skill rather than force.

jiè shǒu 借手 Borrow a hand: when grabbed around the collar, press your adversary's elbow crease, leaving his hand on your collar, and trip. Works with one handed or two-handed grabs.

jiè shǒu bàn zǐ 借手绊子 Borrow a hand trips: the category of trips that pin an adversary's hand to your body to control it during the trip.

jiè shǒu tī 借手踢 Borrow a hand kick throw: control an adversary's elbow, pull it, then twist and kick his leg out and move in to push. From wrestling.

jiè zhù tuǐ jī 借助腿击 Borrow the leg to get the hit: fake a kick or sweep, then move in when your adversary reacts.

斤 (rad.69) jīn   1. A *jin*, a traditional measure of weight, equal to ten *liang*. Equivalent to five hundred grams, or 1.1 pounds. Often translated as a catty. See also liǎng. 2. An axe.

津 (rad.85) jīn   Fluids in the body, the thin, *yang* fluids, such as tears.

jīn yè 津液 The fluids in the body.

筋 (rad.118) jīn   Muscles, tendons, sinews.

jīn lì 筋力 The strength of the sinews: the power of the whole body.

jīn shào 筋梢 The sinew tips: the nails. The visible outer part of the body in which the energy of the sinews is expressed.

jīn suō 筋缩 Acupoint Jinsuo (sinew contraction), DU8. At the back, at the depression below the spinous process of the ninth thoracic vertebra, on the midline. From TCM.

金 (rad.167) jīn   1. Gold. 2. Metal as one of the five elemental phases. Metal relates to the internal organ of the lungs, to the sensing organ of the nose, to the tissue of the skin, and to the season of autumn. Its *yang* expression is weapons, its *yin* is a kettle. See also wǔ xíng. 3. Metal as one of the five phases techniques of Xingyiquan. The mindset of metal is hard headed, defensive moves hold your position, and attacking moves are focussed and controlled. See also pī quán. 4. Money. 5. The Jin dynasty (1115-1234), founded by the Jurchen people of north China. 6. A surname.

jīn bào jiǎn wěi 金豹剪尾 Golden Leopard Slashes its Tail: caught at the shoulder, swing your arm up and over, placing your arm along your adversary's and pressing down.

jīn bào tiào jiàn 金豹跳涧 Golden Leopard Leaps over the Stream: leap forward with a knee butt to close the distance and attack directly.

jīn chā bù 金叉步 Golden fork stance. See jiāo chā bù.

jīn chā shǒu 金叉手 Golden fork hands. See jiǎn shǒu. Also called shuāng yáng tà shǒu.

jīn chán tuō qiào 金蝉脱壳 Golden Cicada Sloughs its Carapace. 1. Escape from a difficult situation by cunning. The twenty-first of the Thirty-six Stratagems of Warfare, which apply to many situations. 2. An opening throw, stepping in, separating the adversary's arms and twisting his body to the side and back. From Baguazhang, one of its sixty-four hands. 3. Drop into a seated cross stance and snap a sword tip up with a scooping action, followed quickly with a snapped down filing action. From Qingping sword.

jīn chǎn zhǐ 金铲指 Golden shovel fingers: strike with four fingers held together.

jīn dī zhé liǔ 金堤折柳 Golden Dyke Breaks the Willow: a swinging kick to waist height combined with a sword slice up above shoulder height. A left kick uses a regular slice, and a right kicks uses a reverse slice. From Qingping sword.

jīn diāo liè tù 金雕猎兔 Golden Vulture Hunts a Rabbit: after controlling the adversary's arm at wrist and elbow, twisting it outwards, reach in to grasp his collar bone.

jīn fèng zhǎn chì 金凤展翅 Golden Phoenix Spreads its Wings: extend an adversary's arm and twist the entire arm to lock out the shoulder, lifting the wrist. From Baguazhang.

jīn fó tuō tiān 金佛托天 Golden Buddha Holds up the Sky: Press both hand directly over the head in a raised knee stance, palms up, fingers pointing to each other. From Shaolinquan.

jīn gāng 金刚 Temple Guard. See sì dà jīn gāng.

jīn gāng chuí 金刚捶 Temple Guard Fists: a routine of Mizongquan, written up as sixty-five moves.

jīn gāng chū dòng 金刚出洞 Temple Guard Emerges from the Cave: in a horse stance, brace the right forearm upward to block over the head. The 38th move of the tiger and crane routine.

jīn gāng dǎo duì 金刚倒碓 Temple Guard Pounds the Pestle: stomp a foot and pound or grind a fist into the other palm. From Chen Taijiquan and southern styles.

jīn gāng dǎo jiù 金刚倒臼 Temple Guard Pounds the Mortar: step into a bow stance and pound the rear fist into the front palm.

jīn gāng guà tuǐ 金刚挂腿 Temple Guard hook kick: a kick combination with one leg, first an inside crescent kick to the front, then a heel kick to the rear. From southern styles

jīn gāng zhǐ 金刚指 Temple Guard finger. 1. A single finger strike. See jīn zhēn zhǐ. 2. The training methods used to develop the one finger strike.

jīn gōu shǒu 金钩手 Golden hook hand, a hand shape. See hè dǐng shǒu.

jīn guī mò 金龟磨 Golden Tortoise Grinds: a front sweep kick with the supporting leg only partly bent, the hands not on the ground. The foot sweeps one or more circles on the ground. From Shaolinquan.

jīn guī tà làng 金龟踏浪 Golden Tortoise Treads on the Waves: hook behind the adversary's heel with your heel and pressure his knee with your hand to take him down backwards.

jīn huā luò dì 金花落地 Golden Flowers Fall to the Ground: a low chop in a hunkered squat stance or a reverse bow stance. From Qingping sword.

jīn jī bào xiǎo 金鸡报晓 Golden Rooster Heralds the Dawn. 1. An advancing high scoop. From Xingyiquan. 2. A lifting wrist lock lifting an adversary's straight arm sharply, twisting his elbow up and reversing his wrist.

jīn jī bù 金鸡步 Golden rooster step: a one-legged stance, varies according to style. In some, the foot is specifically held dorsi-flexed at mid-shin.

jīn jī dēng jiǎo 金鸡蹬脚 Golden Rooster Thrusts a Foot: A front heel thrust kick, with the hands together and lifting up in front of the body. From Xingyiquan.

jīn jī diǎn tóu 金鸡点头 Golden Rooster Nods its Head: a dabbing strike with a straight sword.

jīn jī dǒu líng 金鸡抖翎 Golden Rooster Shakes its Wings. 1. In Xingyiquan, a back horse stance opening snap with the elbow back and a bracing hand in front, either defending high and low or shaking out of a grab. Also called wàng méi zhé jié. 2. In Baguazhang, an opening of the arms with a snap, to ram an adversary's chest with one shoulder. 3. In Tongbeiquan, stepping in with a thrown backhand. 4. To respond to a double strike to the body, grab the little fingers and twist them out, snapping to reverse and break the fingers.

jīn jī dòu zhì 金鸡斗志 Golden Rooster Full of Fight: stepping forward pausing on one leg then the other, advancing four steps, pressing the palms forward alternately with the steps. From Xingyiquan.

jīn jī dú lì 金鸡独立 Golden Rooster Stands on One Leg: a one-legged stance. 1. In Taijiquan, a raised knee stance with the same side hand raised, the other hand pressing down, to control an adversary as the knee strikes. 2. In Liuhe Quan, a raised knee stance with the same side hand hooked behind the raised knee, the other hand held in front. 3. In Xingyiquan, step forward to a raised foot stance, pressing down with one palm. 4. In Chen Taijiquan broadsword, an empty stance holding a broadsword almost vertical in front of the body, left hand on the spine. 5. In Wudangquan, a raised knee stance with the same side hand punching up over the head. 6. In Yiquan, a stake standing posture, see dú lì zhuāng. 7. In Yangjia style, a raised knee stance with the same side fist bracing on the raised knee, the other arm blocking up overhead.

jīn jī jiào dōng 金鸡叫东 Golden Rooster Cries to the East: step back to a reverse bow stance and stab a sword up with the hand reversed, arm and blade aligned with the same line as the leg. Step back and pull the sword back, then step forward to a left raised knee stance and stab straight and high. From Qingping sword.

jīn jī lián huán 金鸡连环 Golden Roosters Interlinked: circle-walking with the hands pushing out away from the body, the inside hand fingers up, palm edge to the centre of the circle, the outside hand fingers down. From Baguazhang.

jīn jī nié sù 金鸡捏嗉 Golden Rooster Wrings the Neck: one hand defends while the other grasps the adversary's neck. From Xingyiquan.

jīn jī sā bǎng 金鸡撒膀 Golden Rooster Shakes its Wings. 1. Squat into a drop stance, threading the same side arm along the extended leg. From Baguazhang. 2. Sit into horse stance with a high block and low press down by the knee. From Wudangquan.

jīn jī shàng jià 金鸡上架 Golden Rooster Blocks Up: snap the hips and block up above the head with the forearm. From Xingyiquan.

jīn jī shí mǐ 金鸡食米 Golden Rooster Pecks Rice: a straight reverse stance driving punch with the other hand covering the forearm. From Xingyiquan. Also called hún yuán chuí.

jīn jī shù chì 金鸡束翅 Golden Rooster Restrains its Wings: tuck the body in, squatting down, crossing one hand down to the opposite knee and one hand up to the opposite jaw. From Xingyiquan.

jīn jī tà xuě 金鸡踏雪 Golden Rooster Treads on Snow: move forward in a semi-crouching chicken stance, alternating the hands with downward presses, threading the hands out along the forearms. From Xingyiquan.

jīn jī zhǎn chì 金鸡展翅 Golden Rooster Spreads its Wings. 1. Settle back, opening the arms out to the sides at head height. From Xingyiquan. 2. Lift the knee in front, swing the same side arm up to

block, and snap the other arm out to the side. From Shaolinquan.

jīn jī zhēng dòu 金鸡挣斗 Golden Rooster Fights: drive forward with a shoving push with both palms, elbows and wrists close together. From Baguazhang.

jīn jī zhuǎn huán 金鸡转环 Golden Rooster Turning: circle-walking with the hands hooked and pushing out away from the body, both hands hooked so the fingers are up. From Baguazhang.

jīn jī zhuó shuǐ 金鸡啄水 Golden Rooster Drinks Water: settle into a low one-legged chicken stance, reaching one hand out with a splitting palm, pulling the other hand back to press down at the hip. From Xingyiquan.

jīn jī zhuó lì 金鸡啄粒 Golden Rooster Pecks Grain: chop and circle the sword, standing up to a raised knee stance, then sit to an empty stance and snap the blade inwards. From Qingping sword.

jīn jiǎn jiǎo bì 金剪绞臂 Golden Scissors Cut the Arm: cross the arms in front of the chest to catch with the forearms, to control or break an adversary's arm. Also called jiǎn zhǒu.

jīn jiǎn zhǐ 金剪指 Golden scissors fingers: a double finger strike, index and middle fingers extended. Used particularly to strike pressure points. From Shaolinquan.

jīn jiāo lóng jiǎn 金蛟龙剪 Golden Flood Dragon Cuts: a trampling kick. From Chuojiao, one of its low-basin kicks.

jīn jiǎo jiǎn 金绞剪 Golden Cutting Scissors. 1. A double weapon similar to double hooks, but without a hooked end. 2. Push the palms forward with the forearms crossed. From Shaolinquan.

jīn jīn 金津 Extraordinary acupoint Jinjin, EX-HN12. Inside the mouth, on the tip of the tongue, to the left of the midline. From TCM.

jīn liáng jià hǎi 金梁架海 Golden Bridge Erected over the Sea: drop to a low crossed stance stabbing a sword out behind, then step towards the blade and lift it to a framing block up settling in a reverse bow stance. From Qingping sword.

jīn lóng bǎi wěi 金龙摆尾 Golden Dragon Lashes its Tail: a spinning back heel kick.

jīn lóng hé fèng 金龙合凤 Golden Dragon Joins the Phoenix: a rear tucked stance with closing palms. From Piguaquan.

jīn lóng hé kǒu 金龙合口 Golden Dragon Closes its Mouth: push the palms forward, heels of the hands together, the top hand fingers pointing up, the lower hand fingers pointing down. From Baguazhang.

jīn lóng jiū dì 金龙揪地 Golden Dragon Drags the Fields: step forward, swinging the left hand and foot back, circling a sword, then land into a reverse stance with a slicing cut across to the forward right. From Qingping sword.

jīn lóng rù hǎi 金龙入海 Golden Dragon Enters the Sea: a drop stance extending the arms to either side rolled over, palms up. From Baguazhang.

jīn lóng xiàn zhǎo 金龙献爪 Golden Dragon Presents its Claws: step across in a front crossing stance, turning back to present dragon claws behind. The 95th move of the tiger and crane routine.

jīn lóng yǐn shuǐ 金龙饮水 Golden Dragon Drinks Water: jump forward with a simultaneous kick to the groin and elbow strike to the head, following up with a knee to the belly.

jīn māo xǐ liǎn 金猫洗脸 Golden Cat Washes its Face: strike an adversary's face with a tiger claw hand, raking downwards. Also called zhuā miàn zhǎo.

jīn mén 金门 Acupoint Jinmen (metal gate), BL63. At the foot, on the outside, directly below the ankle crease, at the talus bone (on each foot). From TCM.

jīn qián 金钱 The Golden Coin. 1. See jīn qián xué. 2. To strike both temples simultaneously.

jīn qián xué 金钱穴 The Golden Coin acupoint. Colloquial term for the acupoint Taiyang, see tài yáng.

jīn qiāng shǒu 金枪手 Golden spear hand. See shuāng zhǐ.

jīn qiáo xiāng dìng 金桥相定 Golden Bridges Settle Each Other: sitting in horse stance, push forward with both palms forward, all fingers extended and pointing up, thumbs tucked. The 19th move of the tiger and crane routine.

jīn rén xiàn jiàn 金人献剑 Jurchen Soldier Presents a Sword: lift and tuck the left knee (or in a reverse bow stance) and strike a sword out at chest height to the right. May stab, keeping the left hand at the hilt, or dab, blocking up with the left. From Qingping sword.

jīn rén yè zhàn 金人夜战 Jurchen Soldier has a Night Battle: step through to a seated cross stance, hands together in front of the chest to point a sword down, then step forward to a bow stance and stab. From Qingping sword.

jīn shān dǎo hǎi 金山倒海 Golden Mountain Falls in the Sea: step to a reverse bow stance, cutting down with an angled chop, sword tip at the apex of the triangle made by the stance, slicing down and through an adversary's head. From Qingping sword.

jīn shé fú dì 金蛇伏地 Golden Snake Lies in Ambush. 1. From a right bow stance drop back on the left leg, taking a sword blade back and down with the action, keeping the tip slightly up. This avoids an attack and prepares for an ambush. 2. Jump forward to a drop stance, brandishing a sword in the air, then cutting out along the extended leg. Both from Qingping sword.

jīn shé pán liǔ 金蛇般柳 Golden Snake Coils around a Willow: enter with a back cross step, squatting and extending the leading hand down close to the body, bringing the rear hand up to protect the face. From Baguazhang.

jīn sī chán bì 金丝缠臂 Golden Thread Coils the Arm, a rope dart technique: circle the dart counter-clockwise, turning and looping the rope around the arm, sending the dart out from the elbow.

jīn sī chán hú lú 金丝缠葫芦 Golden Thread Coils the Gourd, a steel whip technique: vertical circles, bringing the whip around the back of the neck and snapping with the head to keep it spinning.

jīn sī chán wàn 金丝缠腕 Golden Thread Coils the Wrist: if grabbed on the same side (i.e., right grabbing right), use the other hand to fix an adversary's hand, open the grabbed hand to coil around his arm, then press down. From Baguazhang, Qinna, and others. Also called xiǎo chán shǒu in Qinna.

jīn sī huà méi 金丝画眉 Golden Thread Draws the Eyebrows: circle a sword around then slice up above head height, lifting the left knee, then switch feet and slice low. From Qingping sword.

jīn sī mǒ méi 金丝抹眉 Golden Thread Smears the Eyebrows: place the hand to the adversary's forehead and smear his head back, pulling his arm to spread him out. From Baguazhang and Wudangquan, one of Baguazhang's sixty-four hands.

jīn sī pāi zhǒu 金丝拍肘 Golden Thread Elbow Pat: combine a wrist control with a rolling elbow press. From Baguazhang.

jīn suǒ fēng hóu 金锁封喉 Golden Lock Seals the Throat: an upward stab with one finger directly underneath the jaw. From Shaolinquan.

jīn tóng kāi lián 金童开帘 Golden Lad Opens the Shop Curtain: jump forward to land in a bow stance and push forward with clawing hands, the front arm slightly bent, the rear hand at its elbow. From Shaolinquan.

jīn tóng tí lú 金童提炉 Golden Lad Lifts the Oven: a cross sit stance with a lifting slice up with a sword, drawing the blade up to shoulder height on the midline, to cut inside an adversary's arm. From Qingping sword.

jīn xīng guà jiǎo 金星掛角 Golden Star Hangs on the Horn: step into a right bow stance, turning to face that way, and blocking up with the right forearm. The 97th move of the tiger and crane routine.

jīn yú hù lín 金鱼护鳞 Golden Carp Protects its Scales: slice across in front of the body with a double-bladed weapon with a scissors action, finishing with the arms crossed and the weapons back, lying along the body.

jīn yuán lòu bèi 金鼋露背 Golden Turtle Shows its Back: take a digging step forward, lift the back of one hand and lower the other palm in front of the groin. Then shift forward and drop the raised palm down to solar plexus height. From Wudangquan.

jīn zhǎng dī lù 金掌滴露 Golden Palm Drips Dew: a low pierce with a sword, the grip hand held up above shoulder height. From Qingping sword.

jīn zhēn àn dù 金针暗度 Secret Strike from a Golden Needle: sidestep to a low crossed stance, rotating a sword blade and drawing it in, in preparation for a counter attack. From Qingping sword.

jīn zhēn rù dì 金针入地 Golden Needle Enters the Ground: when grabbed with one hand at the shoulder, press your adversary's hand onto your shoulder and swing your arm over and down to lock out his arm.

jīn zhēn zhǐ 金针指 Golden needle finger: a single finger strike, usually with the middle finger. From Shaolinquan. Also called jīn gāng zhǐ.

jīn zhōng chǎn 金钟铲 Golden bell shovel, a shovel weapon with the blade shaped like a bell.

jīn zhōng zhào 金钟罩 Golden bell blanket, a hard skills training method: beat oneself over the whole body daily with a cane, gradually increasing the hardness from wood to iron.

jīn zhòng zhào dǐng 金钟罩顶 Golden Bell Covers the Top: pull an adversary's hand down and out with one hand while pressing his forehead back and down. From Baguazhang.

紧 [緊] (rad.120) jǐn   1. Tight, firm, taut, tense, close. 2. Urgent, critical.

jǐn bā shǒu 紧八手 Jinbashou (tight eight hands), a style from the Qing dynasty, practiced in Hubei province. Its techniques are straightforward, using quick hand and leg combinations.

jǐn bèi 紧背 Taut upper back: spread the upper back in all directions so the skin is stretched taut.

jǐn bī xiān shī 紧逼先施 Press hard, act first: close in on an adversary so that he cannot get in a technique, attack first.

jǐn zhāng 紧张 To tense up, to be tense. Considered a fault in most styles, and likely to lead to defeat in a fight.

锦 [錦] (rad.167) jǐn   1. Brocade. Embroidered. 2. Bright and colourful.

jǐn jī dǒu bǎng 锦鸡抖榜 Golden Pheasant Shakes its Wings: a full body shake emanating into the arms.

jǐn shàng tiān huā 锦上添花 Add Flowers to Brocade (improve on something already good): from a stab, cock the wrist to bring a sword in alongside the arm, also tucking the right knee up, then land forward to a horse stance and cut across. From Qingping sword.

J

劲 [劲] (rad.19) **jìn** 1. Power, trained and harnessed strength. Vigour. Alone, it means a general good feeling of energy and strength combined. With technique specific action words, it means smart strength or trained energy, a combination of structure specific to the action, understanding of the action, proper flow, and the ability to apply the body and mind to the specific action. 2. Pronounced jìng, powerful, sturdy.

jìn dào 劲道 Way of power: the characteristics and skilled use by which power is applied for a specific action.

jìn lì 劲力 Power, strength.

jìn lù 劲路 Route of power: the direction in which power is applied for a specific action.

jìn zhěng 劲整 Power is complete and full. All aspects of power within the body work together, there is a root and a route to each movement. One of the requirements for proper training.

jìn zǒu yuán lì zǒu zhí 劲走圆力走直 Trained power uses circular movement, while brute strength uses straight line movement. A martial saying.

禁 (rad.113) **jìn** 1. To prohibit, forbid; ban. 2. Pronounced jīn, to bear.

jìn jī bù wèi 禁击部位 Out of bounds targets, prohibited targets, disallowed targets. In Sanda they are: the back of the head, the ribs, the throat, the groin, and fingers to the eyes.

jìn yòng fāng fǎ 禁用方法 Prohibited techniques in a Sanda or wrestling match.

近 (rad.162) **jìn** Close, close to.

jìn jù lí 近距离 Close range: attached to an adversary, within range of a knee, elbow, shoulder, or hip strike. See also yuǎn jù lì, zhōng jù lì.

進 [进] (rad.162) **jìn** To enter, advance, move forward. Any advancing footwork.

jìn bī 进逼 To attack; advance on; take the initiative to force a reaction from an adversary.

jìn bù 进步 Advancing step, entry step. 1. Advance: step the lead foot forward. 2. Entry step: any stepping forward entry into an adversary, with either the front or back foot.

jìn bù jiē zhǒu 进步截肘 Advance to Elbow Cut: grab an adversary's arm, press up with the elbow, then turn to roll and press down with the elbow for a break or throw. From Baguazhang, one of its sixty-four hands.

jìn bù tā zhǎng 进步塌掌 Advance Tamping Palm: step directly into a tamping palm. From Baguazhang, one of its sixty-four hands.

jìn bù tiǎo zhǎng 进步挑掌 Advance Scooping Palm: step directly forward into a reverse stance, lifting with one forearm to come through with a push. From Baguazhang, one of its sixty-four hands.

jìn bù tuán zhuàng 进步团撞 Advance to a Joined Shove: step into double shove, trampling into an adversary's feet and shoving his body with the hands connected. From Baguazhang, one of its sixty-four hands.

jìn bù zāi chuí 进步栽捶 Advance to Plant a Mallet. Step in to punch down. From Yang Taijiquan.

jìn bù zhuàng chuí 进步撞捶 Advance to Shove. 1. Step in, coiling to control and shove. 2. Step into a straight punch. From Baguazhang, one of its sixty-four hands.

jìn chǎng 进场 Enter the competition area; step onto the carpet for Taolu events.

jìn gōng zhāo fǎ 进攻招法 Methods of attack: include direct attack, storming, barrage, feint, riposte, and counter attack.

jìn jiāo 进跤 Advancing throw, advancing techniques in wrestling: either directly, angled or stepping to the inside or outside, advancing to prepare for a throw.

jìn mǎ chōng quán 进马冲拳 Enter the Horse and Punch: from a horse stance, shift to left reverse bow stance and punch the right fist out on the line of the stance. The 48th move of the tiger and crane routine.

jìn mǎ chū zhǎng 进马出掌 Enter the Horse and Send out the Palm: from a horse stance, shift to right reverse bow stance and push the left hand forward, elbow straight, fingers turned out. The 36th move of the tiger and crane routine.

jìn qiāng 进枪 Enter a spear: enter from the outside line of an adversary with your body and the spear.

jìn sān tuì èr huó bù tuī shǒu 进三退二活步推手 Three step forward, two steps back, moving step push hands: moving step push hands, with a fixed number and set pattern of stepping, advancing three steps while the partner retreats two steps, using the four square techniques. From Taijiquan. Also called wǔ bù èr rén qiāng. See also àn, jǐ, lǚ, péng.

jìn sān tuì sān huó bù tuī shǒu 进三退三活步推手 Three steps forward, three steps back, moving step push hands: moving step push hands, with a fixed number and set pattern of stepping, using the four square techniques. From Taijiquan. See also àn, jǐ, lǚ, péng.

jìn shēn 进身 Enter: move the body in towards the adversary with footwork (doing an entry technique).

jìn tuì bù tuī shǒu 进退步推手 Enter and retreat step push hands. See dòng bù tuī shǒu.

jìn tuì fǎ 进退法 Enter and retreat techniques: methods of moving back and forth in direct fighting.

jìn tuì lián huán 进退连环 Advance and Retreat Connected: a Xingyiquan routine, written up as eleven moves.

jìn zhāo 进招 Attacking move. 1. Any move that has attacking as its primary goal, either directly or as a counter attack. 2. The technique that serves as the entry portion of a throw.

jìn zhēn 进针 Insert an acupuncture needle. From TCM.

京 (rad.8) jīng   The capital of a country.

jīng gǔ 京骨 Acupoint Jinggu (capital bone), BL64. At the foot, on the outside, below the proximal end of the metatarsals, on the border of the lighter and darker skin (on each foot). From TCM.

jīng mén 京门 Acupoint Jingmen (capital gate), GB25. At the back of the abdomen, at the twelfth, floating, rib, 1.8 *cun* behind acupoint Zhangmen (on each side). From TCM. This is a sensitive point at the tip of the floating ribs. Best to hit with a hard punch, knee, elbow, or foot.

惊 (rad.61) jīng   Surprise, shock. Be startled.

jīng mǎ huí tóu 惊马回头 Startled Horse Looks Back: Step around while opening and circling the hands up and down and around, finishing in a resting stance, one hand pressing down at the hip, the other opened above the head to its side. From Liuhebafa.

jīng shàng qǔ xià 惊上取下 Startle above and get below: fake high and hit low.

睛 (rad.109) jīng   The eyes; pupil of the eye.

jīng míng 睛明 Acupoint Jingming (bright eyes), BL1. At the face, at the upper inside of the eye socket between the eyeball and the bone (on each side). From TCM. Hitting here induces dizziness, blurred vision, or even collapsing from shock.

精 (rad.119) jīng   The essence of a person or thing. The source, essence, of life. A fluid that circulates in the body and is stored in the kidneys. Associated with the Kidney and with the character attribute of the ability to finalize intended actions.

jīng yào chōng pèi qì yí chén 精要充沛气宜沉 The spirit should be vigorous and the *qi* sunken. A martial saying.

jīng shén 精神 1. Spirit; vitality; drive. 2. Lively, spirited, vigorous.

jīng shén chōng pèi 精神充沛 The spirit is brimming with energy: one of the basic qualities of many styles.

jīng wǔ 精武 The spirit of the martial arts, martial essence.

經 [经] (rad.120) jīng   1. To pass through. 2. Warp (of a cloth).

jīng bié 经别 Channel divergences: part of the internal channels of the body that diverge from the main channels. From TCM.

jīng luò 经络 Meridians: the main channels and the collateral channels, through which circulate the *qi*. The *jingluo* wrap around the body. See also jīng mài. From TCM.

jīng luò tōng 经络通 The meridians and collaterals are unimpeded and communicate. For martial arts, this allows training to affect both *qi*

J

and power.

jīng mài 经脉 Meridians, the fourteen main lines of circulation of *qi* and blood. The *jingmai* run vertically through the body, and along the limbs. See also jīng luò. From TCM.

jīng qú 经渠 Acupoint Jingqu (channel ditch), LU8. On the inside of the forearm, in the carpal cavity, about one *cun* up from the wrist crease, level with the styloid process of the radius (on each arm). From TCM.

jīng wài qí xué 经外奇穴 Extraordinary acupoints, acupoints that are not on one of the fourteen main meridians. From TCM.

jīng xué 经穴 Acupoint, meridian point: the three hundred and sixty-one points where the *qi* and blood are transported to the surface, closely related to the circulation of the fourteen main meridians.

井 (rad.7) **jǐng**   1. A well. 2. Something shaped like a well.

jǐng lán zhí rù 井拦直入 Drop the Pulley Rope into the Well: a double elbow strike to the front, the fist surfaces facing each other. From Chen Taijiquan.

jǐng quán gōng 井拳功 Well punching training: sit in horse stance and punch repeatedly (at least a hundred punches each side) down towards the bottom of a well, daily, morning and evening. After years, the water will start to make sounds, and gradually the punches may create waves or even splashing out of the well.

警 (rad.149) **jǐng** 1. To guard. 2. To warn. 3. An alarm. 4. The police.

jǐng gào 警告 A warning, a caution: given to an athlete for an infraction in a Sanda or wrestling match.

jǐng jiè shì 警戒势 A ready stance in sparring. Not a specific posture, but whatever is suitable at the time for your skill and against the skills of an adversary.

頸 [颈] (rad.181) **jǐng**   The neck, the nape of the neck.

jǐng bǎi láo 颈百劳 Extraordinary acupoint Jingbailao, EX-HN15. At the nape of the neck, two *cun* above the spinal protrusion, one *cun* lateral to the midline. From TCM.

jǐng bù 颈部 The neck. Also called jǐng xiàng.

jǐng cè 颈侧 The side of the neck. One of the main targets on the body.

jǐng gǔ 颈骨 Cervical vertebra, the neck bones. Also called jǐng zhuī.

jǐng xiàng 颈项 The neck. Also called jǐng bù.

jǐng zhuī 颈椎 Cervical vertebra. Also called jǐng gǔ.

敬 (rad.66) **jìng**   1. Respect; honour; esteem. 2. To offer politely. 3. Respectful.

jìng dé shàng wǔ 敬德尚武 Respect virtue and value the martial spirit.

jìng dé tuō biān 敬德托鞭 Respect Virtue and Hold up the Whip. 1. An arm bar, lifting an adversary's hand and elbow above shoulder height. From Baguazhang and Qinna. 2. Jump back and land in a bow stance, cutting a sword back aligned with the extended leg, leaning a bit away. This is a cut to the outside of an adversary. From Qingping sword.

競 [竞] (rad.117) **jìng**   To compete; contend.

jìng sài 竞赛 A competition, a contest.

jìng sài guī dìng tào lù 竞赛规定套路 Standardised Competition Routine. Each style that is involved in regulation competition has various levels of these routines.

jìng sài wěi yuán huì 竞赛委员会 Competition committee.

jìng sài xiàng mù 竞赛项目 A competition event (such as Changquan, sword, spear, etc.).

脛 [胫] (rad.130) **jìng**   The shank: the lower leg, including the shin and calf.

jìng féi gǔ gǔ mó yán 胫腓骨骨膜炎 Shin splints, inflammation of the tissue in the shin.

jìng gǔ 胫骨 Tibia: the shinbone. One of the main targets on the body, but also used for striking once this area is toughened up.

jìng gǔ qián jī 胫骨前肌 Tibialis anterior muscle: a shin muscle. Helps to dorsiflex the ankle, extend the toes, and invert the foot.

靜 [静] (rad.174) jìng Stillness; quiet; calm.

jìng gōng 静功 The skill of stillness.

jìng lì zhàn zhuāng 静立站桩 Still standing, various methods of quiet and erect stake standing for *qigong*.

jìng mài 静脉 A vein, the veins; venous.

jìng rú yuè 静如岳 Still like a mountain peak: one of the twelve qualities of movement of Changquan, though these descriptors apply to many other styles.

jìng yún fú shān 静云伏山 Still Clouds Hide the Mountains: lean forward in a right bow stance, snap the wrist up to raise a sword tip after a chop, to attack an adversary's wrist from underneath. From Qingping sword.

jìng zhōng qiú dòng 静中求动 Seek movement in stillness. One of the basic principles of the martial arts.

揪 (rad.64) jiū 1. To hold tight, seize. 2. To pull, tug, drag.

jiū fǎ 揪法 Tugging method: grab tightly and pull with a short, sharp tug.

jiū mén 揪门 Seize the gateway: grab the chest opening of the wrestling jacket in preparation for a throw.

jiū ná bù wèi 揪拿部位 The placement of a hold in preparation for a throw in wrestling.

jiū ná fǎ 揪拿法 Clothing grabbing techniques of wrestling.

jiū xiù 揪袖 Tug the sleeve: grab and tug the sleeve of the wrestling jacket in preparation for a throw.

糾 糺 [纠] (rad.120) jiū 1. To entangle. 2. To gather together.

jiū zhèng 纠正 To correct an error, give corrections.

鳩 [鸠] (rad.196) jiū A turtledove (bird).

jiū wěi 鸠尾 Acupoint Jiuwei (turtledove tail), RN15. At the abdomen, one *cun* below the sternum, on the midline. At the solar plexus. From TCM. A sensitive point, striking it can induce breathlessness. Striking too hard shocks the arteries and veins in the abdominal wall and injures the liver, gallbladder, and heart. Best to hit with a straight punch, a variety of combination parry and punches, push, shove, elbow, or knee. Colloquially called Dangmen, see dāng mén xué. Acupoint Juque is also in the area of the solar plexus, see also jù què.

九 (rad.5) jiǔ Nine.

jiǔ diǎn fēi 九点飞 Nine flying points: a routine of Meishanquan, written up as thirty-nine moves, which are thirteen moves repeated.

jiǔ fèng tǎng 九凤镗 Nine phoenix trident: a long handled weapon shaped like a rake with large tines on both front and back of the rake.

jiǔ gōng bā guà 九宫八卦 Nine palaces of the trigrams: the eight directions of the eight trigrams or the compass, plus the centre.

jiǔ gōng bù 九宫步 Nine palaces stepping: walking pattern around the nine palaces to train agility. Follows the pattern of starting in the South, then NE, West, NW, centre, SE, East, SW, and North, and back in the other direction. From Baguazhang.

jiǔ gōng bù chuān rào fǎ 九宫步穿绕法 Nine palaces threading stepping. See jiǔ gōng bù.

jiǔ gōng jìn 九工劲 Nine skills powers, nine types of power used in Tongbeiquan: crisp, shaking, contained, quick, cold, recoiling, empty, hard. See also cuì, dǒu, hán, jí, lěng, suō, xū, yí, yìng.

jiǔ gōng zhǎng 九宫掌 Nine palaces palm, a hand shape: fingers and thumb naturally straight and slightly separated, palm and wrist inwardly closed. From Tongbeiquan and Piguaquan.

jiǔ jié 九节 Nine sections of the body, the three overall sections each having three sections: root, middle, and tip.

jiǔ jié biān 九节鞭 Nine section whip: a steel whip with nine sections. The standard whip length is to the armpit, holding the grip sideways at the armpit with the whip hanging loose. See biān.

jiǔ pǐn lián tái 九品连台 Low Ranked Officials Give a Performance: Thread through a drop stance, then rise to press down with successive

J

hands. From Liuhebafa.

jiǔ quán 九拳 Nine Fists, a Xingyiquan partner routine, written up as nine moves.

jiǔ tào huán 九套环 Nine Rings. 1. A partner routine of Xinyi Liuhequan. 2. The nine classic partner routines of Xingyiquan. See also āi shēn pào, gǔn fān chuí, jiǎo shǒu pào, jiǔ quán, lián huán chuí, wǔ cǎi liù chuí, wǔ huā pào, wǔ xíng pào, zhǐ zuān chuí.

就 (rad.43) jiù   1. To come near; move towards. 2. To undertake. To accomplish. 3. With regard to; concerning. 4. At once. 5. As early as. 6. In Xingyiquan, to control oneself, uniting upper and lower limbs. 7. As a specific method, to follow an adversary, sticking and controlling.

jiù dì 就地 On the spot, in place.

jiù dì qǔ bǎo 就地取宝 Get the Treasure on the Spot: a drop stance pressing down strike. From Piguaquan.

jiù dì shēng fēng 就地生风 Create Wind on the Spot: a full squat, punching straight down at the side.

jiù dì shí bā gǔn 就地十八滚 Eighteen rolling methods on the spot, training to improve falling and tumbling ability: to undergo a systematic and repetitive variety of tumbling drills. Also called jiē tí gōng.

臼 (rad.134) jiù   1. A mortar. 2. Mortar shaped things. 3. A joint (of the body).

舊 (rad.134) [旧] (rad.72) jiù   1. Past; bygone. 2. Used; worn. 3. Former. 4. Antique. 5. Longstanding.

jiù lì lüè guò xīn lì wèi shēng 旧力略过新力未生 Just as an initial attack has passed and a further attack is not yet initiated. The perfect moment for a counter attack.

居 (rad.44) jū   1. To reside; dwell; live. 2. Residence. 3. Be in a certain place or position.

jū liáo 居髎 Acupoint Juliao (residing bone-hole), GB29. At the hip, at the most protuberant part of the iliac crest, in the body of the tensor fascia latae muscle (on each side). From TCM.

拘 (rad.64) jū   To restrain, seize; detain.

jū mǎ pīn 拘马拚 Restrain the Horse and Risk All. 1. A hand technique where one hand controls an adversary's hand while the other hacks at his head with the palm edge. 2. Both hands shut down an adversary's arms then push him away. Both from Xingyiquan.

jū yì mò sōng 拘意莫松 Control the mind without slackening. A martial saying. Advice for sparring, to pay attention to all opportunities.

局 (rad.44) jú   In sports, a game, set, period, or inning. In martial arts, a round: a two minute round in Sanda. A Sanda match is made up of three rounds with a minute rest between each. Also called huí hé, lún cì.

jú jiān xiū xī 局间休息 Intermission, rest period, break between rounds.

舉 (rad.134) [举] (rad.3) jǔ   1. To hold up (usually palms up). 2. Lift, raise. 3. Manner, deportment.

jǔ dāo mò qí huái bào yuè 举刀磨旗怀抱月 Raise the Blade to Turn the Pennant and Cradle the Moon: holding a halberd, raise the blade, then sit to empty stance and cradle the shaft. From Chen Taijiquan.

jǔ gùn 举棍 Present a staff, usually at the beginning of a routine. May hold the staff in one or both hands, and vertically, horizontally, or diagonally. See also dān shǒu lì jǔ gùn, shuāng shǒu lì jǔ gùn, shuāng shǒu píng jǔ gùn, shuāng shǒu xié jǔ gùn.

jǔ huǒ shāo tiān 举火烧天 Light a Fire to Burn Heaven: shift forward from a low stance to a bow stance, with a double uppercut. From Meishanquan.

jǔ zhàng sōng shēng 举杖松声 Raise the Stick to the Sound of the Pine: a lifting interception with a sword. Retreat a number of steps and set into a horse stance, and snap the blade angled downwards. From Qingping sword.

jǔ zhòng 举重 Weight lifting, training with weights.

巨 (rad.48) **jù** Huge, gigantic, tremendous.

jù gǔ 巨骨 Acupoint Jugu (great bone), LI16. At the top of the shoulder, in the depression between the end of the clavicle and the scapula (on each side). From TCM.

jù liáo 巨髎 Acupoint Juliao (great bone-hole), ST3. At the face, directly below a pupil straight down from ST2, outside the trough at a nostril (on each side). From TCM.

jù mǎng fān shēn 巨蟒翻身 Huge Python Rolls Over: Lift a spear overhead with the right hand (right foot forward), then roll under the shaft to take it in both hands (finishing in left foot forward cross stance). From Shaolinquan.

jù què 巨阙 Acupoint Juque (great tower gate), RN14. At the abdomen, six *cun* above the navel, on the midline. From TCM. The solar plexus, one of the main targets on the body. Striking here induces breathlessness to the point of immobility, and injures the liver, gallbladder, and heart. Striking too hard can cause death. Acupoint Jiuwei is also in the area of the solar plexus, see also jiū wěi.

聚 (rad.128) **jù** To come or put together. To assemble, gather.

jù qì 聚气 Assemble the breath: breathe out, pushing firmly from the abdomen. To give more strength to quick, powerful movement.

jù quán 聚泉 Extraordinary acupoint Juquan, EX-HN10. Inside the mouth, on the tongue, at the middle. From TCM.

jù shǒu pào 聚手炮 Assemble the hands pound: drop into a squat, pounding one hand into the palm of the other in front of the body. From Shaolinquan.

距 (rad.157) **jù** Distance. Be at a distance from.

jù lí gǎn 距离感 Sense of distance, judgement of distance: an essential element of fighting.

鋸 [锯] (rad.167) **jù** 1. A saw. 2. To saw.

jù chǐ láng yá dāo 锯齿狼牙刀 A sawtooth wolf fang halberd: a halberd with teeth on the spine of the blade.

卷 捲 (rad.26, 64) [卷] (rad.26) **juǎn** 1. To roll up; roll. 2. To sweep off (as a wave). 3. As a Qinna technique, to roll up an adversary's wrist.

juǎn dà dāo 卷大刀 Roll with a big cutter: with a two handed cut, settle the blade down, then circle it to slice upward, using power from the waist.

juǎn dì fēng 卷地风 Whirlwind: powerful footwork that drives forward with a trampling force.

juǎn guǒ jìn 卷裹劲 Wrapping power, the power of the arms needed to envelop and control an adversary.

juǎn jìn 卷劲 Rolling up power: to redirect the incoming power and technique of an adversary, changing its direction and sending it back the way it came, like a wave breaking on the shore and sweeping something out to sea.

juǎn lián 卷帘 Roll up the Hanging Curtain: to absorb and shoot back power. Also called juǎn zhū.

juǎn lián dào tuì nán zhē bì 卷帘倒退难遮闭 Roll up the Hanging Curtain, Back off, Hard to Block or Shut Down: retreating rising flowers with a halberd. From Chen Taijiquan.

juǎn ná fǎ 卷拿法 Rolling grappling hold. 1. A rolling snap, like when the arms are wrapped around the neck of the adversary and you roll to get the throw. 2. To squeeze an adversary's neck with the arms. From wrestling.

juǎn quán 卷拳 Fist roll: grab an adversary's fist and hyper-flex his wrist, bowing forward to increase the pressure. From Qinna.

juǎn tǔ 卷土 Rolling dust: coming back with a counter attack.

juǎn wàn 卷腕 Wrist roll: if the adversary puts his hand on your shoulder or chest, press your hand onto his, then twist the little finger side inwards and press down to roll his wrist over. From Qinna.

juǎn xīn quán 卷心拳 Rolled fist: fingers curled tightly, thumb tucked onto them, fist surface flat.

juǎn zhū 卷珠 Roll up (the hanging curtain made of) pearls. See juǎn lián.

J

撅 (rad.64) juē 1. To break, to snap. 2. To protrude. 3. To dig.

juē jìn 撅劲 Breaking power: to control an incoming attack and break it so that it loses effectiveness.

juē shǒu 撅手 Seize, grab, digging hand technique: dig down along with the line of attack.

厥 (rad.27) jué 1. To faint, lose consciousness. 2. Formal: his, her, its, their.

jué yīn 厥阴 Jue Yin, terminal *yin* system: the most *yin* closing nature sub-type of the *yin* meridian channels. In channel theory, it is closing inward, *yin is* retreating to begin to revert to *yang*. This system is the channel of storage and rejuvenation. Diagrammed as one *yang* line under two *yin* lines. Also translated as Reverting Yin. From TCM.

jué yīn shū 厥阴俞 Acupoint Jueyinshu (terminal *yin* transport), BL14. At the back, level with the depression below the spinous process of the fourth thoracic vertebra, 1.5 *cun* lateral to the midline (on each side). From TCM.

抉 (rad.64) jué Original meaning is to pick out; single out. Gouge, pluck out. Martial meaning is often joint control and dislocation methods.

橛 (rad.75) jué A short wooden stake; peg. 1. A weapon about 1.5 metres long, shaped like a chopstick. 2. A shorter weapon, about one metre long, with a wooden handgrip and metal hooks on the tips. Both weapons are usually double weapons, and often have a cord attached through a hole in the grip, which attaches to the wrist.

決 (rad.85) [决] (rad.15) jué 1. To decide; to conclude. 2. To burst (a dike). 3. Certain.

jué jìn 决劲 To burst as water bursting a dike. One of Xingyiquan's five powers. See also cǎi jìn, guǒ jìn, pū jìn and shù jìn.

jué xīn 决心 Determination; resolution. A character trait expected of martial artists.

絕, 絕 [绝] (rad.120) jué 1. To cut off; sever. 2. Exhausted; used up. 3. Desperate. 4. Superb; matchless. 5. Uncompromising. 6. Extremely; most. 7. By any means.

jué lì 绝力 Matchless strength, strength that surpasses most people.

jué zhāo 绝招 Superb skills. A matchless technique. A master stroke.

角 (rad.148) jué 1. Wrestling. 2. A role; character. 3. Pronounced jiǎo, a corner; a horn.

jué dǐ 角抵 Old style Chinese wrestling. Also called jué dǐ, see below.

jué dǐ 角觚 See jué dǐ above.

jué shì 角试 A wrestling or sparring contest in old times.

蹶 (rad.157) juě To kick backward like a horse.

juě zǐ jiǎo 蹶子脚 Mule kick, donkey kick: a side kick with the hip turned into the kick, a rear thrust kick. From Chuojiao, one of its middle-basin kicks. Also called juě zi tuǐ.

juě zǐ tuǐ 蹶子腿 1. A rear thrust kick. From Tongbeiquan. 2. A mule kick, see juě zi jiǎo.

軍 [军] (rad.159) jūn Armed forces; army; troops.

jūn mén sì bì 军门四闭 Close off the Army in Four Directions: chop a sword into a right empty stance, then step the left leg forward and turn into another right empty stance, chopping again. From Qingping sword.

jūn zhàn qiāng 军战枪 Army battle spear: a routine of Yangjia style, written up as forty-three moves.

K

扌卡 (rad.64) **kā**   To grab around something.

kā yāo 扌卡腰 Grab the waist: grab around an adversary's waist to prevent yourself from being thrown.

扌葛 (rad.64) **kā**   To scrape; to scrape with a knife. Pronounced gē, also means to scrape.

kā shǒu 扌葛手 Push hands partner practice. Usually called tuī shǒu. From Taijiquan.

卡 (rad.25) **kǎ**   To block, hit or grab (colloquially used for its sound).

kǎ bó zǐ 卡脖子 Grab the throat. Also called huáng yīng nié sù.

kǎ jīn 卡筋 Grab a tendon: grab a tendon, artery or vein. From Qinna.

kǎ miàn chuí 卡面锤 Hit the Face punch: a rising drilling punch. From Xingyiquan.

開 (rad.169) [开] (rad.55) **kāi**   1. To open. 2. Open to the outside.

kāi bù 开步 Open parallel stance, usually shoulder width, with relatively straight legs. Also called kāi lì bù when the legs are fully straight.

kāi dāng 开裆 Open the crotch: turn the forward knee out in a bow stance, exposing the groin to attack. This is considered an error in most styles, unless the foot and knee are turned out in a specific way to suit a specific technique.

kāi fèng yǎn 开凤眼 Open the phoenix eye. See fèng yǎn quán.

kāi gōng sā jiàn 开弓撒箭 Pull the Bow to Cast Arrows: pull an adversary's arm out and push to strike the throat. From Baguazhang.

kāi gōng shì 开弓式 Pull the Bow stance: extend the fist forward while pulling back the other by the ear, in an open bow stance. From Bajiquan.

kāi gōng zhǒu 开弓肘 Pull the Bow Elbows: open both elbows flat out to the sides with a short power, to strike the ribs.

kāi hé bù 开合步 Open and close stepping: step to the side by first stepping out then stepping in, keeping the feet parallel.

kāi hé shì lì 开合试力 Open and close testing power: stand in sixty-forty stance with the arms in front of the chest, palms facing, open and close the arms. From Yiquan, one of its combat testing moves.

kāi hé zhuāng 开合桩 Open and close stake standing: standing upright with the hands in holding posture, allow the arms to open and close with the breathing.

kāi jìn 开劲 Opening power. 1. Spreading open, a close range technique. 2. A light power that opens out a strong attack, making it fail.

kāi kē 开磕 Knock open (with a broadsword): to strike or block outwards by wrapping the blade around the head. See also guǒ nǎo dāo.

kāi kǒu quán 开口拳 Open mouthed fist, a hand shape: the index and middle fingers are tightly clenched and the thumb presses on the middle segment of the index and middle fingers, the little and ring fingers are only loosely clenched. From Bajiquan.

kāi kuà 开胯 Open the hips 1. Hip joint training to open and release the hip joints, includes kicks and general exercises such as stretching, swinging, pressing. 2. The rear hip splayed out in a bow stance, an error. Also called fàng kuà.

kāi lì bù 开立步 Open parallel standing stance, shoulder width, with straight legs. Also called kāi bù.

kāi mǎ 开马 Open to stance: set up, settle into stance. This refers to horse as in stance, a fighting stance, not to a horse stance.

kāi mén 开门 Open the door. 1. Take a ready stance for fighting. 2. Fakes or actions that make an adversary open his defensive doors, making him vulnerable to getting in close.

kāi mén fǎ 开门法 Open the Door techniques: methods to open up an adversary or make him

K

vulnerable to attack.

kāi mén quán 开门拳 Kaimenquan (open the doors fist). See bā jí quán.

kāi mén yíng kè 开门迎客 Open the Door and Greet the Guest: stand up with double straight palm thrusts, then roll the hands back and do double straight punches, then roll again to punch down. From southern styles.

kāi mén zhuō yǐng 开门捉影 Open the Door and Catch a Shadow. 1. Open out the arms to the sides, exposing the whole torso as an open target, to draw in an adversary in preparation for a counter attack. 2. To take a ready stance while making unnecessary moves as if catching a shadow. An error in most styles.

kāi pì shān chuān 开辟山川 Open up Mountains and Rivers: stand up straight with a large hooking swing, finally chopping down with the arm aligned with the sword blade, to the right. From Qingping sword.

kāi quán 开拳 Kaiquan (opening fist). See bā jí quán.

kāi shān fǔ 开山斧 Mountain opening axe: a long handled axe with a heavy curved blade, a wavy point beyond the blade, and a metal tipped sleeve at the butt end.

kāi shān zhǎng 开山掌 Mountain opening palm: drop to a drop stance, chopping down with the arm extended along the extended leg. From Chuojiao.

kāi shǒu 开手 1. Take a ready stance for sparring. 2. Expand the arms slightly, palms facing each other. From Sun Taijiquan.

kāi shǒu ér dié shǒu 开手而叠手 If an adversary blocks your attack towards the outside, roll back then strike again. From Tanglangquan, one of its twelve soft counters, see also shí èr róu.

kāi zhǎng 开掌 Opening palm: with the palm up or down, strike horizontally outwards to the side.

鎧 [铠] (rad.167) **kǎi** Armour.

kǎi jiǎ 铠甲 A suit of armour.

坎 (rad.32) **kǎn** The Water-as-Rain Trigram, represented by one solid (*yang*) within two broken (*yin*) lines, called 'middle full'. Corresponds to the cloud formation or gate. An opening gate formation. Indicates the attribute of dangerous.

砍 (rad.112) **kǎn** To hack, cut, chop.

kǎn dāo 砍刀 Hack down with a broadsword blade at an angle. The wrist stays cocked so that the blade cuts with the whole blade, not the tip. This may be done holding with one or both hands.

kǎn fǎ 砍法 Hacking methods: to hack flat across with the blade of the palm with full body power.

kǎn zhǎng 砍掌 Hack with the knife edge of the palm.

糠 (rad.119) **kāng** Chaff; bran; husk.

kāng bāo 糠包 A husk filled canvas bag: used for training to develop hard skills, especially fist, palm, and forearm strikes. Normal size is about thirty centimetres square, ten centimetres thick. Used to toss and grab to train grasping skills, to hit to train striking skills and hardness, and to toss back and forth between partners to train strength and coordination.

扛 (rad.64) **káng** 1. To hoist, carry on the shoulder. 2. A hand technique or throw that imitates the action of shouldering a carrying pole, shouldering a long weapon or a hoe to carry it. 3. In wrestling, a throw that first lifts an adversary on the shoulders, and also used for the leg technique of hooking and lifting with the lower leg. 4. Pronounced gāng, to carry between two people, see gāng.

káng biè 扛别 A hoist: a throw that hoists an adversary up, either with the legs or the shoulders.

káng fǎ 扛法 Hoisting: grab an adversary and pull down while reaching forward and setting the shoulders.

káng kǒu dài wán 扛口袋玩 Hoist the Bag Playfully: trap your adversary's arms over the shoulder and step in to throw over the hip. From Baguazhang.

káng tī 扛踢 Hoist and trip: both grabbing and trying to shift the other, quickly drive the head in underneath the adversary's arm and step in, lifting and twisting his body. From wrestling.

káng zhǒu 扛肘 Hoist the elbow: grab your adversary's wrist, turn your back on him while moving in, turning and extending his arm, placing his arm on your shoulder and pulling down to hyper-extend his elbow.

抗 (rad.64) **kàng** 1. To contend with, resist. Fight, combat. Refuse, defy. 2. In wrestling, it is the use of the shoulders and waist in a throw. 3. Contend, the error of over-doing the contention in push hands. From Taijiquan, one of its four defects in push hands. See also sì bìng.

kàng jī 抗击 Resist, beat back.

kàng jīn 抗筋 Test the tensile strength of a tendon: pull on a tendon, artery or vein. From Qinna.

kàng lì 抗力 Ability and strength to fight.

kàng tóu 抗头 Contend with the head: when in a choke hold, press into your adversary's body with the head, neck, and shoulders to gain control.

靠 (rad.175) **kào** 1. The standard meaning is to lean the back against something like a wall; get near to; nearby; depend on. 2. The martial meaning is to lean on, bump: a close strike with the shoulder, upper back, hip, or chest, with the body touching an adversary. 3. In Baguazhang, also an outward parry with the forearm. 4. In wrestling, the category of throws that involve getting down low and leaning the shoulder into an adversary, the body angled (is a throw, not a hit, so the arms are usually hugging an adversary). 5. In Taijiquan, a power issue short force when the body is in contact. 6. To use part of the body to strike the torso of the adversary with power. From Bajiquan, one of its ten major techniques, see also shí dà jī fǎ.

kào bì 靠臂 Arm bumping. See kē bì gōng.

kào fǎ 靠法 Category of counters to attacks from behind, using the back, elbows, or buttocks.

kào jìn 靠劲 Bumping power: the power and skill used to perform any leaning strike or throw with the shoulders, back, hip, etc.

kào shān tàn xué 靠山探穴 Lean on the Mountain to Reach into the Hollow: lean into a bow stance and reach the rear hand over the head, pressing the front hand down at the knee. From Wudangquan.

kào shēn 靠身 Lean on, bump: any strike with the torso, such as shoulder or upper back.

kào shēn tún chuí 靠身臀捶 Lean in and Bump with the Buttocks: step in between your adversary's feet and sit in his thigh for a takedown. From Tanglangquan, one of its eight short techniques.

kào shēn zhǎng 靠身掌 Lean on: in bow stance, a shoulder or upper back strike, the arms angled, front arm up and rear arm down, and extended just past the line of the legs.

kào shēn zhǒu 靠身肘 Leaning elbow: get in close to an adversary and strike with the point of the elbow.

kào shuāi 靠摔 Leaning throw: get in close to an adversary, holding him and setting your shoulder and head into his trunk, pressing forward to take him down backwards.

kào tóu 靠头 Leaning head: lean your head into an adversary's head in a clinch.

kào zhǒu 靠肘 Butt with the elbow: with the elbows tight to the ribs, strike straight back, also moving back with the body. This is the counter to a close hold from behind. Also called shí miàn mái fú.

磕 (rad.112) **kē** To knock hard against something; bump; strike. Used for an abrupt block or strike.

kē bì gōng 磕臂功 Arm knocking training: a pattern of arm strikes done with a partner, working through all sides of the forearms and upper arms, to train the ability to give and take hits with the arms. Also called kào bì.

kē dà tóu 磕大头 Full prostration: a full prostration to extend the body on the ground. Used in Yiquan as an exercise.

kē pèng 磕碰 1. To knock against something. 2. To take a hit.

kē shǒu 磕手 A hard block to the outside, similar to a check. See also bō.

kē shǒu ér rù shǒu 磕手而入手 If your attack is blocked hard, attack with the other hand. From Tanglangquan, one of its twelve soft counters, see also shí èr róu.

kē tóu 磕头 Prostration: to kneel and touch the head to the ground. Called a kowtow in English.

kē xiǎo tuǐ 磕小腿 Lower leg bumping: knocking the shins and calves together with a partner to

K

develop the ability to give and take hits with the lower legs.

kē zhǒu 磕肘 Knock with the elbow. 1. With the elbow bent, a short movement inwards to contact with the forearm. 2. A strike down with the point of the elbow.

可 (rad.30) **kě** 1. Approved. 2. Can; may. 3. Be worth (doing). 4. But; however. 5. Also is used for emphasis in phrases.

kě jī miàn jī 可击面积 Allowable striking area: the parts of the body allowed to be struck during sparring bouts.

剋 [克] (rad.10) **kè** 1. To subdue, restrain, overcome. 2. To restrain, as the five phases are interconnected by engendering and restraining. See also wǔ xíng xiāng kè.

掯 (rad.64) **kèn** To oppress, extort, take by force.

kèn tóu 掯头 A small movement of the head, tucking it to assist power in a throw.

空 (rad.116) **kōng** Empty, hollow, void.

kōng bǎ 空把 Empty butt: in some styles that do not grip the spear at the very end of the shaft, this is the end sticking out. The right hand is a fist-length away from the end of the butt.

kōng chéng fàng jiàn 空城放箭 Shoot Arrows at an Empty City: Fake to keep an adversary's hands up, and kick to his groin. From Shaolinquan.

kōng chéng jì 空城计 The Strategy of the Empty City. Present a bold front to conceal a weakness. The thirty-second of the Thirty-six Stratagems of Warfare, which apply to many situations.

kōng dāng 空裆 Literally means empty groin, but means any unguarded space or opportunity that you give to an adversary. Also called pò zhàn.

kōng jī 空击 Empty striking. 1. A training method for sparring: practise attack and defense together without contact, taking the time to think out each situation. 2. Thinking out defenses for various situations on your own.

kōng jià zǐ 空架子 Empty postures: posing or doing ineffectual moves with no meaning or feeling.

kōng quán 空拳 Empty fist: a loosely clenched fist.

kōng xiōng 空胸 Empty chest. 1. The shoulders settled down and very slightly in, the chest is broad and comfortable, and the breath is unimpeded, so that the chest feels empty rather than full. From Baguazhang. 2. In wrestling, when an adversary is wrapped around your head and chest, empty the chest so that it pulls away from him and allows you to slide out.

kōng zhōng chuí diào 空中垂钓 Go Angling in the Air: bring a sword around with a full chopping circle, hook and continue to circle, ending up piercing directly up. From Qingping sword.

kōng zhōng lǜ qì shì lì 空中滤气试力 Filter air testing power: stand in sixty-forty stance, with the front hand above head height and the rear hand at face height. Clench the fists and lower the hands. From Yiquan, one of its combat testing moves.

孔 (rad.39) **kǒng** 1. A hole, an opening, aperture. 2. A surname.

kǒng mén quán 孔门拳 Kongmenquan (Kong style fist), a hard southern style from Hubei province, spread down to Guangzhou province.

kǒng xué 孔穴 Hole; cavity.

kǒng zuì 孔最 Acupoint Kongzui (collection hole), LU6. On the inside of the forearm, about 7 *cun* up from the wrist bend, 5 *cun* down from the elbow crease (on each arm). From TCM. A sensitive point, pressing here can cause numbness and pain. If more pressure is applied it can shock the Lung and induce unconsciousness.

控 (rad.64) **kòng** To control.

kòng gǔ 控骨 Bone control, a dislocation method, grabbing the joint directly to wrench it.

kòng juǎn 控卷 Clench the fist. Usually called wò quán.

kòng tuǐ 控腿 Leg control training, holding the leg up without support.

kòng zhì jì shù 控制技术 The methods and skills of joint controls.

摳 [抠] (rad.64) **kōu** To dig out with a finger; scratch.

kōu fǎ 抠法 Digging method: grab with the middle finger extended to gouge. Best used on natural depressions like the shoulder depression, behind the knees, etc.

kōu tuǐ 抠腿 Dig up the leg, a throw. See tāo tuǐ.

口 (rad.30) kǒu   1. Mouth. 2. Oral. 3. The lips, one of the five sensory organs, see also wǔ guān.

kǒu hé liáo 口禾髎 Acupoint Kouheliao (mouth's grain bone-hole), LI19. Also called Heliao. Above the upper lip, just below a nostril (on each side). From TCM.

kǒu jué 口诀 Orally transmitted nugget of information pointing out the essentials of the particular style, usually with simple, evocative phrasing, sometimes rhyming.

扣 釦 (rad.64,167) [扣] (rad.64) kòu The basic word has many readings that are all linked in meaning. To tuck in; tucked in. Concave, closed, arced. Hook in. Control. Button up, do up buttons; buckle a belt; latch a door. Place a cup upside down. Tie a knot. Detain, arrest. To deduct; discount. The action done to spike a ball such as in volleyball.
Each meaning gives a nuance to the martial use. The martial meaning is usually: 1. Tuck something in or hook something in. 2. Controlling or grappling technique: crank a joint backwards. 3. One of the eight body requirements of Xingyiquan to keep the shoulders buttoned down, backs of hands and feet arced, and teeth closed. 4. Tucking, one of the sixteen key techniques of Baguazhang, see also shí liù zì jué.

kòu bù 扣步 Hook in step, tuck in step or stance. 1. Step hooking in, a hook-in step, a tucking inward step. 2. The stance resulting from the tucked in step – a T stance, an open V stance, a box stance, or a horse stance. 3. A tucked stance: a stance with one foot tucked in behind the supporting bent knee. See kòu tuǐ.

kòu dāng 扣裆 Tuck in the crotch. 1. Turn in the foot or knee to protect the groin. 2. Close in at the crotch without necessarily turning in the leg. Commonly used in bow stance, empty stance, and knee lifting postures.

kòu fǎ 扣法 Tucking control: category of techniques that circle and press down with the edge of the hand or foot. Also called zhǎng chén xià chā.

kòu fēn 扣分 Deduct points in competition.

kòu jiàn 扣剑 Tuck a sword: hold a sword with the wrist curled underneath the blade.

kòu jīn zhōng 扣金钟 Hit the Golden Bell: a straight legged slap kick, not snapping. From Chuojiao.

kòu jìn 扣劲 Tucking in power.

kòu lǚ 扣将 Tuck onto and pull.

kòu quán 扣拳 Tuck the fist. 1. Tuck with the forearm to block, or grab while tucking to twist. 2. A downward arcing punch with the arm bent, contacting with the fist surface. 3. To grab an adversary's wrist from below, if he is grabbing your sleeve, and pull down while striking above with the other hand.

kòu shǒu 扣手 Tuck the hand. 1. Grab, lock, control, or hook across the back of an adversary's hand to push his hand back on his wrist. 2. Hook the wrist in to control with the palm. From Qinna.

kòu tuǐ 扣腿 Tuck the leg. 1. Using the bottom of the foot to kick inwardly and horizontally. Can hook, catch, or stick in. 2. A stance with the foot tucked in behind the knee of the bent supporting leg, in at least a forty-five degrees squat. The stance is the same as the kòu tuǐ píng héng balance, just not held as a balance. Also called jiāo jiǎo bù, jiāo jiǎo mǎ, kòu bù.

kòu tuǐ píng héng 扣腿平衡 Tucked leg balance, knee lock balance: Squatting on one leg, thigh horizontal, with the other foot hooked behind the knee. In a competition routine, the balance must be held for two seconds.

kòu wàn 扣腕 Tuck the wrist. 1. Grab across the back of your adversary's hand, placing his palm up, and press his hand down towards the forearm, hyper-flexing his wrist. From Qinna. 2. As a wrist movement, to tuck the wrist, bend the wrist and tuck the thumb in for hooking techniques and some grabbing techniques.

kòu xī 扣膝 Tuck in the knee. 1. As a knee technique: tuck in the knee to protect the centre. 2. In stance: in horse stance, fix the feet and hip joints and tuck the knees inwards to round the crotch (from the back) and stabilise the stance.

K

(method used in some styles, in others, the requirement is to brace out the knees, see also chēng xī).

kòu zhǎng 扣掌 Tucked palm, a hand shape. 1. In Shaolinquan, fingers extended and slightly separated, thumb tucked towards the base of the little finger. 2. In Monkey style, the index finger's distal segment is flexed. 3. In Baguazhang, the fingertips and thumb tip are touching, but the palm is open.

kòu zhǒu 扣肘 Tuck the elbow: when an adversary grabs your shoulder or chest, bring your hands up on either side of his elbow and turn it over, pressing down for a takedown.

kòu zhuàn jiě 扣转节 Lock and rotate the joint: when your adversary clenches a fist, hold his wrist in one hand and his little finger or thumb in the other, squeezing it and twisting at its joint. From Qinna.

敂 (rad.66) [叩] (rad.26) kòu 1. To knock. 2. To kowtow (knock the head on the ground).

kòu tuǐ 叩腿 Knock kick: kick to the shin of an adversary behind you. Also called hòu mén kǎn tuǐ.

枯 (rad.75) kū Withered (of a plant); dried up (of a well, river); dull.

kū shù pán gēn 枯树盘根 Withered Tree Twines its Roots. 1. Spin around while lowering the body (may be slicing a sword or broadsword flat), spinning into a crossed sit stance. 2. In wrestling, with your adversary behind you, grab his foot and sit on his leg to take him down, then twist his leg. 3. In Baguazhang, step in behind your adversary's legs and sit into a drop stance, pressing his knee with the hand, then lifting to throw.

苦 (rad.140) kǔ 1. Bitter. 2. Hardship; suffering. 3. To cause suffering. 4. Suffer from. 5. Do one's utmost.

kǔ liàn 苦练 To train hard; to practise diligently; spare no effort.

kǔ ròu jì 苦肉计 The Strategy of Self-inflicted Injury. The thirty-fourth of the Thirty-six Stratagems of Warfare, which apply to many situations.

库 [庫] (rad.53) kù Storeroom, warehouse.

kù fáng 库房 Acupoint Kufang (storeroom), ST14. At the chest, in the first intercostal space beneath the top rib, four *cun* lateral to the midline (on each side). From TCM.

挎 (rad.64) kuà 1. The original, practical, meaning is to carry on the crook of the arm, like carrying a shopping basket. 2. The technique is a close range action that uses the crook of the arm. 3. A hooking strike used to clear the main gateway. From Bajiquan, one of its six main striking techniques, see also liù dà kāi.

kuà hóng 挎肱 Catch with the arm, encircling the torso for an enveloping throw.

kuà jiàn shì 挎剑式 Carry the Sword model. One of twenty-four classic spear moves. Most spear routines will have a move with a like name. In general, this name refers to a large opening dodge.

kuà zhǒu 挎肘 Carrying elbow strike. 1. An upward elbow or forearm strike or block. Can be to first swing the arm up and forward, then bend the elbow to ninety degrees. The movement finishes as if carrying something in the crook of the elbow. 2. Trap an adversary's arm in the crook of your arm to hyper-extend his elbow.

胯 (rad.130) kuà 1. Hip (inside), hip joint, inguinal crease. Note that this is distinguished from the hipbone, see also kuān. 2. The entire groin and pelvis area. 3. Sometimes this character is used for a lower strike.

kuà bēng 胯崩 A hip snapping throw.

kuà fā lì 胯发力 A hip strike, and training for hip strikes. From Yiquan.

kuà guān jié 胯关节 The hip joint, where the leg bone fits into the pelvis. Also referred to as kuān guān jié.

kuà sì bēn mǎ 胯似奔马 The hips are like galloping horses. From Tongbeiquan, one of its requirements.

kuà yào cuī xī ér xī bù ní kuà 胯要催膝而膝不逆胯 Power should flow from the hip joints to the knees, knees should not run counter to the hips. From Xingyiquan.

跨 (rad.157) **kuà** 1. To bestride; straddle. 2. To stride. 3. To cut across.

kuà bù 跨步 Stride, bestride, straddle. 1. Step forward by opening the legs to the side as if stepping over a creek. 2. A fairly large step to the side. Both can be done on the ground or as a leap.

kuà bù yǐn zhǎng 跨步引掌 Stride and Draw: step to the side, then follow in to parallel stance, bracing down with the lead hand while bringing the rear hand over to press the upper arm. From Chaquan.

kuà hǔ 跨虎 Straddle the tiger. This phrase is often used in movement names, to describe a variety of actions.

kuà lán bù 跨栏步 Straddling step: snap the hips and straighten the legs, pivoting on the rear foot and stepping across with the lead foot, so that both feet point the same direction. From wrestling.

kuà mǎ 跨马 Mount the horse: when your adversary is down on his back, move to sit on his chest, holding his wrist and using your legs to gain leverage to break his arm.

kuà mǎ yáng biān 跨马扬鞭 Mount a Horse and Wield a Whip: lift the knee and separate the hands. From Piguaquan.

kuà mǎ yáo qí 跨马摇旗 Mount a Horse and Wave a Banner: a circling kick as the hands also circle. From Piguaquan.

kuà tiào bù 跨跳步 Jumping stride step: take a step forward then push off and stride the other foot forward, landing the push off foot forward.

kuà tuǐ 跨腿 Straddling kick: lift the knee, bending the supporting leg. From Duanquan.

kuà zì gōng 跨字功 Bridging skill: one of Xingyiquan's eight skills. Catch and do a straddling step with a low carrying move into the adversary.

扌 (rad.64) **kuǎi** 1. To scratch. 2. To carry on the arm.

快 (rad.61) **kuài** Fast, quick.

kuài bù 快步 Quick step: move quickly forward, lifting the front foot and drag stepping the rear foot.

kuài dǎ chí 快打迟 Quick beats late. A martial saying. A fast technique will always beat a slow or late defense.

kuài mǎ jiā biān 快马加鞭 Whip a Speeding Horse: drop into a drop stance and send a sword out along the extended leg, to cut to the outside. From Baguazhang sword.

kuài màn xiāng jiàn 快慢相间 Quick and slow alternate: use of speed and slower movement, each serving the other. A quality of rhythm in performance and power generation.

kuài rú fēng 快如风 Quick like the wind: one of the twelve qualities of movement of Changquan, though these descriptors apply to many other styles. Powerful and directed speed.

kuài rù 快入 Quick entry: jump in with both feet to get the hips directly in for a throw. From wrestling.

kuài shuāi fǎ 快摔法 Quick throws. 1. Throws that are done quickly on contact to avoid being grabbed and countered. 2. Within Sanda rules, the throw must be completed within two seconds of taking hold.

髋 [髖] (rad.188) **kuān** Hipbone, pelvis. Note that this is distinguished from the hip joint, see also kuà.

kuān gǔ 髋骨 1. Hipbone. 2. Extraordinary acupoint Kuangu, EX-LE1. A pair of points at the thigh, 1.5 *cun* on either side of acupoint Liangqiu. From TCM.

kuān guān jié 髋关节 The hip joint. Usually referred to as kuà guān jié.

盔 (rad.108) **kuī** A helmet.

kuī jiǎ 盔甲 The full suit of helmet and armour.

奎 (rad.37) **kuí** A constellation in the Chinese zodiac, believed to control literary trends.

kuí xīng 奎星 1. The four stars of the bowl of the big dipper. 2 The star at the tip of the bowl. 3. The God of literature.

kuí xīng chuí 奎星捶 God of Literature punch. See kuí xīng shì.

kuí xīng diǎn dǒu 奎星点斗 The God of Literature Points the Dipper, a pole technique:

stand up in a high empty stance, holding the pole straight up at the side, butt at the waist.

kuí xīng shì 奎星势 God of Literature stance: step back with an elbow cover, then shift forward with an upward scrape. From Xingyiquan. Also called kuí xīng chuí, wū lóng dào qǔ shuǐ.

kuí xīng tī dǒu 奎星踢斗 The God of Literature Kicks the Dipper. 1. A rope dart technique: lay the dart on the foot and kick it out. 2. Block with a sword blade above the head, kicking and striking with the left hand and right foot. From Wu Taijiquan. 3. From a horse stance, kick and tuck the foot back, with both fists at the waist. The 42nd move of the tiger and crane routine.

魁 (rad.194) kuí   1. A chief; head. 2. Outstanding. 3. Stalwart.

kuí xīng 魁星 See kuí xīng 奎星.

kuí xīng shì 魁星势 Big Dipper Stance: push a sword, blade vertical, then raise the knee and lift the sword over the head. From Yang Taijiquan.

坤 (rad.32) kūn   The Earth Trigram, represented by three broken (yin) lines, called 'six broken'. Female. Corresponds to the earthly formation or gate. A closing gate formation. Indicates the attribute of devoted or yielding.

昆 (rad.72) kūn   1. An elder brother. 2. Descendants. 3. Multitudes. 4. In unison.

kūn lún 昆仑 Acupoint Kunlun (Kunlun mountains), BL60. At the ankle, on the outside, at the cavity just above the ankle bone, between the lateral malleolus and the Achilles tendon. From TCM. An easy target. A sharp low kicking sweep here can make the whole lower leg go numb.

kūn lún jiàn 昆仑剑 Kunlun sword, a representative routine of Chaquan, written up in fifty-five moves.

kūn lún quán 昆仑拳 Kunlunquan (Kunlun mountains fist), a style from the Kunlun mountains, developed and spread in northern China. The Kunlun Mountains are the range of mountains between Xinjiang and Tibet.

kūn wú jiàn 昆吾剑 Kunwu sword, a style specialising in the straight sword. It is generally practised in a long routine, written up as one hundred and twenty moves, though it also has more training methods.

捆 (rad.64) kǔn   1. To tie up, bundle up; strap up. 2. A throwing technique: to tie up the adversary. 3. Often refers to a throw that involves holding an adversary's legs. 4. A leg technique, to step in to tie up an adversary's legs.

kǔn shǒu 捆手 Tie up with the arms: to dissolve an attack by turning the body and circling the forearms outwards, elbows at the same height, one forearm turned up, one forearm turned down. From Wing Chun.

廓 (rad.53) kuò   1. Broad, wide, open. 2. Sometimes refers to the neck, as in a broad surface at the rear, when wrapping around it.

闊 [阔] (rad.169) kuò   Wide; broad; vast.

kuò jīn mó zhāng jī 阔筋膜张肌 The iliotibial tract.

L

拉 (rad.64) lā   To pull, draw, tug, drag.

lā fǎ 拉法 Grab and pull sharply back, simultaneously snapping downward.

lā jià zǐ 拉架子 Pull the moves: practice a routine slowly.

lā kāi jià zǐ 拉开架子 Open up the stance: take a ready stance for fighting.

lā lā bù 拉拉步 Pulling steps: take a step in any direction and pull the other foot to follow along.

lā mǎ bù 拉马步 Pulling horse stance.

lā mó 拉磨 Pulling the millstone: circle-walking with the body turned at least one-twenty degrees. From Baguazhang.

lā ná fǎ 拉拿法 Pulling grappling hold: pull an adversary into close contact with your body in preparation for a throw. From wrestling.

lā shāng 拉伤 A strain or sprain injury, a pulled tendon or muscle injury.

lā tuǐ 拉腿 Pull the leg: hook onto your adversary's foot and pull it forward, releasing your grip on him so he falls backwards.

lā tuǐ fān shēn tiào 拉腿翻身跳 Layout body wheel: jump up and turn the body over fully in the air with the arms and legs open, leaving a leg behind so that body appears to float in the air.

lā qiāng 拉枪 Pull a spear: extend the spear behind the body with the shaft on the body.

剌 (rad.18) lá   A cutting slice with a pulling action towards you. To chop and pull simultaneously to increase the depth of the cut, like a cook slicing ham with a sharp knife.

攔 [拦] (rad.64) lán General meaning is to bar, block, hold back; impede; obstruct; hinder. Martial meaning is a circular cover and trap, keeping pressure away from yourself controlling to the outside. When deflecting with a blade, refers to using its rear side. When empty hand, is usually with the forearm. With the leg, is a pressure or kick to trip. One of the sixteen key techniques of Baguazhang, see also shí liù zì jué.

lán dà dāo 拦大刀 Trap with a big cutter: with the right hand near the blade, circle with both hands so that the blade circles horizontally around from one side to the other.

lán dēng tuǐ 拦蹬腿 Trap and Thrust kick: an inward hook kick followed by a side kick with the same leg. From Chuojiao.

lán jié qiāng 拦截枪 Intercepting outer trap with spear: to do an outer trap while bringing the spear back from a stab.

lán mǎ jué 拦马橛 Horse trapping double stick, a representative routine of Chaquan, written up as forty-six moves.

lán mén jiǎo 拦门脚 Trapping kick: trap an adversary with the sole of the foot, contacting his foot, knee, or body. A low kick is specifically also called cǎi jiǎo.

lán mén tuǐ 拦门腿 Trapping kick: hop forward while doing a skimming hook up kick. From Chuojiao.

lán ná qiāng 拦拿枪 1. An outer, then inner trap with a spear. 2. Traditionally, this dual trapping action done as a high defense. See also fēng bì qiāng, tí lū qiāng.

lán ná zhā 拦拿扎 Spear technique of outer trap, inner trap, stab. Also called fēng bì qiāng, yī qiāng fēn xīn. See also lán qiāng, ná qiāng, zhā qiāng.

lán qiāng 拦枪 Outer trap with a spear, circling counter-clockwise with the shaft horizontal. Parry or cover outward. Also traditionally called wài bǎ mén fèng.

lán shǒu 拦手 1. A forearm bar: the forearm in front of the body and horizontal, blocking across the body. This can be single or double arm. From Wing Chun. 2. Close the fist and pull in, turning the fist heart up. From Mojiaquan.

lán shǒu mén 拦手门 Lanshoumen (barring hands style) from Henan province, known since the beginning of the Qing dynasty, and spread across

L

the northern provinces. Known for clear, solid stances and powerful techniques.

lán shǒu quán 拦手拳 Lanshouquan (barring hands fist), a southern style, attributed to Emei mountain.

lán tī 拦踢 Trapping kick, a trip or throw, curling the leg around an adversary's leg and using leverage for a takedown. From wrestling.

lán yāo cáng dāo 拦腰藏刀 Hide a broadsword around the waist: hide a broadsword with the right hand at the left waist, blade flat behind the body, edge out.

lán yāo dāo 拦腰刀 Wrap a broadsword around the waist. Used with the large bladed Bagua broadsword. See lán yāo jiàn.

lán yāo héng sǎo 拦腰横扫 Wrap a broadsword sweeping around the waist: standing still, sweep the blade around at waist height a full circle and a half, cutting edge leading.

lán yāo jiàn 拦腰剑 Wrap a sword around the waist: with the blade flat, grip at the waist, tip out, step around, bringing the edge around flat, pushing into the blade (used with the larger bladed Bagua sword).

lán zhǒu 拦肘 Obstruct with the elbow, trap, hinder.

闌欄 [阑栏] (rad.169, 75) **lán**
1. A fence. 2. A door screen. 3. To block up. 4. Withered.

lán wěi 阑尾 1. Extraordinary acupoint Lanwei (appendix tail), EX-LE7. At the shin, on the external edge of the tibia, five *cun* below acupoint Dubi. From TCM. This is the most sensitive point on the shins, an excellent target. 2. The appendix.

懶 [懒] (rad.61) **lǎn**
Lazy, indolent; sluggish.

lǎn lóng suō shēn 懒龙缩身 Lazy Dragon Tucks In: sit into a low T stance, drawing in the arms and body, front hand with the elbow tucked into the hip, palm up, rear hand palm down at the front elbow. From Baguazhang.

lǎn lóng wò dào 懒龙卧道 Lazy Dragon Lies in the Road: a strike in a low cross step. 1. With a punch to the groin, also called zhǐ dāng chuí. 2. With a chopping hand. From Xingyiquan.

lǎn lóng wò zhěn 懒龙卧枕 Lazy Dragon Lies on the Pillow. 1. Step into the adversary, striking the neck with the forearm, braced with the other hand. 2. Move in on your adversary to hook a hand around his head from the back, pushing his head back and pushing your knee into his lower back. From Baguazhang, one of its sixty-four hands.

lǎn sǎn 懒散 Lazy and scattered: the spirit not focussed. An error in most styles.

lǎn zhā yī 懒扎衣 Tuck in the Robe Lazily, or Casually. 1. A throw across the leg or an on guard position, setting into a comfortable position in a biased horse stance with one arm up smooth to the leg and the other down at the hip. From Chen Taijiquan. 2. The same arm technique, but in a straight standing position. From Taiji Changquan and Wudangquan.

攬 [揽] (rad.64) **lǎn**
1. To pull into one's arms. To take into one's arms, a hand technique. 2. To fasten with a rope.

lǎn què wěi 揽雀尾 Grasp the Sparrow's Tail: to combine ward off, pull, squeeze, and press down in sequence. See also péng, lǚ, jǐ, àn. From Taijiquan.

纜 [缆] (rad.120) **lǎn**
A mooring rope; a hawser. A thick rope; cable.

lǎn shéng 缆绳 A mooring rope; a hawser. A thick rope; cable. Used as a training aid, with one end tied to something, the other end is manipulated to train wrestling actions.

爛 [烂] (rad.86) **làn**
1. To rot; fester; decay. 2. Rotten; soft; mashed. 3. Messy. Ragged.

làn cǎi huā 烂踩花 Trample on rotting blossoms. See luàn cǎi huā.

狼 (rad.94) **láng**
A wolf, wolves.

láng xiǎn 狼筅 A wolf brush, an ancient weapon: a five metre staff with a number of brush-like projections from twenty five to sixty centimetres long covering the end.

láng yá bàng 狼牙棒 A wolf fang cudgel, an ancient weapon: a two metre staff with a huge oval ball on one end, encrusted with protrusions that resemble a wolf's fangs.

浪 (rad.85) **làng** 1. A wave; a breaker. 2. Dissolute; debauched.

làng lǐ pāo qiú 浪里抛球 Throw a Ball into the Waves: in a horse stance, push the right hand forward, elbow straight, heel of palm up, fingers down. The 41st move of the tiger and crane routine.

làng shēn 浪身 To wave with the body, ripple the body like a wave breaking forward.

làng zǐ cù qiú 浪子蹴球 Loafer Stamps a Ball, a rope dart technique: circle the dart to land on the ground, stepping on the dart with the right foot, then send it out with a kick.

làng zǐ tī qiú 浪子踢球 Loafer Kicks a Ball. 1. A steel whip technique: swing the whip and kick the tip out with the foot. 2. A front snap kick with an opposite hand push or punch (not slap). May also pull back with the hands. From Shaolinquan and others.

làng zǐ xì qiú 浪子戏球 Loafer Plays with a Ball, a rope dart technique: circling the dart, lift the left knee and catch the dart across the foot, then shoot the dart out with the foot.

撈 [捞] (rad.64) **lāo** To dredge, scoop out of water. In martial arts, is a movement as if scooping a fish net out of the water.

lāo dāo 捞刀 Dredge with a broadsword: Bring the blade up from the ground to finish with the grip at head height, the blade slightly angled downwards, edge up. Used more with the larger bladed Bagua broadsword.

lāo ná fǎ 捞拿法 Dredging grappling hold: to drop down and pull an adversary's ankle upwards. From wrestling.

lāo shǒu 捞手 Dredge: downward, outward curving block to the sideline, then lift. Sometimes translated as scooping arm. Dissolves and counters, especially kicks, catching and lifting the leg at the same time. From Choylifut and Wing Chun.

lāo xīn zhǒu 捞心肘 Dredge the heart elbow strike: press down with the elbow and forearm, elbow bent, fist heart facing up. Also called zuǒ zhǒu.

lāo yuè 捞月 Dredge the moon. Go through a drop stance, lowering the hands then shifting across and bringing the hands up. A takedown: drop down and pick up an adversary's foot, off-balancing him backwards.

lāo yuè zhǎng 捞月掌 Dredge the moon palm, a circle-walking posture: the reverse of the downward sinking palm, arms in the same position, but palms up. From Baguazhang. See also xià chén zhǎng.

lāo zhǎng 捞掌 Dredging palm: to scoop up, turning the hand over to palm up, as if scooping with a soup ladle.

勞 [劳] (rad.19) **láo** 1. To labour, work. 2. To bother.

láo gōng 劳宫 Acupoint Laogong (palace of toil), PC8. At the palm, between the second and third metacarpal bones, can be found by the tip of the middle finger by clenching the fist (on each hand). From TCM. A crippling point, pressure here can cause loss of strength as well as pain. Striking too hard may cause serious injury. See also cán xué. In internal styles, this point is relaxed to allow *qi* to stay in the palm while the power flows out the inside of the fingers.

láo sǔn 劳损 A strain, a muscular or joint strain.

老 (rad.125) **lǎo** 1. Old; aged; venerable. 2. Always. Very. 3. In martial arts, sluggish, slow to react.

lǎo bā zhǎng 老八掌 Old eight palms: eight palm changes to practice the basics of Baguazhang. Also called bā dà zhǎng, mǔ zhǎng.

lǎo bù 老步 Old steps: sluggish, unstable footwork. An error in most styles.

lǎo hàn bèi yú 老汉背鱼 Old Man Carries a Fish on his Back: from a wrist grab, grab your adversary's hand in both hands, turn and place his arm across your back, his elbow at your shoulder, then bow forward. From Qinna.

lǎo hǔ 老虎 A tiger, often used for movement names See also hǔ.

lǎo hǔ dà wēi wō 老虎大偎窝 Tiger Snuggles in his Den. From Chuojiao, one of its low-basin kicks.

L

lǎo hǔ kào shān 老虎靠山 Tiger Leans on the Mountain: step to bow stance and push, changing to elbow strikes.

lǎo jià 老架 Old frame, Chen Taijiquan branch from Chenjiagou.

lǎo jià èr lù 老架二路 The second routine of Chen Taijiquan old frame.

lǎo jià yī lù 老架一路 The first routine of Chen Taijiquan old frame.

lǎo pǔ 老谱 Old classics: the written classical references to the martial arts. Each style has its own classic writings.

lǎo sēng pāo shí 老僧抛石 Venerable Monk Throws Rocks: pivot around, standing fairly high, sweeping the tip of a sword around a full circle at ankle height, finishing in a left reverse bow stance with the blade extended out to the forward left. From Qingping sword.

lǎo sēng tiǎo bāo 老僧挑包 Venerable Monk Shoulders the Bag: move in on your adversary controlling his arms, turn and throw him over your back, bowing and extending his arms.

lǎo sēng tuō bō 老僧托钵 Venerable Monk Holds up his Alms Bowl. 1. To enter on an adversary leaving an obvious gap to invite him to respond. 2. An on guard position in a seventy-thirty stance, one hand forward and turned up, the other hand at its elbow and turned down.

lǎo sēng tuó mǐ 老僧驼米 Venerable Monk Heaves Rice: when caught from behind, grab your adversary's neck (behind your head) and bow forward to throw him forward on his back. This is a throw like heaving a bag of rice over the shoulder to drop it on the ground after carrying on the back.

lǎo sēng zhuàng zhōng 老僧撞钟 Venerable Monk Strikes the Bell: push forward to elicit a reaction, then step back quickly to off balance your adversary a bit, then step forward again and shove with the whole body. This is like getting the post swinging to strike a large temple bell in the Chinese manner. From Baguazhang.

lǎo shì pī quán 老式劈拳 Old style chopping fist: the chopping strike of Xingyiquan, done with a closed fist. See also pī quán.

lǎo sǒu jiā cuì 老叟挾翠 Old Man Carries Jadeite under his arm: Step into a strong downward strike with a staff butt, both hands on top, tiger mouths facing each other, right hand along the shaft, left hand at the rear hip. From Baguazhang.

lǎo sǒu xié qín 老叟携琴 Old Man Carries a Zither: cut a sword down behind in reverse bow stance, right hand near the left hip, palm in, sword tip lower.

lǎo xióng zhuàng bǎng 老熊撞膀 Old Bear Shoves from the Shoulder: a forward elbow strike. From Xingyiquan. See also dǐng zhǒu.

lǎo yáng shǒu 老阳手 Yang tiger's mouth, as hand placement: forearm rotated so the palm faces out, thumb web up.

lǎo yīn shǒu 老阴手 Yin tiger's mouth, as hand placement: forearm rotated so the palm faces out, thumb web facing down.

lǎo yīng bǔ jī 老鹰捕鸡 Old Eagle Catches a Chicken: chop down in a reverse bow stance, leaning into the chop and keeping the arms in one line. From Shaolinquan.

lǎo yuán guà yìn 老猿挂印 Old Ape Retires from Office. See yuán hóu guà yìn.

勒 (rad.19) lè   1. To coerce; to force. 2. A bridle; a halter. 3. To rein in. 4. Pronounced lēi, to strap tightly, see lēi.

lè mǎ shì 勒马势 Rein in the Horse: draw a sword blade across the front then pull both hands back to either side of the hips, blade pointing forward. From Yang Taijiquan.

lè mǎ tuō qiāng 勒马托枪 Rein in the Horse to Hold a Spear: raise the knee and pull the hands across to its outside, then land forward and bring the hands through as if lifting a spear above the head. From Wudangquan.

lè shǒu xiǎo shù shēn 勒手小束身 Compact the body and rein in: sit back to an empty stance and tuck the arms in, elbows down, fists rotated fist heart up, the extended one at chest height, the other at its elbow. From Shaolinquan.

勒 (rad.19) lēi   1. To tie or strap something tightly. 2. Pronounced lè, to rein in, see lè.

lēi jǐng duàn bì 勒颈断臂 Tie up the neck arm break: with your adversary face down on the ground, kneel on him, twist his arm behind, and apply pressure to his neck with your other arm.

lēi quán 勒拳 Restrain, strap up tight, control: move the fists as if strapping something up.

lēi shǒu 勒手 Restrain, strap up tight, control: move the arms as if strapping something up or reining in a horse.

lēi shuāi zhǎng 勒摔掌 Straight arm swinging strike. From Tongbeiquan. Also called shuāi zhǎng.

lēi zhǒu 勒肘 Restrain the elbow: grab your adversary's hand and wrap your other arm around his arm to hyper-extend his elbow.

雷 (rad.173) léi   Thunder.

léi gōng chuí 雷公锤 The Thunder God's hammer: a short handled hammer with a large head.

léi shēng 雷声 A peal of thunder. 1. A continuous barrage of techniques. From Xingyiquan. 2. A deep sound on power emission.

擂 (rad.64) lèi   To beat, to hit.

lèi quán 擂拳 Downward striking backfist, usually tucking in and striking down with the elbow close to the body.

lèi tái 擂台 Raised sparring platform. Traditionally used for challenge matches, and still used for modern Sanda competition.

lèi tái sài 擂台赛 Challenge match: sparring competition where the winner of each match stays on the platform to fight new challengers.

肋 (rad.130) lèi   The ribs, the costal region, tha flanks.

lèi gǔ shāo 肋骨梢 Tips of the floating ribs. Very sensitive points, one of the main targets on the body. Also called lèi shāo.

lèi jiān jī 肋间肌 Intercostal muscles: the muscles between the ribs.

lèi jiān shén jīng 肋间神经 Intercostal nerves.

lèi ruǎn gǔ 肋软骨 The cartilaginous ribs, the floating ribs.

lèi shāo 肋梢 See lèi gǔ shāo.

冷 (rad.15) lěng   Cold.

lěng bīng qì 冷兵器 Cold weapons: traditional weaponry such as swords and staffs, as distinct from firearms.

lěng jí cuì jìn 冷疾脆劲 Cold, quick break power: a quick snap applied after grabbing an adversary, aiming at breaking a small bone. Used in seizing and controlling methods.

lěng jìn 冷劲 Cold power: a sudden release of power, unexpected, like an ambush. From Tongbeiquan, one of its nine types of power, see also jiǔ gōng jìn. From Baguazhang, one of its distinctive powers.

lěng tán jìn 冷弹劲 Cold snapping power: a sudden snapping release of power, shot from the waist and snapping out to the striking hand.

梨 (rad.75) lí   A pear.

lí huā bā mǔ qiāng 梨花八母枪 Pear Blossoms eight mother techniques of the spear: basic exercises for the spear.

lí huā bǎi tóu 梨花摆头 Pear Blossoms Sway: step in dodging steps, circling a spear tip with outward and inward covering, keeping the right hand at the waist and the tip central.

狸 貍 (rad.94, 153) [貍] (rad.94) lí   A fox; a racoon dog.

lí māo 狸猫 A small wild cat. In movement names is often translated as a leopard cat.

lí māo pū shǔ 狸猫扑鼠 Leopard Cat Pounces on a Rat. 1. Drop into a half squat and, drawing a circle, chop downwards with a staff to eyebrow height. Press the staff butt near the front ankle. From Baguazhang. 2. Drop into a drop stance and slap a spear flat on the ground.

lí māo dǎo shàng shù 狸猫倒上树 Leopard Cat Turns Over whilst Climbing a Tree: turn around to a trampling kick (may kick high, then drop the foot to trample) with a drill then trample to a double split palm. From Xingyiquan.

lí māo pū róng 狸猫扑蝾 Leopard Cat Pounces on a Lizard: continuous advancing stabbing hands, sliding the palms past each other, stepping forward to high empty stances. From Liuhebafa.

L

lí māo shàng shù 狸猫上树 Leopard Cat Climbs a Tree. A forward moving turned out kick combined with a double extension of the hands to cover and strike, landing with a trample. From Baguazhang, Chuojiao, and Xingyiquan.

蠡 (rad.142) **lí**   A calabash shell that serves as a dipper.

lí gōu 蠡沟 Acupoint Ligou (seashell canal), LR5. At the calf, on the inside, 5 *cun* up from the ankle, in the midline of the tibia (on each foot). From TCM.

離 (rad.172) [离] (rad.8) **lí**   1. To leave, depart. 2. To go against. 3. To meet with. 4. The Fire Trigram, represented by one broken (*yin*) line within two solid (*yang*) lines, called 'middle empty'. Corresponds to the circling bird formation or gate. An opening gate formation. Indicates the attribute of light-giving.

lí kōng jìn 离空劲 Disconnecting power: to disconnect from contact with an adversary so that he can no longer feel where you are, causing him to miss his attempt.

李 (rad.75) **lǐ**   1. Plum. 2. A surname.

lǐ dài táo jiāng 李代桃僵 Sacrifice the Plum Tree to Preserve the Peach Tree. The 11th of the Thirty-six Stratagems of Warfare, which apply to many situations.

lǐ guǎng shé shí 李广射石 Li Guang Shoots Stones: block up overhead with a sword, then gather the sword and stab straight forward. Li Guang was a Han dynasty general (- 119 BC). From Wu Taijiquan.

lǐ jiā quán 李家拳 Lijiaquan (Li family fist), a southern style, attributed to the Fujian province Shaolin temple. Popular in Guangdong province, it uses winding small steps and many jumps combined with long range punches.

lǐ shí tài jí quán 李式太极拳 Lishi (Li's) Taijiquan, a style attributed to Li Ruidong.

理 (rad.96) **lǐ**   1. Reason, logic. 2. Principles, theory. 3. To administer, to govern; to manage.

lǐ mài shù 理脉术 Regulating vessel skill: the ability to control the flow of *qi* and blood through the veins and arteries of others.

禮 [礼] (rad.113) **lǐ**   1. Manners: to show courtesy and understand proper etiquette, one of the character traits expected of martial artists. 2. Ceremony, rites.

lǐ jié 礼节 Courtesy; etiquette; protocol; ceremony.

裡 裏 里 (rad.145, 166) [里] (rad.166) **lǐ**   1. Inside. Inner. Within. 2. A traditional unit of length, see shì lǐ.

lǐ bǎ mén fēng 里把门封 Inside sealing off the gate. See ná qiāng.

lǐ biān pào 里边炮 Inside Hits: a coiling double hit bringing the arms from the inside to strike outwards with the fists. From Chen Taijiquan.

lǐ chā tuǐ 里插腿 Inside insertion: step your leg inside your adversary's stance, pressing with the outside of your leg. From Chuojiao, one of its middle-basin kicks.

lǐ chā xiǎo chán sī tuǐ 里插小缠丝腿 Inside coiling insertion: step your leg into your adversary's stance, contacting at the ankle, inside his stance, pressing into your knee to control at the shin. From Chuojiao, one of its middle-basin kicks.

lǐ chāo 里抄 Inward lift: an inward block with the elbow bent, keeping the elbow tucked to the body, forearm level, palm up.

lǐ chāo bào 里抄抱 Inward lifting hold: do an inward lift and trap an adversary in a hugging hold. See also wài chāo bāo.

lǐ cuò wài duò 里挫外跺 Rasp to the Inside and Stamp on the Outside: grab and do repeating low kicks, first turning to rasp or coil an adversary's front leg, then turn the foot to thrust into his rear leg. From Baguazhang, one of its sixty-four hands.

lǐ dāo gōu 里刀勾 Inner cut and hook tripping throw. See dà dé hé. Also called lǐ gōu, sān dào yáo.

lǐ gé 里格 Transverse inner block, with the forearm vertical and the palm in.

lǐ gōu 里勾 1. Inner hooking throw. See dà dé hé. Also called lǐ dāo gōu, sān dào yáo. 2. A hooking deflection of an incoming punch.

lǐ gōu jiǎo 里勾脚 Inner hook throw. See bà zi.

lǐ guà 里挂 Inner hook, a block: to bring the fist down across the body, fist heart facing in.

lǐ hán 里寒 Interior cold, internal cold: a disharmony caused by a pernicious influence. From TCM.

lǐ hé bù 里合步 Inner closing step: a slightly tucked in step, the foot turned in about forty-five degrees. From Baguazhang.

lǐ hé pāi jiǎo 里合拍脚 Inside slap crescent kick: an inside swinging kick, slapping the foot with the opposite side hand. In the category of slap kicks, see also jī xiǎng xìng tuǐ fǎ.

lǐ hé tuǐ 里合腿 Inside crescent kick, a straight swinging kick without a slap. In the category of straight swinging kicks, see also zhí bǎi xìng tuǐ fǎ.

lǐ jiāo 里跤 Inside wrestle. 1. A technique used in wrestling to prevent an adversary from using his legs: slide your leg in between his legs, thigh against thigh. 2. Hook an adversary's front heel to prevent his retreat.

lǐ jiǎo 里脚 The inside foot: used when describing the actions of movements on a circle. From Baguazhang. See also wài jiǎo.

lǐ mén 里门 The inside gate: inside of the arms of an adversary. Also called mén lǐ.

lǐ miàn jià 里面架 Inner face frame: an outward bracing with both arms, palms out, in front of the chest, in horse stance. From Bajiquan. See also wài miàn jià.

lǐ pī 里劈 Inside chop: chop the arm down inside the leg as it does an straight swinging kick to the heel. From Shaolinquan.

lǐ piàn mǎ biān 里骗马鞭 Inward Fool the Horse with the steel whip: swinging the whip in vertical circles, raise the right leg and swing it under, the hand inside the thigh, catching under the thigh.

lǐ rè 里热 Interior heat, internal heat: a disharmony caused by a pernicious influence. From TCM.

lǐ shǒu 里手 The inside hand: used when describing the actions of movements on a circle. From Baguazhang. The outside hand is wài shǒu.

lǐ shǒu huā 里手花 Inside flowers in the hand takedown: grab the back of your adversary's neck and slide your hand in between his thighs, stepping in to lift and pull to throw.

lǐ shǒu huō 里手豁 Inside hand breach takedown: press the back of the hand into the inside of your adversary's knee while pulling on his neck in the opposite direction. See also huō.

lǐ wài guǎi zhǒu 里外拐肘 In and out turning around the elbow: circling method with the steel whip: circling the whip vertically alternating sides of the body, hooking onto the right elbow on each side.

lǐ wài liàn quán 里外练拳 In and Out Fists, the fifth routine of Duanquan, written up as sixteen moves.

鲤 [鯉] (rad.195) lǐ   A carp (fish).

lǐ yú dǎ tǐng 鲤鱼打挺 Carp Straightens Up: a kip up. To pop up directly to the feet from lying on the back. Also called dié jīn, lǐ yú dǎ tǐng zhí lì.

lǐ yú dǎ tǐng zhí lì 鲤鱼打挺直立 Carp Straightens Up. See lǐ yú dǎ tǐng. Also called dié jīn.

lǐ yú gōng bèi 鲤鱼弓背 Carp Arches its Back: trapping an adversary's arm against your chest, bow down to lock it out.

lǐ yú qǐ zōng 鲤鱼起踪 Carp Rises: step forward slicing up with the smooth side arm, thumb turned up. From Xingyiquan.

lǐ yuè lóng mén 鲤跃龙门 Carp Leaps through the Dragon's Gate: lift the right knee and cock a sword in front, then jump forward, lifting the left knee behind and bring the blade over and down to dab with a fully extended arm. From Qingping sword.

利 (rad.18) lì   1. Sharp. In the martial arts, usually means sharp. 2. Favourable. Advantage. 3. Profit.

力 (rad.19) lì   Strength. Unharnessed strength. Force.

lì diǎn 力点 Point of contact, point of focus.

lì duò jīn shí 力剁金石 Forcefully Hash Metal and Stone: a strong downward low hack with a broadsword.

lì fā yú gēn, zhǔ zǎi yú yāo, xíng yú shǒu zhǐ 力

L

发于根，主宰于腰，行于手指 Strength originates in the root, its direction is determined in the waist, and it is carried out in the hands. A martial saying.

lì fǎ 力法 Methods of developing power through the body in conjunction with the mind.

lì liàng 力量 Strength, physical strength.

lì liàng sù zhì 力量素质 The body constitution relating to strength, strength makeup, physical strength.

lì liàng tuō luò 力量脱落 Loss of strength, especially the feeling of weakness caused by being struck at certain points.

lì liàng xùn liàn 力量训练 Strength training. Exercises intended to improve strength.

lì pī huà shān 力劈华山 Forcefully Split Mount Hua: a strong chop. In Taijiquan sword, a chop in a one legged stance. In Baguazhang, a low chop forward with a broadsword, in a deep bow stance. In Piguaquan, a palm chop in a one legged stance. In Yangjia style, a full swinging palm chop.

lì pò bā huāng 力破八荒 Strength Cleaves the Eight Wastelands: an inside crescent kick followed by a spinning back heel kick. From Yangjia style.

lì qì 力气 Physical strength, in the sense of being strong or using physical effort.

lì shì fēn niú 力士分牛 Strongman Separates the Oxen: an empty stance, hooking the hands behind the body.

lì shì quán 力士拳 Strongman fist, the ninth of Chuojiao's nine literary routines, written up as fifty-seven moves. See also wén tàng zi.

lì shì tuī bēi 力士推碑 Strongman Pushes the Stele: a horse stance upper framing block with pushing palm. From Piguaquan.

lì tuī huà shān 力推华山 Forcefully Push Mount Hua: advance into a heavy tamping palm. From Tongbeiquan.

lì yào shùn dá 力要顺达 The strength should arrive smoothly: one of the basic qualities of many styles.

lì zhī qiān jīn 力支千斤 Strength Supports a Thousand Pounds: stand up and stab a spear fully extended at shoulder height with just the right hand holding the butt. From Shaolinquan.

厉 [厉] (rad.27) lì 1. A coarse whetstone. 2. Harsh, severe. Evil. 3. To persuade.

lì duì 厉兑 Acupoint Lidui (severe mouth), ST45. At the outside edge of the second toe, 0.1 *cun* from the root of the toenail (on each foot). This is the last point in the Stomach channel. From TCM.

立 (rad.117) lì 1. Vertical, upright. 2. To stand.

lì bào dāo 立抱刀 Vertical broadsword hold: Hold the grip in the left hand and hold it at the side with the blade's spine along the arm.

lì chán 立禅 Standing meditation. May be done simply standing, or together with stake standing.

lì dì tōng tiān pào 立地通天炮 Blast Straight up through the Sky from the Ground: a strong strike upwards from below with the fist, palm, or elbow. From Bajiquan, one of its eight main concepts, see also bā dà zhāo.

lì duò jīn shí 立剁金石 Hack Straight on Metal and Stone: step directly into a right bow stance and hack a sword down on line with the stance with a straight arm, arm and blade angled downwards, tip about five centimetres from the ground. From Qingping sword.

lì gōu 立勾 Vertical hooking throws in wrestling: the category of throws that involve holding the jacket of an adversary and hooking with the leg, remaining upright throughout the throw.

lì jiàn 立剑 1. A sword with a standing blade. The blade edges are placed vertically, no matter in which direction the blade points. 2. To hold the blade vertically, tip either upwards or downwards.

lì jǔ gùn 立举棍 Raise a staff vertically, holding the shaft upright, usually tip upwards.

lì mǎ bù 立马步 Upright horse stance: a front to back stance, toes of the rear foot tucked in by the arch of the front foot, both feet pointing more or less forward, most weight on the rear leg. From Xingyiquan, especially used with a straight punch.

lì mǎ sān jiàn 立马三箭 Three Arrows on Horseback: three continuous piercing palms. From Piguaquan.

lì pī huà shān 立劈华山 Vertically Split Mount

Hua. 1. A strong chop with a staff. From Shaolinquan staff. 2. A strong chop with a sword, the arms fully extended in a straight line. From Qingping sword.

lì qiāng 立枪 Standing spear. 1. Bring the shaft to vertical with the tip down in order to stab straight down. 2. Stand a spear upright with the butt on the ground.

lì quán 立拳 Upright fist, a placement description. See rì zì quán. Also called zhèng quán.

lì rú jī 立如鸡 Stand (on one leg) like a chicken. Stability, the abilty to stop in the midst of fast movement. One of the twelve qualities of movement of Changquan, though these descriptors apply to many other styles. Also called lì rú sōng, zhàn rú jī, zhàn rú sōng.

lì rú sōng 立如松 Stand (firmly) like a pine tree. See lì rú jī. Also called zhàn rú jī, zhàn rú sōng.

lì sǎo quán 立扫拳 Vertical sweeping punch. From Choylifut.

lì shēn zhōng zhèng 立身中正 Keep the torso upright, centered, and balanced. A common requirement in many styles.

lì tuī dāo 立推刀 Vertical push with a broadsword: push the blade forward with the tip down, the left hand pushing on the spine.

lì wò chēng tiào 立卧撑跳 Burpees: squat, put the hands on the ground, shoot the legs back, then bring the feet back in and jump straight up. A conditioning exercise or warmup.

lì wǔ huā gùn (qiāng) 立舞花棍(枪) Vertical flowers with a staff (or spear): swing the shaft in full circles to that the tip travels down, back, up and forward, repeating at either side of the body. If not specified, flowers are usually vertical.

lì yāo 立腰 Vertical back. 1. To hold the torso straight as a movement is completed. Usually in conjuction with the chest held up. 2. Sometimes means essentially the same thing as a straight back, but usually differentiates between a straight back, seen as an error, and a vertical body, seen as a requirement. See also zhí yāo.

lì yuán 立圆 Vertical circle or circles.

lì yuán dān tuī shǒu 立圆单推手 Vertical circle single hands connected push hands practice drill. From Taijiquan.

lì yuán shuāng tuī shǒu 立圆双推手 Vertical circle both hands connected push hands practice drill. From Taijiquan.

lì yún zhǎng 立云掌 Vertical brandish: circle the hands in a vertical circle in front of the body.

lì zhǎng 立掌 Vertical palm: the palm held with the fingers pointing up. Refers to the hand placement, not the direction of the strike.

lì zhǒu 立肘 Elbow uppercut.

lì zhuāng zhǎng 立桩掌 Upright stake palm, a circle-walking posture: like Point to Heaven and Stab the Ground posture, but with the upper palm facing in, not twisted. From Baguazhang. See also zhí tiān chā dì zhǎng.

荔 (rad.140) lì   Lychee fruit, litchi, usually used in conjunction with zhī.

lì zhī quán 荔枝拳 Lychee fist, a hand shape: the middle finger's knuckle is slightly extended. All the fingers are clenched, the thumb presses on the middle segment of the middle finger to support its slightly sticking out from the fist surface. From southern styles. Also called gǎn lǎn quán, lóng zhū quán.

廉 (rad.53) lián   1. Incorrupt; incorruptible. 2. Inexpensive. 3. To examine.

lián quán (xué) 廉泉(穴) Acupoint Lianquan (ridge spring), RN23. At the throat, just above the larynx, on the midline. From TCM. A sensitive point, to the extent that striking it may cause death.

臁 (rad.130) lián   The shank, the shin.

lián gǔ 臁骨 The shank, the shinbones. Sensitive targets to strike, best hit with short, low kicks. Properly trained, can use them to kick very hard.

連 [连] (rad.162) lián   1. Connected, combine; to connect. 2. Connectedness in push hands. From Taijiquan, one of its four requirements of push hands, see also sì yào.

lián bù fǎ 连步法 Continuous steps method: moving steps to fake to draw out an adversary's attack.

lián dǎ 连打 Continuous attack.

lián guàn 连贯 Connected, continuous. This is a

requirement at the intermediate level of training, movement must linked and flowing.

lián huán diǎn tuǐ 连环点腿 Continuous poking kicks. From Chuojiao, one of its middle-basin kicks.

lián huán fēi jiǎo 连环飞脚 Continuous flying kicks, kicking with both feet when jumping. Used in northern styles. From Chuojiao, one of its high-basin kicks.

lián huán huǒ jiàn 连环火箭 Continuous Fire Arrows: turn to a right reverse bow stance and punch the left fist from the right belly to the front, pulling the right fist back to the waist. The 91st move of the tiger and crane routine.

lián huán jì 连环计 Strategy of Linking. Refers to linking together a number of tactics. From the specific case of linking boats together in the battle of Red Cliff (fooling the enemy into doing something stupid). The thirty-fifth of the Thirty-six Stratagems of Warfare, which apply to many situations.

lián huán kòu zhuàng 连环扣撞 Linking Cover and Bump: step into a right reverse bow stance and swing the right fist through and punch up with the left fist. The 88th move of the tiger and crane routine.

lián huán quán 连环拳 1. Continuous punches, chain punches: a series of at least three straight punches. 2. Continuous Punches, the third of Chuojiao's nine literary routines, written up as thirty-one moves. See also wén tàng zi.

lián huán sǎo 连环扫 Continuous sweeps: a half forward sweep followed immediately by a half back sweep. In the category of sweep kicks, see also sǎo zhuàn xìng tuǐ fǎ.

lián huán sǎo tuǐ 连环扫腿 Continuous sweeps, see lián huán sǎo.

lián huán tōng tiān 连环通天 Continuous Punches Through the Sky: in a right bow stance, from a right uppercut, do a left uppercut and draw the right fist to the waist. The 54th move of the tiger and crane routine.

lián huán tuǐ 连环腿 Continuous Kicks, the fourth of Chuojiao's nine literary routines, written up as forty-one moves. See also wén tàng zi.

lián huán zé xiān 连环责仚 Continuous Duty: move to a bow stance and throw a combination of punches, finishing with the left forward and low. The 87th move of the tiger and crane routine. See also pāo quán.

lián nǔ 连弩 A continuous firing crossbow.

lián quán 连拳 Lianquan (continuous fists): a northern style, considered a branch of Shaolinquan.

lián shǒu duǎn dǎ 连手短打 Continuous Hands Short Fighting. 1. A Shaolinquan routine, written up as thirty-nine moves. 2. Lianshou Duanda (continuous hands short fighting) style, which uses short range techniques.

lián tiǎo 连挑 Continuous leg raises. See wò tī.

lián xù jìn gōng zhāo fǎ 连续进攻招法 Barrage attacking technique: take advantage of a weakening in an adversary, press the attack with a variety of techniques, giving him no chance to recover.

lián zhī bù 连枝步 Continuous branch steps: move sideways by stepping one foot across in front of the other, then stepping the second foot out to the same side.

lián zhū pào 连珠炮 String of Pearls strikes: a barrage of continuous strikes. From Chen Taijiquan.

鐮 鎌 [镰] (rad.167) lián A sickle: a sword length weapon with a hand guard at the grip and turned back hooks near the tip, hooks and tip being equal lengths. A pair is called yuān yāng lián.

斂 [敛] (rad.66) liǎn 1. To gather, collect. 2. To draw back; fold back. 3. To hold back, restrain.

liǎn bù 敛步 Gathering step: bring the front foot back by the rear foot. May be in preparation for a step.

liǎn tún 敛臀 Gather in the buttocks: lightly tuck in the buttocks.

臉 [脸] (rad.130) liǎn 1. The face. 2. The front part of something. 3. Face; self respect.

煉 [炼] (rad.86) liàn To smelt; to refine. To temper.

liàn shí bǔ tiān 炼石补天 Melt down Stones to Repair the Sky (to have supernatural powers): from reaching forward with a sword, lift it up, to a right raised knee stance, hands both on the hilt above the head, blade up and forward. From Qingping sword.

練 [练] (rad.120) liàn
To practice, train. Usually refers to training the body, conditioning.

liàn gōng 练功 To practice to develop deep skills.

liàn gōng shí bā fǎ 练功十八法 Eighteen Training Exercises: simple health exercises of six sections of thirty-six moves, each set aiming at the range of motion of specific body segments.

liàn jīng huà qì 练精化气 To train, or forge, essence to transform to vital energy, or prenatal *qi*.

liàn qì huà shén 练气化神 To train, or forge, vital energy to transform to spirit.

liàn qiāng 练枪 A training spear: a six metre long spear. Used for solo training, not fighting, and seldom for partner work, because of its length. Also called dà qiāng.

liàn quán 练拳 To practice martial arts.

liàn quán bù huó yāo, zhōng jiū yì bù gāo 练拳不活腰，终究艺不高 If you train without enlivening your waist, you will never be highly skilled. A martial saying.

liàn quán bù liàn tuǐ, yī shì mào shī guǐ 练拳不练腿，一世冒失鬼 If you train martial arts without developing your legs, you will pass your whole life haphazardly. A martial saying.

liàn shén huàn xū 练神还虚 To train, or forge, spirit to return to emptiness.

liàn wǔ bù liàn gōng, dào lǎo yī cháng kōng 练武不练功，到老一场空 If you train martial arts without training all the basic conditioning and basic skills, you will end up with nothing. A martial saying.

liàn xí 练习 Practice, to practise.

鏈 [链] (rad.167) liàn
A chain, a cable.

梁 (rad.75) liáng
1. A surname. 2. The Liang kingdom of the Southern dynasties (502-557).

樑 [梁] (rad.75) liáng
1. A roof beam. 2. A bridge. 3. A ridge.

liáng mén 梁门 Acupoint Liangmen (beam gate), ST21. At the abdomen, four *cun* up from the navel, two *cun* lateral to the midline (on each side). From TCM.

liáng qiū 梁丘 Acupoint Liangqiu (beam hill), ST34. At the thigh, the outer and upper edge of the patella (on each leg). From TCM.

兩 (rad.11) [两] (rad.9) liǎng
1. Two; a pair; both. 2. A traditional unit of weight, ten make up a jin. Equivalent to fifty grams. See also jīn.

liǎng gǔ chā 两股叉 A double tipped trident: a long wooden shaft with two sharp, straight, metal tines.

liǎng tóu yuè 两头钺 A two-headed axe: a long handled battle axe with blades on both ends.

liǎng yí 两仪 The pair of appearances: the two polarities of *yin* and *yang* generated from the one *qi* of the Dao.

liǎng yí zhuāng 两仪桩 Paired appearances stake standing: varies with style. May be a half squat with the knees together, arms crossed in front of the chest.

liǎng zhǒu bù lí lèi, liǎng shǒu bù lí xīn 两肘不离肋，两手不离心 The elbows never leave the ribs, the hands never leave the heart. A martial saying. This is particularly used in styles such as Duanquan and Xingyiquan that use tightly-knit methods.

liǎng zhǒu liǎng xī sì chuí 两肘两膝四捶 Four strikes: two elbows, two knees. Four close range techniques to use elbows and knees. From Tanglangquan, one of its eight short techniques.

亮 (rad.8) liàng
1. Bright. Shine. 2. Show, reveal. Usually used for an action that turns the palm away from the body, hence 'flashing' it.

liàng chì 亮翅 Flash the Wings (the arms). Open the arms, turning the palms away from the body.

liàng hóu 亮喉 Flash the throat: lift the chin, exposing the throat to attack. A major error in most styles.

liàng shì 亮势 To pose: to strike a pose during a

liàng tī 亮踢 Flash kick: in a tight clinch, when your adversary sits back to avoid being thrown, do an over the shoulder grab, pressing your armpit into his shoulder and grabbing his belt, twist, trip, and roll. From wrestling.

liàng xiàng 亮相 To strike a pose, especially to open or close a routine.

liàng zhǎng 亮掌 1. Flash the palm: the same as flash the wings, but used for one palm instead of both. Extend one arm above shoulder height with the palm turned away from the body. 2. Flash both palms, one above, one a shoulder height. 3. Flash the sole: the error of flashing the bottom of the leading foot when circle-walking, instead of keeping the foot flat. From Baguazhang. Also called yáng tí.

撩 (rad.64) **liāo** 1. The original, practical, meaning is to lift up something that is hanging, such as curtains or the hem of a skirt. Another meaning is to sprinkle water with the hand. 2. The arm technique is to slice up with the arm held fairly straight. Often it is translated as provoke, in which case it is pronounced liáo. 3. Lift, one of the walking hands of Chuojiao, see also zǒu shǒu.

liāo dāo 撩刀 Vertical slice up with a broadsword. See liāo jiàn.

liāo gōu 撩钩 Slice up with hooks: with the double hooks, slice up vertically beside the body, the crescent blades edge up, keeping the blades close to the body.

liāo gōu 撩勾 Slicing hook throws: various throws involving holding the jacket of an adversary and hooking with the leg. From wrestling.

liāo guà zhǎng 撩挂掌 Slice and hook: in one fluid movement swing the arm up straight, then bend it and hook back by bringing the palm in to the shoulder (often combined with a following push).

liāo gùn 撩棍 Slice up with a staff. See liāo qiāng.

liāo huā 撩花 Slicing up flowers: vertical circles of a bladed weapon, slicing up in front instead of cutting down.

liāo jiàn 撩剑 Vertical slice up with a sword: with the fore-section of the blade, blade edge and palm facing up; uppercut. The action is the same for most bladed weapons. A two handed weapon such as a big cutter is the same, just with a two handed grip. The weapon must pass vertically close by the body.

liāo jīn 撩襟 Lift up the Front Panel (of a robe): hook the hand and swing the arm down then out and up to the side, in an empty stance. From Chaquan.

liāo ná fǎ 撩拿法 Swinging hold: swing a straight arm back to assist power in a tripping takedown. From wrestling.

liāo qiāng 撩枪 Slice up with a spear: slice up with a vertical circle on either side of the body, keeping the shaft close to the body.

liāo quán 撩拳 Slice up with the arm, fist clenched.

liāo rǎo 撩绕 Curl around, entangle, specifically coming up from below.

liāo tī 撩踢 Lifting kick. 1. A kick that swings up behind, contacting with the heel. In the category of straight swinging kicks, see also zhí bǎi xìng tuǐ fǎ. 2. A jump lifting kick: jump up by swinging one leg up, bend the kicking leg underneath and slapping it with a palm behind the body.

liāo tuī zhǎng 撩推掌 Slice and push: swing the arm straight up to shoulder height, then circle it back and push out, all in one smooth action. From Chaquan.

liāo tuǐ 撩腿 Bring the rear foot through to kick up with the knee slightly bent, dorsi-flexed so the sole faces up.

liāo wàn huā 撩腕花 Figure eight; wrist cutting vertical circles, slicing upwards.

liāo yīn 撩阴 An arm slice up into the groin.

liāo yīn jiǎo 撩阴脚 A snap instep kick to groin. From Tanglangquan.

liāo yīn zhǎng 撩阴掌 Slice up into the groin with an open hand.

liāo zhǎng 撩掌 Slice up: swing the straight arm upward to waist or shoulder height with the outer edge leading.

liāo zhǎo 撩爪 Slice up with the hand in a claw shape to grab the groin.

liāo zhī yuǎn wàng 撩枝远望 Lift up the Branch to Gaze in the Distance: swing a staff upwards with a slice, then snap to bring the tip sharply across to hit the head. From Shaolinquan staff.

遼 [辽] (rad.162) **liáo**   1. The Liao dynasty (916-1125). 2. The short name for Liaoning province. 3. Distant, far away.

列 (rad.18) **liè**   1. To arrange, set out. 2. To enter in a list. 3. Row, rank. 4. Categorised by kind, type, sort.

liè quē 列缺 Acupoint Lieque (broken sequence), LU7. On the thumb side of the inside of the forearm, about 1.5 *cun* above the wrist (on each arm). From TCM.

liè zhǎng 列掌 Strike out with the palm to the same side. From Tongbeiquan.

挒 (rad.64) **liè**   1. To splay; split; rend. 2. Lock onto and take an adversary horizontally, to either the inside or outside. 3. Apply two opposing forces by rotating the body and spiraling through the shoulders.

liè jìn 挒劲 Splay, split: the power and skill used to take an adversary horizontally to the outside or to pull horizontally.

liè kuà 挒胯 Splay the hip: in stance, allow the rear thigh to open or leave the ankle splayed out, weakening the stance and the power in the crotch area. Considered an error in most styles.

liè ná fǎ 挒拿法 Splaying hold: when grabbed, pull your adversary's forearm into your chest instead of trying to release his grip, pull him into your centre and use a crossing force to throw him. From wrestling.

liè shǒu pō jiǎo 挒手泼脚 Splaying and sprinkling: in an upright clinch, step to the outside of your adversary, placing your hooked foot by his, and pull the other way, tripping him sideways. From wrestling.

擸 (rad.64) **liè**   1. To hold; to grasp. 2. To hold the hair. 3. To pull out.

liè shǒu 擸手 A deflecting arm. From Wing Chun.

拎 (rad.64) **līn**   1. To carry. 2. To catch and twist an adversary's hand. May twist in either direction, inwards or outwards.

林 (rad.75) **lín**   1. A forest; woods; grove. 2. A group, or circle, of people with similar interests. A group of similar things.

麟 麐 [麟] (rad.198) **lín** Kylin. See qí lín.

lín jiǎo dāo 麟角刀 Kylin antler blade: a single-edged blade with two tips, resembling antlers. Usually used as a double weapon.

lín jiǎo zhǎng 麟角掌 Kylin antler palm: thumb and index finger straight and held open, other fingers tucked. Also called bā zì zhǎng.

凌 淩 (rad.15, 85) [凌] (rad.15) **líng**   1. To insult; maltreat. 2. To ride, rise. 3. To traverse. 4. To soar.

líng kōng jìn 凌空劲 Ride the Skies power. 1. To completely control an adversary, to know what he is going to do before he does it, demoralizing him and making your attack more effective. From Taijiquan. 2. A shout to demoralize an adversary.

菱 (rad.140) **líng** A waternut; water caltrop.

líng xíng jī 菱形肌 The rhomboid muscle: runs from the vertebrae to the inner edge of the scapula (shoulder blade). One on each side of the back. Assists in stabilizing and retracting the scapula.

靈 (rad.173) [灵] (rad.86) **líng**   1. Agile, dexterous, lively, quick, nimble. 2. Clever; effective. Intelligence. 3. Pertaining to the spiritual world.

líng dào 灵道 Acupoint Lingdao (spirit way), HT4. At the palm side of the wrist, up 1.5 *cun* from the wrist crease, along the little finger side (on each arm). From TCM.

líng gēn 灵根 The middle *dantian*, see dān tián.

líng huó 灵活 Nimble; agile; quick; lively. Flexible.

líng huó xìng 灵活性 Flexibility; mobility; elasticity; suppleness.

líng kōng jìn 灵空劲 The skilled power of leading an adversary into empty space.

líng lóng fān shēn 灵龙翻身 Nimble Dragon Rolls Over: lay the shaft of a spear along the body and roll over, sending out the tip to stab.

L

líng māo 灵猫 Often translated as civet cat, which is an arboreal cat. This category of animal includes the mongoose and civet. Used in movement names that call for quick and dexterous action.

líng māo bǔ shǔ 灵猫捕鼠 Civet Cat Catches a Rat. 1. A double pouncing action, moving forward. From Tongbeiquan. 2. Lift the right knee and cut down with a sword, the right hand coming down to the knee, the blade tip lower. Then land and jump forward, circling the blade to the right and up, then cut forward at the hip. From Qingping sword. 3. A rolling out intercepting forearm with a push from the rear hand. From Baguazhang. 4. A dabbing stab with a sword, in a cross stance. From Wu Taijiquan.

líng māo pū shǔ 灵猫扑鼠 Civet Cat Catches a Rat: a double pouncing action, moving forward. From Baguazhang.

líng māo zhuō shǔ shì 灵猫捉鼠式 Civet Cat Clutches a Rat model. One of twenty-four classic spear moves. Most spear routines will have a move with a like name. In general, this name refers to a technique that turns defeat into success, saving you from a bad situation.

líng mǐn 灵敏 Agility, dexterity. Clever, skillful.

líng qiǎo 灵巧 Dexterous, skillful, agile and quick, nimble. This is a requirement at the advanced level of training internal styles, the body should be quick and agile.

líng tāi 灵台 Acupoint Lingtai (spirit tower), DU10. At the back, at the depression below the spinous process of the sixth thoracic vertebra, on the midline. From TCM. A dangerous point, directly opposite the heart, a strike here may cause the heart to contract and may induce a heart attack. In internal styles, this point is expanded slightly.

líng tōng 灵通 Connect to the spirit: the sensitive striking points of the eyes.

líng xū 灵墟 Acupoint Lingxu (spirit ruins), KI24. At the chest, at the third intercostal space, 2 *cun* lateral to the midline (on each side). From TCM.

líng yuán zhāi guǒ 灵猿摘果 Agile Ape Picks Fruit: grasp to groin level in an empty stance, then step forward with multiple stabs. From Liuhebafa.

líng yuán zhǎn bèi 灵猿展臂 Agile Ape Spreads its Arms: when caught on the shoulder, press an adversary's hand on your shoulder and swing that arm over and down, to control and take down.

领 [领] (rad.181) lǐng 1. The neck. 2. The collar; neckband. 3. To guide, lead, drag, receive accept, catch. Use an adversary's oncoming force and changing his direction slightly so that he misses his target. Leading, one of the sixteen key techniques of Baguazhang, see also shí liù zì jué.

lǐng dài 领带 Drag without using force.

lǐng fǎ 领法 Leading, guiding methods, often guiding across the body into a shoulder strike.

lǐng qiāng 领枪 Lead a spear: lead an adversary's spear up with yours.

lǐng shǒu 领手 Drag with a carrying power: with the palm up, take an adversary's high attacking arm upwards and to the side. A drawing pull on the reverse side, crossing the stance.

lǐng tī 领踢 Guiding kick: control and push your adversary above, whilst stepping your foot in close to his foot, then do a lifting kick to throw. Also called bǒ jiǎo.

lǐng zhǎng 领掌 Drag with the palm. See lǐng shǒu.

lǐng zì gōng 领字功 Skill of guiding, one of Xingyiquan's eight skills, involving catching and guiding.

lǐng zuò 领作 Lead and do: a combination of demonstration and commands. A teaching method in the martial arts. The teacher does the moves along with the students while saying the names of the moves or pointers. This method is quite common in the traditional martial arts, but uncommon elsewhere.

令 (rad.9) lìng 1. An order, command. 2. To order, to command. 3. Sometimes used to mean leading, the same as lǐng.

溜 (rad.85) liū 1. To go secretly and quietly, to sneak. 2. To slide. Smooth. 3. Expertness, the ability to move naturally and perfectly.

liū tuǐ 溜腿 Train the legs: practice swinging or snapping kicks, usually standing still and repeating the action, using only the movement of the thigh and hip flexors.

liū tún 溜臀 Settle the buttocks: allow the buttocks

to settle down naturally when bending the knees.

liū tún shōu gāng 溜臀收肛 Settle the buttocks and close the anal sphincter. A common requirement in internal styles.

劉 [刘] (rad.18) liú   Liu, a surname.

liú hǎi xǐ chán 刘海戏蟾 Liu Hai Plays with a Toad: circle the hands in tight opposing circles in front of the body, shifting back and raising one knee, finishing with one hand on the foot and one hand at the head. Liu Hai is a fairy boy in stories, who sits on a toad. From Baguazhang.

liú jiā quán 刘家拳 Liujiaquan (Liu family fist), a southern style, mostly in Guangdong province, which emphasizes quick and agile multi-directional movements.

liú quán jìn guā 刘全进瓜 Liu Quan Offers the Melon: an uppercut to the jaw, also pressing the elbow on the chest. Liu Quan was an official who would offer money hidden in a melon when giving bribes for advancement. From Baguazhang, one of its sixty-four hands.

流 (rad.85) liú   1. To flow. 2. Drifting, wandering. 3. Spread. 4. Degenerate. 5. Banish. 6. Rate, class.

liú shuǐ zhǎng 流水掌 Flowing water palm, a hand shape: see wǔ fēng zhǎng. Also called tiē zhǎng.

liú xīng chuí 流星锤 Meteor hammer: a heavy ball (about five hundred grams) on the end of a rope about five metres long. Also called fēi chuí.

liú xīng gǎn yuè 流星赶月 Shooting Star Chases the Moon. 1. Circle the hands over, down and back, hook at the back, then cross the arms, turning to press both hands down, and then push forward. 2. Flowers with a long weapon. From Shaolinquan. See also wǔ huā. 3. Moving away with front and back cross steps slicing a sword, then turning to come back with a bow stance cut. From Qingping sword. 4. Chopping with a sword. From Taijiquan.

留 (rad.102) liú   1. To remain, to stay. 2. To detain. 3. To leave. 4. To preserve.

liú bà 留把 To leave the base exposed. See lòu bà.

liú shǒu 留手 Detaining hand: having elicited a grab or strike from an adversary, keep his hand and initiate your counter. See also yào shǒu.

柳 (rad.75) liǔ   Willow tree, willow trees.

liǔ yè 柳叶 Willow leaf, used in descriptive names.

liǔ yè zhǎng 柳叶掌 Willow leaf palm, a hand shape: fingers together and straight, thumb tucked in on the thumb web.

六 (rad.12) liù   Six.

liù chǐ pá 六齿耙 A six tined rake. It may also have interspaced teeth on the upper edge.

liù dà kāi 六大开 Six big openings: six main striking techniques that open up an adversary's main gateways. From Bajiquan. See bào, chán, dān, dǐng, kuà, tí.

liù diǎn bàn gùn 六点半棍 Six and half pole: a pole six and a half feet long (two metres). A weapon used in Wing Chun.

liù fēng sì bì 六封四闭 Six sealings and four closings. From Chen Taijiquan. See rú fēng sì bì.

liù hé 六合 Six combinations, the six harmonies: three internal and three external harmonies within the body. External are the hands with the feet, the shoulders with the hips, the elbows with the knees. Internal are the heart with the intent, the intent with the qi, and the qi with the power.

liù hé bā fǎ quán 六合八法拳 Liuhebafa (six harmonies and eight methods fist). 1. A style attributed to the Song dynasty. Also called xīn yì liù hé bā fǎ. 2. A stand alone routine.

liù hé dà qiāng 六合大枪 Six Harmonies big spear, quite a few traditional spear routines go by this name.

liù hé gùn 六合棍 Six Harmonies staff, a Tanglangquan routine, written up as one hundred and twenty-two moves.

liù hé qiāng 六合枪 Six Harmonies spear, a Bajiquan routine.

liù hé quán 六合拳 Six Harmonies Fist. 1. A Shaolinquan two person routine, with six short combinations. 2. A Xingyiquan routine, written up as twelve moves. 3. Liuhequan (six harmonies fist), generally considered a Shaolin style. Thought to be from Hebei province, during the Qing dynasty.

L

liù hé shuāng zhā qiāng 六合双扎枪 Six Harmonies mutual stabbing spear: a partner routine.

liù hé táng láng quán 六合螳螂拳 Liuhe (six harmonies) Tanglangquan style, a branch of Preying Mantis style, which uses fairly soft and long power.

liù hé wéi fǎ 六合为法 Utilize all six combinations (or harmonies) for all techniques: a principle of Xinyiquan and Xingyiquan.

liù hé xīn yì quán 六合心意拳 Liuhe Xinyiquan (six harmonies heart and mind fist), a branch of Xingyiquan from Shanxi province, attributed to Che Yonghong.

liù hé zhuāng 六合桩 Six harmonies stake standing. Varies with style. One version is to sit in a deep squat with the hands crossed in front of the chest, palms pushing out to the sides.

liù hé bù 六和步 Six together stepping: step aside and turn the body, to evade and close off an attack.

liù lù 六路 Six directions: front, back, left, right, up, and down.

liù lù fǎ 六路法 Six directions method. In a fight the eyes are watching the six directions – the front, back, right, left, up, and down. In Baguazhang this is used in conjunction with footwork.

liù miàn lì tóng shí mō jìn 六面力同时摸劲 Seeking power in six directions simultaneously: without moving the torso outwardly, seek out power lines in an all six directions. May be done in different stances or stepping. From Yiquan.

liù pái dāo 六排刀 The six lines broadsword: a Song Xingyiquan routine consisting of six lines back and forth, written up in fifty-seven moves.

liù qì 六气 The six *qi* of nature: wind, cold, fire (dry heat), dampness, summerheat (humid heat), dryness. See also fēng, hán, huǒ, shī, shǔ, zào. See also liù yín.

liù shí sì shǒu 六十四手 Sixty-four hands: a traditional Baguazhang routine, written up as sixty-four moves. It has eight lines of eight practical moves each. Attributed to Liu Dekuan. From Baguazhang. Also called bā bā liù shí sì zhǎng, bā duàn liù shí sì zhǎng, zhí tàng liù shí sì zhǎng.

liù sì bù 六四步 Sixty-forty stance: legs open naturally and weighted sixty percent to the rear leg. See sì liù bù.

liù yín 六淫 The six pernicious influences: the six *qi* of nature when they act in a way that cause illness. Environmental influences that can cause disease when in excess: wind, cold, excessive dry heat, dampness, summerheat, dryness. From TCM. See also liù qì.

碌 (rad.112) liù   A stone roller.

liù shǒu 碌手 Rolling arms exercise: partner training for sensitivity or warm-up, keeping the forearms in contact and rolling. From Wing Chun.

龍 [龙] (rad.212) lóng   A dragon. One of China's four divine creatures, along with the phoenix, tortoise, and kylin. The Chinese consider themselves the descendants of dragons, and the dragon is auspicious. Often used in movement names and to describe qualities of movement. For more movement names using the actions or qualities of the dragon, see also under cāng lóng, chì-, dān-, èr-, fēi-, hēi-, huáng-, jiāo-, jīn-, jīn jiāo-, lǎn-, líng-, pán-, qián-, qīng-, shén-, shuāng-, sì-, wáng-, wò-, wū-, xiǎo-, yóu-, yún-, zhé-. 2. Dragon, as the fifth of the twelve animals from the Chinese zodiac, associated with a twelve year cycle symbolic of the earthly branches. The twelve animals make up a sixty year cycle when combined with the five phases. See also dì zhī, shēng xiào, wǔ xíng.

lóng cáng hǔ yuè 龙藏虎跃 Dragon Hides and Tiger Leaps: a right jumping snap kick with a left descending punch. The 107th move of the tiger and crane routine.

lóng dāo qiāng 龙刀枪 Dragon blade spear, a spear with a long hook in the head that curves forward towards the tip, to be able to catch or do a double stab.

lóng diào bǎng 龙调膀 Dragon Transferring Arms: walking forward in a three step pattern, pressing forward with the same side arm extended down to the knee. From Xingyiquan.

lóng gōng qǔ bǎo 龙宫取宝 Take Treasures from the Dragon's Palace: grab the heel and knee of your adversary, pressing down on his knee while lifting his heel.

lóng hǔ chū xiàn 龙虎出现 Dragon and Tiger Show Themselves: take a high empty stance, right fist and left palm pushing forward in front of the shoulders. The salutation at the beginning of the tiger and crane routine.

lóng hǔ xiāng jiāo 龙虎相交 Dragon and Tiger Contend: a combination heel kick with straight punch from the opposite side, both striking forward together. From Xingyiquan. Also called shí zi bēng quán.

lóng hǔ zhàn 龙虎战 Dragon and tiger fight: a routine of Liuhebafa.

lóng huà jiàn 龙化剑 Dragon sword, a Wudang sword routine, written up with eighteen moves.

lóng mén 龙门 Dragon gate: the back of the torso, upper back and arms, that uses the dragon-like power of expanding and turning.

lóng mén shí sān qiāng 龙门十三枪 Dragon gate thirteen moves spear, a Wudang spear routine.

lóng pán gǔ shù 龙盘古树 Dragon Coils Around the Old Tree: a forearm wrap, controlling an adversary's wrist and pressing down on the forearm.

lóng pán shì 龙盘式 Dragon coiling stance: an elongated sitting cross legged coiled stance.

lóng qǐ yì dì 龙起异地 Dragon Gets up to Change Places: advancing front cross steps hooking the blade in large circles to alternate sides. From Qingping sword.

lóng shēn 龙身 Dragon torso: the body should be agile and able to fold or go in any direction freely. One of the body requirements of Xingyiquan.

lóng tóu gǎn bàng 龙头杆棒 Dragon head stick: a soft weapon made of rope about two metres long, with a dragon head on one end and a tip on the other.

lóng xíng 龙形 1. Dragon form. Reach up and out to catch then drop it into a low extended cross stance, pulling down with the forward hand, the other pressing down behind the hip. Sometimes means this action and stance, but bracing the hands front and rear with the palms rolled. May alternate sides by jumping or stepping forward with a kick. From Xingyiquan. 2. Dragon structure: circle-walking and changes done seeking the structure, posture, and manner of a dragon. From Baguazhang.

lóng xíng hóu xiàng hǔ zuǒ yīng fān 龙形猴相虎坐鹰翻 Have the form of a dragon, the (lively) appearance of a monkey, crouch like a tiger, and wheel like an eagle. A requirement in common with many styles.

lóng xíng quán 龙形拳 Longxing(dragon form fist), a southern style from Guangdong province, thought to have come from the Fujian province Shaolin temple in the mid 1800s.

lóng xíng bù 龙行步 Dragon stepping: stepping forward with the feet moving along an arcing path.

lóng xíng dāo 龙行刀 Dragon walking broadsword: a traditional routine with a large Baguazhang type broadsword, walking quickly, continuously and smoothly.

lóng xíng shì 龙行势 Dragon walking posture: smear a sword blade across in front of the body, from one side to the other. From Yang Taijiquan.

lóng xū chā 龙须叉 Dragon beard (whiskers) fork: a long handled weapon with two thin wavy tines.

lóng xū quán 龙须拳 Dragon beard (whiskers) fist, a hand shape: index finger extended, the other fingers curled to the crease in the palm, thumb pressed on the third segment of the middle finger. Used in southern styles. Also called bǎi hé quán.

lóng yǒu sōu gǔ zhī fǎ 龙有搜骨之法 Dragons have the method of seeking bones. The quality sought in Xingyiquan's dragon form, to control deeply into an adversary, not just grabbing the surface.

lóng yuè tiān mén 龙跃天门 Dragon Leaps through Heaven's Gate: circle a sword to dab up at shoulder height in a raised knee stance, then drop the foot back to a horse stance, cocking the wrist to snap the tip up. From Qingping sword.

lóng zhǎng 龙掌 Dragon palm, a hand shape: all five fingers spread and bent at the second and third joints, palm still fairly open.

lóng zhǎo 龙爪 Dragon claw, a hand shape. 1. In some styles, the same as dragon palm, see lóng zhǎng. 2. Wrist bent, all fingers together and extended, thumb spread out, palm down. 3. In Baguazhang, fingers spread open, index finger fully extended, the others slightly bent.

L

lóng zhǎo zhǎng 龙爪掌 Dragon claw palm. See lóng zhǎng, lóng zhǎo.

lóng zhū quán 龙珠拳 Dragon pearl fist, a hand shape. See lì zhī quán. Also called gǎn lǎn quán.

攏 [拢] (rad.64) **lǒng** To gather or hold together.

摟 [搂] (rad.64) **lōu** 1. To gather up; rake together. 2. Hold up; tuck up. 3. Often used for a movement that brushes aside, across to the outside. 4. In wrestling, refers to a raking action with the leg, stepping inside close to an adversary's front foot, pressing knee to knee, then catching the ankle and raking back with the heel to trip.

lōu gōu 搂钩 Brush with hooks: with the double hooks, sweep across in front of the body and down, the crescent blades edges down.

lōu jiǎo 搂脚 Rake with the foot: to step in to connect the legs and apply pressure with the leg and foot to trip. From wrestling.

lōu shǒu 搂手 1. Brush aside, deflect with the arm. 2. Deflect with the arm and pull.

lōu shǒu ér jìn shǒu 搂手而进手 If grabbed and pulled, go along with the pull, turning it into a punch. From Tanglangquan, one of its twelve soft counters, see also shí èr róu.

lōu tuǐ 搂腿 Raking kick: kick, and then catch an adversary with the flat of the foot and rake while bringing the foot back. From Duanquan.

lōu tuī shuāi 搂推摔 Brush and push takedown: catch an adversary behind the knee and push on the chest to take him down.

lōu xī 搂膝 Brush the knee. 1. Brush the arm out and across at knee level. 2. Push your knee into an adversary's leg to press it offline.

lōu xī ào bù 搂膝拗步 Brush Knee Offset Step, Brush knee with twisted step: step forward with a low parry or catch combined with chest high push or throw from the rear arm. From Taijiquan.

lōu xī dǎ chuí 搂膝打捶 Brush Knee Punch: moving forward with a low parry combined with low punch in reverse stance. One hand parries the attack while the other counter punches. From Taijiquan: Also called zhǐ dāng chuí.

lōu xī kāi bǎng 搂膝开膀 Brush Knee Open Arms: set back, lifting the knee, opening the arms out, front hand pressing by the knee. From Taiji Changquan.

lōu zǐ 搂子 1. A rake. 2. To rake an adversary's leg with your lower leg and foot. Also called guā lōu.

漏 (rad.85) **lòu** 1. To divulge, to disclose. 2. To leak. 3. To neglect.

lòu gǔ 漏谷 Acupoint Lougu (leaking valley), SP7. At the calf, up the inside, six *cun* above the medial malleolus (on each leg). From TCM. A sensitive point, striking here can cause numbness of the leg.

lòu jìn 漏劲 Leaking power: to sneak into an adversary's attack and cause him to make an error of direction or placement.

lòu pàn 漏判 An omission error by a judge or referee; error of omission.

lòu shǒu 漏手 A funneling punch, a reaching, turned over, punch.

露 (rad.173) **lòu** To appear; to emerge; to show. Pronounced lù, dew; distilled syrop or essense of flowers.

lòu bà 露把 To expose the base: to slide the rear hand forward on the spear so that the base is exposed. An error in most styles, especially during a stab, shortening the length of the spear and weakening power transfer. Also called liú bà.

撸 [撸] (rad.64) **lū** 1. To row, a rowing action. Chinese rowing faces forwards, crossing the oars at the chest, then pushing forward. 2. To rub one's palm along something long. 3. To punt, a low block with a long weapon, raising the butt with almost a stirring action.

顱 [颅] (rad.181) **lú** Skull, cranium.

lú xī 颅息 Acupoint Luxi (skull rest), SJ19. At the head, at the hairline behind the ear by the top third of the ear (on each side). From TCM.

擄 [掳] (rad.64) **lǔ** To carry off; capture.

lǔ shǒu 掳手 Catch. 1. Hook onto and grab an adversary's arm and pull him towards your centre.

2. Hook onto an adversary's wrist and press on his elbow with the other hand to control him.

lǔ shǒu tàn tī 掳手弹踢 Catch and snap kick: with one fist extended, circle the other arm around to set at the chest, kicking a low snap kick. From Bajiquan.

橹 [櫓] (rad.75) lǔ   To row, scull, sweep, a rowing action (see lū).

lǔ dāo 橹刀 Row with a broadsword (applied to the longer bagua broadsword): bring the blade across from the right side, blade flat with the edge forward, quite low.

路 (rad.157) lù   1. Road; path. 2. Journey; route. 3. A sequence. 4. A martial arts routine. Often called kata in English, from the Japanese. 5. In some styles, the sections of a routine.

lù gōng 路弓 A long bow, a large bow.

lù mǎ yáng biān 路马扬鞭 Raise the Whip on the Horse Along the Road: lift a foot up behind with the knee bent, and lift a sword up behind with the grip up, tip down. A held balance. From Yangjia style.

lù xiàn 路线 Route, route of movement. Specifically, it is the route taken by the feet. See also guǐ jī. Often drawn out in training manuals.

辘 [轆] (rad.159) lù Used usually in the combined form lù lú, meaning a well-pulley; windlass; winch.

lù lú 辘轳 1. A well-pulley; windlass; winch. 2. Continuous circular punches alternating sides, using the meat of the fist to chop. From Tanglangquan.

露 (rad.173) lù   1. Dew. 2. Syrop distilled from flowers, fruit, or leaves. Pronounced lòu, to appear; to emerge; to show.

lù huā dāo 露花刀 Dew on flowers broadsword, a routine of Liuhebafa.

鹿 (rad.198) lù   A deer.

lù jiǎo dāo 鹿角刀 Deerhorn blades. See yuān yāng yuè. Also called qián kūn jiàn, rì yuè shuāng lián, shuāng yuè, zǐ wǔ yuān yáng yuè.

lù jiǎo gōu 鹿角钩 Deerhorn hooks: a type of double hook with spreading tips. See also shuāng gōu.

吕 [呂] (rad.30) lǚ   A surname.

lǚ bù 吕布 Lü Bu, a general during the late Han period, d. 198 AD. Used in movement names.

lǚ bù jǐ 吕布戟 Lü Bu's Halberd: a halberd with a snaky tip, a snake halberd.

lǚ bù wán jǐ 吕布玩戟 Lü Bu Plays with his Halberd: a release from a belt grab, grab an adversary's wrist and elbow and jam his arm, forcing it upwards. From Baguazhang.

履 (rad.44) lǚ   1. To tread on, walk on. 2. Shoe, shoes.

lǚ báo bīng 履薄冰 Tread on thin ice: to place the front foot flat, keeping the weight on the rear foot, as if testing the ice. One of the metaphors for the circle-walking of Baguazhang.

捋 (rad.64) lǚ   1. To stroke, smooth out with the fingers. 2. Divert, a throwing technique: pull without grabbing, divert an incoming force so that it is sucked into emptiness. Also pronounced luō, see luō.

lǚ dāo 捋刀 Stroke a broadsword: slide the left hand along the spine of a broadsword's blade.

lǚ dài 捋带 Stroking draw.

lǚ gùn 捋棍 Stroke the staff: slide the hand along the shaft. Some styles say this instead of huá bà.

lǚ jìn 捋劲 The power and skill used in doing a stroking draw.

lǚ wàn 捋腕 Divert the wrist: grab an adversary's wrist and pull while twisting.

lǚ zài chǐ zhōng 捋在尺中 The power and efficacy of the stroking pull lies in the ulnar bone (the little finger side of the forearm). A martial saying.

lǚ zhǎng 捋掌 1. To divert back; to stroke and pull without a full grab. 2. A slightly cupping palm shape, suitable for doing the stroking technique.

膂 (rad.130) lǚ   1. The spinal column, the backbone. 2. Physical strength.

L

lǔ lì 膂力 Natural physical strength of the muscles and tendons, implying strength of the torso, where strength is based.

鸞 [鸾] (rad.198) **luán** A mythical bird that resembles a phoenix, and is five coloured like the phoenix (some say that it is a fledgling phoenix, some say it is a different bird). It is said to fly forever without landing, searching for a mate. Some say it is an auspicious bird, while some say that seeing the reflection of a Luan in a mirror is a bad omen. Often translated as fabulous bird. For movement names using the Luan, see ào luán, shùn-.

亂 [乱] (rad.5) **luàn** 1. Chaos; confusion. 2. Confused; agitated. 3. Rebellion. 4. Out of order; to throw into disorder.

luàn cǎi huā 乱踩花 Stomp Randomly on Blossoms: random step push hands practice. From Taijiquan. Also called làn cǎi huā.

luàn chōng 乱冲 To attack wildly.

luàn dǎ 乱打 To hit out wildly. Considered a fault in most styles, and likely to lead to defeat in a fight.

luàn diǎn jīn zhōng 乱点金钟 Hit the Golden Bell in Disorder: lift the knee with continuous strikes. From Piguaquan.

luàn huán 乱环 Random linking: push hands with a random order of techniques.

luàn rén fǎ 乱人法 To throw an adversary into disorder: attack with continuous strikes to the nose and eyes to make his eyes water so he becomes agitated and confused.

luàn tí 乱踢 To kick wildly.

掠 (rad.64) **lüè** 1. To plunder, pillage. 2. To sweep past; graze; skim over. 3. In dialect, pronounced lüě, to pick up. 4. To pull an adversary by the arm, towards you to set up for something else. From Bajiquan, one of its ten major techniques, see also shí dà jī fǎ.

lüè shǒu 掠手 1. To pull down and back. 2. To strike out with the palm, adding a short pull.

掄 [抡] (rad.64) **lūn** To circle, brandish, swing.

lūn bì pāi dì 抡臂拍地 Circle arms to slap the ground: swing both arms in a full circle, then drop to a squat and slap the ground with one hand, the other hooking behind.

lūn bì zá quán 抡臂砸拳 Circle arms to pound the fist: swing both arms in a full circle, then drop to a squat and pound the right fist into the left palm. From Longfist.

lūn biān 抡鞭 Circles with a steel whip: swing the whip vertically at the side, or in front, of the body.

lūn biān rào tóu 抡鞭绕头 Circles with head loop with a steel whip: swing the whip vertically in front of the body, looping it around the back of the neck.

lūn guà dāo (jiàn) 抡挂刀(剑) Swinging hook with broadsword (or sword), circling a full circle at the side with the wrist cocked to catch or dissolve an attack with the blade.

lūn gùn 抡棍 Swing a staff. See lūn qiāng.

lūn kǎn 抡砍 Swinging hack, complete a full circle before hacking with a bladed weapon.

lūn pāi 抡拍 Swinging slap: complete a full circle with the arm and slap the ground.

lūn pī 抡劈 Swinging chop, complete a full circle before chopping.

lūn pī dāo (jiàn) 抡劈刀(剑) Swinging chop with a broadsword (or sword), circling the blade in a vertical circle on either side of the body before chopping.

lūn qiāng 抡枪 Swing a spear: circle the shaft horizontally between shoulder and waist height, with one or two hands. Power goes to the fore-section of the shaft.

輪 [轮] (rad.159) **lún** 1. A wheel. 2. A circular weapon, often used as a pair. 3. Often interchanged with the above 抡 lūn and used as a verb, to wheel around.

lún cì 轮次 A round in a sparring or wrestling match. See also jú. Also called huí hé.

lún cì biǎo 轮次表 A pairing table of the rounds in a sparring or wrestling match.

捋 (rad.64) **luō**   To stroke a beard; smooth out with the fingers. Pronounced luō in many styles, and usually pronounced lǚ in Taijiquan, see lǚ.

luō shǒu 捋手 Divert back; stroke and pull (not grabbing).

luō shǒu chōng chuí 捋手冲捶 Stroke and Pound: pull your adversary's arm across his body and punch the other side of his head. From Baguazhang.

luō shǒu pī chuí 捋手劈捶 Stroke and Chop. See luō shǒu chōng chuí.

luō shǒu piān cǎi 捋手蹁踩 Stroke and Trample: do a pulling arm bar to an adversary combined with a turned out kick to his shin, sliding down onto the foot. From Baguazhang, one of its sixty-four hands.

luō shǒu xī zhuàng 捋手膝撞 Stroke and Knee Strike: pull an adversary into a knee strike. From Baguazhang, one of its sixty-four hands.

luō shǒu xì zhū 捋手戏珠 Stroke and Play with a Pearl: pull the arm and stab the eyes, turning and extending the arm fully. From Baguazhang, one of its sixty-four hands.

luō zhǎng 捋掌 Pull as if stroking, not closing the fingers to grab.

羅 [罗] (rad.122) **luó**   1. Thin, light silk. 2. A net, a snare.

luó hàn 罗汉 Arhat. In Buddhism, the disciples appointed to witness the Buddhist truth and save the world. Often used in movement names.

luó hàn bì fǎ 罗汉避法 Arhat Evades the Law: sit into horse stance, bring the hands in front of the chest, then strike up to the side with an elbow, tucking the hand near the ear. From Shaolinquan.

luó hàn cáng chuí 罗汉藏捶 Arhat Hides his Fist: in a raised knee stance, bring the front fist into the other palm, tucking them in at the rear side. From Shaolinquan.

luó hàn chū dòng 罗汉出洞 Arhat Emerges from the Cave: step into a left bow stance, swing the left fist up in front and the right back behind, leaning into the strike and extending the arms. The 83rd move of the tiger and crane routine, the same as zuì jiǔ bā xiān on the other side.

luó hàn dǒu bì 罗汉抖臂 Arhat Shakes his Arms: retreat with a stamp into a bow stance, snapping the arms straight down at the sides. From Shaolinquan.

luó hàn fú hǔ 罗汉伏虎 Arhat Subdues the Tiger. 1. Catch and reverse an adversary's wrist, pressing down on the pulse point with both thumbs. From Qinna. 2. Trap and press down. From Tongbeiquan.

luó hàn gōng 罗汉功 Arhat training: training the eyes by watching moving lanterns, gradually decreasing their size.

luó hàn jiàng lóng 罗汉降龙 Arhat Subdues the Dragon: starting from an upper block, thrust a sword downwards to chest height in a double handed grip with the thumbs under. From Taijiquan.

luó hàn kāi mén 罗汉开门 Arhat Opens the Door: snap into an open bow stance, opening out the hands with palms out to shoulder height in line with the stance. From Shaolinquan.

luó hàn káng bǎng 罗汉扛膀 Arhat Carries an Arm on his Shoulder: shift to a bow stance, bring the hands in, pressing up the shoulder to hoist something on it. From Shaolinquan.

luó hàn qián 罗汉钱 Arhat's coin: an ancient hidden weapon, a metal coin, often with the edges sharpened, that one could easily hide and throw.

luó hàn quán 罗汉拳 Luohanquan (Arhat fist), considered one of the Shaolin styles, it has eighteen combinations, for the Eighteen Arhats.

luó hàn shài shī 罗汉晒尸 Arhat Airs the Corpse in the Sun: in a left bow stance, punch from overhead with the right fist and underneath with the left fist, leaning into the strike and extending the arms. The 80th move of the tiger and crane routine.

luó hàn shí bā shǒu 罗汉十八手 The eighteen hands of the Arhats: Shaolinquan routines, consisting of eight routines of eighteen postures each.

luó hàn tán tī 罗汉弹踢 Arhat Snaps a Kick: take quick steps in to connect with your adversary's ankle, then a short hook sweep, combined with arm pressure on his back to throw him to the ground.

L

luó hàn zhāi guā 罗汉摘瓜 Arhat Plucks a Melon: move in to grab an adversary's head, twisting it back. From Baguazhang.

luó hàn zhuàng shān 罗汉撞山 Arhat Crashes into the Mountain: a jumping knee and shin strike to the side of an adversary.

luó hàn zuò dèng 罗汉坐凳 Arhat Sits on a Stool: kick forward, then place the foot on the supporting leg's knee and half-sit down. Slice the opposite hand up and hook the same side hand back, looking behind. From Shaolinquan.

螺 (rad.142) **luó** 1. A spiral shell. 2. A spiral; a whorl.

luó bà 螺把 Spiral grip: hold a sword with the index finger curled on the guard and the other fingers on the grip, the thumb tucked on the first joint of the index finger.

luó quān tuǐ 螺圈腿 Bowlegs, bandy legs. Also called ōu xíng tuǐ.

luó sī 螺丝 A screw.

luó sī dào kòu 螺丝倒扣 Spiraling reverse trap: a twisting escape to release a controlling grab of the wrist. From Qinna.

luó sī quán 螺丝拳 Screwing fist, a hand shape: clench the fist and tuck the thumb onto the second segments of the index and third fingers, curling the palm so the fist surface is angled slightly downward. From Xingyiquan.

luó sī shàng kòu 螺丝上扣 Spiraling upper trap: a twisting grab of the hand and wrist. From Qinna.

luó xíng quán 螺形拳 Spiral fist. See luó sī quán.

luó xuán 螺旋 Spiraling, coiling.

luó xuán jìn 螺旋劲 Spiral power, twisting power.

luó xuán quán 螺旋拳 Spiral fist. An upright fist with one joint of the index finger supported and extended. Also called zuàn quán.

luó xuán zhǎng 螺旋掌 Spiraling palm.

络 [絡] (rad.120) **luò** 1. To wrap around. 2. A net or something netlike, a web. 3. Capillaries. 4. The collaterals, the secondary web of the meridians. From TCM.

luò mài 络脉 Collaterals, collateral vessels, the secondary branches of the channels of circulation of qi and blood.

luò què 络却 Acupoint Luoque (declining connection), BL8. At the top of the head, 5.5 *cun* from the front hairline, 1.5 *cun* lateral to the midline (on each side). From TCM.

luò xué 络穴 Collateral acupoint. From TCM.

落 (rad.140) **luò** 1. To fall, drop; go down; set. 2. Land, lower (a technique or step). 3. In Xingyiquan, to complete an attack or hit.

luò bù 落步 To land (a foot when stepping).

luò bù jiǎo 落步脚 Landing trip: the instant that your adversary lands his foot, do a quick tripping kick before his weight is under control. Also called luò bù tī.

luò bù tī 落步踢 Landing kick. See luò bù jiǎo.

luò dì jiǎn chái 落地捡柴 Go to the Ground to Gather Firewood: sit to a drop stance and cut the forward arm out, extending the arm along the extended leg. From southern styles.

luò dì shēng gēn 落地生根 Send in roots on landing: to grip the ground firmly with the feet immediately upon landing while walking. From Baguazhang.

luò huā dài sǎo 落花待扫 Fallen Flowers Await Sweeping: cross step and turn a sword blade tip down, grip reversed, extending the left arm behind, sitting down. From Wu Taijiquan.

luò huā shì 落花式 Falling Flowers posture. 1. Move forward with upward slices of a sword, then turn to stab towards the ground. From Taijiquan. 2. Stepping continuous slices across.

luò kòng 落空 Land in nothingness: completely miss the technique on an adversary.

luò rú què 落如鹊 Land like a magpie: one of the twelve qualities of movement of Changquan, though these descriptors apply to many other styles. Land as lightly as a bird on a branch.

luò shǒu 落手 Falling hands: any dropping strike, such as press down or pound down. From Chuojiao. See also àn, rú, yā, zá, etc. See also qǐ shǒu, zǒu shǒu.

M

扌馬 [扌马] (rad.64) **mā** To pull like pulling a horse.

mā jiān kào 扌马肩靠 Pull into a shoulder strike: if your arm is being pulled, go down and along, moving in to hit with your shoulder. From Xingyiquan.

馬 [马] (rad.187) **mǎ** 1. A horse, horses. 2. Sometimes refers to stances in general. 3. Sometimes refers to the legs or thighs when describing stances or stepping. 4. Horse, as the seventh of the twelve animals from the Chinese zodiac, associated with a twelve year cycle symbolic of the earthly branches. The twelve animals make up a sixty year cycle when combined with the five phases. See also dì zhī, shēng xiào, wǔ xíng.

For more movement names using the actions or qualities of the horse, see also under bái mǎ, èr-, jīng-, kuài-, nù-, shuāng-, tiān-, yě-, yī-, yǐ-. Showing the close relationship of martial artists with horses, many movement names relate actions done to horses or on horseback, see also under cè mǎ-, huí-, jìn-, jū-, kuà-, lā-, lè-, piàn-, qí-, qiān-, tàn-, tuì-, xìn-, zǒu-, zuò-.

mǎ bēn tí 马奔蹄 Horse Charges with its Hooves: driving forward into a seventy-thirty stance with double straight jabs or shoving fists. From Xingyiquan. Also called shuāng mǎ xíng.

mǎ bù 马步 Horse stance, horse riding stance: feet open three foot-lengths apart (distance varies with style), feet parallel, thighs parallel with the ground (height varies with style). Also called qí mǎ, qí mǎ bù, zuò mǎ shì. See also zhèng dāng bù.

mǎ bù dǐng zhǒu 马步顶肘 Horse stance elbow strike: in a horse stance, strike upward at the side with the elbow. From Bajiquan.

mǎ bù jià dǎ 马步架打 Horse stance upper frame and hit: upper frame and punch into a horse stance. In traditional styles the raised arm is often bent and in front of the head. In many northern styles the raised arm is extended above and behind the head.

mǎ bù jiāo chā shǒu 马步交叉手 Horse stance with hands crossed. Often used as a landing from jumps in competition routines.

mǎ bù shuāng tuī dān zhǐ 马步双推单指 Horse stance double push with the single finger palm shape: sit in horse stance and push forward, either slowly with power or quickly. From southern styles.

mǎ bù tuō dǎ 马步托打 Horse stance lift and hit: lift while moving into a horse stance, completing the punch with the stance. From Chaquan.

mǎ chā 马叉 Horse fork: a long handled, three tined fork with flat blades on the outer tines.

mǎ hòu pāo dāo 马后抛刀 Toss the Blade Behind the Horse: stand up straight legged, stepping the right foot in front in a high cross step, cutting a sword downwards behind. Raise the left arm so the left elbow, right arm, and blade form a straight line heading towards a point a few inches from the ground. From Qingping sword.

mǎ jǐ 马戟 Horse halberd: a double weapon, about forty centimetres long with two parallel blades. The second blade is attached out halfway along the shaft, out to the side with a grip so that the weapon can be used double handed, one at the butt and the other on the grip of the second blade.

mǎ shàng jiā biān 马上加鞭 Apply a Whip Mounted on a Steed: strike before and behind, like whipping a horse. From Piguaquan.

mǎ shàng kāi gōng 马上开弓 Pull a Bow Mounted on a Steed: in a horse stance, first cross the arms, bringing the rear arm over to cover, then open out the arms, pulling the rear arm back and up, and bracing forward with the front arm. From Baguazhang.

mǎ xíng 马形 Horse form: charging forward with a double or single straight jab or ram with the fists. From Xingyiquan.

mǎ yá cì 马牙刺 Horse tooth sword: a straight sword with twelve tooth-like protuberances on both sides of the blade, arcing back towards the grip. Used for slashing horses' legs or trapping

M

weapons.

mǎ yǒu jí tí zhī gōng 马有疾蹄之功 Horses have the skill of quick hooves. A quality sought in Xingyiquan's horse form.

麻 (rad.200) má 1. Hemp and the fibre of hemp. 2. Sesame. 3. Numbness, feeling numb or tingling. This is the sensation sought in many control grips.

má gū xiàn shòu 麻姑献寿 Wish your Auntie a Long Life: catch an adversary's hand and twist the wrist little-finger side inwards.

má huā bāi 麻花掰 Break the fried dough twist, a wrestling move. See chán tuǐ.

má huā jìn 麻花劲 Fried dough twist power: a torqueing power within in the body.

má mù 麻木 1. Numb. Numbness. 2. Paralysed.

má què bù 麻雀步 Sparrow stepping: in a half squat with the heel off the ground, kick the other leg forward in a heel kick, alternating legs by jumping to switch them. A training method similar to the Cossack kick squat dancing move.

má zhàng gǎn 麻胀感 To have a tingling and distending feeling, especially in reference to stimulating an acupoint.

埋 (rad.32) mái 1. To cover up (with earth), to bury. 2. To conceal, hide

mái fú 埋伏 To ambush. 1. A sudden, unexpected, strike. 2. Sometimes means a reverse grip stab.

mái fú shì 埋伏式 Ambushing posture: a full squat with one arm protecting the head and the other punching behind. From Wudangquan.

mái gēn 埋根 To Bury the Root: press down on an adversary's foot or leg to control it. Step on, tuck onto and press, or kneel on it, so that he can't move his leg. From Bajiquan, one of its ten major techniques, see also shí dà jī fǎ.

脈 衇 (rad.130, 143) [脉] (rad.130) mài The large blood vessels, arteries and veins.

mài luò 脉络 Blood vessels, arteries and veins.

mài mén 脉门 Pulse gate: on the inside of the wrist, the place where the pulses are taken for diagnosis. This is not quite the same as the pulse point in the Western sense. From TCM.

mài wàn 脉腕 Sensitive point Maiwan, the pulse point on the wrist. Sensitive to the extent that striking it may cause death.

mài xī 脉息 The pulse.

邁 [迈] (rad.162) mài 1. To stride. 2. To pass. 3. To surpass.

mài bù 迈步 Stride, a large step, often a bit to the side.

mài bù rú māo xíng, yùn jìn rú chōu sī 迈步如猫行，运劲如抽丝 Step out as does a cat, move power like reeling silk. A martial saying.

mài bù rú xíng lí, luò bù rú shēng gēn 迈步如行犁，落步如生根 Step out like pushing a plough, land like setting in roots. A martial saying.

mài fǎ 迈法 Footwork: using stepping to move the body to the appropriate position for defense and attack.

瞞 [瞒] (rad.109) mán To fool; deceive. Hide the truth.

mán tiān guò hǎi 瞒天过海 Deceive the Sky to Cross the Sea. The first of the Thirty-six Stratagems of Warfare, which apply to many situations.

蠻 [蛮] (rad.142) mán Savage, rough, barbarous, reckless.

mán lì 蛮力 Brute strength. Not using the body effectively to do a movement, resulting in rough, unconnected movement. One of the elements of awkward brute strength, see also zhuō lì.

滿 [满] (rad.85) mǎn 1. Full; filled. 2. Plentiful. 3. Completely. 4. Haughty.

mǎn bà 满把 Full grip: holding the grip or shaft of a weapon fully, with all fingers and thumb web firmly in contact with it.

慢 (rad.61) màn Slow.

màn rú yīng 慢如鹰 Slow like an eagle. A deliberate, powerful slowness, like a soaring eagle looking for prey, not just moving slowly. See huǎn rú yīng.

màn xìng 慢性 1. Chronic. 2. Slow in taking effect.

màn xìng téng tòng 慢性疼痛 Chronic pain.

鋩 [铓] (rad.167) **máng** The point of a sword; a sharp point.

蟒 (rad.142) **mǎng** A python, a boa constrictor. For movement names using the actions or qualities of the python, see also under dà mǎng, guài-, huáng-, jù-, yù-.

貓 (rad.153) [猫] (rad.94) **māo** 1. A cat, cats. For more movement names using the actions or qualities of the cat, see also under jīn māo, lí-, líng-. 2. Pronounced máo, to stoop.

māo bǔ shǔ 猫捕鼠 Cat catching a rat: a metaphor for a recommended attitude for training. Quick, accurate, and deadly, but playful at the same time. Like how a cat, on catching a rat, plays with it for a while before killing it. This attitude keeps training fresh and interesting, rather than being drudging work.

māo bù 猫步 Catlike stepping: lifting the feet lightly and keeping steady.

māo xǐ liǎn 猫洗脸 Cat Washes its Face. See hǔ xǐ liǎn. Also called yuán hóu xǐ liǎn, zhé jié.

māor xǐ miàn 猫儿洗面 Cat Washes its Face: in horse stance, bring the hands across past the face to press forward in front of the shoulders, palms forward, elbows tucked down. The 29th move of the tiger and crane routine.

máo yāo 猫腰 Arch the back, round the whole back like a cat arches its back before a fight.

毛 (rad.82) **máo** 1. Hair. 2. Feather; down. 3. Wool. 4. Small. 5. A surname.

máo zhì tuō yǐng 毛稚脱颖 Feather Sticks Through a Bag (talent of the young shows itself): drop back to a right empty stance, the arms open to the sides, bend the elbow to bring the tip of a sword in to stab to the midline of the chest. From Qingping sword.

矛 (rad.110) **máo** A lance; a pike. 1. A snake tipped spear: a spear with a long, wavy tip. 2. A straight, sharpened, wooden stick used as a weapon.

máo dūn zhuāng 矛盾桩 Lance and shield stake standing: standing in a sixty-forty stance with the hands up at chest height, forward hand aligned with the forward leg, palms in. From Yiquan.

卯 (rad.26) **mǎo** The fourth of the twelve Terrestrial Branches, used in combination with the ten Celestial Stems to designate years, months, days, and hours. For the sixty year cycles, see also under dīng mǎo, guǐ-, jǐ-, xīn-, yì-. The period of the day from 5:00 a.m. to 7:00 a.m. See also dì zhī, tiān gān.

mǎo gōng 卯功 Training done regularly at the time from 5:00 a.m. to 7:00 a.m.

mǎo shí 卯时 The period of the day from 5:00 a.m. to 7:00 a.m. (5:00 to 7:00).

梅 (rad.75) **méi** Plum, prune.

méi huā bù 梅花步 Plum blossom stepping: stepping diagonally forward or backward to move in at the side, usually taking four quick steps at once.

méi huā lù 梅花路 Plum blossom route: a Tanglangquan routine, written up as thirty-seven moves.

méi huā qiāng 梅花枪 Plum blossom spear, a Shaolinquan spear routine, written up as forty-four moves.

méi huā quán 梅花拳 Meihuaquan (plum blossom fist), which practices on the top of poles planted into the ground. Thought to be from the Ming dynasty.

méi huā táng láng quán 梅花螳螂拳 Meihua (plum blossom) Tanglangquan, a branch of the Preying Mantis style.

méi huā zhuāng 梅花桩 1. Plum blossom stakes: stakes set into the ground in a plum blossom pattern: one in the middle, the other circling around it. Different configurations, but the usual one is four stakes around the central stake, each about two foot-lengths apart. These may be two metres or more long, and of a diameter that the ball or heel of the foot can stand on, but not both. 2. Plum blossom style, see méi huā quán.

méi shān quán 梅山拳 Meishanquan (plum mountain fist): a style from Hunan, in the Meishan area, considered a southern style, thought to be from the Song dynasty. It emphasizes direct and hard techniques.

眉 (rad.109) **méi**   Eyebrow, eyebrows.

méi chōng 眉冲 Acupoint Meichong (eyebrow ascension), BL3. At the head, directly up from the inside corner of the eyebrow, 0.5 *cun* into the hairline, .75 *cun* lateral to the midline (on each side). From TCM.

méi jiān dāo 眉尖刀 Eyebrow blade: a halberd with the blade curved like an eyebrow.

méi xīn 眉心 Centre of the eyebrows: between the eyebrows. One of the main targets on the body.

美 (rad.123) **měi**   1. Beautiful. 2. To beautify. 3. Good.

měi nǚ zhāi huā 美女摘花 Beautiful Woman Arranges Flowers: step forward and stab a sword directly in an angled upward direction. This is used when the sword has cut down and is set with the tip slightly up, so it stabs very directly. From Qingping sword.

měi rén jì 美人计 The Strategy of Using a Beautiful Woman. The thirty-first of the Thirty-six Stratagems of Warfare, which apply to many situations.

měi rén rèn zhèn shì 美人纫针式 Beautiful Woman Threads a Needle model. One of twenty-four classic spear moves. Most spear routines will have a move with a like name. In general, this name refers to a technique that uses the tip of the spear skillfully.

měi rén zhào jìng 美人照镜 Beautiful Woman Looks in the Mirror. 1. Standing up, left fist at the hip, cut across and out with the right forearm, stopping in front of the face. The fourth move of the tiger and crane routine. 2. Move the hands back and forth, one low, one high, repeating and finishing with a high stab. From Meishanquan.

押 [扪] (rad.64) **mén**   Feeling the body surface in channel diagnosis. From TCM.

門 [门] (rad.169) **mén**   1. Gate, door, entrance. 2. Style of martial arts. 3. Gateways to an adversary, especially when referring to the chest, ribs, and groin.

mén dāng gōng 门裆功 Crotch training: practice raising and lowering *qi* in a horse stance, then gradually introducing striking to the groin. Over time, may strike harder or with instruments.

mén hù 门户 1. Style or school of martial art. 2. Gateway to the body, your own to be defended and your adversary's to be attacked.

mén kǎn tuǐ 门坎腿 Destroy the Gate kick: kicks to the shin, either to the front (see also qián mén kǎn) or back (see also hòu mén kǎn).

mén lǐ 门里 Inside the gate: attacks to the inside of the arms of an adversary. See also lǐ mén.

mén pài 门派 Style or school of martial art.

mén qián xióng shī 门前雄狮 Powerful Lion in front of the Gate: step forward into a bow stance, opening the arms, then closing the elbow strike. From Chuojiao.

mén rén 门人 Students of a style or school of martial art.

mén wài 门外 Outside the gate: attacks to the outside the space made by the elbows, outside the arms. See also wài mén.

猛 (rad.94) **měng**   1. Fierce; bold; violent. 2. Energetic; vigorous. 3. Sudden and quick (strikes).

měng gōng zhàn 猛攻战 Vigorous attack tactics: to attack strongly and continuously, not giving an adversary space to react.

měng hǔ bā shā 猛虎扒沙 Ferocious Tiger Rakes Sand: step to a right bow stance and push both palms in tiger claws on line with the stance. The 108th move of the tiger and crane routine.

měng hǔ chū dòng 猛虎出洞 Ferocious Tiger Emerges from its Lair: a low double strike with the base of the hands together.

měng hǔ chū shān 猛虎出山 Ferocious Tiger Emerges from the Mountain: double press down with the hands, circle-walk with the hands settled down in front of the body. From Baguazhang.

měng hǔ chū xiá 猛虎出柙 Ferocious Tiger Escapes from the Cage: Step forward with one hand angled up and out and the lower hand pushing through. From Baguazhang.

měng hǔ chū xué 猛虎出穴 Ferocious Tiger Emerges from its Den: turn around with an upper block and punch. From Tongbeiquan.

měng hǔ fú àn 猛虎伏岸 Ferocious Tiger Hides on the Bank. See měng hǔ fú yú.

měng hǔ fú yú 猛虎伏峪 Ferocious Tiger Hides in the Ravine: in horse stance, punch with the right hand and hold a sword grip in the left hand in front of the chest, in a reverse grip so the sword points flat to the back. From Qingping sword. Also called měng hǔ fú àn.

měng hǔ fú yú 猛虎伏嵎 Ferocious Tiger Hides in the Canyon: sit into horse stance, blocking up over the head with a sword and pressing the left fist into the left knee. From Qingping sword.

měng hǔ fù yú 猛虎负嵎 Ferocious Tiger Fights with its Back to the Canyon: shift back to a back weighted horse stance and tuck the elbows in to bring the hands in tiger claws to set at the shoulders, looking to the forward side. The 45th move of the tiger and crane routine.

měng hǔ huí tóu 猛虎回头 Ferocious Tiger Looks Back. 1. A jumping spin heel kick. 2. A quick turn to a stab.

měng hǔ lā yáng 猛虎拉羊 Ferocious Tiger Drags a Sheep: squat to a drop stance and swing the rear arm up then continue to block up above the head. Chop the front arm down along the extended leg. From Shaolinquan.

měng hǔ pū shí 猛虎扑食 Ferocious Tiger Pounces on its Prey. 1. Step quickly forward into a double shove. 2. Jump forward to a low double grab.

měng hǔ tiào jiàn 猛虎跳涧 Ferocious Tiger Jumps over the Ravine. 1. Drive forward, grabbing and pulling in, the entry prior to a double tiger pounce. From Xingyiquan. 2. Jump forward and land in a drop stance, slapping the ground near the squatting foot. From Shaolinquan. 3. A lean into the body combined with a reaching over punch coming through from above, adding to power with a stamp. From Baguazhang, one of its sixty-four hands. Also called wò hǔ tiào jiàn.

měng hǔ tuī shān 猛虎推山 Ferocious Tiger Pushes the Mountain: step into a right reverse bow stance, turning to face that way and pushing forward with the left palm in a tiger claw. The 98th move of the tiger and crane routine.

měng hǔ xì shān 猛虎戏山 Ferocious Tiger Plays in the Mountain: step forward into a T stance with a rising slice with a sword, the arm fully extended, hand to eye height, the tip slightly lower than the grip. From Qingping sword.

měng hǔ xià shān 猛虎下山 Ferocious Tiger Descends from the Mountain. 1. Trap your foot behind your adversary's and drive your forearm into his hip crease for a direct takedown. 2. Step forward to a right reverse bow stance and push/grab through with the both hands in tiger claws, left forward and high, right near its elbow. Lean into the strike. The 63rd move of the tiger and crane routine. The same as hǔ píng chái láng on the other side. 3. A routine in Meishanquan, emphasizing hard power. Written up as forty-two moves, which is seventeen moves repeated.

měng hǔ yìng pá shān 猛虎硬爬山 Ferocious Tiger Firmly Climbs the Mountain: coming up to attack with the arms and legs together, grabbing and kicking, characteristic of a tiger clambering up a mountain. From Bajiquan, one of its eight main concepts, see also bā dà zhāo.

měng hǔ zuò pō 猛虎坐坡 Ferocious Tiger Sits on the Slope: sit to empty stance and snap down a pressing palm. From Piguaquan.

měng pāi 猛拍 To attack fiercely, lunge.

瞇 [眯] (rad.109) mī   To squint, narrow one's eyes.

mī yǎn fǎ 眯眼法 Squinting method: squint and blink to appear in trouble in fighting, so an adversary attacks without thinking much.

迷 (rad.162) mí   1. To be confused; lost. 2. To confuse; fascinate. 3. To be fascinated by.

mí zōng quán 迷踪拳 Mizongquan (lost track fist), known since the Tang dynasty, considered a Shaolin style. Most famous proponent was Huo Yuanjia. Also called yàn qīng quán.

秘 (rad.115) mì   Secret.

mì mén táng láng quán 秘门螳螂拳 Mimen (secret gate) Tanglangquan, a branch of Mantis style that emphasizes low stances and elbow techniques.

mì zōng lián huán shuò 秘宗连环朔 Mizong rings lance: a long handled weapon with a shovel

M

like blade, spikes out the base of the blade, and rings on the outer edges.

mì zōng quán 秘宗拳 Mizongquan (secret school fist). See mí zōng quán.

mì zōng qiāng 秘宗枪 Mizong spear, a routine for a normal sized spear, written up as sixty-four moves.

綿 [绵] (rad.120) **mián** 1. Silk floss. 2. Continuous; drawn out. 3. Soft; gentle. 4. One of Ziranmen's nineteen main methods.

mián quán 绵拳 Mianquan (soft fist) style, a northern style from Hebei province. It uses expansive movements, mostly soft, but with some hard.

mián zhǎng 绵掌 Mianzhang (soft palm) style, a northern style from Hebei province, spread in Beijing. It emphasizes expansive palm techniques.

勉 (rad.19) **miǎn** 1. To exert oneself; strive. 2. To encourage; urge. 3. To strive to do something beyond one's power. 4. A surname.

miǎn zhāng duǎn dǎ 勉张短打 Mianzhang Duanda (Mian and Zhang's short hits). Also called Short Fist, see duǎn quán.

miǎn zhāng quán 勉张拳 Mianzhangquan (Mian and Zhang's fist). Also called duǎn quán, miǎn zhāng duǎn dǎ. See duǎn quán.

挵 (rad.64) **miǎn** A twisting grab, first grabbing with the thumb web up, then twisting it downward.

苗 (rad.140) **miáo** 1. A young plant, seedling; sprout. 2. The Miao people of Guangxi province.

miáo dāo 苗刀 Miao Broadsword. 1. Sword of the Miao people. A long (about 1.5 metres, with a handgrip about 0.4 metres), thin, single edged, gently curved blade. 2. A short halberd with a similar thin blade, but with a shaft half the length of the total weapon.

miáo quán 苗拳 Miaoquan (Miao nationality fist): style of the Miao people of Guangxi province, which uses short, agile stances with powerful strikes.

秒 (rad.115) **miǎo** A second (in time).

miǎo biǎo 秒表 A stopwatch. Also called pǎo biǎo.

妙 (rad.38) **miào** 1. Wonderful, excellent. 2. Ingenious, clever. One of Ziranmen's nineteen main methods.

miào shǒu 妙手 Excellent hands: an expert.

miào shǒu zhāi xīng 妙手摘星 Expert Hands Pluck the Stars: in a cross sit stance with a reaching low cut with a sword, palm down, flick the blade over to palm up, raising the tip. Then step forward with a reaching stab, palm down. From Wu Taijiquan.

抿 (rad.64) **mǐn** To close lightly; furl; tuck.

mǐn chún 抿唇 Purse the lips lightly.

敏 (rad.66) **mǐn** Sensitive, nimble and agile; alert, reactive. One of the requisite abilities for martial arts. In Xingyiquan, for the heart, eyes, and hands. In Baguazhang, for the body, footwork, eyes, and hands.

名 (rad.30) **míng** 1. Name. Given name. People, particularly in the past, are often referred to by a given name (míng), private name (zì), literary name (hào) and/or nickname (chuò hào). 2. Reputation. 3. Famous.

míng cì 名次 Placing in a competition.

明 (rad.72) **míng** 1. Bright, clear; brilliant. 2. The Ming dynasty (1368-1644).

míng yǎn fǎ 明眼法 Bright looking method: open the eyes wide to carefully observe an adversary's spirit, emotions, and movements.

míng jìn 明劲 Obvious, hard power, evident trained power.

míng tuǐ fǎ 明腿法 Obvious kicks: kicks that are clearly kicks, not hidden in footwork. See also àn tuǐ fǎ.

瞑 (rad.109) **míng** To close the eyes.

míng yǎn fǎ 瞑眼法 Closing eyes method: close the eyes in a fight, as if dim-sighted, to put an adversary off guard.

命 (rad.30) **mìng**   1. Life. 2. Fate; destiny.

mìng mén 命门 Acupoint Mingmen (gate of vitality), DU4. At the lower back, below the spinous process of the second lumbar vertebra, on the midline. From TCM. A good target, and a sensitive point. Hitting too hard may cause paralysis. Best to hit with a pull and short strike or a step around to strike from behind, or elbow, or knee strike from behind. In internal styles, the back is flattened or slightly protruded in this area, allowing for smooth movement and power emission.

摸 (rad.64) **mō**   1. To caress. 2. To feel out, touch. 3. To seek after.

mō gān 磨杆 Sense a pole: practice the power of a pole, twisting to parry back and forth as advancing and retreating. From Yiquan.

mō gān 磨竿 Sense a bamboo pole. See mō gān above.

mō jìn 摸劲 Sensing power. See mō lì.

mō lì 摸力 Sensing strength: to stand in a posture, not moving, or doing micromovements, sensing the lines of power inside. These are exercises for specific components of whole body power, particularly feeling the connections between the hands and between the upper and lower body. From Yiquan.

mō sǎo quán 摸扫拳 An extended sweeping punch. From Choylifut.

摩 (rad.64) **mó**   To rub; scrape. A rubbing, pressuring, hand technique.

mó cā 摩擦 1. Friction. 2. Clash.

mó cā bù 摩擦步 Friction stepping: slow stepping to maintain whole body power. From Yiquan.

mó fǎ 摩法 Massaging methods in treatment, pressing and rubbing, firm but not to the point of injury to the skin. From TCM.

mó suō jìn 摩挲劲 Stroking power: a type of power application that rolls like waves, rising up and dragging down as it drops. From Xingyiquan.

mó tiān guàn yuè zhǎng 摩天观月掌 Rub the Sky and Gaze at the Moon palm. See chēng tiān zhǎng.

mó yǎn bù 摩掩步 Scraping step: the rear foot steps forward with a tucking in step, to a T stance. The other foot lifts and resettles with a turned out step to form another T step. The original (rear) foot then steps in beside the other foot. The body turns around with the steps. From Baguazhang.

磨 (rad.112) **mó**   To rub, wear; polish. Also pronounced mò, see mò.

mó jìng bù 磨胫步 Shin rubbing step: bring the moving rear foot forward to hover beside the supporting ankle before continuing the step forward. From Baguazhang and Xingyiquan. Also called tí bù.

mó lèi zhǎng 磨肋掌 Rib rubbing palm. See mò zhǎng.

抹 (rad.64) **mǒ**   To smear, daub, plaster: move horizontally in an arc as if rubbing a knife on a stone to sharpen it.

mǒ bó 抹脖 Neck smear throw: techniques that involve trapping and manipulating the back of the neck of an adversary, can be combined with various leg techniques. From wrestling.

mǒ bó tī 抹脖踢 Neck smear sweeping throw: grab the back of an adversary's neck, press it one way while doing a hook sweep on his leg the other way. From wrestling.

mǒ dà dāo 抹大刀 Smear with a big cutter: with a two handed cut, turn the right hand palm down to bring the blade to the outside, then extend the blade forward while circling it in a smearing action.

mǒ dāo 抹刀 Smear with broadsword. See mǒ jiàn.

mǒ jiàn 抹剑 Smear with sword: circle with a flat blade at about chest height, the blade travelling in the direction of the edge, force applying to the edge. This may be done with a one-handed or two-handed hold.

mǒ méi duàn jǐng 抹眉断颈 Smear the Eyebrows neck break: from the back, reach over your adversary's head to dig the fingers into his eye sockets and pull his head back.

mǒ méi hóng 抹眉肱 Smear the Eyebrows: turn and forcefully strike to the face. From Chen Taijiquan.

M

mǒ ná fǎ 抹拿法 Smearing grappling hold: use a crossing tearing action while smearing an adversary's neck or forehead. From wrestling.

mǒ pū dāo 抹扑刀 Smear with a horse cutter. See mǒ dà dāo.

mǒ xiù lián chuí 抹袖连捶 Smear the Sleeves Continuing Punches: brush aside an adversary's attack twice, alternating hands, while moving in to punch. From Baguazhang, one of its sixty-four hands.

mǒ zhǎng 抹掌 Smear: slide the hand softly along the other arm, palm down, power to the outer edge.

磨 (rad.112) mò 1. To grind; mill; turn around. 2. A grindstone. 3. A counter to a throw attempt, covering the attack and turning to the back. Also pronounced mó, see mó.

mò pán dāo 磨盘刀 Millstone grinding with a broadsword: See mò pán jiàn.

mò pán jiàn 磨盘剑 Millstone grinding with a sword: holding the blade flat, walk in a circle drawing the blade around at waist height as you go. From Baguazhang and Taijiquan.

mò pán shǒu 磨盘手 Millstone grinding hand: move gently like water in a millstone then change into a crashing wave. From Tanglangquan.

mò shēn dāo 磨身刀 Grinding turn with a broadsword: holding the blade almost vertical, tip down, edge out, handgrip at shoulder height, push a broadsword and step around. Used with the larger bladed Bagua broadsword.

mò shēn zhǎng 磨身掌 Grinding Change: one of the eight mother palms, involving turning on the spot as if grinding. From Baguazhang.

mò yāo dāo huí tóu pán gēn 磨腰刀回头盘根 Turn the Blade around the Waist, Look Back and Coil the Root: holding a halberd with a reverse grip, jump and turn to the right, slicing at waist height. Finish in a resting stance, lifting the blade. From Chen Taijiquan.

mò zhǎng 磨掌 Rubbing palm: bend the elbow, bend and rotate the wrist inward to slide the hand, palm up, back of the hand on the flank, around the ribs to extend out to the rear of the body. Also called mó lèi zhǎng.

莫 (rad.140) mò 1. No one; nothing; none. 2. A surname.

mò jiā quán 莫家拳 Mojiaquan (Mo family fist), a southern style, attributed to the Fujian province Shaolin temple, spread by the Mo family, popular in Guangdong province. Popular in the early 1800s.

拇 (rad.64) mǔ 1. The thumb. 2. The big toe.

mǔ cháng qū jī 拇长屈肌 Flexor pollicis longus muscle: a short muscle in the forearm. Assists in thumb flexion.

mǔ cháng shēn jī 拇长伸肌 Extensor pollicis longus muscle: a short muscle in the forearm. Assists in thumb extension.

mǔ cháng zhǎn jī 拇长展肌 Abductor pollicis longus muscle: a short muscle in the forearm. Assists in thumb abduction.

mǔ duǎn shēn jī 拇短伸肌 Extensor pollicis brevis muscle: a short muscle in the forearm. Assists in thumb extension.

mǔ zhǐ 拇指 The thumb.

mǔ zhǐ 拇趾 The big toe.

mǔ zhǐ yā 拇指压 Thumb press: from a handshake position, press an adversary's thumb joint, step back and press down to the ground if needed. From Qinna.

母 (rad.80) mǔ 1. Mother. 2. Female elders.

mǔ gùn 母棍 Mother staff, a routine using a meridian staff, written up as forty moves. See tài kōng zì wǔ gùn.

mǔ zhǎng 母掌 Mother palms: eight palm changes to practice the basics of Baguazhang. Also called bā dà zhǎng, lǎo bā zhǎng.

踇 (rad.157) mǔ The big toe.

mǔ cháng shēn jī 踇长伸肌 Extensor hallucis longus muscle: in the shin. Assists in dorsiflexion of the ankle and lifting the big toe.

木 (rad.75) mù 1. Tree; timber, wood. 2. Wooden; made of wood. 3. Wood as one of the five elemental phases. Wood relates to the internal organ of the liver, to the sensing organ of the eyes, to the tissue of the tendons, and to the season of spring. Its *yang* expression is fir, its *yin* is bamboo. See also wǔ xíng. 4. Wood as one of the five phases techniques of Xingyiquan. The mindset of wood is alive and aware, defensive moves absorb and recoil directly, and attacking moves sense and react quickly to enter. See also bēng quán.

mù rén zhuāng 木人桩 Wooden dummy, varies in shape and size, usually a head-height post with extended arms and legs.

mù rén zhuāng fǎ 木人桩法 Wooden dummy practice techniques.

mù rén zhuāng gōng 木人桩功 Wooden dummy training methods.

mù zhuāng 木桩 Wooden stake, usually over two metres high and a foot thick, used for conditioning.

mù zhuāng fǎ 木桩法 Wooden stake techniques.

mù zhuāng gōng 木桩功 Wooden stake training methods.

沐 (rad.85) mù   To bathe; to wash.

mù yù gōng 沐浴功 Bathing skill. 1. Training to receive blows. 2. The skill achieved of being able to endure blows.

牧 (rad.93) mù   To herd or tend animals (sheep, cattle, etc.).

mù tóng qiān yáng 牧童牵羊 Shepherd Boy Leads the Sheep: making contact with your adversary's arm, grab his fingers with your other hand, take a step back, and forcibly press his fingers, reversing his joints.

目 (rad.109) mù   1. The eye, the eyes. Also called yǎn. 2. One of the five sensory organs, see also wǔ guān. 3. To look. Used in written descriptions of actions, not normally used in spoken instructions.

mù biāo 目标 A target, an objective. Refers to attack targets on the body, a shooting target, or as a training or planning goal.

mù chuāng 目窗 Acupoint Muchuang (eye window), GB16. At the top of the head, 1.5 *cun* from the front hairline, 2.25 *cun* lateral to the midline (on each side). From TCM.

mù jī 目击 Eye attack: use of the eyes to either to psyche out an adversary or as a fake (looking as if to strike in one way while moving in another).

mù shì (qián fāng) 目视(前方) Look (straight ahead), look at (any descriptor such as the right hand, the sword tip, etc.). Used in written descriptions of actions, not usually used in spoken instructions.

mù xuàn 目眩 To be dizzy, get dizzy (to the extent that the eyes are dazed).

N

拿 挐 [拿] (rad.64) ná   1. To seize and hold; grasp; capture, control; put someone in a difficult situation. 2. A wrestling takedown: a technique that involves grabbing and lifting the foot of an adversary. 3. A controlling or grappling technique: to grasp with a twist. 4. The category of controlling technique that are in each move. See also sì jī. 5. One of the four principles of Taijiquan push hands. See also sì zé. 6. Seize, one of Ziranmen's nineteen main methods.

ná fǎ 拿法   1. Capture techniques, catch techniques, grasping techniques: category of techniques that include joint locks, holds, dislocations, pressure point grips, and counters and escapes from controls. Common to most styles are bì, cuò, diāo, fēng, jié, kòu, ná, xiāo. See also sì jì. 2. Sometimes refers specifically to joint grasping techniques. 3. A treatment method, pinching and pulling firmly. From TCM.

ná gǔ 拿骨 Control a bone: grasp and control an adversary's bone structure or head of a small bone, causing pain, injury, or loss of control. From Qinna.

ná jiān 拿肩 Shoulder controls: a category of Qinna, controlling and using leverage at the shoulder joint.

ná jié 拿节 Control a joint by sticking and coiling. From Qinna.

ná jīn 拿筋 Control a tendon, tendon grasping: grasp and control an adversary's tendon, vein or artery. From Qinna.

ná jīn mài 拿筋脉 Control a tendon or blood vessel: grasp and control an adversary's tendon or blood vessel. From Qinna.

ná jìn 拿劲 Seizing strength: grabbing with the palm rather than a full grip, often used with a two handed control move. Combined with body technique and footwork, used to grab or control an adversary.

ná kòng lèi 拿控类 Grappling methods, the category of methods that include seizing and controlling.

ná qiāng 拿枪 Inner trap with a spear: circle clockwise and press with the shaft horizontal. To parry inward. Also traditionally called lǐ bǎ mén fēng. Traditionally, combined with a stab, called fēng qiāng.

ná tóu jǐng 拿头颈 Head and neck controls: controlling and using leverage at the head and neck. A category of control used in Qinna.

ná wàn 拿腕 Wrist controls: controlling and using leverage at the wrist joint. These are among the most common methods as the wrist is easy to grab and is quite small and mobile. A category of control used in Qinna.

ná xī 拿膝 Knee controls: controlling and throwing by using leverage at the knee joint. A category of control used in Qinna.

ná xióng quán 拿熊拳 Seize the bear routine: a routine of Tongbeiquan, written up as twenty moves.

ná xué 拿穴 Control a pressure point or cavity: to grab or poke a pressure point with a controlling grasp, using a thumb and two fingers. From Qinna.

ná xuè 拿血 Grasp a blood vessel: to grab or pressure over a blood vessel with a controlling grasp. From Qinna.

ná yāo 拿腰 Control the lower back. 1. While the upper body maintains a straight position, the lower back and abdomen swallow in or to left or right. From Tongbeiquan. 2. Waist controls, a category of control, controlling and throwing the waist with leverage.

ná zhǎng gǔ 拿掌骨 Grab the palm bones: when shaking hands, grasp an adversary's fingers very firmly and press down with the thumb. From Qinna.

ná zhǎo 拿爪 To grab and twist inward.

ná zhǐ 拿指 Finger controls: controlling and using leverage at the finger joints. These are among the easiest methods, as the fingers are easily grabbed and separated. A category of control used in Qinna.

N

ná zhǒu 拿肘 Elbow controls: controlling and using leverage at the elbow joint. A category of control used in Qinna.

ná zú huái 拿足踝 Foot and ankle controls: controlling and throwing by using leverage at the foot and ankle joint. A category of control used in Qinna.

捺 (rad.64) **nà**
1. To press down; restrain. 2. The downward right concave character stroke.

nà shǒu 捺手 1. To press down and restrain. 2. A pinning hand: a strong push down with a straight arm at the side of the body. From Wing Chun. Pronounced gun sau in Cantonese.

納 [纳] (rad.120) **nà**
1. To receive; accept. To catch and draw in with hands while rotating the forearm. Uses a smooth power.

乃 (rad.4) **nǎi**
1. Literary, to be. 2. So; therefore. 3. Only then. 4. You, your.

nǎi zì bù 乃字步 1. A hunkered squat (a position that looks like the character 乃), squatting with one foot flat, one heel raised, sitting between the feet. 2. A drop stance, both feet flat on the ground. May be slightly higher than a full drop stance. Also called pū bù. See also dī nǎi zì bù.

耐 (rad.126) **nài**
To be able to endure, bear.

nài lì 耐力 Endurance, stamina.

nài lì xùn liàn 耐力训练 Endurance training; exercises intended to improve overall and specific endurance.

nài xīn 耐心 Patient.

nài xīng 耐性 Patience; endurance.

南 (rad.24) **nán**
South. Southern. Southerly.

nán cháo 南朝 The Southern dynasties of Song, Qi, Liang, and Chen (420-589).

nán dāo 南刀 Southern broadsword. 1. A broadsword used in the southern styles, it is a bit heftier in the blade than a regular broadsword. 2. Southern-style broadsword play: a Taolu competition event, called Nandao in English.

nán fāng 南方 The South. Sometimes written descriptions of routines use compass directions for orientation.

nán gùn 南棍 Southern staff. 1. A staff used in the southern styles, it is a bit heftier than a regular staff. 2. Southern-style cudgel play: a Taolu competition event, called Nangun in English.

nán pài 南派 Southern styles, as differentiated from northern styles. In general, the dividing line between north and south China is the Yangzi river.

nán quán 南拳 1. Southern styles, as differentiated from northern styles. Refers to a large variety of styles. 2. The modern competition Southern-style boxing. Called Nanquan in English.

nán shé tǔ xìn 南蛇吐信 Southern Snake Spits its Tongue: do a bow stance double hack down, then grab and pull with a snap kick. From Meishanquan.

nán sòng 南宋 Southern Song dynasty (1127-1279).

nán yán jīng léi 南岩惊雷 A Clap of Thunder at the Southern Cliff: alternate foot stamps then a squat down, first circling the hands, then lifting them to grab together and pull down to the ground. From Wudangquan.

nán yuè héng shān 南岳衡山 Mount Heng, the Southern of the sacred mountains. See also héng shān, wǔ yuè.

nán zhī quán 南枝拳 Nanzhiquan (southern branch fist), a southern style attributed to Chen Nanzhi, from Guangdong province.

男 (rad.102) **nán**
Male; man, men.

難 [难] (rad.172) **nán**
Difficult.

nán dù 难度 Degree of difficulty: assigned to movements according to difficulty, to give extra points in Taolu competition.

nán dù dòng zuò 难度动作 Degree of difficulty movements: pre-approved optional movements used in Taolu competition wushu to increase the score if successfully completed.

撓 [挠] (rad.64) **náo**
1. To bend; to yield. 2. To hinder; to obstruct. 3. To scratch.

náo shǒu 挠手 Deflect: hook with a straight arm. Similar to brushing aside, but with a straight arm.

See also lōu shǒu.

腦 [脑] (rad.130) nǎo
1. The brain. 2. Often refers to the head.

nǎo hǎi 脑海 Sensitive point Naohai, sea of the brain, behind the head. Best to hit with a pull and short punch, or a step around punch, getting behind an adversary.

nǎo hòu zhāi jīn 脑后摘筋 Pluck Tendons Behind the Head: cock the wrist to bring a sword blade back over the shoulder with a flat snap behind. From Qingping sword.

nǎo hòu zhāi kuī 脑后摘盔 Pluck a Helmet Behind the Head: variously done, but with the action of wrapping the arm around the neck or over the head with a close covering palm, getting power from the back. From Baguazhang.

nǎo hù 脑户 Acupoint Naohu (brain's door), DU17. At the back of the head, just above the protuberance of the occipital bone, 2.5 *cun* up from the hairline, 1.5 *cun* up from acupoint Fengfu, on the midline. From TCM. One of the main targets on the body. Colloquially called hòu nǎo.

nǎo kōng 脑空 Acupoint Naokong (brain hollow), GB19. At the back of the head, in a large depression on the external occipital protuberance, 2.25 *cun* lateral to the midline (on each side). From TCM.

nǎo qiē zǐ 脑切子 Brain cutting, a takedown: grab your adversary's arm, move in and wrap your other arm around his neck, moving forward to take him down backwards. Also called qiē jiān.

nǎo sǔn shāng 脑损伤 Brain damage.

nǎo zhàng 脑胀 The characters literally say brain swelling. The meaning is dizziness; lightheaded; intoxicated.

nǎo zhèn dàng 脑震荡 Cerebral concussion.

臑 (rad.130) nào
Upper arm (literary term, not used in speech).

nào huì 臑会 Acupoint Naohui (upper arm convergence), SJ13. At the arm, the back, in line with the point of the elbow and the tip of the shoulder blade, three *cun* down from acupoint Jianliao (each arm). From TCM.

nào shū 臑俞 Acupoint Naoshu (upper arm transport), SI10. At the back of the shoulder, straight up from the crease of the armpit, in the depression medial to the acromial angle and below the border of the scapula (on each arm). From TCM.

哪 (rad.30) né
Used in the name Nezha, colloquially also called Nazha. Normally pronounced nǎ, meaning which, what.

né zhā 哪吒 Nata, Nezha: a mythical being, an immortal, a divine warrior in the story Journey to the West; A protection deity; Marshal of the Central Altar. Often thought of as troublesome, and sometimes used in movement names.

né zhā nào hǎi 哪吒闹海 Nezha Roils the Sea. 1. Take a double shoulder grab and twist your adversary's arms up and down, finally crossing them for control. 2. Drop back to empty stance, chopping down with the forward fist, guarding with the rear palm. 3. A triple punch: one sweeping flat, one punching straight, then one swinging up. From Meishanquan.

né zhā tàn hǎi 哪吒探海 Nezha Reaches into the Sea: a low stab with a sword. From Taijiquan.

內 (rad.11) [内] (rad.9) nèi
Inside, inner.

nèi bā bù 内八步 Inner character eight (八) stance: feet about a foot-length apart, feet and knees turned in about forty-five degrees.

nèi bà 内把 Inner grip: holding a short weapon in a normal grip, with the weapon turned so the palm faces yourself.

nèi bēng 内绷 Inner draw, a wrist snap with a straight sword to cut an adversary's wrist from the inside. See also wài bēng.

nèi bì hōng mén 内闭鸿门 Close the Inner Door to the Hongmen Feast: retreat to a left bow stance with a low cut with a sword aligned with the extended leg, take a step or two back, then shift forward and come back with a rasping cut in a smooth stance. From Qingping sword. See also hōng mén, wài bì hōng mén.

nèi cuò 内锉 Inner file, an upright filing action with the under edge of a sword blade, in response to a straight flat strike.

N

nèi gōng 内功 Internal training, training of internal strength and health. Also called nèi yáng gōng, nèi zhuāng gōng.

nèi gù jīng shén wài shì ān yì 内固精神外示安逸 Strengthen the spirit on the inside and appear calm on the outside. A quality sought in martial arts training.

nèi guān 内关 Acupoint Neiguan (inner pass), PC6. At the forearm, on the inside, in line with acupoints Quze and Daling, two *cun* above the wrist crease, between the long flexor tendons on the inside of the forearm (on each arm). From TCM. A sensitive point, pressure here can cause loss of strength as well as pain. Hard pressure can also shock the Lung and induce unconsciousness. Best to pressure with an eagle claw grab, and useful to include in a wrist control technique.

nèi huái jiān 内踝尖 Extraordinary acupoint Neihuaijian (tip inside the ankle), EX-LE8. At the ankle, on the medial side where the ankle bone protrudes. From TCM. A crippling point, striking here may cause serious injury. See also cán xué.

nèi jiā quán 内家拳 Internal martial arts, generally considered to be Baguazhang, Liuhebafa, Taijiquan, Wudangquan, and Xingyiquan. Thought to emphasise internal training over physical attributes, or pliancy over strength. This is an artificial division, as many styles include both outer and inner training and utilization, leading to inaccurate categorisation of styles, especially considering Bajiquan and Tongbeiquan.

nèi jiǎo 内脚 The inside foot: used when describing movements such as palm changes that are done following a circle. From Baguazhang. See also wài jiǎo.

nèi jìn 内劲 Internal power: use of deep abdominal breathing, a relaxed body, and at least initial slow training to develop natural, efficient movement and effective techniques. The specifics of power generation differ with the styles.

nèi kāi wài hé 内开外合 To open inside (power) while closing outside (movement).

nèi kuà 内胯 The hip crease, where the leg joins the pelvis. A major area of focus for movements and power flow. The front hip crease is one of the main targets on the body.

nèi lán fǎ 内拦法 Inside barring methods. See also guǒ fǎ.

nèi liàn yī kǒu qì wài liàn jīn gǔ pí 内练一口气外练筋骨皮 Internal training for the *qi* and external training for the muscles, bones, and skin. A martial saying.

nèi mén 内门 The inside gate or indoor area of an adversary: inside the space made by his elbows, the area inside his arms, or in between his legs. Specifically, inside the arms is also called lǐ mén.

nèi pī huá shān 内劈华山 Inside Chop to Mount Hua: move aside by stepping the left foot to the left then crossing the right foot in front of it, then shift back to the right foot into a bow stance, chopping down with a sword in the direction of the stance. From Qingping sword.

nèi qì 内气 Inside *qi*: the *qi* settled in the *dantian* and flowing through the body (as distinguished from air, the *qi* that is breathed in).

nèi róng 内容 Content, substance; details.

nèi sān hé 内三合 Three internal unities or harmonies: will with intent, intent with *qi*, and *qi* with strength.

nèi shāng 内伤 Internal injury, internal damage.

nèi shǒu 内手 The inside hand: used when describing movements such as palm changes that are done following a circle. From Baguazhang. See also wài shǒu.

nèi tíng 内庭 Acupoint Neiting (inner court), ST44. At the top of the foot, between the second and third toes, proximal to the web (on each foot). From TCM.

nèi tuō 内脱 Inside release, an escape from a control: a leverage escape for a wrist grab. Clench the fist and circle outwards to contact an adversary's outer bone and use it as leverage, pressing inwards.

nèi wài jié hé 内外结合 Unite internal and external, integrate the inner and outer body.

nèi wài hé yī 内外合一 Unite internal and external: to move as one, uniting the intent, spirit, will, power, and *qi* with the arms, eyes, torso, and legs (all physical parts of the body) under the control of the mind and movement of *qi*. A quality of movement sought in many styles.

nèi xī yǎn 内膝眼 Extraordinary acupoint Neixiyan, EX-LE4. At the knee, at the depression made by the medial ligament of the patella. From TCM.

nèi xuán 内旋 Internal rotation. This references the rotation of body segments independent of the placement of the segment. For example: turning the arm so that the thumb moves towards the direction of the palm; turning the leg so that the foot rotates inward in relation to the hip.

nèi yáng gōng 内养功 See nèi gōng.

nèi yào tí 内要提 The internal must be held up: to tighten the anal sphincter slightly to raise the *qi* to collect in the *dantian*. From Xingyiquan, one of its essential body positioning requirements.

nèi yīn 内因 Internal causes of disease.

nèi yíng xiāng 内迎香 Extraordinary acupoint Neiyingxiang, EX-HN9. At the face, inside the nostril, on the outer edge. From TCM.

nèi yǒng 内勇 Internal courage: includes qualities of character such as martial virtue, a strong capacity to train, and good moral character.

nèi zhuàng gōng 内壮功 Internal robustness training, training of internal strength and health. Also called nèi gōng.

nèi zhuàng zēng lì gōng 内壮增力功 Training exercises to increase internal robustness: exercises to train internal strength and health.

嫩 (rad.38) **nèn** 1. Tender; delicate. 2. Young, immature. 3. Light (colour). 4. Unskilled, inexperienced, immature.

nèn dāo 嫩刀 Tap with the broadsword: tap the tip of the blade lightly on an adversary's weapon.

泥 (rad.85) **ní** 1. Mud; mire. 2. To daub with plaster.

ní lǐ bá cōng 泥里把葱 Pull Scallions from the Mud: chop one hand down at the side, sitting to a half squat, turning the other palm up to press up in front of the shoulder. From Shaolinquan.

ní mán tóu gōng 泥馒头功 Mud steamed-bun training: increase arm and finger strength by grabbing and performing various exercises with steamed bun sized (about cricket ball size) mud balls of increasingly heavy weights. Usually done with a pair of weights.

ní wán gōng 泥丸宫 Niwan (mud) palace: a colloquial name for the Yintang acupoint, between the eyebrows. See yìn táng.

你 (rad.9) **nǐ** You. Often used in written texts, referring to the writer/reader as I and the adversary as you.

nǐ bǎo wǒ duó 你保我夺 If you protect, I force my way through. From Sanda.

nǐ chāi wǒ xù 你拆我续 If you break down my attack, I continue. From Sanda.

nǐ dā wǒ guò 你搭我过 If you make contact, I pass through. From Sanda.

nǐ duó wǒ chāi 你夺我拆 If you force your way through, I break it down. From Sanda.

nǐ guò wǒ chōu 你过我抽 If you pass through, I draw back. From Sanda.

nǐ huàn wǒ dā 你换我搭 If you switch, I keep contact. From Sanda.

nǐ jià wǒ zhàn 你架我占 If you block, I occupy. From Sanda.

nǐ xù wǒ huàn 你续我换 If you continue, I switch. From Sanda.

nǐ zhàn wǒ bǎo 你占我保 If you occupy, I protect. From Sanda.

逆 (rad.162) **nì** 1. Counter; inverse, converse. 2. Contrary; disobey; rebel. 3. Counter flow, against the current.

nì chán 逆缠 Counter-coiling power: coiling within the legs and body that results in internal rotation of the arm (if starting from palm in beside the body, palm turns backward from the body). In the hand, the thumb leads the movement, rotating towards the palm until the little finger also rotates away from the palm. Through the body, the energy follows meridian lines from the back of either the solid or empty leg (depending on whether the main hand is same or opposite side), waist, shoulder, out to the belly of the thumb, then to the rest of the fingers. Counters an incoming force by sending energy out from the *dantian* to the extremities.

nì huàn bù 逆换步 Counter change step: advancing with a turned out foot then a tucked in step, still advancing. Then turn the first foot out

N

again to go back. From Baguazhang.

nì lì fáng shǒu 逆力防守 Force against force defense: going hard against hard, breaking an adversary's attack with a strong block or cover, with equal force, so that his attack does not succeed.

nì lì gù shǒu fǎ 逆力固手法 See nì lì fáng shǒu.

nì shì fù hū xī 逆式腹呼吸 Reverse abdominal breathing. See fù shì nì hū xī.

nì shí zhēn 逆时针 Counter-clockwise, anti-clockwise.

nì shuǐ xíng zhōu 逆水行舟 Navigate a Boat Against the Current: grab an incoming snap kick, pull and twist the adversary's leg over. From Baguazhang.

拈 (rad.64) **niān** To pick up between thumb and one or two fingers. To take a pinch of.

niān huā gōng 拈花功 Flower pinching training: to rub a bean in the thumb, index, and middle fingers until it is crushed. Can also open sunflower seeds this way.

粘 (rad.119) **nián** To stick. Glue. To attach to. Commonly used in Taijiquan push hands, meaning adhere to. Often used interchangeably with nián 黏. Also pronounced zhān, see zhān.

nián shǒu 粘手 Free form push hands, still maintaining good connection.

nián suí 粘随 Stick and follow: to follow on a horizontal plane in push hands. From Taijiquan.

黏 (rad.202) **nián** 1. To stick; adhere. Sticky. Adhesive. 2. Commonly used in Taijiquan push hands, meaning to adhere to. One of the four requirements of push hands, see also sì yào. Often used interchangeably with the character 粘 above, see nián. 3. Sometimes written 黐 with this meaning, see chī. Also pronounced zhān, see zhān.

nián cuō 黏撮 Sticky leg throw: hook the leg onto your adversary's leg and lift it up in front, bending it to an awkward angle and lifting up into the groin, assisting the takedown by holding his upper body.

撚 [捻] (rad.64) **niǎn** A twisting action with the fingers. Hold onto something and twist with the fingers.

niǎn bàng 捻棒 Twist a stick: holding a short, relatively thick, stick out in front with straight arms, twist the hands in opposite directions. Grip and forearm training.

niǎn zhēn 捻针 Twirl acupuncture needles with the fingers. From TCM.

niǎn zhǐ gōng 捻指功 Finger twirling training: press the thumb on the belly of the extended index and middle fingers, then bend the fingers and rotate the wrist outwards. To develop the strength of the thumb, index and middle fingers, and wrist.

碾 (rad.112) **niǎn** 1. Roller and millstone. 2. Grind with a roller. 3. Roll on the foot, pivot on either the heel or the toe.

niǎn bù 碾步 Pivot step. 1. Pivot one foot inwards or outwards, on either the heel or the toe. 2. Lift one foot and pivot on the other before landing.

niǎn jiǎo 碾脚 Stamp: without lifting the foot, lift the heel for a quick stamp with the heel to an adversary's foot.

niǎn zhèn 碾震 Stomp, thump by lifting the heel and pivoting on the ball of the foot, landing with a thump with the heel turned out.

跈 (rad.157) **niǎn** To pivot; swivel.

niǎn zuān 跈钻 To squirm: to swivel instead of stepping around cleanly. From Baguazhang, where it is considered an error.

鳥 [鸟] (rad.196) **niǎo** A bird, birds.

niǎo nán fēi 鸟难飞 Bird has difficulty flying. A post standing posture done to practise a variety of powers. Standing in fighting stance with loosely held fists as if holding a small bird, imagine moving in the direction opposite from which the bird is attempting to move. From Yiquan.

niǎo nán fēi shì lì 鸟难飞试力 Bird has difficulty flying testing power: stand with the fists at shoulder level, pressing outward with the backfists. From Yiquan, one of its combat testing moves.

揑 [捏] (rad.64) **niē** To knead, pick with fingers, pinch. Hold between finger and thumb. To tweak.

niē fǎ 捏法 Pinching methods of grabbing muscles and tendons: grabbing with the thumb, index and middle fingers, dislocating with a skillful touch, not using a lot of force.

niē mài fǎ 捏脉法 Knead the Vessel: pinching the tendons, arteries or veins. From Qinna.

niē ná fǎ 捏拿法 Kneading grappling hold: hanging onto the clothing of an adversary, readjust your grip to ease the stress on the hands, or to adjust the placement slightly. From wrestling.

niē tóu 捏头 Knead the head lock and strike: shut down an adversary's hand technique and strike high with the knife edge of the other hand. Also called suǒ yáng shǒu.

凝 (rad.15) **níng** To congeal; condense.

níng tǐng jiān 凝挺肩 Condense and thrust the shoulders: close in the body to close both shoulders then open the body to open both shoulders to the rear. Keep the body upright and use the power of the chest and upper back.

擰 [拧] (rad.64) **níng** To twist, to wring. Twist the arm, a Qinna technique. Twist, one of the sixteen key techniques of Baguazhang, see also shí liù zì jué.

níng bāng zi 拧棒子 Twist a stick, a training method for coiling power and controlling ability. See also tài jí bàng zi. From Taijiquan.

níng bēi (bì) shuāi 拧臂摔 Twisting arm throw: grab and extend your adversary's arm over your shoulder, getting the body in close, then pull down and throw him over your shoulder. Can twist the arm inwards or outwards, depending on the situation.

níng bù 拧步 Twisting step. 1. Pivot one foot to prepare for the other to step. 2. Pivot both feet in preparation to move. Also called nuó bù.

níng fǎ 拧法 Grab and twist with a small rotation of the hands, used to control the adversary's arm and possibly dislocate his shoulder. Also called wài piē fǎ, xiè fǎ.

níng huái 拧踝 Twist the ankle: grab an adversary's foot as he tries to kick you, and twist it forcefully outwards. From wrestling.

níng jìn 拧劲 Twisting power.

níng juǎn gōng 拧卷功 Twisting training, various torqueing exercises to train grip strength and forearm twisting ability.

níng ná fǎ 拧拿法 Twisting grappling hold: adding a twist during a throw, using the hands in opposition. From wrestling.

níng shēn 拧身 Twist the torso. 1. Turning to right and left with a relaxed waist and hips. 2. Turn the body without turning or pivoting the feet.

níng xuán tuō 拧旋脱 Twisting release, an escape from a control: twisting the caught segment to make an adversary lose his grip.

níng yāo 拧腰 Waist turning exercise. 1. Standing upright, turn side to side with as much range of motion as possible. 2. Shoot a leg and arm out in opposite directions, laying the body out as flat as possible, then roll over.

níng yāo qiē kuà 拧腰切胯 Turn the waist and cut at the hip joint, which enables one to turn and direct powerful movement into the arms. From Tongbeiquan.

níng yāo shùn jiān 拧腰顺肩 Turn the waist and extend the shoulder. A method of extending a punch or palm strike, gaining distance by fully turning the body and shoulder into the technique to draw a straight line through the shoulder and arm to the hand.

níng zhuǎn bù 拧转步 Turning step: pivot on the heel of both feet to turn towards one side.

níng zǐ 拧子 A twister: a training implement made of brick with a stick threaded lengthways through the middle. Gripping the two ends of the stick, many wrestling type actions can be practised with the weight.

牛 (rad.93) **niú** 1. Ox, cow. Oxen, cows. For movement names using the actions or qualities of the ox, see also under huáng niú, tiě-, wò-, xī-. 2. Stubborn. 3. Ox, as the second of the twelve animals from the Chinese zodiac, associated with a twelve year cycle symbolic of the earthly branches. The twelve animals make up a sixty year cycle when combined with the five phases. See also dì zhī, shēng xiào, wǔ xíng.

niú shé zhǎng 牛舌掌 Ox tongue palm (as hand shape): fingers together and slightly bent, palm tucked, thumb web spread, and thumb tucked near

N

the thumb web. From Baguazhang. 2. Some styles tuck the thumb in tightly. Also called shé tóu zhǎng.

扭 (rad.64) **niǔ** 1. Twisted. To twist; wrench; seize, grasp. 2. Turn back, twist the body to turn. 3. Wrench a joint: grab near a joint and twist that joint. From Qinna.

niǔ bēi yā jiān 扭臂压肩 Twist the arm and press the shoulder: grab an adversary's wrist and move in to press and control his shoulder, pushing and twisting at the wrist. From Qinna.

niǔ bù 扭步 Twisted stance. See ào bù.

niǔ fǎ 扭法 Twisting technique: to grab tightly and tug with a twist.

niǔ guān jié 扭关节 Wrench a joint: any joint control technique that uses understanding of the natural movement of a joint to control an adversary by wrenching or twisting a joint in a way it is not meant to move. May be used to throw, break, press to control, lock out, etc. From Qinna.

niǔ lě yāo 扭了腰 To wrench the back; sprain the lower back.

niǔ mǎ 扭马 Twisted horse: a crossed stance kneel, sitting on the rear heel with the knee almost touching the ground.

niǔ mǎ chōng chuí 扭马冲捶 Twisted horse punch and pound: turn into a crossed kneel and uppercut with the other palm blocking up over the head. The 102nd move of the tiger and crane routine.

niǔ shāng 扭伤 A sprain or wrench injury, a twisted joint, injuring the ligaments and soft tissue of the joint.

niǔ shēn fǎ 扭身法 Method of twisting the body: when an adversary has gotten in very close and you cannot step away or use your hands effectively, suck in your torso and twist to get around to his back. From Baguazhang.

niǔ tóu 扭头 Head twist: push the jaw while pulling the back of the head, thus twisting the neck. From Qinna.

niǔ tún 扭臀 Twisted buttocks: the coccyx is not aligned with the spine, or the buttocks stick out or sway to the side. An error in most styles.

弄 (rad.55) **nòng** To do; to play; to fool around.

nòng quán 弄拳 To play a routine or combinations, not terribly seriously.

努 (rad.19) **nǔ** 1. To put forth, exert, strength. 2. To injure oneself through overexertion.

nǔ lì 努力 Brute strength. Also called zhuō lì.

nǔ qì 努气 Hold the breath to exert force. Often means to lift the breath and hold it in the chest, which is an error in most styles. Holding the breath in a purposeful way is called tuō qì.

弩 (rad.57) **nǔ** Crossbow, an ancient weapon still in use today. A bow and bolt that uses a mechanical system to pull the bow before raising it to aim, so that it may shoot strongly, immediately, and with multiple bolts.

怒 (rad.61) **nù** 1. Temper, anger; rage, angry. 2. Forceful and vigorous (not angry, but having a full spirit). Take from context whether this is being used as angry or showing spirit.

nù mǎ huí tóu 怒马回头 Angry Horse Looks Back: Turn around and sit back to empty stance, opening the arms, one pressing down at the hip, one threading up to head height with the elbow bent, palm in. From Liuhebafa.

nù shī duò jiǎo 怒狮跺脚 Raging Lion Stamps its Foot: from the side, stamp at the rear outside of your adversary's knee with the outer edge of your foot, either as a strike or to press his leg down to the ground as a control.

nù shī kuáng bēn 怒狮狂奔 Raging Lion Gallops: continuous alternating knee strikes.

女 (rad.38) **nǚ** Female, women. For movement names using the actions or abilities of women, see also under měi nǚ, qiǎo-, shén-, yù-.

nǚ rén quán 女人拳 Beautiful woman fist, a routine. See huā quán.

nǚ zì bù 女字步 Character for woman (女) stance: one foot crossed over in front of the other. Usually called gài bù.

挪 (rad.64) **nuó** 1. To move, shift to one side. 2. As general footwork, to shift. 3. As a circular block, to entrap, pull into the body a bit.

nuó bù 挪步 Shifting step. 1. To pivot one foot to prepare for the other to step. 2. To pivot both feet in preparation to move. 3. A general term for shifting around on the feet, not necessarily a specific technique. #1 and #2 also called níng bù.

nuó shēn 挪身 Shifting the body: move with an adversary to get in close, stepping in behind him to avoid his attacks.

O

ōu xíng tuǐ O形腿 Bowlegs, bandy legs. Also called luó quān tuǐ.

P

趴 (rad.157) pā   1. To lie prone. 2. Leaning over, face down, but not lying down.

pā diǎn 趴点 Leaning poke kick: lean forward to place the hands on the ground and poke kick up to the rear, then bring the foot down to 'stab' the ground behind the supporting foot. From Chuojiao, one of its middle-basin kicks.

爬 (rad.87) pá   1. To crawl; creep. 2. To climb; clamber; scramble. 3. In wrestling, a throwing technique.

pá xíng bù 爬行步 Clambering steps: to hop about alternating with the hands and feet on the ground. From Houquan.

耙 鈀 [耙 钯] (rad.127, 167) pá   1. A harrow (a raking plough); a rake. 2. To rake, to smooth with a rake. 3. An ancient weapon resembling a rake: a long wooden shaft with a single or double five to ten tooth metal rake at the end. Pronounced bǎ, a harrow; to draw a harrow over a field.

pá fǎ 耙法 Raking technique, takedowns that use an action similar to raking: combining a twisting of the upper body with a low placement of the foot to trip up an adversary. Usually involves an opposite action of arms with the catching foot. From wrestling.

pá ná 耙拿 Rake and lift, takedowns that combine raking and grabbing: often grabbing and lifting one leg while hooking the other, or grabbing and trapping a foot and applying leverage to the leg. From wrestling.

pá tī 耙踢 Rake and trip, a takedown: catch the foot in behind the ankle of your adversary and rake back towards yourself to trip. From wrestling.

pá zǐ 耙子 1. A harrow: a raking plough. A rake.

2. A takedown, see pá fǎ.

拍 (rad.64) pāi   1. To slap, pat, or control with an open hand. 2. A downward slam with the palm.

pāi dǎ shōu gōng 拍打收功 Patting cool-down: patting the body all over as part of a cool-down.

pāi dǎ fēi dié 拍打飞蝶 Slap the Flying Butterfly, stepping into a bow stance, cut across with the rear hand, slice the front hand up, then pull it in a fist back to the chest. From Shaolinquan.

pāi dǎng 拍挡 Slapping block: block with the palm, using a slapping action.

pāi jī 拍击 A slap hit: a slapping defensive hit on an incoming punch.

pāi jiǎo 拍脚 A slap kick, pat kick.

pāi shǒu 拍手   1. A slap block: control an adversary's forearm with your palm down, usually slapping and recoiling. 2. A slapping attack to the face. 3. A push to the outside with a vertical palm. From Wing Chun.

pāi tuǐ 拍腿 A slap kick, slapping the foot. 1. In competition Taolu, to slap the foot, leg straight, at shoulder height. 2. In Chuojiao, a straight slap kick, one of its middle-basin kicks. Also called kòu jīn zhōng. 3. In wrestling, to quickly slap an adversary's leg to initiate a takedown.

pāi wèi 拍位 A slapping block, usually rebounding into a counter attack.

pāi xiōng pū zhǒu 拍胸扑肘 Pat the Chest with an Elbow Pounce: step in with a turning elbow strike, to strike directly into the chest with the point of the elbow or to press down with the forearm. From Baguazhang, one of its sixty-four hands.

pāi xué 拍穴 Slap a pressure point; hit an acupoint with the heel of the palm. See also dǎ xué.

pāi yā 拍压 Slapping press down: block with the palm, using a slapping action downwards.

pāi zhāng 拍张 Slapping palms: old term for wrestling. Usually called shuāi jiāo.

pāi zhǎng sì xùn diàn 拍掌似迅电 Slap like a shock of electricity. From Tongbeiquan, one of its five requirements, see also wǔ zì yāo qiú.

P

排 (rad.64) **pái** 1. To arrange, put in order. 2. A line. 3. To push.

pái dǎ gōng 排打功 Striking training to develop hard skills. Includes bag striking, grabbing, finger drilling, and iron crotch training.

pǎi tún 排臀 (pronounced pǎi in this context) Press with the buttocks: a counter to a trip or throw. Sit back, rather than down, into an adversary when in very close quarters, to prevent a throw.

派 (rad.85) **pài** 1. A tributary. 2. A school of thought, sect, branch. 3. A branch or school of martial arts.

pài chuí 派捶 A chopping cut with the fist and forearm, turning the fist to strike with the meaty edge of the fist and bone of the forearm. From Mojiaquan.

攀 [扳] (rad.64) **pān** 1. To drag down, seize and pull. 2. Hold onto, to climb. To clamber; climb by pulling oneself up. 3. To grab and kick at the same time. 4. To grab and pull while hooking on behind the neck with the other hand. From Wing Chun. Pronounced bān, to pull; turn; to recoup.

pān jǐng shǒu 扳颈手 Drag the neck: hook the hand onto the nape of an adversary's neck to drag his head towards you.

pān shǒu 扳手 To climb: reach the hands forward, hitting with the backhand, the rear hand palm down at the elbow.

盘 盤 [盘] (rad.108) **pán** 1. Basin, tray, flat dish. 2. Postures or actions that are flat and tucked. 3. Body parts that are shaped like a basin (the shoulder girdle, the pelvic girdle). 4. The guard of a weapon's handle. 5. The measure word for flat objects.

pán biān 盘鞭 Basin whip. See pán qiáo.

pán chán bù 盘禅步 Zen basin stance: fully squat on one leg and sit on the shin of the other.

pán cháng tuǐ 盘肠腿 Basin guts kick: an angled high kick with the foot extended, body twisted in the opposite direction of the kick. From Chuojiao.

pán gēn bù 盘根步 Twine the Root stepping: stepping from a sixty-forty posture to turn completely around in three steps.

pán gēn dāo 盘根刀 Twine the Root with a broadsword: do a full turn and drop down, bringing the blade around with the body, sweeping around and across (term used with the larger Bagua broadsword).

pán huā 盘花 Twist flowers: coil the hands with the wrists together in a twisting control or release action.

pán jià zǐ 盘架子 To practise basic postures.

pán kǒu 盘口 Defensive opening: a gap in defenses that you are trying to find and get in through. Also called dòu kǒu.

pán lóng jìn zhǒu 盘龙进肘 Coiling Dragon Enters an Elbow: in response to a wrist grab and twist, turn and step into it so that the arm is coiled behind your back, allowing you to strike with the other elbow. From Shaolinquan.

pán qiáo 盘桥 Basin bridge, a forearm technique: With bent elbow or straight arm, do a vertical circle inwards rotating around the shoulder, the hand no higher than the head, and no lower than the groin. From southern styles. Also called pán biān.

pán tuǐ 盘腿 Basin squat stance: squat on one leg with the other crossed at the ankle on top of the squatting leg.

pán tuǐ diē 盘腿跌 Fall with legs crossed in sidekick position: jump up and break fall on the side with one leg tucked and the other extended.

pán tuǐ píng héng 盘腿平衡 Basin squat balance: the stance held motionless. If in Taolu competition, held motionless for at least two seconds. See pán tuǐ.

pán tuǐ xiāo 盘腿削 Coil the leg and slice, a takedown: catch your adversary's ankle and lift your leg, bending it and turning the knee out so that the thigh approaches level, while pushing his torso backwards. From wrestling.

pán zhǒu 盘肘 Tuck the elbow. 1. A horizontal, inward forearm strike. 2. To hold an adversary's neck in the crook of the elbow.

蟠 (rad.142) **pán** To coil. To curl.

pán lóng fān gǔn 蟠龙翻滚 Coiling Dragon Rolls Over: a shoulder roll to the ground, finishing with a lying side kick. From Yangjia style.

pán lóng fān tiān 蟠龙翻天 Coiling Dragon Shakes the World: circle-walking with the hands lifted at shoulder height, fingers extending along the line of the circle. From Baguazhang.

判 (rad.18) **pàn** 1. To discriminate; judge; decide. 2. To condemn. 3. A counter to a takedown, when in a head lock, jamming the hand firmly on an adversary's knee to prevent yourself from being thrown.

pàn guān bǐ 判官笔 Judge's pen: a short weapon, usually used as a double weapon. About twenty centimetres long, shaped like a writing brush with a sharpened tip used for accurate stabbing (the judge is the fierce judge in the afterlife court of law).

pàn guān tuō xié 判官脱鞋 Judge Takes off his Shoes, a takedown. 1. A feint to the face followed by a drop to grab an adversary's front heel and pull it strongly back and up, stepping around. 2. To grab the foot of your adversary when he kicks you, then twist his leg to take down.

pàn guān zhí bǐ 判官执笔 Judge Holds his Brush: from a wrist grab, release by twisting the wrist and pressuring with the elbow, grabbing the adversary's thumb or pressuring into his thumb web. From Qinna.

pàn tuǐ 判腿 Judge's leg: a low hooking strike to the shin, using the lower leg for a tripping throw.

旁 (rad.70) **páng** Side. Lateral.

páng qiāo cè jī 旁敲侧击 Sideswipe. 1. The standard phrase means to attack by innuendo, to make oblique references. 2. To step into a straight horse stance punch, keeping a guarding palm. From Meishanquan.

膀 (rad.130) **páng** 1. Swelling. 2. Pronounced bǎng, the upper arm, arm and shoulder.

páng guāng 膀胱 1. The bladder. 2. The Bladder, the organ associated with the Zu Tai Yang channel. It is a *yang* organ.

páng guāng jīng 膀胱经 The Bladder meridian. See zú tài yáng. From TCM.

páng guāng shū 膀胱俞 Acupoint Pangguang (bladder transport), BL28. At the sacrum, level with the second sacral foramina, 1.5 *cun* lateral to the midline (on each side). From TCM.

螃 (rad.142) **páng** A crab, used in conjunction, as páng xiè.

páng xiè quán 螃蟹拳 Crab fist, a hand shape: see wú gong quán.

抛 (rad.64) **pāo** 1. To toss, throw away, cast, fling. 2. A throwing punch. 3. To toss a weapon in the air. 4. To swing a weapon horizontally.

pāo biān 抛鞭 Throw the steel whip: release the whip from being folded in the palm, keeping hold of the grip.

pāo chuí 抛槌 Throwing hammer fist, an extended upward swinging punch, usually swinging the other fist in the opposite direction. From southern styles.

pāo gùn 抛棍 Uppercut with a staff. 1. Holding the shaft in both hands, strike upwards with both hands, putting force to the tip. 2. In context, means to throw the staff up.

pāo jià zǐ 抛架子 Throwing Posture: open the arms with a shake of the body as if flinging a net. From Chen Taijiquan and Wudangquan.

pāo jiǎo 抛脚 Throwing kick: to lift one foot, then jump to switch feet with a snap kick. From Mojiaquan.

pāo jiē 抛接 Toss and catch a weapon.

pāo qiāng 抛枪 Pop up a spear. Holding one end, pop a spear up so that it rotates a half circle, and catch it by the other end. See also dān shǒu pāo qiāng huàn wò.

pāo quán 抛拳 Throwing upper-cut, swinging uppercut: an almost straight arm swinging uppercut with the fist eye or fist back up, usually finishing with the fist well above the head. From southern styles.

pāo tuō 抛托 Uppercut carry: swing one hand up and follow with an uppercut with the other hand. From southern styles.

pāo zhuān yǐn yù 抛砖引玉 Cast out a Brick to Attract Jade. The 17th of the Thirty-six Stratagems of Warfare, which apply to many situations.

pāo zhuàng quán 抛撞拳 Upper-cut ram: uppercut, stopping the arm by a slap to the forearm with the other hand. In this case the uppercut is fist

P

back down, so the catch is on the white meat of the forearm.

刨 (rad.18) **páo**   1. To unearth; to dig. 2. To plane.

páo tuǐ 刨腿 Planing hook kick: a straight hook kick, leaning back and turning. From Mizongquan. Also called gāo gōu.

跑 (rad.157) **pǎo**   To run. To run away.

pǎo bǎn gōng 跑板功 Run the Plank, a light skills training drill: to run up a plank leaning against a wall, gradually raising the angle of the plank until it can be taken away.

pǎo biǎo 跑表 A stopwatch. Also called miǎo biǎo.

pǎo bù 跑步 Run, running. Used in martial arts for aerobic conditioning.

pǎo jiāng hú 跑江湖 To take to the life of the martial wanderer or banditry. See also jiāng hú.

pǎo zhuāng 跑桩 Run the stakes, a light skills training drill: to run on a line of stakes planted in the ground.

炮 (rad.86) **pào**   1. Original meaning is a big gun or cannon, and to bombard with stone balls. To blast. 2. Cannon punch, pounding punch, usually refers to a double punch. 3. A strong slash diagonally with a weapon. From Xingyiquan. 4. Partner routines in Xingyiquan.

pào chuí 炮捶 1. Cannon punch, pounding punch, a double punch. Sometimes one forearm is a high deflection, the other is a straight punch. Sometimes it is a double punch. Sometimes the punches are in hammer fists. 2. A routine of Shaolinquan, also called pào quán.

pào quán 炮拳 1. Pounding fist; cannon punch, blasting punch: an outward deflection combined with a straight punch. From Xingyiquan. It is related to the fire element, see also huǒ. 2. A routine of Shaolinquan, also called pào chuí. 3. Paoquan style, see sān huáng pào chuí.

沛 (rad.85) **pèi**   Copious. Abundant.

pèi gōng zhé shé 沛公折蛇 Duke of Pei Cuts a Snake: slice across with a sword, palm down, then circle the waist to slice back with the palm up. From Wu Taijiquan.

弸 (rad.57) **pēng**   1. Full. 2. Stretched, drawn. 3. A bow stretched to the full. Also pronounced bēng, péng.

掤 (rad.64) **péng**   1. An elastic or resilient power throughout the entire body, a fullness of *qi* that expands in all directions. 2. Ward off: press out with the outside of the forearm with resiliency, using a vertical circular power that contains a spiraling outward. Classed as a throwing technique. (Sometimes printed 棚 when the proper character is not in the keyboard input. This character is often not in dictionaries.)

péng dǎ 掤打 Warding off strike: strike out with the outside of the forearm, elbow a bit bent and palm in, containing an upward element as well.

péng huá 掤化 Using resilient power to defend, in preparation for a counter.

péng jìn 掤劲 An elastic or resilient power throughout the entire body, a fullness of *qi* that expands in all directions. Using power that is neither hard nor slack.

péng ná fǎ 掤拿法 Cupping grappling hold: to cup the hand under the elbow or forearm of an adversary, working together with a higher grab. From wrestling.

péng shǒu 掤手 1. Ward off: press with one forearm. From Taijiquan. 2. A snap from the wrist to do a short, hard punch. From Chuojiao.

鵬 [鹏] (rad.196) **péng**   A Roc, an enormous bird, eagle-like but much bigger. In mythology it was said to carry off elephants or people. For movement names using the actions or qualities of the Roc, see under dà péng, yún-.

捧 (rad.64) **pěng**   1. To cup, carry in both hands (like scooping up water in the hands). 2. A strike with both hands, palms up and usually together as if carrying something.

pěng dà dāo 捧大刀 Present a big cutter: with both hands at the butt, raise it vertically beside the body with the blade edge facing forwards.

pěng dāo 捧刀 Present a broadsword: lift the blade to chest height in front of the body with the edge up, the tip forward, with the left hand cupping the right. May use a double grip or not. This is a defensive action that prepares for a stab.

pěng jiān 捧肩 Shoulder immobilization, shoulder lock: slide the arm under your adversary's armpit and wrap your forearm around his shoulder joint. From wrestling.

pěng tī 捧踢 Carrying kick: in close hold, jam your foot outside an adversary's and execute a twisting throw at the upper body. From wrestling.

掽 碰 [掽 碰] (rad.64, 112) **pèng** 1. To collide with, to hit, to touch, bump. 2. To take a chance. 3. To meet unexpectedly.

pèng shēn 碰身 To bump on the body: to inadvertently allow your weapon to hit your body. An error in all styles.

pèng tuǐ 碰腿 To bump the leg: a knee strike. From Shaolinquan.

pèng zhuàng jìn 碰撞劲 To bounce an adversary off you with a springy internal power.

劈 (rad.18) **pī** 1. To chop vertically, forward and down, with the arm, with a straight arm at the point of impact. May be done with a fully straight arm, or flex and extend the arm to hit. 2. To cleave with a bladed weapon, finishing with the blade extended in a straight line with the arm.

pī bà 劈把 Chop down with the butt of a long weapon.

pī biān 劈鞭 Chop the whip. See pī qiáo.

pī chā xìng tuǐ fǎ 劈叉性腿法 Splits: category of leg techniques that includes all the splits. See also diē chā, héng chā, shù chā.

pī chuí 劈槌 Chopping hammer fist. From southern styles.

pī dǎ dēng 劈打蹬 Chop, Hit, Kick: a combination skipping forward, swinging the arms up, and coming through with a thrust kick and simultaneous push. From Tongbeiquan.

pī dà dāo 劈大刀 Chop down with a big cutter: chop down with the blade edge down, the shaft approaching horizontal, the right hand near the blade, and the left hand near the butt.

pī dāo 劈刀 Chop down with a broadsword. See pī jiàn.

pī guà quán 劈挂拳 Piguaquan (cutting fist), an offshoot style from Tongbeiquan, popular along the Yellow river since the Ming dynasty. Also called pī 披 guà quán.

pī guà zhǎng 劈挂掌 Chop and hook shoulder flexibility exercise. 1. Standing upright, with the arms straight, swing one arm forward or backward. 2. Swing both arms, keeping them in a straight line, both going forward or both going backward.

pī gùn 劈棍 Chop down with a staff. See pī qiāng.

pī jiàn 劈剑 Chop down with a sword with the blade and arm forming a straight line and the blade upright (edges up and down).

pī pū dāo 劈扑刀 Chop down with a horse cutter. See pī dà dāo.

pī qiāng 劈枪 Chop down with a spear: bring the shaft down strongly, keeping both hands on the shaft, sending power to the tip.

pī qiáo 劈桥 Chop the bridge, a forearm technique: chop down with the forearm, contacting with the ulnar edge. May be done straight arm or bent arm, either forward, to the side, or to an angle. From southern styles. Also called pī biān.

pī quán 劈拳 Chopping fist. 1. Chop with a hammer fist, with the heel of the fist, in most styles. 2. The splitting fist of Xingyiquan, a chopping action to chest height, done open hand in most branches, closed fist in some branches. It is related to the metal element, see also jīn.

pī shān duó bǎo 劈山夺宝 Chop the Mountain to Seize the Treasure: a low chop in reverse high empty stance. From Wu Taijiquan.

pī shān jiù mǔ 劈山救母 Chop the Mountain to Save your Mother: take two steps forward to a bow stance and circle the same side hand up to chop down in front, hooking the other hand behind. From Shaolinquan.

pī shān pào 劈山炮 Chop the Mountain explosions: continuous throwing chops with straight arms, striking with backhands, swinging in full circle. For example, left, right, right, left. From Tongbeiquan.

pī xīn chuí 劈心锤 Split the Heart Punch: a straight punch to the heart, stepping into a strong bow stance. From Shaolinquan.

pī tuǐ 劈腿 1. The splits, as a stretching exercise.

2. A straight swinging front kick, ankle dorsi-flexed.

pī zhǎng 劈掌 1. Chop downwards with the edge of the hand, arm quite straight, striking with the palm edge.

pī zhǎng sì léi zhèn 劈掌似雷震 Chop like a clap of thunder. From Tongbeiquan, one of its five requirements, see also wǔ zì yāo qiú.

批 (rad.64) pī   1. To comment, to judge. 2. To slap.

pī zhēng 批睁 Elbow hacking: an elbow strike that curves inward, striking with the forearm edge of the elbow tip. From Wing Chun.

披 (rad.64) pī   1. Original meaning is to drape over one's shoulders, wrap around. 2. A wrestling throw involving wrapping an adversary over your back, throwing him over your shoulder.

pī guà quán 披挂拳 See pī guà quán (劈).

pī hóng 披红 Drape a steel whip or rope dart over the body while spinning it. With the right hand at the back, drape the whip over the left shoulder and turn to the right so that the whip continues to spin and releases from the shoulder.

pī jià zǐ 披架子 Draping posture: snap the arms out to the sides, one high, coiling smoothly, one low, coiling counter. From Chen Taijiquan.

pī shēn chuí 披身捶 Body Draping Mallet: performance varies with style, but involves wrapping the arms around an adversary's arm, controlling or breaking his elbow. From Taijiquan. Also called bì shēn chuí, piē chuí.

pī shēn fú hǔ 披身伏虎 Body Drape to Tame the Tiger. See also fú hǔ. From Sun Taijiquan.

琵 (rad.96) pí   A four stringed Chinese instrument similar to a lute.

pí pá 琵琶 A pipa, a short necked, four stringed, Chinese string instrument, similar to a lute in size. Used in movement names that place the hands in a similar position as if to strum a pipa, hands wrist to elbow length apart.

pí pá shì 琵琶式 Pipa model. One of twenty-four classic spear moves. Most spear routines will have a move with a like name. In general, this name refers to a snapping block then strike. May be high, mid, or low.

pí pá zhē miàn 琵琶遮面 Pipa Hides the Face from View: open the hands then raise one in front of the face and push the other forward. From Liuhebafa.

疲 (rad.104) pí   Tired, fatigued, weary.

pí láo 疲劳 Tired, fatigued, weary.

pí láo xìng 疲劳性 Fatigued: condition caused by over training and fatigue.

皮 (rad.107) pí   1. Skin; fur; hide. 2. Leather. 3. Bark. 4. Rind; peel. 5. A thin sheet.

pí biān 皮鞭 A leather whip.

pí tiáo 皮条 A strap, traditionally made of leather, used for training wrestling techniques.

脾 (rad.130) pí   1. The spleen. 2. The Spleen, the organ associated with the Zu Tai Yin channel. It is a *yin* organ. From TCM. See also zú tài yīn.

pí guān 脾关 Acupoint Piguan (spleen pass), ST31. At the thigh, across from the Huiyin, at the hollow when the hip is flexed (on each side). Also pronounced bì guān. From TCM.

pí jīng 脾经 The Spleen meridian. See zú tài yīn.

pí qì 脾气 Temperament, disposition.

pí shū 脾俞 Acupoint Pishu (spleen transport), BL20. At the back, level with the depression below the spinous process of the 11th thoracic vertebra, 1.5 *cun* lateral to the midline (on each side). From TCM.

痞 (rad.104) pǐ   1. A lump in the abdomen. 2. Constipation; obstruction.

pǐ gēn 痞根 Extraordinary acupoint Pigen (glomus root), EX-B4. At the waist, level with the depression below the spinous process of the first lumbar vertebra, 3.5 *cun* lateral to the midline (on each side). From TCM.

偏 (rad.9) piān   1. Tendency towards one aspect, inclined to one side. 2. Slanting. 3. Partial, prejudiced; favour.

piān chén 偏沉 Favour one aspect of power, position, or part of the body.

piān chuài tuǐ 偏踹腿 Turned heel kick: heel thrust kick in front with the foot turned out. Sometimes written 扁.

piān fú 偏浮 Tendency towards floating: both foot and hand on the same side are empty. From Taijiquan, where it is considered an error.

piān lì 偏历 Acupoint Pianli (veering passageway), LI6. At the outside of the forearm, about three *cun* above the wrist crease (on each arm). From TCM.

piān mǎ bù 偏马步 Partial horse stance: horse stance with weight shifted more towards one leg. The feet may be turned slightly in the direction of the more weighted leg.

piān mén 偏门 Side door. 1. The chest opening to the sleeves of a wrestling jacket (this is the side door for grabbing). 2. To use the side door is to grab with the right hand to the left side of an adversary.

piān mén bà 偏门耙 Side door harrow: grab the chest opening to the sleeves of a wrestling jacket, the right hand to the left side of an adversary, and push while catching with the foot.

piān shēn mǎ 偏身马 Leaning stance: a front facing stance, with the body shifted to one side and turned to the centre. From Wing Chun.

piān zhòng 偏重 Tendency towards heaviness: both foot and hand on the same side are substantial. From Taijiquan, where it is considered an error.

片 (rad.91) **piàn** A flat slice, both as an object as an action.

piàn bǎng 片膀 Scrape the shoulder girdle with a protective movement.

piàn dāo 片刀 Slicing blade: a long handled, thin bladed, single edged broadsword.

piàn mǎ 片马 Mount a horse: an inside crescent kick to waist height. An action that resembles swinging a leg over to mount a horse.

piàn xuán dāo 片旋刀 Flat slice with a broadsword: draw a full circle with the blade to slice flatly in the same direction as the circle.

piàn xuán liǎng mén 片旋两门 Slice to Two Doors. 1. A flat slice with both palm edges to both sides of an adversary's neck, after first coiling the forearms around to reposition. 2. Continuous slices to the neck, cutting in, then cutting out. From Baguazhang, one of its sixty-four hands.

piàn xuán zhǎng 片旋掌 Flat slicing palm: a flat slice with the palm edge, first coiling the forearm in to gain position. Also called yíng fēng huī xiù.

騙 騵 [骗] (rad.187) **piàn** To fool, deceive. As one of the eight attack and defense models, to mix up fakes with real strikes. See also bā zì gōng fáng fǎ zé.

piàn mǎ 骗马 Deceive the Horse: an inside crescent kick to waist height. (Some horses puff up when you are cinching the saddle so that it will slip when you get on. A sharp rap to the body makes him release the air, allowing you to quickly tighten the cinch.) In the category of straight swinging kicks, see also zhí bǎi xìng tuǐ fǎ.

飄 [飘] (rad.182) **piāo** 1. To blow; to float; to drift. 2. In martial arts, often means unrooted, too light, floating.

piāo dǎ jìn 飘打劲 Drifting hit power: a type of power that changes during the action. Includes three uses: 1) to apply an acceleration during movement, 2) to apply a directional change during movement, and 3) to lengthen the time or add pressure to the point of contact. From southern styles.

瓢 (rad.97) **piáo** A ladle, usually made out of a gourd. Can also be a wooden dipper.

piáo zhǎng 瓢掌 Ladle palm, a hand shape: fingers extended and held together, slightly tucked in at the knuckles, the thumb bent. From southern styles.

瞟 (rad.109) **piǎo** To look askance at; glance sideways at.

piǎo tuǐ 瞟腿 Glancing kick: a short, quick kick with the outer edge of the foot. Generally refers to a low kick to the knee.

撇 (rad.64) **piē, piě** 1. The original, practical, meaning is to fling, cast, throw overboard like casting a net. 2. The technique is to strike or throw with this action.

P

piē chuí 撇捶 Cast away, like flinging a fishing net. This move can be a throwing out with both arms to each side. See also pī shēn chuí, piē shēn chuí.

piē shēn chuí 撇身捶 Cast Away Hit: snapping double strike like flinging a large fishing net. See also piē chuí, pī shēn chuí.

piē shǒu 撇手 Cast: meet an adversary without retreating, but turning to the side to avoid his attack and snapping his wrist with yours, and counter attacking.

piē zhǎng 撇掌 Cast: a strike with the palm open, coming in from the side.

piē zhǒu 撇肘 Cast the elbow: grab your adversary's hand at the wrist and twist it outwards, twist his upper arm, bending his elbow. Press his elbow upwards with your forearm while pulling his hand down with both hands. From Qinna.

平 (rad.51) **píng** Level; flat; even; smooth.

píng àn dāo 平按刀 Level press down with a broadsword: Press down to waist height, with the left hand on the spine of the blade or on the right hand, the blade edge down.

píng bào dāo 平抱刀 Level broadsword hold: cross the arms with the spine of the blade on the left arm, grip forward, blade flat in front.

píng bào zhuāng 平抱桩 Level embracing stake standing: standing in a sixty-forty stance with the hands up at chest height, forward hand over the forward leg, palms down. From Yiquan.

píng bēng qiāng 平崩枪 Level snap with a spear: snap a spear, both hands applying an abrupt power horizontally to snap the spear tip up so that it vibrates at chest height.

píng bō qiāng 平拨枪 Level check with a spear: snap the spear from side to side with a quick but steady power, between chest and waist height.

píng bù 平步 Level step, even step: standing with the feet parallel and open. From Yiquan. Usually called kāi bù.

píng cì jiàn 平刺剑 A level pierce with a sword, to shoulder height, blade and extended arm in a straight line.

píng dāo 平刀 Flat broadsword: the blade is sideways, edge outwards. A positional reference, as distinguished from the direction of the strike.

píng dì chā xiāng 平地插香 Insert Incense Sticks on Level Land: do a hooking swing back, then step forward into a low crossed stance, scooping the blade to stick a sword straight up. From Qingping sword.

píng dì fǎn chē 平地反车 Flip the Cart on Level Ground: Spin around and drop to a fully seated cross stance, bringing a sword over to chop down. From Qingping sword.

píng dì fēi lóng 平地飞龙 Flying Dragon on Level Ground: stab forward in a drop stance, leap up, raising a sword, and land back in a drop stance, cocking the sword then stabbing again, shifting forward to bow stance. From Qingping sword.

píng dì fèng wǔ 平地凤舞 Dancing Phoenix on Level Ground: raise the blade then take a long back cross step and slice up. From Qingping sword.

píng dì shēng yān 平地生烟 Generate Smoke on Level Ground: step forward hooking the tip of a sword down, then sit to a crossed stance and roll the blade through, rotating for a straight low pierce behind. From Qingping sword.

píng diǎn qiāng 平点枪 Level dab with spear: a dipping strike with the tip between hip and shoulder height.

píng fēn zhǎng 平分掌 Level separating palms: from crossed, open the arms evenly to their respective sides.

píng fēn qiū sè 平分秋色 Divide the Autumn Colours Evenly: Stand up to a one legged stance, hooked behind the knee, stabbing the raised leg side arm straight up. Then squat into a drop stance, extending the arms out to front and back. From Liuhebafa.

píng gōu quán 平勾拳 A level hooking punch. Usually called a hook in Sanda.

píng héng 平衡 Balance, equilibrium.

píng jiàn 平剑 A flat blade: sword with the blade held flat, the edges to side and side. This is a placement description unrelated to the direction of the strike.

píng jiāo 平跤 No point, clash: during a Sanda or wrestling match, no clear technique is done by either side to earn a point.

píng jú 平局 To tie. A draw in a sparring match.

píng jǔ gùn 平举棍 Raise a staff horizontally over the head, extending the arms straight.

píng lūn gùn 平抡棍 Level swing or brandish with staff: swinging at least a half circle at about chest height.

píng mǎ 平马 Level Horse: a horse stance with the thighs parallel to the ground. See also mǎ bù.

píng qiāng 平枪 A level stab with a spear: a stab with the spear's shaft level.

píng quán 平拳 Flat fist. 1. As a hand shape: tightly held fist with the fist surface flat. 2. As a placement description: a fist held with the fist heart down, knuckles forward.

píng sǎo yān xiá 平扫烟霞 Sweep Aside the Mists and Clouds: step into a full squat, sweeping low with a sword to in front of the stance, both hands on the hilt. From Qingping sword.

píng shā luò yàn 平沙落雁 Wild Goose Lands on Level Sand: bring a staff over as if to slap flat on the ground, but stop at ten centimetres from the ground. From Baguazhang.

píng tuī dāo 平推刀 Level push with a broadsword: push the blade forward, blade flat with tip to the left, with the left hand on the spine of the blade.

píng tuī shì lì 平推试力 Level pushing testing power: stand with slight movement pushing forward and releasing with both arms. From Yiquan.

píng tuī zhǎng 平推掌 Level pushing palm: circle-walking pressing the palms out in front of the chest, with the arms rounded and fingers pointing to each other. The power both embraces and pushes outward. From Baguazhang. Also, with varying emphases, called bào yuè zhǎng, è hǔ bā xīn zhǎng, shuāng zhuàng zhǎng, xiān rén guān qí zhǎng, zhuàng zhǎng.

píng tuǐ 平腿 Level kick: kick upwards with the heel, with the foot turned out. From Duanquan.

píng tuǐ shì 平腿式 Level leg stance: half squat on one leg and tuck the other foot in front of the knee. From Duanquan.

píng tuō qiāng 平托枪 Level carry a spear: snap the shaft strongly upwards, the left hand palm up, shaft horizontal, between waist and chest height.

píng wǔ huā gùn (qiāng) 平舞花棍(枪) Flat flowers with a staff (or spear): with the hands in the middle of the shaft, circle a staff in full circles above the head.

píng xíng bù 平行步 Level stance. See píng xíng mǎ bù.

píng xíng mǎ bù 平行马步 Level horse stance: feet shoulder width apart, feet straight (or one foot may be slightly in front and slightly turned in), knees bent until they are on line with the toes. A high horse stance. Also called píng xíng bù.

píng yuán 平圆 Flat circle or circles.

píng yuán dān tuī shǒu 平圆单推手 Flat circle single hands connected push hands practice drill. From Taijiquan.

píng yuán shuāng tuī shǒu 平圆双推手 Flat circle both hands connected push hands practice drill. From Taijiquan.

píng yuán 平圆 A horizontal, level, circle or circles.

píng yuè sǎo 平月扫 Level moon sweep kick: a front sweep kick. From southern styles. See also qián sǎo tuǐ.

píng yún zhǎng 平云掌 Horizontal brandish: palms down, circle the hands in a flat circle.

píng zhā dāo 平扎刀 A flat stab with a broadsword, blade tip at shoulder height.

píng zhā qiāng 平扎枪 A flat stab with a spear, the arm and spear forming a straight line.

píng zhǎn 平折 A flat cut with a bladed weapon.

píng zhǎn dà dāo 平折大刀 Flat cut with a big cutter: with the right hand near the blade, palm up, cut across, tucking the shaft to the left side with the left hand.

píng zhǒu 平肘 Flat elbow: flat elbow point strike to the side, level with the shoulder.

瓶 (rad.98) **píng** A bottle; vase; jar; flask.

píng huā luò yàn 瓶花落砚 Flowers in a Vase Drop on the Inkstone: Stepping back while lifting the hand to strike or control with the back of the hand upwards, alternating circling the hands down

P

and up, then outwards. From Liuhebafa.

評 [评] (rad.149) **píng**   To comment; criticize; review. Judge; appraise.

píng fēn 评分 To score: a judge in competition gives a score to the competitor.

píng fēn biāo zhǔn 评分标准 Scoring criteria in a test or competition.

píng fēn fāng fǎ 评分方法 Scoring methods in a test or competition.

坡 (rad.32) **pō**   A slope. Sloping; slanted.

pō tuǐ 坡腿 Sloping kick: catch your adversary's lower leg with your shin and reach across his chest with your same side arm. Lift your leg and use an opening, crossing power for a takedown.

泼 (rad.85) **pō**   1. To splash; sprinkle; spill. 2. Shrewish.

pō jiǎo 泼脚 Spilling kick: a sweep kick that uses a full squat, supporting hands, and a full circle of the foot on the ground. From Shaolinquan.

破 (rad.112) **pò**   1. To destroy; break; cleave. 2. Broken; damaged. 3. To break or release a controlling grip.

pò guā shǒu 破瓜手 Cleave the Melon Punch: punch directly to the sensitive point under the nose. From Shaolinquan.

pò huà 破化 Defending by blocking and evading.

pò jiǎo bù 破脚步 Break the foot stepping: walk with continuous front cross steps (see also gài bù), keeping the weight on the crossing foot. From Drunken style.

pò jiě 破解 Release techniques. See jiě fǎ. Also called jiě tuō, tuō ná.

pò jiě qín ná 破解擒拿 Release techniques, techniques to counter controlling grips.

pò xīn zhǒu 破心肘 Break the Heart elbow strike: shift strongly from a bow stance to the other side, driving across with an elbow strike.

pò zhàn 破绽 A break: an unguarded space or opportunity that you give to an adversary, or visa versa. Not a fake to draw him in, but a mistake that lets him get in. Also called kōng dāng.

pò zhāo 破招 Break the attack: defend or counter attack before an adversary has completed his attack, either by guessing what he will do or by using his movement against him. Usually gets in before an adversary, even though reacting to his movement.

迫 廹 (rad.162, 54) [迫] (rad.162) **pò**   To compel; force; press.

pò bù 迫步 Compelling step: stepping in to jam an adversary, staying in stance.

魄 (rad.194) **pò**   1. Vigour; life. 2. Form; shape. 3. Corporeal soul. 4. Associated with the Lung, and with the character attributes of tenacity and physical endurance. 5. The dark side of the moon.

pò hù 魄户 Acupoint Pohu (door of the corporeal soul), BL42. At the back, level with the depression below the spinous process of the third thoracic vertebra, three *cun* lateral to the midline (on each side). From TCM.

pò lì 魄力 Courage; decisiveness; guts; the ability to make quick decisions and act on them.

pò mén 魄门 The anus.

仆 (rad.9) **pū**   To fall forward.

pū bù 仆步 Drop stance: squatting fully on one leg, extend the other straight out to the side, both feet flat on the ground. Also called chā dì lóng, dān chā. Done as a kick, also called pū tuǐ.

pū bù bāo gùn 仆步抱棍 Drop stance hold a staff: in a drop stance, open out the hands and present the staff horizontally across in front of the body.

pū bù chuān zhǎng 仆步穿掌 Drop stance moving through to thread palm. A technique often done in repeats as a basic exercise.

pū bù lún pāi 仆步轮拍 Drop stance swinging slaps on the ground, a basic exercise. Stand up, swinging the arms in full circles, then drop to drop stance, slapping the ground by the foot of the extended leg. Repeat back and forth. Also called pū bù lún pī.

pū bù lún pī 仆步轮劈 Drop stance swinging chops. See pū bù lún pāi.

pū bù shuāi gùn 仆步摔棍 Drop stance smash a

pū bù xià shì 仆步下势 Drop stance lower the position: sit into a drop stance, extend one arm along the outstretched leg and open the other arm in line with the squatting thigh. From Taijiquan.

pū dì bèng 仆地蹦 Hop around prone: holding the body straight, just off the ground, supporting with toes and hands only, hop around in a circle.

pū miàn zhǎng 仆面掌 Pounce on the face: a swinging slap kick, hitting with the opposite hand. From Shaolinquan.

pū qiāng 仆枪 Drop with a spear: sit into a drop stance bringing the shaft near the ground, but not striking it.

pū shēn 仆参 Acupoint Pushen (subservient visitor), BL61. At the ankle, on the outside, just below the ankle bone, directly below acupoint Kunlun, at the border of the lighter and darker flesh (on each leg). May also be pronounced pū cān. From TCM.

pū tuǐ 仆腿 Drop kick, fully squat on one leg and extend the other straight out to the side, sliding on the ground.

pū zhǒu 仆肘 Elbow drop: tuck the elbow in and down to the ribs, the elbow is bent and the palm angled upwards.

撲 [扑] (rad.64) pū 1. To pounce, rush at; to beat strike, pound; to throw oneself on. Often an attack with both arms. 2. As a shield and broadsword technique, pounce: jump forward onto an adversary, using the shield to land on him, combining with a stab or slice.

pū dāo 扑刀 A cutter, a horse cutter: the shaft is the length to the armpit, and the blade is longer, and a bit heftier, than a broadsword blade. Generally, the shaft and blade are of equal length. The horse cutter shaft is shorter than the big cutter, so when held in both hands they can reach comfortably to each end of the shaft. Also called pǔ dāo, shuāng shǒu dài, zhǎn mǎ dāo.

pū dà dāo 扑大刀 Beating cut with a big cutter: with the right hand near the blade, palm down, cut down to waist height from above the head.

pū dì jīng léi 扑地惊雷 A Sudden Clap of Thunder Hits the Ground: drop into a horse stance simultaneously hacking down with the edges of both hands. From Meishanquan.

pū dì jiān xíng shì 扑地肩行式 Shoulder walking: lying face down on the ground, hands at the sides, advancing using only the shoulders to move forward.

pū diāo jiá chì 扑雕夹翅 Pouncing Vulture Squeezes with its Wings. 1. A close range technique: grab the back of the head and pull down into a knee butt to the face. 2. A leaping technique: fake with one knee, then when an adversary moves in, jump and strike with the other knee.

pū diē 扑跌 1. Bumping and falling in wrestling, generalized, not specific techniques. 2. Takedowns applying pressure with the body, rather than foot hooks. From Tanglangquan.

pū fǎ 扑法 Tumbling techniques.

pū guà 扑挂 Arm swing: extend the arms above the body and swing them down to slap the backs of the hands on the thighs. Used as an exercise in many styles, as a technique in Tongbeiquan.

pū hǔ 扑虎 Pounce on the Tiger: a tumbling move, leap up and turn to almost vertical in the air, then land softly, using the arms to absorb the landing, then the stomach, and then the legs.

pū jiǎo 扑脚 Pounce with a foot: come through with the rear foot, sliding with the foot turned to kick an adversary's shin.

pū jìn 扑劲 Pouncing power: land like a tiger pouncing on a prey. From Xingyiquan, one of its five powers. See also cǎi jìn, guǒ jìn, jué jìn, shù jìn.

pū shǒu 扑手 Pounce: a sharp press down, combined with a drop down. From Tanglangquan.

pū shǒu ér jìn shǒu 扑手而进手 If pressed down by an adversary with a sharp power, go into his attack, turning and pressing his arms. From Tanglangquan, one of its twelve soft counters, see also shí èr róu.

pū shǔ 扑鼠 Pounce on a Rat: when an adversary comes in close to grab you, grab around his neck with both hands and pull him forward and down.

pū yì 扑翼 Pounce with the Wings: a double fisted action, upwards like a bird extending its wings.

pū zhǒu 扑肘 Elbow pounce: elbow strike in a

P

reverse stance.

铺 [铺] (rad.167) **pū** To spread; extend; unfold.

pū bù 铺步 Spreading stance: sit on one leg and extend the other straight to the side. About eighty percent of the weight is on the sitting leg, and it is a bit higher than a drop stance (see also pū bù 仆步).

pū dì mián 铺地绵 Spread a Quilt on the Ground. See què dì lóng.

pū dì mián shì 铺地绵式 Spread a Quilt on the Ground model. 1. One of twenty-four classic spear moves. Most spear routines will have a move with a like name. In general, this name refers to a low technique, such as a chop down then stab. 2. Drop down and stab a spear along on the ground, then come up to stab from underneath.

pū dì mián 扑地棉 Spread a Padded Quilt on the Ground. See què dì lóng.

樸 [朴] (rad.75) **pǔ** Simple.

pǔ dāo 朴刀 A horse cutter. See pū dāo. Also called shuāng shǒu dài, zhǎn mǎ dāo.

譜 [谱] (rad.149) **pǔ** A record or register. A manual; guidebook.

pǔ yuē 谱曰 As it says in the classics. The classic manual says. This is a standard phrase used in writing when quoting from a classic.

Q

七 (rad.1) **qī**   Seven.

qī cháng 七长 Seven long: the seven long range techniques of Tanglangquan. See also chán fēng shuāng zhǎng, fān shēn jí rù, hán tōng tōng bèi, jiǎo shǒu kǎn zhǎng, shùn bù qiàn shǒu, yáo bù rù shǒu, yíng miàn tōng chuí.

qī chōng mén 七冲门 Seven gateways to attack: painful targets on the body, related to midline acupoints. The philtrum, jaw, throat, solar plexus, navel, belly, and groin. See also chǎn mén, fèi mén, guàn mén, hù mén, hún mén, xī mén, yōu mén.

qī cūn kào 七寸靠 Seven Inch Lean: drop, move in, and contact an adversary's shin with your shoulder. From Chen Taijiquan.

qī cūn tuǐ 七寸腿 Seven Inch Kick: lift the knee, turn the foot out and stamp downwards. The foot should lift only about seven inches. From Duanquan.

qī jí 七疾 The seven things that must be quick: eyes, hands, feet, mind, initiation of attack, entry, and bodywork. From Xingyiquan.

qī qiào 七窍 The seven orifices: the mouth and two each of nostrils, ears, and eyes.

qī quán 七拳 Seven fists. See qī xīng.

qī shùn 七顺 Seven flows: seven requirements of smooth power flow: the power flows from shoulders to elbows, from elbows to hands, from hands to fingers, from waist to hips, from hips to knees, from knees to feet, and from head to body. From Xīngyiquan.

qī xīng 七星 Seven stars: the seven striking parts of the body: feet, knees, hips, hands, elbows, shoulders, head. Also called qī quán, qī yào.

qī xīng bù 七星步 Seven stars stepping: advance on a zigzag line, not turning on each step, but on every few steps.

qī xīng diǎn zǐ 七星点子 Seven stars dot. See dǔ mén tuǐ.

qī xīng gānr 七星杆 1. Seven star stick: a thin stick, usually about 1.2 metres long. 2. In Baguazhang, a thin, whippy, hollow bamboo pole, containing mercury inside that slides back and forth with the movement, making the whipping strikes very heavy.

qī xīng jiàn 七星剑 Seven stars sword. 1. A straight sword with the seven stars engraved on the blade. 2. A traditional sword routine.

qī xīng luò dì 七星落地 Seven Stars Land on the Ground: thread the palms forward stepping forward, then set to horse stance pressing down at the thighs. From Wudangquan.

qī xīng quán 七星拳 Seven Stars Punch: a straight punch past the crossing forearm of the other arm.

qī xīng táng láng quán 七星螳螂拳 Qixing (seven stars) Tanglangquan, a branch of Preying Mantis style, known for quick movement.

qī xīng zhuāng 七星桩 1. Seven star stakes: seven stakes set into the ground (usually wrapped in hemp rope) about three feet (one metre) apart in the shape of the seven stars (three in straight line then four in a square). Used to practice sweep kicks and develop the lower legs to take the impact of sweep kicks. 2. Seven star stake standing. Varies with style, may be sitting in a seventy-thirty stance, turned around to face the rear, the rear hand up and the front hand at the ribs.

qī yào 七曜 The seven luminaries. 1. The sun, moon, metal, wood, water, fire, and earth. 2. In Xingyiquan, see qī xīng.

qī zì bù 七字步 Character seven (七) step: take a long step forward with the rear foot and draw the other foot a half step to the side, so the body has turned to present the side to an adversary while advancing.

期 (rad 74) **qī**   A period of time; phase; stage. A measure word for periods of time, cycles.

qī mén 期门 Acupoint Qimen (cycle gate), LR14. At the chest, below the nipple, in the sixth intercostal space, four *cun* from the midline (on each side). From TCM. Sensitive to the extent that striking it may cause death. This point facilitates

Q

qi flow through the body – when open, the cycle can be completed.

欺 (rad.76) **qī**   1. To deceive. 2. To bully. 3. To take advantage of someone's weakness.

qī shēn 欺身 Move in close to take advantage or cause weakness in an adversary, to initiate or prevent a throw.

qī xiōng 欺胸 Chest press: when in contact, press forward on an adversary with the chest using all the power of the body. From wrestling.

奇 (rad.37) **qí**   1. Strange; rare. 2. Wonderful. 3. To feel strange about something.

qí fāng 奇方 Unconventional tactics.

qí jīng bā mài 奇经八脉 The eight extraordinary vessels: the grouping of acupoints that are not within the twelve channels that relate to the organs. From TCM.

qí quán 奇拳 Unusual fist: a fist shape, pressing the thumb on the second joint of the middle and ring fingers, leaving the index finger bent but unsupported. From Tongbeiquan.

qí xíng jiàn 奇行剑 Remarkable sword, a traditional sword routine, written up as sixty-nine moves.

qí zhāo 奇招 An unusual move. 1. A sudden attack, launched before an adversary can defend. 2. An unusual, unexpected attack.

qí zhèng zhuǎn huàn 奇正转换 To alternate between unexpected techniques and straight-forward techniques in fighting. See also zhèng zhāo.

脐 (rad.130) **qí**   The navel, the belly button.

qí mén 脐门 The sensitive point at the navel. See also chǎn mén.

騎 [骑] (rad.187) **qí**   1. To ride (when using an action of straddling, like on a horse or bicycle). 2. Ride, a counter to a leg hooking takedown: leaving the hooked leg in contact, turn the throw into a sideways lean.

qí lóng bù 骑龙步 1. Dragon riding stance: a half-squat on the front leg with the rear leg bent behind with the heel up, feet about two foot-lengths apart. The rear knee and shin are parallel to the ground, not touching it. From southern styles. Also called tuō lí bù. 2. Similar to #1, but with the weight two thirds forward and the rear foot flat. 3. Dragon walking: a training walking method, circle-walking using this stance, keeping the hips at the height of the knees. From Baguazhang.

qí lóng shì 骑龙式 Ride the Dragon model. One of twenty-four classic spear moves. Most spear routines will have a move with a like name. In general, this name refers to a coiling and controlling move that sets up a stab.

qí lǘ bù 骑驴步 Donkey riding stance: sit with the feet front and back, about two foot-lengths apart with the weight more on the front leg, both heels off the ground. From southern styles.

qí mǎ 骑马 Ride a horse. See mǎ bù. Also called qí mǎ bù, zuò mǎ shì.

qí mǎ bù 骑马步 Horse riding stance. See mǎ bù. Also called qí mǎ, zuò mǎ shì.

qí mǎ héng sǎo 骑马横扫 Sweep across on Horseback: step into horse stance and sweep the butt of a staff around to eyebrow height in a reverse grip. From Baguazhang.

麒 (rad.198) **qí**   A kylin, usually used in combination as qí lín.

qí lín 麒麟 Kylin, a mythical animal with a dragon-like head with two antlers, the body of a powerful animal much like a horse, the tail of a bull (though sometimes it is a thick tail), and cloven hooves like a deer. Its body is covered in scales, but is often depicted covered in flames or waves. One of China's four divine creatures, along with the dragon, phoenix, and tortoise, it is a symbol of auspiciousness. It can walk on water and spit fire, and its roar is like thunder. Often translated as Chinese unicorn, but this is misleading, as it has two antlers and is nothing like a unicorn.

qí lín bù 麒麟步 Kylin step. 1. Take two firm steps forward, crossing the feet with each step. From southern styles. 2. A follow step, see gēn bù. 3. Sometimes the same as the dragon riding stance, see qí lóng bù.

qí lín dān shān 麒麟担山 Kylin Carries a Mountain: circle-walking with the elbows bent so that the hands push up at the ears, palms up, fingers pointing behind. From Baguazhang.

qí lín dǒu zhuō 麒麟抖爪 Kylin Shakes its Feet: a low snap kick combined with a opening of the arms then a shake of the shoulders and elbows to flash the palms. From Shaolinquan.

qí lín liàng zhǎng 麒麟亮掌 Kylin Flashes its Palms: sit into empty stance and flash the palms in front, in a fighting ready stance. From Shaolinquan.

qí lín tǔ shū 麒麟吐书 Kylin Tells a Story: step to a one legged stance, extending the palm out to the front. From Baguazhang.

qí lín tuō tiān 麒麟托天 Kylin Carries the Sky: circle-walking with the hands pushing up above the head, palms up, fingers pointing to each other. From Baguazhang.

qí lín tuò dì 麒麟拓地 Kylin Opens up the Land: circle-walking with the hands pushing down at the hips, curving in. From Baguazhang.

qí lín xiàn shū 麒麟献书 Kylin Presents a Book: Squat to lower the body, separating the hands. From Piguaquan.

齊 [齐] (rad.210) qí 1. In order, orderly. Neat, even. Equal, uniform. To be level with. 2. The Qi of the Southern Dynasties (479-502).

qí méi gùn 齐眉棍 Eyebrow-level staff. 1. A short staff, the length is from the ground to eyebrow height. 2. A routine of Mojiaquan using this staff, written up as twenty moves.

起 (rad.156) qǐ 1. To rise, get up, stand up. 2. To initiate action. 3. To initiate the attack, enter.

qǐ fú zhuàn zhé 起伏转折 Take off, landing, rotation, and change of direction: four qualities of skill and rhythm in a routine.

qǐ píng luò kòu 起平落扣 Rise level and land tucked. Refers to circle-walking in Baguazhang: the feet lift flatly, the toes coming up first, the outside foot lands turned onto the line of the circle. The degree of turn in depends on the size of the circle. In some styles, tuck refers to the arching of the foot as it grabs.

qǐ rú yuán 起如猿 Initiate action like an ape, or Rise like an ape: one of the twelve qualities of movement of Changquan, though these descriptors apply to many other styles.

qǐ shì 起势 First movement of a routine, starting posture.

qǐ shǒu 起手 Rising hand: any strike that involves striking upwards from below. See, for example, liāo, tiǎo, tuō, yáng. From Chuojiao.

qǐ zhēn 起针 Remove an acupuncture needle. From TCM.

qǐ zuān luò fān 起钻落翻 Rise with a drilling action, lower with a turning action. A martial saying. When the hands rise the arms externally rotate and extend, when the hands lower the arms internally rotate and come back in with a settling of the wrists. From Baguazhang and Xingyiquan.

器 (rad.30) qì An implement; utensil.

qì xiè 器械 1. Implements, apparatus. 2. A machine. 3. In martial arts, weapons.

qì xiè biàn xíng 器械变形 Deformation, or bending, of a weapon. An ordinary deduction (0.1) in Taolu competition.

qì xiè diào dì 器械掉地 Drop a weapon. A major deduction (0.3) in Taolu competition.

qì xiè pèng shēn 器械碰身 Hit yourself with your weapon. An ordinary deduction (0.1) in Taolu competition.

qì xiè zhé duàn 器械折断 Break a weapon. A serious deduction (0.2) in Taolu competition.

棄 (rad.75) [弃] (rad.55) qì To throw away; discard; abandon.

qì quán 弃权 To forfeit; waive the right to compete (due to injury or some other problem).

qì shí qiú yù 弃石求玉 Discard the Stone to Seek Jade: set back to a raised knee stance, pushing both hands out to the sides to draw a sword back, tip still pointing forward. From Qingping sword.

氣 [气] (rad.84) qì 1. Vital energy, both energy and matter that carries vital energy. 2. Air; breath.

qì chén dān tián 气沉丹田 Settle the *qi* to the *dantian*: breathe deeply with abdominal breathing so that the lower belly feels full, giving a feeling of filling up with *qi*.

Q

qì chōng 气冲 Acupoint Qichong (surging qi), ST30. At the abdomen, five *cun* below the navel, two *cun* lateral to the midline (on each side). From TCM. In internal styles, relaxing the hips allows *qi* to flow through this point, enabling the *qi* to settle into the legs and bring stability.

qì duān 气端 Extraordinary acupoint Qiduan, EX-LE12. At the foot, five points, one at the tip of each toe, 0.1 *cun* from the toenail. From TCM.

qì fǎ 气法 Breathing techniques used to improve power, stability, etc., of movement.

qì gēn 气根 The root of *qi*: the belly, the *dantian*. Thought to be the storage place for *qi*, and where it starts out from.

qì gōng 气功 Various methods to train the *qi* within the body. Called chi gong or *qigong* in English.

qì hǎi 气海 Acupoint Qihai (sea of qi), RN6. At the abdomen, 1.5 *cun* below the navel, on the midline. From TCM. A sensitive point, striking hard damages *qi* generation and may cause death. In internal styles, this point is lightly lifted during practice, to keep the body core firm.

qì hǎi shū 气海俞 Acupoint Qihaishu (sea of qi transport). BL24. At the lower back, level with the depression below the spinous process of the third lumbar vertebra, 1.5 *cun* lateral to the midline (on each side). From TCM. A sensitive point.

qì hé yú shén 气合于神 *Qi* combines with the spirit. From Liuhebafa, one of its principles.

qì hù 气户 Acupoint Qihu (air door), ST13. At the chest, just under the clavicle, about four *cun* lateral to the midline (on each side). From TCM. A sensitive point, pressure here can induce coughing. Excess pressure can seal the breath.

qì jī 气机 The *qi* dynamic within the body.

qì lì 气力 Strength, vigour, overall energy.

qì liǎn 气敛 The *qi* is collected: the *qi* is not scattered, but is gathered. In terms of breathing: breathing in closes and gathers and breathing out opens and releases power. One of the requirements for proper training.

qì mén 气门 The front of the throat, or larynx. A sensitive point, colloquially called the gateway to *qi*. Best to hit with a grab, a stab, or character eight palm. Not to be confused with acupoint Qīmén, LR14, on the chest.

qì pò 气魄 Courage; daring; boldness of vision or spirit. Grandeur.

qì shě 气舍 Acupoint Qishe (qi abode), ST11. At the neck, just above the proximal end of the clavicle (on each side). From TCM.

qì shì 气势 1. An imposing manner. 2. Momentum (in a fight).

qì shū 气俞 Sensitive point Qishu (colloquial for the Shenzhu point). Behind the neck, at the depression under the third cervical vertebra. Best to hit with a pull and short strike or a step around to strike from behind.

qì yào chén 气要沉 The *qi* must be settled. A common requirement of many styles, one of Tongbeiquan's requirements.

qì xué 气穴 Acupoint Qixue (qi point), KI13. At the abdomen, three *cun* below the navel, 0.5 *cun* lateral to the midline (on each side). From TCM.

qì yí chén 气宜沉 The *qi* should be settled down: one of the basic qualities of many styles.

qì yí gǔ dàng shén yí nèi liǎn 气宜鼓荡神宜内敛 The *qi* should flow freely while the spirit should be restrained.

qì yú lì hé 气与力合 The *qi* harmonizes, or works together with, the strength. One of the six harmonies. See also liù hé.

qì zhì 气至 Arrival of *qi*: to feel that the *qi* has taken the acupuncture needle. A feeling of the person administering the needling. From TCM.

qì zhì 气质 Temperament; disposition. Qualities; makings.

qì zhì 气滞 1. Stagnant *qi*, *qi* that is sluggish. 2. Stagnation of the circulation of *qi*. 3. Postures and movements that show blockage and lack of flow.

掐 (rad.64) **qiā** 1. To pinch; nip. Clutch. 2. A bunch, a pinch.

qiā diǎn 掐点 Pinch and dab, the eighth of Chuojiao's nine literary routines, written up as sixty-two moves. See also wén tàng zi.

qiā dù shuāng zhuàng 掐肚双撞 Grab the belly and double shove.

qiā fǎ 掐法 Clutching techniques: clutch with the thumb web open, using all fingers and thumb to grip. Used mainly on the throat or belly of muscles.

qiā hú lǔ 掐葫芦 Grab the gourd, a grip: grabbing the elbow just at the joint. From wrestling.

qiā ná fǎ 掐拿法 Clutching hold: to grab putting all the strength of the arm into the hand. From wrestling.

髂 (rad.188) qià   The ilium.

qià gǔ 髂骨 Ilium bone: the largest bone in the pelvic girdle.

千 (rad.24) qiān   A thousand.

qiān céng zhǐ 千层纸 Thousand layered paper: a training tool for developing punches. Start by punching a thick pile of papers. The sheets of paper are gradually worn away, so that eventually one is punching the wall directly. Can use to train punches, finger strikes, palm edge strikes, and palm slaps.

qiān jīn bàng 千斤棒 Thousand pounds stick. For rollups, grip and forearm training: holding a short, relatively thick stick in front with straight arms, with a weight attached by a rope, and wind the weight up and down. See also jiǎo bàng gōng, tuó bàng.

qiān jīn zhá 千斤闸 Thousand pounds plank: a large plank used for training by holding overhead while sitting in horse stance. When very heavy, may be suspended between supports.

qiān jīn zhuì dì 千斤坠地 A Thousand Pounds Crash to the Ground. 1. Using an adversary's force, go along with him locking his arm with your arms to quickly throw. 2. Grab your adversary's arm and drop into a full squat (or step back) pressuring down to drop him, a takedown. From Baguazhang, one of its sixty-four hands. 3. Stand up straight and swing a sword's blade in a large circle to chop down. From Qingping sword.

qiān jūn gùn 千军棍 A Thousand Troops Staff: a routine of Yangjia style, written up as twenty-three moves.

扦 (rad.64) qiān   1. A short, slender, pointed piece of metal or bamboo. 2. To stick in, insert.

qiān biè 扦别 Inserting throw: grab the front of the jacket, quickly and forcefully step in to take your adversary's legs out from under him, swinging your leg up and pulling him to spin him down. From wrestling.

牵 [牽] (rad.93) qiān   To pull, drag; lead by hand (as leading an animal on a rope).

qiān lā diē 牵拉跌 Dragging takedown: type of takedown that pulls back to take an adversary down on his face, setting your foot to prevent him from stepping out of the pull.

qiān mǎ pīn 牵马拚 Lead the Horse and Risk All: retreating, hook onto your adversary's hand near your body and punch his arm. From Xingyiquan.

qiān shǒu 牵手 Lead: to use the incoming power of an adversary, using the hands to lead him in and on.

qiān yán shǒu 牵沿手 Lead along: switch the hand in front of the body so that when you grasp your adversary with both hands you can do a variety of techniques involving rotation. From Shaolinquan.

乾 (rad.5) qián   1. The Heaven, Sky, Trigram, represented by three solid (yang) lines, called 'three connected'. Male. Corresponds to heaven, or the heavenly formation or gate. A closing gate formation. Indicates the attribute of 'strong'. 2. Pronounced gān, dry, see gān.

qián kūn 乾坤 Heaven and earth; the cosmos.

qián kūn jiàn 乾坤剑 Heaven and Earth sword. See yuān yáng yuè. Also called lù jiǎo dāo, rì yuè shuāng lián, shuāng yuè, zǐ wǔ yuān yáng yuè.

qián kūn quān 乾坤圈 Heaven and earth ring: a hidden weapon. Worn as a bracelet, most the outer edge has sharp teeth, with a quarter of the circumference left clear as a grip.

qián kūn shǒu 乾坤手 Heaven and earth hands: the front hand high and turned up, the other hand low and turned down. A ready position, a defensive posture able to turn to attack in an instant.

Q

前 (rad.18) **qián** Front, fore. In front of. Towards the front.

qián bì or **bēi** 前臂 Forearm.

qián diǎn bù 前点步 Front touch stance or step.

qián diǎn gùn 前点棍 Front dab with a staff: slide the front hand back to meet the rear hand, at the butt, and lift both to dab downwards with the tip of the staff.

qián dǐng 前顶 Acupoint Qianding (before the peak), DU21. At the top of the head, 3.5 up from the front hairline, 1.5 *cun* forward of acupoint Baihui, on the midline. From TCM.

qián duàn 前段 1. Fore-section of the blade or shaft of a weapon, the third nearest the tip. 2. The section of a three-section staff that is used most as its fore-section.

qián é 前额 The forehead.

qián fān zhǒu 前翻肘 Forward elbow flip: grab your adversary's wrist in one hand and his elbow in the other, rotating the arm and pulling the elbow towards you. Continue on to take down. From Qinna.

qián fǔ 前俯 To lean forward, bend forward.

qián fǔ yāo 前俯腰 Forward stretch, toe touches. Place the hands flat on the floor or grab the legs, keeping the legs straight and the back flat.

qián gōng bù 前弓步 Front bow stance. See **gōng bù**. Also called **gōng dēng bù**, **gōng jiàn bù**, **jiàn mǎ**.

qián gǔ 前谷 Acupoint Qian'gu (front valley), SI2. At the outer edge of the proximal segment of the little finger, at the joint, at the border of the darker and lighter skin (on each hand). From TCM.

qián gǔn fān 前滚翻 Front somersault, front roll. Also called **qián máo**.

qián hòu diǎn tuǐ 前后点腿 Continuous poke kicks to front then rear. From Chuojiao, one of its middle-basin kicks.

qián hòu jī zhǎng 前后击掌 Back and front slaps, a shoulder flexibility exercise used in Tongbeiquan: swing straight arms to slap with the palms and then with the backs of the hands.

qián hòu liāo yīn tuǐ 前后撩阴腿 Continuous swinging kicks to the groin. From Chuojiao, one of its middle-basin kicks.

qián hòu mō jìn 前后摸劲 To stand with the arms rounded in front of the chest and search for a feeling of power moving forwards and backwards within the body. From Yiquan.

qián hòu xuán zhuàn 前后旋转 Rotation within the body on the forward to back plane.

qián jiāo chā bù 前交叉步 Front crossing step: starting from an open stance, step the lead foot across in front of the rear foot, stepping the rear foot immediately to return to the original stance.

qián jiǎo zhǎng 前脚掌 The ball of the foot.

qián jìn bù 前进步 Advancing step: push off the rear foot to step the lead foot forward, then follow in with the rear foot, to advance without changing stance.

qián jǔ tuǐ dǐ shì píng héng 前举腿底式平衡 Front leg raised low balance: fully squat on the supporting leg and extend the other straight out in front without touching the ground.

qián jǔ tuǐ píng héng 前举腿平衡 Front leg raised supine balance.

qián kōng fān 前空翻 Front aerial somersault.

qián kōng tuǐ píng héng 前空腿平衡 Front leg raised vertical balance: with the body upright, lift the leg straight in front.

qián kòng tuǐ 前控腿 Front leg hold: standing holding the leg to the front without support.

qián liāo yīn tuǐ 前撩阴腿 Front straight swing kick to the groin with the foot dorsi-flexed. A common kick, one of Chuojiao's middle-basin kicks, also called **dōu dāng tuǐ**.

qián máo 前毛 Traditional name for a front somersault. Also called **qián gǔn fān**.

qián mén 前门 The Front Gate: the distance of an outstretched hand.

qián mén kǎn tuǐ 前门坎腿 Destroy the Front Gate kick: a kick to the shin. Also called **cǎi tuǐ**. See also **mén kǎn tuǐ**.

qián ná shǒu 前捺手 Front Pinning Hand: a straight arm low thrust forward with the wrist hyper-flexed to contact with the heel of the palm. From Wing Chun.

qián pō tuǐ 前坡腿 Forward sloping kick: drop to

squat fully on one leg and outstretch the other with the heel on the ground and toes up. From Chuojiao. Similar to què dì lóng.

qián ruǎn fān 前软翻 A front walkover.

qián sǎo tuǐ 前扫腿 Front sweep kick, in full squat with the hands off the ground. Also specifically called zhí shēn qián sǎo when the body is absolutely upright. In the category of sweep kicks, see also sǎo zhuàn xìng tuǐ fǎ.

qián shān shì 前搧式 Forward fanning strike: starting with the arms crossed, move forward, pulling one hand back while simultaneously slicing forward with the other hand.

qián shǒu fān 前手翻 Front somersault, touching the hands down before landing.

qián suǒ hóu 前锁喉 Front choke hold: from the front, press with the forearm or with both hands around the neck of your adversary. Can be done with the thumb and index joints on the larynx, if wanting total control or to break the larynx. From Qinna.

qián táng ǎo bù 前堂拗步 Front Chamber Reverse Stance: brush knee and open up, with the body open and the weight on the rear leg. From Chen Taijiquan.

qián tàng ǎo bù 前趟拗步 Wade Forward to Reverse Stance: advancing with a brush knee, finishing in a reverse bow stance. From Chen Taijiquan.

qián tī tuǐ 前踢腿 Front straight kick, swing a straight leg up in front with the foot plantar flexed. In the category of straight swinging kicks, see also zhí bǎi xìng tuǐ fǎ.

qián tí xī píng héng 前提膝平衡 Front knee raised balance: raise one knee in front of the body, the supporting leg straight.

qián yín 前阴 The groin. See dāng bù. Also called dāng, xià yín.

qián zhāo 前招 Front Provocation, Forward Beckoning, Take Care of the Front, Maneuver to the Front: raise one hand and lower the other to the sides, turning forward. A throw or defence against an attack from the front. From Chen Taijiquan.

qián zhǒu 前肘 Forward elbow: strike the elbow forward horizontally, contacting with the forearm. In a routine, drive the forearm near the elbow into the other hand.

qián zhuā yāo dài 前抓腰带 Grasp the belt at the front: a grip in wrestling or in practicing releases.

qián zhuō 前啄 Forward peck: attack an adversary's eyes with the finger tips in a hooked hand.

qián zuǐ 前嘴 Forward beak: strike to the front with the finger tips in a hooked hand. Usually, but not specifically, to the eyes.

拑 (rad.64) **qián** See qián 鉗 [钳].

潜 (rad.85) **qián** 1. Latent, hidden. 2. Stealthy, secretly.

qián fú 潜伏 To duck, bend the body down to avoid a high attack.

qián lóng dài shí 潜龙待时 Hidden Dragon Bides its Time: lift a spear up and back, fully extending the arms and opening the chest, then come down with a big chop.

qián rén xìng lín 潜人杏林 Someone Hidden in the Apricot Orchard: drop to a seated cross stance and slice a sword out low to the right, tip reaching almost to the ground, left hand curved above the head. From Qingping sword.

qián shì fáng shǒu 潜势防守 Evasion: an evasive maneuver to cause your attacker to miss.

鉗 [钳] (rad.167) **qián** 1. Pincers; pliers; tongs. 2. To grip with pincers; to clamp onto with the hands. 3. To clamp onto with the thighs. Also written 拑.

qián bǎ 钳把 Pincer grip: grasp the grip of a short weapon firmly with the thumb and index finger, allowing the other fingers to loosen on the grip. Used when need to allow more movement from the wrist.

脥 (rad.130) **qiǎn** The lower abdomen. The pelvic cavity.

qiǎn dǐ jiàn quán 脥底箭拳 Belly Arrow Punch: step into a left reverse bow stance and punch the right fist from the belly to the front, pulling the left fist back to the waist. The 89th move of the tiger and crane routine.

Q

槍 [枪] (rad.75) **qiāng** 1. A gun; a firearm. 2. A spear. The spear is often called a red tasselled spear, to differentiate between a spear and a gun. See also hóng yīng qiāng.

qiāng bà 枪把 Spear base or butt, the end of the aft-section, where the right hand grips.

qiāng chū rú fēi jiàn 枪出如飞箭 The spear should shoot out like a flying arrow. A martial saying.

qiāng dāo bù rù fǎ 枪刀不入法 The training method so that spears and broadsword can't get in. A soft training to help dodging skills, building up the ability to see and judge by counting first simple things like roof tiles, working up to flocks of birds on the ground, then on the wing, then moving groups of insects.

qiāng gǎn 枪杆 Spear shaft. Also called qiāng shēn.

qiāng gēn hé yī 枪棍合一 Spear and staff combined. To use the shaft of the spear with moves that are usually more characteristic of the staff.

qiāng jiān 枪尖 The spear tip. See qiāng tóu.

qiāng pà yáo tóu 枪怕摇头 The worst thing for the spear is to have a wobbly head. A martial saying.

qiāng shēn 枪身 Spear shaft. Also called qiāng gǎn.

qiāng shì chán yāo suǒ 枪是缠腰锁 The spear is like a lock and chains around the waist. A martial saying. Describes the necessary closeness of the spear to the body.

qiāng shù 枪术 1. Spear skill. 2. Spearplay: a Taolu competition event, called Qiangshu in English.

qiāng sì yóu lóng gùn ruò yǔ 枪似游龙棍若雨 The spear is like a swimming dragon and the staff is like falling rain. A martial saying. Describes the difference between the spear and the staff.

qiāng tóu 枪头 Spear head, the sharp metal tip that is attached to the thin end of the shaft. Also called qiāng jiān.

qiāng tuō zhǎng 枪托掌 Spear carrying palm. See tuō qiāng zhǎng.

qiāng yīng 枪缨 Spear tassel. Made of horse's tail hairs or synthetic. Traditionally dyed red.

qiāng wěi 枪尾 Spear tail: the very end of the aft-section.

qiāng zhā yī tiáo xiàn 枪扎一条线 The spear stabs in a straight line. A martial saying. Describes the essence of the spear.

强 [强] (rad.57) **qiáng** Strong, powerful. Also pronounced qiǎng.

qiáng jiān 强间 Acupoint Qiangjian (strong space), DU18. At the back of the head, four *cun* up from the hairline, 1.5 *cun* up from acupoint Naohu, on the midline. Midway between acupoints Fengfu and Baihui. From TCM.

qiáng yìng 强硬 Hard; strong; stiff; tough.

强 [强] (rad.57) **qiǎng** To force, make an effort. Also pronounced qiáng.

qiǎng gōng zhāo fǎ 强攻招法 Storming attack moves: techniques that take an adversary by storm, taking his position.

qiǎng pò jū gōng 强迫鞠弓 Force the Bow: from behind, wrap your arms around under your adversary's armpits, to press your hands on the back of his head, forcing him down.

搶 [抢] (rad.64) **qiǎng** To steal in; rob, plunder; scramble for, vie for; rush; snatch, grab. In martial arts, means to 'steal' the place where an adversary was, or to control the positioning.

qiǎng bèi 抢背 Forward back roll, shoulder roll: jump up and somersault forward, landing on the back without using the hands to support.

qiǎng bèi wò niú 抢背卧牛 Forward Roll to make the Ox Lie Down, a throw. See bái yuán káng qí.

qiǎng bì 抢臂 Rushing arms: move forward swinging the arms vertically, one after the other.

qiǎng bù 抢步 Stealing step: stepping into an adversary's stance.

qiǎng bù bēng quán 抢步崩拳 Stealing step crushing punch: drive into an adversary with the fist, a long step into a short stance. From Xingyiquan.

qiǎng bù qiǎng shuāi 抢步抢摔 Stealing throw:

step quickly to the outside of your adversary's leg, grabbing that side's wrist and the opposite side's shoulder. Use the other foot to trip and throw with the hips. From wrestling.

qiǎng bù tuī shuāi 抢步推摔 Stealing step pushing throw: step quickly in between your adversary's legs, grabbing and pulling one foot while pushing his chest with the other hand. From wrestling.

qiǎng hào 抢号 To draw lots for a bye in Sanda or wrestling competition.

qiǎng jiǎo 抢角 Steal the angle: take the optimum angle during fighting, not allowing your adversary to do so.

qiǎng kuà 抢胯 To steal in with the hips, changing place with a snap of the waist, in a tight clinch.

qiǎng pāi 抢拍 Steal the initiative: to take the initiative in a fight, pressing your adversary or countering his attacks before he can complete them.

qiǎng shǒu 抢手 Stealing hand: stab forward to nose height, often palm up. From Shaolinquan.

qiǎng wèi 抢位 Steal the position: to control the optimum position during fighting.

蹺 蹻 [跷] (rad.157) qiāo   To raise the foot; dorsi-flex.

qiāo guà diē 跷挂跌 Hooking takedown: category of takedown that hooks and lifts with the foot behind an adversary's ankle, lifting it to take him down on his back.

qiāo tuǐ 跷腿 Raise the foot kick: catch behind the ankle and lift a bit, a short hooking sweep kick. From Tanglangquan.

樵 (rad.75) qiáo   A woodsman; a woodcutter.

qiáo fū dān chái 樵夫但柴 Woodsman Carries the Firewood over his Shoulder: Advance with finger stabs, then turn and circle the arms up and over to settle into a horse stance with the arms to shoulder height. From Liuhebafa.

qiáo fū kǎn chái 樵夫砍柴 Woodsman Chops the Firewood: a bow stance hacking palm. From Piguaquan.

qiáo fū wèn chái 樵夫问柴 Woodsman Asks about Firewood: step into a right empty stance and reach forward with a sword blade higher than the head, with the right palm turned out, left hand at the armpit. From Wu Taijiquan.

橋 [桥] (rad.75) qiáo   1. A bridge. 2. In martial arts, the arm or forearm. It is so called because when two adversaries face off they stretch their arms out towards each other, forming a bridge.

qiáo fǎ 桥法 1. Bridge techniques, forearm techniques. Usually are circling techniques, and can be done with straight or bent arms. Also called biān fǎ. 2. Defensive posture taken with the arms.

qiáo shǒu 桥手 Bridge arm, the arm.

翹 [翘] (rad.124) qiáo   To raise the head.

qiáo jiǎo bù 翘脚步 Raised foot step: a long empty stance with the forward knee straight and heel on the ground. From Tanglangquan.

巧 (rad.48) qiǎo   Skillful, ingenious force or technique. Ingenuity. One of Ziranmen's nineteen main methods.

qiǎo jìn 巧劲 Ingenious power: skillful use of techniques to win a fight.

qiǎo nǚ rèn zhēn 巧女纫针 Ingenious Woman Threads a Needle: roll the right hand to pierce with a sword three times while stepping in low crossed stances. From Qingping sword.

qiǎo nǚ rèn zhēn 巧女认针 Ingenious Woman Knows her Needle: a sweeping stab with a sword, holding the wrist cocked, bringing the sword in a full circle with the tip leading. From Wudang sword.

qiǎo pò yāo suǒ 巧破腰索 Cleverly Break the Rope around the Waist: in response to a full grab from behind, drop down and brace the hands on your thighs to aid in snapping the elbows upward and outward to loosen the grip. then turn and deliver an elbow strike. From Shaolinquan.

qiǎo zhàn méi huā zhuāng 巧站梅花桩 Skillfully stand on plum blossom stakes: a stance and stepping training method. Lay a foundation by holding horse stance on plum blossom stakes, then undergo moving stances. See also méi huā zhuāng.

Q

撬 (rad.64) **qiào** To pry. To lift.

qiào shǒu 撬手 Prying control: hook away, bending the elbow, to trap and pull. From Chuojiao.

撒 (rad.64) **qiào** To beat from one side; to hit sideways.

qiào tī 撒踢 Sideways hook kick: a low snapping hook kick inwards to the heel of the adversary. From Mizongquan. Also called dī gōu.

窾 [窍] (rad.116) **qiào** An aperture, hole, opening.

qiào yīn 窍阴 Acupoint Qiaoyin (orifice yin), GB44. See zú qiào yīn. From TCM.

鞘 (rad.177) **qiào** Scabbard, sheath, snug carrying case that protects the blade of a short weapon.

切 (rad.18) **qiē** 1. To cut, slash (with weapon, blade of hand, or edge of foot); mince. 2. Slicing, whether with the palm or a weapon, usually involves a bending of the arm then a sharp extension to snap the cut. A sheering cut, angled like cutting cabbage from a field. 3. Shear, a grappling technique. 4. Taking the radial pulse, using the separation method in classical channel diagnosis. From TCM. 5. A close range short, sharp, low kick up with the heel.

qiē biān 切鞭 Whip slice. See qiē qiáo.

qiē biè 切别 Cutting throw: move the hip in and swing the leg to throw over the hip, holding one arm and grabbing over the shoulder to the back. From wrestling.

qiē fǎ 切法 Cutting. 1. Control the adversary's wrist by coiling and cutting. 2. Sharp cutting techniques to the wrist, elbow, shoulder, belly, or neck.

qiē jiān 切肩 Cut the shoulder, a takedown. See nǎo qiē zi.

qiē jiǎo 切脚 Cut with the foot, a short, sharp, low kick.

qiē kuà 切胯 Cut in at the hip joint. 1. In stances that are front and back, to keep the rear thigh tucked in and the ankle aligned to move forward, so that the hip is rolled inward, protecting the groin and keeping the body upright. 2. To cut in at the inguinal crease to keep the legs pulled into the pelvis and coil the torso naturally.

qiē lì 切力 Shearing force.

qiē qiáo 切桥 Bridge slice, a forearm technique: cut forward and down sharply with the forearm, pushing the palms down at an angle. From southern styles. Also called qiē biān.

qiē shǒu 切手 Cut with the hand: strike sharply with the blade of the hand, often sliding along the other arm. A similar action to hacking with a machete. Also called qiē zhǎng. Also called zhuó shǒu, when downward.

qiē shuāi 切摔 Shearing throw: draw your adversary's hand to the outside while sliding your foot behind him, then do a hip throw while pushing with the arm. From Sanda.

qiē tuǐ 切腿 Shearing kick: a snap kick with the foot hooked and rotated inward, to kick forward and down with the outer edge of the foot, doing a cutting action. See also qiē jiǎo.

qiē wàn 切腕 Cut the wrist: a short, sharp strike at your adversary's wrist with the edge of your hand in order to block an acupoint or break the tendons or blood vessels.

qiē zhǎng 切掌 Cut with the palm. See qiē shǒu.

qiē zǐ 切子 Shearing throws: throws that involve using the upper thigh as the pivot point to take the adversary horizontally around and down. This is a takedown that takes advantage of an opportunity and moves in quickly. From wrestling.

怯 (rad.61) **qiè** 1. Timid; nervous. 2. Timidity, a pattern applied in channel diagnosis. From TCM.

qiè chǎng 怯场 To have stage fright: nervousness before competition or performance.

鍥 [锲] (rad.167) **qiè** 1. A sickle. 2. To cut with an action similar to using a sickle. 3. To carve, engrave.

qiè jiǎo 锲脚 A cutting kick: an inward hooking kick, kicking with the outer edge of the foot. See also qiē jiǎo, qiē tuǐ.

擒 (rad.64) **qín** 1. To seize, catch, capture, grab, grasp. 2. To arrest. 3. Catch, one of Ziranmen's nineteen main methods.

qín dǎ 擒打 Seize and hit.

qín dí quán 擒敌拳 Seize the Enemy fist: a basic routine of Yangjia style, written up as twenty-five moves.

qín fǎ 擒法 Seizing, grabbing techniques.

qín ná 擒拿 Seize and control, grab and control, catch and capture, locking techniques. Includes joint locks, breaks, dislocations, pressure points, and many other close range techniques that make use of the body's weak points and leverage. Usually called Qinna or Chin na in English, for want of a translation.

qín xué 擒穴 Seize a pressure point or acupoint, grabbing with all fingers. See also dǎ xué.

qín zéi qín wáng 擒贼擒王 Seize the Leader to Catch the Bandits. The 18th of the Thirty-six Stratagems of Warfare, which apply to many situations.

秦 (rad.115) **qín** 1. The Qin dynasty (221-207 BC). 2. The traditional name for the area of Shaanxi (shǎn xī) province, used as its short name. 3. A surname.

撳 [揿] (rad.64) **qìn** 1. To press with the hand, push down. 2. An upper body throw: to throw without use of a foot hook, sweep, or lift. From wrestling.

qìn dāo 揿刀 To press down with the blade of a broadsword.

清 [清] (rad.85) **qīng** 1. Clear; pure; clean. 2. Honest. 4. Simple, understandable. 5. The Qing dynasty (1644-1911).

qīng fēng chuān táng 清风穿堂 A Clean Breeze Goes through the Hall: lift the right knee and stand up straight, circle the right wrist to sweep a sword blade flat, then extend, land the foot and step forward to a left bow stance, circling the blade again and extending the blade forward. From Qingping sword.

qīng fēng jiàn 清风剑 Clean Breeze sword: a routine of Yangjia style, emphasizing light and quick movements. Written up as thirty-one moves.

qīng lěng yuān 清冷渊 Acupoint Qinglengyuan (clear cold abyss), SJ11. At the arm, on the back, two *cun* up from the elbow point when it is bent (each arm). From TCM.

qīng qì 清气 Clear *qi*.

蜻 [蜻] (rad.142) **qīng** Dragonfly, usually used in combination as qīng tíng.

qīng tíng diǎn shuǐ 蜻蜓点水 Dragonfly Touches Down on the Pond: dab with a sword, generally in a closed stance, a low T stance or tucked knee stance. From Qingping, Taiji, and Wudang swords.

輕 [轻] (rad.159) **qīng** 1. Lightweight, light. 2. Simple. 3. Gentle. 4. Flippant. 5. To slight, to neglect, to take lightly.

qīng dí 轻敌 To take your adversary (too) lightly.

qīng gōng 轻功 Light skills, jumping and body weightless ability. For example, the ability to do three hits in one jump, or running on the rim of a basket. Also called qīng shēn fǎ, qīng shēn gōng.

qīng líng 轻灵 Light and agile, easy movement in both mind and body.

qīng rú yè 轻如叶 Light like a leaf. Land from jumps lightly, like a leaf floating soundlessly to the ground. One of the twelve qualities of movement of Changquan, though these descriptors apply to many other styles.

qīng shēn fǎ 轻身法 Lightness training methods. See qīng gōng. Also called qīng shēn gōng.

qīng shēn gōng 轻身功 Lightness training, see qīng gōng. Also called qīng shēn gōng.

qīng sōng 轻松 Light. This is a requirement at the advanced level of training internal styles, the body should be light and relaxed.

qīng zhòng 轻重 Both light and heavy.

青 [青] (rad.174) **qīng** 1. A natural colour. May be green, blue, or even black, but most commonly is the green of fresh crops. 2. Young.

qīng fēng chuān táng 青风穿堂 A Fresh Breeze Goes through the Hall: a slight circle to press down, then a direct stab with a staff. From

Q

qīng líng 青灵 Acupoint Qingling (green spirit), HT2. Along the inside of the arm, three *cun* above the elbow crease, on the inner side of the biceps brachii muscle, in a straight line between acupoints Jiquan and Shaohai (on each arm). From TCM. A sensitive point, pressing or striking here can cause numbness in the arm. Too much pressure, however, may induce a heart attack.

qīng lóng bǎi wěi 青龙摆尾 Green Dragon Slashes its Tail. 1. A kick combination with the same leg, inside crescent kick followed by an outside crescent kick. The kicks are no higher than the shoulder, swing to shoulder width, and the kicks are slapped. 2. A flicking kick behind, slapping the foot with the opposite hand. From Shaolinquan. 3. A turning upward slashing move with a sword. From Taijiquan. 4. A full circle slash around and back to the same place with the butt of a staff, hands together at the tip. From Shaolinquan.

qīng lóng chū shuǐ 青龙出水 Green Dragon Emerges from the Water. Usually refers to a punch combination, the exact configuration differs with styles. 1. In Xingyiquan, a retreating straight punch, see bēng quán. 2. In southern styles, a front heel kick from a side lying position on the ground. 3. In Taijiquan, a punch combination or a straight stab with a sword or broadsword. 4. In Baguazhang, a full stepping turning stab with a broadsword. 5. In Chuojiao, a kick behind while double punching in front, laying into the kick with the torso horizontal. 6. In Piguaquan, a raised knee palm chop.

qīng lóng fǎn shēn 青龙返身 Green Dragon Returns: turn the body around to the Green Dragon Reaches Out its Claws position, either standing in place or starting to walk around the circle. From Baguazhang. Also called qīng lóng zhuàn shēn. See also qīng lóng tàn zhuā.

qīng lóng fǎn shǒu 青龙返首 Green Dragon Looks Back. 1. Step out with a turned out foot, while bracing out with the hands, the leading hand at shoulder height, the following hand near the elbow. From Baguazhang. 2. Turn around with a stabbing palm. From Tongbeiquan.

qīng lóng fēi shēng 青龙飞升 Green Dragon Flies Up: staying in character eight (八) stance, turn around while extending the arms to the sides from a crossed position to lift up at shoulder height. From Baguazhang.

qīng lóng huí shǒu 青龙回首 Green Dragon Looks Back: advance the left foot and turn into a T stance, slicing a sword blade to the left, chopping as the right foot touches down, to cut the adversary's head or outside arm. From Qingping sword.

qīng lóng jiàn 青龙剑 Green Dragon sword: a sword routine of Yangjia style that uses many characteristics of the spear. Written up as thirty-six moves.

qīng lóng kàn sǐ rén 青龙看死人 Green Dragon Looks at the Corpse: rising slices with a big cutter, finishing with a strong push. From Chen Taijiquan.

qīng lóng quán 青龙拳 Green Dragon fist, a routine of Piguaquan.

qīng lóng tàn hǎi 青龙探海 Green Dragon Reaches into the Sea. 1. A horse stance snapping palm. From Piguaquan. 2. A balance with the leg lifted straight to the rear, the body leaning forward, a sword stabbing forward and down, such that the leg, body, and sword form one line. From Yangjia sword.

qīng lóng tàn zhuā 青龙探爪 Green Dragon Reaches out its Claws. 1. Reach out with one hand, keeping the other at the elbow. A common on guard or attacking position in Baguazhang, often held in circle-walking. 2. To lift the knee and extend the same palm forward, extending the other palm to the rear. 3. To grab the floating ribs. 4. A threading strike to the throat. 5. A reaching grab to the face. From Baguazhang, one of its sixty-four hands.

qīng lóng tǔ wù 青龙吐雾 Green Dragon Spits Out a Mist: shoot a spear out, leaning forward and lifting a straight leg behind for full reach.

qīng lóng tǔ xū 青龙吐鬚 Green Dragon Spits its Beard: a stab, either in straight or reverse grip, bringing a sword from high to stab low and moving to bow stance, extending the sword. From Wudang sword.

qīng lóng xiàn zhuā 青龙现爪 Green Dragon Shows its Claws: reach the left hand forward, stepping into it and stabbing straight forward with a sword. From Yang Taijiquan.

qīng lóng xiàn zhuā shì 青龙现爪式 Green Dragon Shows its Claws model. One of twenty-four classic spear moves. Most spear routines will have a move with a like name. In general, this name refers to a one handed stab done with the shaft of the spear lying along the arm and back.

qīng lóng yǎn yuè dāo 青龙偃月刀 Green Dragon Lying Moon Blade: a halberd with the blade in the shape of a new moon.

qīng lóng zhuàn shēn 青龙转身 Green Dragon Turns Around: see qīng lóng fǎn shēn.

qīng píng jiàn 青平剑 Qingping straight sword. 1. A traditional sword routine. 2. A traditional style of swordplay, with six routines. Also written 青萍剑.

qīng píng jiàn 青萍剑 Qingping straight sword. See qīng píng jiàn above.

qīng shào nián sài 青少年赛 Junior category competition: competition for ages twelve to eighteen.

qīng shé chū dòng 青蛇出洞 Green Snake Emerges from its Hole: Step to horse stance, gathering the fist to the shoulder, then turn to bow stance and punch directly (in reverse stance). From Meishanquan and other southern styles.

擎 (rad.64) **qíng**   To lift up; to prop up; to hold up.

qíng tiān zhù 擎天柱 Pillar Supporting the Sky: in reverse bow stance, push the hand directly upwards, the other at the hip. From Wudangquan.

請 [请] (rad.149) **qǐng**   1. To invite. 2. To request.

qǐng shǒu 情手 Inviting Hands: holding the hands out in front, elbows bent, palms up. The front hand is at throat height, the rear hand is at its elbow. From Shaolinquan.

丘 (rad.1) **qiū**   A hillock; mound.

qiū xū 丘墟 Acupoint Qiuxu (hill ruins), GB40. At the foot, on the outside, in the depression under the ankle bone, at the insertion of the extensor digitorum longus (on each foot). From TCM.

秋 (rad.115) **qiū**   1. Autumn. 2. Harvest time.

qiū fēng sǎo yè 秋风扫叶 Autumn Breeze Sweeps the Leaves. 1. A back sweep kick. 2. Starting with the hands at the tip of a staff, slide the left hand then switch the right hand also to the butt, swinging across horizontally with both hands, in a cross grip. From Shaolinquan staff.

qiū shuǐ qiě liàn 秋水且练 Autumnal Waters (limpid eyes of a woman) Practise: retreat with a hooking sweep of the blade out to the side, blade handing vertically, standing up with both arms extended out to shoulder height at the sides. From Qingping sword.

求 (rad.85) **qiú**   1. To strive for. 2. To beg, request. 3. To seek, try.

qiú jìn fǎ 求进法 Seek to enter method: to keep very close to the adversary in defense.

球毬 (rad.96, 82) [球] (rad.96) **qiú** A ball, a sphere. Things that are shaped like a ball.

qiú hòu 球后 Extraordinary acupoint Qiuhou (behind the ball), EX-HN7. At the face, on the lower eye socket, about three fourths towards the outside (on each side). From TCM.

屈 (rad.44) **qū**   1. To bend. 2. Bent, crooked, curved.

qū dūn dīng bù 屈蹲丁步 Squatting T stance: a T stance with the legs bent.

qū shēn xìng tuǐ fǎ 屈伸性腿法 Snap kicks, cocked kicks: the category of kicks that goes from flexion to extension. See, for example, cǎi tuǐ, chán tuǐ, chǎn tuǐ, chuài tuǐ, dēng tuǐ, diǎn tuǐ, fēn jiǎo, gōu tī, héng dīng tuǐ, hòu guà tuǐ, hǔ wěi tuǐ, quān tuǐ, tán tuǐ.

qū tuǐ píng héng 屈腿平衡 Bent leg balances: in competition styles, balances when the supporting leg is bent, usually at least to thigh parallel to the ground.

qū tuō 屈脱 Flexing release, an escape from a wrist grab and control: first rotate outwards then bend the elbow forcefully to bring the forearm in.

qū yāo 屈腰 Flex the back: to tuck in the trunk.

qū zhǒu 屈肘 Flex the elbow. 1. From a straight

Q

arm, snap the fist in, leaving the bent elbow forward. 2. Bend the elbow to press down with the forearm.

曲 麯 (rad.73, 199) [曲] (rad.73) **qū** 1. To bend, flex. 2. Bent, flexed, curved. 3. One of Xingyiquan's eight requirements, for the elbows, knees, and wrists.

qū bìn 曲鬢 Acupoint Qubin (temporal hairline curve), GB7. At the head, at the hairline above and in front of the ear, at the height of the top of the ear (on each side). From TCM.

qū chā 曲差 Acupoint Qucha (deviating turn), BL4. At the head, 0.5 *cun* into the hairline, 1.5 *cun* lateral to the midline, 0.5 *cun* lateral to acupoint Meichong (on each side). From TCM.

qū chí (xué) 曲池(穴) Acupoint Quchi (pool at the bend), LI11. At the elbow crease, on the midline of the arm (on each arm). From TCM. A sensitive point, pressing or striking here can cause numbness and pain. In internal styles it is thought that keeping the elbow joints slightly bent allows the *qi* to flow along the arms through to the wrists and hands.

qū gǔ 曲骨 Acupoint Qugu (curved bone), RN2. At the abdomen, at the level of the hip joints, 5 *cun* below the navel, on the midline. From TCM.

qū quán 曲泉 Acupoint Ququan (spring at the bend), LR8. At the knee, on the inside, near the end of the femur, in front of the tendons of the semi-membranosus and semi-tendinosus (on each leg). From TCM.

qū xī bù 曲膝步 Bent knees stance: a hunkered squat, tucking the rear knee at the front ankle.

qū xī kāi kuà 曲膝开胯 Bend the knees and open the hip area. A requirement of Chen Taijiquan, among others.

qū yāo 曲腰 Bent waist: to lean over at the waist or hump the upper back. An error in most styles.

qū yuán 曲垣 Acupoint Quyuan (crooked wall), SI13. At the upper back, in the depression at the medial end of the supraspinous fossa (on each side). From TCM.

qū zé (xué) 曲泽(穴) Acupoint Quze (marsh at the bend), PC3. At the elbow, on the crease, in the depression on the inside of the biceps brachii tendon (on each arm). From TCM.

趨 [趋] (rad.156) **qū** To hasten, go quickly.

qū bù 趋步 Hastening step: step forward, then bring the rear foot quickly in to hit the front foot, hastening the lead foot forward with a low skip/hop action.

qū gōng bù 趋弓步 Hastening bow step: bring the rear foot quickly in to hit the front foot, hastening it forward into a bow stance.

軀 [躯] (rad.158) **qū** The human body.

qū gàn 躯干 The torso, the trunk of the body.

圈 (rad.31) **quān** 1. A circle. 2. To encircle; an encircling hand technique. 3. A circular quality of movement. 4. A ring: a circular bladed weapon about thirty centimetres in diameter. Traditional rings have curved blades on the outside, performance rings just have silk flags. 5. The category of circling kicks of Chuojiao. 6. Pronounced juān, to open in, shut in a pen; lock up, put in jail.

quān bì 圈臂 Arm wrap. 1. A wrestling grip: tuck the arm around the adversary's arms to throw. Also referred to as quān. Also called sǐ gē bei. 2. A release from a grab on the back of the belt. Encircle the grabbing arm with your near arm, turning and extending your leg to trip and throw.

quān biān 圈鞭 Encircling whip: see quān qiáo.

quān bù 圈步 Circling steps: circle the foot in then outward as it steps forward, to intrude into your adversary's stance. Used for close contact attacking.

quān chuài tuǐ 圈踹腿 Encircle with the leg then side kick: trap then side kick. From Chuojiao, one of its middle-basin kicks.

quān chuí 圈捶 Encircling punch: a hook punch to the ear, hitting inward with the fist centre down and the wrist cocked, using the waist to swing the arm with the elbow slightly bent. From Piguaquan.

quān diǎn tuǐ 圈点腿 Encircle with the leg then poke kick: trap then poke. From Chuojiao, one of its middle-basin kicks.

quān duò tuǐ 圈跺腿 Encircle with the leg then low side kick: trap then side kick to the knee. From Chuojiao, one of its middle-basin kicks.

quān gē shǒu 圈割手 Circling cut: hook and circle the hand and forearm. From Wing Chun.

quān jiàn 圈剑 Encircle with a sword blade.

quān jiǎo 圈脚 Encircle with the lower leg, hooking in.

quān kòu bù 圈扣步 Circling hook in step: step the rear foot forward with a curving hook in step.

quān nèi 圈内 Inside the circle, within range: within the range of your ability or your weapon's ability to strike immediately.

quān qiāng 圈枪 Encircle with a spear.

quān qiáo 圈桥 Encircling bridge. 1. A vertical circle of the forearm with the elbow bent, pivoting around the elbow, rotating inward or outward. 2. Bend the elbow to bring the fist back horizontally, leaving the elbow out in front of the body. From southern styles. Also called quān biān.

quān shǒu 圈手 Circling hand. 1. Raise and circle the hand. 2. In Wing Chun: with an extended arm, turn the palm up, hook the wrist and circle until the palm is down, and finish with a straight punch.

quān tiào bù 圈跳步 Circling jump step: push off with the feet and snap the waist to turn ninety degrees, barely leaving the ground with the feet. The front foot turns on the spot and the rear foot turns and comes in closer to the front foot. From wrestling.

quān tuǐ 圈腿 Circling leg: an inside crescent kick with the knee bending then curling inward. In the category of snap kicks, see also qū shēn xìng tuǐ fǎ.

quān wài 圈外 Outside the circle, not within range: outside the range of you or your weapon's ability to strike immediately.

quān zhǒu 圈肘 Elbow circle: draw a vertical circle with the elbow bent, applying power to the forearm. Used to control a straight punch.

全 (rad.11) quán   1. Complete. 2. To make complete. 3. Whole; entire.

quán dūn 全蹲 A full squat: with the heels on the ground, squat down to sit on them.

quán néng 全能 All-round event at a competition, for the title of the all-round champion.

quán néng guān jūn 全能冠军 All-round champion: leader in points of Taolu competition, adding up the scores of all the events (or a specific number of events, determined by the organization).

quán wǔ huā 全舞花 Complete flourishing of the flowers: turning flowers with a big cutter, turning a full circle to both the left and the right. From Chen Taijiquan.

拳 (rad.64) quán   1. Fist. 2. Bare-handed training. 3. Martial arts and martial arts styles in general. 4. With the name of a routine indicates that it is bare hand.

For names of punches that use this term for fist, see also under bā quán, bǎi-, bān-, bào-, bēng-, biān-, biāo-, bō-, cè bēng-, cè shēn-, chāo-, chē zuān-, chēng-, chōng diǎn-, chōng-, chōu zhuàng-, chuí-, chuō-, cì-, cuán-, dīng-, dǐng-, dǒu-, duì-, fǎn bèi-, fǎn chōng-, fēi-, fēn zhuàng-, gài-, gōu-, guà gài-, guà pī-, guà-, guàn-, guàn-, gǔn léi-, héng chōng-, hēng kòu-, héng-, hù xīn-, huò xīn-, jī sān-, jiǎ-, jià chōng-, jià-, jiàn-, jiàn-, jié-, jiǔ-, juǎn-, kāi mén-, kòu-, lēi-, lèi-, lián huán-, liāo-, lūn bì zá-, mō sǎo-, pāo-, pāo zhuàng-, pào-, pī-, rì zì chōng-, sǎo-, shàng bù duì-, shàng duì-, shàng gōu-, shí zì bēng-, shí zì dé-, shuāng chōng-, shuāng-, shuāng zhū-, tán-, tàn hǎi-, tāo-, tí-, tí xī chōng-, tí xī tiào chōng-, tiē kào-, tōu gǔ-, wō dù-, xié sǎo-, yán shǒu chōng-, yāo bù-, yē-, yíng miàn-, zá-, zāi-, zhǎn-, zhé shǒu-, zhèng-, zhí-, zhōng-, zhuàng-, zuān-, zuàn-.

quán bèi 拳背 Fist's back surface.

quán chǎng 拳场 A training ground, a place generally accepted in a park where the martial artists practice.

quán dǎ qiān biàn shēn fǎ zì rán 拳打千遍身法自然 You must do a move a thousand times before the bodywork becomes natural. A martial saying.

quán fǎ 拳法 1. Bare-handed methods, as distinguished from weapons methods. 2. Fist techniques as distinguished from palm or forearm techniques.

quán fēng 拳锋 Fist's peak edge, the knuckles.

quán gēn 拳根 The fist's meaty part, at the base,

Q

the heel of the fist.

quán jīng 拳经 Martial classics, the classic written texts of the martial arts.

quán jué 拳诀 Martial formula or verse. See gē jué.

quán lǐ 拳礼 Salute. Right fist in left palm is a common salute. In Chinese martial arts the salute is given at attention, not bowing.

quán lǐ 拳理 Martial theory: the theoretical foundation behind a system or style of martial art.

quán liàn qiān biàn shēn fǎ zì rán 拳练千遍身法自然 A martial saying. See quán dǎ qiān biàn shēn fǎ zì rán.

quán lún 拳轮 The meaty part of the fist.

quán mén 拳门 A style, or type, of martial art.

quán miàn 拳面 Fist face, first finger segments surface, the normal punching surface of the knuckles.

quán pài 拳派 A school or branch of martial art that differs from other styles.

quán pǔ 拳谱 Martial record, classic manual of a style: a record of the lineage, technique names, methods and other information on a style for posterity.

quán shī 拳师 A colloquial term for a martial arts master, especially one who has students.

quán shì 拳势 1. Martial movements, postures. 2. The momentum of a fight.

quán shù 拳术 1. A style of martial art. 2. The category of empty hand routines in competition.

quán sì líu xīng 拳似流星 The fist is like a shooting star: one of the basic qualities of many styles.

quán sì liú xīng yǎn sì diàn 拳似流星眼似电 The fists should be like shooting stars and the eyes should be like lightning. A martial saying. See also shǒu sì liú xīng yǎn sì diàn.

quán tán 拳坛 Martial circles, the martial community. See wǔ lín.

quán wáng 拳王 King of the ring, a fighting champion.

quán wú quán yì wú yì, wú yì zhī zhōng shì zhēn yì 拳无拳意无意,无意之中是真意 When the techniques have no planned technique, and the mind has no set ideas, then within this mindlessness lies the real mind. A martial saying.

quán xì 拳系 A style of martial art that has an organized syllabus of theory and techniques.

quán xīn 拳心 Fist heart, fist centre, fist core (the palm side of a clenched fist).

quán yǎn 拳眼 Fist eye: the thumb side of the fist, where the thumb and index finger curl together, looking like an eye.

quán yàn 拳谚 Martial saying, an adage, a saying: short, pithy explanations of martial theory, to aid understanding and memory.

quán zhǒng 拳种 A style, or type, of martial art.

quán zhǒu zǔ dǎng 拳肘阻挡 Fist and elbow block: with the arms held up in on guard position, lift the arms to cover up to absorb an incoming punch.

颧 [颧] (rad.181) quán Relating to the cheek bone or cheek area.

quán liáo 颧髎 Acupoint Quanliao (cheek bone-hole), SI19. At the face, down from the corner of the eye, in the depression just below the cheekbone (on each side). From TCM.

犬 (rad.94) quǎn 1. A dog (literary, not normally used in speech). 2. Dog, as the eleventh of the twelve animals from the Chinese zodiac, associated with a twelve year cycle symbolic of the earthly branches. The twelve animals make up a sixty year cycle when combined with the five phases. See also dì zhī, shēng xiào, wǔ xíng.

quǎn quán 犬拳 Dog fist, a hand shape: fingers bent just up to the crease of the palm, thumb pressed on the distal segment of the middle finger, so that the second segment of the fingers and the outer edge of the thumb form a flat punching surface. From southern styles.

勸 [劝] (rad.19) quàn Advice. To urge. Try to persuade.

quàn gào 劝告 Admonish: the stage prior to giving a warning to an athlete in a Sanda or wrestling match, for a minor infraction of the rules.

缺 (rad.121) quē 1. To be short of, lack. 2. Incomplete, imperfect. 3. Be absent.

quē dé 缺得 Lack (martial) virtue, wicked, villainous.

quē pén 缺盆 Acupoint Quepen (empty basin), ST12. At the depression above the clavicle, about 4 *cun* lateral to the midline, directly above the nipples (on each side). From TCM. A sensitive point, pressure here can induce coughing. This is a good point to hook the fingers in to catch the collarbone.

雀 (rad.172) què 1. A sparrow. 2. In Chen village dialect it means to tunnel forward.

què bù 雀步 Sparrow steps: hop forward on the balls of the feet, both taking off and landing on both feet.

què dì lóng 雀地龙 Dragon on the Ground, Dragon Dive, Tunnel After Worms: drop to squat on one leg with the other outstretched with the heel on the ground, toes up. This is properly done with the supporting knee on the ground in a hurdler's position, but may be done without putting it down. Used as a counter attack. From Chen Taijiquan. Similar to qián pō tuǐ. Also called yuè cèn, pū dì mián. In other styles the whole foot may be on the ground, instead of lifting the toes.

què tiào 雀跳 Sparrow hop: jump forward, pushing off with the balls of the feet, jumping and landing with both feet simultaneously. From southern styles.

鵲 [鹊] (rad.196) què A magpie.

què yuè bù 鹊跃步 Magpie leaping steps. 1. A long leap forward, raising the knee while pushing off with the other leg. 2. Continuous jumps on one leg with the other bent to keep off the ground.

群 (rad.123) qún 1. A group, a multitude. 2. A flock, a herd.

qún yáng gùn 群羊棍 Flock of sheep staff, a representative routine of Chaquan, written up as fifty-eight moves.

裙 (rad.145) qún A skirt.

qún tuǐ 裙腿 Skirt kick: hook up the foot and kick out, scraping the heel on the ground, kicking the adversary's shin with the sole of the foot. From Chuojiao.

qún lán 裙拦 Skirt trap: a large opening dodge with a spear.

Q

R

然 (rad.86) **rán**   1. Right, correct. 2. So; like that.

rán gǔ 然谷 Acupoint Rangu (blazing valley) KI2. At the foot, on the inside, at the proximal end of the big toe's metatarsal bone, at the line of the lighter and darker skin (on each foot). From TCM.

讓 [让] (rad.149) **ràng**   1. To give way; give ground; yield; concede. 2. Let, allow. Offer. 3. As one of the eight attack and defense models, to move to the side, not engaging on the midline. See also bā zì gōng fáng fǎ zé.

ràng tī 让踢 Conceding kick: immediately on making contact, pull across to twist your adversary and kick behind his ankle, twisting to take him down on his back. From wrestling.

橈 [桡] (rad.75) **ráo**   An oar, oars.

ráo cè wàn cháng shēn jī 桡侧腕长伸肌 Extensor carpi radialis longus muscle: a forearm muscle, on the outside, the backhand side. Assists in wrist and finger extension, pulling the back of the hand up towards the forearm.

ráo cè wàn qū jī 桡侧腕屈肌 Flexor carpi radialis muscle: a forearm muscle, on the inside, the palm side. Assists in wrist and finger flexion, pulling the palm and fingers towards the forearm.

ráo gǔ 桡骨 Radius, one of the principle bones of the forearm. The radius is smaller at the elbow and becomes the principle bone at the wrist, at the thumb side. It pivots around the ulna for supination and pronation of the hand. See also chǐ gǔ.

繞 [绕] (rad.120) **rào**   1. To go around, detour. 2. To move around; circle. 2. To wind, coil.

rào bì 绕臂 Wind around the upper arm, into the armpit, to control it while moving in for a throw. From wrestling.

rào bù 绕步 Step around, roundabout step.

rào fǎ 绕法 Detouring methods: Stepping around to avoid or counter attack. Also called guǎi fǎ.

rào hóu chuān gùn (qiāng) 绕喉穿棍(枪) Thread a staff (or spear) past your throat: with the shaft horizontal, bring the tip towards the throat, sliding it through the left hand, then shoot it past to the back.

rào mǎ tuǐ 绕码腿 1. Roundabout kick: cock the leg with the foot turned out and up, then thrust to knee height. This will, for example, kick your adversary's left knee to his left with your right foot. 2. Roundabout Kicks, the fifth of Chuojiao's nine literary routines, written up as thirty-nine moves. See also wén tàng zi.

rào tuǐ huàn bà chuān qiāng 绕腿换把穿枪 Thread a spear past the leg, switching grip: lift a leg and thread the spear tip out through underneath it. Start out holding a spear in both hands, and switch grips quickly as the spear passes under the leg.

rào tóu guà bì 绕头挂臂 Coil the head and hook the arm, a steep whip technique: vertical circles in front of the body, bring the whip to the neck but lifting the hand so that it continues and hooks to the elbow, continuing the circles.

rào yāo chuān qiāng 绕腰穿枪 Thread a spear past the waist: thread the left hand from behind the back to take the spear tip on the right side and pull it back to the left. Slide the right hand and push the spear to the left so that the spear tip and shaft stabs out sticking close to the back. When the spear butt reaches the left hand, turn and take it in the right hand.

熱 [热] (rad.86) **rè**   1. Hot. Heat. 2. Fever. 3. Summerheat, humid heat: one of the six *qi* of nature, environmental influences that can cause disease when in excess. Also called shǔ. See also liù qì, liù yín.

rè shēn liàn xí 热身练习 Warm-up exercises. More commonly called zhǔn bèi huó dòng.

R

人 (rad.9) **rén** Person; people, humanity.

rén bù zhī wǒ, wǒ dú zhī rén 人不知我我独知人 Only I figure out my adversary, he must not figure me out. A martial saying.

rén qiāng wéi yī tǐ, yóu rú qīng lóng xì shuǐ 人枪为一体犹如青龙戏水 Man and spear move as one, moving as smoothly as a green dragon playing in water. A martial saying.

rén suí dāo zǒu, dāo suí rén zhuàn 人随刀走刀随人转 The person follows the broadsword, the broadsword turns with the person. From Baguazhang. Describes the harmony of movement required with the broadsword.

rén suí jiàn zǒu, jiàn suí rén xuàn 人随剑走剑随人旋 The person follows the sword, the sword whirls with the person. From Baguazhang. Describes the harmony of movement required with the sword.

rén yíng 人迎 Acupoint Renying (person's welcome), ST9. At the neck, about 1.5 *cun* behind the larynx, at the forward border of the sternocleidomastoid muscle (on each side). From TCM. Hitting here causes blockage of *qi* and blood and induces dizziness.

rén zhōng 人中 Sensitive point Renzhong (person's centre), colloquial term for acupoint Shuigou. See shuǐ gōu.

rén zì shì 人字式 Character for person position: standing with the legs open to shoulder width, hands down at the sides, held out at a forty-five degree angle, similar to the character 人. Used during *qigong* training.

仁 (rad.9) **rén** Kindness, humaneness, benevolence, kind-heartedness.

rén yì 仁义 Benevolence and virtue. A character trait expected of martial artists.

壬 (rad.33) **rén** The ninth of the ten Celestial Stems, used in combination with the twelve Terrestrial Branches to designate years, months, days, and hours. See also dì zhī, tiān gān. 2. Ninth in a list when listing using the celestial stems, equivalent to I in English when listing alphabetically.

rén chén 壬辰 The years 2012, 1952 and so on, for sixty year cycles.

rén shēn 壬申 The years 1992, 1932 and so on, for sixty year cycles.

rén wǔ 壬午 The years 2002, 1942, and so on, for sixty year cycles.

rén yín 壬寅 The years 1962, 1902, and so on, for sixty year cycles.

rén xū 壬戌 The years 1982, 1922, and so on, for sixty year cycles.

rén zǐ 壬子 The years 1972, 1912, and so on, for sixty year cycles.

忍 (rad.61) **rěn** 1. To endure; tolerate; bear. 2. Tolerance.

任 (rad.9) **rèn** 1. A duty. 2. To bear (a burden). 3. To take control. 4. An official post.

rèn mài 任脉 Conception vessel (CV), Ren meridian (RN). Flows up from the Mingmen to the Huiyin, in the front of the body. From TCM. In most internal styles, at least, the torso is held straight to allow the flow of *qi* in this important channel, which regulates the *yin* channels in the body.

刃 [刃] (rad.18) **rèn, rènr** The sharp edge, or cutting edge, of a bladed weapon.

韌 [韧] (rad.178) **rèn** Elastic; soft but tough; pliable and strong.

rèn dài 韧带 Ligament, ligaments.

rèn dài niǔ shāng 韧带扭伤 A strained ligament; a ligament strain.

rèn dài sī liè 韧带撕裂 A torn ligament; a ligament tear.

扔 (rad.64) **rēng** Throw; toss.

rēng gōu zǐ 扔勾子 Toss the hook. See tiāo tuǐ.

rēng shā dài 扔砂袋 Toss a sandbag: a training method for grip, wrist, and arm strength. There are a variety of methods, including tossing one handed to yourself and tossing back and forth between people.

rēng zhì zǐ 扔制子 Toss the implement: tossing a

stone lock, to train grip strength, power and hand eye coordination. Nowadays we use kettlebells in the same way. See also shí suǒ.

日 (rad.72) **rì** Sun. Daytime; day.

rì kuà shuāng ěr 日挎双耳 Sun Carries the Ears: circle-walking with the inside hand pressing down at the hip, the outside hand pressing up over the head, both arms slightly bent. From Baguazhang.

rì tào sān huán 日套三环 Three Rings around the Sun: sweep a broadsword around at knee height, turning around fully, step into back cross stance lifting the blade, then chop. From Taijiquan.

rì yuè 日月 Acupoint Riyue (sun and moon), GB24. At the abdomen, at the level of the seventh intercostal space, four *cun* lateral to the midline (on each side). From TCM.

rì yuè bìng xíng 日月并行 Sun and Moon Move Together. 1. A double pushing shove, hands held together, palms forward, fingers up and down. 2. A simultaneous direct strike with the hands together, one open palm and one fist, or open hands. From Baguazhang, one of its sixty-four hands. 3. Holding the deerhorn blades out in ready posture, hooks forward. From Baguazhang. 4. An expressive term for the category of pushing methods, see also tuī fǎ.

rì yuè shuāng lián 日月双链 Sun and Moon sickle. See yuān yáng yuè. Also called lù jiǎo dāo, qián kūn jiàn, shuāng yuè, zǐ wǔ yuān yáng yuè.

rì zì chōng quán 日字冲拳 Sun character punch: a thrusting punch with an upright fist. The fist placement is called lì quán, rì zì quán.

rì zì měng jiàn 日字猛箭 Fierce Arrow Sun Punch: a horse stance with a right upright punch. The 99th move of the tiger and crane routine.

rì zì quán 日字拳 Sun character fist, a placement description: a punch with an upright fist, fist eye up, knuckles forward. Looked at head on, resembles the character 日. Also called lì quán, zhèng quán.

揉 (rad.64) **róu** To knead, rub.

róu cuǒ 揉搓 Knead: grab an adversary and extend one segment of his body outwards while withdrawing another.

róu fǎ 揉法 Kneading methods of healing. From TCM.

róu qiú gōng 揉球功 Ball rolling training: rolling a small ball or balls in the palm of the hand or hands. The balls are usually stone or metal, sometimes with bells inside. The size and weight of the balls is as you prefer.

róu qiú shì lì 揉球试力 Ball rolling testing power: stand in sixty-forty stance, hold the arms in front of the chest as if holding a ball, press forward with the back of the front hand. From Yiquan, one of its combat testing moves.

róu qiú zhǎng 揉球掌 Trundle the ball palm, a circle-walking posture: the reverse of the carry the spear palm, arms in the same position, but palms in as if holding a ball. From Baguazhang. See also tuō qiāng zhǎng.

róu yāo 揉腰 Trundle the waist, a stretching exercise: the athlete lies face up across a bench, legs straight and arms extended overhead. A helper presses the chest and thighs and rolls the victim back and forth to loosen the waist.

柔 (rad.75) **róu** Soft; supple, flexible; yielding, gentle. Pliant, pliable like bamboo.

róu jìn 柔劲 Soft, rounded, gentle, pliant power.

róu rèn 柔韧 Supple. This is a requirement at the intermediate level of training, the body must be pliable yet tough.

róu rèn xìng 柔韧性 Flexibility and strength of the tendons and ligaments.

róu shǒu 柔手 1. Push hands practice. From Taijiquan. 2. Soft connected partner practice.

róu zhōng yǒu gāng gōng bù pò 柔中有刚攻不破 When there is a core of hardness within pliancy, no attack can break it. A martial saying.

肉 (rad.130) **ròu** 1. Flesh. 2. Meat. 3. Pulp of fruit.

ròu shāo 肉梢 The muscle tip: the tongue. The visible part of the body in which the energy of the muscles is expressed.

儒 (rad.9) **rú** 1. Scholars, learned people. 2. Confucian.

rú bù 儒步 Glide walking, walking with an entering step. From Baguazhang.

如 (rad.38) **rú** 1. As if; like. 2. Supposing. 3. In compliance with.

rú fēng sì bì 如封似闭 Apparent Close-off, Seal off, Shut down: a counter attack that gathers and then closes the door, or shuts down an adversary. The final action is some version of moving forward and pressing down and away. From Taijiquan. Also called liù fēng sì bì.

蠕 (rad.142) **rú** 1. A worm. 2. To wiggle; squirm.

rú xíng bù 蠕行步 Worm walking: stand firmly on one leg, kick just under the belly of the calf by hooking the other foot and bringing it in to kick lightly. The impetus of the kick moves the supporting foot forward. Continue, alternating feet. Both toughens the legs and relaxes them.

乳 (rad.5) **rǔ** Nipples of the breast.

rǔ fáng 乳房 A breast.

rǔ fáng gēn 乳房根 Colloquial term for acupoint Rugen. See rǔ gēn.

rǔ gēn 乳根 Acupoint Rugen, (root of the nipples) (ST18). Under the nipples, in the fifth intercostal space, four *cun* lateral to the midline (on each side). From TCM.

rǔ tóu 乳头 The nipples, a colloquial term.

rǔ yàn xié fēi 乳燕斜飞 Fledging Swallow Tilts in Flight: a turning slice up with one arm (thumb web up) while pulling down with the other. From Baguazhang.

rǔ zhōng 乳中 Acupoint Ruzhong (centre of the nipples) (ST17). At the nipples, in the fourth intercostal space, four *cun* lateral to the midline (on each side). From TCM. A sensitive point, striking it can induce breathlessness.

入 (rad.11) **rù** 1. To enter. 2. To arrive at. 3. To put in. 4. To get inside. 5. To join, become a member. 6. One of the falling hands in Chuojiao, see also luò shǒu.

rù jìn 入劲 Entry power: to enter into gaps or weakness left by the adversary in his attack.

rù kōng 入空 Enter empty, a wrestling basics exercise done solo to develop footwork, coordination, and waist strength. Step in with a cross-step as if grabbing an adversary and execute a full bowing throw. Repeat. From wrestling.

rù mén 入门 Entered the door: to have a basic knowledge of, to be ready for more profound study of something. Said of someone who shows some ability and basic mastery of skills.

rù qiāng 入枪 Enter a spear: enter the inside line of your adversary with your body and the spear.

rù shǒu ér tōu shǒu 入手而偷手 Steal in to an entering hand: counter attack before the adversary's attack has landed, so he cannot react. From Tanglangquan, one of its twelve soft counters, see also shí èr róu.

撋 (rad.64) **ruán** To rub between the hands. Also written with 日 instead of 王, but there is no character like this in the keyboard entry system.

ruán shǒu 撋手 Rubbing hands: a crossing block down in front of the body with the forearms and edge of palm. A mid to low level block. From Wing Chun. Pronounced gaun-sau in Cantonese.

軟 [软] (rad.159) **ruǎn** 1. Soft, supple, pliable. 2. Pliability, one of Ziranmen's nineteen main methods. 3. Mild. 4. Weak.

ruǎn gōng 软功 Flexibility exercises.

ruǎn gǔ 软骨 Cartilage.

ruǎn gǔ gōng 软骨功 Cartilage training, flexibility training. Various stretching exercises, especially for the hips and back.

ruǎn jìn 软劲 Soft power, relaxed and smooth.

ruǎn mén 软门 Soft door: the front edges of a wrestling jacket, at the belt. Also called xiǎo mén.

ruǎn qì xiè 软器械 Soft weapons: the category of weapons that are constructed with iron links or ropes, that can be folded or rolled up.

ruǎn shé quán 软蛇拳 Pliable snake routine: a routine of Tongbeiquan, written up as twenty-one moves.

ruǎn shǒu 软手 Flaccid hands: overly soft, all *yin*

with little *yang* power.

ruǎn tuǐ 软腿 Flaccid legs: no strength in the legs, unstable stances. An error in most styles.

銳 [锐] (rad.167) ruì   1. Sharp. 2. A blade, usually on a double weapon.

潤 [润] (rad.85) rùn 1. Moist; smooth. 2. To moisten, lubricate. 3. Moistening treatment of channels. From TCM.

S

S xíng bù S 行步 Walking in an S shape. See chuān lín bù.

撒 (rad.64) sā, sǎ 1. To scatter; to disperse; cast. 2. An expansive throw, swinging the adversary horizontally.

sǎ dà wǎng 撒大网 Cast a Big Net, a large throw, holding your adversary's belt and swinging him horizontally (this needs a fair bit of strength and good timing).

sǎ shǒu 撒手 Block by hitting your adversary's attacking hand (with an action like scattering seeds).

腮 顋 (rad.130, 181) [腮] (rad.130) sāi The cheeks (of the face).

sāi gǔ 腮骨 The cheek bones.

三 (rad.1) sān Three. Thrice.

sān bǎo 三宝 The three treasures, or valuable things. In nature, the sun, moon, and stars. In humans, essence (see jīng), qi (see qì), and spirit (see shén).

sān bào 三抱 Three holdings: the *dantian* holds the qi, bravery holds the body, and the elbows hold the ribs. From Xingyiquan, one of its requirements

sān bìng 三病 Three diseases: see sān jí.

sān bù gòu 三不够 Three Insufficiencies: inadequate duration of training, inadequate angle of stance, inadequate intent. Any one of these three may prevent you from advancing in stake standing. From Yiquan.

sān bù luò 三不落 Three Without Landing: a three kick combination – front slap kick, landing with a hop slap to the other foot kicked up to the buttocks, then a flying outside crescent kick. From northern styles.

sān bù wěn 三不紊 The three 'not disorderly': the mind must not be flustered, the hands must not be rushed, and the feet must not be confused.

sān cái 三才 The three attributes, three powers. 1. Heavens, humanity, and earth. 2. Head, hands, and feet; the upper, middle, and lower basins of the body. 3. Body, spirit, and *qi*.

sān cái bù 三才步 Three attribute stepping: advance the lead foot at an angle, bring the rear foot to the ankle and advance it at an angle. Also called shé xíng qián bù.

sān cái zhuāng 三才桩 Three attribute standing. Varies with style, usually is a seventy-thirty stance with the front hand forward at eyebrow height and the rear hand at the *dantian*. The name 'three attributes' emphasizes the internal meaning, that it is not just a posture, but is a type of training to develop deep ability. From Xingyiquan. Some branches of Xingyiquan use this name instead of sān tǐ shì. Also called sān tǐ shì zhuāng, zǐ wǔ zhuāng.

sān chā pá 三叉耙 A three tined rake.

sān chuān zhǎng 三穿掌 Three piercing palms: three quick stabs with alternate hands. From Baguazhang and Wudangquan.

sān chuí 三垂 Three hangings, three sinkings: the qi, shoulders, and elbows should be dropped or sunken. From Xingyiquan, one of its requirements.

sān cuī 三催 Three Urgings, or Three Pushes: pressing the distal segments of the body forward from the proximal segments to create a whole body power. The waist urges the shoulders forward, the shoulders urge the elbows, and the elbows urge the hands.

sān dào 三到 The three arrivals: in completion of a move, the eyes, hands, and feet must arrive together in a coordinated way.

sān dào yāo 三道腰 Three Ways with the Waist, a takedown. See dà dé hé Also called lǐ dāo gōu, lǐ gōu.

sān diǎn yī xiàn 三点一线 Three points one line: a reference to spear technique. The tip and both hands should form a straight line.

sān dīng zhǎng 三丁掌 Three T palm, a hand shape: thumb tucked in, fingers separated, index and middle fingers extended, ring and small fingers bent.

sān dǐng 三顶 Three presses, three pressings, three pushing against: the crown of the head should press up, the palms should press forward or outward, and the tongue should press up to the palate. From Baguazhang and Xingyiquan.

sān dú 三毒 Three poisonous things: the heart/mind, the eyes, and the hands should be fierce. From Xingyiquan, one of its requirements.

sān guān 三关 Three passes. 1. Three ways in that must be protected or that give a way in on the adversary. The shoulders, elbows, and wrists are the three passes of the upper limbs. The hips, knees and ankles are the three passes of the lower limbs. 2. The three passes in meridian flow in the torso: three sets of acupoints in the torso that must be unblocked to allow the others to flow (the Spine Squeezing pass, the Coccyx pass, and the Jade Pillow pass). See also jiā jǐ guān, wěi lū guān, yù zhěn guān.

sān guó 三国 Three Kingdoms period (220-280). See also shǔ hàn, wèi, wú.

sān hài 三害 Three calamities: to hold the breath, to use brute strength, and to puff up the chest and suck in the belly. The internal styles consider that these three actions infringe on the natural flow in the body.

sān hé 三合 The three unities: three things that are united or in harmony, divided into the three internal and three external unities. See also liù hé, sān nèi hé, sān wài hé.

sān huán dāo 三环刀 Three ringed blade: a halberd with three rings attached to the spine of its blade.

sān huán tào yuè 三环套月 Three Rings Cover the Moon. 1. In bow stance, press a spear tip down, then advance in a rear cross step, stabbing low while rotating the shaft so the right hand is underneath. Repeat three times. From Shaolinquan. 2. Continuous chopping palms, also insertion step with double chops. From Piguaquan. 3. Continuous sword attacks. From Yang Taijiquan.

sān huán tuǐ 三换腿 Triple leg exchange: three advancing slap kicks in sequence, alternating feet. From Taiji Changquan.

sān huàn zhǎng 三换掌 Triple palm exchange: three pushes in sequence, alternating hands. From Chen Taijiquan.

sān huáng pào chuí 三皇炮捶 Sanhuang Paochui (three sovereigns pounding) style, an old Longfist style, popular in the northern provinces. Sometimes translated as Paochui style.

sān huí dǎ 三回打 Three Retreating Hits: stepping back while doing three double handed strikes, pushing, cutting, and slapping. From Taiji Changquan.

sān jí 三疾 Three diseases, three major errors in internal styles particularly: holding the breath, using brute force, and puffing up the chest while pulling in the belly. Also called sān bìng.

sān jí cái pàn yuán 三级裁判员 Level three judge: a basic level judge, qualified to judge at provincial level competitions. A classification within China,

sān jí jiào liàn yuán 三级教练员 Level three coach: a basic level coach, qualified to coach amateur athletes. A classification within China,

sān jí wǔ shì 三级武士 A level three martial artist: a mid-level athlete who has achieved high scores and placings in three events at local or county level competitions. A classification within China.

sān jiān 三间 Acupoint Sanjian (third space), LI3. At the proximal end of the index finger joint (on each hand). From TCM.

sān jiān 三尖 The three tips. 1. The three tips or points: nose, hands, and feet. 2. The alignment of these tips.

sān jiān liǎng rèn dāo 三尖两刃刀 Three-tip two-edge blade: a halberd with a straight edged blade, sharp on both edges, with three tips.

sān jiān yào duì 三尖要对 The three points must be aligned: the tips of the nose, hands, and feet should be aligned. From Xingyiquan, one of its essential requirements. Also called sān jiān yào zhào.

sān jiān yào zhào 三尖要照 See sān jiān yào duì.

sān jiāo 三焦 The Triple Burner, the organ associated with the Shou Shao Yang channel. It is a *yang* organ. It is not an organ in the Western, anatomical, sense. It is the surrounding tissue in the chest area, the stomach area, and the lower abdomen area, and also includes the interstitial fluid of the entire body. It is considered to take part in regulation of the body. From TCM.

sān jiāo jīng 三焦经 The triple burner meridian. See shǒu shào yáng. From TCM.

sān jiāo shū 三焦俞 Acupoint Sanjiaoshu (triple burner transport), BL22. Also called the triple warmer in English. At the waist, level with the depression below the spinous process of the first lumbar vertebra, 1.5 *cun* lateral to the midline (on each side). From TCM.

sān jiǎo bù 三角步 Triangle stance or stepping. 1. In some styles, a stance with the feet shoulder width apart, one foot-length between the feet, front foot and knee turned in, rear foot turned out forty-five degrees, weight about two thirds to the rear leg. 2. In some styles, a stance with normal horse stance distance, with the rest the same as above. Also called sān jiǎo mǎ bù. 3. Triangle stepping, which differs according to style, but generally uses a pattern of triangulation to step. In Baguazhang, one foot comes in to the other, out to the point of a triangle, then back along the same lines to the original spot, then the other foot does the same, so stepping is along the lines of a triangle.

sān jiǎo jī 三角肌 Deltoid muscle: the muscle that runs across the top of the shoulder. Because it has individual tendon groups attaching to the clavicle and scapula to the humerus at different angles, it assists in abduction, extension, flexion, medial rotation, and lateral rotation.

sān jiǎo mǎ bù 三角马步 Triangle horse stance. See #2 of sān jiǎo bù.

sān jié 三节 The three sections: a description that likens the body to a tree, which is divided into root, trunk, and branch tips. 1. The waist is the root, the spine is the middle, and feet and hands are the tips. 2. The legs are the root, the body the middle, and the arms the tips. 3. The legs are the root, the waist the middle, and the head the tip. 4. Each segment is split into sections: the sections of the arm are the shoulder the root, the elbow the middle, and the hand is the tip. The sections of the leg are the hip is the root, the knee the middle, and the foot the tip. The sections of the torso are the *dantian* is the root, the heart is the middle, and the head is the tip.

sān jié gùn 三节棍 Three section staff: three even length (length about shoulder width) wooden sticks attached by metal links.

sān kōng 三空 Three empties: the palms, the soles of the feet, and the chest should be empty. From Baguazhang, one of its requirements.

sān kòu 三扣 Three tucks, also translated as concavities: the shoulders should be closing in together, the hands and feet should be rounded to tuck in, and teeth should be closed together, so that strength can get through to the arms, hands, and feet, and the power of the tendons and bones is connected. From Baguazhang and Xingyiquan.

sān lǐ (xué) 三里(穴) Acupoint Sanli. See zú sān lǐ. From TCM.

sān liàn sān bù liàn 三练三不练 Three Train, Three Don't Train: three conditions that are conducive for training, and three that are not. Train when the air is fresh and the environment is pleasant. Train when not hungry, full, or tired. Train when feeling stable or content. Do not train when very hungry, very full, or very tired or unhappy.

sān lù 三路 Three routes. 1. Three sections of the body: the upper is the head and shoulders area, the middle is the chest and waist area, and the lower is the legs area. This term is used more to indicate the three routes into the body than to divide the body into sections. See also sān pán. 2. Third path, refers to the third routine of many styles. For example, sān lù chá quán, sān lù huá quán, the third routines of Chaquan and Huaquan.

sān mǐn 三敏 Three agilities, three sensitivities: the mind/heart, the eyes, and the hands should be quick to respond. From Xingyiquan.

sān nèi hé 三内合 The three internal unities: three things that are united or in harmony within the non-physical body. The heart with the intent, the intent with the *qi*, and the *qi* with the power. See also liù hé, sān hé, sān wài hé.

sān níng 三拧 Three twisting, three twisted: the neck, the waist, and the arms must be torqued. From Baguazhang.

sān pán 三盘 Three basins. 1. Three basins of the body: the upper is above the solar plexus, the middle around the waist area, and the lower is below the groin. See also sān lù. 2. Three heights of walking. High is the height of normal walking, middle is sitting into the legs, and low is sitting fully with the hips level with the knees. From Baguazhang. See also dī pán, shàng pán, zhōng pán.

sān pán luò dì 三盘落地 Three Basins Land on the Ground. 1. In Xingyiquan, a horse stance with a brace to both sides at knee height. 2. In Chen Taijiquan, a drop stance, bringing the hips, elbows with the forearms crossed, and the chest or shoulder to the ground.

sān pán shí èr shì 三盘十二势 Three Basins Twelve Models: a routine of Liuhebafa, using twelve animal models.

sān qī bù 三七步 Three-seven stance: legs open naturally front to back and weighted seventy percent to the rear leg. Usually called seventy-thirty stance. Sometimes the same as bù dīng bù bā, liù sì bù. Also called sān qī mǎ bù.

sān qī mǎ bù 三七马步 Three-seven horse stance. See sān qī bù.

sān qiǎng shǒu 三抢手 Three stealing hands: three quickly alternating finger strikes, palms up. From Shaolinquan.

sān qū 三曲 Three bends, three curves: the knees, elbows, and wrists should be bent to half-moon shape, neither straight nor fully flexed, so that they may move easily with power. From Xingyiquan.

sān shèng qiāng 三胜枪 A three victories spear, a spear with a combination of spear head, axe head, and a crescent moon blade, all at the same end.

sān shí qī shì 三十七势 The thirty-seven moves: a Yang Taijiquan routine.

sān shì 三势 Three types of power: walk as if through mud, arms connected as a twisted rope, walk the circle like pushing a millstone. From Baguazhang.

sān tǐ shì 三体式 The three bodies stake standing of Xingyiquan. Setting the position and power of Xingyiquan by standing in seventy-thirty or sixty-forty stance with strict requirements for body positioning and power flow. The name 'three bodies' emphasizes the outer structure of the head, hands, and feet, the upper, middle, and lower parts of the body. Also called sān cái zhuāng, sān tǐ shì zhuāng, zǐ wǔ zhuāng.

sān tǐ shì zhuāng 三体式桩 See sān tǐ shì.

sān tǐng 三挺 Three straightenings, three extensions: the nape of the neck, the spine, and the knees are extending to straighten. Although the knees remain slightly bent, they are extending, or lengthening, not collapsing. From Xingyiquan.

sān tōng bèi 三通背 Three Through the Back. 1. Open up the arms and shift forward to a bow stance. See also shǎn tōng bì. Also called shān tōng bì. 2. Catch and spin around, bringing the arms around to throw and strike. Both from Taijiquan.

sān wài hé 三外合 The three external unities: three parts of the bdoy that are united or in harmony within the physical body. The hands with the feet, the shoulders with the hips, and the elbows with the knees. See also liù hé, sān hé, sān nèi hé.

sān xīn yào bìng 三心要并 Three centres must join: power returns to the centre of the body from the centre of the top of the head, from the centre of the feet, and from the centres of the hands. From Xingyiquan, one of its essential requirements.

sān xīng 三星 Three stars: the depressions seen at the shoulder, elbow, and wrist joints when the arm is extended and twisted as in Xingyiquan.

sān xīng zhuāng 三星桩 Three star dummy: a tripodal wooden training dummy. Typically used in Wing Chun training.

sān xíng 三形 Three likenesses: walk like a dragon, move like a monkey, change like an eagle. From Baguazhang.

sān yáng luò 三阳络 Acupoint Sanyangluo (three *yang* connection), SJ8. At the forearm, on the outside, four *cun* up from the wrist crease, between the ulna and the radius (each arm). From TCM.

sān yáng zhǐ 三阳指 Three *yang* fingers, a hand shape: index, middle, and ring fingers extended, thumb pressing on the little finger in the palm. Used particularly to strike pressure points. From Shaolinquan.

sān yì yào lián 三意要连 Three minds must be combined: the ability to think, activate, and express should coordinate. There should be no hesitation between comprehending and moving. One of the eight essential requirements of Xingyiquan.

sān yīn jiāo 三阴交 Acupoint Sanyinjiao (intersection of three *yins*), SP6. At the calf, up the inside, three *cun* above the medial malleolus (on each leg). From TCM. A crippling point, striking here may cause serious injury. Vulnerable to a low kick. See also cán xué.

sān yīn zhǐ 三阴指 Three *yin* fingers. See dǐng zǔ zhǐ.

sān yuán 三圆 Three rounded, three roundings. 1. Rounded upper back, chest, and thumb web. 2. Rounded upper back, elbows, and thumb web. Both from Baguazhang and Xingyiquan.

sān zhàn 三战 Three fights, see sān zhèng.

sān zhǎng 三掌 Triple palm strikes: two lighter, or feinting, strikes, followed by a final strong strike.

sān zhēn sì dào 三真四到 Three are true and four arrive. When the eyes, hands, waist and legs arrive as one, and the heart, spirit and strength are true, you have complete control. From Baguazhang.

sān zhèng 三正 Three uprights: the body is upright, the head is upright, and the horse stance is upright. From southern styles. Also called sān zhàn.

散 散 [散] (rad.66) **sǎn** 1. Scattered, dispersed. Come loose; fall apart. 2. In a positive sense, to disperse energy from the centre out in all directions.

sǎn dǎ 散打 Sparring event with modern Chinese rules, which includes kicks, punches, takedowns, and pushes out of bounds, but not ground grappling. The modern event is called Sanda in English.

sǎn luàn 散乱 Scattered and confused, an error in performance of any style.

sǎn shǒu 散手 Sparring, as a general classification for sparring training.

sǎn shǒu dàn 散手弹 Scattering pellets: an ancient throwing weapon. See fēi huáng shí. Also called fēi shí.

sǎn shǒu hù jù 散手护具 Protective equipment for sparring. Includes head guards, mouth guards, chest protectors, jock straps, shin guards, gloves, foot protectors, etc.

sǎn zhāo 散招 Random moves: in performance of a routine, disorganized movements or techniques without proper execution.

掃 [扫] (rad.64) **sǎo** 1. The original, practical, meaning is to sweep. A Chinese broom is a long branch held almost horizontally, and the sweeping action is a long, flat, action from back to front. 2. A kick: sweep the leg across low to trip. 3. Any sweeping action with the arms, legs, or weapon.

sǎo bà 扫把 Sweep with the butt of a long weapon, between ankle and knee height.

sǎo dāo 扫刀 Sweep with a broadsword. See sǎo jiàn.

sǎo dì jīn bō 扫地金波 Sweep the Ground with a Golden Wave: step into a smooth stance with a sword slice up to head height. From Qingping sword.

sǎo dòng jīn guāng 扫动金光 Sweep aside the Golden Rays: a low sword sweep to the side. In a drop stance, shift from the right leg to the left while sweeping the blade flat across in front, tip away from the body. From Qingping sword.

sǎo ěr dān chuí 扫耳单捶 Sweep the Ear with a Single Strike: a sweeping punch to the ear. From Baguazhang, one of its sixty-four hands.

sǎo gōu 扫钩 Sweep with double hooks: hook one onto the other at the hooked ends, and swing the blades around in a full circle, sending power to the drill end of the furthest hook.

sǎo gùn 扫棍 Sweep with a staff: swing the staff with the tip level below the waist or angled down, not necessarily touching the ground.

sǎo jiàn 扫剑 Sweep with a sword. 1. A horizontal hack at ankle height, blade flat, edge in the direction of the sweep. 2. A sweeping cut at about waist height.

sǎo jìng 扫胫 A sweeping kick to the shin.

sǎo jìng xún méi 扫经寻梅 Sweep the Path to Seek Plums: turn around with a block with a sword blade, extending the arm low and raising the tip. From Qingping sword.

sǎo pū dāo 扫扑刀 Sweep with a horse cutter: holding the shaft horizontal and tight to the belly, turn around to cut in a sweeping action with the blade. May be done as a mid-height or a low sweep.

sǎo qiāng 扫枪 Sweep with a spear: swing the spear with the shaft near the ground, but not touching.

sǎo quán 扫拳 Sweeping punch: swing a straight arm either flat or angled, power to the fist back, eye, or heel. Can swing either inwards or outwards. From southern styles.

sǎo táng tuǐ 扫堂腿 Sweep the Hall: a back sweep kick. From Shaolinquan.

sǎo táng tuǐ 扫膛腿 Sweep the Chest. 1. A sweep kick. From Chen Taijiquan. 2. The category of all sweep kicks. From Mizongquan. See also sǎo zhuàn xìng tuǐ fǎ.

sǎo tī 扫踢 Sweeping kick: cock the knee and lean back, swing the leg across, contacting with the top of the foot. The category of kicks that are done with this sweeping action.

sǎo tuǐ 扫腿 Sweep kicks. See sǎo zhuàn xìng tuǐ fǎ.

sǎo zhǒu 扫肘 Elbow sweep: bend the elbow in front of your chest and drive it quickly across to either side.

sǎo zhuàn tuǐ fǎ 扫转腿法 Sweep kicks. See sǎo zhuàn xìng tuǐ fǎ.

sǎo zhuàn xìng tuǐ fǎ 扫转性腿法 Sweep kicks: the category of kicks that squat on one leg to sweep close to the ground with the other. Also called sǎo tuǐ, sǎo zhuàn tuǐ fǎ. See also fú dì hòu sǎo, héng sǎo tuǐ, lián huán sǎo, zhí shēn qián sǎo.

sǎo zhuàng 扫桩 Sweep stakes: a leg training method. Move between and kick posts set in the ground (not just sweep kicks, but all sorts of kicks). Often done with nine poles set in three rows of three.

僧 (rad.9) sēng 1. A monk; a Buddhist priest or monk. 2. One of the four big family branches of Emeiquan, see also sì dà jiā.

sēng dào 僧道 Buddhist monks and Daoist priests.

殺 (rad.79) [杀] (rad.4) shā 1. To kill, to put to death. 2. To destroy. 3. To fight.

shā gùn 杀棍 To chop down firmly with a pole while simultaneously standing up, not changing the hand position.

shā jī niú tóu 杀鸡扭头 Kill the Chicken with a Twist of the Neck: control your adversary's arm and get in behind, grabbing his hair or neck with one hand while placing the other on his chin. Apply a sharp snap to break his neck. From Qinna.

shā jiē 杀揭 To chop down then cut up with a pole.

shā jǐng shǒu 杀颈手 Throat cut: a side strike to the neck with the blade of the hand.

shā shǒu jiān 杀手锏 An unexpected thrust with a mace, but the term is used to mean an unexpected and overpowering thrust with any weapon.

shā shǒu jìn 杀手劲 Killing power: to launch power in between breaths. From Xingyiquan.

沙 (rad.85) shā Sand; grit.

shā bāo gōng 沙包功 Sandbag training: hitting and kicking a large sandbag.

shā dài 沙袋 Sandbag. 1. Generally refers to a small bag used for tossing. 2. A sandbag set on a table for striking. 3. A larger hanging punching or kicking bag.

扇 (rad.63) shān 1. A fan. 2. As a hand technique, a fanning action or slap. With this meaning, should be written 搧.

shān tōng bì 扇通臂 Fan Out the Arms, see shǎn tōng bì. Also called sān tōng bèi. Also pronounced shān tōng bēi.

shān zǐ 扇子 A fan. When used as a weapon, is usually made of metal or is metal edged.

搧 (rad.64) shān 1. To fan. 2. To slap on the face. To strike sideways with the palm. 3. To stir up, incite.

shān bǎng 搧膀 To incite with the arms, when getting the body in close for a throw.

shān ěr guāng 搧耳光 To box the ear.

shān kuà tiě shā zhǎng 搧跨铁沙掌 Fan and Stride Iron Sand Palms, the seventh routine of Duanquan, written up as twelve moves.

shān tuǐ 搧腿 Fanning kick. 1. In Chuojiao, an inside crescent kick, also called lǐ hé tuǐ. A mid-height kick, see also zhōng pán tuǐ fǎ. 2. In

Duanquan, an outside crescent kick.

膻 (rad.130) **shān** This character means the musky odour of sheep, but is more often used in combination as shān zhōng in TCM. Also pronounced dàn.

shān zhōng 膻中 Acupoint Shanzhong (chest centre), RN17. At the chest, between the nipples, level with the fourth intercostal space, on the midline. From TCM. One of the main targets on the body, a sensitive point. Striking here scatters *qi* and induces confusion or even unconsciousness. Best to hit with the head, shoulder, elbow, tiger pouncing, shoving punch, or carrying palm. Also pronounced dàn zhōng.

閃 [闪] (rad.169) **shǎn** 1. To dodge, get out of the way. As general footwork, to step to evade. As one of the eight attack and defense models, to evade attacks completely. See also bā zì gōng fáng fǎ zé. Dodging, one of Ziranmen's nineteen main methods. 2. Twist, sprain.

shǎn bù 闪步 Dodging step: quickly move to either side to evade an attack. One foot takes a small step then the other follows with a larger step.

shǎn diàn 闪电 Lightning. Used in movement names or sayings to infer quickness.

shǎn qiāng 闪枪 Dodge with a spear: dodge to either side, controlling an attack with the shaft of the spear.

shǎn shēn 闪身 Dodge, move a bit to the side, usually just with the body. Sometimes includes small steps.

shǎn tōng bì 闪通臂 Dodge with Connected Arms: varies with the styles, but involves opening the arms out like a fan, sending the power out through the upper back and arms. From Taijiquan. Other names are similar, and it is hard to say which are mistakes and which come from other interpretations. Also called sān tōng bèi, shān tōng bì. Also pronounced shǎn tōng bēi.

shǎn zhǎn bù 闪展步 Dodging step. 1. Lift the front foot and hop forward from the rear leg, both feet landing at the same time. 2. A sideways bridging step done with or without a jump.

shǎn zhǎn téng nuó 闪展腾挪 Dodging, opening, jumping, and moving: four basic and specialist skills needed in many styles. Dodging is the ability to dodge the body, opening is the ability to open up fully, jumping is the ability to jump, and moving is the ability to move with footwork.

shǎn zhàn 闪战 The ability to change direction, angle, and point of focus suddenly with the slightest adjustment.

shǎn zhàn gōng 闪战功 Dodging training: set up hanging sandbags in a large frame, strike them to get them swinging, and move amongst them, both striking and avoiding swinging ones.

shǎn zhàn fǎ 闪占法 Dodge and occupy techniques: methods of evading and sliding in to strike.

傷 [伤] (rad.9) **shāng** 1. An injury, wound. 2. To injure, to wound. To hurt.

商 (rad.30) **shāng** 1. To discuss, consult. 2. Trade, business. Merchant. 3. A note in the Chinese scale. 4. A surname. 5. The Shang dynasty (c. 1600-1046 BC).

shāng qiū 商丘 Acupoint Shangqiu (market hill), SP5. At the inside of the ankle, just below and to the front of the medial malleolus, in the depression (on each foot). From TCM.

shāng qū 商曲 Acupoint Shangqu (commerce bend), KI17. At the abdomen, two *cun* above the navel, 0.5 *cun* lateral to the midline (on each side). From TCM.

shāng yáng 商阳 Acupoint Shangyang (commerce yang), LI1. At the index finger, at the distal segment, about 0.1 *cun* from the root of the fingernail (on each hand). From TCM. Pinching the side of the finger tip while applying the control can add considerable pain to the technique, even to the extent of inducing unconsciousness.

shāng yáng wǔ yǔ 商羊舞雨 Goat at the Market Dances in the Rain: raised knee reaching cut with a sword. Lifting the left knee, sweeping the blade around to the side with an extended arm. From Qingping sword.

上 (rad.1) **shàng** 1. Upper; higher. 2. First of something divided into parts. 3. Most recent; former. 3. To get up, go up. 4. To get onto, board, as in board a train. 4. Advance, go ahead. 5. To enter a competition area.

S

shàng bà 上把 The upper grip: the third of the shaft closest to the blade on a long bladed weapons such as a big cutter.

shàng bēng qiāng 上崩枪 Upward snap with a spear: pull the right hand back, sliding the shaft through the left hand, then stop the right hand, both hands applying an abrupt power to snap the spear tip up so that it vibrates at head height.

shàng bì 上臂 The upper arm.

shàng bō qiāng 上拨枪 Upper check with a spear: snap the spear from side to side with a quick but steady power, a bit above head height.

shàng bù 上步 Step forward, bring the rear foot through to step ahead of the lead foot.

shàng bù cǐ bù 上步趾步 Step forward the rear foot then shift step, staying in stance. From Chuojiao, usually in thrusting stance, see also dēng jī bù.

shàng bù duì quán 上步对拳 Step forward to facing fists. 1. Step the left foot forward, often a bit to the side, extending the palms up. Then step the right foot forward and bring the left to a closed parallel stance, placing the fists in front of the belly, fist centres down. 2. The same stepping, but finishing with a double straight punch to the front. Both from Chaquan.

shàng bù qī xīng 上步七星 Step Forward to Seven Stars: step the right foot forward to touch the toes or heel down, cross the forearms in front of the body, hands about shoulder height. This parries up and prepares the foot for kicking, but also prepares any of the seven stars for use. From Taijiquan. See also qī xīng.

shāng bù zhèn 上步震 Stomp while advancing. See also zhèn jiǎo.

shàng chǎng 上场 To enter the competition area for your turn at performance, to take to the field.

shàng chuān 上穿 Thread a hand upwards, usually sliding along the other arm.

shàng cì jiàn 上刺剑 Upwards pierce straight to the tip with a sword, forming a straight line with the arm and blade, tip at head height.

shàng cuò 上锉 Upwards file, a flat filing action with the under edge of a sword blade, in response to a chop.

shàng dà tuǐ fǎ 上大腿法 Methods for replacing a dislocated hip.

shàng dān tián 上丹田 Upper cinnabar field: centred in the head. See also dān tián, xià dān tián, zhōng dān tián.

shàng diǎn qiāng 上点枪 High dab with spear: lift the grip and dab with the tip between shoulder and head height.

shàng dòng bù tíng 上动不停 Continue on from the previous movement without stopping. A phrase often used in training manuals.

shàng duì quán 上对拳 Upper facing fists: punch both fists towards each other, knuckles facing each other, over head height.

shàng è fǎ 上颚法 Methods for replacing a dislocated jaw.

shàng fēn zhǐ 上分指 Upward finger separation: grab and lock one or more of the adversary's fingers, then rotate and lift. From Qinna.

shàng fū fǎ 上跗法 Methods for replacing a dislocated foot.

shàng fú 上浮 1. Upward floating: with a long weapon such as pole or spear, lower the rear hand, holding the front hand firm, to lift the tip. 2. Float upwards, a pattern applied in channel diagnosis. From TCM.

shàng gōu quán 上勾拳 An uppercut: punch upwards with the knuckles, elbow bent.

shàng gōu tī 上勾踢 Hooked roundhouse kick: a high roundhouse kick with the foot dorsi-flexed.

shàng gǔ fǎ 上骨法 Joint replacement methods. A subcategory of dislocation methods. See also xiè gǔ fǎ.

shàng guà dāo 上挂刀 Upper hooking parry with a broadsword: hooking up and back, contacting with the spine of a broadsword blade.

shàng guān 上关 Acupoint Shangguan (upper pass), GB3. At the face, just at the hairline of the sideburn, directly above acupoint Xiaguan (on each side). From TCM.

shàng guàn gōng 上罐功 Jar rollups training: attach a jar to a stick by a rope, hold the stick out from the shoulders, and work the wrists to roll the jar up and down.

shàng hòu jù jī 上后锯肌 Superior serratus posterior muscle: thin muscles that insert into the ribs from the spine.

shàng jià 上架 An upward propping frame: from on guard position, lift the front arm with the elbow bent to contact and lift up with the forearm.

shàng jià zhǒu 上架肘 Prop up the elbow: grab your adversary's wrist with your same side hand (right to right), step in and slide your other arm under his elbow (your elbow bent, controlling with your upper arm), rotate and straighten his arm, pressing the elbow up while pulling his hand down. From Qinna.

shàng jiān fǎ 上肩法 Methods for replacing a dislocated shoulder.

shàng guà jiàn 上挂剑 Upper hooking parry with a sword: hooking up and back, contacting with the thumb edge of a sword blade.

shàng jié dāo (jiàn) 上截刀(剑) High intercept with broadsword (or sword): a diagonal cut up with the arm on a straight line with the blade, a flat blade, cutting with the fore-edge.

shàng jù xū 上巨虚 Acupoint Shangjuxu (upper great hollow), ST37. At the shin, just to the outside of the shin bone, six *cun* below acupoint Dubi (on each side). From TCM.

shàng kàng 上亢 Ascendant hyperactivity, a pattern applied in channel diagnosis. From TCM.

shàng lián 上廉 Acupoint Shanglian (upper ridge), LI9. At the outer edge of the forearm, about three *cun* down from the elbow crease. From TCM.

shàng liáo 上髎 Acupoint Shangliao (upper bonehole), BL31. At the sacrum, the top sacral formina, 0.8 *cun* lateral to the midline (on each side). From TCM.

shàng lù 上路 1. The upper level of the body: the shoulders, neck and head. 2. The upper level route for striking. Also called shàng sān lù.

shàng mén 上门 The upper gate: above an adversary's outstretched arm.

shàng nì 上逆 Counterflowing upward, a pattern applied in channel diagnosis. From TCM.

shàng pán 上盘 The upper basin, higher basin. 1. The upper body: head, neck, shoulders, arms. 2. The shoulder girdle. 3. A high height used whilst training, at the height of normal walking. From Baguazhang.

shàng pán bǎi zhī yáo, xià pán sì shēng gēn 上盘百枝摇，下盘似生根 The upper basin moves like branches, the lower basin sets down roots.

shàng pán tuǐ 上盘腿 The high basin kicks, a series of short routines of Chuojiao. See also bā pán tuǐ, xià pán tuǐ, zhōng pán tuǐ.

shàng pán tuǐ fǎ 上盘腿法 High-basin kicks: nine kicks that use jumping and upper levels to strike. From Chuojiao. See also xià pán tuǐ fǎ, zhōng pán tuǐ fǎ.

shàng pāo 上抛 Toss up: toss a spear with one hand so that it spins vertically.

shàng píng qiāng 上平枪 A high level stab with a spear: the shaft is horizontal, above chest height. Usually the outer cover is to chest height, the inner cover is to jaw height, then the stab is to head height.

shàng qiāng 上枪 A high stab with a spear: the stab is between shoulder and head height.

shàng rèn 上刃 The upper edge of a double-edged bladed weapon, the thumb side of the blade when holding with a normal grip.

shàng sān dāo xià shā xǔ chū 上三刀吓杀许褚 Three Rising Blades to Scare General Xu Chu to Death: advancing with turning steps, spinning and slicing up three times with a halberd. From Chen Taijiquan.

shàng sān lù 上三路 Upper three routes. See shàng lù.

shàng shǒu 上手 The upper hand: the pro-active person in a fight, the first to attack (getting the upper hand), the fighter in the offensive position. Also called xiān shǒu. See also xià shǒu.

shàng shǒu huā 上手花 Raised hands flowers: spin a long weapon horizontally above the head, alternating hands to keep it spinning.

shàng tǐ 上体 The upper body, the torso.

shàng tǐ huàng dòng 上体晃动 Swaying of the upper body: indicates imperfect balance. An ordinary deduction (0.1) in Taolu competition.

shàng tuō qiāng 上托枪 High carry a spear: snap the shaft strongly upwards, the left hand palm up, shaft horizontal, shoulder height.

S

shàng wǎn 上脘 Acupoint Shangwan (upper stomach duct), RN13. At the abdomen, five *cun* above the navel, on the midline. From TCM.

shàng wū chōu tī 上屋抽梯 Remove the Ladder Once (the enemy has) Ascended the Roof. The twenty-eighth of the Thirty-six Stratagems of Warfare, which apply to many situations.

shàng xī fǎ 上膝法 Methods for replacing a dislocated knee.

shàng xià mō jìn 上下摸劲 Seeking power up-down: without moving the torso outwardly, seek out power lines in an upward-downward direction. May be done in different stances or stepping. From Yiquan.

shàng xià xiāng suí 上下相随 Upper and lower body work together; upper and lower in mutual accord. A requirement in many styles.

shàng xiāo 上削 An upward paring slice, usually angled.

shàng xīng 上星 Acupoint Shangxing (upper star), DU23. At the head, one *cun* up from the front hairline, on the midline. From TCM.

shàng yā wàn 上压腕 Rising wrist lock: grab your adversary's hand and elbow and press his hand to his forearm, pushing straight upwards until you have full control. From Qinna.

shàng yā zhǒu 上压肘 Rising elbow lock: grab your adversary's hand and elbow, straighten and turn his arm and press his elbow up, pulling his hand down. From Qinna.

shàng yán 上炎 Flare upwards, a pattern applied in channel diagnosis. From TCM.

shàng yíng xiāng 上迎香 Extraordinary acupoint Shangyingxiang (greeting fragrance), EX-HN8. At the face, where the bone meets the cartilage of the nose, above the nostrils. From TCM.

shàng zhā dāo 上扎刀 Upwards stab with a broadsword, blade tip at head height.

shàng zhī 上肢 The upper limbs, the arms.

shàng zhī fáng shǒu 上肢防守 Blocking and protective techniques using the upper limbs, the arms.

shàng zhǐ kòu 上指扣 Upward finger twist: grab and rotate one or more of the adversary's fingers at the joint, pressing upwards. From Qinna.

shàng zhòng xià qīng 上重下轻 The upper body is heavy while the lower body is light; top-heavy with a light base. An error in most styles.

shàng zhǒu fǎ 上肘法 Methods for replacing a dislocated elbow.

尚 (rad.42) shàng   1. To uphold; to honour. 2. A surname.

shàng shì xíng yì quán 尚氏形意拳 Shang family Xingyiquan, a branch of Xingyiquan attributed to Shang Yunxiang.

shàng wǔ jīng shén 尚武精神 Martial spirit.

shàng wǔ zūn dé 尚武尊德 Encourage martial spirit and venerate morals.

弰 (rad.57) shāo   The tips of a bow.

梢 (rad.75) shāo   1. The tip of a branch. 2. The tip of something that thins towards the end.

shāo bà bìng yòng 梢把并用 Use the tip and the butt equally. A saying about the staff. One should be able to use both ends of the staff effectively.

shāo gōng yáo lǔ 梢公摇橹 Helmsman Sculls: push the blade of a sword forward with the grip held at chest height, blade hanging vertically pointing down, left hand pushing on the grip. From Wu Taijiquan.

shāo jié lǐng 梢节领 The extremities lead: the distal segments of the body lead the way for the proximal segments. See also sān jié.

shāo zǐ gùn 梢子棍 Long flail: a two-section staff that is made up of one longer and one shorter section, linked with metal links. May either be a long staff (see cháng shāo zi gùn) or short (see duǎn shāo zi gùn).

杓 (rad.75) sháo   1. A big spoon, a ladle. 2. The handle of a cup or ladle. 3. Pronounced biāo, the constellation the Big Dipper. Also pronounced dī, shuó, zhuó.

sháo jiǎo 杓脚 Ladle foot, a tripping technique: hooking with the leg and lifting with the foot turned out. From wrestling.

sháo tuǐ 杓腿 Ladle leg, a tripping technique: a level crossing hook of the leg to throw. From wrestling.

芍 (rad.140) **sháo**   Peony, a flower.

sháo shǒu 芍手 Peony hand, a hand shape: the first segment of the thumb, index and middle fingers held together, the ring and little fingers pressed on the palm heel, the wrist bent and curled in. From Tongbeiquan.

少 (rad.42) **shǎo, shào**   1. Few; little. 2. Less. 3. Lack. 4. Lose, be missing. 5. Young.

shào chōng 少冲 Acupoint Shaochong (lesser surge), HT9. At the distal segment of the little finger, on the edge of the finger nail (on each hand). This is the final acupoint in the Heart meridian. From TCM. Pinching the side of the finger tip while applying an extra control can add considerable pain to the technique, even to the extent of inducing unconsciousness.

shào fǔ 少府 Acupoint Shaofu (lesser mansion), HT8. At the palm, between the ring and middle fingers, the point that the middle finger touches when curled (on each hand). From TCM.

shào hǎi (xué) 少海(穴) Acupoint Shaohai (lesser sea), HT3. At the crook of the elbow, in the depression just in front of the medial epicondyle of the humerus (on each arm). From TCM. A sensitive point, pressure can induce numbness. Best to hit with an eagle claw grab, and handy to use in 'lead the sheep' and other hooking techniques. Too much pressure, however, may induce a heart attack.

shǎo lín bǎn fǔ 少林板斧 Shaolin plank axe: a short handled axe with a relatively long, thick blade. The total is a bit less than one metre, with the head a bit over thirty centimetres.

shǎo lín èr shí sì pào dǎ fǎ 少林二十四炮打法 Shaolin Twenty-four Fighting methods: a routine of twenty-four practical combinations practiced in Shaolinquan.

shǎo lín kǎn shǒu 少林砍手 Shaolin chopping hand, a hard skills training method to develop the palm edge and wrist. to strike bricks with the palm edge, gradually increasing the number and/or hardness of the bricks. Also called táng láng zhuā.

shǎo lín lián huán quán 少林连环拳 Shaolin Connected Fists: a Shaolinquan routine, written up as sixty-four moves.

shǎo lín quán 少林拳 Shaolinquan (young forest fist), refers to a range of styles, but most commonly to those done in the Shaolin Songshan temple in Henan province.

shǎo lín rú yì quān 少林如意圈 Shaolin bracelet: a double weapon with a circular blade and a grip at a part of the blade. About twenty five centimetres across.

shǎo lín sān shí èr hé shàng fǎ 少林三十二合上法 Shaolin Thirty-two methods: a routine of thirty-two head attacking combinations practiced in Shaolinquan.

shǎo lín sì 少林寺 The Shaolin temple. Refers to all the Shaolin temples, but most commonly to the Songshan temple in Henan province.

shǎo lín wǔ quán 少林五拳 Shaolin Five Fists: Shaolinquan routines, five routines of the dragon, tiger, panther, snake, and crane.

shǎo nián sài 少年赛 A junior age competition: ages twelve to seventeen inclusive.

shǎo nián zǔ 少年组 The junior age group at a competition: ages twelve to seventeen inclusive.

shǎo shāng 少商 Acupoint Shaoshang (lesser commerce), LU11. At the inside edge of the distal segment of the thumb, at the nail (on each hand). This is the last point of the Lung meridian. From TCM. Pinching the side of the thumb tip while applying a control can add considerable pain to the technique, even to the extent of inducing unconsciousness.

shào yáng 少阳 Shao Yang, the Lesser Yang: the mid-*yang* pivot nature sub-type of meridian channels, an outwardly expanding level, but less so than Tai Yang. Containing the triple burner and the gallbladder, this system regulates physiology within the body. It governs the *yang* pivot. Diagrammed as one *yin* line between two *yang* lines.

shào yīn 少阴 Shao Yin, the Lesser Yin: the mid-*yin* pivot nature sub-type of the *yin* meridian channels. Containing the heart and kidneys, this system regulates extreme heat of the external environment and is the source of blood in the internal environment. This system governs the *yin* pivot. Diagrammed as one *yang* line between two *yin* lines.

S

shào zé 少泽 Acupoint Shaoze (lesser marsh), SI1. At the distal segment of the little finger, the outside of the base of the finger nail (on each hand). From TCM. Pinching the side of the finger tip while applying a control can add considerable pain to the technique, even to the extent of inducing unconsciousness.

舌 (rad.135) **shé** 1. The tongue. 2. One of the five sensory organs, see also wǔ guān. 3. Something shaped like a tongue. 4. The clapper of a bell.

蛇 虵 [蛇] (rad.142) **shé** 1. Snake, serpent. For more movement names using the actions or qualities of the snake, see also under bái shé, dú-, è-, fēi-, jīn-, nán-, qīng-, shuāng-, yín-. 2. Snake, as the sixth of the twelve animals from the Chinese zodiac, associated with a twelve year cycle symbolic of the earthly branches. The twelve animals make up a sixty year cycle when combined with the five phases. See also dì zhī, shēng xiào, wǔ xíng. Also called xiǎo lóng.

shé quán 蛇拳 Shequan (snake fist), an animal imitative style, generally considered a Shaolinquan style, uses hand techniques extensively.

shé shì 蛇式 Snake model: circle-walking and changes done seeking the movement and manner of a snake. From Baguazhang.

shé tóu zhǎng 蛇头掌 Snake head palm, a hand shape: fingers together and relatively straight, palm tucked, thumb tucked in tight.

shé xíng qián bù 蛇行前步 Snake advancing step. See sān cái bù.

shé xíng 蛇形 Snake form: coil into a low protective stance, then step to a forearm scoop or full arm upward slice. From Xingyiquan.

shé xíng shù 蛇行术 Snake walking skill: planking on the elbows, popping up while keeping the body straight. May pop up to the hands and back to the elbows, and can add weight on the back.

shé yǒu bō cǎo zhī jīng 蛇有拨草之精 Snakes have the essence of sliding through grass. A quality sought in Xingyiquan's snake form.

shé zhǎng 蛇掌 Snake palm: index and middle fingers extended, not quite straight, other fingers curled. From Xingyiquan, used in the snake form.

射 (rad.41) **shè** 1. To shoot, fire. Discharge. 2. To send out.

shè jī shù 射击术 Marksmanship.

shè jiàn 射箭 1. To shoot an arrow. 2. Archery.

shè qǐ jiān 射起肩 Shoot the shoulder. A shoulder technique: close in the body and shoulders, then expand so that the shoulder hits the adversary.

shè tiē 射帖 An archery target.

shè yàn shì 射雁势 Shoot the Wild Goose: open out the arms then slice a sword forward and down, then pull the blade back to sit in empty stance. From Yang Taijiquan.

shè zhòng 射中 To hit the target; to score a hit.

伸 (rad.9) **shēn** To extend, stretch out, lengthen out.

shēn jīn 伸筋 Stretch out the sinews. With the back flat and arms extended, lean over to press the hands into the ground or wrap the arms around the legs.

shēn jīn bá gǔ 伸筋拔骨 Stretch out the sinews and draw out the bones.

shēn qū tuǐ fǎ 伸屈腿法 Snap kicks, cocked kicks: category of kicks that first bend and lift the knee then extend the knee to kick.

shēn yāo 伸腰 Lengthen the waist, straighten the back. Used in wrestling actions to apply power through the body. Also called cháng yāo.

申 (rad.102) **shēn** 1. The ninth of the twelve Terrestrial Branches, used in combination with the ten Celestial Stems to designate years, months, days, and hours. For the sixty year cycles, see also under bǐng shēn, gēng-, jiǎ-, rén-, wù-. The period of the day from 3:00 p.m. to 5:00 p.m. See also dì zhī, tiān gān. 2. To state, express.

shēn mài 申脉 Acupoint Shenmai (Ninth branch vessel), BL62. At the ankle, on the outside, in the depression 0.5 *cun* below the lateral malleolus, or ankle bone (on each leg). From TCM.

shēn shí 申时 The period of the day from 3:00 p.m. to 5:00 p.m. (15:00 – 17:00).

shēn sù 申诉 To appeal: to petition for a change in a judge's or referee's score or opinion in a competition.

shēn sù chéng xù 申诉程序 The appeal procedure at a competition.

身 (rad.158) shēn   1. Body, torso, trunk of the body. 2. The body of the blade of a bladed weapon, the whole blade, but not the grip.

shēn fǎ 身法 Body technique, bodywork: use of the chest, back, lower back, abdomen, and hips area, as differentiated from leg and arm techniques.

shēn gōng 身弓 The torso bow: the waist is likened to the central grip, the first cervical vertebra and sacrum to the upper and lower tips. When the bow is pulled the intent is focussed at the Mingmen (see also mìng mén) so the body remains upright and centered, the upper and lower pull apart slightly to balance.

shēn líng 身灵 The body is agile: the body is not stiff, and is able to adjust appropriately for each movement, each part of it working as whole. One of the requirements for proper training.

shēn tǐ 身体 The whole body.

shēn tǐ sù zhì 身体素质 Physical constitution, physique, fitness.

shēn xíng 身型 Body posture: the positions taken by the entire body when still.

shēn xīn hé yī 身心合一 Body and mind as one; unity of body and mind. A goal in most styles.

shēn zhǔ 身柱 Acupoint Shenzhu (body pillar), DU12. At the back, at the depression below the spinous process of the third thoracic vertebra, on the midline. From TCM. A good target.

神 (rad.113) shén   Spirit. Consciousness. Vitality of the mind and body, awareness of life, the soul. Divinity. Associated with the Heart, and with character attributes related to the spark of intelligence. Awareness, one of Ziranmen's nineteen main methods.

shén cáng 神藏 Acupoint Shencang (storehouse of the spirit), KI25. At the chest, at the second intercostal space, 2 *cun* lateral to the midline (on each side). From TCM.

shén chū guǐ mò 神出鬼没 The spirit goes out and erases the ghost: to put your spirit into your weapon, to better beat the adversary.

shén dào 神道 Acupoint Shendao (path of the spirit), DU11. At the back, at the depression below the spinous process of the fifth thoracic vertebra, on the midline. From TCM.

shén fēng 神封 Acupoint Shenfeng (spirit seal), KI23. At the chest, at the fourth intercostal space, 2 *cun* from the midline (on each side). From TCM.

shén guī chū shuǐ shì lì 神龟出水试力 Celestial turtle emerges from water testing power. Moving the body down as the hands move above it, circling and moving the body in coordination with the hand movement, a method of finding balancing power in the body. Can be done with fixed stance or moving steps. From Yiquan.

shén hé yú dòng 神合于动 The spirit combines with movement. From Liuhebafa, one of its principles.

shén jù 神聚 The spirit gathers everything together. One of the requirements for proper training.

shén lóng bǎi wěi 神龙摆尾 Mystical Dragon Slashes its Tail. 1. A jump spin back kick to land on the ground. From Yangjia style. 2. A full circle high sweep with the shaft of a spear.

shén lóng diào yǐ 神龙掉尾 Mystical Dragon Sheds its Tail Hairs: extend the right foot in front of the left to aid leaning back, circling up to the rear left with a reverse chop with a sword, also raising the left arm to aid extension. From Qingping sword.

shén mén 神门 Acupoint Shenmen (gate of the spirit), HT7. At the palm side of the wrist, in the depression just above the crease, at the little finger side (on each arm). From TCM. A crippling point, striking here may cause serious injury. See also cán xué.

shén miào 神妙 Wonderful, marvelous. Often used to describe people with high level skills.

shén nǚ xiàn ruì 神女献瑞 Goddess Presents the Jade Token: lift a sword up in empty stance. Sit to a right empty stance and push the hilt up in front of the face, to lift above the head with a standing blade horizontal on the plane of the body. From

S

Qingping sword.

shén qì 神气 The vigorous spirit.

shén què 神阙 Acupoint Shenque (gate tower of the spirit), RN8. At the abdomen, at the navel, on the midline. From TCM. An easy target.

shén tài 神态 Spirit; expression; bearing; mien. Also called shén yǔ.

shén táng 神堂 Acupoint Shentang (hall of the spirit), BL44. At the back, level with the depression below the spinous process of the fifth vertebra, three *cun* lateral to the midline (on each side). From TCM.

shén tíng 神庭 Acupoint Shenting (court of the spirit), DU24. At the head, 0.5 *cun* up from the front hairline, on the midline. From TCM. Hitting can induce dizziness and light-headedness.

shén wú xíng zé bù cún, xíng wú shén zé dāi zhì 神无形则不存，形无神则呆滞 The spirit cannot exist without form, form without spirit is lifeless. A martial saying.

shén yào qīng 神要清 The spirit must be clear. A focussed mind and stable emotions are necessities in fighting.

shén yì 神意 The intent spirit, power of the mind, intention put into movements.

shén yǔ 神宇 Spirit. See shén tài.

shén zhì bù qīng 神志不清 To be unconscious.

審 [审] (rad.40) **shěn**
1. To examine; go over. 2. Observation of channel pathways, part of channel diagnosis. From TCM.

慎 (rad.61) **shèn**
Cautious; careful.

shèn zhòng 慎重 Cautiousness, using mostly defensive and feinting actions in sparring.

腎 [肾] (rad.130) **shèn**
1. The kidneys. Colloquially called yāo zi. 2. The Kidney, the organ associated with the Zu Shao Yin channel. It is a *yin* organ.

shèn jīng 肾经 The Kidney meridian. See zú shào yīn. From TCM.

shèn shū 肾俞 Acupoint Shenshu (kidney transport), BL23. At the waist, level with the depression below the spinous process of the second lumbar vertebra, 1.5 *cun* lateral to the midline (on each side). From TCM. These are good targets but should not be hit too hard, as this may cause kidney damage or even paralysis.

生 (rad.100) **shēng**
1. To give birth to. To be born. 2. To grow. 3. Life. Alive. 4. To be afflicted with. 5. Unripe. 6. Uncooked. Unrefined. 7. Unfamiliar, strange. 8. To engender, as the five phases are interconnected by engendering and restraining (see also wǔ xíng). 9. One of Ziranmen's nineteen main methods.

shēng xiào 生肖 A zodiac animal. The twelve zodiac animals are associated with a twelve year cycle, and combined with the five phases, a sixty year cycle. See also shǔ, niú, hǔ, tù, lóng, shé, mǎ, yáng, hóu, jī, quǎn, zhū. See also dì zhī, wǔ xíng.

聲 (rad.128) [声] (rad.33) **shēng**
1. A sound. 2. To make a sound. 3. In the martial arts, often means to shout. 4. To sound out (an adversary): feint towards or hit a target before hitting your main objective.

shēng dōng 声东 Shout to the East: draw the adversary into guarding in the wrong place.

shēng dōng dǎ xī 声东打西 Shout to the East and Hit to the West: a back cross step stab with a sword, then stepping to horse stance chop in the opposite direction. From Yangjia style.

shēng dōng jī xī 声东击西 Shout to the East and Hit to the West. 1. The sixth of the Thirty-six Stratagems of Warfare, which apply to many situations. 2. Feint or actually hit in one direction or part of the body to draw the attention of the adversary there, then hit the other direction or body part (such as kicking the leg a couple of times to get his mind there, then attacking the head). From Baguazhang. Also called zhǐ dōng dǎ xī, zhǐ shàng dǎ xià. 3. Moving forward to slicing strike and pull down, one on each side. From Liuhebafa.

shēng jī 声击 Strike with sound: shout to psyche out the adversary, combined with an attack.

繩 [绳] (rad.120) **shéng**
1. A rope, cord. 2. To restrain.

shéng biāo 绳镖 Rope dart: a metal dart about sixteen to twenty centimetres long attached to a rope about four metres long.

失 (rad.37) shī   1. To lose. 2. To miss. 3. A mistake.

shī fēn 失分 To lose a point (in competition).

shī jī 失机 To lose your opportunity in a fight.

shī shǒu 失手 1. To be unexpectedly defeated. 2. To accidentally drop something.

shī tiáo 失调 Loss of regulation, a pattern applied in channel diagnosis. From TCM.

shī xiān 失先 To lose the advantage in fight, to be too slow in setting up.

師 [师] (rad.50) shī   1. Teacher; tutor; master. 2. A person skilled in his/her profession.

shī fù 师傅 Master worker: a term of respect for a master, especially a skilled artisan.

shī fù 师父 1. One's tutor, to whom one is officially apprenticed, and so considered one of his martial family. In English, often called sifu or shirfu. 2. A term of respect for a monk or nun.

shī mǔ 师母 The wife of one's tutor.

shī tú 师徒 A master and his apprentices.

shī xiōng dì 师兄弟 Elder and younger brothers within one's apprenticed lineage.

shī zǐ mèi 师姊妹 Elder and younger sisters within one's apprenticed lineage.

施 (rad.70) shī   1. To act, to do, bring into effect. 2. To bestow, to grant. 3. To apply.

shī lǐ 施礼 To bow, to salute in curtesy.

shī páo huán lǐ 施袍还礼 Send a Return Present Out from your Gown. 1. A throat thread of a spear to a direct stab. 2. A throat thread of a spear to get the right hand to the tip, then a full overhead swinging smash to the ground.

shī yòng 施用 To use; to employ.

濕 [湿] (rad.85) shī   1. Damp, wet, humid. 2. Dampness: one of the six *qi* of nature, environmental influences that can cause disease when in excess. See also liù qì, liù yín.

shī rè 湿热 Damp heat, a pattern applied in channel diagnosis. From TCM.

shī shèng 湿胜 Dampness prevailing, a pattern applied in channel diagnosis. From TCM.

shī yù 湿郁 Damp depression, a pattern applied in channel diagnosis. From TCM.

shī zǔ 湿阻 Dampness obstructing, a pattern applied in channel diagnosis. From TCM.

獅 [狮] (rad.94) shī   A lion. For more movement names using the actions or qualities of the lion, see also under nù shī, xióng-.

shī bǔ shuāng bào 狮捕双豹 Lion Seizes Two Leopards: with one adversary in front and one behind, kick forward to one adversary's belly, then kick back to the other adversary's belly, without turning the body.

shī tùn shǒu 狮吞手 Lion Swallows: use the hands as if the arms were a lion playing with a big ball – the hands facing, palm up and palm down. The hand technique comes from the body, and can go in most any direction.

shī xíng 狮形 Lion structure: circle-walking and changes done seeking the structure, posture, and manner of a lion. From Baguazhang.

shī zǐ bǎi tóu 狮子摆头 Lion Swings its Head: a spinning backfist, ending in a raised knee stance. From Baguazhang.

shī zǐ bǎi wěi 狮子摆尾 Lion Swings its Tail: turn and step out with one hand raised, fingers up, the other moving with the knee, bracing out, fingers down. From Baguazhang.

shī zǐ bào qiú 狮子抱球 Lion Carries a Ball. 1. Hold the arms as if carrying a huge ball between them, in circle-walking: outside hand over the head, inside hand in front of the shoulder. Also applies to the same movement with small double weapons. From Baguazhang. Also called hé bào zhuàn zhǎng, shī zi zhāng zuǐ. 2. Hold the arms as if carrying a large barrel in front of the chest, outside hand at belly height, inside hand at chest height, in circle-walking. From Baguazhang.

shī zǐ chī shí 狮子吃食 Lion Eats a Meal: A circular punch, bringing the hands together to punch into the palm above the head, in a bow stance. From Chuojiao.

shī zǐ gǔn qiú 狮子滚球 Lion Rolls a Ball. 1. A rolling action, either maintaining a ball-holding posture, or bringing the hands together. From Baguazhang. 2. To maintain the ball holding position while stepping and rolling over and through with the whole body. From Baguazhang. Also called hé bào zhuàn zhǎng. 3. A large lifting rolling action with the arms combined with a low turned out kick. From Wudangquan. 4. Circle-walking with the arms bracing out at chest height. From Baguazhang. 5. Rolling the arms to control, then stepping through to a low double connected shove. From Baguazhang, one of its sixty-four hands.

shī zǐ huí tóu 狮子回头 Lion Turns its Head: turn around, tucking in a broadsword beside the body in preparation for a stab.

shī zǐ pán qiú 狮子盘球 Lion Dribbles a Ball. 1. Retreat with a pressing down palm. From Tongbeiquan. 2. Step forward, drawing the blade back, keeping it vertical and pointing down, then step forward into an empty stance and pierce low. From Qingping sword.

shī zǐ pū qiú 狮子扑球 Lion Pounces on a Ball. 1. Step forward with a pouncing action of the arms. This is normally thought of as a tiger pounce, but when done within other lion actions, is a lion pounce. From Baguazhang. 2. Step forward and back with alternate hand pouncing actions. From Wudangquan. 3. Circle-walking with the hands pressing down at hip height. From Baguazhang.

shī zǐ yáo tóu 狮子摇头 Lion Shakes its Head. 1. Step forward with a covering step with an outer spear circle, then to a bow stance inner circle. Repeat, then shift back and snap the spear to press down aligned with the extended leg. From Shaolinquan. 2. Set to empty stance with a sword. From Yang Taijiquan.

shī zǐ zhāng kǒu 狮子张口 Lion Opens its Mouth. 1. Holding the arms up as if holding a large ball. From Baguazhang and Wudangquan. Also called shī zi zhāng zuǐ. 2. Circle the hands and strike downwards with one hand palm in, whilst blocking upwards with the other hand palm out. From Shaolinquan.

shī zǐ zhāng zuǐ 狮子张嘴 Lion Opens its Mouth. 1. Clenching fists, and bending the elbows, open them up to the sides above shoulder height, dropping down at the same time. 2. A movement forward with a rotated brace out and a lift, also called zhāng zhǒu. 3. Holding the arms as if holding a large ball, the same as #1 of shī zi bào qiú or #1 of shī zi zhāng kǒu.

十 (rad.24) shí 1. Ten. 2. Often used in movement names where the action takes the shape of a cross that looks like the character 十.

shí bā bān wǔ yì 十八般武义 The eighteen weapons skills: the techniques and skills of operating the eighteen weapons. See also shí bā qì xiè.

shí bā diǎn 十八点 The eighteen points, the seventh of Chuojiao's nine literary routines, written up as fifty-nine moves. See also wén tàng zi.

shí bā qì xiè 十八器械 The eighteen weapons. Not always the same listing, but often refers to broadsword, spear, straight sword, crescent halberd, stave, pole, lance, trident, axe, battle axe, shovel, rake, whip, mace, mallet, harpoon, dagger axe, and pike. See also dāo, qiāng, jiàn, jǐ, gùn, bàng, shuò, tǎng, fǔ, yuè, chǎn, bǎ, biān, jiǎn, chuí, chā, gē, máo.

shí bā tī 十八踢 The eighteen kicks, the sixth of Chuojiao's nine literary routines, written up as thirty-one moves. See also wén tàng zi.

shí bā yào 十八要 The eighteen requirements of Tongbeiquan for the body positions and power through each joint. These are listed throughout the dictionary.

shí dà jī fǎ 十大技法 The ten major techniques of Bajiquan. To the upper body: peck, graze, carry, sweep across, see diǎn, lüè, tí, yún. To the mid body: close in, poke, crowd, bump, see āi, chuō, jǐ, kào. To the lower body: eat the root, bury the root, see chī gēn, mái gēn.

shí èr hóng chuí 十二洪捶 Twelve Flooding Fists, a routine of Xingyiquan, written up as fifty-eight moves.

shí èr róu 十二柔 Twelve softs: twelve counter attacks, deflecting and countering hard attacks. From Tanglangquan. See also cǎi shǒu ér rù shǒu, hùn shǒu ér lòu shǒu, jiàn gāng ér huí shǒu, jié shǒu ér gǔn shǒu, kāi shǒu ér dié shǒu, kē shǒu ér rù shǒu, lōu shǒu ér jìn shǒu, pū shǒu ér jìn shǒu, rù shǒu ér tōu shǒu, shí tōng ér gòu shǒu, tiāo shǒu ér rù shǒu, zhān shǒu ér pò shǒu.

shí èr xíng 十二型 The twelve qualities of movement sought in many styles: moving, stillness, initiation, landing, standing (on one leg), standing, rotating, bending, lightness, heaviness, speed, and leisureliness. See also dòng, jìng, qǐ, luò, lì, zhàn, zhuàn, zhé, qīng, zhòng, kuài, màn (huǎn).

shí èr xíng 十二形 The twelve qualities of movement modeled on animals of Xingyiquan (the branches that have twelve): dragon, tiger, monkey, horse, alligator, chicken, sparrow hawk, swallow, snake, wedge-tailed hawk, eagle, and bear. See also lóng, hǔ, hóu, mǎ, guī, jī, yào, yàn, shé, tài, yīng, xióng.

shí èr xíng dà hé lián 十二形大合练 Twelve Models Combined: a Xingyiquan routine combining the twelve animals, written up as eighty-nine moves.

shí fāng 十方 The ten directions: East, West, South, North, SE, NE, SW, NW, up, down.

shí liù bǎ 十六把 The sixteen grabs partner routine of Song Xingyiquan. Written up as twelve moves.

shí liù zì jué 十六字诀 The sixteen word formula: the sixteen basic attack and defense manoeuvres of some schools of Baguazhang: penetrate, drag, cut, trap, wring, wheel, walk, revolve, push, carry, drag, guide, coil, tuck, hook, and bore. See also chuān, bān, jié, lán, níng, fān, zǒu, zhuàn, tuī, tuō, dài, lǐng, chán, kòu, diāo, zuān.

shí miàn mái fú 十面埋伏 Ambush from all sides. 1. With the elbows tight to the ribs, strike straight back, also moving back with the body. Also called kào zhǒu. 2. Advancing hook to one side with a sword then slice up to the other side. From Qingping sword.

shí miàn mái fú shì 十面埋伏式 Ambush from All Sides model. One of twenty-four classic spear moves. Most spear routines will have a move with a like name. In general, this name refers to a low level stab.

shí qī zhàn qiāng 十七战枪 Seventeen battle spear: a routine of Yangjia style, written up as seventeen moves.

shí qī zhuī xué 十七椎穴 Extraordinary acupoint Shiqizhuixue (17th vertebra point), EX-B8. At the waist, at the depression under the fifth lumbar vertebra, on the midline. From TCM.

shí sān shì 十三势 The thirteen postures, a routine of Taijiquan.

shí tàng tán tuǐ 十趟弹腿 The ten spring legs, a set of ten short routines used for basics in many northern styles.

shí xuān 十宣 Extraordinary acupoint Shixuan (ten diffusing points), EX-UE11. Five points at the tips of the fingers (with both hands, ten altogether), 0.1 *cun* from the fingernails. From TCM.

shí yào 十要 Ten essentials: intent, *qi*, rotation, sinking, lifting, wrapping, hanging, expanding, releasing, and sequential smoothness. From Baguazhang.

shí zhǐ shēn chū rú zhuī 十指伸出如锥 The ten fingers must extend like awls. From Tongbeiquan, one of its requirements.

shí zì bān lōu 十字搬搂 Remove with a Cross. 1. Cross the arms to block, forming a cross 2. Control the adversary's body to take down in such a way that his arms and raised leg form a cross. From Baguazhang.

shí zì bēng quán 十字崩拳 Crossed crushing punch. See lóng hǔ xiāng jiāo.

shí zì cǎi jiǎo 十字采脚 Crossed Plucking Kick: a front snap kick combined with a finger stab with the opposite hand. From Shaolinquan.

shí zì chā 十字叉 Crossed Fork: block downwards with double weapons crossed. 2. A front split, also called shù chā.

shí zì chuí 十字捶 Crossed strikes: in bow stance, punch straight to each side, to form a cross if seen from above.

shí zì dà lóng xíng 十字大龙形 Crossing Dragon form: walking forward with a three step pattern, hanging the opposite arm down beside the front knee, pressing forward. From Xingyiquan.

shí zì dǎng tuǐ 十字挡腿 Crossing block kick: jump straight up into full splits to kick forward and backward. From Chuojiao.

shí zì dāo pī kǎn xiōng huái 十字刀劈砍胸怀 Crossing Blade Chops and Hacks the Chest: a flat blade hack with a big cutter strongly across the body, the shaft forming a cross shape with the body. From Chen Taijiquan.

shí zì dé quán 十字迭拳 Crossed Folding Fists: rolling punches, pulling in and punching out, alternating rotation. From Wudangquan.

shí zì duǎn jiàn 十字短剑 Double daggers.

shí zì fēn jīn 十字分金 Split Metal with a Cross: step into a horse stance, cross the arms in front of the chest, then bring the fists over and down to punch with backfists at the sides. The 96th move of the tiger and crane routine.

shí zì guǒ héng 十字裹横 Crossing envelop: stepping to the side with a crosscut, doing a circling pull with the arms to change sides. From Xingyiquan.

shí zì hǔ pū bà 十字虎扑把 Crossing tiger pounce and grab: practicing the tiger pounce and grab exercise with a cross shaped stepping pattern. From Xingyiquan. See also hǔ pū bà.

shí zì jià 十字架 Block up with a Cross: block upward with double weapons crossed above the head.

shí zì jiǎo 十字脚 Crossed kick: see shí zì tuǐ.

shí zì kūn shǒu 十字捆手 Bind up the Hands in a Cross: draw your adversary in, trapping his arms extended and crossed, then controlling them with one hand to strike with the other. From Baguazhang.

shí zì lóng xíng héng 十字龙形横 Crossing Dragon form: stepping forward pressing with the arm down by the front knee, pull back and lift the same side foot to cut in, and continue to move forward. From Xingyiquan.

shí zì pāi jiǎo 十字拍脚 Crossing hands slap kick. From Wu Taijiquan.

shí zì píng héng 十字平衡 Cross balance: balance with arms spread to either side of the body, torso no lower than horizontal.

shí zì shǒu 十字手 Crossed arms: cross the arms in front of the body.

shí zì tú 十字图 Cross chart: a cross that indicates north, south, east and west, used for teaching. In the Chinese manner, the South is usually at the top, and the students start standing facing the South. The other directions then follow from there.

shí zì tuǐ 十字腿 Crossed kick. 1. An inside crescent kick with the arms crossed to slap same side hand and foot. 2. An open kick to the side with the arms opened out to the sides. 3. A crossing kick straight to the opposite ear.

實 [实] (rad.40) shí
1. Substantial, solid. Often used in relation to empty, see also xū. 2. True; real. Reality. 3. Repletion, a pattern applied in channel diagnosis. From TCM.

shí yǎn fǎ 实眼法 Solid look method: fix your eyes on your adversary in a fight, showing full confidence, so that he becomes uncertain.

shí fù 实腹 Solid abdomen: using abdominal breathing, settle the *qi* to the *dantian*, pulling the diaphragm down so that the lower belly feels full.

shí fù chàng xiōng 实腹畅胸 To keep the abdomen solid and the chest unimpeded.

shí gōu 实钩 Solid hook, as hand shape: fingers held together. When the arm is rotated so the hook points up, the hand needs to be in a solid hook.

shí lì 实力 Actual strength.

shí lì xiāng dāng 实力相当 Well matched strength (between adversaries).

shí zhàn 实战 Fighting.

shí zhàn bù 实战步 Sparring stance, on guard stance. 1. A natural, upright stance with the hands held up in front. 2. A natural bow stance with the feet open front to back, the front foot turned in slightly, the rear knee bent, heel off the ground, weighted a bit to the front leg.

shí zhāo 实招 Good, solid techniques.

拾 (rad.64) shí
1. To pick up something (like your weapon) from the ground. 2. To tidy up; put in order.

時 [时] (rad.72) shí
1. Time; times. 2. Opportunity, chance.

shí jī 时机 Opportunity, opportune moment. One strategy of fighting is to wait for this opportune instant to attack, defend, or counter attack.

shí jiān chā 时间差 Timing. An essential element of fighting.

石 (rad.112) shí   Stone, rock.

shí bí qí gōng 石筚齐功 Stone ball training, mostly for hand and wrist strength. Stone balls come in a variety of sizes and weights. The lighter ones are rolled in the palm, the heavier ones are carried in the palm while walking. They may reach weights of over twenty kilograms.

shí dān 石担 A stone barbell, used for strength training. Also called shuāng shí tóu.

shí gē 石戈 A stone dagger: a thick dagger made of stone.

shí gǔ 石鼓 A stone drum, used for strength training, especially enveloping type throws.

shí guān 石关 Acupoint Shiguan (stone pass), KI18. At the abdomen, three *cun* above the navel, 0.5 *cun* lateral to the midline (on each side). From TCM.

shí mén 石门 Acupoint Shimen (stone gate), RN5. At the abdomen, two *cun* below the navel, on the midline. From TCM.

shí suǒ 石锁 A stone lock. Come in various weights, and able to carry out a variety of exercises such as lifting and swinging. They are similar in shape and exercise methods to kettlebells, intended to develop a connected power through the body. See also rēng zhì zi, zhì zi, zuān tuī zi.

shí xiù pī chái 石秀劈柴 Stone Talent Chops Wood: a repeating full arm chopping to the head. From Tongbeiquan.

shí zhuāng gōng 石桩功 Stone stance training: sit in horse stance with flat stones on the thighs. Gradually increase the size and weight, and may change to one big stone plank across both thighs.

食 (rad.184) shí   1. To eat. 2. A meal. 3. To feed. 4. Edible.

shí dòu 食窦 Acupoint Shidou (food hole), SP17. At the chest, the fifth intercostal space, six *cun* lateral to the midline (on each side). From TCM.

shí zhǐ 食指 The index finger, index fingers.

矢 (rad.111) shǐ   1. An arrow. 2. A dart. 3. To vow.

shǐ dí 矢镝 An arrowhead.

shǐ fú 矢服 A quiver for arrows.

shǐ liàng 矢量 A vector.

shǐ zhóu 矢轴 The coronal, frontal plane. Divides the body into front and back parts, called anterior and posterior.

shǐ zhuàng miàn 矢状面 A vector.

世 (rad.1) shì   1. A generation. 2. A life span. 3. An age. 4. The world.

shì jiè bēi sài 世界杯赛 World Cup competition.

shì jiè jǐn biāo sài 世界锦标赛 World championship competition, world championships.

市 (rad.8) shì   1. A market, a market town. 2. City; municipality.

shì chǐ 市尺 A market foot: the traditional distance of a *chi*. One *chi* is about 1.1 feet, or one third of a metre. Ten *chi* make up the distance of one *zhang*. Also called chǐ.

shì cùn 市寸 A market inch: the traditional distance of a *cun*. One *cun* is generally measured out by the width of the thumb. Two *cun* is the width of the index and middle fingers together. Three *cun* is the width of four fingers. Four *cun* is palm width. From the ankle bone to the ground is three *cun*, from the ankle bone to the middle of the knee is sixteen *cun*. Also called cùn.

shì lǐ 市里 A market mile: the traditional distance of a *li*. One *li* is about five hundred metres, or a third of a mile. More traditionally, the distance was 300 or 360 paces. Also called lǐ.

shì zhàng 市丈 The traditional distance of a *zhang*, a unit of length about 3.3 metres. One hundred and fifty *zhang* make up the distance of one *li*. Also called zhàng.

勢 [势] (rad.19) shì   1. The outward appearance of a natural object. 2. Often used in martial arts to refer to stances or movements that are modeled on the shape of something or some animal. 3. To emulate the essence or being of an animal. 4. Power; force.

shì jiàn 势剑 Postural sword: sword methods that emphasize moving crisply to hit poses and balances rather than continuous movement. Also called zhàn jiàn.

shì shì xiāng chéng 势势相承 Each and every move follows from the previous, with very few pauses in a routine. A characteristic of Tongbeiquan.

shì yào wěn 势要稳 The postures and power must be stable. From Tongbeiquan, one of its requirements.

式 (rad.56) shì 1. Type, style. A pattern, a type, a model. 2. Often used in martial arts to refer to stances or movements that are modeled after the character of an animal. To emulate the type of movement or style of an animal.

示 (rad.113) shì To show; notify; make known.

shì fàn 示范 1. To demonstrate; to show how to do something; to teach by showing a move physically. 2. A model example. To set an example.

shì fēn 示分 Display the score: openly show the score of a competitor at Taolu competition.

shì fēn yuán 示分员 Person responsible for publicly displaying the score at a competition.

视 [視] (rad.147) shì To look at; to regard. Used in written descriptions of eye movement, not normally used in spoken instructions.

试 [試] (rad.149) shì To try, to test; a trial, a test. To examine. To sound out.

shì dí 试敌 A test match; to test each other within restricted rules.

shì jiàn 试剑 1. To test the sharpness of a blade of a sword. 2. To try out a new sword.

shì lì 试力 To test out power developed from standing training, either with slow, gentle movements or with a partner. From Yiquan.

shì shēng 试声 1. To emit a sound from the *dantian* simultaneous with, and assisting, power moves. 2. Exercises to improve breathing musculature to augment strength. Both from Yiquan.

shì tàn 试探 To test, explore the abilities of an adversary.

收 (rad.66) shōu 1. To gather in. Receive; accept. 2. To put away; take in. 3. Contraction treatment of channels. From TCM.

shōu biān 收鞭 Gather the steel whip: gather the entire whip into the palm of the right hand, folding it cleanly.

shōu biāo 收镖 Gather a dart; snap the dart of a rope dart back into the right hand.

shōu fàng 收放 Gather and release: body technique of gathering in before an explosive technique. The gather is soft and the release is hard. The body technique first swallows in then opens up.

shōu gāng 收肛 Gather the anal sphincter. See tí gāng. Also called bì dì hū.

shōu gōng 收功 To do a cool-down after training.

shōu jiǎo 收脚 Gather the foot, a defensive method: bring the lead foot back, sitting back.

shōu kuà 收胯 Gather in the hip joint: gather the femur into the joint to keep the pelvis straight and upright and stabilise the leg. This allows a straighter line for the hip flexors and delivers clean performance of stances and kicks. Also called chōu kuà.

shōu shì 收势 The final movement of a routine, to close the routine.

shōu shì bìng bù 收势并步 The final movement of a routine when it closes in a closed parallel stance to indicate full completion. Also called shōu shì.

shōu shì huán yuán 收势还原 The final movement of a routine, going back to the original position. Usually the same as shōu shì, shōu shì bìng bù.

shōu tún 收臀 Gather in the buttocks: lightly tuck in the buttocks.

shōu yāo 收腰 Gather the lower back, a method of exploding power: while the torso expands to its fullest, one or both sides of the lower back muscles suddenly tighten, causing the lower back to close down and in.

手 (rad.64) **shǒu**   Hand, hands.

For more hand and arm techniques named by hand rather than palm or fist, see also under àn shǒu, bāi-, bān-, bǎng-, bào pāi-, bī-, biāo zhǐ-, bó-, cǎi-, cāo-, chā-, chāi-, cháng qiā-, chán-, chǎn-, chāo-, chén-, chèn-, chī dān-, chī-, chōu-, chū-, chū-, chuī-, cuō-, cuō-, dā-, dǎ yǎn-, dài-, dān-, dān tuī-, dān yún-, dī bǎng-, diǎn jīng-, diàn diāo-, diào-, dié-, dǒu-, duǎn-, fā-, fān-, fǎn chán-, fēng-, fú-, fú-, fù zǐ gōng-, gān-, gōu-, gòu-, guàn táng-, gǔn-, guò-, hé-, héng-, hú dié-, hù-, huàn zhěn-, huō-, huò-, jǐ-, jiǎ-, jiǎn-, jiāo chā-, jiāo-, jiāo-, jiē-, jiè-, jīn chā-, jǐn bā-, juē-, kā-, kāi-, kē-, kòu-, kǔn-, lán-, lāo-, lēi-, liè-, lǐng-, lòu-, lǔ-, lǚ-, lüè-, luò-, nà-, náo-, nián-, pāi-, pān-, pān jǐng-, péng-, piē-, pò guā-, pū-, qī-, qiān-, qián kūn-, qiǎng-, qiāo-, qiē-, qīng-, quān gē-, quán-, ruǎn-, sǎ-, shī tùn-, shí zì-, shuāi-, shuǎi-, shuāng gōu-, shuāng guān-, shuāng tuī-, sōng-, suí-, suǒ-, tān-, tàn-, tí-, tiē sǎo-, tiě zhǒu-, tú-, tuī-, tūn-, tuō-, tuō tiān-, tōu-, tuō-, wài kē-, wǔ huā-, xià ná-, xiǎo chán-, xiè-, xū-, yǐn-, yòu-, yuán-, yún-, yún mó-, yún-, yùn-, zhà-, zhào fēng-, zhěn-, zhì-, zhuǎn shēn wò-, zhuǎn shēn yún-, zhān-, zhuàn-, zhuàng bēi-, zhuì-, zhuó-, zǒu-, zuān-.

shǒu bǎ 手靶 Hand pad: a small hand held pad used by a trainer for punching practice.

shǒu bān dān guì 手扳丹桂 Pull the Orange Osmanthus Tree: step to a left reverse bow stance and strike across the front with the right elbow. The 66th move of the tiger and crane routine. The same as dài mǎ guī cáo on the other side.

shǒu bào huàn xióng 手抱浣熊 Hug the Racoon: twist the arm behind the back in a policeman's grip. From wrestling. Also called fǎn bèi zhuàn.

shǒu bào dà xióng 手抱大熊 Hug the Bear: hug an adversary around his waist from the front and bow forward until he falls back. From wrestling.

shǒu bèi rú tiě 手背如铁 The backs of the hands must be like iron. From Tongbeiquan, one of its requirements.

shǒu bì 手臂 The arm, arms: the arm in general, including the upper arm and the forearm.

shǒu biè 手别 Hand pinning throw: throws that off balance an adversary by use of mostly the hands rather than trips or close hip contact, often catching behind the knee as one pivot point. From wrestling.

shǒu bù guò jiǎo, zhǒu bù guò xī 手不过脚肘不过膝 The hands do not pass the feet, the elbows do not pass the knees. A classic requirement of compact styles.

shǒu dǎ sān fēn jiǎo dǎ qī 手打三分脚打七 The hands hit three tenths worth while the feet are used for seven tenths worth. A martial saying.

shǒu dāo 手刀 A hand blade: a broadsword with a slightly shorter and thicker blade than a normal broadsword. See also dāo.

shǒu dǎo lì 手倒立 A handstand. Also called shǒu dǐng.

shǒu dào jiǎo bù yí, quán quán dǎ zì jǐ. shǒu dào jiǎo yě dào, jīn gāng yě diē dǎo 手到脚不移拳拳打自己。手到脚也到，金刚也跌倒 If you don't move your feet and only hit with your hands, you might as well be fighting yourself. If your hands and feet arrive together, even a temple guard will fall. A martial saying.

shǒu dào yāo bù dào, fàng rén bù dé miào. shǒu dào yāo yě dào, fàng rén rú bá cǎo 手到腰不到放人不得妙。手到腰也到放人如拔草 If you hit with your hands without your waist, you won't achieve anything against your adversary. If your hands and waist arrive together, beating him is as easy as pulling grass. A martial saying.

shǒu dé 手得 Ethical hands: to not apply more violence to an adversary than necessary, to not injure needlessly.

shǒu dǐng 手鼎 A handstand. Also called shǒu dǎo lì.

shǒu fǎ 手法 Hand and arm techniques, handwork.

shǒu fēng 手峰 Point of contact of the hand: includes all the striking surfaces of the fist, palm, hook, and grabbing shapes.

shǒu gé 手格 Bare knuckle fighting. Also called tú bó.

shǒu gōng 手弓 The hand bow: the elbow is the central grip, the collar bone and wrist are the tips. When the bow is pulled the elbow is settled and the direction is set, the hand settles at the wrist, the collar bone is stabilised, so that the entire unit is balanced from proximal to distal.

shǒu huī pí pa 手挥琵琶 Strum the Pipa. Usually an empty stance with the hands placed in front, one at the elbow of the other, palms facing. To bend an adversary's arm and apply pressure on his elbow down and away while hyper-flexing and pressing up the wrist.

shǒu jué yīn 手厥阴 Hand Jue Yin. Together with the Foot Jue Yin, this is a deep *yin* channel that collects and transmits blood, collecting it for later use. From TCM. See also shǒu jué yīn xīn bāo jīng, zú jué yīn.

shǒu jué yīn xīn bāo jīng 手厥阴心包经 Shou Jue Yin (Hand Faint Yin) Pericardium channel, PC. Full name of the shǒu jué yīn. From TCM.

shǒu lèi 手擂 Striking throw techniques of wrestling: throws that involve driving the hands forcefully in on an adversary, using mostly the hands as pivot points, rather than trips or the body.

shǒu pái 手牌 A hand shield: a light shield made of wood, meant to be carried in one hand. Almost six feet long and about a foot wide.

shǒu pò pái 手破排 Hand Breaks the Platoon: shifting from horse stance to bow stance, turn and push one hand forward with the elbow bent, bracing the other to the side. The left is the 26th move of the tiger and crane routine, the right is the 27th.

shǒu sān lǐ 手三里 Acupoint Shousanli, (hand three miles) (LI10). About two *cun* down from the elbow crease, on line between acupoints LI5 and LI11 (on each arm). From TCM. A sensitive point. Best to hit with a chop or a grab and knife edge strike. A crippling point, striking here may cause serious injury. See also cán xué.

shǒu shào yáng 手少阳 Hand Shao Yang. Together with the Foot Shao Yang, it regulates the flow of *qi* and blood between exterior and interior. From TCM. See also shǒu shào yáng sān jiāo jīng, zú shào yáng.

shǒu shào yáng sān jiāo jīng 手少阳三焦经 Shou Shao Yang (Hand Lesser Yang) San Jiao (Triple Energizer or Triple Warmer) channel, SJ. Full name of shǒu shào yáng. From TCM.

shǒu shào yīn 手少阴 Hand Shao Yin. Together with the Foot Shao Yin, it communicates between the Tai Yin channels and the Jue Yin channels, regulating *qi*, blood, and heat. From TCM. See also shǒu shào yīn xīn jīng, zú shào yīn.

shǒu shào yīn xīn jīng 手少阴心经 Shou Shao Yin (Hand Lesser Yin) Heart channel, HT. Full name of shǒu shào yīn. From TCM.

shǒu shì 手势 Hand signals (of a referee).

shǒu shì liǎng shàn mén, quán píng jiǎo dǎ rén 手是两扇门, 全凭脚打人 The hands are like hinged gates (for protection), but success against an adversary depends on the feet. A martial saying.

shǒu sì liú xīng yǎn sì diàn 手似流星眼似电 The hands should be like shooting stars and the eyes should be like lightning. A martial saying. Also called quán sì liú xīng yǎn sì diàn.

shǒu suí bù kāi 手随步开 Hands open with the feet: The hands do not move on their own, nor do they move while the feet are stationary, they move as the feet move. From Baguazhang, one of its main requirements.

shǒu tài yáng 手太阳 Hand Tai Yang. Together with the Foot Tai Yang, it covers the back of the torso and back of the legs and arms. From TCM. See also shǒu tài yáng xiǎo cháng jīng, zú tài yáng.

shǒu tài yáng xiǎo cháng jīng 手太阳小肠经 Shou Tai Yang (Hand Greater Yang) Small Intestine channel, SI. Full name of shǒu tài yáng. From TCM.

shǒu tài yīn 手太阴 Hand Tai Yin. Together with the Foot Tai Yin, it is a superficial channel that opens to the inside, transforms and delivers blood and fluids. From TCM. See shǒu tài yīn fèi jīng, also zú tài yīn.

shǒu tài yīn fèi jīng 手太阴肺经 Shou Tai Yin (Hand Greater Yin) Lung channel, LU. Full name of shǒu tài yīn. From TCM.

shǒu tào 手套 Sparring gloves. Boxing gloves.

shǒu wàn 手腕 The wrist. An easy target for control techniques.

shǒu wò dà liáng 手握大梁 Grab the Big Beam: grab your adversary's wrist and curl your other arm over then under his arm, press up on his elbow and pull his hand down. From Qinna.

shǒu wò lóng tóu 手握龙头 Grab the Dragon's Head: grab around your adversary's neck, wrapping your arm around from the front, getting your hand behind his neck. From Qinna.

shǒu wǔ lǐ 手五里 Acupoint Shouwuli (hand five li), LI13. At the outside of the arm, 3 *cun* up from the lateral epicondyle of the humerus, about the midpoint of the biceps (on each arm). From TCM.

shǒu xíng 手型 The hand shape used in a technique (palm, fist, hook, finger placement, etc.).

shǒu yáng míng 手阳明 Hand Yang Ming. Together with the Foot Yang Ming, it runs inside the body and is involved with digestion and movement of nutrients and fluids. From TCM. See also shǒu yáng míng dà cháng jīng, zú yáng míng.

shǒu yáng míng dà cháng jīng 手阳明大肠经 Shou Yang Ming (Hand Bright Yang) Large Intestine channel, LI. Full name of shǒu yáng míng. From TCM.

shǒu yào cuī zhǐ ér zhǐ bù ní shǒu 手要催指而指不逆手 Power should flow from hands to fingers, the fingers should not run counter to the hands. From Xingyiquan.

shǒu yào jí 手要疾 The hands must be quick. Speed and accuracy of the hands in attack and defense are necessities in fighting.

shǒu yú zú hé 手与足合 The hands harmonise, or work together with, the feet. One of the six harmonies. See also liù hé.

shǒu zhǐ 手肢 Finger, fingers.

首 (rad.185) **shǒu** 1. Head. 2. First. 3. The tip of the grip of a short weapon.

shǒu yào cuī shēn ér shēn bù ní shǒu 首要催身而身不逆首 Power should flow from head to body, the body should not run counter to the head. A principle of Xingyiquan.

受 (rad.87) **shòu** To receive; to accept; to get. To take; to tolerate.

shòu shāng 受伤 To get injured.

獸 (rad.94) [兽] (rad.30) **shòu** A beast, animal. Bestial.

shòu tóu shì 兽头式 Beast's Head posture. 1. See hù xīn quán. 2. A vertical elbow tuck in front combined with a sweeping punch to the rear. From Wudangquan.

樞 [枢] (rad.75) **shū** 1. Pivot; hub; centre. This character is used in names for acupoints, so watch for the difference between this shū and the shū 腧 输 俞 below. From TCM.

殳 (rad.79) **shū** A ancient long weapon in the halberd class, generally about four metres long. It is wooden and may have two metal tips, either plain or with large spiked oblongs.

腧 (rad.130) **shū** A depression. This character is used in names for acupoints that involve transport or conveyance through muscle. From TCM.

shū xué 腧穴 Acupoint. The 'holes' where the *qi* and blood are transported to the surface, closely related to the circulation of the meridians and collaterals. From TCM.

shū fǔ 腧府 Acupoint Shufu (transport mansion), KI27. At the chest, in the depression under the collar bone, two *cun* lateral to the midline (on each side). This is the final point of the Kidney channel. Sometimes written 输, which is also pronounced shū. From TCM.

舒 (rad.135) **shū** 1. Easy, leisurely. 2. Unfold, stretch.

shū chàng 舒畅 Comfortable and unimpeded, calm and pleasant. A comfortable feeling sought in internal styles.

shū fú 舒服 Comfortable.

shū xiōng 舒胸 Comfortable chest: the chest is held open, expanded, and natural, not stuck out or puffed out. This is a common requirement for internal styles.

shū zhǐ 舒指 Spread the fingers open.

輸 [输] (rad.159) **shū** 1. To transport; to convey. 2. Often acupoints are written with 俞 or 腧 when the final word in an acupoint name is shū. All three characters are pronounced shū. Watch also for the difference between this shū and 樞shū above in acupoint names. From TCM.

S

暑 (rad.72) **shǔ** 1. Heat; hot weather. 2. Summerheat: one of the six *qi* of nature, environmental influences that can cause disease when in excess. See also liù qì, liù yín.

蜀 (rad.142) **shǔ** 1. Shu kingdom (221-263), one of the Three Kingdoms. 2. The traditional name for the area of Sichuan province, used as its short name.

shǔ hàn 蜀汉 The Shu kingdom (221-263), one of the Three Kingdoms. See also sān guó.

鼠 (rad.208) **shǔ** 1. Rat, mouse. 2. Rat as the first of the twelve animals from the Chinese zodiac, associated with a twelve year cycle symbolic of the earthly branches. The twelve animals make up a sixty year cycle when combined with the five phases. See also dì zhī, shēng xiào, wǔ xíng.

束 (rad.75) **shù** 1. To bind. 2. A bundle. 3. To control, restrain.

shù gǔ 束骨 Acupoint Shugu (bundle bone), BL65. At the foot, on the outer edge, at the proximal joint of the little toe, at the border of the lighter and darker skin (on each foot). From TCM.

shù jìn 束劲 Binding power: the upper and lower body bind together as one. One of Xingyiquan's five powers. See also cǎi jìn, guǒ jìn, jué jìn, pū jìn.

shù shēn 束身 1. To tuck in the body while gathering expanding power. 2. To sit back to a gathered stance, making oneself smaller.

shù shēn qǐng shǒu 束身情手 Tuck in with Inviting Hands: sit back to empty stance, holding the hands out palm up, front at throat height, rear at its elbow. From Shaolinquan.

樹 [树] (rad.75) **shù** 1. A tree. 2. To plant. 3. To set up; establish. For movement names using the quality of trees, see also under gū shù-, gǔ-, kū-.

shù shàng kāi huā 树上开花 Deck the Tree with False Blossoms. The twenty-ninth of the Thirty-six Stratagems of Warfare, which apply to many situations.

竪 [竖] (rad.117) **shù** Upright, vertical, perpendicular. Erect, upright.

shù chā 竖叉 Front splits. In the category of the splits leg techniques. See also pī chā xìng tuǐ fǎ. Also called shí zì chā.

shù dǐng 竖顶 Upright crown of head: keep the nape of the neck straight so that the head stays level.

shù wàn 竖腕 Set the wrist so that the palm is upright.

shù zhǎng 竖掌 Vertical palm, upright palm.

shù zhǒu 竖肘 Vertical elbow: the forearm is held vertically with the elbow bent.

術 (rad.144) **[术]** (rad.75) **shù** 1. Art; skill; technique. 2. Methods, tactics.

shù yǔ 术语 Specialised terminology, technical terms.

摔 (rad.64) **shuāi** 1. To throw, to take down. 2. The category of throws or takedowns in each move. See also sì jī.

shuāi bà 摔把 Slap the butt end of a long weapon: Strike the shaft quickly and strongly flat on the ground, holding at the tip end.

shuāi biān 摔鞭 A takedown controlling just the wrist, taking down and continuing to control the wrist for a lockout.

shuāi dǎo 摔倒 To be thrown down, be taken down.

shuāi diē lèi 摔跌类 Throwing methods, the category of methods that include throwing and takedowns.

shuāi fǎ 摔法 Throws, takedowns: category of techniques that include all throwing techniques that take an adversary to the ground (though generally not including sweep kicks, which are within the category of kicks). Common to most styles are hip throws, knock downs, jerks, hooks, shoots, traps, rakes, and bounces. See also chuāi, dǎo, gǒng, gōu, huá, ná, pá, péng. See also sì jī.

shuāi gùn 摔棍 Smash a staff: Strike the shaft quickly and strongly flat on the ground. Usually done either in drop stance or a squat. Usually following a large circling swing.

shuāi jiāo 摔跤 Chinese wrestling. Also called jiāo shù, pāi zhǎng.

shuāi ké zǐ 摔壳子 A back break fall.

shuāi pāi zhǎng 摔拍掌 Throwing slap palms: throw the back of the palm out to strike to eyebrow height, then throw the other palm out to strike with the palm. From Tongbeiquan.

shuāi pī zhǎng 摔劈掌 Throwing chop: to chop down with a straight arm, relaxed shoulder and palm. From Tongbeiquan.

shuāi qiāng 摔枪 Smash a spear: holding near the tip, strike the shaft quickly and strongly flat on the ground. Double handed is usually done in a drop stance, single handed is usually done in a bow stance.

shuāi shǒu 摔手 Throw the hand, a backhand slap: a flinging technique with a relaxed wrist, to snap a backhand to an adversary's face, especially to the nose, in preparation for a following attack. In Tongbeiquan, also called shuǎi shǒu.

shuāi shǒu jiàn 摔手剪 Throwing darts, a hidden weapon made of iron or bamboo.

shuāi shǒu táng láng quán 摔手螳螂拳 Shuaishou (throwing hands) Tanglangquan, a branch of Preying Mantis that uses reverse hand techniques and backhands extensively.

shuāi tóu 摔投 Takedowns and throws.

shuāi tóu jì shù 摔投技术 The methods and skills of takedowns and throws.

shuāi zhǎng 摔掌 Throw the palm. 1. As an exercise, swing a straight arm in a full circle to slap the thigh with the back of the hand. 2. Swing the arm in a large circle to contact with the palm or back of the hand, depending on the direction of the swing. Also called lēi shuāi zhǎng. 3. Snap the arm out to contact with a backhand. From Tongbeiquan. 4. A slap on the ground. 5. A sudden snap of the wrist to strike with the hand or fist. From Duanquan.

shuāi zhǎng sì zhà dàn 摔掌似炸弹 Throw the palm like a missile. From Tongbeiquan, one of its five requirements, see also wǔ zì yāo qiú.

甩 (rad.101) shuǎi 1. To throw away, discard. 2. To swing, throw, fling.

shuǎi biān 甩鞭 Fling the Whip: catch an adversary's wrist with both hands and fling his arm sharply to take him down.

shuǎi bì 甩臂 To throw out the arms.

shuǎi chuí 甩捶 1. A throwing punch. 2. A full circle backfist.

shuǎi fǎ 甩法 Flailing methods in general. See also shuǎi jī, shuǎi ná.

shuǎi jī 甩击 Evade and turn around to throw a flailing strike like a spinning backfist.

shuǎi ná 甩拿 Grab and yank outwards to throw down or dislocate.

shuǎi shǒu 甩手 1. Free-hand sparring practice. From Wing Chun. 2. A loosely thrown backhand strike. From Tongbeiquan. Also called shuāi shǒu, shuāi zhǎng.

shuǎi tóu 甩头 Throw the head: to initiate a throw from a movement of the head, to assist power to the arms.

shuǎi tóu yī zhī 甩头一枝 Throw the Head like a Branch, a rope dart technique: circle the rope dart clockwise, turn and lift the dart to the shoulder and across the back, turning again to bring it around in front of the belly, then shoot it out across the back from under the left armpit.

shuǎi yāo 甩腰 Waist swinging: standing with the legs astride, extend the arms forward and backward, bending forward and backward at the waist, or circling around.

率 (rad.95) shuài To lead, command.

shuài gǔ 率谷 Acupoint Shuaigu (commanding the valley), GB8. At the head, 1.5 cun from the hairline directly above the ear (on each side). From TCM.

栓 (rad.75) shuān 1. To bind, fasten. 2. As a hand technique, an action binding an adversary as if with a rope.

涮 (rad.85) shuàn To rinse. Scald.

shuàn bà 涮把 Scald the butt: holding the shaft vertical, draw the tip of a long weapon sharply across the ground to check at ground level.

shuàn hú lǔ 涮葫芦 Scald the Gourd, a takedown:

when grasped head on, grab behind your adversary's neck and at his belt, hook his leg, and lean forward, pushing him down while swinging his leg up.

shuàn yāo 涮腰 1. A rolling snap of the waist used particularly to switch places in a throw, both preventing a throw and getting into position for a throw yourself. 2. Waist rolling: standing with the legs astride, do big waist circles around the hip joints. 3. Walk the circle, turning and rolling at the waist as if throwing an adversary. Done in a number of different ways to emphasis different power. From Baguazhang.

shuàn yāo lūn gùn 涮腰抡棍 Waist roll with staff swing: standing with the legs astride, circle and roll around the waist, swinging the staff so that it swings around behind and then across in front as you lean back.

雙 [双] (rad.29) shuāng A pair; double.

shuāng àn zhǎng 双按掌 Double press down. 1. Press down with both hands. 2. The pressing down circle-walking posture of Baguazhang. Also called àn zhǎng, xià chén zhǎng.

shuāng bǎ 双把 Double Grab: drill up the midline to grab, pull down while lifting the knee to strike, then land to pounce forward. From Xingyiquan.

shuāng bǎi zhǎng 双摆掌 Double arm swing: swing both arms together in a full circle from one side to strike downwards at shoulder height on the other side.

shuāng bān jǐng 双扳颈 Double Twist to the Neck: grab the back of the head and the cheeks of an adversary and twist.

shuāng bǐ shǒu 双匕首 Double daggers: a pair of double edged daggers. Also called bǐ shǒu.

shuāng bì gōng 双臂功 Handstand pushups.

shuāng bì huán rào cè pī fā lì 双臂环绕侧劈发力 Double arm circles to sideways cutting, alternating the arms. From Yiquan.

shuāng bì jiāo chā rào huán 双臂交叉绕环 Double arm crossing swings, a shoulder warm-up exercise, circling the arms in opposite directions.

shuāng bì rào huán 双臂绕环 Double arm swings, a shoulder warm-up exercise.

shuāng biān suǒ bì 双鞭索臂 Double Whips use the Arm like a Cable: an arm bar, reversing your adversary's elbow and placing his arm over your shoulder.

shuāng biān yā zhǒu 双鞭压肘 Double Whips Press the Elbow: an arm bar, reversing your adversary's elbow and pressing down. From Baguazhang, one of its sixty-four hands.

shuāng chā zhǎng 双插掌 Double palm insertion: drive the hands forward as if smashing a double door open.

shuāng chén 双沉 Double settled, when both hands or feet are settled and sunk.

shuāng chōng quán 双冲拳 Double punch: punch both fists simultaneously forward at shoulder width.

shuāng dā shǒu 双搭手 Double hand contact: in partner training such as push hands, contacting with two arms.

shuāng dāo 双刀 Double broadswords. A pair usually has the inside of the guard flat so that they can be pressed together when carried. See also dāo.

shuāng dāo kàn zhǒu 双刀看肘 (To judge the skill of) the double broadsword, watch the elbows. A martial saying.

shuāng dāo shā yā 双刀杀鸭 Double Blades Kill the Duck: one hand grabs the adversary while the other chops his throat, retreating to put more power into the strike.

shuāng dāo tiào bā guà 双刀跳八卦 Double Blades Jump the Trigrams. A routine in Duanquan for double broadswords, written up as eight moves.

shuāng dāo zhé shǔ 双刀折鼠 Double Blades Chop the Rat: a double palm strike to both sides of the neck.

shuāng dì chuí 双地捶 Double Mallets to the Ground: a full squat with punches straight down at the sides. From Chuojiao.

shuāng dié bù 双蝶步 Double butterfly stance: kneel with the knees close together and the inside of the shins on the ground. From southern styles.

shuāng dié fēi wǔ 双蝶飞舞 A Pair of Butterflies Dance in Flight: pivot on a foot to turn a full circle, bringing a sword all the way around, and landing into a bow stance low pierce. From Qingping sword.

shuāng fǎn dāo 双反刀 Double reverse blades: a chop to the throat with both hands, using the root of the palms. This is done when your adversary has a close hold on you from the front, to release his grip.

shuāng fēi fú dié 双飞蚨蝶 A Pair of Butterflies Fly: sit into a low horse stance and settle under an uppercut. Protect the head with the other hand blocking up. The 101st move of the tiger and crane routine.

shuāng fēi wō 双飞挝 Double flying grips: an ancient soft weapon made of a double rope with two hand-shaped metal pieces at the ends.

shuāng fēn tuǐ 双分腿 Double separating legs: sit to a full squat, legs together, and pound down on either side with the forearms, fist hearts turns in. From Shaolinquan.

shuāng fāng huà jǐ 双方画戟 Double sided design crescent headed spear: a spear with a crescent hook on each side of the tip. See also dān fāng huà jǐ, jǐ.

shuāng fēng guàn ěr 双峰贯耳 Two Peaks Pierce the Ears. 1. Step forward and circle the fists to finish facing each other at ear height, punching with the knuckles, fists rolled over. From Taijiquan. 2. Stand up and hit to the ears with the meaty part of the fists, fist hearts up. From Shaolinquan.

shuāng fēng wò yuè 双峰卧月 Two Peaks Lay Down the Moon: Stand on one leg with double chopping palms. From Piguaquan.

shuāng fèng cháo yáng 双凤朝阳 Two Phoenix Face the Sun: double punch to the temples. From Liuhebafa.

shuāng fèng yǎn 双凤眼 A pair of Phoenix Eyes. See shuāng zhū quán.

shuāng fèng zhǎn chì 双凤展翅 A Pair of Phoenixes Spread their Wings. See #5 of fèng huáng zhǎn chì.

shuāng fú 双浮 Double lightness: both hands or feet are overly empty. From Taijiquan, where it is considered an error causing instability. See also shuāng zhòng.

shuāng fǔ 双斧 Double axes, a short heavy weapon similar to an ax, but chunkier, wielded as a pair.

shuāng gōng qián zì 双工千字 A Pair of Workers Write the Character Qian (千): from a horse stance, shift to right reverse stance and push the right palm forwards, turned to strike with the edge, blocking up with the left forearm. The 50th move of the tiger and crane routine.

shuāng gōng bào yuè 双弓抱月 Two Bows Cradle the Moon: step to a bow stance and push the palms down in front, elbows slightly bent, fingers pointing to each other. The 43rd move of the tiger and crane routine.

shuāng gōng bù 双弓步 Double bow stance. 1. A bow stance with the front foot tucked in, shin vertical, the rear leg bent with the thigh vertical, foot aligned straight, both heels on the ground. From southern styles. 2. A bow stance with a raised rear heel, pressing into the ground with the ball of the foot. See also gōng bù.

shuāng gōng chā huā 双弓插花 Double Bows Insert Flowers: in a horse stance with the elbows out to each side, push the palms down in front of the hips, fingers pointing to each other. The 16th move of the tiger and crane routine.

shuāng gōng fú hǔ 双弓伏虎 A Pair of Bows Ambush the Tiger: shifting from bow stance to horse stance, push both palms forward with the elbows bent, hands both turned so the little finger is on top. The left hand is at neck height, the right below. The 28th move of the tiger and crane routine.

shuāng gōu shǒu 双勾手 Double hook hands: usually means hooking both hands and swinging the arms down behind the body.

shuāng gōu guà yù píng 双勾挂玉瓶 Double Hooks Hook onto the Jade Vase: jump forward, bringing the hands forward, then hook them and set them in front of the chest. From Shaolinquan.

shuāng gōu 双钩 Double hooks: the standard double hooks have a double edged blade with a hook at the tip, grips near the end with a protecting and sharp crescent moon shaped hand guard, and a sharp drill at the grip end. They are the length of a normal sword. Non-standard double hooks include hǔ tóu gōu, hù shǒu gōu, lù jiǎo gōu.

S

shuāng guà chuí fǎ 双掛搥法 Double Hook Punches: from a right reverse stance, step to a right empty stance and hook the elbows to bring the fists up. The right forearm is across the chest and the left fist is tucked up at the side. The 51st move of the tiger and crane routine.

shuāng guān shǒu 双关手 A double hit with the hands.

shuāng guān tiē mén 双关铁门 Close the Iron Paired Doors: lift the knee and turn around, pressing the hands together in front of the chest. From Shaolinquan.

shuāng gǔn chuí 双滚搥 Trundle to control, then double strike. Also called gǔn shǒu pào.

shuāng hèn jiǎo 双恨脚 Double stamp on the spot: a quick unweighting to come down with a double stamp in a low squat. From Shaolinquan.

shuāng hǔ bào tóu 双虎抱头 A pair of tigers wrap the head: step forward gathering the hands up the midline, bring the same side hand up close to the head, which presses forward. Gather both fists at the chest and step forward, pulling the hands down to the knee in a bow stance. From Xingyiquan.

shuāng huā duì wǔ 双花对舞 Two Flowers Dance Together: step back and forth using back cross steps, bringing a sword over with each step to cut down extending out with the extended leg. From Qingping sword.

shuāng huán shǒu 双环手 Double rings: with the hands in front of the body, circle one hand in then out, then the other hand, finishing with both palms extended in front of the shoulders. From southern styles.

shuāng huàn bù 双换步 Double change step: tuck in step, then turned out step, then continue to tuck in step to the other foot, then turn out step again, continuing in the same direction. From Baguazhang. Also called fù huàn bù.

shuāng huàn zhǎng 双换掌 Double Change: the second of the eight mother palms, involving the double changing stepping. From Baguazhang.

shuāng jiā zhǒu 双挟肘 Cover up: tuck the elbows together in front of the chest as a protective move.

shuāng jiǎn 双锏 Double rulers, wielded as a pair, one in each hand. See also jiǎn.

shuāng jiàn 双剑 Double swords, wielded as a pair, one in each hand. See also jiàn.

shuāng jiàn qiē qiáo 双剑切桥 Double Swords Cut the Bridge: sitting in horse stance, stab the hands forward with the elbows bent so that the forearms are horizontal, fingers forward, palms facing each other. The 25th move of the tiger and crane routine.

shuāng kòu bù 双扣步 Double tucked stance: Feet and knees tucked in, one foot slightly in front of the other. Also called bāo mǎ bù.

shuāng kòu zǎo 双扣枣 Double Pick the Date. See shuāng zhū quán.

shuāng kǔn tuǐ 双捆腿 Double leg binding takedown: a category of takedown that involves grabbing around both legs of an adversary.

shuāng lóng bǎi wěi 双龙摆尾 A Pair of Dragons Slash their Tails: a leg technique to deal with two adversaries. Kick the one in front of you with a turned out kick to the shin, then immediately kick the one behind you with a rear thrust kick with the same leg.

shuāng lóng chū hǎi 双龙出海 A Pair of Dragons Emerge from the Sea: sitting in horse stance, stab both palms forward, palms down. The 18th move of the tiger and crane routine.

shuāng lóng jiǎo wěi 双龙绞尾 A Pair of Dragons Wring their Tails: a shoulder exercise. Stand with arms stretched out to the sides, roll the palms up, one normal and one rolled under, rolling from the shoulders, alternating back and forth.

shuāng lóng rù hǎi 双龙入海 A Pair of Dragons Enter the Sea: circle-walking with the hands both stabbing down, palms facing the centre of the circle. From Baguazhang.

shuāng lóng tàn hǎi 双龙探海 A Pair of Dragons Reach into the Sea: a double straight high thrust with the hands. From Wing Chun.

shuāng lún chuí 双抡搥 Double swinging beating, an arm training exercise: swinging the arms loosely from the shoulders in a full circle, one going forwards and the other going backwards from the top.

shuāng mǎ xíng 双马形 Double horse form: moving into a seventy-thirty stance with double ramming fists or straight jabs. From Xingyiquan.

Also called mǎ bēn tí.

shuāng ná 双拿 Double control: grasp an adversary with both hands by the shoulders, hips, or other large joint, or the wrist or elbow, or to poke a pressure point with a double grasp. From Qinna.

shuāng pāi hú dié 双拍蝴蝶 Double Pat the Butterflies: sit to an empty stance and circle the hands in front, patting downwards together near the front knee. From Shaolinquan.

shuāng qí kāi dào 双旗开道 Two Banners Clear the Way: lift the left knee and intercept with a sword to the left, then lift the right knee and intercept to the right. From Qingping sword. See also jié jiàn.

shuāng qì xiè 双器械 Double weapons. 1. A pair of the same weapons, holding one in each hand, such as double swords, double broadswords, double hooks, double daggers. 2. Two different weapons wielded together, one in each hand, such as broadsword and whip.

shuāng qiāng 双枪 Double spears: a pair of double-headed spears that are wielded simultaneously. They are smaller than a normal spear. One alone is called a shuāng tóu qiāng.

shuāng qín 双擒 Double grasp: to grab an adversary with both hands, usually to prevent him from escaping and prepare for a control technique. From Qinna.

shuāng quán 双拳 Double simultaneous punch, usually high and low.

shuāng rén duì liàn 双人对练 A two person partner routine.

shuāng shé chán shēn 双蛇缠身 A Pair of Snakes Coil their Bodies: circle-walking in a high and extended spear carrying posture, inside hand palm up over shoulder height, outside hand up behind palm up, reaching forward over the head. From Baguazhang.

shuāng shé tù xìn 双蛇吐信 A Pair of Snakes Spit their Tongues: turning reaching out with the palms up, stepping around and reaching behind in a fairly low stance. From Baguazhang.

shuāng shí tóu 双石头 A stone barbell, used for strength training. Also called shí dān.

shuāng shǒu 双手 Two-handed, as in a two-handed push or a two-handed grasp on a weapon.

shuāng shǒu dài 双手带 1. A two handed cutter, a horse cutter. See pū dāo. Also called pǔ dāo, zhǎn mǎ dāo. 2. A representative routine of Chaquan horse cutter, written up as fifty-one moves.

shuāng shǒu guān mén 双手关门 Close the Door with Both Hands: sit to a squatting stance, bringing the hands together in front of the chest. From Shaolinquan.

shuāng shǒu huā 双手花 Double handed flowers, a steel whip technique: holding the whip in the middle with both hands, circle it forward vertically to the left and right of the body.

shuāng shǒu jià gùn (qiāng) 双手架棍(枪) Framing block up double handed with a staff (or spear): lift the shaft above the head, hands spread with one hand at the butt and the other along the shaft, shaft horizontal or angled down.

shuāng shǒu jiàn 双手剑 Double handed sword: a sword with a slightly longer grip, and usually also a longer blade, made for wielding with both hands.

shuāng shǒu lì jǔ gùn 双手立举棍 Double handed present the staff vertically: Stand at attention, holding the base of the staff with the right hand in front the body, the left hand holding the shaft, staff vertical. This is usually at the beginning of a routine.

shuāng shǒu ná wò dān shǒu 双手拿握单手 Double handed grab on one arm: grab the forearm with both hands. A wrestling grip, or for practicing releases.

shuāng shǒu píng jǔ gùn 双手平举棍 Double handed present the staff flatly: stand holding near the base of the staff with the right hand in front the body, the left hand holding the shaft, staff horizontal above the head.

shuāng shǒu píng tuī zhǎng 双手平推掌 Two handed level push: circle-walking with the palms turned out away from the body, towards the circle centre. From Baguazhang. See also bào yuè zhǎng.

shuāng shǒu qí chū 双手齐出 Two handed attack: to strike simultaneously with both hands. An error in many styles, though not all.

shuāng shǒu tí liāo huā gùn 双手提撩花棍 Two handed vertical rising flowers with a staff: circle the staff repeatedly with rising circles towards the front, hands together.

shuāng shǒu shuāi qiāng 双手摔枪 Double handed spear slap: Strike the shaft quickly and strongly flat on the ground, holding the butt in the right hand and pressing down on the shaft with the left hand, in a drop stance.

shuāng shǒu tuī chuāng 双手推窗 Open a Window with Two Hands: bring the feet together in a half squat and push forward with both palms. From Shaolinquan.

shuāng shǒu tuō tǎ 双手托塔 Support a Pagoda in Two Hands: step into a bow stance and lift with the palms to shoulder height, extending the same side hand and placing the rear hand at its elbow. From Shaolinquan.

shuāng shǒu tuō yuè 双手托月 Support the Moon in Two Hands: step to a bow stance, circling the hands then snap the wrists over to push upwards above head height with both palms up, fingers forward. From Shaolinquan.

shuāng shǒu wò wàn 双手握腕 Two-handed wrist grab. When differentiating types of grabs, this is with both hands. See also wò wàn.

shuāng shǒu wǔ huā biān 双手舞花鞭 Double handed flowers with the steel whip: spinning vertical flowers with both hands at the middle of the whip.

shuāng suǒ gōng 双锁功 Double lock training: various training to toughen the body without equipment. For example, knock your forearms together, or lift your knees and knock your thighs with your fists.

shuāng tí rì yuè 双提日月 Lift the Sun and Moon: in a horse stance, punch the fists up to nose height, knuckles up, fist hearts in. The 14th move of the tiger and crane routine.

shuāng tóng bài fó 双童拜佛 Two Children Bow to Buddha: pull your adversary's arm across your body, slide your arm through to his stomach, and press your shoulder behind his, bowing forward. From Qinna.

shuāng tóu gùn 双头棍 A double headed staff: a staff with both ends of the same thickness.

shuāng tóu qiāng 双头枪 A double headed spear. Usually a bit shorter and lighter than a regular spear. Also called shuāng tóu shé. A pair is called shuāng qiāng.

shuāng tóu shé 双头蛇 Double haaded snake. See shuāng tóu qiāng.

shuāng tóu shé zhuàn qiāng 双头蛇转枪 Double Headed Snake Turning Spear, a Baguazhang routine, written up with twenty-two moves.

shuāng tóu shí dàn 双头石担 A barbell with stone weights.

shuāng tuī dān zhǐ 双推单指 Double push with hands in single finger shape. If in horse stance the double push is together. If in bow stance, one is forward and the other to the head. From southern styles.

shuāng tuī shǒu 双推手 Double Push: push levelly with both hands. From Chen Taijiquan.

shuāng tuī zhǎng 双推掌 1. Double handed push. 2. Sometimes used for the double pushing circle-walking posture of Baguazhang.

shuāng tuō zhǎng 双托掌 1. Double handed lift. 2. The raised hands circle-walking posture of Baguazhang. See tuō tiān zhǎng.

shuāng tuō zhuàn zhǎng 双托转掌 Double handed lifting palm while circle-walking. From Baguazhang. See tuō tiān zhǎng.

shuāng xié zhǒu 双携肘 Double elbow block: hold the forearms up in front of the chest with the elbows tucked in to cover attacks.

shuāng xīng pěng yuè 双星捧月 Two Stars Carry the Moon: low intercepting left and right with a sword while stepping the left, then right foot forward. From Qingping sword.

shuāng yáng bǎ 双阳把 Double *yang* grip: holding a long weapon with both hands palm up.

shuāng yáng tà shǒu 双阳踏手 Double *Yang* Stamping Hands. From Shaolinquan. See jiǎn shǒu. Also called jīn chā shǒu.

shuāng yīn bǎ 双阴把 Double *yin* grip: holding a long weapon with both hands palm down.

shuāng yuè 双钺 Double blades. See yuān yáng yuè. Also called lù jiǎo dāo, qián kūn jiàn, rì yuè shuāng lián, zǐ wǔ yuān yáng yuè.

shuāng zhèn jīng léi 双震惊雷 Two Claps of Startling Thunder: a double stamp, timed to hit one, two.

shuāng zhèn jiǎo 双震脚 Double stamp: a slight jump and land with either a simultaneous double stamp or a double stamp timed to hit one, two.

shuāng zhèng bǎ 双正把 Double normal grip: holding a long weapon with both hands tiger's mouths on top.

shuāng zhǐ 双指 Double fingers, a hand shape: index and middle fingers extended (either together or slightly separated), remaining fingers bent, thumb tucked by the thumb web or onto the bent fingers' fingernails. From southern styles. Also called jiǎn dāo zhǐ, jīn qiāng shǒu, shuāng zhǐ kuài.

shuāng zhǐ chā 双指插 To stab with double finger shape.

shuāng zhǐ kuài 双指筷 Double finger chopsticks, a hand shape. See shuāng zhǐ.

shuāng zhī zhāo yáng 双枝昭阳 Two Branches Seek the Sun: raise the palms with the wrists crossed in front of the chest, then push forward together. From Wing Chun.

shuāng zhòng 双重 Double heavy, double weighted: both hands or feet are solid, with no distinction between *yin* and *yang*. From Taijiquan, where it is considered an error bringing stiffness. See also shuāng fú.

shuāng zhǒu zǔ dǎng 双肘阻挡 Double elbow block: from ready stance, block outwards with both forearms, keeping the elbows tucked.

shuāng zhū quán 双珠拳 Double pearl fist, a hand shape: the fingers tightly clenched, the index and middle fingers protruding and the thumb tucked into their distal segments. From southern styles. Also called shuāng fèng yǎn, shuāng kòu zǎo.

shuāng zhuàn bù 双转步 Double pivot on the balls of both feet.

shuāng zhuàng chuí 双撞捶 Double ramming punches. From Sun Taijiquan.

shuāng zhuàng zhǎng 双撞掌 Double ramming palm. 1. See píng tuī zhǎng. 2. To ram with both hands, keeping the arms straight for a heavy hit.

shuāng zhuàng zhuàn zhǎng 双撞转掌 Holding a double ramming palm posture, arms slightly bent, while circle-walking. From Baguazhang.

shuāng zú zhèn jiǎo 双足震脚 Stomp with both feet. See shuāng zhèn jiǎo.

水 (rad.85) shuǐ 1. Water. 2. Water, as one of the five elemental phases. Water relates to the internal organ of the kidneys, to the sensing organ of the ears, to the tissue of the bones, and to the season of winter. Its *yang* expression is waves, its *yin* is brooks. See also wǔ xíng. 3. Water as one of the five phases techniques of Xingyiquan. The mindset of water is flowing and soft, defensive moves dodge and avoid head-on force, and attacking moves redirect softly and enter by an unseen way. See also zuān quán.

shuǐ dào 水道 Acupoint Shuidao (waterway), ST28. At the abdomen, three *cun* below the navel, two *cun* lateral to the midline (on each side). From TCM.

shuǐ dǐ lāo yuè 水底捞月 Scoop the Moon from the Water: sitting in horse stance, cut down with the forearms as if holding the moon in the arms in front of the belly, forearms crossed, palms up. The 22nd move of the tiger and crane routine.

shuǐ fēn 水分 Acupoint Shuifen (water divide), RN9. At the abdomen, one *cun* above the navel, on the midline. From TCM.

shuǐ gōu 水沟 Acupoint Shuigou (water trough), DU26. At the face, two thirds of the way up between the top lip and the nose, in the midline of the philtrum. From TCM. A sensitive point, striking it may induce dizziness or even unconsciousness. Best hit with a direct punch. Colloquially called Renzhong, see rén zhōng.

shuǐ hǔ zhuàn 水湖传 The story A Water Margin, The Outlaws of the Marsh. A popular martial arts classic about one hundred and eight outlaw heroes of Mount Liang, in Shandong province. Originally told by story tellers, gradually became a novel.

shuǐ làng pāo qiú 水浪抛球 Throw a Ball into the Waves: switch from a right open bow stance to the left, swinging the right fist upwards with a thrown uppercut to the left, and the left fist back, leaning a bit into the strike. The 70th move of the tiger and crane routine.

shuǐ mó gāng biān 水磨钢鞭 A steel knobbed whip stick.

shuǐ quán 水泉 Acupoint Shuiquan (water spring), KI5. At the foot, on the inside of the ankle, in the concavity one *cun* below acupoint Taixi (on each foot). From TCM.

S

shuǐ tū 水突 Acupoint Shuitu (water prominence), ST10. At the neck, below and behind the larynx, on line between acupoints ST9 and ST11 (on each side). From TCM.

瞬 (rad.109) shùn   A wink. A twinkle.

shùn jiān 瞬间 An instant. In the twinkling of an eye. In a flash.

shùn xī qiú shēng 瞬息求生 Seek Survival in a Flash: snap from an empty stance, turning to empty stance on the other side, snapping a sword quickly from one side to the other. From Qingping sword.

順 [顺] (rad.181) shùn   Smooth power transfer, no blockages. Flow, go along the natural path or follow the direction of an action. In the same direction as. Take the opportunity to. With the current. To take an opportunity that presents itself.

shùn bǎ 顺把 Aligned grip. 1. Holding a staff with both hands aligned smoothly to the direction of the strike. 2. Holding a short weapon's grip with a natural grip, thumb web on top, fingers curled under.

shùn bù 顺步 Aligned stance or stepping: same hand and foot move or land forward.

shùn bù qián shǒu 顺步扞手 Smooth step grip: take a long step out to control and strike with a smooth technique. From Tongbeiquan, one of its seven long range techniques. Also called shùn bù qǐng zhǎng.

shùn bù qǐng zhǎng 顺步请长 Smooth Step Invite the Chief. See shùn bù qián shǒu.

shùn chán 顺缠 Smooth coiling power. 1. Smooth coiling within the legs and body that results in external rotation of the arm (if starting from palm in beside the body, palm turns forward and out away from the body). In the hand, the little finger leads the movement, rotating towards the palm until the thumb also rotates away from the palm. Through the body, the energy follows meridian lines from the inside of either the solid or empty leg (depending on whether the main hand is same or opposite side), waist, shoulder, out to the back of the hand and to the little finger, then to the rest of the fingers. 2. To neutralize incoming force by absorbing back into the *dantian*.

shùn fēng 顺风 A favourable wind; a tail wind; the wind at the back.

shùn fēng bǎi liǔ 顺风摆柳 Tail Wind makes the Willow Sway: a large swinging hook movement with deerhorn blades back over the head. From Baguazhang.

shùn fēng chě qí 顺风扯旗 Tail Wind Tears a Banner. 1. Grab an oncoming punch and continue its movement, twisting it and pulling it forward and down. 2. With a big Bagua broadsword, step around a full circle and a half while wielding a broadsword at waist height, first spinning it to turn, and completing by leading into the grip end.

shùn fēng dǎ qí 顺风打旂 Tail Wind Strikes a Banner: stand up, lifting the right knee, and scoop at an angle until the sword blade is straight up, hands at the hilt in front of the face. From Qingping sword.

shùn fēng gǎn yuè 顺风赶月 Tail Wind Chases the Moon: with a raised staff, step forward to bow stance and chop down forcibly to eyebrow height, rear hand at the hip, front hand bracing the shaft. From Baguazhang.

shùn fēng lǐng yī 顺风领衣 Tail Wind Tugs the Clothes. 1. Move forward in alternating low cross stances, rolling and circling the hands to press across, down, and forward. From Wudangquan. 2. Draw the blade back while stepping back, then turn and advance to a horse stance stab. From Qingping sword.

shùn fēng sǎo lián 顺风扫莲 Tail Wind Sweeps the Lotus. 1. Step into a low bow stance and chop down with a sword, leaning into the strike. From Qingping sword. Also called shùn fēng sǎo yè. 2. A front sweep kick, not full circle. From Yangjia style.

shùn fēng sǎo yè 顺风扫叶 Tail Wind Sweeps the Leaves. 1. Use an adversary's force and line of attack, pull and twist him down, tripping as well. From Baguazhang and wrestling. 2. See shùn fēng sǎo lián. 3. A full swinging sweep of a spear, going around in two full circles over the head. From Shaolinquan.

shùn hū xī 顺呼吸 Smooth breathing. 1. Allowing the abdomen to protrude when breathing in and come in when breathing out. 2. Performing a routine with natural breathing, breathing in when movements close in and breathing out when movements open out.

shùn jià 顺架 Smooth frame faceoff in wrestling, adversaries have the same feet forward (right to right, or left to left).

shùn jiān 顺肩 Put the shoulder into an action.

shùn jìn 顺劲 Following power, smooth power: to keep an adversary's movement going the same way and add to it, leading him into emptiness and difficulty.

shùn lì fáng shǒu 顺力防守 Smooth defense, absorbing, following: defending with an action that goes along the same direction of the incoming attack, so that an adversary loses balance and loses the impetus of the attack. Also called shùn lì gù shǒu fǎ.

shùn lì gù shǒu fǎ 顺力固手法 See shùn lì fáng shǒu.

shùn luán zhǒu 顺弯肘 Smooth Luan (a mythical bird) Elbow. In horse stance, strike with the elbows bent, one forearm horizontal, the other elbow at its fist and angled in front of the chest. From Wudangquan. See also luán.

shùn rén zhī shì, jiè rén zhī lì 顺人之势借人之力 Take advantage of an adversary's technique, borrow his strength. A martial saying.

shùn shí zhēn 顺时针 Clockwise.

shùn shì 顺势 1. A position based on an aligned stance – same hand and foot forward. 2. To follow the line of an adversary's attack.

shùn shì huà lì 顺势化力 Disperse force with smooth action: to meet oncoming force by going along with it, not meeting it head on.

shùn shì lǐng yī 顺势领衣 Take the Chance to Pull the Cloak: turn, swinging the arm up. From Baguazhang.

shùn shì sì liǎng bō qiān jīn 顺势四两拨千斤 When you use an adversary's moves smoothly you can brush aside a thousand pounds with four ounces of effort. A martial saying.

shùn shì zhǎng 顺势掌 Following Change: one of the mother palms, stepping and turning using smooth stance or aligned actions. From Baguazhang.

shùn shǒu 顺手 Aligned hands. 1. To face off with sparring partner with the hands along the same line touching (i.e. right and left). 2. Smoothly; handy; to do something as you go without any extra trouble.

shùn shǒu bān zhuàng 顺手搬撞 Smoothly Remove and Bump: an expressive term for the category of controlling moves. See also bān fǎ.

shùn shǒu qiān yáng 顺手牵羊 1. Take the Opportunity to Steal the Goat. The 12th of the Thirty-six Stratagems of Warfare, which apply to many situations. 2. Lead the Sheep Along: pull along with the line of attack to pull an adversary off balance. There are a variety of ways of doing this, depending on the style, but most take an adversary down onto his belly. Can be done with both palms up, with the hands turned to grab, and with one palm down on an adversary's wrist, the other palm up under his elbow. 3. In Tongbeiquan, a pull back combined with a hooking thrust kick. 4. In Shaolinquan, to hyper-flex the wrist of an adversary's attacking hand and take him down. 5. In Qingping sword, advancing turning slices that turn smoothly into chops. 6. An expressive term for the category of dragging methods, see also dài fǎ.

shùn shǒu tóu jǐng 顺手投井 Smoothly Throw Down a Well: Step forward into a bow stance with double punches to rib height. From Liuhebafa.

shùn shuǐ 顺水推 Go downstream, go with the current.

shùn shuǐ tuī zhōu 顺水推舟 Push a Boat Downstream: used for many techniques that take an adversary smoothly or move smoothly forward. 1. In Qinna, grab your adversary's wrist in both hands, twist and take down, turning your body. 2. With a rope dart, trap the dart with the left hand prior to shooting it out. 3. In Xingyiquan and Liuhebafa, enter pulling softly down, then advance while pushing forward. 4. In Baguazhang, walk forward while pushing a large broadsword straight with the left hand on the end of the butt or the deerhorn blades pushing into the main blades, held vertically. 5. In Qingping sword, push a sword out to the side at shoulder height. 6. In Wu Taiji sword, pull a sword in on the left side while kicking with the left foot. 7. In Yangjia sword, step into a crossed sitting stance and push with the flat blade. 8. In Yiquan, a testing power exercise, opening the hands when sitting back and closing the hands forward with shifting forward.

shùn tuǐ liāo dāng 顺腿撩裆 Smoothly hit the groin: step in with the same side leg to strike an adversary's groin. From Baguazhang.

shùn xiàng tí dǐng 顺项提顶 Place the nape of the neck smoothly and carry the crown of the head. A common requirement in internal styles.

shùn zhuā 顺抓 Aligned grab: grabbing or holding the opposite side of an adversary (left hand grabs right shoulder, arm, or hand), so that you are both aligned smoothly, the arms do not cross.

說 [说] (rad.149) shuō   To say, speak, talk. Explain.

shuō míng 说明 Explanation; description. Explain.

搠 (rad.64) shuò   To thrust; stab.

shuò quán 搠拳 A stabbing punch: a quick, fully extended but relaxed, snapping punch that bounces back. From Tongbeiquan.

槊 (rad.75) [朔] (rad.74) shuò   A lance, a long pike: an ancient weapon with a wooden shaft over two metres long. May have one long rounded iron head surrounded by rows of spikes, like those of a wolf-teeth club. May have a spear head on one end and a wolf-teeth club on the other end. May have a rounded blade with a spike out the base of the blade.

撕 (rad.64) sī   To tear; rip.

sī chì 撕翅 Tear the Wingtips: grasp your adversary's hand in both hands and hyper-extend his wrist, pressing on the back of his hand with your thumbs and twisting as well. From Qinna.

sī chuí 撕锤 Tearing punch: cross the arms, then step out to horse stance and punch with the fists as if drawing a bow, fist hearts down, one extended to the side, the other bent in front of the chest. The bent arm protects from a strike to the ribs while the extended fist strikes back.

sī ná fǎ 撕拿法 Tearing grappling hold: grab with both hands and pull horizontally to the sides. From wrestling.

sī tuǐ 撕腿 Tear the legs: the splits, specifically when using assisted stretching. See also zhèng sī tuǐ.

絲 [丝] (rad.120) sī   1. Silk. 2. Any threadlike thing. 3. A tiny bit, a trace.

sī zhú kōng 丝竹空 Acupoint Sizhukong (silk bamboo hole), SJ23. At the face, at depression at the outer point of the eyebrow (on each side). This is the final acupoint of the Triple Burner (Sanjiao) channel. From TCM.

死 (rad.78) sǐ   1. To die. To be dead. Dead. Death. 2. Very, extremely. 3. Inanimate; inert. 4. Obstinate; resolute. 5. Rigid, fixed.

sǐ bà 死把 Fixed grip: holding a long weapon without changing the position of the hands at all. See also huó bà.

sǐ gē bèi 死胳臂 To kill the arms, an arm wrap: wrap around an adversary's arms to immobilize him. Used for takedowns and throws. Also called quān, quān bì.

sǐ lǐ táo shēng 死里逃生 To Escape from Certain Death, a counter: when you have been taken to the ground, grip your adversary's leg between your lower legs and take him down.

sǐ lì 死力 Rigid strength: the inability to change with the situation when issuing power, the inability to bring it back or adjust the direction or amount. The opposite of lively power, see also huó jìn.

sǐ xué 死穴 Death Acupoints: points on the body that attacking may cause death: Fengfu, Lianquan, Maiwan, Qimen, Taiyang, Tianzhu, Zhangmen. These are points to avoid when fighting unless driven to absolute extremity. See also fēng fǔ, lián quán, mài wàn, qī mén, tài yáng, tiān zhù, zhāng mén.

四 (rad.31) sì   Four.

sì bà quán 四把拳 Four Grabbing routine: a routine of Xinyi Liuhequan, written up as twelve moves.

sì bái 四白 Acupoint Sibai (four whites), ST2. At the face, directly under a pupil, under the bone, directly below Chengqi (on each side). From TCM.

sì bìng 四病 Four diseases, four defects of push

hands: awkwardness, to butt against, to lose contact, and to contend. From Taijiquan. See also biăn, dĭng, diū, kàng.

sì dà jiā 四大家 The four big family styles of Emei school. See also dù, sēng, yuè, zhào.

sì dà jīn gāng 四大金刚 The four Deva Kings, the four temple guards. Four huge statues of fierce guardians that stand at the entrance gate of Buddhist temples. Also called jīn gāng, sì dà tiān wáng.

sì dà tiān wáng 四大天王 The four Heavenly Kings. See sì dà jīn gāng.

sì dū 四都 Acupoint Sidu (four rivers), SJ9. At the forearm, on the back, in line with acupoint Yangchi and the tip of the elbow, five *cun* distal to the point of the elbow, between the radius and the ulna (each arm). From TCM.

sì duàn gōng 四段功 Four section training: a short basics training, developing mostly horse stance, bow stance, and punching, a routine of Shaolinquan.

sì fă 四法 The four methods: outwardly, every movement can be defined and described by hand method, eye method, body method, and footwork.

sì fāng sān jiăo mă 四方三角马 Square and triangular horse stance: the feet about shoulder width, the front foot turned slightly in, the rear foot aligned to face forward, the front knee aligned with the front toes, the body turned towards the front foot. The weight may also be shifted back so that the front shin is vertical and the rear knee is above the toes. From southern styles.

sì fèng 四缝 Extraordinary acupoint Sifeng (four seams), EX-UE10. At the fingers, four points on the bellies of the proximal segments the fingers (four on each hand). From TCM.

sì hăi bīn fú shì 四海宾服式 All in the World Submit model. One of twenty-four classic spear moves. Most spear routines will have a move with a like name. In general, this name refers to a mid level stab. See also zhōng píng qiāng.

sì huán săo 四环扫 Four Rings sweep: a back sweep kick. From southern styles. See also hòu săo tuĭ.

sì jī 四击 The four strikes. the four categories of techniques. Kick (any leg technique: tī), hit (arm, hand, and body strikes: dă), throw (throws and takedowns: shuāi), and control (joint locks, breaks, and pressure points: ná). In most Chinese styles, you can apply at least one of each within each move. Also called sì jì.

sì jì 四技 The four skills. See sì jī.

sì jié tăng 四节镋 Four-section fork: an ancient weapon with four metal linked sections and fork shaped tines at the tip.

sì liăng bō qiān jīn 四两拨千斤 Four Ounces Move Aside a Thousand Pounds: to use little force to off balance someone coming in with great force.

sì liù bù 四六步 Four-six stance: feet open to front and back, about shoulder width apart, front foot tucked in slightly, rear foot open about thirty degrees, weight sixty percent towards the rear leg. In some styles also called bàn mă bù, bù dīng bù bā, dīng bā bù, liù sì bù. Sometimes considered the same as sān qī bù.

sì lóng qŭ shuĭ 四龙取水 Four Dragons Fetch Water. 1. Advancing continuous finger strikes to the eyes with the fingers spread open. From Baguazhang, one of its sixty-four hands. 2. To absorb a kick with the upper arm in order to move in and control an adversary's arm for a throw or strike. From Baguazhang.

sì lù 四路 Fourth path, refers to the fourth routine of many styles. For example, sì lù chá quán, sì lù huá quán, the fourth routines of Chaquan and Huaquan.

sì lù bēn dă 四路奔打 Fourth path quick hits: a routine of Mizongquan, written up as eighty moves.

sì măn 四满 Acupoint Siman (fourfold fullness), KI14. At the abdomen, two *cun* below the navel, 0.5 *cun* lateral to the midline (on each side). From TCM.

sì mĭn 四敏 Four agile things: the hands, the footwork, the body, and the eyes. Four things that need to be alert and reactive, moving with agility. From Baguazhang.

sì píng 四平 Four levels: a common requirement with varying references. 1. When referring to the body position: the top of the head, the eyes, the shoulders, and the hips should be level. 2. When referring to spear skills: the crown of the head, shoulders, spear, and feet should be level. This is so the eyes can see clearly, the body stays erect, the spear stabs effectively, and the feet connect firmly to the ground.

sì píng bù 四平步 Four levels stepping: step evenly to the side, continuing for several steps.

sì píng dà mǎ 四平大马 Four Levels Big Horse: sit into a horse stance and pull the fists to the sides. The 13th move of the tiger and crane routine.

sì píng chā 四平叉 Four leveled fork: a long handled, four tined fork with the tips all aligned.

sì píng jià 四平架 Four levels frame. See sì píng.

sì píng mǎ 四平马 Four levels horse. See sì píng mǎ bù.

sì píng mǎ bù 四平马步 Four levels horse stance: feet three foot-lengths apart, sit with the peak of the head level, the shoulders level, the thighs level, and the heart level (calm).

sì píng quán 四平拳 Four levels fist, a hand shape: all fingers tightly clenched, the thumb pressed on the outer edge of the second segment of the index finger. From Shaolinquan.

sì shāo 四梢 The four tips, four extremities. 1. The tip of the blood is the hair, the tip of the bones is the teeth, the tip of the muscles is the tongue, and the tip of the tendons is the nails. 2. The tip of the blood is the hair, the tip of *qi* is the hands, the tip of the spirit is the eyes, and the tip of strength is the feet.

sì shāo yào jì 四梢要齐 The four tips must be kept in order. The tongue should press on the palate, the teeth should touch together, the fingers and toes should grip, and the hair follicles should be tight. See also sì shāo.

sì shén cōng 四神聪 Extraordinary acupoint Sishentong (four alert spirits), EX-HN1. On the top of the head, four points, in cardinal directions one *cun* from acupoint Baihui. From TCM.

sì shí bā shì tài jí quán 四十八式太极拳 The forty-eight move Taijiquan routine. A standardised intermediate level routine based on Yang style, mixed with others.

sì shǒu 四手 Four hand techniques of linked push hands. Done as either the four direct techniques of ward off, stroke, press, and push, or the four corner techniques pluck, splay, elbow, and lean. From Taijiquan. See also péng, lǚ, jǐ, àn, of cǎi, liè, zhǒu, kào.

sì xiàng 四象 The four images. 1. The first split of Yin and Yang creates the four symbols; Greater Yang (two solid lines), Lesser Yin (solid underneath, broken above), Lesser Yang (solid above, broken underneath), and Greater Yin (two broken lines). 2. The four imitative or four mimics in the postures of Xingyiquan: the chicken legs, dragon body, bear shoulders, and tiger holding its head. 3. The four viscera: heart, liver, lung, and kidney.

sì xiàng zhuāng 四象桩 Four symbols stake standing. Varies with style, but may be a horse stance with the palms bracing forward at chest height, elbows out.

sì xiǎo jiā 四小家 The four small family styles of Emei school: see also hóng, huá, yú, zì.

sì yào 四要 The four requirements of push hands: stick, adhere, connect, and follow. See also zhān, nián, lián, suí.

sì yú fāng xiàng 四隅方向 The four non-cardinal directions: South-west, North-west, North-east, South-east.

sì yú shǒu fǎ 四隅手法 The four cornered techniques of pluck, splay, elbow, and lean, which supplement the four direct techniques. From Taijiquan. See also sì zhèng shǒu fǎ, cǎi, liè, zhǒu, kào.

sì yú shǒu tuī shǒu 四隅手推手 Four corner push hands: push hands using the techniques of pluck, splay, elbow, and lean in moving step. From Taijiquan. See also cǎi, liè, zhǒu, kào. Also called dà lǚ.

sì zé 四则 The four principles of push hands: neutralize, draw in, seize, and send out. From Taijiquan. See also huà, yǐn, ná, fā.

sì zhèng fāng xiàng 四正方向 The four cardinal directions: East, West, South, North (in the Chinese order).

sì zhèng shǒu fǎ 四正手法 The four direct, frontal, or square, techniques of: ward off, stroke, press, and push. These techniques work with the vertical circle, and tend not to be influenced by other forces. From Taijiquan. See also péng, lǚ, jǐ, àn.

sì zhèng shǒu tuī shǒu 四正手推手 Four square

push hands: push hands using the techniques of ward off, stroke, press, and push in fixed or moving step. From Taijiquan. See also péng, lǔ, jǐ, àn.

sì zhǐ chēng tiān 四指撑天 Four Fingers Prop up the Sky: standing up, left fist at the hip, right hand forward, snap the wrist down to bring the fingers up. The ninth move of the tiger and crane routine.

sì zhuì 四坠 Four weighed down: four body parts that should hang as if weighed down into the next body part. The shoulders weigh down into the lumbar area, the lumbar area weighs down into the hip joints (inguinal creases), the hip joints weigh down into the knees, and the knees weigh down into the feet. This allows the shoulders to settle, the waist to sink, the hip joints to sit, the knees to shear, and the feet to trample. From Baguazhang.

巳 (rad.49) **sì**
The sixth of the twelve Terrestrial Branches, used in combination with the ten Celestial Stems to designate years, months, days, and hours. For the sixty year cycles, see also under dīng sì, guǐ-, jǐ-, xīn-, yì-. The period of the day from 9:00 a.m. to 11:00 a.m. See also dì zhī, tiān gān.

sì shí 巳时 The period of the day from 9:00 a.m. to 11:00 a.m. (9:00 to 11:00).

崧 嵩 [崧] (rad.46) **sōng** Lofty; high.

sōng shān 崧山 Mount Song, Song Shan, in Henan province. The central of the five sacred mountains. One of the famous mountains of martial lore, home of the northern Shaolin temple. See also wǔ yuè, zhōng yuè sōng shān.

鬆 (rad.190) [松] (rad.75) **sōng**
1. To relax and extend; release tension; disengage; be prepared for action but not tense; loosen. The supple balance between tense and slack. 2. A pine tree.

sōng bǎng 松膀 Release tension through the shoulder girdle.

sōng chí 松迟 Soft and flabby; slack, lax.

sōng jiān 松肩 Release the shoulders, relax the shoulders: the shoulders are settled and natural, and move easily. This is a requirement common to many styles.

sōng jiān chén zhǒu 松肩沉肘 Release the shoulders and settle the elbows. This is a requirement common among many styles.

sōng kuà 松胯 Release tension through the hip joints, relax the hips: release tension and settle in the hip socket to allow the pelvis and greater trochanter of each leg to move easily. This is a requirement common to many styles.

sōng róu zé zhǎng, jiāng jìn zé zhì 松柔则长,僵劲则滞 If you are soft and pliable you will progress, if you are hard and rigid you will stagnate. A martial saying.

sōng shǒu 松手 Release the grip of the hand or hands.

sōng xiōng 松胸 Relaxed chest: the chest is held open, expanded, and natural, not stuck out or puffed out. This is a requirement common among many styles.

sōng xuán gāo kōng 松悬高空 Pine Tree Hangs at High Altitude: thrust kick to the side, throwing both fists out to the sides at shoulder height, followed by a lowering stamp to a horse stance, cutting the forearms across to finish with one pressing down and one blocking up. From Wudangquan.

sōng yāo 松腰 Release the lower back: the lower back is relaxed and moves easily, allowing the upper and lower body to interact and power to flow unimpeded. This is a requirement common to many styles.

竦 [耸] (rad.128) **sǒng** Towering, lofty.

sǒng jiān 耸肩 Shrug the shoulders. An error in most styles.

宋 (rad.40) **sòng**
1. The Song dynasty (960-1279). 2. The Song of the Southern dynasties (420-479). 3. A surname.

sòng jiàng jiē yìn 宋将接印 Song General Takes his Turn with the Seal: an inward hooking punch in front of the body. From Shaolinquan.

sòng tài zǔ cháng quán 宋太祖长拳 Songtaizu Changquan (ancestor Song's longfist) style: a style known in the Ming dynasty, attributed to Zhao Kuangyin, the founder of the Song dynasty. Also called zhào jiā quán.

S

送 (rad.162) sòng   1. To send. To present. To deliver. 2. To send someone off. 3. In wrestling, to send someone off with a long power rather than a short snapping throw.

sòng bào jìn dòng 送暴进洞 Send the Savage into the Cave: snap the wrists at the chest then stab one hand out strongly in front of the chest, the other tucked at its elbow. From Shaolinquan.

sòng fó shàng tiān 送佛上天 See Buddha off to Heaven: grab your adversary's wrist and step to the side, swinging his arm upwards while rolling under, twisting and controlling the wrist. From Qinna.

sòng kè chū mén 送客出门 See the Guest Out the Door: a turning forearm press to shoulder height, the rear hand assisting at the wrist. From Baguazhang.

sòng kè guān mén 送客关门 See the Guest Off and Close the Door: a double push to the front with the knee lifted, followed by a snap kick then land forward to cover and push in a reverse bow stance. From Meishanquan.

sòng mó shàng tiān 送魔上天 See the Devil off to Heaven. See sòng fó shàng tiān.

搜 (rad.64) sōu   1. To search for, look for. 2. In martial arts, a penetrating technique.

sōu dāng tuǐ 搜裆腿 Seek the groin kick. See tán tuǐ.

sōu lèi tuǐ 搜肋腿 Seek the ribs kick. See cè chuāi tuǐ.

sōu tī 搜踢 Searching kicks. See also qū shēn xìng tuǐ fǎ. From Mizongquan.

sōu tiān 搜天 Seek the Sky. See #1 of wū lóng jiǎo zhù.

蘇 [苏] (rad.140) sū   1. To revive. 2. A surname.

sū qín 苏秦 Su Qin: a political strategist (340-284 BC) during the Warring States period. Sometimes used in movement names.

sū qín bēi dāo 苏秦背刀 Su Qin Shoulders his Blade: sit back to empty stance and place the blade of a broadsword in front of the body, the spine on the right shoulder. From Taijiquan.

sū qín bēi jiàn 苏秦背剑 Su Qin Shoulders his Sword. Drop into a squat and strike with the tip of a staff high and behind with a reverse slice, the right arm extended along the length of the shaft, the left hand tucked at the shoulder. From Baguazhang. 2. Nestle a spear on the back, shaft running along the right arm. You can then take the shaft in the left hand near the tip, and bring it over to strike with the butt. From Shaolinquan.

宿 (rad.40) sù   To lodge for the night; stay overnight.

sù niǎo tóu lín 宿鸟投林 Nesting Bird Drops into the Woods: a quick run forward into a bow stance sword pierce. From Qingping sword and Taijiquan sword.

sù wū tóu lín 宿乌投林 Nesting Crow Drops into the Woods: a backfist with the wrist, the hand in a firm hook shape. From Baguazhang.

素 (rad.120) sù   White; unbleached; undyed. Plain, simple.

sù liáo 素髎 Acupoint Suliao (white bone-hole), DU25. At the face, on the tip of the nose. From TCM. A sensitive point, when hitting basically just hit right on the nose. Best to hit with the head, rising drill, backfist, or direct upright punch.

速 (rad.162) sù   Speed, quick; prompt.

sù dù 速度 Speed, velocity. Fast, quick.

sù dù xùn liàn 速度训练 Speed training: exercises intended to improve speed.

酸 (rad.164) suān   1. Sour; tart. Acid. 2. An aching pain.

suān téng 酸疼 1. A muscular pain from exertion, 2. An aching pain reaction during acupuncture or tuina. From TCM.

隋 (rad.170) suí   1. The Sui dynasty (581-618). 2. A surname.

隨 [随] (rad.170) suí   1. To follow. 2. Specifically, to follow along with any changes of an adversary and eventually find his weaknesses. 3. As one of the eight attack and defense models, to grab an adversary's attacking hand or leg and attack just as his attack dissipates and before he can launch a new attack. See also bā zì gōng fáng fǎ zé. 4. To follow in push hands, one of the four requirements, see also sì yào.

suí bù 随步 Following step: bring the lead foot back towards the rear foot after the rear foot has stepped backwards. Also called gēn bù, though that can mean in either direction, and usually means forwards.

suí fēng bǎi liú 随风摆柳 Willow Fronds Swing with the Wind: retreat with chopping palms. From Piguaquan.

suí fēng zhuǎn duò 随风转舵 Trim the Sails According to the Wind: a series of high and low stabs with a sword, stepping to four directions. From Qingping sword.

suí jī yìng biàn 随机应变 Change according to the situation; take advantage of presented opportunities.

suí qiāng 随枪 Following spear: a close range stabbing method.

suí shì 随视 Following regard. 1. To follow one's movements in a routine with the eyes. 2. To follow one's adversary's moves.

suí shǒu 随手 1. Follow: to go along in the same direction as an adversary and turn that to your advantage. 2. Following Hands, the second routine of Duanquan, written up as fifty-three moves.

suí xíng bù 随形步 Follow the Form stepping: step following along to the leanings of the body and shifts of the weight. From Drunken boxing.

suí yì huó bù tuī shǒu 随意活步推手 Freely moving step push hands: no set patterns, free practice of push hands. From Taijiquan.

髓 (rad.188) suǐ   Marrow, bone marrow.

suǐ hǎi 髓海 Sea of marrow, the brain.

碎 (rad.112) suì   1. To break to pieces; smash. 2. Broken; fragmentary.

suì bù 碎步 Quick stepping, moving continuously forward.

孫 [孙] (rad.39) sūn   1. Grandchild, the generation of or below grandchildren. 2. Second growth of plants. 3. A surname.

sūn bìn 孙膑 Sun Bin, a military strategist (-316 BC) during the Warring States period (475-221 BC).

sūn bìn guǎi 孙膑拐 Sun Bin's crutch: a short double weapon, about the length of a sword, with grips and crescent moon blades on the ends.

sūn bìn quán 孙膑拳 Sunbinquan (Sun Bin's style), attributed to Sun Bin.

sūn shì tài jí quán 孙式太极拳 Sunshi (Sun's) Taijiquan style, attributed to Sun Lutang, who combined Wu Taijiquan with Baguazhang and Xingyiquan.

sūn wǔ 孙武 Sun Wu. See sūn zǐ.

sūn zǐ 孙子 Sun Tzu, a military strategist (c. 500 BC) during the Spring and Autumn period (700-475 BC). (The pinyin is Sun Zi, but he is best known as Sun Tzu because his book was translated quite early on, using the Wade Giles system). Also known as sūn wǔ.

sūn zǐ bīng fǎ 孙子兵法 Sun Tzu's book the Art of War, one of the most famous works on martial tactics. The thirty-six stratagem of warfare are each in this dictionary.

娑 (rad.38) suō   The onomatopoeic word *suosuo* imitates the sound of the feet shuffling.

suō suō bù 娑娑步 Shuffling steps: Move the front foot forward before advancing, or move the rear foot backward before retreating. This footwork is common, though this term is not often used.

縮 [缩] (rad.120) suō   1. To contract; to shorten; to shrink. 2. To draw back; to recoil. 3. To bind.

suō jiān 缩肩 Draw back the shoulders: draw the arms into the shoulder sockets to keep the body connected. From Baguazhang, one of its requirements.

suō jìn 缩劲 1. Shrinking power, reduce size of movement. 2. Compressing power. 3. Recoiling power. From Tongbeiquan, one of its nine types of power.

suō kuà gēn 缩胯根 Draw back the hip roots: draw the legs into the hip sockets to keep the body connected. From Baguazhang, one of its requirements.

S

suō qiāng 缩枪 Draw in a spear: bring the spear back, the hands sliding to near the spear tassel.

suō shēn 缩身 Contract or draw in the torso. 1. Fold in on oneself; compress the torso. 2. Lower the body, dropping down into a squatting stance, pulling the arms as well.

鎖 [锁] (rad.167) suǒ
1. A lock; shackles. 2. To lock. 3. In martial arts, locking techniques.

suǒ fǎ 锁法 Locking techniques: blocking or pressing techniques that prevent an adversary from fighting back.

suǒ gǔ 锁骨 Clavicle, collar bone.

suǒ hóu 锁喉 Choke hold: grab the adversary and apply an arm bar around his neck. Can be done with the thumb and index joints on the larynx, if wanting total control or to break the larynx. In routines, this name is given to an eagle claw extended to throat height. From Qinna.

suǒ hóu bào jī 锁喉暴击 Throat lock to sudden hit: thread a spear past the throat, going directly into a low stab, right hand at the tip, left arm extended along the shaft.

suǒ jiān 锁肩 Shoulder crank, shoulder hold or lock: using the head and shoulder to control an adversary's arm, press his elbow and shoulder down and lean forward. From Qinna and wrestling.

suǒ jiāo lóng 锁蛟龙 Lock up the Flood Dragon: a thrust kick combined with a throat lock. From Tongbeiquan.

suǒ jǐng 锁颈 Neck lock techniques.

suǒ kǒu qiāng 锁口枪 Lock up openings spear, a routine of Chaquan, written up in fifty-four moves.

suǒ ná fǎ 锁拿法 Locking grappling hold: press an adversary's hand onto your body to negate his grab. From wrestling.

suǒ shǒu 锁手 Lock: use an open palm to lock down an adversary's hand technique.

suǒ tóu 锁头 Head lock, neck crank. From wrestling.

suǒ yān hóu 锁咽喉 Lock the Throat: a spear technique, pulling the tip in towards the throat, then shooting it out through to the rear.

suǒ yáng shǒu 锁阳手 Lock and strike. See niē tóu.

suǒ zhǒu 锁肘 Arm bar, elbow lock.

suǒ zhù 锁住 To lock on, to control an adversary by pressing his limb onto your body.

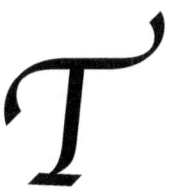

塌 (rad.32) tā 1. To collapse; fall down; cave in. 2. To implode. Sink. 3. To settle down, sink down.

tā jī bù 塌鸡步 Settling chicken stance: with the feet front and back, sit on the rear leg and extend the front leg straight with the heel on the ground. Similar to an empty stance but for the extension and placement of the heel.

tā wàn 塌腕 Sit the wrist, settle the wrist down (with the arm extended).

tā yāo 塌腰 Flatten the lower back to form a straight line up to the head, aligning the vertebrae. In some styles this means that the lumbar vertebrae are pulled in so that the lower back is slightly arched.

tā zhǎng 塌掌 1. To tamp with the palm to cause an adversary to cave in. Sometimes used to mean the same as a push, but should be used for a heavier, dropping shock, not a push. Sometimes written 搨 or 踏 for this technique, see also tà below.

搨 (rad.64) tà 1. The original meaning is to make rubbings from stone inscriptions, an action that is a rolling pat, or tamping. 2. To crush, stamp, tamp with the hand.

tà zhǎng 搨掌 To shock with the palm, tamp firmly with the palm. Could almost be translated as bounce, but is a heavier power that comes from the body. Sometimes written 塌 or 踏 for this technique, see also tā above and tà below.

撻 [挞] (rad.64) tà To whip; flog.

tà qiáo 挞桥 Whipping bridge, a forearm technique: with an internal rotation, snap the forearm down.

踏 (rad.157) tà To step on, tread, stamp. Sometimes written 蹋 with the same meaning.

tà bù 踏步 Stomp, a stamp that drives forward. Bring in the rear foot, plant it on the ground beside the front foot, then move the front foot forward.

tà jìn 踏劲 Stamping power: settle the body down heavily.

tà jiān xiè bì 踏肩卸臂 Stand on the shoulder to dislocate the arm: when your adversary is face down on the ground, put your foot on the back of his shoulder/armpit and pull his arm back.

tà zhǎng 踏掌 Tamp with the palm: place the palm down then apply abrupt, shocking power down.

蹋 (rad.157) tà See tà 踏.

胎 (rad.130) tāi Embryo, foetus.

tāi lì 胎力 Natural strength. See běn lì. Also called xiān tiān lì.

tāi xī 胎息 Embryo breathing: easy breathing that cannot be heard.

擡 [抬] (rad.64) tái To raise, lift, carry.

tái jiǎo 抬脚 1. Raise the foot. 2. Often refers to dorsi-flexing the foot to raise the toes, in an action like hooking onto an adversary for a trip.

tái tóu 抬头 Raise the head. 1. If lying on the stomach, lift the head up off the ground. 2. If standing up, raise the chin.

tái zhǒu 抬肘 Raise the elbow: grab your adversary's hand at the wrist and pull it forward, turning and using your forearm to lift his elbow, reversing it. From Qinna.

太 (rad.37) tài 1. Great, to the extreme. 2. Highest, more or most. 3. Excessively; extremely.

tài bái 太白 Acupoint Taibai (supreme white), SP3. At the foot, behind the proximal segment of the big toe (on each foot). From TCM.

tài chōng 太冲 Acupoint Taichong (great surge), LR3. At the foot, on the top, between the tendons of the big and second toes, near where the metacarpals come together (on each foot). From TCM.

tài gōng chuí diào 太公垂钓 Great-grandfather Goes Fishing: step forward into a high empty stance and lift the butt of a staff up over the head with the right hand, sweeping and chopping with the tip down, the left hand just past midway along the staff. From Baguazhang.

tài gōng diào yú shì 太公钓鱼式 Great-grandfather Goes Fishing model. One of twenty-four classic spear moves. Most spear routines will have a move with a like name. In general, this name refers to smooth techniques such as rubbing with the shaft.

tài gōng zhí gān 太公执竿 Great-grandfather Holds the Rod: step to an empty stance and dab with a sword. From Qingping sword.

tài hé jiàn 太和剑 Great Peace sword, a Wudang sword routine, written up as sixty moves.

tài jí 太极 The supreme ultimate, the undifferentiated whole of the universe sorted into *yin* and *yang*.

tài jí bàng (zǐ) 太极棒(子) Taiji stick: a short stick, about the length and thickness of a forearm, attributed to the original use of a rolling pin for training. Used in Taijiquan to train coiling power and controlling ability.

tài jí bǔ xīn 太极补心 The Supreme Ultimate Fills the Heart: snap from a bow stance to the other side bow stance, to stab a sword forward in a reverse bow stance. From Qingping sword.

tài jí cháng quán 太极长拳 Taiji Changquan (taiji longfist), a traditional routine, attributed to Guo Yunshen, which combines the feeling of Taijiquan, the footwork of Baguazhang, and the structural lines of Xingyiquan. Written up as one hundred and fifty-eight moves.

tài jí chū shǒu 太极出手 Taijiquan Opening Move: the opening move of Wu Taijiquan.

tài jí dāo 太极刀 Taiji broadsword. 1. A normal broadsword used for Taiji practice, see *dāo*. 2. A longer and thinner broadsword than usual, with a guard with the top curving towards the blade spine and the bottom curving towards the grip to protect the fingers.

tài jí jiàn 太极剑 Taijijian (taiji sword), a normal straight sword, used for Taiji sword practice. 2. The competition event of Taiji Sword, called Taiji Jian in English.

tài jí quán 太极拳 Taijiquan (taiji fist). 1. The system of Taijiquan, which has a number of branches. The standard five are Chen, Sun, Wu/Hao, Wu, and Yang. Among less well known styles are Dong, Fu, Li, and Zhaobao. Often written as T'ai Chi Ch'uan, from the old Wade Giles romanization system. In English, often called Tai Chi. 2. The modern competition event of Taijiquan.

tài jí shì 太极式 Position of Taiji, or order, taken before starting a Taijiquan routine. Usually sitting a bit, with the hands pressing down to the sides.

tài jí tú 太极图 The Taiji diagram, the *yin-yang* symbol, the *yin-yang* fish drawing.

tài jí zhuāng 太极桩 Taiji stake standing: varies with style. May be standing up with the palms covering the *dantian*.

tài kōng zǐ wǔ gùn 太空子午棍 Great firmament meridian staff. 1. A traditional staff eight to ten centimetres longer than an outstretched arm above the head, the shape and diameter of a spear. Its methods derive from spear methods, and it is used with the hand at the butt similar to a spear. Also called *zǐ wú gùn*. 2. The name of its routine, written up as forty-six moves.

tài shàng fǎ 太上法 Methods and techniques have reached the top: one has mastered the techniques and the ability to use them.

tài shī biān 太师鞭 Taishibian (grandmaster's whip) style: a style from the Tang dynasty done with a three foot rod the diameter of a duck's egg, the tip thinner. Practised in sixty-six and forty-two move routines. Also called *tài shī hǔ wěi gāng biān*, *tài shī shí sān biān*.

tài shī hǔ wěi gāng biān 太师虎尾钢鞭 Grandmaster's tiger tail steel whip. See *tài shī biān*.

tài shī shí sān biān 太师十三鞭 Grandmaster's thirteen move whip. See *tài shī biān*.

tài shū quán 太淑拳 Highly Refined fist, a routine of Piguaquan.

tài xī 太溪 Acupoint Taixi (great ravine), KI3. At the ankle, on the inside behind the ankle bone, between the medial malleolus and the Achilles tendon (on each leg). From TCM.

tài yáng 太阳 1. The sun. 2. The temples of the head. 3. Tai Yang, Greater Yang: the expanding *yang* nature sub-type of meridian channels, the most outwardly expanding level. It governs opening to the outside. This system, containing the bladder and small intestine, keeps the outside of the body comfortable. Diagrammed as one *yin* line over two *yang* lines. From TCM.

tài yáng gōng 太阳功 Solar meditation, internal training basking in the sun. From Liuhebafa.

tài yáng (xué) 太阳(穴) Extraordinary acupoint Taiyang (greater *yang*), EX-HN5. At the temple, the depression between the hairline and the tip of the eyebrow. From TCM. A good target, but a very sensitive point, striking can induce unconsciousness. Striking too hard and accurately may cause death. May be hit with the head, a backfist, or a knife edge hand. Colloquially also called jīn qián, jīn qián xué.

tài yǐ 太乙 Acupoint Taiyi (supreme unity), ST23. At the abdomen, two *cun* above the navel, two *cun* lateral to the midline (on each side). From TCM.

tài yǐ rì yuè qián kūn quān 太乙日月乾坤圈 Supreme-unity sun-moon earth-heaven ring: a double weapon with a ringed blade, with crescent moon shaped blades inside protecting the grips. About thirty centimetres across.

tài yīn 太阴 1. Tai Yin, Greater Yin: the most outward expanding *yin* nature sub-type of the *yin* meridian channels. It governs opening of the interior levels of the body towards the external level. This system, containing the spleen and lungs, regulates dampness and distributes nutrition. Diagrammed as one *yang* line over two *yin* lines. 2. Sometimes specifies the right temple.

tài yuān 太渊 Acupoint Taiyuan (great abyss), LU9. At the inside of the wrist, just at the crease above the thumb, just inside the abductor pollicis longus tendon (on each wrist). From TCM. Hard pressure or a strike here may injure the entire network of channels.

tài zǐ shàng diàn 太子上殿 The Crown Prince Enters the Palace: first kick to the groin, then step in and push the chest for a takedown.

tài zǐ xià pō 太子下坡 The Crown Prince Goes down the Hill: turn and sit to horse stance, cutting one hand around, circling and chopping down with the other. From Wudangquan.

tài zǔ quán 太祖拳 Taizuquan (great ancestor fist), a Longfist style known since the Song dynasty, from Shandong province, and later spread quite extensively.

泰 (rad.85) tài 1. Safe; peaceful. 2. Extreme; most.

tài qióng liú mǎ 泰琼骝马 Great Jade Bay Horse: circle walk with a sword flat at chest height, palm up to cut into the leading edge. From Baguazhang sword.

tài shān 泰山 Mount Tai, Tai Shan, in Shandong province. The Eastern of the five sacred mountains. Often used in movement names. See also dōng yuè tài shān, wǔ yuè.

tài shān yā dǐng 泰山压顶 Mount Tai Bears Down its Weight. 1. Bring the hand from above the head to press down in front. From Baguazhang. 2. Hard palm edge strikes, inward and outward, hitting both above and below. From Tanglangquan.

tài shān yā luǎn shì 泰山压卵式 Mount Tai Bears Down on an Egg model. One of twenty-four classic spear moves. Most spear routines will have a move with a like name. In general, this name refers to a technique that shows overwhelming superior force, like a big sweep.

鳥台 [鸟台] (rad.196) tài Wedge-tailed hawk. Also called a mythical Tai bird. Sometimes printed as 骀 or 胎 because the correct character is not available in typing input programs.

tài xíng 鸟台形 Wedge-tailed hawk form, mythical Tai bird form: a high clearing with the forearms then a low double shoving fist to hip level. When referring to the mythical bird, the technique of the hands imitates the bird's power of raising the tail. When referring to the real bird, the power is that of catching a rabbit with a scoop of the tail and wings. From Xingyiquan.

tài yǒu bēng zhuàng zhī xíng 鸟台有崩撞之形 The Wedge-tailed hawk has the form of bracing out. From Xingyiquan, a quality sought in its Wedge-tailed hawk form.

T

攤 [摊] (rad.64) **tān** To open and spread out.

tān lì 摊力 Opening power, to open out once the arms control across the adversary' chest, for a takedown. From Baguazhang.

tān shǒu 摊手 Opening hand: a palm up cross with the forearm, drop the elbow down at the side, palm crossing to the opposite side. The action presses down with the forearm, either inward or outward for a mid-level defense. From Wing Chun.

癱 [瘫] (rad.104) **tān** 1. To be physically paralysed. 2. Numb; numbness. This includes the temporary state brought on by a strike to a pressure point.

tān huàn 瘫痪 Paralyse; paralysis.

彈 [弹] (rad.57) **tán** 1. Elastic, snap. 2. To shoot. 3. A chambered kick: a snap kick, first cocking the knee, then snapping out to contact with the top of the foot and/or shin. 4. To flick the skin, a palpation method. Flick the acupuncture needle to encourage the *qi* to take it. From TCM. 5. To take the pulse, using the plucking method to look for elasticity along channels. From TCM. 6. Pronounced dàn, a pellet, see dàn.

tán diǎn 弹点 A snapping poke kick. From Chuojiao, one of its middle-basin kicks.

tán dòu jìn 弹抖劲 Elastic shaking power: gather and release the full force of the body into a focused shake, either for attack or defense.

tán gōng 弹弓 1. A bow. 2. Pronounced dàn gōng, a catapult, a slingshot.

tán huáng bàng 弹簧棒 Stick on a spring: a short stick jammed into a large metal spring, attached horizontally on a backing. Used to train gripping, pulling, and twisting.

tán huáng jìn 弹簧劲 Elastic power; elastic, springy force. Also called tán jìn.

tán jìn 弹劲 Elastic power; elastic, springy force. Also called tán huáng jìn.

tán níng zǐ 弹拧子 Snap and Twist, a type of throw in wrestling: as soon as the hands grab, quickly jerk and twist.

tán quán 弹拳 Snapped punch. 1. To snap out a punch with a shake of the body. Also called dǒu quán. 2. In Sanda, a snapped backfist.

tán tī 弹踢 1. A low front snap instep kick, a hidden kick done almost as a step. 2. In wrestling, using a low stepping kick to move in, causing an adversary to react and allow for a following trip.

tán tiào xùn liàn 弹跳训练 Spring training: exercises intended to improve jumping ability.

tán tuǐ 弹腿 1. Front snap kick, a chambered spring kick contacting with the top of the foot. In the category of snap kicks, see also qū shēn xìng tuǐ fǎ. 2. Spring kick drills: a set of ten or twelve basic drills that emphasize stances and spring kicks, popular in Shandong, Hebei and Henan provinces, and used by many northern styles.

tán tuǐ jī zhǎng 弹腿击掌 Front snap kick palm strike: a front snap instep kick combined with a push from the opposite palm, the other hand usually clenching a fist at the hip. From Chaquan.

tán tún 弹臀 Snap the buttocks: when the buttocks are in contact with the belly of an adversary during a throw, snap the hips to assist in the throw.

潭 (rad.85) **tán** A pond; a deep pool.

tán tuǐ 潭腿 The set of basic drills, essentially the same as this meaning of the above spring kick drills. When this character is used, it often means a set of twelve basic drills, rather than ten. See tán tuǐ above.

tán tuǐ duì liàn 潭腿对练 A traditional partner routine based on the spring legs short routines.

罎 (rad.121) [坛] (rad.32) **tán** 1. An altar. 2. A raised plot of land. 3. A platform. 4. An earthen jar.

tán zǐ 坛子 An earthen jar; a jug; a vat. Often used for training grip and arm strength.

錟 [锬] (rad.167) **tán** A long spear, a lance.

鐔 [镡] (rad.167) **tán** 1. A small dagger. 2. The tip of the handgrip of a sword.

探 (rad.64) **tàn** 1. To reach out to grab or as if to grab. 2. To explore. 3. As one of the eight attack and defense models, to stretch out the hand to clarify empty and solid (see also bā zì gōng fáng fǎ zé). 4. In Qinna, to get a sense of whether or not an adversary can escape your grasp, to help decide whether or not to fully put on a controlling technique.

tàn bù 探步 Reaching step: sit back, lifting and turning the front heel in, then turn and stomp the front heel to set to a bow stance. From Bajiquan.

tàn cì jiàn 探刺剑 Reaching pierce straight to the tip with a sword, with the arm rotated over so the thumb is down, reaching out with the shoulder.

tàn dà dāo 探大刀 Reach a big cutter: with the right hand near the hilt and the left along the shaft, reach forward with the blade with the edge up. This can be a stab or a feint.

tàn hǎi píng héng 探海平衡 Reach into the Sea balance: supporting leg straight, the body prone with the front arm extended downward and the other leg extended straight behind.

tàn hǎi quán 探海拳 Reach into the Sea punch: a straight punch to the head with the fist heart down, hitting from the shoulder with a snap from the hip, extending well out. From Tongbeiquan and Piguaquan.

tàn lí dé zhú 探骊得珠 Pat the Black Horse to get the Pearls. 1. To be focused, without digression. 2. Slap the ground in a squatting stance. From Liuhequan. 3. Step into a direct, fully extended, sword stab. From Qingping sword.

tàn mǎ shì 探马式 Pat the Horse: a reverse bow stance punching directly upwards, the other fist at the waist. From Wudangquan.

tàn náng qǔ wù 探囊取物 Reach to Pick-Pocket: a rolled reverse sword stab in a right empty stance. From Qingping sword.

tàn shēn 探身 Reach the body: extend the torso forward, also forward and up or down.

tàn shǒu 探手 To reach out to test an adversary, get a feel for him without yet doing a technique.

tàn xué 探穴 Reach into the hole: strike the depression of the shoulder joint.

tàn zhǎng 探掌 Reaching palm: extend the arm, palm down, fingers forward, to strike with the fingers or palm heel.

蹚 (rad.157) **tāng** 1. To wade, to ford (a stream). 2. To turn the soil (with a hoe). 3. To trample.

tāng hé 蹚河 Ford the Stream, a trip: grab your adversary and push until his body is at an angle, then kick his ankle, snapping the push. From wrestling. Also called chǎn tī.

tāng jìn 趟劲 Wading power: stepping by pushing forward strongly from the rear foot, springing the front foot forward. From Baguazhang and Xingyiquan.

tāng ní bù 蹚泥步 Mud-wading step. 1. Stepping by lifting and landing the feet flatly, hovering the landing foot forward and gripping the ground, as if walking in a muddy stream, unsure of unseen footing. From Baguazhang. 2. Technique to walk through small sharp objects thrown down on the ground to injure the feet, by keeping the feet flat along the ground. Sometimes written 趟, with the walking radical instead of the foot radical, see tàng.

tāng pá 蹚耙 Trampling rake: step in with a push to the chest while catching your adversary's ankle with your foot, then rake back while pushing forward.

tāng shuǐ bù 蹚水步 Water wading step, see tāng ní bù.

堂 (rad.32) **táng** 1. Hall, the main room of a house. 2. In martial arts, the chest. The acupoint point in the centre of the chest is called the Jade Hall, see also yù táng.

唐 (rad.53) **táng** 1. The Tang dynasty (618-907). 2. A surname. 3. The Chinese in general.

táng rén jiē 唐人街 Chinatown. The first kungfu clubs in the West were often in the traditional Chinatowns of the larger cities.

膛 (rad.130) **táng** The thorax, the chest.

螳 (rad.142) **táng** Mantis, an insect.

táng láng 螳螂 A praying mantis: a large insect capable of capturing or fighting off larger animals.

táng láng bǔ chán 螳螂捕蝉 Praying Mantis Catches the Cicada. 1. After controlling your adversary's arm, reach in to grasp his armpit. 2. The mantis stalks the cicada (unaware of the oriole behind, stalking it). This is a Daoist saying, warning against pursuing small gains while

T

neglecting a greater danger.

táng láng bù 螳螂步 Praying mantis stance: the front leg bent to half squat, the rear leg fully bent about a half step behind and to the side, the knee open and not touching the ground. From Tanglangquan.

táng láng dāo 螳螂刀 Praying mantis broadsword. 1. A broadsword with a number of two-centimeter long teeth along the blade and a long hinged hooked tip. Operated as a pair. 2. A routine of Tongbeiquan, with a pair of this type of broadsword, written up as eighteen moves.

táng láng gōu shǒu 螳螂勾手 Praying mantis hook, a hand shape: thumb, index, and middle fingers lightly gathered, ring and little fingers pulled back, wrist bent. From Tanglangquan.

táng láng quán 螳螂拳 Tanglangquan (praying mantis) style. There are many branches of this style. The northern style originated from Shandong province during the Ming dynasty.

táng láng shǒu 螳螂手 Praying mantis hands, a double grab during wrestling, elbows down, one hand on each of the upper arms of an adversary.

táng láng zhuǎ 螳螂爪 Praying mantis claw, a hard skills training method. See shào lín kǎn shǒu.

躺 (rad.158) **tǎng**   To lie down; recline.

tǎng bà 躺耙 Lying harrow: in close clinch, to harrow low with the foot and lean back. A takedown.

tǎng dāo 躺刀 Lying Blade: step in between your adversary's legs and lean directly with your shoulder, falling back on him as he goes down. A takedown.

tǎng dǎo 躺倒 Lie down throw: the category of throws that involve lying back on an adversary to take him down, as a counter measure. From wrestling.

鐺 [铛] (rad.167) **tǎng**   Trident, bladed fork: a long weapon with curving or straight spikes out to the side at the tip. The handle is about 2.5 metres and the tip about .5 metres. Differentiated from a fork in that the tines do not point straight forward, but form a crescent.

趟 (rad.156) **tàng**   1. A grammatical measure word that applies to the number of times you make a trip and to things that are lined up. 2. In martial arts, usually refers to a sliding action of the feet. 3. Also used the same as tāng 蹚, to press forward from the back foot to spring the front foot forward in a step.

tàng guà tuǐ 趟挂腿 Sliding sweep kick: slide the foot on the ground and extend the leg to sweep the heel out and across, pushing into the calf.

tàng jìn 趟劲 The energy of a foot pushing off the ground hard to spring the body forward.

tàng ní bù 趟泥步 Mud sliding step. See tāng ní bù.

tàng tī tuǐ 趟踢腿 Sliding side kick: a chambered side kick.

tàng tuǐ 趟腿 Sliding kick: a low kick, hooking in to trap an adversary's shin. From Baguazhang.

tàng zǐ 趟子 A short combination of moves.

掏 (rad.64) **tāo**   1. To take out; pull out; clean out; fish out. 2. In push hands, to step or press the leg on the outside of an adversary's lead lower leg to restrict his stepping.

tāo dāng shuāi 掏裆摔 Pull out the groin: drop down and dodge behind to the side, pushing down with one hand on your adversary's jaw and up with the other in his groin. A quick throw used in Sanda.

tāo ná fǎ 掏拿法 Taking out grappling hold: a digging action, controlling your adversary's back or legs and pushing on his chest to topple him.

tāo quán 掏拳 An uppercut punch.

tāo tī tuǐ 掏踢腿 Kick step: a low abrupt hook kick: circle in and forward to hook up with the foot, leaving the heel on or near the ground. The kick is to an adversary's lower leg or ankle. From Chuojiao, one of its middle-basin kicks.

tāo tuǐ 掏腿 Pull out the leg: grab and lift an adversary's leg or use it as leverage to take down. Also called kōu tuǐ.

tāo xīn chuí 掏心锤 Pull out the heart punch. 1. A straight punch to the heart. From Xingyiquan. Also called bēng quán, but that is less specific as to the target. 2. An upper framing block with an uppercut. From Tongbeiquan. 3. An uppercut. From Shaolinquan.

淘 (rad.85) táo   1. To rinse in a pan or basket. 2. To seek and buy second-hand. 3. To clean out, dredge.

táo tài 淘汰 1. Elimination through selection or competition. 2. To die out; fall into disuse.

táo tài sài 淘汰赛 Elimination series; a direct elimination competition; a knock-out competition.

陶 (rad.170) táo   1. Pottery, earthenware. To make pottery. 2. A surname.

táo dào 陶道 Acupoint Taodao (kiln path), DU13. At the back, at the depression below the spinous process of the first thoracic vertebra, on the midline. From TCM.

套 (rad.37) tào   1. A set; case, cover. 2. A trap, placing the forward foot outside an adversary's foot to control it (in a non-stepping situation).

tào bù 套步 Continuous cross stepping: move to the side with a number of back crossing steps.

tào kuà 套胯 To slide the hips, changing place with a snap of the waist, in a tight clinch.

tào kuà rù 套胯入 To step in, slide the hips into an adversary, and throw over the hips with a snapping bowing action.

tào lù 套路 1. A routine, a form. Also called tào zi. In English a routine is also often called a kata, from the Japanese. 2. The routine performance division of modern competition wushu, called Taolu in English.

tào lù biān pái 套路编排 Choreography of a routine: refers to Taolu competition routines.

tào tuǐ 套腿 Trapping kick: a hidden kick, stepping into an adversary to trap his lower limbs. From Baguazhang.

tào zhù 套住 To trap.

tào zi 套子 A routine, see #1 of tào lù.

特 (rad.93) tè   Special; particular.

tè diǎn 特点 Characteristics, of a style, a person, or thing.

籘 (rad.118) [藤] (rad.140) téng   Vines; cane plants; rattans; climbing plants.

téng luó guà bì 藤萝掛壁 Purple-vine Hangs on the Wall: step back into an open bow stance to the side with a rising cut to press up with a sword above the head. This dodges back, bars an incoming chop, and cuts an adversary's wrist. From Qingping sword.

騰 [腾] (rad.187) téng   1. To fly; rise, soar. 2. To gallop; prance; run. 3. As general footwork, to charge. 4. As a shield and broadsword technique, gallop: charge forward, landing with a chop.

téng kōng 腾空 1. To soar in the air: complete a technique in flight, applied to aerial kicking techniques, usually those where the body remains upright. 2. Be airborne during a throw (getting thrown).

téng kōng bǎi lián 腾空摆莲 Aerial outside crescent kick, aerial lotus kick: turn the pushing off foot out, jump up, swing one leg inward, then swing the other outward, slapping the outward foot with both hands.

téng kōng bǎi lián sān bǎi liù 腾空摆莲360 Aerial outside crescent kick three-sixty, lotus kick with a full three-sixty degrees circle turn.

téng kōng bēi gùn tí xī 腾空背棍提膝 Flying raise knee shoulder a staff: moving forward with a skip jump, knee held high, with the staff tucked on the back. Used to gain momentum for a jump kick, often combining a punch with the left fist while in the air.

téng kōng cè chuài 腾空侧踹 Aerial side kick, completing the kick in the air.

téng kōng dǎo tī 腾空倒踢 Aerial back kick, two-footed jump up with a one-legged swinging kick towards the back of the head.

téng kōng dēng tī 腾空蹬踢 Aerial thrust kick, completing the kick in the air.

téng kōng fǎ 腾空法 Aerial techniques: leaping to strike an adversary in flight.

téng kōng fēi jiǎo 腾空飞脚 Flying slap kick: swing one leg up and push off the other, extend the pushing off leg to a snap kick, slapping the foot. From Chuojiao, one of its high-basin kicks.

In competition Longfist routines, must slap at least to shoulder height and land on the kicking leg.

téng kōng fēi jiǎo xiàng nèi zhuàn tǐ yī bǎi bā 腾空飞脚向内转体180 Flying slap kick one-eighty, turning inside to land facing back; kick in flight with half inward turn.

téng kōng guà mián tuǐ 腾空挂面腿 Aerial hook the face kick: turn the push off foot in, jump up, swing one leg outward, then swing the other inward, slapping the inward kicking foot with the opposite hand, turning one-eighty degrees.

téng kōng hòu fān 腾空后翻 Aerial back summersault, with two-footed take off and landing.

téng kōng jiǎn tuǐ 腾空剪腿 Aerial scissor splits: leap up, lifting the left leg straight, then switch the legs to perform the front splits in the air.

téng kōng jiàn tán 腾空箭弹 Aerial snap kick, jumped front snap kick. Usually done with the palm pushing forward.

téng kōng lián huán fēi jiǎo 腾空连环飞脚 Aerial consecutive slap kicks: swing the left leg up, push off the right leg and swing it up as well. Slap the feet, left then right.

téng kōng pán tuǐ sān bǎi liù cè pū 腾空盘腿360侧仆 Aerial cross-legged kick with a full three-sixty twist, landing on the side. From southern styles.

téng kōng qián fān 腾空前翻 Aerial forward summersault, with two-footed take off and landing.

téng kōng shān jiǎo 腾空搧脚 Aerial fanning kick. From Chuojiao, for the tornado kick. See also xuàn fēng jiǎo.

téng kōng shù chā yuè bù 腾空竖叉跃步 Aerial front split leap.

téng kōng shuāng cè chuài 腾空双侧踹 Aerial double side kick: double side kicks in flight.

téng kōng shuāng dēng 腾空双蹬 Aerial double heel kick: double front heel kicks in flight.

téng kōng shuāng fēi jiǎo 腾空双飞脚 Aerial double slap kick, slapping both feet. See also téng kōng fēi jiǎo.

téng kōng wài bǎi lián 腾空外摆莲 Aerial outside crescent kick. Also called téng kōng wài bǎi tuǐ.

téng kōng wài bǎi tuǐ 腾空外摆腿 Aerial outside crescent kick, outward kick in flight. Also called téng kōng wài bǎi lián.

téng kōng wài bǎi tuǐ qī bǎi èr 腾空外摆腿720 Aerial outside crescent kick seven-twenty: outward kick in flight with two full rotations.

téng kōng wài bǎi tuǐ sān bǎi liù 腾空外摆腿360 Aerial outside crescent kick three-sixty: outward kick in flight with one full rotation.

téng kōng wài bǎi tuǐ wǔ bǎi sì 腾空外摆腿540 Aerial outside crescent kick five-forty: outward kick in flight with one and a half rotations.

téng kōng xié pāi jiǎo 腾空斜拍脚 Flying angled slap kick, the same as the flying slap kick, but with the opposite leg. See also téng kōng fēi jiǎo.

téng kōng zhèng tī tuǐ 腾空正踢腿 Aerial front straight kick with hanging leg straight.

téng kōng zhuàn shēn dēng tuǐ 腾空转身蹬腿 Aerial turning heel kick: jump up, turn one-eighty degrees in the air and heel thrust kick while still in the air.

téng kōng zhuàn shēn fēi jiǎo 腾空转身飞脚 Aerial turning snap kick: jump up, turn one-eighty degrees in the air and snap kick while still in the air.

téng kōng zǒu 腾空走 Walk in the air: a training method, walking on bricks or pillars. From Baguazhang.

téng nuó 腾挪 Preparedness to move, the intent to move has occurred but movement has not yet taken place.

téng nuó fǎ 腾挪法 Shifting techniques: methods of getting around to the back of an adversary.

téng nuó liè 腾挪挒 Shift aside while splaying an adversary. From Taijiquan push hands.

téng shǒu zhèn xīn 腾手震心 Charging hand to shock the heart: an expressive term for the category of hand techniques that use hooking. See also diāo fǎ.

剔 (rad.18) **tī**　1. To clean with a pointed instrument; to pick. 2. To pick out and throw away.

tī dà dāo 剔大刀 Pick with a big cutter: with both

hands mid-shaft, bring the butt of a cutter over then stab forward with it. Used with a butt that has a pointed metal sheath.

踢 (rad.157) tī   1. To kick. 2. The category of strikes using the legs (such as kicks, sweeps, not leg throws), see also sì jī. 3. In throwing styles, the category of throws using mostly the leg.

tī dēng 踢灯 Kick the Lamp: bring the foot up from the side or back to kick an adversary's kidney with the heel. The name is because the kidney is known as the 'fire' at the Mingmen acupoint. From Shaolinquan.

tī èr qǐ 踢二起 Two jump kick: a jump front slap kick. See èr qǐ jiǎo. Also called fān shēn èr qǐ, when there is a turn before the kick.

tī fǎ 踢法 Kicking methods, category of leg strikes referring to all types of kicks. Common to most styles are bǎi, chán, chuāi, dēng, diǎn, guà, sǎo, tán. See also sì jī. See also the lists linked to jiǎo and tuǐ.

tī jiàn 踢毽 Kick the shuttlecock, a trip: a counter to your adversary coiling a leg around your leg. Swing your leg straight up between his legs, taking his leg along with yours. From wrestling.

tī mén kǎn 踢门坎 Kick the doorstep: to kick the front foot out as if it is kicking through the Chinese doorstep (an old style door is set into a frame, with a heavy sill) instead of stepping over it. A metaphor describing the walking of Baguazhang.

tī mù zhuāng 踢木桩 Kick the wooden stake: kick a tree or planted stump to develop the foot (not shin kicking). Also called tī zhuāng gōng.

tī tuǐ 踢腿 Kick. 1. Often refers to straight legged kicks or to ballistic stretching kicks. 2. Kicks in general: may be a dorsi-flexed ankle, kicking with the outside of the foot, or a basic snap kick.

tī tuǐ liāo zhǎng 踢腿撩掌 Straight kick with lifting palm: raise the leg in an oblique straight kick and swing the opposite arm up alongside the outside of the leg.

tī zhuāng gōng 踢桩功 Kick the stake training: see tī mù zhuāng.

提 (rad.64) tí   1. Basic meaning to lift, raise, take up. Carry in one's hand with the arm down. 2. A lifting strike used to clear the main gateway. From Bajiquan, one of its six main striking techniques, see also liù dà kāi. 3. Raise. From Bajiquan, one of its ten major techniques, see also shí dà jī fǎ. 4. The category of chambered kicks of Chuojiao.

tí bào zhuāng 提抱桩 Lift and hug stake standing: sitting slightly with the elbows open to the sides, palms up, fingers pointing to the hips, combining the power of lifting up and embracing, as if carrying barrels. From Yiquan.

tí bì bǎn zhǒu 提臂扳肘 Carry the arms and pull the elbows: get under the elbows to straighten the arms and lift them, jamming them up. From wrestling.

tí bù 提步 1. A step or a stance with the suspended foot raised to the ankle of the supporting leg. 2. The same, with the suspended foot dorsi-flexed. From Xingyiquan. Also called mó jìng bù. 2. A quick lift of the knee with the foot pointed down, then landing back to the same spot, just before stepping forward. From northern styles.

tí chā zhuāng 提插桩 Lift and stab stake standing: sitting slightly with the arms slightly open at the sides, fingers down, combining the powers of lifting up the elbows and stabbing down through the fingers. From Yiquan.

tí dài tī 提带踢 Lift the Belt and Kick: grab your adversary's belt with one hand and his sleeve with the other and lift and twist him while placing your foot outside his and controlling his leg with the inside of your foot. From wrestling.

tí dāo 提刀 Lift a broadsword: lift the grip above the head, slicing up as it moves, and finishing with the blade angled down, cutting edge up.

tí dà dāo 提大刀 Lift a big cutter: with the right hand at the butt and the left along the shaft, lift the butt behind the body, angling the blade down to knee height, edge up.

tí dēng 提登 Raised knee stance. See tí xī. Also called tí xī dú lì bù, tí xī dú lì shì.

tí dǐng shùn xiàng 提顶顺项 Lift the head and keep the nape of the neck naturally erect. A basic requirement of many styles.

tí gāng 提肛 Raise the anal sphincter: lightly close the anal sphincter when training. This aids to collect the qi in the dantian, prevent qi from dissipating, connect the groin and head in a direct line, and improve the *qi* circulation. This is a common requirement in many styles, the effort is light, like closing the eyes. Also called bì dì hū, shōu gāng.

tí huáng chuài tuǐ 提皇踹腿 Lift the Emperor Side Kick: a chambered side kick, lifting the knee both before and after the kick. From Chuojiao, one of its middle-basin kicks.

tí huáng diǎn tuǐ 提皇点腿 Lift the Emperor Poke Kick: a chambered poke kick, lifting the knee both before and after the kick. From Chuojiao, one of its middle-basin kicks.

tí huáng tuǐ 提皇腿 Lift the Emperor Kick: lift the knee, either as a defensive move or a knee strike. From Chuojiao, one of its middle-basin kicks.

tí jiàn 提剑 Lift a sword, tip angled down.

tí jīn 提筋 Lift the tendon: grab and lift a tendon, artery or vein, pulling it away from the body. From Qinna.

tí jìn 提劲 Lifting power: disturb the balance of an adversary with a lifting intent. Usually changing the direction of his attack, absorbing and lifting so he loses balance.

tí liáo gùn 提撩棍 Rising slice with a staff: raise the butt of the staff over the head, swinging the tip of the staff upwards in front of the body.

tí liáo huā gùn 提撩花棍 Rising flowers with a staff, rising figure eights: circle the staff repeatedly with rising circles close to the sides of the body, the tip lifting in front.

tí liáo wǔ huā gùn 提撩舞花棍 See tí liáo huā gùn.

tí lū qiāng 提撸枪 Lift and rub a spear. 1. Lift the right hand to circle the tip down. 2. Traditionally, this dual trapping action done as a low defense. See also fēng bì qiāng, lán ná qiāng.

tí qì 提气 Lift the breath: to breathe into the chest to lighten the body. Used to assist rising movements such as coming up from a low stance or moving into jumps.

tí qiān jīn 提千斤 Lift a thousand pounds: hold a jar or stone lock with the fingers or full grip, releasing and catching with the other hand repeatedly. For grip and arm strength training, usually done in horse stance to develop connected body power.

tí quán 提拳 Lift with the fist, raise up with the fist.

tí shǒu 提手 Lift the hand. 1. In a tight situation, bend the elbow and wrist to lift the hand straight up to strike an adversary's jaw with a wrist or backhand. 2. A straight arm lift, hand hooked to hit the jaw of an adversary with a wrist strike. From Wing Chun.

tí shuǐ shì 提水式 Lift the Water: a step into a half-horse stance with a low rolled over punch. From Xingyiquan.

tí wàn 提腕 Lift the wrist: grab the back of your adversary's hand and press his hand to hyper-flex the wrist. From Qinna.

tí xī 提膝 Raise the knee, a knee technique: lift the knee to protect the high centre. A raised knee brings the knee up as high as possible, and the supporting leg should be straight. Also called tí dēng, tí xī dú lì bù, tí xī dú lì shì.

tí xī chōng quán 提膝冲拳 Raised knee punch: stand in a straight one legged stance with the knee raised and punch forward with the same side fist as the raised knee.

tí xī dú lì bù 提膝独立步 Raised knee stance. See tí xī. Also called tí dēng, tí xī dú lì shì.

tí xī dú lì shì 提膝独立式 Raised knee position. See tí xī. Also called tí dēng, tí xī dú lì bù.

tí xī píng héng 提膝平横 One legged stance with back and supporting leg straight and the suspended knee raised at least to waist height. In Taolu competition, must be held for two seconds. See also tí dēng, tí xī, tí xī dú lì bù, tí xī dú lì shì.

tí xī tàn hǎi 提膝探海 Raised Knee Reach into the Sea: a straight legged stance with the knee raised, torso leaning forward to reach a sword to cut downward. From Wudang sword.

tí xī tiào chōng quán 提膝跳冲拳 Jumping raised knee punch: jump and complete a raised knee stance in the air, punching while still airborne. Often a hop skip step to gain momentum for a jump.

tí xī wàng yuè 提膝望月 Raised Knee Look at the Moon: a straight one legged stance with the knee raised, sword blocking above the head, left hand extended. From Wudang sword.

tí zhǎng 提掌 Lift with the palm, raise up with the hand.

tí zhǒu 提肘 Lift the elbow: with the arm bent, raise the tip of the elbow, either to the front or to the side. In many styles, the elbow stays low and the strike is done with the forearm or fist. The final posture is as if holding something in the crook of the elbow.

tí zhuàn dāo 提转刀 Lift a broadsword while turning: circle-walk while holding a broadsword in a lifting up posture. From Baguazhang. See tí dāo.

體 (rad.188) [体] (rad.9) tǐ 1. The body or part of the body. 2. Substance.

tǐ hé yú xīn 体合于心 The body combines with the heart. From Liuhebafa, one of its principles.

tǐ lì 体力 The strength and endurance of the body, conditioning. Includes power and aerobic conditioning.

tǐ yòng jiān bèi 体用兼备 To have both conditioning and ability to apply the techniques.

tǐ zhòng 体重 The body weight.

tǐ zhòng fēn jí 体重分级 Weight category; weight categories. Used for Sanda and wrestling competitions.

tǐ zhòng qì 体重器 Scales (to measure body weight).

天 (rad.37) tiān 1. The sky. Heavens. 2. Day. 3. Natural; inborn. 4. Weather.

tiān biān guà yuè 天边掛月 Hang the Moon at the Horizon: from a bow stance straight stab, cross step and bring a sword over with a hooking slice up and back. From Qingping sword.

tiān chèng 天秤 Sky balance: an apparatus for training grip strength and power, consisting of a large tripod with a weight hanging from the middle, with a pole attached to the hanging rope. The pole is manipulated from the other end in exercises to strengthen the grip, the wrist, and twisting power particularly.

tiān chí 天池 Acupoint Tianchi (celestial pool), PC1. At the chest, at the fourth intercostal space, one *cun* outside and slightly above the centre of the nipple, five *cun* lateral to the midline (on each side). From TCM.

tiān chōng 天冲 Acupoint Tianchong (celestial hub), GB9. At the head, two *cun* from the hairline, drawing a line up from the root of the ear (on each side). From TCM.

tiān chuāng 天窗 Acupoint, Tianchuang (celestial window), SI16. At the outside edge of the neck, just behind the line of the large muscle (the sternocleidomastoid), at the level of the laryngeal prominence (on each side). From TCM.

tiān dì tóng shòu 天地同寿 Heaven and Earth Share the same Age: a snap kick with a finger thrust, landing to a horse stance upper framing block and punch. From Yangjia style.

tiān dǐng 天鼎 Acupoint Tianding (celestial tripod), LI17. At the outside edge of the neck, just behind the line of the sternocleidomastoid muscle (on each side). From TCM.

tiān fǔ 天府 Acupoint Tianfu (celestial storehouse), LU3. At the upper arm, on the outside line of the biceps, about three *cun* down from the outer edge of the armpit (on each arm). From TCM. A sensitive point. Best to hit with a chop or hack.

tiān gān 天干 The ten Celestial Stems, used as numbers in listings, and in combination with the twelve Terrestrial Branches to designate years, months, days, and hours. See also bǐng, dīng, gēng, guǐ, jǐ, jiǎ, rén, wù, xīn, yǐ. See also dì zhī.

tiān gāng jiàn 天罡剑 Big Dipper sword: a long tasseled sword routine of Mizongquan, written up as seventy-nine moves.

tiān gōng zhāi xīng 天宫摘星 Picking Stars at the Heavenly Palace: Press up with one palm and step through to trip. From Liuhebafa.

tiān jǐng 天井 Acupoint Tianjing (celestial well), SJ10. At the elbow, on the outside, one *cun* proximal to the tip of the elbow (each arm). From TCM.

tiān liáo 天髎 Acupoint Tianliao (celestial bonehole), SJ15. At the upper back/shoulders, in the body of the trapezius muscle, the upper edge of the scapula, between acupoints Tianjing and Quyuan (each side). From TCM.

tiān líng gài 天灵盖 Celestial spirit cover: colloquial term for the acupoint Baihui, see bǎi huí.

tiān luó dì wǎng 天罗地网 Snares above and Nets below: to set a dragnet from which no one can escape. In Yangjia style, a side kick followed by a front sweep kick.

tiān mǎ 天马 1. A celestial, or heavenly, steed, from Chinese mythology. 2. A superior horse. Often used in movement names. May be translated as Pegasus, but that is from Western mythology.

tiān mǎ fēi bào 天马飞报 Celestial Steed Flies with the Report: step into an empty stance low chop with a sword. From Yang Taijiquan.

tiān mǎ fēi pù 天马飞瀑 Celestial Steed Flies over the Waterfall, a rising sword technique. From Yang Taijiquan.

tiān mǎ xíng kōng 天马行空 Celestial Steed Moves across the Sky. 1. In Taijiquan, a moving smear with a sword. 2. In Baguazhang, a posture held while circle-walking, the inside hand raised and inwardly rotated, the outside hand placed below the elbow. 3. As a standard idiom, a bold, powerful, and uncontrained style.

tiān péng chā 天蓬叉 A large trident.

tiān quán 天泉 Acupoint Tianquan (celestial spring), PC2. At the arm, two *cun* from the crease at the armpit, between the two bellies of the biceps brachii muscle (on each arm).

tiān róng 天容 Acupoint Tianrong (celestial countenance), SI17. At the outside of the neck, just behind the jawbone, just in front of the large muscle (on each side). From TCM.

tiān shū 天枢 Acupoint Tianshu (celestial pivot), ST25. At the abdomen, at the height of the navel, two *cun* lateral to the midline (on each side). From TCM. A sensitive point, striking it can induce breathlessness.

tiān tíng 天庭 The middle of the forehead. A sensitive point where many meridians meet or pass.

tiān tū (xué) 天突(穴) Acupoint Tiantu (celestial chimney), RN22. At the chest, at the depression of the manubrium (the suprasternal notch), on the midline. From TCM. Striking here can cause a lot of pain and damage, so it should not be hit too hard.

tiān wáng dǎ sǎn 天王打伞 Celestial King Opens his Umbrella: thread one arm upwards, spiraling the forearm, placing the other palm at the raised elbow. This is used as an arm jam. From Baguazhang.

tiān wáng tuō tǎ 天王托塔 Celestial King Carries the Pagoda (he always carried a small pagoda to protect himself from Nezha, but that is a long story). 1. Step forward with a lifting palm (see tuō). This is a direct strike to the jaw or neck, or a lifting reversal of the wrist. From Baguazhang and Shaolinquan, one of Baguazhang's sixty-four hands. 2. An expressive term for the category of hand techniques that use drilling. See also zuān fǎ.

tiān xī 天溪 Acupoint Tianxi (celestial ravine), SP18. At the chest, the fourth intercostal space, six *cun* lateral to the midline (on each side). From TCM.

tiān xiān zhǎng 天仙掌 Goddess palm: punch and kick, then pull back the foot, leaving the knee up. Stand on one leg, one arm extended up, the other extended forward. From Chuojiao.

tiān xuán dì zhuàn 天旋地转 Heaven and Earth Revolve: when grabbed on the shoulder from behind, turn completely around, raising your arms, trapping your adversary's hand between your shoulder and neck. Lock his elbow with one arm and take him down. You can also assist with the other arm. From Qinna.

tiān yǒu 天牖 Acupoint Tianyou (celestial window), SJ16. At the head, at the highest insertion of the levator scapula, level with the angle of the jawbone, down and below acupoint Kongtu (on each side). From TCM.

tiān zhù (xué) 天柱(穴) Acupoint Tianzhu (celestial pillar), BL10. At the nape of the neck, about at the rear hairline, 1.3 *cun* lateral to the midline, at the lateral side of the trapezius muscle, on each side. From TCM. A sensitive point, to the extent that striking it may cause death.

tiān zhù yíng rì 天柱迎日 Celestial Pillar Greets the Sun: move forward to a ready stance, same side hand chopping to head height, rear hand at the belly. From Wudangquan.

tiān zōng 天宗 Acupoint Tianzong (celestial gathering), SI11. At the upper back, in the cavity of the shoulder blade, across from the armpit, level with the depression below the fourth thoracic vertebra (on each side). From TCM. Pressure here can induce numbness, so helps to control an adversary.

填 (rad.32) **tián** 1. To fill; to stuff. 2. To write, to fill in.

tián hǎi shì 填海式 Fill the Sea: a high snap up with a spear, first scooping, then snapping.

tián yāo 填腰 To fill in with the waist: set the waist into an adversary with a back step and a twist of the hips.

田 (rad.102) **tián** A field. Farmland; cropland.

tián liè 田猎 1. To go hunting. 2. To busk, to perform martial arts in the street for money.

tián zì zhuāng 田字桩 Character for field stake: a basic routine of Meishanquan, written up as forty-three moves. The route of the steps follows the lines of the 田 character.

腆 (rad.130) **tiǎn** 1. Prosperous; sumptuous. 2. Virtuous. 3. Protruding; thrust out.

tiǎn xiōng 腆胸 Stick out the chest: puff up the chest. An error in many styles.

條 (rad.9) [条] (rad.34) **tiáo** 1. A twig. 2. Measure word for long narrow things. 3. A strip. 4. An item. Order of items.

tiáo jiàn 条件 Condition, term, factor. Requirement, qualification.

tiáo jiàn shí zhàn 条件实战 Conditional sparring drills: sparring drills with predetermined techniques, to repeat certain techniques (i.e. a specific kick) or methods (ie. head attacks).

tiáo kǒu 条口 Acupoint Tiaokou (ribbon opening), ST38. At the shin, eight *cun* below the acupoint Dubi (on each side). From TCM.

調 [调] (rad.149) **tiáo** 1. To regulate; to mediate. 2. To mix, blend, adjust. 3. Balance; regular. 4. Fit in, suit well. 5. Pronounced diào, to transfer, see diào.

tiáo dāng 调裆 To adjust the crotch area to a certain position to collect the *qi* in the *dantian*. Includes tucking the buttocks, lightly closing the anal sphincter, lightly lifting the Huiyin point, and lightly turning up the abdomen. From Taijiquan.

tiáo jìn 调劲 To regulate power: the adjustments that a teacher makes to help a student to use power correctly.

tiáo shè shù 调摄术 Regulate oneself: the technique of regulating one's veins and arteries.

tiáo yáng gōng 调养功 A standing *qigong* method to adjust and cultivate the health.

挑 (rad.64) **tiǎo** 1. The original, practical, meaning is to push something up with a stick, such as hanging a lantern up from the end of a pole or pushing a bale of hay up to a hay rack with the end of a pitchfork. 2. To stir up, instigate. 3. The rising stroke in Chinese writing. 4. An arm technique: to scoop, the action of slicing the arm or a weapon up with the elbow and wrist held cocked like shoveling or using a pitchfork. 5. In Changquan, a lifting arm flicking the wrist at the end of the action. 6. As a leg technique, to hook the foot up, or dorsi-flex. 7. As a throw, to scoop up with the thigh to off balance an adversary. 8. Rising, one of the walking hands of Chuojiao, see also zǒu shǒu.

tiǎo bà 挑把 Scoop up with the butt end of a long weapon.

tiǎo dǎ 挑打 1. A scooping up strike, uppercut. 2. An upper jamming block and punch combination.

tiǎo dǎ chuí 挑打捶 Scooping punch: a sweeping upper block and punch in horse stance. From Chuojiao. Usually called jià dǎ in other styles.

tiǎo dǎ shuāi 挑打摔 Scooping and hitting throws, the category of throws that involve moving in tight, turning to place the hip on the adversary, and lifting his leg for a high flying throw, often involving holding around the neck or waist.

tiǎo dāo 挑刀 Scoop with a broadsword. See tiǎo jiàn.

tiǎo dà dāo 挑大刀 Scoop with a big cutter: swing the blade upward, rotating the right arm to bring the cutting edge up.

tiǎo dēng guān zhàn 挑灯观战 Lift the Lamp to Observe the Battle: continuous rising chopping palms. From Piguaquan.

tiǎo dòu 挑逗 To provoke: to stir up an excitable adversary to cause him to make errors.

tiǎo gōu 挑勾 Scooping throw: category of throws that involve pulling the jacket of an adversary and hooking his thigh with the leg. From wrestling.

tiǎo gōu 挑钩 Scoop with hooks: with the double hooks, circle the blades vertically from one side to the other, starting and finishing with the hooks up, slicing with the forward edge of the blades.

tiǎo gōu zǐ 挑勾子 Scooping throw: catch your adversary's arm and move in to grasp around his neck, stepping in and turning to tuck your hip into him. Catch his leg and lift your leg high to take his leg up, at the same time dropping his neck, so that he does a high flying fall. Also called jiā jǐng tiāo.

tiǎo gùn 挑棍 Scoop up with either end of a staff.

tiǎo huá chē 挑滑车 Raise with a Pulley: send a spear forward to its full length, stabbing down, then move forward into a crossed stance (or empty stance) and snap the spear tip up. From Shaolinquan.

tiǎo jiàn 挑剑 Scoop with a sword: snap up the blade, putting power to the tip.

tiǎo jìn 挑劲 Power used to generate the scooping strike.

tiǎo lián shì 挑帘势 Push up the Shop Sign: circle a sword around then lift the blade in front of the body in a raised knee stance.

tiǎo má jīn 挑麻筋 Dig into the numbness tendons: grab and apply strong pressure to the acupoints on the back of the hand in between the tendons of the fingers, at the tiger's mouth, or between the index and middle, middle and ring, or ring and little finger. This can induce numbness of the hand and arm.

tiǎo qiāng 挑枪 Scoop up with either end of a spear, though scooping with the butt is usually called tiǎo bà.

tiǎo shǒu ér rù shǒu 挑手而入手 If your adversary lifts under your attack, slide under to keep his arm lifting, punching with the other hand. From Tanglangquan, one of its twelve soft counters, see also shí èr róu.

tiǎo tiān pī dì 挑天劈地 Scoop the Sky and Chop the Earth: single chopping palms to left and right, or continuous chopping palms. From Piguaquan.

tiǎo tuǐ 挑腿 Scooping kick. 1. A straight swinging back kick with the foot dorsi-flexed. 2. A wrestling leg exercise, swinging the leg up behind while leaning forward, as if throwing with the leg.

Also called rēng gōu zi.

tiǎo zì gōng 挑字功 Skill of scooping, one of Xingyiquan's eight skills, using a bent arm scoop with full body power.

tiǎo zhǎng 挑掌 1. In most traditional styles: scoop, a scooping strike upwards with the arm slightly bent and the wrist cocked, hitting with the forearm or palm. 2. In Changquan, flick, an upward flick of the wrist to present the palm. 3. In southern styles, stir, a strike in front of the body, power going outwards at chest height, palm up.

tiǎo zhǒu 挑肘 Upward strike with the elbow, fist heart facing in.

跳 (rad.157) **tiào** To jump, spring, bounce. Skip over something. Usually used for vertical jumps more than jumps for distance.

tiào bā miàn 跳八面 Jump to the eight directions, a leg training exercise. Standing in one place, jump up and land in bow stance, jump up and land in horse stance, then repeat to the other side. Repeat. Also called tiào bā shān.

tiào bā shān 跳八扇 Jump the eight fans. See tiào bā miàn.

tiào biè 跳别 Jumping throw: jump both feet in, getting your hips onto those of your adversary, then swing one leg up and throw him over your hip. From wrestling.

tiào bīng bù 跳并步 Jump off one foot and bring the legs together in mid-air to land with the feet together.

tiào bù 跳步 1. A jumping step, may tuck the heels up. 2. A rebounding jump upwards while completing a move.

tiào bù dān tī 跳步单踢 Jump step single kick: lift up a knee, push off with the other leg and kick with that leg while landing the lifted foot. From Bajiquan.

tiào bù fēi jiǎo 跳步飞脚 Jump step flying kick: jump forward and do a snap kick on landing. From Shaolinquan.

tiào bù jiàn tán 跳步箭弹 Jump arrow kick: a jumping snap kick, pushing forward with the opposite hand. From Chaquan.

tiào chā bù 跳插步 Jumping back cross step: jump up, completing the posture of a back cross stance while airborne.

tiào dān pāi jiǎo 跳单拍脚 Jumping slap kick: jump up for a quick slap kick with no run-up.

tiào kēng 跳坑 Jump the pit, a light skills training method: jump out of a pit dug into the ground, gradually increasing the depth of the pit.

tiào shǎn 跳闪 Jumping dodging: jump to the side, pushing off both feet to change position, to avoid an attack without making contact.

tiào shéng 跳绳 Skipping rope: often used in sparring training for aerobic conditioning and agility training.

tiào tī bù 跳踢步 Jumping kick step: from a half horse stance, lift the leading knee and push off from the rear leg, jumping forward to kick with it. Land on the original lead leg and land the rear leg still behind. From Duanquan.

tiào tí xī gōu shǒu tuī zhǎng 跳提膝勾手推掌 Jumping raised knee with hook and push: jump up, raising the knee, hooking the rear hand to the back and pushing forward with the leading palm. From Changquan.

tiào tuǐ 跳腿 Bouncing kick: set on one leg and extend the other, sliding the foot to the rear. From Duanquan.

tiào yuè 跳跃 Leap, jump in the air. The jump category of movements in Taolu competition.

tiào zhuàn shēn 跳转身 Leaping turn, jumping turn: to emphasize the jump up when turning around.

tiào zhuàn shēn pū bù qiē zhǎng 跳转身仆步切掌 Leaping turn to drop stance cut: leap up and fully turn in the air, landing in a drop stance with the arms crossed, slicing down with the outside arm. From Changquan.

贴 [贴] (rad.154) **tiē**　　To stick to; keep close to; glue.

tiē ěr chuān chuí 贴耳穿捶 Stick to the ear thread a mallet: from a raised fist start, drive a rolled over punch from your ear and directly to your adversary. From Baguazhang, one of its sixty-four hands. Also called guàn ěr chuān chuí.

tiē kào 贴靠 Stick and lean: stick to an adversary's chest and strike or throw with the body.

tiē kào quán 贴靠拳 Sticking Fist, the eighth routine of Duanquan, written up as fifteen moves.

tiē xiōng 贴胸 Stick the chest: stick the entire chest firmly on an adversary in preparation for a throw. From wrestling.

tiē shēn 贴身 Stick the body: stick close to an adversary to use elbows, knees, shoulders, and hips.

tiē shēn fǎ 贴身法 Pressing techniques: methods of getting in close and engaging an adversary.

tiē shēn shuāi 贴身摔 Close throws: a category of throws that are used in a clinch, with the body in contact, generally using small forces and skillful actions to use an adversary's strength against him.

tiē zhǎng 贴掌 Sticking palm, a hand shape: see wǔ fēng zhǎng. Also called liú shuǐ zhǎng.

鐵 [铁] (rad.167) **tiě**　　1. Iron. 2. Hard like iron.

tiě bǎn qiáo 铁板桥 Iron plate bridge. 1. As a throw: shoot into an adversary's legs to grab one, drop and lean back, lifting it to throw and land backwards on top of him. One of the leg threading type of throws, see also chuān tuǐ. From wrestling. 2. A hard skills planking method: lie face up with the body straight, supported only at the head and heels.

tiě bì gōng 铁臂功 Iron arm training: various exercises involving hitting the forearms to toughen them.

tiě biān 铁鞭 An iron whip: a sword-length stick with a grip, made of iron.

tiě bù shān 铁布衫 Iron shirt training: a hard skills training method, beating the chest and back with a wooden hammer progressively harder, to develop resistance to injury. May involve wrapping the torso in strips of cloth.

tiě chǐ 铁尺 Iron ruler: a short weapon, an iron bar, straight like a ruler.

tiě dāng gōng 铁裆功 Iron crotch skill. The training methods to develop the ability of the crotch to take hits.

tiě fān gān shì 铁翻杆式 Iron Pole Rolls Over model. 1. One of twenty-four classic spear moves. Most spear routines will have a move with a like name. In general, this name refers to a large circling trap and cover outwards. 2. A large outer trap, followed by shifting the hands to about an arm length apart in the middle of the shaft for a stab.

tiě kuài zǐ 铁筷子 Iron chopsticks: an iron weapon the same size and shape as chopsticks, used for close range, accurate striking, especially for acupoints. Also called diǎn xué zhēn.

tiě lí fān dì 铁犁翻地 Iron Plough Turns the Furrow: powerful footwork that drives forward with a trampling force. From Xingyiquan.

tiě mén shuān chuí 铁门闩捶 Beat the Iron Latch on the Gate: a right bow stance double pounding punches, right hand up to head height, left to belly height. The 59th move of the tiger and crane routine.

tiě niú gēng dì 铁牛耕地 Iron Ox Ploughs a Furrow: walk forward with a long Bagua broadsword tip lowered to point towards the ground, cutting edge forward. From Baguazhang.

tiě niú gēng dì shì 铁牛耕地式 Iron Ox Ploughs a Furrow model. 1. One of twenty-four classic spear moves. Most spear routines will have a move with a like name. In general, this name refers to a hard hacking technique. 2. From a low stance with the spear tip down, stab upwards and forward, keeping the right hand back near the front knee of a low bow stance.

tiě niú gōng 铁牛功 Iron ox training, to develop the torso to take blows. Gradually increase from massaging the belly and chest, to striking them, to lying with weights on the abdomen.

tiě quán 铁拳 An iron fist: a powerful punch.

tiě sǎo bà jiǎo 铁扫把脚 Iron Sweep the Foot: from a right reverse bow stance snap a low kick and bring it back, pushing the palms forward, right on top, fingers up, left below, fingers down. The 92nd move of the tiger and crane routine.

tiě sǎo shǒu 铁扫手 Iron Sweep: a swinging strike at the eyes with the fingers. From Shaolinquan.

tiě sǎo zhǒu gōng 铁扫帚功 Iron Sweeping training: kicking poles and trees to toughen the shins.

tiě shā zhǎng 铁沙掌 Iron sand palm. See tiě shā zhǎng below.

tiě shā zhǎng 铁砂掌 Iron pellet palm: training of the hand by slapping with the palm and the back of the hand on a bean filled pad, working up to an iron pellet filled pad.

tiě shàn zǐ 铁扇子 Iron fan, a fan made out of iron or other metal.

tiě shū zǐ 铁梳子 Iron comb: a double weapon shaped like a comb with four pointed tips and a range of pointed teeth.

tiě tóu gōng 铁头功 Iron head training, a hard qigong: involves striking the head and striking with the head to develop the ability to take hits and use it as a weapon.

tiě xī gōng 铁膝功 Iron knee training, a hard qigong: involves striking the knees, gradually increasing from slapping to striking with iron rods, to develop their hardness for striking.

tiě zhǒu shǒu 铁帚手 Iron Broom: a swinging strike at the eyes, either to hit the eyes or as a feint. From Shaolinquan.

tiě zhū dài 铁珠袋 Iron bead sack: a training bag filled with iron beads or ball bearings, used for tossing to train grip and arm strength.

tiě zhuó zǐ 铁镯子 Iron bracelet: hoist using the wrist and palm edge, a quick, strong, and short hook without grabbing, to send an adversary off.

聽 (rad.128) [听] (rad.30) **tīng** 1. To listen; hear. 2. To listen to; obey. 3. To hear through touching someone.

tīng fēng dú lì 听风独立 Hear the Wind and Stand Alone: Stand up and raise a sword blade to point straight up over the head, raising the left knee and placing the left hand at the foot. From Qingping sword.

tīng gōng 听宫 Acupoint Tinggong (auditory palace), SI19. At the face, just in front of the ear, behind the cavity made by the jawbone with the jaw open (on each side). This is the final acupoint in the Small Intestine meridian. From TCM.

tīng huì 听会 Acupoint Tinghui (auditory convergence), GB2. At the face, in the cavity made when the jaw opens, in front of the ear (on each side). From TCM.

tīng jìn 听劲 Listening power: when in contact with an adversary (usually in a gentle contact situation), using kinesthetic awareness to know what an adversary is about to do.

tīng jìn dǒng jìn shǒu shú wéi néng 听劲懂劲手熟为能 To be able to listen and understand an adversary's power you must have mastered your own practice.

停 (rad.9) **tíng**   1. To stop; to halt. To delay. 2. In martial arts, usually means to stop an adversary before they are fully engaged in your space.

tíng chē wèn lù 停车问路 Stop the Cart to Ask the Way: circle the hands then place them in ready fighting stance, taking an empty stance. From Liuhebafa.

tíng qiāng 停枪 Stop a spear: to wait, watching to defend with the spear.

挺 (rad.64) **tǐng**   1. To hold erect. 2. Upright, straight. 3. Thrust outwards. 4. Straighten. 5. One of the eight body requirements of Xingyiquan: straight or straightening the nape of the neck, the spinal column and lower back, and the knees.

tǐng bēi (or bì) 挺臂 Straighten the arm: to lock out the arm straight for a throw or takedown. From wrestling.

tǐng shī 挺尸 Hold the Corpse: jump up to thrust kick with both legs, laying the body flat, face up in the air.

tǐng xiōng 挺胸 Hold up the chest. 1. When as a requirement for some styles, this means to hold the abdomen in, the head up, the shoulders slightly back, and the chest naturally up. 2. In wrestling, to press the chest into an adversary to assist in takedowns and throws. 3. When referred to as an error, it means to thrust out the chest.

tǐng xiōng shōu fù 挺胸收腹 Hold up the chest and pull in the belly. An error in internal styles. Also called diān xiōng tí fù.

通 (rad.162) **tōng**   1. To connect through, pass through, communicate. 2. Clear, in the sense that a passage is clear to pass through.

tōng bēi (bì) sǎn tào 通臂散套 Connected Arms Scattered routine, a Tongbeiquan routine, written up as thirty-nine moves.

tōng bēi (bì) quán 通臂拳 Tongbeiquan (connected arms) a style from the area of Hebei, Shandong and Shanxi provinces. Also called bái yuán tōng bēi quán.

tōng bèi quán 通背拳 Tongbeiquan (through the back fist). See tōng bēi quán.

tōng gǔ 通谷 Acupoint Tonggu (valley passage), BL66. See zú tōng gǔ. From TCM.

tōng lǐ 通里 Acupoint Tongli (connecting inside), HT5. At the palm side of the wrist, one *cun* up from the wrist crease, on the little finger side (on each arm). From TCM.

tōng tiān 通天 Acupoint Tongtian (celestial connection), BL7. At the top of the head, four *cun* from the front hairline, 1.5 *cun* lateral to the midline, a slight depression (on each side). From TCM.

tōng tiān pào 通天炮 Punch Through the Sky. 1. A swinging uppercut to above head height. 2. A normal uppercut. From Tongbeiquan.

tōng tiān quán shì 通天拳势 Punch Through the Sky: in a right bow stance, do an uppercut with the right fist and draw the left fist back behind the body. The 53rd move of the tiger and crane routine.

tōng zhě bù tòng 通者不痛 Those with clear passages don't have pain. A martial saying. Expresses the belief that training the martial arts keeps the *qi*, blood, tendons, and ligaments smooth and connected, thus keeping the joints pain free.

同 (rad.30) **tóng**   1. To be the same as, similar to. Same, equal, identical. 2. Together. 3. To share; to agree.

tóng gāo 同高 The same height as. Often used in written training manuals when describing actions.

tóng shí 同时 At the same time as. Often used in written training manuals when describing actions.

tóng shí wán chéng 同时完成 Complete all movement simultaneously. Often used in written training manual when describing actions.

tóng xué 同学 Classmates. This use of the word same can be applied to many categories: work, age, school, for workmates, age cohorts, school mates, etc.

瞳 (rad.109) **tóng**   The pupil of the eye.

tóng zǐ liáo 瞳紫髎 Acupoint Tongziliao (pupil

bone-hole), GB1. At the face, 0.5 *cun* outside the eye socket, in the temporal fossa (on each side). From TCM.

童 (rad.117) **tóng**   1. A child. Often refers to a young boy, translated as a lad. 2. Virgin. 3. Bare; bald. For more movement names using the actions or abilities of young lads, see also jīn tóng, mù-, xiān-, yù-.

tóng zǐ bài fó 童子拜佛 Lad Bows to Buddha. 1. When the adversary grabs your shirt at the chest, press and twist his hand into your chest and bow. 2. Contacting an adversary's forearm with a block, grab the blade of his hand with your blocking hand, then grab his hand with the other hand and hyper flex his wrist, lifting his elbow above his head. 3. Done in a routine, flower hands, wrists together in front of the chest. 4. Leaning into a bow stance, stab to head height with the palms together. The 44th move of the tiger and crane routine.

tóng zǐ bài guān yīn 童子拜观音 Lad Bows to Guan Yin: when an adversary attacks, grab his thumb in one hand and little finger in the other hand, pull his hand along into your chest, simultaneously pressing down on his wrist and fingers, stepping back, and bowing. From Qinna.

tóng zǐ bào qín 童子抱琴 Lad Holds the Guqin (Chinese zither): reach out to grab, then pull back to the hips while kicking forward with a low turned out kick. From Liuhebafa.

tóng zǐ fēn duì 童子分队 Lad Splits the Troops: sit to horse stance and cut flat out to the sides with both arms. From Shaolinquan.

tóng zǐ sǎo xuě 童子扫雪 Lad Sweeps the Snow: step away, then come back to a long bow stance, cutting a sword back then slicing forward at an angle. From Qingping sword.

tóng zǐ sòng shū 童子松书 Lad Delivers a Book: Pull back, then step into a parallel stance and present the palm up to shoulder height, tucking the other palm at the wrist. From Liuhebafa.

tóng zǐ wā ěr 童子挖耳 Lad Picks the Ears: three quick finger strikes in succession. From Shaolinquan.

tóng zǐ xiàn shū 童子献书 Lad Presents a Book: Pull a sword back, then step into a parallel stance and present the palms together at shoulder height, stabbing straight forward. From Qingping sword.

箇 [筒] (rad.118) **tóng**   1. A bamboo pipe; a section of thick bamboo. 2. A thick tube-shaped object. 3. A case made of leather, shaped like a bamboo tube, for carrying arrows.

捅 (rad.64) **tǒng**   1. A poke or stab. To push. To nudge. 2. A direct attack, combined with a strong push off to get the body in, turning the body to wedge in presenting a small surface.

tǒng mén 捅门 Push to the chest.

tǒng ná fǎ 捅拿法 Pushing grappling hold: grab the front of the wrestling jacket and shove to prevent an adversary from getting in or applying a technique. From wrestling.

偷 媮 (rad.9, 38) [偷] (rad.9) **tōu**   1. To steal, burglarize. 2. Surreptitiously, on the sly.

tōu bù 偷步 Stealing step. 1. A back cross step: step the rear foot forward behind the front foot to move in on an adversary (similar to an insertion step, see also chā bù). Also called xí bù. 2. When stepping forward, turning the foot out into a slightly crossed stance. 3. The stance resulting from this step.

tōu bù fēng bì qiāng 偷步封闭枪 Stealing step closing spear: a back cross step with an outward cover, then step to bow stance with an inward cover and stab.

tōu kuà 偷胯 To steal with the hips, changing place with a snap of the waist, in a tight clinch.

tōu lì 偷力 Steal strength: to meet a fiercely oncoming adversary with strikes to his soft points or joints to take away his strength.

tōu liáng huàn zhù 偷梁换柱 Steal the Beams and Change the Pillars. Perpetrate a fraud. The twenty-fifth of the Thirty-six Stratagems of Warfare, which apply to many situations.

tōu shǒu 偷手 Stealing hand: get in a direct counter, without blocking, before an adversary can react.

頭 (rad.181) [头] (rad.37) **tóu**   1. The head. 2. Hair. 3. Top. 4. Leading. 5. Before.

tóu dǐng 头鼎 Headstand.

tóu fā lì 头发力 1. A head strike. 2 Training for head strikes. From Yiquan.

tóu fān 头翻 1. A head flip: a tumbling move. Bend the knees to touch down the head in front, then push off with the feet to flip over to land on both feet. 2. A headstand without using the hands as support.

tóu lín qì 头临泣 Acupoint Toulinqi (overlooking tears), GB15. At the head, above the eye, 0.5 *cun* into the front hairline, above acupoint Tongkong (on each side). From TCM.

tóu lù chá quán 头路查拳 The first routine of Chaquan. Also called yī lù chá quán.

tóu qiào yīn 头窍阴 Acupoint Touqiaoyin (head orifice yin), GB11. At the head, on the temporal bone, on an arc with acupoints Tianchong and Wangu, one third up from Wangu (on each side). From TCM.

tóu shǒu fān 头手翻 1. A supported head flip: a tumbling move. Bend the knees to touch down the head and hands in front, then push off with the feet to flip over to land on both feet. 2. A normal headstand, using the hands as support. Also called dà dǐng, tóu shǒu dào lì.

tóu shǒu dào lì 头手倒立 A headstand using the hands as support. Also called dà dǐng, tóu shǒu fān.

tóu wéi 头维 Acupoint Touwei (head corner), ST8. At the side of the head, about 0.5 *cun* behind the hairline, 4.5 *cun* lateral to the midline of the top of the head (on each side). From TCM.

tóu yūn 头晕 To get dizzy, to feel dizzy.

tóu zhǒu 头肘 An elbow to the head. From Tanglangquan, one of its eight short techniques.

透 (rad.162) tòu   To penetrate, pass through; seep through.

tòu gǔ 透骨 Penetrate the bones.

tòu gǔ quán 透骨拳 Penetrating bone fist, a hand shape: the fist is tightly clenched with the middle finger slightly protruding. From Tongbeiquan.

tòu jìn 透劲 Penetrating power. 1. The ability to apply direct strikes that penetrate deeply into an adversary. Also called tòu lì. 2. When performing a routine, the connection and coordination of completely unimpeded power throughout the body.

tòu lì 透力 Penetrating strength: see tòu jìn.

凸 (rad.17) tū   To protrude, bulge out, convex. Raised.

tū āo 凸凹 Convexity and concavity: movement and structure that bulges out and collapses in, losing the fullness that most styles require.

tū āo chù 凸凹处 Places in the body that protrude and cave in. Used in the sense that these places shoud not protrude or cave in.

突 (rad.116) tū   1. To dash forward; charge. 2. Projecting.

tū jī 突击 Sudden attack; unexpected attack (in a fighting match).

圖 [图] (rad.31) tú   A picture; drawing; chart; map.

tú jiě 图解 Illustrated explanations of techniques in martial arts manuals.

徒 (rad.60) tú   1. On foot. 2. Empty. 3. Pupil. Follower.

tú bó 徒搏 Bare knuckle fighting. See shǒu gé.

tú dǐ 徒弟 Apprentice, disciple.

tú shǒu 徒手 Barehanded, unarmed.

tú shǒu bèi 徒手背 Empty handed back throw: a wresting exercise. Lower the hands and cross the feet, then reach up and over, pulling and snapping the body to end up head and hands down, legs straight. Also called bēng zi.

tú shǒu duì liàn 徒手对练 Barehanded partner routine.

tú shǒu tào lù 徒手套路 Barehanded solo routine.

tú shǒu yǔ qì xiè duì liàn 徒手与器械对练 Barehanded versus weapon(s) partner routine.

吐 (rad.30) tǔ   1. To spit. 2. Often used in martial arts to mean the body technique of expelling energy. Often used in conjunction with tūn, first gathering in, then expelling power. One of Ziranmen's nineteen main methods.

tǔ nà 吐纳 Expelling and drawing energy, deep

breathing exercises to draw in fresh air and expel stale air.

土 (rad.32) **tǔ** 1. Earth, soil; ground. 2. Local; native. 3. Earth as one of the five elemental phases. Earth relates to the internal organ of the spleen, to the sensing organ of the mouth, to the tissue of the flesh, and to the season of Indian summer. Its *yang* expression is a hill, its *yin* is a plain. See also wǔ xíng. 4. Earth as one of the five phase techniques of Xingyiquan. The mindset of earth is centred and calm, defensive moves cover and neutralize, and attacking moves sense and redirect the adversary. See also héng quán.

兔 [兔] (rad.10) **tù** 1. A rabbit; hare. 2. Hare, as the fourth of the twelve animals from the Chinese zodiac, associated with a twelve year cycle symbolic of the earthly branches. The twelve animals make up a sixty year cycle when combined with the five phases. See also dì zhī, shēng xiào, wǔ xíng.

tù gǔn yīng fān 兔滚鹰翻 Rabbit Rolls and Eagle Flips over: from a two handed neck grab, drop backwards onto your back, holding the adversary's wrists still at your throat, setting a foot into his belly and rolling back so that he flies over you. From Shaolinquan.

tù zǐ dēng yīng 兔子蹬鹰 Rabbit Kicks the Eagle. 1. In a backing up, falling down situation, grab hold and throw a forward thrust kick. 2. In Sanda, an adversary's momentum may be used to push kick him off the platform.

團 [团] (rad.31) **tuán** 1. A group; society. 2. To unite. 3. Round.

tuán jiá 团胛 Rounded shoulder blades: curve the chest and upper back. From southern styles.

tuán tǐ sài 团体赛 Team competition: compete for results of the overall team.

推 (rad.64) **tuī** 1. To push with one or both hands; shove. 2. A push. One of the sixteen key techniques of Baguazhang, see also shí liù zì jué.

tuī bà 推把 Push with the butt: push with the shaft of a long weapon, power to the base end, shaft held level or slightly tilted (butt no lower than the knee). Not a stab, but a push to the end portion of the shaft.

tuī chuāng wàng yuè 推窗望月 Push Open the Shutter to Gaze at the Moon. 1. A horse or half-horse stance with one arm blocking up in front and the other coming through to push, the body tilted back. This references the Chinese type shutter with the hinge on top, so that it opens upwards. From Baguazhang and Xingyiquan. 2. Similar movements involving stepping forward placing one arm up and the other coming through with a strike, but not tilting. 3. A reverse grip slice up behind with a short weapon, looking up under the weapon. 4. A horse stance with a double opening palm. From Piguaquan.

tuī cuò 推挫 Shove, a pushing shove.

tuī dāo 推刀 Push a broadsword: push the blade forward with the left hand on the spine.

tuī dǎo jīn shān 推倒金山 Overturn the Golden Mountain: step back to a left bow stance, turning the torso left and intercepting with a sword pointing downwards so the tip is quite low. From Qingping sword.

tuī dǐng 推鼎 Handstand pushups, whether against a wall or freestanding.

tuī è 推颚 Push the jaw: grab around an adversary's back with one arm and shove his jaw with the other. From Qinna.

tuī fǎ 推法 Pushing methods. 1. A manipulative methods of healing, specifically a slightly rubbing firm push. From TCM. 2. Pushing methods of wrist control and dislocation. 3. Explosive techniques for pushing an adversary far away without striking or throwing to the ground.

tuī gōu 推钩 Push with hooks: with the double hooks, place the blades upright and push forward with the crescent blades at the grips.

tuī gùn 推棍 Push a staff: with the hands apart, straighten the arms to push with the shaft. The shaft may be horizontal or vertical, and the push may be to the front or to the side.

tuī hǎi shí léi 推海十雷 Push Back the Sea with Ten Claps of Thunder: a strong push.

tuī lán mǎ bàng 推拦马棒 Hold Back a Horse with a Pole: step into horse stance and press down with the shaft of a long weapon, left hand at the tip (just behind the body), right hand halfway down the shaft (just in front of the knee). From Shaolinquan.

tuī lóng 推龙 Push the Dragon: training with a stone lock, swinging it between the legs with an extended arm, swinging it up, releasing at the high point, re-catching and swinging back down. The swing, with a kettlebell, done with one or two hands, and with or without a release.

tuī mò zhǎng 推磨掌 Millstone pushing palm: holding the upper hand in front of the face and the lower hand at the elbow (especially while circle-walking). The power both wraps and extends outward. Both palms face the centre of the circle, or are slightly angled to cut to the blades of the palms. From Baguazhang, particularly for circle-walking. Also called hōng yàn chū qún, huái bào dān yú, tuī zhuàn zhǎng, zhuǎn shēn zhǎng.

tuī ná 推拿 Hands on method of healing that includes manipulation of the bones, muscles, tendons, and use of pressure points to both unblock the *qi* of the body and place structures in the body properly. Often called Tuina or Chinese massage in English.

tuī ná fǎ 推拿法 Pushing grappling hold: when the adversary is not allowing you to grab his wrestling jacket for a throw, push directly with both hands on his elbow or shoulder. From wrestling.

tuī shān gōng 推山功 Push the Mountain training: put bricks or flat stones on a table and push them with a sharp push so that they slide away. Gradually increase the weight. May also gradually add an uprooting to the push, so that they fly back through the air.

tuī shān kāi dào 推山开道 Push the Mountain to Clear the Way: step around, then advance directly into a push with deerhorn blades, one high one low, both blades vertical. From Baguazhang.

tuī shān rù hǎi 推山入海 Push the Mountain into the Sea: a strong one handed push or strike. The other hand assists by clearing above or holding behind an adversary's back. From Baguazhang.

tuī shān sè hǎi shì 推山赛海式 Push the Mountain to Block up the Sea model. One of twenty-four classic spear moves. Most spear routines will have a move with a like name. In general, this name refers to techniques that attack the knees.

tuī shǒu 推手 1. To push. 2. Push hands training in Taijiquan.

tuī sòng 推送 To push away, push for distance.

tuī tuō zhuāng 推托桩 Push and carry stake standing: sitting slightly with the hands at head height, palms out, combining the powers of pushing and carrying. From Yiquan.

tuī xī bō yāo 推膝拨腰 Push the knee and check the waist: from a clinch, with your adversary beside you with his arm around your neck, drop down, pushing his knee and checking his waist to the outside, dropping him face down. A throw or takedown.

tuī yá záo jiè 推崖凿界 Push the Cliff to Bore a Hole in the Boundary: jump forward to a bow stance and push forward with both palms at chest height, both palms vertical. From Shaolinquan.

tuī zhǎn 推斩 Pushing cut: a push to the forward edge of a blade that also contains a cutting action.

tuī zhǎn pū dāo 推斩扑刀 Pushing cut with a horse cutter: chop horizontally with a short strong action, with the blade edge in the direction of travel, the shaft horizontal, with the right hand near the hilt and the left hand along the shaft. The hands apply force in opposite directions, the right pushing into the cut and the left pulling inwards.

tuī zhǎng 推掌 To push with the palm. Normally the push is with the heel of the hand, the wrist is settled down, the fingers are vertical, and the palm is directly forward or slightly angled.

tuī zhǎng chōng quán 推掌冲拳 To push and punch. 1. Thrust the right fist and left palm forward at shoulder height and width. 2. As well as a double strike, this is used as a salute in southern styles, so may also be done slowly.

tuī zhuān 推砖 A pushing brick: a stone lock made out of brick instead of stone. Also called zuān tuī zi.

tuī zhuàn zhǎng 推转掌 See tuī mò zhǎng.

腿 骽 (rad.130,188) [腿] (rad.130) **tuǐ** 1. Leg, the legs. 2. Stances and kicks in general.

For more kicks and leg techniques that use tuǐ rather than jiǎo, see also under bā guà tuǐ, bǎi lián-, bǎi-, bān-, bào dān-, bào-, bēng-, biān chuāi-, bō-, bǒ-, cǎi-,

T

cè bǎi-, cè bān-, cè biāo-, cè chǎn-, cè chēng-, cè chuāi-, cè sī-, cè tī-, cè wō jié-, cèng-, chā-, chán sī-, chán-, chǎn-, chēng-, chōu bō-, chōu chuài-, chuāng qiāng-, chuān-, cùn tī-, cùn-, cuò-, dài bù-, dào chā-, dào sǎo-, dào tī-, dēng-, dī gòu tī-, diān tī-, diān-, diǎn-, dīng chāi-, dīng gāo-, dīng zǐ-, dōu dāng-, dǒu-, dǔ mén-, duò zǐ-, èr huàn-, fā hòu-, fān huán diǎn-, fēi diǎn-, fēi gē-, fēi yàn-, fú dì hòu dēng-, fǔ rèn tuǐ-, gōu bàn-, gōu-, guà-, guǎi-, guī táng-, guì-, gǔn jiǎn-, héng bǎi sǎo-, héng cǎi-, héng dīng-, héng liáng-, héng sǎo-, hóu tán-, hòu bǎi-, hòu bān-, hòu biāo-, hōu dēng-, hòu guà-, hòu kòng-, hòu liāo-, hòu liāo yīn-, hòu mén kǎn-, hòu sǎo-, hóu tán-, hóu tiǎo-, hóu yā-, hù-, jī xiǎng wài bǎi-, jī dēng-, jī-, jiā jiǎn-, jiāo-, jiē tuǐ lōu-, jié-, jié tuǐ lōu-, juē zǐ-, kòng-, kōu-, kòu-, kuà-, lā-, lán dēng-, lán mén-, lǐ chā-, lǐ chā xiǎo chán-, lǐ hé-, lián huán diǎn-, lián huán sǎo-, lián huán-, liào-, liū-, lōu-, luó quān-, mén kǎn-, pāi-, pán cháng-, pán-, páo-, pèng-, pī-, piān chuāi-, piǎo-, píng-, pū-, qī cūn-, qián hòu liāo yīn-, qián kòng-, qián mén kǎn-, qián sǎo-, qián tī-, qiāo-, qiē-, quān diǎn-, quān duò-, quān-, qún-, rào mǎ-, sān huàn-, sǎo táng-, sǎo-, shān-, sháo-, shí zì dǎng-, shí zì-, shuāng fēn-, shuāng kǔn-, sī-, sōu dāng-, sōu lèi-, tán-, tán-, tàng guà-, tàng tī-, tàng-, tāo tī-, tāo-, tào-, téng kōng jiǎn-, téng kōng wài bǎi-, téng kōng zhèng tī-, téng kōng zhuàn shēn dēng-, tī-, tí huáng chuài-, tí huáng diǎn-, tí huáng-, tiǎo-, tiào-, wài bǎi-, wài biāo-, wài chā-, wài gòu-, wò niú-, wú yǐng-, xià chuài-, xiān-, xiǎo guǐ dēng-, xié shān-, xié tī-, xū-, xuàn fēng-, yā-, yáng jiǎo chǎn-, yī zǐ-, yǐn-, yíng miàn-, yǒng-, yuān yāng-, yuè pán-, zhèng bān-, zhèng sǎo-, zhèng sī-, zhèng tī-, zhǐ-, zhuā xiū chuān-, zhuǎn shēn biāo-, zhuǎn zhǐ-, zhuàng-, zuān-, zuò-.

tuǐ fǎ 腿法 Leg techniques, legwork: kicks and stances.

tuǐ gōng 腿功 1. Leg training exercises. 2. The skill of the legs.

tuǐ quán 腿拳 Leg routines, the foundational routines of Chaquan, the first and second routines.

tuǐ sì hán jī 腿似寒鸡 The legs are like cold chickens. From Tongbeiquan, one of its requirements.

tuǐ tī gōng 腿踢功 Leg training for kicks: catch sand bags on the shins, kicking them up to catch again or with the other leg. Gradually increase the weight of the sand bags.

tuǐ wài cè biē 腿外侧憋 Smother with the leg: smother an incoming attack with your leg, stepping and moving the body quickly forward and using whatever part of your leg you can.

tuǐ yào hěn 腿要狠 The legs must be relentless: speed and severity of the kicks in attack and defense are necessities in fighting.

退 (rad.162) tuì 1. To retreat, move back; withdraw from; recede. 2. Cancel. 3. An army retreat. 4. Any retreating footwork.

tuì bù 退步 Retreat. 1. Specifically, to step back without stepping through, step the rear foot a half-step back or step the front foot back. 2. Can also refer to any movement or stepping backwards to create distance from an adversary.

tuì bù dǎ hǔ 退步打虎 Retreat to Hit the Tiger, step back to a tiger hitting stance. From Wu Taijiquan. See also dǎ hǔ.

tuì bù kuà hǔ 退步跨虎 Retreat to Mount the Tiger. From Taijiquan. See tuì bù dǎ hǔ.

tuì bù mái fú 退步埋伏 Retreating Ambush: a long cross stance with the sword blade rolled over to lie aligned with the extended leg. From Qingping sword.

tuì bù qiān yáng 退步牵羊 Retreat Leading the Sheep: sit back and pull an adversary's arm down. From Baguazhang, one of its sixty-four hands.

tuì bù yā zhǒu 退步压肘 Retreat to Press the Elbow: step back with a rolling elbow press down. From Chen Taijiquan.

tuì bù zhǎng 退步掌 Retreating palm: drop back to horse stance, pushing forward to the side (front), pulling back the other hand to block up at the head. From Bajiquan.

tuì bù zhèn 退步震 Retreating stomp, thump the foot while retreating. See also zhèn jiǎo.

tuì chǎng 退场 Leave the competition area; leave the carpet or performance area after a performance. Also called xià chǎng. 2. To march off after an athletes' parade.

tuì cǐ 退跐 Retreating stomp: slide the front foot back a short way, landing with a thump, maintaining a rearward power on landing.

tuì mǎ jù kè 退马拒客 Back the Horse to Repel the Guest: from a horse stance, step back, snapping to horse stance on the other side with an inward sweeping punch. From Meishanquan.

tuì qiāng 退枪 Retreat with a spear: fall back, feinting defeat, maintaining the opportunity to counter attack.

tuì shēn 退身 Retreat the body by stepping back.

tuì shēn fǎ 退身法 Body retreating methods. See xiā fǎ.

吞 (rad.30) tūn   1. To swallow; gulp down. 2. Used for body movement that closes in as if the body were swallowing. The hands also trap while the feet step back and the body tucks in. 3. To suck in an adversary's attack, sticking and circling to dissipate it and make him lose balance. 4. One of Ziranmen's nineteen main methods.

tūn shǒu 吞手 Swallowing hands: defensive moves while retreating, preparing for a counter attack.

tūn tiān pào 吞天炮 Swallow the Sky Pound: use one hand to pull an adversary's arm while the other fist slides up your arm and does a straight punch to his head. From Tongbeiquan.

tūn tǔ 吞吐 Swallow and spit. 1. A body technique of closing in and snapping back. 2. Combine the hands and feet closing in then advancing. 3. To gather immediately after an attack.

囤 (rad.31) tún   1. To store up, hoard. 2. Pronounced dùn, a grain bin.

tún bù fǎ 囤步法 Hoarding stance, storing power stance: setting into a stance open front to back with the weight slightly into the rear leg, with both legs ready for action.

臀 (rad.130) tún   The buttocks.

tún bù 臀部 The buttocks.

tún dà jī 臀大肌 Gluteus maximus muscle: a large muscle at the buttocks. Assists in stabilisation, extension, and rotation of the hip joint.

tún wěi 臀尾 Tailbone. The normal focus is in keeping it tucked in, but can also be used in striking and throwing.

tún xiǎo jī 臀小肌 Gluteus minimus muscle: a muscle at the buttocks. Assists in stabilisation, rotation, and abduction of the hip joint.

tún zhōng jī 臀中肌 Gluteus medius muscle: a muscle at the buttocks, attaching to the iliac crest. Assists in stabilisation, rotation, and abduction of the hip joint.

褪 (rad.145) tùn   1. To slip out of something. 2. To hide something in one's sleeve. 3. Pronounced tuì, to take off clothes or shed feathers.

tùn zhǒu 褪肘 Slip out with the elbows: with the elbows bent so the fists are in front, fist hearts up, step back quickly or spin around, applying power through the whole body. This is an escape from a strike that hides a counter attack. From Duanquan.

托 託 (rad.64, 149) [托] (rad.64) tuō 1. The original, practical, meaning is to carry a tray with one or both hands. 2. The technique is to carry, with one or both hands, usually fingers down and palm up, though they do not need to be held flat. 3. One of the sixteen key techniques of Baguazhang, see also shí liù zì jué. 4. One of the walking hands of Chuojiao, see also zǒu shǒu.

tuō bào zhuāng 托抱桩 Carry a ball stake standing: Standing with the legs naturally apart and slightly bent, hold the hands as if carrying a ball, the palms up at the belly wrists straight and fingers open, breathing into the belly. The position moves slightly with the breathing.

tuō dāo shì 托刀式 Carry the broadsword posture: lift a broadsword in the right hand, palm in, with the cutting edge up, slicing so the grip is higher than the tip.

tuō dù sǎo dāng 托肚扫裆 Carry the Belly and Sweep the Groin: drop down, hooking between an adversary's legs with your foot, simultaneously striking his belly with the hand. A throw or takedown.

tuō fǎ 托法 1. Carrying joint control: place a hand palm up under a joint such as the elbow, controlling the elbow against its natural movement. 2. Lifting, carrying techniques. Also called yù tóng sòng shù.

tuō gōu 托钩 Carry with double hooks: lift the blades up to shoulder height, laying the blades along the arms, crescent blades up.

tuō huái 托踝 Carry the ankle: grab your adversary's foot as he tries to kick you with an instep kick, and push down on his foot while lifting up his ankle. This hyper-extends his ankle while putting him off balance. From wrestling.

tuō jiàn 托剑 Carry a sword: with a horizontal blade, edges vertical, lift the blade up to head height, palm in. Power goes to the middle of the blade, as a defensive move.

tuō ná fǎ 托拿法 Carrying grappling hold: a short, sharp, carrying action that balances and initiates a throw. From wrestling.

tuō qì 托气 Carry the breath: to hold the breath briefly, by shutting the throat, after inhaling. Used to stabilise high balance techniques in routines performance.

tuō qiān jīn 托千斤 Carry a Thousand Pounds: lift the knee and hold a sword horizontally with the tip pointing forward, bringing the sword across in a smearing action. From Taijiquan.

tuō qiāng 托枪 Carry a spear: snap the shaft strongly upwards over the head, the left hand palm up, shaft horizontal.

tuō qiāng dǎ hǔ 托枪打虎 Carry a Spear to Hit the Tiger: jam an adversary's arm, controlling at the wrist and elbow and raising the arm as a unit. From Baguazhang.

tuō qiāng zhǎng 托枪掌 Carry a spear palm: extend the palms as if carrying a spear in front of the chest, the lower arm at chest height with the fingers tilted down, the upper arm above the head with the palm up. The power both lifts and extends. From Baguazhang, as a circle-walking posture. Also called chā zi zhǎng, qiāng tuō zhǎng.

tuō shǒu 托手 Carry: one hand carries like serving a tray. This lifts an adversary's arm. This is often combined with your other hand hooking down to strike his ribs. Also called tuō tiān shǒu.

tuō shǒu shì 托手式 Carrying posture: during *qigong* training, standing with the legs open to shoulder width, hands facing up in front of the abdomen.

tuō tiān gài dì 托天盖地 Carry the Sky and Cover the Ground: thread an arm straight up in a one legged stance then drop down to a horse stance with a press down to the side. From Liuhebafa.

tuō tiān shì 托天式 Carry the Sky posture: hold the hands as if carrying something heavy, then turn them as if pushing something down. From Yiquan.

tuō tiān shǒu 托天手 Carry the Sky. See tuō shǒu.

tuō tiān zhǎng 托天掌 Heaven Upholding Palm. 1. A strike upward with the palm up. 2. A circle-walking posture: extending the palms out to the sides, with the arms at least shoulder height, palms up. The power both lifts and extends. From Baguazhang. Also called dà péng zhǎn chì, shuāng tuō zhuàn zhǎng, and sometimes called tuō zhǎng.

tuō tiān zhuāng 托天桩 Carry the Heaven stake standing: Standing with the legs naturally apart and slightly bent, hold the hands up over the head, arms curved, shoulders settled, palms up, as if holding a ball up to the sky. Look up and breathe naturally.

tuō yáng zhǎng 托阳掌 Carry the Sun: with the palm up, lift up no higher than the head.

tuō zhǎng 托掌 Carrying strike with the palm. 1. Lift the palm up with the shoulder and elbow settled down. Strike is usually angled forward and up, though it may be upwards or downwards. Often used to lift the adversary's arm to allow for counter attack. It can also be an attack itself, with less upward action. 2. Place the fist in the palm and lift the fist. 3. A circle-walking posture, see tuō tiān zhǎng.

tuō zhèng zhì shǒu 托睜窒手 Carry the elbow and stop the hand.

tuō zhǒu 托肘 Carry the elbow: lift the elbow of an adversary while jamming his wrist downwards, to break the arm or snap the elbow. From Qinna. See also tuō zhèng zhì shǒu.

tuō zhuàn dāo 托转刀 Carry the broadsword while turning: circle-walk while holding the Bagua broadsword in a carrying posture, palm in, grip up, and blade tip slightly down, pointing into the centre of the circle.

拖 (rad.64) **tuō** 1. To pull; drag; haul. 2. To mop. 3. To drag on, delay.

tuō bù 拖步 Dragging step: advance the lead foot, then do a follow step with the rear foot, dragging it on the ground.

tuō dà dāo 拖大刀 Drag a big cutter: let the blade touch or drag on the ground, holding the shaft with one hand. This is an invitation for an adversary to try something.

tuō lí bù 拖犁步 Drag the plough stance. See qí lóng bù.

tuō qiāng 拖枪 Drag a spear: holding a spear in one hand, allow the tip to lie on the ground, or even drag it along the ground. This is in preparation for a counter attacking move.

tuō tiào bù 拖跳步 Jump to dragging stance: jump up and land in with the rear shin on the ground in a dragging stance. See also tuō lí bù.

tuō yāo 拖腰 Drag the waist: shifting back and forth in stake standing. From Yiquan.

tuō zhù 拖住 To pin down.

脱 [脫] (rad.130) **tuō** 1. To release, escape from, get out of. 2. Take off, cast off. 3. Dislocation of a joint (such as the shoulder).

tuō bà 脱把 Released grip: lose hold of your weapon or release one hand from a long weapon. A 'feared error' in sparring. An ordinary deduction (0.1) in Taolu competition.

tuō gǔ 脱骨 Released from the bones: the muscles slide freely with no obstructions. This is a goal in internal styles, that the *qi* and muscles move freely, as if released from the skeleton.

tuō jiān tuán jiǎ 脱肩团胛 Released shoulder and united shoulder blades: pulling the shoulders down firmly and pulling the shoulder blades slightly forward to form an arc, keeping the upper back tight. From southern styles.

tuō jiù 脱臼 Joint dislocation, to dislocate a joint.

tuō ná 脱拿 Release techniques. See jiě fǎ. Also called jiě tuō, pò jiě.

tuō shēn huà yǐng 脱身化影 Change your Body for a Shadow: see tuō shēn huàn yǐng.

tuō shēn huàn yǐng 脱身换影 Trade your Body for a Shadow. 1. To dissolve an attack almost before it begins, getting away from an attack, seeming to leave just your shadow behind. A characteristic of Baguazhang. 2. Step away, turning and lifting, then come back into a horse stance brace. From Baguazhang, one of its sixty-four hands. Also called tuō shēn huà yǐng.

tuō shēn huàn yǐng fǎ 脱身换影法 The footwork of becoming the shadow of your adversary – not leaving space but not opposing.

tuō shǒu 脱手 Release from being grabbed on the wrist. 1. Roll and turn the arm. 2. Slide the palm down the held arm, starting with the palm up and slicing to palm down, simultaneously pulling the held hand back. From Wing Chun.

tuō shǒu biāo 脱手镖 Throwing dart. See fēi biāo.

tuō shǒu gùn 脱手棍 Pop up the staff: with the right hand at the butt or the tip, pop the staff up, releasing it so that it spins in the air and comes back to the right hand, to catch at the opposite end.

tuō xuē gài miàn 脱靴盖面 Kick off your Boots to Hit the Face: a swinging kick to the head with the sole of the foot.

tuō zhǒu 脱肘 (Appear like a) dislocated elbow: the elbow is lax and hanging, the armpits are empty, and no power is in the arm. An error in most styles.

砣鉈 [砣铊] (rad.112, 167) **tuó** A stone roller, a heavy stone.

tuó bàng 砣棒 A heavy stone attached to a short stick by a rope. Used for wrist and forearm rollups. See also jiǎo bàng gōng, qiān jīn bàng.

鴕 [鸵] (rad.196) **tuó** An ostrich.

tuó xíng bù 鸵形步 Ostrich stepping: circle-walking with a rubbing step going into full bow stance on each step before bringing the rear foot in. From Baguazhang.

鼉 [鼍] (rad.205) **tuó** 1. A Chinese alligator. 2. A large water lizard.

tuó xíng 鼍形 Alligator form: bracing out to the side, sidestepping, either moving forward, backward, or just to the side. From Xingyiquan.

tuó yǒu fú shuǐ zhī líng 鼍有浮水之灵

T

Alligators have the effectiveness of floating on water. A quality sought in Xingyiquan's alligator form.

tuó zhǎng 鼍掌 Alligator palm: as hand shape. The thumb and index finger stretched open, the other fingers slightly curled. From Xingyiquan.

椭 [楕] (rad.75) tuǒ Oval-shaped, elliptical. Sometimes used in movement descriptions in training manuals.

W

哇 (rad.30) wā Original meaning is the sound of crying. In the martial arts, especially in southern styles, it is a shout to gain or express power in a technique.

挖 (rad.64) wā To dig, excavate.

wā gùn 挖棍 Uproot with a staff: chop across from the side with a staff, stopping sharply when extended in front.

wā jīn 挖筋 Uproot a tendon: dig into an adversary to grasp and pull a tendon, artery, or vein. From Qinna.

wā xíng bù 挖行步 Digging steps: walking away (walking forwards but looking back), legs bent, digging into the ground with the balls of the feet as if kicking sand in an adversary's eyes as you get away.

瓦 (rad.98) wǎ Tile, roof tile made of clay.

wǎ léng quán 瓦棱拳 Roof ridge fist, a hand shape. 1. In Tongbeiquan, the thumb is tucked on the index finger, the fist is clenched but the other fingers spread the knuckles outward. 2. In Shaolinquan, the fist is tightly clenched and the thumb tucked along the index finger eye.

wǎ léng zhǎng 瓦棱掌 Roof ridge palm, a hand shape: the fingers are together and naturally straight, drawing the palm in. The thumb and index finger are spread apart, and the thumb is tucked in. From Piguaquan.

wǎ lǒng zhǎng 瓦拢掌 Roof tile palm, a hand shape: thumb and little finger gathered slightly, middle, index and ring fingers pulled back slightly, palm centre slightly hollow, all fingers slightly gathered. From Chen Taijiquan.

wǎ miàn zhǎng 瓦面掌 Tile face palm, a hand shape: the fingers are together and bent at the second joint. The thumb is tucked into the thumb web. From Piguaquan. In some styles, the fingers are straight.

扚外 (rad.64) wāi 1. Using the whole of the foot to pivot with a short, sharp movement, keeping firmly on the ground. 2. Wrestling throws that use this movement (pivoting whilst keeping the feet on the ground).

扚歪 (rad.64) wāi A torqueing takedown, using twisting from the side to take an adversary into an awkward position. From wrestling.

歪 (rad.77) wāi Crooked, askew, inclined. In martial arts, often meaning as an error.

wāi xié 歪斜 Crooked and tilted: the neck, head, or body tilted to the side. An error in many styles.

外 (rad.36) wài Outside; outer; outward.

wài bǎ 外把 Outer grip: holding a short weapon in a normal grip, turning the palm facing away from yourself.

wài bǎ mén fēng 外把门封 Outside sealing off the gate. See lán qiāng.

wài bǎ mén jiù hù 外把门救护 Outside gate save: retreat doing an outer cover with a spear, then retreat again with a stab.

wài bāi 外掰 Outward break off. 1. Grab an adversary's hand in a reverse grip, turn it over and hyper-flex his wrist, taking him down. You can add to the effect by flexing his fingers as well. Also called chè chǐ. 2. Step out, pressing the thighs outward.

wài bǎi 外摆 Outer step, outer circling step: step out, turning the leg and foot outward.

wài bǎi lián 外摆莲 Outer Swinging Lotus. 1. An outside crescent kick, without a slap. Also called wài bǎi tuǐ, wài biāo tuǐ. 2. A jumping outside crescent kick.

wài bǎi pāi jiǎo 外摆拍脚 Outside slapping crescent kick.

wài bǎi tuǐ 外摆腿 Outer crescent kick, a straight swinging kick to the outside, without a slap. From Chuojiao, one of its middle-basin kicks. In the category of straight swinging kicks, see also zhí bǎi xìng tuǐ fǎ. Also called wài bǎi lián, wài biāo tuǐ.

wài bì hóng mén 外闭鸿门 Close the Outer Door to the Feast. 1. Circle the tip of a staff, then strike sharply across to the outside. From Baguazhang. 2. Move forward to a rasping sword strike in a reverse bow stance. From Qingping sword. See also hóng mén yàn, nèi bì hóng mén.

wài bēng 外弸 Outer draw, a wrist snap with a straight sword to cut an adversary's wrist from the outside. See also nèi bēng.

wài biāo tuǐ 外摽腿 Outward waving leg: a straight swing kick outwards. From Mizongquan. Also called wài bǎi lián, wài bǎi tuǐ.

wài cǎi 外采 Outer pluck: use the forearm to cover up a punch to the head, circle outwards and turn the hand to grab an adversary's wrist.

wài chā bù 外插步 Outside insertion step: lift the leading foot and bring it from the inside to step into your adversary's stance, from the outside.

wài chā tuǐ 外插腿 Outside insertion kick: step your leg into your adversary's stance, outside his stance, pressing with the inside of your leg. From Chuojiao, one of its middle-basin kicks.

wài chā xiǎo chán sī tuǐ 外插小缠丝腿 Outside coiling insertion: step your leg into your adversary's stance, contacting at his ankle, outside his stance, pressing into your knee to control at the shin. From Chuojiao, one of its middle basin kicks.

wài chāo 外抄 Outward lift: an outward block with the elbow bent, keeping the elbow tucked to the ribs, forearm level, palm up.

wài chāo bāo 外抄抱 Outward lifting hold: do an outward lift and trap an adversary in a hugging hold. See also lǐ chāo bāo.

wài cuò 外锉 Outer file, an upright filing action with the under edge of a sword blade, in response to a stab from the outside.

wài duò 外跥 Outward stamp: a low kick to the knee or shin with the foot hooked in, kicking with the outer edge, often also sliding down to stamp on the foot.

wài gé 外格 Outward transverse block, with the forearm vertical and the palm in.

wài gōng 外功 External training. 1. Training of strength and hardness. Includes the ability to hit, fall, and take hits, and is meant to build strong tendons and bones. Also called wài zhuàng gōng. 2. Overall conditioning, which includes speed, endurance, agility, flexibility, coordination, strength and power.

wài gōu jiǎo 外勾脚 Outer hook throw. See cuō wō.

wài gōu tuǐ 外勾腿 Outer leg hook throw: step in to control your adversary above, hooking your leg around the outside of his lead leg, so your leg is between his legs, hooking his lead lower leg to assist your throw.

wài guà 外挂 Outer hook, a block: to bring the fist across and down to the outside.

wài guān 外关 Acupoint Waiguan (outer pass), SJ5. At the forearm, on the outside, in line with acupoint Yangchi and the tip of the elbow, two *cun* up from the wrist crease (in each arm). From TCM. A crippling point, striking here may cause serious injury. See also cán xué.

wài guǎn 外管 Outer trip, a tripping throw: see wài jiāo.

wài huái jiān 外踝尖 Extraordinary acupoint Waihuaijian (outer ankle tip), EX-LE9. At the ankle, on the lateral side where the ankle bone protrudes. From TCM. A crippling point, striking here may cause serious injury. See also cán xué.

wài jiā quán 外家拳 External martial styles: styles that emphasize strength over softness, or physical attributes over internal health. Normally Shaolinquan, Chaquan, Longfist styles, and most southern styles are classified as external. This is an artificial division, as many styles include both outer and inner training and utilization, leading to inaccurate categorisation of styles.

wài jiāo 外跤 Outer throw, a tripping throw: step to the outside of your adversary, trapping his leading heel with your foot to prevent him from taking a step back. Then you can hook and pull him so he falls face down. Also called wài guǎn.

wài jiǎo 外脚 The outside foot: used when describing movements such as palm changes that are done following a circle. From Baguazhang. See also nèi jiǎo.

wài kē shǒu 外磕手 Outward check: an abrupt block or strike moving towards the outside, arm extended, fist heart down.

wài láo gōng 外劳宫 Extraordinary acupoint Wailaogong (outer palace of toil), EX-UE8. At the back of the hand, between the second and third metacarpals, 0.5 *cun* behind the knuckles. From TCM.

wài lì 外力 Basic muscular strength.

wài liàn jīn gǔ pí, nèi liàn yī kǒu qì 外练筋骨皮，内练一口气 Outwardly train sinews, bones, and skin, inwardly train *qi*. A martial saying.

wài liàn shǒu yǎn shēn fǎ bù, nèi xiū jīng shén qì lì gōng 外练手眼身法步，内修精神气力功 Outwardly train hands, eyes, bodywork, and footwork, inwardly cultivate essence, spirit, *qi*, strength and skill. A martial saying.

wài líng 外陵 Acupoint Wailing (outer mound), ST26. At the abdomen, one *cun* below the navel, two *cun* lateral to the midline (on each side). From TCM.

wài mén 外门 The outside gate or outdoor area of an adversary: outside the space made by his elbows, outside his arms. Also called mén wài.

wài miàn jià 外面架 Face out frame: an outward bracing with both arms, palms out, in front of the chest, in bow stance. From Bajiquan. See also lǐ miàn jià.

wài pī huá shān 外劈华山 Outside chop to Mount Hua: shift back, pulling a sword back, then shift to a left bow stance, chopping down in the apex of the triangle of the stance. From Qingping sword.

wài piàn mǎ biān 外骗马鞭 Outward Deceive the Horse with the steel whip: swinging the whip in vertical circles, raise the right leg and swing it under, the hand outside the thigh, catching under the thigh.

wài piē fǎ 外撇法 Outward casting. See níng fǎ. Also called xiè fǎ.

wài qiū 外丘 Acupoint Waiqiu (outer hill), GB36. At the calf, on the outside, seven *cun* up from the ankle, on the front edge of the fibula, on the front edge of the peroneus brevis muscle (on each leg). From TCM.

wài sān hé 外三合 The three external unities, or harmonies: shoulders with hips, elbows with knees, and hands with feet.

wài shāng 外伤 An external injury, external damage.

wài shì ān yì 外示安逸 Show an appearance of being settled and calm. A martial saying. Describes how a martial artist should be in a fight.

wài shǒu 外手 The outside hand: used when describing movements such as palm changes that are done following a circle. From Baguazhang. See also nèi shǒu.

wài tuō 外脱 Outer release, an escape from a control: a leverage escape for a wrist grab. Clench the fist and circle inwards to contact an adversary's inside bone and use it as leverage, pressing outwards.

wài xuán 外旋 External rotation. This references the rotation of body segments independent of the placement of the segment, as if the body were standing straight with the hands at the sides. For example: turning the arm so that the thumb moves away from the direction of the palm; turning the leg so that the foot rotates outward in relation to the hip.

wài yīn 外因 External causes of disease. Including, but not limited to, wind, cold, dry heat, humid heat damp. See also liù qì, liù yín.

wài zhuàng gōng 外壮功 See wài gōng.

彎 [弯] (rad.57) wān
Bent, curved; crooked. To bend; flex. A curve, a bend.

wān gōng shè hǔ 弯弓射虎 Draw the Bow to Shoot the Tiger: used in many styles to describe a final position resembling drawing a bow. The raised hand is either a block or a twist if the hand is grabbed. The extended hand is a punch or control. Both can be moving in the same direction, or the hands may separate as if drawing a bow. One of Baguazhang's sixty-four hands. Also called dǎ hǔ shì, fú hǔ.

wān qū 弯曲 Bent; curved; zigzag; crooked.

wān yāo 弯腰 1. To bend the waist, to bend down. 2. In wrestling, to bend the waist for a throw, but not as deeply as bowing throws. See also gōng yāo.

完 (rad.40) wán
1. Intact, whole. 2. Use up, used up. 3. Finish.

W

wán gǔ 完骨 Acupoint Wangu (bone completion), GB12. At the neck, under the occipital bone, on the lower back edge of the mastoid process (on each side). From TCM.

wán zhěng 完整 Whole, integrated. This is a requirement at the intermediate level of training, the body must be well integrated.

挽 輓 (rad. 64, 159) [挽] (rad. 64) wǎn
1. To draw; pull. Roll up. 2. In wrestling, a rolling throw, gripping and controlling on the leg to roll an adversary down rather than lifting to throw.

wǎn gōng shè diāo 挽弓射雕 Draw a Bow to Shoot a Condor: sit into a back weighted bow stance, pulling back to the chest with one hand while pushing forward with the other, aligning with the stance. From Shaolinquan.

腕 (rad.130) wàn
The wrist, wrists.

wàn dǎ 腕打 Wrist hits, striking methods using the end of the arm at the wrist.

wàn fǎ 腕法 Wrist techniques: striking or controlling methods using the wrist.

wàn gǔ 腕骨 Acupoint Wangu, (wrist bone), SI4. At the heel of the hand, in the small depression near the wrist (on each hand). From TCM.

wàn guān jié 腕关节 The wrist joint.

wàn mài xué 腕脉穴 Pulse point: meeting place of Shenmen, Yinxi, Tongli, and Lingdao points. Sensitive to a grab or strike. Not where you feel your pulse, but on the little finger side of that area.

wàn rú mián 腕如绵 The wrists must be like silk floss. From Tongbeiquan, one of its requirements.

萬 (rad.140) [万] (rad.1) wàn
1. Ten thousand. 2. Innumerable, a great many, a myriad. 3. A surname.

王 (rad.96) wáng
1. The king, monarch, emperor. 2. A duke, prince. 3. A chieftain, head. 4. A surname.

wáng lóng nào hǎi 王龙闹海 Dragon King Roils the Sea: repeated low kicks behind, with the soles of the feet, while stepping forward. From Chuojiao.

wáng lóng tàn zhuā 王龙探爪 Dragon King Reaches to Grab: standing with the legs a bit open, and straight, punch one fist down to the ground and extend the other upwards. From Chuojiao.

wáng mǔ guǎi xiàn 王母拐线 The Queen Mother Winds the Thread: holding an adversary's hand, pressing it on your forearm, pull in, bend and roll your elbow over to control and break. This is an action similar to winding a skein of yarn around the arm. From Baguazhang, one of its sixty-four hands.

望 [望] (rad.74) wàng
To gaze, look at from a distance.

wàng méi zhé jié 望眉折截 Gaze at the Eyebrow Breaking Interception: back horse stance opening snap with the forearm back and a bracing hand in front. Protects the head and groin. Also called jī jī dǒu líng in Xingyiquan.

wàng mén cuán 望门攒 Watch the Gate Strike: strike to the ear with the palm rolled over, turning the body away to get more reach. From Chen Taijiquan.

wàng yuè 望月 Gaze at the Moon, used in posture descriptions, often involving an angled posture looking back or looking through under an arm.

wàng yuè píng héng 望月平衡 Gaze at the Moon balance: standing on one leg, the other foot suspended behind and hooked, looking back over the shoulder.

偎 (rad.9) wēi
1. To snuggle up to; to lean close to, cling to, cuddle. 2. A close range leaning takedown which uses the front more than does a normal lean. See also kào.

wēi shēn kào dǎ 偎身靠打 Snuggle, Lean, and Strike: step in to an adversary, raising one arm to enable pressing with the whole body while pushing with rear hand. From Baguazhang.

圍 [围] (rad.31) wéi
1. To enclose; besiege; surround. 2. Around; all round.

wéi wèi jiù zhào 围魏救赵 Besiege the kingdom of Wei to rescue the kingdom of Zhao. The second of the Thirty-six Stratagems of Warfare, which apply to many situations.

維 [维] (rad.120) wéi
1. To tie up; hold together. 2. To maintain; preserve.

wéi dào 维道 Acupoint Weidao (maintaining path), GB28. At the abdomen, at the iliac crest, 0.5 *cun* below acupoint Wushu (on each side). From TCM.

韋 [韦] (rad.178) **wéi**   1. Tanned leather, the leather radical. 2. A surname. 3. Used for the Wei sound in foreign names.

wéi tuó 韦驼 Wei Tuo, Skanda: a Bodhisattva guardian of temples. Used in movement names.

wéi tuó bìng zhǎng 韦驼并掌 Wei Tuo Brings his Palms Together: empty stance with the palms up, one extended, one tucked in at the forearm. From Chuojiao.

wéi tuó gōng 韦驼功 Wei Tuo's training, a standing meditation. From Liuhebafa.

委 (rad.38) **wěi**   1. To entrust, appoint. 2. Throw away. 3. Indirect. 4. End. 5. Actually. 6. Listless.

wěi yáng 委阳 Acupoint Weiyang (bend *yang*), BL39. At the back of the knee, at the outer edge of the popliteal crease, just inside the insertion of the biceps femoris tendon (on each leg). From TCM.

wěi zhōng 委中 Acupoint Weizhong (bend centre), BL40. At the back of the knee, in the popliteal crease, in the middle between the two large tendons. From TCM. A crippling point, striking here may cause serious injury. See also cán xué. In internal styles, these points are kept full, to keep strength in the knees. If the backs of the knees are slack the knees are weak and the legs are unsupported.

尾 (rad.44) **wěi**   1. A tail. 2. Something tail-like. 3. Pronounced yǐ, the hairs on a horse's tail.

wěi gǔ 尾骨 The coccyx.

wěi jiān 尾尖 Tail tip: pointed metal tip at the butt end of a long handled weapon.

wěi lú 尾闾 The tailbone. Sometimes translated as the sacrum, sometimes as the coccyx, the tailbone is a combination of both, but the tip is the coccyx. This is an easy target but should not be hit too hard. Striking here inhibits *qi* circulation.

wěi lú guān 尾闾关 Coccyx pass. See also sān guān, wěi lú.

wěi lú zhèng zhōng 尾闾正中 The tailbone is straight: the pelvis is slightly tucked to align the spine. A requirement of many styles.

wěi gōng 尾宫 The Tail Palace. Right on the tip of the coccyx. A crippling point, striking here may cause serious injury. See also cán xué.

喂 (rad.30) **wèi**   1. To feed. 2. Feed techniques: training sparring or push hands by feeding techniques to a lesser skilled partner, to help them find the proper reactions and techniques.

wèi jìn 喂劲 Feed power and techniques to help a training partner in sparring.

未 (rad.75) **wèi**   1. Have not, did not; not. 2. The eighth of the twelve Terrestrial Branches, used in combination with the ten Celestial Stems to designate years, months, days, and hours. For the sixty year cycles, see also under dīng wèi, guǐ-, jǐ-, xīn-, yǐ-. The period of the day from 1:00 p.m. to 3:00 p.m. See also dì zhī, tiān gān.

wèi céng xí wǔ xiān míng dé 未曾习武先明德 Before learning the martial arts first learn virtue. A martial saying.

wèi céng xué yì xiān shí lǐ 未曾学艺先识礼 Before learning the art first learn courtesy. A martial saying.

wèi xí dǎ xiān xué zhuāng 未习打先学桩 Before learning to fight, first sit in your stances. A martial saying.

wèi xí quán xiān xué bù 未习拳先学步 Before learning any techniques, first study your stances. A martial saying.

wèi xí quán xiū xí xiè 未习拳休习械 Don't learn weapons before learning barehand techniques. A martial saying.

wèi shí 未时 The period of the day from 1:00 p.m. to 3:00 p.m. (13:00 – 15:00).

胃 (rad.130) **wèi**   1. The stomach. 2. The Stomach. The Stomach includes more than the stomach in the Western meaning. It is a *yang* organ. It is the organ associated with the Zu Yang Ming channel.

wèi cāng 胃仓 Acupoint Weicang (stomach

granary), BL50. At the back, level with the depression below the spinous process of the twelfth thoracic vertebra, three *cun* lateral to the midline (on each side). From TCM.

wèi guǎn xià shù 胃管下俞 Extraordinary acupoint Weiguanxiashu (below the stomach duct), EX-B3. At the back, at the depression under the eighth thoracic vertebra, 1.5 *cun* lateral to the midline (on each side). From TCM.

wèi jīng 胃经 The stomach meridian. See zú yáng míng. From TCM.

wèi shù 胃俞 Acupoint Weishu (stomach transport), BL21. At the back, level with the depression below the spinous process of the twelfth thoracic vertebra, 1.5 *cun* lateral to the midline (on each side). From TCM.

衛 (rad.144) [卫] (rad.26) **wèi** To defend; guard; protect.

wèi duì 卫队 Bodyguards, armed escort. See also bǎo biāo, biāo jú, biāo kè, biāo shī.

wèi qì 卫气 Protective *qi*: generated in the Kidney, nourishes the muscles, skin, and interstices. Gives resistance against outer pernicious influences.

wèi shēng 卫生 1. Hygiene; health; sanitation. 2. To cultivate the life force, protect life, build the health.

魏 (rad.194) **wèi** 1. The Wei kingdom (220-263), one of the Three Kingdoms, see also sān guó. 2. A surname.

温 (rad.85) **wēn** 1. Warm, mild. 2. Soft, tender. 3. A surname.

wēn jiā quán 温家拳 Wenjiaquan (Wen family fist), a style popular during the Ming dynasty. The style used both long and short range techniques.

wēn liū 温溜 Acupoint Wenliu (warm dwelling), LI7. At the outer edge of the forearm, about five *cun* up from the wrist crease (on each arm). From TCM.

文 (rad.67) **wén** 1. Culture. Character. 2. Writing. Language. Literary composition, writing. 3. Liberal arts.

wén wáng lā qiàn 文王拉扦 King Wen Pulls the Towrope: Grab your adversary's wrist and shoulder and jerk firmly downwards, as he leans forward, switch the grip to his head and belt at the back to continue to pull down. From Shaolinquan.

wén tàng zǐ 文趟子 The cultural routines, a grouping of nine routines of Chuojiao. See also lì shí quán, lián huán quán, lián huán tuǐ, qiā diǎn, rào mǎ tuǐ, shí bā diǎn, shí bā tī, yù huán bù èr, yù huán bù yī.

wén zhuāng 文桩 Cultured stake standing: stake standing postures with the feet apart and legs straight, with the emphasis on relaxing. From Yiquan.

吻 (rad.30) **wěn** 1. The lips. 2. To kiss.

wěn xuē 吻靴 Kiss the shoes, a stretching method: standing on one leg slightly bent or sitting, with the other leg extended, hold the extended foot with the hands and pull the lips to the toes.

穩 [稳] (rad.115) **wěn** 1. Stable; firm; steady. 2. Certain.

wěn bù fǎ 稳步法 Method for stepping with stability: step forward as if trampling on someone, step back raising the heel, and turn around always with a hook in step.

wěn dìng 稳定 Stable, steady. This is a requirement at the basic level of training, balance must be under control.

wěn gōng zhàn 稳攻战 Steady attack tactics: to wait and watch in a fight, testing and observing an adversary to find his weaknesses before committing to an attack.

搵 [揾] (rad.64) **wèn** 1. To wipe off; press down with the knuckle. 2. A category of throw that sends an adversary flipping over or rolling down.

wèn biè 揾别 A hip throw, stepping in across the adversary's legs and flipping him upright over the hips.

問 [问] (rad.169) **wèn** 1. To ask, inquire. Interrogate. Ask after. 2. To test out an adversary. To try out pressure while in contact, to see how an adversary will react.

wèn jìn 问劲 Examining power: when connecting to an adversary, testing him out to feel what kind of power he has.

wèn shǒu 问手 Examining hand. 1. Stretching the arm out to judge distance. 2. In Wing Chun, extending the arm to head height, palm out, thumb down. 3. Using the first hand as a feint or a setup for a following attack.

挝 [挝] (rad.64) wō 1. To grip, gripping actions (colloquial). 2. An eagle claw shaped bladed weapon. 3. Pronounced zhuā, to beat.

wō biān shǒu 挝边手 A hooking strike to the gap under the ribs or between the lower ribs.

窝 [窝] (rad.116) wō 1. Nest. Lair, den. 2. Pit; hollow part of the body (such as armpit or pit of the stomach).

wō dǐ pào 窝底炮 Punch in the Pit: a punch to the groin. From Chen Taijiquan.

wō dù quán 窝肚拳 Fist in the pit of the belly: roll and tuck the fist at the ribs in front of the hip, fist heart up.

wō gōu 窝勾 Hook to the Den, a wrestling move. See chán tuǐ.

wō lǐ pào 窝里炮 Double Punch into the Pit: a double punch to the armpits. From Chen Taijiquan.

wō xīn chuí 窝心捶 Mallet to the Solar Plexus, a direct punch to the solar plexus. From Shaolinquan.

握 (rad.64) wò 1. To grip something, to grasp. 2. The grip or handle of a short weapon.

wò bēi quán 握杯拳 Holding a cup fist shape: the thumb and index finger are rounded as if holding a small cup, the other fingers are tightly clenched. From Zuiquan.

wò dāo 握刀 Method of gripping the handgrip of a broadsword. See wò jiàn.

wò fǎ huó biàn 握法活便 Have a dexterous grip. A saying about the staff. One should be able to move the hands around freely on the staff to be in the best position for each technique.

wò gùn zhuàn jiān 握棍转肩 Shoulder rotations with a bar: holding a short stick at each end, circle the stick up over the head to the back, keeping the arms straight, rotating in the shoulders.

wò jiàn 握剑 Method of gripping the handgrip of a sword. This changes according to the technique, to keep power transfer to the blade smooth.

wò jǐng 握颈 Neck grab, neck control: wrap the hand around the nape of an adversary's neck and tuck the forearm firmly onto his chest. From wrestling.

wò lì 握力 Grip strength.

wò quán 握拳 Clench the fist. Sometimes called kòng juǎn.

wò shǒu ná wàn 握手拿腕 Shake the hand and control the wrist: hold the adversary's hand as if shaking hands, grab his wrist with the other hand and rotate, then quickly extend the first hand to his wrist to control his wrist and elbow. From Qinna.

wò wàn 握腕 Wrist grab. When differentiating types of grabs, this one is a simple grab, your thumb web aligned to the adversary's elbow. See also fǎn wò wàn.

wò zhǐ fān 握指翻 Grab finger and flip over: grab one or more fingers and turn counter to the natural position, backwards or sideways both work. A category of controlling technique.

wò zhǒu 握肘 Elbow grab: grip an adversary's upper arm firmly, tucking the point of his elbow into your palm. From wrestling.

卧 [卧] (rad.131) wò To lie down. Applied to sleeping. When used with animals, often means crouching.

wò chā 卧叉 Lying splits: in the side splits, press the torso onto one leg.

wò chuāi 卧踹 Lying side kick.

wò fú shì 卧佛式 Lying Buddha posture: squatting on one leg, extend the other through behind, horizontal to, but not touching, the ground. The body is laid back but not touching the ground, supported by the elbow, and the head is placed in that hand.

wò gōng shè hǔ 卧弓射虎 Shoot the Tiger from a Lying Position: a roll and punch. From Chen Taijiquan. Usually called dǎ hǔ shì.

wò hǔ dāng mén 卧虎当门 Crouching Tiger Blocks the Gateway: pull a sword in to in front of the chest, palm turned in, blade horizontal. From

W

Wu Taijiquan. Also called dāng mén jiàn.

wò hǔ fān shēn 卧虎翻身 Crouching Tiger Rolls Over: step through in a cross stance, turning the body back to strike with a staff behind, arms crossed, then continue to step forward and strike forward. From Baguazhang.

wò hǔ gōng 卧虎功 Crouching tiger training: all types of flat pushups, includes normal flat hand, fist, fingers, extended, one legged, weight on back, switching from one to another, etc.

wò hǔ juǎn wěi 卧虎卷尾 Crouching Tiger Curls its Tail: step back to drop stance, cocking the wrist to set the sword blade up, arm extended along the extended leg. From Qingping sword.

wò hǔ tiào jiàn 卧虎跳涧 Crouching Tiger Leaps the Ravine. See #3 of měng hǔ tiào jiàn.

wò lóng téng kōng 卧龙腾空 Crouching Dragon Takes to the Air: draw a staff back behind the body, slide the hands to the tip, then slice upward with the butt to head height. From Shaolinquan staff.

wò niú tuǐ 卧牛腿 Lying Ox Kick: lean forward and execute a back thrust kick, reaching out with the palms as well. From Baguazhang.

wò shì zhuāng 卧式桩 Lying stake training. Doing the various stake standing postures in a lying position. Used by people who cannot manage sitting or standing postures. From Yiquan.

wò tī 卧踢 Lying leg raises: lying on the ground, alternately lift the legs, feet dorsi-flexed. Also called lián tiǎo.

wò tí 卧蹄 Make the Hoof Lie Down. The category of Qinna techniques that involve controlling an adversary's wrist, hyper-extending, hyper-flexing, or flexing it to the side.

wò xuē 卧靴 Lying foot self pulling stretch: standing with the knee bent, holding the other foot dorsi flexed in front on the ground. Lean forward, gripping the foot with the opposite hand and turning the body to the side, lying along the extended leg.

wò zhěn 卧枕 Lie on a Pillow: a close range technique, leaning in with the head and torso, punching to jaw height with the front hand and down to the groin with the rear hand. From Shaolinquan.

屋 (rad.44) **wū** 1. A small house. 2. A room.

wū yì 屋翳 Acupoint Wuyi (roof of the house), ST15. At the chest, in the second intercostal space, four *cun* lateral to the midline (on each side). From TCM.

烏 [乌] (rad.86) **wū** 1. A crow, raven, or rook. For more movement names using the actions of the crow, see bǎi wū, sù-. 2. Black; a natural dark colour. 3. A surname.

wū lóng 乌龙 Black dragon, often used in technique and movement names.

wū lóng bǎi wěi 乌龙摆尾 Black Dragon Slashes its Tail. 1. A swinging back kick. 2. Raise the knee and snap the hand up, hooking the other behind. 3. A low intercept or downward slash with a sword or palm in a moving empty stance. 4. An extending arm strike to the rear. 5. A swinging low palm strike. 6. Snap a spear side to side. 7. Alternating uppercuts with a swinging arm and elbow snap. 8. A low rear cross step into low pounding backfists behind. The 79th move of the tiger and crane routine.

wū lóng chán shēn 乌龙缠身 Black Dragon Coils its Body: retreating alternate crossing forearm covers in front of the face and torso. From Wudangquan.

wū lóng chán yāo 乌龙缠腰 Black Dragon Coils its Waist. 1. Stand with the feet close together, coil the arms, the front arm first lifting (tuō) then coming down beside the head, the rear arm coiling behind the back. Also, to walk around, following the coiling arm behind. 2. Step in an encircle an adversary's waist around from the front for a throw off the hip, pulling his arm across your shoulder. From Baguazhang.

wū lóng dào qǔ shuǐ 乌龙倒取水 Black Dragon Tips to Drink Water. See kuí xīng shì.

wū lóng fān jiāng 乌龙翻江 Black Dragon Overturns the River, a smooth step, aligned, crossing punch. From Xingyiquan.

wū lóng jiǎo shuǐ 乌龙搅水 Black Dragon Stirs the Water: advance while stirring with a sword tip. From Taijiquan.

wū lóng jiǎo zhù 乌龙绞柱 Black Dragon Wraps around a Pillar. 1. A tumbling move: from a lying position, swing the legs to gain momentum to rise to a hand stand, and then land on the feet. From Chuojiao, one of its low-basin kicks. Also called jiǎo tuǐ, sōu tiān, yè jī sōu tiān. 2. As #1, but as a basic exercise, popping up to the back but lying down again, not rising to stand. 3. Stab the arm up behind in a low squat stance, then stand up, extending the arm upwards and spinning to roll the shoulder to normal. From Baguazhang.

wū lóng pán dǎ 乌龙盘打 Black Dragon Coils to Strike: a full arm swing slapping palm. From Piguaquan.

wū lóng qǔ shuǐ 乌龙取水 Black Dragon Draws Water: step forward to press down, then shift to the back leg and block up. From Xingyiquan.

wū lóng sǎo dì 乌龙扫地 Black Dragon Sweeps the Ground: turn and side kick an adversary's supporting knee when he is attempting a high kick.

wū lóng tǔ zhū 乌龙吐珠 Black Dragon Spits a Pearl: standing up, pull the right fist in and punch the left fist out with a hammer fist. The 11th move of the tiger and crane routine.

wū lóng xì qiú 乌龙戏球 Black Dragon Plays with a Ball: control an adversary's arm and press into his throat, twisting and pushing it over. From Baguazhang.

wū lóng xì shuǐ 乌龙戏水 Black Dragon Plays in Water: standing up, left fist at the hip, stab the right hand directly forward, palm down. The eighth move of the tiger and crane routine.

wū yā liàng yì 乌鸦晾翼 Crow Dries its Wings: in a horse stance with the fists up, strike out with the elbows to each side at shoulder height. The 15th move of the tiger and crane routine.

wū yā luò dì 乌鸦落地 Crow Lands on the Ground: step into a closed parallel stance, swinging a sword in a full circle to finish chopping down to the right, left hand blocking up behind. From Qingping sword.

wū yā pū chì 乌鸦扑翅 Crow Pounces with its Wings: step forward to a bow stance double pounce with palms. From Wudangquan.

wū yā yuè lǐng 乌鸦越岭 Crow Crosses the Mountain Range: a low thrust kick to the rear combined with a brace high to the front (same side hand) and low to the rear (opposite hand). From Wudangquan.

wū yún zhào dǐng 乌云罩顶 Dark Clouds Cover the Peak: with the right hand near the butt of a staff, hold it overhead while walking in a full circle. From Baguazhang.

wū yún zhào tiān 乌云罩天 Dark Clouds Cover the Sky: sit to empty stance, circling the palms to block up overhead and hook back behind. From Shaolinquan.

吳 [吴] (rad.30) wú 1. The Wu kingdom (222-280) of the Three Kingdoms period, see also sān guó. 2. The abbreviation for the region of Shanghai and Suzhou. 3. A surname.

wú shì tài jí quán 吴式太极拳 Wushi (Wu's) Taijiquan, attributed to Quan You, who learned from Yang Luchan and Yang Banhou. This style is called Wu from his son, who took the name Wu Jianquan.

無 (rad.86) [无] (rad.71) wú 1. Nothing; nil. 2. Not have; without.

wú chù bù shì quān 无处不是圈 There is no part of the body that is not a circle. A martial saying.

wú chù bù shì quán 无处不是拳 There is no part of the body that is not a fist. A martial saying.

wú jí 无极 The primordial void, chaos, nothingness.

wú jí gōng 无极功 See wú jí shì.

wú jí shì 无极势 Primordial posture: position taken in internal power training, the position of chaos before the separation of yin and yang, standing upright with the hands at the sides. Also called wú jí gōng.

wú jiān jù 无间距 1. Contact range (in fighting). 2. No distance between two points. 3. No space between two objects.

wú míng zhǐ 无名指 The ring finger, ring fingers.

wú xiào fēn 无效分 Invalid points: the high and low judges' scores in Taolu competition that are taken out (not all competitions do this). See also yǒu xiào fēn.

wú yǐng tuǐ 无影腿 Shadowless kick: jump thrust kicks, hitting the adversary's chest three times before landing.

wú zhōng shēng yǒu 无中生有 Create Something

out of Nothing. To save yourself from a seemingly hopeless situation. The seventh of the Thirty-six Stratagems of Warfare, which apply to many situations.

蜈 (rad.142) **wú**   A centipede, usually used in combination as wú gong.

wú gǒng quán 蜈蚣拳 Centipede fist, a hand shape: the middle, ring, and little fingers are curled tightly to the crease of the palm. The thumb and index fingers are bent to form a circle. From southern styles. Also called páng xiè quán.

wú gǒng tiào 蜈蚣跳 Jumping pushups, a training method: repeatedly jumping up and forward from pushups position, keeping the body straight.

五 (rad.7) **wǔ**   Five.

wǔ bù 五步 Five steps: five main footwork options: advance, retreat, step to either side, and stay put. From Taijiquan.

wǔ bù èr rén qiāng 五步二人抢 Five step partner pushing. From Taijiquan. Also called jìn sān tuì èr huó bù tuī shǒu.

wǔ bù quán 五步拳 Five stance fist: a short routine that trains the five basic stances of bow, horse, drop, resting, and empty. See also gōng bù, mǎ bù, pū bù, xiē bù, xū bù.

wǔ cǎi liù chuí 五踩六捶 Five Steps and Six Hits, a Xingyiquan partner routine, written up as sixteen moves.

wǔ chù 五处 Acupoint Wuchu (fifth place), BL5. At top of the head, one cun in from the hairline, 1.5 cun out lateral to the midline (on each side). From TCM.

wǔ dài 五代 The Five dynasties period: Later Liang (907-923), Later Tang (923-936), Later Jin (936-947), Later Han (947-951), and Later Zhou (951-960).

wǔ fēng zhǎng 五峰掌 Five peaks palm, a hand shape: all fingers and thumb extended and slightly separated. Used in southern styles. Also called liú shuǐ zhǎng, tiě zhǎng.

wǔ gōng 五弓 The five bows of the body: the torso, two legs, and two arms. The structures of the body that gather and release force like drawing a bow to release an arrow. Also called yī shēn bèi

wǔ gōng. See also shēn gōng, shǒu gōng, zú gōng.

wǔ guān 五官 1. The five sensory organs: the five organs of the face – nose, ears, lips, eyes, and tongue. See also bí, ěr, kǒu, mù, shé, 2. Facial features.

wǔ huā 五花 Five Flowers: alternate circling forearm cuts following one after the other, and to different directions. From Shaolinquan.

wǔ huā bàn zhǎng 五花瓣掌 Five Flower Petals Palm, a palm shape: all fingers and thumb bent.

wǔ huā pào 五花炮 Five Flowers Barrage, a Xingyiquan routine, written up as eight moves, considered to have essentially five moves.

wǔ jiā 五夹 Five presses, five scissor clips: power created by a scissoring effect between the legs, twisting the lower limbs and body to create a force through the body. From Xingyiquan.

wǔ jìn 五劲 Five powers: five types of power– trampling, enveloping, cutting, pouncing, binding. A categorisation used in Xingyiquan. See also cǎi, guǒ, jué, pū, shù.

wǔ lǐ 五里 Acupoint Wuli (fifth inner), LV10. At the abdomen, three cun below the Qichong. See also qì chōng. From TCM.

wǔ lù tuǐ 五路腿 Five roads kick, a stretching exercise: swing a straight leg up to your face, with the ankle dorsi-flexed. As a kick, also called yíng miàn tuǐ, zhèng tī tuǐ.

wǔ qín xī 五禽戏 The five animal frolics: internal health and regulation exercises that imitate the actions of the tiger, deer, bear, ape, and bird.

wǔ rèn 五刃 The five bladed weapons: generally refers to the broadsword, dagger-axe, halberd, straight sword, and pike. See also dāo, gē, jǐ, jiàn, máo.

wǔ shèng cháo tiān 五圣朝天 Five Sages Look Skyward: a heel kick combined with a covering press at the groin with the opposite hand, the other hand lifted straight up above the head. From Liuhebafa.

wǔ shǒu quán 五手拳 Wushouquan (five hands fist), a style from the docks of Shandong province. It uses short routines to practice straight forward techniques.

wǔ shū 五枢 Acupoint Wushu (fifth pivot), GB27.

At the abdomen, at the iliac crest, three *cun* below the level of the navel (on each side). From TCM.

wǔ xīn zhuāng 五心桩 Five hearts stake. See wǔ xīng zhuāng.

wǔ xīng zhuāng 五星桩 Five star stake. Varies with style. One version is sitting in seiza, the hands palm up at the belly. Also called wǔ xīn zhuāng.

wǔ xíng 五行 The five elemental phases of metal, water, wood, fire and earth that interact with each other in generating and controlling cycles to maintain balance. Combined with the twelve zodiac animals make up a sixty year cycle. See also huǒ, jīn, mù, shuǐ, tǔ, wǔ xíng xiāng kè, wǔ xíng xiāng shēng.

wǔ xíng dāo (jiàn, gùn, qiāng) 五行刀(剑,棍,枪) Five phase broadsword (sword, staff, and spear): Xingyiquan's five basic techniques for weapons, based on the five phases. See also wǔ xíng quán.

wǔ xíng lián huán quán (dāo, jiàn, gùn, qiāng) 五行连环拳(刀,剑,棍,枪) Five phases connected routines of Xingyiquan's five basic techniques, based on the five phases, for empty hand (broadsword, sword, staff, and spear).

wǔ xíng pào 五行炮 Five Phase Barrage, a basic partner routine of Xingyiquan, written up as eight to thirteen moves.

wǔ xíng quán 五行拳 Five phases fists: Xingyiquan's five basic techniques, based on the five phases. See also pī quán, zuān quán, bēng quán, pào quán, héng quán, and jīn, shuǐ, mù, huǒ, tǔ.

wǔ xíng xiāng kè 五行相克 The controlling order of the five phases, the order of subjugating, restraining, or controlling within the five phases. Metal controls, limits, or contracts wood; wood controls earth; earth controls water; water controls fire; fire controls metal.

wǔ xíng xiāng shēng 五行相生 The generating order of the five phases, the order of engendering or supporting within the five phases. Metal generates, enables, or expands water; water generates wood; wood generates fire; fire generates earth; earth generates metal.

wǔ xíng yào shùn 五行要顺 The five elemental phases must flow smoothly: the five basic techniques should flow externally and the five visceral organs should be unimpeded internally. From Xingyiquan, one of its essential body positioning requirements.

wǔ zàng 五脏 The five visceral organs: Lungs, Liver, Spleen, Kidney, Heart, and Pericardium. See also fèi, gān, pí, shèn, xīn, xīn bāo, zàng.

wǔ zǐ dēng kē 五子登科 Five Sons Pass the Imperial Exams: a classic five kick combination. Alternating legs each time: a same side slap kick, the other side same side slap kick, a turning inside slap crescent kick, a slapping flick kick behind, then a double slapped outside crescent kick.

wǔ zì yāo qiú 五字要求 The five requirements of Tongbeiquan for palm techniques, describing their speed and power. See also chuān, cuán, pāi, pī, shuāi.

wǔ zǔ quán 五祖拳 Wuzuquan (five ancestors fist): a southern style from Fujian province.

午 (rad.24) wǔ The seventh of the twelve Terrestrial Branches, used in combination with the ten Celestial Stems to designate years, months, days, and hours. For the sixty year cycles, see also under bǐng wǔ, gēng-, jiǎ-, rèn-, wù-. The period of the day from 11:00 a.m. to 1:00 p.m. See also dì zhī, tiān gān.

wǔ gōng 午功 Training done regularly at the time from 11:00 a.m. to 1:00 p.m. (11:00 to 13:00).

wǔ shí 午时 The period of the day from 11:00 a.m. to 1:00 p.m. (11:00 to 13:00).

捂 搗 [捂] (rad.64) wǔ 1. To seal, cover, muffle. 2. Slap kicks.

wǔ cuō 捂撮 Muffle trip: catch an adversary's leg with your foot and pull it directly upwards while pushing his body back.

武 (rad.77) wǔ Martial; military. Connected with martial arts.

wǔ dǎ piàn 武打片 A kungfu movie.

wǔ dāng cháng quán 武当长拳 Wudang Longfist, a Wudang routine, written up as thirty-four moves.

wǔ dāng jiàn 武当剑 1. Wudang style sword. 2. A Xingyiquan sword routine, written up as fifty-

W

three moves.

wǔ dāng quán 武当拳 Wudangquan (Wudang mountain fist), attributed to the Wudang mountain temple.

wǔ dāng shān 武当山 Wudang mountain. One of the famous mountains in martial lore, the location of the Wudang temple, in northwest Hubei province.

wǔ dé 武得 Martial virtue. A fighter who does not hold to martial ethics is considered a thug rather than a martial artist.

wǔ hún 武魂 Martial spirit.

wǔ jìn shì 武进士 Successful candidate at the highest level of the imperial examinations for military knowledge and skill.

wǔ jǔ 武举 1. The imperial examinations for military knowledge and skill. The exams changed over the years, but usually included archery, horse riding and shooting, and other tests of skill. Sometimes the exams contained a written component. Also called wǔ kē. 2. A person who has passed these exams.

wǔ jǔ rén 武举人 Successful candidate at the township level (lower level) of the imperial examinations for military knowledge and skill.

wǔ kē 武科 The imperial examinations for military knowledge and skill. See also wǔ jǔ.

wǔ lín 武林 The martial world; in martial circles; the community of martial artists. Also called quán tán, wǔ tán.

wǔ shì tài jí quán 武式太极拳 Wushi (Wu's) Taijiquan, attributed to Wu Yuxiang. Sometimes called Hao style, to differentiate it from the other Wu style, since it was spread by Hao Weizhen.

wǔ sōng 武松 Wu Song, a martial hero turned outlaw from the novel the Water Margin. One of its more popular stories is how he kills a tiger with his bare hands. See also shuǐ hǔ zhuàn.

wǔ sōng dǎ hǔ 武松打虎 Wu Song Hits the Tiger: a high and low strike, varies with styles. Normally one hand will be low as if holding the tiger and the other hand will be high as if hitting it in the head. See also dǎ hǔ shì.

wǔ sōng shàng kào 武松上铐 Wu Song Puts on the Handcuffs: step to horse stance, cross the wrists above the head, then set them down in front of the groin. From Shaolinquan.

wǔ sōng tuō kào 武松脱铐 Wu Song Escapes from the Handcuffs. 1. A traditional routine, written up as sixty-six moves. Most of the routine is done with the hands together, releasing near the end. 2. A move separating the hands with a knee strike.

wǔ shù 武术 1. Chinese martial arts, often called wushu or kungfu in English. 2. In English wushu often refers to the modern Taolu performance style of Changquan and its performance weapons. See also gōng fu.

wǔ shù duì 武术队 Chinese martial arts team.

wǔ shù guǎn 武术馆 Chinese martial arts hall or club.

wǔ tán 武坛 The martial world. See wǔ lín. Also called quán tán.

wǔ tàng zǐ 武趟子 The martial routines, a grouping of nine routines of Chuojiao. They are named simply by number.

wǔ tóng 武童 A martial child, a level of athlete classification for children within China: an athlete under eighteen who has achieved high scores in two events of a Taolu competition.

wǔ wǔ 武舞 Performance martial arts. This an old term, referring to busking on street corners with martial routines. Also called xiàng wǔ.

wǔ xiá 武侠 1. A martial hero, often translated as a knight errant: usually a transient martial artist in the old times who would help the weak and fight against injustice. Also called xiá kè. 2. Popular novels about martial heroes.

wǔ yì 武艺 Martial artistry, martial skill.

wǔ yīng 武英 A martial hero, the highest level of athlete classification within China: an athlete who has achieved high scores and placings in national competitions.

wǔ zhuāng 武桩 Martial stake standing: stake standing postures with the feet set front to back and legs straight. From Yiquan.

wǔ zhuàng yuǎn 武状元 The top martial scholar of the imperial examinations for military knowledge and skill, that is, the person with the highest score in the highest level examinations.

舞 (rad.136) wǔ   1. To dance; move about as dancing. 2. To flourish; brandish.

wǔ huā 舞花 Dancing flowers: circular entrapment with hands or weapon.

wǔ huā bēi gùn (qiāng) 舞花背棍(枪) Flowers to the back, with a staff (or spear): swing the shaft in full vertical circles to that the tip travels down in front of the body, circles at either side of the body, staying close to the body, and stops by laying the shaft on the back.

wǔ huā gùn (qiāng) 舞花棍(枪) Flowers, figure eights, with a long weapon such as staff (or spear): rotate the shaft in full vertical circles to that the tip travels down when in front of the body, repeating vertical circles at either side of the body, staying close to the body.

wǔ huā guò bèi 舞花过背 Flowers around the back, figure eights, continuing on the back, with a staff or spear: swing the shaft in full vertical circles to that the tip travels down when in front of the body, circle at either side of the body, staying close to the body, and continuing on by laying the shaft on the back, still turning and continuing on.

wǔ huā pū dāo 舞花扑刀 Flowers, figure eights, with a horse cutter: rotate the shaft in full vertical circles to that the tip travels down when in front of the body, repeating vertical circles at either side of the body, staying close to the body. With bladed weapons such as the horse cutter and halberd, the sharp edge of the blade must be turned to travel into the cut.

wǔ huā shuāng jiǎo shéi gān zǔ 舞花双脚谁敢阻 Flowers, Two Feet, Who Dares Obstruct Me: Do flowers with a big cutter, then place it on the shoulder to do two slap kicks. From Chen Taijiquan.

wǔ huā tí liáo gùn 舞花棍提撩 Reverse flowers, rising figure eights: continuously swing the shaft in vertical rising circles so that the tip travels upwards in front of the body.

wǔ huā shǒu 舞花手 Flowers with the hands: first cross the arms, then circle with the wrists still together.

wǔ xiù tuī shān 舞袖推山 Flourish the Sleeves and Push the Mountain: turn and stamp, rolling the arms over, trap the left hand inside the right, then snap out a fist. From Chen Taijiquan.

悟 (rad.61) wù   To realize; awaken.

wù dào 悟到 To intuit; to understand through the body, mind, and soul, not intellectually.

戊 (rad.62) wù   1. The fifth of the ten Celestial Stems, used in combination with the twelve Terrestrial Branches to designate years, months, days, and hours. See also dì zhī, tiān gān. 2 Fifth in a list when listing using the celestial stems, equivalent to E in English when listing alphabetically.

wù chén 戊辰 The years 1988, 1928, and so on, for sixty year cycles.

wù shēn 戊申 The years 1968, 1908, and so on, for sixty year cycles.

wù wǔ 戊午 The years 1978, 1918, and so on, for sixty year cycles.

wù yín 戊寅 The years 1998, 1938, and so on, for sixty year cycles.

wù xū 戊戌 The years 2018, 1958, and so on, for sixty year cycles.

wù zǐ 戊子 The years 2008, 1948, and so on, for sixty year cycles.

誤 [误] (rad.149) wù An error, mistake. By mistake.

wù chā 误差 Errors and shortcomings.

wù shāng 误伤 1. An accidental injury. 2. To accidentally injure someone in a sparring or wrestling match.

X

吸 (rad.30) **xī** 1. To breathe in, inhale. 2. As body technique, to absorb; to suck in. 3. To absorb an adversary's attempt at a throw and prevent the throw.

xī huà zhǎng 吸化掌 Absorbing palm: absorb and alter the incoming force by sticking to and following an adversary. Used in Baguazhang.

xī kuà 吸胯 To absorb into the hip joints, 'breathe' into the hip joints.

xī mén 吸门 Sensitive point Ximen (breathing gateway). The softest point of the throat, at the depression between the two collarbones, on the midline. One of seven painful gateways to attack that are related to midline acupoints. See also qī chōng mén.

xī yāo 吸腰 To absorb into the waist, suck in the waist.

扱 (rad.64) **xī** To collect; draw in; gather; receive.

xī zhēng 扱睁 Collecting elbow: a vertical downward block with the elbow and forearm.

犀 (rad.93) **xī** 1. Sharp-edged and hard (weapons). 2. A rhinoceros. 3. The reference is often to a water buffalo, which is common in Chinese fields, and a natural analogy to use. It has large side horns rather than the single nose horn of the rhinoceros.

xī bīng 犀兵 Sharp weapons.

xī niú biè jiǎo 犀牛别角 Rhinoceros Jams with its Horn: drive your knee into the thigh or groin of an adversary as he does a high kick.

xī niú dǐng jiǎo 犀牛顶角 Rhinoceros Stabs with its Horn: a snap kick punch landing into a horse stance elbow strike. From Yangjia style.

xī niú fēn shuǐ 犀牛分水 Water Buffalo Splits the Water: a bow stance double stabbing palm. From Piguaquan.

xī niú gēng tián 犀牛耕田 Water Buffalo Tills the Field: lower the tip of a pole and push it forward, both hands with the palms up, rear hand at the butt, front hand extended along the shaft. From Ziwu pole.

xī niú gōng jiǎo 犀牛攻角 Rhinoceros Attacks with its Horn: drive your knee into the belly of an adversary.

xī niú shuāi jiǎo 犀牛甩角 Water Buffalo Swings its Horns: turn around with a snapping palm strike. From Piguaquan.

xī niú wàng yuè 犀牛望月 Water Buffalo Gazes at the Moon. 1. In an open horse stance, brace high with one arm while pushing though underneath with the other, tilting the body. 2. Sit into a resting stance with the arms embracing to tuck and press with the deerhorn blades at shoulder height. From Baguazhang. 3. Cover and strike through over top the forward hand. From Liuhebafa. 4. A long back cross step with a high reverse slice up behind with a sword, leaning forward to get more height. From Qingping sword.

xī niú xià shuǐ 犀牛下水 Water Buffalo Goes into the Water: sit back to empty stance, pulling and pressing down. From southern styles.

xī niú yǐn shuǐ 犀牛饮水 Rhinoceros Drinks Water: a knee butt to the groin.

xī niú zhēng jiǎo 犀牛攻角 Water Buffalo Gores with its Horns: butt with the elbow and knee simultaneously.

膝 (rad.130) **xī** Knee, the knees. Often pronounced qī in the martial arts in colloquial speech.

xī bì gōng 膝臂功 1. Training the knee and elbow strikes. 2. The skill of the knees, shins, and elbow strikes.

xī bìn gǔ 膝膑骨 The patella, the knee cap. An easy target, but a very sensitive point. Alright to strike with hammer fist, but kick to this point only in extremity.

xī cè 膝侧 The side of the knee. An easy target, but crippling. Kick to this point only if in real danger.

X

xī fā lì 膝发力 A knee strike, and training for knee strikes. From Yiquan.

xī fǎ 膝法 Knee striking techniques.

xī fàn guī 膝犯规 A knee foul in a Sanda or wrestling competition.

xī gài 膝盖 The patella, the knee cap. See xī bìn gǔ.

xī guān 膝关 Acupoint Xiguan (knee pass), LR7. At the calf, behind the head of the tibia, in the medial head of the gastrocnemius, one *cun* behind acupoint Yinlingquan (on each leg). From TCM.

xī guān jié 膝关节 The knee joint.

xī wō 膝窝 The depression behind the knee. An easy target.

xī yǎn 膝眼 Extraordinary acupoint Xiyan (eye of the knee), EX-LE5. At the knee, at the depressions made on either side of the patellar ligament (two on each leg, inside and outside). From TCM. When used in movement descriptions, usually refers to the inner depressions.

xī yáng guān 膝阳关 Acupoint Xiyangguan (knee *yang* joint), GB33. At the knee, on the outside, three *cun* above acupoint Yanglingquan (on each leg). From TCM.

xī yào cuī zú ér zú bù nì xī 膝要催足而足不逆膝 Power should flow from knees to feet, the feet should not run counter to the knees. From Xingyiquan.

西 (rad.146) xī   West, Western, Westerly.

xī fāng 西方 The West. Sometimes written descriptions of routines use compass directions for orientation.

xī hàn 西汉 The Western Han dynasty (221 BC – 24 AD).

xī jìn 西晋 The Western Jin dynasty (265-316).

xī wèi 西魏 The Western Wei dynasty (535-556) of the northern dynasties.

xī yuè huà shān 西岳华山 Mount Hua, the Western of the sacred mountains. See also huà shān, wǔ yuè.

xī zhōu 西周 The Western Zhou dynasty (1027-771 BC).

xī zǐ pěng xīn 西子捧心 Xizi Holds the Heart in her Hands: a straight, palm up, double stab to the chest. Xizi was a famous beauty of the Spring and Autumn period.

郤 (rad.163) xī   1. Cleft, more often seen in combination as xī mén for an acupoint. 2. A surname.

xī mén 郤门 Acupoint Ximen (cleft gate), PC4. At the forearm, on the inside, between acupoints Quze and Daling, five *cun* up from the wrist crease, between the two long tendons on the inside of the forearm (on each arm). From TCM.

襲 (rad.145) xí   To make a surprise attack on; raid.

xí bù 襲步 A raiding step, a stealing step. See tōu bù.

喜 (rad.30) xǐ   1. A happy event, especially a wedding. 2. To be fond of, to like. 3. To be happy; to feel pleased.

xǐ què guò zhī 喜鹊过枝 Magpie Passes the Branch, a pole technique. Pull a pole back, tuck the base at the shoulder to press down, then snap it up.

xǐ què xián méi 喜鹊衔梅 Magpie Holds a Plum in its Mouth: to escape from a double handed grab to shoulder and opposite wrist, swing the loose arm up and over an adversary's arm, trapping his hand with your shoulder and head.

洗 (rad.85) xǐ   To wash; bathe.

xǐ jiàn 洗剑 Wash with a straight sword: a traditional term for the class of techniques that use the edges of the blade, such as slicing up, drawing, pulling back, intercepting, cutting, and sweeping.

xǐ suǐ 洗髓 Wash the marrow. The third stage of training, to cleanse the inside and lighten the body. See also yì gǔ, yì jīn.

細 [细] (rad.120) xì   1. Thin, slender. 2. Fine. Delicate. 3. Careful; meticulous; detailed (this is the usual meaning when used in martial arts).

蝦 [虾] (rad.142) xiā   A shrimp, shrimp.

xiā fǎ 虾法 Shrimp method: retreating constantly from an attack (like a shrimp squirting backwards in the water), with a hidden defensive maneuver each time, while preparing for a counter attack. Also called tuì shēn fǎ.

俠 [侠] (rad.9) xiá   1. Martial chivalry; chivalrous. 2. A martial artist who does chivalrous deeds.

xiá jiā quán 侠家拳 See xiá quán.

xiá kè 侠客 A Chinese knight errant, an independent, usually itinerant, martial artist in the old society who did chivalrous deeds (in stories more than in reality). Also called wǔ xiá.

xiá kè cáng jiàn 侠客藏剑 Knight Errant Hides his Sword: step forward with a front cross step kick, pulling back with the hands. From Shaolinquan.

xiá quán 侠拳 Xiaquan (hero fist). Attributed to the hero Li Huzi, who brought it from Emei mountain to Guangdong province. Uses strong stances and full power. Also called xiá jiā quán.

xiá yì 侠义 Chivalrous. Willing to fight for justice for those unable to help themselves.

暇 (rad.72) xiá   Leisurely, unhurried.

狹 [狭] (rad.94) xiá   Narrow.

xiá bái 狭白 Acupoint Xiabai (guarding white), LU4. At the inside of the upper arm, on the line of the biceps, about four *cun* down from the outside of the armpit (on each arm). From TCM.

xiá xī 狭溪 Acupoint Xiaxi (pinched ravine), GB43. At the foot, on the top, between the tendons of the fourth and fifth toes, just at the web between the toes (on each foot). From TCM.

下 (rad.1) xià   1. Lower, underneath, below. 2. To go down, get off.

xià bā kē 下巴颏 The chin.

xià bǎ 下把 The lower grip: the aft-section of a long handled bladed weapon such as a halberd.

xià bēng qiāng 下崩枪 Low snap with a spear: snap a spear, both hands applying an abrupt power horizontally to snap the spear tip up so that it shudders at knee height.

xià bō qiāng 下拨枪 Low check with a spear: snap a spear from side to side with a quick but steady power, below knee height.

xià bù kuà hóng 下步挎肱 Drop down and wrap the arm around, like setting to pick up a bale of hay to swing up onto the shoulder.

xià chǎng 下场 To leave the competition area, to leave the playing field. Also called tuì chǎng.

xià chén 下沉 Downward sinking: with a long weapon such as pole or spear, lift the rear hand, pressing down with the front hand, to press down with the tip of the weapon.

xià chén zhǎng 下沉掌 Downward sinking palm: pressing the palms down in front of the hips, fingers pointing to each other. The power is like pushing a ball down in water, with additional outward and inward balancing rotations. From Baguazhang, especially for set circle-walking. Sometimes called àn zhǎng, shuāng àn zhǎng.

xià chuài tuǐ 下踹腿 Downward thrust kick: a turned out kick to the knee. From Wing Chun. Also called yí bù, yí mǎ.

xià cì jiàn 下刺剑 Downward pierce to the tip of a sword to knee height, forming a straight line with the arm and blade.

xià dān tián 下丹田 Lower cinnabar field: centred in the pelvis. See dān tián. See also shàng dān tián, zhōng dān tián.

xià diǎn qiāng 下点枪 Low dab with a spear: a dipping action with the tip of a spear, lifting the grip to dip the tip between ankle and knee height.

xià duǒ shǎn 下躲闪 Dropping evasion: duck downwards to avoid attack without making contact.

xià gōu shǒu jiē tuǐ shuāi fǎ 下勾手接腿摔法 Hook the leg throw: catch an incoming kick by hooking the arm under the leg, then bring it to your body for a throw or takedown.

xià gōng fū 下功夫 Put in a lot of time and energy towards a goal; devote a lot of effort towards mastery of something.

xià guà dāo (jiàn) 下挂刀（剑）Lower parrying hook with a broadsword (or sword), hooking

X

down and back, contacting with the spine of a broadsword blade or thumb edge of a sword blade.

xià guān 下关 Acupoint Xiaguan (below the pass), ST7. At the face, at the jaw depression in front of the ear hole, directly above Jiache (on each side). From TCM.

xià héng bēng 下横崩 Low crossing snap: with a long weapon, snap sharply to the side with the tip angled down.

xià hòu jù jī 下后锯肌 Inferior serratus posterior muscle: thin muscles that insert into the ribs from the spine, at the lower edge of the ribcage.

xià jí shū 下极俞 Extraordinary acupoint Xiajishu, EX-B5. At the waist, level with the depression under the third lumbar vertebra, on the midline of the spine. From TCM.

xià jié dāo (jiàn) 下截刀（剑）Low intercept with broadsword (or sword): a diagonal cut down with the arm on a straight line with the blade, a flat blade, cutting with the fore-edge.

xià jù xū 下巨虚 Acupoint Xiajuxu (lower great hollow), ST39. At the shin, nine *cun* below acupoint Dubi (on each leg). From TCM.

xià lián 下廉 Acupoint Xialian (lower ridge), LI8. At the outer edge of the forearm, about four *cun* up from the wrist crease (on each arm). From TCM.

xià liáo 下髎 Acupoint Xialiao (lower bone-hole), BL34. At the sacrum, the fourth sacral formina, just below acupoint Zhongliao, 0.5 *cun* lateral to the midline (on each side). From TCM.

xià lù 下路 1. The lower part of the body: thighs, knees, lower legs, ankles. Also called xià sān lù. 2. Lower level route for striking.

xià mén 下门 The lower gate: under the outstretched arm of a standing adversary.

xià ná shǒu 下捺手 Back Pinning Hand: a straight arm thrust to the rear with the wrist hyper-flexed to hit with the heel of the palm. From Wing Chun.

xià nèi yā wàn 下内压腕 Inner dropping wrist lock: grab the adversary's hand and elbow and press the hand to the forearm, continuing to press until he is on the ground. From Qinna.

xià pán 下盘 1. The lower body: hips, legs. 2. The lower basin: the legs. 3. A low height used whilst moving, keeping the hips at knee level. From Baguazhang.

xià pán tuǐ 下盘腿 The low basin kicks, a series of short routines of Chuojiao. See also bā pán tuǐ.

xià pán tuǐ fǎ 下盘腿法 Low-basin kicks: nine kicks that use low positions and strike low. From Chuojiao. See also shàng pán tuǐ fǎ, zhōng pán tuǐ fǎ.

xià pī 下劈 Chop down to knee height with a broadsword, sword, or double hooks, with the blade and arm forming a straight line and the blade upright (edges up and down).

xià píng qiāng 下平枪 A low level stab with a spear: the shaft is horizontal, at waist height.

xià qiāng 下枪 A low stab with a spear: the stab is between knee and foot height, the shaft angled downwards.

xià qiáo 下桥 Bridge: supporting yourself on hands and feet, arched backwards with straight arms and legs. Done from standing, called xià yāo.

xià qiē tuǐ 下切腿 Low cutting kick. See cèng tuǐ. Also called duò zi tuǐ.

xià rèn 下刃 The under edge of a bladed weapon, the little finger side of the blade, when held in normal grip.

xià sān dāo jīng tuì cáo cāo 下三刀惊退曹操 Three Blades from below to Startle Cao Cao into Retreating: Three right turning flowers with a big cutter, with emphasis on the low slices up on the left side. Cao Cao was a real general and warlord (155–220), but is better known as the villain in the Romance of the Three Kingdoms. From Chen Taijiquan.

xià sān lù 下三路 See xià lù.

xià shǎn 下闪 Duck down: bend the knees and drop down, tucking in the neck and covering up with the forearms, to protect the body.

xià shì 下式 Closing move of a routine.

xià shì 下势 Low posture: squat on one leg while extending the other, extending one arm along the extended leg and the other arm up behind. From Taijiquan. Also called chuān quán xià shì, chuān zhǎng xià shì.

xià shǒu 下手 1. The re-active person in a fight, the fighter put on the defensive. Also called hòu shǒu. See also shàng shǒu. 2. The next player, the following player in a game. 3. To put one's hand to something, set about doing something.

xià wài yā wàn 下外压腕 Outer dropping wrist lock: grab an adversary's hand, turn it palm up, and press his elbow down to the floor. From Qinna.

xià wǎn 下脘 Acupoint Xiawan (lower stomach duct), RN10. At the abdomen, two *cun* above the navel, on the midline. From TCM.

xià yā zhǐ 下压指 Low finger press: rotate one or more fingers of an adversary and press down to the ground. From Qinna.

xià yāo 下腰 Bridge, a waist exercise: Standing, lean back to place the hands on the ground, arching the back. The posture is also called xià qiáo.

xià yín chǔ 下阴处 The groin. See dāng bù. Also called qián yīn.

xià zhā dāo 下扎刀 Downward stab with a broadsword, the tip at knee height.

xià zhī 下肢 The lower limbs, the legs.

xià zhī fáng shǒu 下肢防守 Blocking techniques using the lower limbs, the legs.

夏 (rad.34) xià 1. Summer. 2. The Xia dynasty (c. 2000 BC). 3. A surname.

仙 僊 [仙] (rad.9) xiān An immortal; a deity: a celestial being.

xiān gū tuō pán 仙姑托盘 Sorceress Carries the Plates: lift a knee and lift the hands in front, opposite hand high, same side hand near the knee. From Shaolinquan.

xiān gū zhào jìng 仙姑照镜 Sorceress Looks in the Mirror: sit to an empty stance and chop the front arm down, bend the elbow of the rear arm to grab and place the hand in front of the shoulder. From Shaolinquan.

xiān rén 仙人 An immortal; a deity; a celestial being. Often used in movement names.

xiān rén bǒ mǐ 仙人簸米 Immortal Winnows the Chaff: A low double lift. May cup an adversary's elbows in the palms and shove back and up. The action is like tossing rice in a basket to winnow away the chaff. From Baguazhang, one of its sixty-four hands.

xiān rén chēng yāo 仙人撑腰 Immortal Supports the Waist: control an adversary and step in to trip while pressing his waist and shoulder from behind, to twist and take down. From Baguazhang.

xiān rén chuān zhǎng 仙人穿掌 Immortal Pierces with a Palm: slice a palm up then turn it into a stab, hitting the other palm into its forearm. From Shaolinquan.

xiān rén dǎn chén 仙人掸尘 Immortal Whisks the Dust: lift the knee with double hooking hands. From Piguaquan.

xiān rén guān qí 仙人观棋 Immortal Watches a Chess Game. See xiān rén guān qí 旗.

xiān rén guān qí 仙人观旗 Immortal Watches a Banner: open your elbows to cross or control your adversary, then shove to his chest. From Baguazhang, one of its sixty-four hands. Also called píng tuī zhǎng, xiān rén guān qí 棋.

xiān rén guò qiáo 仙人过桥 Immortal Crosses a Bridge. 1. Lying down, hook one leg and kick with the other. From Chuojiao, one of its low-basin kicks. 2. Deal with an incoming attack by stepping around and kicking to the back of an adversary's knee. From Baguazhang.

xiān rén huà tú 仙人画图 Immortal Draws a Picture: coil a sword blade twice to control an adversary's blade, then stab. From Qingping sword.

xiān rén mō miàn 仙人摸面 Immortal Strokes the Face: Retreat with continuous chopping palms. From Piguaquan.

xiān rén mò méi 仙人抹眉 Immortal Smears the Eyebrows: reaching from behind, hook into an adversary's eye sockets with your fingers and pull back.

xiān rén shuì chuáng 仙人睡床 Immortal Sleeps in a Bed: lying down, with one foot on the ground, kick with the other from underneath. From Chuojiao, one of its low-basin kicks.

xiān rén tuī bēi 仙人推碑 Immortal Pushes a Stele: a sliding step into a push. From Tongbeiquan.

xiān rén yíng pán 仙人迎盘 Immortal Receives the Basin: sit into a resting stance while blocking up over the head with a pole. From Ziwu pole.

xiān rén zhāi qié 仙人摘茄 Immortal Picks an Aubergine (eggplant): come up to a raised knee stance, with a strong stab to the front, palm up. From Shaolinquan.

xiān rén zhāi táo 仙人摘桃 Immortal Plucks a Peach: a slice up followed by a hook, then a reverse slice up. From Tongbeiquan.

xiān rén zhǐ 仙人指 Immortal's finger, a hard skills training method to strengthen the fingertips for striking: striking gradually increasing hardness of surfaces with the fingers.

xiān rén zhǐ guǒ 仙人指果 Immortal Points to the Fruit: step around hooking a sword tip down, then sit to empty stance and cock the blade up. From Qingping sword.

xiān rén zhǐ lù 仙人指路 Immortal Points the Way. 1. In Liuhequan, a raised knee stance with the leading hand stabbing forward. 2. In Taijiquan sword, a raised knee stance stabbing with the blade angled downwards. 3. In Wudang sword, point with the left fingers while holding a sword at the side, or point with the sword grip while the sword lies on the right forearm. 4. With a rope dart, throw the dart out and finish with the arm extended, in bow stance. 5. In Baguazhang and Shaolinquan, a direct stab with the fingers. 6. In Qingping sword, an angled pierce to along the line of the straight leg in a back weighted bow stance. 7. In Yangjia sword, pointing with the left fingers while pulling a sword back to hide behind.

xiān rén zhǐ yuè 仙人指月 Immortal Points at the Moon: a one legged stance with the foot tucked in at the knee, stabbing a sword to chest height with a standing blade. From Qingping sword.

xiān tóng bǔ què 仙童捕雀 Celestial Youth Catches a Sparrow: move forward into a high bow stance or a half squat stance, punching down with both hands, above knee height. From Shaolinquan.

xiān tóng xiàn guǒ 仙童献果 Celestial Youth Catches Presents Fruit: bow stance double piercing palm. From Piguaquan.

xiān wēng fú zhàng 仙翁扶杖 Celestial Elder Uses a Cane: a low check with a sword, stepping forward to land in a right bow stance, sweeping the blade angled to the lower right. From Qingping sword.

xiān yuán tuī bēi 仙猿推碑 Celestial Ape Pushes a Tablet: circle-walking with the hands held with their bases together, fingers spread away, pushing out from the belly. From Baguazhang.

先 (rad.10) xiān 1. Ahead of, earlier, before. 2. In advance. 3. The elder generation.

xiān fā zhì rén 先发制人 Strike first to win. A martial saying. Whoever strikes first gains the initiative. Forestall an adversary with a pre-emptive strike.

xiān kàn yī bù zǒu, zài kàn yī shēn shǒu 先看一步走，再看一伸手 (To judge skill) first look at someone's footwork, and only then look at his hand techniques. A martial saying.

xiān qiú kāi zhǎn hòu qiú jǐn còu 先求开展后求紧凑 First try to be large and expansive, and then try to be compact. A martial saying.

xiān shǒu 先手 The pro-active person a fight, the one with the upper hand, the one in the offensive position. See shàng shǒu. See also hòu shǒu.

xiān tiān 先天 Congenital; innate; prior to birth. Refers to a person's inherited qualities, nature (vs nuture). Often translated as pre-heaven.

xiān tiān bā guà 先天八卦 Innate eight trigrams: the trigram order of qián, xùn, kǎn, gèn, kūn, zhèn, lí, duì. See also hòu tiān bā guà.

xiān tiān lì 先天力 Natural strength. See běn lì. Also called tāi lì.

xiān tiān qì 先天气 A person's inherited *qi*. This *qi* can be trained to improve on one's inherited qualities.

xiān tiān zuò 先天座 Pre-heaven seated meditation. From Liuhebafa.

xiān zhào 先兆 To telegraph moves: give away your attack with a preparatory action, such as moving the shoulder before a punch.

掀 (rad.64) xiān 1. To lift, as if lifting the lid off a pot or lifting a door curtain. 2. A lifting sidekick: a sidekick with the outer edge of the foot, not completely chambered before the kick. 3. A takedown, starting as if taking down to the front, then reversing the action to take down to the rear.

xiān jīn 掀筋 Lift a tendon: grab and lift a tendon,

artery or vein away from its normal location. From Qinna.

xiān ná fǎ 掀拿法 Lifting grappling hold. 1. As a hand technique, pull sideways, coordinating a low grip with a covering grip, to twist an adversary. 2. As an arm technique, a strong and direct takedown controlling an adversary's chest and back. From wrestling.

xiān tuǐ 掀腿 Lifting kick: a lifting kick to the side or rear with the foot hooked inward to kick with the outer edge. From Chuojiao, one of its middle-basin kicks.

xiān xiāng qǔ bǎo 掀箱取宝 Lift the Lid (of a box) to Pick out the Treasure: an empty stance with the back of the leading hand on the leading knee. From Liuhequan.

xiān zhǎng 掀掌 Lift the sole. See hǔ zhāng kǒu.

弦 (rad.57) **xián** A bowstring.

顯 (rad.181) [**显**] (rad.72) **xiǎn** 1. To be apparent; be obvious. 2. To show; display. Expose.

xiǎn hóu 显喉 Expose the throat: lift the chin, exposing the throat to attack. A major error in most styles.

獻 [**献**] (rad.94) **xiàn** 1. To present; offer. 2. To donate. 3. To put on display. 4. Often used for movements in martial arts where the action looks like holding something up with both hands, as if presenting it to someone as a gift.

xiàn dāo 献刀 To present the blade of a broadsword or halberd, the blade held up horizontally, not necessarily flat.

xiàn zūn 献鐏 To present the sharp metal capped end of a halberd shaft, to lift the shaft with the blade held flat, prior to stabbing with that end.

陷 (rad.170) **xiàn** 1. Pitfall; trap. 2. Get bogged down. 3. Sink, cave in.

xiàn gǔ 陷谷 Acupoint Xiangu (sunken valley), ST43. At top of the foot, between the bones of the second and third toes (on each foot). From TCM.

相 (rad.75) **xiāng** 1. Each other; one another; mutually. 2. Pronounced xiàng, looks, appearance;

X

bearing, posture, see xiàng.

xiāng chā 相叉 Wrestling.

xiāng fǎ 相法 Assessment of one another, observation: to calculate the weaknesses of your adversary before committing to action.

xiāng pū 相扑 1. Old style wrestling. Also called xiāng sǎn shǒu. 2. Sumo wrestling.

xiāng pū péng 相扑朋 Old style wrestling ground.

xiāng sǎn shǒu 相散手 Old style wrestling. Also called xiāng pū.

香 (rad.186) **xiāng** 1. Fragrant; aromatic. 2. Savoury; appetizing. 3. With relish, enjoy (a good sleep, a good meal).

xiāng shān duǎn dǎ 香山短打 Xiangshanduanda (fragrant mountain short hits) style, a southern style.

祥 (rad.113) **xiáng** Auspicious.

xiáng yún tuō yuè 祥云托月 Auspicious Clouds Hold the Moon: If grabbed at the wrist, twist your wrist to reverse your adversary's grip, then press his fingers with your other hand to overextend them. From Baguazhang.

降 (rad.170) **xiáng** 1. To subdue; vanquish. 2. To surrender; capitulate. 3. Pronounced jiàng, to fall or lower.

xiáng lóng qiāng 降龙枪 Subdue the dragon spear: a routine of Yangjia style, written up as forty moves.

xiáng lóng zhuāng 降龙桩 Subdue the dragon post standing: a stance training to lower the fire in the body. In an extended insertion stance turn the body around towards the back, extending the opposite arm along the line of the extended leg. The other arm is bent with the palm out at head height. From Xingyiquan and Yiquan. In Xingyiquan there will be moving intent, while in Yiquan there will be micro movements putting power out in all directions. Also pronounced jiàng lóng zhuāng.

向 嚮 [**向**] (rad.30) **xiàng** 1. To turn towards; to face. 2. A direction. 3. To guide, direct, lead. 4. To lean toward.

X

xiàng cè dǎo 向侧倒 To fall towards the side.

xiàng hòu 向后 To the rear, towards the back.

xiàng hòu dǎo 向后倒 To fall towards the back.

xiàng qián 向前 To the front, towards the front.

xiàng qián dǎo 向前倒 To fall towards the front.

xiàng yòu 向右 To the right, towards the right.

xiàng zuǒ 向左 To the left, towards the left.

相 (rad.75) **xiàng** 1. Looks, appearance; bearing, posture. 2. Pronounced xiāng, mutual, see xiāng.

象 (rad.152) **xiàng** 1. Appearance; shape. 2. Imitate. 3. Like, such as. 4. An elephant.

xiàng bí dà dāo 象鼻大刀 Elephant trunk cutter: a halberd with a curvy blade, rounded at the tip. Also called xiàng bí dāo.

xiàng bí dāo 象鼻刀 Elephant trunk blade. See xiàng bí dà dāo.

xiàng wǔ 象舞 Performance martial arts (old term, referring to busking). See also wǔ wǔ.

xiàng xíng 象形 1. As one word means a pictograph. 2. As two words means to imitate the form or appearance of something.

xiàng xíng qǔ yì 象形取意 Apply meaning to the model: take the inner meaning of the model, do not just imitate its outward appearance. A principle of Xingyiquan, but can be applied to any imitation style.

项 [項] (rad.181) **xiàng** The nape of the neck, back of the neck. Also called hòu jǐng.

xiàng mù 项目 1. An item; a project. 2. In sports means a competition or performance event.

削 (rad.18) **xiāo** 1. To pare, peel, whittle with a knife. 2. As a hand technique, to slice across with the palm down, hitting strongly with the palm edge. 3. To cut at a bit of an angle, as if taking a slice out of something. Sometimes pronounced xuē.

xiāo dà dāo 削大刀 Slice with a big cutter: with a two handed cut, slice the blade across with the edge towards the direction of travel.

xiāo jiàn 削剑 Slice with a sword: with a flat blade, take the blade across from the offside, upwards to head height with the palm up, putting power to the front third of the blade.

xiāo zhǎng 削掌 1. Slice across with the arm, palm down, laterally rotating the arm to apply a horizontal force to the ulnar edge of the palm or forearm. 2. An angled slice upwards or downwards slice, palm up or down.

xiāo zhú lián zhī 削竹连枝 Slice a row of Bamboo Branches: in a horse stance, cut the right forearm downward and across, slicing with the outer edge. The 39th move of the tiger and crane routine.

枭 [梟] (rad.75) **xiāo** 1. An owl, owls. 2. Brave, valiant. 3. Also used in phrases related to decapitation.

xiāo dà dāo 枭大刀 Decapitating slice with a big cutter: with a two handed cut, slice the blade across with the edge towards the direction of travel, moving the blade from the lower rear to the upper front with an angled cut.

消 (rad.85) **xiāo** 1. To disperse, dispel. 2. To disappear; vanish. 3. To pass time, while away time.

xiāo bǎi bù 消摆步 To step aside to avoid an attack then step back in to counter.

xiāo jí 消极 Passivity in a Sanda match, deliberately wasting time.

xiāo jí lōu bào 消极搂抱 Passive clinch, tying up without attempting a throw.

xiāo luò 消泺 Acupoint Xiaoluo (dispersing riverbed), SJ12. At the arm, on the back, at the midpoint between acupoints Qinglengyuan and Xuhui (each arm). From TCM.

销 [銷] (rad.167) **xiāo** 1. To pin: a controlling technique. 2. A choke hold.

小 (rad.42) **xiǎo** 1. Small, little. 2. Young.

xiǎo bàng 小棒 Small club, a short stick used for training, about twenty-eight centimetres long with a circumference appropriate for gripping.

xiǎo bì 小臂 The forearm.

X

xiǎo bì xià zá 小臂下砸 Low forearm jam: block with the forearm, striking a low incoming kick with the outside of the forearm.

xiǎo bù fǎ 小步法 Small step method: use small steps to move and turn around in order to be agile and to not give away in which direction you are going.

xiǎo chà 小衩 Small vents: the sides of a short sleeved wrestling jacket, just under the armpit.

xiǎo chán dǎ 小缠打 Small coil and hit: coil one arm around an adversary and punch with the other. From Tongbeiquan.

xiǎo chán shǒu 小缠手 Small coiling of the hand. See jīn sī chán wàn.

xiǎo chán zhǒu 小缠肘 Small coiling of the elbow: if grabbed on the same side (i.e. right grabbing right), use the grabbed hand to coil the adversary's wrist, press your other elbow on his elbow, turning to lift his elbow, then press down. This is either an elbow lock or a shoulder dislocation, depending on the angle you use. From Qinna.

xiǎo cháng 小肠 1. The small intestine. 2. The Small Intestine, the organ associated with the Shou Tai Yang channel. It is a *yang* organ.

xiǎo cháng jīng 小肠经 The small intestine meridian. See shǒu tài yáng. From TCM.

xiǎo cháng shū 小肠俞 Acupoint Xiaochang (small intestine transport), BL27. At the sacrum, at the top sacral foramina, 1.5 *cun* lateral to the midline (on each side). From TCM.

xiǎo dé hé 小得合 Little achievement takedown: a type of takedown that involves dropping down to a kneel to complete the throw. From wrestling. Also called guì tuǐ.

xiǎo fù 小腹 The lower abdomen, the belly.

xiǎo gǔ kōng 小骨空 Extraordinary acupoint Xiaogukong (little finger bone hollow), EX-UE6. At the back of the hand, the middle of the interphalangeal joint at the distal end of the proximal phalanx of the little finger. From TCM.

xiǎo guàng yāo 小逛腰 Little Stroll for the Waist, a warm-up exercise: legs together and straight, hands on head, move the waist side to side and front to back in small, gentle movements.

xiǎo guǐ dēng tuǐ 小鬼蹬腿 Imp Thrust Kick: in a low squat stance, lift the leg to kick out the heel then pull it immediately back, still in a low stance. From Shaolinquan.

xiǎo guǐ diē jīn gāng 小鬼跌金刚 Imp Throws the Temple Guard. 1. A leg throw: when caught from behind, drop and grab your adversary's feet and lift them, sitting down into him. 2. A head on attack, scooping up an adversary's legs for a takedown.

xiǎo guǐ liàng pái 小鬼亮牌 Imp Shows his Cards: stand up, slice the left hand out to the side and circle the right hand around to flash at the chest. Used as a salutation for the ending of a routine. From Shaolinquan.

xiǎo guǐ tiào shéng 小鬼跳绳 Imp Skips Rope: jump up and turn around, kicking one leg up behind, hooking the same side hand back with it. From Shaolinquan.

xiǎo hǎi 小海 Acupoint Xiaohai (small sea), SI8. At the elbow, the outside, at the space between the heads of the ulna and radius that appears flat when the elbow is bent (on each arm). From TCM.

xiǎo hēi hǔ fān shēn 小黑虎翻身 Black Tiger Cub Rolls Over: in a hunkered squat, circle a pole low, then pop it up.

xiǎo hóng quán 小洪拳 Little Resonant Fist: A routine of Shaolinquan, written up as fifteen moves. May also be called 小红拳 xiǎo hóng quán.

xiǎo hóng quán 小红拳 Little Red Fist: A routine of Shaolinquan, written up as sixty moves. May also be called 小洪拳 xiǎo hóng quán.

xiǎo hóng 小肱 1. Forearm (normally pronounced gōng, often pronounced hóng in the martial arts). 2. Can also mean the shin, or lower leg.

xiǎo hóu qiǎng guā 小猴抢瓜 Cheeky Boy Vies for a Melon: turn into a horse stance, grabbing and pulling, then pressing inwards in front of the chest, palms in. From Shaolinquan.

xiǎo hǔ yàn 小虎燕 Tiger Cub and Swallow: a routine of Mizongquan, to train agility, written up as fifty-seven moves.

xiǎo huā qiāng 小花枪 Little flowers spear: a routine of Yangjia style, written up as forty moves.

xiǎo huàn zhuāng 小换桩 Small changing stances.

X

See xiǎo zhuàn jiǎo. Also called xiǎo zuān zi.

xiǎo jià 小架 Small frame. 1. Styles that use compact movements. 2. A branch of Chen Taijiquan.

xiǎo jiàng diǎn bīng 小将点兵 Young General Musters the Troops: standing in closed parallel stance, strike to the side with the right hand, left fist at the waist. From Shaolinquan.

xiǎo jié quán 小结拳 Small knotted fist, a hand shape: all five fingers tightly clenched, thumb pressed on the middle joints of the index and middle fingers, the other fingers tucked further in. The wrist may be slightly tucked in as well. From southern styles.

xiǎo jìn 小劲 Small force, shrinking a move to increase efficiency.

xiǎo kuí xīng 小魁星 Little Dipper: sweep a sword around flat then lift it over the head in empty stance. From Yang Taijiquan.

xiǎo liù hé qiāng 小六合枪 Little six combined spear, a routine of Mizongquan, written up as forty moves.

xiǎo lóng 小龙 Snake, as the sixth of the twelve animals from the Chinese zodiac, associated with a twelve year cycle symbolic of the earthly branches. The twelve animals make up a sixty year cycle when combined with the five phases. See also dì zhī, shēng xiào, wǔ xíng. Also called shé.

xiǎo lóng xíng 小龙形 Snake form: from dragon moving arms, 'wash the face', then step forward and double strike to the head. From Xingyiquan.

xiǎo mén 小门 The small gate. 1. The small gate of an adversary: between the legs, or the groin. 2. A setup stance standing shoulder to shoulder, each with different foot forward so that you present a small frontal surface. 3. The front edges of a wrestling jacket, at the belt, also called ruǎn mén.

xiǎo mǔ zhǐ 小拇指 The little finger. Also called xiǎo zhǐ.

xiǎo niàn tóu 小念头 Little Idea: a routine of Wing Chun, written up as about forty moves.

xiǎo qiāng 小枪 Small spear: Two metres long, with a base circumference smaller than a circle made with the thumb and forefinger.

xiǎo qín dǎ 小禽打 Little Grapple and Hit: a release from a wrist grab, with a follow-up control and hit. From Chen Taijiquan.

xiǎo shāo zǐ gùn 小梢子棍 Short handled flail. See duǎn shāo zi gùn.

xiǎo shuàn yāo 小涮腰 Small waist circles, a warm up exercise.

xiǎo tuǐ 小腿 Shank, shin and calf, lower leg.

xiǎo tuǐ gē dǎng 小腿格挡 Block or jam with the lower leg: lift the knee and jam an incoming kick either with the inside or the outside of the lower leg, depending on the angle of attack.

xiǎo xiù 小袖 Small sleeve of a wrestling jacket, especially where it is used for grabs. A Chinese wrestling jacket has short sleeves.

xiǎo xún huán fǎ 小循环法 Small cycle changeover: in Baguazhang, changing from one side to the other of the eight circle-walking fixed postures, completing both sides of each posture before going on to the next posture. See also dà xún huán fǎ, zhōng xún huán fǎ.

xiǎo yáng huí huà 小羊回话 Lamb Responds: grab the hair of an adversary and pull directly down and forward. From Qinna.

xiǎo yuán jī 小园肌 Teres minor muscle: one of the muscles of the shoulder girdle, runs from the lower scapula to the humerus. Active in arm lateral rotation.

xiǎo zhǐ 小指 The little finger. Also called xiǎo mǔ zhǐ.

xiǎo zhōu tiān 小周天 The small heavenly circulation: moving the *qi* through the torso in a small circle down the front of the body and up the back.

xiǎo zhuàn jiǎo 小转脚 Small turns, a leg training exercise: sit down into a full squat cross stance, stand and turn to sit from one side to the other repeatedly. Also called xiǎo zuān zi, xiǎo huàn zhuāng.

xiǎo zuān zǐ 小钻子 Small drills. See xiǎo zhuàn jiǎo. Also called xiǎo huàn zhuāng.

笑 (rad.118) xiào   To smile.

xiào lǐ cáng dāo 笑里藏刀 Hide a Dagger behind a Smile. The tenth of the Thirty-six Stratagems of Warfare, which apply to many situations.

楔 (rad.75) xiē   Wedge: to use the body to directly knock over an adversary. From wrestling.

歇 (rad.76) xiē   To rest; stop over.

xiē bù 歇步 Resting stance, legs crossed and sitting, rear knee tucked into the hollow of the front knee. A fully seated cross stance, sitting on the rear leg. Also called zuò bù. 2. The same stance, a bit higher. Also called jiǎn zi gǔ bù.

蠍 [蝎] (rad.142) xiē   A scorpion. For more movement names using the scorpion, see also under dú xié.

xiē zǐ bèi zhuō 蝎子背啄 Scorpion Pecks Behind: a straight swing kick behind the body to groin level. From Chuojiao. Also called hòu liāo yīn tuǐ.

xiē zǐ shì 蝎子势 Scorpion spear: a four-section spear, 2.25 metres long overall, with sections of eighty-one, fifty-three, forty-one, and thirty-five centimetres, the longest attached to the tip. 2. A routine of Tongbeiquan with the scorpion spear, written up as twenty-one moves.

xiē zǐ shì 蝎子势 Scorpion position: a rear poke kick with the hands on the ground. From Chuojiao.

協 [协] (rad.24) xié   1. Joint; common. 2. To assist.

xié tiáo 协调 Coordinated.

xié tiáo xìng 协调性 Coordination.

挾 [挟] (rad.64) xié   1. To hold something under the arm. 2. To trap. Coerce.

xié zhǒu 挟肘 Elbow lock: with a bent and raised elbow, hook and hold the adversary's neck for a throw or arm for an arm bar.

xié zhù 挟住 Seize and control.

攜 攜 [携] (rad.64) xié   To carry; take along. Take by the hand.

xié dài 携带 1. The usual meaning is to take along, carry on oneself. 2. The martial meaning can be to wear as a belt: a method of carrying a soft weapon such as a steel whip.

斜 (rad.68) xié   Diagonal, oblique, slanted, tilted.

xié chā jīn huā 斜插金花 Stick the Golden Flower in at an Angle: press the sword grip down by the hip, tip angled down, then step forward into a half squat and snap the blade forward and in, cocking the wrist with the grip down low. From Qingping sword.

xié chén bù 斜沉步 Angled settled stance: sitting in horse stance but with one knee on the ground.

xié chū zhēng rù 斜出正入 Avoid to the angle and attack directly. From Baguazhang.

xié dāng 斜裆 See xié dāng bù.

xié dāng bù 斜裆步 Slanted crotch stance: feet opened to front and back, about two foot-lengths apart. The lead leg is bent with the foot turned in, the rear leg is straight with the foot lined up straight. The lead knee must not go past the toes, and both heels must be on the ground. From Duanquan. Also called xié dāng.

xié fāng jī 斜方肌 Trapezius muscle: runs from the vertebrae to the scapula, starting quite low down and ending in the head, it spreads out to the acromial tip of the scapula. Its various branches assist in retracting, elevating, depressing, and rotating the shoulder blades.

xié fēi shì 斜飞势 Oblique Flying, Slant Flying, Tilt in Flight, Diagonal Flying: an open throwing movement, shifting to a wide bow stance while angling the arms outward, one forward and up, the other rearward and down. From Taijiquan.

xié fēn zhǎng 斜分掌 Slanted separation: open the hands angled up and down or front and back.

xié fēng bǎi liǔ 斜风摆柳 Gentle Wind Sways the Willow: standing up, left fist at the hip, pull the right hand in to the right hip, palm out, fingers down. The fifth move of the tiger and crane routine.

xié pāi jiǎo 斜拍脚 Diagonal slap kick, single foot slap kick, slapping the foot with the opposite side hand. In the category of slap kicks, see also jī xiǎng xìng tuǐ fǎ.

xié sǎo quán 斜扫拳 A slanted sweeping punch. From Choylifut.

xié shǎn 斜闪 Turn to angle the body to the side.

X

A weave to present less body to an adversary.

xié shēn 斜身 Angle the body: turn the body angled away from an adversary, presenting a small surface.

xié shēn rào bù 斜身绕步 Step around with body angled: Step around keeping the body angled to the line of defence.

xié tiǎo 斜挑 Angled raise: a high strike with the forearm, using the thumb edge, palm up. From Choylifut.

xié tī tuǐ 斜踢腿 Diagonal straight kick: a straight kick to the opposite ear. In the category of straight swinging kicks, see also zhí bǎi xìng tuǐ fǎ.

xié xià pī 斜下劈 Angled low chop: a low strike with the forearm, using the little finger edge, palm down. From Choylifut.

xié wāi 斜歪 Slightly dislocated, sprained (joint).

xié xíng 斜行 Diagonal Stepping, Stepping to the Corner: advance into bow or reverse bow stance, slightly circling the feet in stepping. Stepping to the corner. From Chen Taijiquan. Sometimes called xié xíng 形.

xié xíng 斜形 Diagonal Stepping, Diagonal Model. See the two different xié xíng above and below.

xié xíng 斜型 Diagonal Model: step into a reverse bow stance, punching out front and back with the arms bent, hitting with the meat of the fist heels. From Shaolinquan. Sometimes called xié xíng 形.

脇 脅 [胁] (rad.130) xié The flank; the side of the body from the armpit to the waist. May refer to armpits, ribs, or the whole flank, depending on context.

xié zhǒu 胁肘 An elbow to the flank. From Tanglangquan, one of its eight short techniques.

邪 (rad.163) xié 1. Evil. 2. Irregular. 2. Unhealthy environmental influences that cause disease. From TCM.

xié liú 邪留 Evils retained, a pattern applied in channel diagnosis. From TCM.

xié qì 邪气 Pathogenic *qi*.

卸 (rad.26) xiè 1. To unload, discharge; lay down. 2. To remove, strip. 3. To get rid of, dissipate an attack.

xiè bù 卸步 Unloading step or stance. 1. Step the feet open (either to the sides or to front and back), slide the rear foot back, bringing the lead foot along to touch down beside it. This is a quick step and should not cause the body to move off balance. 2. A one legged stance with the raised foot tucked in to touch the inside of the supporting knee.

xiè fǎ 卸法 Dislocation methods. 1. When used specifically, is the method of striking a joint with the palm, fingers, or knuckles to knock it out of place. 2. Dislocating the arm at the shoulder. Also called níng fǎ, piē bì fǎ, wài piē fǎ.

xiè fū fǎ 卸跗法 Foot dislocation methods.

xiè gǔ fǎ 卸骨法 Bone manipulation methods. Includes both dislocation and healing manipulation of the joints. See also shàng gǔ fǎ.

xiè hé fǎ 卸颌法 Jaw dislocation methods.

xiè jiān fǎ 卸肩法 Shoulder dislocation methods.

xiè shǒu 卸手 1. As a technique, lay down, pound: backfist downwards with the elbow bent, fist heart up. In routines, lay the punching right forearm into the left hand. Also called xiè zá. 2. As a release from a grab, strip: when your front arm is grabbed, slide your rear hand under your adversary's elbow, extend your rear arm and pull back your grabbed arm, to strip the grab off.

xiè wàn fǎ 卸腕法 Wrist dislocation methods.

xiè xī fǎ 卸膝法 Knee dislocation methods.

xiè zá 卸砸 See xiè shǒu.

xiè zhǒu fǎ 卸肘法 Elbow dislocation methods.

蟹 蠏 [蟹] (rad.142) xiè A crab, crabs.

xiè xíng 蟹形 Crab structure: circle-walking and changes done seeking the structure, posture, and manner of a crab. From Baguazhang.

心 (rad.61) xīn 1. The heart. 2. The heart, mind, feeling, intention, will. The part of the mind that intends to do something. The source of a person's being. Sometimes translated as the emotional mind. 3. The Heart, the organ associated with the Shou Shao Yin channel. It is a *yin* organ.

xīn bāo 心包 The Pericardium, the organ associated with the Shou Jue Yin channel. It is a *yin* organ.

xīn bāo jīng 心包经 The Pericardium meridian. See shǒu jué yīn. From TCM.

xīn hé yú yì 心合于意 The heart combines with intent. From Liuhebafa, one of its principles.

xīn huāng yì luàn 心慌意乱 To be alarmed and confused; to be nervous and flustered.

xīn jīng 心经 The heart meridian. See shǒu shào yīn. From TCM.

xīn jìng 心静 The heart is quiet: one of the requirements for proper training.

xīn kǒu 心口 The heart's mouth: see xīn wōr. Also called xīn kǒu wō, xiōng gǔ xià jiǎo.

xīn kǒu wō 心口窝 The heart's mouth den: see xīn wōr. Also called xīn kǒu, xiōng gǔ xià jiǎo.

xīn shù 心俞 Acupoint Xinshu (heart transport), BL15. At the back, level with the depression below spinous process of the fifth thoracic vertebra, 1.5 *cun* lateral to the midline (on each side). From TCM. These points are good targets but should not be hit too hard, especially on the side directly behind the heart. Best to hit with a pull and short strike or a step around to strike from behind.

xīn wōr 心窝儿 The heart's den: the solar plexus, pit of the stomach. This is an easy target but should not be hit too hard. Also called xīn kǒu, xīn kǒu wō, xiōng gǔ xià jiǎo.

xīn yán fǎ 心眼法 Mindful eyes method: to keep calm and use the eyes in coordination with the whole body, to wait patiently for the right opportunity.

xīn yào xì 心要细 The heart must be meticulous. A clear and thinking mind is a necessity in fighting.

xīn yào xiá 心要暇 The heart must be leisurely: in practice or a fight, one should not be hurried or worried, and have no fear. This is one of the eight essentials of Xingyiquan, but applies to most styles.

xīn yì bǎ 心意把 Purposeful set: a set of line exercises to practice individual techniques. From Shaolinquan.

xīn yì gùn 心意棍 Purposeful staff: a routine of Liuhebafa.

xīn yì liù hé bā fǎ quán 心意六合八法拳 Xinyi Liuhebafa (heart and mind six harmonies fist). See liù hé bā fǎ quán.

xīn yì liù hé quán 心意六合拳 Xinyi Liuhequan. See xīn yì quán.

xīn yì quán 心意拳 Xinyiquan (heart and mind fist). Attributed to the early 1600s. Also called xīn yì liù hé quán.

xīn yú yì hé 心与意合 The heart harmonizes, or works together, with the intent. One of the six harmonies. See also liù hé.

新 (rad.69) xīn   New; fresh.

xīn jià 新架 New frame, a branch of Chen Taijiquan attributed to Chen Fake.

xīn jià èr lù 新架二路 Second routine of Chen Taijiquan new frame.

xīn jià yī lù 新架一路 First routine of Chen Taijiquan new frame.

辛 (rad.160) xīn   1. The eighth of the ten Celestial Stems, used in combination with the twelve Terrestrial Branches to designate years, months, days, and hours. See also dì zhī, tiān gān. 2 Eighth in a list when listing using the celestial stems, equivalent to H in English when listing alphabetically.

xīn chǒu 辛丑 The years 1961, 1901, and so on, for sixty year cycles.

xīn hài 辛亥 The years 1971, 1911, and so on, for sixty year cycles.

xīn mǎo 辛卯 The years 2011, 1951, and so on, for sixty year cycles.

xīn sì 辛巳 The years 2001, 1941, and so on, for sixty year cycles.

xīn wèi 辛未 The years 1991, 1931, and so on, for sixty year cycles.

xīn yǒu 辛酉 The years 1981, 1921, and so on, for sixty year cycles.

信 (rad.9) xìn   True. Trust. Honesty. Trustworthiness, a character trait expected of martial artists. 2. Believe 3. Evidence. 4. A letter.

X

5. A message. 6. Core, a variant of xìn 芯. In this sense, often used to mean 'snake's tongue' in movement names.

xìn xīn 信心 Self confidence.

xìn mǎ yóu jiāng 信马由缰 Trust the Horse to Ride without Holding the Reins: an arm bar. From blocking an adversary's arm, reach for his fingers with that hand, pressing his elbow with the other hand. Continue to lift and twist, bending his elbow and lifting his hand so he is locked out at shoulder, elbow and wrist.

囟 顖 (rad.31,181) [囟] (rad.31) xìn The top of the head, fontanel, where the bones fuse gradually after birth.

xìn huì 囟会 Acupoint Xinhui (fontanel meeting), DU22. At the top of the head, two *cun* back from the front hairline, three *cun* forward of acupoint Baihui. From TCM.

芯 (rad.140) xìn Pith from rush. Core. In movement names, means the tongue of a snake.

形 (rad.59) xíng 1. Form, shape; body. 2. External structure and/or action of the body. 3. To emulate the structure or posture of an animal.

xíng tǐ tōng 形体通 Form and structure communicate: all the joints are relaxed and the whole body works together.

xíng yì bā shì 形意八势 Eight models routine of Xingyiquan, see bā shì quán.

xíng yì hé yī 形意合一 United, with form and intent as one. This is a requirement at the advanced level of training internal styles.

xíng yì lián huán dāo (jiàn, gùn, qiāng) 形意连环刀(剑,棍,枪) Xingyiquan linking routines for broadsword (sword, staff, and spear).

xíng yì mǔ quán 形意母拳 Xingyiquan mother fists, the basic techniques of the style.

xíng yì quán 形意拳 Xingyiquan (form and intent fist), a style developed from Xinyiquan. This is the standard name, and use of this name emphasizes the structure. Best known branches are Che, Dai, Hebei province, and Shang. See also xíng 行 yì quán.

xíng yì shí qī shì 形意十七势 Form and intent seventeen postures: a Xingyiquan routine of the Song branch.

xíng yì zōng hé quán 形意综合拳 Form and intent composite routine, a modern routine of Xingyiquan, written up as fifty-one moves.

行 (rad.144) xíng 1. Stepping, walking. 2. Travel. 3. To walk, go. 4. To do; perform a task. 5. To be alright. 6. To be competent. 7. Pronounced háng, a line, row; trade, profession; business firm; seniority.

xíng bù 行步 1. Stepping in general. 2. In Baguazhang refers both to plain stepping without an entry push, and to mud wading step. 3. In Longfist, refers to a quick, smooth, steady, slightly lowered walking.

xíng bù guà dāo 行步挂刀 Hook a broadsword while walking: hook back with the spine of the blade while walking forward.

xíng bù liāo dāo 行步撩刀 Slice up with a broadsword while walking: slice up with the cutting edge of the blade while walking forward.

xíng bù liāo yī 行步撩衣 Pull up the Cloak while Walking Along: a reverse slice up while stepping, or while stepping out into an open horse stance. From Baguazhang. See also fǎn liāo.

xíng bù tuī shǒu 行步推手 Moving step push hands. From Taijiquan.

xíng chuán yáo lǔ 行船摇橹 Scull a Boat with One Oar: pull with hands down while doing a turned out stomping kick. From Wudangquan.

xíng jiàn 行剑 Moving sword: sword methods that involve moving continuously, with few pauses. Bagua sword and Dragon walking sword are the best known of these.

xíng jiān 行间 Acupoint Xingjian (moving between), LR2. At the foot, on top, just proximal to the web between the big and second toes (on each foot). From TCM.

xíng qì 行气 Move the *qi*: manipulate the acupuncture needle to move the *qi* along the channel. From TCM.

xíng quán 行拳 To practice moves. Also called dǎ quán, yǎn liàn, yǎn quán.

xíng yì quán 行意拳 Xingyiquan (phases and intent fist). Use of this name for Xingyiquan emphasizes the five phases. See also xíng 形 yì quán.

xíng zhě qín yāo 行者擒妖 Passerby Catches a Goblin: catch an adversary at the wrist and elbow, twisting the arm over and down, keeping it extended to lock out.

胸 胷 [胸] (rad.130) xiōng The chest.

xiōng bèi huā 胸背花 Chest to back flowers: spin a long weapon in front of and behind the body, leaning backwards (spinning in front) and forwards (spinning behind) and alternating hands to keep it spinning.

xiōng dà jī 胸大肌 Pectoralis major muscle: one of the muscles in the front of the torso that runs out to the arms. Assists in shoulder adduction, extension, flexion, and medial rotation.

xiōng gǔ 胸骨 Sternum, breastbone. Also called xiōng jī.

xiōng gǔ xià jiǎo 胸骨下角 Corner under the breastbone, the solar plexus. See xīn wōr. Also called xīn kǒu, xīn kǒu wō.

xiōng jī 胸齐 See xiōng gǔ.

xiōng qián guà yìn 胸前挂印 Hang a Seal on the Chest: a thrust kick directly to the chest. See also dēng jiǎo.

xiōng suǒ rǔ tū jī 胸锁乳突肌 Sternocleidomastoid muscle: a major neck muscle, attaching two tendons to the clavicle and running up to behind the ear.

xiōng xiāng 胸乡 Acupoint Xiongxiang (chest village), SP19. At the chest, the third intercostal space, six *cun* lateral to the midline (on each side). From TCM.

xiōng yāo zhé dié 胸腰折叠 Folding action of the chest and waist.

xiōng zhuī 胸椎 Thoracic vertebra, vertebrae.

熊 (rad.86) xióng A bear. For movement names using the actions or qualities of the bear, see also under hēi xióng, lǎo- .

xióng bǎng 熊膀 Shoulder girdle of a bear, one of the body requirements of Xingyiquan: both chest and upper back are naturally rounded, the nape of the neck held vertical, the shoulders and elbows set down. Imitates how a bear lifts its head by depressing its shoulders, when standing on all four feet.

xióng xíng 熊形 Bear form. 1. Stepping forward with a drilling punch that braces into the forearm. From Xingyiquan. 2. Bear structure: circle-walking and changes done seeking the structure, posture, and manner of a bear. From Baguazhang.

xióng yǒu shù xiàng zhī lì 熊有竖项之力 Bears have the strength of the upright nape of the neck. A quality sought in Xingyiquan's bear form.

雄 (rad.172) xióng 1. Having great power. 2. Manly. 3. The male of a species.

xióng shī kāi kǒu 雄狮开口 Male Lion Opens its Mouth: bow stance framing upper block push forward. From Piguaquan.

休 (rad.9) xiū Stop; cease. Rest.

xiū xī 休息 To take a rest.

修 脩 [修] (rad.9) xiū 1. To study; to repair. 2. To cultivate. Includes external training and internal nurturing.

xiū gōng 修功 To refine skills.

袖 (rad.145) xiù Sleeve; sleeves. Often used in movement names when the action is similar to actions one would do with the extra long sleeves of a traditional Chinese robe.

xiù jiàn 袖箭 Sleeve arrow: an ancient weapon, a bamboo arrow about fifteen centimetres long with an iron tip that one hid in a quiver up the sleeve and shot by means of a spring in the quiver.

xiù kǒu 袖口 Sleeve mouth: the opening of the sleeves on a wrestling jacket.

xiù lǐ cáng huā 袖里藏花 Hide a Flower in the Sleeve: standing up, left fist at the hip, push the right hand across to the left shoulder, palm left, index finger up. The sixth move of the tiger and crane routine.

xiù lǐ chōng chuí 袖里冲搥 Punch into the Sleeve: in a left open bow stance to the left, punch the right hand with an upright fist out on the midline of the stance, leaning onto the left thigh a bit. The 71st move of the tiger and crane routine.

xiù lǐ qiāng 袖里枪 Spear in the sleeve: a short

X

range spear stab with the arms crossed, the left hand tucked at the right armpit.

戌 (rad.62) **xū** The eleventh of the twelve Terrestrial Branches, used in combination with the ten Celestial Stems to designate years, months, days, and hours. For the sixty year cycles, see also under bǐng xū, gēng-, jiǎ-, rén-, wù-. The period of the day from 7:00 p.m. to 9:00 p.m. See also dì zhī, tiān gān.

xū shí 戌时 The period of the day from 7:00 p.m. to 9:00 p.m. (19:00 to 21:00).

虛 [虚] (rad.141) **xū** 1. Empty, clear, hollow. 2. Void, emptiness. Often used in relation to solid, see also shí. 3. False. 4. Vacuity, a pattern applied in channel diagnosis. From TCM.

xū bù 虚步 Empty stance: sitting on one leg with the heel on the ground, the other touching the toes on the ground in front but not weighted. In competition Longfist the thigh must be parallel to the ground. In competition southern styles, the thigh must approach forty-five degrees. In many styles the angle is not as acute as the competition style. Also called hán jī bù, xū mǎ.

xū bù huō dǎ 虚步豁打 Empty stance slitting hit: in an empty stance straight punches to the front and back. From Bajiquan.

xū bù liàng zhǎng 虚步亮掌 Empty stance flash the palm: in empty stance, flash one palm and hook the other behind the body.

xū fā 虚发 Shoot in vain, shoot into a void; send out (an arrow, a punch) in vain, missing the target.

xū yǎn fǎ 虚眼法 Empty eyes method: show a lack of spirit in the eyes to draw in an adversary, in preparation for a strong counter attack.

xū gōu 虚钩 Hollow hook hand shape: the finger tips hanging downwards, but not touching.

xū hán 虚寒 Vacuity cold, a pattern applied in channel diagnosis. From TCM.

xū jìn 虚劲 Empty power. From Tongbeiquan, one of its nine types of power, see also jiǔ gōng jìn.

xū jìng 虚静 Empty and still. This is a requirement at the advanced level of training internal styles, the body should be empty, containing a stillness in movement.

xū mǎ 虚马 Empty stance. See xū bù.

xū shí 虚实 Insubstantial and substantial: either end of a continuum of emptiness and solidity, in terms of weight balance, stance structure and power output. There is a balance of some of each in every movement, otherwise movement would be floating or stiff.

xū shí fēn míng 虚实分明 Insubstantial and substantial are clearly distinguished.

xū shí xiāng shēng 虚实相生 Insubstantial and substantial produce each other: a fake may turn into a real strike; a real strike may turn into a fake. A fake may hide a real technique, a real technique may contain a fake.

xū shǒu 虚手 A feint with the hands. Also called xū zhāo.

xū tuǐ 虚腿 A feint with the legs. Also called xū zhāo.

xū zhāo 虚着 An empty move, a feint. With the hands, also called xū shǒu. With the feet, also called xū tuǐ.

續 [续] (rad.120) **xù** To continue; to extend. Continuous; successive.

xù bù 续步 Continuing step: a type of circle-walking step containing three powers – contained, stable, and continuing. From Baguazhang.

xù lì fǎ 续力法 Continuing power method: to continue an attack when an adversary is slightly off balance, pressing your advantage.

xù qiáo 续桥 Continuous bridging. See huàn qiáo.

蓄 (rad.140) **xù** 1. To collect, store; reserve. 2. To raise, rear. 3. To wait, expect.

xù jìn 蓄劲 To gather or store power in order to release it.

xù jìn rú zhāng gōng, fā jìn rú fàng jiàn 蓄劲如张弓，发劲如放箭 Gather power like drawing a bow, launch power like releasing an arrow. A martial saying.

xù shì 蓄势 A hoarding stance, a ready stance. 1. Sitting in a seventy-thirty stance with a pole held fairly flat in readiness in front of the body. 2. Sitting in empty stance with a pole held vertically in front of the body. From Ziwu pole.

xù xī fā hū 蓄吸发呼 Breathe in to gather and breathe out to issue power.

宣 (rad.40) xuān
1. To declare. 2. To lead off liquids; drain. 3. Diffusion treatment of channels. From TCM.

xuān gào yuán 宣告员 The announcer at a competition or event.

懸 [悬] (rad.61) xuán
1. Suspended, hung. 2. To suspend, hang.

xuán dǐng 悬顶 To suspend the top of the head. To hold the head straight and relaxed. A required position for many styles.

xuán lí 悬厘 Acupoint Xuanli (suspended tuft), GB6. At the head, just inside the hairline, in from the temple (on each side). From TCM.

xuán lú 悬颅 Acupoint Xuanlu (suspended skull), GB5. At the head, just inside the hairline, in from the temple where the hair curves out, above acupoint Xuanli (on each side). From TCM.

xuán shū 悬枢 Acupoint Xuanshu (suspended pivot), DG5. At the lower back, below the spinous process of the first lumbar vertebra, on the midline. From TCM.

xuán tóu shù xiàng 悬头竖项 Suspended head and straight neck. A required posture in many styles.

xuán yá lè mǎ 悬崖勒马 Rein in the Horse at the Brink of the Cliff. 1. Brandish deerhorn blades to both sides, at eyebrow and shoulder height, stepping around, then lifting the knee and pushing one dagger forward. From Baguazhang. 2. A brush knee and twist step, followed by a pullback and placement back in fighting stance. From Liuhebafa.

xuán zhōng 悬钟 Acupoint Xuanzhong (suspended bell), GB39. At the calf, on the outside, three *cun* above the ankle, on the front edge of the fibula, between it and the peroneus brevis tendon (on each leg). From TCM.

旋 (rad.70) xuán
To rotate, spin, circle. The simplified character for xuàn is also written with this character.

xuán qián fāng jī 旋前方肌 Pronator quadratus muscle: wraps the forearm. Serves to pronate (rotate the hand to palm down position).

xuán qián yuán jī 旋前园肌 Pronator Teres muscle: wraps the forearm. Serves to pronate (rotate the hand to palm down position).

xuán zhuàn 旋转 Rotate, spin, usually involving at least one full rotation.

xuán zhuàn bù 旋转步 Rotating step: rotate on the ball of one foot with the leg straight, lifting the other knee, so that the rotation is made in the knee raised position.

xuán zhuàn mǒ dāo 旋转抹刀 Circling Smear with a broadsword: draw a full circle with a flat blade at about chest height.

xuán zhuàn sǎo dāo 旋转扫刀 Circling sweep with a broadsword. See xuán zhuàn sǎo jiàn.

xuán zhuàn sǎo jiàn 旋转扫剑 Circling sweep with a sword: draw a full three-sixty circle whilst sweeping with the blade at ankle height.

xuán zhuàn sōng huó 旋转松活 Turning fluidly with a relaxed and sunken waist.

xuán zhuàn zì rú 旋转自如 Turning fluidly and naturally, the whole body turning from the waist.

玄 (rad.95) xuán
1. Black, dark. 2. Profound, abstruse. 3. Unreliable.

xuán kōng quán 玄空拳 Profound empty fist: a punching training method. 1. Stand over a well, punching five hundred times each session, until the water at the bottom makes sounds and ripples. 2. Stand facing the sun or moon, and punch five hundred times towards the sun at dawn and towards the moon in the evening.

xuán tán fú hǔ 玄坛伏虎 Ambush the Tiger from the Dark Alter: from a right bow stance, shift to horse stance and brace the right hand forward at belly height, fingers turned in. The 37th move of the tiger and crane routine.

xuán wǔ gùn 玄武棍 Profound martial staff, a Wudang staff routine, written up as ninety-six moves.

璇 (rad.96) xuán
Fine jade.

xuán jī 璇玑 Acupoint Xuanji (jade swivel), RN21. At the chest, about one *cun* below the suprasternal notch, one *cun* below acupoint

X

Tiantu, on the midline. From TCM.

選 [选] (rad.162) **xuǎn** To select; choose; pick. Elect.

xuǎn shǒu 选手 An elite athlete; a team member.

眩 (rad.109) **xuàn** Dizzy; giddy. To be dazed, disoriented.

xuàn yùn 眩晕 Dizziness; vertigo. To feel dizzy.

鏇 (rad.167) [旋] (rad.70) **xuàn** 1. To whirl, like turning on a lathe. 2. Twist a limb in its socket, a Qinna technique. The simplified character is also pronounced xuán, see xuán.

xuàn fǎ 旋法 Twisting methods: to cup the hand softly around a joint and turn the palm over, controlling the joint. Works especially well on the elbow.

xuàn fǎ fā lì 旋法发力 Release of power with a rotation. From Yiquan.

xuàn fēng bù 旋风步 Whirlwind stepping: 1. The first foot does a tuck in step to ninety degrees across the other foot so the heel passes the toes, then the second foot hooks out to ninety degrees, placing the heel near the toes. The body has turned one-eighty degrees. 2. The first foot turns out, the second foot does a tuck in step in the same direction, then the second foot turns out again and first foot steps to hook in again. Continuing, the line of walking is placing regular and reverse character eight stances along a straight line. From Baguazhang.

xuàn fēng jiǎo 旋风脚 1. Tornado kick, jumping inside crescent kick, whirlwind kick. Also called xuàn fēng tuǐ. Common in northern styles, one of Chuojiao's high-basin kicks. 2. A rotating inside crescent kick without a jump.

xuàn fēng jiǎo qī baǐ èr 旋风脚720 Jumping inside crescent kick seven-twenty, a tornado kick with a double turn.

xuàn fēng jiǎo sān bǎi liù 旋风脚360 Jumping inside crescent kick three-sixty, a tornado kick with a full three-sixty turn.

xuàn fēng jiǎo wǔ baǐ sì 旋风脚540 Jumping inside crescent kick five forty, a tornado kick with full turn and a half.

xuàn fēng sǎo dì 旋风扫地 Whirlwind Sweeps the Ground: drop into a drop stance and sweep a deerhorn blade past the extended leg, sweep kick and bring the other blade around, and continue to turn and bring the blades around keeping the arms extended. From Baguazhang.

xuàn fēng tuǐ 旋风腿 See xuàn fēng jiǎo.

xuàn fēng zhǎng 旋风掌 Whirlwind palm, a training method: in horse stance, stab the fingers into a pot of sand. Gradually add a twist as you pull out, so that the sand scatters. Increase the coarseness of the sand.

xuàn zǐ 旋子 Butterfly kick: jump up and float the body horizontally while swinging the legs up and around, at least the same height as the torso.

xuàn zǐ sǎo biān 旋子扫鞭 Butterfly kick sweep the steel whip: do a butterfly kick, sweeping the whip horizontally under the body whilst hovering in mid air.

xuàn zǐ sǎo gùn 旋子扫棍 Butterfly kick sweep the staff. See xuán zi sǎo biān.

xuàn zǐ zhuàn tǐ 旋子转体 Butterfly twist: a butterfly kick with a full turn at the horizontal. Also called zhuàn tǐ.

xuàn zǐ zhuàn tǐ qī bǎi èr 旋子转体720 Butterfly double twists, butterfly seven-twenty: a butterfly kick with two full turns at the horizontal.

學 [学] (rad.39) **xué** To study; to learn. Learning.

xué huì qiān zhāo bù rú liàn shú yī zhāo 学会千招不如练熟一招 It is better to master one technique than to learn a thousand. A martial saying.

xué jià zǐ 学架子 To learn the postures, to use the external form to lead the internal energy.

xué quán róng yì gǎi quán nán 学拳容易改拳难 It is easy to learn skills but hard to change them later. A martial saying. A warning against learning too much and too quickly without paying attention to the details.

xué yǒu dìng shì yòng wú dìng fǎ 学有定势用无定法 When learning practise set stances, when applying, there is no set technique. A martial saying. From Xingyiquan.

穴 (rad.116) **xué** 1. A hole; cave; den. 2. An acupuncture point, meridian point, acupoint. From TCM.

xué dào 穴道 Sensitive points on the body. Points that cause more pain than usual when struck. Often, but not always, acupoints. Colloquial term for xué wèi.

xué wèi 穴位 Meridian point, called acupoint or point for short. The spaces where the *qi* and blood are transported to the surface, closely related to the circulation of the meridians and collaterals, and linked to the organs, nerves, and joints. From TCM. For martial artists, important in healing and smoothing out the body and for points of attack (and some points that should not be attacked).

雪 (rad.173) **xuě** Snow.

xuě huā gài dǐng 雪花盖顶 Snowflakes Cover the Roof: swing a steel whip horizontally over the head, then bowing to pass it over the back.

血 (rad.143) **xuè** Blood.

xuè hǎi 血海 Acupoint Xuehai (sea of blood), SP10. At the inside of the thigh, about two *cun* above the inside edge of the top of the patella, on the vastus medialis muscle (on each leg). From TCM. A sensitive point, striking here can cause numbness of the leg. Care must be taken, as it is also a crippling point, striking here may cause serious injury. See also cán xué.

xuè shāo 血梢 The blood tip: hair. The visible part of the body in which the energy of the blood is expressed.

薰 (rad.140) **xūn** 1. Warm. 2. Fragrance.

xūn fēng sǎo yè 薰风扫叶 Fragrant Breeze Sweeps the Leaves: press through and out with a forearm while pushing with the other hand, repeating by stepping out in different directions. From Liuhebafa.

尋 [寻] (rad.41) **xún** To look for; to seek; search.

xún qiáo 寻桥 Arm seeking routine: a Wing Chun routine, written up as about sixty-four moves. It is trained to seek the bridge arm of an adversary.

xún xū jī shí 寻虚击实 Seek out the empty and hit the solid. A martial saying. This refers to the fighting method of the broadsword, to avoid rather than block, and attack the most advantageous spot.

循 (rad.60) **xún** 1. To follow; abide by. 2. To take the pulse, using the method of going along the channel. From TCM.

xún guī 循规 Follow the rules; abide by the rules of competition.

xún guī dòng bù tuī shǒu 循规动步推手 Moving step push hands by the rules: following a set stepping pattern during push hands practice, such as three retreat and three advances. From Taijiquan.

xún huán sài 循环赛 A round robin competition.

巽 (rad.49) **xùn** The Wind Trigram, two solid (*yang*) lines over one broken (*yin*) line, called 'lower broken'. Corresponds to the wind formation or gate. A closing gate formation. Indicates the attribute of penetrating.

訓 [训] (rad.149) **xùn** 1. To instruct. Instructions. 2. Standard; model.

xùn liàn 训练 Training, to train; to drill under instruction.

xùn liàn fāng fǎ 训练方法 Training methods, training regime.

xùn liàn fù hè 训练负荷 Training load.

xùn liàn qiáng dù 训练强度 Training intensity.

xùn liàn xiào guǒ 训练效果 Training effects.

X

Y

壓 [压] (rad.32) yā   1. To press down; hold down; weigh down. 2. In wrestling includes pressing down with the entire body. 3. Press, one of the falling hands in Chuojiao, see also luò shǒu. 4. To grasp and press down on an acupuncture needle and turn clockwise slowly, then hold, to encourage the *qi* to arrive at the needle. From TCM.

yā àn 压按 Press with the fingers, a channel palpation method. From TCM.

yā bà 压把 Press down with the base. 1. Press down with the butt of a long weapon. 2. Press down with the palm on the handgrip of a short weapon, opening your grip slightly at the little finger to ensure a solid push down with the palm.

yā bì tuō wàn 压臂脱腕 Press the arm wrist release: press down on the forearm when gripped with a one handed grab on the wrist. From wrestling.

yā biān 压鞭 Press the whip. See yā qiáo.

yā fǎ 压法 Pressing methods: press down on an adversary's joint with whatever part your body is in contact. Also called gài fǎ.

yā jiān 压肩 Shoulder press. 1. Press the shoulder: grab an adversary's wrist and twist it over while pressing down on his shoulder from the back. 2. A shoulder press exercise: lean forward with the hands on a support, using the upper body weight to open the shoulder joints. 3. A close range, controlling, move, pressing with the shoulder.

yā jiàn 压剑 Press down with the flat of the blade of a sword, palm down, tip forward.

yā jǐng tuī xī 压颈推膝 Press down the neck and push the knee: in a clinch, with an adversary embracing your knees from the front, press down on his neck with one hand and push and lift his knee, dropping to take him down on his face.

yā qiáo 压桥 Press the bridge: press down with the forearm with the elbow bent, the forearm flat. A defensive move. Also called yā biān.

yā tuǐ 压腿 Press the legs: stretch the legs and back by setting one leg straight on a support and pressing down, a passive or rocking stretch.

yā wàn 压腕 Pressing wrist lock. 1. If an adversary's hand is on your shoulder, reach across to press one hand to keep his hand there, lift the same side arm then bring it down to control his wrist with a shearing force. 2. Non-twisting wrist pressure techniques, pressing the hand directly to the forearm. From Qinna.

yā wàn dān tuī shǒu 压腕单推手 Wrist press down push hands: fixed step push hands with single hand connection, back and forth pressing down. From Taijiquan.

yā xià jiān 压下肩 Press the shoulder down: press down with the head of your shoulder on an incoming attack, applying pressure from the whole body.

yā xiōng 压胸 Chest press: when in contact, press down on an adversary with the chest using all the power of the body. From wrestling.

yā xué fǎ 压穴法 Cavity press methods. See diǎn xué fǎ.

yā zhǒu 压肘 Elbow press, arm bar. Lift the bent elbow and press down to the opposite side. One way is to get an adversary's arm across your shoulder, roll your arm over his arm to press down the elbow with the arm trapped.

yā zhuàn dāo 压转刀 Turning press down with a broadsword: circle-walking pressing the blade flat down in front of the body. From Baguazhang.

鴉 鵶 [鸦] (rad.196) yā   A crow, crows. For movement names referencing crows, see under wū yā.

yā zuǐ 雅咀 Crow beak: a fist with the index finger slightly extended, the thumb pressing on its first segment. Used in Shaolinquan, particularly for hitting pressure points.

鴨 [鸭] (rad.196) yā   A duck, ducks. For movement names referencing ducks, see under bǎo yā.

Y

yā xíng quán 鸭形拳 Yaxingquan (duck form fist). An imitative style with short and solid techniques.

牙 (rad.92) yá   1. Tooth, teeth. 2. Tooth-like thing. 3. Ivory.

yá chǐ 牙齿 Tooth, teeth.

yá hù shì 牙笏势 Ivory Tablet posture: drop back, pressing a sword blade down at the side, then step forward and stab directly to the throat. From Yang Taijiquan.

yá sāi 牙腮 The cheek at the teeth: a sensitive point on the cheek, below the cheekbone.

啞 [哑] (rad.30) yǎ   1. Dumb, mute. 2. Cries of a crow. 3. Hoarse, husky.

yǎ mén 哑门 Acupoint Yamen (mute's gate), DU15. At the nape of the neck, 0.5 *cun* into the rear hairline, in the depression below the first cervical vertebra, on the midline. From TCM. A sensitive point, striking it may induce temporary dumbness, dizziness, or even unconsciousness.

yǎ xué 哑穴 Dumbness points: pressure points that striking can cause so much pain the person cannot even call out. Lightly striking the death or crippling points may cause this. See also cán xué, sǐ xué.

咽 (rad.30) yān   The pharynx.

yān hóu 咽喉 The throat, larynx.

研 [研] (rad.112) yán   1. To grind. 2. A pestle. 3. To study; to investigate.

yán mó zhǒu 研磨肘 Grinding elbows: move in with both elbows rolling and coiling to attack an adversary's chest.

閻 [阎] (rad.169) yán   1. The gate of a village. 2. A surname. 3. Yama, the King of Hell.

yán wáng sān diǎn shǒu 阎王三点手 The three strikes of the King of Hell. From Bajiquan, one of its eight main concepts, see also bā dà zhāo. Also called yán wáng shǎn diàn shǒu, yǎn wàng shǎn diàn shǒu.

yán wáng shǎn diàn shǒu 阎王闪电手 The three lightning hands of the King of Hell. See yán wáng sān diǎn shǒu.

偃 (rad.9) yǎn   1. To fall on one's back. 2. To lie on one's back.

yǎn yuè dāo 偃月刀 1. A moon halberd. Often called a Guan's halberd (see guān dāo), though there is a slight difference between the blade shape of the two, the back of the moon halberd being slightly more crescent moon shaped. 2. A representative routine of Chaquan with a halberd, written up as fifty-five moves.

掩 (rad.64) yǎn   1. To cover up, conceal, a hooking cover. 2. To shut; close. 3. In martial arts is often an inward parry with the elbow and forearm, or a tucking in action of the elbow that initiates a circling of a weapon. This meaning is an action of covering up or closing in for protection.

yǎn dāo 掩刀 Cover with a broadsword: place the flat blade on the arm, holding the left hand on the right wrist, turning the blade over with the tip down, doing an elbow cover with the blade leading. Used with the larger blade of the Bagua broadsword.

yǎn jié 掩截 Tuck in the elbow to intercept and control with the forearm.

yǎn mén 掩门 Cover the door: technique of protecting the chest by turning sideways, covering with the hands, or squeezing the elbows.

yǎn ná fǎ 掩拿法 Clinch: cover up, wrapping the arms around an adversary to avoid being grabbed. From wrestling.

yǎn shǒu chōng quán 掩手冲拳 Hide the Fist and Punch: tuck the fist in by the lead hand, then punch. From Liuhebafa.

yǎn shǒu dāo 掩手刀 Tuck in the hand to hook a broadsword: tuck the elbow and hand in to bring a broadsword in to tuck in at the chest, edge up.

yǎn shǒu hóng chuí 掩手肱捶 Hide the Fist and Punch, Tuck in the Hand and Unfurl a Mallet: tuck in the elbow while pulling back the fist, then punch. A fast punch done either unfurling or direct. From Chen Taijiquan. May also be pronounced yǎn shǒu gōng chuí.

yǎn zhǒu 掩肘 Elbow cover, cutting in with the forearm to roll with the upper arm and down with the elbow, controlling with the forearm.

yăn zhŏu chā lèi tuī shŏu 掩肘插肋推手 Elbow cover push hands: fixed step push hands, one arm with wrists connected, the other hand at the elbow of the partner, horizontal circles with pressure on the elbow. From Taijiquan.

yăn zhŏu tuī shān 掩肘推山 Tuck with the Elbows and Push the Mountain: advance into a double shove, controlling with, then keeping the elbows tucked for protection. From Baguazhang, one of its sixty-four hands.

演 (rad.85) **yăn** 1. To develop. 2. To drill; practise. 3. To perform, play for entertainment.

yăn liàn 演练 To perform, play; drill. Practice. Also called dă quán, xíng quán, yăn quán.

yăn liàn shuǐ píng 演练水平 Quality, or level, of performance of a performance.

yăn qiāng 演枪 A practice spear: a four metre long spear used for training and partner work. It is too long for practical fighting. Also called dà qiāng.

yăn quán 演拳 To practice, specific to martial arts. See yăn liàn. Also called dă quán, xíng quán.

眼 (rad.109) **yăn** The eye, eyes. In written text, also called mù.

yăn fă 眼法 Eye technique, eye work. 1. Using the eyes and turning of the head to indicate direction of looking. In a routine, shows spirit, power, and knowledge of applications. 2. In sparring, using the eyes to intimidate or fake.

yăn guān liù lù 眼观六路 The eyes watch in six directions: in a fight the eyes watch the front, back, right, left, up, and down.

yăn huā 眼花 Have dim eyesight; have blurred vision. This includes getting blurred vision as a result of being hit.

yăn jīng 眼睛 The eye, eyes. In written text, also called mù.

yăn mào jīn xīng 眼冒金星 To see stars (from a blow to the head).

yăn wàng sān diăn shŏu 眼望三点手 Three Strikes in One Glance. See yán wáng sān diăn shŏu.

yăn wéi xīn zhī miáo 眼为心之苗 The eyes are the seedlings of the heart. A martial saying. You can see the mind through the eyes.

yăn wú shé quán wú hún 眼无神拳无魂 When the eyes lose their spirit so do the fists. A martial saying. Also used to describe someone who has lost the will to fight, he has no spirit in the eyes or fists.

yăn yào dú 眼要毒 The eyes must be poisonous (fierce). From Xingyiquan, one of its essential body positioning requirements.

yăn yào lì 眼要利 The eyes must be sharp. Seeing and understanding clearly what an adversary is doing is a necessity in fighting.

燕 鷰 (rad.86, 196) [燕] (rad.86) **yàn** A swallow, swallows. For more movement names using the actions or qualities of the swallow, see also under fēi yàn, hēi-, rŭ-, zǐ-.

yàn chì tăng 燕翅镗 Swallow wing trident: a long handled weapon with three prongs, the middle straight forward and the outer two straight out like soaring wings.

yàn pū hú dié 燕扑蝴蝶 Swallow Jumps on the Butterfly: kick one leg up behind and reach the hands up to grab then slap each other. From Shaolinquan.

yàn qīng quán 燕青拳 Yanqingquan (fledgling swallow fist). See mí zōng quán.

yàn shì píng héng 燕式平衡 Swallow balance: the supporting leg is straight, the torso leans forward to just above level, the other leg is raised straight out to the rear, above horizontal. The arms are usually held straight to the sides.

yàn wěi tăng 燕尾镗 Swallow tail trident: a long handled weapon with three prongs, the middle straight and the outer smaller and curved, one forwards, one backwards.

yàn xíng 燕形 Swallow form of Xingyiquan, involving a short sequence of leaping and dropping.

yàn yŏu chāo shuǐ zhī qiăo 燕有抄水之巧 Swallows have the agility of swooping over water. A quality sought in Xingyiquan's swallow form.

yàn zǐ bié chì 燕子别翅 Swallow Pins its Wings: from a raised knee stance, snap a slapped kick directly and open the other palm out behind. From

Y

Shaolinquan.

yàn zǐ chāo shuǐ 燕子抄水 Swallow Skims the Water. 1. Squat into a drop stance, extending one arm out along the extending leg, the other back. 2. Jump for distance, raising the hands with the jump and separating them front and back upon landing. From Xingyiquan. 3. From a wrist grab, rotate your arm to reverse your adversary's elbow, grabbing and pressing down. 4. To snap a spear up, raise it to block over the head, then stab low. From Shaolinquan.

yàn zǐ chuān yún 燕子穿云 Swallow Pierces the Clouds: Step up to a one legged stance, extending the opposite hand forward with a rotated reversed stab to shoulder height. From Liuhebafa.

yàn zǐ hán ní 燕子含泥 Swallow Holds Mud in its Beak: circle both hands, pressing outwards, then step forward and press out with the forearm to chest height. From Liuhebafa.

yàn zǐ qǔ shuǐ 燕子取水 Swallow Scoops Water: a drop stance with a threading palm along the outstretched leg. In Xingyiquan, also includes a rise into a groin strike.

yàn zǐ rù lín 燕子入林 Swallow Enters the Forest: step forward with a threading palm strike. From Baguazhang.

yàn zǐ rù yún 燕子入云 Swallow Enters the Clouds: a raised knee stance with an upward threading palm. From Xingyiquan.

yàn zǐ xì shuǐ 燕子戏水 Swallow Plays over the Water: a forward jump into a drop stance, threading the palms up during the jump then threading both palms along forward and back in the drop stance. From Xingyiquan.

yàn zǐ xián ní 燕子衔泥 Swallow Gathers Mud: a low stabbing palm or punch in a closed squat stance. From Xingyiquan.

yàn zǐ xié fēi 燕子斜飞 Swallow Tilts in Flight: drop stance thread the hand along the leg. Similar to yàn zi chāo shuǐ but with the palms facing down. From Liuhebafa.

yàn zǐ zhǎn chì 燕子展翅 Swallow Spreads its Wings: move forward, threading the palms up, then land and open the arms out to front and back at shoulder height. From Wudangquan and Xingyiquan.

yàn zǐ zhuó ní 燕子啄泥 Swallow Dunks its Beak in Mud. 1. Step forward with a low dab with a sword tip. 2. Punch downward in a closed squat stance.

雁 鴈 (rad.172, 196) [雁] (rad.172) **yàn**
 A wild goose, wild geese. For movement names using the actions or qualities of the wild goose, see also under gū yàn.

yàn biè jīn chì 雁别金翅 Wild Goose Pins with its Golden Wing: swing a broadsword, lifting the left knee, then land, swing the blade so that it finishes upright at the left side, tucked behind the shoulder, lifting the right knee and raising the left arm in an upward block. From Taijiquan.

yàn líng dāo 雁翎刀 A goose feather blade: a large broadsword with the tip curved to the point.

yàn luò hé tān 雁落河滩 Wild Goose Lands on the Riverbank: sit into a cross sit stance, opening the arms out to the sides with lifting palms. From Shaolinquan.

yàn luò píng shā 雁落平沙 Wild Goose Lands on the Beach: sit into a cross sit stance and brace out with the forward hand, rolling the shoulder to press the palm out reversed. Protect the face with the other palm. The 100th move of the tiger and crane routine.

佯 (rad.9) **yáng** To feign, pretend; sham.

yáng gōng zhāo fǎ 佯攻招法 Feign with follow up: realistically feign an attack to draw a reaction from an adversary then take advantage with a real attack.

揚 [扬] (rad.64) **yáng** 1. To raise. 2. To throw upwards and scatter; winnow. 3. To spread, one of the walking hands of Chuojiao, see also zǒu shǒu.

yáng biān fú hǔ 扬鞭伏虎 Raise a Whip to Subdue a Tiger: open up the arms, slicing a sword blade out and up to the right side, pointing forward with the left hand. From Wu Taijiquan.

yáng ná fǎ 扬拿法 Winnowing grappling. 1. With the hands or arms, a long, angled power applied to a big leverage throw, wheeling an adversary over. 2. With the legs, also a long swing up, using with the leg to catch an adversary's leg and throw.

From wrestling.

yáng tí 扬蹄 Raise the hooves: to allow the heels to lift when walking. From Baguazhang, where it is considered an error. Also called liàng zhǎng.

楊 [杨] (rad.75) yáng   1. A poplar tree. 2. A surname.

yáng jiā jiàng 杨家将 Yangjiajiang (general Yang) style, a style from Shaanxi province, dating from the northern Song dynasty, mainly practising weapons.

yáng jiā qiāng 杨家枪 Yangjiaqiang (Yang family spear), a style that specialized in the spear, noted as the best in the Ming dynasty book of general Qi Jiguang.

yáng shì tài jí quán 杨式太极拳 Yangshi (Yang's) Taijiquan, attributed to Yang Luchan.

羊 (rad.123) yáng   1. Sheep; goat; ram; ewe. 2. Sheep, as the eighth of the twelve animals from the Chinese zodiac, associated with a twelve year cycle symbolic of the earthly branches. The twelve animals make up a sixty year cycle when combined with the five phases. See also dì zhī, shēng xiào, wǔ xíng. 3. A surname.

yáng jiǎo guǎi 羊角拐 Goat horn flail. See guǎi zi.

yáng jiǎo chǎn tuǐ 羊角铲腿 Goat Horn Digging Leg: slide a kick into the adversary's supporting thigh whilst he is kicking you.

yáng jiǎo zhǎng 羊角掌 Goat horn palm, a hand shape: the index and thumb are open and extended while the other fingers are tucked. From Xingyiquan. Also called bā zì zhǎng, though that is usually something else.

yáng wěi bā zhuì 羊尾巴坠 Hang the Sheep's Tail. See yuán bǎo jiǎo. Also called dǎo jiǎo.

陽 [阳] (rad.170) yáng   Yang (in the continuum of yin and yang). Originally meant the sunny side. Represents the sun, light, masculine, positive principle in nature. The south side of a hill or north bank of a river (where the sun hits from the south). The generative power of the sun. Of the human body, it refers to the back, the parts that would be in the sun if one stood with one's back to the sun, palms turned forward.

yáng bǎ 阳把 Yang grip: holding a short weapon with one hand, palm down, hand on top of the handgrip.

yáng bái 阳白 Acupoint Yangbai (*yang* white), GB14. At the face, one *cun* above the eyebrow, one third up from the eyebrow to the hairline, directly below acupoint Tongkong (on each side). From TCM.

yáng chí (xué) 阳池(穴) Acupoint Yangchi (*yang* pool), SJ4. At the hand, on the back at the wrist crease, in the depression between the tendons of the extensor digitorum and the extensor digiti minimi (on each hand). From TCM.

yáng fǔ 阳辅 Acupoint Yangfu (*yang* assistance), GB38. At the calf, on the outside, four *cun* up from the ankle, in front of the fibula or peroneus brevis muscle (on each leg). From TCM.

yáng gāng 阳纲 Acupoint Yanggang (*yang* headrope), BL48. At the back, level with the depression below the spinous process of the ninth thoracic vertebra, three *cun* lateral to the midline (on each side). From TCM.

yáng gǔ 阳谷 Acupoint Yanggu (*yang* valley), SI5. At the wrist, the outer edge, in the depression between the ulna and the carpals (on each wrist). From TCM.

yáng jiāo 阳交 Acupoint Yangjiao (*yang* intersection), GB35. At the calf, on the outside, seven *cun* up from the ankle, on the rear edge of the fibula, in the groove between the peroneus and soleus muscles (on each leg). From TCM.

yáng jìn 阳劲 *Yang* power: hard power. In contrast to soft power, see also yīn jìn. See also gāng jìn.

yáng líng quán 阳灵泉 Acupoint Yanglingquan (*yang* mound spring), GB34. At the calf, on the outside, at the triangle formed by the head of the fibula with the head of the tibia (on each leg). From TCM. In internal styles, the knees are kept slightly bent to maintain a smooth *qi* flow between upper and lower leg.

yáng míng 阳明 Yang Ming, *Yang* Brightness: the closing *yang* nature sub-type of the *yang* channels, the level between Shao Yang and Tai Yin. It governs uniting of the external level to the interior levels of the body. Containing the stomach and the large intestine, this system regulates digestion and fluid balance. Diagrammed as one *yin* line under two *yang* lines. From TCM.

Y

yáng quán 阳拳 Yang fist, a placement description. See yǎng quán.

yáng xī 阳溪 Acupoint Yangxi (*yang* ravine), LI5. At the wrist crease, where the thumb root protrudes on the back of the wrist. The anatomical snuffbox (on each wrist). From TCM. A sensitive point, pressure here can cause loss of strength as well as pain.

yáng yīn bǎ 阳阴把 Yang Yin grip: holding a long weapon with the hand at the butt palm down and the hand along the shaft palm up.

yáng zhǎng 阳掌 Yang hand. 1. A hand placement description: see yǎng zhǎng. 2. As a technique, in some styles, any strike that uses a backhand.

仰 (rad.9) **yǎng** 1. To face upward. 2. Facing upward.

yǎng dāo 仰刀 Face up broadsword: the blade is edge up. A positional reference, separate from the direction of the strike.

yǎng diǎn 仰点 Facing up poke kick: lean back, pushing the hips into a front poke kick. From Chuojiao, one of its middle-basin kicks.

yǎng quán 仰拳 Facing up fist, a placement description. Fist held horizontal with the fist heart side up, fist back down, knuckles forward. See also yáng quán.

yǎng shēn 仰身 Supine torso, a placement description: position the body face up by leaning back.

yǎng shēn diē 仰身跌 Back drop: drop back so only the upper back contacts the ground, usually kicking with one raised leg in front.

yǎng shēn gǔn dòng xià sǎo biān 仰身滚动下扫鞭 Face up rolling low sweep with the steel whip: on the ground on the back, sweep the whip around low to the ground, pushing up with the right foot to allow the whip to pass beneath the body.

yǎng shēn píng héng 仰身平衡 Supine balance, back lean balance, face up balance: supporting leg straight, lean back to horizontal, lifting the suspended leg straight in front to at least horizontal.

yǎng shēn shàng jià 仰身上架 Leaning framing block up: lean well back and bring a weapon or double weapons up and back, blocking up, the hands behind the head, the weapons higher than the head.

yǎng shēn xià sǎo biān 仰身下扫鞭 Supine low sweep with the steel whip: on the ground on the back, sweep the whip around low to the ground, popping up to allow the whip to pass beneath the body.

yǎng shuāi 仰摔 A back drop, a back fall.

yǎng tóu 仰头 Lift the head: when the head is in contact with an adversary in a clinch, lean the head back to assist in a backwards throw.

yǎng zhǎng 仰掌 Face up palm, supine palm. Refers to a hand placement with the palm up, separate from the direction of the strike. Also called yáng zhǎng.

yǎng zhǎo 仰爪 Bring the arm up, hand in claw shape, palm up, to grab under an adversary's arm.

養 (rad.184) [养] (rad.123) **yǎng** 1. To support, provide for. 2. To raise, grow. 3. To maintain, keep in good repair. 4. To rest, convalesce.

yǎng gōng 养功 Training to nurture health, to nurture, to cultivate, to continue to develop.

yǎng lǎo 养老 1. Acupoint Yanglao (nursing the aged), SI6. At the wrist, where the distal end of the ulna protrudes, 1.5 *cun* up from SI5 (on each hand). From TCM. 2. To provide for one's parents, or for the elderly. 3. To live in retirement.

yǎng shén zhuāng 养神桩 Cultivating spirit stake standing: standing with the backs of the hands at the kidneys, breathing deeply and relaxing. From Yiquan.

yǎng shēn 养身 To enhance health. As training, to continue to develop.

yǎng shēng 养生 To preserve one's health, keep in good health. Life enhancing.

yǎng shēng gōng 养生功 Maintain life training: health exercises for internal regulation, focussing on the meridians and organs. Also called bǎo jiàn gōng.

腰 (rad.130) **yāo** The waist, which includes the lower back, small of the back, kidney area, lumbar area, lumbar sacral area, waist, the entire area between the hips and the ribs (front and back). Sometimes translated as lumbosacral fascial region, but usually simply as waist. In some styles movement of the waist refers to the movement of the muscles in the area between hips and ribs, thus movement of the ribs. In some styles, movement of the waist refers to deep, largely unseen, movement in the lumbar area. In some styles, movement of the waist refers to adjustments between the hip crease and the torso.

yāo bà lán qiāng 腰把拦枪 Waist outer trap with a spear: counter-clockwise circle with press down, keeping the base of the spear at the waist, the shaft on the waist. The spear tip draws a small circle, between hip and shoulder height.

yāo bà ná qiāng 腰把拿枪 Waist inner trap with a spear: clockwise circle with press down, keeping the base of the spear at the waist. The spear tip draws a small circle, between shoulder and hip height.

yāo bù quán 腰步拳 Waist stance punch: turn from horse stance to bow stance, punching forward in a reverse stance. Usually done as a training exercise. From Tantui.

yāo dài 腰带 A belt, a sash.

yāo dāo 腰刀 A waist blade; a broadsword with a long, straight, narrow blade, curving only towards the end to the tip.

yāo gōng 腰功 Back skill. 1. Training of the lower back, waist. 2. The result of a well trained waist area, a strong and skilled waist and back.

yāo jī 腰肌 Lumbar muscles.

yāo kuà 腰胯 Lumbar area, waist to hip joints area.

yāo qí 腰奇 Extraordinary acupoint Yaoqi (lumbar extra), EX-B9. At the buttocks, in the anal cleft, two *cun* above the coccyx, on the midline. From TCM.

yāo rú shé xíng bù sài zhān 腰如蛇行步赛粘 When the waist moves like a snake, the footwork is sticky. A martial saying.

yāo rú zhóu lì, shǒu sì lún xíng 腰如轴立手似轮行 The waist is like an upright axis, and the hands move like the wheel. A martial saying.

yāo shū 腰俞 Acupoint Yaoshu (lumbar transport), DU2. At the buttocks, just at the top of the crack, at the sacro-coccygeal joint, on the midline. From TCM.

yāo sì shé 腰似蛇 The waist is like a snake. From Tongbeiquan, one of its requirements.

yāo suān 腰酸 An aching back, a sore lower back.

yāo tòng 腰痛 Extraordinary acupoint Yaotong (lumbar pain), EX-UE7. Two points at the back of the hand, midpoint between the wrist crease and the knuckles, one between the second and third metacarpals, and one between the fourth and fifth metacarpals (two in each hand, total of four points). From TCM.

yāo wéi shé xíng 腰为蛇行 Waist (torso technique) like a moving snake: one of the basic qualities of many styles.

yāo wéi zhǔ zǎi 腰为主宰 The waist dictates the movement: the movement and power of the waist controls the movement and power of the rest of the body. A requirement in many styles.

yāo yǎn 腰眼 Extraordinary acupoint Yaoyan (lumbar eye), EX-B7. At the waist, level with the depression under the fourth lumbar vertebra, shows as a dimple below the iliac crest, 3.5 *cun* lateral to the midline (on each side). From TCM. One of the main targets on the body.

yāo yáng guān 腰阳关 Acupoint Yaoyangguan (lumbar yang pass), DU3. At the lower back, below the spinous process of the fourth lumbar vertebra, on the midline. From TCM.

yāo yào cuī kuà ér kuà bù nì yāo 腰要催胯而胯不逆腰 Power should flow from the waist to the hip joints, the hips should not run counter to the waist. From Xingyiquan.

yāo yí 腰宜 Extraordinary acupoint Yaoyi, EX-B6. At the waist, level with the depression under the fourth lumbar vertebra, three *cun* lateral to the midline (on each side). From TCM.

yāo zhǎn bái shé 腰斩白蛇 Cut the White Snake around the Waist: a level cut at waist height. May be a bow stance level cut with a sword or a turning level cut with a broadsword into a horse stance.

yāo zhuī 腰椎 Lumbar vertebra, lumbar vertebrae.

yāo zǐ 腰子 The kidneys (colloquial). See also shèn.

Y

摇 [摇] (rad.64) **yáo** To swing, wag; shake; scull.

yáo bǎi 摇摆 To weave: ducking and swinging the body side to side to avoid an attack or grab.

yáo bù rù shǒu 摇步入手 Weaving step entry, a turned out step then a step straight into the centre, shutting down with the lead hand and attacking with the follow-up hand. From Tongbeiquan, one of its seven long range techniques.

yáo chē jiǎo 摇车脚 Swing the Chariot trip: stretch a leg out to throw an adversary, then, when he steps around it to avoid the throw, change grip and use his momentum, sticking your foot in front of his landing foot to trip. From wrestling.

yáo dāo 摇刀 Swing a broadsword: lift the hand to bring the blade around the back, left to right. Used with the larger Bagua broadsword, which cannot roll tightly around the head. From Baguazhang.

yáo fǎ shì lì 摇法试力 Testing power with waving. Can be done in different standing postures or moving steps. From Yiquan.

yáo lóng guī dòng 摇龙归洞 Swaying Dragon Returns to its Cave: standing up, left fist at the hip, right hand forward, snap the elbow to bring the fist in towards the chest. The tenth move of the tiger and crane routine.

yáo lǔ 摇橹 To row, scull. Often used for large circular motions with a big broadsword, when the hand draws a small circle and the tip draws a large circle. This is reminiscent of a rowing action but on a different plane in order to slice. Chinese rowing is done standing up and pushing the oars, then circling back in.

yáo shān shǒu 摇扇手 Wave the Fan hand. See hú dié shǒu.

yáo shēn 摇身 Shake the body, snap. Dodge.

yáo shēn zhǎng 摇身掌 Shake the body palm, one of the palm changes of Baguazhang.

yáo shēn dǐng zhuàng 摇身顶撞 Shake the body, stab and ram with the elbows: with a powerful snap of the body, do a simultaneous forward elbow strike and backwards ramming strike with the elbows.

yáo tóu bǎi wěi 摇头摆尾 Shake the Head and Wag the Tail: fighting by following along naturally with whatever an adversary is doing, faking to be like a fawning dog. Also called yú fǎ.

yáo tuō 摇托 Shake and carry: grab the adversary's arm with one hand while the other hand strikes it upwards strongly, with the palm up.

yáo zhǒu 摇肘 Shake the elbow: bend the elbow and draw a full circle down and out, using the shoulder. Use to encircle and press down on an adversary's arm to prepare a counter attack.

齩 (rad.211) **[咬]** (rad.30) **yǎo** 1. To bite. 2. To snap at.

yǎo yá qiē chǐ 咬牙切齿 To clench and grind the teeth, gnash the teeth. An error in most styles.

要 (rad.146) **yào** 1. Important, essential. 2. To ask for. 3. To want. Need.

yào diǎn 要点 Important points: pointers in written text of details to watch out for, often following the description of movements.

yào jué 要诀 Essentials: concise phrase that reminds the student of something essential to the style. Usually called poems or verses in English because they are often rhyming, as they were originally passed down orally.

yào lǐng 要领 Important points, essentials, requirements.

yào shǒu 要手 Asking hand: to extend a hand in a certain way to elicit a predicted response from your adversary, thus reducing your possible choice of reactions. See also liú shǒu.

鹞 [鷂] (rad.196) **yào** A sparrow hawk, goshawk. Used in movement names, particularly those that combine agility with speed and power.

yào luò píng shā 鹞落平沙 Sparrow Hawk Lands on the Sandy Beach: retreat to a drop stance and push out along the extended leg, punching the other fist behind. From Wudangquan.

yào xíng 鹞形 Sparrow hawk, or Goshawk, form of Xingyiquan, containing a short combination of moves with a smooth cannon punch, a high drill, and a rolling body escape.

yào yǒu zuān tiān zhī shì 鹞有钻天之势 Sparrow hawks have the power of spiraling to the heavens. A quality sought in Xingyiquan's sparrow hawk form.

yào zǐ chuān lín 鹞子穿林 Sparrow Hawk Threads through the Woods. 1. Advancing piercing palms connected to turning piercing palms. From Wudangquan. 2. Empty stance high frame piercing palm. From Piguaquan.

yào zǐ fān shēn 鹞子翻身 Sparrow Hawk Wheels Over. 1. In Xingyiquan, a bracing, coiling turn, finishing with an extended fist. 2. In Baguazhang, an elbow control, grabbing an adversary's wrist and twisting his elbow with pressure from your elbow to take down. 3. In Shaolinquan, with the right hand near the tip of a spear and the left hand back along the shaft, jump up and spin around to strike down behind with the butt.

yào zǐ pū ān chún shì 鹞子扑鹌鹑式 Sparrow Hawk Pounces on a Quail model. One of twenty-four classic spear moves. Most spear routines will have a move with a like name. In general, this name refers to low drawing actions near the ground, as if pushing aside grass.

yào zǐ pū chún 鹞子扑鹑 Sparrow Hawk Pounces on a Quail: lift the left knee and hook a staff tip by it, then land and bring the staff around to strike downward. From Baguazhang.

yào zǐ rù lín 鹞子入林 Sparrow Hawk Enters the Woods. 1. An advancing step into an aligned stance pounding punch, see also pào quán. From Xingyiquan. 2. A knee strike with an upper block, landing to bow stance with a pull down. From Chuojiao.

yào zǐ shù shēn 鹞子束身 Sparrow Hawk Folds its Wings: a forward driving shin rubbing step with a crossing straight or dropping punch. From Xingyiquan.

yào zǐ zhǎn chì 鹞子展翅 Sparrow Hawk Spreads its Wings: drop to a horse stance and brace out with both arms, palms over the knees. From Xingyiquan.

yào zǐ zhuā jiān 鹞子抓肩 Sparrow Hawk Grabs the Shoulder: step in to trap an adversary's leg, grabbing his shoulder and pulling it down to the side. From Baguazhang.

yào zǐ zuān lín 鹞子钻林 Sparrow Hawk Enters the Woods: a flat stab with a broadsword, first rolling the body under the blade.

yào zǐ zuān tiān 鹞子钻天 Sparrow Hawk Pierces the Sky: a rising drilling fist or palm, may be up to a raised knee stance. From Baguazhang and Xingyiquan.

掖 (rad.64) yē To steal in, tuck in, thrust in between.

yē quán 掖拳 Thrust in fist: punch with the arm rolled, the fist eye down, knuckles forward.

yē ná fǎ 掖拿法 Stealing grappling hold: whether grabbed or grabbing, quickly sneak the hand into a place inconvenient to an adversary, like down behind his back. From wrestling.

yē zhǎng 掖掌 Stealing palm: slide the hand along the ribs then strike low to the side with the heel of the palm, palm forward and down. In some styles, first extend the arm, then suddenly change direction, rotating the arm to strike with the palm. In Baguazhang, rotate and slide the hand on the ribs, then drop it down to the side, striking with the heel of the palm to the hip crease of an adversary.

yē zhǒu 掖肘 Stealing elbow: to press the elbow into an adversary's chest at the collar bone to directly take him down backwards. From wrestling.

野 (rad.166) yě 1. Wild; untamed; undomesticated. 2. Open country; the open.

yě jī ào chì 野鸡拗翅 Break the Wild Chicken's Wing: with an arm lock, take an adversary face down to the ground, then twist his arm, pulling his wrist up and pushing his elbow down. From Qinna.

yě jī sōu tiān 野鸡搜天 Wild chicken seeks the sky. See #1 of wū lóng jiǎo zhǔ.

yě mǎ chuǎng cáo 野马闯槽 Wild Horse Charges a Manger. 1. Drive forward to get in close with a scooping punch, often to the groin. From Baguazhang. 2. Charge forward pulling an adversary's arm down while shoving with the shoulder. From Baguazhang, one of its sixty-four hands 3. Drive forward with a double shoving palm, heels of the palms together. From Wudangquan.

yě mǎ fēn fēng 野马分风 Wild Horse Separates the Wind: Separate the hands forward and back, angled high and low, while moving forward to

yě mǎ fēn zōng 野马分鬃 Wild Horse Tosses its Mane. 1. Separate the hands forward and back, angled high and low, while moving forward to bow stance. From Taijiquan. 2. In some styles: move forward maintaining pressure with both hands forward. Used either as a control or a throw.

yě mǎ jié jiǎo 野马截脚 Wild Horse Jams with its Foot: a transversely turned kick to the knee or shin to jam a kick.

yě mǎ shàng cáo 野马上槽 Wild Horse Advances on its Manger: sit to empty stance, circle, then push the hands forward, front (smooth side) hand palm forward at shoulder height, rear hand at its elbow. From Shaolinquan.

yě mǎ tán tí 野马弹蹄 Wild Horse Snaps out a Hoof: a strong jamming side kick to stomach height.

yě mǎ tiào dòng 野马跳洞 Wild Horse Leaps the Ravine: jumping forward, pushing a sword forward with the action. From Taijiquan. Also called yú tiào lóng mén. There is more emphasis on a long leap with the horse name.

yě mǎ zhuàng cáo 野马撞槽 Wild Horse Rams the Manger. See #2 of yě mǎ chuǎng cáo.

yě yuán xiàn guǒ 野猿献果 Wild Ape Presents Fruit: step up on one leg, presenting the fists, fist hearts up.

夜 [夜] (rad.8) **yè** Night; evening.

yè chā 夜叉 Yecha, Yaksha: a malevolent spirit in Buddhism; a ferocious looking person. In Buddhism, also guardians of temples. A broad class of nature-spirits. Also translated as sea monsters and night ghosts. Used in movement names.

yè chā chū shǒu 夜叉出手 Yaksha Puts out his Hand: step forward with a stomp, pushing forward with the edge of the palm. While doing this, slice the other hand up then pull it back to the waist. From Shaolinquan.

yè chā guò hé 夜叉过河 Yaksha Crosses the River: step to reverse bow stance and swing the reverse hand up with a lifting palm, swinging the other back with a hook hand. From Shaolinquan.

yè chā nào fáng 夜叉闹房 Yaksha Teases on a Wedding Night: jump lightly forward and sit to a full squat kicking stance, circling and swinging the arms, ending with the rear arm blocking up above the head. From Shaolinquan.

yè chā tàn hǎi 夜叉探海 Yaksha Reaches into the Sea. 1. A low striking palm or dab with a sword. 2. A high reaching palm. 3. An arm lock. 4. A squat with a hooking push. From Piguaquan.

yè chā tàn hǎi shì 夜叉探海式 Yaksha Reaches into the Sea model. One of twenty-four classic spear moves. Most spear routines will have a move with a like name. In general, this name refers to holding a spear ready for defense.

yè chā tàn lù 夜叉探路 Yaksha Explores the Road: a high extended stab with a spear, standing up high and moving forward.

yè xíng gōng 夜行功 Night walking skill. See fēi xíng shù.

液 (rad.85) **yè** Liquid; fluid; juice. The thick *yin* fluids, such as mucus, often translated as humours when referring to the fluids in the body.

yè kuī 液亏 Humour depletion, a pattern applied in channel diagnosis. From TCM.

yè mén 液门 Acupoint Yemen (humour gate), SJ2. At the hand, on the back between the knuckles of the ring and little finger, proximal to the web, level to where the knuckle bends (on each hand). From TCM.

腋 (rad.130) **yè** The armpit, armpits; axilla.

yè wō 腋窝 The armpit, armpits, axilla. An easy target. Also called yè xià.

yè xià 腋下 See yè wō.

yè xià qiāng 腋下枪 Spear under the armpit: from crossed arms, stab out with the left hand, sliding the right to the butt, stepping forward. Also called huáng lóng chū dòng.

葉 (rad.140) [叶] (rad.30) **yè** A leaf, leaves; foliage. A leaf-like thing.

yè dī cáng huā 叶低藏花 Hide a Flower under a Leaf. 1. A poking technique of the hand under the armpit, also a close jamming technique in preparation for a throw. Sometimes also refers to a similar hand placement down at the waist. 2. A poking kick to the armpit. From Baguazhang and Chuojiao. Also called zhèng tuō diǎn. 3. To swing a steel whip, sliding it from left to right across the back and head, finishing with it wrapped around the waist. 4. Sometimes used for the Taijiquan move Fist under Elbow: see zhǒu dǐ chuí. 5. A drop stance holding a broadsword or sword behind the body. 6. To tuck a broadsword in close to the body prior to a stab. 7. A cross sit stance, extending a sword blade out flat behind.

yè dī cáng lián 叶低藏莲 Hide a Flower under a Lotus: stepping forward to punch out from under a stab. From Liuhebafa.

yè dǐ tōu táo 叶低偷桃 Steal a Peach from Under a Leaf. 1. Extend the adversary's arm and slide your other hand in to strike his groin. 2. Grab the adversary's wrist by crossing the hands then twist it over. Both from Baguazhang.

yè lǐ cáng huā tuǐ 叶里藏花腿 Hide a Flower in a Leaf kick: poke kick with the hands forward to hold or strike an adversary.

yè luò guī gùn 叶落归棍 Falling Leaves Settle: drop into a drop stance and sweep the staff fully around high then across at shin height. From Shaolinquan staff.

yè xià cáng huā 叶下藏花 Hide a flower under a leaf: swing an arm up to clear and push the other hand out, then bring it back to hide under at the armpit. From Shaolinquan. Also often interchangeable with yè dī cáng huā.

一 (rad.1) yī   One; single; alone; whole.

yī cùn cháng yī cùn qiáng 一寸长一寸强 An inch longer is an inch stronger. A martial saying. Whoever can get in the furthest will get in first and have the advantage. This applies to bare hand or the length of a weapon.

yī cùn xiǎo yī cùn qiǎo 一寸小一寸巧 An inch shorter is an inch smarter. A martial saying. A small weapon is agile.

yī dòng wú yǒu bù dòng, yī jìng wú yǒu bù jìng 一动无有不动，一静无有不静 Once you start moving there is nothing that does not move, once you stop there is nothing that keeps moving. A martial saying. Describes full body coordination.

yī jí cái pàn yuán 一级裁判员 Level one judge: a classification within China, a mid level judge, qualified to judge at provincial level competitions.

yī jí jiào liàn yuán 一级教练员 Level one coach: a classification within China, a mid level coach, qualified to coach both full time and spare time athletes.

yī jí wǔ shì 一级武士 A level one martial artist, a high level of athlete classification within China: an athlete who has achieved high scores and placings in national competitions (but a lower level than martial hero, see also wǔ yīng).

yī lù 一路 The first route, a name in some styles for the first routine of the style. Used in Chen Taijiquan, Chaquan, Huaquan, Shaolin, Tongbeiquan routines, among others.

yī mǎ dāng xiān 一马当先 One horse comes first. 1. To gallop at the head, to take the lead. 2. A horse stance outer block.

yī mǎ sān jiàn 一马三箭 Three Arrows Shot from One Horse: a combination of three quick upright punches (see also bēng quán): advancing in short stance, retreating in cross stance, then advancing in smooth step. From Xingyiquan.

yī péng hǔ jiù dì fēi lái 一掤虎就地飞来 A Quiver of Tigers Flies On the Spot: swing a big cutter in a full circle over the head, holding the base end with both hands together. From Chen Taijiquan.

yī qì guàn tōng 一气贯通 Qi permeates the whole body, uniting all.

yī qì hē chéng 一气呵成 Completed in one breath: no break in continuity during the performance of a sequence of movements, each movement flowing smoothly to the next, power maintained in held postures.

yī mèn 一闷 A quick snap and bend of the waist to initiate a throw.

yī qiāng fēn xīn 一枪分心 Split the Heart with One Spear. See lán ná zhā.

yī rì liàn yī rì gōng, yī rì bù liàn shí rì kōng 一日练一日功，一日不练十日空 For one day's training you gain one day's skill, if you miss a day you've wasted ten. A martial saying.

yī sǎo sān xián 一扫三贤 Take out Three Worthies with One Sweep: walk around cutting with a sword blade angled upwards. From Qingping sword.

Y

yī shēn bèi wǔ gōng 一身备五弓 The body is made of five bows. See wǔ gōng.

yī tiáo biān 一条鞭 One whip: a backfist. Also called fǎn bèi chuí.

yī xiàn chuān 一线穿 Pierce in one line: a light skills training method. Start with running with weights strapped to the forearms and shins, then walk around a filled tub gradually emptying the tub. Another is to walk a tightrope, gradually loosening it or speeding up.

yī xīng pāo chuí 一星抛捶 The first Star Throwing Punch: shift into a left bow stance and do a swinging rising punch almost on line with the front leg with the right fist, the left swinging behind. The 85th move of the tiger and crane routine. The same as èr xīng pāo chuí on the other side.

yī zhǐ méi 一指梅 One finger plum, a hand shape. See dān zhǐ. Also called dān zhǐ kuài.

yī zhī bù 一枝步 One branch stance: like a drop stance, but with the feet slightly closer than a full drop stance, and the stance slightly higher. See also pū bù 仆步 and pū bù 铺步.

yī zhù dǐng tiān 一柱顶天 Support the Sky with One Post: grab the adversary's wrist in the same hand (right to right), step in and tuck your shoulder under his armpit, stretching his arm out and twisting it palm out. Lift and pull down to control or dislocate the shoulder. From Qinna.

yī zì bù 一字步 Character One (straight line) stance: 1. An empty stance with the front heel on the ground. 2. A category of stances that have the feet in line, such as horse, bow, empty, drop.

yī zì chā 一字叉 Character One (straight line) splits: side splits. See héng chā.

yī zì jīn qiāng 一字金枪 Character One (straight line) Golden Spear: a jump back spin kick, first tucking the knees up, then shooting out a leg to connect with the outer edge of the heel.

yī zì mǎ bù 一字马步 Character One (straight line) horse stance: a horse stance with the feet turned out to form a straight line. From southern styles.

yī zì tuǐ 一字腿 Character One (straight line) legs: walking forwards, every fourth step swing one leg up to the nose with the sole of the foot up, both legs straight, so that the legs form a straight line. A leg training exercise from Tongbeiquan.

醫 (rad.164) [医] (rad.22) yī   1. Medical service; medical science. 2. Doctor. 3. Medicine.

yī shēng 医生 A doctor.

yī wù rén yuán 医务人员 The medical team at an event.

yī yuàn 医院 A hospital, clinic.

挜 (rad.64) yí   To hit, to slap.

移 (rad.115) yí   To move, remove, shift.

yí bù 移步 Move the stance. See xià chuài tuǐ.

yí mǎ 移马 Move the stance. See xià chuài tuǐ.

yí huā jiē mù 移花接木 Move a Flower to Graft a Branch. 1. Hook out the foot, lifting and rotating the same side arm, palm up, sliding the other hand through. From Baguazhang. 2. To respond to a direct attack with a piercing palm. 3. Respond to a wrist grab by grabbing an adversary's wrist then using both hands to reverse his grip and force a release. 4. Pull back and punch immediately.

乙 (rad.5) yǐ   1. The second of the ten Celestial Stems, used in combination with the twelve Terrestrial Branches to designate years, months, days, and hours. Someone. See also dì zhī, tiān gān. 2. Second in a list when listing using the celestial stems, equivalent to B in English when listing alphabetically.

yǐ chǒu 乙丑 The years 1985, 1925, and so on, for sixty year cycles.

yǐ hài 乙亥 The years 1995, 1935, and so on, for sixty year cycles.

yǐ mǎo 乙卯 The years 1975, 1915, and so on, for sixty year cycles.

yǐ sì 乙巳 The years 1965, 1905, and so on, for sixty year cycles.

yǐ wèi 乙未 The years 2015, 1955, and so on, for sixty year cycles.

yǐ yǒu 乙酉 The years 2005, 1945, and so on, for sixty year cycles.

yǐ zǔ 乙组 The B level athletes at a competition, if the competition is organized by skill level.

yǐ zǔ tào lù 乙组套路 The B level routines of the compulsory performance wushu routines.

以 (rad.9) yǐ   1. By means of. 2. Because of.

yǐ gāng wéi zhǔ 以刚为主 To emphasise hardness; to rely on strength.

yǐ gōng dài shǒu 以攻代守 To use attack as a defense: to defend against an attack with attacking techniques, both breaking the attack and attacking at the same time.

yǐ jìng dài dòng 以静待动 To wait calmly for an adversary to make the first move.

yǐ kuài zhì màn 以快制慢 To move quickly to beat an adversary who hesitates. To beat slowness with speed.

yǐ nèi qì cuī wài xíng 以内气催外形 To use internal *qi* to drive the external form.

yǐ qì yùn shēn 以气运身 To move the body by means of *qi*: to permeate the body with *qi* through intent, thus enabling movement.

yǐ róu jì gāng 以柔济刚 To prepare a hard counter attack with absorption of the attack.

yǐ róu kè gāng 以柔克刚 To overcome hard attacks with pliancy.

yǐ róu wéi zhǔ 以柔为主 To emphasise softness; to rely on pliancy.

yǐ tuì wéi jìn 以退为进 To advance by means of retreating. 1. Step and dissipate an attack while preparing the counter. 2. Block overhead with a spear, then take it down to the chest in the right hand, then spin around and stab out with full extension with just the right hand. From Shaolinquan.

yǐ xiǎo zhì dà 以小制大 To use small efficient movements to control a larger attack.

yǐ xīn xíng yì, yǐ yì dǎo qì, yǐ qì yùn shēn 以心形意, 以意导气, 以气运身 The heart gives form to the intent, the intent leads the *qi*, and the *qi* moves the body.

yǐ yì dài láo 以逸待劳 Wait at Ease for Exhaustion. To stay calm while the enemy exhausts himself. The fourth of the Thirty-six Stratagems of Warfare, which apply to many situations.

yǐ yì dǎo qì 以意导气 To permeate the body with *qi* through intent; use intent to lead *qi*.

yǐ yì xíng qì 以意行气 To control the movement of *qi* through intent; use intent to lead *qi*.

yǐ zhèng qū xié 以正驱斜 Use the direct to drive the angle: position yourself to face directly to the side or back of an adversary to attack. From Baguazhang.

yǐ zhuān cháng jìn gōng 以专长进攻 The tactic of using your strengths to attack: to focus on using the techniques at which you excel.

yǐ zǒu wéi yòng 以走为用 Use walking as your technique. A martial saying, particularly in Baguazhang.

yǐ zǒu zhì dí 以走制敌 Use movement to control your adversary. A martial saying. Also means to use walking to control your adversary.

倚 (rad.9) yǐ   1. To lean on or against; rest on or against. 2. Sometimes means leaning as an error in a stance that should be upright.

yǐ mǎ wèn lù 倚马问路 Lean on a Horse to Ask the Way: reach out with the palms up, one in front of the other, the rear hand under the front elbow. From Baguazhang and Wudangquan.

yǐ shān jǐ kào 倚山挤靠 Lean on a Mountain: step in to press with arms and body to throw. From Baguazhang, one of its sixty-four hands.

億 [亿] (rad.9) yì   A hundred million.

yì xī 億僖 Acupoint Yixi (millionfold happiness), BL45. At the back, level with the depression below the spinous process of the sixth thoracic vertebra, three *cun* lateral to the midline (on each side). From TCM.

意 (rad.61) yì   Will, intent; meaning; idea. The intentional mind, 'mind intention', the part of your mind that expresses your intentions. Associated with the Spleen, and with the character attributes of organized, logical thought.

yì bù kōng huí 意不空回 Don't retract without intent. A martial saying. Strike with purpose, retract with purpose. Don't strike out blindly, don't retract without thinking.

yì dào qì dào, qì dào shēn dòng 意到气到, 气

Y

到身动 Where the intent goes the *qi* goes, and when the *qi* arrives the body can move. A martial saying.

yì duàn shén lián 意断神连 When the intent is interrupted the spirit goes on smoothly. A quality sought in martial movement.

yì fā shén chuán, xīn dòng xíng suí 意发神传，心动形随 When the intent initiates the spirit permeates, the will acts and the body follows. A martial saying.

yì hé yú qì 意合于气 Intent combines with *qi*. From Liuhebafa, one of its principles.

yì niàn 意念 An idea; thought.

yì qì fēng fā 意气风发 The wind of mind and *qi* issues forth. 1. High-spirited and vigorous. 2. Jump up, turning and stabbing a spear behind, the left knee tucked up and the right leg straight.

yì qì jūn lái gǔ ròu chén 意气君来骨肉臣 The will and *qi* rule the muscles and bones. A martial saying.

yì quán 意拳 Yiquan (intention fist), attributed to Wang Xiangzhai, developed from Xingyiquan. Usually called Yiquan in English. Also known as **dà chéng quán**.

yì shè 意舍 Acupoint Yishe (abode of intent), BL49. At the back, level with the depression below the spinous process of the eleventh thoracic vertebra, three *cun* lateral to the midline (on each side). From TCM.

yì shí sàng shī 意识丧失 To lose consciousness.

yì xíng tōng 意形通 Mind and structure communicate: the intent controls the mechanical body, and the body reciprocates with kinesthetic awareness.

yì yú qì hé 意与气合 The intent harmonizes, or works together with, the *qi*. One of the six harmonies. See also **liù hé**.

易 (rad.72) **yì** 1. To change. 2. Easy.

yì gǔ 易骨 Change the bones. The first stage of training, to become strong. See also **xǐ suǐ**, **yì jīn**.

yì jīn 易筋 Change the tendons. The second stage of training, to clear and lengthen muscle, tendon, and ligament. See also **xǐ suǐ**, **yì gǔ**.

yì jīn gōng 易筋功 Training to change the tendons, make them strong. The hard skills of striking with bone edges of the body.

yì jīn jìng shí èr shì 易筋经十二势 The twelve exercises of the Classic of Tendon Changing, internal strength and health exercises.

嗌 (rad.108) **yì** 1. The original meaning is the throat, or to quarrel, or to choke. 2. Specifically in the martial arts, a shout used in southern styles to gain or express power in a technique.

義 (rad.123) [**义**] (rad.3) **yì** 1. Justice. 2. Righteous; just. 3. Righteousness, one of the character traits expected of martial artists.

翳 (rad.124) **yì** 1. Nebula, corneal opacity. 2. A screen.

yì fēng 翳风 Acupoint Yifeng (wind screen), SJ17. At the head, just under the ear lobe, in the depression between two tendons, between the mandible and the mastoid process (on each side). From TCM. A sensitive point, striking too hard and accurately can rupture the artery.

yì míng 翳明 Extraordinary acupoint Yiming (bright screen), EX-HN14. At the nape of the neck, one *cun* behind acupoint Yifeng. From TCM.

藝 [**艺**] (rad.140) **yì** Skill. Art. Talent. Craft.

yì gāo dǎn dà 艺高胆大 When people are skilled they are bold. A martial saying.

言意 (rad.149) **yì** Used in acupoint Yixi.

yì xī 言意 言喜 Acupoint Yixi (BL45). On the back, to each side, three *cun* lateral to the spine, below the sixth thoracic protrusion. From TCM.

殷 (rad.79) **yīn** 1. Abundance; abundant. 2. Rich. 3. Eager; ardent.

yīn mén 殷门 Acupoint Yinmen (gate of abundance), BL37. At the back of the thigh, in the belly of the hamstring, six *cun* under acupoint Chengfu (on each leg). From TCM.

陰 [阴] (rad.170) **yīn** *Yin* (in the continuum of *yin* and *yang*). Originally meant the shady side. Represents the moon, darkness, the feminine, negative principle in nature. The back side; hidden; private parts. The north of a hill or south bank of a river (in the shade with the sun in the south). The reflective power of the moon. On the human body, it refers to the front, the parts that would be in shade if one stood with one's back to the sun, palms turned forward.

yīn bǎ 阴把 *Yin* grip. 1. Holding the shaft of a long weapon with the palms down, thumb webs pointing towards each other. 2. Holding a short weapon with the thumb web away from the guard, towards the base. Both also called fǎn bà. 3. Holding a short weapon's grip with the palm up, hand under the grip.

yīn bāo 阴包 Acupoint Yinbao (*yin* bladder), LR9. At the thigh, on the inside, four *cun* above the end of the femur, between the vastus medialis and the sartorius (on each leg). From TCM.

yīn dū 阴都 Acupoint Yindu (*yin* metropolis), KI19. At the abdomen, four *cun* above the navel, 0.5 *cun* lateral to the midline (on each side). From TCM.

yīn gǔ 阴谷 Acupoint Yingu (*yin* valley), KI10. At the knee, in the depression behind, to the medial end of the popliteal crease, between the tendons of the semitendinosus and semi-membranosus muscles (on each leg). From TCM.

yīn jiāo 阴交 Acupoint Yinjiao (*yin* intersection), RN7. At the abdomen, one *cun* below the navel, on the midline. From TCM.

yīn jìn 阴劲 Hidden, unexpressed power. See also yáng jìn.

yīn lián 阴髎 Acupoint Yinlian (*yin* corner), LR11. At the groin, the root of the thigh, below the hip joint, the outer edge of the adductor longus, two *cun* below acupoint Qichong (on each side). From TCM.

yīn líng quán 阴陵泉 Acupoint Yinlingquan (*yin* mound spring), SP9. At the calf, just inside the knee by the depression between the back edge of the tibia and the front edge of the gastrocnemius muscle (on each leg). From TCM.

yīn quán 阴拳 *Yin* fist, placement description: fist held horizontally with the fist heart down.

yīn shì 阴市 Acupoint Yinshi (*yin* market), ST33. At the thigh, three *cun* up from the outer edge of the patella (on each leg). From TCM.

yīn xī 阴郄 Acupoint Yinxi (*yin* cleft), HT6. At the palm side of the wrist, 0.5 *cun* up from the wrist crease, on the little finger side (on each arm). From TCM.

yīn yáng 阴阳 *Yin* and *Yang*, the foundation theory of much of Chinese thought, and particularly the root concept of many styles of wushu. See also yīn and yáng separately.

yīn yáng bā pán zhǎng 阴阳八盘掌 *Yinyang Bapanzhang* (*yinyang* eight basins palm), a branch of Baguazhang. Attributed to Liu Baozhen, a student of Dong Haichuan, from Hebei province.

yīn yáng bǎ 阴阳把 1. *Yin Yang* grip: holding a long weapon with the hand at the butt end palm up and the hand along the shaft palm down. 2. *Ying Yang* hand strike: palms together, striking out to the side. Commonly used in Che style Xingyiquan.

yīn yáng kāi hé shǒu 阴阳开合手 *Yin Yang* open and close hands: intercept an attack with the palms up and close, then turn the palms down and open them so one keeps defending and the other strikes. From Xingyiquan.

yīn yáng wéi mǔ 阴阳为母 Utilize *yin* and *yang* as the foundation for all body structures, movements and techniques. One of the principles of Xingyiquan, also applies to many styles.

yīn yáng yú shì 阴阳鱼式 *Yin Yang* fish model: circle-walking and changes done seeking the movement and manner of the *Yin Yang* fish. From Baguazhang. See also yīn yáng yú zhǎng.

yīn yáng yú zhǎng 阴阳鱼掌 *Yin Yang* fish palm: pressing the front palm out in front of the chest (or higher) and the rear palm out from the lower back (especially while circle-walking). The power both wraps and presses outward. From Baguazhang. Also called hēi xióng bèi guān, hù xīn zhǎng, yīn yàng zhuǎn zhǎng (specific to circle-walking).

yīn yáng zhuàn zhǎng 阴阳转掌 *Yin Yang* turning palm, specific to circle-walking. From Baguazhang. See yīn yáng yú zhǎng.

yīn zhǎng 阴掌 *Yin* palm. 1. As hand placement:

palm held face down, irrespective of the direction of the strike. 2. As a technique (in some styles), any technique that strikes with the palm centre.

寅 (rad.40) **yín**   The third of the twelve Terrestrial Branches, used in combination with the ten Celestial Stems to designate years, months, days, and hours. For the sixty year cycles, see also under bǐng yín, gēng-, jiǎ-, rèn-, wù-. The period of the day from 3:00 a.m. to 5:00 a.m. See also dì zhī, tiān gān.

yín shí 寅时 The period of the day from 3:00 a.m. to 5:00 a.m. (3:00 to 5:00).

銀 [银] (rad.167) **yín**   Silver.

yín shé pán shēn 银蛇盘身 Silver Snake Coils around the Body: tie up strikes to front and rear. From Piguaquan.

yín shé rù dòng 银蛇入洞 Silver Snake Enters its Hole: spin to a crossed seated stance, spinning a sword in a full circle, tip leading, completing with a low stab. From Yangjia sword.

yín shé tù xìn 银蛇吐信 Silver Snake Spits its Tongue: press an adversary's wrist back to hyper-flex it.

齦 [龈] (rad.211) **yín**   Gum, the gums (in the mouth).

yín jiāo 龈交 Acupoint Yinjiao (gum intersection), DU28. Inside the upper lip, just above the gum, on the midline. This is the final point on the Governor Vessel channel. From TCM.

引 (rad.57) **yǐn**   1. To lead, guide. To pull; to attract. To draw; stretch. 2. To draw an adversary in once it is clear he cannot escape your grasp. 3. Draw in. From Taijiquan, one of its four principles of push hands, see also sì zé. 4. To lure in, entice.

yǐn gōng 引弓 To draw a bow.

yǐn jìn 引劲 Guiding power: a power that leads or guides an adversary's by sticking to his attack and adding to it. Uses the same direction and level of power of an adversary to redirect him past his target.

yǐn jìn luò kōng 引劲落空 To draw an adversary's attack into emptiness.

yǐn jǐng 引颈 To jut the neck forward, stick out the jaw. An error in most styles.

yǐn shǒu 引手 Lure: feint with the hand or hands to draw an attack from an adversary.

yǐn shǒu zhǎng 引手掌 Luring palm, a hand shape: the fingers together and naturally straight, slightly closed towards the palm, the thumb tucked in. From Tongbeiquan.

yǐn tuǐ 引腿 Enticing leg: a kick used as a fake. From Chuojiao, one of its middle-basin kicks.

yǐn tuǐ hòu chuài 引腿后踹 Enticing leg and back kick: a fake followed by a back thrust kick. From Chuojiao, one of its middle-basin kicks.

yǐn yòu 引诱 To lure, to entice. In martial arts, yǐn often has this meaning when used alone.

yǐn zhǎng 引掌 Guiding palm: bring the hand over to the opposite shoulder in an upright palm. From Chaquan.

隱 [隐] (rad.170) **yǐn**   Hidden, concealed. Lurking.

yǐn bái 隐白 Acupoint Yinbai (hidden white), SP1. At the inside of the big toe, 0.1 *cun* from the toenail (on each foot). From TCM.

yǐn shēn kào 隐身靠 Hidden body lean, a shoulder technique: open up the adversary's arms, quickly get the body in close and strike his chest with the shoulder.

印 (rad.26) **yìn**   1. A seal, a stamp, a chop. 2. To print, to stamp. 3. An imprint. The traditional and simplified characters have a slight difference, but the input system doesn't make the distinction.

yìn táng 印堂 Extraordinary acupoint Yintang (hall of impression), EX-HN3. At the face, on the forehead between the eyebrows. From TCM. A sensitive point and an easy target. Striking here induces dizziness, but too hard may cause death. Colloquially called ní wán gōng.

yìn zhǎng 印掌 Stamping palm: a forward thrust to strike with the heel of the palm, palm open. From Wing Chun.

應 (rad.61) [应] (rad.53) **yīng**   1. Answer; respond. 2. Comply with. 3. Suit. 4. Deal with, cope with. 5. Should, ought to, must. Also pronounced yìng.

yīng dé fēn 应得分 The deserved score: the score of a Taolu competitor before the possible extra points are taken off by the head judge.

膺 (rad.130) **yīng**   1. The breast (formal). 2. To bear; to receive (formal).

yīng chuāng 膺窗 Acupoint Yingchuang (breast window), ST16. At the chest, on the chest plate, in the third intercostal space, four *cun* lateral to the midline (on each side). From TCM. A sensitive point, striking it can induce breathlessness and can shock the arteries, veins, and nerves in the chest. Hitting too hard may shock the heart and stop the blood supply.

鶯 [莺] (rad.196) **yīng**   Oriole; greenfinch. For more movement names using the oriole, see also under huáng yīng.

yīng bǔ yàn què 莺捕燕雀 Oriole Catches Swallows and Sparrows: step forward into a full squat empty stance, reaching the body forward, rounding the back, and dropping the head to reach a sword as far forward as possible. From Qingping sword.

鷹 [鹰] (rad.196) **yīng**   An eagle, eagles. For more movement names using the actions or qualities of the eagle, see also under huáng yīng, lǎo-.

yīng shì 鹰势 Eagle essence: circle-walking and changes done seeking the essence and being of the eagle. From Baguazhang.

yīng xíng 鹰形 Eagle form: stepping into a dragon riding stance, pulling down with both hands, front hand at the apex of the triangulation to take down the adversary. From Xingyiquan.

yīng xióng dǒu zhì 鹰熊斗智 Eagle and Bear in a Battle of Wits: bring a sword in a full circle then lift the knee and draw back at head height, looking down to the angle. From Taijiquan.

yīng yì gōng 鹰翼功 Eagle wings training method. 1. Stand in horse stance holding sandbags up on the elbows, which are extended out to the side, flexed, with the fists facing each other in front of the body. May also toss the bags. 2. Stand between two large hanging sandbags and strike them with the backs of the elbows.

yīng yǒu zhuō ná zhī jì 鹰有捉拿之技 Eagles have the talent of grasping. A quality sought in Xingyiquan's eagle form.

yīng zhuā gōng 鹰爪功 Eagle talon skills and training methods. Usually called eagle claw training in English.

yīng zhuǎ quán 鹰爪拳 Yingzhuaquan (eagle talon fist), an animal imitative style originating in Hebei province, related to Fanzi style. Usually called eagle claw in English.

yīng zhuā zhǎng 鹰爪掌 Eagle talon palm, as hand shape: fingers slightly spread and extended, palm rounded, thumb web open. Usually called eagle claw in English.

yīng zhuō 鹰捉 Eagle grasp. 1. As a hand shape: fingers and thumb bent, palm and thumb spread, fingers together. 2. As a technique: grasping using the eagle hand shape. 3. One of the body requirements of Xingyiquan: the hand goes out like a grappling iron and never comes back empty.

鸚 [鹦] (rad.196) **yīng**   A parrot, parrots.

yīng wǔ zhuó lì 鹦鹉啄粒 Parrot Pecks Grain: turn and shift back, cut with the side of a sword blade to the outside of the knee as the right foot touches down in empty stance, left hand pointing forward above the head, to cut the adversary's arm or wrist. From Qingping sword.

營 (rad.86) [营] (rad.140) **yíng**   1. A camp. Barracks. 2. To build. 3. To manage.

yíng qì 营气 Managing *qi*, operational *qi*: liquid that is generated in the spleen/ stomach area and moves into the blood stream. It serves to nourish and manage the whole body.

迎 (rad.162) **yíng**   1. To welcome; go to meet; greet. 2. As one of the eight attack and defense models, to meet the attack head on. See also bā zì gōng fáng fǎ zé.

yíng fēng zhāo yáng zhǎng 迎封朝阳掌 Welcome the Rising Sun: any palm strike that angles upwards. Often strikes softer targets such as temple, groin, or larynx. From Bajiquan, one of its eight main concepts, see also bā dà zhāo.

yíng fēng chǐ qí 迎风扯旗 Banner Tears in the Wind: raise the left knee, circle a staff tip then

Y

scoop it up on the left side, right hand at the waist, left hand extended along the shaft. From Baguazhang.

yíng fēng chuān xiù 迎风穿袖 Wind Penetrates the Sleeve: slide the rear palm out under the front arm, turning the palm down for a piercing strike. May be repeated. From Wudangquan.

yíng fēng dǎn chén 迎风掸尘 Dust Stirs up in the Wind. 1. Encircle with a sword tip. From Taijiquan. 2. A low slice in line with the extended leg in an open bow stance. From Wu Taijiquan.

yíng fēng huī shàn 迎风挥扇 Fan Waves in the Wind: a large extended slice up with a sword blade. From Qingping sword.

yíng fēng huī xiù 迎风挥袖 Sleeves Wave in the Wind: Walking forward, slice one arm in across the body palm down, then bring the palm in turning it over, and then cut forward with the palm up. From Baguazhang. Also called piàn xuán zhǎng.

yíng fēng xià jié 迎风下截 Wind Cuts Down: in a one legged stance, pivot fully around and bring a sword blade down to cut around. From Baguazhang sword.

yíng fēng gǔn bì 迎峰滚闭 Welcome a Blade with a Roll and a Close: with the left hand on the spine and flat of the blade, holding the blade angled in front of the body, roll a broadsword to the left or right to neutralize an incoming stabbing attack.

yíng jī 迎击 Greeting Strike, to meet head on: to quickly strike or kick an adversary as he attacks, combining your defense with an attack to a gap in his defenses. This is a simultaneous defense and attack.

yíng mén 迎门 Greet at the Door: movements using the name 'greet the door' involve a frontal attack, through the main door. This often means attacking straight in without extra defensive moves.

yíng mén bào jiàn 迎门抱剑 Greet at the Door Cradling a Sword: tuck a sword into the midline in a protective stance.

yíng mén diǎn tuǐ 迎门点腿 Greet at the Door Poke Kick: poke kick holding onto an adversary with both hands, usually high.

yíng mén duǎn tuǐ 迎门短腿 Greet at the Door Short Kick: jam an advancing leg with a low kick to the shin.

yíng mén huī shān 迎门挥扇 Greet at the Door Waving a Fan: first step forward and cut across with the hand, then step back around with the foot and slice across horizontally with the same arm. From Baguazhang.

yíng mén kāi pào 迎门开炮 Open Fire at the Doorway: a strong punch to the chest, with the other hand clearing up and out.

yíng mén pào 迎门炮 Open Fire at the Doorway: hop forward directly into a straight punch. From Tongbeiquan.

yíng mén sān bù gù 迎门三不顾 Greet at the Door Ignoring Everything: to go straight in without bothering to defend, to enter hard and fast. From Bajiquan, one of its eight main concepts, see also bā dà zhāo.

yíng mén tōng chuí 迎门通捶 Greet at the Door throwing out the fists: direct punches to front and rear. From Tongbeiquan, one of its seven long range techniques.

yíng mén tóu chuí 迎门头捶 Greet at the Door with a Head Strike: pull an adversary's arm down and go in for a head butt. From Tanglangquan, one of its eight short techniques.

yíng mén zhōng cì 迎门中刺 Greet at the Door straight stab: a direct, level stab to the midline.

yíng miàn 迎面 Greet the Face: head-on, in one's face.

yíng miàn duǎn tuǐ 迎面短腿 Head-on short leg: bring the rear leg through to a low, sliding kick to the shin. This is a long range kick, as the body leans back to put the hip into the kick and keep the torso away from counter attack.

yíng miàn quán 迎面拳 Head-on fist: attack to the face with a backfist, striking downwards.

yíng miàn shǒu 迎面手 Head-on hand: attack to the face with a hand, usually with a backhand.

yíng miàn tán xī 迎面弹膝 Head-on Kick to the Knee: simultaneously strike the face and do a low snap kick towards the knee. From Baguazhang, one of its sixty-four hands.

yíng miàn tiē jīn 迎面贴金 Cover the Face with

Gold Leaf: press your adversary's arm upwards with a framing block, with a simultaneous sliding grab to his face. From Hongquan.

yíng miàn tuǐ 迎面腿 Head-on kick. 1. A straight front swing kick, the foot reaching the face. Also called zhèng tī tuǐ. 2. This kick done as a training exercise, also called lù tuǐ.

yíng miàn zhǎng 迎面掌 Head-on palm: attack to the face with a push. From Wu Taijiquan.

yíng miàn zhí tǒng 迎面直统 Head-on and Straight Through: advancing elbow strikes followed with a head butt. From Tanglangquan.

yíng xiāng 迎香 Acupoint Yingxiang (welcome fragrance), LI20. Beside the outer edge of a nostril. This is the last point of the Large Intestine meridian (on each side). From TCM.

yíng zhāo 迎招 To meet an attack.

硬 (rad.112) yìng   1. Hard, as relating to a force or object. 2. Stiff, tough. 3. Hardness. From Tongbeiquan, one of its nine types of power, see also jiǔ gōng jìn.

yìng biān 硬鞭 A hard whip: a sword length stick with a grip, usually with striations or knobs.

yìng gōng 硬功 Hard skills: the ability to make and take hard hits.

yìng jìn 硬劲 Hard power: a strong, direct, focused attacking force.

yìng mén quán 硬门拳 Yingmenquan (hard gate fist): a southern style from Jiangxi.

yìng pīn 硬拼 To fight all out, even against a stronger adversary.

yìng shǒu 硬手 A hard hand: someone who is hard with no softness.

yìng táng láng quán 硬螳螂拳 Ying (hard) Tanglangquan, a branch of Preying Mantis style that emphasizes hard strikes and power.

擁 [拥] (rad.64) yōng   1. To hug. To wrap around. 2. To possess. 3. To gather around.

yōng huā yāo zǐ 拥花腰子 Flower gathering kidneys, a weapon. See jī dāo lián.

yōng jìn 拥进 To swarm forward.

yōng tuǐ 拥腿 A direct side kick across the shin. From Xingyiquan.

勇 (rad.19) yǒng   Brave, courageous: one of the character traits expected of martial artists.

永 (rad.85) yǒng   Long; lasting; eternal.

yǒng chūn quán 永春拳 Wing Chun, see 詠 yǒng chūn quán.

泳 (rad.85) yǒng   To swim.

yǒng chūn quán 泳春拳 Wing Chun, see 詠 yǒng chūn quán.

涌 (rad.85) yǒng   To gush; pour; surge. Rise; spring; well; emerge.

yǒng quán 涌泉 Acupoint Yongquan (gushing spring, often translated as bubbling), KI1. At the foot, the depression made when the toes are curled, in the centre of the sole, between the second and third toes, one third of the way in along the foot (on each foot). From TCM. In internal styles, these points are not pressed hard to the ground, but kept open to allow circulation. Striking here disrupts *qi* flow.

詠 (rad.149) [咏 詠] (rad.30, 149) yǒng   To chant; intone. Express in poetic form.

yǒng chūn quán 詠春拳 Yongchunquan (singing spring fist), a style from the Fujian province Shaolin temple, attributed to Yan Yongchun, a female monk. Known in English as Wing Chun, from the Cantonese pronunciation. The character yǒng in the name is also written 永 or 泳.

用 (rad.101) yòng   To use; employ; apply.

yòng fǎ 用法 Use, usage. 1. Applications of techniques. 2. Specifically, strategic methods to defend in the most effective way according to an adversary, taking into consideration height, size, etc.

yòng yì bù yòng lì 用意不用力 Use intent, not force. A common dictum in martial arts, especially internal styles.

幽 (rad.52) yōu   Deep and remote. Secluded. Dim. Hidden. Quiet; serene.

yōu mén 幽门 Acupoint Youmen (secret gate),

Y

KI21. The belly, six *cun* above the navel, 0.5 *cun* lateral to the midline (on each side). From TCM. One of seven painful gateways to attack that are related to midline acupoints. See also qī chōng mén.

悠 (rad.61) **yōu** 1. Leisurely. 2. Long. 3. Remote, distant. 4. Drawn out.

yōu chuí 悠锤 Distance punch. 1. Step the rear foot through and forward and swing that fist over from behind, towards the top of an adversary's head. 2. A horizontally swung straight arm strike. Both from Bajiquan and Xingyiquan. Also called yōu shǒu pào.

yōu shǒu pào 悠手炮 See yōu chuí.

游 遊 (rad.85, 162) [**游**] (rad.85) **yóu** 1. A stretch of river. 2. To saunter, stroll. 3. Moving around; floating.

yóu jī zhàn 游击战 Guerilla warfare. In a fight, to use the terrain, keep moving, and look for opportunities for a quick attack.

yóu lóng bǎi wěi 游龙摆尾 Swimming Dragon Lashes its Tail: swing the arm from the outside, wrapping with a straight arm to swing an adversary's arm upwards, then grab with the other hand to press down behind his shoulder.

有 (rad.74) **yǒu** To have; to be present; to exist.

yǒu xiào fēn 有效分 Valid points, useable score: the remaining judges' scores in Taolu competition after the high and low have been taken out (not all competitions do this). See also wú xiào fēn.

酉 (rad.164) **yǒu** The tenth of the twelve Terrestrial Branches, used in combination with the ten Celestial Stems to designate years, months, days, and hours. For the sixty year cycles, see also under dīng yǒu, guǐ-, jǐ-, xīn-, yì-. The period of the day from 5:00 p.m. to 7:00 p.m. (17:00 to 19:00). See also dì zhī, tiān gān.

yǒu gōng 酉功 Training done regularly at the time from 5:00 p.m. to 7:00 p.m. (17:00 to 19:00).

yǒu shí 酉时 The period of the day from 5:00 p.m. to 7:00 p.m. (17:00 to 19:00).

右 (rad.30) **yòu** The right side, to the right, on the right.

yòu chán bó biān 右缠脖鞭 Right coil the neck with the steel whip: swinging the whip vertically at the right side of the body, loop it over the neck and turn to continue swinging.

yòu gōng bù 右弓步 Right bow stance. 1. A right bow stance, a normal bow stance, weighted to the forward right leg. See also gōng bù. 2. In some Chen Taijiquan schools, this is a turned bow stance weighted to the right leg. The bow stance faces in the direction of a biased horse stance, but the feet are turned as in a bow stance.

yòu jià 右架 A right wrestling hold: right foot forward, usually right hand high and left hand low. See also zuǒ jià.

yòu mǎ 右马 Right horse: the right leg. Sometimes used in describing stances and stepping.

yòu pàn 右盼 To retreat sideways, rather than straight back. See also zuǒ gù, zuǒ gù yòu pàn.

yòu shǎn zuǒ dǎ 右闪左打 Dodge Right and Hit Left: sit to a cross stance elbow tuck and pull on the right, then come up with a left hit and kick. From Taiji Changquan.

yòu xié bù 右斜步 Angled step to the right: in a fighting ready stance with the left foot forward, step the right foot out at an angle, advancing to the right. The left foot may just pivot or may also step forward, but the body has changed the angle of defense or attack.

诱 [誘] (rad.149) **yòu** 1. To guide, lead, direct. 2. To lure, entice. 3. To induce, cause.

yòu gōng zhàn 诱攻战 Enticement attacking tactics: to use fakes to draw an adversary into making errors.

yòu shǒu 诱手 Enticing hand: a feint. Also called jiǎ shǒu.

yòu shǒu tí liāo 诱手提撩 Entice and Slice Up: extend one hand then swing the other up to strike with the wrist. From Baguazhang, one of its sixty-four hands.

瘀 (rad.104) **yū** Stasis of blood. From TCM.

yū rè 瘀热 Heat stasis, static heat, a pattern applied

in channel diagnosis. From TCM.

迂 (rad.162) yū 1. Roundabout, indirect, circuitous. 2. Make a detour. 3. Impractical; unrealistic.

yū huí bù 迂回步 Indirect returning step: pivot the leading foot on the ball to turn the body to a smooth stance, lift the rear foot and step it into an adversary from the side. From Che Xingyiquan.

漁 [渔] (rad.85) yú To fish; fishing; fishery.

yú láng wèn jīn 渔郎问津 Fisherman Makes Inquiries: a hop step advance while circling a sword tip in front of the chest, landing with a chop, the arm on a straight line with the blade. From Qingping sword.

yú wēng sā wǎng 渔翁撒网 Old Fisherman Casts his Net: a sweeping flat slice, usually with a double weapon, like throwing out a Chinese style fishing net. From Baguazhang.

隅 (rad.170) yú A corner. An angle. A nook.

yú bù 隅步 Corner stance: both feet pointing straight ahead, the distance between them about a foot-length and a half in width and about a half foot-length in length.

餘 (rad.184) [余 (rad.9) yú 1. Surplus, spare, remaining. 2. More than; beyond. 3. A surname. 4. One of the small family styles of Emei, see also sì xiǎo jiā.

yú liàng jù lí 余量距离 Extra distance: to keep more distance between you and an adversary than is optimal for attack, used to keep safe from unexpected attack.

魚 [鱼] (rad.195) yú 1. A fish, fish. 2. To fish. For more movement names using the actions of fish, or things you do to fish, see also under děng yú, diào-, hēi-, jīn-, lǐ-, yīn yáng-.

yú cháng 鱼肠 Fish guts: refers to the 'fish gut sword', a short and sharp blade that was hidden inside a fish at a banquet in order to assassinate a king during the Spring and Autumn period. There are a great many famous swords, too many to include in the dictionary.

yú fǎ 鱼法 Fish technique: fighting by following along naturally with whatever an adversary is doing, like a fish swimming in water. Also called yáo tóu bǎi wěi.

yú jì 鱼际 Acupoint Yuji (fish border), LU10. At the belly of the thumb, at the border of lighter and darker flesh (on each hand). From TCM.

yú tiào lóng mén 鱼跳龙门 Fish Jumps the Dragon's Gate. See yě mǎ tiào dòng. There is more emphasis on a high jump with the fish name.

yú wěi fǔ 鱼尾斧 Fish tail axe: a long handled axe with the flat side of the head shaped like a fish tail.

yú yāo 鱼腰 Extraordinary acupoint Yuyao (fish's back), EX-HN4. At the head, on the forehead, above the pupil, in the middle of the eyebrow (on each side). From TCM.

yú yuè cè gǔn fān 鱼跃侧滚翻 Fish jumping side roll: leap forward and tuck to land with a side roll.

yú yuè qián gǔn fān 鱼跃前滚翻 Fish jumping forward roll: leap forward and tuck to land with a forward roll.

羽 (rad.124) yǔ A feather.

yǔ kè huī zhǔ 羽客挥麈 Daoist Priest Brandishes: from an empty stance, snap to the other leg to take an empty stance on the other side, turning and sweeping a sword across with the shift. The right arm, front leg, and blade are aligned. From Qingping sword.

yǔ shàn huà jiāng 羽扇画江 Feather Fan Draws the River: draw back to an empty stance and open both hands out to the sides at shoulder height, palms back, dropping a sword tip downwards below the right hand. From Qingping sword. The feather fan is a reference to Zhuge Liang, indicating the move is a tactical one, to draw someone in, see zhū gě liàng.

彧 (rad.59) yù To have literary talent (formal).

yù zhōng 彧中 Acupoint Yuzhong (talented centre), KI26. At the chest, at the first intercostal space, 2 *cun* from the midline (on each side). From TCM.

Y

御禦 [御] (rad.60) **yù** 1. To drive. 2. To manage, govern. 3. Imperial. 4. To resist.

yù huán bù èr 御环步二 The Second Imperial Linking Steps: the second of the cultured routines of Chuojiao, written up in forty-four moves. See also wén tàng zi.

yù huán bù yī 御环步一 The First Imperial Linking Steps: the first of the cultured routines of Chuojiao, written up in thirty-six moves. See also wén tàng zi.

玉 (rad.96) **yù** 1. Jade. 2. Beautiful.

yù chuān jiàn 玉川剑 Jade river sword, a routine of Liuhebafa.

yù dài chán yāo 玉带缠腰 Jade belt Encircles the Waist: step from forward a half horse through to a half horse stance on the other side, bring the staff around flat. Start with the left hand at the waist and finish with the right hand at the waist, striking around with the staff following the movement of the waist. From Baguazhang.

yù dài gōng 玉带功 Jade belt training: a training method for arm and back strength. Embrace a tree and try to pull it up, continuing to exhaustion each session. Can also be done with a large stone pillar or large barrel until it can be lifted and carried.

yù gē 玉戈 A jade dagger: a thick dagger made of jade.

yù hǔ xuàn fēng 玉虎旋风 Jade Tiger Whirlwind: raise the right knee, slicing strongly upwards with the blade in front of the knee to shoulder height. From Qingping sword.

yù huán bù 玉环步 Jade belt stance or stepping. 1. As a stance, the feet about three foot-lengths apart, front leg squatting so the thigh is parallel to the ground, rear leg squatting with the knee tucked in and the heel off the ground, weight between the feet, knees held in. 2. As stepping, advancing stepping with a dragging step, drawing the character 人 with each step. From Duanquan.

yù huán bù quán 玉环步拳 Jade Belt Stepping Fists, the fourth routine of Duanquan, written up as eleven moves.

yù huán táng láng quán 玉环螳螂拳 Yuhuan (jade belt) Tanglangquan, a branch of Preying Mantis style that uses the jade belt stepping extensively.

yù mǎng fān shēn 玉蟒翻身 Jade Python Rolls Over: step the hip close into an adversary, laying the body and arm across his chest to take him directly back and down.

yù nǚ 玉女 Jade girl, Fair lady: often used in movement names. Light coloured jade is thought to be the best quality, so jade girl refers to the paleness of a woman's face, which was thought to be most beautiful.

yù nǚ chuān suō 玉女穿梭 Fair Lady Works at Shuttles, Jade Girl Throws the Shuttle 1. An upper framing deflection combined with a push. From Taijiquan. 2. Step forward with a double push. From Wudangquan. 3. An advancing weaving movement into a sword pierce. From Qingping sword. 4. A long back cross step, leaning to swing one arm up to clear as the other comes through low. From Baguazhang, one of its sixty-four hands.

yù nǚ shuǎi xiù 玉女甩袖 Fair Lady Throws her Sleeves: bow stance throwing palms. From Piguaquan. See also shuāi shǒu.

yù nǚ sòng shū 玉女送书 Fair Lady Delivers a Book: step into a smooth stance, reaching the body forward and slicing a sword up in line, reaching to lift up over head height, cutting an adversary's torso or arm. From Qingping sword.

yù nǚ tàn huā 玉女探花 Fair Lady Reaches for Flowers: move into an empty stance and stab a sword forward in a rolled over grip, right arm and blade forming a straight line, tip below knee height, blocking up with the left arm. From Qingping sword.

yù nǚ tóu hú 玉女投壶 Fair Lady Plays Pitch-pot (tosses arrows into a vase). 1. A charging sword pierce to shoulder height with a fully extended arm and a standing blade, leaning into the strike in a bow stance. This chases down an adversary. From Qingping sword. 2. Raise a sword, then sit to a cross stance, stabbing straight down behind. From Wu Taijiquan.

yù nǚ xiàn qín 玉女献琴 Fair Lady Presents the Qin (Chinese zither): from a back cross step cradling a sword, tip down a bit, lunge to a bow stance and pierce straight. From Qingping sword.

yù nǚ xiàn shū 玉女献书 Fair Lady Presents a

Book: An advancing palm lift. From Baguazhang.

yù táng 玉堂 Acupoint Yutang (jade hall), RN18. At the chest, level with the third intercostal space, on the midline. From TCM.

yù tóng xiàn shū 玉童献书 Fair Lad Presents a Book: step forward to a lifting palm. From Tongbeiquan.

yù tóng sòng shū 玉童送书 Fair Lad Delivers a Book: an expressive term for the category of hand techniques that use lifting and supporting methods. See also tuō fǎ.

yù xiàng juǎn bí 玉象卷鼻 Jade Elephant Curls its Trunk: advance and retreat doing large hooking slices with a sword, completing each slice with a reverse pierce. From Qingping sword.

yù yè 玉液 Extraordinary acupoint Yuye (jade humour), EX-HN13. Inside the mouth, under the tongue, just off the midline (on each side). From TCM.

yù zhěn 玉枕 Acupoint Yuzhen (jade pillow), BL9. At the back of the head, 2.5 *cun* up from the rear hairline, in a depression just on top of the external occipital protuberance, 1.3 *cun* lateral to the midline (on each side). From TCM. In internal styles, these points are relaxed to help relax the neck and allow *qi* to flow between the head and body. One of the three passes of meridian flow, see also sān guān.

yù zhěn guān 玉枕关 Jade Pillow Pass. See yù zhěn. See also #2 of sān guān.

yù zhù qíng tiān 玉柱擎天 Jade Pillar Supports the Sky: Stand straight up and scoop up a sword until it is stabbing directly upwards, a strong clearing move. From Qingping sword.

欲 慾 (rad.150,61) [欲] (rad.150) yù 1. Wish; desire; longing. 2. About to; on the point of.

yù dòng xiān jìng, yù gāng xiān róu; yù qǔ zhī bì xiān yǔ zhī 欲动先静，欲刚先柔；欲取之必先予之 Be still before moving, be pliant before hitting hard; if you want to take someone you must first give a bit. A martial saying.

yù qín gù zòng 欲擒故纵 Leave some Latitude if you wish to Apprehend. The 16th of the Thirty-six Stratagems of Warfare, which apply to many situations.

预 [预] (rad.181) yù In advance; beforehand.

yù bèi 预备 Prepare, get ready.

yù bèi shì 预备势 Position of preparation. Usually is standing upright, feet together, before starting a routine.

渊 (rad.85) yuān A deep pool. Deep.

yuān yè 渊腋 Acupoint Yuanye (armpit abyss), GB22. At the torso, three *cun* directly under the armpit, at the level of the fourth rib (on each side). From TCM.

yuān zhōng qiú zhū 渊中求珠 Seek Pearls in a Deep Pool: turn and lift the left knee, rolling the right hand over to do a reversed sword stab forward at shoulder height. From Qingping sword.

鴛 [鸳] (rad.196) yuān A male mandarin duck. Usually used in combination as yuān yáng for a pair of mandarin ducks.

yuān yāng 鸳鸯 A pair of mandarin ducks. Used in movement names either for the curved shape of the wings or for the belief that they mate for life (thus used for a pair of things).

yuān yāng jiǎo 鸳鸯脚 Mandarin duck kick. 1. A swinging kick to the rear with the leg slightly bent, slapping the foot near the head, From Chuojiao, one of its middle-basin kicks. Also called fā hòu tuǐ. 2. Usually means this kick in other styles, but sometimes means a barrage of front kicks, taking the paired meaning.

yuān yāng lián 鸳鸯镰 Mandarin duck sickle: a pair of sickles. See lián.

yuān yāng liàng chì yuān yāng fú wō 鸳鸯亮翅 鸳鸯伏窝 Mandarin Duck Flashes its Wings while the Other Hides in the Nest: brace the arms out to the sides at head height while kicking straight on low to the shin. From Xinyi Liuhequan.

yuān yāng quán 鸳鸯拳 Mandarin duck fists: an on guard position. In a normal fighting stance with the weight evenly placed, place the leading hand, elbow bent and down, fist at nose height, fist heart angled downwards. Place the rear fist inside the lead elbow, elbow down, fist heart angled down.

yuān yāng tuǐ 鸳鸯腿 Mandarin duck kick: start

with a hooked in kick, then turn to a hooked out kick before landing. When the left foot lands, it is pointing in the opposite direction as the right foot, so both the action and the final placement is crossing. From Duanquan.

yuān yāng yuè 鸳鸯钺 Mandarin duck blades. A relatively small double weapon, with curving blades each with nine edges and four tips. The outer tips may be the same length or the forward tip may be longer. The spread from the forward tip to the hook tip is usually about twenty-two to thirty-two centimetres. The inner tips are usually shorter than the outer tips, with a spread just past the handgrip width. Often called deerhorn blades or deerhorn knives in English. Also called lù jiǎo dāo, qián kūn jiàn, rì yuè shuāng lián, shuāng yuè, zǐ wǔ yuān yāng yuè. See also under yuè for the names of its parts.

yuān yāng zhǎng 鸳鸯掌 Mandarin duck palms: the same on guard position as Mandarin duck fists, but with the palms held open with the palm edges forward. See yuān yāng quán.

元 (rad.10) **yuán** 1. First, primary; chief, principal; basic, fundamental. 2. The Yuan dynasty (1271-1368), founded by the Mongols.

yuán bǎo jiǎo 元宝脚 Silver Ingot Trip. A tripping throw at the back of the calf, which makes an adversary lands on his back. Move the foot into your adversary's stance so that he shifts his foot. Then hook that lower leg and lift, simultaneously settling your body and pulling back with your arms. Landing on his back with the feet and hands in the air, the adversary resembles an old style silver ingot. Also called dǎo jiǎo, yáng wěi bǎ zhuì.

yuán shī guàn zhèn 元师观阵 Master Yuan Surveys the Battle Array: closed parallel stance press the palm down. From Piguaquan.

原 (rad.27) **yuán** Source, origin, beginning. Primary; original.

yuán bù 原步 Stationary, fixed step, do a move without stepping.

yuán dì 原地 On the spot: an action done essentially remaining in the same place.

yuán dì dǒu 原地抖 On the spot shaking, a wrestling throw training: holding a belt at each end, snap side to side. When turning to the left, the left hand pulls down to the left hip and the right hand snaps up to the upper left.

yuán dì hòu kōng fān 原地后空翻 A stationary back flip.

yuán dì tiào 原地跳 Jump on the spot: jump up and land in the same place. May land with a thump, but not necessarily.

yuán qì 原气 Source *qi*, original *qi*, unprocessed *qi*. The first breath of life that infuses all other types of *qi* in the body.

圆 [圓] (rad.31) **yuán** 1. A circle; round, circular. 2. Refers to the roundness of the upper back, the chest, and the thumb web when used as one of the eight body requirements of Xingyiquan. 3. One of Ziranmen's nineteen main methods.

yuán bèi 圆背 To make the upper back rounded.

yuán dāng 圆裆 Round the groin area, keeping it relaxed and, in conjunction with releasing the hips, allowing communication between the upper and lower body.

yuán huó 圆活 Round, smooth; round and lively. This is a requirement at the intermediate level of training, movement must be rounded and smooth.

yuán xíng zhǎng 圆形掌 Rounded palm shape. Five fingers naturally separated and slightly bent, index finger pulled slightly up, thumb web spread, palm heart concave.

yuán xiōng 圆胸 Rounded chest: draw in the chest. From southern styles.

援 (rad.64) **yuán** 1. To pull by hand; hold. 2. Help, aid; rescue.

yuán shǒu 援手 Rescuing hand: when one hand misses its goal, use the other to help out.

猿 猨 [猿] (rad.94) **yuán** An ape, apes. Translated either as ape or monkey. Yuán generally refers to larger species, while hóu refers to smaller species. For more movement names using the actions or qualities of the ape, see also under bái yuán, lǎo-, líng-, xiān-, yě-.

yuán hóu bān zhī 猿猴般枝 Ape Removes a Branch: step forward with the foot turned out, swinging the arm around with the action of the body to clear the way.

yuán hóu bāo zhuāng 猿猴抱桩 Ape Embraces a Pillar: lower your body and grab an adversary around the waist, trapping his leg with your leg for a takedown.

yuán hóu bào gāng 猿猴抱缸 Ape Cradles a Vat: circle-walking with the hands cradling in front of the belly. From Baguazhang.

yuán hóu dáo shēng 猿猴捯绳 Ape Pulls at its Leash: multiple reaching, threading forward with the hands while sitting back. From Xingyiquan.

yuán hóu dēng zhī 猿猴蹬枝 Ape Kicks a Branch: a heel kick, lifting in front and drawing back with the rear hand. From Baguazhang and Xingyiquan. In Baguazhang it may be a push kick or a heel kick.

yuán hóu guà yìn 猿猴挂印 Ape Hangs up its Seal (retires from office): step around in hooked out step then hooked in step (see also bǎi bù, kòu bù) drilling the fist up the centre, a dodging block, followed by a reaching palm. In Wong Kar Wai's film The Grandmaster, it was said that the value of the move is not the drilling up to protect, but the turning around to look back. From Xingyiquan. Also called lǎo yuán guà yìn. Sometimes called yuán hóu tuō yìn.

yuán hóu pá gān 猿猴爬杆 Ape Clambers up the Pole: catch an adversary's arm and pull to bar the arm, repeat on the other side. From Baguazhang, one of its sixty-four hands.

yuán hóu rēng shéng 猿猴扔绳 Ape Throws a Rope: step in arcing steps forward and back while alternating multiple palm strikes. From Wudangquan.

yuán hóu tōu táo 猿猴偷桃 Ape Steals a Peach: poking under the armpit similar to Hide a Flower Under a Leaf (see yè dī cáng huā), but with both palms turned down. From Baguazhang.

yuán hóu tuō yìn 猿猴托印 Ape Raises its Seal. See yuán hóu guà yìn.

yuán hóu xǐ liǎn 猿猴洗脸 Ape Washes its Face: bring alternating hand and forearm across and down in front of the face. From Wudangquan. Also called hǔ xǐ liǎn, māo xǐ liǎn, zhé jiē.

yuán hóu xiān guǒ 猿猴献果 Ape Offers Fruit. 1. Lift near the jaw with the hands close together, palms up. From Baguazhang. 2. Sit into a cross legged stance, cocking a sword up. From Qingping sword.

yuán hóu zhāi guǒ 猿猴摘果 Ape Picks Fruit: reach out with the palm up, bringing back the other hand. From Baguazhang.

yuán hóu zhuì zhī 猿猴坠枝 Ape Drops off a Branch: step forward with a crossing cover step, lifting in front and drawing back with the rear hand, to control an adversary's elbow while moving in. From Xingyiquan.

yuán hóu zuò dòng 猿猴坐洞 Ape Sits in its Cave: drop back to a tucked squat. From Baguazhang.

轅 [辕] (rad.159) **yuán**
1. The shafts of a cart. 2. The outer gate of a government office (ancient, the magistrate's office is often called the Yamen in English translations).

yuán mén shè jǐ 辕门射戟 Shoot a Halberd at the Yamen's Gate: an aerial snap kick. From Liuhequan.

遠 [远] (rad.162) **yuǎn**
Far, distant, remote.

yuǎn dǎ jìn ná tié shēn shuāi 远打近拿贴身摔 When far, hit; when close, grab; when in tight, throw. A martial saying.

yuǎn jiāo jìn gōng 远交近攻 Befriend Those at Distance while Attacking Those Nearby. The twenty-third of the Thirty-six Stratagems of Warfare, which apply to many situations.

yuǎn jiǎo jìn xī tié shēn kuà 远脚近膝贴身胯 When far, use the feet; when close, use the knees; when in tight, use the hips. A martial saying.

yuǎn jù lí 远距离 Long range: distant from an adversary; within striking range of a quick attack involving footwork to move in. See also jìn jù lí, zhōng jù lì.

yuǎn zhǎng jìn zhǒu tié shēn kào 远掌近肘贴身靠 When far, use the hands; when close, use the elbows; when in tight, use the shoulder and back. A martial saying.

岳 嶽 [岳] (rad.46) **yuè**
1. A high mountain. 2. A mountain range. 3. A surname. In

movement names, often refers to General Yue Fei. 4. One of the four big family branches of Emeiquan, see also sì dà jiā.

yuè fēi 岳飞 Yue Fei (1103-1142), a Song dynasty general, famous in folklore for his patriotism and loyalty.

yuè jiā quán 岳家拳 Yuejiaquan (Yue family fist), attributed to General Yue Fei.

yuè shèng dāo 岳胜刀 Victorious Yue cutter. Also translated as big cutter, halberd, Guan's halberd. See guān dāo. Also called chūn qiū dāo, dà dāo, dìng sòng dāo.

月 (rad.74) yuè   The moon. Month. Monthly.

yuè guà sōng shāo 月挂松梢 Moon Hooks the Branches of the Pine: turn and advance with multiple alternating stabs and pushes, finishing with a hooked knee stab. From Liuhebafa.

yuè pán tuǐ 月爿腿 Moon kick: a jumping inside crescent kick with a one-eighty turn.

yuè yá 月牙 1. Usually refers to the crescent moon, the new moon. 2. The crescent shaped blade of a double hook, acts as a hand guard and additional blade. Also called gōu yuè.

yuè yá chǎn 月牙铲 Crescent moon shovel. 1. A long weapon, one end with a crescent moon shaped blade and the other with a shovel shaped blade. 2. A long weapon with a crescent shaped shovel at one end and nothing at the butt. 3. A long handled trident with just two prongs.

yuè yá cì 月牙刺 Crescent moon dagger: a double weapon. A double ended dagger with a hand guard in the middle that is a bladed crescent moon.

yuè yá fǔ 月牙斧 Crescent moon axe: a long handled axe with a curved crescent blade.

yuè yǐng shǒu jiǎo 月影手脚 Hands and Feet like the Moon's Shadow: step with a left front crossing step, swinging the left fist up over the head and bringing the right palm forward, index finger extended. The 106th move of the tiger and crane routine.

躍 [跃] (rad.157) yuè   1. To leap; jump. 2. As a shield and broadsword technique, leap: leap to the front, side, or rear with a slicing broadsword technique.

yuè bù 跃步 Leap, a leaping step. 1. Pushing off the lead foot, bringing the rear foot through to land first. 2. A jump straight up, opening and switching the foot position.

yuè cén 跃岑 Hurdle the Mountain Peak: half split on the ground, which looks like a hurdling position. Also called pū dì mián, què dì lóng.

yuè pū shì 跃扑式 Leaping to pounce.

鉞 [钺] (rad.167) yuè   1. A battle-axe. An axe is called fǔ. In general, a fǔ has an axe blade with a flat back for pounding, a yuè is larger and the blade may have a decorative back. The yuè can have a double pointed blade at the end, extended, instead of placed like an axe. 2. The short name for deerhorn blades. See yuān yáng yuè. Also called lù jiǎo dāo, qián kūn jiàn, rì yuè shuāng lián, shuāng yuè, zǐ wǔ yuān yáng yuè.

yuè bǐng 钺柄 Handgrip of the deerhorn blades.

yuè chā 钺叉 Fork of the deerhorn blades: the edge where the two blades meet at the index finger side.

yuè dāo 钺刀 Blade of the deerhorn blades: the forward blade at the index finger side. This is the longer blade on some types.

yuè gōu 钺勾 Hook of the deerhorn blades: the forward tip at the little finger side.

yuè jiānr 钺尖 Tip of the deerhorn blades: the forward tip on the index finger blade.

yuè jiǎo 钺角 Corner of the deerhorn blades: the inside tip at the index finger side.

yuè wěi 钺尾 Tail of the deerhorn blades: the inside blade at the little finger side.

暈 [晕] (rad.72) yūn   To faint, swoon. To get dizzy. Also pronounced yùn, see yùn.

yūn jué 晕厥 To faint, swoon.

紜 [纭] (rad.120) yún   Diverse and confused.

yún shǒu 纭手 Diverse hands, a move of Wu Taijiquan: similar to cloud hands, done with Wu style characteristics. See also yún 云 shǒu.

耘 (rad.127) yún   1. To weed. 2. A weeding power: a rounded crossing power used to pull an adversary over. From wrestling.

yún zhèng 耘挣 To snap with a crossing power for a throw or takedown.

雲 (rad.173) [云] (rad.7) **yún** 1. Cloud, clouds. For more movement names evocatively using clouds, see also under bái yún, fēi-, jìng-, wū-, xiáng-. 2. To pass, swing by, swing overhead. 3. A flat slice of the palm edge, pivoting the forearm around the elbow with the palm up throughout. 4. Brandish a weapon, swing it in a horizonal circle, usually over the head. 5. Twirl, if the action is rotating around the wrist. 6. Sweep across. From Bajiquan, one of its ten major techniques, see also shí dà jī fǎ.

yún bō 云拨 A brandishing check.

yún dāo 云刀 Pass a broadsword overhead. See yún jiàn.

yún dǐng qī xīng 云顶七星 Clouds Press Seven Stars: press one hand up over the head and the other down at the hip, turning into the upper arm to punch in seven stars formation. From Shaolinquan.

yún gùn 云棍 Twirl a staff: a horizontal circle over the head or in front of the head. If the shaft passes near the head, duck back or to the side. The staff may be swung with one or both hands.

yún hóng zhèn yǔ 云鸿振羽 Cloud Swan Flaps its Wings: Move in sideways, turning around to the back, and advancing to cut upwards to the wrist. From Qingping sword.

yún jiàn 云剑 Pass a sword overhead: a near horizontal circle over and in front of the head, leaning back and turning the wrist to pivot at the blade in front of the guard. If the blade passes near the head, duck back or to the side.

yún lǐ fān shēn 云里翻身 Wheel around in the clouds: jump up, pulling both feet and knees up, to turn around and land on both feet.

yún lǐ xiǎn shèng 云里显圣 Sage Shows himself in the Clouds: hit an adversary's head with a reaching palm strike, then immediately turn the body and circle the arm to strike the groin. This works as a feint and attack. From Hongquan.

yún lóng xiàn zhǎo 云龙献爪 Cloud Dragon Presents its Claws. 1. A cover combined with a reaching finger stab and possible grab into the face. From Baguazhang, one of its sixty-four hands. 2. A reaching strike with deerhorn blades. From Baguazhang.

yún lóng xiàn zhǒu 云龙现肘 Cloud Dragon Shows its Elbow: pull back then step into a bow stance same side elbow strike. From Wudangquan.

yún lóng zuān xīn 云龙钻心 Cloud Dragon Drills into the Heart: a full sweep of a spear over the body, leaning back, then followed by an outward cover, inward cover, stab.

yún mén 云门 Acupoint Yunmen (cloud gate), LU2. At the chest, in a depression just under the lateral tip of the collarbone, about 6 *cun* lateral to the midline (on each side). From TCM.

yún mó dāo 云磨刀 Grinding brandish with a broadsword: starting with the spine of the blade near the left shoulder, roll under the blade so that it passes behind the body across to the right side. The grip passes behind and over the head. Used with the larger bladed Bagua broadsword.

yún mó pū dāo 云磨扑刀 Grinding brandish with a horse cutter: circle the weapon flatly over the head with the edge up then bring it down in front of the body, crossing the arms to complete a low chop to the right. Usually includes a full one-eighty degree turn of the body.

yún mó shǒu 云磨手 Grinding hands: alternating horizontal, grinding circles with the hands. From Chuojiao.

yún nèi chā huā 云内插花 Stick the Flowers into the Clouds: Scoop up with the blade, turning stepping forward to a left empty stance, the right arm extended downwards, sword tip up at eyebrow height. From Qingping sword.

yún péng mó kōng 云鹏摩空 The Roc in the Clouds Rubs the Void: raise a sword to cut the neck, in a high crossed stance, reach the blade out angled to the side with the arm straight and aligned with the flat blade, to cut out towards an adversary's neck. From Qingping sword.

yún péng pán huā 云鹏盘花 The Roc in the Clouds Twists Flowers: cross the arms low and coil them at the wrist with a grappling action. From Wudangquan.

yún pū dāo 云扑刀 Brandish a horse cutter: horizontal circle over the head or in front of the head. If the shaft passes near the head, duck back or to the side.

yún shǒu 云手 Cloud Hands: stepping sideways continuously, drawing circles on a plane across in front of the body, to draw across, like the clouds moving across the sky. Also called yùn 运 shǒu and yún 纭 shǒu.

yún wài chā huā 云外插花 Stick the Flowers Beyond the Clouds: Scoop up with a sword, turn and step forward to a right empty stance, the right arm extended downwards, the sword tip up at eyebrow height. From Qingping sword.

yún wài zhǎn cǎo 云外斩草 Cut the Grass Beyond the Clouds: drop to a full squat and push/cut a sword forward, hands together at waist height. From Qingping sword.

yún wù zhào dǐng 云雾罩顶 Clouds and Mist Cover the Peaks: sit into horse stance with a crossing downwards strike with the butt of a long weapon, front hand palm down, halfway along the shaft. From Shaolinquan.

yún yān gài dǐng 云烟盖顶 Clouds and Mist Cover the Peaks: sit into horse stance and snap the wrist to reverse chop a sword up at the side at shoulder height, hand turned palm up, tip back. From Qingping sword.

yún zhǎng 云掌 Brandish the palm: with the palm up, a flat circle above the head. Used to redirect and then come in from the other side.

yún zì gōng 云字功 Passing skill, one of Xingyiquan's eight skills, using a soft passing double deflection combined with a hard counter attack.

暈 [晕] (rad.72) yùn   To faint, swoon. Dizzy. A mist. Also pronounced yūn, see yūn.

yùn dǎo 晕倒 To faint.

yùn xué 晕穴 Fainting points: pressure points that striking can cause fainting. Lightly striking the death or crippling points may cause fainting. See also cán xué, sǐ xué.

yùn zhēn 晕针 To faint when needled.

運 [运] (rad.162) yùn   1. Motion; movement. 2. To transfer, transport.

yùn dòng 运动 Movement, motion in general. Sports, athletics.

yùn dòng huì 运动会 Sports meet; games.

yùn dòng liàng 运动量 Training intensity, in terms of training workload.

yùn dòng lù xiàn 运动路线 The route, path, line of movement. The movement of each hand and foot, as drawn out in instructional manuals.

yùn dòng yuán 运动员 Athlete, player; competitor.

yùn jīn chéng fēng 运斤成风 Whirl the Hatchet like the Wind. 1. Jump forward, spinning around and landing to stab with a sword. From Qingping sword. 2. The phrase comes from a story of a carpenter who whirled his hatchet to slice a bit of mud from someone's nose, so it means to wield a weapon with great skill.

yùn jìn 运劲 Move power, energy; how to apply energy, power.

yùn qì 运气 Move *qi*; how to move, and the process of moving, *qi* around the whole body.

yùn róu qiáo 运柔桥 Move the Supple Bridges: sitting in horse stance, palms pushing forward, move them to extend one to the side, the other to the opposite shoulder, palms facing to the side, index finger pointing up. To the left is the 20th move of the tiger and crane routine, to the right is the 21st.

yùn shǒu 运手 Travelling hands, similar to Cloud hands (see yún 云 shǒu) but using Chen coiling energy, usually with cross stepping, and with the palms out. From Chen Taijiquan.

韻 [韵] (rad.180) yùn   Rhyme. Harmony. Refined; polished. Musical sound.

yùn dù 韵度 The quality of harmony: a combination of rhythm and bearing. All movements within a routine need to done with harmony, balance of qualities.

Z

砸 (rad.112) zá   1. To break, smash. Shatter. 2. As a hand technique: to pound, tamp. 3. Pound, one of the falling hands in Chuojiao, see also luò shǒu.

zá fǎ 砸法 Smashing method: to pound the fist down, especially onto a joint.

zá quán 砸拳 Smashing punch, a hammer fist downwards with a backfist.

zá zhǒu 砸肘 Smash with the elbow. 1. An arcing strike upwards with the elbow bent. 2. A strong press with the forearm to an adversary's elbow, as a takedown.

zá zhuāng 砸桩 Tamping stake stance and power training. In a sixty-forty stance with the arms in a pressing position, compress slightly back and forth, with a tamping action with the front or rear foot to find whole body power. From Xingyiquan.

雜 (rad.172) [杂] (rad.75) zá   Mixed; miscellaneous; sundry.

zá shì chuí 杂势捶 Mixture of moves fists: a routine of Xingyiquan, written up as forty-one to forty-seven moves. Also called zhá shì quán.

栽 (rad.75) zāi   1. To stick in, insert. 2. To plant; to grow a plant.

zāi bēi 栽碑 A straight front break fall: a straight forward fall, breaking with the forearms, keeping the body straight.

zāi chuí 栽捶 A planting hammer fist, a downward punch, landing low. From Wu Taijiquan.

zāi quán 栽拳 A planting punch, a downward punch with the knuckles, landing low.

zāi quán fā lì 栽拳发力 A planting punch: a dropping punch, but remaining in a high stance. From Yiquan.

zāi zhǒu 栽肘 To plant the elbow: a downward strike with the point of the elbow.

載 [载] (rad.159) zài   1. To carry, hold. 2. To be loaded with.

zài zhǒu 载肘 Stab down with the elbow in a cocked position.

攢 [攒] (rad.64) zǎn   To accumulate; hoard; save. Also pronounced cuán, see cuán.

zǎn zhú 攒竹 Acupoint Zanzhu (bamboo gathering), BL2. At the face, at the inside corner of the eyebrow (on each side). From TCM.

暫 [暂] (rad.72) zàn   Of short duration. Temporary.

zàn tíng 暂停 Time out in a competition.

鏨 [錾] (rad.167) zàn   1. To engrave. 2. To chisel.

zàn tuǐ 錾腿 Chisel kick: a poke kick leaning back to put the hip into it. From Baguazhang. Usually called diǎn tuǐ.

臟 [脏] (rad.130) zàng   The yin organs of the body, the viscera: Lungs, Liver, Spleen, Kidney, Heart, and Pericardium. The yin organs deal with the inside environment of the body, produce and store qi, and generate the fluids of the body. From TCM. Also called wǔ zàng. See also fèi, gān, pí, shèn, xīn, xīn bāo. See also fǔ.

燥 (rad.86) zào   1. Dry. 2. Dryness: one of the six qi of nature, environmental influences that can cause disease when in excess. See also liù qì, liù yín. From TCM.

造 (rad.162) zào   1. The standard meaning is to make; build; create. 2. To create an opening: feint intended to draw a counter, to prepare the way for one's own counter attack.

仄 (rad.9) zè   1. Narrow. 2. To tilt.

zè diǎn tuǐ 仄点腿 Slanting poke kick. From Chuojiao, one of its middle-basin kicks.

Z

扎 紮 (rad.64, 120) [**扎**] (rad.64) **zhā** To stab, plunge into. Usually used for thick blades such as spear and broadsword rather than thin blades such as straight sword.

zhā dāo 扎刀 Stab with a broadsword. The edge may be in any direction, as long as the tip is stabbing straight ahead, the arm and blade forming a straight line.

zhā gōu 扎钩 Stab with hooks: with the double hooks, turn the blades to strike with the sharpened tips at the grip end.

zhā mǎ 扎马 Stab the stance: regularly sit in horse stance for extended periods of time to build up the endurance and conditioning for the stance.

zhā qiāng 扎枪 Stab with a spear: the spear travels in a straight line to the tip, the left hand slides to meet the right hand. Sometimes called cì qiāng.

zhā zuò mǎ shì 扎坐马势 Stab the horse sitting stance: sit firmly into a horse stance.

挓 (rad.64) **zhā** 1. To spread one's fingers. 2. To pick up something with the fingers.

閘 [闸] (rad.169) **zhá** 1. The standard meaning is a floodgate; a break; a switch. 2. A charging technique of Baguazhang.

zhá shì quán 闸势拳 Floodgates fists: a routine of Xingyiquan. See zá shì chuí.

乍 (rad.4) **zhà** 1. First, for the first time. 2. Suddenly; abruptly. 3. Spread (like wings).

zhà shǒu 乍手 Straight stab with the fingers, palms up.

zhà zhǒu 乍肘 Spread the elbows away from the ribs (like opening wings, but can leave a relatively small space as well).

炸 (rad.86) **zhà** 1. To burst, explode. Bursting. A type of sudden power that is released without warning. From Xingyiquan. 2. Pronounced zhá, to deep fry.

詐 [诈] (rad.149) **zhà** To feign; fake. To cheat, swindle. To bluff.

zhà bài 诈败 To feign defeat.

摘 (rad.64) **zhāi** To pluck, pick. Thus, an action like picking fruit: one hand holds on while the other grasps and pulls.

zhāi bì 摘臂 Pluck the arm: when your adversary raises his arm to grab your neck, reverse grab his wrist with the same hand and reverse grab his forearm from underneath with the opposite hand, pull down while turning. From wrestling.

zhāi jiě fǎ 摘解法 Release methods for grabs: to raise and twist the hand above the head or attack directly to an adversary's face to gain release from a grab.

zhāi jìn 摘劲 Plucking power: to use vertical power, accumulating through the upper and lower body, the ribs and belly. It comes from the *dantian*, and the body core lengthens, compresses, and shakes. From Xingyiquan.

zhāi kuī 摘盔 Pluck the helmet: move in and grab an adversary's head in your hands or in the crook of the arm, twisting the neck.

zhāi xīn chuí 摘心捶 Pluck the Heart punch: a downward pound with a bent elbow, into the heart area, rotating the fist so that the knuckles and back of the fist hit. From Shaolinquan.

zhāi xīng huàn dǒu 摘星换斗 Pluck the Stars to Exchange the Dipper. 1. A horse stance with a strong push of a sword, blade vertical. From Taijiquan. 2. A pull down to a resting stance, followed by a rising stab to a one legged stance. From Liuhebafa.

粘 (rad.119) **zhān** 1. To stick, sticky. 2. Glue. Also pronounced nián.

zhān bù 粘步 Sticking step: sit back onto the rear leg without moving the foot and turn the body to evade a punch, bringing the front foot back slightly. When your adversary pulls back, immediately counter attack, advancing your front foot.

zhān jìn 粘劲 Sticking power: to adhere to an adversary in order to follow and control his actions without having to fight with strength. From Taijiquan push hands. Also called zhān zhān jìn.

zhān ná xiōng chuí 粘拿胸捶 Stick and hit with the chest: from a full grab, step to the outside of your adversary's legs, press your chest across his arms, and turn to take him down around your leg. From Tanglangquan, one of its eight short techniques.

zhān shēn 粘身 Stick close to an adversary and control him, staying at his side, not allowing him to escape.

zhān shǒu 粘手 Grab hard and hold on.

zhān shǒu ér pò shǒu 粘手而破手 If you are grabbed hard near your wrist, press your adversary's hand to your arm, then apply a wrist lock. From Tanglangquan, one of its twelve soft counters, see also shí èr róu.

霑 (rad.173) [沾] (rad.85) zhān 1. To wet; moisten. 2. To touch. 3. Commonly used to mean stick like water wetting clothing, not shedding off. From Taijiquan, one of its four requirements for push hands, see also sì yào.

zhān lián 沾连 Stick and connect when joined; a push hands method, to follow on a vertical plane.

zhān lián nián suí 沾连黏随 Stick, connect, adhere, and follow: the principles of push hands.

zhān zhān jìn 沾粘劲 Sticking power. See zhān jìn.

黏 (rad.202) zhān   See nián.

展 (rad.44) zhǎn 1. To spread, open up, unfurl. 2. To let go. 3. To stretch an adversary out.

zhǎn kuà 展胯 Throw the hips, put the hips into a kick: sending the kicking leg's hip into the kick to get more reach and power, for kicks such as side kick, poke kick, roundhouse kick etc. . Also called fàng kuà.

zhǎn zì gōng 展字功 Skill of spreading, one of Xingyiquan's eight skills, that involves stepping in to open out an adversary.

斬 [斩] (rad.69) zhǎn 1. To cut, chop, slay, cut down an adversary. 2. To cut off. 3. A high horizontal hack, often implies an arcing action.

zhǎn dāo 斩刀 Hack with a broadsword, cutting horizontally at shoulder height.

zhǎn mǎ dāo 斩马刀 A horse cutter. See pū dāo. Also called pǔ dāo, shuāng shǒu dài. 2. A long bladed sword similar to a Miao broadsword, but thicker, see also miáo dāo.

zhǎn pū dāo 斩扑刀 Hack with a horse cutter: chop horizontally with a short strong action, with the blade edge in the direction of travel, the shaft horizontal, with the right hand near the hilt and the left hand along the shaft. Both hands apply force towards the cut.

zhǎn shǒu quán 斩手拳 Cutting punch fist shape: a tight fist, fully closed, with the thumb pressing on only the second segment of the forefinger.

zhǎn quán 斩拳 Cutting punch: swing the forearm down at an angle to cut with the heel of the fist. From Piguaquan.

占 佔 (rad.25, 9) [占] (rad.25) zhàn To seize; to occupy; to take by force.

zhàn xiān 占先 To lead in a contest, to be ahead in points during a match.

戰 [战] (rad.62) zhàn To fight. War; warfare; battle.

zhàn guó 战国 Warring States Period (475-221 BC).

zhàn shù 战术 Strategy.

站 (rad.117) zhàn   To stand; be on one's feet.

zhàn hǎo zhuāng kǒu 站好桩口 Take a ready stance for sparring.

zhàn jiàn 站剑 Standing sword practice. See shì jiàn.

zhàn qiāng 站枪 Standing spear: drop down and drive the spear upwards.

zhàn rú jī 站如鸡 Stand like a chicken. See lì rú jī. Also called lì rú sōng, zhàn rú sōng.

zhàn rú sōng 站如松 Stand like a pine tree. See lì rú jī. Also called lì rú sōng, zhàn rú jī.

zhàn zhuāng 站桩 Post standing or Standing pole stance training, to set into the ground like a pile or stake and develop the postural and internal alignment appropriate to the style being trained.

zhàn zhuāng rú shān yuè nán hàn, xíng bù rú shuǐ zhōng yóu lóng 站桩如山岳难撼, 行步如水中游龙 Do stake standing like an immovable

Z

mountain, walk like a dragon swimming in water. A martial saying.

顫 [颤] (rad.181) **zhàn** To shiver; shake; shudder; vibrate.

zhàn qiāng 颤枪 To jerk or snap a spear so that it quivers.

zhàn yāo 颤腰 To shudder, or shake from the waist.

張 [张] (rad.57) **zhāng** 1. To open, spread, stretch. 2. To display. 3. A surname.

zhāng fēi 张飞 Zhang Fei (-221) a famous general from the Three Kingdoms period, one of the sworn brothers (with Guan Yu and Liu Bei) in the novel Romance of the Three Kingdoms. Best known for rash bravery rather than brilliance. Often used in movement names.

zhāng fēi héng máo 张飞横矛 Zhang Fei Snaps his Pike Sideways: grab an adversary's wrist and hit his forearm sharply with yours.

zhāng fēi léi gǔ 张飞擂鼓 Zhang Fei Beats the Drum: trip and extend an adversary to enable a punch in the back. From Baguazhang.

zhāng fēi piàn mǎ 张飞骗马 Zhang Fei Tricks the Horse. 1. A knee strike to the belly, the foot also lifting to hit the groin. 2. A side thrust kick coming up from a resting stance. 3. A knee strike to the groin or an inside crescent kick to the flank combined with a high cutting strike. From Baguazhang, one of its sixty-four hands.

zhāng fēi xià mǎ 张飞下马 Zhang Fei Dismounts from his Horse: Respond to an incoming punch directly with a spinning kick to the head.

zhāng zhǒu 张肘 Open the elbows: clenching fists, and bending the elbows, open them up to the sides above shoulder height, dropping down at the same time. Usually used to escape an enveloping hold from the back. Also called shī zi zhāng zuǐ.

章 (rad.117) **zhāng** 1. Chapter, section. 2. Rules. 3. A seal; stamp.

zhāng mén 章门 Acupoint Zhangmen (seal gate), LR13. At the torso, the tip of the 11th, floating, rib (on both sides). From TCM. A sensitive point, to the extent that striking it may cause death. If it absolutely must be hit, best to hit with a low punch, knee, elbow, or foot. In internal styles, focus in on relaxing these points, to allow the *qi* to settle down from the chest. If not relaxed, the chest can feel tense and tight.

掌 (rad.64) **zhǎng** Palm, palms; open hand. For techniques specific to the palms, see also under àn zhǎng, bǎi-, bān-, bào lián-, bào qiú-, bào yīng-, bào yuè-, bào-, bèi shēn tàn-, biǎn xuàn-, biāo-, bō-, cè shēn-, cè-, chā zǐ-, chā-, chā-, chāo-, chē lún-, chēng tiān-, chèng-, chóng-, chuān-, chuō-, cuán-, cuò-, dān tuī-, dǎn-, dǐ-, diǎn jīng-, dōu-, dùn-, fǎn bèi pī-, bǎn bèi-, fǎn è-, fǎn gài-, fǎn liāo-, fǎn-, fēn-, fēng lún pī-, fú-, fú yún fǎn-, gài shǒu-, gài-, gōng guà-, gǔn qiú-, hé pán-, hé-, hé zǐ-, hè zhuā-, héng qié-, héng-, hóu-, hú dié-, hù shēn-, huì-, jī-, jǐ-, kāi shān-, kāi-, kǎn-, kào shēn-, kòu-, lāo-, lēi shuāi-, lì yún-, lì zhuāng-, liàng-, liāo guà-, liāo tuī-, liāo yīn-, liāo-, liè-, líng-, lǚ-, luō-, mó lèi-, mǒ-, mò-, pāi-, pī-, piàn xuán-, piáo-, piē-, píng chuān-, píng fēn-, píng tuī-, pū miàn-, qián hòu jī-, qián jiǎo-, qiāng tuō-, qiē-, róu qiú-, sān chuān-, sān huàn-, sān-, shuāi pī-, shuāi-, shàng àn-, shuāng bǎi-, shuāng chā-, shuāng hé-, shuāng tuō-, shuāng zhuàng-, tā-, tà-, tà-, tàn-, tí xī tiǎo-, tí-, tiān xiān-, tiǎo-, tuī mò-, tuī-, tuì bù-, tuō tiān-, tuō yáng-, tuō-, xī huà-, xià chén-, xià tà-, xiān-, xiāo-, xié fēn-, xū bù liàng-, xuàn fēng-, yáng-, yē-, yīn-, yǐn-, yìn-, yuān yāng-, yún-, zhē yáng-, zhèng è-, zhī zì dié-, zhōng xīn-, zhuàng-, zhuó-.

zhǎng bēi 掌背 The back of the hand.

zhǎng cháng jī 掌长肌 Palmaris longus muscle: a long muscle in the inside of the forearm, runs from the medial epicondyle of the humerus to merge with the palmar connective tissue. Assists in wrist flexion.

zhǎng chén xià chā 掌沉下插 Palm settles and stabs: an expressive term for the category of hand techniques that use tucking actions. See also kòu fǎ.

zhǎng fā lì 掌发力 A palm strike, and training for palm strikes. From Yiquan.

zhǎng fǎ 掌法 The category of open hand techniques.

zhǎng gēn 掌根 The base of the palm.

zhǎng gǔ 掌骨 Metacarpal bone, five main bones

of the hand.

zhǎng suí bù fǎ fān, bù àn zhǎng dòng xíng 掌随步法翻，步按掌动行 The hands follow the footwork, and the footwork works with the movement of the hands.

zhǎng wài yán 掌外沿 The knife edge of the palm, the blade of the hand.

zhǎng wò 掌握 To grasp; master; get a good grip on (not literally). To get a good command of something.

zhǎng xīn 掌心 Palm heart, the centre of the palm, the hollow of the palm.

zhǎng xīn zǔ dǎng 掌心阻挡 Palm block: with the arms held up in on guard position, tap an incoming attack with a palm to push it slightly aside.

zhǎng xíng 掌型 Hand shape, configuration held by the hand (other than as a fist).

丈 (rad.1) **zhàng** A *zhang*, a traditional unit of measure for distance, see *shì zhàng*.

仗 (rad.9) **zhàng** 1. Usually refers to weaponry in general. 2. Sometimes refers specifically a rod or staff. 3. To hold a weapon, to be armed. 4. Battle.

zhàng jiàn 仗剑 To hold a sword, do battle with a sword.

杖 (rad.75) **zhàng** A rod, stick, or cane. It is twelve grips long, a bit shorter than a normal Shaolinquan staff (which is thirteen grips), with a crossing piece at one end.

招 (rad.64) **zhāo** One move, one posture, one technique (in martial arts). One move means the entire move – hand technique, footwork, bodywork, method, initial and final stance. Also written 着.

zhāo fǎ 招法 A move, a technique: a name that describes the entire movement and posture, taking the name sometimes from the application, sometimes from the shape or the feeling. Traditionally, moves have evocative descriptive names, often involving animals, renowned people, and cultural references. The names are a method of referring to a technique such that outsiders will not understand the meaning.

zhāo fēng shǒu 招风手 Move like the Wind punch. See *zhào fēng shǒu*.

zhāo jià 招架 A defensive move, specifically, the proper defensive move for a particular attack.

zhāo qián bì hòu 招前避后 Defend Ahead and Evade Behind: a flick kick to the rear, slapping with the opposite hand, swinging the other hand up in front. From Shaolinquan.

zhāo shù 招术 Techniques, methods, moves.

着 (rad.109) **zhāo** A technique; a trick. One move (as in chess, so applies to martial arts and other moves). One move means the entire move – hand technique, footwork, bodywork, stance, eyes, etc. Also pronounced zhe, zháo, and zhuó, with other meanings. Also written 招, see *zhāo* above.

爪 (rad.87) **zhǎo** 1. A claw; talon. 2. Hands in a clawing shape, fingers flexed. Also pronounced zhuǎ.

zhǎo fǎ 爪法 Clawing techniques: techniques done with the hand in a claw shape, such as eagle claw, tiger claw, dragon claw, etc..

照 炤 [照] (rad.86) **zhào** 1. To shine, illuminate. 2. To reflect. 3. To take a photograph. 4. To take care of.

zhào fēng shǒu 照风手 Light up the Wind punch: cover an attack with one hand and do a roundhouse knuckle punch to the adversary's ear with the other. From Shaolinquan. Similar to a roundhouse punch, but specifically hitting with the knuckles like a normal punch. Also called *zhāo fēng shǒu*. See also *guàn ěr*.

zhào hǎi 照海 Acupoint Zhaohai (shining sea), KI6. At the foot, on the inside, just below the ankle bone, below the tibialis posterior tendon (on each foot). From TCM.

趙 [赵] (rad.156) **zhào** 1. To surpass. 2. One of the Warring States during the Warring States period (c 475-221 BC), in what is now Shanxi and Hebei provinces. 3. The traditional name for the area of Hebei province, used as its short name. 4. A surname. 5. One of the four big

Z

family branches of Emeiquan, see also sì dà jiā.

zhào bǎo tài jí quán 赵堡太极拳 Zhaobao Taijiquan, a branch of Taijiquan from Zhaobao village, Henan province.

zhào jiā quán 赵家拳 Zhaojiaquan (Zhao family fist). See sòng tài zǔ cháng quán.

遮 (rad.162) **zhē** 1. To block, obstruct, impede. 2. To cover, screen, hide from view.

zhē lán 遮拦 A covering block: cross the arms and bring them down in front of the body.

zhē yáng zhǎng 遮阳掌 Block the Sun palm, a circle-walking posture like the heaven supporting palm, but reversed, arms in the same position, palms down. From Baguazhang. See also chēng tiān zhǎng.

折摺 [折] (rad.64) **zhé** 1. To break, snap. 2. To bend; twist. 3. To turn back; change direction. Also pronounced shé.

zhé biè jìn 折别劲 Breaking power: to point forward and hit back, rolling and turning to shoot. From Xingyiquan.

zhé dāo 折刀 Horizontal cut with broadsword. See zhé jiàn.

zhé dié 折叠 Fold; folding motion, particularly when the movement is within the torso.

zhé duàn 折断 Break, a general term for breaking.

zhé fǎ 折法 Breaking technique: to grab firmly and twist the little finger inwards while snapping the thumb web to push forward and down. From Qinna.

zhé jiàn 折剑 Horizontal cut with a sword: cut about shoulder height, arm straight, blade flat, palm down. May be towards the back.

zhé jié 折截 Breaking interception. See hǔ xǐ liǎn. Also called māo xǐ liǎn, yuán hóu xǐ liǎn.

zhé liè qīng shí 折裂青石 Rend the Bluestone: swing a sword overhead to chop down strongly with an extended arm in a horse stance. From Qingping sword.

zhé mǔ zhǐ 折拇指 Thumb break: grab an adversary's thumb and pull it straight up while pushing down at the root of the thumb. From Qinna.

zhé rú gōng 折如弓 Bend like a bow. Supple and elastic, one of the twelve qualities of movement of Changquan, though these descriptors apply to many other styles.

zhé shǒu quán 折手拳 Bent hand fist: a fist shape: fingers tightly clenched, giving a flat surface, thumb bent and pressing on the second section of only the index finger.

zhé wàn 折腕 Wrist break: grab an adversary's hand with both hands, place his palm towards you, and press his hand forward and down to hyperextend his wrist. From Qinna.

zhé wàn tiǎo zhǒu 折腕挑肘 Elbow scoop escape from a wrist break, an escape from a double wrist grab: bend the legs a bit and drive the elbow upwards.

zhé yāo 折腰 Break at the back. 1. Losing the connection between the upper and lower body at the waist. The waist is bent, often with the buttocks sticking out, so that the power is broken. This is seen as a major error in most styles. 2. A waist exercise, bending to the side.

zhé zhǎn 折展 To bend and open out, one of the techniques of the body.

zhé zhǐ 折指 Finger break: grab an adversary's finger and pull it straight up. From Qinna.

蛰 (rad.142) **zhé** To hibernate.

zhé lóng chū xiàn 蛰龙出现 Hibernating Dragon Appears: a same side straight punch, a punch that shoots out directly. From Xingyiquan.

zhé lóng fān shēn 蛰龙翻身 Hibernating Dragon Rolls Over: send a sword out then roll under, finishing with the sword raised up. From Baguazhang

zhé lóng xiàn shēn 蛰龙现身 Hibernating Dragon Shows Itself: Gather the hands in front of the chest, then turn around and lift the hands above the head, turning them out. This is a flower action at the wrists. From Liuhebafa.

zhé lóng yóu 蛰龙游 Hibernating dragon swims: a routine of Liuhebafa.

輒 [辄] (rad.159) **zhé** 1. The sides of a carriage. 2. The luggage rack for weapons.

zhé jīn 辄筋 Acupoint Zhejin (sinew seat), GB23.

At the torso, at the level of the fourth rib, one *cun* in front of acupoint Yuanye (on each side). From TCM.

真 (rad.109) zhēn   True; real; genuine.

zhēn qì 真气 Genuine *qi*, see zhèng qì.

枕 (rad.75) zhěn   1. A pillow. 2. To use something as a pillow. 3. In wrestling, to settle the head firmly into an adversary, pressing to assist with the throw.

zhěn gǔ 枕骨 Pillow bone: the occipital bone.

zhěn shǒu 枕手 Settling block: lower the elbow and turn the arm outward to release a grip on the wrist, circle and extend the arm forward, cutting with the blade of the hand. From Wing Chun.

zhěn tóu 枕头 Pillow with the head: in a clinch, nestle the head into the adversary to assist in applying leverage.

震 (rad.173) zhèn   1. The Thunder Trigram, represented by two broken (*yin*) lines over one solid (*yang*) line, called 'upturned cup'. Corresponds to the flying dragon formation or gate. An opening gate formation. Indicates the attribute of movement. 2. To shake; shock; vibrate. 3. A shocking technique used in Baguazhang.

zhèn bù 震步 See zhèn jiǎo.

zhèn jiǎo 震脚 1. To stomp, thump with the foot, a heavy stamp. Can be used to stamp on an adversary's feet or to gain power. Also called duò zi jiǎo, hèn jiǎo, zhèn bù. 2. In southern styles, usually means to stamp simultaneously with both feet.

zhèn jiǎo àn zhǎng 震脚按掌 Stamp and press: stamp a foot and press down with one palm, tucking the other foot behind the knee of the stamping leg. From Longfist.

zhèn jiǎo bào quán 震脚抱拳 Stamp the feet with the fists clenched: holding the fists at the waist, pop up to stamp both feet strongly. In competition Southern style, often used to begin a routine.

zhèn jiǎo cáng dāo 震脚藏刀 Stamp the feet with a broadsword hidden: pulling a broadsword back behind the body to the right, pop up to stamp both feet strongly. From southern styles.

Z

爭 [争] (rad.87) zhēng   To contend; to struggle. To fight.

zhēng jiāo 争交 Old style wrestling.

zhēng jìn 争劲 Press or brace outwards, keeping a closing energy within the body. Used in conjunction with rolling power to keep power balanced during opening movements. See also gǔn jìn.

㨃 (rad.64) zhěng   A wrestling throw; to throw someone down.

撜 (rad.64) zhěng   To grab and tug, a setup for a throw in wrestling.

zhěng dài jià liáng jiǎo 撜带架梁脚 Tug and Support the Beam: tug and pull the adversary's upper body while hooking the ankle with the foot.

zhěng kāi 撜开 Tug out of a grab.

zhěng fǎ 撜法 Tugging grappling hold: tug downwards to release from a grip, or tug to fake and set up a throw. From wrestling.

整 (rad.66) zhěng   Whole; complete; full; entire.

zhěng jìn 整劲 Whole body power: use of maximum power, obtained by relaxing, sinking, and connecting the body throughout, clearing all blockages, to obtain a full and direct power.

zhěng qí 整齐 Orderly. This is a requirement at the basic level of training, the movements must be done in an orderly fashion.

zhěng quān shǒu fǎ 整圈手法 Full-circle methods: against a multi-person attack when you are surrounded, to keep moving, always aiming to either to counter or attack, not just to avoid.

zhěng tào 整套 A complete routine from beginning to end.

zhěng tào xùn liàn 整套训练 Whole routine training: to train repetitions of a complete routine.

zhěng tǐ jìn 整体劲 Whole body power.

掙 [挣] (rad.64) zhèng   To contend; struggle; throw off.

zhèng jìn 挣劲 Opposing power, contending power: to use the midline of the spine, pulling

Z

open to the sides with a right and left opening power, to give balanced power to the limbs. From Xingyiquan. See also gǔn jìn, guǒ jìn, zuān jìn.

zhèng ná fǎ 挣拿法 1. Opposing grappling hold: an angled, crossing grip, pulling in opposing directions. 2. An arm technique, a powerful shake side to side, utilizing the full power of the arms. Both from wrestling.

zhèng wàn 挣腕 Throw off the wrist: when one wrist is grabbed with one hand, jerk it sharply downward to release the grab.

正 (rad.77) **zhèng** 1. Upright, straight; 2. Situated in the middle. 3. Honest. 4. Precisely. 5. Correct, right, proper.

zhèng bǎ 正把 Standard grip, normal grip. Grip the shaft of a long weapon with the thumb web pointing forward. Grip a short weapon with the thumb web at the guard. See also zhèng wò.

zhèng bā zì bù 正八字步 Normal Character Eight stance: feet form the shape of the character eight (八) with the toes pointing towards each other, usually a foot-length apart, sitting on both legs, knees aligned with the feet.

zhèng bān tuǐ 正搬腿 Partner assisted front straight stretch: leaning against a wall, the partner pushes your leg up, then straight towards the wall.

zhèng bù 正步 Straight stance: both feet pointing forward, a foot-length apart both by length and width. From Wu Taijiquan.

zhèng cuò dāo 正错刀 Straight rub with a broadsword: a quick backward press followed by a forward push, with the palm up, the edge forward, and the tip to the right.

zhèng dāng 正裆 See zhèng dāng bù.

zhèng dāng bù 正裆步 Middle crotch stance: sit with the feet open and parallel, weight in the middle. The feet are two foot-lengths apart, the shins upright, the knees above the toes, so that the stance is square. This stance is a fairly high horse stance. In Duanquan, also called zhèng dāng, fāng dāng.

zhèng dāo 正刀 Conventional broadsword: the blade is level with the edge down. A positional reference, separate from the direction of the strike.

zhèng dīng zì bù 正丁字步 Normal T stance: both feet flat on the ground, one foot pointing to the instep of the other, feet about a foot-length apart. From Baguazhang.

zhèng è zhǎng 正扼掌 Normal guarding palm: palm extended with the fingers down, palm facing away from the body, arm externally rotated. See also fǎn è zhǎng.

zhèng fāng 正方 1. Conventional tactics. 2. Setting up facing straight onto an adversary, or coming straight in at an adversary.

zhèng gōu shǒu 正勾手 Upright hooked hand, a hand positioning: a hooked hand with the fingers pointing down, top of wrist on the top.

zhèng jí bù 正疾步 Normal quick step. See jí bù.

zhèng jiǎo 正搅 Normal stirring: circle the tip of a sword clockwise.

zhèng jiǎo 正脚 Main gate kick: a front heel kick, either straight or slightly turned out. From Wing Chun.

zhèng liāo dāo (jiàn) 正撩刀(剑) Upright slice up with a broadsword (or sword): slice up with the forearm externally rotated (turn the thumb away from the palm), cutting with the little finger edge of the blade.

zhèng lūn biān 正抡鞭 Normal circles with a steel whip: swing the whip vertically at the right side of the body, the whip circling down in front, then up behind.

zhèng mén 正门 The main gate of an adversary: his chest, abdomen, and groin.

zhèng miàn 正面 From the front: in illustrated books, looking straight on at the posture as if seated to watch as the routine is presented, the presenter standing facing the viewer at the beginning. See also cè miàn, hòu miàn.

zhèng miàn fǎn lūn biān 正面反抡鞭 Reverse circles in front of the body with a steel whip: swing the whip vertically, anticlockwise, in front of the body.

zhèng miàn zhèng lūn biān 正面正抡鞭 Normal circles in front of the body with a steel whip: swing the whip vertically, clockwise, in front of the body.

zhèng pī fā lì 正劈发力 Release of power with a straight cut: vertical cutting, one arm moving up while the other arm moves down. From Yiquan.

zhèng pū 正扑 Front fall: fall straight forward, breaking the fall with the forearms, swinging them to hit as you land.

zhèng qì 正气 1. Healthy *qi*, correct *qi*. 2. The combination of innate *qi* and absorbed *qi*, responsible for physiological function and resistance to disease. Also called zhēn qì. 3. Morality or righteousness.

zhèng qín 正擒 Straight seize, normal grab: grabbing an adversary with your thumb web forward.

zhèng quán 正拳 Upright fist: fist eye on top, knuckles forward. When used in a punch, there is no rotation of the arm. Also called lì quán, rì zì quán.

zhèng què 正确 Correct. This is a requirement at the basic level of training, the positions must be learned correctly.

zhèng sǎo tuǐ 正扫腿 Front sweep kick. From Chuojiao, one of its middle-basin kicks.

zhèng shēn 正身 Face an adversary straight on. As a positional description: stand with the body facing straight forward.

zhèng shēn fǎ 正身法 Keep the body upright: the torso needs to stay upright and centered to allow stable, agile, and effective movement.

zhèng shēn mǎ 正身马 Front facing horse stance: stand facing straight on, the legs slightly apart, open front to back. From Wing Chun.

zhèng shuāi 正摔 Direct Fall: a direct and full slap on the ground with a long weapon, held at the end in one hand, in a deep bow stance to take the hand to the ground.

zhèng sī tuǐ 正撕腿 The front splits ('tear' the legs), sitting with the legs straight and extended to front and back.

zhèng tī tuǐ 正踢腿 Front straight kick: a direct swinging kick with the foot dorsi-flexed, both legs kept straight. A representative move of Longfist. In the category of straight swinging kicks, see also zhí bǎi xìng tuǐ fǎ. As a stretch, also called wǔ lù tuǐ, and as a kick, also called yíng mén tuǐ.

zhèng tuō diǎn 正托点 Straight poke and lift: a poke kick with the hands forward to hold an adversary. From Chuojiao, one of its middle-basin kicks. Also called yè dī cáng huā.

zhèng wò 正握 Standard grip: holding a weapon normally, such as a steel whip with the whip coming out from the thumb side, or a sword with the thumb web at the hilt, the blade coming out normally. Also called zhèng bǎ.

zhèng wò tuǐ 正卧腿 Lying front stretch: grab the foot of one leg extended (foot on the ground, dorsi-flexing the ankle), bend the supporting leg, and pull the chin to the toes, lying along the leg.

zhèng yā tuǐ 正压腿 Front straight leg pressing stretch: place the heel of one leg on a surface and press the body forward, trying to touch the chin to the toes.

zhèng yǎo 正咬 Frontal bite, a counter takedown: when grabbed, slide in tight to an adversary, catching low on behind his ankle, hook and turn, pressing out with the knee.

zhèng yíng 正营 Acupoint Zhengying (upright construction), GB17. At the top of the head, 2.5 *cun* in from the front hairline, 2.25 *cun* lateral to the midline (on each side). From TCM.

zhèng zhǎng 正掌 Upright palm: fingers pointing up, palm forward.

zhèng zhāo 正着 Proper moves. See zhèng zhāo below.

zhèng zhāo 正招 1. Proper movement: doing a movement as taught, not changing the movement. 2. Straightforward techniques in sparring, using direct lines, hard techniques, with a tendency of force against force.

月争 [胂] (rad.130) **zhèng** The elbow, particulary when used as a weapon. Usually called zhǒu, see zhǒu.

之 (rad.3) **zhī** 1. A possessive particle, the literary equivalent of de 的. 2. In movement names sometimes used for its Z shape.

zhī zì dié zhǎng 之字蝶掌 Character Z Butterfly palm: in a straight bow stance, circle the hands, right hand palm out, left hand palm angled near the right elbow to make a Z shape with the forearms. The 104th move of the tiger and crane routine.

Z

支 (rad.65) **zhī** 1. To prop up. To support. 2. To protrude. 3. A branch, an offshoot. 4. The twelve Earthly Branches. See dì zhī.

zhī bié 支别 1. Propping pin, holding tight and shoving an adversary away with the forearm. Used to keep an adversary away or to prepare for a takedown, as it easily changes to a pull. 2. A direct hip throw, stepping in and swinging your leg up to throw your adversary on your hip. Both from wrestling.

zhī chēng 支撑 To support; prop up. Strut; brace.

zhī chēng bā miàn 支撑八面 Braced to the eight directions: to guard in all directions.

zhī gōu 支沟 Acupoint Zhigou (branch ditch), SJ6. At the forearm, on the outside, in line with acupoint Yangchi and the tip of the elbow, between the radius and the ulna, three *cun* up from the wrist crease (in each arm). From TCM.

zhī ná fǎ 支拿法 Propping grappling hold. 1. Grab the adversary's jacket opening and sleeve and jerk to get a reaction from him so that you can use his power for the throw. 2. Grab the adversary's belt or lower jacket and brace to prevent him from getting in on you. Both from wrestling.

zhī tuǐ 支腿 Propping leg: firm up the supporting leg when doing a throw or trip with the other leg, giving support to the technique and withstanding any attack to the supporting leg. From wrestling.

zhī zhèng 支正 Acupoint Zhizheng (branch to the upright), SI6. At the forearm, along the outer edge, on the anterior edge of the ulna, five *cun* above the wrist (in each arm). From TCM. A crippling point, striking here may cause serious injury. See also cán xué.

zhī zhǒu 支肘 Prop with the elbow: press up and out with the elbow when in close contact and an adversary is trying to squeeze your elbows in.

肢 (rad.130) **zhī** Limb, limbs, the extremities (the arms and legs).

直 [直] (rad.109) **zhí** 1. Straight, a straight line. 2. To straighten. 3. Vertical.

zhí bǎi tuǐ fǎ 直摆腿法 See zhí bǎi xìng tuǐ fǎ.

zhí bǎi xìng tuǐ fǎ 直摆性腿法 Straight swinging kicks: a category of kicks that use straight legs, swinging the leg from the hip. Also called zhí bǎi tuǐ fǎ. See also cè tī tuǐ, dào tī tuǐ, hòu bǎi tuǐ, hòu liào tuǐ, lǐ hé tuǐ, liào tī, piàn mǎ, qián tī tuǐ, wài bǎi tuǐ, xié tī tuǐ, zhēng tī tuǐ. Sometimes called biāo tī.

zhí chòng quán 直冲拳 A straight punch. Also called zhí quán.

zhí dāo 直刀 Upright broadsword: the blade is vertical with the tip up. A positional reference, separate from the direction of the strike.

zhí dǎo huáng lóng 直捣黄龙 Directly Attack Huanglong. This is the capital of the Nuzhen Tartars, so the phrase means to drive straight on towards the enemy, or to directly deal with a problem. 1. Step into a bow stance elbow strike. From Baguazhang. 2. Step into a bow stance reverse punch. From Yangjia style.

zhí fān shēn 直翻身 Straight line roll over. See diào yāo.

zhí jiān 直肩 Straight shoulder, a shoulder technique: to ram with the head of the shoulder in any level direction.

zhí jiē huán jī 直接还击 Direct counter attack. 1. To counter as an adversary attacks, striking directly to the attacking segment. 2. To sidestep or dodge and directly counter an attack.

zhí jiē jìn gōng zhāo fǎ 直接进攻招法 Direct attacking moves: techniques that are short, direct, and quick, used to directly attack, most commonly fist or palm strikes.

zhí lì 直力 1. Straight strength: obvious strength with no subtlety. 2. Vertical strength: the strength involved in lifting a heavy object straight above the head. Also called guò dǐng lì.

zhí lì 直立 Standing upright: to do all stances with straight legs, not sitting into stances. An error in most styles.

zhí lì píng héng 直立平衡 Straight standing balances: in competition styles, the category of balances with a straight supporting leg.

zhí lì zhǎng 直立掌 Upright vertical palm: fingers pointing up, wrist straight. The position is when the hand is held up from a bent elbow, or when the arm is extended straight up. A positional reference, separate from the direction of the strike.

zhí mén 直门 Straight gateway: grab with right

hand to the right side of an adversary.

zhí pū hǔ 直扑虎 Straight Pounce on the Tiger. See cuān pū hǔ.

zhí quán 直拳 A straight punch. In Sanda, this usually refers to a reverse stance punch. A smooth stance straight punch is called cì quán. Also called zhí chòng quán.

zhí quán fā lì 直拳发力 A straight punch. From Yiquan.

zhí rù 直入 Direct entry: a straight stab with a spear, without the usual covering moves preceding it.

zhí shēn 直身 Straight body, a positional description. 1. The whole body is upright and straight, the head up, the jaw tucked in, the back flat, the legs straight. 2. When used with other stances and techniques, the torso is upright.

zhí shēn qián sǎo 直身前扫 Front sweep kick with the body upright, specifically not touching the hands down. Also called qián sǎo tuǐ. In the category of sweep kicks, see also sǎo zhuàn xìng tuǐ fǎ.

zhí shēn qián sǎo wǔ bǎi sì 直身前扫540 Front sweep five-forty: a front sweep kick with the body upright, not touching the hands down, covering one and a half rotations.

zhí shēn qián sǎo jiǔ bǎi 直身前扫900 Front sweep nine-hundred: a front sweep kick with the body upright, not touching the hands down, covering two and a half rotations.

zhí tàng liù shí sì zhǎng 直趟六十四掌 Straight-line sixty-four palms. See liù shí sì shǒu. Also called bā bā liù shí sì zhǎng, bā duàn liù shí sì zhǎng.

zhí tōng 直通 A straight punch. From Tanglangquan.

zhí tōng ér gōu shǒu 直通而勾手 Hook away a straight punch. From Tanglangquan, one of its twelve soft counters, see also shí èr róu.

zhí xiàn dà lóng xíng 直线大龙形 Straight line Dragon form: walking forward with a three step pattern, alternating the same side arm and opposite arm down beside the front knee, pressing forward. From Xingyiquan.

zhí xíng bù 直行步 Straight-line walking: footwork done in a certain way appropriate to the style. Not usually just walking in a straight line.

zhí yāo 直腰 Straight back. 1. Holding the torso straight, usually in conjunction with the chest held up. A requirement in many styles. Sometimes means as an error, holding the body too straight. 2. To straighten the back and chest in a close clinch, a wrestling technique.

蹠 (rad.157) **zhí** The metatarsus, sole of the foot (formal).

zhí gǔ 蹠骨 Metatarsals, the five long bones in the feet. Also called zhǐ gǔ.

只 (rad.30) **zhǐ** Only; merely. But, yet.

zhǐ yā bù liù bù zhōng yòng, zhǐ liù bù yā bèn rú niú 只压不遛不中用，只遛不压笨如牛 If you just stretch your legs and don't kick, they will be useless; if you just kick and don't stretch, they will be clumsy as an ox. A martial saying.

指 (rad.64) **zhǐ** A finger, fingers. To point at.

zhǐ chuō yī diǎn, quán dǎ yī piàn 指戳一点，拳打一片 A finger stabs a point, while a fist hits a wide area. A martial saying.

zhǐ dāng chuí 指裆锤 Mallet to the Groin: a punch to the groin, usually a swinging up punch like a backfist or hammer fist.

zhǐ dāng shì 指裆式 Point to the Groin: see zhǐ dāng chuí.

zhǐ dì chéng gāng 指地成刚 Point to the Ground to become Steel: stab down in a reverse grip, then swing a sword overhead, turning around to chop high in a raised knee stance. From Qingping sword.

zhǐ dìng zhōng yuán 指定中原 Finger Sets to the Centre: standing up, left fist at the hip, push the right hand forward, palm forward, index finger up. The seventh move of the tiger and crane routine.

zhǐ dōng dǎ xī 指东打西 Point to the East and Hit to the West. 1. Fake or actually hit in one direction or part of the body to draw the attention of an adversary there, then hit the other direction or body part. Also called shēng dōng jī xī, zhǐ shàng dǎ xià. 2. Extending a grabbed hand away while striking with the other hand. From Baguazhang.

Z

zhǐ gǔ 指骨 Phalanx, phalanges (there are fourteen in the hand and fourteen in the foot), finger and toe bones.

zhǐ guān jié 指关节 Finger joints.

zhǐ jiān 指尖 The tip of a finger, the finger tips.

zhǐ lù duǎn dǎ 指路短打 Point the way short strikes: a basic routine of Mizongquan, to train mobility and quickness. Written up as forty-six moves.

zhǐ lù wéi mǎ 指鹿为马 Call a Deer a Horse (to mislead): walk away, slicing a sword fully up, then turn and dab down to the front. From Qingping sword.

zhǐ nán jīn zhēn 指南金针 Golden Needle Guides you South: from a reverse empty stance, pressing a sword flat in front of the belly, tip slightly up, step forward and stab straight. From Qingping sword.

zhǐ nán zhēn shì 指南针式 Needle Guides you South model. 1. One of twenty-four classic spear moves. Most spear routines will have a move with a like name. In general, this name refers to a high level stab. See also shàng píng qiāng. 2. To stab with a sword. From Yang Taijiquan.

zhǐ qiǎn qū jī 指浅屈肌 Flexor digitorum superficialis muscle: a shallow muscle on the inside of the forearm. Assists in wrist and finger flexion.

zhǐ rì gāo shēng 指日高升 Point to the Sun on High: sit to a right empty stance and stab a sword up to the forward right, palm up, left hand over the head and also turned to point to the forward right. From Qingping sword.

zhǐ sāng mà huái 指桑骂槐 Point at the Mulberry but Curse the Locust tree. The twenty-sixth of the Thirty-six Stratagems of Warfare, which apply to many situations.

zhǐ shān dǎ mò 指山打磨 Point at the Mountain to Get the Millstone: feint then attack with multiple strikes. From Baguazhang.

zhǐ shān mài mò 指山卖磨 Point at the Mountain to Sell the Millstone: pull the adversary's arm down, then use the force and power line as he pulls back to move forward and strike. From Baguazhang.

zhǐ shàng dǎ xià 指上打下 Point High and Hit Low. 1. In general, to feint high to draw an opening for a low attack. Also called shēng dōng jī xī, zhǐ dōng, dǎ xī. 2. A high stab in reverse stance followed with a low punch, snapping to horse stance. From Meishanquan.

zhǐ shēn qū jī 指深屈肌 Flexor digitorum profundus muscle: a deep muscle on the inside of the forearm. Assists in wrist and finger flexion.

zhǐ shǒu wèn tí 指手问题 Point the Finger to Ask a Question: in a right open bow stance push the left palm forward down the midline, index finger extended. Extend the left fist out behind and lean onto the thigh. The 69th move of the tiger and crane routine.

zhǐ tiān chā dì 指天插地 Point to the Sky and Stab to the Ground: stab the inside arm straight up by the head and stab the outside arm straight down by the hip of the raised arm. Palms may be rotated to face either out or in. Used especially during circle-walking, combining twisting and extending powers. From Baguazhang. Also called zhǐ tiān huà dì, zhǐ tiān zhǐ dì.

zhǐ tiān chā dì shì 指天插地式 Point to the Sky and Stab to the Ground model: circle-walking and changes done seeking the movement and manner of Point to the Sky and Stab to the Ground. From Baguazhang. See also zhǐ tiān chā dì.

zhǐ tiān huà dì 指天画地 Point to the Sky and Draw the Ground: see zhǐ tiān chā dì.

zhǐ tiān zhǐ dì 指天指地 Point to the Sky and Point to the Ground: See zhǐ tiān chā dì.

zhǐ yǐ chēng tiān 指尾撑天 Fingertips Brace the Sky: in a right reverse bow stance, settle the left hand down then push it forward, fingers up as if supporting the sky, elbow bent a bit. The 34th move of the tiger and crane routine.

zhǐ yuè guān huī 指月观辉 Point to the Moon to View the Splendour: circle a sword tip then stab downwards at an angle, with the hand rotated thumb down. From Qingping sword.

zhǐ zǒng shēn jī 指总伸肌 Extensor digitorum muscle: a forearm muscle running from the lateral epicondyle of the humerus to open out to tendons attached to the middle and distal phalanges (of the fingers). Assists in wrist and finger extension.

止 (rad.77) **zhǐ** 1. To stop. 2. Up until. 3. Only.

zhǐ diǎn 止点 Final placement of a movement of the hand or foot.

紙 [纸] (rad.120) **zhǐ** 1. Paper. 2. Measure word for documents.

zhǐ péng gōng 纸蓬功 Paper clumps training: pound a many layered pile of paper to develop the fists.

趾 (rad.157) **zhǐ** 1. Toe, toes. 2. Foot.

zhǐ cháng shēn jī 趾长伸肌 Extensor digitorum longus muscle: in the shin. Assists in lifting the toes and dorsiflexing the ankle.

zhǐ gǔ 趾骨 Metatarsals, the five long bones in the feet. Also called zhí gǔ.

志 (rad.61) **zhì** Will; aspiration; ideal. Associated with the Kidney, and with the character attribute of the ability to finalise intended actions.

zhì shì 志室 Acupoint Zhishi (residence of the will), BL52. At the back, level with the spinous process of the second lumbar vertebra, three *cun* lateral to the midline (on each side). From TCM. Striking here injures the arteries, veins, and nerves in the waist, and shocks the kidneys.

擲 [掷] (rad.64) **zhì** To throw; to cast; to hurl.

zhì jī 掷击 To punch with a throwing action.

智 (rad.72) **zhì** Wisdom, knowledge, resourcefulness, intelligence. One of the character traits expected of martial artists.

治 (rad.85) **zhì** 1. Rule; govern; administer. 2. To treat, cure (a disease). 3. To control; harness.

zhì fǎ 治法 Treatment methods. It is handy for martial artists to know the treatment after damaging someone.

滯 [滞] (rad.85) **zhì** 1. Stagnant, sluggish. 2. Blocked, obstructed.

秩 (rad.115) **zhì** Order (formal).

zhì biān 秩边 Acupoint Zhibian (border of the sequence), BL54. At the sacrum, level with the fourth sacral foramina, level with the sacrococcygeal joint, at the level of the top of the crack of the buttocks, three *cun* lateral to the midline (on each side). From TCM.

窒 (rad.116) **zhì** To block, stop up, obstruct.

zhì shǒu 窒手 Obstructing hand, jerk hand: a downward forward block together with a quick downward push. Both forearms gather in, palms down, elbows down, pressure on the thumb side. From Wing Chun.

至 (rad.133) **zhì** 1. To, until. 2. Extremely, most. 3. To arrive; reach.

zhì wēi fǎn tài 至危反泰 Turn Danger into Safety: from a bow stance stab, sit and lean back and snap the wrist to snap a sword tip up to block. From Qingping sword.

zhì yáng 至阳 Acupoint Zhiyang (yang extremity), DU9. At the back, at the depression under spinous process of the seventh thoracic vertebra, on the midline, on a direct line between the lower tips of the shoulder blades. From TCM. One of the main targets on the body.

zhì yīn 至阴 Acupoint Zhiyin (reaching yin), BL67. At the foot, on the outside, at the border of the base of the toenail of the little toe (on each foot). This is the final acupoint of the Bladder channel. From TCM.

製 (rad.145) [制] (rad.18) **zhì** To make; produce; manufacture.

zhì zǐ 制子 Implement: a stone with a grip cut into it, used to train grip strength, power and hand eye coordination. Similar to a stone lock or kettlebell. See also shí suǒ.

中 (rad.2) **zhōng** 1. Middle, centre; central. 2. Mathematical mean. 3. Fit for. 4. Pronounced zhòng, to hit exactly, hit the mark. See zhòng.

zhōng bǎ 中把 The middle grip: the mid-section, the middle third of a long handled weapon such as a staff.

Z

zhōng chōng 中冲 Acupoint Zhongchong (central charging), PC9. At the tip of the middle finger, on the radial side (on each hand). This is the final acupoint in the Pericardium channel. From TCM. Pinching the side of the finger tip while applying a control can add considerable pain to the technique, even to the extent of causing unconsciousness.

zhōng dān tián 上丹田 Upper cinnabar field: centred in the chest. See also dān tián, shàng dān tián, xià dān tián.

zhōng dìng 中定 Setting upright and vertical; resting at the central equilibrium.

zhōng dū 中都 Acupoint Zhongdu (central metropolis), LR6. At the calf, on the inside, seven *cun* up from the ankle, on the midline of the tibia (on each leg). From TCM.

zhōng dú 中渎 Acupoint Zhongdu (central river), GB32. At the thigh, on the midline down the outside, in the vastus lateralis muscle, two *cun* below acupoint Fengshi, five *cun* up from the popliteal crease, between the iliotibial tract and the biceps femoris muscle (on each leg). From TCM.

zhōng duàn 中段 1. The mid-section of the blade or shaft of a long handled weapon. 2. The middle section of a sectioned weapon such as the three-section staff.

zhōng fēng 中封 Acupoint Zhongfeng (central mound), LR4. At the foot, one *cun* in front of the ankle, in the depression made by the tendon of the tibialis anterior, between acupoints Shangqiu and Jiexi (on each foot). From TCM.

zhōng fǔ 中府 Acupoint Zhongfu (central treasury), LU1. At the chest, 6 *cun* lateral to the midline, just under the top rib, under the lateral tip of the clavicle (on each side). From TCM. In internal styles, these points are relaxed, to help relax the collar bones and shoulders.

zhōng gōu 中勾 Middle hook: a short mid height hook kick to the thigh, dorsi-flexing the ankle to hook. Also called gōu tī.

zhōng guǎn zhī fǎ 中管之法 Take the middle method: step directly in between an adversary's feet, getting the body in close to his body. Also called zǒu zhōng pán.

zhōng guó 中国 China, in general, and historically.

zhōng huá rén mín gòng hé guó 中华人民共和国 The People's Republic of China (1949-).

zhōng huá mín guó 中华民国 The Republic of China 1. China (1911-1949). 2. Taiwan (1949-).

zhōng jí 中极 Acupoint Zhongji (central pole), RN3. At the abdomen, four *cun* below the navel, on the midline. From TCM. Striking here shocks the arteries and veins in the abdominal wall and may damage the colon.

zhōng jí cháng (nán) quán 中级长（南）拳 Intermediate level standardized long (or Southern) fist routine.

zhōng jí dāo (jiàn) shù 中级刀（剑）术 Intermediate level standardized broadsword (or sword) routine.

zhōng jí gùn (qiāng) shù 中级棍（枪）术 Intermediate level standardized staff (or spear) routine.

zhōng jí tào lù 中级套路 Intermediate level standardized routine. In Longfist, refers to the B level routines. These are usually about fifty moves.

zhōng jié bù míng quán shēn xuán kōng 中节不明全身悬空 If the middle sections are not understood, the whole body will be unsettled. A martial saying.

zhōng jié suí 中节随 The middle sections of the body follow. See also sān jié.

zhōng jù lí 中距离 Mid-range, fairly close to an adversary: within striking range of a punching or kicking attack without needing to step in. See also jì jù lí, yuán jù lí.

zhōng kuí 中魁 Extraordinary acupoint Zhongkui (central eminence), EX-UE4. At the back of the hand, on the interphalangeal joint at the distal end of the proximal phalanx of the middle finger (on each hand). From TCM.

zhōng liáo 中髎 Acupoint Zhongliao (central bone-hole), BL33. At the sacrum, the third sacral formina, just below acupoint Ciliao, 0.6 *cun* lateral to the midline (on each side). From TCM.

zhōng lù 中路 1. The midsection of the body: abdomen and chest. 2. Mid-level route for striking, going for the midsection of the body. Also called zhōng sān lù.

zhōng lǚ shū 中膂俞 Acupoint Zhonglushu (central backbone transport), BL29. At the sacrum, level with the third sacral foramina, 1.5 *cun* lateral to the midline (on each side). From TCM.

zhōng pán 中盘 1. The midsection of the body: torso, belly. 2. The middle basin of the body: the pelvic girdle. 3. A mid-height posture used whilst training moving. From Baguazhang. 4. Centered Basins: a move that finishes in a low horse stance opening the arms, with shoulder girdle, pelvic girdle, and lower legs aligned. From Chen Taijiquan.

zhōng pán bù 中盘步 Centered stance: a natural fighting stance, similar to a sixty-forty or seventy-thirty, but less set. See sān tǐ shì.

zhōng pán tuǐ 中盘腿 The mid basin kicks, a series of short routines of Chuojiao. See also bā pán tuǐ, shàng pán tuǐ, xià pán tuǐ.

zhōng pán tuǐ fǎ 中盘腿法 Middle-basin kicks: fifty-three kicks that strike at mid-height, or high but grounded, to the front, rear, and side. From Chuojiao. See also shàng pán tuǐ fǎ, xià pán tuǐ fǎ.

zhōng píng qiāng 中平枪 A mid-level stab with a spear: the shaft is horizontal, at chest height. Also called sì hǎi bīn fú shì.

zhōng qì 中气 Inside *qi*, Middle Burner *qi*. middle *qi*: the *qi* settled in the *dantian* and flowing through the body.

zhōng qiāng 中枪 Midsized spear: three metres long, base circumference is that of a circle made with the thumb and forefinger.

zhōng quán 中拳 Central punch: a straight upright punch to the centre of the chest. From Wing Chun.

zhōng quán 中泉 Extraordinary acupoint Zhongquan (central spring), EX-UE3. At the back of the hand, the wrist crease, the depression between the thumb and index finger extensor tendons. From TCM.

zhōng sān lù 中三路 The middle of three routes. See zhōng lù.

zhōng shū 中枢 Acupoint Zhongshu (central pivot), DU7. At the back, at the depression below the spinous process of the tenth thoracic vertebra, on the midline. From TCM.

zhōng tíng 中庭 Acupoint Zhongting (central palace), RN16. At the chest, at the sternum, level with the fifth intercostal space, on the midline. From TCM.

zhōng wǎn 中脘 Acupoint Zhongwan (central stomach duct), RN12. At the abdomen, four *cun* above the navel, on the midline. From TCM.

zhōng xiàn 中线 Midline, median line. Central line. Also called zhōng xīn xiàn.

zhōng xīn xiàn 中心线 Midline. See zhōng xiàn.

zhōng xīn zhǎng 中心掌 Palm to the centre: a strike to the solar plexus with the palm or backhand.

zhōng xún huán fǎ 中循环法 Mid-cycle change-over: when changing from one side to the other of circle-walking set postures, going on to the following fixed posture, instead of to the other side of the same posture. From Baguazhang. See also dà xún huán fǎ, xiǎo xún huán fǎ.

zhōng yī 中医 Chinese traditional medicine. Often, and in this dictionary, referred to as TCM.

zhōng yuè sōng shān 中岳嵩山 Mount Song, the central of the sacred mountains. See also sōng shān, wǔ yuè.

zhōng zhèng 中正 Centered and erect.

zhōng zhǐ 中指 The middle finger, middle fingers.

zhōng zhǔ 中渚 Acupoint Zhongzhu (central islet), SJ3. At the hand, on the back between the metacarpal bones and the tendons of the ring and little finger, proximal to the knuckles (on each hand). From TCM. A sensitive point, pressing here can cause numbness, pain, and loss of strength. If more pressure is applied it can shock the brain and induce unconsciousness.

zhōng zhù 中注 Acupoint Zhongzhu (central flow), KI15. At the abdomen, one *cun* below the navel, 0.5 *cun* lateral to the midline (on each side). From TCM.

忠 (rad.61) **zhōng** Loyal, faithful, devoted.

zhōng yì 忠义 Loyal and righteous. A character trait expected of martial artists.

zhōng yì quán 忠义拳 Loyal fist: a basic routine of Yangjia style, written up as twenty-six moves.

Z

鐘 [钟] (rad.167) **zhōng** 1. A bell. 2. A clock. 3. A surname.

zhōng kuí 钟魁 Zhong Kui: a guardian spirit, the demon queller. Used in movement names.

zhōng kuí zhèng jiàn 钟魁仗剑 Zhong Kui Holds his Sword: hold a sword in a ready posture. From Taijiquan.

中 (rad.2) **zhòng** 1. To hit the mark, to hit exactly. 2. Pronounced zhōng, the middle, see zhōng,

重 (rad.166) **zhòng** 1. Weight. 2. Heavy. 3. Important. 3. Pronounced chóng, to repeat.

zhòng lì 重力 Gravity; gravitational pull or force.

zhòng mù gùn 重木棍 Weighted stick: a stick with a weighted ball at one end, used for grip, wrist, and upper body training.

zhòng rú tiě 重如铁 Heavy like iron: one of the twelve qualities of movement of Changquan, though these descriptors apply to many other styles. When are in a stance that is supposed to be solid, you should settle like a block of lead.

周 週 (rad 30, 162) **[周]** (rad.30) **zhōu** 1. Circumference; periphery. 2. Make a circuit. 3. All over; all around. 4. A week. 5. The Zhou dynasty (1046-256 BC). 6. A surname.

zhōu cāng káng dāo 周倉扛刀 Zhou Cang Shoulders his Cutter: hoist the adversary's arm using the elbow, then place it over the shoulder. From Baguazhang, one of its sixty-four hands.

zhōu róng 周荣 Acupoint Zhourong (circumference flourishing), SP20. At the chest, the second intercostal space, six *cun* lateral to the midline (on each side). From TCM.

zhōu shēn xiāng suí 周身相随 The whole body moves in full coordination, with mutual accord and support of all its segments. A common requirement, especially in internal styles.

捌 (rad.64) **zhōu** A strong lift with both hands held close to the body, palms usually up, lifting at waist height to maintain maximum power.

zhōu tī 捌踢 Lift and kick, a trip: drag an adversary's collar down, then use his reaction to step in and trip him backwards. From wrestling.

軸 [轴] (rad.159) **zhóu** 1. Axis. 2. An axle; a shaft.

肘 (rad.130) **zhǒu** 1. The elbow. The elbow is sometimes written zhèng when referring to techniques, see zhèng.

zhǒu cè 肘侧 The elbow joint. One of the main targets on the body, and also a strong striking implement.

zhǒu dǐ chuí 肘底捶 Mallet Under Elbow: one fist punches from under the forward elbow, usually in an empty stance, a controlling close strike. From Taijiquan. Also called zhǒu dǐ kàn chuí, zhǒu dǐ kàn quán. Sometimes called yè dǐ cáng huā.

zhǒu dǐ jìn chuí 肘底进捶 Mallet Advances under the Elbow: get in close, wedging a tightly bent arm with the fist up, and punch with the other under its elbow. From Baguazhang, one of its sixty-four hands. Also called zhǒu dǐ kàn chuí.

zhǒu dǐ kàn chuí 肘底看捶 See the Mallet under the Elbow. See zhǒu dǐ jìn chuí.

zhǒu dǐ kàn quán 肘底看拳 See the Fist under the Elbow. See zhǒu dǐ chuí.

zhǒu dǐng 肘鼎 An elbow stand.

zhǒu fā lì 肘发力 An elbow strike, and training for elbow strikes. From Yiquan.

zhǒu fàn guī 肘犯规 An elbow foul in a Sanda or wrestling competition.

zhǒu guān jié 肘关节 The elbow joint.

zhǒu jìn 肘劲 Elbow power: the power and skill used to strike or control with the forearm and elbow. Usually setting up the elbow strike with a forearm control.

zhǒu jiān 肘尖 Extraordinary acupoint Zhoujian (elbow tip), EX-UE1. Behind the elbow, at the very tip of the bone. From TCM.

zhǒu liáo 肘髎 Acupoint Zhouliao (elbow bone-hole), LI12. On the outside edge of the arm, one *cun* up from acupoint Quchi (on each arm). From TCM.

zhǒu rú huán 肘如环 The elbows must be like bracelets. From Tongbeiquan, one of its requirements.

zhǒu yào cuī shǒu ér shǒu bù nì zhǒu 肘要催手而手不逆肘 Power should flow from the elbows to the hands, the hands should not run counter to the elbows. From Xingyiquan, one of its principles.

zhǒu yú xī hé 肘与膝合 The elbows harmonize, or work together with, the knees. One of the six harmonies. See also liù hé.

zhǒu zǔ dǎng 肘阻挡 Elbow block: with the arms held up in on guard position, cut them to the inside or the outside to parry with the forearms, keeping the elbows down.

朱 (rad.75) zhū 1. Vermilion; bright red. 2. A surname.

zhū jiā quán 朱家拳 Zhujiaquan (Zhu family fist), a southern style from Guangdong province.

zhū shā zhǎng 朱砂掌 Vermillion sand palm. A hard skill developed by driving the hands into sand and later pebbles over a long period of training. Also called hóng shā zhǎng.

柱 (rad.75) zhū 1. The trunk of a tree; stem of a plant. 2. Pillar; post. 3. To plant.

zhū zǐ zhǎng 柱子掌 Trunk hand, a hand shape: fingers together and slightly bent, thumb tucked on the second joint of the middle finger. This makes a firm shape for poking.

諸 [诸] (rad.149) zhū 1. All; various. 2. A surname.

zhū gě liàng 诸葛亮 Zhuge Liang (181-234), a strategist in the Three Kingdoms period (230-265). In literature and folklore, and the novel Romance of the Three Kingdoms, considered as a military genius, almost a magician. Movement names invoking his name (often by referencing his feather fan) usually imply particular tactical cleverness.

豬 (rad.152) [猪] (rad.94) zhū 1. Pig, hog, swine, boar. 2. Hog, boar, as the twelfth of the twelve animals from the Chinese zodiac, associated with a twelve year cycle symbolic of the earthly branches. The twelve animals make up a sixty year cycle when combined with the five phases. See also dì zhī, shēng xiào, wǔ xíng.

竹 (rad.118) zhú Bamboo.

zhú jié biān 竹节鞭 A bamboo whip: a short stick that is a piece of unworked bamboo, still with the natural knobs.

主 (rad.3) zhǔ 1. A host. 2. Owner. 3. Main; primary.

zhǔ dòng 主动 Take the initiative, initiate an attack.

拄 (rad.64) zhǔ To lean on, support oneself with (a stick, a cane).

zhǔ dì gùn 拄地棍 Lean on a staff: set the butt on the ground to brace to do a movement, such as a cartwheel or hook an ankle on the staff for a balanced kick.

zhǔ ná fǎ 拄拿法 Leaning grappling hold: shove down with a straight arm, as on an adversary's neck once it is low enough. From wrestling.

注 (rad.85) zhù To concentrate; fix.

zhù shì 注视 Fixed regard: to fix one's eyes on one point. Used in routines during stationary postures to show spirit and to help balance.

zhù yì 注意 1. To pay attention. 2. Watch out!

築 筑 [筑] (rad.118) zhù To build; construct.

zhù bīn 筑宾 Acupoint Zhubin (guest house), KI9. At the calf, on the inside, just inside and down from the medial head of the gastrocnemius, five *cun* above acupoint Taixi (on each leg). From TCM.

zhù jī 筑基 Build the Foundation: a routine of Liuhebafa.

抓 (rad.64) zhuā 1. To grab; seize; clutch. 2. A weapon with a grappling hook on the end.

zhuā fā 抓发 Grab the hair, usually means to lock the fingers into the hair at the top of the head (not just pull on long hair).

zhuā fǎ 抓法 Grabbing technique: to grab with the fingers together, closing firmly.

zhuā gōng 抓功 Grip strength training.

Z

zhuā jīn 抓筋 Grab a tendon, muscle, or blood vessel. A Qinna term.

zhuā miàn zhǎo 抓面爪 Grab the face claw. See jīn māo xǐ liǎn.

zhuā piān mén 抓偏门 Grab the side door. To grab with the right hand to the left side (or visa versa) of an adversary's chest opening at the sleeve area of a wrestling jacket. From wrestling.

zhuā qiāng 抓抢 A grappling spear: a spear with a heavier tip than an ordinary spear, and with teeth along the shaft behind the tip.

zhuā sāi zhǎo 抓腮爪 Grab the Cheek Claw: strike the cheek with a claw hand.

zhuā tán zǐ 抓坛子 Grip a large jug by the rim and lift, to train grip and arm strength.

zhuā wàn 抓腕 Grab the wrist, wrist grab, control techniques on the wrist joint.

zhuā wàn fǎ 抓腕法 Wrist controls: any of the wrist control techniques that involve grabbing near on on the wrist.

zhuā xiù chuān tuǐ 抓袖穿腿 Grab the sleeve and thread the leg: grab an adversary's arm or sleeve, move in tight to thread your other arm through his legs, set into a strong stance to lift on your shoulder and back, and throw.

zhuā yīn 抓阴 Grab the *yin*: grab the eyes.

zhuā zǐ 抓子 A grappling hook.

zhuā zǐ bàng 抓子棒 A grappling pole: a long pole with grappling hook or number of hooks on the end.

zhuā zhǎo 抓爪 To grab.

撾 [挝] (rad.64) zhuā 1. A grappling hook: grappling hook or hooks attached to a rope. 2. To knock at; beat. 3. The same as 抓 zhuā. Also pronounced wō.

爪 (rad.87) zhuǎ See zhǎo.

拽 (rad.64) zhuāi To hurl, fling, throw; tug, tow, drag. Also pronounced zhuài or yè.

zhuāi ná fǎ 拽拿法 Throwing grapping move: the final snap of a throw, putting the hips and waist into the throw. This is used in many types of throw.

zhuāi pí tiáo 拽皮条 Tugging the leather belt: using a leather strap, tugging on each end and snapping the belt while doing moves, to train for punches and throws.

甎 (rad.98) [砖] (rad.112) zhuān 1. A brick. 2. Something shaped like a brick. Either can be used for training grip and arm strength.

轉 [转] (rad.159) zhuǎn 1. To turn; change. 2. To pass on, transfer. 3. Pronounced zhuàn, to rotate, see zhuàn.

zhuǎn mǎ 转马 Turn the stance: pivot a full one-eighty turn, and staying in the same stance (weight on the rear leg, and shifting to the rear leg on the turn). From Wing Chun.

zhuǎn shēn 转身 Turn around, usually by pivoting.

zhuǎn shēn biāo tuǐ 转身摽腿 Turning waving leg: a half circle turn, swinging leg kick. From Mizongquan. Also called hǔ wěi tuǐ.

zhuǎn shēn bù 转身步 Turn around by stepping around in two steps and pivoting.

zhuǎn shēn dǐng zhǒu 转身顶肘 Turn and Elbow Strike: step as if going away, then turn and come back to drive the elbow into the adversary's head or chest. From Baguazhang, one of its sixty-four hands.

zhuǎn shēn léi yāo 转身擂腰 Turn around Beat the Waist: step around to the back and come back with a strong backfist into an adversary's body. From Baguazhang, one of its sixty-four hands.

zhuǎn shēn lún gùn 转身抡棍 Turning swing with the staff: turn while swinging the staff strongly in a full circle horizontally at about shoulder height.

zhuǎn shēn piē zhú 转身撇竹 Turn around and Throw the Bamboo: from a hanging squat on the right leg, sit and turn to a hunkered squat, left knee up, right knee down, and cut across with the right forearm. The 58th move of the tiger and crane routine.

zhuǎn shēn wò shǒu 转身握手 Turn around and shake hands: while shaking hands, grab tightly, extend your adversary's elbow, and trap the arm, turning to control his arm. From Qinna.

zhuǎn shēn yún shǒu 转身云手 Turn around

brandishing the hands: spin the body while circling the hands over the head, the wrists remaining connected. From Longfist.

zhuǎn shēn zhǎng 转身掌 1. Spinning Change: one of the eight palm changes, most branches have this name for one. From Baguazhang. 2. The same as millstone pushing palm, either in posture or circle-walking. From Baguazhang. See also tuī mò zhǎng.

zhuǎn tǐ bō bèi biān 转体拨背鞭 Turn back spin with the steel whip: spinning the whip vertically beside the body, looping it over the left arm then over the back, turning and continuing the spin.

zhuǎn tǐ fēi jiǎo 转体飞脚 Turning jump kick, kicking on the same side as turning, the turn completed before the kick.

zhuǎn zhǐ bù 转趾步 Turn the feet: pivot the feet a full one-eighty degrees without turning the head, in preparation for a throw.

zhuǎn zhǐ tuǐ 转趾腿 Turn the foot: a defensive move, turning the leading foot and leg to present the back of the body.

傳 [传] (rad.9) zhuàn

1. Commentaries on classics. 2. A biography. 3. A story or novel. 4. Pronounced chuán, to pass on, to hand down. See chuán.

轉 [转] (rad.159) zhuàn

1. To turn, revolve, rotate. 2. To rotate a joint or segment of the body. 3. One of the sixteen key techniques of Baguazhang, see also shí liù zì jué. 4. Pronounced zhuǎn, to turn, see zhuǎn.

zhuàn bù 转步 Pivot on the ball of the foot (dān zhuàn bù) or a double pivot on the balls of both feet (shuāng zhuàn bù).

zhuàn fēn zhǐ 转分指 Turn and separate the fingers: grab one finger of an adversary's hand in each hand, then twist your hands to cross his fingers, pressing your thumb forward. From Qinna.

zhuàn huán shǒu 转环手 See zhuàn shǒu.

zhuàn mó 转磨 Turning the millstone. circle-walking in the millstone pushing posture with the upper body turned ninety degrees so the head can face the centre. From Baguazhang

zhuàn qiāng 转枪 Turning spear: turn to strike behind.

zhuàn rú lún 转如轮 Turn like a wheel: one of the twelve qualities of movement of Changquan, though these descriptors apply to many other styles. To have a good, pivotal, centre.

zhuàn shǒu 转手 Rotating hand: rotate the forearm to turn the palm or fist to change from upwards to downwards or visa versa, while striking. From Chuojiao. Also called zhuàn huán shǒu.

zhuàn tǐ 转体 Butterfly twist. See xuàn zi zhuàn tǐ.

zhuàn zhǎng 转掌 1. To circle-walk while holding a posture. From Baguazhang. 2. The posture held while circle-walking. From Baguazhang. 3. Zhuanzhang (turning palms), the original name of Baguazhang. See also bā guā zhǎng.

zhuàn zhǎng shì 转掌式 Turning posture, the posture held while circle-walking. From Baguazhang. Some branches differentiate between the feeling in the postures by using shì 式, shì 势, and xíng 形. Also called bā guā zhuāng.

椿 [桩] (rad.75) zhuāng

1. Stake, pile, post. 2. A wooden dummy used to practice techniques. 3. A knee strike. 4. A ready stance in Wing Chun. 5. A routine, especially one that trains the basics.

zhuāng bù 桩步 Stance for stake standing.

zhuāng gōng 桩功 1. Stake standing training for stances and internal power. 2. The skill to withstand pushing or kicking.

裝 [装] (rad.145) zhuāng

1. Outfit, clothing. 2. To load, pack. 3. A wrestling throw that involves holding an adversary in the arms, lifting him up completely, quite high, then dropping him.

zhuāng dǐng 装顶 A wrestling throw that involves holding an adversary in the arms, lifting him up completely, then dropping him (similar to the #3 above, but lifting less and using more twist) lifting both feet of an adversary off the ground by driving your thigh into his thighs.

Z

撞 (rad.64) **zhuàng** 1. To shove, charge, ram, barge into, collide with. Classified as a hand technique, but is often with the body or shoulders, or wedging with the arms, not just with the end of the arms, fists or palms. 2. As a shield and broadsword technique, collide: bump into an adversary with the shield, combining this with a hack.

zhuàng bēi shǒu 撞碑手 Ram the Tablet: ram directly to the chest.

zhuàng fǎ 撞法 Ramming techniques, bumping or barging techniques: hard close range techniques with the knees, elbows, torso, shoulders or head.

zhuàng jiān 撞肩 Shoulder barging: knocking the front of the shoulders together with a partner to develop the ability to give and take hits with the shoulders.

zhuàng jiǎo 撞脚 Ramming kick. From Chuojiao, one of its middle-basin kicks.

zhuàng quán 撞拳 Ramming punch. 1. A strong punch straight forward. 2. A strong swinging punch with the arm straight. When to the front it is essentially a straight arm uppercut, the fist heart up. When to the back, the fist heart faces down.

zhuàng tuǐ 撞腿 Knee strike. See zhuàng xī.

zhuàng tuǐ gōng 撞腿功 Leg bumping training: a pattern of stepping and leg strikes done by partners, combining stepping with lower leg controls and kicks to develop agility and understanding of use of the legs.

zhuàng tún 撞臀 Charge with the buttocks: during a throw, put the full power of the hips, waist, and buttocks and drive into an adversary with a sudden action.

zhuàng xī 撞膝 Knee strike upwards and forward. Also called zhuàng tuǐ.

zhuàng xiōng 撞胸 Chest barging: knocking the chests together with a partner to develop the ability to give and take hits with the chest.

zhuàng zhǎng 撞掌 1. Shove, ram, with the hand or hands or end of the arm. 2. In some styles, means a double shove with the fingers pointing to each other. 3. Sometimes refers to circle-walking with the arms held in this double shove position, see also píng tuī zhǎng.

zhuàng zhǎng gōng 撞掌功 Palm bumping training: a pattern of stepping and forearm strikes done by partners to train the arms.

zhuàng zhǒu 撞肘 Shove, bump, with the elbow: holding fists, bend the elbows and strike directly with the tips, using a full, short force.

狀 [壯] (rad.90) **zhuàng** 1. Strong; robust; sturdy. 2. To strengthen, make better.

zhuàng shì jī gǔ 壮士击鼓 Sturdy Warrior Hits the Drum: starting with the staff on your shoulder, step forward with a swinging chop down to the head, both hands at the base of the staff. From Shaolinquan staff.

追 (rad.162) **zhuī** 1. To chase after; pursue. 2. To seek; go after.

zhuī dì fēng bō 追地风波 Chase the Land, Wind, and Waves: shift from a front weighted bow stance to a back weighted bow stance, leaning back and chopping a sword down aligned to the extended leg. Then step forward three times, spinning around, and finally sitting into an empty stance with the blade held in front of the chest. Finally, pierce forward. From Qingping sword.

zhuī fēng chuān xīn 追风穿心 Chase the Wind and Pierce the Heart: advancing with a spear, first a back cross step with an outer cover then bow stance stab, then a front crossing jump step with an inner cover then bow stance stab.

zhuī fēng gǎn yuè 追风赶月 Chase the Wind and Catch the Moon. 1. Quick, smooth, walking steps used within a routine. Common to Chaquan and Liuhequan. 2. Step forward to a stamping palm. From Tongbeiquan.

zhuī mǎ bù 追马步 Chasing stance step: to step forward from one small horse stance to another, circling the feet. From Wing Chun.

zhuī xīng gǎn yuè 追星赶月 Chase the Stars and Catch the Moon: a front kick followed by a turning side kick with the other leg, in the same direction. From Yangjia style.

錐 [锥] (rad.167) **zhuī** An awl; anything awl shaped.

zhuī kǒng 锥孔 To bore a hole with an awl.

墜 [坠] (rad.32) **zhuì** 1. To hang, drop, settle down. Fall. 2. Weight; a hanging object. 3. To weigh down.

zhuì shǒu 坠手 Dropping hand: rake down an adversary's face with a clawing palm (in dragon or tiger shape).

zhuì zhǒu 坠肘 Hang the elbow: settle the elbow down as if it were a heavy fruit on a branch.

肫 (rad.130) **zhūn** The gizzard of a fowl. Used colloquially to refer to the throat of a person.

準 (rad.85) [准] (rad.15) **zhǔn** 1. Level, even. 2. A rule. 3. To aim. 4. Certainly. 5. Standard, criterion. The proper way, as in complying with the standard posture.

zhǔn bèi 准备 Prepare, get ready. Intend, plan.

zhǔn bèi huó dòng 准备活动 Warm-ups, warm-up exercises, limbering up exercises. Sometimes called rè shēn liàn xí.

拙 (rad.64) **zhuō** Brute. Crude; stupid. Clumsy.

zhuō jìn 拙劲 Clumsiness, a combination of musclebound, poorly coordinated, and slow-witted. See also biǎn, dāi lì, jiāng lì.

zhuō lì 拙力 Brute strength. Awkward, clumsy, hard, inappropriate application of strength. Also called bèn lì, nǔ lì.

捉 (rad.64) **zhuō** To clutch; grasp; capture; seize. One of Ziranmen's nineteen main methods.

啄 (rad.30) **zhuó** To peck.

zhuó mù zhǐ 啄目指 Eye pecking fingers. See diǎn jīng zhǎng.

斫 (rad.69) **zhuó** To hack, a strong cut with the edge, particularly with a heavy blade.

zhuó shǒu 斫手 Hack with the hand: strike downwards with the outer edge of the hand. The action is similar to cutting, see also qiē shǒu.

zhuó xué 斫穴 Hack a pressure point: strike it with the palm edge. See also dǎ xué.

zhuó zhǎng 斫掌 Hack with the palm: see zhuó shǒu.

濁 [浊] (rad.85) **zhuó** Turbid; muddy. Chaotic.

zhuó qì 浊气 Turbid qi.

着 (rad.109) **zhuó** 1. To touch; come in contact with. 2. Pronounced zhāo, a move; a trick.

zhuó lì 着力 To exert oneself, put effort into something.

zhuó lì diǎn 着力点 The effective point of contact on an adversary, where you can gain control when you apply your technique.

子 (rad.39) **zǐ** 1. The first of the twelve Terrestrial Branches, used in combination with the ten Celestial stems to designate years, months, days, and hours. For the sixty year cycles, see also under bǐng zǐ, gēng-, jiǎ-, rèn-, wù-. The period of the day from 11:00 p.m. to 1:00 a.m. (23:00 to 1:00). See also dì zhī, tiān gān. 2. Son; child. 3. Person. 4. Seed.

zǐ gōng 子宫 Extraordinary acupoint Zigong (child's palace), EX-CA1. At the abdomen, four *cun* below the level of the navel, three *cun* lateral to the midline (on each side). From TCM.

zǐ mǔ dāo 字母刀 Paired bladed weapons.

zǐ shí 子时 The period of the day from 11:00 p.m. to 1:00 a.m. (23:00 to 1:00).

zǐ wǔ 子午 Midnight and noon, meridian. *Zi* is the first of the twelve Earthly Branches, midnight. *Wu* is the seventh, noon. Commonly translated as midnight-midday in ordinary use.

zǐ wǔ diào tí mǎ 子午吊提马 Meridian half-hanging horse stance: a high horse stance.

zǐ wǔ gùn 子午棍 Meridian staff. 1. See tài kōng zǐ wú gùn. 2. A short staff routine of Mizongquan, written up as fifty-five moves.

zǐ wǔ mǎ 子午马 Meridian horse stance. A turned combination of horse and bow stance. The legs are essentially in bow stance (one straight, more weighted to the bent leg), but the technique is done to the front as if it were a horse stance (instead of aligning with the legs as in a bow or reverse bow stance), and so the body angles to apply power in that direction.

zǐ wǔ yuān yāng yuè 子午鸳鸯钺 Midnight-midday mandarin duck daggers. See yuān yāng yuè. Also called lù jiǎo dāo, qián kūn jiàn, rì yuè shuāng lián, shuāng yuè.

zǐ wǔ zhū qiáo 子午珠桥 Meridian stance Pearl Bridge: in a right reverse bow stance, push the left hand forward, index finger extended up. The 32nd move of the tiger and crane routine.

zǐ wǔ zhuāng 子午桩 Meridian standing. 1. One name for the trinity stance in Xingyiquan. Using the word meridian emphasizes the importance of post standing in Xingyiquan, that it is the foundation of the foundation. See also sān tǐ shì. 2. In other styles usually means to stand straight up with the feet together.

zǐ xū guò guān 子胥过关 Zi Xu Goes Through the Pass: a foot jam to the knee while blocking above. From Baguazhang.

紫 (rad.120) zǐ   Purple; violet.

zǐ gōng 紫宫 Acupoint Zigong (purple palace), RN19. At the chest, level with the second intercostal space, on the midline. From TCM.

zǐ xiāo héng yún 紫霄横云 Violet Clouds Float Across the Sky. 1 Circle the hand horizontally twice, then do a double hooking in punch, one fist at waist height, one fist high. 2. A straight heel kick with a same side pounding punch, the other fist out behind. Both from Wudangquan.

zǐ yàn chōng tiān 紫燕冲天 Violet Swallow Charges up to Heaven: aerial double chopping palms. From Piguaquan.

zǐ yàn lüè shuǐ 紫燕掠水 Violet Swallow Skims over the Water: move forward with front cross steps and forward steps with flat side to side cuts. From Qingping sword.

zǐ yàn pāo jiǎn 紫燕抛翦 Violet Swallow Tosses its Wings. 1. Step forward with a crossing action of the arms. From Baguazhang. 2. Step into a low reverse bow stance with an angled low sword chop, a few inches off the ground. From Qingping sword.

zǐ yàn zhāi chì 紫燕侧翅 Violet Swallow Tilts its Wings: drop to a low crossed stance and do a reverse stab upwards with a sword, leaning onto the leg, tucking the head down and tucking the left arm around the head, looking up behind at the sword tip. A dodge to cut under to an adversary's wrist. From Qingping sword.

釨 (rad.167) zǐ   A halberd with a dull edged blade.

字 (rad.39) zì   1. Character; word. 2. Private name, name taken at twenty, often translated as 'styled'. People, particularly in the past, are often referred to by a given name (míng), private name (zì), literary name (hào) and/or nickname (chuò hào). 3. One of the small family styles of Emei, see also sì xiǎo jiā.

自 (rad.132) zì   1. Self; oneself. 2. Naturally.

zì rán 自然 Nature; natural.

zì rán bù 自然步 1. Natural stance: feet about a foot-length apart, parallel, legs naturally straight. 2. Natural stepping: short steps, with sunken qi, and naturally comfortable. From Baguazhang.

zì rán hū xī 自然呼吸 Natural breathing pattern: to breathe naturally, though deeply, during practice.

zì rán jià 自然架 A natural wrestling hold: feet on a line, a couple of feet apart, legs naturally bent about one-twenty degrees, body leaning forward a bit, arms bent and extended, ready for attack.

zì rán mén 自然门 Ziranmen (natural way), a style from Hunan attributed to Du Xinwu.

zì rán quán 自然拳 Ziranquan (natural fist), see zì rán mén.

zì rán shì 自然式 Natural position: during qigong training, standing with the legs open to shoulder width, arms hanging at the sides.

zì tuì fǎ 自退法 Technique of retreating yourself: to retreat more than seems necessary from an attack, to give oneself the opportunity to counter.

zì xuán tào lù 自选套路 Optional routine in Taolu competition.

zì xuán xiàng mù 自选项目 Optional events in Taolu competition.

zì xué 自学 To study on one's own, self teach. To learn through books and videos instead of from a teacher.

zì yóu bó jī 自由博击 Freestyle wrestling.

zì yóu shí zhàn 自由实战 Free fighting: free

sparring, though still within predetermined rules.

宗 (rad.40) **zōng** 1. Ancestor. 2. Sect. 3. Clan. 4. School.

zōng qì 宗气 Ancestral *qi*: the mix of fluid microscopic particles with natural air that is breathed in. Strengthens the throat and the ability to move the blood supply of oxygen throughout the body.

綜 [综] (rad.120) **zōng** To put together; sum up.

zōng hé bó jī 混合式格斗 Mixed martial arts, MMA. Not Chinese style Sanda or wrestling, but sparring specifically with MMA rules. Also called hún hé shì gé dòu, hún hé shì wǔ shù, zōng hé gé dòu.

zōng hé gé dòu 混合式格斗 Mixed martial arts. See zōng hé bó jī.

總 (rad.120) [总] (rad.61) **zǒng** 1. To assemble; put together. 2. General; overall. 3. Chief; head.

zǒng cái pàn 总裁判 Head judge; chief referee of a competition.

zǒng cái pàn zhǎng 总裁判长 See zǒng cái pàn.

縱 [纵] (rad.120) **zòng** 1. Lengthwise, longitudinal, vertical. 2. From north to south. 3. To jump up.

zòng bù 纵步 Driving step forward: lift the front foot and push off the rear foot to drive forward.

zòng héng pī jī 纵横劈击 Chop from North to South and from East to West: a cloud hands action with the hands whilst stepping in a pattern that takes each to a different cardinal point. From Chen Taijiquan.

zòng pī 纵劈 A lengthwise chop, cleave something straight down the median plane. Also called zòng qiē.

zòng qiē 纵切 See zòng pī.

zòng tiào bù 纵跳步 Hop forward: lift the front foot and push off the rear foot, hopping forward on the rear foot.

zòng zhóu 纵轴 Median plane: the vertical line that divides the body into left and right parts.

走 (rad.156) **zǒu** 1. To walk; run; go. 2. Go away. 3. One of the sixteen key techniques of Baguazhang, see also shí liù zì jué.

zǒu biān pán 走边盘 Walk the side basin: step around to the outside of an adversary's leading foot.

zǒu biāo 走镖 Act as armed escort, especially for a convoy of goods.

zǒu bù 走步 1. To walk. 2. To do actions or exercises with moving steps instead of fixed stances.

zǒu bù fā lì xùn liàn 走步发力训练 Moving step power exertion training. From Yiquan.

zǒu chǎng 走场 Walk the field: to move around the sparring ring, watching each other and preparing to fight.

zǒu jià 走架 To practise a routine, to do individual practice of sequences of moves, not necessarily the whole routine.

zǒu jià shí wú rén ruò yǒu rén, duì dí shí yǒu rén ruò wú rén 走架时无人若有人，对敌时有人若无人 In forms practice act as if there is someone before you, in fighting act as if there is no one there. A martial saying.

zǒu jiāo 走跤 Tripping throws: using the feet, moving to trip while throwing.

zǒu jìn 走劲 Walking power: a defensive energy, going along softly with a hard adversary, moving gradually away and eventually drawing him in.

zǒu jiǔ gōng 走九宫 Do Baguazhang circle-walking on the nine palaces pattern. See jiǔ gōng bù.

zǒu mǎ 走马 Walking stance: see zǒu mǎ bù.

zǒu mǎ bù 走马步 Walking stance stepping: a training method of changing repeatedly from one stance to another, not just horse stance. This is the name for this training in southern styles, but most styles use this training.

zǒu mǎ guān huā 走马观花 View the Flowers on Horseback. an instep kick to waist height combined with a circling slice up with opposite hand, circling the other hand up and back. From Liuhebafa.

zǒu mǎ huí tóu 走马回头 Look Back on

Z

Horseback, or Departing Horse Looks Back. 1. Turn fully around by stepping and bringing the hand over to cover, then drop and extend the other leg, extending the other hand along that leg. 2. Turn back a bit, catch and pull on the adversary's arm, and strike directly with the other hand. From Baguazhang.

zǒu mǎ huó xié 走马活携 Grab an Adversary on Horseback. 1. A combination of a brushing out to the side with a scooping in to the ribs, contacting the full arm around the chest or head and coiling around the back to catch and throw. From Baguazhang. 2. Step through behind your adversary's legs, control his front elbow and slide an arm bar across his chest and neck. From Baguazhang. 3. A raised knee stance with the same side hand up, palm forward, and the rear hand down, palm down, closing the arms in slightly. From Wudangquan.

zǒu mǎ sǎo chéng 走马扫城 Raze the City on Horseback: drive forward into a bow stance, extending fully into a head high stab, blocking up with the left hand. This is a direct counter, so must be quick. From Qingping sword.

zǒu qí lín bù 走麒麟步 Walking Kylin steps: step with low front crossing steps, extending the arms to sweep across below the knees. The 103rd move of the tiger and crane routine.

zǒu quān 走圈 Just means to walk in a circle, but usually refers to the circle-walking of Baguazhang.

zǒu sān bù 走三步 Walking three steps: taking three steps whilst doing a power searching or expression technique. From Yiquan.

zǒu shēng mǎ 走生马 Walking horse stance: a training method of changing repeatedly from one stance to another, sometimes including kicks in the stepping. This is the name for this training in Choylifut, and refers to stepping between eight specific stances. Less specifically, and without kicks, also called zǒu mǎ, zǒu mǎ bù.

zǒu shǒu 走手 Walking hands: any rising strike in Chuojiao. Includes liāo, tiǎo, tuō, yáng, etc.. See also luò shǒu.

zǒu wéi shàng jì 走为上计 The Best Strategy is Running Away. The thirty-sixth of the Thirty-six Stratagems of Warfare, which apply to many situations.

zǒu yī bù 走一步 Walking one step: taking one step whilst doing a power searching or expression technique. From Yiquan.

zǒu yīn yáng tú 走阴阳图 Walk the *Yin Yang* chart: while circle-walking, repeatedly cross through the centre in a curved line to change directions and continue walking. From Baguazhang.

zǒu zhōng pán 走中盘 Go into the middle basin. See zhōng guǎn zhǐ fǎ.

足 (rad.157) zú 1. Foot, feet. 2 Leg, legs. Used in written Chinese, seldom in spoken. See also jiǎo, tuǐ.

zú gōng 足弓 The foot bow. 1. The knee is the central grip; the hip and foot are the tips. When the bow is pulled the knee has power forward, the hip is settled with a backward bracing power, and the heel is set down to send power back. The power is balanced and connected to the body. 2. The arch of the foot.

zú jué yīn 足厥阴 Foot Jue Yin. Together with the Hand Jue Yin, this is a deep *yin* channel that collects and transmits blood, collecting it for later use. See also shǒu jué yīn, zú jué yīn gān jīng.

zú jué yīn gān jīng 足厥阴肝经 Zu Jue Yin (Foot Faint Yin) Liver channel, LR. Full name for zú jué yīn.

zú lín qì 足临泣 Acupoint Zulinqi (foot overlooking tears), GB41. At the foot, on the top, at the proximal end of the metatarsal of the fourth toe, on the outside of the extensor digitorum longus tendon (on each foot). From TCM.

zú qiào yīn 足窍阴 Acupoint Zuqiaoyin (foot orifice yin), GB44. At the foot, on the upper tip of the fourth toe, 0.1 *cun* from the toenail (on each foot). This is the final point of the Gall Bladder channel. Also called qiào yīn. From TCM.

zú sān lǐ 足三里 Acupoint Zusanli (foot three miles), ST36. At the shin just below the knee, 3 *cun* below acupoint Dubi (on each leg). From TCM. A crippling point, striking here induces numbness, and too hard may cause serious injury. Also called sān lǐ. See also cán xué.

zú shào yáng 足少阳 Foot Shao Yang. Together with the Hand Shao Yang, it regulates the flow of *qi* and blood between exterior and interior. See also shǒu shào yáng, zú shào yáng dǎn jīng. From TCM.

zú shào yáng dǎn jīng 足少阳胆经 Zu Shao Yang (Foot Lesser Yang) Gallbladder channel, GB. Full name for zú shào yáng. From TCM.

zú shào yīn 足少阴 Foot Shao Yin. Together with the Hand Shao Yin, it communicates between the Tai Yin channels and the Jue Yin channels, regulating *qi*, blood, and heat. See also shǒu shào yīn, zú shào yīn shèn jīng. From TCM.

zú shào yīn shèn jīng 足少阴肾经 Zu Shao Yin (Foot Lesser Yin) Kidney channel, KI. Full name for zú shào yīn. From TCM.

zú shè gōng 足射功 Foot Shooting training: kick bricks and stones with the toes to toughen them.

zú tài yáng 足太阳 Foot Tai Yang. Together with the Hand Tai Yang, it covers the back and back of the legs and arms. See also shǒu tài yáng, zú tài yáng páng guāng jīng. From TCM.

zú tài yáng páng guāng jīng 足太阳膀胱经 Zu Tai Yang (Foot Greater Yang) Bladder channel, BL. Full name for zú tài yáng. From TCM.

zú tài yīn 足太阴 Foot Tai Yin. Together with the Hand Tai Yin, it is a superficial channel that opens to the inside, transforms and delivers blood and fluids. See also shǒu tài yīn, zú tài yīn pí jīng. From TCM.

zú tài yīn pí jīng 足太阴脾经 Zu Tai Yin (Foot Greater Yin) Spleen channel, SP. Full name for zú tài yīn. From TCM.

zú tōng gǔ 足通谷 Acupoint Zu Tonggu (foot valley passage), BL66. At the foot, on the outside, at the middle phalanx of the little toe (on each foot). Also called tōng gǔ. From TCM.

zú wǔ lǐ 足五里 Acupoint Zuwuli (foot five li), LR10. At the groin, at the root of the thigh, the head of the hip joint, the outer edge of the adductor longus, three *cun* below acupoint Qichong (on each side). From TCM.

zú xīn hán kōng 足心涵空 Heart of the foot hollowed and empty: when the foot grips the ground firmly, the arch is hollowed. A requirement in Baguazhang.

zú yáng míng 足阳明 Foot Yang Ming. Together with the Hand Yang Ming, it runs inside the body and is involved with digestion and movement of nutrients and fluids. See also shǒu yáng míng, zú yáng míng wèi jīng. From TCM.

zú yáng míng wèi jīng 足阳明胃经 Zu Yang Ming (Foot Bright Yang) Stomach channel, ST. Full name for zú yáng míng. From TCM.

阻 (rad.170) **zǔ** To hinder; block; obstruct. To jam, to set into the root of an adversary's attack, such as the hip socket, shoulder socket, or elbow.

zǔ ài 阻碍 1. To block; impede. 2. Defensive moves that mostly involve obstructing your adversary.

zǔ dǎng 阻挡 To jam. 1. A blocking technique: to use the shoulder and hand to prevent your adversary from getting in. 2. Refers to blocks in general.

zǔ jié 阻接 Jamming interception, a blocking technique: a low pressuring kick to jam your adversary's leg with the sole or edge of the foot.

zǔ kuà 阻胯 Jam the hip: in a close situation, push your hands into your adversary's hip socket to prevent him from kicking or kneeing you.

zǔ zhǒu 阻肘 Jam the elbow: jam your forearm into the crook of your adversary's elbow to prevent a swinging punch from getting in.

躜 [躦] (rad.157) **zuān** 1. To jump up; to dash forward. 2. In Xingyiquan, to enter the body like an arrow, with agile footwork and bodywork.

鑽 [钻] (rad.167) **zuān** 1. To penetrate, pierce, drill through; bore. 2. Quickness, as in the ability to penetrate. 3. One of the sixteen key techniques of Baguazhang, see also shí liù zì jué. 4. The sharpened butt end of a metal weapon. 5. The sharpened metal tip on the butt of a wooden shafted long weapon. When not sharpened, called zūn. 6. Pronounced zuàn, a drill or auger, so refers to drilling actions and power.

zuān dǎ 钻打 A drilling hit.

zuān fǎ 钻法 Drilling methods: techniques that enter with a drilling strike or control prior to a final strike or throw.

zuān jiǎo 钻脚 Drill in with the foot: send the foot into an adversary's legs in preparation for a trip or throw.

Z

zuān jìn 钻劲 Drilling power. 1. To pierce, drill, bore through something. With this meaning, it is part of piercing power. See also chuān. 2. Pronounced zuàn, a drilling, screwing power. Used in conjunction with rolling power to keep the power balanced during advancing movement. See also gǔn jìn, guǒ jìn, zhèng jìn. 3. In Xingyiquan, see zuān quán.

zuān quán 钻拳 Drilling fist. 1. Rotate and extend the arm with a spiralling punch. 2. The drilling fist of Xingyiquan, twisting the fist over with the elbow tucked in, little finger side twisted up. See zuān jìn. It is related to the water element, see also shuǐ. 3. A straight punch, but twisting the forearm inward, so the thumb side is down. From Tongbeiquan.

zuān quán fā lì 钻拳发力 A drilling punch. From Yiquan.

zuān shǒu 钻手 Drilling hand: to drill out from a hidden place, passing either over or under the leading arm. From Chuojiao.

zuān tuī zǐ 钻推子 A drilled pusher: a stone lock, for training arms and grip. When made of brick, also called tuī zhuān. See also shí suǒ.

zuān tuǐ 钻腿 Penetrating kick: a poke kick with the leg externally rotated to use either the toes or the outer edge of the foot. From Baguazhang.

zuān zǐ jiǎo 钻子脚 Drilling step: slide the foot into your adversary in preparation for a throw, but not touching the heel down yet, so that the leg can still turn for the throw.

攥 (rad.64) zuàn To grip; grasp; hold.

zuàn quán 攥拳 Gripping fist, a hand shape. See luó xuán quán.

zuàn wàn 攥腕 To grasp the wrist, not as a controlling technique, but in preparation for a throw.

嘴 (rad.30) zuǐ 1. The mouth. 2. A beak.

zuǐ bā 嘴巴 The mouth.

zuǐ zhǒu 嘴肘 An elbow to the mouth. From Tanglangquan, one of its eight short techniques.

最 (rad.73) zuì The most.

zuì hòu dé fēn 最后得分 The final score: the final score of a Taolu competitor after all the possible extra deductions are made by the head judge.

zuì jiā jù lí 最佳距离 Optimal distance: to keep distance between you and an adversary that is optimal for you to attack. This varies for each fighter, depending on their size and preferred methods.

醉 (rad.164) zuì Drunk, drunken.

zuì bā xiān 醉八仙 Eight drunken immortals, a Wudang routine, written up as thirty-two moves.

zuì bù 醉步 Drunken stepping: to step quickly in the direction opposite from where the body is leaning. From Zuiquan.

zuì dǎ shān mén 醉打山门 Drunkenly Hit the Mountain Gate, Drunkard Hits the Mountain Gate: continuous strikes to an adversary's face, a finger stab turning into a backhand strike. From Baguazhang.

zuì fú gǔ sōng 醉扶古松 Drunkenly Lean on the Old Pine Tree, Drunkard Leans on the Old Pine Tree: flick the leg back and dab a sword forward, jump forward with a flick back, circling the blade to draw it up, then land with another circle and block. From Qingping sword.

zuì huàn yāo 醉晃腰 Drunken waist shake: in a horse stance with raised heels, circle the waist while 'holding the cup' in front of the body. From Zuiquan.

zuì jiǔ bā xiān 醉酒八仙 Eight Drunken Immortals: step into a right bow stance, swing the right fist up in front and the left back behind, leaning into the strike and extending the arms. The 82nd move of the tiger and crane routine. The same as luó hàn chū dòng on the other side.

zuì quán 醉拳 Zuiquan (drunken fist), hides techniques in feigned drunkenness to confuse an adversary.

zuì wò yá chuáng 醉卧牙床 Drunkenly Lie on the Ivory-inlaid Bed, Drunkard Lies on the Ivory-inlaid Bed: the body extended just off the ground, propped up on one elbow, the same side leg extended parallel to the ground, the opposite side leg bent with the foot supporting on the ground.

鐏 (rad.167) **zūn** 1. The metal capped sleeve on the shaft of a long bladed weapon such as a spear or halberd. When sharpened, called zuān. 2. May mean the butt end of a spear without the metal sleeve, but not usually.

左 (rad.48) **zuǒ** Left (side), on the left, to the left.

zuǒ gōng bù 左弓步 A left bow stance. 1. A normal bow stance, with the left leg forward. See also gōng bù. 2. A turned bow stance weighted to the left leg: the bow stance faces in the direction of a biased horse stance, but the feet are turned as in a bow stance. From Chen Taijiquan.

zuǒ gù 左顾 To advance sideways, rather than head on. See also yòu pàn, zǒu gù yòu pàn.

zuǒ gù yòu pàn 左顾右盼 Take care of the left and gaze to the right. Guard the left and anticipate the right. 1. To move with footwork to the left and right. 2. To use both movement and stillness. 3. To use both structure and intent. 4. To pay attention to all directions, be aware of your position and that of an adversary. 5. To defend to the left and watch to the right to prepare.

zuǒ jià 左架 A left wrestling hold: left foot forward, usually left hand high and right hand low. See also yòu jià.

zuǒ mǎ 左马 Left horse: the left leg. Sometimes used in describing stances and stepping.

zuǒ pán zhǒu biān 左盘肘鞭 Left coil around the elbow with the steel whip: loop the whip around the left elbow and circle it to both sides of the body.

zuǒ piē zǐ 左撇子 A left handed person; often called a southpaw in a sparring situation.

zuǒ shǎn yòu dǎ 左闪右打 Dodge Left and Hit Right: sit to a cross stance elbow tuck and pull left, then come up with a right strike and right kick. From Taiji Changquan.

zuǒ xié bù 左斜步 Left angled step: in a fighting ready stance with the left foot forward, step the left foot to the left at an angle, advancing to the left. The right foot may also step forward, but the body has changed the angle of defense or attack.

zuǒ yòu chā huā 左右插花 Arrange Flowers Left and Right: from blocking a punch, bring the other hand up to grab the blade of an adversary's hand, then grab with both hands and hyper-flex his wrist, pressing it back towards him.

zuǒ yòu chuān suō 左右穿梭 Thread the Shuttle left and right: an upper framing block combined with a push, repeating on both sides. From Taijiquan.

zuǒ yòu diǎn gùn 左右点棍 Back and forth dabbing with the staff: using the wrists as pivot, hands together, quickly hit the ground to either side with the tip of the staff.

zuǒ yòu jiāo zhǒu 左右交肘 Cross the elbows over: if you manage to get an adversary's arms crossed (often by pulling down on one, he will punch with the other), grab both and twist one over top of the other, pressing his forearm down on his other elbow. From Qinna.

zuǒ yòu lūn biān 左右抡鞭 Left-right circles with a steel whip: swing the whip vertically, alternating sides of the body.

zuǒ yòu mō jìn 左右摸劲 Seeking power side to side: without moving the torso outwardly, seek out power lines in a left-right direction. May be done in different stances or stepping. From Yiquan.

zuǒ yòu shuǎi shēn fǎ 左右甩身法 Method of throwing back and forth with the waist: grab an adversary and snap the waist back and forth to first push then pull an adversary.

zuǒ yòu yìng kāi mén 左右硬开门 Firmly Open the Door Side to Side: continuous defense side to side or back and forth, intended to open up an adversary to allow for direct attack. The defense is already preparing for the offense, and both are hard. From Bajiquan, one of its eight main concepts, see also bā dà zhāo.

作 (rad.9) **zuò** 1. To do. 2. To grow. 3. To feel. 4. To make. 5. To work.

zuò yòng 作用 1. To act on; to affect. 2. Action. Result. 3. The application of a move, applications.

zuò yòng diǎn 作用点 The point of action, fulcrum, force on a lever, point of control on an adversary.

zuò yòng lì 作用力 Acting force, effective force. Applied force.

Z

坐 (rad.32) **zuò** To sit.

zuò bài 坐拜 Seated bows: straight leg sit-ups, straight arms as well, reaching to the feet.

zuò bù 坐步 Sitting stance. 1. Sitting to the back leg with the front heel on the ground, toes pulled up. 2. Sitting in a crossed stance. Also called xiē bù.

zuò chán 坐禅 Sit in meditation; meditate. Called zazen in English, from the Japanese.

zuò dēng bù 坐蹬步 Full squat kicking stance: sitting on one leg, extend the other straight in front with a heel hick.

zuò dì 坐地 The literal meaning is to sit on the ground, but the martial meaning is to sit in horse stance. From southern styles.

zuò gǔ 坐骨 The ischium, the sitting bone in the pelvis.

zuò hǔ lǐng yī 坐虎领衣 Draw the Clothes across whilst Seated on a Tiger: step back to right back-weighted bow stance and draw a sword down, then up to above the head, left hand at the right wrist, keeping the blade aligned with the left leg. From Qingping sword.

zuò kuà 坐胯 1. Set into the hip joints: set into a horse stance, keeping the hip joints strong and stable so the stance does not waver. 2. Set the hip joints: move from the waist rather than the hip joints. 3. Sit down into the hip joints, allow the hips to move back in a horse stance so that the weight moves back and the torso leans forward to balance. #3 is an error in most styles, and is also called zuò kuān.

zuò kuān 坐髋 Sit into the hip bones, allow the hips to move back in a horse stance so that the weight moves back and the torso leans forward to balance, an error. Also called zuò kuà.

zuò lián bù 坐莲步 Lotus sitting stance: kneeling on the ground with the lower legs crossed behind the body, sitting on the lower legs. Also called dié zuò bù.

zuò mǎ dān qiáo 坐马单桥 Horse Stance Single Bridge: from a right reverse bow stance, shift to horse stance and push the right hand out to the side, index finger extended, elbow settled. The 35th move of the tiger and crane routine.

zuò mǎ guān shān 坐马观山 View the Mountain on Horseback: step to a transverse bow stance and chop a sword down on line with the extended leg. From Qingping sword.

zuò mǎ shì 坐马势 Horse sitting stance. See mǎ bù. Also called qǐ mǎ, qǐ mǎ bù.

zuò mǎ yáng dāo 坐马扬刀 Yield blades on horseback: sit in horse stance and thrust the palms to the same side, fingers up. From southern styles.

zuò pán 坐盘 Cross-legged sitting stance, see zuò pán bù.

zuò pán bù 坐盘步 Cross-legged sitting stance. 1. Sit completely on the ground with the legs curled and crossed. Also called zuò pán. 2. A low crossed stance, the legs crossed and sitting close to the rear leg. Also called xiē bù. 3. Sometimes this name also used for the low cross stance used for dragon form in Xingyiquan, which is more extended.

zuò pán cǎi shì 坐盘踩势 Sitting trample stance: the dragon stance of Xingyiquan: a full squat on one leg, heel off the ground, with the front foot extended, foot turned out with a forward trampling power. In some styles the legs are crossed at the knees, in some style the knees are together but not crossed. Sometimes called zuò pán bù.

zuò shān dān biān 坐山单鞭 Mountain sitting Single Whip: a horse stance with the arms extended to the sides in straight punches. From Shaolinquan.

zuò shān bù 坐山步 Mountain sitting stance. 1. The feet point forward, front to back about one to two foot-lengths apart, sitting low with the weight between the feet, the front foot dorsi-flexed to place just the heel on the ground. 2. A horse stance. From Shaolinquan.

zuò shān jià 坐山架 Mountain sitting frame: a horse stance with one arm doing a framing block up over the head, the other with the same shape blocking down at the knee. From Shaolinquan.

zuò shēn 坐身 Sit the body: lower the body further into an already sitting stance.

zuò shì 坐式 Sitting posture: sitting on a chair or stool while doing power searching training. From Yiquan.

zuò tuǐ 坐腿 Sit into the legs. 1. Shift from a front weighted stance to a back weighted stance, keeping the buttocks tucked and hips settled. 2. Grab the adversary's kicking leg, swing yours over it, and sit on it for a takedown.

zuǒ tuǐ diǎn zú 坐腿点足 Sit and point the foot: sit onto one leg and touch the other foot's toes on the ground.

zuò tún 坐臀 Sit with the buttocks: a counter to a trip or throw. Drop down on an adversary to prevent his throwing you.

zuò wàn 坐腕 Sit the wrist: settle the wrist to send power to the palm.

zuò yāo 坐腰 Sit the back, a method of applying explosive power: quickly sit down and tuck in and down so that the torso sits down (see also zuò shēn), exhaling with power. Commonly used for dropping techniques such as tā zhǎng and àn zhǎng, and for setting up throws.

zuò zhǒu 坐肘 Sit the elbow. See lāo xīn zhǒu.

Z

Notes on Looking up Characters by Radical

List of shorter, simplified, or variations of radicals. Radical order in the index is by the fullest form of the radical.

Common use	Number of strokes on radical chart	Original form of radical, thus official stroke count.
忄	four strokes	心 (61, heart)
扌	four strokes	手 (64, hand)
曰	four strokes	曰 (73, say) May have vertical lines through it.
氵	four strokes	水 (85, water)
火 灬	four strokes	火 (86, fire)
犭	four strokes	犬 (94, dog)
王	five strokes	玉 (96, jade)
纟	six strokes	糸, 糹 (120, silk)
艹	six strokes	艸 (140, grass)
见	seven strokes	見 (147, see)
讠	seven strokes	言, 訁 (149, speech)
贝	seven strokes	貝 (154, shell)
车	seven strokes	車 (159, cart)
辶	seven strokes	辵 (162, walk)
阝 (on right)	seven strokes	邑 (163, city)
钅	eight strokes	金, 釒 (167, gold)
长	eight strokes	長, 镸 (168, long)
门	eight strokes	門 (169, gate)
阝 (on left)	eight strokes	阜 (170, mound)
韦	nine strokes	韋 (178, tanned leather)
页	nine strokes	頁 (181, leaf)
风	nine strokes	風 (182, wind)
饣	nine strokes	食, 飠 (184, eat)
马	ten strokes	馬 (187, horse)
鱼	eleven strokes	魚 (195, fish)
鸟	eleven strokes	鳥 (196, bird)
麦	eleven strokes	麥 (199, wheat)
黾	thirteen strokes	黽 (205, frog)
斉 齐	fourteen strokes	齊 (210, even)
齿	fifteen strokes	齒 (211, tooth)
龙	sixteen strokes	龍 (212, dragon)

NOTES ON LOOKING UP CHARACTERS BY RADICAL
List of characters having obscure radicals:

丘	radical 1	一
举 and 义	radical 3	丶
杀	radical 4	丿
乾	radical 5	乙
离	radical 8	亠
刁	radical 18	刀
半 and 单	radical 24	十
商 命 and 周	radical 30	口
平	radical 51	干
开	radical 55	廾
或	radical 59	彡
曲	radical 73	曰
朢 [望]	radical 74	月
束	radical 75	木
歪	radical 77	止
烏 [乌]	radical 86	火	This is not radical 196 鳥鸟, the character has one less stroke.
爭 [争]	radical 87	爪 爫
王	radical 96	玉 王	A five stroke radical, although it has only four strokes.
琵	radical 96	玉 王
申	radical 102	田
直	radical 109	目	From its old writing 直
养	radical 123	羊 䒑
聚	radical 128	耳
舒	radical 135	舌
斗	radical 191	鬥	Because the meaning of the radical is simplified as 斗. Not radical 68, which is more logical for the character itself.
齐	radical 210	齊	Because the radical is simplified as 齐.
龟	radical 213	龜	Because the radical is simplified as 龟.

Be careful to differentiate these radicals:

匚	(22, right open box)	and	匸	(23, hiding enclosure)	
土	(32, earth)	and	士	(33, scholar)	
幺	(52, short thread)	and	纟	(120, silk)	
日	(72, sun)	and	曰	(73, say)	
礻	(113, spirit)	and	衤	(145, clothes)	
钅	(167, gold)	and	饣	(184, eat)	
門	(169, gate)	and	鬥	(191, fight)	

Characters with 月 on the left that refer to body parts are radical 肉, 月 (130, flesh), not 月 (74, moon).
Watch out for the line length difference between the characters 末 mò and 未 wèi.

RADICAL INDEX

1 stroke

1	一	one
2	丨	line
3	丶	dot
4	丿	slash
5	乙 乚	second
6	亅	hook

2 strokes

7	二	two
8	亠	lid
9	人 亻	man
10	儿	legs
11	入	enter
12	八	eight
13	冂	down box
14	冖	cover
15	冫	ice
16	几	table
17	凵	open box
18	刀 刂	knife
19	力	power
20	勹	wrap
21	匕	spoon
22	匚	right open box
23	匸	hiding enclosure
24	十	ten
25	卜	divination
26	卩	seal
27	厂	cliff
28	厶	private

29	又	again

3 strokes

30	口	mouth
31	囗	enclosure
32	土	earth
33	士	scholar
34	夂	go
35	夊	go slowly
36	夕	evening
37	大	big
38	女	woman
39	子 孑	child
40	宀	roof
41	寸	inch
42	小	small
43	尢	lame
44	尸	corpse
45	屮	sprout
46	山	mountain
47	巛 川	river
48	工	work
49	己 巳	oneself
50	巾	turban
51	干	dry
52	幺 彡	short thread
53	广	dotted cliff
54	廴	long stride
55	廾	two hands
56	弋	shoot
57	弓	bow
58	彐 彑	snout

59	彡	bristle
60	彳	step

4 strokes

61	心 忄	heart
62	戈	halberd
63	戶 户	door
64	手 扌	hand
65	支	branch
66	支 攵	rap
67	文	script
68	斗	dipper
69	斤	axe
70	方	square
71	无 旡	not
72	日	sun
73	曰	say
74	月	moon
75	木	tree
76	欠	lack
77	止	stop
78	歹	death
79	殳	weapon
80	毋	do not
81	比	compare
82	毛	fur
83	氏	clan
84	气	steam
85	水 氵	water
86	火 灬	fire
87	爪 爫	claw
88	父	father
89	爻	double x

90	爿 丬	half tree trunk
91	片	slice
92	牙	fang
93	牛 牜	cow
94	犬 犭	dog

5 strokes

95	玄	profound
96	玉 王	jade
97	瓜	melon
98	瓦	tile
99	甘	sweet
100	生	life
101	用	use
102	田	field
103	疋	bolt of cloth
104	疒	sickness
105	癶	dotted tent
106	白	white
107	皮	skin
108	皿	dish
109	目	eye
110	矛	spear
111	矢	arrow
112	石	stone
113	示 礻	spirit
114	禸	track
115	禾	grain
116	穴	cave
117	立	stand

423

RADICAL INDEX

6 strokes

118	竹	bamboo
119	米	rice
120	糸 糹 纟	silk
121	缶	jar
122	网 罒	net
123	羊 𦍌	sheep
124	羽	feather
125	老 耂	old
126	而	and
127	耒	plough
128	耳	ear
129	聿	brush
130	肉 月	flesh
131	臣	minister
132	自	self
133	至	arrive
134	臼	mortar
135	舌	tongue
136	舛	oppose
137	舟	boat
138	艮	stopping
139	色	colour
140	艸 艹	grass
141	虍	tiger
142	虫	insect
143	血	blood
144	行	walk enclosure
145	衣	clothes
146	西 覀 西	west

7 strokes

147	見 见	see
148	角	horn
149	言 訁 讠	speech
150	谷	valley
151	豆	bean
152	豕	pig
153	豸	badger
154	貝 贝	shell
155	赤	red
156	走	run
157	足 𧾷	foot
158	身	body
159	車 车	cart
160	辛	bitter
161	辰	morning
162	辵 辶	walk
163	邑 阝	(on right) city
164	酉	wine
165	采	distinguish
166	里	village

8 strokes

167	金 釒 钅	gold
168	長 镸 长	long
169	門 门	gate
170	阜 阝	(on left) mound
171	隶	slave
172	隹	short tailed bird
173	雨	rain
174	青	blue
175	非	wrong

9 strokes

176	面	face
177	革	leather
178	韋 韦	tanned leather
179	韭	leek
180	音	sound
181	頁 页	leaf
182	風 风	wind
183	飛	fly
184	食 飠 饣	eat
185	首	head
186	香	fragrant

10 strokes

187	馬 马	horse
188	骨	bone
189	高	tall
190	髟	hair
191	鬥 斗	fight
192	鬯	sacrificial wine
193	鬲	cauldron
194	鬼	ghost

11 strokes

195	魚 鱼	fish
196	鳥 鸟	bird
197	鹵	salt
198	鹿	deer
199	麥 麦	wheat
200	麻	hemp

12 strokes

201	黃	yellow
202	黍	millet
203	黑	black
204	黹	embroidery

13 strokes

205	黽 黾	frog
206	鼎	tripod
207	鼓	drum
208	鼠	rat

14 strokes

209	鼻	nose
210	齊 斉 齐	even

15 strokes

211	齒 齿	tooth

16 strokes

212	龍 龙	dragon
213	龜 龟	turtle

17 strokes

214	龠	flute

Character Index by Radical Order

Each column: Added strokes | Traditional character | Simplified (~ if the same) | Pinyin | Page number

一 丨 丶 丿 乙 亅 二 亠 人

1 stroke radicals

一 (1)

0	一 ~	yī	373
1	丁 ~	dīng	82
	七 ~	qī	239
2	三 ~	sān	263
	上 ~	shàng	269
	萬 万	wàn	332
	下 ~	xià	345
	丈 ~	zhàng	395
3	不 ~	bù	37
	丑 ~	chǒu	55
4	丙 ~	bǐng	35
	丘 ~	qiū	251
	世 ~	shì	281
5	丟 丢	diū	84

丨 (2)

3	丰	fēng	103
	中 ~	zhōng,	403
		zhòng	406
5	并	bìng	35
6	串 ~	chuàn	57
7	並	bìng	35

丶 (3)

2	义	yì	376
3	卞 ~	biàn	33
	丹 ~	dān	68
	之 ~	zhī	399
4	主 ~	zhǔ	407
8	舉 举	jǔ	174

丿 (4)

1	乃 ~	nǎi	218
4	乏 ~	fá	95
	乍 ~	zhà	392
5	殺 杀	shā	268
9	乘 ~	chéng	52

乙 乚 (5)

0	乙 ~	yǐ	374
1	九 ~	jiǔ	173
6	亂 乱	luàn	204
7	乳 ~	rǔ	260
10	乾	gān	111
	乾	qián	243
12	亂	luàn	204

亅 (6)

2 stroke radicals

二 (7)

0	二 ~	èr	92
1	干 ~	gān	111
2	互 ~	hù	140
	井 ~	jǐng	172
	五 ~	wǔ	338
	云	yún	389

亠 (8)

3	市 ~	shì	281
4	亥 ~	hài	127
	交 ~	jiāo	160
6	京 ~	jīng	171
	夜 ye	yè	372
7	亮 ~	liàng	195
	亱	yè	372
8	离	lí	190

人 亻 (9)

0	人 ~	rén	258
1	个	gè	114
	亿	yì	375
2	化 ~	huà	142
	内	nèi	219
	仆 ~	pū	236
	仁 ~	rén	258
	以 ~	yǐ	375
	仄 ~	zè	391
3	代 ~	dài	67
	令 ~	lìng	198
	仙 ~	xiān	347
	仗 ~	zhàng	395
4	伐 ~	fá	95
	仿 ~	fǎng	100
	伏 ~	fú	106
	合 ~	hé	128
	會 会	huì	146
	任 ~	rèn	258
	傷 伤	shāng	269
	休 ~	xiū	357
	仰 ~	yǎng	368
5	傳 传	chuán	57
	低 ~	dī	76
	佛 ~	fó	106
	兩 两	liǎng	195
	你 ~	nǐ	221
	伸 ~	shēn	274
	體 体	tǐ	313
	余	yú	383
	佔	zhàn	393
	傳 传	zhuàn	409
	作 ~	zuò	417
6	併	bìng	35
	側	cè	43
	俠	jiā	154
	俠	xiá	345
	佯 ~	yáng	366
7	保 ~	bǎo	25
	俠	xiá	345
	信 ~	xìn	355
	修 ~	xiū	357
8	倒 ~	dǎo,	73
		dào	74
	倣	fǎng	100
	俯 ~	fǔ	108
	個	gè	114
	借 ~	jiè	164
	條	tiáo	315
	脩	xiū	357
	倚 ~	yǐ	375
9	偪	bī	31
	側	cè	43
	假 ~	jiǎ	154
	偏 ~	piān	232
	停 ~	tíng	319
	偷 ~	tōu	320
	偎 ~	wēi	332
	偃 ~	yǎn	364
11	傳	chuán	57
	催 ~	cuī	60
	傷	shāng	269
	傳	zhuàn	409
12	僧 ~	sēng	268
	僊	xiān	347
13	僵 ~	jiāng	159
	億	yì	375

425

Character Index by Radical Order

Each column: Added strokes | Traditional character | Simplified (~ if the same) | Pinyin | Page number

人 儿 入 八 冂 冖 冫 几 凵 刀 力 勹 匕 匸 匚 十

| 14 | 儒 | ~ | rú | 260 |

儿 (10)

0	儿		ér	92
2	元	~	yuán	386
4	充	~	chōng	54
	光	~	guāng	122
	先	~	xiān	348
5	兑	~	duì	88
	克		kè	180
	兎		tù	322
6	兒		ér	92
	兔		tù	322
7	剋		kè	180
9	兜	~	dōu	85

入 (11)

0	入	~	rù	260
2	內		nèi	219
4	全	~	quán	253
6	兩		liǎng	195

八 (12)

0	八	~	bā	15
2	公	~	gōng	115
	六	~	liù	199
6	典	~	diǎn	78

冂 (13)

| 2 | 冈 | | gāng | 112 |
| 6 | 岡 | | gāng | 112 |

冖 (14)

冫 (15)

4	冲	chōng	54
	决	jué	176
5	冷	~	lěng	189
8	准	zhǔn	411
	凌	~	líng	197
14	凝	~	níng	223

几 (16)

凵 (17)

3	凹	~	āo	14
	出	~	chū	55
	击	jī	151
	凸	~	tū	321

刀 刂 (18)

0	刀	~	dāo	73
	刁	~	diāo	80
1	刃	刄	rèn	258
2	分	~	fēn	102
	切	~	qiē	248
4	刚	gāng	112
	划	huá	141
	列	~	liè	197
	刘	liú	199
5	別	别	bié	34
	別		biè	34
	刜	~	fú	107
	刔		jié	163
	刧		jié	163
	利	~	lì	191
	判	~	pàn	229
	刨	~	páo	230
6	刺	~	cì	59
	剁	~	duò	89
	刮	~	guā	119
	刼		jié	163
7	剝	bō	36
	剑	jiàn	158
	剌	~	lá	185
	前	~	qián	244
	削	~	xiāo	350
	制	zhì	403
8	剥	bō	36
	剛	gāng	112
	剔	~	tī	310
9	副	~	fù	108
	剪	~	jiǎn	157
11	剿	~	jiǎo	161
12	劃	huá	141
13	劐	~	huō	147
	劍	jiàn	158
	劉	liú	199
	劈	~	pī	231
14	劎	jiàn	158
	劔	jiàn	158

力 (19)

0	力	~	lì	191
2	劝	quàn	254
3	功	~	gōng	115
4	动	dòng	84
5	劫	~	jié	163
	劲	jìn	170
	劳	láo	187
	努	~	nǔ	224
6	势	shì	281
7	勁	jìn	170
	勉	~	miǎn	212
	勇	~	yǒng	381
9	動	dòng	84
	勒	~	lè,	188
			lēi	188
10	勞	láo	187
11	勦	jiǎo	161
	勢	shì	281
17	勸	quàn	254

勹 (20)

| 2 | 勾 | ~ | gōu | 117 |
| 3 | 包 | ~ | bāo | 25 |

匕 (21)

| 0 | 匕 | ~ | bǐ | 31 |
| 3 | 北 | ~ | běi | 28 |

匸 (22)

| 5 | 医 | yī | 374 |

匚 (23)

| 9 | 匾 | ~ | biǎn | 33 |

十 (24)

0	十	~	shí	278
1	千	~	qiān	243
2	午	~	wǔ	339
3	半	~	bàn	24
4	华	huá	141
	协	xié	353
6	協	xié	353
	单	dān	68
7	南	~	nán	218
8	華	huá	141

Character Index by Radical Order

Each column: Added strokes | Traditional character | Simplified (~ if the same) | Pinyin | Page number

卜 阝 厂 厶 又 口 囗 土 士 夂

卜 (25)

| 3 | 卡 | ~ | kǎ | 177 |
| 3 | 占 | ~ | zhàn | 393 |

阝 (26)

1	卫	wèi	334
3	叩	kòu	182
	卯	~	mǎo	209
	印	印	yìn	378
6	卷	~	juǎn	175
7	卸	~	xiè	354

厂 (27)

3	厉	lì	192
4	后	hòu	136
8	原	~	yuán	386
10	厥	~	jué	176
13	厲	lì	192

厶 (28)

又 (29)

1	叉	~	chā	44
2	反	~	fǎn	97
	鳳	fèng	105
	雙	shuāng	288
3	发	fā	95
6	变	biàn	37
11	叠	dié	81
16	雙	shuāng	288

3 stroke radicals

口 (30)

0	口	~	kǒu	181
2	古	~	gǔ	118
	号	hào	128
	可	~	kě	180
	叶	yè	372
	右	~	yòu	382
	只	~	zhǐ	401
3	吃	~	chī	52
	吕	lǚ	203
	名	~	míng	212
	同	~	tóng	319
	吐	~	tǔ	321
	向	~	xiàng	349
4	呆	~	dāi	67
	含	~	hán	127
	呂	lǚ	203
	听	tīng	318
	吞	~	tūn	325
	吻	~	wěn	334
	吴	吴	wú	337
	吸	~	xī	343
5	呼	~	hū	138
	命	~	mìng	213
	咏	yǒng	381
	周	~	zhōu	406
6	哈	~	hā	127
	哪	~	né	219
	哇	~	wā	329
	啞	yǎ	364
	咽	~	yān	364
	咬	~	yǎo	370
7	哼	~	hēng	132

8	商	~	shāng	269
	兽	shòu	285
	啞	yǎ	364
	啄	~	zhuó	411
9	喘	~	chuǎn	57
	單	dān	68
	喉	~	hóu	135
	喂	~	wèi	333
	喜	~	xǐ	344
10	喙	~	huì	146
11	嘑	hū	138
12	嘿	~	hēi	130
	嘴	~	zuǐ	416
13	器	~	qì	241
14	嚮	xiàng	349

囗 (31)

2	四	~	sì	296
3	回	~	huí	145
	团	tuán	322
	囟	~	xìn	356
4	囮	~	é	91
	囤	~	tún	325
	围	wéi	332
5	固	~	gù	119
	国	guó	125
	图	tú	321
7	圆	yuán	386
8	國	guó	125
	圈	~	quān	252
10	圍	wéi	332
	圓	yuán	386
11	圖	tú	321
	團	tuán	322

土 (32)

0	土	~	tǔ	322
3	地	~	dì	77
	压	yā	363
4	场	chǎng	49
	坎	~	kǎn	178
	坛	tán	306
	坠	zhuì	411
	坐	~	zuò	418
5	坤	~	kūn	184
	坡	~	pō	236
6	垫	diàn	79
7	埋	~	mái	208
8	堵	~	dǔ	87
	基	~	jī	151
	堂	~	táng	307
9	報	bào	25
	場	chǎng	49
10	塌	~	tā	303
	填	~	tián	315
11	墊	diàn	79
	墜	zhuì	411
12	墩	~	dūn	89
14	壓	yā	363

士 (33)

1	壬	~	rén	258
4	声	shēng	276
5	垂	~	chuí	58
7	壶	hú	138
10	壺	hú	138

夂 (34)

| 2 | 处 | chǔ | 56 |
| 4 | 条 | tiáo | 315 |

427

Character Index by Radical Order

Each column: Added strokes | Traditional character | Simplified (~ if the same) | Pinyin | Page number

夂 夊 夕 大 女 子 宀 寸 小 尢 尸 屮 山 巛 工 己 巾 干

6	復 复 fù	108,109
7	夏 ~ xià	347

夊 (35)

夕 (36)

2	外 ~ wài	329
3	多 ~ duō	89

大 (37)

0	大 ~ dà	64
1	太 ~ tài	303
	天 ~ tiān	313
2	奔 ~ bèn, hāng	30, 128
	失 ~ shī	277
	头 tóu	320
3	夺 duó	89
	关 guān	121
	夹 jiā	154
4	夾 jiā	154
5	奇 ~ qí	240
	奔 ~ bēn	30
6	奎 ~ kuí	183
7	套 ~ tào	309
11	奪 duó	89

女 (38)

0	女 ~ nǚ	224
3	如 ~ rú	260
4	妙 ~ miào	212
5	委 ~ wěi	333
7	娑 ~ suō	301
9	媮 tōu	320
11	嫦 ~ cháng	48

	嫩 ~ nèn	221

子 孑 (39)

0	子 ~ zǐ	411
1	孔 ~ kǒng	180
3	存 ~ cún	60
	孙 sūn	301
	字 ~ zì	412
5	孤 ~ gū	118
	学 xué	360
7	孫 sūn	301
13	學 xué	360

宀 (40)

3	安 ~ ān	13
4	宋 ~ sòng	299
	完 ~ wán	331
5	宝 bǎo	25
	定 ~ dìng	83
	审 shěn	276
	实 shí	280
	宗 ~ zōng	413
6	宣 ~ xuān	359
8	宿 ~ sù	300
	寅 ~ yín	378
9	寒 ~ hán	128
12	審 shěn	276
	實 shí	280
17	寶 bǎo	25

寸 (41)

0	寸 ~ cùn	60
2	对 duì	88
3	导 dǎo	74
	寻 xún	361

6	封 ~ fēng	103
	将 jiàng	160
7	射 ~ shè	274
8	將 jiàng	160
9	尋 xún	361
11	對 duì	88
12	導 dǎo	74

小 (42)

0	小 ~ xiǎo	350
1	少 ~ shǎo,shào	273
3	当 dāng	72
	尖 ~ jiān	156
5	尚 ~ shàng	272

尢 (43)

9	就 ~ jiù	174

尸 (44)

1	尺 ~ chǐ	53
4	局 ~ jú	174
	尾 ~ wěi	333
5	居 ~ jū	174
	屈 ~ qū	251
6	屋 ~ wū	336
7	展 ~ zhǎn	393
12	履 ~ lǚ	203

屮 (45)

山 (46)

5	岳 ~ yuè	387
7	峨 ~ é	91
	峩 ~ é	91

8	崩 ~ bēng	30
	崧 ~ sōng	299
10	嵩 ~ sōng	299
14	嶽 yuè	387

巛 川 (47)

0	川 ~ chuān	56

工 (48)

2	巧 ~ qiǎo	247
	巨 ~ jù	175
	左 ~ zuǒ	417
3	巩 gǒng	116

己 巳 (49)

0	己 ~ jǐ	153
	巳 ~ sì	299
1	巴 ~ bā	17
9	巽 ~ xùn	361

巾 (50)

2	布 ~ bù	38
3	吊 ~ diào	80
	师 shī	277
6	带 dài	67
7	帮 bāng	25
	師 shī	277
8	帶 dài	67
14	幫 bāng	25

干 (51)

2	平 ~ píng	234

Character Index by Radical Order

Each column: Added strokes | Traditional character | Simplified (~ if the same) | Pinyin | Page number

幺广廴廾弋弓彐彡彳心戈戶手

幺 乡 (52)

6	幽 ~	yōu	381

广 (53)

4	庇 ~	bì	32
	库	kù	182
	应	yīng	378
5	底 ~	dǐ	77
	府 ~	fǔ	108
	庚 ~	gēng	114
7	庫	kù	182
	唐 ~	táng	307
10	廉 ~	lián	193
	廓 ~	kuò	184

廴 (54)

5	迫	pò	236
6	建 ~	jiàn	158

廾 (55)

1	开	kāi	177
4	弄 ~	nòng	224
	弃	qì	241

弋 (56)

3	式 ~	shì	282

弓 (57)

0	弓 ~	gōng	115
1	弔	diào	80
	引 ~	yǐn	378
4	弝	bà	18
5	弣 ~	fǔ	108
	弧 ~	hú	138

	弩 ~	nǔ	224
	弦 ~	xián	349
	张	zhāng	394
6	弯	wān	331
7	弰 ~	shāo	272
8	弸 ~	bēng, pēng	31, 230
	弹	dàn, tán	72, 306
	强	qiáng, qiǎng	246, 246
	張	zhāng	394
9	強	qiáng, qiǎng	246, 246
12	彆	biè	34
	彈	dàn, tán	72, 306
19	彎	wān	331

彐 彑 (58)

2	归	guī	122

彡 (59)

4	形 ~	xíng	356
5	参	cān	42
7	彧 ~	yù	383
8	彩	cǎi	41
	參	cān	42

彳 (60)

4	彻	chè	50
	彼 ~	bǐ	31
6	待 ~	dài	68
	後	hòu	136
7	徒 ~	tú	321

8	得 ~	dé	76
9	循 ~	xún	361
	復	fù	108
	御 ~	yù	384
12	徹	chè	50
14	禦	yù	384

4 stroke radicals

心 忄 (61)

0	心 ~	xīn	354
3	忌 ~	jì	153
	忍 ~	rěn	258
	志 ~	zhì	403
4	怀	huái	142
	忠 ~	zhōng	405
	快 ~	kuài	183
5	怪 ~	guài	120
	急 ~	jí	152
	怒 ~	nù	224
	怯 ~	qiè	248
	总	zǒng	413
6	恶	è	91
	恠	guài	120
	恨 ~	hèn	132
	恆 恒	héng	132
7	悟 ~	wù	341
	悬	xuán	359
	悠 ~	yōu	382
8	惊	jīng	171
9	惯	guàn	121
	慌 ~	huāng	144
	意 ~	yì	375
10	恶	è	91
	慎 ~	shèn	276

11	慢 ~	màn	208
	慾 ~	yù	385
12	憋 ~	biē	34
	懂 ~	dǒng	84
	慣	guàn	121
13	懒	lǎn	186
	應	yīng	378
16	懷	huái	142
	懶	lǎn	186
	懸	xuán	359

戈 (62)

0	戈 ~	gē	113
1	戊 ~	wù	341
2	成 ~	chéng	52
	戍 ~	xū	358
5	战	zhàn	393
8	戟 ~	jǐ	153
10	截 ~	jié	163
12	戰	zhàn	393
14	戳 ~	chuō	58
	戴 ~	dài	68

戶 户 (63)

0	戶 户	hù	140
5	扁 ~	biǎn	33
6	扇 ~	shān	268

手 扌 (64)

0	手 ~	shǒu	283
1	扎 ~	zhā	392
2	扒 ~	bā	17
	打 ~	dǎ	63
	扑	pū	237
	扔 ~	rēng	258

429

CHARACTER INDEX BY RADICAL ORDER
EACH COLUMN: ADDED STROKES | TRADITIONAL CHARACTER | SIMPLIFIED (~ IF THE SAME) | PINYIN | PAGE NUMBER

手

3	扠	~	chā	44	5	拗	~	ào	14		持	~	chí	53		挽	~	wǎn	332
	扛	~	gāng,	112		拔	~	bá	17		挡		dǎng	72		捂	~	wǔ	339
			káng	178		拌	~	bàn	24		挆	~	duò	89		挾		xié	353
	扣	~	kòu	181		抱	~	bào	25		拱	~	gǒng	116		捉	~	zhuō	411
		扬	mā	207			拨	bō	36		挂		guà	119	8	掰	~	bāi	19
		扪	mén	210		拆	~	chāi	46		挥		huī	145		掤	~	bīng	35
	扦	~	qiān	243		抻		chēn	50		挤		jǐ	153		採		cǎi	41
	扫		sǎo	267		抽	~	chōu	54		挾		jiā	154		掣	~	chè	50
	托	~	tuō	325		担		dān	71		挎	~	kuà	182		捵		chēn	50
4	把	~	bǎ,	18		抵	~	dǐ	77		挒	~	liè	197		捶	~	chuí	58
			bà	18		拂	~	fú	107		拿	~	ná	217		撢		dǎn	71
	扳	~	bān	23		拐	~	guǎi	120		挠		náo	218		捯	~	dáo	73
		报	bào	25		拘	~	jū	174		挪	~	nuó	225		捣		dǎo	74
	抄	~	chāo	49		扡	~	kā	177		拳	~	quán	253		掉	~	diào	81
		扯	chě	50		扤	~	kuǎi	183		拾	~	shí	280		掛		guà	119
	承	~	chéng	52		拉	~	lā	185		挞		tà	303		捆	~	hùn	147
	扽	~	dèn	76		拦		lán	185		挑	~	tiǎo	315		接	~	jiē	163
	抖	~	dǒu	85		拎	~	līn	197		挖	~	wā	329		捲		juǎn	175
	扼	~	è	91		拢		lǒng	202		挝	wō,	335		掯	~	kèn	180
	扶	~	fú	107		抿	~	mǐn	212				zhuā	408		控	~	kòng	180
		护	hù	140		抹	~	mǒ	213		挟		xié	353		擄		lǔ	202
	技	~	jì	153		拇	~	mǔ	214		挒	~	yí	374		掠	~	lüè	204
	抉	~	jué	176		拏	~	ná	217			挣	zhèng	397		掄		lūn	204
	抗	~	kàng	179		拈	~	niān	222		指	~	zhǐ	401		捫		mén	210
		抠	kōu	180		拧		níng	223		拽	~	zhuāi	408		捺	~	nà	218
		抡	lūn	204		拍	~	pāi	227	7	挨	~	āi	13		捻		niǎn	222
	抟	~	miǎn	212		披	~	pī	232		挫	~	cuò	61		捏		niē	222
	扭	~	niǔ	224		拑	~	qián	245			换	huàn	143		排	~	pái	228
		扳	pān	228		抬		tái	303		挾		jiā	154		掤	~	péng	230
	抛	~	pāo	229		拖	~	tuō	327		捆	~	kǔn	184		捧	~	pěng	230
	批	~	pī	232		拽	~	wāi	329			捞	lāo	187		搒 掽	pèng	231
		抢	qiǎng	246		擁		yōng	381		捋	~	lǚ,	203		掐	~	qiā	242
	扱	~	xī	343		招	~	zhāo	395				luō	205			扫	sǎo	267
		扬	yáng	366		注	~	zhǔ	407		捏		niē	222		探	~	tàn	306
	折	~	zhé	396		拙	~	zhuō	411		挺	~	tǐng	319		掏	~	tāo	308
	抓	~	zhuā	407	6	按	~	àn	13		捅	~	tǒng	320		推	~	tuī	322

430

CHARACTER INDEX BY RADICAL ORDER
EACH COLUMN: ADDED STROKES | TRADITIONAL CHARACTER | SIMPLIFIED (~ IF THE SAME) | PINYIN | PAGE NUMBER

手 支 攴

	掀	~	xiān	348
	掩	~	yǎn	364
	掖	~	yē	371
	掌	~	zhǎng	394
	掟	~	zhěng	397
	掙		zhèng	397
		掷	zhì	403
	掫	~	zhōu	406
9	揹		bēi	28
	插	~	chā	45
		搀	chān	46
	揣	~	chuāi	56
	搥		chuí	58
	搓	~	cuō	61
	搭	~	dā	63
		掼	guàn	121
	換		huàn	143
	揮		huī	145
		搅	jiǎo	161
	揭	~	jiē	163
	揪	~	jiū	173
		揽	lǎn	186
		搂	lōu	202
	媽		mā	207
		揿	qìn	249
	揉	~	róu	259
	搜	~	sōu	300
	提	~	tí	311
	揋	~	wāi	329
		揾	wèn	334
	握	~	wò	335
	搗		wǔ	339
	揚		yáng	366
	援	~	yuán	386
	揸	~	zhā	392
10	擺	摆	bǎi	22

	搬	~	bān	23
	搏	~	bó	37
	搗		dǎo	74
	搤	~	è	91
	搿	~	gé	113
	搆		gòu	118
	搟		huàng	145
	摸	~	mō	213
	搶		qiǎng	246
	搧		shān	268
	搠	~	shuò	296
	搨	~	tà	303
	摊		tān	306
	搵		wèn	334
	携		xié	353
	搖	摇	yáo	370
11	摽	~	biāo	34
	撦		chě	50
	摧	~	cuī	60
	摳		kōu	180
	摟		lōu	202
	摩	~	mó	213
	摔	~	shuāi	286
	摘	~	zhāi	392
	摺		zhé	396
12	撥	拨	bō	36
	撤	~	chè	50
	撐 撑		chēng	51
	撮	~	cuō	61
	撣		dǎn	71
	撢		dǎn	71
	撐	~	dēng	76
	撘	~	gě,	114
			kā	177
	摜		guàn	121
	攪		jiǎo	161

	撅	~	juē	176
	撈		lāo	187
	撩	~	liāo	196
	撸		lū	202
	擄		lǔ	202
	撓		náo	218
	撚		niǎn	222
	撇	~	piē, piě	233
	撲		pū	237
	撬	~	qiào	248
	撳		qìn	249
	擎	~	qíng	251
	撋	~	ruán	260
	(also 日 inside, instead of 王)			
	撒	~	sā, sǎ	263
	撕	~	sī	296
	撻		tà	303
	撾		wō,	335
			zhuā	408
	撜	~	zhěng	397
	撞	~	zhuàng	410
13	操	~	cāo	43
	擔	担	dān	71
	擋	挡	dǎng	72
	攉		huò	149
	擊	击	jī	151
	擂	~	lèi	189
	撽		qiào	248
	擒	~	qín	249
	撷		xié	353
	擁	拥	yōng	381
14	擦	~	cā	41
	擠	挤	jǐ	153
	擰	拧	níng	223
	擡	抬	tái	303
15	擺	摆	bǎi	22

	擼	撸	lū	202
	攀	~	pān	228
	擷	撷	liè	197
	擲	掷	zhì	403
16	攢	攒	cuán, zǎn	60, 391
	攉	~	huō	147
	攏	拢	lǒng	202
17	攙	搀	chān	46
	攔	拦	lán	185
18	攜	携	xié	353
19	攢	攒	cuán, zǎn	60, 391
	攤	摊	tān	306
20	攥	~	zuàn	416
21	攬	揽	lǎn	186

支 (65)

| 0 | 支 | ~ | zhī | 400 |

攴 攵 (66)

2	收	~	shōu	282
3	改	~	gǎi	111
	攻	~	gōng	116
4	敗		bài	23
	放	~	fàng	100
5	敂		kòu	182
6	敵		dí	77
7	敗		bài	23
	教	~	jiāo, jiào	160, 162
	敛		liǎn	194
	敏	~	mǐn	212
8	敬	~	jìng	172
	散	~	sǎn	267

431

Character Index by Radical Order
Each column: Added strokes | Traditional character | Simplified (~ if the same) | Pinyin | Page number

攴 文 斗 斤 方 无 日 曰 月 木

	散	sǎn	267
11	敵	dí	77
	敷	~	fū	106
	整	~	zhěng	397
13	斂	liǎn	194

文 (67)
| 0 | 文 | ~ | wén | 334 |

斗 (68)
| (0 | 斗 | dòu | 85 |

In simplified with the meaning of fighting is radical 191)

| 7 | 斜 | ~ | xié | 353 |

斤 (69)
0	斤	~	jīn	165
4	斧	~	fǔ	108
	斬	zhǎn	393
5	斫	~	zhuó	411
7	斷	duàn	88
	斬	zhǎn	393
9	新	~	xīn	355
14	斷	duàn	88

方 (70)
0	方	~	fāng	99
5	施	~	shī	277
6	旁	~	páng	229
7	旋	~	xuán	359
	旋	xuàn	360

无 旡 (71)
| 0 | 无 | ~ | wú | 337 |

日 (72)
0	日	~	rì	259
1	旧	jiù	174
3	时	shí	280
4	畅	chàng	49
	昆	~	kūn	184
	明	~	míng	212
	易	~	yì	376
5	春	~	chūn	58
	显	xiǎn	349
6	晃	~	huǎng	145
	晃	~	huàng	145
	時	shí	280
	晕	yūn,	388
		yùn	390
7	晨	~	chén	50
8	暑	~	shǔ	286
	暂	zàn	391
	智	~	zhì	403
9	暗	~	àn	14
	暇	~	xiá	345
	暈	yūn,	388
		yùn	390
10	暢	chàng	49
11	暴	~	bào	28
	暫	zàn	391

曰 (73)
1	电	diàn	80
2	曲	~	qū	252
8	最	~	zuì	416
9	會	huì	146

月 (74)
0	月	~	yuè	388
2	有	~	yǒu	382
4	服	~	fú	107
6	朔	~	shuò	296
7	望	~	wàng	332
8	朝	~	cháo	49
	期	~	qī	239
10	朢	wàng	332

木 (75)
0	木	~	mù	214
1	本	~	běn	30
	東	dōng	84
	術	shù	286
	未	~	wèi	333
2	朴	~	pǔ	238
	雜	zá	391
	朱	~	zhū	407
3	杜	~	dù	87
	杆	gān	111
	杠	gàng	112
	李	~	lǐ	190
	杓	sháo	272
	束	~	shù	286
	杖	~	zhàng	395
4	板	~	bǎn	24
	杵	~	chǔ	56
	東	dōng	84
	枫	fēng	103
	極	jí	152
	林	~	lín	197
	枪	qiāng	246
	樞	shū	285
	松	~	sōng	299
	梟	xiāo	350
	杨	yáng	367
	枕	~	zhěn	397
5	标	biāo	34
	柄	~	bǐng	35
	查	~	chá	46
	架	~	jià	155
	枯	~	kū	182
	栏	lán	186
	柳	~	liǔ	199
	柔	~	róu	259
	树	shù	286
	相	~	xiāng,	349
		xiàng	350
	柱	~	zhū	407
6	格	~	gē,	113
		gé	113
	根	~	gēn	114
	核	~	hé	129
	桥	qiáo	247
	桡	ráo	257
	栓	~	shuān	287
	梟	xiāo	350
	栽	~	zāi	391
	桩	zhuāng	409
7	桿	gān	111
	梗	~	gěng	115
	检	jiǎn	157
	梨	~	lí	189
	梁	~	liáng	195
	梅	~	méi	209
	梢	~	shāo	272
8	棒	~	bàng	25
	棍	~	gùn	124
	極	jí	152
	棄	qì	241
	椭	tuǒ	328
9	槌	~	chuí	58
	楓	fēng	103

Character Index by Radical Order

Each column: Added strokes | Traditional character | Simplified (~ if the same) | Pinyin | Page number

木欠止歹殳毋比毛氏气水

	楔 ~ xiē 353
	楊 yáng 367
10	槓 gàng 112
	槐 ~ huái 143
	槍 qiāng 246
	槊 shuò 296
11	標 ~ biāo 34
	橫 ~ héng 132
	樑 liáng 195
	樞 shū 285
	橢 tuǒ 328
	椿 zhuāng 409
12	橄 ~ gǎn 112
	橛 ~ jué 176
	櫓 lǔ 203
	樸 pǔ 238
	樵 ~ qiáo 247
	橋 qiáo 247
	橈 ráo 257
	樹 shù 286
13	檢 jiǎn 157
15	櫓 lǔ 203
17	欄 lán 186
19	欑 cuán 60
21	欛 bà 18

欠 (76)

2	次 ~ cì 59
8	欺 ~ qī 240
9	歇 ~ xiē 353
10	歌 ~ gē 113

止 (77)

0	止 ~ zhǐ 403
1	正 ~ zhèng 398

3	步 ~ bù 38
4	武 ~ wǔ 339
5	歪 ~ wāi 329
14	歸 guī 123

歹 (78)

2	死 ~ sǐ 296
5	殘 cán 42
8	殘 cán 42

殳 (79)

0	殳 ~ shū 285
5	段 ~ duàn 88
6	殷 ~ yīn 376
	殺 shā 268

毋 (80)

1	母 ~ mǔ 214
4	毒 ~ dú 86

比 (81)

0	比 ~ bǐ 31

毛 (82)

0	毛 ~ máo 209
6	毬 qiú 251

氏 (83)

气 (84)

0	气 ~ qì 241
6	氣 qì 241

水 氵 (85)

0	水 ~ shuǐ 293
1	永 ~ yǒng 381
2	漢 hàn 128
	求 ~ qiú 251
3	江 ~ jiāng 160
4	沈 ~ chén 50
	決 jué 176
	沐 ~ mù 215
	沙 ~ shā 268
5	波 ~ bō 37
	法 ~ fǎ 95
	泥 ~ ní 221
	沛 ~ pèi 230
	潑 pō 236
	泰 ~ tài 305
	泳 ~ yǒng 381
	沾 zhān 393
	治 ~ zhì 403
	注 ~ zhù 407
6	洪 ~ hóng 134
	渾 hún 147
	活 ~ huó 148
	津 ~ jīn 165
	派 ~ pài 228
	洗 ~ xǐ 344
	濁 zhuó 411
7	滌 dí 77
	浮 ~ fú 107
	海 ~ hǎi 127
	浪 ~ làng 187
	流 ~ liú 199
	潤 rùn 261
	消 ~ xiāo 350
	涌 ~ yǒng 381

8	涵 ~ hán 128
	混 ~ hún 146
	凌 líng 197
	清 清 qīng 249
	涮 ~ shuàn 287
	淘 ~ táo 309
	液 ~ yè 372
	漁 yú 383
	淵 yuān 385
9	渾 hún 147
	濺 jiàn 159
	濕 shī 277
	溫 ~ wēn 334
	游 ~ yóu 382
	滯 zhì 403
10	滌 dí 77
	滾 gǔn 123
	滑 ~ huá 141
	溜 ~ liū 198
	滿 mǎn 208
	準 zhǔn 411
11	滴 ~ dī 77
	滾 gǔn 123
	漢 hàn 128
	漏 ~ lòu 202
	滿 mǎn 208
	演 ~ yǎn 365
	漁 yú 383
	滯 zhì 403
12	潛 ~ qián 245
	潤 rùn 261
	潭 ~ tán 306
13	激 ~ jī 151
	濁 zhuó 411
14	濕 shī 277
15	濺 jiàn 159

433

Character Index by Radical Order

Each column: Added strokes | Traditional character | Simplified (~ if the same) | Pinyin | Page number

水 火 爪 父 爻 爿 片 牙 牛 犬 玄 玉 瓜 瓦 甘 生 用 田 疋 广

17	灌 ~	guàn	122

火 灬 (86)

0	火 ~	huǒ	148
3	灵	líng	197
	乌	wū	336
5	点	diǎn	79
	烂	làn	186
	炼	liàn	194
	炮 ~	pào	230
	烏	wū	336
	炸 ~	zhà	392
	炤	zhào	395
6	热	rè	257
8	然 ~	rán	257
	無	wú	337
9	煉	liàn	194
	照 ~	zhào	395
10	熊 ~	xióng	357
11	熱	rè	257
12	燕 ~	yàn	365
13	營	yíng	379
	燥 ~	zào	391
15	爆 ~	bào	28
17	爛	làn	186

爪 爫 (87)

0	爪 ~	zhǎo, zhuǎ	395, 408
4	爬 ~	pá	227
	受 ~	shòu	285
	争 争	zhēng	397

父 (88)

0	父 ~	fù	108

爻 (89)

爿 丬 (90)

3	壮	zhuàng	410
4	狀	zhuàng	410

片 (91)

0	片 ~	piàn	233

牙 (92)

0	牙 ~	yá	364

牛 牛 (93)

0	牛 ~	niú	223
4	牧 ~	mù	215
5	牵	qiān	243
6	特 ~	tè	309
7	牽	qiān	243
8	犇	bēn	30
	犊 ~	dú	86
	犀 ~	xī	343

犬 犭 (94)

0	犬 ~	quǎn	254
2	犯 ~	fàn	99
6	独	dú	86
	狠 ~	hěn	132
	狮	shī	277
	狭	xiá	345
7	狼 ~	láng	186
	狸 ~	lí	189
	狹	xiá	345
8	猫	māo	209
	猛 ~	měng	210
	猪	zhū	407
9	猴 ~	hóu	135
	獻	xiàn	349
	猨	yuán	386
10	獃	dāi	67
	獅	shī	277
	猿 ~	yuán	386
13	獨	dú	86
15	獸	shòu	285
	獻	xiàn	349

5 stroke radicals

玄 (95)

0	玄 ~	xuán	359
6	率 ~	shuài	287

玉 王 (96)

0	王 ~	wáng	332
	玉 ~	yù	384
4	环	huán	143
6	球 ~	qiú	251
7	理 ~	lǐ	190
8	琵 ~	pí	232
11	璇	xuán	359
13	環	huán	143

瓜 (97)

11	瓢 ~	piáo	233

瓦 (98)

0	瓦 ~	wǎ	329
6	瓶 ~	píng	235
11	甄	zhuān	408

甘 (99)

生 (100)

0	生 ~	shēng	276

用 (101)

0	用 ~	yòng	381
	甩 ~	shuǎi	287

田 (102)

0	田 ~	tián	315
	甲 ~	jiǎ	155
	申 ~	shēn	274
2	男 ~	nán	218
3	画	huà	142
4	畊	gēng	115
5	留 ~	liú	199
7	畫	huà	142
8	當	dāng	72
17	疊	dié	81

疋 (103)

广 (104)

5	疾 ~	jí	152
	疲 ~	pí	232
7	痞 ~	pǐ	232
8	瘀 ~	yū	382
9	瘦 ~	chì	53
10	癱	tān	306
19	癱	tān	306

癶 (105)

4	癸 ~	guǐ	122
7	登 ~	dēng	76
	發	fā	95

白 (106)

0	白 ~	bái	19
1	百 ~	bǎi	22
3	的 ~	dì	78

皮 (107)

0	皮 ~	pí	232

皿 (108)

6	蓋 gài		111
	盔 ~	kuī	183
	盘 ~	pán	228
8	嗌 ~	yì	376
10	盤	pán	228
12	盪 ~	dàng	72

目 (109)

0	目 ~	mù	215
3	直 ~	zhí	400
4	盾 ~	dùn	89
	眉 ~	méi	210
5	眩 ~	xuàn	360
	真 ~	zhēn	397
6	眯	mī	211
	眼 ~	yǎn	365
	着 ~	zhāo, zhuó	395 411
8	督 ~	dū	86
	睛 ~	jīng	171
9	瞇	mī	211
10	瞒	mán	208
	瞑 ~	míng	212
11	瞞	mán	208
	瞟 ~	piǎo	233
12	瞳 ~	tóng	319
13	瞬 ~	shùn	294

矛 (110)

0	矛 ~	máo	209

矢 (111)

0	矢 ~	shǐ	281
7	短 ~	duǎn	87
8	矮 ~	ǎi	13

石 (112)

0	石 ~	shí	281
4	砍 ~	kǎn	178
	研	yán	364
5	破 ~	pò	236
	砣 ~	tuó	327
	砸 ~	zá	391
	砖	zhuān	408
6	研	yán	364
7	硬 ~	yìng	381
8	碌 ~	liù	200
	碰 碰	pèng	231
	碎 ~	suì	301
9	碧 ~	bì	32
10	磕 ~	kē	179
	碾 ~	niǎn	222
11	磨 ~	mó, mò	213 214

示 礻 (113)

0	示 ~	shì	282
1	礼	lǐ	190
5	神 ~	shén	275
	祥 ~	xiáng	349
8	禁 ~	jìn	170
	禅	chán	46
12	禪	chán	46
13	禮	lǐ	190

宀 (114)

禾 (115)

0	禾 ~	hé	129
3	秉 ~	bǐng	35
	和 ~	hé	129
4	秒 ~	miǎo	212
	秋 ~	qiū	251
5	称	chèn, chēng	51 52
	秘 ~	mì	211
	秦 ~	qín	249
	秩 ~	zhì	403
6	移 ~	yí	374
9	稱	chèn, chēng	51 52
	稳	wěn	334
10	穀	gǔ	118
14	穩 ~	wěn	334
17	穲 ~	chī	53

穴 (116)

0	穴 ~	xué	361
3	空 ~	kōng	180
4	穿 ~	chuān	56
	突 ~	tū	321
5	窍	qiào	248
6	窒 ~	zhì	403
7	窜	cuàn	60
	窝	wō	335
9	窩	wō	335
13	竄	cuàn	60
	竅	qiào	248

立 (117)

0	立 ~	lì	192
4	竖	shù	286
5	竝 ~	bìng	35
	站 ~	zhàn	393
6	竟	jìng	172
	章 ~	zhāng	394
7	童 ~	tóng	320
8	竪	shù	286
9	端 ~	duān	87
15	競	jìng	172

6 stroke radicals

竹 (118)

0	竹 ~	zhú	407
3	竿 ~	gān	112
4	笑 ~	xiào	352
5	笨 ~	bèn	30
	第 ~	dì	78
6	策 ~	cè	44
	等 ~	děng	76
	筋 ~	jīn	165
	筒 ~	tǒng	320
	筑 ~	zhù	407

435

Character Index by Radical Order

Each column: Added strokes | Traditional character | Simplified (~ if the same) | Pinyin | Page number

竹米糸缶网羊羽老而耒耳聿肉

7	简 jiǎn 158
	節 jié 164
	箎 tóng 320
8	管 ~ guǎn 121
	箕 ~ jī 151
9	箭 ~ jiàn 159
10	築 zhù 407
12	簡 jiǎn 158
15	籐 téng 309

米 (119)

5	粘 ~ nián, 222
		zhān 392
8	精 ~ jīng 171
11	糠 ~ kāng 178

糸 糹 纟 (120)

1	紀 jiū 173
2	糾 纠 jiū 173
3	紅 红 hóng 135
	丝 sī 296
4	紧 jǐn 169
	納 纳 nà 218
	素 ~ sù 300
	紜 纭 yún 388
	紮 zhā 392
	紙 纸 zhǐ 403
	纵 zòng 413
5	絆 绊 bàn 24
	经 jīng 171
	练 liàn 195
	細 细 xì 344
6	絞 绞 jiǎo 161
	絕 绝 jué 176
	絶 jué 176

	絡 络 luò 206
	绕 rào 257
	絲 sī 296
	紫 ~ zǐ 412
7	經 jīng 171
8	綳 绷 bēng 31
	綵 cǎi 41
	綽 绰 chāo, 49
		chuò 59
	緊 jǐn 169
	綿 绵 mián 212
	绳 shéng 276
	維 维 wéi 332
	续 xù 358
	綜 综 zōng 413
9	編 编 biān 32
	緩 缓 huǎn 143
	缆 lǎn 186
	練 liàn 195
10	缠 chán 46
	縫 缝 fèng 105
11	繃 bēng 31
	縮 缩 suō 301
	總 zǒng 413
	縱 zòng 413
	繞 rào 257
	繩 shéng 276
15	纏 chán 46
	續 xù 358
21	纜 lǎn 186

缶 (121)

3	缸 ~ gāng 112
4	缺 ~ quē 255
12	罈 tán 306

网 罒 (122)

3	罗 luó 205
14	羅 luó 205

羊 羊 (123)

0	羊 ~ yáng 367
3	美 ~ měi 210
	养 yǎng 368
7	群 ~ qún 255
	義 yì 376

羽 (124)

0	羽 ~ yǔ 383
4	翅 ~ chì 53
	翄 chì 53
6	翘 qiáo 247
9	翦 jiǎn 158
11	翳 yì 376
12	翻 fān 95
	翹 qiáo 247

老 耂 (125)

0	老 ~ lǎo 187

而 (126)

3	耐 ~ nài 218

耒 (127)

4	耙 ~ bà, 18
		pá 227
	耕 ~ gēng 115
	耗 ~ hào 128
	耘 ~ yún 388
6	耠 ~ huō 147

耳 (128)

0	耳 ~ ěr 92
4	耸 sǒng 299
8	聚 ~ jù 175
11	聲 shēng 276
	聳 sǒng 299
16	聽 tīng 318

聿 (129)

肉 月 (130)

0	肉 ~ ròu 259
2	肋 ~ lèi 189
	肌 ~ jī 151
3	肚 ~ dù 87
	肝 ~ gān 112
	肛 ~ gāng 112
	肓 ~ huāng 144
	肘 ~ zhǒu 406
4	肠 cháng 48
	肱 ~ gōng, 116
		hóng 135
	股 ~ gǔ 118
	肩 ~ jiān 156
	肾 shèn 276
	胁 xié 354
	肢 ~ zhī 400
	肫 ~ zhūn 411
5	胞 ~ bāo 25
	背 ~ bèi 29
	胆 dǎn 71
	肺 ~ fèi 101
	胛 ~ jiǎ 155
	胫 jìng 172
	脉 mài 208

436

Character Index by Radical Order

Each column: Added strokes | Traditional character | Simplified (~ if the same) | Pinyin | Page number

肉臣自至臼舌舛舟艮色艸虍虫

	胎	~	tāi	303		腧	~	shū	285	**舌 (135)**			
	胃	~	wèi	333		腿	~	tuǐ	323				
6	脆	~	cuì	60		腰	~	yāo	368	0	舌	~	shé	274
	胳	~	gē	113	10	膀	~	bǎng,	25	6	舒	~	shū	285
	脊	~	jǐ	153				páng	229				
	胯	~	kuà	182		膏	~	gāo	112	**舛 (136)**			
	脈	脉	mài	208		膈	~	gé	113				
	腦	脑	nǎo	219		膂	~	lǚ	203	8	舞	~	wǔ	341
	臍	脐	qí	240		膝	~	xī	343				
	脇	胁	xié	354	11	膕	腘	guó	125	**舟 (137)**			
	脅	胁	xié	354		膛	~	táng	307				
	胸	~	xiōng	357	13	臂	~	bēi, bì	28	**艮 (138)**			
	胷	~	xiōng	357		膽	胆	dǎn	71				
	臟	脏	zàng	391		膻	~	dàn,	72	0	艮	~	gěn	114
	睜	睁	zhēng	399				shān	269				
						臁	~	lián	193	**色 (139)**			
7	脖	~	bó	37		臉	脸	liǎn	194				
	腳	脚	jiǎo	161		臀	~	tún	325	**艸 艹 (140)**			
	脛	胫	jìng	172		膺	~	yīng	379	1	艺	yì	376
	脸	脸	liǎn	194	14	臑	~	nào	219	2	节	jié	164
	脥	~	qiǎn	245	17	臟	脏	zàng	391	3	芍	~	sháo	273
	脫	脱	tuō	327						4	苍	cāng	42
8	腓	~	féi	101	**臣 (131)**						花	~	huā	141
	腑	~	fǔ	108							苏	sū	300
	腘	guó	125	2	臥	卧	wò	335		芯	~	xìn	356
	腎	肾	shèn	276						5	苌	cháng	48
	腆	~	tiǎn	315	**自 (132)**						苦	~	kǔ	182
	腕	~	wàn	332							苗	~	miáo	212
	腋	~	yè	372	0	自	~	zì	412	6	荔	~	lì	193
	腈	zhēng	399						7	荡	dàng	72
9	腸	肠	cháng	48	**至 (133)**						荷	~	hé	130
	腠	~	còu	59	0	至	~	zhì	403		获	huò	149
	腹	~	fù	108							莫	~	mò	214
	脚	jiǎo	161	**臼 (134)**					8	萇	cháng	48
	腦	nǎo	219	0	臼	~	jiù	174		菱	~	líng	197
	脾	~	pí	232	10	舉	jǔ	174		营	yíng	379
	腮	~	sāi	263	12	舊	jiù	174	9	落	~	luò	206

	萬	wàn	332	
	葉	yè	372	
10	蒼	cāng	42	
	蓋	gài	111	
	蓄	~	xù	358
11	蔡	~	cài	42
12	蕩	dàng	72	
	蕺	~	hāo	128
14	藏	~	cáng	42
	薰	~	xūn	361
15	藤	~	téng	309
	藝	yì	376	
16	蘇	sū	300	
17	蘱	~	huā	141

虍 (141)

2	虎	~	hǔ	138
5	處	chǔ	56	
	虛	xū	358	
6	虚	xū	358	
7	號	hào	128	

虫 (142)

3	虵	shé	274	
	虾	xiā	345	
4	蚨	~	fú	107
5	蛇	~	shé	274
6	蛤	~	há	127
	蛟	~	jiāo	160
	蛮	mán	208	
	蜇	~	zhé	396
7	蜀	~	shǔ	286
	蜈	~	wú	338
8	蜻	qīng	249	
9	蝙	~	biān	32

437

Character Index by Radical Order

Each column: Added strokes | Traditional character | Simplified (~ if the same) | Pinyin | Page number

虫血行衣西見角言谷豆豕豸貝赤走足

	蝶 ~ dié	82
	蝴 ~ hú	138
	蝦 xiā	345
	蠍 xiē	353
10	蟒 ~ mǎng	209
	螃 ~ páng	229
11	螺 ~ luó	206
	螳 ~ táng	307
12	蟠 ~ pán	228
13	蠍 xiē	353
	蟹 ~ xiè	354
	蟹 xiè	354
14	蠕 ~ rú	260
15	蠡 ~ lí	190
19	蠻 mán	208

血 (143)

0	血 ~ xuè	361
6	衄 mài	208

行 (144)

0	行 ~ háng, xíng	128, 356
5	術 shù	286
9	衝 chōng	54
10	衡 ~ héng	134
	衛 wèi	334

衣 衤 (145)

2	補 bǔ	37
	初 ~ chū	55
3	表 ~ biǎo	34
5	袋 ~ dài	68
	袖 ~ xiù	357
6	裁 ~ cái	41

	襠 dāng	72
	裝 zhuāng	409
7	補 bǔ	37
	裡 lǐ	190
	裏 lǐ	190
	裙 ~ qún	255
	裝 zhuāng	409
9	複 fù	109
	褪 ~ tùn	325
	製 zhì	403
10	裹 ~ guǒ	125
13	襠 dāng	72
16	襲 ~ xí	344

西 西 覀 (146)

0	西 ~ xī	344
3	要 ~ yào	370

7 stroke radicials

見 见 (147)

0	見 见 jiàn	159
2	观 guān	120
4	規 规 guī	122
	視 视 shì	282
17	觀 guān	120

角 (148)

0	角 ~ jiǎo, jué	162, 176
6	解 ~ jiě	164

言 言 讠 (149)

2	計 计 jì	154

3	記 记 jì	154
	让 ràng	257
	託 tuō	325
	訓 训 xùn	361
5	評 评 píng	236
	詠 ~ yǒng	381
	詐 诈 zhà	392
6	試 试 shì	282
7	說 说 shuō	296
	誤 误 wù	341
8	調 调 diào, tiáo	81, 315
	請 请 qǐng	251
	誘 诱 yòu	382
	諸 诸 zhū	407
9	謊 谎 huǎng	145
10	謌 gē	113
12	警 ~ jǐng	172
	譜 谱 pǔ	238
13	護 hù	140
	言意 ~ yì	376
16	變 biàn	33
17	讓 ràng	257

谷 (150)

0	谷 gǔ	118
4	欲 ~ yù	385
10	豁 ~ huō	148

豆 (151)

11	豐 fēng	103

豕 (152)

5	象 ~ xiàng	350
8	豬 zhū	407

豸 (153)

3	豹 ~ bào	28
7	狸 lí	189
8	貌 ~ mào	209

貝 贝 (154)

2	負 负 fù	109
5	貫 贯 guàn	122
	貼 贴 tiē	317

赤 (155)

0	赤 ~ chì	53

走 (156)

0	走 ~ zǒu	413
2	赵 zhào	395
3	赶 gǎn	112
	起 ~ qǐ	241
5	超 ~ chāo	49
	趁 ~ chèn	51
	趋 qū	252
7	趕 gǎn	112
	趙 zhào	395
8	趟 ~ tàng	308
10	趨 qū	252

足 ⻊ (157)

0	足 ~ zú	414
2	趴 ~ pā	227
4	跃 yuè	388
	趾 ~ zhǐ	403
5	跛 ~ bǒ	37
	跌 ~ diē	81
	跗 fū	106

438

Character Index by Radical Order

Each column: Added strokes | Traditional character | Simplified (~ if the same) | Pinyin | Page number

足 身 車 辛 辰 辵 邑 酉

	踐	jiàn	159	14	躍	yuè	388	11	轆	辘	lù	203	7	遞	dì	78
	距	~	jù	175	16	躦	zuān	415		轉	zhuǎn,	408		連	lián	193
	跈	~	niǎn	222	18	躥	cuān	59			zhuàn	409		速	~	sù	300
	跑	~	pǎo	230	19	躜	zuān	415	14	轟	hōng	134		通	~	tōng	319
6	跐	~	cǐ	59										透	~	tòu	321
	跺	~	duò	89		**身 (158)**				**辛 (160)**				造	~	zào	391
	跟	~	gēn	114	0	身	~	shēn	275	0	辛	~	xīn	355	8	逮	~	dài	68
	跪	~	guì	123	3	躬	~	gōng	116						進	jìn	170
	跤	~	jiāo	161	4	軀	qū	252		**辰 (161)**				週	zhōu	406
	跨	~	kuà	183	6	躲	duǒ	89	0	辰	~	chén	51	9	逼	~	bī	31
	路	~	lù	203		躳	gōng	116						達	dá	63
	跷	qiāo	247	7	躱	duǒ	89		**辵 辶 (162)**				道	~	dào	75
	跳	~	tiào	316	8	躺	~	tǎng	308	2	边	biān	32		過	guò	125
7	踇	~	mǔ	214	11	軀	qū	252		辽	liáo	197		遊	yóu	382
8	踩	~	cǎi	41							达	dá	63		運	yùn	390
	踔	~	chuō	59		**車 车 (159)**			3		过	guò	125	10	遞	dì	78
	踮	~	diǎn	78	0	車	车	chē	50			迈	mài	208		遠	yuǎn	387
	踝	~	huái	143	2	軌	轨	guǐ	123		迂	~	yū	383	11	遮	~	zhē	396
	踐	jiàn	159		軍	军	jūn	176		迟	chí	53	12	遲	chí	53
	踏	~	tà	303	4	轟	hōng	134	4	返	~	fǎn	99		遼	liáo	197
	踢	~	tī	311		輪	lún	204		还	huán	143		邁	mài	208
9	踹	~	chuài	56		軟	软	ruǎn	260		近	~	jìn	170		選	xuǎn	360
	蹉	~	cuō	61	5	輕	轻	qīng	249		进	jìn	170	13	避	~	bì	32
	踺	jiàn	159		軸	轴	zhóu	406		连	lián	193		還	huán	143
10	蹋	~	tà	303		转	zhuǎn,	408		迎	~	yíng	379	14	邊	biān	32
11	蹦	~	bèng	31			zhuàn	409		远	yuǎn	387				
	蹩	~	bié	34	6	較	较	jiào	162		运	yùn	390		**邑 阝 (163)**		
	蹚	~	tāng	307		載	载	zài	391	5	迫	~	pò	236		**(on right)**		
	蹠	~	zhí	401	7	輔	辅	fǔ	108	6	迴	huí	145	4	邪	~	xié	354
12	蹭	~	cèng	44		輕	qīng	249		迷	~	mí	211	7	郗	~	xī	344
	蹲	cuān	59		輓	wǎn	332		逆	~	nì	221				
	蹬	~	dēng	76		輒	辄	zhé	396		送	~	sòng	300		**酉 (164)**		
	蹲	~	dūn	89	8	輪	lún	204		退	~	tuì	324	0	酉	~	yǒu	382
	蹶	~	jué	176	9	輸	输	shū	285		选	xuǎn	360	7	酸	~	suān	300
	蹺	qiāo	247	10	轅	辕	yuán	387		追	~	zhuī	410	8	醉	~	zuì	416
	蹻	qiāo	247											11	醫	yī	374

439

CHARACTER INDEX BY RADICAL ORDER
Each column: Added strokes | Traditional character | Simplified (~ if the same) | Pinyin | Page number

采里金長門阜隶隹雨

采 (165)

0	采	cǎi	41

里 (166)

0	里 ~	lǐ	190
2	重 ~	chóng,	54
		zhòng	406
4	野 ~	yě	371

8 stroke radicials

金金钅 (167)

0	金	~	jīn	165
2	釘	钉	dīng	82
3	釣	钓	diào	81
	釦		kòu	181
	釨	~	zǐ	412
4	鈀	钯	bǎ,	18
			pá	227
	鈍	钝	dùn	89
	釜	~	fǔ	108
	鈎	钩	gōu	117
	鈒	~	jí	152
		钟	zhōng	406
5	鉍	铋	bì	32
	鈸	钹	bó	37
	鉤		gōu	117
	鉗	钳	qián	245
		铁	tiě	317
	鉈	铊	tuó	327
	鉞	钺	yuè	388
		钻	zuān	415
6		铲	chǎn	47
		铠	kǎi	178

	鋩	铓	máng	209
	銀	银	yín	378
7	銼	锉	cuò	62
	鋌	铤	dìng	84
	鋒	锋	fēng	103
		铜	jiǎn	158
		链	liàn	195
	鋪	铺	pū	238
	銳	锐	ruì	261
		锁	suǒ	302
	銷	销	xiāo	350
8	錘	锤	chuí	58
	錯	错	cuò	62
	錞	~	duì	88
	錦	锦	jǐn	169
	鋸	锯	jù	175
	錟	锬	tán	306
		錾	zàn	391
	錐	锥	zhuī	410
9	鍥	锲	qiè	248
10	鎧	铠	kǎi	178
	鎌		lián	194
	鏈	链	liàn	195
	鎖	锁	suǒ	302
	鎧	锐	tǎng	308
11	鏢	镖	biāo	34
		铲	chǎn	47
		镟	xuàn	360
		錾	zàn	391
12	鐧		jiǎn	158
	鐔	镡	tán	306
		鐘	zhōng	406
	鐏	~	zūn	417
13	鐮	镰	lián	194
	鐵		tiě	317
19			zuān	415

長镸长 (168)

0	長	长	cháng	48

門门 (169)

0	門	门	mén	210
2	閃	闪	shǎn	269
3	閉	闭	bì	32
		闯	chuǎng	58
	問	问	wèn	334
4	間	间	jiān,	157
			jiàn	159
		开	kāi	177
5	閘	闸	zhá	392
6	閣		hé	130
8		闡	chǎn	48
	閻	阎	yán	364
9	闊	阔	kuò	184
	蘭	阑	lán	186
10	闖		chuǎng	58
	闔	阖	hé	130
11	關		guān	121
12	闡		chǎn	48

阜阝 (170)
(on left)

2		队	duì	88
4	防	~	fáng	99
		阳	yáng	367
		阴	yīn	377
5		陈	chén	51
	附	~	fù	109
	阻	~	zǔ	415
7	陡	~	dǒu	85
	降	~	jiàng,	160
			xiáng	349

8	陶	~	táo	309
	陷	~	xiàn	349
	陰		yīn	377
9	陳	陈	chén	51
	隊		duì	88
	隋		suí	300
		随	suí	300
	陽		yáng	367
		隐	yǐn	378
	隅	~	yú	383
10	隔	~	gé	114
12	隨		suí	300
14	隱		yǐn	378

隶 (171)

隹 (172)

2		难	nán	218
3	雀	~	què	255
4	集	~	jí	152
	雄	~	xióng	357
	雁	~	yàn	366
10	雞		jī	151
	離		lí	190
		雜	zá	391
11	難		nán	218

雨 (173)

3	雪	~	xuě	361
4	雲		yún	173
5	電		diàn	80
	雷		léi	189
7	震	~	zhèn	397
8	霑		zhān	393
13	露	~	lòu,	202

440

Character Index by Radical Order

Each column: Added strokes | Traditional character | Simplified (~ if the same) | Pinyin | Page number

雨靑非面革韋韭音頁風飛食首香馬骨高髟鬥鬯鬲鬼魚

		lù	203
	霸	~ bà	18
16	靈	líng	197

靑 青 (174)

0	靑	青 qīng	249
6		静 jìng	173
8	靜	jìng	173

非 (175)

0	非	~ fēi	100
7	靠	~ kào	179

9 stroke radicals

面 (176)

革 (177)

4	靶	~ bǎ	18
6	鞏	gǒng	116
7	鞘	~ qiào	248
9	鞭	~ biān	33

韋 韦 (178)

0	韋	韦 wéi	333
3	韌	韧 rèn	258
8	韓	韩 hán	128

韭 (179)

音 (180)

4		韵 yùn	390
10	韻	yùn	390

頁 页 (181)

2	頂	顶 dǐng	83
3	順	顺 shùn	294
	項	项 xiàng	350
4	頓	顿 dùn	89
	顧	顾 gù	119
	預	预 yù	385
5		颈 jǐng	172
	領	领 lǐng	198
		颅 lú	202
6	頜	颌 gé, hé	114, 130
		颊 jiá	154
7	頷	颔 hàn	128
	頰		154
	頸		jǐng	172
	頭		tóu	320
9	額	额 é	91
	顋		sāi	263
10	顛	颠 diān	78
	顖		xìn	356
12	顧		gù	119
13	顫	颤 zhàn	394
14	顯		xiǎn	349
16	顱		lú	202
17	顴	颧 quán	254

風 风 (182)

0	風	风 fēng	103
11	飄	飘 piāo	233

飛 (183)

| 0 | 飛 | 飞 fēi | 100 |

食 飠 (184)

0	食	~ shí	281
6	養		yǎng	368
7	餓	饿 è	91
	餘		yú	383

首 (185)

| 0 | 首 | | shǒu | 285 |

香 (186)

| 0 | 香 | | xiāng | 349 |

10 stroke radicals

馬 马 (187)

0	馬	马 mǎ	207
3	馳	驰 chí	53
6		骄 jiāo	161
8	騎	骑 qí	240
9		骗 piàn	233
	騙		piàn	233
10	騰	腾 téng	309
12	驕		jiāo	161
17	驊	~ huān	143

骨 (188)

0	骨	~ gǔ	119
5	骶	~ dǐ	77
7	骽	~ tuǐ	323
9	髂	~ qià	243
10		髌 bìn	35
	髖		kuān	183
12	髓	~ suǐ	301
13	體		tǐ	313

14	髕	bìn	35
	髖	kuān	183

高 (189)

| 0 | 高 | ~ gāo | 112 |

髟 (190)

7		鬓 bìn	35
8	鬆	sōng	299
14	鬢	bìn	35

鬥 斗 (191)

0	鬥	斗 dòu	85
4	鬧	dòu	85
14	鬭	dòu	85

鬯 (192)

鬲 (193)

鬼 (194)

4	魂	~ hún	147
	魁	~ kuí	184
5	魄	~ pò	236
8	魏	~ wèi	334

11 stroke radicals

魚 鱼 (195)

0	魚	鱼 yú	383
7	鯉	鲤 lǐ	191

441

Character Index by Radical Order

Each column: Added strokes | Traditional character | Simplified (~ if the same) | Pinyin | Page number

鳥 鹵 鹿 麥 麻 黃 黍 黑 黹 黽 鼎 鼓 鼠 鼻 齊 齒 龍 龜 龠

鳥 鸟 (196)

0	鳥 鸟	niǎo	222
2	鸡	jī	151
	鳩 鸠	jiū	173
3	鳳	fèng	105
4	鴉 鸦	yā	363
	鴈	yàn	366
5	鳹 鸰	tài	305
	鴕 鸵	tuó	327
	鴨 鸭	yā	363
	莺	yīng	379
	鴛 鸳	yuān	385
6	鴻 鸿	hóng	135
	鸾	luán	204
7	鵝 鹅	é	91
	鵞	é	91
	鶩	é	91
8	鵬 鹏	péng	230
	鵲 鹊	què	255
	鵐	yā	363
10	鶴 鹤	hè	130
	鷂 鹞	yào	370
	鶯	yīng	379
11	鸚	yīng	379
12	鷰	yàn	365
13	鷹 鹰	yīng	379
17	鸚	yīng	379
19	鸞	luán	204

鹵 (197)

鹿 (198)

0	鹿	~ lù	203
7	麐	lín	197
8	麒	~ qí	240
12	麟	~ lín	197

麥 麦 (199)

6	麯	qū	252

麻 (200)

0	麻	~ má	208

12 stroke radicals

黃 (201)

0	黃	~ huáng	144

黍 (202)

5	黏	~ nián, zhān	222, 393

黑 (203)

0	黑	~ hēi	130
5	點	diǎn	79

黹 (204)

13 stroke radicals

黽 黾 (205)

12	鼉 鼍	tuó	327

鼎 (206)

0	鼎	~ dǐng	83

鼓 (207)

0	鼓	~ gǔ	119

鼠 (208)

0	鼠	~ shǔ	286

14 stroke radicals

鼻 (209)

0	鼻	~ bí	31

齊 齐 (210)

0	齊 齐	qí	241

15 stroke radicals

齒 齿 (211)

0	齒 齿	chǐ	53
6	齩	yǎo	370
	齦 龈	yín	378

16 stroke radicals

龍 龙 (212)

0	龍 龙	lóng	200

龜 龟 (213)

0	龟	guī	122
2	龜	guī	122

17 stroke radicals

龠 (214)

Looking up by Stroke Order

If you can't figure out the radical of a character, you can find the character by counting its strokes.

Looking up characters by stroke order charts, you need to know how to write characters – which type of lines take one or two strokes to write. A curvy or bent line is often one stroke. For example, ⌐, ⌐, ⌐ are each two strokes because one stroke goes around the corner. Boxes such as ☐ are three strokes – the first down, the second across the top then down, and the third closes the bottom. Lines with a final hook are one stroke. For example, ⌐ is two strokes, one on the left and one along the top that is completed with a flourish.

List of non-radical part of the character having unclear stroke numbers:

乃 is three strokes.
专 is five strokes.
长 is five strokes.
亞 is eight strokes.

To use the Stroke Order index:

1. Count the number of strokes used in writing the character. Then go to the list of characters with that number of strokes. The characters are listed as their actual number of stroke it takes to write them, whether modern or traditional characters.

2. The characters with the same number of strokes are grouped together under their radicals. For the stroke order, the radicals are counted as the number of strokes in which they are actually written. Some radicals are officially a different number of strokes than they are written. For example, water is officially four strokes, but when it is written as three dots, its stroke order is three. The Radical Index for Stroke Order lists the radicals in their normal order, with the ordered radicals at the end of their stroke count when that differs from the normal radical order.

I included the simplified characters as best I could. A bit of running the finger down the column will always be necessary. I don't think anyone else has tried to incorporate both traditional characters and simplified characters independently in the same lookup indices.

RADICAL INDEX FOR STROKE ORDER

1 stroke radicals		**3 stroke radicals**		94	犭	89	爻	114	肉
1	一	30	口	120	纟	90	爿	115	禾
2	丨	31	囗	140	艹	91	片	116	穴
3	丶	32	土	162	辶	92	牙	117	立
4	丿	33	士	169	门	93	牛 牜	----	
5	乙	34	夂	184	饣	94	犬	145	衤
6	亅	35	夊	187	马	----		167	钅
2 stroke radicals		36	夕	183	飞	96	王	196	鸟
7	二	37	大	**4 stroke radicals**		113	礻	212	龙
8	亠	38	女	61	心	130	月	**6 stroke radicals**	
9	人 亻	39	子 孑	62	戈		(from 肉)	118	竹
10	儿	40	宀	63	戶 户	147	见	119	米
11	入	41	寸	64	手	154	贝	120	糸 纟
12	八	42	小	65	支	159	车	121	缶
13	冂	43	尢	66	攴 攵	168	长	122	网 罒
14	冖	44	尸	67	文	178	韦	123	羊 䒑
15	冫	45	屮	68	斗	182	风	124	羽
16	几	46	山	69	斤	**5 stroke radicals**		125	老
17	凵	47	巛 川	70	方	95	玄	126	而
18	刀 刂	48	工	71	无, 旡	96	玉	127	耒
19	力	49	己 巳	72	日	97	瓜	128	耳
20	勹	50	巾	73	曰	98	瓦	129	聿
21	匕	51	干	74	月	99	甘	130	肉
22	匚	52	幺	75	木	100	生	131	臣
23	匸	53	广	76	欠	101	用	132	自
24	十	54	廴	77	止	102	田	133	至
25	卜	55	廾	78	歹	103	疋	134	臼
26	卩	56	弋	79	殳	104	疒	135	舌
27	厂	57	弓	80	毋	105	癶	136	舛
28	厶	58	彐 彑	81	比	106	白	137	舟
29	又	59	彡	82	毛	107	皮	138	艮
----		60	彳	83	氏	108	皿	139	色
49	讠	----		84	气	109	目	140	艸
163	阝 (on right)	61	忄	85	水	110	矛	141	虍
170	阝 (on left)	64	扌	86	火 灬	111	矢	142	虫
		85	氵	87	爪 爫	112	石	143	血
		90	犭	88	父	113	示	144	行

444

RADICAL INDEX FOR STROKE ORDER

145	衣	175	非	**12 stroke radicals**	
146	西 西 覀	----		201	黃
----		184	食	202	黍
181	頁	195	鱼	203	黑
210	齐	205	黾	204	黹
7 stroke radicals		210	斉	**13 stroke radicals**	
147	見	211	齿	205	黽
148	角	**9 stroke radicals**		206	鼎
149	言 讠	176	面	207	鼓
150	谷	177	革	208	鼠
151	豆	178	韋	**14 stroke radicals**	
152	豕	179	韭	209	鼻
153	豸	180	音	210	齊
154	貝	181	頁	**15 stroke radicals**	
155	赤	182	風	211	齒
156	走	183	飛	**16 stroke radicals**	
157	足 ⻊	184	食	212	龍
158	身	185	首	213	龜
159	車	186	香	**17 stroke radicals**	
160	辛	**10 stroke radicals**		214	龠
161	辰	187	馬		
162	辵	188	骨		
163	邑	189	高		
164	酉	190	髟		
165	采	191	鬥		
166	里	192	鬯		
----		193	鬲		
213	龟	194	鬼		
8 stroke radicals		**11 stroke radicals**			
167	金 钅	195	魚		
168	長 镸	196	鳥		
169	門	197	鹵		
170	阜	198	鹿		
171	隶	199	麥		
172	隹	200	麻		
173	雨				
174	青 靑				

CHARACTER INDEX BY STROKE ORDER
Each column: Character | Pinyin | Radical | Page number

1, 2, 3, 4 & 5 strokes

1 stroke characters

一	yī	1	373
乙	yǐ	5	374

2 stroke characters

丁	dīng	1	82
七	qī	1	239
乃	nǎi	4	218
九	jiǔ	5	173
二	èr	7	92
人	rén	9	258
儿	ér	10	92
入	rù	11	260
八	bā	12	15
刀	dāo	18	73
刁	diāo	18	80
力	lì	19	191
匕	bǐ	21	31
十	shí	24	278

3 stroke characters

三	sān	1	263
上	shàng	1	269
万	wàn	1	332
下	xià	1	345
丈	zhàng	1	395
义	yì	3	376
干	gān	7	111
个	gè	9	114
亿	yì	9	375
刃	rèn	18	258
刄	rèn	18	258
千	qiān	24	243
卫	wèi	26	334
叉	chā	29	44
口	kǒu	30	181
土	tǔ	32	322
大	dà	37	64
女	nǚ	38	224
子	zǐ	39	411
寸	cùn	41	60
小	xiǎo	42	350
川	chuān	47	56
己	jǐ	49	153
巳	sì	49	299
弓	gōng	57	115
门	mén	169	210
飞	fēi	183	100
马	mǎ	187	207

4 stroke characters

不	bù	1	37
丑	chǒu	1	55
中	zhōng, zhòng	2	403, 406
丰	fēng	2	103
卞	biàn	3	33
丹	dān	3	68
之	zhī	3	399
互	hù	7	140
井	jǐng	7	172
五	wǔ	7	338
云	yún	7	389
化	huà	9	142
内	nèi	9	219
仆	pū	9	236
仁	rén	9	258
以	yǐ	9	375
仄	zè	9	391
元	yuán	10	386
內	nèi	11	219
公	gōng	12	115
六	liù	12	199
冈	gāng	13	112
分	fēn	18	102
切	qiē	18	248
劝	quàn	19	254
勾	gōu	20	117
午	wǔ	24	339
反	fǎn	29	97
风	fēng	29	105
双	shuāng	29	288
壬	rén	33	258
太	tài	37	303
天	tiān	37	313
孔	kǒng	39	180
少	shǎo, shào	42	273
尺	chǐ	44	53
巴	bā	49	17
开	kāi	55	177
引	yǐn	57	378
弔	diào	57	80
心	xīn	61	354
戈	gē	62	113
户	hù	63	140
户	hù	63	140
手	shǒu	64	283
扎	zhā	64	292
支	zhī	65	400
文	wén	67	334
斤	jīn	69	165
方	fāng	70	99
无	wú	71	337
日	rì	72	259
月	yuè	74	388
木	mù	75	214
止	zhǐ	77	403
殳	shū	79	285
比	bǐ	81	31
毛	máo	82	209
气	qì	84	241
水	shuǐ	85	293
火	huǒ	86	148
乌	wū	86	336
爪	zhǎo, zhuǎ	87	395, 408
父	fù	88	108
片	piàn	91	233
牙	yá	92	364
牛	niú	93	223
犬	quǎn	94	254
王	wáng	96	332
艺	yì	140	376
见	jiàn	147	159
计	jì	149	154
车	chē	159	50
队	duì	170	88
韦	wéi	178	333
风	fēng	182	103
斗	dòu	191	85

5 stroke characters

丙	bǐng	1	35
丘	qiū	1	251
世	shì	1	281
主	zhǔ	3	407
乍	zhà	4	392
乏	fá	4	95
市	shì	8	281
代	dài	9	67
令	lìng	9	198
仙	xiān	9	347
仗	zhàng	9	395

446

Character Index by Stroke Order
Each column: Character | Pinyin | Radical | Page number

5 & 6 strokes

凹	āo	17	14	扒	bā	64	17	丝	sī	120	296	列	liè	18	197
出	chū	17	55	打	dǎ	64	63	节	jié	140	164	刘	liú	18	199
击	jī	17	151	扑	pū	64	237	记	jì	149	154	动	dòng	19	84
凸	tū	17	321	扔	rēng	64	258	让	ràng	149	257	华	huá	24	141
功	gōng	19	115	旧	jiù	72	174	训	xùn	149	361	协	xié	24	353
包	bāo	20	25	电	diàn	73	80	长	cháng	162	48	后	hòu	27	136
北	běi	21	28	本	běn	75	30	边	biān	162	32	吃	chī	30	52
半	bàn	24	24	东	dōng	75	84	辽	liáo	168	197	吕	lǚ	30	203
卡	kǎ	25	177	术	shù	75	286	闪	shǎn	169	269	名	míng	30	212
占	zhàn	25	393	未	wèi	75	333	鸟	niǎo	196	222	同	tóng	30	319
叩	kòu	26	182	正	zhèng	77	398	龙	lóng	212	200	吐	tǔ	30	321
卯	mǎo	26	209	母	mǔ	80	214					向	xiàng	30	349
印	yìn	26	378	汉	hàn	85	128	**6 stroke characters**				回	huí	31	145
厉	lì	27	192	永	yǒng	85	381	丢	diū	1	84	团	tuán	31	322
发	fā	29	95	犯	fàn	94	99	丢	diū	1	84	囟	xìn	31	356
古	gǔ	30	118	玄	xuán	95	359	并	bìng	2	35	地	dì	32	77
号	hào	30	128	玉	yù	96	384	杀	shā	4	268	压	yā	32	363
可	kě	30	180	瓦	wǎ	98	329	亥	hài	8	127	多	duō	36	89
叶	yè	30	372	生	shēng	100	276	交	jiāo	8	160	夺	duó	37	89
右	yòu	30	382	甩	shuǎi	101	287	伐	fá	9	95	关	guān	37	121
只	zhǐ	30	401	用	yòng	101	381	仿	fǎng	9	100	夹	jiā	37	154
四	sì	31	296	甲	jiǎ	102	155	伏	fú	9	106	如	rú	38	260
处	chǔ	34	56	申	shēn	102	274	合	hé	9	128	存	cún	39	60
外	wài	36	329	田	tián	102	315	会	huì	9	146	孙	sūn	39	301
夯	bèn	37	30	白	bái	106	19	任	rèn	9	258	字	zì	39	412
	hāng	37	128	皮	pí	107	232	伤	shāng	9	269	安	ān	40	13
失	shī	37	277	目	mù	109	215	休	xiū	9	357	导	dǎo	41	74
头	tóu	37	320	矛	máo	110	209	仰	yǎng	9	368	寻	xún	41	361
对	duì	41	88	矢	shǐ	111	281	充	chōng	10	54	当	dāng	42	72
巨	jù	48	175	石	shí	112	281	光	guāng	10	122	尖	jiān	42	156
巧	qiǎo	48	247	礼	lǐ	113	190	先	xiān	10	348	巩	gǒng	48	116
左	zuǒ	48	417	示	shì	113	282	全	quán	11	253	吊	diào	50	80
布	bù	50	38	禾	hé	115	129	冲	chōng	15	54	师	shī	50	277
平	píng	51	234	穴	xué	116	361	决	jué	15	176	式	shì	56	282
归	guī	58	122	立	lì	117	192	刚	gāng	18	112	成	chéng	62	52
戊	wù	62	341	纠	jiū	120	173	划	huá	18	141	戌	xū	62	358

447

Character Index by Stroke Order
Each column: Character | Pinyin | Radical | Page number

6 & 7 strokes

扠	chā	64	44	芍	sháo	140	273	作	zuò	9	417	条	tiáo	34	315
扛	gāng,	64	112	血	xuè	143	361	兑	duì	10	88	夾	jiā	37	154
	káng	64	178	行	háng,	144	128	克	kè	10	180	妙	miào	38	212
扣	kòu	64	181		xíng	144	356	兎	tù	10	322	宋	sòng	40	299
扤	mā	64	207	西	xī	146	344	冷	lěng	15	189	完	wán	40	331
扪	mén	64	210	观	guān	147	120	别	bié	18	34	局	jú	44	174
扦	qiān	64	243	负	fù	154	109	别	bié, biè	18	34	尾	wěi	44	333
扫	sǎo	64	267	轨	guǐ	159	123	刜	fú	18	107	庇	bì	53	32
托	tuō	64	325	军	jūn	159	176	刦	jié	18	163	库	kù	53	182
收	shōu	66	282	达	dá	162	63	刧	jié	18	163	应	yīng	53	378
曲	qū	73	252	过	guò	162	125	利	lì	18	191	弄	nòng	55	224
有	yǒu	74	382	迈	mài	162	208	判	pàn	18	229	弃	qì	55	241
朴	pǔ	75	238	迂	yū	162	383	刨	páo	18	230	弝	bà	57	18
杂	zá	75	391	邪	xié	163	354	劫	jié	19	163	形	xíng	59	356
朱	zhū	75	407	闭	bì	169	32	劲	jìn	19	170	彻	chè	60	50
次	cì	76	59	闯	chuǎng	169	58	劳	láo	19	187	怀	huái	61	142
死	sǐ	78	296	问	wèn	169	334	努	nǔ	19	224	忌	jì	61	153
江	jiāng	85	160	防	fáng	170	99	医	yī	22	374	快	kuài	61	183
求	qiú	85	251	阳	yáng	170	367	呆	dāi	30	67	忍	rěn	61	258
争	zhēng	87	397	阴	yīn	170	377	含	hán	30	127	志	zhì	61	403
壮	zhuàng	90	410	驰	chí	187	53	吕	lǚ	30	203	把	bǎ,	64	18
百	bǎi	106	22	齐	qí	210	241	听	tīng	30	318		bà	64	18
竹	zhú	118	407					吞	tūn	30	325	扳	bān,	64	23
红	hóng	120	135	**7 stroke characters**				吻	wěn	30	334		pān	64	228
羊	yáng	123	367	串	chuàn	2	57	吴	wú	30	337	报	bào	64	25
羽	yǔ	124	383	乱	luàn	5	204	吳	wú	30	337	抄	chāo	64	49
老	lǎo	125	187	传	chuán	9	57	吸	xī	30	343	扯	chě	64	50
耳	ěr	128	92	低	dī	9	76	呃	é	31	91	扽	dèn	64	76
肌	jī	130	151	佛	fó	9	106	囤	tún	31	325	抖	dǒu	64	85
肋	lèi	130	189	两	liǎng	9	195	围	wéi	31	332	扼	è	64	91
肉	ròu	130	259	你	nǐ	9	221	场	chǎng	32	49	扶	fú	64	107
自	zì	132	412	伸	shēn	9	274	坎	kǎn	32	178	护	hù	64	140
至	zhì	133	403	体	tǐ	9	313	坛	tán	32	306	技	jì	64	153
臼	jiù	134	174	余	yú	9	383	坠	zhuì	32	411	抉	jué	64	176
舌	shé	135	274	佔	zhàn	9	393	坐	zuò	32	418	抗	kàng	64	179
艮	gěn	138	114	传	zhuàn	9	409	声	shēng	33	276	抠	kōu	64	180

448

Character Index by Stroke Order
Each column: Character | Pinyin | Radical | Page number
7 & 8 strokes

Char	Pinyin	Rad	Pg	Char	Pinyin	Rad	Pg	Char	Pinyin	Rad	Pg	Char	Pinyin	Rad	Pg
抡	lūn	64	204	肘	zhǒu	130	406	阻	zǔ	170	415	图	tú	31	321
扂	miǎn	64	212	苍	cāng	140	42	韧	rèn	178	258	坤	kūn	32	184
扭	niǔ	64	224	花	huā	140	141	鸡	jī	196	151	坡	pō	32	236
抛	pāo	64	229	苏	sū	140	300	鸠	jiū	196	173	垂	chuí	33	58
批	pī	64	232	芯	xìn	140	356	龟	guī	213	122	奔	bēn	37	30
抢	qiǎng	64	246	补	bǔ	145	37	**8 stroke characters**				奇	qí	37	240
扱	xī	64	343	初	chū	145	55					委	wěi	38	333
扬	yáng	64	366	見	jiàn	147	159	並	bìng	2	35	孤	gū	39	118
折	zhé	64	396	角	jiǎo, jué	148	162	乳	rǔ	5	260	学	xué	39	360
抓	zhuā	64	407			148	176	京	jīng	8	171	宝	bǎo	40	25
改	gǎi	66	111	评	píng	149	236	夜	yè	8	372	定	dìng	40	83
攻	gōng	66	116	诈	zhà	149	392	併	bìng	9	35	审	shěn	40	276
时	shí	72	280	谷	gǔ	150	118	侧	cè	9	43	实	shí	40	280
杜	dù	75	87	赤	chì	155	53	侠	jiā, xiá	9	154	宗	zōng	40	413
杆	gān	75	111	走	zǒu	156	413			9	345	尚	shàng	42	272
杠	gàng	75	112	足	zú	157	414	佯	yáng	9	366	居	jū	44	174
李	lǐ	75	190	身	shēn	158	275	兒	ér	10	92	屈	qū	44	251
杓	sháo	75	272	車	chē	159	50	兔	tù	10	322	岳	yuè	46	387
束	shù	75	286	辛	xīn	160	355	兩	liǎng	11	195	底	dǐ	53	77
杖	zhàng	75	395	辰	chén	161	51	典	diǎn	12	78	府	fǔ	53	108
步	bù	77	38	迟	chí	162	53	岡	gāng	13	112	庚	gēng	53	114
沈	chén	85	50	返	fǎn	162	99	刺	cì	18	59	迫	pò	54	236
决	jué	85	176	还	huán	162	143	剁	duò	18	89	弣	fǔ	57	108
沐	mù	85	215	近	jìn	162	170	刮	guā	18	119	弧	hú	57	138
沙	shā	85	268	进	jìn	162	170	刼	jié	18	163	弩	nǔ	57	224
灵	líng	86	197	连	lián	162	193	势	shì	19	281	弦	xián	57	349
男	nán	102	218	迎	yíng	162	379	单	dān	24	68	张	zhāng	57	394
紀	jiū	120	173	远	yuǎn	162	387	協	xié	24	353	参	cān	59	42
纳	nà	120	218	运	yùn	162	390	卷	juǎn	26	175	彼	bǐ	60	31
纭	yún	120	388	酉	yǒu	164	382	变	biàn	29	33	怪	guài	61	120
纸	zhǐ	120	403	采	cǎi	165	41	呼	hū	30	138	怯	qiè	61	248
纵	zòng	120	413	里	lǐ	166	190	命	mìng	30	213	忠	zhōng	61	405
肚	dù	130	87	钉	dīng	167	82	咏	yǒng	30	381	拗	ào	64	14
肝	gān	130	112	间	jiān, jiàn	169	157	周	zhōu	30	406	拔	bá	64	17
肛	gāng	130	112			169	159	固	gù	31	119	拌	bàn	64	24
肓	huāng	130	144	附	fù	170	109	国	guó	31	125	抱	bào	64	25

449

Character Index by Stroke Order
Each column: Character | Pinyin | Radical | Page number

8 & 9 strokes

拨	bō	64	36	明	míng	72	212	秉	bǐng	115	35	闸	zhá	169	392
拆	chāi	64	46	易	yì	72	376	和	hé	115	129	陈	chén	170	51
抻	chēn	64	50	服	fú	74	107	空	kōng	116	180	靑	qīng	174	249
承	chéng	64	52	板	bǎn	75	24	绊	bàn	120	24	青	qīng	174	249
抽	chōu	64	54	杵	chǔ	75	56	经	jīng	120	171	非	fēi	175	100
担	dān	64	71	東	dōng	75	84	纠	jiū	120	173	顶	dǐng	181	83
抵	dǐ	64	77	枫	fēng	75	103	练	liàn	120	195	鱼	yú	195	383
拂	fú	64	107	极	jí	75	152	细	xì	120	344	齿	chǐ	211	53
拐	guǎi	64	120	林	lín	75	197	罗	luó	122	205				
拘	jū	64	174	枪	qiāng	75	246	肠	cháng	130	48	**9 stroke characters**			
咔	kā	64	177	枢	shū	75	285	肱	gōng,	130	116	举	jǔ	3	174
㧟	kuǎi	64	183	松	sōng	75	299		hóng	130	135	亮	liàng	8	195
拉	lā	64	185	枭	xiāo	75	350	股	gǔ	130	118	亱	yè	8	372
拦	lán	64	185	杨	yáng	75	367	肩	jiān	130	156	保	bǎo	9	25
拎	līn	64	197	枕	zhěn	75	397	肾	shèn	130	276	俠	xiá	9	345
拢	lǒng	64	202	武	wǔ	77	339	胁	xié	130	354	信	xìn	9	355
抿	mǐn	64	212	毒	dú	80	86	肢	zhī	130	400	修	xiū	9	357
抹	mǒ	64	213	波	bō	85	37	肫	zhūn	130	411	剋	kè	10	180
拇	mǔ	64	214	法	fǎ	85	95	臥	wò	131	335	剥	bō	18	36
拈	niān	64	222	泥	ní	85	221	卧	wò	131	335	剑	jiàn	18	158
拧	níng	64	223	沛	pèi	85	230	苌	cháng	140	48	剌	lá	18	185
拍	pāi	64	227	泼	pō	85	236	苦	kǔ	140	182	前	qián	18	244
披	pī	64	232	泳	yǒng	85	381	苗	miáo	140	212	削	xiāo	18	350
拑	qián	64	245	沾	zhān	85	393	虎	hǔ	141	138	制	zhì	18	403
抬	tái	64	303	治	zhì	85	403	表	biǎo	145	34	劲	jìn	19	170
拖	tuō	64	327	注	zhù	85	407	规	guī	147	122	勉	miǎn	19	212
歪	wāi	64	329	爬	pá	87	227	视	shì	147	282	勇	yǒng	19	381
拥	yōng	64	381	受	shòu	87	285	试	shì	149	282	南	nán	24	218
招	zhāo	64	395	争	zhēng	87	397	轰	hōng	159	134	卸	xiè	26	354
拄	zhǔ	64	407	狀	zhuàng	90	410	轮	lún	159	204	哈	hā	30	127
拙	zhuō	64	411	牧	mù	93	215	软	ruǎn	159	260	哪	né	30	219
败	bài	66	23	环	huán	96	143	迫	pò	162	236	哇	wā	30	329
放	fàng	66	100	画	huà	102	142	钓	diào	167	81	哑	yǎ	30	364
斧	fǔ	69	108	的	dì	106	78	金	jīn	167	165	咽	yān	30	364
斩	zhǎn	69	393	直	zhí	109	400	長	cháng	168	48	咬	yǎo	30	370
昆	kūn	72	184	直	zhí	109	400	門	mén	169	210	垫	diàn	32	79

450

Character Index by Stroke Order
Each column: Character | Pinyin | Radical | Page number

9 strokes

复	fù	34	108,	拾	shí	64	280	派	pài	85	228	养	yǎng	123	368
		34	109	挞	tà	64	303	泰	tài	85	305	耐	nài	126	218
奎	kuí	37	183	挑	tiǎo	64	315	洗	xǐ	85	344	胞	bāo	130	25
宣	xuān	40	359	挖	wā	64	329	浊	zhuó	85	411	背	bèi	130	29
封	fēng	41	103	挝	wō,	64	335	点	diǎn	86	79	胆	dǎn	130	71
将	jiàng	41	160		zhuā	64	408	烂	làn	86	186	肺	fèi	130	101
屋	wū	44	336	挟	xié	64	353	炼	liàn	86	194	胛	jiǎ	130	155
带	dài	50	67	挤	yí	64	374	炮	pào	86	230	胫	jìng	130	172
幽	yōu	52	381	挣	zhèng	64	397	乌	wū	86	336	脉	mài	130	208
建	jiàn	54	158	指	zhǐ	64	401	炸	zhà	86	392	胎	tāi	130	303
弯	wān	57	331	拽	zhuāi	64	408	炤	zhào	86	395	胃	wèi	130	333
待	dài	60	68	敂	kòu	66	182	牵	qiān	93	243	荔	lì	140	193
後	hòu	60	136	斫	zhuó	69	411	独	dú	94	86	虵	shé	142	274
怪	guài	61	120	施	shī	70	277	狠	hěn	94	132	虾	xiā	142	345
恨	hèn	61	132	畅	chàng	72	49	狮	shī	94	277	要	yào	146	370
恆	héng	61	132	春	chūn	72	58	狭	xiá	94	345	計	jì	149	154
恒	héng	61	132	显	xiǎn	72	349	畊	gēng	102	115	说	shuō	149	296
急	jí	61	152	标	biāo	75	34	癸	guǐ	105	122	误	wù	149	341
怒	nù	61	224	柄	bǐng	75	35	盾	dùn	109	89	負	fù	154	109
总	zǒng	61	413	查	chá	75	46	眉	méi	109	210	贯	guàn	154	122
战	zhàn	62	393	架	jià	75	155	砍	kǎn	112	178	贴	tiē	154	317
扁	biǎn	63	33	枯	kū	75	182	研	yán	112	364	赵	zhào	156	395
按	àn	64	13	栏	lán	75	186	神	shén	113	275	趴	pā	157	227
持	chí	64	53	柳	liǔ	75	199	秒	miǎo	115	212	軌	guǐ	159	123
挡	dǎng	64	72	柔	róu	75	259	秋	qiū	115	251	軍	jūn	159	176
挆	duò	64	89	树	shù	75	286	穿	chuān	116	56	轻	qīng	159	249
拱	gǒng	64	116	相	xiāng,	75	349	突	tū	116	321	轴	zhóu	159	406
挂	guà	64	119		xiàng	75	350	竖	shù	117	286	转	zhuǎn,	159	408
挥	huī	64	145	柱	zhū	75	407	竿	gān	118	112		zhuàn	159	409
挤	jǐ	64	153	歪	wāi	77	329	紅	hóng	120	135	迴	huí	162	145
挟	jiā	64	154	残	cán	78	42	绞	jiǎo	120	161	迷	mí	162	211
挎	kuà	64	182	段	duàn	79	88	绝	jué	120	176	逆	nì	162	221
挒	liè	64	197	洪	hóng	85	134	络	luò	120	206	送	sòng	162	300
拏	ná	64	217	浑	hún	85	147	绕	rào	120	257	退	tuì	162	324
挠	náo	64	218	活	huó	85	148	缸	gāng	121	112	选	xuǎn	162	360
挪	nuó	64	225	津	jīn	85	165	美	měi	123	210	追	zhuī	162	410

451

Character Index by Stroke Order
Each column: Character | Pinyin | Radical | Page number

9 & 10 strokes

Char	Pinyin	Rad	Pg		Char	Pinyin	Rad	Pg		Char	Pinyin	Rad	Pg		Char	Pinyin	Rad	Pg
郗	xī	163	344		准	zhǔn	15	411		拿	ná	64	217		消	xiāo	85	350
重	chóng,	166	54		剝	bō	18	36		捏	niē	64	222		涌	yǒng	85	381
	zhòng	166	406		剛	gāng	18	112		拳	quán	64	253		热	rè	86	257
钯	bǎ,	167	18		剔	tī	18	310		挺	tǐng	64	319		特	tè	93	309
	pá	167	227		華	huá	24	141		捅	tǒng	64	320		狼	láng	94	186
钝	dùn	167	89		原	yuán	27	386		挽	wǎn	64	332		狸	lí	94	189
钩	gōu	167	117		哼	hēng	30	132		捂	wǔ	64	339		狹	xiá	94	345
钟	zhōng	167	406		圓	yuán	31	386		挾	xié	64	353		球	qiú	96	251
陡	dǒu	170	85		埋	mái	32	208		捉	zhuō	64	411		留	liú	102	199
降	jiàng,	170	160		壺	hú	33	138		敌	dí	66	77		疾	jí	104	152
	xiáng	170	349		夏	xià	34	347		旁	páng	70	229		疲	pí	104	232
韋	wéi	178	333		套	tào	37	309		晃	huǎng,	72	145		眩	xuàn	109	360
顺	shùn	181	294		娑	suō	38	301			huàng	72	145		真	zhēn	109	397
项	xiàng	181	350		孫	sūn	39	301		時	shí	72	280		破	pò	112	236
風	fēng	182	103		射	shè	41	274		晕	yūn,	72	388		砣	tuó	112	327
飛	fēi	183	100		展	zhǎn	44	393			yùn	72	390		砸	zá	112	391
食	shí	184	281		峨	é	46	91		朔	shuò	74	296		砖	zhuān	112	408
首	shǒu	185	285		峩	é	46	91		格	gē,	75	113		祥	xiáng	113	349
香	xiāng	186	349		帮	bāng	50	25			gé	75	113		称	chèn,	115	51
骄	jiāo	187	161		師	shī	50	277		根	gēn	75	114			chēng	115	52
鸦	yā	196	363		庫	kù	53	182		核	hé	75	129		秘	mì	115	211
					唐	táng	53	307		桥	qiáo	75	247		秦	qín	115	249
10 stroke characters					哨	shào	57	272		桡	ráo	75	257		秩	zhì	115	403
					或	yù	59	383		栓	shuān	75	287		窍	qiào	116	248
乘	chéng	4	52		徒	tú	60	321		栽	zāi	75	391		立	bìng	117	35
离	lí	8	190		恶	è	61	91		桩	zhuāng	75	409		站	zhàn	117	393
倒	dǎo,	9	73		悟	wù	61	341		殺	shā	79	268		笑	xiào	118	352
	dào	9	74		扇	shān	63	268		殷	yīn	79	376		紧	jǐn	120	169
倣	fǎng	9	100		挨	āi	64	13		毬	qiú	82	251		納	nà	120	218
俯	fǔ	9	108		挫	cuò	64	61		氣	qì	84	241		素	sù	120	300
個	gè	9	114		换	huàn	64	143		滌	dí	85	77		紜	yún	120	388
借	jiè	9	164		挾	jiā	64	154		浮	fú	85	107		紮	zhā	120	392
條	tiáo	9	315		捆	kǔn	64	184		海	hǎi	85	127		紙	zhǐ	120	403
修	xiū	9	357		捞	lāo	64	187		浪	làng	85	187		缺	quē	121	255
倚	yǐ	9	375		挶	lǚ,	64	203		流	liú	85	199		翅	chì	124	53
凌	líng	15	197			luō	64	205		润	rùn	85	261		翄	chì	124	53

452

Character Index by Stroke Order
Each column: Character | Pinyin | Radical | Page number
10 & 11 strokes

Char	Pinyin	Rad	Pg	Char	Pinyin	Rad	Pg	Char	Pinyin	Rad	Pg	Char	Pinyin	Rad	Pg
耙	bà,	124	18	躬	gōng	158	116	**11 stroke characters**				弹	dàn,	57	72
	pá	127	227	较	jiào	159	162						tán	57	306
耕	gēng	127	115	载	zài	159	391	乾	gān,	5	111	強	qiáng,	57	246
耗	hào	127	128	递	dì	162	78		qián	5	243		qiǎng	57	246
耘	yún	127	388	連	lián	162	193	偪	bī	9	31	張	zhāng	57	394
耸	sǒng	128	299	速	sù	162	300	側	cè	9	43	彩	cǎi	59	41
脆	cuì	130	60	通	tōng	162	319	假	jiǎ	9	154	參	cān	59	42
胳	gē	130	113	透	tòu	162	321	偏	piān	9	232	得	dé	60	76
脊	jǐ	130	153	造	zào	162	391	停	tíng	9	319	惊	jīng	61	171
胯	kuà	130	182	铋	bì	167	32	偷	tōu	9	320	悬	xuán	61	359
脉	mài	130	208	钹	bó	167	37	偎	wēi	9	332	悠	yōu	61	382
脑	nǎo	130	219	钉	dīng	167	82	偃	yǎn	9	364	掤	bīng	64	35
脐	qí	130	240	钳	qián	167	245	兜	dōu	10	85	採	cǎi	64	41
胁	xié	130	354	铁	tiě	167	317	副	fù	18	108	捵	chēn	64	50
脅	xié	130	354	铊	tuó	167	327	剪	jiǎn	18	157	捶	chuí	64	58
胷	xiōng	130	357	钺	yuè	167	388	動	dòng	19	84	掸	dǎn	64	71
胸	xiōng	130	357	钻	zuān	167	415	勒	lè,	19	188	捯	dáo	64	73
脏	zàng	130	391	閃	shǎn	169	269		lēi	19	188	搗	dǎo	64	74
脀	zhēng	130	399	陶	táo	170	309	匾	biǎn	23	33	掉	diào	64	81
荡	dàng	140	72	陷	xiàn	170	349	商	shāng	30	269	掛	guà	64	119
荷	hé	140	130	陰	yīn	170	377	兽	shòu	30	285	掍	hùn	64	147
获	huò	140	149	难	nán	172	218	啞	yǎ	30	364	接	jiē	64	163
莫	mò	140	214	顿	dùn	181	89	啄	zhuó	30	411	捲	juǎn	64	175
蚨	fú	142	107	顾	gù	181	119	國	guó	31	125	掯	kèn	64	180
袖	xiù	145	357	预	yù	181	385	圈	quān	31	252	控	kòng	64	180
调	diào,	149	81	饿	è	184	91	堵	dǔ	32	87	掳	lǔ	64	202
	tiáo	149	315	馬	mǎ	187	207	基	jī	32	151	掠	lüè	64	204
記	jì	149	154	骨	gǔ	188	119	堂	táng	32	307	掄	lūn	64	204
请	qǐng	149	251	高	gāo	189	112	宿	sù	40	300	捫	mén	64	210
託	tuō	149	325	鬥	dòu	191	85	寅	yín	40	378	捺	nà	64	218
訓	xùn	149	361	鸟	tài	196	305	將	jiàng	41	160	捻	niǎn	64	222
诱	yòu	149	382	鸵	tuó	196	327	崩	bēng	46	30	捏	niē	64	222
诸	zhū	149	407	鸭	ya	196	363	崧	sōng	46	299	排	pái	64	228
豹	bào	153	28	莺	yīng	196	379	帶	dài	50	67	掤	péng	64	230
赶	gǎn	156	112	鸳	yuān	196	385	绷	bēng,	57	31	捧	pěng	64	230
起	qǐ	156	241						pēng	57	230	掽	pèng	64	231

453

Character Index by Stroke Order
Each column: Character | Pinyin | Radical | Page number

11 & 12 strokes

Char	Pinyin	Rad	Pg	Char	Pinyin	Rad	Pg	Char	Pinyin	Rad	Pg	Char	Pinyin	Rad	Pg
掽	pèng	64	231	清	qīng	85	249	細	xì	120	334	釦	kòu	167	181
掐	qiā	64	242	涮	shuàn	85	287	續	xù	120	358	铓	máng	167	209
掃	sǎo	64	267	淘	táo	85	309	綜	zōng	120	413	銀	yín	167	378
探	tàn	64	306	液	yè	85	372	脖	bó	130	37	釨	zǐ	167	412
掏	tāo	64	308	漁	yú	85	383	腳	jiǎo	130	161	閉	bì	169	32
推	tuī	64	322	淵	yuān	85	385	脛	jìng	130	172	閘	chǎn	169	48
掀	xiān	64	348	牽	qiān	93	243	臉	liǎn	130	194	問	wèn	169	334
掩	yǎn	64	364	猫	māo	94	209	腴	qiǎn	130	245	閻	yán	169	364
掖	yē	64	371	猛	měng	94	210	脫	tuō	130	327	隊	duì	170	88
掟	zhěng	64	397	猪	zhū	94	407	脫	tuō	130	327	隋	suí	170	300
掙	zhèng	64	397	率	shuài	95	287	萇	cháng	140	48	隨	suí	170	300
掷	zhì	64	403	理	lǐ	96	190	菱	líng	140	197	陽	yáng	170	367
捆	zhōu	64	406	瓶	píng	98	235	營	yíng	140	379	隱	yǐn	170	378
敗	bài	66	23	蓋	gài	108	111	處	chǔ	141	56	隅	yú	170	383
教	jiāo,	66	160	盔	kuī	108	183	虛	xū	141	358	雀	què	172	255
	jiào	66	162	盤	pán	108	228	蛇	shé	142	274	雪	xuě	173	361
斂	liǎn	66	194	眯	mī	109	211	術	shù	144	286	頂	dǐng	181	83
敏	mǐn	66	212	眼	yǎn	109	365	袋	dài	145	68	頸	jǐng	181	172
斜	xié	68	353	着	zhāo,	109	395	襠	dāng	145	72	領	lǐng	181	198
斷	duàn	69	88		zhuó	109	411	規	guī	147	122	頗	lú	181	202
斬	zhǎn	69	393	研	yán	112	364	視	shì	147	282	騎	qí	187	240
旋	xuán,	70	359	移	yí	115	374	謊	huǎng	149	145	魚	yú	195	383
	xuàn	70	360	窒	zhì	116	403	欲	yù	150	385	鴻	hóng	196	135
晨	chén	72	50	竟	jìng	117	172	躍	yuè	157	388	鸞	luán	196	204
望	wàng	74	332	章	zhāng	117	394	趾	zhǐ	157	403	鳥	niǎo	196	222
桿	gān	75	111	笨	bèn	118	30	軀	qū	158	252	鹿	lù	198	203
梗	gěng	75	115	第	dì	118	78	輔	fǔ	159	108	麻	má	200	208
檢	jiǎn	75	157	粘	nián,	119	222	軟	ruǎn	159	260				
梨	lí	75	189		zhān	119	392	輒	zhé	159	396	**12 stroke characters**			
梁	liáng	75	195	絆	bàn	120	24	逮	dài	162	68				
梅	méi	75	209	繃	bēng	120	31	進	jìn	162	170	勞	láo	19	187
梢	shāo	75	272	綽	chāo,	120	49	週	zhōu	162	406	厥	jué	27	176
涵	hán	85	128		chuò	120	59	野	yě	166	371	喘	chuǎn	30	57
混	hún	85	146	綿	mián	120	212	鏟	chǎn	167	47	單	dān	30	68
凌	líng	85	197	繩	shéng	120	276	釣	diào	167	81	喉	hóu	30	135
清	qīng	85	249	維	wéi	120	332	鎧	kǎi	167	178	喂	wèi	30	333

454

CHARACTER INDEX BY STROKE ORDER
EACH COLUMN: CHARACTER | PINYIN | RADICAL | PAGE NUMBER

12 strokes

喜	xǐ	30	344	搜	sōu	64	300	犀	xī	93	343	腋	yè	130	372
報	bào	32	25	提	tí	64	311	猴	hóu	94	135	掙	zhèng	130	399
場	chǎng	32	49	揞	wāi	64	329	猨	yuán	94	386	舒	shū	135	285
偷	tōu	38	320	揾	wèn	64	334	琵	pí	96	232	落	luò	140	206
寒	hán	40	128	握	wò	64	335	畫	huà	102	142	萬	wàn	140	332
尋	xún	41	361	搗	wǔ	64	339	痞	pǐ	104	232	葉	yè	140	372
就	jiù	43	174	揚	yáng	64	366	登	dēng	105	76	虛	xū	141	358
巽	xùn	49	361	援	yuán	64	386	發	fā	105	95	蛤	há	142	127
強	qiáng,	57	246	揸	zhā	64	392	短	duǎn	111	87	蛟	jiāo	142	160
	qiǎng	57	246	掌	zhǎng	64	394	硬	yìng	112	381	蠻	mán	142	208
復	fù	60	108	敬	jìng	66	172	禪	chán	113	46	蟄	zhé	142	396
循	xún	60	361	散	sǎn	66	267	竄	cuàn	116	60	脈	mài	143	208
御	yù	60	384	散	sǎn	66	267	窩	wō	116	335	補	bǔ	145	37
慣	guàn	61	121	暑	shǔ	72	286	童	tóng	117	320	裁	cái	145	41
慌	huāng	61	144	暫	zàn	72	391	策	cè	118	44	裡	lǐ	145	190
戟	jǐ	62	153	智	zhì	72	403	等	děng	118	76	裏	lǐ	145	190
掰	bāi	64	19	最	zuì	73	416	筋	jīn	118	165	裙	qún	145	255
揹	bēi	64	28	朝	cháo	74	49	筒	tóng	118	320	裝	zhuāng	145	409
插	chā	64	45	期	qī	74	239	筑	zhù	118	407	評	píng	149	236
搀	chān	64	46	棒	bàng	75	25	編	biān	120	32	詠	yǒng	149	381
掣	chè	64	50	棍	gùn	75	124	緩	huǎn	120	143	詐	zhà	149	392
揣	chuāi	64	56	極	jí	75	152	絞	jiǎo	120	161	象	xiàng	152	350
搥	chuí	64	58	棄	qì	75	241	絕	jué	120	176	貫	guàn	154	122
搓	cuō	64	61	椭	tuǒ	75	328	絶	jué	120	176	貼	tiē	154	317
搭	dā	64	63	欺	qī	76	240	纜	lǎn	120	186	超	chāo	156	49
掼	guàn	64	121	殘	cán	78	42	絡	luò	120	206	趁	chèn	156	51
換	huàn	64	143	渾	hún	85	147	絲	sī	120	296	趨	qū	156	252
揮	huī	64	145	濺	jiàn	85	159	紫	zǐ	120	412	跛	bǒ	157	37
攪	jiǎo	64	161	濕	shī	85	277	翹	qiáo	124	247	跌	diē	157	81
揭	jiē	64	163	溫	wēn	85	334	耠	huō	127	147	趺	fū	157	106
揪	jiū	64	173	游	yóu	85	382	腓	féi	130	101	踐	jiàn	157	159
攬	lǎn	64	186	滯	zhì	85	403	腑	fǔ	130	108	距	jù	157	175
摟	lou	64	202	然	rán	86	257	膕	guó	130	125	跈	niǎn	157	222
搗	mā	64	207	無	wú	86	337	腎	shèn	130	276	跑	pǎo	157	230
揿	qìn	64	249	犇	bēn	93	30	脾	tiǎn	130	315	軸	zhóu	159	406
揉	róu	64	259	犊	dú	93	86	腕	wàn	130	332	逼	bī	162	31

455

Character Index by Stroke Order
Each column: Character | Pinyin | Radical | Page number

12 & 13 strokes

達	dá	162	63	順	shùn	181	294	摸	mō	64	213	睛	jīng	109	171
道	dào	162	75	項	xiàng	181	350	搶	qiǎng	64	246	矮	ǎi	111	13
過	guò	162	125	骗	piàn	187	233	搧	shān	64	268	碌	liù	112	200
遊	yóu	162	382	鹅	é	196	91	搠	shuò	64	296	碰	pèng	112	231
運	yùn	162	390	黃	huáng	201	144	搨	tà	64	303	碰	pèng	112	231
鈀	bǎ,	167	18	黑	hēi	203	130	攤	tān	64	306	碎	suì	112	301
	pá	167	227					搵	wèn	64	334	禁	jìn	113	170
銼	cuò	167	62	**13 stroke characters**				攜	xié	64	353	竪	shù	117	286
铤	dìng	167	84					搖	yáo	64	370	简	jiǎn	118	158
鈍	dùn	167	89	亂	luàn	5	204	搖	yáo	64	370	節	jié	118	164
鋒	fēng	167	103	傳	chuán	9	57	新	xīn	69	355	筒	tóng	118	320
釜	fǔ	167	108	催	cuī	9	60	暗	àn	72	14	缠	chán	120	46
鈎	gōu	167	117	傷	shāng	9	269	暇	xiá	72	345	缝	fèng	120	105
鈒	jí	167	152	傳	zhuàn	9	409	暈	yūn,	72	388	經	jīng	120	171
铜	jiǎn	167	158	剿	jiǎo	18	161		yùn	72	390	群	qún	123	255
链	liàn	167	195	勦	jiǎo	19	161	會	huì	73	146	義	yì	123	376
铺	pū	167	238	勢	shì	19	281	槌	chuí	75	58	腸	cháng	130	48
锐	ruì	167	261	疊	dié	29	81	楓	fēng	75	103	腠	còu	130	59
锁	suǒ	167	302	喙	huì	30	146	楔	xiē	75	353	腹	fù	130	108
销	xiāo	167	350	圍	wéi	31	332	楊	yáng	75	367	腳	jiǎo	130	161
間	jiān,	169	157	圓	yuán	31	386	歇	xiē	76	353	腦	nǎo	130	219
	jiàn	169	159	塌	tā	32	303	滌	dí	85	77	脾	pí	130	232
開	kāi	169	177	填	tián	32	315	滚	gǔn	85	123	腮	sāi	130	263
阔	kuò	169	184	壺	hú	33	138	滑	huá	85	141	腧	shū	130	285
闌	lán	169	186	嵩	sōng	46	299	溜	liū	85	198	腿	tuǐ	130	323
陳	chén	170	51	廓	kuò	53	184	滿	mǎn	85	208	腰	yāo	130	368
隔	gé	170	114	廉	lián	53	193	準	zhǔn	85	411	蒼	cāng	140	42
集	jí	172	152	慎	shèn	61	276	煉	liàn	86	194	蓋	gài	140	111
雄	xióng	172	357	意	yì	61	375	照	zhào	86	395	蓄	xù	140	358
雁	yàn	172	366	摆	bǎi	64	22	獅	shī	94	277	號	hào	141	128
雲	yún	173	389	搬	bān	64	23	獻	xiàn	94	349	蜀	shǔ	142	286
韩	hán	178	128	搏	bó	64	37	猿	yuán	94	386	蜈	wú	142	338
韌	rèn	178	258	搗	dǎo	64	74	當	dāng	102	72	裝	zhuāng	145	409
頜	gé,	181	114	搤	è	64	91	瘀	yū	104	382	解	jiě	148	164
	hé	181	130	搆	gòu	64	118	嗌	yì	108	376	試	shì	149	282
颊	jiá	181	154	提	huàng	64	145	督	dū	109	86	跐	cǐ	157	59

456

Character Index by Stroke Order
Each column: Character | Pinyin | Radical | Page number

13 & 14 strokes

Char	Pinyin	Rad	Pg	Char	Pinyin	Rad	Pg	Char	Pinyin	Rad	Pg	Char	Pinyin	Rad	Pg
跺	duò	157	89	馳	chí	187	53	暢	chàng	72	49	綜	zōng	120	413
跟	gēn	157	114	騰	téng	187	309	朢	wàng	74	332	聚	jù	128	175
跪	guì	157	123	鳳	fèng	196	105	槓	gàng	75	112	膀	bǎng,	130	25
跤	jiāo	157	161	鳩	jiū	196	173	槐	huái	75	143		páng	130	229
跨	kuà	157	183	鵬	péng	196	230	槍	qiāng	75	246	膏	gāo	130	112
路	lù	157	203	鵲	què	196	255	槊	shuò	75	296	膈	gé	130	113
跷	qiāo	157	247	鼎	dǐng	206	83	歌	gē	76	113	膂	lǔ	130	203
跳	tiào	157	316	鼓	gǔ	207	119	滴	dī	85	77	膝	xī	130	343
躲	duǒ	158	89	鼠	shǔ	208	286	滾	gǔn	85	123	蔡	cài	140	42
躬	gōng	158	116					漢	hàn	85	128	蜻	qīng	142	249
較	jiào	159	162	**14 stroke**				漏	lòu	85	202	蜻	qīng	142	249
輸	shū	159	285	**characters**				滿	mǎn	85	208	複	fù	145	109
載	zài	159	391					演	yǎn	85	365	裹	guǒ	145	125
遞	dì	162	78	僧	sēng	9	268	漁	yú	85	383	褪	tùn	145	325
遠	yuǎn	162	387	僊	xiān	9	347	滯	zhì	85	403	谱	pǔ	149	238
鉍	bì	167	32	劃	huá	18	141	熊	xióng	86	357	說	shuō	149	296
鈸	bó	167	37	嘑	hū	30	138	獃	dāi	94	67	誤	wù	149	341
錘	chuí	167	58	圖	tú	31	321	瘈	chì	104	53	狸	lí	153	189
错	cuò	167	62	團	tuán	31	322	瞇	mī	109	211	赶	gǎn	156	112
鉤	gōu	167	117	墊	diàn	32	79	碧	bì	112	32	趙	zhào	156	395
锦	jǐn	167	169	墜	zhuì	32	411	稱	chèn,	115	51	踇	mǔ	157	214
锯	jù	167	175	奪	duó	37	89		chēng	115	52	躲	duǒ	158	89
鉗	qián	167	245	嫦	cháng	38	48	穩	wěn	115	334	輔	fǔ	159	108
锬	tán	167	306	嫩	nèn	38	221	窩	wō	116	335	輕	qīng	159	249
鉈	tuó	167	327	對	duì	41	88	端	duān	117	87	輓	wǎn	159	332
鉞	yuè	167	388	惡	è	61	91	管	guǎn	118	121	辕	yuán	159	387
錐	zhuī	167	410	慢	màn	61	208	箕	jī	118	151	輒	zhé	159	396
閡	hé	169	130	截	jié	62	163	精	jīng	119	171	遮	zhē	162	396
閘	zhá	169	392	摽	biāo	64	34	綳	bēng	120	31	酸	suān	164	300
電	diàn	173	80	摺	chě	64	50	綵	cǎi	120	41	鋩	máng	167	209
雷	léi	173	189	摧	cuī	64	60	綽	chāo,	120	49	鍥	qiè	167	248
靶	bǎ	177	18	搿	gé	64	113		chuò	120	59	銀	yín	167	378
韵	yùn	180	390	摳	kōu	64	180	緊	jǐn	120	169	閤	hé	169	130
頓	dùn	181	89	搜	lōu	64	202	綿	mián	120	212	隨	suí	170	300
颔	hàn	181	128	摔	shuāi	64	286	缩	suō	120	301	静	jìng	174	173
预	yù	181	385	摘	zhāi	64	392	維	wéi	120	332	領	lǐng	181	198
				摺	zhé	64	396								

Character Index by Stroke Order
Each column: Character | Pinyin | Radical | Page number
14 & 15 strokes

Char	Pinyin	Rad	Pg	Char	Pinyin	Rad	Pg	Char	Pinyin	Rad	Pg	Char	Pinyin	Rad	Pg
養	yǎng	184	368	撢	dǎn	64	71	橢	tuǒ	75	328	諸	zhū	149	407
鬥	dòu	191	85	撣	dǎn	64	71	椿	zhuāng	75	409	豬	zhū	152	407
魂	hún	194	147	扚等	dēng	64	76	潛	qián	85	245	貌	mào	153	209
魁	kuí	194	184	扌葛	gē,	64	114	潤	rùn	85	261	趟	tàng	156	308
鼻	bí	209	31		kā	64	177	潭	tán	85	306	踩	cǎi	157	41
齊	qí	210	241	摜	guàn	64	121	熱	rè	86	257	踔	chuō	157	59
齦	yín	211	378	攪	jiǎo	64	161	璇	xuán	96	359	踮	diǎn	157	78
15 stroke characters				撅	juē	64	176	甎	zhuān	98	408	踝	huái	157	143
				撈	lāo	64	187	瘫	tān	104	306	踐	jiàn	157	159
				撩	liāo	64	196	盤	pán	108	228	踏	tà	157	303
僵	jiāng	9	159	撸	lū	64	202	瞞	mán	109	208	踢	tī	157	311
億	yì	9	375	擄	lǔ	64	202	瞑	míng	109	212	躺	tǎng	158	308
劐	huō	18	147	摩	mó	64	213	磕	kē	112	179	輥	lù	159	203
劍	jiàn	18	158	撓	náo	64	218	碾	niǎn	112	222	輪	lún	159	204
劉	liú	18	199	撚	niǎn	64	222	穀	gǔ	115	118	遲	chí	162	53
劈	pī	18	231	撇	piē, piě	64	233	箭	jiàn	118	159	遼	liáo	162	197
厲	lì	27	192	撲	pū	64	237	編	biān	120	32	邁	mài	162	208
嘿	hēi	30	130	撬	qiào	64	248	緩	huǎn	120	143	選	xuǎn	162	360
嘴	zuǐ	30	416	撳	qìn	64	249	練	liàn	120	195	醉	zuì	164	416
墩	dūn	32	89	撋	ruán	64	260	翦	jiǎn	124	158	銼	cuò	167	62
審	shěn	40	276	(also 日 inside, not 王)				膕	guó	130	125	鋌	dìng	167	84
實	shí	40	280	撒	sā, sǎ	64	263	膛	táng	130	307	鋒	fēng	167	103
導	dǎo	41	74	撕	sī	64	296	舞	wǔ	136	341	鋪	pū	167	238
履	lǚ	44	203	撻	tà	64	303	蕩	dàng	140	72	銳	ruì	167	261
彆	biè	57	34	撾	wō,	64	335	蕎	hāo	140	128	锃	zèng	167	308
彈	dàn,	57	72		zhuā	64	408	蝙	biān	142	32	销	xiāo	167	350
	tán	57	306	撜	zhěng	64	397	蝶	dié	142	82	震	zhèn	173	397
徹	chè	60	50	撞	zhuàng	64	410	蝴	hú	142	138	靠	kào	175	179
懂	dǒng	61	84	敵	dí	66	77	蝦	xiā	142	345	鞏	gǒng	177	116
慣	guàn	61	121	敷	fū	66	106	蝎	xiē	142	353	額	é	181	91
慾	yù	61	385	暴	bào	72	28	衝	chōng	144	54	領	gé,	181	114
撥	bō	64	36	暫	zàn	72	391	製	zhì	145	403		hé	181	130
撤	chè	64	50	標	biāo	75	34	調	diào,	149	81	飄	piāo	182	233
撐	chēng	64	51	橫	héng	75	132		tiáo	149	315	餓	è	184	91
撑	chēng	64	51	樑	liáng	75	195	請	qǐng	149	251	餘	yú	184	383
撮	cuō	64	61	樞	shū	75	285	誘	yòu	149	382	骶	dǐ	188	77

458

Character Index by Stroke Order
Each column: Character | Pinyin | Radical | Page number

15, 16 & 17 strokes

魄	pò	194	236	橋	qiáo	75	247	閻	yán	169	364	盪	dàng	108	72
鯉	lǐ	195	191	橈	ráo	75	257	隱	yǐn	170	378	瞳	tóng	109	319
鶴	hè	196	130	樹	shù	75	286	霑	zhān	173	393	禮	lǐ	113	190
鴉	yā	196	363	激	jī	85	151	靜	jìng	174	173	糠	kāng	119	178
鴈	yàn	196	366	濁	zhuó	85	411	鞘	qiào	177	248	繃	bēng	120	31
鷂	yào	196	370	燕	yàn	86	365	顛	diān	181	78	縮	suō	120	301
齒	chǐ	211	53	獨	dú	94	86	領	hàn	181	128	總	zǒng	120	413
				瓢	piáo	97	233	頰	jiá	181	154	縱	zòng	120	413
16 stroke				瞞	mán	109	208	頸	jǐng	181	172	翳	yì	124	376
characters				瞟	piǎo	109	233	頭	tóu	181	320	聲	shēng	128	276
儒	rú	9	260	磨	mó,	112	213	鮐	tái	196	305	聳	sǒng	128	299
凝	níng	15	223		mò	112	214	鮀	tuó	196	327	臂	bēi, bì	130	28
劍	jiàn	18	158	禪	chán	113	46	鴨	yā	196	363	膽	dǎn	130	71
劒	jiàn	18	158	築	zhù	118	407	鸚	yīng	196	379	膻	dàn,	130	72
器	qì	30	241	縫	fèng	120	105	鴛	yuān	196	385		shān	130	269
學	xué	39	360	舉	jǔ	134	174	龍	lóng	212	200	臁	lián	130	193
憋	biē	61	34	蟒	mǎng	142	209					臉	liǎn	130	194
懶	lǎn	61	186	螃	páng	142	229	**17 stroke**				膺	yīng	130	379
戰	zhàn	62	393	衡	héng	144	134	**characters**				臀	tún	130	325
操	cāo	64	43	衛	wèi	144	334	嚮	xiàng	30	349	藏	cáng	140	42
擔	dān	64	71	謊	huǎng	149	145	壓	yā	32	363	薰	xūn	140	361
擋	dǎng	64	72	踹	chuài	157	56	嶽	yuè	46	387	螺	luó	142	206
攫	huò	64	149	蹉	cuō	157	61	幫	bāng	50	25	螳	táng	142	307
擂	lèi	64	189	踺	jiàn	157	159	禦	yù	60	384	謌	gē	149	113
撬	qiào	64	248	輸	shū	159	285	應	yīng	61	378	豁	huō	150	148
擒	qín	64	249	避	bì	162	32	擦	cā	64	41	趨	qū	156	252
擎	qíng	64	251	還	huán	162	143	擊	jī	64	151	蹋	tà	157	303
攜	xié	64	353	鏢	biāo	167	34	擠	jǐ	64	153	轅	yuán	159	387
擁	yōng	64	381	錘	chuí	167	58	擰	níng	64	223	邊	biān	162	32
擲	zhì	64	403	錯	cuò	167	62	擡	tái	64	303	鍥	qiè	167	248
整	zhěng	66	397	錞	duì	167	88	斂	liǎn	66	194	鐔	tán	167	306
橄	gǎn	75	112	錦	jǐn	167	169	檢	jiǎn	75	157	闊	kuò	169	184
橛	jué	75	176	鋸	jù	167	175	濕	shī	85	277	闌	lán	169	186
樐	lǔ	75	203	錟	tán	167	306	營	yíng	86	379	韓	hán	178	128
樸	pǔ	75	238	鏨	zàn	167	391	燥	zào	86	391	骸	tuǐ	188	323
樵	qiáo	75	247	錐	zhuī	167	410	環	huán	96	143	鴻	hóng	196	135

459

Character Index by Stroke Order

Each column: Character | Pinyin | Radical | Page number

17, 18, 19 & 20 strokes

Char	Pinyin	Rad	Pg
麴	qū	199	252
黏	nián,	202	222
	zhān	202	393
點	diǎn	203	79

18 stroke characters

Char	Pinyin	Rad	Pg
雙	shuāng	29	288
戳	chuō	62	58
戴	dài	62	68
擺	bǎi	64	22
擷	liè	64	197
擼	lū	64	202
斷	duàn	69	88
歸	guī	77	122
濺	jiàn	85	159
瞬	shùn	109	294
竄	cuàn	116	60
竅	qiào	116	248
簡	jiǎn	118	158
繞	rào	120	257
繩	shéng	120	276
罎	tán	121	306
翻	fān	124	95
翹	qiáo	124	247
臑	nào	130	219
舊	jiù	134	174
藤	téng	140	309
藝	yì	140	376
蟠	pán	142	228
襠	dāng	145	72
豐	fēng	151	103
蹦	bèng	157	31
蹚	tāng	157	307
蹠	zhí	157	401
軀	qū	158	252
轆	lù	159	203
轉	zhuǎn,	159	408
	zhuàn	159	409
醫	yī	164	374
鎧	kǎi	167	178
鎌	lián	167	194
鐮	lián	167	194
鏈	liàn	167	195
鎖	suǒ	167	302
鏜	tāng	167	308
闖	chuǎng	169	58
闔	hé	169	130
雞	jī	172	151
離	lí	172	190
雜	zá	172	391
鞭	biān	177	33
額	é	181	91
顋	sāi	181	263
騎	qí	187	240
鬆	sōng	190	299
魏	wèi	194	334
鯉	lǐ	195	191
鵝	é	196	91
鵝	é	196	91
鵝	é	196	91
鶩	é	196	91
鷹	yīng	196	379
麋	lín	198	197
龜	guī	213	122

19 stroke characters

Char	Pinyin	Rad	Pg
勸	quàn	19	254
懷	huái	61	142
懶	lǎn	61	186
攢	cuán,	64	60
	zǎn	64	391
攉	huō	64	147
攏	lǒng	64	202
攀	pān	64	228
櫓	lǔ	75	203
爆	bào	86	28
獸	shòu	94	285
獻	xiàn	94	349
穩	wěn	115	334
羅	luó	122	205
蘇	sū	140	300
蠍	xiē	142	353
蟹	xiè	142	354
蟹	xiè	142	354
警	jǐng	149	172
譜	pǔ	149	238
鱉	bié	157	34
蹭	cèng	157	44
蹿	cuān	157	59
蹬	dēng	157	76
蹲	dūn	157	89
蹶	juě	157	176
蹺	qiāo	157	247
蹻	qiāo	157	247
鏢	biāo	167	34
鏟	chǎn	167	47
鏇	xuàn	167	360
鏨	zàn	167	391
關	guān	169	121
難	nán	172	218
韻	yùn	180	390
顛	diān	181	78
顖	xìn	181	356
顫	zhàn	181	394
騙	piàn	187	233
騸	piàn	187	233
骼	qià	188	243
鵬	péng	196	230
鵲	què	196	255
鴉	yā	196	363
麒	qí	198	240

20 stroke characters

Char	Pinyin	Rad	Pg
寶	bǎo	40	25
懸	xuán	61	359
攙	chān	64	46
攔	lán	64	185
灌	guàn	85	122
競	jìng	117	172
蘤	huā	140	141
蠕	rú	142	260
護	hù	149	140
譩	yì	149	376
鐧	jiǎn	167	158
鐔	tán	167	306
鐘	zhōng	167	406
鐏	zūn	167	417
闡	chǎn	169	48
飄	piāo	182	233
騰	téng	187	309
髕	bìn	188	35
髖	kuān	188	183
鬢	bìn	190	35
鼉	tuó	205	327

Character Index by Stroke Order
Each column: Character | Pinyin | Radical | Page number
21, 22, 23, 24, 25, 26, 27, 28 & 30 strokes

21 stroke characters

攜	xié	64	353
欄	lán	75	186
爛	làn	86	186
籐	téng	118	309
纏	chán	120	46
續	xù	120	358
臟	zàng	130	391
蠡	lí	142	190
躍	yuè	157	388
轟	hōng	159	134
鐮	lián	167	194
鐵	tiě	167	317
霸	bà	173	18
露	lòu,	173	202
	lù	173	203
顧	gù	181	119
鶴	hè	196	130
鷂	yào	196	370
鶯	yīng	196	379
齩	yǎo	211	370
齦	yín	211	378

22 stroke characters

彎	wān	57	331
攢	cuán,	64	60
	zǎn	64	391
攤	tān	64	306
疊	dié	102	81
穮	chī	115	53
聽	tīng	128	318
襲	xí	145	344
顫	zhàn	181	394
驕	jiāo	187	161
髓	suǐ	188	301

23 stroke characters

攥	zuàn	64	416
欑	cuán	75	60
變	biàn	149	33
躦	zuān	157	415
顴	quán	181	254
顯	xiǎn	181	349
體	tǐ	188	313
鷰	yàn	196	365
麟	lín	198	197

24 stroke characters

攬	lǎn	64	186
癱	tān	104	306
觀	guān	147	120
讓	ràng	149	257
靈	líng	173	197
鬢	bìn	188	35
髖	kuān	188	183
鬢	bìn	190	35
鬥	dòu	191	85
鷹	yīng	196	379

25 stroke characters

欛	bà	75	18
躥	cuān	157	59
蠻	mán	142	208
顱	lú	181	202
鼉	tuó	205	327

26 stroke characters

躦	zuān	157	415
顴	quán	181	254

27 stroke characters

纜	lǎn	120	186
鑽	zuān	167	415
驩	huān	187	143

28 stroke characters

鸚	yīng	196	379

30 stroke characters

鸞	luán	196	204

PRONUNCIATION GUIDE FOR CHINESE IN PINYIN

CONSONANTS

p	similar to the 'p' in <u>p</u>et, with a considerable puff of air.
b	similar to the *pinyin* "p" but without the puff of air (unvoiced, neither <u>p</u>et nor <u>b</u>et).
t	similar to the 't' in <u>t</u>ag, with a considerable puff of air.
d	similar to the *pinyin* "t" but with no puff of air (unvoiced, not <u>d</u>og).
k	similar to the 'k' in <u>k</u>ill, with a considerable puff of air.
g	similar to the *pinyin* "k" but with no puff of air (unvoiced, not <u>g</u>et).
c	like exaggerating the 'ts' in ca<u>ts</u>, with a considerable puff of air.
z	like the *pinyin* "c" but without the puff of air (unvoiced).
ch	somewhat similar to <u>ch</u>at with a puff of air, but with the tip of the tongue rolled back.
zh	like the *pinyin* "ch" but with no puff of air (unvoiced).
q	somewhat similar to the 'ch' in <u>ch</u>at with a puff of air, but with the front of the tongue raised and the tip on the lower teeth.
j	like the *pinyin* "q" but without the puff of air (unvoiced).
m	similar to the 'm' in <u>m</u>et.
n	similar to the 'n' in <u>n</u>et.
ng	similar to the 'ng' in si<u>ng</u>.
f	similar to the 'f' in <u>f</u>at, but with the teeth just touching lightly behind the lower lip.
s	similar to the 's' in <u>s</u>et.
sh	somewhat similar to the 'sh' in <u>sh</u>ow, but with the same tongue placement as the *pinyin* "ch" and "zh."
x	somewhat similar to <u>sh</u>ine but with the same tongue placement as the *pinyin* "q" and "j."
h	raise the back of the tongue and let the breath come through the obstructed passage without vibrating the vocal cords.
l	similar to the 'l' in <u>l</u>et.
r	like the *pinyin* "sh" but with voicing.

	manner of articulation						
place of articulation	Unaspirated Stops	Aspirated Stops	Unaspirated Affricates	Aspirated Affricates	Nasals	Fricatives	Voiced Continuants
bilabials	b	p			m		
labio-dentals						f	
dental-alveolars	d	t	z	c	n	s	l
retroflexes			zh	ch		sh	r
palatals			j	q		x	
velars	g	k				h	

VOWELS

a	usually close to f<u>a</u>r (not p<u>a</u>t). Like <u>y</u>et when written "-ian" or "yan."
e	usually similar to p<u>e</u>t.
i	usually similar to b<u>ee</u>. Similar to <u>w</u>et when written "ui." After c, s, s, and z is similar to sk<u>i</u>ll. After ch, zh, sh, and r it is similar to s<u>i</u>r.
o	usually close to r<u>o</u>ll. Similar to c<u>o</u>w when written "ao," and <u>ow</u>e when in "ou." After bilabial and labio-denatal consonants (b-, p-, m-, f-) it is ʷo.
u	usually similar to b<u>oo</u>t. After the *pinyin* "x", "q", and "j" and in the vowel groups starting with these consonants, it is pronounced "ü."
ü	pronounced <u>ü</u>. It is written after "n" or "l," because these are the only positions where both "u" and "ü" are possible.

When written together, vowels are not a diphthong, but more a combination of 'w' or 'y' with a clean vowel. The tone marker is placed over the clean vowel.

ai	similar to 'b<u>uy</u>'
ao	similar to 'c<u>ow</u>'
ei	similar to 'h<u>ey</u>'
ia	similar to '<u>y</u>et'
iao	similar to '<u>yow</u>'
ie	similar to '<u>y</u>es'
io	similar to '<u>y</u>onder'
iu	similar to '<u>y</u>our'
ou	similar to '<u>oh</u>'
ua	similar to '<u>wa</u>nt'
uai	similar to '<u>wi</u>se'
ui	similar to '<u>w</u>et', verging towards 'way'
uo	similar to '<u>wo</u>rn'

TONES

#	pinyin	name	range
1	v̄	high level	55
2	v́	high rising	35
3	v̌	dipping	214
4	v̀	high falling	51

In a normal vocal range, 5 is high and 1 is low.

When combined as one word, two third tones together are pronounced as a second and a third tone. A third tone followed by any other tone is pronounced as a half-third tone – 21 – not rising.

The symbol ° indicates a neutral tone.

trois   gros   lapins   traversent   le   chemin

ISBN 978-0-9879028-5-6

www.ingramcontent.com/pod-product-compliance
Lightning Source LLC
Chambersburg PA
CBHW080532300426
44111CB00017B/2687